А
Б
В
Г
Д
Е
Ж
З
И
ЙК
Л
М
Н
О
П
Р
С
Т
У
Ф
Х
Ц
Ч
Ш-Я

Berlitz®

# Russian Concise Dictionary

Russian – English
English – Russian

**Berlitz Publishing**
New York · Munich · Singapore

Edited by the Langenscheidt editorial staff

Based on a dictionary compiled with contributions by Irina A. Walshe

Activity section by Olga Layer

Book in cover photo: © Punchstock/Medioimages



Berlitz Publishing
193 Morris Avenue
Springfield, NJ 07081
USA

Printed in Germany
ISBN 978-981-268-058-7

1. 2. 3. 4. 5. 11 10 09 08 07

# Preface

This new dictionary of English and Russian is a tool with more than 45,000 references for learners of the Russian language at beginner's or intermediate level.

A large number of idiomatic expressions has been included. The user-friendly layout with all headwords in blue allows the user to have quick access to all the words, expressions and their translations.

Clarity of presentation has been a major objective. Is *flimsy* referring to furniture the same in Russian as *flimsy* referring to an excuse? This dictionary is rich in sense distinctions like this – and in translation options tied to specific, identified senses.

Vocabulary needs grammar to back it up. In this dictionary you will find extra grammar information on the conjugation and declension of Russian verbs, nouns and adjectives.

The additional activity section provides the user with an opportunity to develop language skills with a selection of engaging word puzzles. The games are designed specifically to improve vocabulary, spelling, grammar and comprehension in an enjoyable style.

Designed for a wide variety of uses, this dictionary will be of great value to those who wish to learn Russian and have fun at the same time.

# Contents

# How to Use the Dictionary

1. **Arrangement.** Strict alphabetical order has been maintained throughout the dictionary.

   A number of prefixed words, especially verbs, are not explicitly listed because of the limited size of the dictionary, and in such cases it may prove useful to drop the prefix and look up the primary form, e. g.:

   по̲благодари́ть → благодари́ть

   Compounds not found at their alphabetical place should be reduced to their second component in order to find out their main meaning, e. g.:

   термоя́дерный → я́дерный = nuclear

   The tilde (~) serves as a mark of repetition. The tilde in bold type replaces either the headword or the part of the headword preceding the vertical bar; e. g.:

   **иди́лл|ия** ...; **~и́ческий** = **идилли́ческий**

   In the English-Russian part the tilde in multi-word lexical units is used to replace the whole headword, e.g.:

   **mobil|e** ...; ***~ phone*** = ***mobile phone***

   In the Russian-English part the tilde in idioms is used to relace the part preceding the vertical bar, e. g.:

   **коль|циво́й** ...; **~цо́** ...; ***обруча́льное ~цо́*** = ***обруча́льное кольцо́***

   The tilde with a circle (~̊): when the first letter changes from a capital to a small letter or vice-versa, the usual tilde is replaced by the tilde with a circle.

   In brackets a hyphen (-) has been used instead of the tilde, e. g.:

   **брать** [беру́, -рёшь; брал, -а́ ...] = [беру́, берёшь; брал, брала́ ...]

   Of the two main aspects of a Russian verb the imperfective form appears first, in boldface type, followed, in acute-angled brackets < >, by its perfective counterpart.

2. **Pronunciation.** As a rule the pronunciation of individual Russian headwords has been given only in cases and places that differ from the standard pronunciation of Russian vowel and consonant letters, e. g.:

   **лёгкий** (-xk-) - «гк» is pronounced «хк».

3. **Stress.** The accent mark (´) is placed above the stressed vowel of a Russian entry (or any other) word with more than one syllable and printed in full, as well as of run-on words, provided their accentuated vowel is not covered by the tilde or hyphen (= marks of repetition), e. g.:

   **дока́з|ывать** ..., <~а́ть> = <доказа́ть>

   Since ë is always stressed the two dots over it represent implicitly the accent mark.

   Wherever the accent mark precedes the tilde (´~) the second-last syllable of the part for which the tilde stands is stressed, e. g.:

   **уведом|ля́ть** ..., <´~ить> = <уве́домить>

An accent mark over the tilde (~́) implies that the last (or sole) syllable of the part replaced by the tilde is to be stressed.

Example:

**наход|и́ть** ...; **~́ка** = **нахо́дка**
**прода|ва́ть** ..., <~́ть> = <прода́ть>

In special cases of phonetic transcription, however, the accent mark precedes the stressed syllable, cf. **анте́нна** (-ˈtɛn-). This usage is in accordance with IPA rules.

Two accents in a word denote two equally possible modes of stressing it, thus:

**и́на́че** = **ина́че** *or* **и́наче**

Quite a number of predicative (or short) adjectives show a shift, or shifts, of stress as compared with their attributive forms. Such divergences are recorded as follows:

**хоро́ший** [17; хоро́ш, -а́] = [17; хоро́ш, хороша́, хорошо́ (*pl.* хороши́)]

The same system of stress designation applies, to accent shifts in the preterite forms of a number of verbs, e. g.:

**да|ва́ть** ..., <~ть> [... дал, -а́, -о; ... (дан, -а́)] = [... дал, дала́, да́ло (*pl.* да́ли); ... (дан, дана́, дано́, даны́)]

Insertion of the "epenthetic" о, е, between the two last stem consonants in masculine short forms has been noted in all adjectives where this applies, e. g.:

**лёгкий** ... [16; лёгок, легка́; *a.* лёгки] = [16; лёгок, легка́, легко́ (*pl.* легки́ *or* лёгки)]

If the stress in all short forms conforms to that of the attributive adjective the latter is merely provided with the abbreviation *sh.* (for *short form*) which indicates at the same time the possibility of forming such predicative forms, e. g.:

**бога́тый** [14 *sh.*] = [14; бога́т, бога́та, бога́то, бога́ты]

4. **Inflected forms.** All Russian inflected parts of speech appearing in the dictionary are listed in their appropriate basic forms, i. e. nominative singular (nouns, adjectives, numerals, certain pronouns) or infinitive (verbs). The gender of Russian nouns is indicated by means of one of three abbreviations in italics (*m*, *f*, *n*) after the headword.* Each inflected entry is followed, in square brackets [ ], by a figure which serves as reference to a definite paradigm within the system of conjugation and declension listed at the end of this book. Any variants of these paradigms are stated after the reference figure of each headword in question.

---

* For users of part II: Any Russian noun ending in a consonant *or* -й is of masculine gender;
those ending in -а *or* -я are of feminine gender;
those ending in -о *or* -е are of neuter gender.
In cases where this rule does not apply, as well as in nouns ending in -ь, the gender is indicated.

# How to Use the Dictionary

1. **Arrangement.** Strict alphabetical order has been maintained throughout the dictionary.

   A number of prefixed words, especially verbs, are not explicitly listed because of the limited size of the dictionary, and in such cases it may prove useful to drop the prefix and look up the primary form, e. g.:

   поблагодари́ть → благодари́ть

   Compounds not found at their alphabetical place should be reduced to their second component in order to find out their main meaning, e. g.:

   термоя́дерный → я́дерный = nuclear

   The tilde (~) serves as a mark of repetition. The tilde in bold type replaces either the headword or the part of the headword preceding the vertical bar; e. g.:

   **иди́лл|ия** ...; **~и́ческий** = **идилли́ческий**

   In the English-Russian part the tilde in multi-word lexical units is used to replace the whole headword, e.g.:

   **mobil|e** ...; ***~ phone*** = ***mobile phone***

   In the Russian-English part the tilde in idioms is used to relace the part preceding the vertical bar, e. g.:

   **коль|цево́й** ...; **~цо́** ...; ***обруча́льное ~цо́*** = ***обруча́льное кольцо́***

   The tilde with a circle (≗): when the first letter changes from a capital to a small letter or vice-versa, the usual tilde is replaced by the tilde with a circle.

   In brackets a hyphen (-) has been used instead of the tilde, e. g.:

   **брать** [беру́, -рёшь; брал, -á ...] = [беру́, берёшь; брал, брала́ ...]

   Of the two main aspects of a Russian verb the imperfective form appears first, in boldface type, followed, in acute-angled brackets < >, by its perfective counterpart.

2. **Pronunciation.** As a rule the pronunciation of individual Russian headwords has been given only in cases and places that differ from the standard pronunciation of Russian vowel and consonant letters, e. g.:

   **лёгкий** (-xk-) - «гк» is pronounced «хк».

3. **Stress.** The accent mark (´) is placed above the stressed vowel of a Russian entry (or any other) word with more than one syllable and printed in full, as well as of run-on words, provided their accentuated vowel is not covered by the tilde or hyphen (= marks of repetition), e. g.:

   **дока́з|ывать** ..., <~а́ть> = <доказа́ть>

   Since ё is always stressed the two dots over it represent implicitly the accent mark.

   Wherever the accent mark precedes the tilde (´~) the second-last syllable of the part for which the tilde stands is stressed, e. g.:

   **уведом|ля́ть** ..., <´~ить> = <уве́домить>

An accent mark over the tilde (~́) implies that the last (or sole) syllable of the part replaced by the tilde is to be stressed.

Example:

**наход|и́ть** ...; ~́**ка** = **нахо́дка**
**прода|ва́ть** ..., <~́ть> = <прода́ть>

In special cases of phonetic transcription, however, the accent mark precedes the stressed syllable, cf. **анте́нна** (-ˈtɛn-). This usage is in accordance with IPA rules.

Two accents in a word denote two equally possible modes of stressing it, thus:

**и́на́че** = **ина́че** *or* **и́наче**

Quite a number of predicative (or short) adjectives show a shift, or shifts, of stress as compared with their attributive forms. Such divergences are recorded as follows:

**хоро́ший** [17; хоро́ш, -а́] = [17; хоро́ш, хороша́, хорошо́ (*pl.* хороши́)]

The same system of stress designation applies, to accent shifts in the preterite forms of a number of verbs, e. g.:

**да|ва́ть** ..., <~ть> [... дал, -а́, -о; ... (дан, -а́)] = [... дал, дала́, да́ло (*pl.* да́ли); ... (дан, дана́, дано́, даны́)]

Insertion of the "epenthetic" о, е, between the two last stem consonants in masculine short forms has been noted in all adjectives where this applies, e. g.:

**лёгкий** ... [16; лёгок, легка́; *a.* лёгки] = [16; лёгок, легка́, легко́ (*pl.* легки́ *or* лёгки)]

If the stress in all short forms conforms to that of the attributive adjective the latter is merely provided with the abbreviation *sh.* (for *short form*) which indicates at the same time the possibility of forming such predicative forms, e. g.:

**бога́тый** [14 *sh.*] = [14; бога́т, бога́та, бога́то, бога́ты]

4. **Inflected forms.** All Russian inflected parts of speech appearing in the dictionary are listed in their appropriate basic forms, i. e. nominative singular (nouns, adjectives, numerals, certain pronouns) or infinitive (verbs). The gender of Russian nouns is indicated by means of one of three abbreviations in italics (*m*, *f*, *n*) after the headword.* Each inflected entry is followed, in square brackets [ ], by a figure which serves as reference to a definite paradigm within the system of conjugation and declension listed at the end of this book. Any variants of these paradigms are stated after the reference figure of each headword in question.

---

* For users of part II: Any Russian noun ending in a consonant *or* -й is of masculine gender;
those ending in -а *or* -я are of feminine gender;
those ending in -о *or* -е are of neuter gender.
In cases where this rule does not apply, as well as in nouns ending in -ь, the gender is indicated.

Example:

**ло́жка** *f* [5; *g/pl.*: -жек], like ло́жа *f* [5], is declined according to paradigm 5, except that in the genitive plural the former example inserts the "epenthetic" e between the two last stem consonants: ло́жек; cf. **ло́дка** *f* [5; *g/pl.*: -док] = [*g/pl.*: ло́док].

**кусо́к** *m* [1; -ска́] = the "epenthetic" o is omitted in the oblique cases of the singular and in all cases of the plural; cf. **коне́ц** *m* [1; -нца́] = [конца́, концу́, etc.].

As the prefixed forms of a verb follow the same inflection model and (with the exception of perfective aspects having the stressed prefix вы́-) mode of accentuation as the corresponding unprefixed verb, differences in stress, etc. have in cases of such aspect pairs been marked but once, viz. with the imperfective form.

5. **Government.** Case government, except for the accusative, is indicated with the help of Latin and Russian abbreviations. Emphasis has been laid on differences between the two languages, including the use of prepositions. Whenever a special case of government applies only to one of several meanings of a word, this has been duly recorded in connection with the meaning concerned. To ensure a clear differentiation of person and thing in government, the English and Russian notes to that effect show the necessary correspondence in sequence.

6. **Semantic distinction.** If a word has different meanings and, at the same time, different forms of inflection or aspect, this has been indicated by numbers (e. g. бить, коса́, коси́ть); otherwise a semicolon separates different meanings, a comma mere synonyms. Sense indicators in italics serve to specify individual shades of meanings, e. g. **поднима́ть** ... *трево́гу, пла́ту* raise; *ору́жие* take up; *флаг* hoist; *я́корь* weigh; *паруса́* set; *шум* make; **приёмный** ... *часы́* office; *экза́мен* entrance; *оте́ц, сын* foster.

   In a number of Russian verbs the perfective aspect indicated (particularly with the prefixes <за-> and <по->) has, strictly speaking, the connotations "to begin to do s. th." (the former) and "to do s. th. for a (little) while" (the latter); but since these forms are very often rendered in English by means of the equivalent verb without any such additions they have occasionally been given as simple aspect counterparts without explicit indication as to their aforesaid connotations.

7. **Orthography.** In both the Russian and English parts newest spelling standards have been applied, and in the latter differences between American and British usage noted wherever possible and feasible.

   Words at the end of a line which are always hyphenated are indicated by repetition of the hyphen (at the end of the first line and the beginning of the next line).

   In parts of words or additions given in brackets a hyphen is placed within the bracket.

# Abbreviations Used in the Dictionary
## English Abbreviations

| | | |
|---|---|---|
| also | *a.* | та́кже |
| abbreviation | *abbr.* | сокраще́ние |
| accusative (case) | *ac.* | вини́тельный паде́ж |
| adjective | *adj.* | и́мя прилага́тельное |
| adverb | *adv.* | наре́чие |
| aeronautics | *ae.* | авиа́ция |
| agriculture | *agric.* | се́льское хозя́йство |
| Americanism | *Am.* | американи́зм |
| anatomy | *anat.* | анато́мия |
| architecture | *arch.* | архитекту́ра |
| astronomy | *astr.* | астроно́мия |
| attributive usage | *attr.* | атрибути́вное употребле́ние (т. е. в ка́честве определе́ния) |
| Biblical | *Bibl.* | библе́йский |
| biology | *biol.* | биоло́гия |
| British (English) usage | *Brt.* | брита́нское (англи́йское) словоупотребле́ние |
| botany | *bot.* | бота́ника |
| bad sense | *b.s.* | в дурно́м смы́сле |
| chemistry | *chem.* | хи́мия |
| cinema | *cine.* | кинематогра́фия |
| conjunction | *cj.* | сою́з |
| colloquial usage | *coll.* | разгово́рный язы́к |
| collective (noun) | *collect.* | собира́тельное и́мя (существи́тельное) |
| commonly | *com.* | обыкнове́нно |
| commercial term | *comm.* | торго́вля |
| comparative (form) | *comp.* | сравни́тельная сте́пень |
| compounds | *compds.* | сло́жные слова́ |
| computer | *comput.* | компью́терная те́хника |
| contemptuously | *contp.* | пренебрежи́тельно |
| culinary term | *cul.* | кулина́рия |
| dative (case) | *dat.* | да́тельный паде́ж |
| diminutive | *dim.* | уменьши́тельная фо́рма |
| diplomacy | *dipl.* | диплома́тия |
| endings stressed (throughout) | *e.* | ударе́ние (сплошь) наоконча́ниях |
| ecclesiastical term | *eccl.* | церко́вное выраже́ние |
| economy | *econ.* | эконо́мика |
| education | *educ.* | шко́ла, шко́льное де́ло, педаго́гика |

| | | |
|---|---|---|
| for example | *e.g.* | напримéр |
| electrical engineering | *el.* | электротéхника |
| especially | *esp.* | осóбенно |
| et cetera (and so on) | *etc.* | и т. д. (и так дáлее) |
| euphemism | *euph.* | эвфеми́зм |
| feminine (gender) | *f* | жéнский род |
| figurative usage | *fig.* | в перенóсном значéнии |
| financial term | *fin.* | финáнсы, бáнковое дéло |
| feminine plural | *f/pl.* | мнóжественное числó жéнского рóда |
| future (tense) | *ft.* | бýдущее врéмя |
| genitive (case) | *gen.* | роди́тельный падéж |
| geography | *geogr.* | геогрáфия |
| geology | *geol.* | геолóгия |
| gerund | *ger.* | герýндий (деепричáстие) |
| genitive plural | *g/pl.* | роди́тельный падéж мнóжественного числá |
| present (past) gerund | *g. pr.* (*pt.*) | деепричáстие настоя́щего (прошéдшего) врéмени |
| grammar | *gr.* | граммáтика |
| history | *hist.* | истóрия |
| horticulture | *hort.* | садовóдство |
| hunting | *hunt.* | охóта |
| impersonal (form) | *impers.* | безли́чная фóрма, безли́чно |
| imperfective (aspect) | *impf.* | несовершéнный вид |
| imperfective and perfective (aspect) | (*im*)*pf.* | несовершéнный и совершéнный вид |
| indeclinable word | *indecl.* | несклоня́емое слóво |
| infinitive | *inf.* | инфинити́в, неопределённая фóрма глагóла |
| instrumental (case) | *instr.* | твори́тельный падéж |
| interjection | *int.* | междомéтие |
| interrogative(ly) | *interr.* | вопроси́тельная фóрма, вопроси́тельно |
| ironically | *iro.* | ирони́чески |
| irregular | *irr.* | непрáвильная фóрма |
| iterative, frequentative (aspect) | *iter.* | многокрáтный вид |
| jocular | *joc.* | шутли́во |
| linguistics | *ling.* | лингви́стика |
| literary | *lit.* | кни́жное выражéние |
| masculine (gender) | *m* | мужскóй род |
| mathematics | *math.* | матемáтика |
| medicine | *med.* | медици́на |

| | | |
|---|---|---|
| military term | *mil.* | вое́нный те́рмин |
| mineralogy | *min.* | минерало́гия |
| motoring | *mot.* | автомобили́зм |
| masculine plural | *m/pl.* | мно́жественное число́ мужско́го ро́да |
| mostly | *mst.* | бо́льшей ча́стью |
| musical term | *mus.* | му́зыка |
| neuter (gender) | *n* | сре́дний род |
| nautical term | *naut.* | судохо́дство |
| number | *no.* | но́мер |
| nominative (case) | *nom.* | имени́тельный паде́ж |
| neuter plural | *n/pl.* | мно́жественное число́ сре́днего ро́да |
| one another | *o. a.* | друг дру́га, друг дру́гу |
| obsolete | *obs.* | устаре́вшее сло́во, выраже́ние |
| semelfactive (aspect) | *once* | однокра́тный вид |
| oneself | *o. s.* | себя́, себе́, -ся |
| popular | P | просторе́чие |
| participle | *p.* | прича́стие |
| person | *p.* | лицо́ |
| person | *P.* | челове́к |
| painting | *paint.* | жи́вопись |
| 1. particle; 2. particular(ly) | *part.* | 1. части́ца; 2. осо́бенно |
| partitive genitive | *part. g.* | роди́тельный раздели́тельный |
| pejorative | *pej.* | пейорати́вно, неодобри́тельно |
| person(al form) | *pers.* | лицо́, ли́чная фо́рма |
| perfective (aspect) | *pf.* | соверше́нный вид |
| pharmacy | *pharm.* | фармаце́втика |
| philosophy | *philos.* | филосо́фия |
| photography | *phot.* | фотогра́фия |
| physics | *phys.* | фи́зика |
| plural | *pl.* | мно́жественное число́ |
| poetic | *poet.* | поэти́ческое сло́во, выраже́ние |
| politics | *pol.* | поли́тика |
| possessive (form) | *poss.* | притяжа́тельная фо́рма |
| present participle active (passive) | *p. pr. a.* (*p.*) | действи́тельное (страда́тельное) прича́стие настоя́щего вре́мени |

| | | |
|---|---|---|
| past participle active (passive) | *p. pt. a.* (*p.*) | действи́тельное (страда́тельное) прича́стие проше́дшего вре́мени |
| present (tense) | *pr.* | настоя́щее вре́мя |
| predicative usage | *pred.* | предикати́вное употребле́ние (т. е. в ка́честве именно́й ча́сти сказу́емого) |
| prefix | *pref.* | приста́вка |
| pronoun | *pron.* | местоиме́ние |
| preposition | *prp.* | предло́г |
| preterite, past (tense) | *pt.* | проше́дшее вре́мя |
| railway | *rail.* | железнодоро́жное де́ло |
| reflexive (form) | *refl.* | возвра́тная фо́рма |
| rhetoric | *rhet.* | рито́рика |
| somebody | *s. b.* | кто-(кого́-, кому́-)нибудь |
| somebody's | *s. b. 's.* | че́й-нибудь |
| sewing | *sew.* | шве́йное де́ло |
| singular | *sg.* | еди́нственное число́ |
| short (predicative) form | *sh.* | кра́ткая фо́рма |
| slang | *sl.* | жарго́н |
| stem stressed (throughout) | *st.* | ударе́ние (сплошь) на осно́ве |
| something | *s. th.* | что́-либо |
| substantive, noun | *su.* | и́мя существи́тельное |
| technical | *tech.* | техни́ческий те́рмин |
| telephony | *tel.* | телефо́н |
| thing | *th.* | вещь, предме́т |
| theater | *thea.* | теа́тр |
| typography | *typ.* | типогра́фское де́ло |
| university | *univ.* | университе́т |
| usually | *usu.* | обы́чно |
| auxiliary verb | *v/aux.* | вспомога́тельный глаго́л |
| verb | *vb.* | глаго́л |
| intransitive verb | *v/i.* | неперехо́дный глаго́л |
| reflexive verb | *v/refl.* | возвра́тный глаго́л |
| transitive verb | *v/t.* | перехо́дный глаго́л |
| zoology | *zo.* | зооло́гия |

# Russian Abbreviations

| | | |
|---|---|---|
| имени́тельный паде́ж | И | nominative (case) |
| роди́тельный паде́ж | Р | genitive (case) |
| да́тельный паде́ж | Д | dative (case) |
| вини́тельный паде́ж | В | accusative (case) |
| твори́тельный паде́ж | Т | instrumental (case) |
| предло́жный паде́ж | П | prepositional or locative (case) |
| и так да́лее | и т. д. | etc. (et cetera) |
| и тому́ подо́бное | и т. п. | and the like |
| лати́нский язы́к | лат. | Latin |
| та́кже | тж. | also |

# Russian Pronunciation

## I. Vowels

1. All vowels in stressed position are half-long in Russian.

2. In unstressed position Russian vowels are very short, except in the first pretonic syllable, where this shortness of articulation is less marked. Some vowel letters (notably о, е, я), when read in unstressed position, not only differ in length (quantity), but also change their timbre, i.e. acoustic quality.

| Russian letter | Explanation of its pronunciation | | Transcription symbol |
|---|---|---|---|
| **а** | stressed | = **a** in 'f**a**ther', but shorter:<br>ма́ма ['mamə] *mamma* | a |
| | unstressed | 1. = **a** in the above examples, but shorter – in first pretonic syllable:<br>карма́н [kar'man] *pocket* | a |
| | | 2. = **a** in '**a**go, **a**bout' – in post-tonic or second, etc. pretonic syllable(s):<br>ата́ка [a'takə] *attack*<br>каранда́ш [kəran'daʃ] *pencil* | ə |
| | | 3. = **i** in 's**i**t' – after ч, щ in first pretonic syllable:<br>часы́ [ţʃ̡ɪ'sɨ] *watch*<br>щади́ть [ʃ̡ţʃ̡ɪ'd̡iţ] *spare* | ɪ |
| **е** | Preceding consonant (except ж, ш, ц) is soft. | | |
| | stressed | 1. = **ye** in '**ye**t' – in initial position, i.e. at the beginning of a word, or after a vowel, ъ, ь (if not ё) before a hard consonant:<br>бытие́ [bɨţi'jɛ] *existence*<br>ел [jɛɫ] (*I*) *ate*<br>нет [ņɛt] *no* | jɛ/ɛ |
| | | 2. = **e** in 's**e**t' – after consonants, soft or hard (ж, ш, ц), before a hard consonant, as well as in final position, i.e. at the end of a word, after consonants:<br>на лице́ [naļi'tsɛ] *on the face*<br>шест [ʃɛst] *pole* | ɛ |
| | | 3. = **ya** in **Ya**le; before a soft consonant:<br>ель [jeļ] *fir*<br>петь [p̡eţ] *to sing* | je/e |
| | unstressed | 1. = sit; in initial position and after a vowel preceded by (j)<br>ещё [jɪ'ʃ̡ţʃ̡ɔ] *still*<br>зна́ет ['znajɪt] (*he*, *she*, *it*) *knows*<br>река́ [r̡ɪ'ka] *river* | jɪ/ɪ |

| Russian letter | Explanation of its pronunciation | Transcription symbol |
|---|---|---|
| | 2. = **ы** (cf.) after ж, ш, ц:<br>жена́ [ʒɨ'na] *wife*<br>цена́ [tsɨ'na] *price* | ɨ |
| **ё** | Preceding consonant (except ж, ш, ц) is soft. | |
| | only stressed = **yo** in be**yo**nd<br>ёлка ['jɔłkə] *fir tree*<br>даёт [da'jɔt] (*he*, *she*, *it*) *gives*<br>лёд [ļɔt] *ice* | jɔ/ɔ |
| **и** | Preceding consonant (except ж, ш, ц) is soft. | |
| | 1. stressed = like **ee** in s**ee**n, but shorter – in the instr/sg. of он/оно́ and the oblique forms of они́ initial и- may be pronounced (ji-):<br>и́ва ['ivə] *willow*<br>юри́ст [ju'ŗist] *lawyer*<br>их [ix] *or* [jix] *of them* (*g/pl.*) | i/ji |
| | 2. unstressed = like **ee** in s**ee**n, but shorter – in first pretonic syllable:<br>мину́та [m̧i'nutə] *minute* | i |
| | = **i** in s**i**t – in post-tonic or second, etc. pretonic syllable(s):<br>хо́дит ['xɔḑit] (*he*, *she*, *it*) *goes* | ı |
| | 3. stressed and unstressed = **ы** (cf.) after ж, ш, ц:<br>ши́на ['ʃɨnə] *tire*<br>цили́ндр [tsɨ'ļindr] *cylinder* | ɨ |
| **о** | stressed = **o** in **o**bey: том [tɔm] *volume* | ɔ |
| | unstressed 1. = **o** in **o**bey; in final position of foreign words<br>кака́о [ka'kaɔ] *cocoa* | ɔ |
| | 2. = **a** in f**a**ther, but shorter – in first pretonic syllable:<br>Москва́ [mas'kva] *Moscow* | a |
| | 3. = **a** in **a**go, **a**bout – in post-tonic or second, etc. pretonic syllable(s):<br>со́рок ['sɔrək] *forty*<br>огоро́д [əga'rɔt] *kitchen garden* | ə |
| **у** | stressed and unstressed= like **oo** in b**oo**m, but shorter<br>бу́ду ['budu] (*I*) *will be* | u |
| **ы** | stressed and unstressed= a retracted variety of **i**, as in h**i**ll; no English equivalent:<br>вы [vɨ] *you* | |
| **э** | stressed and unstressed 1. = **e** in s**e**t<br>э́то ['ɛtə] *this*<br>эско́рт [ɛs'kɔrt] *escort* | |

| Russian letter | | Explanation of its pronunciation | Transcription symbol |
|---|---|---|---|
| | | 2. = resembles the English sound **a** in p**a**le (but without the i-component) – before a soft consonant<br>э́ти ['eţı] *these* | e |
| **ю** | Preceding consonant is soft. | | |
| | stressed and unstressed | = like **yu** in **yu**le, but shorter<br>рабо́таю [ra'bɔtəju] (*I*) *work*<br>сюда́ [şu'da] *here* | ju/u |
| **я** | Preceding consonant is soft. | | ja/a |
| | stressed | 1. = **ya** in **ya**rd, but shorter – in initial position, after a vowel and before a hard consonant:<br>я́ма ['jamə] *pit*<br>моя́ [ma'ja] *my*<br>мя́со ['m̦asə] *meat* | |
| | | 2. = **a** in b**a**d – in interpalatal position, i.e. between soft consonants:<br>пять [pæţ] *five* | æ |
| | unstressed | 1. = **a** in '**a**go' (preceded by j after vowels) – in final position:<br>со́я [sɔjə] *soya bean*<br>неде́ля [ņı'ḑeļə] *week* | jə/ə |
| | | 2. = **i** in 's**i**t', but preceded by (j) – in initial position, i.e. also after a vowel and ъ:<br>язы́к [jı'zɨk] *tongue*<br>та́ять ['tajıţ] *to thaw*<br>мясни́к [m̦ış'ņik] *butcher* | jı/ı |

## II. Semivowel

| Russian letter | | Explanation of its pronunciation | Transcription symbol |
|---|---|---|---|
| **й** | | 1. = **y** in **y**et – in initial position, i.e. also after a vowel, in loan words:<br>йод [jɔt] *iodine*<br>майо́р [ma'jɔr] *major* | j |
| | | 2. = in the formation of diphthongs as their second element: | j |
| **ай** | | = (i) of (ai) in t**i**me: май [maj] *May* | aj |
| **ой** | stressed | = **oi** in n**oi**se: бой [bɔj] *fight* | ɔj |
| | unstressed | = **i** in t**i**me: война́ [vaj'na] *war* | aj |
| **уй** | | = **u** in r**u**le + (j): бу́йвол ['bujvəɫ] *buffalo* | uj |
| **ый** | | = ы (cf.) + (j):<br>вы́йти ['vɨjţı] *to go out*<br>кра́сный ['krasnɨj] *red* | ɨj |

| Russian letter | | Explanation of its pronunciation | Transcription symbol |
|---|---|---|---|
| **ий** | | = и (cf.) + (j): | ij |
| | stressed | австри́йка [af'stŗijkə] *Austrian woman* | |
| | unstressed | си́ний ['şiņıj] *blue* | |
| **ей** | stressed | = (j+) **a** in p**a**le:<br>ей [jej] *to her*<br>ле́йка ['ļejkə] *watering-can* | jej/ej |
| | unstressed | = **ee** in s**ee**n, but shorter + (j):<br>сейча́с [şı(j)'ţ∫as] *now* | ıj |
| **юй** | | = to (cf.) + (j):<br>малю́й! [ma'ļuj] *paint!* | juj/uj |
| **яй** | stressed | = (j+) **a** in b**a**d + (j):<br>я́йца ['jæjtsə] *eggs*<br>лентя́й ['ļın'ţæj] *lazy bones* | jæj/æj |
| | unstressed | **yi** in **Yi**ddish:<br>яйцо́ [jı(j)'tsɔ] *egg* | jı |

## III. Consonants

1. As most Russian consonants may be palatalized (or 'softened') there is, in addition to the series of normal ('hard') consonants, an almost complete set of 'soft' parallel sounds. According to traditional Russian spelling, in writing or printing this 'softness' is marked by a combination of such palatalized consonants with the vowels е, ё, и, ю, я or, either in final position or before a consonant, the so-called 'soft sign' (ь). In phonetic transcription palatalized consonants are indicated by means of a small hook, or comma, attached to them. As a rule a hard consonant before a soft one remains hard; only з, с may be softened before palatalized з, с, д, т, н.
2. The following consonants are always hard: ж, ш, ц.
3. The following consonants are always soft: ч, щ.
4. The voiced consonants б, в, г, д, ж, з are pronounced voicelessly (i.e. = п, ф, к, т, ш, с) in final position.
5. The voiced consonants б, в, г, д, ж, з, when followed by (one of) their voiceless counterparts п, ф, к, т, ш, с, are pronounced voicelessly (regressive assimilation) and vice versa: voiceless before voiced is voiced (except that there is no assimilation before в).
6. The articulation of doubled consonants, particularly those following a stressed syllable, is marked by their lengthening.

| Russian letter | | Explanation of its pronunciation | Transcription symbol |
|---|---|---|---|
| **б** | hard | = **b** in **b**ad: брат [brat] *brother* | b |
| | soft | = as in al**b**ion:<br>бе́лка ['ḅełkə] *squirrel* | ḅ |

| Russian letter | | | Explanation of its pronunciation | Transcription symbol |
|---|---|---|---|---|
| **в** | hard | | = **v** in **v**ery: вода́ [va'da] *water* | v |
| | soft | | = as in **v**iew: ве́на ['v̡ɛnə] *vein* | v̡ |
| **г** | hard | | = **g** in **g**un: газ [gas] *gas* | g |
| | soft | | = as in ar**g**ue: гимн [g̡imn] *anthem* | g̡ |
| | | *Note*: | = (v) in endings -ого, -его: больно́го [bal̡'nɔvə] *of the sick* си́него ['s̡in̡ɪvə] *of the blue* ничего́ [n̡ɪt̡ʃ̡ɪ'vɔ] *nothing* | v |
| | | | = (x) in бог *God* and in the combination -гк-, -гч-: мя́гкий ['m̡axk̡ɪj] *soft* мя́гче ['m̡axt̡ʃ̡ɛ] *softer* | x |
| **д** | hard | | = **d** in **d**oor: да́ма ['damə] *lady* | d |
| | soft | | = as in **d**ew: дю́на ['d̡unə] *dune* In the combination -здн- д is mute: по́здно ['pɔznə] *late* | d̡ |
| **ж** | hard | | = **s** in mea**s**ure, but hard: жа́жда ['ʒaʒdə] *thirst* | ʒ |
| | | **жч** | = щ: мужчи́на [mu'ʃ̡t̡ʃ̡inə] *man* | ʃ̡t̡ʃ̡ |
| **з** | hard | | = **z** in **z**oo: зако́н [za'kɔn] *law* | z |
| | soft | | = as in pre**s**ume: зелёный [z̡ɪ'l̡ɔnɨj] *green* | z̡ |
| | | **зж** | = hard or soft doubled ж: по́зже ['pɔʒʒɛ] *or* ['pɔʒ̡ʒ̡ɛ] *later* | ʒʒ/ʒ̡ʒ̡ |
| | | **зч** | = щ: изво́зчик [iz'vɔʃ̡t̡ʃ̡ɪk] *coachman* | ʃ̡t̡ʃ̡ |
| **к** | hard | | = **c** in **c**ome (unaspirated!): как [kak] *how* | k |
| | soft | | = like **k** in **k**ey: ке́пка ['k̡ɛpkə] *cap* | k̡ |
| **л** | hard | | = **ll** in General American call: ла́мпа ['ɫampə] *lamp* | ɫ |
| | soft | | = **ll** in mi**ll**ion: ли́лия ['l̡il̡ɪjə] *lily* | l̡ |
| **м** | hard | | = **m** in **m**an: мать [mat̡] *mother* | m |
| | soft | | = as in **m**ute: метр [m̡ɛtr] *meter* | m̡ |
| **н** | hard | | = **n** in **n**oise: нос [nɔs] *nose* | n |
| | soft | | = **n** in **n**ew: не́бо ['n̡ɛbə] *heaven* | n̡ |
| **п** | hard | | = **p** in **p**art (unaspirated!): па́па ['papə] *daddy* | p |
| | soft | | = as in scor**p**ion: пить [p̡it̡] *to drink* | p̡ |
| **р** | hard | | = trilled **r**: рот [rɔt] *mouth* | r |
| | soft | | = as in O**r**ient: ряд [r̡at] *row* | r̡ |

| Russian letter | | Explanation of its pronunciation | Transcription symbol |
|---|---|---|---|
| **с** | hard | = **s** in **s**ad: сорт [sɔrt] *sort* | s |
| | soft | = as in a**ss**ume: си́ла ['ş̡iłə] *force* | ş |
| | **сч** | = щ: сча́стье ['ʃ̡t̡ʃ̡æşt̡jɛ] *happiness* | ʃ̡t̡ʃ̡ |
| **т** | hard | = **t** in **t**ent (unaspirated!): такт [takt] *measure* | t |
| | soft | = as in **t**une: тепе́рь [t̡ɪ'p̡er̡] *now* | t̡ |
| | | = -стн-, -стл- – in these combinations -т- is mute: изве́стно [iz'v̡ɛsnə] *known* счастли́вый [ʃ̡t̡ʃ̡ɪş'l̡ivɨj] *happy* | |
| **ф** | hard | = **f** in **f**ar: фо́рма ['fɔrmə] *form* | f |
| | soft | = as in **f**ew: фи́рма ['f̡irmə] *firm* | f̡ |
| **х** | hard | = **ch** as in Scottish lo**ch**: ах! [ax] *ah!* | x |
| | soft | = like **ch** in German i**ch**, no English equivalent: хи́мик ['x̡im̡ɪk] *chemist* | x̡ |
| **ц** | nur hard | = **ts** in **ts**ar: царь [tsar̡] *tsar* | ts |
| **ч** | nur soft | = **ch** in **ch**eck: час [t̡ʃ̡as] *hour* | t̡ʃ̡ |
| **ш** | nur hard | = **sh** in **sh**ip, but hard: шар [ʃar] *ball* | ʃ |
| **щ** | nur soft | = **sh** + **ch** in **ch**eck, cf. fre**sh** **ch**eeks, or = doubled (ʃ̡ʃ̡) as in sure: щи [ʃ̡t̡ʃ̡i] *or* [ʃ̡ʃ̡i] *cabbage soup* | ʃ̡t̡ʃ̡ *or* ʃ̡ʃ̡ |

## IV. Surds

| | | | |
|---|---|---|---|
| **ъ** | hard sign | = The *jer* or 'hard sign' separates a hard (final) consonant of a prefix and the initial vowel, preceded by (j), of the following root, thus marking both the hardness of the preceding consonant and the distinct utterance of (j) before the vowel: предъяви́ть [pr̡ɪdjɪ'v̡it̡] 'to show, produce' съезд [sjɛst] 'congress'. | |
| **ь** | soft sign | = The *jer* or 'soft sign' serves to represent the palatal or soft quality of a (preceding) consonant in final position or before another consonant, cf.: брат [brat] 'brother' and брать [brat̡] 'to take' по́лка ['pɔłkə] 'shelf' and по́лька ['pɔl̡kə] 'polka, Pole (= Polish woman)'. | |

| Russian letter | Explanation of its pronunciation | Transcription symbol |
|---|---|---|
| | It is also used before vowels to indicate the softness of a preceding consonant as well as the pronunciation of (j) with the respective vowel, e.g.:<br>семья́ [ş̧ım̧'ja] ‘family’ – *cf.* се́мя ['ş̧em̧ə] ‘seed’,<br>and in foreign words, such as батальо́н [bəta'l̦jɔn] ‘battalion’. | |

# English Pronunciation

## Vowels

| | |
|---|---|
| [ɑː] | *father* ['fɑːðə] |
| [æ] | *man* [mæn] |
| [e] | *get* [get] |
| [ə] | *about* [ə'baʊt] |
| [ɜː] | *first* [fɜːst] |
| [ɪ] | *stick* [stɪk] |
| [iː] | *need* [niːd] |
| [ɒ] | *hot* [hɒt |
| [ɔː] | *law* [lɔː] |
| [ʌ] | *mother* ['mʌðə] |
| [ʊ] | *book* [bʊk] |
| [uː] | *fruit* [fruːt] |

## Diphthongs

| | |
|---|---|
| [aɪ] | *time* [taɪm] |
| [aʊ] | *cloud* [klaʊd] |
| [eɪ] | *name* [neɪm] |
| [eə] | *hair* [heə] |
| [ɪə] | *here* [hɪə] |
| [ɔɪ] | *point* [pɔɪnt] |
| [əʊ] | *oath* [əʊθ] |
| [ʊə] | *tour* [tʊə] |

## Consonants

| | |
|---|---|
| [b] | *bag* [bæg] |
| [d] | *dear* [dɪə] |
| [f] | *fall* [fɔːl] |
| [g] | *give* [gɪv] |
| [h] | *hole* [həʊl] |
| [j] | *yes* [jes] |
| [k] | *come* [kʌm] |
| [l] | *land* [lænd] |
| [m] | *mean* [miːn] |
| [n] | *night* [naɪt] |
| [p] | *pot* [pɒt] |
| [r] | *right* [raɪt] |
| [s] | *sun* [sʌn] |
| [t] | *take* [teɪk] |
| [v] | *vain* [veɪn] |
| [w] | *wait* [weɪt] |
| [z] | *rose* [rəʊz] |
| [ŋ] | *bring* [brɪŋ] |
| [ʃ] | *she* [ʃiː] |
| [tʃ] | *chair* [tʃeə] |
| [dʒ] | *join* [dʒɔɪn] |
| [ʒ] | *leisure* ['leʒə] |
| [θ] | *think* [θɪŋk] |
| [ð] | *the* [ðə] |
| ['] | means that the following syllable is stressed: *ability* [ə'bɪlətɪ] |

# The Russian Alphabet

| printed | | written | | pronounced | transcribed | printed | | written | | pronounced | transcribed |
|---|---|---|---|---|---|---|---|---|---|---|---|
| А | а | *А* | *а* | а | a | П | п | *П* | *п* | пэ | pɛ |
| Б | б | *Б* | *б* | бэ | bɛ | Р | р | *Р* | *р* | эр | ɛr |
| В | в | *В* | *в* | вэ | vɛ | С | с | *С* | *с* | эс | ɛs |
| Г | г | *Г* | *г* | гэ | gɛ | Т | т | *Т* | *т* | тэ | tɛ |
| Д | д | *Д* | *д* | дэ | dɛ | У | у | *У* | *у* | у | u |
| Е | е | *Е* | *е* | е | jɛ | Ф | ф | *Ф* | *ф* | эф | ɛf |
| Ё | ё | *Ё* | *ё* | ё | jɔ | Х | х | *Х* | *х* | ха | xa |
| Ж | ж | *Ж* | *ж* | жэ | ʒɛ | Ц | ц | *Ц* | *ц* | цэ | tsɛ |
| З | з | *З* | *з* | зэ | zɛ | Ч | ч | *Ч* | *ч* | че | t̡ʃ̡e |
| И | и | *И* | *и* | и | i | Ш | ш | *Ш* | *ш* | ша | ʃa |
| Й | й | *Й* | *й* | и[1]) | | Щ | щ | *Щ* | *щ* | ща | ʃ̡t̡ʃ̡a |
| К | к | *К* | *к* | ка | ka | Ъ | ъ | – | *ъ* | [2]) | |
| Л | л | *Л* | *л* | эль | ɛl̦ | Ы | ы | – | *ы* | ы[3]) | ɨ |
| М | м | *М* | *м* | эм | ɛm | Ь | ь | – | *ь* | [4]) | |
| Н | н | *Н* | *н* | эн | ɛn | Э | э | *Э* | *э* | э[5]) | ɛ |
| О | о | *О* | *о* | о | ɔ | Ю | ю | *Ю* | *ю* | ю | iu |
| | | | | | | Я | я | *Я* | *я* | я | ia |

[1]) и кра́ткое short i
[2]) твёрдый знак hard sign
[3]) *or* еры́
[4]) мя́гкий знак soft sign
[5]) э оборо́тное reversed e

# Important English Irregular Verbs

| | | |
|---|---|---|
| **alight** | alighted, alit | alighted, alit |
| **arise** | arose | arisen |
| **awake** | awoke | awoken, awaked |
| **be** (am, is, are) | was (were) | been |
| **bear** | bore | borne |
| **beat** | beat | beaten |
| **become** | became | become |
| **begin** | began | begun |
| **behold** | beheld | beheld |
| **bend** | bent | bent |
| **beseech** | besought, beseeched | besought, beseeched |
| **bet** | bet, betted | bet, betted |
| **bid** | bade, bid | bidden, bid |
| **bind** | bound | bound |
| **bite** | bit | bitten |
| **bleed** | bled | bled |
| **blow** | blew | blown |
| **break** | broke | broken |
| **breed** | bred | bred |
| **bring** | brought | brought |
| **broadcast** | broadcast | broadcast |
| **build** | built | built |
| **burn** | burnt, burned | burnt, burned |
| **burst** | burst | burst |
| **bust** | bust(ed) | bust(ed) |
| **buy** | bought | bought |
| **cast** | cast | cast |
| **catch** | caught | caught |
| **choose** | chose | chosen |
| **cleave** (*cut*) | clove, cleft | cloven, cleft |
| **cling** | clung | clung |
| **come** | came | come |
| **cost** | cost | cost |
| **creep** | crept | crept |
| **crow** | crowed, crew | crowed |
| **cut** | cut | cut |
| **deal** | dealt | dealt |
| **dig** | dug | dug |
| **do** | did | done |
| **draw** | drew | drawn |
| **dream** | dreamt, dreamed | dreamt, dreamed |
| **drink** | drank | drunk |
| **drive** | drove | driven |
| **dwell** | dwelt, dwelled | dwelt, dwelled |
| **eat** | ate | eaten |
| **fall** | fell | fallen |
| **feed** | fed | fed |
| **feel** | felt | felt |
| **fight** | fought | fought |
| **find** | found | found |
| **flee** | fled | fled |

| | | |
|---|---|---|
| **fling** | flung | flung |
| **fly** | flew | flown |
| **forbear** | forbore | forborne |
| **forbid** | forbad(e) | forbidden |
| **forecast** | forecast(ed) | forecast(ed) |
| **forget** | forgot | forgotten |
| **forgive** | forgave | forgiven |
| **forsake** | forsook | forsaken |
| **freeze** | froze | frozen |
| **get** | got | got, *Am.* gotten |
| **give** | gave | given |
| **go** | went | gone |
| **grind** | ground | ground |
| **grow** | grew | grown |
| **hang** | hung, (*v/t*) hanged | hung, (*v/t*) hanged |
| **have** | had | had |
| **hear** | heard | heard |
| **heave** | heaved, hove | heaved, hove |
| **hew** | hewed | hewed, hewn |
| **hide** | hid | hidden |
| **hit** | hit | hit |
| **hold** | held | held |
| **hurt** | hurt | hurt |
| **keep** | kept | kept |
| **kneel** | knelt, kneeled | knelt, kneeled |
| **know** | knew | known |
| **lay** | laid | laid |
| **lead** | led | led |
| **lean** | leaned, leant | leaned, leant |
| **leap** | leaped, leapt | leaped, leapt |
| **learn** | learned, learnt | learned, learnt |
| **leave** | left | left |
| **lend** | lent | lent |
| **let** | let | let |
| **lie** | lay | lain |
| **light** | lighted, lit | lighted, lit |
| **lose** | lost | lost |
| **make** | made | made |
| **mean** | meant | meant |
| **meet** | met | met |
| **mow** | mowed | mowed, mown |
| **pay** | paid | paid |
| **plead** | pleaded, pled | pleaded, pled |
| **prove** | proved | proved, proven |
| **put** | put | put |
| **quit** | quit(ted) | quit(ted) |
| **read** [riːd] | read [red] | read [red] |
| **rend** | rent | rent |
| **rid** | rid | rid |
| **ride** | rode | ridden |
| **ring** | rang | rung |
| **rise** | rose | risen |
| **run** | ran | run |
| **saw** | sawed | sawn, sawed |

| | | |
|---|---|---|
| **say** | said | said |
| **see** | saw | seen |
| **seek** | sought | sought |
| **sell** | sold | sold |
| **send** | sent | sent |
| **set** | set | set |
| **sew** | sewed | sewed, sewn |
| **shake** | shook | shaken |
| **shear** | sheared | sheared, shorn |
| **shed** | shed | shed |
| **shine** | shone | shone |
| **shit** | shit(ted), shat | shit(ted), shat |
| **shoe** | shod | shod |
| **shoot** | shot | shot |
| **show** | showed | shown |
| **shrink** | shrank | shrunk |
| **shut** | shut | shut |
| **sing** | sang | sung |
| **sink** | sank | sunk |
| **sit** | sat | sat |
| **slay** | slew | slain |
| **sleep** | slept | slept |
| **slide** | slid | slid |
| **sling** | slung | slung |
| **slink** | slunk | slunk |
| **slit** | slit | slit |
| **smell** | smelt, smelled | smelt, smelled |
| **smite** | smote | smitten |
| **sow** | sowed | sown, sowed |
| **speak** | spoke | spoken |
| **speed** | sped, speeded | sped, speeded |
| **spell** | spelt, spelled | spelt, spelled |
| **spend** | spent | spent |
| **spill** | spilt, spilled | spilt, spilled |
| **spin** | spun, span | spun |
| **spit** | spat | spat |
| **split** | split | split |
| **spoil** | spoiled, spoilt | spoiled, spoilt |
| **spread** | spread | spread |
| **spring** | sprang, sprung | sprung |
| **stand** | stood | stood |
| **stave** | staved, stove | staved, stove |
| **steal** | stole | stolen |
| **stick** | stuck | stuck |
| **sting** | stung | stung |
| **stink** | stunk, stank | stunk |
| **strew** | strewed | strewed, strewn |
| **stride** | strode | stridden |
| **strike** | struck | struck |
| **string** | strung | strung |
| **strive** | strove | striven |
| **swear** | swore | sworn |
| **sweep** | swept | swept |
| **swell** | swelled | swollen |

| | | |
|---|---|---|
| **swim** | swam | swum |
| **swing** | swung | swung |
| **take** | took | taken |
| **teach** | taught | taught |
| **tear** | tore | torn |
| **tell** | told | told |
| **think** | thought | thought |
| **thrive** | throve | thriven |
| **throw** | threw | thrown |
| **thrust** | thrust | thrust |
| **tread** | trod | trodden |
| **understand** | understood | understood |
| **wake** | woke, waked | woken, waked |
| **wear** | wore | worn |
| **weave** | wove | woven |
| **wed** | wed(ded) | wed(ded) |
| **weep** | wept | wept |
| **wet** | wet(ted) | wet(ted) |
| **win** | won | won |
| **wind** | wound | wound |
| **wring** | wrung | wrung |
| **write** | wrote | written |

# Russian – English

# Russian – English

## A

**а 1.** *cj.* but; ***а то*** or (else), otherwise; ***а что?*** why (so)?; **2.** *int.* ah!; **3.** *part.*, *coll.* eh?
**аб|ажу́р** *m* [1] lampshade; **~ба́т** *m* [1] abbot; **~ба́тство** *n* [9] abbey; **~за́ц** *m* [1] paragraph; **~онеме́нт** *m* [1] subscription; **~оне́нт** *m* [1] subscriber; **~о́рт** *m* [1] abortion; **~рико́с** *m* [1] apricot; **~солю́тный** [14; -тен, -тна] absolute; **~стра́ктный** [14; -тен, -тна] abstract; **~су́рд** *m* [1] absurdity; ***довести́ до ~су́рда*** carry to the point of absurdity; **~су́рдный** [14; -ден, -дна] absurd; **~сце́сс** *m* [1] abscess
**аван|га́рд** *m* [1] avant-garde; **~по́ст** *m* [1] outpost; **~с** *m* [1] advance (of money); **~сом** (payment) in advance; **~тю́ра** *f* [5] adventure, shady enterprise; **~тюри́ст** *m* [1] adventurer; **~тюри́стка** *f* [5; *g/pl.*: -ток] adventuress
**авар|и́йный** [14] emergency…; **~ия** *f* [7] accident; *mot.*, *ae.* crash; *tech.* breakdown
**а́вгуст** *m* [1] August
**авиа|ба́за** *f* [5] air base; **~биле́т** *m* [1] airline ticket; **~констру́ктор** *m* [1] aircraft designer; **~ли́ния** *f* [7] airline; **~но́сец** *m* [1; -сца] aircraft carrier; **~по́чта** *f* [5] air mail; **~тра́сса** *f* [5] air route; **~цио́нный** [14] air-(craft)…; **~ция** *f* [7] aviation, aircraft *pl.*
**аво́сь** *part. coll.* perhaps, maybe; ***на ~*** on the off chance
**австр|али́ец** *m* [1; -и́йца], **~али́йка** *f* [5; *g/pl.*: -и́ек], **~али́йский** [16] Australian; **~и́ец** *m* [1; -и́йца], **~и́йка** *f* [5; *g/pl.*: -и́ек], **~и́йский** [16] Austrian
**автобиогр|афи́ческий** [16], **~афи́чный** [14; -чен, -чна] autobiographic(al); **~а́фия** *f* [7] autobiography
**авто́бус** *m* [1] (motor) bus
**авто|вокза́л** *m* [1] bus *or* coach station; **~го́нки** *f/pl.* [5; *gen.*: -нок] (car) race; **~граф** *m* [1] autograph; **~заво́д** *m* [1] car factory, automobile plant; **~запра́вочный** [14] ***~запра́вочная ста́нция*** filling station; **~кра́тия** *f* [7] autocracy; **~магистра́ль** *f* [8] highway; **~ма́т** *m* [1] automaton; *игорный* slot machine; *mil.* submachine gun; *coll.* telephone box *or* booth; **~мати́ческий** [16], **~мати́чный** [14; -чен, -чна] automatic; **~ма́тчик** *m* [1] submachine gunner; **~маши́на** *f* [5] → ***~моби́ль***; **~мобили́ст** *m* [1] motorist; **~моби́ль** *m* [4] (motor-) car; ***го́ночный ~моби́ль*** racing car, racer; **~но́мия** *f* [7] autonomy; **~отве́тчик** *m* [1] answering machine; **~портре́т** *m* [1] self-portrait
**а́втор** *m* [1] author; **~изова́ть** [7] *(im)pf.* authorize; **~ите́т** *m* [1] authority; **~ский** [16] author's; ***~ское пра́во*** copyright; **~ство** *n* [9] authorship
**авто|ру́чка** *f* [5; *g/pl.*: -чек] fountain pen; **~стоя́нка** *f* [5; *g/pl.*: -нок] parking (space); **~стра́да** *f* [5] high-speed, multilane highway
**ага́** (*int.*) aha!; (oh,) I see!
**аге́нт** *m* [1] agent; **~ство** *n* [9] agency
**агити́ровать** [7], ⟨c-⟩ *pol.* carry on agitation, campaign; *coll.* (*убеждать*) (try to) persuade
**агра́рный** [14] agrarian
**агрега́т** *m* [1] *tech.* unit, assembly
**агресс|и́вный** [14; -вен, -вна] aggressive; **~ия** *f* [7] aggression
**агро|но́м** *m* [1] agronomist; **~номи́ческий** [16] agronomic(al); **~но́мия** *f* [7] agronomy
**ад** *m* [1; в ~у́] hell
**ада́птер** (-tɛr) *m* [1] *el.* adapter
**адвока́т** *m* [1] lawyer, attorney (at law), *Brt.* barrister; solicitor; **~у́ра** *f* [5] the legal profession

**адеква́тный** [14; -тен, -тна] (*совпадающий*) coincident; adequate
**адми|нистрати́вный** [14] administrative; **~нистра́ция** *f* [7] administration; **~ра́л** *m* [1] admiral
**а́дрес** *m* [1; *pl.*: -á, *etc. e.*] address (**не по** Д at wrong); **~а́т** *m* [1] addressee; (*грузополучатель*) consignee; **~ова́ть** [7] (*im*)*pf.* address, direct
**а́дски** *coll.* awfully, terribly
**а́дский** [16] hellish, infernal
**адъюта́нт** *m* [1] aide-de-camp
**адюльте́р** *m* [1] adultery
**ажиота́ж** *m* [1] hullabaloo; **~ный** [14; -жен, -жна]: ***~ный спрос*** unusually high demand (for **на** B)
**аз** *m* [1 *e.*]: **~ы́** *pl.* basics, elements; *coll.* **с *~о́в*** from scratch
**аза́рт** *m* [1] passion, heat, enthusiasm; ***войти́ в ~*** get excited; **~ный** [14; -тен, -тна] passionate, enthusiastic; ***~ные и́гры*** games of chance
**а́збу|ка** *f* [5] alphabet; **~чный** [14] alphabetic(al); ***~чная и́стина*** truism
**азербайджа́|нец** *m* [1; -нца], **~нка** *f* [5; *g*/*pl.*: -нок] Azerbaijani(an); **~нский** [16] Azerbaijani(an)
**азиа́т** *m* [1], **~ка** *f* [5; *g*/*pl.*: -ток], **~ский** [16] Asian, Asiatic
**азо́т** *m* [1] nitrogen; **~ный** [14] nitric
**а́ист** *m* [1] stork
**ай** *int.* ah! oh!; *при боли* ouch!
**айва́** *f* [5] quince
**а́йсберг** *m* [1] iceberg
**акаде́м|ик** *m* [1] academician; **~и́ческий** [16] academic; **~ия** *f* [7] academy; ***Акаде́мия нау́к*** academy of sciences; ***Акаде́мия худо́жеств*** academy of arts
**ака́ция** *f* [7] acacia
**аквала́нг** *m* [1] aqualung
**акваре́ль** *f* [8] water colo(u)r
**акклиматизи́ровать(ся)** [7] (*im*)*pf.* acclimatize
**аккомпан|еме́нт** *m* [1] *mus.*, *fig.* accompaniment; **~и́ровать** [7] *mus.* accompany
**акко́рд** *m* [1] *mus.* chord
**аккредит|и́в** *m* [1] letter of credit; **~ова́ть** [7] (*im*)*pf.* accredit
**аккумул|и́ровать** [7] (*im*)*pf.* accumulate; **~я́тор** *m* [1] battery
**аккура́тный** [14; -тен, -тна] (*исполнительный*) accurate; punctual; *работа и т. д.* tidy, neat
**аксессуа́ры** *m* [1] accessories
**акт** *m* [1] act(ion); *thea.* act; document; *parl.* bill; **~ёр** *m* [1] actor
**акти́в** *m* [1] *fin.* asset(s); **~ный** [14; -вен, -вна] active
**актри́са** *f* [5] actress
**актуа́льный** [14; -лен, -льна] topical, current
**аку́ла** *f* [5] shark
**аку́сти|ка** *f* [5] acoustics; **~ческий** [16] acoustic(al)
**акуше́р|ка** *f* [5; *g*/*pl.*: -рок] midwife; **~ство** *n* [9] obstetrics, midwifery
**акце́нт** *m* [1] accent; (*ударение*) stress
**акци|оне́р** *m* [1] stockholder, *Brt.* shareholder; **~оне́рный** [14] jointstock (company); **~они́ровать** [7] turn into a joint-stock company; **~я**[1] *f* [7] share; *pl. a.* stock; **~я**[2] *f* [7] action, démarche
**алба́н|ец** *m* [1; -ца], **~ка** *f* [5; *g*/*pl.*: -ок], **~ский** [16] Albanian
**а́лгебра** *f* [5] algebra
**алеба́стр** *m* [1] alabaster
**але́ть** [8] blush, grow red; *заря и т. д.* glow
**алиме́нты** *m*/*pl.* [1] alimony
**алкого́л|ик** *m* [1] alcoholic; **~ь** *m* [4] alcohol
**аллегори́ческий** [16] allegorical
**аллерг|е́н** *m* [1] allergen; **~ик** *m* [1] one prone to allergy; **~и́ческий** [16] allergic; **~и́я** *f* [7] allergy
**алле́я** *f* [6; *g*/*pl.*: -е́й] avenue, lane
**алма́з** *m* [1], **~ный** [14] *uncut* diamond
**алта́рь** *m* [4 *e.*] altar
**алфави́т** *m* [1] alphabet; **~ный** [14] alphabetical
**а́лчн|ость** *f* [7] greed(iness); **~ый** [14; -чен, -чна] greedy (of, for **к** Д)
**а́лый** [14 *sh.*] red
**альбо́м** *m* [1] album; sketchbook
**альмана́х** *m* [1] literary miscellany
**альпини́|зм** *m* [1] mountaineering; **~ст** *m* [1], **~стка** *f* [5; *g*/*pl.*: -ток] mountain climber

**альт** *m* [1 *e*.] alto; *инструмент* viola
**алюми́ний** *m* [3] alumin(i)um
**амба́р** *m* [1] barn; *для хранения зерна* granary
**амбулато́рный** [14]: **~ *больно́й*** outpatient
**америка́н|ец** *m* [1; -нца], **~ка** *f* [5; *g/pl.*: -ок], **~ский** [16] American
**ами́нь** *part.* amen
**амнисти́|ровать** [7] *(im)pf.*; **~я** *f* [7] amnesty
**амортиз|а́тор** *m* [1] shock absorber; **~а́ция** *f* [7] amortization, depreciation
**амо́рфный** [14; -фен, -фна] amorphous
**амплиту́да** *f* [5] amplitude
**амплуа́** *n* [*indecl.*] *thea.* type, role
**а́мпула** *f* [5] ampoule
**ампут|а́ция** *f* [7] amputation; **~и́ровать** [7] *(im)pf.* amputate
**амфи́бия** *f* [7] amphibian
**амфитеа́тр** *m* [1] amphitheater (-tre); *thea.* circle
**ана́ли|з** *m* [1] analysis; **~зи́ровать** [7] *(im)pf.*, ⟨про-⟩ analyze, -se
**аналог|и́чный** [14; -чен, -чна] analogous, similar; **~ия** *f* [7] analogy
**анана́с** *m* [1] pineapple
**ана́рхия** *f* [7] anarchy
**анато́мия** *f* [7] anatomy
**анга́р** *m* [1] hangar
**а́нгел** *m* [1] angel
**анги́на** *f* [5] tonsillitis
**англи́|йский** [16] English; **~ст** *m* [1] specialist in English studies; **~ча́нин** *m* [1; *pl.*: -ча́не, -ча́н] Englishman; **~ча́нка** *f* [5; *g/pl.*: -нок] Englishwoman
**анекдо́т** *m* [1] anecdote; **~и́чный** [14; -чен, -чна] anecdotal; (*маловероятный*) improbable
**ане|ми́я** *f* [7] anemia; **~стези́я** (-nɛstɛ-) *f* [7] anaesthesia
**ани́с** *m* [1] anise
**анке́та** *f* [5] questionnaire; (*бланк*) form
**аннекс|и́ровать** [7] *(im)pf.* annex; **~ия** *f* [7] annexation
**аннули́ровать** [7] *(im)pf.* annul, cancel
**анома́лия** *f* [7] anomaly
**анони́мный** [14; -мен, -мна] anonymous
**анса́мбль** *m* [4] ensemble, *thea.* company
**антагони́зм** *m* [1] antagonism
**антаркти́ческий** [16] antarctic
**анте́нна** (-'tɛn-) *f* [5] aerial, antenna
**антибио́тик** *m* [1] antibiotic
**антиква́р** *m* [1] antiquary; dealer in antique goods; **~иа́т** *m* [1] antiques; **~ный** [14] antiquarian
**антило́па** *f* [5] antelope
**анти|пати́чный** [14; -чен, -чна] antipathetic; **~па́тия** *f* [7] antipathy; **~санита́рный** [14] insanitary; **~семити́зм** *m* [1] anti-Semitism; **~се́птика** *f* [5] antisepsis, *collect.* antiseptics
**анти́чн|ость** *f* [8] antiquity; **~ый** [14] ancient, classical
**антоло́гия** *f* [7] anthology
**антра́кт** *m* [1] *thea.* intermission, *Brt.* interval
**антропо́л|ог** *m* [1] anthropologist; **~о́гия** *f* [7] anthropology
**анчо́ус** *m* [1] anchovy
**аню́тины** [14]: **~ *гла́зки*** *m/pl.* [1; *g/pl.*: -зок] pansy
**апат|и́чный** [14; -чен, -чна] apathetic; **~ия** *f* [7] apathy
**апелл|и́ровать** [7] *(im)pf.* appeal (to **к** Д); **~яцио́нный** [14] (*court*) of appeal; **~яцио́нная жа́лоба** = **~я́ция** *f* [7] *law* appeal
**апельси́н** *m* [1] orange
**аплоди́|ровать** [7], ⟨за-⟩ applaud; **~сме́нты** *m/pl.* [1] applause
**апло́мб** *m* [1] self-confidence, aplomb
**апоге́й** *m* [3] *ast.* apogee; *fig.* climax
**апо́стол** *m* [1] apostle
**апофео́з** *m* [1] apotheosis
**аппара́т** *m* [1] apparatus; *phot.* camera; **~у́ра** *f collect.* [5] apparatus, gear, *comput.* hardware
**аппе́нд|икс** *m* [1] *anat.* appendix; **~ици́т** *m* [1] appendicitis
**аппети́т** *m* [1] appetite; ***прия́тного ~а!*** bon appetite!; **~ный** [14; -и́тен, -и́тна] appetizing
**апре́ль** *m* [4] April
**апте́ка** *f* [5] drugstore, *Brt.* chemist's shop; **~рь** *m* [4] druggist, *Brt.* (pharmaceutical) chemist
**апте́чка** *f* [5; *g/pl.*: -чек] first-aid kit
**ара́|б** *m* [1], **~бка** *f* [5; *g/pl.*: -бок] Arab;

**~бский** (**~вийский**) [16] Arabian, Arabic, Arab (*League*, *etc.*); **~п** *m* [1] *obs.* Moor, Negro
**арби́тр** *m* [1] arbiter; umpire, referee; **~а́ж** *m* [1] *law* arbitration, arbitrage
**арбу́з** *m* [1] watermelon
**аргенти́н|ец** *m* [1; -нца], **~ка** *f* [5; *g/pl.*: -нок], **~ский** [16] Argentine
**аргуме́нт** *m* [1] argument; **~а́ция** *f* [7] reasoning, argumentation; **~и́ровать** [7] (*im*)*pf.* argue
**аре́на** *f* [5] arena
**аре́нд|а** *f* [5] lease, rent; ***сдава́ть*** (***брать***) ***в ~у*** lease (rent); **~а́тор** *m* [1] lessee, tenant; **~ова́ть** [7] (*im*)*pf.* rent, lease
**аре́ст** *m* [1] arrest; **~о́ванный** *su.* [14] prisoner; **~о́вывать** [1], ⟨**~ова́ть**⟩ [7] arrest
**аристокра́тия** *f* [7] aristocracy
**аритми́я** *f* [7] *med.* arrhythmia
**арифме́т|ика** *f* [5] arithmetic; **~и́ческий** [16] arithmetic(al)
**а́рия** *f* [7] aria
**а́рка** *f* [5; *g/pl.*: -рок] arc; arch
**арка́да** *f* [5] arcade
**аркти́ческий** [16] arctic
**армату́ра** *f* [5] fittings, armature
**а́рмия** *f* [7] army
**армян|и́н** *m* [1; *pl.*: -мя́не, -мя́н], **~ка** *f* [5; *g/pl.*: -нок], **~ский** [16] Armenian
**арома́т** *m* [1] aroma, perfume, fragrance; **~и́ческий** [16], **~ный** [14; -тен, -тна] aromatic, fragrant
**арсена́л** *m* [1] arsenal
**арте́ль** *f* [8] workmen's *or* peasants' cooperative, association
**арте́рия** *f* [7] artery
**арти́кль** *m* [4] *gr.* article
**артилле́р|ия** *f* [7] artillery; **~и́ст** *m* [1] artilleryman; **~и́йский** [16] artillery…
**арти́ст** *m* [1] artist(e); actor; **~ка** *f* [5; *g/pl.*: -ток] artist(e); actress
**артишо́к** *m* [1] artichoke
**а́рфа** *f* [5] harp
**архео́лог** *m* [1] archeologist; **~и́ческий** [16] archeologic(al); **~ия** *f* [7] archeology
**архи́в** *m* [1] archives *pl.*
**архиепи́скоп** *m* [1] archbishop
**архипела́г** *m* [1] archipelago
**архите́кт|ор** *m* [1] architect; **~у́ра** *f* [5] architecture; **~у́рный** [14] architectural
**арши́н** *m* [1; *g/pl.*: арши́н]: ***ме́рить на свой ~*** measure by one's own yardstick
**асбе́ст** *m* [1] asbestos
**аске́т** *m* [1] ascetic; **~и́ческий** [16] ascetic(al)
**аспира́нт** *m* [1] postgraduate; **~у́ра** *f* [5] postgraduate study
**ассамбле́я** *f* [6; *g/pl.*: -ле́й]: ***Генера́льная ~ Организа́ции Объединённых На́ций*** United Nations' General Assembly
**ассигнова́|ть** [7] (*im*)*pf.* assign, allocate, allot; **~ние** *n* [12] assignment, allocation, allotment
**ассимил|и́ровать** [7] (*im*)*pf.* assimilate, (**-ся** o.s.); **~я́ция** *f* [7] assimilation
**ассисте́нт** *m* [1], **~ка** *f* [5; *g/pl.*: -ток] assistant; *univ.* junior member of research staff
**ассортиме́нт** *m* [1] assortment, range
**ассоци|а́ция** *f* [7] association; **~и́ровать** [7] associate
**а́стма** *f* [5] asthma
**а́стра** *f* [5] aster
**астроно́м** *m* [1] astronomer; **~и́ческий** [16] astronomic(al) (*a. fig.*); **~ия** *f* [7] astronomy
**асфа́льт** *m* [1] asphalt
**ата́к|а** *f* [5] attack, charge; **~ова́ть** [7] (*im*)*pf.* attack, charge
**атама́н** *m* [1] ataman (*Cossack chieftan*)
**ателье́** (-tɛ-) *n* [*indecl.*] studio, atelier
**атланти́ческий** [16] Atlantic…
**а́тлас**[1] *m* [1] atlas
**атла́с**[2] *m* [1] satin
**атле́т** *m* [1] athlete; **~ика** *f* [5] athletics; **~и́ческий** [16] athletic
**атмосфе́р|а** *f* [5] atmosphere; **~ный** [16] atmospheric
**а́том** *m* [1] atom; **~ный** [14] atomic
**атрибу́т** *m* [1] attribute
**аттеста́т** *m* [1] certificate; ***~ зре́лости*** school-leaving certificate
**ауди|е́нция** *f* [7] audience; **~то́рия** *f* [7] lecture hall; (*слушатели*) audience
**аукцио́н** *m* [1] auction (**с** P by)
**афе́р|а** *f* [5] speculation, fraud, shady

deal; **~и́ст** *m* [1], **~и́стка** *f* [5; *g/pl.*: -ток] speculator, swindler
**афи́ш|а** *f* [5] playbill, poster; **~и́ровать** [7] *impf.* parade, advertise, make known
**афори́зм** *m* [1] aphorism
**африка́н|ец** *m* [1; -нца], **~ка** *f* [5; *g/pl.*: -нок], **~ский** [16] African
**ах** *int.* ah!; **~́ать** [1], *once* ⟨~́нуть⟩ [20] groan, sigh; (*удивиться*) be amazed
**ахине́|я** *f* [7] *coll.* nonsense; ***нести́ ~ю*** talk nonsense
**ацетиле́н** *m* [1] acetylene
**аэро́|бус** *m* [1] airbus; **~дина́мика** *f* [5] aerodynamics; **~дро́м** *m* [1] airdrome (*Brt.* aero-); **~по́рт** *m* [1] airport; **~сни́мок** *m* [1; -мка] aerial photograph; **~ста́т** *m* [1] balloon; **~съёмка** *f* [5; *g/pl.*: -мок] aerial survey

# Б

**б** → ***бы***
**ба́б|а** *f* [5] married peasant woman; ***сне́жная ~а*** snowman; **~а-яга́** *f* old witch (*in Russian folk-tales*), hag; **~ий** [18]: ***~ье ле́то*** Indian summer; ***~ьи ска́зки*** *f/pl.* old wives' tales; **~ка** *f* [5; *g/pl.*: -бок] grandmother; **~очка** *f* [5; *g/pl.*: -чек] butterfly; **~ушка** *f* [5; *g/pl.*: -шек] grandmother, granny
**бага́ж** *m* [1 *e.*] baggage, *Brt.* luggage; ***ручно́й ~*** small baggage; ***сдать в ~*** check one's baggage, *Brt.* register one's luggage; **~ник** *m* [1] *mot.* trunk, *Brt.* boot; **~ный** [14]: ***~ый ваго́н*** baggage car, *Brt.* luggage van
**багров|е́ть** [8], ⟨по-⟩ turn crimson, purple; **~́ый** [14 *sh.*] purple, crimson
**бадминто́н** *m* [1] badminton
**ба́за** *f* [5] base, basis, foundation; *учреждение* depot, center (-tre)
**база́р** *m* [1] market, bazaar; *coll.* uproar, row; **~ный** [14] market…
**бази́ровать** [7] *impf.* base (***на*** П on); **~ся** rest *or* base (***на*** П on)
**ба́зис** *m* [1] basis
**байда́рка** *f* [5; *g/pl.*: -рок] canoe, kayak
**ба́йка** *f* [5] flannelette
**байт** *m* [1] *comput.* byte
**бак** *m* [1] *naut.* forecastle; container, receptacle; tank, cistern
**бакал|е́йный** [14]: ***~е́йный магази́н*** grocery, grocer's store (*Brt.* shop); ***~е́йные това́ры*** *m/pl.* = **~е́я** *f* [6] groceries *pl.*
**ба́кен** *m* [1] beacon
**бак|енба́рды** *f/pl.* [5], **~и** *m/pl.* [1; *gen.*: бак] side-whiskers
**баклажа́н** *m* [1] aubergine
**баклу́ши**: ***бить ~*** *coll.* idle, dawdle, fritter away one's time
**бактерио́лог** *m* [1] bacteriologist; **~и́ческий** [16] bacteriological; **~́ия** *f* [7] bacteriology
**бакте́рия** *f* [7] bacterium
**бал** *m* [1; на ~у́; *pl. e.*] ball, dance (***на*** П at)
**балага́н** *m* [1] booth (*at fairs*); *fig.* farce; noise and bustle
**балагу́р** *m* [1] *coll.* joker; **~ить** *coll.* [13] jest, crack jokes
**балала́йка** *f* [5; *g/pl.*: балала́ек] balalaika
**баламу́тить** [15], ⟨вз-⟩ *coll.* stir up, trouble
**бала́нс** *m* [1] balance (*a. comm.*); ***торго́вый бала́нс*** balance of trade; **~и́ровать** [7] balance; **~овый** [14] balance…
**балахо́н** *m* [1] *coll.* loose overall; shapeless garment
**балбе́с** *m* [1] *coll.* simpleton, booby
**балда́** *m/f* [5] sledgehammer; *coll.* blockhead, dolt
**бале|ри́на** *f* [5] (female) ballet dancer; **~́т** *m* [1] ballet
**ба́лка**[1] *f* [5; *g/pl.*: -лок] beam, girder
**ба́лка**[2] *f* [5; *g/pl.*: -лок] gully, ravine
**балка́нский** [16] Balkan…
**балко́н** *m* [1] balcony

Б

**балл** *m* [1] grade, mark (*in school*); point (*sport*)
**балла́да** *f* [5] ballad
**балла́ст** *m* [1] ballast
**баллисти́ческий** [16] ballistic
**балло́н** *m* [1] balloon (*vessel*); container, cylinder
**баллоти́роваться** [7] run (**в** B for), be a candidate (**в, на** B for)
**ба́лов|анный** [14 *sh.*] *coll.* spoiled; **~а́ть** [7] (*a.* **-ся**) be naughty; trifle with; ⟨из-⟩ spoil, coddle; **~ень** *m* [4; -вня] darling, pet; **~ство́** *n* [9] mischievousness; spoiling, pampering
**балти́йский** [16] Baltic…
**бальза́м** *m* [1] balsam, balm
**балюстра́да** *f* [5] balustrade
**бамбу́к** *m* [1] bamboo
**бана́ль|ность** *f* [8] banality; commonplace; **~ный** [14; -лен, -льна] banal, trite
**бана́н** *m* [1] banana
**ба́нда** *f* [5] band, gang
**банда́ж** *m* [1 *e.*] bandage; truss
**бандеро́ль** *f* [8] wrapper for mailing (*newspapers*, *etc.*); designation for printed matter, book post
**банди́т** *m* [1] bandit, gangster; **~и́зм** *m* [1] gangsterism
**банк** *m* [1] bank
**ба́нка** *f* [5; *g/pl.*: -нок] jar; (***консе́рвная***) ~ can, *Brt.* tin
**банке́т** *m* [1] banquet
**банки́р** *m* [1] banker
**банкно́т** *m* [1] bank note
**банкро́т** *m* [1] bankrupt; **~иться** [15], ⟨о-⟩ go bankrupt; **~ство** *n* [9] bankruptcy
**бант** *m* [1] bow
**ба́нщик** *m* [1] bathhouse attendant
**ба́ня** *f* [6] (Russian) bath(s)
**бапти́ст** *m* [1] Baptist
**бар** *m* [1] (snack) bar; **~мен** *m* [1] barman
**бараба́н** *m* [1] drum; **~ить** [13], ⟨про-⟩ (beat the) drum; **~ный** [14]: ***~ный бой*** beat of the drum; ***~ная перепо́нка*** eardrum; **~щик** *m* [1] drummer
**бара́к** *m* [1] barracks; hut
**бара́н** *m* [1] ram; P idiot, ass; **~ий** [18] sheep's; mutton; ***согну́ть в ~ий рог*** to make s.b. knuckle under; **~ина** *f* [5] mutton
**бара́нка** *f* [5; *g/pl.*: -нок] ringshaped roll; *coll.* steering wheel
**барахло́** *n* [9] old clothes; disused goods and chattels, *Brt.* lumber; trash, junk
**бара́хтаться** [1] *coll.* flounder
**барбари́с** *m* [1] barberry
**бард** *m* [1] bard (*poet and singer*)
**барда́к** *m* [1] *coll.* complete chaos; P brothel
**барелье́ф** *m* [1] bas-relief
**ба́ржа** *f* [5] barge
**ба́рий** *m* [3] barium
**ба́рин** *m* [1; *pl.*: ба́ре *or* ба́ры, бар] member of landowning gentry in prerevolutionary Russia; *coll.* refers to s.b. affecting an air of superiority
**барито́н** *m* [1] baritone
**барка́с** *m* [1] launch, long boat
**баро́кко** *n* [*indecl.*] baroque
**баро́метр** *m* [1] barometer
**баррика́да** *f* [5] barricade
**барс** *m* [1] snow leopard
**ба́р|ский** [16] lordly; ***жить на ~скую но́гу*** live in grand style
**барсу́к** *m* [1 *e.*] badger
**ба́рхат** *m* [1] velvet; **~ный** [14] velvet(y)
**ба́рыня** *f* [6] barin's wife; *coll.* refers to s.b. acting in a haughty manner
**бары́ш** *m* [1 *e.*] profit, gain(s)
**ба́рышня** *f* [6; *g/pl.*: -шень] *iro. or joc.* young lady, miss
**барье́р** *m* [1] barrier
**бас** *m* [1; *pl. e.*] *mus.* bass
**баск** *m* [1] Basque
**баскетбо́л** *m* [1] basketball
**басно|пи́сец** *m* [1; -сца] fabulist; **~сло́вный** [14; -вен, -вна] legendary; *coll.* fabulous, incredible
**ба́сня** *f* [6; *g/pl.*: -сен] fable
**бассе́йн** *m* [1]: ***~ реки́*** river basin; ***пла́вательный ~*** swimming pool
**ба́ста** that will do; no more of this!
**бастио́н** *m* [1] bastion
**бастова́ть** [7], ⟨за-⟩ (be *or* go on) strike
**батальо́н** *m* [1] battalion
**батаре́|йка** *f* [5; *g/pl.*: -ре́ек] (dry cell) battery; **~я** *f* [6; *g/pl.*: -е́й] *mil.*, *tech.* battery; ***~я парово́го отопле́ния*** (central

heating) radiator
**бати́ст** *m* [1] cambric; **~овый** [14] of cambric
**бато́н** *m* [1] long loaf of bread
**ба́тюшка** *m* [5; *g/pl.*: -шек] *coll.* father; (*as mode of address to priest*) father
**бахва́л** P *m* [1] braggart; **~иться** [13] boast, brag; **~ьство** *n* [9] bragging, vaunting
**бахрома́** *f* [5] fringe
**бахчево́дство** *n* [9] melon growing
**бациллоноси́тель** *m* [4] bacilluscarrier
**ба́шенка** *f* [5; *g/pl.*: -нок] turret
**башка́** P *f* [5] head, noddle
**башкови́тый** [14 *sh.*] *coll.* brainy
**башма́к** *m* [1 *e.*] shoe; ***быть под ~о́м*** be under the thumb of
**ба́шня** *f* [6; *g/pl.*: -шен] tower; *mil.* turret
**баю́кать** [1], ⟨у-⟩ lull; rock (to sleep)
**бая́н** *m* [1] (*kind of*) accordion
**бде́ние** *n* [12] vigil, watch
**бди́тель|ность** *f* [8] vigilance; **~ный** [14; -лен, -льна] vigilant, watchful
**бег** *m* [1; на -у́] run(ning); *pl.* [**бега́** *etc. e.*] race(s); ***~ с барье́рами*** hurdle race; ***~ на коро́ткие диста́нции*** sprint; ***на ~у́*** while running → ***бего́м***
**бе́гание** *n* [12] running (*a. for s.th., on business*)
**бе́гать** [1], ⟨по-⟩ run (around); *coll.* shun (*a.* p. **от** P); *fig.* run after (*a.* p. **за** T); ***~ вза́пуски*** *coll.* race, vie in a run
**бегемо́т** *m* [1] hippopotamus
**бегле́ц** *m* [1 *e.*] runaway
**бе́гл|ость** *f* [8] *речи* fluency; cursoriness; **~ый** [14] fluent; cursory
**бег|ово́й** [14] race…; **~о́м** on the double; **~отня́** *coll. f* [6] running about, bustle; **~́ство** *n* [9] flight, escape; *паническое* stampede; ***обрати́ть в ~́ство*** put to flight
**бегу́н** *m* [1 *e.*] runner, trotter
**беда́** *f* [5; *pl.*: бе́ды] misfortune, disaster, trouble; ***что за ~?*** what does it matter?; ***не беда́*** it doesn't matter; ***~ не велика́*** there's no harm in that; ***в то́м-то и ~*** that's the trouble; the trouble is (that)…; ***на беду́*** *coll.* unluckily; ***про́сто ~!*** it's awful!
**бе́д|ненький** [16] poor, pitiable; **~не́ть** [8], ⟨о-⟩ grow (become) poor; **~ность** *f* [8] poverty; **~нота́** *f* [5] *collect.* the poor; **~ный** [14; -ден, -дна́, -дно] poor (T in); **~ня́га** *coll. m/f* [5], **~ня́жка** *coll. m/f* [5; *g/pl.*: -жек] poor fellow, wretch; **~ня́к** *m* [1 *e.*] poor man, pauper
**бедро́** *n* [9; бёдра, -дер, -драм] thigh; hip; loin
**бе́дств|енный** [14 *sh.*] disastrous, calamitous; ***~енное положе́ние*** disastrous situation; **~ие** *n* [12] distress, disaster; ***стихи́йное ~ие*** natural calamity; **~овать** [7] suffer want, live in misery
**бежа́ть** [4; бегу́, бежи́шь, бегу́т; беги́; бегу́щий] ⟨по-⟩ (be) run(ning *etc.*); flee; avoid, shun (*a. p.* **от** P); ***~ сломя́ го́лову*** *coll.* run for one's life *or* head over heels
**бе́жевый** [14] beige
**бе́женец** *m* [1; -нца], **~ка** *f* [5; *g/pl.*: -нок] refugee
**без, ~о** (P) without; in the absence of; less; (*in designations of time*) to: ***~ четверти час*** a quarter to one; ***~о всего́*** without anything; ***без вас*** *a.* in your absence
**безавари́йный** [14; -и́ен, -и́йна] *tech.* accident-free
**безала́берный** *coll.* [14; -рен, -рна] disorderly, slovenly
**безалкого́льный** [14] nonalcoholic
**безапелляцио́нный** [14; -о́нен, -о́нна] categorical, peremptory
**безбе́дный** [14; -ден, -дна] welloff, comfortable
**безбиле́тный** [14] ticketless; ***~ пасса-жи́р*** *на корабле* stowaway, passenger traveling without a ticket
**безбо́жн|ый** [14; -жен, -жна] irreligious; *coll.* shameless, scandalous; ***~ые це́ны*** outrageous prices
**безболе́зненный** [14 *sh.*] painless
**безборо́дый** [14] beardless
**безбоя́зненный** [14 *sh.*] fearless
**безбра́чие** *n* [12] celibacy
**безбре́жный** [14; -жен, -жна] boundless
**безве́рие** *n* [12] unbelief
**безве́стный** [14; -тен, -тна] unknown, obscure
**безве́тр|енный** [14 *sh.*], **~ие** *n* [12] calm

**безви́нный** [14; -и́нен, -и́нна] guiltless, innocent
**безвку́с|ица** *f* [5] tastelessness, bad taste; **~ный** [14; -сен, -сна] tasteless, insipid
**безвла́стие** *n* [12] anarchy
**безво́дный** [14; -ден, -дна] arid
**безвозвра́тный** [14; -тен, -тна] irrevocable, irretrievable
**безвозме́здный** (-mezn-) [14] gratuitous; without compensation
**безволо́сый** [14] hairless, bald
**безво́льный** [14; -лен, -льна] lacking willpower, weak-willed
**безвре́дный** [14; -ден, -дна] harmless
**безвре́менный** [14] premature, untimely
**безвы́ездный** (-jiznyj) [14] uninterrupted, continuous
**безвы́ходный** [14; -ден, -дна] **1.** permanent; **2.** desperate, hopeless
**безголо́вый** [14] headless; *fig.* stupid, brainless
**безгра́мотн|ость** *f* [8] illiteracy, ignorance; **~ый** [14; -тен, -тна] illiterate, ignorant
**безграни́чный** [14; -чен, -чна] boundless, limitless
**безда́рный** [14; -рен, -рна] untalented, ungifted; (*of a work of art*) feeble, undistinguished
**безде́йств|ие** *n* [12] inaction; **~овать** [7] be inactive, idle
**безде́л|ица** *f* [5], **~ка** *f* [5; *g/pl.*: -лок] trifle, bagatelle; **~у́шка** *f* [5; *g/pl.*: -шек] knickknack
**безде́ль|е** *n* [12] idleness; **~ник** *m* [1], **~ница** *f* [5] idler; good-for-nothing; **~ничать** [1] idle, lounge
**безде́нежье** *n* [10] lack of money, impecuniousness
**безде́тный** [14; -тен, -тна] childless
**безде́ятельный** [14; -лен, -льна] inactive, sluggish
**бе́здна** *f* [5] abyss, chasm; *fig. coll.* lots (of)
**бездоказа́тельный** [14; -лен, -льна] unsubstantiated
**бездо́мный** [14; -мен, -мна] homeless
**бездо́нный** [14; -до́нен, -до́нна] bottomless; *fig.* unfathomable
**бездоро́жье** *n* [12] impassability; absence of roads; prohibitive road conditions
**бездохо́дный** [14; -ден, -дна] unprofitable
**безду́мный** [14; -мен, -мна] unthinking, thoughtless
**безду́шный** [14; -шен, -шна] heartless, soulless
**безе́** *n* [*indecl.*] meringue
**безжа́лостный** (biʒʒ-sn-) [14; -тен, -тна] ruthless, merciless
**безжи́зненный** (biʒʒ-) [14] lifeless; inanimate; *fig.* dull
**беззабо́тный** [14; -тен, -тна] carefree, lighthearted; careless
**беззаве́тный** [14; -тен, -тна] selfless; unreserved
**беззако́н|ие** *n* [12] lawlessness; unlawful act; **~ность** *f* [8] illegality; **~ный** [14; -о́нен, -о́нна] illegal, unlawful
**беззасте́нчивый** [14 *sh.*] shameless; impudent; unscrupulous
**беззащи́тный** [14; -тен, -тна] defenseless; unprotected
**беззвёздный** (-zn-) [14; -ден, -дна] starless
**беззву́чный** [14; -чен, -чна] soundless, silent, noiseless
**беззло́бный** [14; -бен, -бна] good-natured, kind
**беззу́бый** [14] toothless; *fig.* feeble
**безли́кий** [16 *sh.*] featureless, faceless
**безли́чный** [14; -чен, -чна] without personality; impersonal
**безлю́дный** [14; -ден, -дна] deserted, uninhabited; (*малонаселённый*) sparsely populated
**безме́рный** [14; -рен, -рна] immeasurable; immense
**безмо́зглый** [14] *coll.* brainless, stupid
**безмо́лв|ие** *n* [12] silence; **~ный** [14; -вен, -вна] silent, mute
**безмяте́жный** [14; -жен, -жна] serene, tranquil, untroubled
**безнадёжный** [14; -жен, -жна] hopeless
**безнадзо́рный** [14; -рен, -рна] uncared for; neglected
**безнака́занный** [14 *sh.*] unpunished

**безнали́чный** [14] without cash transfer; **~ расчёт** *fin.* clearing
**безнра́вственный** [14 *sh.*] immoral
**безоби́дный** [14; -ден, -дна] inoffensive; harmless
**безо́блачный** [14; -чен, -чна] cloudless; serene
**безобра́з|ие** *n* [12] ugliness; outrage; disgrace; **~ие!** scandalous! shocking!; **~ничать** [1] behave outrageously; get up to mischief; **~ный** [14; -зен, -зна] ugly; shameful, disgusting
**безоговоро́чный** [14; -чен, -чна] unconditional, unreserved
**безопа́с|ность** *f* [8] safety; security; **Сове́т** **Ѻности** Security Council; **~ный** [14; -сен, -сна] safe, secure (**от** P from); **~ная бри́тва** safety razor
**безору́жный** [14; -жен, -жна] unarmed; *fig.* defenseless
**безостано́вочный** [14; -чен, -чна] unceasing; nonstop…
**безотве́тный** [14; -тен, -тна] without response; *любовь* unrequited; (*кроткий*) meek
**безотве́тственный** [14 *sh.*] irresponsible
**безотка́зный** [14; -зен, -зна] without a hitch; croublefree; *tech.* faultless; reliable
**безотлага́тельный** [14; -лен, -льна] undelayable, urgent
**безотноси́тельно** *adv.* irrespective (of **к** Д)
**безотра́дный** [14; -ден, -дна] cheerless
**безотчётный** [14; -тен, -тна] not liable to account; not subject to control; inexplicable: *e.g.*, **~ страх** unaccountable fear
**безоши́бочный** [14; -чен, -чна] faultless; correct; unerring
**безрабо́т|ица** *f* [5] unemployment; **~ный** [14] unemployed
**безра́достный** [14; -тен, -тна] joyless; dismal
**безразде́льный** [14; -лен, -льна] individed; whole-hearted
**безразли́ч|ие** *n* [12] (**к** Д) indifference; **~ный** [14; -чен, -чна] indifferent; **это мне ~но** it is all the same to me
**безрассу́дный** [14; -ден, -дна] reckless, rash
**безрезульта́тный** [14; -тен, -тна] futile, unsuccessful, ineffectual
**безро́потный** [14; -тен, -тна] uncomplaining humble, meek, submissive
**безрука́вка** *f* [5; *g/pl.*: -вок] sleeveless jacket *or* blouse
**безуда́рный** [14; -рен, -рна] unaccented unstressed
**безу́держный** [14; -жен, -жна] unrestrained; impetuous
**безукори́зненный** [14 *sh.*] irreproachable, impeccable
**безу́м|ец** *m* [1; -мца] *fig.* madman, lunatic; madcap; **~ие** *n* [12] madness, folly; **~ный** [14; -мен, -мна] crazy, insane; nonsensical, absurd; ill-considered, rash
**безумо́лчный** [14; -чен, -чна] incessant, uninterrupted
**безу́мство** *n* [9] madness; foldhardiness
**безупре́чный** [14; -чен, -чна] blameless, irreproachable
**безусло́в|но** certainly, surely; **~ный** [14; -вен, -вна] absolute, unconditional; (*несомненный*) indisputable, undoubted
**безуспе́шный** [14; -шен, -шна] unsuccessful
**безуста́нный** [14; -а́нен, -а́нна] tireless; indefatigable
**безуте́шный** [14; -шен, -шна] inconsolable
**безуча́стный** [14; -тен, -тна] apathetic, unconcerned
**безъя́дерный** [14] nuclear-free
**безымя́нный** [14] nameless, anonymous; **~ па́лец** ring finger
**безыску́сный** [14; -сен, -сна] artless, unaffected, unsophisticated
**безысхо́дный** [14; -ден, -дна] hopeless, desperate
**бейсбо́л** *m* [14] baseball
**беко́н** *m* [1] bacon
**белёсый** [14] whitish
**беле́ть** [8], ⟨по-⟩ grow *or* turn white; *impf.* (*a.* **-ся**) appear *or* show white
**белиберда́** *f* [14] *coll.* nonsense, rubbish

**белизна́** *f* [5] whiteness
**бели́ла** *n/pl.* [9]: ***свинцо́вые ~*** white lead; ***ци́нковые ~*** zinc white
**бели́ть** [13; белю́, бели́шь, белённый] **1.** ⟨вы́-⟩ bleach; **2.** ⟨по-⟩ whitewash
**бе́лка** *f* [5; *g/pl.*: -лок] squirrel
**белко́вый** [14] albuminous
**беллетри́стика** *f* [5] fiction
**белобры́сый** [14] *coll.* flaxenhaired, tow-haired
**белова́тый** [14 *sh.*] whitish
**бело|ви́к** *m* [1 *e.*], **~во́й** [14], ***~во́й экземпля́р*** fair copy; **~гварде́ец** *m* [1; -е́йца] White Guard (*member of troops fighting against the Red Guards and the Red Army in the Civil War 1918-1920*)
**бело́к** *m* [1; -лка́] albumen, protein; white (*of egg or eye*)
**бело|кро́вие** *n* [12] leukemia; **~ку́рый** [14 *sh.*] blond, fair; **~ру́с** *m* [1], **~ру́ска** *f* [5; *g/pl.*: -сок], **~ру́сский** [16] Byelorussian; **~сне́жный** [14; -жен, -жна] snowwhite
**белу́га** *f* [5] white sturgeon
**бе́л|ый** [14; бел, -á, -о] white; ***~ый свет*** (wide) world; ***~ые стихи́*** *m/pl.* blank verse; ***средь ~а дня*** *coll.* in broad daylight
**бель|ги́ец** *m* [1; -ги́йца], **~ги́йка** *f* [5; *g/pl.*: -ги́ек], **~ги́йский** [16] Belgian
**бельё** *n* [12] linen; ***ни́жнее ~*** underwear
**бельмо́** *n* [9; *pl.*: бе́льма, бельм] walleye; ***она́ у меня́ как ~ на глазу́*** she is an eyesore to me
**бельэта́ж** *m* [1] *thea.* dress circle; second (*Brt.* first) floor
**бемо́ль** *m* [4] flat
**бенефи́с** *m* [1] benefit(-night)
**бензи́н** *m* [1] gasoline, *Brt.* petrol
**бензо|ба́к** *m* [1] gasoline *or* petrol tank; **~коло́нка** (*a.* ***запра́вочная ~коло́нка***) [5; *g/pl.*: -нок] gas *or* petrol pump, *coll.* gas *or* filling station
**бенуа́р** *m* [1] *thea.* parterre box
**бе́рег** [1; на -гу́; *pl.*: -гá, *etc. e.*] bank, *морской*, shore, coast; (*суша*) land; ***вы́йти (вы́ступить) из ~о́в*** overflow the banks; ***приста́ть к ~у*** land; **~ово́й** [14] coast(al), shore…
**бережли́вый** [14 *sh.*] economical
**бе́режный** [14; -жен, -жна] cautious, careful
**берёза** *f* [5] birch tree; rod *or* bundle of twigs for flogging
**березня́к** *m* [1 *e.*] birch grove
**берёзовый** [14] birch(en)
**бере́мен|ная** [14] pregnant; **~ность** *f* [8] pregnancy
**бере́т** *m* [1] beret
**бере́чь** [26 г/ж: берегу́, бережёшь] **1.** ⟨по-⟩ guard, watch (over); **2.** ⟨по-, с-⟩ spare, save, take care of; **3.** ⟨с-⟩ [сбережённый] keep; preserve; **-ся** take care (of o.s.); ***береги́сь!*** take care! look out!
**берло́га** *f* [5] den, lair
**берцо́|вый** [14]: ***~вая кость*** shinbone
**бес** *m* [1] demon, evil spirit
**бесе́д|а** *f* [5] conversation, talk; **~ка** *f* [5; *g/pl.*: -док] arbo(u)r, summerhouse; **~овать** [7] converse
**бесёнок** *m* [2; -нка; *pl.*: бесеня́та] imp
**беси́ть** [15], ⟨вз-⟩ [взбешённый] enrange, madden; **-ся** (fly into a) rage; (*резвиться*) romp
**бесконе́ч|ность** *f* [8] infinity; ***до ~ности*** endlessly; **~ный** [14; -чен, -чна] разгово́р и т. д. endless, infinite; простра́нство, любо́вь unlimited, boundless, eternal; ***~но ма́лый*** infinitesimal
**бесконтро́льный** [14; -лен, -льна] uncontrolled, unchecked
**бескоры́ст|ие** *n* [12] unselfishness; **~ный** [14; -тен, -тна] disinterested
**бескра́йний** [15; -áен, -áйна] boundless
**бескро́вный** [14; -вен, -вна] anemic, pale, lacking vitality
**бескульту́рье** *n* [10] lack of culture
**бесновáться** [7] be possessed, rage, rave
**бесо́вщина** *f* [5] devilry
**беспа́мятство** *n* [9] unconsciousness, frenzy, delirium
**беспарти́йный** [14] *pol.* independent; non-party (man)
**бесперебо́йный** [14; -бо́ен, -бо́йна] uninterrupted, regular
**беспереса́дочный** [14] direct (*as a train*), through…
**бесперспекти́вный** [14; -вен, -вна]

having no prospects, hopeless
**беспе́ч|ность** *f* [8] carelessness; **~ный** [14; -чен, -чна] careless
**беспла́т|ный** [14; -тен, -тна] free (of charge), gratuitous; **~но** gratis
**беспло́д|ие** *n* [12] barrenness, sterility; **~ный** [14; -ден, -дна] barren, sterile; *fig*. fruitless, vain
**бесповоро́тный** [14; -тен, -тна] unalterable, irrevocable, final
**бесподо́бный** [14; -бен, -бна] incomparable, matchless
**беспозвоно́чный** [14] invertebrate
**беспок|о́ить** [13], ⟨(п)о-⟩ upset, worry; (*мешать*) disturb, bother, trouble; **-ся** worry, be anxious (**о** П about); **~о́йный** [14; -ко́ен, -ко́йна] restless; uneasy; **~о́йство** *n* [9] unrest; trouble; anxiety; ***прости́те за ~о́йство*** sorry to (have) trouble(d) you
**бесполе́зный** [14; -зен, -зна] useless
**беспо́мощный** [14; -щен, -щна] helpless
**беспоря́до|к** *m* [1; -дка] disorder, confusion; *pl*. disturbances, riots; **~чный** [14; -чен, -чна] disorderly, untidy
**беспоса́дочный** [14]: ~ ***перелёт*** nonstop flight
**беспо́чвенный** [14 *sh*.] groundless, unfounded
**беспо́шлинный** [14] duty-free
**беспоща́дный** [14; -ден, -дна] pitiless, ruthless, relentless
**беспреде́льный** [14; -лен, -льна] boundless, infinite, unlimited
**беспредме́тный** [14; -тен, -тна] aimless
**беспрекосло́вный** [14; -вен, -вна] absolute, unquestioning, implicit
**беспрепя́тственный** [14 *sh*.] unhampered, unhindered, free
**беспреры́вный** [14; -вен, -вна] uninterrupted, continuous
**беспреста́нный** [14; -а́нен, -а́нна] incessant, continual
**беспри́быльный** [14; -лен, -льна] unprofitable
**беспризо́рный** [14; -рен, -рна] homeless, uncared-for
**бесприме́рный** [14; -рен, -рна] unprecedented, unparalleled
**беспринци́пный** [14; -пен, -пна] unprincipled, unscrupulous
**беспристра́ст|ие** *n* [12] impartiality; **~ный** (-sn-) [14; -тен, -тна] impartial, unprejudiced, unbias(s)ed
**беспричи́нный** [14; -и́нен, -и́нна] groundless; unfounded
**бесприю́тный** [14; -тен, -тна] homeless
**беспробу́дный** [14; -ден, -дна] *сон* deep; *пьянство* unrestrained
**беспросве́тный** [14; -тен, -тна] pitch-dark; *fig*. hopeless
**беспроце́нтный** [14] interest-free; bearing no interest
**беспу́тный** [14; -тен, -тна] dissolute
**бессвя́зный** [14; -зен, -зна] incoherent, rambling
**бессерде́чный** [14; -чен, -чна] heartless, unfeeling, callous
**бесси́|лие** *n* [12] debility; impotence; **~льный** [14; -лен, -льна] weak, powerless, impotent
**бессла́вный** [14; -вен, -вна] infamous, ignominious, inglorious
**бессле́дный** [14; -ден, -дна] without leaving a trace, complete
**бесслове́сный** [14; -сен, -сна] speechless, dumb; silent
**бессме́нный** [14; -е́нен, -е́нна] permanent
**бессме́рт|ие** *n* [12] immortality; **~ный** [14; -тен, -тна] immortal
**бессмы́сл|енный** [14 *sh*.] senseless; meaningless; **~ица** *f* [5] nonsense
**бессо́вестный** [14; -тен, -тна] unscrupulous
**бессодержа́тельный** [14; -лен, -льна] empty, insipid, dull
**бессозна́тельный** [14; -лен, -льна] unconscious; (*непроизвольный*) involuntary
**бессо́нн|ица** *f* [5] insomnia, **~ый** [14] sleepless
**бесспо́рный** [14; -рен, -рна] indisputable; doubtless, certain
**бессро́чный** [14; -чен, -чна] without time-limit; indefinite
**бесстра́ст|ие** *n* [12] dispassionateness, impassiveness; **~ный** [14; -тен, -тна] dispassionate, impassive
**бесстра́ш|ие** *n* [12] fearlessness; **~ный**

[14; -шен, -шна] fearless, intrepid
**бессты́д|ный** [14; -ден, -дна] shameless, impudent; (*непристойный*) indecent; **~ство** *n* [9] impudence, insolence
**бессчётный** [14] innumerable
**беста́ктн|ость** *f* [8] tactlessness; tactless action; **~ый** [14; -тен, -тна] tactless
**бестала́нный** [14; -а́нен, -а́нна] untalented; ill-starred
**бе́стия** *f* [7] brute, beast; rogue
**бестолко́вый** [14 *sh.*] muddleheaded, confused; *человек* slowwitted
**бе́столочь** *f* [8] *coll.* nitwit
**бестре́петный** [14; -тен, -тна] intrepid, undaunted
**бестсе́ллер** *m* [1] bestseller
**бесхара́ктерный** [14; -рен, -рна] lacking character, weak-willed
**бесхи́тростный** [14; -тен, -тна] artless, naive, ingenuous, unsophisticated
**бесхо́зный** [14] *coll.* having no owner
**бесхозя́йствен|ность** *f* [8] careless and wasteful management; **~ный** [14] thriftless
**бесцве́тный** [14; -тен, -тна] colo(u)rless, insipid
**бесце́льный** [14; -лен, -льна] aimless; *разговор* idle
**бесце́н|ный** [14; -е́нен, -е́нна] invaluable, priceless; **~ок** *m* [1; -нка]: ***за ~ок*** *coll.* for a song or a trifling sum
**бесцеремо́нный** [14; -о́нен, -о́нна] unceremonious, familiar
**бесчелове́чн|ость** *f* [8] inhumanity; **~ый** [14; -чен, -чна] inhuman, cruel
**бесче́ст|ный** [14; -тен, -тна] dishonest; (*непорядочный*) dishono(u)rable; **~ье** *n* [10] dishono(u)r, disgrace
**бесчи́нство** [9] excess, outrage; **~вать** [7] behave outrageously
**бесчи́сленный** [14 *sh.*] innumerable, countless
**бесчу́вств|енный** [14 *sh.*] insensible, callous, hard-hearted; **~ие** *n* [12] insensibility (***к*** Д); unconsciousness, swoon
**бесшаба́шный** [14; -шен, -шна] *coll.* reckless, careless; wanton
**бесшу́мный** [14; -мен, -мна] noiseless, quiet
**бето́н** *m* [1] concrete; **~и́ровать** [7], ⟨за-⟩ concrete; **~ный** [14] concrete…
**бечёвка** *f* [5; *g/pl.*: -вок] string
**бе́шен|ство** *n* [9] **1.** *med.* hydrophobia; **2.** fury, rage; **~ый** [14] **1.** *собака* rabid; **2.** furious, frantic, wild; **3.** *цена* enormous
**библе́йский** [16] Biblical; Bible…
**библиографи́ческий** [16] bibliographic(al)
**библиоте́|ка** *f* [5] library; **~карь** *m* [4] librarian; **~чный** [14] library…
**би́блия** *f* [7] Bible
**би́вень** *m* [4; -вня] tusk
**бигуди́** *n/pl.* [*indecl.*] hair curlers
**бидо́н** *m* [1] can, churn; milkcan
**бие́ние** *n* [12] beat, throb
**бижуте́рия** *f* [7] costume jewel(le)ry
**би́знес** *m* [1] business; **~ме́н** *m* [1] businessman
**бизо́н** *m* [1] bison
**биле́т** *m* [1] ticket; card; note, bill; ***обра́тный ~*** round-trip ticket, *Brt.* return-ticket
**билья́рд** *m* [1] billiards
**бино́кль** *m* [4] binocular(s), ***театра́льный ~*** opera glasses; ***полево́й ~*** field glasses
**бинт** *m* [1 *e.*] bandage; **~ова́ть** [7], ⟨за-⟩ bandage, dress
**био́граф** *m* [1] biographer; **~и́ческий** [16] biographic(al); **~ия** *f* [7] biography
**био́лог** *m* [1] biologist; **~и́ческий** [16] biological; **~ия** *f* [7] biology
**биори́тм** *m* [1] biorhythm
**биохи́мия** *f* [7] biochemistry
**би́ржа** *f* [5] (stock) exchange; ***~ труда́*** labor registry office, *Brt.* labour exchange
**биржеви́к** *m* [1 *e.*] → ***бро́кер***
**би́рка** *f* [5; *g/pl.*: -рок] label-tag, nameplate
**бирюза́** *f* [5] turquoise
**бис** *int.* encore!
**би́сер** *m* [1] *coll.* (glass) beads *pl.*
**бискви́т** *m* [1] sponge cake
**бит** *m* [1] *comput.* bit
**би́тва** *f* [5] battle
**бит|ко́м** → ***наби́тый***; **~о́к** *m* [1; -тка́] (mince) meat ball
**бить** [бью, бьёшь; бей!; би́тый] **1.** ⟨по-⟩ beat; **2.** ⟨про-⟩ [проби́л, -би́ла, проби́-

ло] *часы* strike; **3.** ⟨раз-⟩ [разобью́, -бьёшь] break, smash; **4.** ⟨у-⟩ shoot, kill, trump (*card*); **5.** *no pf.* spout; ***~ в глаза́*** strike the eye; ***~ трево́гу*** *fig.* raise an alarm; ***~ отбо́й*** *mst. fig.* beat a retreat; ***~ ключо́м*** **1.** bubble; **2.** boil over; **3.** sparkle; **4.** abound in vitality; ***про́бил его́ час*** his hour has struck; ***би́тый час*** *m* one solid hour; **-ся** fight; *сердце* beat, struggle, toil (***над*** Т); ***~ся голово́й о(б) сте́ну*** *fig.* beat one's head against a brick wall; ***~ся об закла́д*** bet; ***она́ бьётся как ры́ба об лёд*** she exerts herself in vain

**бифште́кс** *m* [1] (beef) steak

**бич** *m* [1 *e.*] whip; *fig.* scourge

**бла́го** *n* [9] good; blessing; ***всех благ!*** *coll.* all the best; **2вещение** *n* [12] Annunciation

**благови́дный** [14; -ден, -дна] *fig.* seemly, *предлог* specious

**благоволи́ть** [13] *old use* be favourably disposed (***к*** Д); ⟨со-⟩ *iro.* deign

**благово́н|ие** *n* [12] fragrance; **~ный** [14] fragrant

**благого|ве́йный** [14; -ве́ен, -ве́йна] reverent, respectful; **~ве́ние** *n* [12] awe (of), reverence, respect (for) (***пе́ред*** Т); **~ве́ть** [8] (***пе́ред*** Т) worship, venerate

**благодар|и́ть** [13], ⟨по-, от-⟩ (В ***за*** В) thank (*a. p.* for s.th.); **~ность** *f* [8] gratitude; thanks; ***не сто́ит ´~ности*** you are welcome, don't mention it; **~ный** [14; -рен, -рна] grateful, thankful (to *a. p.* for s.th. Д / ***за*** В); **~я́** (Д) thanks *or* owing to

**благода́т|ный** [14; -тен, -тна] *климат* salubrious; *край* rich; **~ь** *f* [8] blessing; ***кака́я тут ~ь!*** it's heavenly here!

**благоде́тель** *m* [4] benefactor; **~ница** *f* [5] benefactress

**благодея́ние** *n* [12] good deed

**благоду́ш|ие** *n* [12] good nature, kindness; **~ный** [14; -шен, -шна] kindhearted, benign

**благожела́тель|ность** *f* [8] benevolence; **~ный** [14; -лен, -льна] benevolent

**благозву́ч|ие** *n* [12], **~ность** *f* [8] euphony, sonority; **~ный** [14; -чен, -чна] sonorous, harmonious

**благ|о́й** [16] good; ***~о́е наме́рение*** good intentions

**благонадёжный** [14; -жен, -жна] reliable, trustworthy

**благонаме́ренный** [14; *sh.*] well-meaning, well-meant

**благополу́ч|ие** *n* [12] well-being, prosperity, happiness; **~ный** [14; -чен, -чна] happy; safe

**благоприя́т|ный** [14; -тен, -тна] favo(u)rable, propitious; **~ствовать** [7] (Д) favo(u)r, promote

**благоразу́м|ие** *n* [12] prudence, discretion; **~ный** [14; -мен, -мна] prudent, judicious

**благоро́д|ный** [14; -ден, -дна] noble; *идеи и т. д.* lofty; *металл* precious; **~ство** *n* [9] nobility

**благоскло́нный** [14; -о́нен, -о́нна] favo(u)rable, well-disposed (to [-ward(s)] a p. ***к*** Д)

**благосло|ве́ние** *n* [12] benediction, blessing; **~вля́ть** [28], ⟨**~ви́ть**⟩ [14 *e.*; -влю́, -ви́шь] bless; ***~вля́ть свою́ судьбу́*** thank one's lucky stars

**благосостоя́ние** *n* [12] prosperity

**благотвори́тельный** [14] charitable, charity…

**благотво́рный** [14; -рен, -рна] beneficial, wholesome, salutary

**благоустро́енный** [14 *sh.*] well-equipped, comfortable; with all amenities

**благоуха́|ние** *n* [12] fragrance, odo(u)r; **~ть** [1] to be fragrant, smell sweet

**благочести́вый** [14 *sh.*] pious

**блаже́н|ный** [14 *sh.*] blissful; **~ство** *n* [9] bliss; **~ствовать** [7] enjoy felicity

**блажь** *f* [8] caprice, whim; *дурь* folly

**бланк** *m* [1] form; ***запо́лнить ~*** fill in a form

**блат** Р *m* [1] profitable connections; ***по ~у́*** on the quiet, illicitly, through good connections; **~но́й** Р [14]: ***~но́й язы́к*** thieves' slang, cant

**бледне́ть** [8], ⟨по-⟩ turn pale

**бледнова́тый** [14 *sh.*] palish

**бле́д|ность** *f* [8] pallor; **~ный** [14; -ден, -дна́, -о] pale, *fig.* colo(u)rless, insipid;

**~ный как полотно́** as white as a sheet
**блёк|лый** [14] faded, withered; **~нуть** [21], ⟨по-⟩ fade, wither
**блеск** *m* [1] luster, shine, brilliance, glitter; *fig.* splendo(u)r
**блест|е́ть** [11; *a.* бле́щешь], *once* ⟨блеснуть⟩ shine; glitter; flash; ***не всё то зо́лото, что ~и́т*** all is not gold that glitters; **блёстки** (bl̥oski) *f/pl.* [5; *gen.*: -ток] spangle; **~я́щий** [17 *sh.*] shining, bright; *fig.* brilliant
**блеф** *m* [1] bluff
**бле́ять** [27], ⟨за-⟩ bleat
**ближ|а́йший** [17] (→ ***бли́зкий***) the nearest, next; **~е** nearer; **~ний** [15] near(by); *su.* fellow creature
**близ** (Р) near, close; **~иться** [15; 3rd *p. only*], ⟨при-⟩ approach (a p. ***к*** Д); **~кий** [16; -зок, -зка́, -о; *comp.*: бли́же], (***к*** Д) near, close; **~кие** *pl.* folk(s), one's family, relatives; ***~ко от*** (Р) close to, not far from; **~колежа́щий** [17] nearby, neighbo(u)ring
**близне́ц** *m* [1 *e.*] twin
**близору́кий** [16 *sh.*] shortsighted
**бли́зость** *f* [8] nearness, proximity; *об отношениях* intimacy
**блин** *m* [1 *e.*] kind of pancake; **~чик** *m* [1] pancake
**блиста́тельный** [14; -лен, -льна] brilliant, splendid, magnificent
**блиста́ть** [1] shine
**блок** *m* [1] **1.** bloc, coalition; **2.** *tech.* pulley; unit
**блок|а́да** *f* [5] blockade; **~и́ровать** [7] (*im*)*pf.* block (up)
**блокно́т** *m* [1] notebook, writing pad
**блонди́н** *m* [1] blond; **~ка** *f* [5; *g/pl.*: -нок] blonde
**блоха́** *f* [5; *nom/pl.*: бло́хи] flea
**блуд** *m* [1] *coll.* fornication; **~ный** [14]: ***~ный сын*** prodigal son
**блужда́ть** [11], ⟨про-⟩ roam, wander
**блу́з|а** *f* [5] (working) blouse, smock; **~ка** *f* [5; *g/pl.*: -зок] (ladies') blouse
**блю́дечко** *n* [9; *g/pl.*: -чек] saucer
**блю́до** *n* [9] dish; *еда* course
**блю́дце** *n* [11; *g/pl.*: -дец] saucer
**блюсти́** [25], ⟨со-⟩ observe, preserve, maintain; **~тель** *m* [4]: ***~тель поря́дка*** *iro.* arm of the law
**бля́ха** *f* [5] name plate; number plate
**боб** *m* [1 *e.*] bean; haricot; ***оста́ться на ~а́х*** get nothing for one's pains
**бобёр** [1; -бра] beaver (*fur*)
**боби́на** *f* [5] bobbin, spool, reel
**бобо́в|ый** [14]: ***~ые расте́ния*** *n/pl.* legumes
**бобр** *m* [1 *e.*], **~о́вый** [14] beaver
**бо́бсле́й** *m* [3] bobsleigh
**бог** (bɔx) *m* [1; *vocative*: бо́же *from g/pl. e.*] God; god, idol; ***~ весть, ~ (его́) зна́ет*** *coll.* God knows; ***Бо́же (мой)*** oh God!, good gracious!; ***дай ~*** God grant; I (let's) hope (so); ***ра́ди ~а*** for God's (goodness') sake; ***сла́ва ~!*** thank God!; ***сохрани́ (не дай, изба́ви, упаси́) ~ (бо́же)*** God forbid!
**богат|е́ть** [8], ⟨раз-⟩ grow (become) rich; **~ство** *n* [9] wealth; **~ый** [14 *sh.*; *comp.*: бога́че] rich, wealthy
**богаты́рь** *m* [4 *e.*] (epic) hero
**бога́ч** *m* [1 *e.*] rich man
**боге́ма** *f* [5] (artists leading a) Bohemian life
**боги́ня** *f* [6] goddess
**Богома́терь** *f* [8] the Blessed Virgin, Mother of God
**Богоро́дица** *f* [5] the Blessed Virgin, Our Lady
**богосло́в** *m* [1] theologian; **~ие** *n* [12] theology, divinity; **~ский** [16] theological
**богослуже́ние** *n* [12] divine service; worship, liturgy
**боготвори́ть** [13] worship, idolize; deify
**бода́ть** [1], ⟨за-⟩, *once* ⟨боднуть⟩ [20] (*a.* **~ся**) butt (*a.* o.a.)
**бо́др|ость** *f* [8] vivacity, sprightliness; **~ствовать** [20] be awake; **~ый** [14; бодр, -а́, -о] sprightly, brisk, vigorous
**боеви́к** *m* [1 *e.*] member of revolutionary fighting group; *coll.* hit; ***~ сезо́на*** hit of the season
**боев|о́й** [14] battle…, fighting, war…, military; live (*shell etc.*); pugnacious, militant; ***~ы́е де́йствия*** operations, hostilities; ***~о́й па́рень*** dashing fellow
**бое|голо́вка** *f* [5; *g/pl.*: -вок] warhead;

**~припа́сы** *m/pl.* [1] ammunition; **~спосо́бный** [14; -бен, -бна] battleworthy, effective

**бое́ц** *m* [1; бойца́] soldier, fighter

**Бо́же** → ***бог***; **ᘐский** [16] fair, just; **ᘐственный** [14 *sh.*] divine, **~ство́** *n* [9] deity, devinity

**бо́ж|ий** [18] God's, divine; ***я́сно как ~ий день*** as clear as day

**божи́ться** [16 *e.*; -жу́сь, -жи́шься], ⟨по-⟩ swear

**бо́жья коро́вка** *f* [5; *g/pl.*: -вок] ladybird

**бой** *m* [3; бо́я, в бою́; *pl.*: бои́, боёв, *etc. e.*] battle, combat, fight; ***брать*** (***взять***) ***бо́ем*** *or* **с бо́ю** take by assault (storm); ***рукопа́шный ~*** close fight; ***~ часо́в*** the striking of a clock; **ᘐкий** [16; бо́ек, бойка́, бо́йко; *comp.*: бо́йч(é)е] brisk, lively; *место* busy; *речь* voluble, glib; **ᘐкость** *f* [8] liveliness

**бойкоти́ровать** [7] *(im)pf.* boycott

**бо́йня** *f* [6; *g/pl.*: бо́ен] slaughterhouse; *fig.* massacre, slaughter

**бок** *m* [1; на боку́; *pl.*: бока́, *etc. e.*] side; ***на́ ~, ᘐом*** sideways; ***~ о́ ~*** side by side; ***под бо́ком*** *coll.* close by

**бока́л** *m* [1] wineglass, goblet

**боково́й** [14] side, lateral

**бокс** *m* [1] boxing; **~ёр** *m* [1] boxer; **~и́ровать** [7] box

**болва́н** *m* [1] dolt, blockhead

**болга́р|ин** *m* [4; *pl.*: -ры, -р] Bulgarian; **~ка** *f* [5; *g/pl.*: -рок], **~ский** [16] Bulgarian

**бо́лее** (→ ***бо́льше***) more (than P); ***~ высо́кий*** higher; ***~ или ме́нее*** more or less; ***~ того́*** what is more; ***тем ~, что*** especially as; ***не ~*** at (the) most

**боле́зненный** [14 *sh.*] sickly, ailing; *fig.* morbid; painful (*a. fig.*)

**боле́знь** *f* [8] sickness, illness; disease; (*mental*) disorder; sick (*leave*… **по** Д)

**боле́льщик** *m* [1] *sport*: fan

**боле́ть** [8] **1.** be sick, be down (with T); *за дело; о ком-то* be anxious (for, about **за** В, **о** П), apprehensive; *sport* support, be a fan (of **за** В); **2.** [9; 3rd *p. only*] hurt, ache; ***у меня́ боли́т голова́*** (***зуб, го́рло***) I have a headache (a toothache, a sore throat)

**болеутоля́ющ|ий** [17]: ***~ее сре́дство*** anodyne, analgesic

**боло́т|истый** [14 *sh.*] boggy, swampy; **~ный** [14] bog…, swamp…; **~о** *n* [9] bog, swamp

**болт** *m* [1 *e.*] bolt

**болта́ть** [1] **1.** ⟨вз-⟩ shake up; **2. (-ся)** dangle; **3.** *coll.* ⟨по-⟩ [20] chat(ter); **~ся** *coll.* loaf *or* hang about

**болтли́вый** [14 *sh.*] talkative

**болтовня́** *f* [6] *coll.* idle talk, gossip

**болту́н** *m* [1; -на] *coll.*, **~ья** *f* [6] babbler, chatterbox

**боль** *f* [8] pain, ache

**больни́|ца** *f* [5] hospital; ***вы́писаться из ~цы*** be discharged from hospital; ***лечь в ~цу*** go to hospital; **~чный** [14] hospital…; ***~чный лист*** medical certificate

**бо́льн|о** painful(ly); P very; ***мне ~о*** it hurts me; ***глаза́м бо́льно*** my eyes smart; **~о́й** [14; бо́лен, больна́] sick, ill, sore; *su.* patient; *fig.* delicate, burning; tender; ***стациона́рный ~о́й*** inpatient

**бо́льше** bigger, more; ***~ всего́*** most of all; above all; ***~ не*** no more *or* longer; ***как мо́жно ~*** as much (many) as possible; **~ви́зм** *m* [1] Bolshevism; **~ви́к** *m* [1 *e.*] Bolshevik; **~ви́стский** (-visski-) [16] Bolshevist(ic)

**бо́льш|ий** [17] bigger, greater; ***по ~ей ча́сти*** for the most part; ***са́мое ~ее*** at most; **~инство́** *n* [9] majority; most; **~о́й** [16] big, large, great; *coll.* ***взро́слый*** grown-up; **~у́щий** [17] *coll.* huge

**бо́мб|а** *f* [5] bomb; **~ардирова́ть** [7] bomb, shell; bombard (*a. fig.*); **~ардиро́вка** *f* [5; *g/pl.*: -вок] bombardment, bombing; **~ардиро́вщик** *m* [1] bomber; **~ёжка** *coll.* *f* [5; *g/pl.*: -жек] → ***~ардиро́вка***; **~и́ть** [14; *e.*; -блю́, -би́шь (раз-) бомблённый], ⟨раз-⟩ bomb

**бомбоубе́жище** *n* [11] air-raid *or* bombproof shelter

**бор** *m* [1; в бору́] pine wood or forest; ***разгоре́лся сыр ~*** passions flared up

**бордо́** *n* [*indecl.*] claret; **~вый** [14] dark purplish red

Б

**бордю́р** *m* [1] border, trimming
**боре́ц** *m* [1; -рца́] fighter, wrestler; *fig.* champion, partisan
**борза́я** *f* [14] *su.* borzoi, greyhound
**бормота́ть** [3], ⟨про-⟩ mutter
**бо́ров** *m* [1; *from g/pl. e.*] boar
**борода́** *f* [5; *ac/sg.*: бо́роду; *pl.* бо́роды, боро́д, -а́м] beard
**борода́вка** *f* [5; *g/pl.*: -вок] wart
**борода́|тый** [14 *sh.*] bearded; **~ч** *m* [1 *e.*] bearded man
**борозд|а́** *f* [5; *pl.*: бо́розды, боро́зд, -да́м] furrow; **~и́ть** [15 *e.*; -зжу́, -зди́шь], ⟨вз-⟩ furrow
**борон|а́** *f* [5; *ac/sg.*: бо́рону; *pl.*: бо́роны, боро́н, -на́м] harrow; **~ни́ть** [13], **~нова́ть** [7], ⟨вз-⟩ harrow
**боро́ться** [17; боря́сь] fight, struggle (for ***за*** B, against ***про́тив*** P, wrestle)
**борт** *m* [1; на ~у́; *nom/pl.*: -та́] *naut.* side; board; ***на ~у́ су́дна*** on board a ship; ***бро́сить за ~*** throw overboard; ***челове́к за ~о́м!*** man overboard!
**борщ** *m* [1 *e.*] borsch(t), red-beet soup
**борьба́** *f* [5] *sport* wrestling; *fig.* fight, struggle
**босико́м** barefoot
**бо́сой** [14; бос, -а́, -о] barefooted; ***на босу́ но́гу*** wearing shoes on bare feet
**босоно́гий** [16] → ***босо́й***
**босоно́жка** *f* [5; *g/pl.*: -жек] sandal
**бота́ни|к** *m* [1] botanist; **~ка** *f* [5] botany; **~ческий** [16] botanic(al)
**ботва́** *f* [5] leafy tops of root vegetables, *esp.* beet leaves
**боти́нок** *m* [1; *g/pl.*: -нок] shoe, *Brt.* (lace) boot
**бо́цман** *m* [1] boatswain
**бо́чк|а** *f* [5; *g/pl.*: -чек] cask, barrel; **~ово́й** [14]: ***~ово́е пи́во*** draught beer
**бочко́м** sideway(s), sidewise
**бочо́нок** *m* [1; -нка] (small) barrel
**боязли́вый** [14 *sh.*] timid, timorous
**боя́зн|ь** *f* [8] fear, dread; ***из ~и*** for fear of, lest
**боя́р|ин** *m* [4; *pl.*: -ре, -р], **~ыня** *f* [6] boyar(d) (*member of old nobility in Russia*)
**боя́рышник** *m* [1] hawthorn
**боя́ться** [бою́сь, бои́шься; бо́йся, бо́йтесь!], ⟨по-⟩ be afraid (of P), fear; ***бою́сь сказа́ть*** I don't know exactly, I'm not quite sure
**бра** *n* [*indecl.*] lampbracket, sconce
**бра́во** *int.* bravo
**бразды́** *f/pl.* [5] *fig.* reins
**брази́|лец** *m* [1; -льца] Brazilian; **~льский** [16], **~лья́нка** *f* [5; *g/pl.*: -нок] Brazilian
**брак**[1] *m* [1] marriage; matrimony
**брак**[2] *m* [1] (*no pl.*) defective articles, rejects, spoilage
**бракова́ть** [7], ⟨за-⟩ scrap, reject
**браконье́р** *m* [1] poacher
**бракосочета́ние** *n* [12] wedding
**брани́ть** [13], ⟨по-, вы́-⟩ scold, rebuke; **~ся** quarrel; swear
**бра́нн|ый** [14] abusive; ***~ое сло́во*** swearword
**брань** *f* [8] abuse, invective
**брасле́т** *m* [1] bracelet; watchband
**брат** *m* [1; *pl.*: бра́тья, -тьев, -тьям] brother; (*mode of address*) old boy!; ***на ~а*** a head, each
**бра́тец** *m* [1; -тца] *iro.* dear brother
**бра́тия** *f* [7] *coll. joc.* company, fraternity
**бра́т|ский** [16; *adv.*: (по-)бра́тски] brotherly, fraternal; ***~ская моги́ла*** communal grave; **~ство** *n* [9] brotherhood, fraternity, fellowship
**брать** [беру́, -рёшь; брал, -а́, -о; … бра́нный], ⟨взять⟩ [возьму́, -мёшь; взял, -а́, -о; взя́тый (взят, -а́, -о)] take; ***~ напрока́т*** hire; ***~ приме́р*** (**с** P) take (*a p.*) for a model; ***~ верх над*** (T) be victorious over, conquer; ***~ обра́тно*** take back; ***~ сло́во*** take (have) the floor; (**с** P) ***~ сло́во*** make (s.o.) promise; ***~ свой слова́ обра́тно*** withdraw one's words; ***~ себя́ в ру́ки*** *fig.* collect o.s., pull o.s. together; ***~ на себя́*** assume; ***~ за пра́вило*** make it a rule; ***он взял и уе́хал*** he left unexpectedly; ***возьми́те напра́во!*** turn (to the) right!; → *a.* ***взима́ть***; ***с чего́ ты взял?*** what makes you think that?; **-ся** [бра́лся, -ла́сь, -ло́сь] ⟨взя́ться⟩ [взя́лся, -ла́сь, взя́ло́сь, взя́ли́сь] (***за*** B) undertake; (*приступить*) set about; (*хватать*) take hold

of, seize; **~ся за́ руки** join hands; **~ся за кни́гу** (**рабо́ту**) set about or start reading a book (working); **отку́да это берётся?** where does that come from?; **отку́да у него́ де́ньги беру́тся?** wherever does he get his money from?; **отку́да ни возьми́сь** all of a sudden
**бра́чн|ый** [14] matrimonial, conjugal; **~ое свиде́тельство** marriage certificate
**брев|е́нчатый** [14] log…; **~но́** *n* [9; *pl*.: брёвна, -вен, -внам] log; beam
**бред** *m* [1] delirium; *coll*. nonsense; **~ить** [15], ⟨за-⟩ be delirious; *fig*. rave; be crazy, dream (about **о** П); **~ни** *f/pl*. [6; *gen*.: -ней] nonsense
**бре́зг|ать** [1] (T) be squeamish, fastidious (about); (*гнушаться*) disdain; **~ли́вость** *f* [8] squeamishness, disgust; **~ли́вый** [14 *sh*.] squeamish, fastidious (in **к** Д)
**брезе́нт** *m* [1] tarpaulin
**бре́зжить** [16], **~ся** glimmer; (*рассветать*) dawn
**бре́мя** *n* [3; *no pl*.] load, burden (*a. fig*.)
**бренча́ть** [4 *e*.; -чу́, -чи́шь] clink, jingle; *на гитаре* strum
**брести́** [25], ⟨по-⟩ drag o.s. along; saunter
**брете́лька** *f* [5; *g/pl*.: -лек] shoulder strap
**брешь** *f* [8] breach; gap
**брига́|да** *f* [5] brigade (*a. mil*.), team, group of workers; **~ди́р** *m* [1] foreman
**бри́джи** *pl*. [*gen*.: -жей] breeches
**бриллиа́нт** *m* [1], **~овый** [14] brilliant, (cut) diamond
**брита́н|ец** *m* [1; -нца] Briton, Britisher; **~ский** [16] British
**бри́тва** *f* [5] razor; **безопа́сная ~** safety razor
**брить** [бре́ю, бре́ешь; брей(те)!; бре́я; брил; бри́тый], ⟨вы-, по-⟩ shave; **~ся** *v/i*. get shaved, (have a) shave; **~ё** *n* [10] shaving
**бри́финг** *m* [1] *pol*. briefing
**бров|ь** *f* [8; *from g/pl. e*.] eyebrow; **хму́рить ~и** frown; **он и ~ью не повёл** *coll*. he did not turn a hair; **попа́сть не в ~ь, а в глаз** *coll*. hit the nail on the head
**брод** *m* [1] ford
**броди́ть¹** [15], ⟨по-⟩ wander, roam
**броди́ть²** [15] (*impers*.) ferment
**бродя́|га** *m* [5] tramp, vagabond; **~чий** [17] vagrant; *собака* stray
**броже́ние** *n* [12] fermentation; *fig*. agitation, unrest
**бро́кер** *m* [1] broker
**бром** *m* [1] bromine
**броне|та́нковый** [14]: **~та́нковые ча́сти** *f/pl*. armo(u)red troops; **~транспортёр** *m* [1] armo(u)red personnel carrier
**бро́нз|а** *f* [5] bronze; **~овый** [14] bronze…
**брони́ровать** [7], ⟨за-⟩ reserve, book
**бро́нх|и** *m/pl*. [1] bronchi *pl*. (*sg*. **~** bronchus); **~и́т** *m* [1] bronchitis
**броня́** *f* [6; *g/pl*.: -не́й] armo(u)r
**бро́ня** *f* [6; *g/pl*.: -ней] reservation
**броса́ть** [1], ⟨бро́сить⟩ throw, (*a. naut*.) cast, fling (*a. out*) (s.th. at В *or* Т/**в** В); (*покинуть*) leave, abandon, desert; (*прекратить делать*) give up, quit, leave off; **~ взгля́д** cast a glance; **бро́сь(те)…!** *coll*. (oh) stop…!; **-ся** dash, rush, dart (off **~ся бежа́ть**); fall up(on) (**на** В); go to (**в** В); **~ в глаза́** strike the eye
**бро́ский** [16] bright, loud
**бро́совый** [14] catchpenny; under (price)
**бросо́к** *m* [1; -ска́] hurl, throw; (*рывок*) spurt
**бро́шка** *f* [5; *g/pl*.: -шек] brooch
**брошю́ра** *f* [5] brochure, pamphlet
**брус** *m* [1; *pl*.: бру́сья, бру́сьев, бру́сьям] (square) beam; bar; *pl*. **паралле́льные бру́сья** parallel bars
**брусни́ка** *f* [5] cowberry
**брусо́к** *m* [1; -ска́] **1.** bar, ingot; **2.** (*a*. **точи́льный ~**) whetstone
**бру́тто** [*indecl*.] gross (weight)
**бры́з|гать** [1 *or* 3], *once* ⟨**~нуть**⟩ [20] splash, spatter, sprinkle; gush; **~ги** *f/pl*. [5] splashes, spray
**брык|а́ться** [1], *once* ⟨**~ну́ться**⟩ [20] kick; *fig*. rebel
**брюз|га́** *m/f* [5] *coll*. grumbler, grouch; **~гли́вый** [14 *sh*.] peevish, grouchy;

**~жа́ть** [4 *e.*; -жу, -жи́шь], ⟨за-⟩ grumble, grouch
**брю́ква** *f* [5] swede
**брю́ки** *f/pl.* [5] trousers, pants
**брюне́т** *m* [1] dark-haired man, brunet; **~ка** *f* [5; *g/pl.*: -ток] brunette
**брюссе́ль|ский** [16]: ***~ская капу́ста*** *f* Brussels sprouts
**брю́хо** P *n* [9] belly, paunch
**брюш|и́на** *f* [5] peritoneum; **~но́й** [14] abdominal; ***~но́й тиф*** *m* typhoid fever
**бря́кать** [1], *once* ⟨бря́кнуть⟩ [20] *v/i.* clink, clatter; *v/t. fig. coll.* drop a clanger
**бу́бен** *m* [1; -бна; *g/pl.*: бу́бен] (*mst. pl.*) tambourine; **~чик** *m* [1] jingle, small bell
**бу́блик** *m* [1] slightly sweetened ring-shaped bread roll
**бу́бны** *f/pl.* [5; *g/pl.*: бубён, -бнам] (*cards*) diamonds
**буго́р** *m* [1; -гра́] hill(ock)
**бугри́стый** [14] hilly; *доро́га* bumpy
**бу́дет** (→ ***быть***) (*impers.*): ***~ тебе́ ворча́ть*** stop grumbling
**буди́льник** *m* [1] alarm clock
**буди́ть** [15] **1.** ⟨раз-⟩ (a)wake, waken; **2.** ⟨про-⟩ [пробуждённый] *fig.* (a)rouse; ***~ мысль*** set one thinking
**бу́дка** *f* [5; *g/pl.*: -док] booth, box
**бу́дни** *m/pl.* [1; *gen.*: -дней] weekdays; *fig.* everyday life, monotony; **~чный** [14] everyday; humdrum
**будора́жить** [16], ⟨вз-⟩ excite
**бу́дто** as if, as though (*a.* ***~ бы, ~ б***) that, allegedly
**бу́дущ|ее** *n* [17] future; ***в ближа́йшем ~ем*** in the near future; **~ий** [17] future (*a. gr.*) ***в ~ем году́*** next year; **~ность** *f* [8] future
**бу́ер** *m* [1; *pl.*: -ра, *etc. e.*] iceboat, ice yacht
**бузина́** *f* [5] elder, elderberries
**буй** *m* [3] buoy
**бу́йвол** *m* [1] buffalo
**бу́йный** [14; бу́ен, буйна́, -о] violent, vehement; (*необу́зданный*) unbridled; *расти́тельность* luxuriant
**бу́йство** *n* [9] rage, violence; **~вать** [7] behave violently, rage
**бук** *m* [1] beech
**бу́к|ва** *f* [5] letter; ***прописна́я*** (***строчна́я***) ***~ва*** upper-(lower)case letter (with **с** P); **~ва́льный** [14] literal, verbal; **~ва́рь** *m* [4 *e.*] primer; **~вое́д** *m* [1] pedant
**буке́т** *m* [1] bouquet (*a. of wine*), bunch of flowers
**букини́ст** *m* [1] secondhand bookseller; **~и́ческий** [16]: ***~и́ческий магази́н*** secondhand bookshop
**бу́ковый** [14] beechen, beech…
**букси́р** *m* [1] tug(boat); ***взять на букси́р*** take in tow; **~ный** [14] tug…; **~ова́ть** [7] tow
**була́вка** *f* [5; *g/pl.*: -вок] pin; ***англи́йская ~*** safety pin
**була́т** *m* [1] Damascus steel *fig.* sword; **~ный** [14] steel…; damask…
**бу́лка** *f* [5; *g/pl.*: -лок] small loaf; roll; white bread
**бу́лоч|ка** *f* [5; *g/pl.*: -чек] roll; bun; **~ная** *f* [14] bakery, baker's shop
**булы́жник** *m* [1] cobblestone
**бульва́р** *m* [1] boulevard, avenue; **~ный** [14]: ***~ный рома́н*** dime novel, *Brt.* penny dreadful; ***~ная пре́сса*** tabloids; gutter press
**бу́лькать** [1] gurgle
**бульо́н** *m* [1] broth; stock
**бума́|га** *f* [5] paper; document; ***це́нные ~ги*** securities; **~жка** *f* [5; *g/pl.*: -жек] slip of paper; **~жник** *m* [1] wallet; **~жный** [14] paper…
**бундеста́г** *m* [1] Bundestag
**бунт** *m* [1] revolt, mutiny, riot; **~а́рь** *m* [4 *e.*] → ***~овщи́к***
**бунтов|а́ть** [7] rebel, revolt; ⟨вз-⟩ instigate; **~ско́й** [14] rebellious, mutinous; **~щи́к** *m* [1 *e.*] mutineer, rebel
**бура́в** *m* [1 *e.*] gimlet, auger; **~ить** [14], ⟨про-⟩ bore, drill
**бура́н** *m* [1] snowstorm, blizzard
**бурда́** *coll. f* [5] slops, wish-wash
**буреве́стник** *m* [1] (storm) petrel
**буре́ние** *n* [12] drilling, boring
**буржуаз|и́я** *f* [7] bourgeoisie; **~ный** [14] bourgeois
**бури́ть** [13], ⟨про-⟩ bore, drill
**бу́ркать** [1], *once* ⟨-кнуть⟩ mutter

**бурли́ть** [13] rage; (*кипеть*) seethe
**бу́рный** [14; -рен, -рна] stormy, storm…; *рост* rapid; boisterous, violent (*a. fig.*)
**буру́н** *m* [1 *e.*] surf, breaker
**бурча́|нье** *n* [12] grumbling; *в животе* rumbling; **~ть** [4 *e.*; -чу́, -чи́шь] (*бормотать*) mumble; (*ворчать*) grumble; rumble
**бу́рый** [14] brown, tawny; **~ медве́дь** brown bear; **~ у́голь** brown coal, lignite
**бурья́н** *m* [1] tall weeds
**бу́ря** *f* [6] storm (*a. fig.*); **~ в стака́не воды́** storm in a teacup
**бу́сы** *f/pl.* [5] *coll.* (glass)beads
**бутафо́рия** *f* [7] *thea.* properties *pl.*; *в витрине* dummies; *fig.* window dressing
**бутербро́д** (-tɛr-) *m* [1] sandwich
**буто́н** *m* [1] bud
**бу́тсы** *f/pl.* [5] football boots
**буты́л|ка** *f* [5; *g/pl.*: -лок] bottle; **~очка** *f* [5; *g/pl.*: -чек] small bottle; **~ь** *f* [8] large bottle; *оплетённая* carboy
**бу́фер** *m* [1; *pl.*: -pá, *etc. e.*] buffer
**буфе́т** *m* [1] sideboard; bar, lunchroom, refreshment room; **~чик** *m* [1] counter assistant; barman; **~чица** *f* [5] counter assistant; barmaid
**бух** *int.* bounce!, plump!
**буха́нка** *f* [5; *g/pl.*: -нок] loaf
**бу́хать** [1], *once* ⟨бу́хнуть⟩ thump, bang
**бухга́лтер** (bu'ha) *m* [1] bookkeeper; accountant; **~ия** *f* [7] bookkeeping; **~ский** [16] bookkeeper('s)…, bookkeeping…; **~ский учёт** accounting
**бу́хнуть** [21] **1.** ⟨раз-⟩ swell; **2.** → **бу́хать**
**бу́хта**[1] *f* [5] bay
**бу́хта**[2] *f* [5] coil (of rope)
**бушева́ть** [6; бушу́ю, -у́ешь] roar, rage, storm
**бушла́т** *m* [1] (sailor's) peajacket
**буя́нить** [13] brawl, kick up a row
**бы**, *short* **б**, *is used to render subjunctive and conditional patterns*: *a) with the preterite*, *e.g.* **я сказа́л ~, е́сли ~ (я) знал** I would say it if I knew it; (*similary*: *should*, *could*, *may*, *might*); *b) with the infinitive*, *e.g.*: **всё ~ ему́ знать** *iro.* he would like to know everything; **не вам ~ говори́ть!** you had better be quiet; c) *to express a wish* **я ~ съел чего́нибудь** I could do with s.th. to eat
**быва́лый** [14] experienced
**быва́|ть** [1] **1.** occur, happen; **как ни в чём не ~ло** as if nothing had happened; **она́ ~ло, гуля́ла** she would (*or* used to) go for a walk; **бо́ли как не ~ло** *coll.* the pain had (or has) entirely disappeared; **2.** ⟨по-⟩ (**у** P) be (at), visit, stay (with)
**бы́вший** [17] former, ex-…
**бык**[1] *m* [1 *e.*] *моста* pier
**бык**[2] *m* [1 *e.*] bull
**были́на** *f* [5] Russian epic
**были́нка** *f* [5; *g/pl.*: -нок] blade of grass
**бы́ло** (→ **быть**) (*after verbs*) already; **я уже́ заплати́л ~ де́ньги** I had already paid the money, (but)…; almost, nearly, was (were) just going to…; **я чуть ~ не сказа́л** I was on the point of saying, I nearly said
**был|о́й** [14] bygone, former; **~о́е** *n* past; **~ь** *f* [8] true story *or* occurence
**быстро|но́гий** [16] swift(-footed); **~та́** *f* [5] quickness, swiftness, rapidity; **~хо́дный** [14; -ден, -дна] fast, high-speed
**бы́стрый** [14; быстр, -á, -o] quick, fast, swift
**быт** *m* [1; в быту́] everyday life; **семе́йный ~** family life; **~ дереве́нской жи́зни** way of life in the country; **~ие́** *n* [12] existence, social being; **Кни́га** ♀**ия́** *Bibl.* Genesis; **~ность** *f* [8] **в мою́ ~ность** in my time; **~ово́й** [14] everyday, social, popular, genre; **~овы́е прибо́ры** household appliances
**быть** [3rd *p. sg. pr.*: → **есть**; 3rd *p. pl.*: суть; *ft.*: бу́ду, -дешь; бу́дь[те]!; бу́дучи; был, -á, -o; не́ был, -o, -и] be; (→ **бу́дет, быва́ть, бы́ло**); **~** (Д) **…** will (inevitably) be or happen; **мне бы́ло (бу́дет) … (го́да** *or* **лет**) I was (I'll be) … (years old); **как же ~?** what is to be done?; **так и ~!** all right! agreed!; **будь что бу́дет** come what may; **будь пова́шему** have it your own way!; **бу́дьте добры́ (любе́зны)**, … be so kind as…, would your please…; **у меня́ бы́ло мно́го свобо́дного вре́мени** I had a lot of time
**бюдже́т** *m* [1], **~ный** [14] budget
**бюллете́нь** *m* [4] bulletin; ballot paper;

*coll.* sick-leave certificate

**бюро́** *n* [*indecl.*] office, bureau; ***спра́вочное ~*** inquiry office; information; ***~ путеше́ствий*** travel agency *or* bureau

**бюрокра́т** *m* [1] bureaucrat; **~и́ческий** [16] bureaucratic; ***~и́ческая волоки́та*** *f* [5] red tape; **~и́я** *f* [7] bureaucracy

**бюст** *m* [1] bust; **~га́льтер** (-'haļtɛr) *m* [1] bra(ssiere)

**бязь** *f* [8] calico

# В

**в**, **во 1.** (В); (*direction*) to, into; for; ***в окно́*** out of (in through) the window; (*time*) in, at, on, within; ***в сре́ду*** on Wednesday; ***в два часа́*** at two o'clock; (*measure, price, etc.*) at, of; ***в день*** a *or* per day; ***длино́й в четы́ре ме́тра*** four meters long; ***в де́сять раз бо́льше*** ten times as much; **2.** (П): *положение* in, at, on; *время* in; ***в конце́ (нача́ле) го́да*** at the end (beginning) of the year; (*расстояние*) ***в пяти́ киломе́трах от*** (Р) five kilometers from

**ва-ба́нк**: (*cards*) ***идти́ ~*** stake everything

**ваго́н** *m* [1] car(riage *Brt.*); **~овожа́тый** [14] (*Brt.* tram) driver; **~-рестора́н** *m* dining car

**ва́жн|ичать** [1] put on (*or* give *o.s.*) airs; **~ость** *f* [8] importance; conceit; **~ый** [14; ва́жен, -жна́, -о, ва́жны] important, significant; *надменный и т. д.* haughty, pompous; *coll.* ***не ~о*** rather bad; ***э́то не ~о*** that doesn't matter *or* is of no importance

**ва́за** *f* [5] vase, bowl

**вазели́н** *m* [1] vaseline

**вака́н|сия** *f* [7] vacancy; **~тный** [14; -тен, -тна] vacant

**ва́куум** *m* [1] vacuum

**вакци́на** *f* [5] vaccine

**вал** *m* [1; на ~у́; *pl. e.*] **1.** *крепостной* rampart; *насыпь* bank; **2.** billow, wave; **3.** *tech.* shaft

**вале́жник** *m* [1] brushwood

**ва́ленок** *m* [1; -нка] felt boot

**валерья́н|ка** *coll.* *f* [5], **~овый** [14]: ***~овые ка́пли*** *f/pl.* tincture valerian

**вале́т** *m* [1] (*cards*) knave, jack

**ва́лик** *m* [1] **1.** *tech.* roller; **2.** bolster

**вал|и́ть** [13; валю́, ва́лишь; ва́ленный], ⟨по-, с-⟩ **1.** overturn, tumble (down; *v/i.* **-ся**), *лес* fell; *в кучу* heap (up) dump; **2.** [3rd *p. only*: -и́т] *о толпе* flock, throng; ***снег ~и́т*** it is snowing heavily

**валово́й** [14] gross, total

**валто́рна** *f* [5] French horn

**валу́н** *m* [1 *e.*] boulder

**ва́льдшнеп** *m* [1] woodcock

**ва́льс** *m* [1] waltz; **~и́ровать** [7], ⟨про-⟩ waltz

**валю́т|а** *f* [5] (foreign) currency; ***твёрдая ~а*** hard currency; **~ный** [14] currency…, exchange…; ***~ный курс*** *m* rate of exchange

**валя́ть** [28], ⟨по-⟩ roll, drag; Р ***валя́й!*** OK go ahead!; ***валя́й отсю́да!*** beat it!; ***~ дурака́*** idle; play the fool; **-ся** *о человеке* wallow, loll; *о предметах* lie about (in disorder)

**вандали́зм** *m* [1] vandalism

**вани́ль** *f* [8] vanilla

**ва́нн|а** *f* [5] tub; bath; ***со́лнечная ~а*** sun bath; ***приня́ть ~у*** take a bath; **~ая** *f* [14] bath(room)

**ва́рвар** *m* [1] barbarian; **~ский** [16] barbarous; **~ство** *n* [9] barbarity

**ва́режка** *f* [5; *g/pl.*: -жек] mitten

**вар|е́ние** *n* [12] → ***ва́рка***; **~е́ник** *m* [1] (*mst. pl.*) boiled pieces of dough with stuffing; **~ёный** [14] cooked, boiled; **~е́нье** *n* [10] jam, confiture

**вариа́нт** *m* [1] variant, version

**вари́ть** [13; варю́, ва́ришь; ва́ренный], ⟨с-⟩ cook, boil; brew; *v/i.* **~ся**: ***~ в со́бственном соку́*** stew in one's own juice

**ва́рка** *f* [5] cooking, boiling

**варьете́** *n* (-tɛ) [*indecl.*] variety show
**варьи́ровать** [7] vary
**варя́г** *m* [1] *hist.* Varangian; *coll., joc.* alien, stranger
**василёк** *m* [1; -лька́] cornflower
**ва́та** *f* [5] absorbent cotton, *Brt.* cotton wool
**ватага** *f* [5] gang, band, troop
**ватерли́ния** (-tɛ-) *f* [7] water-line
**ва́тный** [14] quilted; wadded
**ватру́шка** *f* [5; *g/pl.*: -шек] curd tart, cheese cake
**ва́фля** *f* [6; *g/pl.*: -фель] waffle, wafer
**ва́хт|а** *f* [5] *naut.* watch; ***стоя́ть на ~е*** keep watch; **~енный** [14] sailor on duty; **~ёр** *m* [1] janitor, *Brt.* porter
**ваш** *m*, **~a** *f*, **~e** *n*, *pl.* **~и** [25] your; yours; ***по ~ему*** in your opinion (*or* language); **(*пусть бу́дет*) *по ~ему*** (have it) your own way, (just) as you like; ***как по-~ему?*** what do you think?; → ***наш***
**вая́|ние** *n* [12] sculpture; **~тель** *m* [4] sculptor; **~ть** [28], ⟨из-⟩ sculpture, cut, model
**вбе|га́ть** [1], ⟨**~жа́ть**⟩ [4; -гу́, -жи́шь, -гу́т] run *or* rush into
**вби|ва́ть** [1], ⟨**~ть**⟩ [вобью́, вобьёшь; вбе́й(те)!; вбил; вби́тый]; drive (*or* hammer) in; ***~ть себе́ в го́лову*** get/take into one's head; **~ра́ть** [1], ⟨вобра́ть⟩ [вберу́, -рёшь] absorb, imbibe
**вблизи́** nearby; close (to P)
**вбок** to one side, sideways
**вброд**: ***переходи́ть ~*** ford, wade
**вва́л|ивать** [1], ⟨**~и́ть**⟩ [ввалю́, вва́лишь; вва́ленный] throw, heave (in[-to]), dump; **-ся** fall or tumble in; burst in(to); *толпой* flock in
**введе́ние** *n* [12] introduction
**ввезти́** → ***ввози́ть***
**ввер|га́ть** [1], ⟨**~ну́ть**⟩ [21]: ***~а́ть в отча́яние*** drive to despair
**ввер|я́ть** [14], ⟨**~ить**⟩ entrust, commit, give in charge
**ввёртывать** [1], ⟨ввертéть⟩ [11; вверчу́, вве́ртишь] *once* ⟨ввернýть⟩ [20; ввёрнутый] screw in; *fig.* put in (a word *etc.*)
**вверх** up(ward[s]); ***~ по ле́снице*** upstairs; ***~ дном*** (*or* ***нога́ми***) upside down; ***~ торма́шками*** head over heels; ***ру́ки ~!*** hands up!; ***~у́*** above; overhead
**ввести́** → ***вводи́ть***
**ввиду́** in view (of P), considering; ***~ того́, что*** as, since, seeing
**вви́н|чивать** [1], ⟨**~ти́ть**⟩ [15 *e.*; -нчу́, -нти́шь] screw in
**ввод** *m* [1] *tech.* input
**ввод|и́ть** [15], ⟨ввести́⟩ introduce; bring *or* usher (in); ***~и́ть в заблужде́ние*** mislead; ***~и́ть в курс де́ла*** acquaint with an affair; ***~и́ть в строй*** (*or* ***де́йствие, эксплуата́цию***) put into operation; **~ный** [14] introductory; ***~ное сло́во*** *or* ***предложе́ние*** *gr.* parenthesis
**ввоз** *m* [1] import(s); importation; **~и́ть** [15], ⟨ввезти́⟩ [24] import
**вво́лю** (P) *coll.* plenty of; to one's heart's content
**ввя́з|ываться** [1], ⟨**~а́ться**⟩ [3] meddle, interfere (with ***в*** B); get involved (in)
**вглубь** deep into, far into
**вгля́д|ываться** [1], ⟨**~е́ться**⟩ [11] (***в*** B) peer (into), look narrowly (at)
**вгоня́ть** [28], ⟨вогна́ть⟩ [вгоню́, вго́нишь; вогна́л, -а́, -о; во́гнанный (во́гнан, -а́, -о)] drive in (to)
**вдава́ться** [5], ⟨вда́ться⟩ [вда́мся, вда́шься, *etc.* → ***дать***] jut out into; ***~ в подро́бности*** go (into)
**вда́в|ливать** [1], ⟨**~и́ть**⟩ [14] press (in)
**вдал|еке́**, **~и́** far off, far (from **от** P); **~ь** into the distance
**вдви|га́ть** [1], ⟨**~нуть**⟩ [20] push in
**вдво́|е** twice (as ..., *comp.*: ***~е бо́льше*** twice as much *or* many); *vb.* + **~е** *a.* double; **~ём** both *or* two (of us, *etc.*, *or* together); **~йне́** twice (as much, *etc.*) doubly
**вде|ва́ть** [1], ⟨**~ть**⟩ [вде́ну, вде́нешь; вде́тый] (***в*** B) put into, thread
**вде́л|ывать**, ⟨**~ать**⟩ [1] set (in[to])
**вдоба́вок** in addition (to); into the bargain, to boot
**вдов|а́** *f* [5; *pl. st.*] widow; **~е́ц** *m* [1; -вца́] widower
**вдо́воль** *coll.* in abundance; quite enough; plenty of
**вдо́вый** [14 *sh.*] widowed

**вдого́нку** after, in pursuit of
**вдоль** (Р, ***по*** Д) along; lengthwise; ***~ и поперёк*** in all directions, far and wide
**вдох** *m* [1] breath, inhalation; ***сде́лайте глубо́кий ~*** take a deep breath
**вдохнов|е́ние** *n* [12] inspiration; **~е́нный** [14; -ве́нен, -ве́нна] inspired; **~ля́ть** [28], ⟨**~и́ть**⟩ [14 *e*.; -влю́, -ви́шь] inspire; **-ся** get inspired (with *or* by T)
**вдре́безги** to smithereens
**вдруг** **1.** suddenly, all of a sudden; **2.** what if, suppose
**вду|ва́ть** [1], ⟨**~ть**⟩ [18] blow into, inflate
**вду́м|чивый** [14 *sh*.] thoughtful; **~ываться**, ⟨**~аться**⟩ [1] (***в*** В) ponder (over), reflect ([up]on)
**вдыха́ть** [1], ⟨**вдохну́ть**⟩ [20] inhale; *fig*. inspire (with)
**вегета|риа́нец** *m* [1; -нца] vegetarian; **~ти́вный** [14] vegetative
**ве́д|ать** [1] **1.** know; **2.** (T) be in charge of, manage; **~е́ние**[1] *n* [12] running, directing; ***~е́ние книг*** bookkeeping; **~ение**[2] *n* [12]: ***в его́ ~ении*** in his charge, competence; **~омо** known; ***без моего́ ~ома*** without my knowledge; **~омость** *f* [8; *from g/pl. e*.] list, roll, register; *периодическое издание* bulletin; ***инвента́рная ~омость*** inventory; **~омство** *n* [9] department
**ведро́** *n* [9; *pl*.: вёдра, -дер, -драм] bucket, pail; ***~ для му́сора*** garbage can, *Brt*. dustbin
**веду́щий** *m* [17] leading; basic
**ведь** indeed, sure(ly); why, well; then; you know, you see; ***~ уже́ по́здно*** it is late, isn't it?
**ве́дьма** *f* [5] witch, hag
**ве́ер** *m* [1; *pl*.: -ра́ *etc. e*.] fan
**ве́жлив|ость** *f* [8] politeness; **~ый** [14 *sh*.] polite
**везде́** everywhere; **~хо́д** *m* [1] allterrain vehicle
**везе́ние** *n* [12] luck; ***како́е ~*** what luck!
**везти́** [24], ⟨по-, с-⟩ *v/t*. drive (be driving, *etc*.), transport; *санки и т. д.* pull; ***ему́ (не) везёт*** *coll*. he is (un)lucky
**век** *m* [1; на веку́; *pl*.: века́, *etc. e*.] **1.** century; age; **2.** life (time); ***сре́дние ~а́*** *pl*. Middle Ages; ***на моём ~у́*** in my life (-time); ***~ с тобо́й мы не вида́лись*** we haven't met for ages
**ве́ко** *n* [9; *nom/pl*.: -ки] eyelid
**веково́й** [14] ancient, age-old
**ве́ксель** *m* [4; *pl*.: -ля́, *etc. e*.] bill of exchange, promissory note
**веле́ть** [9; ве́ленный] (*im*)*pf*.; *pt. pf. only* order, tell (p. s.th. Д/В)
**велика́н** *m* [1] giant
**вели́к|ий** [16; вели́к, -а́, -о] great; (too) large or big; *only short form*; ***от ма́ла до ~а*** everybody, young and old; ***Пётр ~ий*** Peter the Great
**велико|ду́шие** *n* [12] magnanimity; **~ду́шный** [14; -шен, -шна] magnanimous, generous; **~ле́пие** *n* [12] splendo(u)r, magnificence; **~ле́пный** [14; -пен, -пна] magnificent, splendid
**велича́вый** [14 *sh*.] majestic, stately
**вели́ч|ественный** [14 *sh*.] majestic, grand, stately; **~ество** *n* [9] majesty; **~ие** *n* [12] grandeur; greatness; **~ина́** *f* [5; *pl. st*.: -чи́ны] size; magnitude, quantity; *math*. value; *об учёном и т. д.* celebrity; ***~ино́й в*** *or* (**с** В) … big *or* high
**вело|го́нки** *f/pl*. [5; *gen*.: -нок] cycle race; **~дро́м** *m* [1] cycling truck
**велосипе́д** *m* [1] bicycle; ***е́здить на ~е*** cycle; **~и́ст** *m* [1] cyclist; **~ный** [14] (bi)cycle…, cycling…
**вельве́т** *m* [1], **~овый** [14] velveteen
**ве́на** *f* [5] *anat*. vein
**венг|е́рка** *f* [5; *g/pl*.: -рок], **~е́рский** [16]; **~р** *m* [1] Hungarian
**венери́ческий** [16] venereal
**вене́ц** *m* [1; -нца] crown; *ореол* halo; *fig*. consummation
**венециа́нский** [16] Venetian
**ве́нзель** *m* [4; *pl*.: -ля́] monogram
**ве́ник** *m* [1] broom, besom
**вено́к** *m* [1; -нка́] wreath, garland
**вентил|и́ровать** [7], ⟨про-⟩ ventilate, air; **~я́тор** *m* [1] ventilator, fan
**венча́|льный** [14] wedding…, **~ние** *n* [12] wedding (ceremony); **~ть** [1] **1.** ⟨у-⟩ crown; **2.** ⟨об-, по-⟩ marry; **-ся** get married (in church)
**ве́ра** *f* [5] faith, belief, trust (in ***в*** В); religion
**вера́нда** *f* [5] veranda(h)

**ве́рба** *f* [5] willow
**верблю́|д** *m* [1] camel; **~жий** [18]: ***~жья шерсть*** *f* camel's hair
**ве́рбн|ый** [14]: ***2ое воскресе́нье*** *n* Palm Sunday
**вербов|а́ть** [7], ⟨за-, на-⟩ enlist, recruit; *на работу* engage, hire; **≈ка** *f* [5; -вок] recruiting
**верёв|ка** *f* [5; *g/pl.*: -вок] rope, cord, string; **~очный** [14] rope…
**верени́ца** *f* [5] row file, line
**ве́реск** *m* [1] heather
**вереща́ть** [16 *e.*; -щу́, -щи́шь] chirp; *coll.* squeal
**верзи́ла** *coll. m* [5] ungracefully tall fellow
**ве́рить** [13], ⟨по-⟩ believe (in **в** В); believe, trust (acc. Д); ***~ на́ слово*** take on trust; **-ся** (*impers.*): ***(мне) не ве́рится*** one (I) can hardly believe (it)
**вермише́ль** *f* [8] *coll.* vermicelli
**ве́рно** *adv.* **1. & 2.** → ***ве́рный*** **1. 2.**; **3.** probably; **~сть** *f* [8] **1.** faith(fulness), fidelity, loyalty; **2.** correctness, accuracy
**верну́ть(ся)** [20] *pf.* → ***возвраща́ть(ся)***
**ве́рн|ый** [14; -рен, -рна́, -о] **1.** *друг* faithful, true, loyal; **2.** (*правильный*) right, correct; (*точный*) accurate, exact; **3.** (*надёжный*) safe, sure, reliable; **4.** (*неизбежный*) inevitable, certain; ***~ée (сказа́ть)*** or rather
**вероиспове́дание** *n* [12] creed; denomination
**вероло́м|ный** [14; -мен, -мна] perfidious, treacheorus; **~ство** *n* [9] perfidy, treachery
**веротерпи́мость** *f* [8] toleration
**вероя́т|ность** *f* [8] probability; ***по всей ~ности*** in all probability; **~ный** [14; -тен, -тна] probable, likely
**ве́рсия** *f* [7] version
**верста́к** *m* [1 *e.*] workbench
**ве́рт|ел** *m* [1; *pl.*: -ла́] spit, skewer; **~е́ть** [11; верчу́, ве́ртишь], ⟨по-⟩ turn, twist; **-ся 1.** turn, revolve; **2.** *на стуле* fidget; ***~е́ться на языке́*** be on the tip of one's tongue; ***~е́ться под нога́ми*** be (or get) in the way; **~ика́льный** [14; -лен, -льна] vertical; **~олёт** *m* [1] helicopter
**ве́рующий** *m* [17] *su.* believer
**верфь** *f* [8] shipyard
**верх** *m* [1; на верху́; *pl. e.*] top, upper part; *fig.* height; ***взять ~*** gain the upper hand, win; **~и́** *pl.* top-rank officials **1.** ***в ~а́х*** summit…; **2.** *о знаниях* superficial knowledge; **≈ний** [15] upper
**верхо́в|ный** [14] supreme, high; ***~ная власть*** supreme power; ***~ный суд*** supreme court; **~о́й** [14] riding…; rider; horseman; ***~ая езда́*** *f* riding; **~ье** *n* [10; *g/pl.*: -ьев] upper reaches
**верхо́м** *adv.* astride, on horseback; ***е́здить ~*** ride, go on horseback
**верху́шка** *f* [5; *g/pl.*: -шек] top, apex; high-rank officials
**верши́на** *f* [5] peak, summit
**верши́ть** [16 *e.*; -шу́, -ши́шь; -шённый], ⟨за-, с-⟩ **1.** manage, control; **2.** run (Т); **3.** accomplish, decide
**вес** *m* [1] weight; ***на ~*** by weight; ***уде́льный ~*** *phys.* specific gravity; ***име́ть ~*** *fig.* carry weight; ***на ~ зо́лота*** worth its weight in gold; ***≈ом в*** (В) weighting…
**вес|ели́ть** [13], ⟨раз-⟩ amuse, divert, (**-ся** enjoy o.s.); **~ёлость** *f* [8] gaeity, mirth; **~ёлый** [14; ве́сел, -á, -о] gay, merry, cheerful; ***как ≈ело!*** it's such fun!; ***ему́ ≈ело*** he is enjoying himself, is of good cheer; **~е́лье** *n* [10] merriment, merrymaking, fun; **~ельча́к** *m* [1 *e.*] convivial fellow
**весе́нний** [15] spring…
**ве́с|ить** [15] *v/i.* weigh; **~кий** [16; ве́сок, -ска] weighty
**весло́** *n* [9; *pl.*: вёсла, -сел] oar
**весн|а́** *f* [5; *pl.*: вёсны, вёсен] spring (in [the] Т); **~у́шка** *f* [5; *g/pl.*: -шек] freckle
**весов|о́й** [14] **1.** weight…; balance…; **2.** sold by weight; **~щи́к** *m* [1 *e.*] weigher
**весо́мый** [14] *fig.* weighty
**ве́сти**[1] *f/pl.* [8] news
**вести́**[2] [25], ⟨по-⟩ **1.** (be) lead(ing *etc.*), conduct, guide; **2.** *разговор* carry on; **3.** *дневник* keep; **4.** *машину* drive; ***~ (своё) нача́ло*** spring (from **от** Р); ***~ себя́*** behave (*o.s.*); ***и у́хом не ведёт*** pays no attention at all; **~сь** be conducted *or* carried on; ***так уж у нас повело́сь*** that's a custom among us

**вестибю́ль** *m* [4] entrance hall
**ве́ст|ник** *m* [1] bulletin; **~очка** *f* [5; *g/pl.*: -чек] *coll.* news; **~ь** *f* [8; *from g/pl. e.*] news, message; ***пропа́сть без ~и*** be missing
**весы́** *m/pl.* [1] scales, balance; ♎ Libra
**весь** *m*, **вся** *f*, **всё** *n*, *pl.*: **все** [31] **1.** *adj.* all, the whole; full, life (size; at **в** B); **2.** *su. n* all over; everything, *pl. e.* everybody; ***вот и всё*** that's all; ***лу́чше всего́*** (***всех***) best of all, the best; ***пре́жде всего́*** first and foremost; ***при всём том*** for all that; ***во всём ми́ре*** all over the world; ***по всей стране́*** throughout the country; ***всего́ хоро́шего!*** good luck!; ***во всю*** → ***си́ла***; **3. всё** *adv.* always, all the time; only, just; ***всё*** (***ещё***) ***не*** not yet; ***всё бо́льше*** (***и бо́льше***) more and more; ***всё же*** nevertheless, yet
**весьма́** very, extremely, highly; ***~ вероя́тно*** most probably
**ветв|и́стый** [14 *sh.*] branchy, spreading; **~ь** *f* [8; *from g/pl. e.*] branch (*a. fig.*), bough
**ве́тер** *m* [1; -тра] wind; ***встре́чный ~*** contrary *or* head wind; ***попу́тный ~*** fair wind; ***броса́ть де́ньги*** (***слова́***) ***на ~*** waste money (words); *old use* ***держа́ть нос по ве́тру*** be a timeserver
**ветера́н** *m* [1] veteran
**ветерина́р** *m* [1] veterinary surgeon, *coll.* vet; **~ный** [14] veterinary
**ветеро́к** *m* [1; -рка́] light wind, breeze, breath
**ве́тка** *f* [5; *g/pl.*: -ток] branch(let), twig; *rail.* branch line
**ве́то** *n* [*indecl.*] veto; ***наложи́ть ~*** veto
**ве́тр|еный** [14 *sh.*] windy (*a. fig.* = flippant); **~яно́й** [14] wind…; ***~яна́я ме́льница*** windmill; **~яный** [14]: ***~яная о́спа*** chicken pox
**ве́тх|ий** [16; ветх, -á, -о; *comp.*: ве́тше] *дом* old, dilapidated; *одежда* worn out, shabby; decrepit; **~ость** *f* [8] decay, dilapidation; ***приходи́ть в ~ость*** fall into decay
**ветчина́** *f* [5] ham
**ветша́ть** [1], ⟨об-⟩ decay, become dilapidated
**ве́ха** *f* [5] landmark, milestone *mst. fig.*
**ве́чер** *m* [1; *pl.*: -pá, *etc. e.*] **1.** evening; **2. *~ па́мяти*** commemoration meeting; **~ом** in the evening; ***сего́дня ~ом*** tonight; ***вчера́ ~ом*** last night; ***по́д ~*** toward(s) the evening; **~е́ть** [8; *impers.*] decline (of the day); **~и́нка** *f* [5; *g/pl.*: -нок] (evening) party, soirée; **~ко́м** *coll.* = **~ом**; **~ний** [15] evening…, night…; **~я** *f* [6]: ***Та́йная ~я*** the Last Supper
**ве́чн|ость** *f* [8] eternity; (***це́лую***) ***~ость*** *coll.* for ages; **~ый** [14; -чен, -чна] eternal, everlasting; perpetual
**ве́ша|лка** *f* [5; *g/pl.*: -лок] (coat) hanger; (*петля*) tab; peg, rack; *coll.* cloakroom; **~ть** [1] **1.** ⟨пове́сить⟩ [15] hang (up); **-ся** hang o.s.; **2.** ⟨взве́сить⟩ [15] weigh
**веща́ние** *n* [12] → *радио~*
**вещ|е́ственный** [14] material, substantial; **~ество́** *n* [9] matter, substance; **~и́ца** *f* [8] knickknack; piece; **~ь** *f* [8; *from g/pl. e.*] thing; object; (*произведение*) work, piece, play; *pl.* belongings; baggage, *Brt.* luggage
**ве́я|ние** *n* [12] *fig.* trend, tendency, current; ***~ние вре́мени*** spirit of the times; **~ть** [27] *v/i.* blow, flutter, ⟨по-⟩ smell, breathe of
**вжи|ва́ться** [1], ⟨**~ться**⟩ [-ву́сь, *etc.* → ***жить***] accustom o.s. (**в** B to)
**взад** *coll.* back(ward[s]); ***~ и вперёд*** back and forth, to and fro; up and down
**взаимн|ость** *f* [8] reciprocity; **~ый** [14; -мен, -мна] mutual, reciprocal
**взаимо|вы́годный** [14; -ден, -дна] mutually beneficial; **~де́йствие** *n* [12] interaction; *сотрудничество* cooperation; **~де́йствовать** [7] interact, cooperate; **~отноше́ние** *n* [12] interrelation; *людей* relationship, relations *pl.*; **~по́мощь** *f* [8] mutual aid; **~понима́ние** *n* [12] mutual understanding
**взаймы́**: ***брать ~*** borrow (***у, от*** P from); ***дава́ть ~*** lend
**вза|ме́н** (P) instead of, in exchange for; **~перти́** locked up, under lock and key
**взба́л|мошный** *coll.* [14; -шен, -шна] eccentric, extravagant; **~тывать**, ⟨взболта́ть⟩ [1] shake *or* stir up

**взбе|га́ть** [1], ⟨**~жа́ть**⟩ [4; взбегу́, -жи́шь, -гу́т] run up
**взбива́ть** [1], ⟨взби́ть⟩ [взобью́, -бьёшь; взбил, -а; взби́тый] whip, beat up
**взбира́ться**, ⟨взобра́ться⟩ [взберу́сь, -рёшься; взобрался, -ла́сь, -ло́сь] climb, clamber up (***на*** В s.th.)
**взби́ты|й** [14]: ***~е сли́вки*** whipped cream
**взболта́ть** → ***взба́лтывать***
**взбудора́живать** [1] → ***будора́жить***
**взбунтова́ться** → ***бунтова́ть***
**взбух|а́ть** [1], ⟨**~́нуть**⟩ [21] swell
**взва́ливать** [1], ⟨взвали́ть⟩ [13; взвалю́, -а́лишь; -а́ленный] load, lift, hoist (onto), *обязанности и т. д.* charge (***на*** В with)
**взвести́** → ***взводи́ть***
**взве́|шивать** [1], ⟨**~сить**⟩ [15] weigh; **-ся** weigh o.s.
**взви|ва́ть** [1], ⟨**~ть**⟩ [взовью́, -вьёшь, *etc.* → ***вить***] whirl up; **-ся** soar up, rise; *fig.* flare up
**взви́зг|ивать** [1], ⟨**~нуть**⟩ [20] cry out, squeak, scream; *о собаке* yelp
**взви́н|чивать** [1], ⟨**~ти́ть**⟩ [15 *e.*; -нчу́, -нти́шь; -и́нченный] excite; *цены* raise
**взвить** → ***взвива́ть***
**взвод** *m* [1] platoon
**взводи́ть** [15], ⟨взвести́⟩ [25]: ***~ куро́к*** cock (*firearm*)
**взволно́|ванный** [14 *sh.*] excited; *испытывающий беспокойство* uneasy; **~ва́ть(ся)** → ***волнова́ть***
**взгля|д** *m* [1] look; glance; gaze, stare; *fig.* view, opinion; ***на мой ~д*** in my opinion; ***на пе́рвый ~д*** at first glance; ***с пе́рвого ~́да*** at first sight; *любовь* at first sight, at once; **~́дывать** [1], *once* ⟨**~ну́ть**⟩ [19] (***на*** В) (have a) look, glance (at)
**взгромо|жда́ть** [1], ⟨**~зди́ть**⟩ [15 *e.*; -зжу́, -зди́шь, -мождённый] load, pile up; **-ся** clamber, perch (on ***на*** В)
**взгрустну́ть** [20; -ну, -нёшь] *coll.* feel sad
**вздёр|гивать** [1], ⟨**~нуть**⟩ [20] jerk up; ***~нутый нос*** *m* turned-up nose
**вздор** *m* [1] nonsense; ***нести́ ~*** talk nonsense; **~́ный** [14; -рен, -рна] foolish, absurd; *coll.* (*сварливый*) quarrelsome, cantankerous
**вздорожа́|ние** *n* [12] rise in price(s); **~ть** → ***дорожа́ть***
**вздох** *m* [1] sigh; ***испусти́ть после́дний ~*** breathe one's last; **~ну́ть** → ***вздыха́ть***
**вздра́гивать** [1], *once* ⟨вздро́гнуть⟩ [20] start, wince; shudder
**вздремну́ть** *coll.* [20] *pf.* have a nap, doze
**взду|ва́ть** [1], ⟨**~ть**⟩ [18] **1.** *цены* run up; **2.** *v/i.* **-ся** swell; **3.** *coll.* give a thrashing; **~́тие** *n* [12] swelling
**взду́ма|ть** [1] *pf.* conceive the idea, take it into one's head; **-ся**; ***ему́ ~лось = он ~л***; ***как ~ется*** at one's will
**взды|ма́ть** [1] raise, *клубы дыма* whirl up; **~ха́ть** [1], *once* ⟨вздохну́ть⟩ [20] sigh; ***~ха́ть*** (***по, о*** П) long (for); *pf. coll.* pause for breath
**взи|ма́ть** [1] levy, raise (from ***с*** Р); ***~ма́ть штраф*** collect; **~ра́ть** [1] (***на*** В) look (at); ***невзира́я на*** without regard to, notwithstanding
**взла́мывать**, ⟨взлома́ть⟩ [1] break *or* force open
**взлёт** *m* [1] upward flight; *ae.* take off; ***~но-поса́дочная полоса́*** landing strip, runway
**взлет|а́ть** [1], ⟨**~е́ть**⟩ [11] fly up, soar; *ae.* take off
**взлом** *m* [1] breaking in; **~́ать** → ***взла́мывать***; **~́щик** *m* [1] burglar
**взмах** *m* [1] *руки пловца* stroke; *косы* sweep; **~́ивать** [1], *once* ⟨**~ну́ть**⟩ [20] swing, *рукой* wave, *крыльями* flap
**взмет|а́ть** [3], *once* ⟨**~ну́ть**⟩ [20] *пыль* whirl *or* throw up
**взмо́рье** *n* [10] seashore, seaside
**взнос** *m* [1] payment; fee; *при покупке в рассрочку* installment
**взну́зд|ывать** [1], ⟨**~а́ть**⟩ bridle
**взобра́ться** → ***взбира́ться***
**взойти́** → ***восходи́ть & всходи́ть***
**взор** *m* [1] look; gaze; eyes *pl.*
**взорва́ть** → ***взрыва́ть***
**взро́слый** [14] grown-up, adult
**взрыв** *m* [1] explosion; *fig.* outburst;

**~áтель** *m* [4] (detonating) fuse; **~áть** [1], ⟨взорвáть⟩ [-вý, -вёшь; взóрванный] blow up; *fig.* enrage; **-ся** explode; fly into a rage; **~нóй** [14], **~чатый** [14] explosive (*su.*: ***~чатое веществó***), *coll.* **~чáтка**

**взрыхлять** [28] → ***рыхлить***

**взъе|зжáть** [1], ⟨~хать⟩ [взъéду, -дешь; въезжай(те)!] ride *or* drive up; **~рóшивать** [1], ⟨~рóшить⟩ [16 *st.*] dishevel, tousle; **-ся** become dishevel(l)ed

**взывáть** [1], ⟨воззвáть⟩ [-зовý, -зовёшь; -звáл, -á, -о] appeal (to ***к*** Д); ***~ о пóмощи*** call for help

**взыск|áние** *n* [12] **1.** penalty, exaction, levy; **2.** (*выговор*) reprimand; **~áтельный** [14; -лен, -льна] exacting, exigent; **~ивать** [1], ⟨~áть⟩ [3] (**с** Р) levy, exact

**взя́т|ие** *n* [12] seizure, capture; **~ка** *f* [5; *g/pl.*: -ток] **1.** bribe; ***дать ~ку*** bribe; **2.** *карты* trick; **~очник** *m* [1] bribe taker, corrupt official; **~очничество** *n* [9] bribery; **~ь** → ***брать***

**вибр|áция** *f* [7] vibration; **~и́ровать** [7] vibrate

**вид** *m* [1] **1.** look(s), appearance, air; **2.** sight, view; **3.** kind, sort; species; **4.** *gr.* aspect; ***в ~е*** (Р) in the form of, as, by way of; ***в любóм ~е*** in any shape; ***под ~ом*** under the guise (of Р); ***при ~е*** at the sight of; ***на ~ý*** (***у*** Р) in sight; visible (to); ***с*** (*or* ***по***) ***~у*** by sight; judging from appearance; ***ни под каки́м ~ом*** on no account; ***у негó хорóший ~*** he looks well; ***дéлать ~*** pretend; (***не***) ***теря́ть*** *or* ***выпускáть из ~у*** (not) lose sight of (keep in view); **~ы** *pl.* prospects (for ***на*** В)

**видáть** *coll.* [1], ⟨у-, по-⟩ see; ***егó давнó не ~*** I *or* we haven't seen him for a long time; **~ся** (*iter.*) meet, see (o.a.; *a p.* **с** Т)

**ви́дение**[1] *n* [12] vision, view; ***моё ~ проблéмы*** the way I see it

**видéние**[2] *n* [12] vision, apparition

**видео|зáпись** *f* [8] video (tape) recording; **~кассéта** *f* [5] video cassette; **~магнитофóн** *m* [1] video (tape) recorder

**ви́деть** [11 *st.*], ⟨у-⟩ see; catch sight of; ***~ во сне*** dream (of В); ***ви́дишь*** (***-ите***) ***ли?*** you see?; **-ся** → ***видáться*** (*but a. once*)

**ви́дим|о** apparently, evidently; ***~о-не~о*** *coll.* lots of, immense quantity; **~ость** *f* [8] **1.** visibility; **2.** *fig.* appearance; ***всё это однá ~*** there is nothing behind this; **~ый** [14 *sh.*] **1.** visible; **2.** [14] apparent

**видн|éться** [8] be visible, be seen; **~о** it can be seen; it appears; apparently; (***мне***) ***ничегó не ~о*** I don't *or* can't see anything; **~ый** **1.** [14; -ден, -днá, -дно] visible, conspicuous; **2.** [14] distinguished, prominent; *coll. мужчина* portly

**видоизмен|éние** *n* [12] modification, alteration; variety; **~я́ть** [1], ⟨~и́ть⟩ [13] alter, change

**ви́за** *f* [5] visa

**визави́** [*indecl.*] **1.** opposite; **2.** person face-to-face with another

**византи́йский** [16] Byzantine

**виз|г** *m* [1] scream, shriek; *животного* yelp; **~гли́вый** [14 *sh.*] shrill; given to screaming; **~жáть** [4 *e.*; -жý, -жи́шь], ⟨за-⟩ shriek; yelp

**визи́ровать** [7] (*im*)*pf.* visa

**визи́т** *m* [1] visit, call; ***нанести́ ~*** make an official visit; **~ный** [14]: ***~ная кáрточка*** *f* calling *or* visiting card

**ви́л|ка** *f* [5; *g/pl.*: -лок] **1.** fork; **2.** (***штéпсельная***) ***~ка*** *el.* plug; **~ы** *f/pl.* [5] pitchfork

**ви́лла** *f* [5] villa

**виля́ть** [28], ⟨за-⟩, *once* ⟨вильнýть⟩ [20] wag (one's tail *хвостом*); *о дороге* twist and turn; *fig.* prevaricate; be evasive

**вин|á** *f* [5; *pl. st.*] **1.** guilt; fault; blame; **2.** (*причина*) reason; ***вменя́ть в ~ý*** impute (to Д); ***свáливать ~ý*** lay the blame (on ***на*** В); ***э́то не по моéй ~é*** it's not my fault

**винегрéт** *m* [1] Russian salad with vinaigrette

**вини́т|ельный** [14] *gr.* accusative (case); **~ь** [13] blame (***за*** В for), accuse (***в*** П of)

**ви́н|ный** [14] wine…; **~ó** *n* [9; *pl. st.*] wine

**винов́ат|ый** [14 *sh.*] guilty (of ***в*** П); ***~!*** sorry!, excuse me!; (I beg your) pardon!; ***вы в э́том*** (***не***) ***~ы*** it's (not) your

fault; ***я ~ перед ва́ми*** I must apologize to you, (*a.* ***кругóм ~***) it's all my fault
**винóв|ник** *m* [1] **1.** culprit; **2. *~ник торжества́*** hero; **~ный** [14; -вен, -вна] guilty (of **в** П)
**виногра́д** *m* [1] **1.** vine; **2.** *collect.* grapes *pl.*; **~арство** *n* [9] viticulture; **~ник** *m* [1] vineyard; **~ный** [14] (of) grape(s), grape…
**виноде́лие** *n* [12] winemaking
**винт** *m* [1 *e.*] screw; **ҳик** *m* [1] small screw; ***у негó ҳиков не хвата́ет*** *coll.* he has a screw loose; **~óвка** *f* [5; *g/pl.*: -вок] rifle; **~овóй** [14] screw…; spiral; ***~ова́я ле́стница*** spiral (winding) stairs
**виньéтка** *f* [5; *g/pl.*: -ток] vignette
**виолонче́ль** *f* [8] (violon)cello
**вира́ж** *m* [1 *e.*] bend, curve, turn
**виртуóз** *m* [1] virtuoso; **~ный** [14; -зен, -зна] masterly
**ви́рус** *m* [1] virus
**ви́селица** *f* [5] gallows
**висе́ть** [11] hang
**ви́ски** *n* [*indecl.*] whisk(e)y
**вискóза** *f* [5] *tech.* viscose; *ткань* rayon
**ви́снуть** *coll.* [21], ⟨по-⟩ *v/i.* hang
**висóк** *m* [1; -ска́] *anat.* temple
**високóсный** [14]: ***~ год*** leap year
**вися́чий** [17] hanging; suspension…; ***~ замóк*** padlock
**витами́н** *m* [1] vitamin; **~ный** [14] vitaminic
**вит|а́ть** [1]: ***~а́ть в облака́х*** have one's head in the clouds; **~иева́тый** [14] affected, bombastic
**витóк** *m* [1; -тка] coil, spiral
**витра́ж** *m* [1] stained-glass window
**витри́на** *f* [5] shopwindow; showcase
**вить** [вью, вьёшь; ве́й(те)!; вил, -а́, -о; ви́тый], ⟨с-⟩ [совью́, совьёшь] wind, twist; ***~ гнездó*** build a nest; **-ся 1.** wind; *о пыли* spin, whirl; **2.** *о растении* twine, creep; *о волосах* curl; **3.** *о птице* hover
**ви́тязь** *m* [4] *hist.* valiant warrior
**вихóр** *m* [1; -хра́] forelock
**вихрь** *m* [4] whirlwind
**ви́це-…** (*in compds.*) vice-…
**вишн|ёвый** [14] cherry…; **ҳя** *f* [6; *g/pl.*: -шен] cherry
**вка́пывать** [1], ⟨вкопа́ть⟩ dig in; *fig.* ***как вкóпанный*** stock-still, rooted to the ground
**вка́т|ывать** [1], ⟨**~ить**⟩ [15] roll in, wheel in
**вклад** *m* [1] deposit; *капитала* investment; *fig.* contribution (**в** В to); **ҳка** *f* [5; *g/pl.*: -док] insert; **ҳчик** *m* [1] depositor; investor; **ҳывать** [1], ⟨вложи́ть⟩ [16] put in, insert, enclose; *деньги* invest; deposit
**вкле́|ивать** [1], ⟨**~ить**⟩ [13] glue *or* paste in; **~йка** *f* [5; *g/pl.*: -е́ек] gluing in; sheet, *etc.*, glued in
**вкли́ни|вать(ся)** [1], ⟨**ҳть(ся)**⟩ [13; *a. st.*] drive a wedge into
**включ|а́ть** [1], ⟨**~и́ть**⟩ [16 *e.*; -чу́, -чи́шь; -чённый] include; insert; *el.* switch *or* turn on; **-ся** join (**в** В s.th.); **~а́я** including; **~е́ние** *n* [12] inclusion; insertion; *el.* switching on, **~и́тельно** included
**вкол|а́чивать** [1], ⟨**~оти́ть**⟩ [15] drive *or* hammer in
**вконе́ц** *coll.* completely, altogether
**вкопа́ть** → ***вка́пывать***
**вкось** askew, aslant, obliquely; ***вкривь и ~*** pell-mell; amiss
**вкра́|дчивый** [14 *sh.*] insinuating, ingratiating; **~дываться** [1], ⟨**~сть(ся)**⟩ [25] creep *or* steal in; *fig.* insinuate o.s.
**вкра́тце** briefly, in a few words
**вкруту́ю**: ***яйцó ~*** hard-boiled egg
**вкус** *m* [1] taste (*a. fig.*), flavo(u)r; ***прия́тный на ~*** savo(u)ry; ***быть*** (***прийти́сь***) ***по вку́су*** be to one's taste; relish (*or* like) s.th.; ***име́ть ~*** (P) taste (of); ***о ҳах не спóрят*** tastes differ; ***э́то де́ло ҳа*** it is a matter of taste; **ҳный** [14; -сен, -сна́] tasty; (***э́то***) ***ҳно*** it tastes good *or* nice
**вла́га** *f* [5] moisture
**владе́|лец** *m* [1; -льца] owner, proprietor, possessor; **~ние** *n* [12] ownership, possession (of T); **~ть** [8], ⟨за-, о-⟩ (T) own, possess; *ситуацией* control; *языком* have command (T of); ***~ть собóй*** control o.s.
**влады́ка** *m* [5] *eccl.* Reverend
**вла́жн|ость** *f* [8] humidity; **~ый** [14;

-жен, -жна́, -о] humid, damp, moist
**вла́мываться** [1], ⟨вломи́ться⟩ [14] break in
**вла́ст|вовать** [7] rule, dominate; **~ели́н** *m* [1] *mst. fig.* lord, master; **~и́тель** *m* [4] sovereign, ruler; **~ный** [14; -тен, -тна] imperious, commanding, masterful; ***в э́том я не ~ен*** I have no power over it; **~ь** *f* [8; *from g/pl. e.*] authority, power; rule, regime; control; *pl.* authorities
**влачи́ть** [16 *e.*; -чу́, -чи́шь]: ***~ жа́лкое существова́ние*** hardly make both ends meet, drag out a miserable existence
**вле́во** (to the) left
**влез|а́ть** [1], ⟨~ть⟩ [24 *st.*] climb *or* get in(to); climb up
**влет|а́ть** [1], ⟨~е́ть⟩ [11] fly in; *вбежать* rush in
**влеч|е́ние** *n* [12] inclination, strong attraction; *к кому-л.* love; **~ь** [26], ⟨по-, у-⟩ drag, pull; *fig.* attract, draw; ***~ь за собо́й*** involve, entail
**вли|ва́ть** [1], ⟨~ть⟩ [волью́, -льёшь; вле́й(те)!; вли́тый (-та́, -о)] pour in; **-ся** flow *or* fall in; **~па́ть** *coll.* [1], ⟨~пнуть⟩ [20] *fig.* get into trouble; find o.s. in an awkward situation; **~я́ние** *n* [12] influence; **~я́тельный** [14; -лен, -льна] influential; **~я́ть** [28], ⟨по-⟩ (have) influence
**влож|е́ние** *n* [12] enclosure; *fin.* investment; **~и́ть** → ***вкла́дывать***
**вломи́ться** → ***вла́мываться***
**влюб|лённость** *f* [8] (being in) love; **~лённый** enamo(u)red; *su.* lover; **~ля́ться** [28], ⟨~и́ться⟩ [14] fall in love (***в*** В with); **~чивый** [14 *sh.*] amorous
**вмен|я́емый** [14 *sh.*] responsible, accountable; **~я́ть** [28], ⟨~и́ть⟩ [13] consider (***в*** В as), impute; ***~я́ть в вину́*** blame; ***~я́ть в обя́занность*** impose as duty
**вме́сте** together, along with; ***~ с тем*** at the same time
**вмести́|мость** *f* [8] capacity; **~тельный** [14; -лен, -льна] capacious, spacious; **~ть** → ***вмеща́ть***
**вме́сто** (Р) instead, in place (of)
**вмеш|а́тельство** *n* [9] interference, intervention; *хирургическое* operation; **~ивать** [1], ⟨~а́ть⟩ [1] (В/***в*** В) (in; with); *fig.* involve (in); **-ся** interfere, intervene, meddle (***в*** В in)
**вме|ща́ть** [1], ⟨~сти́ть⟩ [15 *e.*; -ещу́, -ести́шь; -ещённый] **1.** (*поместить*) put, place; **2.** *зал и т. д.* hold, contain, accommodate; **-ся** find room; hold; go in
**вмиг** in an instant, in no time
**вмя́тина** *f* [5] dent
**внача́ле** at first, at the beginning
**вне** (Р) out of, outside; beyond; ***быть ~ себя́*** be beside o.s.; ***~ вся́ких сомне́ний*** beyond (any) doubt
**внебра́чный** [14] extramarital; *ребёнок* illegitimate
**внедр|е́ние** *n* [12] introduction; **~я́ть** [28], ⟨~и́ть⟩ [13] introduce; **-ся** take root
**внеза́пный** [14; -пен, -пна] sudden, unexpected
**внекла́ссный** [14] out-of-class
**внеочередно́й** [14] out of turn, extra(ordinary)
**внес|е́ние** *n* [12] entry; **~ти́** → ***вноси́ть***
**вне́шн|ий** [15] outward, external; *pol.* foreign; **~ость** *f* [8] (*наружность*) appearance, exterior
**внешта́тный** [14] *сотрудник* not on permanent staff, freelance
**вниз** down(ward[s]); **~у́ 1.** (Р) beneath, below; **2.** down(stairs)
**вник|а́ть** [1], ⟨~нуть⟩ [19] (***в*** В) get to the bottom (of), fathom
**внима́|ние** *n* [12] attention; care; ***приня́ть во ~ние*** take into consideration; ***принима́я во ~ние*** taking into account, in view of; ***оста́вить без ~ния*** disregard; **~тельность** *f* [8] attentiveness; **~тельный** [14; -лен, -льна] attentive; **~ть** [1], ⟨внять⟩ [*inf. & pt. only*; внял, -а́, -о] (Д) *old use.* hear *or* listen (to)
**вничью́**: (*sport*) ***сыгра́ть ~*** draw
**вновь 1.** again; **2.** newly
**вноси́ть** [15], ⟨внести́⟩ [25; -с-: -су́, -сёшь; внёс, внесла́] carry *or* bring in; *в список и т. д.* enter, include; *деньги* pay (in); contribute; *поправки* make (correction); *предложение* submit, put forward

**внук** *m* [1] grandson; **~и** grandchildren

**вну́тренн|ий** [15] inner, inside, internal, interior; *море и т. д.* inland…; (*отечественный*) home…; **~ость** *f* [8] interior; (*esp. pl.*) internal organs, entrails

**внутр|и́** (P) in(side); within; **~ь** (P) in(-to), inward(s), inside

**внуч|а́та** *m/f pl.* [2] → ***вну́ки***; **~ка** *f* [5; *g/pl.*: -чек] granddaughter

**внуш|а́ть** [1], ⟨-и́ть⟩ [16 *e.*; -шу́, -ши́шь; -шённый] (Д/В) suggest; *надежду, страх* inspire (*a p.* with); *уважение и т. д.* instill; **~е́ние** *n* [12] suggestion; *выговор* reprimand; **~и́тельный** [14; -лен, -льна] imposing, impressive; **~и́ть** → ***~а́ть***

**вня́т|ный** [14; -тен, -тна] distinct, intelligible; **~ь** → ***внима́ть***

**вобра́ть** → ***вбира́ть***

**вовл|ека́ть** [1], ⟨-е́чь⟩ [26] draw in; (*впутывать*) involve

**во́время** in *or* on time, timely

**во́все**: ~ ***не(т)*** not (at all)

**вовсю́** *coll.* with all one's might; ***стара́ться ~*** do one's utmost

**во-вторы́х** second(ly)

**вогна́ть** → ***вгоня́ть***

**во́гнутый** [14] concave

**вод|а́** *f* [5; *ac/sg.*: во́ду; *pl.*: во́ды, вод, во́дам] water; ***в му́тной ~е́ ры́бу лови́ть*** fish in troubled waters; ***вы́йти сухи́м из ~ы́*** come off cleanly; ***как в ~у опу́щенный*** dejected, downcast; ***толо́чь ~у (в сту́пе)*** beat the air

**водвор|я́ть** [28], ⟨~и́ть⟩ [13] *порядок* establish

**водеви́ль** *m* [4] vaudeville, musical comedy

**води́тель** *m* [4] driver; **~ский** [16]: ***~ские права́*** driving licence

**вод|и́ть** [15], ⟨по-⟩ **1.** lead, conduct, guide; **2.** *машину* drive; **3.** move (T); **-ся** be (found), live; ***как ~ится*** as usual; ***э́то за ним ~ится*** *coll.* that's typical of him

**во́дка** *f* [5; *g/pl.*: -док] vodka

**во́дный** [14] water…; ***~ спорт*** aquatic sports

**водо|воро́т** *m* [1] whirpool, eddy; **~ём** *m* [1] reservoir; **~измеще́ние** *n* [12] *naut.* displacement, tonnage

**водо|ла́з** *m* [1] diver; **♒ле́й** *m* [3] Aquarius; **~лече́ние** *n* [12] hydropathy, water cure; **~напо́рный** [14]: ***~напо́рная ба́шня*** *f* water tower; **~непроница́емый** [14 *sh.*] watertight, waterproof; **~па́д** *m* [1] waterfall; **~по́й** *m* [3] watering place; watering (*of animals*); **~прово́д** *m* [1] water supply; *в доме* running water; **~прово́дчик** *coll. m* [1] plumber; **~разде́л** *m* [1] watershed; **~ро́д** *m* [1] hydrogen; **~ро́дный** [14]: ***~ро́дная бо́мба*** hydrogen bomb; **~росль** *f* [8] alga, seaweed; **~снабже́ние** *n* [12] water supply; **~сто́к** *m* [1] drain(age), drainpipe; **~сто́чный** [14]: ***~сто́чный жёлоб*** gutter; **~храни́лище** *n* [11] reservoir

**водру|жа́ть** [1], ⟨~зи́ть⟩ [15 *e.*; -ужу́, -узи́шь; -ужённый] hoist

**вод|яни́стый** [14 *sh.*] watery; wishy-washy; **~я́нка** *f* [5] dropsy; **~яно́й** [14] water…

**воева́ть** [6] wage *or* carry on war, be at war

**воеди́но** together

**военача́льник** *m* [1] commander

**военизи|а́ция** *f* [7] militarization; **~и́ровать** [7] (*im*)*pf.* militarize

**вое́нно|-возду́шный** [14]: ***´~-возду́шные си́лы*** *f/pl.* air force(s); **´~-морско́й** [14]: ***´~-морско́й флот*** navy; **~пле́нный** *m* [14] *su.* prisoner of war; **~слу́жащий** [17] serviceman

**вое́нн|ый** [14] **1.** military, war…; **2.** military man, soldier; ***~ый врач*** *m* medical officer; ***~ый кора́бль*** *m* man-of-war, warship; ***~ое положе́ние*** martial law (under ***на*** П); ***поступи́ть на ~ую слу́жбу*** enlist, join; ***~ые де́йствия*** *n/pl.* hostilities

**вож|а́к** *m* [1 *e.*] (gang) leader; **~дь** *m* [4 *e.*] chief(tain); leader; **~жи** *f/pl.* [8; *from g/pl. e.*] reins; ***отпусти́ть ~жи*** *fig.* slacken the reins

**воз** *m* [1; на -у́; *pl. e.*] cart(load); *coll. fig.* heaps; ***а ~ и ны́не там*** nothing has changed

**возбу|ди́мый** [14 *sh.*] excitable; **~ди́тель** *m* [4] stimulus, agent; **~жда́ть**

[1], ⟨~ди́ть⟩ [15 *e.*; -ужу́, -уди́шь] excite, stir up; *интерес, подозрение* arouse; incite; *надежду* raise; *law* **~ди́ть де́ло про́тив кого́-л.** bring an action against s.o.; **~жда́ющий** [17] stimulating; **~жде́ние** *n* [12] excitement; **~ждённый** [14] excited

**возвести́** → ***возводи́ть***

**возв|оди́ть** [15], ⟨~ести́⟩ [25] (**в** *or* **на** В) put up, raise, erect; *в сан* elect; *на престол* elevate (to)

**возвра́|т** *m* [1] **1.** → **~ще́ние**; ***1. & 2.***; **2.** relapse; **~ти́ть(ся)** → **~ща́ть(ся)**; **~тный** [14] back…; *med.* recurring; *gr.* reflexive; **~ща́ть** [1], ⟨~ти́ть⟩ [15 *e.*; -ащу́, -ати́шь; -ащённый] return; give back; *владельцу* restore; *долг* reimburse; *здоровье* recover; **-ся** return, come back (***из*** *or* **с** P from); revert (***к*** Д to); **~ще́ние** *n* [12] **1.** return; **2.** *об имуществе* restitution

**возв|ыша́ть** [1], ⟨~ы́сить⟩ [15] raise, elevate; **-ся** rise; tower (over ***над*** T); **~ыше́ние** *n* [12] rise; elevation; **~ы́шенность** *f* [8] **1.** *fig.* loftiness; **2.** *geogr.* height; **~ы́шенный** [14] high, elevated, lofty

**возгл|авля́ть** [28], ⟨~а́вить⟩ [14] (be at the) head

**во́зглас** *m* [1] exclamation, (out)cry

**возд|ава́ть** [5], ⟨~а́ть⟩ [-да́м, -да́шь, *etc.* → ***дава́ть***] render; (*отплатить*) requite; ***~а́ть до́лжное*** give s.b. his due (Д for)

**воздвиг|а́ть** [1], ⟨~нуть⟩ [21] erect, construct, raise

**возде́йств|ие** *n* [12] influence, pressure; **~овать** [7] (*im*)*pf.* (**на** В) (*оказывать влияние*) influence; (*действовать, влиять*) act upon, affect

**возде́л|ывать**, ⟨~ать⟩ [1] cultivate, till

**воздержа́ние** *n* [12] abstinence; abstention

**возде́рж|анный** [14 *sh.*] abstemious, temperate; **~иваться** [1], ⟨~а́ться⟩ [4] abstain (**от** P from); ***при двух ~а́вшихся*** *pol.* with two abstentions

**во́здух** *m* [1] air; ***на откры́том*** (***све́жем***) ***~е*** in the open air, outdoors; **~оплава́ние** *n* [12] aeronautics

**возду́ш|ный** [14] air…, aerial **1.** ***~ная трево́га*** *f* air-raid warning; ***~ное сообще́ние*** aerial communication; ***~ные за́мки*** *m/pl.* castles in the air; **2.** [14; -шен, -шна] airy, light

**воззва́|ние** *n* [12] appeal; **~ть** → ***взыва́ть***

**вози́ть** [15] carry, transport; *на машине* drive; **-ся** (**с** T) busy o.s. with, mess (around) with; (*делать медленно*) dawdle; *о детях* romp, frolic

**возл|ага́ть** [1], ⟨~ожи́ть⟩ [16] (**на** В) lay (on); entrust (with); ***~ага́ть наде́жды на*** (В) rest one's hopes upon

**во́зле** (P) by, near, beside

**возложи́ть** → ***возлага́ть***

**возлю́блен|ный** [14] beloved; *m* (*su.*) lover; **~ная** *f* [14] mistress, sweetheart

**возме́здие** *n* [12] requital

**возме|ща́ть** [1], ⟨~сти́ть⟩ [15 *e.*: -ещу́, -ести́шь; -ещённый] compensate, make up (for); **~ще́ние** *n* [12] compensation, indemnity; *law* damages

**возмо́жн|о** it is possible; possibly; ***о́чень ~о*** very likely; **~ость** *f* [8] possibility; ***по*** (***ме́ре***) ***~ости*** as (far as) possible; **~ый** [14; -жен, -жна] possible; ***сде́лать всё ~ое*** do everything possible

**возмужа́лый** [14] mature, grown up

**возму|ти́тельный** [14; -лен, -льна] scandalous, shocking; **~ща́ть**, ⟨~ти́ть⟩ [15 *e.*: -щу́, -ути́шь] rouse indignation; **-ся** be shocked *or* indignant (T at); **~ще́ние** *n* [12] indignation; **~щённый** [14] indignant (at)

**вознагра|жда́ть** [1], ⟨~ди́ть⟩ [15 *e.*; -ажу́, -ади́шь; -аждённый] (*наградить*) reward; recompense (for); **~жде́ние** *n* [12] reward, recompense; (*оплата*) fee

**вознаме́ри|ваться** [1], ⟨~ться⟩ [13] form the idea of, intend

**Вознесе́ние** *n* [12] Ascension

**возник|а́ть** [1], ⟨~нуть⟩ [21] arise, spring up, originate, emerge; ***у меня́ ~ла мысль …*** a thought occurred to me …; **~нове́ние** *n* [12] rise, origin, beginning

**возня́** *f* [6] **1.** fuss; bustle; romp; ***мыши́-***

**ная ~** petty intrigues; **2.** (*хлопоты*) trouble, bother

**возобнов|ле́ние** *n* [12] renewal; (*продолжение*) resumption; **~ля́ть** [28], 〈**~и́ть**〉 [14 *e.*; -влю́, -ви́шь; -влённый] *знакомство*, *усилия* renew, resume

**возра|жа́ть** [1], 〈**~зи́ть**〉 [15 *e.*; -ажу́, -ази́шь] **1.** object (to **про́тив** Р); **2.** return, retort (**на** В to); **(я) не ~жа́ю** I don't mind; **~же́ние** *n* [12] objection; rejoinder

**во́зраст** *m* [1] age (**в** П at); **~а́ние** *n* [12] growth, increase; **~а́ть** [1], 〈**~и́**〉 [24; -ст-; -расту́; -ро́с, -ла́; -ро́сший] grow, increase, rise

**возро|жда́ть** [1], 〈**~ди́ть**〉 [15 *e.*; -ожу́, -оди́шь; -ождённый] revive (*v/i.* **-ся**); **~жде́ние** *n* [12] rebirth, revival; **эпо́ха** **2жде́ния** Renaissance

**во́ин** *m* [1] warrior, soldier; **~ский** [16] military; **~ская обя́занность** service; **~ственный** [14 *sh.*] bellicose

**вои́стину** in truth

**вой** *m* [3] howl(ing), wail(ing)

**во́йло|к** *m* [1]: **~чный** [14] felt

**войн|а́** *f* [5; *pl. st.*] war (**на** П at); warfare; **идти́ на ~у́** go to war; **объяви́ть ~у́** declare war; **втора́я мирова́я ~а́** World War II

**во́йска́** *n* [9; *pl. e.*] army; *pl.* troops, (land, *etc.*) forces

**войти́** → **входи́ть**

**вокза́л** [1]: **железнодоро́жный ~** railroad (*Brt.* railway) station; **морско́й ~** port arrival and departure building; **речно́й ~** river-boat station

**вокру́г** (Р) (a)round; **(ходи́ть) ~ да о́коло** beat about the bush

**вол** *m* [1 *e.*] ox

**волды́рь** *m* [4 *e.*] blister; bump

**волейбо́л** *m* [1] volleyball

**во́лей-нево́лей** willy-nilly

**во́лжский** [16] (of the) Volga

**волк** *m* [1; *from g/pl. e.*] wolf; **смотре́ть ~ом** *coll.* scowl

**волн|а́** *f* [5; *pl. st.*, *from dat. a. e.*] wave; **дли́нные, сре́дние, коро́ткие ~ы** long, medium, short waves; **~е́ние** *n* [12] agitation, excitement; *pl.* disturbances, unrest; *на море* high seas; **~и́стый** [14 *sh.*] *волосы* wavy; *местность* undulating; **~ова́ть** [7], 〈**вз-**〉 (**-ся** be[come]) agitate(d), excite(d); (*тревожиться*) worry; **~у́ющий** [17] disturbing; exciting, thrilling

**волоки́та** *f* [5] *coll.* red tape; a lot of fuss and trouble

**волокн|и́стый** [14 *sh.*] fibrous; **~о́** *n* [9; *pl.*: -о́кна, -о́кон, *etc. st.*] fiber, *Brt.* fibre

**во́лос** *m* [1; *g/pl.*: -ло́с; *from dat. e.*] (*a. pl.*) hair; **~а́тый** [14 *sh.*] hairy; **~о́к** *m* [1; -ска́] hairspring; **быть на ~о́к** (*or* **на ~ке́**) **от сме́рти** *coll.* be on the verge (within a hair's breadth *or* within an ace) of death; **висе́ть на ~ке́** hang by a thread

**волосяно́й** [14] hair…

**волочи́ть** [16], 〈**по-**〉 drag, pull, draw; **-ся** drag o.s., crawl along

**во́лч|ий** [18] wolfish; wolf('s)…; **~и́ца** *f* [5] she-wolf

**волчо́к** *m* [1; -чка́] top (*toy*)

**волчо́нок** *m* [2] wolf cub

**волше́б|ник** *m* [1] magician; **~ница** *f* [5] sorceress; **~ный** [14] magic, fairy…; [-бен, -бна] *fig.* enchanting; **~ство́** *n* [9] magic, wizardry; *fig.* enchantment

**волы́нк|а** *f* [5; *g/pl.*: -нок] bagpipe

**во́льн|ость** *f* [8] liberty; **позволя́ть себе́ ~ости** take liberties; **~ый** [14; -лен, -льна́] free, easy, unrestricted; **~ая пти́ца** one's own master

**вольт** *m* [1] volt

**вольфра́м** *m* [1] tungsten

**во́л|я** *f* [6] **1.** will; **си́ла ~и** willpower; **2.** liberty, freedom; **~я ва́ша** (just) as you like; **не по свое́й ~е** against one's will; **по до́брой ~е** of one's own free will; **отпусти́ть на ~ю** set free; **дать ~ю** give free rein

**вон 1.** there; **~ там** over there; **2. ~!** get out!; **пошёл ~!** out *or* away (with you)!; **вы́гнать ~** turn out; **~ (оно́) что!** you don't say!; so that's it!

**вонза́ть** [1], 〈**~и́ть**〉 [15 *e.*; -нжу́, -зи́шь; -зённый] thrust, plunge, stick (into)

**вон|ь** *f* [8] stench, stink; **~ю́чий** [17 *sh.*] stinking; **~я́ть** [28] stink, reek (of T)

**вообра|жа́емый** [14 *sh.*] imaginary; fictitious; **~жа́ть** [1], 〈**~зи́ть**〉 [15 *e.*; -ажу́,

В

-ази́шь; -ажённый] (*a.* **~жа́ть себе́**) imagine, fancy; **~жа́ть себя́** imagine o.s. (T s.b.); **~жа́ть о себе́** be conceited; **~же́ние** *n* [12] imagination; fancy

**вообще́** in general, on the whole; at all

**воодушев|ле́ние** *n* [12] enthusiasm; **~ля́ть** [28], ⟨**~и́ть**⟩ [14 *e.*; -влю́, -ви́шь; -влённый] (**-ся** feel) inspire(d by T)

**вооруж|а́ть** [1], ⟨**~и́ть**⟩ [16 *e.*; -жу́, -жи́шь; -жённый] **1.** arm, equip (T with); **2.** stir up (**про́тив** P against); **~е́ние** *n* [12] armament, equipment

**воо́чию** with one's own eyes

**во-пе́рвых** first(ly)

**вопи́|ть** [14 *e.*; -плю́, -пи́шь], ⟨за-⟩ cry out, bawl; **~ющий** [17] crying, flagrant

**вопло|ща́ть** [1], ⟨**~ти́ть**⟩ [15 *e.*; -ощу́, -оти́шь, -ощённый] embody, personify; **~щённый** *a.* incarnate; **~ще́ние** *n* [12] embodiment, incarnation

**вопль** *m* [4] howl, wail

**вопреки́** (Д) contrary to; in spite of

**вопро́с** *m* [1] question; **под ~ом** questionable, doubtful; **~ не в э́том** that's not the question; **спо́рный ~** moot point; **что за ~!** of course!; **~и́тельный** [14] interrogative; **~и́тельный знак** question mark; **~и́тельный взгляд** inquiring look; **~ник** *m* [1] questionnaire

**вор** *m* [1; *from g/pl. e.*] thief

**ворва́ться** → **врыва́ться**

**ворковáть** [7], ⟨за-⟩ coo; *fig.* bill and coo

**вороб|е́й** *m* [3 *e.*; -бья́] sparrow; **стре́ляный ~е́й** *coll.* old hand

**ворова|́ть** [7] steal; **~ка** *f* [5; *g/pl.*: -вок] (female) thief; **~ско́й** [16] thievish; thieves'…; **~ство́** *n* [9] theft; *law* larceny

**во́рон** *m* [1] raven; **~а** *f* [5] crow; **бе́лая ~а** rara avis; **воро́н счита́ть** *coll. old use* stand about gaping

**воро́нка** *f* [5; *g/pl.*: -нок] **1.** funnel; **2.** *от бомбы, снаряда* crater

**вороно́й** [14] black; *su. m* black horse

**во́рот** *m* [1] **1.** collar; **2.** *tech.* windlass; **~а** *n/pl.* [9] gate; **~и́ть** [15]: **~и́ть нос** turn up one's nose (at); **~ни́к** *m* [1 *e.*] collar; **~ничо́к** *m* [1; -чка́] (small) collar

**во́рох** *m* [1; *pl.*: -ха́; *etc. e.*] pile, heap; *coll.* lots, heaps

**воро́|чать** [1] **1.** move, roll, turn; **2.** *coll.* manage, boss (T); **-ся** toss; turn; stir; **~ши́ть** [16 *e.*; -шу́, -ши́шь; -шённый] turn (over)

**ворч|а́ние** *n* [12] grumbling; *животного* growl; **~а́ть** [4 *e.*; -чу́, -чи́шь], ⟨за-, п(р)о-⟩ grumble; growl; **~ли́вый** [14 *sh.*] grumbling, surly; **~у́н** *m* [1 *e.*], **~у́нья** *f* [6] grumbler

**восвоя́си** *coll. iro.* home

**восемна́дцa|тый** [14] eighteenth; **~ть** [35] eighteen; → **пять**, **пя́тый**

**во́семь** [35; восьми́, *instr.* во́семью] eight; → **пять**, **пя́тый**; **~десят** [35; восьми́десяти] eighty; **~со́т** [36; восьмисо́т] eight hundred; **~ю** eight times

**воск** *m* [1] wax

**воскл|ица́ние** *n* [12] exclamation; **~ица́тельный** [14] exclamatory; **~ица́тельный знак** exclamation mark; **~ица́ть** [1], ⟨**~и́кнуть**⟩ [20] exclaim

**восково́й** [14] wax(en)

**воскр|еса́ть** [1], ⟨**~е́снуть**⟩ [21] rise (from **из** P); recover; **Христо́с ~е́с(е)!** Christ has arisen! (*Easter greeting*); (*reply*:) **вои́стину ~е́с(е)!** (He has) truly arisen!; **~есе́ние** *n* [12] resurrection; **~есе́нье** *n* [10] Sunday (on: **в** В; *pl.* **по** Д); **~еша́ть** [1], ⟨**~еси́ть**⟩ [15 e.; -ешу́, -еси́шь; -ешённый] resurrect, revive

**воспал|е́ние** *n* [12] inflammation; **~е́ние лёгких (по́чек)** pneumonia (nephritis); **~ённый** [14 *sh.*] inflamed; **~и́тельный** [14] inflammatory; **~я́ть** [28], ⟨**~и́ть**⟩ [13] inflame; (*v/i.* **-ся**)

**воспе|ва́ть** [1], ⟨**~ть**⟩ [-пою́, -поёшь; -пе́тый] sing of, praise

**воспит|а́ние** *n* [12] education, upbringing; (good) breeding; **~анник** *m* [1], **~анница** *f* [5] pupil; **~анный** [14 *sh.*] well-bred; **пло́хо ~анный** ill-bred; **~а́тель** *m* [4] educator; (private) tutor; **~а́тельный** [14] educational, pedagogic(al); **~ывать** [1], ⟨**~а́ть**⟩ bring up; educate; *прививать* cultivate, foster

**воспламен|я́ть** [28], ⟨**~и́ть**⟩ [13] set on fire (*v/i.* **-ся**) *a fig.*; inflame

**восполн|я́ть** [28], ⟨**~ить**⟩ [13] fill in; make up (for)

**воспо́льзоваться** → ***по́льзоваться***

**воспомина́ние** *n* [12] remembrance, recollection, reminiscence; *pl. a.* memoirs

**воспрепя́тствовать** [7] *pf.* hinder, prevent (from Д)

**воспре|ща́ть** [1], ⟨~ти́ть⟩ [15 *e.*; -ещу́, -ети́шь; -ещённый] prohibit, forbid; ***вход ~щён!*** no entrance!; ***кури́ть ~ща́ется!*** no smoking!

**воспри|и́мчивый** [14 *sh.*] receptive, impressionable; *к заболеванию* susceptible (**к** Д to); **~нима́ть** [1], ⟨~ня́ть⟩ [-приму́, -и́мешь; -и́нял, -а́, -о; -и́нятый] take in, understand; **~я́тие** *n* [12] perception

**воспроизв|еде́ние** *n* [12] reproduction; **~оди́ть** [15], ⟨~ести́⟩ [25] reproduce

**воспря́нуть** [20] *pf.* cheer up; ***~ ду́хом*** take heart

**воссоедин|е́ние** *n* [12] reun(ificat)ion; **~я́ть** [28], ⟨~и́ть⟩ [13] reunite

**восста|ва́ть** [5], ⟨~́ть⟩ [-ста́ну, -ста́нешь] rise, revolt

**восстан|а́вливать** [1], ⟨~ови́ть⟩ [14] **1.** reconstruct, restore; **2.** *против* antagonize; **~́ие** *n* [12] insurrection, revolt; **~ови́ть** → ***~а́вливать***; **~овле́ние** *n* [12] reconstruction, restoration

**восто́к** *m* [1] east; the East, the Orient; ***на ~*** (to[ward] the) east, eastward(s); ***на ~е*** in the east; ***с ~а*** from the east; ***к ~у от*** (Р) (to the) east of

**восто́р|г** *m* [1] delight, rapture; ***я в ~ге*** I am delighted (**от** Р with); ***приводи́ть*** (***приходи́ть***) ***в ~г*** = ***~га́ть***(***ся***) [1] *impf.* be delight(ed) (Т with); **~женный** [14 *sh.*] enthusiastic, rapturous

**восто́чный** [14] east(ern, -erly); oriental

**востре́бова|ние** *n* [12]: ***до ~ния*** to be called for, poste restante; **~ть** [7] *pf.* call for, claim

**восхвал|е́ние** *n* [12] praise, eulogy; **~я́ть** [28], ⟨~и́ть⟩ [13; -алю́, -а́лишь] praise, extol

**восхи|ти́тельный** [14; -лен, -льна] delightful; **~ща́ть** [1], ⟨~ти́ть⟩ [15 *e.*; -ищу́, -ити́шь; -ищённый] delight, transport; **-ся** (Т) be delighted with; admire; **~ще́ние** *n* [12] admiration; delight; ***приводи́ть*** (***приходи́ть***) ***в ~ще́ние*** → ***~ща́ть***(***ся***)

**восхо́|д** *m* [1] rise; ascent; **~ди́ть** [15], ⟨взойти́⟩ [взойду́, -дёшь; взошёл] rise, ascend; go back to; ***э́тот обы́чай ~дит*** (**к** Д) this custom goes back (to); **~жде́ние** *n* [12] sunrise

**восьм|ёрка** *f* [5; *g/pl.*: -рок] eight (→ ***дво́йка***); **~́еро** [37] eight (→ ***дво́е***)

**восьми|деся́тый** [14] eightieth; → ***пя́т***(***идеся́т***)***ый***; **~ле́тний** [14] eight-year-old; **~со́тый** [14] eight hundredth

**восьмо́й** [14] eighth; → ***пя́тый***

**вот** *part.* here (is); there; now; well; that's…; ***~ и всё*** that's all; ***~*** (***оно́***) ***как*** *or* ***что́*** you don't say!, is that so?; ***~ те***(***бе́***) ***раз*** *or* ***на́*** well I never!; a pretty business this!; ***~ како́й …*** such a …; ***~ челове́к!*** what a man!; ***~-~!*** yes, indeed!; ***~-~*** (at) any moment

**воткну́ть** → ***втыка́ть***

**во́тум** *m* [1]: ***~*** (***не***)***дове́рия*** (Д) vote of (no) confidence (in)

**воцар|я́ться** [28], ⟨~и́ться⟩ [13] (*fig.*, *third person only*) set in; ***~и́лось молча́ние*** silence fell

**вошь** *f* [8; вши; во́шью] louse

**вощи́ть** [16 *e.*], ⟨на-⟩ wax

**вою́ющий** [17] belligerent

**впа|да́ть** [1], ⟨~сть⟩ [25; впал, -а] (**в** В) fall (flow, run) in(to); **~де́ние** *n* [12] flowing into; *реки* mouth, confluence; **~́дина** *f* [5] cavity; *глазная* socket; *geogr.* hollow; **~́лый** [14] hollow, sunken; **~сть** → ***~да́ть***

**впервы́е** for the first time

**вперёд** forward; ahead (Р of), on(ward); *заранее* in advance, beforehand; → *a.* ***взад***

**впереди́** in front, ahead (Р of); before

**впереме́жку** alternately

**впечатл|е́ние** *n* [12] impression; **~и́тельный** [14; -лен, -льна] impressionable, sensitive; **~я́ющий** [17 *sh.*] impressive

**впи|ва́ться** [1], ⟨~́ться⟩ [вопью́сь, -пьёшься; впи́лся, -а́сь, -ось] (**в** В) stick (into); *укусить* sting, bite; ***~ва́ться глаза́ми*** fix one's eyes (on)

**впи́с|ывать** [1], ⟨~а́ть⟩ [3] enter, insert

**впи́т|ывать** [1], ⟨~а́ть⟩ soak up *or* in;

*fig.* imbibe, absorb
**впи́х|ивать** *coll.* [1], *once* ⟨**~ну́ть**⟩ [20] stuff *or* cram in(to) (**в** В)
**вплавь** by swimming
**впле|та́ть** [1], ⟨**~сти́**⟩ [25; -т-: вплету́, -тёшь] interlace, braid
**вплот|ну́ю** (**к** Д) close, (right) up to; *fig. coll.* seriously; **~ь** *fig.* (**до** Р) (right) up to; even (till)
**вполго́лоса** in a low voice
**вполз|а́ть** [1], ⟨**~ти́**⟩ [24] creep *or* crawl in(to), up
**вполне́** quite, fully, entirely
**впопыха́х** → ***второпя́х***
**впо́ру**: ***быть ~*** fit
**впорхну́ть** [20; -ну́, -нёшь] *pf.* flutter *or* flit in(to)
**впосле́дствии** afterward(s), later
**впотьма́х** in the dark
**впра́вду** *coll.* really, indeed
**впра́ве**: ***быть ~*** have a right
**вправля́ть** [28], ⟨вправить⟩ [14] *med.* set; *рубашку* tuck in; ***~ мозги́*** make s.o. behave more sensibly
**впра́во** (to the) right
**впредь** henceforth, in future; ***~ до*** until
**впро́голодь** half-starving
**впрок 1.** for future use; **2.** to a p.'s benefit; ***э́то ему́ ~ не пойдёт*** it will not profit him
**впроса́к**: ***попа́сть ~*** make a fool of o.s.
**впро́чем** however, but; or rather
**впры́г|ивать** [1], *once* ⟨**~нуть**⟩ [20] jump in(to) *or* on; (***в, на*** В)
**впры́с|кивать** [1], *once* ⟨**~нуть**⟩ [20] *mst. tech.* inject
**впря|га́ть** [1], ⟨**~чь**⟩ [26 г/ж; → ***напря́чь***] harness, put to (**в** В)
**впус|к** *m* [1] admission; **~ка́ть** [1], ⟨**~ти́ть**⟩ [15] let in, admit
**впусту́ю** in vain, to no purpose
**впу́т|ывать**, ⟨**~ать**⟩ [1] entangle, involve (**в** В in); **-ся** become entangled
**впя́теро** five times (→ ***вдво́е***); **~́м** five (together)
**враг** *m* [1 *e.*] enemy
**враж|да́** *f* [5] enmity; **~де́бность** *f* [8] animosity; **~де́бный** [14; -бен, -бна] hostile; **~дова́ть** [7] be at odds (**с** Т with); **~́еский** [16], **~́ий** [18] (the) enemy('s)…
**вразбро́д** *coll.* separately; without coordination
**вразре́з**: ***идти́ ~*** be contrary (**с** Т to)
**вразум|и́тельный** [14; -лен, -льна] intelligible, clear; **~ля́ть** [1], ⟨**~и́ть**⟩ [14] make understand, make listen to reason
**враньё** *n coll.* [12] lies, fibs *pl.*, idle talk
**врас|пло́х** unawares, by surprise; **~сыпну́ю**: ***бро́ситься ~сыпну́ю*** scatter in all directions
**враст|а́ть** [1], ⟨**~и́**⟩ [24 -ст-: -сту́; врос, -ла́] grow in(to)
**врата́рь** *n* [4 *e.*] goalkeeper
**врать** *coll.* [вру, врёшь; врал, -а́, -о], ⟨со-⟩ lie; (*ошибиться*) make a mistake; *о часах и т. д.* be inaccurate
**врач** *m* [1 *e.*] doctor, physician; ***зубно́й ~*** dentist; **~е́бный** [14] medical
**вращ|а́ть** [1] (В *or* Т) turn, revolve, rotate; (*v/i.* **-ся в** П associate with); **~а́ющийся** revolving; moving; **~е́ние** *n* [12] rotation
**вред** *m* [1 *e.*] harm, damage; ***во ~*** (Д) to the detriment (of); **~и́тель** *m* [4] *agric.* pest; **~и́ть** [15 *e.*; -ежу́, -еди́шь], ⟨по-⟩ (do) harm, (cause) damage (Д to); **~́ный** [14; -ден, -дна́, -о] harmful, injurious (Д *or* ***для*** Р to)
**врез|а́ть** [1], ⟨**~́ать**⟩ [3] (**в** В) cut in(to); set in; **-ся** run in(to); project into; *в память* impress (on)
**вре́менный** [14] temporary, transient, provisional
**вре́м|я** *n* [13] time; *gr.* tense; ***~я го́да*** season; ***во ~я*** (Р) during; ***в настоя́щее ~я*** at (the) present (moment); ***в пе́рвое ~я*** at first; ***~я от ~́ени, ~ена́ми*** from time to time, (every) now and then, sometimes; ***в ско́ром ~́ени*** soon; ***в то (же) ~я*** at that (the same) time; ***в то ~я как*** whereas; ***за после́днее ~я*** lately, recently; ***на ~я*** for a (certain) time, temporarily; ***со ~́енем, с тече́нием ~́ени*** in the course of time, in the long run; ***тем ~́енем*** meanwhile; ***ско́лько ~́ени?*** what's the time?; ***ско́лько ~́ени э́то займёт?*** how long will it take?; ***хорошо́ провести́ ~я*** have a good time; ***~яисчисле́ние*** *n* [12] chronology; ***~я(пре)провожде́ние*** *n* [12]

pastime
**вро́вень** level with, abreast (with **с** T)
**вро́де** like, such as, kind of
**врождённый** [14 *sh.*] innate; *med.* congenital
**вроз(н)ь** separately, apart
**врун** *coll. m* [1 *e.*], **∴ья** *coll. f* [6] liar
**вруч|а́ть** [1], ⟨**~и́ть**⟩ [16] hand over; deliver; (*вверить*) entrust
**вры|ва́ть** [1], ⟨**~ть**⟩ [22; -ро́ю, -ро́ешь] dig in(to); **-ся**, ⟨ворваться⟩ [-вусь, -вёшься; -вался, -лась] rush in(to); enter (by force)
**вряд**: **~ ли** hardly, scarcely
**вса́дни|к** *m* [1] horseman; **~ца** *f* [5] horsewoman
**вса́|живать** [1], ⟨**~ди́ть**⟩ [15] thrust *or* plunge in(to); hit; **~сывать** [1], ⟨всоса́ть⟩ [-су́, -сёшь] suck in *or* up; absorb
**всё**, **все** → ***весь***
**все|ве́дущий** [17] omniscient; **~возмо́жный** [14] of all kinds *or* sorts, various
**всегда́** always; **~шний** *coll.* [15] usual, habitual
**всего́** (-vɔ) altogether, in all; sum, total; **~** (***то́лько, лишь, -на́всего***) only, merely; ***пре́жде ~*** above all
**всел|е́нная** *f* [14] universe; **~я́ть** [28], ⟨**~и́ть**⟩ [13] settle, move in(to) (*v/i.* **-ся**); *fig.* inspire
**все|ме́рный** every (or all) … possible; **~ме́рно** in every possible way; **~ми́рный** [14] world…; universal; **~могу́щий** [17 *sh.*] → ***~си́льный***; **~наро́дный** [14; -ден, -дна] national, nationwide; *adv.*: **~наро́дно** in public; **∴нощная** *f* [14] vespers *pl.*; **~о́бщий** [17] universal, general; **~объе́млющий** [17 *sh.*] comprehensive, all-embracing; **~ору́жие** *n* [12]: ***во ~ору́жии*** fully prepared (for), in full possession of all the facts; **~росси́йский** [16] All-Russian
**всерьёз** *coll.* in earnest, seriously
**все|си́льный** [14; -лен, -льна] all-powerful; **~сторо́нний** [15] all-round, thorough
**всё-таки** for all that, still
**всеуслы́шанье**: ***во ~*** publicly
**всеце́ло** entirely, wholly
**вска́|кивать** [1], ⟨вскочи́ть⟩ [16] jump *or* leap (***на*** B up/on); start (**с** P from); *о прыщике, шишке* come up, swell (up); **~пывать**, ⟨вскопа́ть⟩ [1] dig up
**вскара́бк|иваться**, ⟨**~аться**⟩ [1] (***на*** B) scramble, clamber (up, onto)
**вска́рмливать** [1], ⟨вскорми́ть⟩ [14] raise, rear *or* bring up
**вскачь** at full gallop
**вскип|а́ть** [1], ⟨**~е́ть**⟩ [10 *e.*; -плю́, -пи́шь] boil up; *fig.* fly into a rage
**вскло́(ко́)|чивать** [1], ⟨**~чить**⟩ [16] tousle; ***~ченные*** *or* ***~чившиеся во́лосы*** *m/pl.* dishevel(l)ed hair
**всколыхну́ть** [20] stir up, rouse
**вскользь** in passing, cursorily
**вскопа́ть** → ***вска́пывать***
**вско́ре** soon, before long
**вскорми́ть** → ***вска́рмливать***
**вскочи́ть** → ***вска́кивать***
**вскри́|кивать** [1], ⟨**~ча́ть**⟩ [4 *e.*; -чу́, -чи́шь], *once* ⟨**~кнуть**⟩ [20] cry out, exclaim
**вскружи́ть** [16; -жу́, -у́жи́шь] *pf.*; **~** (Д) ***го́лову*** turn a p.'s head
**вскры|ва́ть** [1], ⟨**~ть**⟩ **1.** open; (*обнаружить*) *fig.* reveal; **2.** *med.* dissect; **-ся 1.** open; be disclosed; **2.** *med.* burst, break; **∴тие** *n* [12] *mst. med.* dissection, autopsy
**всласть** *coll.* to one's heart's content
**вслед** (***за*** T, Д) (right) after, behind, following; **∴ствие** (P) in consequence of, owing to; ***∴ствие э́того*** consequently
**вслепу́ю** *coll.* blindly, at random
**вслух** aloud
**вслу́ш|иваться**, ⟨**~аться**⟩ [1] (***в*** B) listen attentively (to)
**всма́триваться** [1], ⟨всмотре́ться⟩ [9; -отрю́сь, -о́тришься] (***в*** B) peer (at); observe closely, scrutinize
**всмя́тку**: ***яйцо́ ~*** soft-boiled egg
**всо́|вывать** [1], ⟨всу́нуть⟩ [20] put, slip (**в** B into); **~са́ть** → ***вса́сывать***
**вспа́|хивать** [1], ⟨**~ха́ть**⟩ [3] plow (*Brt.* plough) *or* turn up; **~шка** *f* [5] tillage
**всплес|к** *m* [1] splash; **∴кивать** [1], ⟨**~ну́ть**⟩ [20] splash; ***~ну́ть рука́ми*** throw up one's arms
**всплы|ва́ть** [1], ⟨**∴ть**⟩ [23] rise to the

surface, surface; *fig.* come to light, emerge

**всполоши́ть** [16 *e.*; -шу́, -ши́шь; -шён-ный] *pf.* alarm; (*v/i.* **-ся**)

**вспом|ина́ть** [1], ⟨**∠нить**⟩ [13] (В *or* **о** П) remember, recall; (Д + **-ся** = И + *vb.*); **∼ога́тельный** [14] auxiliary

**вспорхну́ть** [20] *pf.* take wing

**вспоте́ть** [8] (break out in a) sweat

**вспры́г|ивать** [1], *once* ⟨**∼нуть**⟩ [20] jump *or* spring (up/on **на** В)

**вспры́с|кивать** [1], ⟨**∼нуть**⟩ [20] sprinkle; wet; *coll. покупку* celebrate

**вспу́г|ивать** [1], *once* ⟨**∼ну́ть**⟩ [20] frighten away

**вспух|а́ть** [1], ⟨**∠нуть**⟩ [21] swell

**вспыл|и́ть** [13] *pf.* get angry, flare up; **∠ьчивость** *f* [8] irascibility; **∠ьчивый** [14 *sh.*] hot-tempered

**вспы́|хивать** [1], ⟨**∼хнуть**⟩ [20] **1.** burst into flames; blaze up, flare up; *огонёк* flash; (*покраснеть*) blush; **2.** *от гнева* burst into a rage; *о войне* break out; **∼шка** *f* [5; *g/pl.*: -шек] flare, flash; outburst; outbreak

**вста|ва́ть** [5], ⟨**∼ть**⟩ [вста́ну, -нешь] stand up; get up, rise (from **с** Р); arise; **∠вка** *f* [5; *g/pl.*: -вок] insertion; insert; **∼вля́ть** [28], ⟨**∠вить**⟩ [14] set *or* put in, insert; **∼вно́й** [14] inserted; ***∼вны́е зу́бы*** *m/pl.* false teeth

**встрепену́ться** [20] *pf.* start; (*оживиться*) become animated

**встрёпк|а** Р *f* [5] reprimand; ***зада́ть ∼у*** (Д) bawl out, scold (a p.)

**встре́|тить(ся)** → ***∼ча́ть(ся)***; **∼ча** *f* [5] meeting, encounter; *приём* reception; ***тёплая ∼ча*** warm welcome; **∼ча́ть** [1], ⟨**∼тить**⟩ [15 *st.*] **1.** meet (*v/t.*, with В) encounter; *случайно* come across; **2.** *прибывших* meet, receive, welcome ***∼ча́ть Но́вый год*** see the New Year in; celebrate the New Year; *v/i.* **-ся 1.** meet (**с** Т o.a., with); **2.** (*impers.*) occur, happen; there are (were); **∼чный** [14] counter…; contrary; head (*wind*); (coming from the) opposite (direction); *машина* oncoming; ***пе́рвый ∼чный*** the first person one meets; anyone; ***пе́рвый ∼чный и попере́чный*** every Tom, Dick and Harry

**встря́|ска** *f* [5; *g/pl.*: -сок] shock; **∼хивать** [1], *once* ⟨**∼хну́ть**⟩ [20] shake (up); *fig.* stir (up); **-ся** *v/i. coll.* cheer up

**вступ|а́ть** [1], ⟨**∼и́ть**⟩ [14] *стать членом* (**в** В) enter, join; set foot in, step (into); *в должность* assume; ***∼и́ть в брак*** marry; ***∼и́ть в де́йствие*** come into force; ***∼и́ть на трон*** ascend the throne; **-ся** (***за*** В) intercede (for), project; take a p.'s side; **∼и́тельный** [14] introductory; opening; *экзамен и т. д.* entrance…; **∼ле́ние** *n* [12] *на престол* accession; *в книге и т. д.* introduction

**всу́|нуть** → ***всо́вывать***; **∼чивать** *coll.* [1], ⟨**∼чи́ть**⟩ [16] foist (В/Д s.th. on)

**всхлип** *m* [1], **∠ывание** *n* [12] sob(bing); **∠ывать** [1], *once* ⟨**∠нуть**⟩ [20 *st.*] sob

**всход|и́ть** [15], ⟨**взойти́**⟩ [взойду́, -дёшь; взошёл; *g. pt.*: взойдя́] go *or* climb (***на*** В [up] on), ascend, rise; *agric.* come up, sprout; **∼ы́** *m/pl.* [1] standing *or* young crops

**всхо́жесть** *f* [8] germinating capacity

**всхрапну́ть** [20] *coll. joc. pf.* have a nap

**всыпа́ть** [1], ⟨**∠ать**⟩ [2 *st.*] pour *or* put (**в** В into); Р upbraid; give s.b. a thrashing

**всю́ду** everywhere, all over

**вся́|кий** [16] **1.** any; every; anyone; everyone; ***без ∼кого сомне́ния*** beyond any doubt; ***во ∼ком слу́чае*** at any rate; **2.** = **∼ческий** [16] all kinds *or* sorts of, sundry; every possible; **∼чески** in every way; ***∼чески стара́ться*** try one's hardest, try all ways; **∼чина** *coll. f* [5]: ***∼кая ∼чина*** odds and ends

**вта́|йне** in secret; **∼лкивать** [1], ⟨**втолкну́ть**⟩ [20] push *or* shove in(to); **∼птывать** [1], ⟨**втопта́ть**⟩ [3] trample into; **∼скивать** [1], ⟨**∼щи́ть**⟩ [16] pull *or* drag in, into, up

**вте|ка́ть** [1], ⟨**∼чь**⟩ [26] flow in(to)

**вти|ра́ть** [1], ⟨**втере́ть**⟩ [12; вотру́, -рёшь; втёр] rub in; ***∼ра́ть очки́*** (Д) throw dust in (p.'s) eyes; **-ся** *coll.* ***в дове́рие*** worm into; **∠скивать** [1], ⟨**∠снуть**⟩ [20] squeeze o.s. in(to)

**втихомо́лку** *coll.* on the sly

**втолкну́ть** → ***вта́лкивать***

**втоптáть** → ***втáптывать***

**втор|гáться** [1], ⟨**~гнуться**⟩ [21] (**в** В) intrude, invade, penetrate; *в чужие дела* meddle (with); **~жéние** *n* [12] invasion, incursion; **~ить** [13] *mus.* sing (*or* play) the second part; echo; repeat; **~úчный** [14] second, repeated; *побочный* secondary; **~úчно** once more, for the second time; **~ник** *m* [1] Tuesday (**в** В, *pl.*: **по** Д on); **~óй** [14] second; ***из ~ы́х рук*** second-hand; → ***пéрвый & пя́тый***; **~окýрсник** *m* [1] sophomore, *Brt.* secondyear student

**второпя́х** hurriedly, in haste

**второстепéнный** [14; -éнен, -éнна] secondary, minor

**в-трéтьих** third(ly)

**втрúдорога**: *coll.* triple the price; ***платúть ~*** pay through the nose

**втрó|е** three times (as ..., *comp.*: → ***вдвóе***); *vb.* **~е** *a.* treble; **~ём** three (of us *or* together); **~йнé** three times (as much *etc.*), treble

**втýлка** *f* [5; *g/pl.*: -лок] *tech.* sleeve

**втыкáть** [1], ⟨воткнýть⟩ [20] put *or* stick in(to)

**втя́|гивать** [1], ⟨**~нýть**⟩ [19] draw *or* pull in(to), on; *вовлечь* involve, engage; **-ся** (**в** В) *fig. в работу* get used (to)

**вуáль** *f* [8] veil

**вуз** *m* [1] (***вы́сшее учéбное заведéние*** *n*) institution of higher education

**вулкáн** *m* [1] volcano; **~úческий** [16] volcanic

**вульгáрный** [14; -рен, -рна] vulgar

**вундеркúнд** *m* [1] child prodigy

**вход** *m* [1] entrance; entry; ***~а нет*** no entry; ***плáта за ~*** entrance *or* admission fee

**входúть** [15], ⟨войтú⟩ [войдý, -дёшь; вошёл, -шлá; вошéдший *g. pt.*: войдя́] (**в** В) enter, go, come *or* get in(to); (*помещаться*) go in(to), have room for; hold; be a member of; be included in; ***~ во вкус*** (Р) take a fancy to; ***~ в довéрие к*** (Д) gain a p.'s confidence; ***~ в положéние*** (Р) appreciate a p.'s position; ***~ в привы́чку*** (*в поговорку*) become a habit (proverbial); ***~ в*** (***состáв*** Р) form part (of), belo (to)

**входнóй** [14] entrance..., admission...

**вхолостýю**: ***рабóтать ~*** run idle

**вцеп|ля́ться** [28], ⟨**~úться**⟩ [14] (**в** В) grasp, catch hold of

**вчерá** yesterday; **~шний** [5] yesterday's, of yesterday

**вчернé** in rough; in draft form

**вчéтверо** four times (as ..., *comp.*: → ***вдвóе***); **~м** four (of us *etc.*)

**вчúтываться** [1] (**в** В) *impf. only* try to grasp the meaning of

**вшéстеро** six times (→ ***вдвóе***)

**вши|вáть** [1], ⟨**~ть**⟩ [вошью́, -шьёшь; → ***шить***] sew in(to); **~вый** [14] *mst. coll. fig.* lousy

**въе|дáться** [1], ⟨**~сться**⟩ [→ ***есть***] eat (in[to]); **~дливый** [14 *sh.*] *coll.* corrosive, acid

**въе|зд** *m* [1] entrance, entry; **~зднóй** [14]: ***~здна́я вúза*** entry visa; **~зжáть** [1], ⟨**~хать**⟩ [въéду, -дешь; въезжáй(-те)!] enter, ride *or* drive in(to), up, on (**в, на** В); move in(to); **~сться** → ***~дáться***

**вы** [21] you (polite form *a.* ♀); ***~ с ним*** you and he; ***у вас*** (***был***) you have (had)

**выб|áлтывать** *coll.* [1], ⟨**~олтать**⟩ blab *or* let out; **~егáть** [1], ⟨**~ежать**⟩ [4; вы́бегу, -ежишь] run out; **~ивáть** [1], ⟨**~ить**⟩ [вы́бью, -бьешь, *etc.* → ***бить***] beat *or* knock out; *стекло и т. д.* break; smash; (*изгнать*) drive out, *mil.* dislodge; ***~ить из колеи*** unsettle; **-ся** break out *or* forth; ***~ивáться из сил*** be(come) exhausted, fatigued; ***~ивáться из колеи*** go off the beaten track; **~ирáть** [1], ⟨**~рать**⟩ [вы́беру, -решь; -бранный] choose, pick out; (*избирать*) elect; take out; *минутку* find; **-ся** get out; *на концерт и т. д.* find time to go; **~ить** → ***~ивáть***

**вы́боина** *f* [5] dent; *на дороге* pothole; rut

**вы́бор** *m* [1] choice, option; (*отбор*) selection; *pl.* election(s); ***на ~*** (*or* ***по ~у***) at a p.'s discretion; random (*test*); ***всеóбщие ~ы*** *pl.* general election; ***дополнúтельные ~ы*** by-election; **~ка** *f* [5; *g/pl.*: -рок] selection; *pl.* excerpts; *statistics* sample; **~ный** [14] electoral; elected

**выбр|а́сывать** [1], ⟨**ꙫосить**⟩ [15] throw (out *or* away); discard; (*исключить*) exclude, omit; **~а́сывать (зря) де́ньги** waste money; **-ся** throw o.s. out; **ꙫать** → **выбира́ть**; **ꙫить** [-ею, -еешь; -итый] *pf.* shave clean; (*v/i.* **-ся**); **ꙫосить** → **~а́сывать**

**выб|ыва́ть** [1], ⟨**ꙫыть**⟩ [-буду, -будешь] leave; *из игры* drop out

**выв|а́ливать** [1], ⟨**ꙫалить**⟩ [13] discharge, throw out; **-ся** fall out; **~а́ривать** [1], ⟨**ꙫарить**⟩ [13] (*экстрагировать*) extract; boil (down); **~е́дывать**, ⟨**ꙫедать**⟩ [1] find out, (try to) elicit; **ꙫезти** → **~ози́ть**

**выв|ёртывать** [1], ⟨**ꙫернуть**⟩ [20] unscrew; *дерево* tear out; *руку и т. д.* dislocate; *наизнанку* turn (inside out); *v/i.* **-ся**; slip out; extricate o.s.

**вы́вес|ить** → **выве́шивать**; **~ка** *f* [5; *g/pl.*: -сок] sign(board); *fig.* screen, pretext; **~ти** → **выводи́ть**

**выв|е́тривать** [1], ⟨**ꙫетрить**⟩ [13] (remove by) air(ing); **-ся** *geol.* weather; disappear **~е́триваться из па́мяти** be effaced from memory; **~е́шивать** [1], ⟨**ꙫесить**⟩ [15] hang out *or* put out; **~и́нчивать** [1], ⟨**ꙫинтить**⟩ [15] unscrew

**вы́вих** *m* [1] dislocation; **~нуть** [20] *pf.* dislocate, put out of joint

**вы́вод** *m* [1] **1.** *войск* withdrawal; conclusion; **сде́лать ~** draw a conclusion; **~и́ть** [15], ⟨**вы́вести**⟩ [25] **1.** take, lead *or* move (out, to); **2.** conclude; **3.** *птенцов* hatch; *сорт растения* cultivate; **4.** *пятно* remove, *насекомых* extirpate; **5.** *буквы* write *or* draw carefully; **6.** *образ* depict; **~и́ть** (B) **из себя́** make s.b. lose his temper; **-ся**, ⟨-сь⟩ disappear; **~ок** *m* [1; -дка] brood

**вы́воз** *m* [1] export; *мусора* removal; **~и́ть** [15], ⟨**вы́везти**⟩ [24] remove, take *or* bring out; export

**выв|ора́чивать** *coll.* [1], ⟨**ꙫоротить**⟩ [15] → **вывёртывать**

**выг|а́дывать**, ⟨**ꙫадать**⟩ [1] gain *or* save (B/**на** П s.th. from)

**вы́гиб** *m* [1] bend, curve; **~а́ть** [1], ⟨**вы́гнуть**⟩ [20] *о кошке* arch; curve, bend

**вы́гля|деть** [11 *st.*] *impf.* look (s.th. T, like **как**); **как она́ ~дит?** what does she look like?; **он ~дит моло́же свои́х лет** he doesn't look his age; **ꙫдывать** [1], *once* ⟨**~нуть**⟩ [20 *st.*] look *or* peep out (of **в** B, **из** P)

**вы́гнать** → **выгоня́ть**

**вы́гнуть** → **выгиба́ть**

**выгов|а́ривать** [1], ⟨**´~орить**⟩ [13] **1.** pronounce; utter; **2.** *impf. coll.* (Д) tell off; **´~ор** *m* [1] **1.** pronunciation; **2.** reproof, reprimand

**вы́год|а** *f* [5] (*прибыль*) profit; (*преимущество*) advantage; (*польза*) benefit; **~ный** [14; -ден, -дна] profitable; advantageous (Д, **для** P to)

**вы́гон** *m* [1] pasture; **~я́ть** [28], ⟨**вы́гнать**⟩ [**вы́гоню**, **-нишь**] turn *or* drive out; *coll. с работы* fire

**выгор|а́живать** [1], ⟨**´~одить**⟩ [15] fence off; P shield, absolve from blame; **~а́ть** [1], ⟨**´~еть**⟩ [9] **1.** burn down; **2.** (*выцвести*) fade; **3.** *coll.* (*получиться*) click, come off

**выгр|ужа́ть** [1], ⟨**ꙫузить**⟩ [15] unload, discharge; *с судна* disembark; (*v/i.* **-ся**); **ꙫузка** [5; *g/pl.*: -зок] unloading; disembarkation

**выдава́ть** [5], ⟨**вы́дать**⟩ [-дам, -дашь, *etc.* → **дать**] **1.** give (out), pay (out); **2.** *пропуск* issue; **3.** *предать* betray; **4.** *другому государству* extradite; **~ (себя́) за** (B) pass (o.s. off) as; **~ (за́муж) за** (B) give (a girl) in marriage to; **-ся 1.** (*выступать*) stand out; **2.** *coll. день и т. д.* happen *or* turn out

**выд|а́вливать** [1], ⟨**ꙫавить**⟩ [14] press *or* squeeze out (*a. fig.*); **ꙫавить улы́бку** force a smile; **~а́лбливать** [1], ⟨**ꙫолбить**⟩ [14] hollow out, gouge out

**вы́да|ть** → **~ва́ть**; **~ча** *f* [5] **1.** (*раздача*) distribution; *сдача* delivery; *денег* payment; **2.** issue; **3.** disclosure; **4.** extradition; **день ~чи зарпла́ты** payday; **~ю́щийся** [17; -щегося *etc.*] outstanding, prominent, distinguished

**выдви|га́ть** [1], ⟨**´~нуть**⟩ [20] **1.** pull out; **2.** *предложение* put forward, propose; *на должность* promote; *кандидата* nominate; **-ся 1.** slide in and out; **2.** *esp. mil.* move forward; **3.** *по службе* advance; **4.** *impf.* → **~жно́й** [14] pull-out…, sliding; (*tech.*) telescopic

**выд|еле́ние** *n* [12] discharge, secretion; **~е́лка** *f* [5; *g/pl.*: -лок] *о качестве* workmanship; *кожи* dressing; **~е́лывать**, ⟨**~елать**⟩ [1] work, make *кожу*; **~еля́ть** [28], ⟨**~елить**⟩ [13] **1.** mark out, single out; (*отметить*) emphasize; **2.** *землю и т. д.* allot; satisfy (*coheirs*); **3.** *med.* secrete; **4.** *chem.* isolate; **-ся** *v/i.* 1, 4; (*отличаться*) stand out, rise above; excel; **~ёргивать**, ⟨**~ернуть**⟩ [20] pull out

**выде́рж|ивать** [1], ⟨**´~ать**⟩ [4] stand, bear, endure; *экзамен* pass; *размеры и т. д.* observe; ***´~ать хара́ктер*** be firm; **´~анный** self-possessed; (*последовательный*) consistent; *о вине* mature; **´~ка** *f* [5; *g/pl.*: -жек] **1.** self-control; **2.** (*отрывок*) excerpt, quotation; **3.** *phot.* exposure

**выд|ира́ть** *coll.* [1], ⟨**~рать**⟩ [-деру, -ерешь] tear out; *зуб* pull; *pf.* thrash; **~олбить** → ***~а́лбливать***; **~охнуть** → ***~ыха́ть***; **~ра** *f* [5] otter; **~рать** → ***~ира́ть***; **~умка** *f* [5; *g/pl.*: -мок] invention; made-up story, fabrication; **~у́мывать**, ⟨**~умать**⟩ [1] invent, contrive, devise

**выд|ыха́ть** [1], ⟨**~охнуть**⟩ [20] breathe out; **-ся** become stale; *fig.* be played out

**вы́езд** *m* [1] departure; *из города* town/city gate

**выезжа́ть** [1], ⟨**вы́ехать**⟩ [вы́еду, -едешь; -езжа́й(те)!] *v/i.* (**из/с** Р) **1.** leave, depart; **2.** *на машине, лошади* drive *or* ride out, on(to); **3.** *из квартиры* leave *or* move (from)

**вы́емка** *f* [5; *g/pl.*: -мок] excavation; *ямка* hollow

**вы́ехать** → ***выезжа́ть***

**вы́ж|ать** → ***~има́ть***; **~дать** → ***выжида́ть***; **~ива́ние** *n* [12] survival; **~ива́ть** [1], ⟨**~ить**⟩ [-иву, -ивешь; -итый] survive; go through; stay; *coll. из дома и т. д.* oust, drive out; ***~ить из ума́*** be in one's dotage; *fig.* take leave of one's senses; **~ига́ть** [1], ⟨**~ечь**⟩ [26 г/ж: -жгу, -жжешь, -жгут; -жег, -жженный] burn out; burn down; scorch; **~ида́ть** [1], ⟨**~дать**⟩ [-жду, -ждешь; -жди(те)!] (Р *or* В) wait for *or* till (after); **~има́ть** [1], ⟨**~ать**⟩ [-жму, -жмешь; -жатый] squeeze, press *or о белье* wring out; *sport* lift (weights); **~ить** → ***~ива́ть***

**вы́звать** → ***вызыва́ть***

**выздор|а́вливать** [1], ⟨**´~оветь**⟩ [10] recover; **~а́вливающий** [17] convalescent; **~овле́ние** *n* [12] recovery

**вы́з|ов** *m* [1] call, summons; (*приглашение*) invitation; *mst. fig.* challenge; **~у́бривать** [1] → ***зубри́ть*** *2*; **~ыва́ть** [1], ⟨**~вать**⟩ [-ову, -овешь] **1.** call (to; for *thea.*; up *tel.*); *врача* send for; **2.** summon (**к** Д to, **в суд** before a court); **3.** challenge (to **на** В); **4.** (*приводить*) rouse, cause; *воспоминания* evoke; **-ся** undertake *or* offer; **~ыва́ющий** [17] defiant, provoking

**выи́гр|ывать**, ⟨**´~ать**⟩ [1] win (from **у** Р); (*извлечь выгоду*) gain, benefit; **´~ыш** *m* [1] win(ning[s]), gain(s), prize; profit; ***быть в ´~ыше*** have won (profited); **´~ышный** [14] *положение* advantageous, effective

**вы́йти** → ***выходи́ть***

**вык|а́лывать** [1], ⟨**~олоть**⟩ [17] put out; prick out; **~а́пывать**, ⟨**~опать**⟩ [1] dig out *or* up; **~ара́бкиваться**, ⟨**~арабкаться**⟩ [1] scramble *or* get out; **~а́рмливать** [1], ⟨**~ормить**⟩ [14] bring up, rear; **~а́тывать** [1], ⟨**~атить**⟩ [15] push *or* wheel out; ***~атить глаза́*** P stare

**выки́|дывать** [1], *once* ⟨**´~нуть**⟩ [20] **1.** throw out *or* away; discard; (*опустить*) omit; **2.** *белый флаг* hoist (up); **3.** *coll. фокус* play (trick); **´~дыш** *m* [1] miscarriage

**вы́кл|адка** *f* [5; *g/pl.*: -док] *math.* computation, calculation; *mil.* pack *or* kit; **~а́дывать** [1], ⟨**вы́ложить**⟩ [16] **1.** *деньги* lay out; tell; **2.** (*отделать*) face with masonry

**выключ|а́тель** *m* [4] *el.* switch; **~а́ть** [1], ⟨**´~ить**⟩ [16] switch *or* turn off; *двигатель* stop; **~е́ние** *n* [12] switching off, stopping

**вык|о́вывать** [1], ⟨**~овать**⟩ [7] forge; *fig.* mo(u)ld; **~ола́чивать** [1], ⟨**~олотить**⟩ [15] *ковёр* beat *or* knock out; *долги и т. д.* exact; **~олоть** → **~алывать**; **~опать** → **~апывать**; **~ормить** → **~армливать**; **~орчёвывать** [1], ⟨**~орчевать**⟩ [7] root up *or* out

**выкр|а́ивать** [1], ⟨**~оить**⟩ [13] *sew.* cut out; *coll. время* spare; *деньги* find; **~а́шивать** [1], ⟨**~асить**⟩ [15] paint, dye; **~и́кивать** [1], *once* ⟨**~икнуть**⟩ [20] cry *or* call (out); **~оить** → **~а́ивать**; **~ойка** *f* [5; *g/pl.*: -оек] pattern

**выкр|ута́сы** *coll. m/pl.* [1] *о поведении* vagaries, crotchets; **~у́чивать** [1], ⟨**~утить**⟩ [15] twist; *бельё* wring (out); *coll.* unscrew; **-ся** *coll. лампочку и т. д.* slip out

**вы́куп** *m* [1] redemption; *заложника и т. д.* ransom; **~а́ть** [1], ⟨**~ить**⟩ [14] *вещь* redeem; ransom; **~ать** → **купа́ть**

**выку́р|ивать** [1], ⟨**´~ить**⟩ [13] smoke

**выл|а́вливать** [1], ⟨**~овить**⟩ [14] fish out, draw out; **~азка** *f* [5; *g/pl.*: -зок] *mil.* sally; **~а́мывать**, ⟨**~омать**⟩ [1] break open

**выл|еза́ть** [1], ⟨**~езть**⟩ [24] climb *or* get out; *о волосах* fall out; **~епля́ть** [28], ⟨**~епить**⟩ [14] model, fashion

**вы́лет** *m* [1] *ae.* taking off, flight; **~а́ть** [1], ⟨**~еть**⟩ [11] fly out; *ae.* take off, (**в** В for); rush out *or* up; (*вывалиться*) fall out; slip (a *p.'s* memory **~еть из головы́**); **~еть в трубу́** go broke

**выл|е́чивать** [1], ⟨**~ечить**⟩ [16] cure, heal (*v/i.* **-ся**); **~ива́ть** [1], ⟨**~ить**⟩ [-лью, -льешь; → **лить**] pour out; **~итый** [14] the image of, just like (И s.b.)

**вы́л|овить** → **~а́вливать**; **~ожить** → **выкла́дывать**; **~омать** → **~а́мывать**; **~упля́ться** [28], ⟨**~иться**⟩ [14] hatch

**вым|а́зывать** [1], ⟨**~азать**⟩ [3] smear; daub (**-ся** o.s.) (T with); **~а́ливать** [1], ⟨**~олить**⟩ [13] get *or* obtain by entreaties; **~а́ливать проще́ние** beg for forgiveness; **~а́нивать** [1], ⟨**~анить**⟩ [13] lure (**из** P out of); coax *or* cheat (**у** P/B a p. out of s.th.); **~а́ривать** [1], ⟨**~орить**⟩ [13] exterminate; **~а́чивать** [1], ⟨**~очить**⟩ [16] *дождём* drench; *в жидкости* soak; **~а́щивать** [1], ⟨**~остить**⟩ [15] pave **~е́нивать** [1], ⟨**~енять**⟩ [28] exchange (for **на** В); **~ереть** → **~ира́ть**; **~ета́ть** [1], ⟨**~ести**⟩ [25; -т- *st.*: -ету, -етешь] sweep (out); **~еща́ть** [1], ⟨**~естить**⟩ [15] avenge o.s. (on Д); *злобу* vent (**на** П on p.); **~ира́ть** [1], ⟨**~ереть**⟩ [12] die out, become extinct

**вымога́т|ельство** *n* [9] blackmail, extortion; **~ь** [1] extort (В *or* Р/**у** Р s.th. from)

**вым|ока́ть** [1], ⟨**~окнуть**⟩ [21] get wet through; **~окнуть до ни́тки** get soaked to the skin; **~олвить** [14] *pf.* utter, say; **~олить** → **~а́ливать**; **~орить** → **~а́ривать**; **~остить** → **~а́щивать**; **~очить** → **~а́чивать**

**вы́мпел** *m* [1] pennant, pennon

**вым|ыва́ть** [1], ⟨**~ыть**⟩ [22] wash (out, up); **~ысел** *m* [1; -сла] invention; fantasy; *ложь* falsehood; **~ыть** → **~ыва́ть**; **~ышля́ть** [28], ⟨**~ыслить**⟩ [15] think up, invent; **~ышленный** *a.* fictitious

**вы́мя** *n* [13] udder

**вын|а́шивать** [1]: **~а́шивать план** nurture a plan; **~ести** → **~оси́ть**

**вын|има́ть** [1], ⟨**~уть**⟩ [20] take *or* draw out, produce

**вын|оси́ть** [15], ⟨**~ести**⟩ [24; -с-: -су, -сешь; -с, -сла, -сло] **1.** carry *or* take out (away), remove; **2.** (*терпеть*) endure, bear; **3.** *благодарность* express; pass (*a. law*); **~оси́ть сор из избы́** wash one's dirty linen in public; **~о́сливость** *f* [8] endurance; **~о́сливый** [14 *sh.*] sturdy, hardy, tough

**вын|ужда́ть** [1], ⟨**~удить**⟩ [15] force, compel; extort (В/**у** *or* **от** Р s.th. from); **~ужденный** [14 *sh.*] forced; of necessity; **~ужденная поса́дка** emergency landing

**вы́нырнуть** [20] *pf.* come to the surface, emerge; *coll.* turn up (unexpectedly)

**вы́пад** *m* [1] *fencing* lunge; thrust; *fig.* attack

**выпа|да́ть** [1], ⟨**´~сть**⟩ [25] **1.** fall *or* drop (out); (*выскользнуть*) slip out; **2.** fall (Д to, *a.* **на до́лю** to *a p.'s* lot); devolve on

**вып|а́ливать** [1], ⟨**~алить**⟩ [13] *coll.*

blurt out; shoot (***из*** P with); **~áлывать** [1], ‹**∻олоть**› [17] weed (out); **~áривать** [1], ‹**∻арить**› [13] steam; clean, disinfect; (*chem.*) evaporate

**вып|екáть** [1], ‹**∻ечь**› [26] bake; **~ивáть** [1], ‹**∻ить**› [-пью, -пьешь; → ***пить***] drink (up); *coll.* be fond of the bottle; ***∻ить*** (***ли́шнее***) *coll.* have one too many; ***∻ить чáшку чáю*** have a cup of tea; **∻ивка** *coll. f* [5; *g/pl.*: -вок] booze

**вы́п|иска** *f* [5; *g/pl.*: -сок] **1.** writing out, copying; **2.** *из текста* extract; statement (of account *из счёта*); **3.** order; subscription; **4.** *из больницы* discharge; *с места жительства* notice of departure; **~и́сывать** [1], ‹**∻исать**› [3] **1.** write out (*or* down); copy; **2.** → ***выводи́ть 6.***; **3.** *журнал и т. д.* order; subscribe; **4.** discharge; **-ся** sign out; ***~и́сываться из больни́цы*** leave hospital

**вы́пла|вка** *f* [5] smelting; **~кать** [3] *pf.* cry (one's eyes *глаза*) out; **~та** *f* [5] payment; **∻чивать** [1], ‹**~тить**› [15] pay (out *or* off)

**выпл|ёвывать** [1], *once* ‹**∻юнуть**› [20] spit out; **~ёскивать** [1], ‹**∻ескать**› [3], *once* ‹**∻еснуть**› [20] dash *or* splash (out); ***∻еснуть с водо́й ребёнка*** throw the baby out with the bathwater

**выпл|ывáть** [1], ‹**∻ыть**› [23] swim out; surface; emerge, appear

**выпол|áскивать** [1], ‹**ʹ~оскать**› [3] rinse; *горло* gargle; **~зáть** [1], ‹**ʹ~зти**› [24] creep *or* crawl out; **~нéние** *n* [12] fulfil(l)ment, execution, realization; **~нять** [1], ‹**ʹ~нить**› [13] carry out, fulfil(l); execute; **ʹ~оть** → ***выпáлывать***

**вы́пр|авка** *f* [5; *g/pl.*: -вок]: ***воéнная ~авка*** soldierly bearing; **~авля́ть** [28], ‹**~авить**› [14] set right *or* straighten out; *рукопись и т. д.* correct; **~áшивать** [1], ‹**~осить**› [15] try to get *or* obtain, solicit; **~овáживать** *coll.* [1], ‹**~оводить**› [15] send s.o. packing, turn out; **~ыгивать** [1], ‹**~ыгнуть**› [20] jump out; **~ягáть** [1], ‹**~ячь**› [26 г/ж: -ягу, -яжешь; -яг] unharness; **~ямля́ть** [28], ‹**~ямить**› [14] straighten; **-ся** become straight; *спину* straighten

**вы́пукл|ость** *f* [8] protuberance; prominence, bulge; **~ый** [14] convex; prominent; *fig.* expressive; distinct

**вы́пуск** *m* [1] output; issue; publication; (*часть романа*) instal(l)ment; *о студентах* graduate class; **~áть** [1], ‹**вы́пустить**› [15] let out; *law* release; *товары* produce, issue, publish; (*исключить*) omit, leave out; graduate; ***~áть в продáжу*** put on sale; **~ни́к** *m* [1 *e.*] graduate; **~нóй** [14] graduate…, graduation…, final, leaving; *tech.* discharge…; exhaust…

**вып|ýтывать**, ‹**∻утать**› [1] disentangle *or* extricate (**-ся** o.s.); **~ýчивать** [1], ‹**∻учить**› [16] **1.** bulge; **2.** P → ***тарáщить***

**вып|ы́тывать**, ‹**∻ытать**› [1] find out, (try to) elicit

**выпя́|ливать** P [1], ‹**∻лить**› [13] → ***тарáщить***; **~чивать** *coll.* [1], ‹**ʹ~тить**› [15] stick *or* thrust out; *fig.* emphasize

**выраб|áтывать**, ‹**ʹ~отать**› [1] manufacture, produce; *план и т. д.* elaborate, work out; develop; **ʹ~отка** *f* [15; *g/pl.*: -ток] manufacture, production; output

**выр|áвнивать** [1], ‹**∻овнять**› [28] **1.** level; smooth out; **2.** align; (*уравнивать*) equalize; **-ся** straighten; become even

**выра|жáть** [1], ‹**ʹ~зить**› [15] express, show; ***~жáть словáми*** put into words; **~жáться** [1], ‹**ʹ~зиться**› [15] **1.** express o.s.; **2.** manifest itself (**в** П in); **~жéние** *n* [12] expression; **~зи́тельный** [14; -лен, -льна] expressive; *coll.* significant

**выр|астáть** [1], ‹**∻асти**› [24 -ст-: -асту; → ***расти́***] **1.** grow (up); increase; (*превратиться*) develop into; **2.** (*появиться*) emerge, appear; **~áщивать** [1], ‹**∻астить**› [15] *растение* grow; *животных* breed; *ребёнка* bring up; *fig. чемпиона* train; **∻вать 1.** → ***~ывáть***; **2.** → ***рвать 3***

**вы́рез** *m* [1] notch; cut; ***плáтье с глубóким ~ом*** low-necked dress; **~áть** [1], ‹**~ать**› [15] **1.** cut out, clip; **2.** *из дерева* carve; (*гравировать*) engrave; **3.** slaughter; **~ка** *f* [5; *g/pl.*: -зок] cutting out, clipping; *cul.* tenderloin; **~нóй** [14] carved

**вы́ро|док** *m* [1; -дка] *coll.* monster;

**~ждáться** [1], ⟨**~диться**⟩ [15] degenerate; **~ждéние** *n* [12] degeneration
**вы́ронить** [13] *pf.* drop
**вы́росший** [17] grown
**выр|убáть** [1], ⟨**~́убить**⟩ [14] cut down *or* fell; **~учáть** [1], ⟨**~́учить**⟩ [16] **1.** come to s.o.'s help *or* rescue; **2.** *за товар* make, net; **~́учка** *f* [5] rescue; assistance, help; *comm.* proceeds; ***прийти́ на ~́учку*** come to the aid (Д of)
**выр|ывáть** [1], ⟨**~́вать**⟩ [-ву, -вешь] **1.** pull out; tear out; **2.** snatch (***из*** P, ***у*** P from); *fig.* extort (В/***у*** P s.th. from a p.); **-ся** break away; tear o.s. away (***из*** P from); break loose; escape; **~ывáть,** ⟨**~́ыть**⟩ [22] dig out, up
**вы́с|адка** *f* [5; *g/pl.*: -док] disembarkation, landing; **~áживать** [1], ⟨**~адить**⟩ [15] **1.** land, disembark; **2.** help out; make *or* let a p. get off; **3.** *растения* transplant; **-ся** *v/i.*; *a.* get out, off
**выс|áсывать** [1], ⟨**~́осать**⟩ [-осу, -осешь] suck out; **~вéрливать** [1], ⟨**~́верлить**⟩ [13] bore, drill; **~вобождáть** [1], ⟨**~́вободить**⟩ [15] free, disentangle
**выс|евáть** [1], ⟨**~́еять**⟩ [27] sow; **~екáть** [1], ⟨**~́ечь**⟩ [26] **1.** hew, carve; **2.** → ***сечь***; **~елéние** *n* [12] eviction; **~елять** [28], ⟨**~́елить**⟩ [13] evict; **~́еять** → ***~евáть***; **~и́живать** [1], ⟨**~́идеть**⟩ [11] sit out, stay; *яйцо* hatch
**выск|áбливать** [1], ⟨**~́облить**⟩ [13] scrape clean; *удалить* erase; **~áзывать** [1], ⟨**~́азать**⟩ [3] express, tell, state; ***~́азать предположéние*** suggest; **-ся** express o.s.; express one's opinion, thoughts, *etc.* (***о*** П about); speak (***за*** В for; ***прóтив*** P against); **~áкивать** [1], ⟨**~́очить**⟩ [16] jump, leap *or* rush out; **~áльзывать, ~ользáть** [1], ⟨**~́ользнуть**⟩ [20] slip out; **~́облить** → ***~áбливать***; **~́очить** → ***~áкивать***; **~́очка** *m/f* [5; *g/pl.*: -чек] upstart; **~ребáть** [1], ⟨**~́рести**⟩ [25 -б-: → ***скрести́***] scrape out (off); (*удалить*) scratch out
**вы́сл|ать** → ***высылáть***; **~éживать** [1], ⟨**~едить**⟩ [15] track down; **~у́живать** [1], ⟨**~ужить**⟩ [16] obtain by *or* for service; **-ся** curry favo(u)r (***пéред*** T with s.b.); **~у́шивать,** ⟨**~ушать**⟩ [1] listen (to), hear (out); *med.* auscultate
**высм|éивать** [1], ⟨**~́еять**⟩ [27] deride, ridicule
**выс|óвывать** [1], ⟨**~́унуть**⟩ [20 *st.*] put out; **-ся** lean out
**высóкий** [16; высóк, -á, -óкó; *comp.*: вы́ше] high; tall (*a.* ***~ рóстом***); *fig.* lofty
**высоко|кáчественный** [14] (of) high-quality; **~квалифици́рованный** [14] highly skilled; **~мéрие** *n* [12] haughtiness; **~мéрный** [14; -рен, -рна] haughty, arrogant; **~пáрный** [14; -рен, -рна] bombastic, high-flown; **~превосходи́тельство** [9] *hist.* Excellency; **~производи́тельный** [14; -лен, -льна] *работа* highly productive; *оборудование* high-efficiency
**вы́сосать** → ***высáсывать***
**высо|тá** *f* [5; *g/pl.*: -óты, *etc. st.*] height; *mus.* pitch; *geogr.* eminence; hill; altitude; *уровень* level; ***оказáться на ~тé*** be equal to (the occasion); ***высотóй в*** (В) … or …; ***в ~тý …*** high
**вы́сох|нуть** → ***высыхáть***; **~ший** [17] dried up, withered
**выс|очáйший** [17] highest; *достижение* supreme; **~óчество** *n* [9] *hist.* Highness; **~́паться** → ***высыпáться***
**вы́спренний** [15] bombastic
**вы́став|ить** → ***~лять***; **~ка** *f* [5; *g/pl.*: -вок] exhibition, show; **~лять** [28], ⟨**~ить**⟩ [14] **1.** (*вынуть*) put (take) out; **2.** *картину и т. д.* exhibit, display; represent (***себя*** o.s.); **3.** *оценку* give a mark; *mil.* post; *выгнать* turn out; ***~лять напокáз*** show, parade; **-ся** exhibit; **~очный** [14] (of the) exhibition, show…
**выстр|áивать(ся)** [1] → ***стрóить(ся)***; **~́ел** *m* [1] shot; (noise) report; ***на*** (***расстоя́ние, -ии***) ***~́ел(а)*** within gunshot; **~́елить** → ***стреля́ть***
**вы́ступ** *m* [1] projection; **~áть** [1], ⟨**~ить**⟩ [14] **1.** step forth, forward; come *or* stand out; *слёзы и т. д.* appear; **2.** *в поход* set out; **3.** speak (sing, play) in public; ***~áть с рéчью*** (***в прéниях***) address an audience, deliver a speech; take the floor; **~лéние** *n* [12] setting out; *pol.* speech; appearance (in public); *thea.*

performance, turn
**вы́сунуть(ся)** → ***высо́вывать(ся)***
**высу́ш|ивать** [1], 〈´~ить〉 [16] dry up, *coll.* emaciate
**выс|чи́тывать** [1], 〈´~читать〉 calculate, compute; *coll.* deduct
**вы́сш|ий** [17] highest, supreme, higher (*a. educ.*), superior; ***~ая ме́ра наказа́ния*** capital punishment
**выс|ыла́ть** [1], 〈´~лать〉 [вы́шлю, -лешь] send, send out, *pol.* exile; *из страны* deport; **´~ылка** *f* [15] dispatch; exile, expulsion; **~ыпа́ть** [1], 〈´~ыпать〉 [2] pour out *or* in, on; *v/i. о людях* spill out; **~ыпа́ться** [1], 〈вы́спаться〉 [-сплюсь, -спишься] sleep one's fill, have a good night's rest; **~ыха́ть** [1], 〈´~охнуть〉 [21] dry up, wither; **~ь** *f* [8] height, summit
**выт|а́лкивать**, *coll.* 〈´~олкать〉 [1], *once* 〈´~толкнуть〉 [20 *st.*] throw out; **~а́пливать** [1], 〈´~опить〉 [14] **1.** heat; **2.** *о жире* melt (down); **~а́скивать** [1], 〈´~ащить〉 [16] drag off *or* out; *coll. украсть* pilfer
**выт|ека́ть** [1], 〈´~ечь〉 [26] flow out; *fig.* follow, result; **´~ереть** → ***~ира́ть***; **´~ерпеть** [14] *pf.* endure, bear; ***не ´~ерпел*** couldn't help; **~есня́ть** [28], 〈´~еснить〉 [13] force, push out; *оппонента* oust, supplant; **´~ечь** → ***~ека́ть***
**выт|ира́ть** [1], 〈´~ереть〉 [12] dry, wipe (**-ся** o.s.); wear out
**вы́точенный** [14] chiseled; *tech.* turned
**вы́тр|ебовать** [7] *pf.* ask for, demand, order, summon; *добиться требованием* obtain on demand; **~яса́ть** [1], 〈´~ясти〉 [24 -с-] shake out
**выть** [22], 〈вз-〉 howl
**выт|я́гивать** [1], 〈´~януть〉 [20 *st.*] draw, pull *or* stretch (out); elicit; *сведения* endure, bear; **-ся** stretch, extend (o.s.); *вырасти* grow (up); **´~яжка** *f chem.* extract
**выу́|живать** [1], 〈´~дить〉 [15] catch, dig out (*a. fig.*)
**выу́ч|ивать** [1], 〈´~ить〉 [16] learn, memorize (В + *inf. or* Д); teach (a p. to … *or* s.th.); **-ся** learn (Д/**у** Р s.th. from); ***~иваться на врача́*** become a doctor
**вых|а́живать** [1], 〈´~одить〉 [15] *больного* nurse, restore to health; **~а́тывать** [1], 〈´~ватить〉 [15] snatch away, from, out; pull out, draw
**вы́хлоп** *m* [1] exhaust; **~но́й** [14] exhaust…
**вы́ход** *m* [1] **1.** exit; way out (*a. fig.*); *чувствам* outlet; **2.** departure; withdrawal, *на пенсию* retirement; **3.** *книги* appearance, publication; *thea.* entrance (on stage); **4.** *продукции* yield, output; ***~ за́муж*** marriage (of woman); ***~ в отста́вку*** retirement, resignation; **~ец** *m* [1; -дца] immigrant, native of; ***быть ~цем из*** come from
**выходи́ть** [15], 〈вы́йти〉 [вы́йду, -дешь; вы́шел] **1.** go *or* come out; leave; withdraw; retire; **2.** *о книге* appear, be published *or* issued; **3.** *получиться* come off; turn out, result; happen, arise, originate; ***вы́шло!*** it's worked!; ***вы́йти в отста́вку*** (***на пе́нсию***) retire, resign; ***~ за преде́лы*** (Р) transgress the bounds of; ***~*** (***за́муж***) ***за*** (В) marry (*v/t.*; *of woman*); ***~ из себя́*** be beside o.s.; ***~ из терпе́ния*** lose one's temper (patience); ***окно́ выхо́дит на у́лицу*** window facing the street; ***~ из стро́я*** fail; be out of action; ***из него́ вы́шел …*** he has become …; ***из э́того ничего́ не вы́йдет*** nothing will come of it
**вы́ход|ить** → ***выха́живать***; **~ка** *f* [5; *g/pl.*: -док] trick, prank; excess; **~но́й** [14] exit…; outlet…; ***~но́й день*** *m* day off; (have a ***быть*** Т); ***~но́е посо́бие*** gratuity
**вы́холенный** [14] well-groomed
**выцве|та́ть** [1], 〈´~сти〉 [25 -т-: -ету] fade
**выч|ёркивать** [1], 〈´~еркнуть〉 [20] cross *or* strike out; *из памяти* erase, obliterate; **~е́рпывать**, 〈´~ерпать〉 [1], *once* 〈´~ерпнуть〉 [20 *st.*] bail, scoop (out); **´~есть** → ***~ита́ть***; **´~ет** *m* [1] deduction; ***за ´~ом*** (Р) less, minus
**вычисл|е́ние** *n* [12] calculation; **~я́ть** [1], 〈´~ить〉 [13] calculate, compute
**вы́чи|стить** → ***~ща́ть***; **~та́емое** *n* [14] subtrahend; **~та́ние** *n* [12] subtraction; **~та́ть** [1], 〈вы́честь〉 [25 -т-: -чту; -чел, -чла; *g. pt.*: вы́чтя] deduct; subtract;

Г

**~щáть** [1], ⟨′~стить⟩ [15] clean, scrub, scour; brush
**вы́чурный** [14; -рен, -рна] ornate, flowery; fanciful
**вы́швырнуть** [20 *st.*] *pf.* throw out
**вы́ше** higher; above; *сил и т. д.* beyond; ***онá ~ меня́*** she is taller than I (am); ***э́то ~ моегó понимáния*** that's beyond my comprehension
**вы́ше...** above...
**выш|ибáть** [1], ⟨**~́ибить**⟩ [-бу, -бешь; -б, -бла; -бленный] *coll.* (*выбить*) knock out; (*выгнать*) kick out; **~ивáние** *n* [12] embroidery; **~ивáть** [1], ⟨**~́ить**⟩ [-шью, -шьешь] embroider; **~́ивка** *f* [5; *g/pl.*: -вок] embroidery
**вышинá** *f* [5] height; → ***высотá***
**вы́шка** *f* [5; *g/pl.*: -шек] tower; ***буровáя ~*** derrick; ***диспéтчерская ~*** *ae.* control tower
**выяв|ля́ть** [28], ⟨′~ить⟩ [14] display, make known; uncover, reveal
**выясн|éние** *n* [12] clarification; **~я́ть** [28], ⟨′~ить⟩ [13] clear up, find out, ascertain; **-ся** turn out; come to light
**вью́|га** *f* [5] snowstorm; **~щиийся** [17] curly; ***~щееся растéние*** *n* creeper, climber
**вя́жущий** [17] astringent
**вяз** *m* [1] elm
**вязáльн|ый** [14] knitting...; ***~ый крючóк*** crochet hook; ***~ая спи́ца*** knitting needle
**вя́зан|ка** *f* [5; *g/pl.*: -нок] knitted garment; fag(g)ot; **′~ный** [14] knitted; **~ье** *n* [10] (*a.* **~ие** *n* [12]) knitting; *крючком* crochet
**вяз|áть** [3], ⟨с-⟩ **1.** tie, bind (together); **2.** knit; *крючком* crochet; **-ся** *impf.* (*соответствовать*) agree, be in keeping; ***разговóр не ~áлся*** the conversation flagged; **~́кий** [16; -зок, -зкá, -о] viscous; *о почве* swampy, marshy; **~́нуть** [21], ⟨за-, у-⟩ get stuck in; sink into
**вя́лить** [13], ⟨про-⟩ dry; dry-cure, jerk (*meat, fish*)
**вя́|лый** [14 *sh.*] *цветок* withered, faded; *физически* flabby; *fig.* sluggish; dull (*a. comm.*); **~нуть** [20], ⟨за-, у-⟩ wither, fade

# Г

**габари́т** *m* [1] *tech.* clearance-related dimension, size
**гáвань** *f* [8] harbo(u)r
**гáга** *f* [5] *zo.* eider
**гадá|лка** *f* [5; *g/pl.*: -лок] fortuneteller; **~ние** *n* [12] fortune-telling; *догадка* guessing, conjecture; **~ть** [1] **1.** ⟨по-⟩ tell fortunes (with cards ***на кáртах***); **2.** *impf.* guess, conjecture
**гáд|ина** *f* [5] *coll.* loathsome person, cur; **~ить** [15] **1.** ⟨на-, за-⟩ soil; (Д) harm; **2.** ⟨из-⟩ P botch; **~кий** [16; -док, -дкá, -о; *comp.*: гáже] nasty, ugly, disgusting, repulsive; **~ли́вый** [14 *sh.*]: ***~ли́вое чу́вство*** feeling of disgust; **~ость** *f* [8] *coll.* filth; low *or* dirty trick; **~ю́ка** *f* [5] *zo.* viper (*a.* P *fig.*), adder
**гáечный ключ** *m* [1; *g/pl.*: -éй] spanner, wrench
**газ** *m* [1] **1.** gas; ***дать ~*** *mot.* step on the gas; ***на пóлном ~у́*** at full speed (throttle); *pl. med.* flatulence; **2.** *ткань* gauze
**газéль** *f* [8] gazelle
**газéт|а** *f* [5] newspaper; **~ный** [14] news...; ***~ный киóск*** *m* newsstand, *Brt.* news stall; **~чик** *m* [1] *coll.* journalist
**газирóван|ный** [14]: ***~ная водá*** soda water
**гáз|овый** [14] **1.** gas...; ***~овая колóнка*** geyser; water heater; ***~овая плитá*** gas stove; **~ови́к** *m* [1] *coll.* gasman
**газóн** *m* [1] lawn; **~окоси́лка** *f* [5; *g/pl.*: -лок] lawnmower
**газо|обрáзный** [14; -зен, -зна] gaseous; **~прóвод** *m* [1] gas pipeline

**га́йка** *f* [5; *g*/*pl*.: га́ек] *tech*. nut
**галантер|е́йный** [14]: **~е́йный магази́н** notions store, haberdashery; **~е́йные това́ры** *m*/*pl*. = **~е́я** *f* [6] notions *pl*., haberdashery
**галд|ёж** *m* [1 *e*.] row, hubbub; **~е́ть** [11], ⟨за-⟩ clamo(u)r, din
**гал|ере́я** *f* [6] gallery; **~ёрка** *coll*. *f* [5] *thea*. gallery, "the gods" (*occupants of gallery seats*)
**галиматья́** *f* [7] *coll*. balderdash, nonsense; **сплошна́я ~** sheer nonsense
**галифе́** *pl*. [*indecl*.] riding breeches *pl*.
**га́лка** *f* [5; *g*/*pl*.: -лок] jackdaw
**гало́п** *m* [1] gallop; **~ом** at a gallop; **~и́ровать** [7] gallop
**га́лочк|а** *f* [5] tick; **для ~и** for purely formal purposes
**гало́ши** *f*/*pl*. [5] galoshes, rubbers
**га́лстук** *m* [1] (neck)tie
**галу́н** *m* [1 *e*.] galloon, braid
**гальван|изи́ровать** [7] (*im*)*pf*. galvanize; **~и́ческий** [16] galvanic
**га́лька** *f* [5; *g*/*pl*.: -лек] pebble
**гам** *m* [1] *coll*. din, row, rumpus
**гама́к** *m* [1 *e*.] hammock
**га́мма** *f* [5] *mus*. scale; *красок* range; **´~-излуче́ние** gamma rays
**гангре́на** *f* [5] gangrene
**га́нгстер** *m* [1] gangster
**гандбо́л** *m* [1] handball
**ганте́ли** (-'tɛ-) *f*/*pl*. [8] (*sport*) dumbbells
**гара́ж** *m* [1 *e*.] garage
**гарант|и́ровать** [7] (*im*)*pf*., **´~ия** *f* [7] guarantee
**гардеро́б** *m* [1] wardrobe, *a*. *collect*.; **~ная** *f* [14] check-, cloakroom; **~щик** *m* [1], **~щица** *f* [5] cloakroom attendant
**гарди́на** *f* [5] curtain
**гармо́|ника** *f* [5] (*kind of*) accordion; **губна́я ~** mouth organ, harmonica; **~ни́ровать** [7] harmonize, be in harmony (**с** T with); **~ни́ст** *m* [1] accordionist; harmonist; **~ни́чный** [14; -чен, -чна] harmonious; **~ния** *f* [7] harmony; **~нь** *f* [8], **~шка** *f* [5; *g*/*pl*.: -шек] → **~ника**
**гарни|зо́н** *m* [1] garrison; **´~р** *m* [1], **´~ровать** [7] (*im*)*pf*., *cul*. garnish; **~ту́р** *m* [1] set; *мебели* suite
**гарпу́н** *m* [1 *e*.], **~ить** [13] harpoon
**гарь** *f* [8] (s.th.) burnt, chared; **па́хнет ´~ю** there is a smell of smoke
**гаси́ть** [15], ⟨по-, за-⟩ extinguish, put *or* blow out; *известь* slake; **~ почто́вую ма́рку** frank a postage stamp
**га́снуть** [21], ⟨по-, у-⟩ grow feeble, die away; *fig*. fade, wither
**гастрол|ёр** *m* [1] guest actor *or* artiste; *coll*. casual worker moving from town to town; **~и́ровать** [7] tour; perform on tour; **´~и** *f*/*pl*. [8] tour
**гастроно́м** *m* [1] *a*. = **~и́ческий магази́н** *m* grocery store *or* shop; **~и́ческий** [16] gastronomic(al); **~ия** *f* [7] provisions; delicacies *pl*.
**гвалт** *coll*. *m* [1] rumpus, uproar
**гвард|е́ец** *m* [1; -е́йца] guardsman; **´~ия** *f* [7] Guards *pl*.
**гво́зд|ик** *dim*. → **~ь**; **~и́ка** *f* [5] carnation, pink; (spice) clove; **~ь** *m* [4 *e*.; *pl*.: гво́зди, -де́й] tack, nail; *fig*. *программы* main feature
**где** where; *coll*. → **куда́**; **~-~** = **ко́е-где́**; → **ни**; **~** = **´~-либо, ´~-нибудь, ´~-то** anywhere; somewhere; **´~-то здесь** hereabout(s)
**гей!** *int*. hi!
**гекта́р** *m* [1] hectare
**ге́лий** *m* [3] helium
**ген** *m* [1] gene
**генеоло́гия** *f* [7] genealogy
**генера́|л** *m* [1] general; **~лите́т** *m* [1] *collect*. generals; *coll*. top brass; **~льный** [14] general; **~льная репети́ция** *f* dress rehearsal; **~тор** *m* [1] generator
**гене́ти|ка** *f* [5] genetics; **´~ческий** [16] genetic, genic
**ген|иа́льный** [14: -лен, -льна] of genius; ingenious; **´~ий** *m* [3] genius
**гените́лии** *m*/*pl*. [3] genitals
**геноци́д** *m* [1] genocide
**гео́|граф** *m* [1] geographer; **~графи́ческий** [16] geographic(al); **~гра́фия** *f* [7] geography; **~ло́г** *m* [1] geologist; **~ло́гия** *f* [7] geology; **~ме́трия** *f* [7] geometry
**георги́н(а** *f* [5]) *m* [1] dahlia
**гера́нь** *f* [8] geranium
**герб** *m* [1 *e*.] (coat of) arms; emblem;

Г

Г

**∼овый** [14] heraldic; stamp(ed)
**геркуле́с** *m* [1] **1.** man of herculian strength; **2.** rolled oats; porridge
**герма́нский** [16] German, *ling.* Germanic
**гермети́ческий** [16] airtight
**герои́зм** *m* [1] heroism
**герои́н** *m* [1] heroin
**геро|и́ня** *f* [6] heroine; **∼и́ческий** [16] heroic; **∼й** *m* [3] hero; **∼йский** [16] heroic
**гиаци́нт** *m* [1] hyacinth
**ги́бель** *f* [8] death; *корабля и т. д.* loss; (*разрушение*) ruin, destruction; **∼ный** [14; -лен, -льна] disastrous, fatal
**ги́бк|ий** [16; -бок, -бка́, -о́; *comp*.: ги́бче] supple, pliant, flexible (*a. fig.*); **∼ость** *f* [8] flexibility
**ги́б|лый** [14]: ***∼лое де́ло*** hopeless case; ***∼лое ме́сто*** godforsaken place; **∼нуть** [21], ⟨по-⟩ perish
**гига́нт** *m* [1] giant; **∼ский** [16] gigantic, huge
**гигие́н|а** *f* [5] hygiene; **∼и́ческий** [16], **∼и́чный** [14; -чен, -чна] hygienic
**гигроскопи́ческий** [16; -чен, -чна] hygroscopic
**гид** *m* [1] guide
**гидравли́ческий** [16] hydraulic
**гидро|пла́н** *m* [1] seaplane, hydroplane; **∼(электро)ста́нция** *f* [7] hydroelectric (power) station
**гие́на** *f* [5] hyena
**ги́льза** *f* [5] (cartridge) case; (cylinder) sleeve
**гимн** *m* [1] hymn; *государственный* anthem
**гимна|зи́ст** *m* [1] pupil; **∼зия** *f* [7] high school, *Brt.* grammar school; **∼ст** *m* [1] gymnast; **∼стёрка** *f* [5; *g/pl.*: -рок] *mil.* blouse, *Brt.* tunic; **∼стика** *f* [5] gymnastics; **∼сти́ческий** [16] gymnastic; ***∼сти́ческий зал*** gymnasium
**гипе́рбола¹** *f* [5] *math.* hyperbola
**гипе́рбол|а²** *f* [5] hyperbole; exaggeration; **∼и́ческий** [16] hyperbolic, exaggerated
**гипертони́я** *f* [7] high blood-pressure, hypertension
**гипно́|з** *m* [1] hypnosis; **∼тизи́ровать** [7], ⟨за-⟩ hypnotize
**гипо́теза** *f* [5] hypothesis
**гипс** *m* [1] *min.* gypsum; *tech.* plaster of Paris; **∼овый** [14] gypseous, plaster…
**гирля́нда** *f* [5] garland
**ги́ря** *f* [6] weight
**гита́р|а** *f* [5] guitar; **∼и́ст** *m* [1] guitarist
**глава́¹** *f* [5; *pl. st.*] chapter
**глав|а́²** *f* [5; *pl. st.*] head; (***быть, стоя́ть***) ***во ∼е́*** (be) at the head; lead (**с** T by); ***поста́вить во ∼у́ угла́*** consider to be of the greatest importance; **∼а́рь** *m* [4 *e.*] (ring-) leader
**главе́нство** *n* [9] supremacy; domination; **∼вать** [7] command, hold sway (over)
**главнокома́ндующий** *m* [17] commander in chief; ***Верхо́вный ∼*** Commander in Chief; Supreme Commander
**гла́вн|ый** [14] chief, main, principal, central; head…; … in chief; ***∼ое*** (***де́ло***) the main thing; above all; ***∼ым о́бразом*** mainly, chiefly
**глаго́л** *m* [1] *gr.* verb; **∼ьный** [14] verbal
**глад|и́льный** [14] ironing; ***∼и́льная доска́*** ironing board; **∼ить** [15] **1.** ⟨вы́-⟩ iron, press; **2.** ⟨по-⟩ stroke, caress; *coll.* ***∼ить по голо́вке*** indulge; favo(u)r; ***∼ить про́тив ше́рсти*** rub the wrong way; **∼кий** [16; -док, -дка́; *comp.*: гла́же] smooth (*a. fig.*); *волосы* lank; *ткань* plain; **∼ко** smoothly, successfully; ***всё прошло́ ∼ко*** everything went off smoothly; **∼ь** *f* [8] smoothness; smooth surface; ***тишь да ∼ь*** *coll.* peace and quiet
**глаз** *m* [1; в ∼у́; *pl.*: -а́, глаз, -а́м] eye; look; *зрение* (eye)sight; *coll. присмотр* heed, care; ***в ∼а́*** (Д) to s.b.'s face; ***в мои́х ∼а́х*** in my view *or* opinion; ***за ∼а́*** in s.b.'s absence, behind one's back; more than enough; ***на ∼*** approximately, by eye; ***на ∼а́х*** (*poss. or* **у** P) in s.b.'s presence; ***не в бровь, а в ∼*** *coll.* hit the mark; ***с ∼у на ∼*** privately, tête-à-tête; ***невооружённым ∼ом*** with the naked eye; ***темно́, хоть ∼ вы́коли*** *coll.* it is pitch-dark; **∼а́стый** *coll.* [14 *sh.*] sharp-sighted; **∼е́ть** P [8] stare, gape; **∼но́й** [14] eye…, optic; ***∼но́й врач*** *m*

ophthalmologist; **~но́е я́блоко** eyeball; **~о́к** *m* [1; -зка́] **1.** [*pl. st.*: -зок] *dim.* → **глаз**; **аню́тины ~ки** *pl.* pansy; **2.** [*pl. e.*: -зки́, -зко́в] *bot.* bud; *в двери* peephole
**глазоме́р** *m* [1]: **хоро́ший ~** good eye
**глазу́нья** *f* [6] fried eggs *pl.*
**глазур|ова́ть** [7] (*im*)*pf.* glaze; **~ь** *f* [8] glaze, icing
**гла́нда** *f* [5] tonsil
**глас** *m* [1]: **~ вопию́щего в пусты́не** voice of one crying in the wilderness
**гла|си́ть** [15 *e.*; *3. sg. only*] say, read, run; **~сность** *f* [8] public(ity), openness; **~сный** [14] open, public; (*a. su.*) vowel
**гле́тчер** *m* [1] glacier
**гли́н|а** *f* [5] clay; loam; **~истый** [14 *sh.*] clayey; loamy; **~озём** *m* [1] *min.* alumina; **~яный** [14] clay- *or* earthenware-related
**глист** *m* [1 *e.*], **~а́** *f* [5] (intestinal) worm; (**ле́нточный**) **~** tapeworm
**глицери́н** *m* [1] glycerin(e)
**глоб|а́льный** [14; -лен, -льна] global, worldwide; **~ус** *m* [1] globe
**глода́ть** [3], ⟨об-⟩ gnaw (at, round)
**глот|а́ть** [1], ⟨про~и́ть⟩ [15], *once* ⟨~ну́ть⟩ [20] swallow; *coll. жадно* devour; **~ка** *f* [5; *g/pl.*: -ток] throat; **во всю ~ку** → **го́лос**; **~о́к** *m* [1; -тка́] mouthful, gulp (Т of)
**гло́хнуть** [21] **1.** ⟨о-⟩ grow deaf; **2.** ⟨за-⟩ *о звуке* fade, die away; *о саде и т. д.* grow desolate, become wild
**глуб|ина́** *f* [5] depth; *веков* antiquity *fig.* profundity; *леса* heart of the forest; Т/**в** В ..., *or* ... **в** В ... deep; **~и́нка** *f* [5] remote places; **~о́кий** [16; -бо́к, -бока́, -бо́ко́; *comp.*: глу́бже] deep; low; remote; *fig.* profound; complete; *старость* extreme old age; **~о́кой зимо́й** (**но́чью**) in the dead of winter (late at night)
**глубоко|мы́сленный** [14 *sh.*] thoughtful, profound; **~мы́слие** *n* [12] thoughtfulness, profundity; **~уважа́емый** [14] highly-esteemed; *в письме* dear
**глубь** *f* [8] → **глубина́**
**глум|и́ться** [14 *e.*; -млю́сь, -ми́шься] sneer, mock, scoff (**над** Т at); **~ле́ние** *n* [12] mockery
**глуп|е́ть** [8], ⟨по-⟩ become stupid; **~е́ц** *m* [1; -пца́] fool, blockhead; **~и́ть** [14 *e.*; -плю́, -пи́шь] fool; **~ость** *f* [8] stupidity, foolishness; nonsense; **~ый** [14; глуп, -а́, -о] foolish, silly, stupid
**глух|а́рь** *m* [4 *e.*] wood grouse; **~о́й** [14; глух, -а́, -о; *comp.*: глу́ше] deaf (*a. fig.*; **к** Д to; → **слепо́й**); *звук* dull, muffled; *место* desolate, wild; out-of-the-way; *arch.* solid, blind; **~о́й но́чью** late at night, in the dead of night; **~онемо́й** [14] deaf-mute; **~ота́** *f* [5] deafness
**глуш|и́тель** *m* [4] *tech.* silencer, muffler; **~и́ть** [16 *e.*; -шу́, -ши́шь, -шённый] **1.** ⟨о-⟩ deafen, stun; **2.** ⟨за-⟩ *о звуке* muffler; *боль* mitigate; *подавить* smother, suppress (*a. bot.*); *tech.* switch off, throttle; **~и́ть мото́р** stop the engine; **~ь** *f* [8] out-of-the-way place
**глы́ба** *f* [5] lump, clod; block
**глюко́за** *f* [5] glucose
**гля|де́ть** [11; гля́дя], ⟨по-⟩, *once* ⟨~нуть⟩ [20] look, glance (**на** В at); peep (**из** Р out of, from); **того́ и ~ди́ ...** it looks as though; **идти куда́ глаза́ ~дя́т** follow one's nose; **на ночь ~дя** late in the evening
**гля́н|ец** *m* [1; -нца] luster; polish; **~цев(и́т)ый** [14 (*sh.*)] glossy, lustrous; glazed paper; **~уть** → **гляде́ть**
**гнать** [гоню́, го́нишь; гони́мый; гнал, -а́, -о, ⟨по-⟩ **1.** *v/t.* drive; urge on; *из дома* turn out; **2.** *hunting* pursue, chase; (*a.* **~ся за** Т; *fig.* strive for); **3.** *coll. v/i.* speed along
**гнев** *m* [1] anger; **~аться** [1], ⟨раз-, про-⟩ be(come) angry (**на** В with); **~ный** [14; -вен, -вна́, -о] angry
**гнедо́й** [14] sorrel, bay
**гнезд|и́ться** [15] nest; **~о́** *n* [9; *pl.*: гнёзда, *etc. st.*] nest, aerie; *el.* socket
**гнёт** *m* [1] *fig.* oppression, yoke
**гни|е́ние** *n* [12] decay, rot, putrefaction; **~ло́й** [14; гнил, -а́, -о] rotten, putrid; **~ль** *f* [8] rottenness; **~ть** [гнию́, -ёшь; гнил, -а́, -о], ⟨с-⟩ rot, decay, putrefy
**гно|и́ть, (-ся)** [13] let rot, fester; **~й** *m* [3] pus; **~йный** [14] purulent
**гнуса́вить** [14] snuffle; twang

**гну́сн|ость** *f* [8] vileness; **~ый** [14; -сен, -сна́, -о] vile, foul
**гнуть** [20], ⟨со-⟩ bend, curve; bow; *coll.* *клонить* drive (**к** Д at)
**гнуша́ться** [1], ⟨по-⟩ (P *or* T) scorn, despise, disdain
**гобеле́н** *m* [1] tapestry
**гобо́й** *m* [3] oboe
**го́вор** *m* [1] talk; hum; murmur; accent; dialect; **~и́ть** [13], ⟨по-, сказа́ть⟩ [3] speak *or* talk (**о** П, **про** В about, of; **с** T to *or* with p.); say, tell; **~я́т, ~и́тся** they say, it is said; **~и́ть по-ру́сски** speak Russian; **ина́че ~я́** in other words; **не ~я́ уже́ о** (П) let alone; **по пра́вде** (**со́вести**) **~я́** tell the truth; **что вы ~и́те!** you don't say!; **что** (**как**) **ни ~и́** whatever you (one) may say; **что и ~и́ть, и не ~и́**(**те**)**!** yes, of course!, sure!; **~ли́вый** [14 *sh.*] talkative
**говя́|дина** *f* [5], **~жий** [18] beef
**го́голь-мо́голь** *m* [4] eggflip
**го́гот** *m* [1], **~а́ть** [3], ⟨за-⟩ *гусей* cackle; P roar (with laughter)
**год** *m* [1; *pl.*: -ды, -да́, *from g/pl. e.* & лет, *etc.* 9 *e.*] year (**в ~** a year, per annum); **в ~а́х** elderly, old; **в ~ы** during; **в те ~ы** in those days; **в э́том** (**про́шлом**) **~у́** this (last) year; **из ~а в ~** year in year out; **~ от ~у** year by year; **кру́глый ~** all (the) year round; (**с**) **~а́ми** for years; as years went on; **спустя́ ~** a year later
**годи́т|ься** [15 *e.*; гожу́сь, годи́шься], ⟨при-⟩ be of use (**для** P, **к** Д, **на** B for), do; fit; *pf.* come in handy; **э́то** (**нику́да**) **не ~ся** that's no good (for anything), that won't do, it's (very) bad
**годи́чный** [4] annual
**го́дный** [14; -ден, -дна́, -о, го́дны́] fit, suitable; *действующий* valid; *полезный* useful, good; **ни на что не ~** good-for-nothing
**годов|а́лый** [14] one-year-old, yearling; **~о́й** [14] annual, yearly; **~щи́на** *f* [5] anniversary
**гол** *m* [1] *sport* goal; **заби́ть ~** score (a goal)
**гол|ени́ще** *n* [11] bootleg; **~ень** *f* [8] shin, shank
**голла́нд|ец** *m* [1; -дца] Dutchman; **~ка** *f* [5; *g/pl.*: -док] Dutchwoman; **~ский** [16] Dutch
**голов|а́** *f* [5; *ac/sg.*: ~у; *pl.*: го́ловы, голо́в, -ва́м] head; mind, brain; **как снег на́ ~у** all of a sudden; **лома́ть ´~у** rack one's brains; **с ~ы́ до ног** from head to toe; **на свою́ ´~у** *coll.* to one's own detriment; **пове́сить ´~у** become discouraged *or* despondent; **~а́ идёт кру́гом** (**у** P s.b.'s) thoughts are in a whirl; **~ка** *f* [5; *g/pl.*: -вок] small head; *винта* head; *лука и т. д.* bulb, clove; **~но́й** [14] head…; **~на́я боль** *f* headache; **~но́й плато́к** head-scarf; **~но́й убо́р** headgear, head-dress
**голово|круже́ние** *n* [12] giddness; **~кружи́тельный** [14] dizzy, giddy; **~ло́мка** [5; *g/pl.*: -мок] puzzle; **~мо́йка** [5; *g/pl.*: -мо́ек] *coll.* dressing-down; **~ре́з** *coll.* *m* [1] daredevil; *бандит* cutthroat, thug; **~тя́п** *coll.* *m* [1] booby, bungler
**го́лод** *m* [1] hunger; starvation; famine; **~а́ть** [1] hunger, starve; go without food, fast; **~ный** [14; го́лоден, -дна́, -о, го́лодны́] hungry, starving; **~о́вка** *f* [5; *g/pl.*: -вок] hunger strike
**гололе́дица** *f* [5] ice-crusted ground
**го́лос** *m* [1; *pl.*: -са́, *etc. e.*] voice; *на выборах* vote; **пра́во ~а** suffrage; **во весь ~** at the top of one's voice; **в оди́н ~** unanimously; **~а́ за и про́тив** the yeas (ayes) & nays; **~ло́вный** [14; -вен, -вна] unfounded; **~ова́ние** *n* [12] voting, poll(ing); **та́йное ~ова́ние** secret vote; **~ова́ть** [7], ⟨про-⟩ vote; *coll.* thumb a lift (by raising one's hand); **~ово́й** [14] vocal (cords **свя́зки** *f/pl.*)
**голуб|е́ц** *m* [1; -бца́] cabbage-roll; **~о́й** [14] (sky) blue; **~ушка** *f* [5; *g/pl.*: -бок(шек)], **~чик** *m* [1] *often iro.* (my) dear; **´~ь** *m* [4] pigeon; **~я́тня** *f* [6; *g/pl.*: -тен] dovecote
**го́л|ый** [14; гол, -á, -о] naked, nude; bare (*a. fig.*); **~ь** *f* [8]: **~ь на вы́думки хитра́** necessity is the mother of invention
**гомеопа́тия** *f* [7] homeopathy
**го́мон** *coll.* *m* [1] din, hubbub
**гондо́ла** *f* [5] gondola (*a. ae.*)
**гон|е́ние** *n* [12] persecution; **~ка** *f* [5;

*g/pl.*: -нок] rush; chase; *coll.* haste; *pl.* race(s); *naut.* regatta; ***~ка вооружéний*** arms race
**гóнор** *m* [1] *coll.* arrogance, airs *pl.*
**гонорáр** *m* [1] honorarium, fee; *авторский* royalties
**гóночный** [14] race…, racing
**гончáр** *m* [1 *e.*] potter; **~ный** [14] potter's; ***~ные издéлия*** *n/pl.* pottery
**гóнчая** *f* [17] hound
**гонять(ся)** [1] drive, *etc.*, → ***гнать***
**гор|á** *f* [5; *ac/sg.*: гóру, *pl.*: гóры, гор, горáм] mountain; *куча* heap, pile; ***катáться с ~ы́*** toboggan; ***в ~у*** *or* ***нá ~у*** uphill; *fig.* up(ward); ***пóд ~у*** *or* ***с ~ы́*** downhill; ***под ~óй*** at the foot of a hill (*or* mountain); ***не за ~áми*** not far off, soon; ***пир ~óй*** sumptuous feast; ***стоять ~óй*** (***за*** В) defend s.th. *or* s.b. with might & main; ***как у меня ~á с плеч свалилась*** as if a load had been taken off my mind
**горáздо** *used with the comp.* much, far
**горб** *m* [1 *e.*; на ~ý] hump, hunch; **~áтый** [14 *sh.*] humpbacked; curved; *нос* aquiline; **~ить** [14], ⟨с-⟩ stoop, bend, curve (*v/i.* **-ся**); **~ýн** *m* [1 *e.*] hunchback; **~ýша** *f* [5] humpback salmon; **~ýшка** *f* [5; *g/pl.*: -шек] crust (*of a loaf*)
**горд|еливый** [14 *sh.*] haughty, proud; **~éц** *m* [1 *e.*] proud man; **~иться** [15 *e.*; горжýсь, гордишься], ⟨воз-⟩ be(-come) proud (T of); **~ость** *f* [8] pride; **~ый** [14; горд, -á, -о] proud (T of)
**гóр|е** *n* [10] grief, sorrow; misfortune, disaster; ***с ~я*** out of grief; ***емý и ~я мáло*** *coll.* he doesn't care a bit; ***с ~ем пополáм*** *coll.* hardly, with difficulty; **~евáть** [6], ⟨по-⟩ grieve; (*сожалеть*) regret (**о** П s.th.)
**горéл|ка** *f* [5; *g/pl.*: -лок] burner; **~ый** [14] burnt
**гóрест|ный** [14; -тен, -тна] sorrowful, mournful; **~ь** *f* [8] → ***гóре***
**гор|éть** [9], ⟨с-⟩ burn (*a. fig.*), be alight, be on fire; (*светиться*) glow, gleam; ***не ~ит*** *coll.* there's no hurry; ***дéло ~ит*** *coll.* the matter is very urgent
**гóрец** *m* [1; -рца] mountain-dweller; highlander
**гóречь** *f* [8] bitter taste; *fig.* bitterness; *утраты* grief
**горизóнт** *m* [1] horizon; skyline; **~áльный** [14; -лен, -льна] horizontal, level
**гористый** [14 *sh.*] mountainous; hilly
**гóрка** *f* [5; *g/pl.*: -рок] *dim.* → ***горá*** hillock
**горлáнить** P [13], ⟨за-, про-⟩ bawl
**гóрл|о** *n* [9] throat; gullet; *сосуда* neck (*a.* **~ышко** *n* [9; *g/pl.*: -шек]); ***дел по ~о*** *coll.* up to the eyes in work; ***я сыт по ~о*** *coll.* I've had my fill (*fig.* I'm fed up with [T]); ***во всё ~о*** → ***гóлос***
**горн** *m* [1] horn, bugle; **~ист** *m* [1] bugler
**гóрничная** *f* [14] (house)maid
**горнопромы́шленный** [14] mining
**горностáй** *m* [3] ermine
**гóрн|ый** [14] mountain(ous), hilly; *min.* rock…; mining; ***~ое дéло*** *n* mining; **~я́к** *m* [1 *e.*] miner; mining engineer
**гóрод** *m* [1; *pl.*: -дá, *etc. e.*] town; city (large town; *coll.* downtown); ***за ~(ом)*** go (live) out of town; **~ить** P [15], ⟨на-⟩ *вздор etc.* talk nonsense; **~óк** *m* [1; -дкá] small town; **~скóй** [14] town…, city…, urban, municipal; → ***горсовéт***
**горожáн|ин** *m* [1; *pl.*: -жáне, -жáн] townsman; *pl.* townspeople; **~ка** *f* [5; *g/pl.*: -нок] townswoman
**горó|х** *m* [1] *растение* pea; *collect.* peas *pl.*; **~ховый** [14] pea(s)…; ***чýчело ~ховое*** *n*, ***шут ~ховый*** *m coll. fig.* scarecrow; buffoon, merryandrew; **~шек** *m* [1; -шка] *collect.* green peas *pl.*; **~шин(-к)а** *f* [5 (*g/pl.*: -нок)] pea
**горсовéт** (**городскóй совéт**) *m* [1] city *or* town council
**гóрст|очка** *f* [5; *g/pl.*: -чек] very small group of people, *dim. of* **~ь** *f* [8; *from g/pl. e.*] *о ладони* hollow; *земли и т. д.* handful (*a. fig.*)
**гортáн|ный** [14] guttural; **~ь** *f* [8] larynx
**горчи|чник** *m* [1] mustard poultice; **~ца** *f* [5] mustard
**горшóк** *m* [1; -шкá] pot, jug
**гóрьк|ий** [16; -рек, -рькá, -о; *comp.*: гóрьче, гóрше] bitter (*a. fig.*); ***~ий пья́ница*** *coll. m* inveterate drunkard
**горю́ч|ее** *n* [17] liquid fuel; gasoline, *Brt.*

Г

petrol; **~ий** [17 *sh.*] combustible; *old use* bitter (tears)

**горя́ч|ий** [17; горя́ч, -а́] hot (*a. fig.*); (*вспыльчивый*) fiery, hot-tempered; *любовь, поклонник* ardent, passionate; *спор* heated; *след* warm; *приём* hearty; *время* busy; ***~ая то́чка***; ***по ~им следа́м*** hot on the trail; *fig.* without delay; **~и́ть** [16 *e.*; -чу́, -чи́шь], ⟨раз-⟩ excite, irritate; (*a. fig.*); **-ся** get *or* be excited; **~ка** *f* [5] fever (*a. fig.*); ***поро́ть ~ку*** *coll.* act impetuosly; **~ность** *f* [8] zeal, enthusiasm; impulsiveness

**гос = госуда́рственный** state…

**госпитал|изи́ровать** [7] hospitalize; **~ь** *m* [4] *esp. mil.* hospital

**господ|и́н** *m* [1; *pl.*: -пода́, -по́д, -да́м] gentleman; Mr.; *pl.* (ladies &) gentlemen; ***уважа́емые ~а́*** *в письме* Dear Sirs; **~ство** *n* [9] rule; (*превосходство*) supremacy; (*преобладание*) predominance; **~ствовать** [7] rule, reign; (pre)dominate, prevail (***над*** T over); (*возвышаться*) command; **~ь** *m* [Го́спода, -ду; *vocative*: -ди] Lord, God (*a. as int.*, → ***Бог***)

**госпожа́** *f* [5] Mrs.; Miss

**гостеприи́м|ный** [14; -мен, -мна] hospitable; **~ство** *n* [9] hospitality

**гост|и́ная** *f* [14] drawing room, living room; **~и́нец** *m* [1; -нца] present, gift; **~и́ница** *f* [5] hotel; inn; **~и́ть** [15 *e.*; гощу́, гости́шь] be on a visit, stay with (***у*** P); **~ь** *m* [4; *from g/pl. e.*] guest; visitor (*f* **~ья** [6]); ***идти́ (е́хать) в ~и*** go to see (***к*** Д s.b.); ***быть в ~я́х*** (***у*** P) → ***~и́ть***

**госуда́рственн|ый** [14] state…; public; *измена* high (*treason*); ***~ый переворо́т*** *m* coup d'état; ***~ый строй*** *m* political system, regime: ***~ая слу́жба*** public *or* civil service

**госуда́р|ство** *n* [9] state; **~ь** *m* [4] *hist.* sovereign

**готова́льня** *f* [6; *g/pl.*: -лен] (case of) drawing utensils *pl.*

**гото́в|ить** [14] **1.** ⟨при-⟩ cook; prepare (**-ся *к*** Д o.s. *or* get ready for); **2.** ⟨под-⟩ prepare, train; **3.** ⟨за-⟩ store up; lay in (stock); **~ность** *f* [8] readiness; preparedness, willingness; **~ый** [14 *sh.*] ready (***к*** Д *or inf.* for), on the point of; finished; willing; *одежда* ready-made

**гофриро́ванн|ый** [14]: ***~ое желе́зо*** corrugated iron

**граб** *m* [1] hornbeam

**граб|ёж** *m* [1 *e.*] robbery; **~и́тель** *m* [4] robber; **~и́тельский** [16] *цены* exorbitant; **~ить** [14], ⟨о-⟩ rob, plunder

**гра́бли** *f/pl.* [6; *gen.*: -бель, -блей] rake

**грав|ёр** *m* [1] engraver; **~ий** *m* [3] gravel; **~ирова́ть** [7], ⟨вы-⟩ engrave; **~иро́вка** *f* [5; *g/pl.*: -вок] engraving, etching, print, (*a.* **~ю́ра** *f* [5])

**град** *m* [1] hail (*a. fig.* = shower); ***вопро́сы посы́пались ~ом*** he was showered with questions; ***~ идёт*** it is hailing; ***~ом*** thick and fast, profusely

**гра́дус** *m* [1] degree (***в*** B of); ***под ~ом*** P under the weather; **~ник** *m* [1] thermometer

**гражд|ани́н** *m* [1; *pl.*: гра́ждане, -ан], **~а́нка** *f* [5; *g/pl.*: -нок] citizen (*address mst. without name*); **~а́нский** [16] civil (*a. war*); civic (*a. right*); **~а́нство** *n* [9] citizenship; citizens *pl.*: ***дать (получи́ть) пра́во ~а́нства*** give or (be given) civic rights; (*fig.*) gain general (public) recognition; ***приня́ть … ~а́нство*** become a … citizen

**грамм** *m* [1] gram(me)

**грамма́т|ика** *f* [5] grammar; **~и́ческий** [16] grammatical

**гра́мот|а** *f* [5] reading & writing; ***вери́тельная ~а*** credentials; ***э́то для меня́ кита́йская ~а*** *coll.* it's Greek to me; **~ность** *f* [8] literacy; **~ный** [14; -тен, -тна] literate; *специалист* competent, expert

**грана́т** *m* [1] pomegranate; *min.* garnet; **~а** *f* [5] shell; *ручная* grenade

**грандио́зный** [14; -зен, -зна] grandiose; mighty, vast

**гранёный** [14] facet(t)ed; cut

**грани́т** *m* [1] granite

**грани́|ца** *f* [5] border, frontier; boundary; *fig.* limit, verge; ***за ~цу (~цей)*** (go, be) abroad; ***из-за ~цы*** from abroad; ***перейти́ все ~цы*** pass all bounds; **~чить** [16] border *or* verge (***с*** T [up]on)

**гра́н|ка** *f* [5; *g/pl.*: -нок] *typ.* galley

(proof); **~ь** *f* [8] → **грани́ца**; *math.* plane; *драгоценного камня* facet; edge; *fig.* verge

**граф** *m* [1] earl (*Brt.*); count

**граф|á** *f* [5] column; **˷ик** *m* [1] diagram, graph; *временной* schedule; **˷ика** *f* [5] graphic arts; (*произведения*) drawings

**графи́н** *m* [1] decanter, carafe

**графи́ня** *f* [6] countess

**графи́|т** *m* [1] graphite; **~ть** [14 *e.*; -флю́, -фи́шь; -флённый], ⟨раз-⟩ line *or* rule (paper); **~ческий** [16] graphic(al)

**граци|óзный** [14; -зен, -зна] graceful; **˷я** *f* [7] grace(fulness)

**грач** *m* [1 *e.*] *zo.* rook

**греб|ёнка** *f* [5; *g/pl.*: -нок] comb; ***стри́чь всех под одну́ ~ёнку*** reduce everyone to the same level; **˷ень** *m* [4; -бня] comb; *волны, горы* crest; **~éц** *m* [1; -бцá] oarsman; **~ешóк** *m* [1; -шкá] → **˷ень**; **˷ля** *f* [6] rowing; **~нóй** [14] row(-ing)…

**грёза** *f* [5] *rare* (day) dream

**грéзить** [15] *impf.* dream (**о** П of)

**грéйдер** *m* [1] *tech.* grader; *coll.* earth road

**грейпфру́т** *m* [1] grapefruit

**грек** *m* [1] Greek

**грéлка** *f* [5; *g/pl.*: -лок] hot-water bottle; ***электри́ческая ~*** heating pad, electric blanket

**грем|éть** [10 *e.*; гремлю́, -ми́шь], ⟨про-, за-⟩ thunder, peal (*a. о голосе, колоколах, etc.*); *телега, ключи* rattle, clank, tinkle; *посудой* clatter; **~у́чий** [17]: ***~у́чая змея́*** *f* rattlesnake

**грéнки** *m/pl.* [1 *e.*] toast (*sg.*: -нок)

**грести́** [26 -б-: гребу́; грёб, греблá], ⟨по-⟩ row; scull; *граблями* rake

**греть** [8; …грéтый], ⟨со-, на-, разо-, обо-, подо-⟩ warm (**-ся** o.s.) (up); heat; ***-ся на сóлнце*** sun

**грех** *m* [1 *e.*] sin; (*недостаток*) fault; *coll.* → **грешнó**; ***с ~óм пополáм*** just manage; → **гóре**; ***есть такóй ~*** *coll.* well, I own it; ***как на ~*** *coll.* unfortunately

**грé|цкий** [16]: ***~цкий орéх*** *m* walnut; **~чáнка** *f* [5; *g/pl.*: -нок], **~ческий** [16] Greek

**греч|иха, ˷ка** *f* [5] buckwheat; **˷невый** [14] buckwheat…

**греш|и́ть** [16 *e.*; -шу́, -ши́шь], ⟨со-⟩ sin (**прóтив** Р *a.* against); ***~и́ть прóтив и́стины*** distort the truth; **˷ник** *m* [1], **˷ница** *f* [5] sinner; **~нó** (it's a) shame (on Д); **˷ный** [14; -шен, -шнá, -ó] sinful; F *sh.*: sorry

**гриб** *m* [1 *e.*] mushroom; **~óк** *m* [1; -бкá] *dim.* → **гриб**; fungus

**гри́ва** *f* [5] mane

**гри́венник** *coll. m* [1] ten-kopeck coin

**гриль** *m* [4] grill

**грим** *m* [1] *thea.* makeup

**гримáс|а** *f* [5] grimace; **~ничать** [1] make faces *or* grimaces

**гримировáть** [7], ⟨за-, на-⟩ make up (*v/i.* **-ся**)

**грипп** *m* [1] influenza

**гриф** *m* [1]: ***~ секрéтности*** inscription designating the degree of confidentiality

**гроб** *m* [1; в -у́ *pl.*: -ы́, -а, *etc. e.*] coffin; **~ни́ца** *f* [5] tomb; **~ово́й** [14] coffin…; tomb…; ***~ово́е молчáние*** deathly silence

**грозá** *f* [5; *pl. st.*] (thunder) storm (*a. fig.*); menace; terror

**грозд|ь** *m* [4; *pl.*: -ди, -дей, *etc. e.*, -дья, -дьев] *винограда* bunch; *ягод, цветов* cluster

**грози́ть** [15 *e.*; грожу́, -зи́шь], ⟨по-⟩ threaten (Д/Т a p. with) (*a.* **-ся**)

**грóз|ный** [14; -зен, -знá, -о] menacing, threatening; *человек* formidable; *coll. голос* stern, severe; **~ово́й** [14] stormy; ***~ова́я ту́ча*** thundercloud

**гром** *m* [1; *from g/pl. e.*] thunder (*a. fig.*); ***~ греми́т*** it thunders; ***как ~ среди́ я́сного нéба*** like a bolt from the blue; ***как ˷ом поражённый*** *fig.* thunderstruck

**громáд|а** *f* [5] bulk, mass of; **~ный** [14; -ден, -дна] vast, huge; *успех и т. д.* tremendous

**громи́|ть** [14 *e.*; -млю́, -ми́шь; -млённый], ⟨раз-⟩ smash, crush; *врага* rout, smash

**грóмк|ий** [16; -мок, -мкá, -о; *comp.*: грóмче] loud; noisy; *fig.* famous, great,

Г

noted; *слова* pompous
**громо|во́й** [14] thunder…; *голос* thunderous; **~гла́сный** [14; -сен, -сна] loud; *mst. adv.* publicly, openly; **~зди́ть(ся)** [15 *e.*; -зжу́, -зди́шь] → ***взгроможда́ть*(ся)**; **≈здкий** [16; -док, -дка] bulky, cumbersome; **~отво́д** *m* [1] lightning rod *or* conductor
**громыха́ть** *coll.* [1] rumble; *посудой* clatter; *о пушках* boom
**гроссме́йстер** *m* [1] *chess* grand master
**грот** *m* [1] grotto
**гроте́ск** *m* [1], **~ный** [14] grotesque
**гро́х|нуть** *coll.* [20] *pf.* crash, bang down (*v/i.* **-ся** fall with a crash); **~от** *m* [1] din; **~ота́ть** [3], ⟨за-⟩ rumble; *пушек* roar
**грош** *m* [1 *e.*]: ***ни ~а́*** not a farthing; ***~ цена́*** *or* ***~а́ ло́маного не сто́ит*** not worth a pin; ***ни в ~ не ста́вить*** not care a straw (В for); **~о́вый** [14] *fig.* (dirt-)cheap
**груб|е́ть** [8], ⟨за-, о-⟩ coarsen, become rude; **~и́ть** [14 *e.*; -блю́, -би́шь], ⟨на-⟩ be rude (Д to); **~ия́н** *coll. m* [1] rude fellow, boor; **≈ость** *f* [8] rudeness; **≈ый** [14; груб, -а́, -о] *материал* coarse; *игра*, *работа* rough; rude; *ошибка и т. д.* gross
**гру́да** *f* [5] pile, heap
**груд|и́нка** *f* [5; *g/pl.*: -нок] brisket; bacon; **~но́й** [14]: ***~на́я кле́тка*** *f* thorax; ***~но́й ребёнок*** infant in arms; **~ь** *f* [8; в, на -ди́; *from g/pl. e.*] breast; chest; ***стоя́ть ≈ью*** (***за*** В) champion, defend
**груз** *m* [1] load (*a. fig.*); *перевозимый* freight; *naut.* cargo
**грузи́н** *m* [1; *g/pl.*: грузи́н], **~ка** *f* [5; *g/pl.*: -нок] Georgian; **~ский** [16] Georgian
**грузи́ть** [15 *e.*; -ужу́, -у́зишь], ⟨на-, за-, по-⟩ load, freight
**гру́з|ный** [14; -зен, -зна́, -о] massive, heavy; **~ови́к** *m* [1 *e.*] truck, *Brt.* lorry; **~ово́й** [14] freight…, goods…; *naut.* cargo; ***~ово́й автомоби́ль*** *m* → ***~ови́к***; **~оподъёмность** *f* [8] carrying capacity; *naut.* tonnage; **~получа́тель** *m* [4] consignee; **~чик** *m* [1] loader; *naut.* docker, stevedore
**грунт** *m* [1] soil, earth; ground (*a. paint.*); **~ово́й** [14] *о воде* subsoil; *дорога* dirt road

**гру́пп|а** *f* [5] group; **~ирова́ть(ся)** [7], ⟨с-⟩ (form a) group
**груст|и́ть** [15 *e.*; -ущу́, -сти́шь], ⟨взгрустну́ть⟩ [20] be sad; long for (***по*** П); **≈ный** [14; -тен, -тна́, -о] sad, sorrowful; *coll.* grievous, distressing; ***мне ≈о*** I feel sad; **~ь** *f* [8] sadness, grief, melancholy
**гру́ша** *f* [5] pear (*a.* tree)
**гры́жа** *f* [5] hernia, rupture
**грыз|ня́** *f* [6] squabble; **~ть** [24; *pt. st.*] gnaw (*a. fig.*), nibble; bite; *орехи* crack; **-ся** fight, squabble; **~у́н** *m* [1 *e.*] *zo.* rodent
**гряд|а́** *f* [5; *nom/pl. st.*] ridge, range; *agric.* bed (*a.* **≈ка** *f* [5; *g/pl.*: -док])
**гряду́щий** [17] future, coming; ***на сон ~*** before going to bed
**гряз|ево́й** [14] mud…; **~езащи́тный** [14] antisplash; **~елече́бница** *f* [5] therapeutic mud baths; **≈и** *f/pl.* [8] (curative) mud; **~ни́ть** [13], ⟨за-⟩ soil (*a. fig.*); **-ся** get dirty; **≈нуть** [21], ⟨по-⟩ sink (mud, *etc.*, *fig.*); **≈ный** [14; -зен, -зна́, -о, грязны́] dirty (*a. fig.*); muddy; **~ь** *f* [8; в -зи́] dirt, mud; ***в ~и́*** dirty; ***не уда́рить лицо́м в ~*** manage to do s.th. successfully; ***смеша́ть с ≈ью*** sling mud (В at)
**гря́нуть** [19 *st.*] *pf. гром* burst out; *выстрел* ring, roar; *война* break out; *песня* burst, start
**губ|а́** *f* [5; *nom/pl. st.*] lip; *залив*, *устье* bay; ***у него́ ~а́ не ду́ра*** his taste isn't bad; he knows which side his bread is buttered on
**губерн|а́тор** *m* [1] governor; **≈ия** *f* [7] *hist.* province
**губи́т|ельный** [14; -лен, -льна] ruinous; pernicious; **~ь** [14], ⟨по-, с-⟩ destroy, ruin; *время* waste
**гу́б|ка** *f* [5; *g/pl.*: -бок] **1.** *dim.* → ***~а́***; **2.** sponge; **~но́й** [14] labial; ***~на́я пома́да*** *f* lipstick
**гуд|е́ть** [11], ⟨за-⟩ buzz; *о гудке* honk, hoot, whistle; *coll. болеть* ache; **~о́к** *m* [1; -дка́] honk, hoot, signal; horn; siren; whistle
**гул** *m* [1] boom, rumble; *голосов* hum; **≈кий** [16; -лок, -лка́, -о] *громкий* booming, loud; resonant
**гуля́|нье** *n* [10] walk(ing); *массовое*

open-air merrymaking, fête; **~ть** [28], ⟨по-⟩ [20] go for a walk (*a.* ***идти́ ~ть***), stroll; *fig. о ветре и т. д.* sweep; *coll.* carouse, go on a spree
**гуля́ш** *m* [1; *g/pl.*: -е́й] goulash, stew
**гуманита́рны|й** [14]: ***~е нау́ки*** the humanities
**гума́нн|ость** *f* [8] humanity; **~ый** [14; -а́нен, -а́нна] humane
**гурма́н** *m* [1] gourmet
**гур|т** *m* [1 *e.*] herd, drove (cattle); **~ьба́** *f* [5] crowd (T in)
**гу́сеница** *f* [5] caterpillar
**гуси́ный** [14] goose (*a.* gooseflesh *кожа*)
**густ|е́ть** [8], ⟨за-⟩ thicken; **~о́й** [14; густ, -á, -о; *comp.*: гу́ще] thick, dense; deep, rich (*colo(u)r, sound*)
**гус|ь** *m* [4; *from g/pl. e.*] goose; *fig.* ***хоро́ш ~ь*** *b.s.* fine fellow indeed!; ***как с ~я́ вода́*** like water off a duck's back, thick-skinned; ***~ько́м*** in single file
**гу́ща** *f* [5] grounds *pl.*; *осадок* sediment; *леса* thicket; *fig.* in the center (-tre) of things

# Д

**да 1.** *part.* yes; oh (yes), indeed (*a. interr.*); (oh) but, now, well; *imperative* do(n't)…!; *tags*: aren't, don't, *etc.*; may, let; **2.** *cj.* (*a.* ***~ и***) and; but; ***~ и то́лько*** nothing but; and that's all; ***~ что вы!*** you don't say!
**да́бы** *old use* (in order) that *or* to
**да|ва́ть** [5], ⟨**~ть**⟩ [дам, дашь, даст, дади́м, дади́те, даду́т (…-) дал, -á, -о; (…)да́нный (дан, -á)] give; (*позволить*) let; (*даровать*) bestow; *клятву* take, pledge; make (way); ***~ва́й(те)!*** come on!; *with vb.* (*a.* ***~́й[те]***) let us (me); ***ни ~ть ни взять*** exactly alike; ***~ва́ть ход де́лу*** set s.th. going; further s.th.; **-ся** let o.s. (**в** В *be caught, cheated*); *с трудом и т. д.* (turn out to) be (*e.g.* hard for Д); (can) master (И s.th.)
**дави́ть** [14] **1.** ⟨на-⟩ press; squeeze (⟨вы́-⟩ out); **2.** ⟨за-, раз-⟩ crush; P (*сбить машиной*) run over, knock down; **3.** ⟨по-⟩ oppress; suppress; **4.** ⟨при-, с-⟩ press (down *or* together), jam, compress; crush, trample; **5.** ⟨у-⟩ strangle; **-ся** choke; (*повеситься*) hang o.s.
**да́в|ка** *f* [5] throng, jam; **~ле́ние** *n* [12] pressure (*a. fig.*)
**да́вн|(ишн)ий** [15] old; of long standing; **~о́** long ago; for a long time, long since; **~опроше́дший** [17] remote, long past; **~́ость** *f* [8] antiquity; *law* prescription; ***срок ~́ости*** term of limitation; ***~ы́м-~о́*** very long ago, ages ago
**да́же** (*a.* **~ и**) even; ***~ не*** not even
**да́л|ее** → ***да́льше***; ***и так ~ее*** and so on (*or* forth); **~ёкий** [16; -лёк, -лека́, -леко́ -лёко; *comp.*: да́льше] far (away), distant (**от** P from); long (way); *fig.* wide (of); strange (to); ***он не о́чень ~ёкий челове́к*** he is not very clever; **~еко́, ~ёко** far (off, away); a long way (**до** P to); (Д) ***~еко́ до*** (P) far from, much inferior to; ***~еко́ не*** by no means; ***~еко́ за*** (B) long after; *о возрасте* well over; **~еко́ иду́щий** [17] farreaching; **~ь** *f* [8; в **~и́**] distance; open space; **~ьне́йший** [17] further; ***в ~ьне́йшем*** in future, henceforth; **~ьний** [15] distant (*a. kin*); remote; → *a.* ***~ёкий***; ***~ьневосто́чный*** [14] Far Eastern
**дально|бо́йный** [14] *mil.* long range; **~ви́дность** *f* [8] foresight; **~ви́дный** [14; -ден, -дна] *fig.* farsighted; **~зо́ркий** [16; -рок, -рка] far-, long-sighted; **´~сть** *f* [8] distance; *mil., tech.* (long-)range
**да́льше** farther; further (more); then, next; (**чита́йте**) ***~!*** go on (reading)
**да́м|а** *f* [5] lady; (dance) partner; *cards* queen; **~ба** *f* [5] dam, dike; **~ка** *f* [5; *g/pl.*: -мок] king (*in draughts*); **~ский**

Д

[16] ladies', women's
**да́н|ный** [14] given, present, in question; **~ные** *pl.* data, facts; statistics; ***обрабо́тка ~ных*** data processing
**дань** *f* [8] tribute (*a. fig.*); ***отдава́ть ~*** appreciate, recognize
**дар** *m* [1; *pl. e.*] gift (*a. fig.*); **~и́ть** [13], ⟨по-⟩ give (Д/В a p. s.th.), present (В/Т a p. with); **~мое́д** *coll. m* [1] sponger; **~ова́ние** *n* [12] donation, giving; talent; **~ови́тый** [14 *sh.*] gifted, talented; **~ово́й** [14] gratis, free
**да́ром** *adv.* gratis, for nothing; (*напрасно*) in vain; ***пропа́сть ~*** be wasted; ***э́то ему́ ~ не пройдёт*** he will smart for this
**да́т|а** *f* [5] date; **~ельный** [14] *gr.* dative (*case*); **~и́ровать** [7] (*im*)*pf.* (*задним числом* ante)date
**да́т|ский** [16] Danish; **~ча́нин** *m* [1; *pl.*: -ча́не, -ча́н], **~ча́нка** *f* [5; *g/pl.*: -нок] Dane
**да́тчик** *m* [1] *tech.* sensor
**да́ть(ся)** → ***дава́ть(ся)***
**да́ч|а** *f* [5] dacha, cottage, summer residence, villa; ***на ~е*** in a dacha; out of town; in the country; **~ник** *m* [1] summer resident; **~ный** [14] suburban; country…; garden (suburb *посёлок*)
**два** *m, n,* **две** *f* [34] two; → ***пять, пя́тый***; ***в ~ счёта*** *coll.* in a jiffy
**двадцат|иле́тний** [15] twenty-year; twenty-year-old; **~́ый** [14] twentieth; → ***пя́т(идеся́т)ый***; **´~ь** [35; -ти́] twenty; → ***пять***
**два́жды** twice; ***~ два*** *math.* two by two; ***я́сно как ~ два (четы́ре)*** plain as day
**двена́дцат|и…** (*in compds.*) twelve…; dodec(a)…; duodecimal, duodenary; **~ый** [14] twelfth; → ***пя́тый***; **~ь** [35] twelve; → ***пять***
**двер|но́й** [14] door…; ***~но́й проём*** doorway; **~́ца** *f* [5; *g/pl.*: -рец] (*cupboard, etc.*) door; **~ь** *f* [8; в -ри́; *from g/pl. e.; instr. a.* -рьми́] door (*a. pl.* **~́и**)
**двéсти** [36] two hundred
**дви́|гатель** *m* [4] engine, motor; **~гать** [13], ⟨**~нуть**⟩ [20] (В/Т) move, set in motion; stir; **-ся** move, advance; *отправиться* set out; start; **~же́ние** *n* [12] movement (*a. pol.*); stir; *phys.* motion; traffic; *fig.* emotion; ***приводи́ть (приходи́ть) в ~же́ние*** set going (start [moving]); **~жимый** [14 *sh.*] prompted, moved; movable; **~жущий** [17]: ***~жущая си́ла*** driving force; **~нуть** → ***~гать***
**дво́е** [37] two (in a group, together); ***нас бы́ло ~*** there were two of us; **~то́чие** *n* [12] *gr.* colon
**двои́т|ься** [13], ⟨раз-⟩ divide into two; ***у меня́ в глаза́х ~ся*** I see double
**дво́й|ка** *f* [5; *g/pl.*: дво́ек] two (*a.* boat; team; bus, *etc.*, *no.* 2; cards; *a.* deuce); pair; (mark) = ***пло́хо***; **~ни́к** *m* [1 *e.*] double; **~но́й** [14] double (*a. fig.*); **~ня** *f* [6; *g/pl.*: дво́ен] twins *pl.*; **~ственный** [14 *sh.*]; ***~ствнное отноше́ние*** mixed feelings
**двои́чный** [14; -чен, -чна] binary
**двор** *m* [1 *e.*] (court) yard; farm (-stead); *королевский* court; ***на ~е́*** outside, outdoors; **~е́ц** *m* [1; -рца́] palace; ***♀ бракосочета́ний*** Wedding Palace; ***♀ культу́ры*** Palace of Culture; **~́ник** *m* [1] janitor, (yard and) street cleaner; *mot.* windshield (*Brt.* windscreen) wiper; **~ня́га** *coll. f* [5], **~ня́жка** *coll. f* [5; *g/pl.*: -жек] mongrel; **~цо́вый** [14] court…, palace…; ***~цо́вый переворо́т*** palace revolution; **~яни́н** *m* [1; *pl.*: -я́не, -я́н] nobleman; **~я́нка** *f* [5; *g/pl.*: -нок] noblewoman; **~я́нский** [16] of the nobility; of noble birth; **~я́нство** *n* [9] nobility
**двою́родн|ый** [14]: ***~ый брат*** *m*, ***~ая сестра́*** *f* cousin
**двоя́к|ий** [16 *sh.*] double, twofold; **~о** in two ways
**дву|бо́ртный** [14] double-breasted; **~гла́вый** [14] double-headed; **~жи́льный** [14] sturdy, tough; *tech.* twin-core; **~кра́тный** [14] double; done twice; **~ли́чие** *n* [12] duplicity, double-dealing; **~ли́чный** [14; -чен, -чна] two-faced; **~смы́сленный** [14 *sh.*] ambiguous; **~ство́лка** *f* [5; *g/pl.*: -лок] double-barrel(l)ed gun; **~ство́льный** [14]: ***~ство́льное ружьё*** *n* → ***~ство́лка***; **~створчатый** [14]: ***~ство́рчатая дверь*** *f* folding doors; **~сторо́нний**

[15] bilateral; *движение* two-way; *ткань* reversible

**двух|...** (→ *a.* **дву...**): **~днéвный** [14] two days; **~колéйный** [14] double-track; **~колёсный** [14] two-wheel(ed); **~лéтний** [15] two-years-old; two-years'; **~мéстный** [14] two-seat(er); **~мéсячный** [14] two months' *or* two-months-old; **~motóрный** [14] twin-engine(d); **~недéльный** [14] two weeks', *Brt. a.* a fortnight's; **~сóтый** [14] two hundredth; **~этáжный** [14] two-storied (*Brt.* -reyed)

**двуязы́чный** [14; -чен, -чна] bilingual

**дебáты** *m/pl.* [1] debate

**дéбет** *m* [1] *comm.* debit; ***занести́ в ~*** = **~овáть** [7] (*im*)*pf.* debit (sum against *or* to a p. В/Д)

**дебитóр** *m* [1] debtor

**дебóш** *m* [1] shindy, riot

**дéбр|и** *f/pl.* [8] thickets; the wilds; ***запу́таться в ~ях*** get bogged down (P in)

**дебю́т** *m* [1] debut; *chess* opening

**дéва** *f* [5]: ♀ ***Мари́я*** the Virgin; ♀ Virgo; (***стáрая***) **~** (old) maid

**девальвáция** *f* [7] devaluation

**девáть** [1], ⟨деть⟩ [дéну, -нешь] put, leave, mislay; ***кудá ~*** *a.* what to do with, how to spend; **-ся** go, get; *vb.* + И = put, leave + *obj.*; be (*pr.*); ***кудá мне ~ся?*** where shall I go *or* stay?; ***кудá он дéлся?*** what has become of him?

**дéверь** *m* [4; *pl.*: -рья́, -рéй, -рья́м] brother-in-law (*husband's brother*)

**деви́з** *m* [1] motto

**дев|и́ца** *f* [5] *iro.* young lady, girl; **~и́чий** [18] maidenly; girlish; **~очка** *f* [5; *g/pl.*: -чек] (little) girl; **~ственный** [14 *sh.*] maiden, virgin...; *лес и т. д.* primeval; **~ушка** *f* [5; *g/pl.*: -шек] young lady, unmarried girl (*a. form of address*); **~чóнка** *f* [5; *g/pl.*: -нок] girl

**девя|нóсто** [35] ninety; **~нóстый** [14] ninetieth; → ***пят(идеся́т)ый***; **~тисóтый** [14] nine hundredth; **~тка** [5; *g/pl.*: -ток] nine (→ ***двóйка***); **~нáдцатый** [14] ninetieth; → ***пять***, ***пя́тый***; **~нáдцать** [35] nineteen; → ***пять***; **~тый** [14] ninth; → ***пя́тый***; **´~ть** [35] nine; → ***пять***; **~тьсóт** [36] nine hundred; **´~тью** nine times

**дегенерáт** *m* [1] degenerate

**деград|áция** *f* [7] degradation; **~и́ровать** [7] (*im*)*pf.* degrade

**дéд|(ушка** *m* [5; *g/pl.*: -шек]) *m* [1] grandfather; old man; *pl.* **~ы** *a.* forefathers; **~-морóз** *m* Santa Claus, Father Christmas

**деепричáстие** *n* [12] *gr.* gerund

**дежу́р|ить** [13] be on duty; be on watch; **~ный** *m* [14] (*p.*) duty..., on duty; **~ство** *n* [9] duty, (night) watch

**дезерти́р** *m* [1] deserter; **~овать** [7] (*im*)*pf.* desert; **~ство** *n* [9] desertion

**дезинф|éкция** *f* [7] disinfection; **~ици́ровать** [7] (*im*)*pf.* disinfect

**дезинформ|áция** *f* [7] misinformation; **~и́ровать** [7] (*im*)*pf.* misinform

**дезодорáнт** *m* [1] deodorant; air freshener

**дезорганизовáть** [7] (*im*)*pf.* disorganize

**дéйств|енный** [14 *sh.*] effective; *средство* efficacious; **~ие** *n* [12] action; activity; *mil.*, *tech.*, *math.* operation; *thea.* act; *лекарства и т. д.* effect; (*влияние*) influence, impact; ***мéсто ~ия*** scene; ***свобóда ~ий*** free play; **~и́тельно** really, indeed; **~и́тельность** *f* [8] reality, (real) life; **~и́тельный** [14; -лен, -льна] real, actual; *билет и т. д.* valid; *mil.*, *gr.* active (*service*; *voice*); **~овать** [7], ⟨по-⟩ act, work (**на** В on); operate, function; apply; have effect (**на** В on); get (on one's nerves); **~ующий** [17] active; acting; ***~ующее лицó*** character, personage

**декáбрь** *m* [4 *e.*] December

**декáда** *f* [5] decade

**декáн** *m* [1] *acad.* dean; **~áт** *m* [1] dean's office

**декла|ми́ровать** [7], ⟨про-⟩ recite, declaim; **~мáция** *f* [7] declaration

**декольт|é** (dɛ-'tɛ) *n* [*indecl.*] décolleté; **~и́рованный** [14 *sh.*] lowcut; *thea.*

**декорá|тор** *m* [1] (interior) decorator; *thea.* scene-painter; **~ция** *f* [7] decoration; *thea.* scenery

**декрéт** *m* [1] decree, edict; *coll.* maternity leave

Д

**де́ла|нный** [14 *sh.*] affected, forced; **~ть** [1], ⟨с-⟩ make, do; *coll.* **~ть не́чего** it can't be helped; **-ся** (Т) become, grow, turn; happen (**с** T with, to), be going on; ***что с ним сде́лалось?*** what has become of him?
**делега́|т** *m* [1] delegate; **~ция** *f* [7] delegation
**дел|ёж** *coll. m* [1 *e.*] distribution, sharing; **~е́ние** *n* [12] division (*a. math.*); *на шкале* point, degree (*scale*)
**деле́ц** *m* [1; -льца́] *mst. pej.* smart operator; *pers.* on the make
**деликате́с** *m* [1] *cul.* delicatessen
**делика́тн|ость** *f* [8] tact(fulness), delicacy; **~ый** [14; -тен, -тна] delicate
**дели́|мое** *n* [14] *math.* dividend; **~тель** *m* [4] *math.* divisor; **~ть** [13; делю́, де́лишь] **1.** ⟨раз-, по-⟩ (***на*** В) divide (in[-to]), *a.* by; **2.** ⟨по-⟩ share (*a.* **-ся** [Т/**с** Т s.th. with s.b.], exchange; confide [s.th. to], tell; *math.* be divisible)
**де́л|о** *n* [9; *pl. e.*] affair, matter, concern; affair(s), work, business (***по*** Д on); (*деяние*) deed, act(ion); *law* case, (*a. fig.*) cause; ***говори́ть ~о*** talk sense; ***де́лать ~о*** *fig.* do serious work; ***то и ~о*** continually, time and again; ***в чём ~о?*** what's the matter?; ***в том то и ~о*** that's just the point; ***како́е вам ~о?, э́то не ва́ше ~о*** that's no business of yours; ***ме́жду ~ом*** in between; ***на ~е*** in practice; ***на*** (*or* ***в***) ***са́мом ~е*** in reality, in fact; really, indeed; ***пусти́ть в ~о*** use; ***по ~а́м*** on business; ***как ~а́?*** how are you?; ***~о идёт → идти́***
**делов|и́тый** [14 *sh.*], **~о́й** [14] businesslike; efficient; *a.* business…; work(ing)
**де́льный** [14] businesslike; (*разумный*) sensible
**де́льта** *f* [5] delta
**дельфи́н** *m* [1] dolphin
**демаго́г** *m* [1] demagogue; **~ия** *f* [7] demagoguery
**демаркацио́нный** [14] (*adj. of*) demarcation
**демилитаризова́ть** [7] (*im*)*pf.* demilitarize
**демобилизова́ть** [7] (*im*)*pf.* demobilize
**демокра́т** *m* [1] democrat; **~и́ческий** [16] democratic; **~ия** *f* [7] democracy
**демонстр|ати́вный** [14; -вен, -вна] demonstrative, done for effect; **~а́ция** *f* [7] demonstration; **~и́ровать** [7] (*im*)*pf.*, *a.* ⟨про-⟩ demonstrate; *фильм* show
**демонта́ж** *m* [1] dismantling
**де́мпинг** *m* [1] *econ.* dumping
**де́нежный** [14] money…, monetary, pecuniary; currency…; *coll.* moneyed
**день** *m* [4; дня] day; ***в ~*** a *or* per day; ***в э́тот ~*** (on) that day; ***~ за днём*** day after day; ***изо дня́ в ~*** day by day; ***~ ото дня́*** with every passing day; ***весь ~*** all day (long); ***на днях*** the other day; in the next few days (*a.* ***со дня на́ ~***); ***три часа́ дня*** 3 p.m., 3 o'clock in the afternoon; ***→ днём***; ***~ рожде́ния*** birthday
**де́ньги** *f/pl.* [*gen.*: де́нег; *from. dat. e.*] money
**департа́мент** *m* [1] department
**депози́т** *m* [1] deposit
**депута́т** *m* [1] deputy, delegate
**дёр|гать** [1], *once* ⟨~нуть⟩ [20] pull, tug (*a.* ***за*** В at), jerk; *о теле* twitch; *отрывать от дела* worry, harrass; ***чёрт меня́ ~нул*** why the devil did I do it
**дерев|ене́ть** [8], ⟨за-, о-⟩ stiffen; grow numb; **~е́нский** [16] village…, country…, rural, rustic; ***~е́нский жи́тель*** *m* villager; **~ня** *f* [6; *g/pl.*: -ве́нь, *etc. e.*] village; *не город* country(side); **´~о** *n* [9; *pl.*: -е́вья, -е́вьев] tree; *sg.* wood; ***кра́сное ´~о*** mahogany; ***чёрное ´~о*** ebony; ***резьба́ по ´~у*** wood carving; **~я́нный** [14] wooden (*a. fig.*)
**держа́ва** *f* [5] *pol.* power
**держа́ть** [4] hold; keep; support; have (*a. comm.* in stock); ***~ пари́*** bet; ***~ в ку́рсе*** keep posted; ***~ в неве́дении*** keep in the dark; ***~ себя́*** (***кого́-либо***) ***в рука́х*** (have) control (over) o.s. (*a p.*); ***~ себя́*** conduct o.s., behave = **-ся 1.** ***~ся язы́к за зуба́ми*** hold one's tongue; **2.** ⟨у~ся⟩ (***за*** В, Р) hold (on[to]); *fig.* stick (to); keep; (*выдерживать*) hold out, stand
**дерз|а́ть** [1], ⟨~ну́ть⟩ [20] dare, venture; **~кий** [16; -зок, -зка́, -о; *comp.* -зче] impudent, insolent; (*смелый*) bold, daring, audacious; **~ость** *f* [8] impudence,

cheek; daring, audacity
**дёрн** *m* [1] turf
**дёрнуть** → ***дёргать***
**дес|áнт** *m* [1] landing; troops *pl.* (landed) (***áвиа…*** airborne); **~éрт** *m* [1] dessert; **~нá** *f* [5; *pl.*: дёсны, -сен, *etc. st.*] *anat.* gum; **~éртный** [14] (*adj. of*) dessert; *вино* sweet; **ˆпот** *m* [1] despot
**десяти|днéвный** [14] ten days; **~крáтный** [14] tenfold; **~лéтие** *n* [12] decade; *годовщина* tenth anniversary; **~лéтний** [15] ten-years; ten-year-old
**десят|íчный** [14] decimal; **ˆка** *f* [5; *g/pl.*: -ток] ten (→ ***двóйка***); **ˆок** *m* [1; -тка] ten; *pl.* dozens of, many; → ***идтú***; ***не рóбкого ˆка*** plucky, not a coward; **ˆый** [14] tenth (*a.*, *f.*, part; 3, 2-read: ***три цéлых и две ˆых*** = *3. 2*); → ***пят***(***идесят***)***ый***; ***с пятого на ˆое*** discursively, in a rambling manner; **ˊь** [35 *e.*] ten; → ***пять & пятый***; **~ью** ten times
**детáль** *f* [8] detail; *tech.* part, component; **~но** in detail; **~ный** [14; -лен, -льна] detailed, minute
**дет|ворá** *f* [5] *coll.* → **ˆи**; **~ёныш** *m* [1] young one; cub, *etc.*; **ˆи** *n/pl.* [-éй, -ям, -ьмú, -ях] children, kids; ***двóе*** (***трóе, чéтверо***, *etc.*) **~éй** two (three, four) children; *sg.*: ***дитя*** (*a.* ***ребёнок***); **ˆский** [16] child(ren)'s, infant(ile); childlike; childish; ***ˆский дом*** children's home; ***ˆский сад*** kindergarten; **ˆская** *f* nursery; **ˆство** *n* [9] childhood
**дéть**(**ся**) → ***девáть***(***ся***)
**дефéкт** *m* [1] defect; **~ный** [14] defective, faulty
**дефицúт** *m* [1] *econ.* deficit; *товаров* shortage; *товар* commodity in short supply; **~ный** [14; -тен, -тна] *econ.* showing a loss; in short supply, scarce
**деш|евéть** [8], ⟨по-⟩ fall in price; become cheaper; **~евúзна**, **~ёвка** *f* [5] cheapness, low price(s); ***купúть по ~ёвке*** buy cheap; **~ёвый** [14; дёшев, дешевá, дёшево; *comp.*: дешéвле] cheap (*a. fig.*)
**дéятель** *m* [4]: ***государственный ~*** statesman; ***научный ~*** scientist; ***общéственный ~*** public figure; ***политúческий ~*** politician; **~ность** *f* [8] activity, -ties *pl.*; work; **~ный** [14; -лен, -льна] active
**джин** *m* [1] gin
**джúнсы** [1] *pl.* jeans
**джýнгли** *f/pl.* [*gen.*: -лей] jungle
**диабéт** *m* [1] diabetes; **~ик** *m* [1] diabetic
**диá|гноз** *m* [1] diagnosis; **~гонáль** *f* [8] diagonal; **~лéкт** *m* [1] dialect; **~лéктный** [14] dialect…, dialectal; **~лóг** *m* [1] dialogue; **~метр** *m* [1] diameter; **~пазóн** *m* [1] range (*a. fig.*); **~позитúв** *m* [1] *phot.* slide; **~фрáгма** *f* [5] diaphragm; *phot.* aperture
**дивáн** *m* [1] divan, sofa
**дивéрсия** *f* [7] *mil.* diversion; sabotage
**дивидéнд** *m* [1] dividend
**дивúзия** *f* [7] *mil.* division
**дúвный** [14; -вен, -вна] wonderful; amazing
**диéт|а** (-'ɛta) *f* [5] diet; **~úческий** [16] dietetic
**дúзель** *m* [4] diesel engine; **~ный** [14] diesel…
**дизентерúя** *f* [7] dysentery
**дик|áрь** *m* [4 *e.*] savage (*a. fig.*); *coll.* shy, unsociable person; **ˆий** [16; дик, -á, -о] wild; savage (*a. fig.*); *поведение и т. д.* odd, bizarre, absurd; **ˆость** *f* [8] wildness; savagery; absurdity
**дикт|áнт** *m* [1] → **~óвка**; **~áтор** *m* [1] dictator; **~áторский** [16] dictatorial; **~атýра** *f* [5] dictatorship; **~овáть** [7], ⟨про-⟩ dictate; **~óвка** *f* [5; *g/pl.*: -вок] dictation; **ˆор** *m* [1] (radio, TV) announcer
**дúкция** *f* [7] articulation, enunciation
**дилéмм|а** *f* [5] dilemma; ***стоять пéред дилéммой*** face a dilemma
**дилетáнт** *m* [1] dilettante, dabbler; **~ский** [16] dilettantish
**динам|úзм** *m* [1] dynamism; **ˆика** *f* [5] dynamics; **~úт** *m* [1] dynamite; **~úчный** [14; -чен, -чна] dynamic
**динáстия** *f* [7] dynasty
**дипл*óм** *m* [1] diploma; *univ.* degree; *coll.* degree work, research
**дипломáт** *m* [1] **1.** diplomat; **2.** *coll.* (attaché) case; **~úческий** [16] diplomatic; **~úчный** [14; -чен, -чна] *fig.* diplomatic, tactful; **~ия** *f* [7] diplomacy
**дирéк|тор** *m* [1; *pl.*: -рá, *etc. e.*] manager,

director; (*школы*) principal, headmaster; **~ция** *f* [7] management, directorate

**дириж|а́бль** *m* [4] dirigible, airship; **~ёр** *m* [1] *mus.* conductor; **~и́ровать** [7] (T) conduct

**дисгармо́ния** *f* [7] *mus. and fig.* disharmony, discord

Д

**диск** *m* [1] disk

**диск|валифици́ровать** [7] (*im*)*pf.* disqualify; **~редити́ровать** [7] (*im*)*pf.* discredit; **~римина́ция** *f* [7] discrimination

**диску́ссия** *f* [7] discussion

**дисп|ансе́р** (-'sɛr) *m* [1] health clinic; **~е́тчер** *m* [1] (traffic) controller; *ae.* flight control officer; **~ут** *m* [1] dispute, disputation

**дис|серта́ция** *f* [7] dissertation, thesis; **~сона́нс** *m* [1] *mus. and fig.* dissonance, discord; **~та́нция** *f* [7] distance; ***сойти́ с ~та́нции*** withdraw; **~тилиро́ванный** [14 *sh.*] distilled; **~ципли́на** *f* [5] discipline

**дитя́** *n* [-я́ти; *pl.* → ***де́ти***] child

**диф|ира́мб** *m* [1] dithyramb; (*fig.*) eulogy; ***петь ~ира́мбы*** sing praises (to Д); **~тери́т** *m* [1], **~тери́я** *f* [7] diphtheria

**дифференц|иа́л** *m* [1], **~иа́льный** [14] *math*, *tech.* differential; **~и́ровать** [7] (*im*)*pf.* differentiate

**дич|а́ть** [1], ⟨о-⟩ run wild, grow wild; *fig.* become unsociable; **~и́ться** [16 *e.*; -чу́сь, -чи́шься] be shy *or* unsociable; shun (a p. P); **~ь** *f* [8] game, wild fowl; *coll.* (*чушь*) nonsense, bosh

**длин|а́** *f* [5] length; ***в ~у́*** (at) full length, lengthwise; ***~о́й в*** (В) **...** *or* **...** ***в ~у́*** long; **~но...** (*in compds.*) long-...; **~ный** [14; -и́нен, -и́нна, -и́нно́] long, too long; *coll.* (*высокий*) tall

**дли́т|ельный** [14; -лен, -льна] long, protracted, lengthy; **~ься** [13], ⟨про-⟩ last

**для** (Р) for, to; because of; ***~ того́, что́бы*** (in order) to, that... may; ***~ чего́?*** what for; ***я́щик ~ пи́сем*** mail (*Brt.* letter) box

**днев|а́ть** [6]: ***~а́ть и ночева́ть где́-л.*** spend all one's time somewhere; **~ни́к** *m* [1 *e.*] journal, diary (*vb.*: ***вести́*** keep); **~но́й** [14] day('s), daily; day(light **свет** *m*)

**днём** by day, during the day

**дн|о** *n* [9; *pl.*: до́нья, -ньев] bottom; ***вверх ~ом*** upside down; ***золото́е ~о*** *fig.* gold mine; ***вы́пить до ~а*** drain to the dregs; ***идти́ ко ~у*** *v/i.* (***пусти́ть на ~о*** *v/t.*) sink

**до** (Р) *place*: to, as far as, up (*or* down) to; *time*: till, until, to; before; *degree*: to, up to; *age*: under; *quantity*: up to, about; ***~ того́*** so (much); (Д) ***не ~ того́*** not be interested in, have no time, *etc.*, for, to

**доба́в|ить** → ***~ля́ть***; **~ле́ние** *n* [12] addition; supplement; **~ля́ть** [28], ⟨~ить⟩ [14] add; **~очный** [14] additional, extra; supplementary, accessory

**добе|га́ть** [1], ⟨~жа́ть⟩ [-егу́, -ежи́шь, -егу́т] run up to, reach (***до*** Р)

**доб|ива́ть** [1], ⟨~и́ть⟩ [-бью́, -бьёшь, -бе́й(те)!; -би́тый] deal the final blow, kill, finish off; completely smash; **-ся** (Р) (try to) get, obtain *or* reach; (*стремиться*) strive for; *правды и т. д.* find out (about); ***он ~и́лся своего́*** he gained his ends; **~ира́ться** [1], ⟨~ра́ться⟩ [-беру́сь, -рёшься] (***до*** Р) get to, reach

**до́блест|ный** [14; -тен, -тна] valiant, brave; **~ь** *f* [8] valo(u)r

**добро́** *n* [9] good deed; *coll.* property; **~м** kindly, amicably; ***~ бы*** it would be a different matter if; ***~ пожа́ловать!*** welcome!; ***жела́ть добра́*** wish *s.o.* well; **~во́лец** *m* [1; -льца] volunteer; **~во́льный** [14; -лен, -льна] voluntary; **~де́тель** *f* [8] virtue; **~ду́шие** *n* [12] good nature; **~ду́шный** [14; -шен, -шна] good-natured; **~жела́тельный** [14; -лен, -льна] benevolent; **~жела́тельство** *n* [9] benevolence; **~ка́чественный** [14 *sh.*] of good quality; *med.* benign; **~серде́чный** [14; -чен, -чна] good-hearted; **~со́вестный** [14; -тен, -тна] conscientious; **~сосе́дский** [16] friendly, neighbo(u)rly

**добр|ота́** *f* [5] kindness; **~о́тный** [14; -тен, -тна] of good *or* high quality; **~ый** [14; добр, -а́, -о, добры́] kind, good; *coll.* solid; ***~ых два часа́*** two solid hours; ***~ое у́тро*** (***~ый день, ве́чер***)!

good morning (afternoon, evening); ***в ~ый час!, всегó ~ого!*** good luck!; ***по ~ой вóле*** of one's own free will; ***чегó ~ого*** after all; ***бýдь(те) ~(ы)!*** would you be so kind as to

**добы|вáть** [1], ⟨~ть⟩ [-бýду, -бýдешь; добы́л, -á, дóбытый (добы́т, добы́та, добы́то)] get, obtain, procure; extract, mine, quarry; **~ча** *f* [5] procurement; extraction, mining; (*награбленное*) booty, spoils; *животного* prey (*a. fig.*); *hunt.* bag, catch

**довезтú** → ***довозúть***

**довéр|енность** *f* [8] (***на*** В) power of attorney; → ***~ие***; **~енный** [14] person empowered to act for s.b.; proxy, agent; ***~енное дéло*** work entrusted; **~ие** *n* [12] confidence, trust (***к*** Д in); **~úтельный** [14; -лен, -льна] confidential; **~ить** → ***~ять***; **~чивый** [14 *sh.*] trusting, trustful; **~шáть** [1], ⟨~шúть⟩ [16 *e.*; -шý, -шúшь] finish, complete; **~шéние** *n* [12]: ***в ~шéние всегó*** to crown it all, to boot; **~ять** [28], ⟨~ить⟩ [13] trust (Д a p.); confide *or* entrust (В/Д s.th. to); entrust (Д/В a p. with); **-ся** (Д) *a.* trust, rely on

**дов|естú** → ***~одúть***; **~од** *m* [1] argument; **~одúть** [15], ⟨~естú⟩ [25] (***до*** Р) see (a p. to); lead (up [to]); *до конца* bring (to); *до отчаяния и т. д.* drive, make; ***~естú до свéдения*** inform, bring to the notice (Р of)

**довоéнный** [14] prewar

**дов|озúть** [15], ⟨~езтú⟩ [24] (***до*** Р) take *or* bring ([right up] to)

**довóль|но** enough, sufficient; (*до некоторой степени*) rather, pretty, fairly; **~ный** [14; -лен, -льна] content(ed), satisfied (with Т); **~ствие** *n* [12] *mil.* ration, allowance; **~ствоваться** [7] content o.s. (Т with)

**догад|áться** → ***~ываться***; **~ка** *f* [5; *g/pl.*: -док] guess, conjecture **~ливый** [14 *sh.*] quick-witted; **~ываться**, ⟨~áться⟩ [1] (**о** П) guess, surmise

**дóгма** *f* [5], **~т** *m* [1] dogma

**догнáть** → ***догонять***

**догов|áривать** [1], ⟨~орúть⟩ [13] finish saying *or* telling; **-ся** (**о** П) agree (upon), arrange; ***~áривающиеся стóроны*** *f/pl.* contracting parties; **~óр** *m* [1] contract; *pol.* treaty; **~орúть(ся)** → ***~áривать(ся)***; **~óрный** [14] contract(ual); *цена* agreed

**дог|онять** [28], ⟨~нáть⟩ [-гоню́, -гóнишь; → ***гнать***] catch up (with); ***до какóго-л. мéста*** drive *or* bring to; *impf. a.* pursue, try to catch up, be (on the point of) overtaking; **~орáть** [1], ⟨~орéть⟩ [9] burn down; *fig.* fade, die out

**дод|éлывать**, ⟨~éлать⟩ [1] finish, complete; **~ýмываться**, ⟨~ýматься⟩ [1] (***до*** Р) find, reach; hit upon (*s.th.*, by thinking)

**доезжá|ть** [1], ⟨доéхать⟩ [-éду, -éдешь] (***до*** Р) reach; ***не ~я*** short of

**дожд|áться** → ***дожидáться***; **~евúк** *m* [1 *e.*] raincoat; **~евóй** [14] rain(y); ***~евóй червь*** earthworm; **~лúвый** [14 *sh.*] rainy; **~ь** *m* [4 *e.*] rain (***под*** Т, ***на*** П in); ***~ь идёт*** it is raining

**дож|ивáть** [1], ⟨~úть⟩ [-живý, -вёшь; дóжил, -á, -о (дожúт, -á, -о)] *impf.* live out (one's time, years, *etc.*); (***до*** Р) *pf.* live (till *or* up to); *до события* (live to) see; (*докатиться*) come to; **~идáться** [1], ⟨~дáться⟩ [-дýсь, -дёшься; → ***ждать***] (Р) wait (for, till); *pf. a.* see

**дóза** *f* [5] dose

**дозвонúться** [13] *pf.* ring s.b. (***до*** *or* ***к***) by means of telephone or doorbell until one gets an answer; get through to s.b. by telephone; gain access to s.b. by doorbell

**доигр|ываться** [1; -áюсь, -áешься], ⟨~áться⟩ get o.s. into *or* land o.s. in trouble

**доиск|иваться** *coll.* [1], ⟨~áться⟩ [3] (Р) (try to) find (out)

**доúть(ся)** [13], ⟨по-⟩ (give) milk

**дойтú** → ***доходúть***

**док** *m* [1] *naut.* dock

**доказ|áтельство** *n* [9] proof, evidence; **~ывать** [1], ⟨~áть⟩ [3] prove; argue

**док|áнчивать** [1], ⟨~óнчить⟩ [16] finish, complete

**докá|тываться** [1], ⟨~тúться⟩ [15; -ачýсь, -áтишься] roll up to; *о звуке* reach; *о человеке* come to (Р)

**до́кер** *m* [1] docker
**докла́д** *m* [1] report; lecture (**о** П on); paper; address, talk; **~на́я** [14] (*a.* **за-пи́ска** *f*) memorandum, report; **~чик** *m* [1] lecturer; speaker; **~ывать** [1], ⟨доложи́ть⟩ [16] report (В s.th. *or* **о** П on); announce (**о** П a p.)
**доко́нчить** → **дока́нчивать**
**до́ктор** *m* [1; *pl*.: -ра, *etc. e*.] doctor
**доктри́на** *f* [5] doctrine
**докуме́нт** *m* [1] document, paper
**долби́ть** [14 *e*.; -блю́, -би́шь, -блённый] **1.** ⟨вы́-, про-⟩ hollow (out); chisel; *о птице* peck (*bird*); **2.** P ⟨в-⟩ *в голову* inculcate, cram
**долг** *m* [1; *pl. e*.] debt; *sg*. duty; (*последний*) (last) respects *pl*.; **в ~** → **взаймы́**; **в ~у́** indebted (*a. fig*., **у** Р, **пе́ред** Т to); **~ий** [16; до́лог, долга́, -о; *comp*: до́льше] long; **~о** long, (for) a long time *or* while
**долго|ве́чный** [14; -чен, -чна] perennial, lasting; **~во́й** [14]: **~во́е обяза́тельство** *n* promissory note; **~вре́менный** [14 *sh*.] (very) long; **~вя́зый** [14] *coll*. lanky; **~жда́нный** [14] long--awaited; **~ле́тие** *n* [12] longevity; **~ле́тний** [15] longstanding; of several years; **~сро́чный** [14] long-term; **~та́** *f* [5; *pl*.: -го́ты, *etc. st*.] duration; *geogr*. longitude
**дол|ета́ть** [1], ⟨~ете́ть⟩ [11] (**до** Р) fly (to, as far as), reach; *a*. = **доноси́ться**
**до́лж|ен** *m*, **~на́** *f*, **~но́** *n* (→ **~но**), **~ны́** *pl*. **1.** must [*pt*.: **~**ен был, **~**на́ была́, *etc*. had to]; **2.** (Д) owe (a p.)
**долж|ни́к** *m* [1 *e*.] debtor; **~но́** one (it) should *or* ought to (be…); proper(ly); **~но́** = **~но́ быть** probably, apparently; **~ностно́й** [14] official; **~ность** *f* [8] post office; **~ный** [14] due (*a. su*. **~ное** *n*), proper; **~ным о́бразом** duly
**доли|ва́ть** [1], ⟨**~**ть⟩ [-лью́, -льёшь; → **лить**] fill (up), add
**доли́на** *f* [5] valley
**до́ллар** *m* [1] dollar
**доложи́ть** → **докла́дывать**
**доло́й** *coll*. off, down; **~ …** (В)! down *or* off with …!; **с глаз ~ из се́рдца вон** out of sight, out of mind
**долото́** *n* [9; *pl. st*.: -ло́та] chisel
**до́льше** (*comp*. of **до́лгий**) longer
**до́ля** *f* [6; *from g/pl. e*.] **1.** lot, fate; **2.** part, portion; share; *правды* grain; **льви́ная ~** the lion's share
**дом** *m* [1; *pl*.: -á, *etc. e*.] house, building; *очаг* home; (*домашние*) household; **вы́йти из ~у** leave (one's home), go out; **на́ ~** = **~о́й**; **на ~у́** = **~а** at home; **как ~а** at one's ease; (**у** Р) **не все ~а** (be) a bit off (one's head), nutty; **~ о́тдыха** holiday home; **~а́шний** [15] home…, house(hold)…, private; *животное* domestic; *pl. su*. folks; **~а́шняя еда́** home cooking; **~енный** [14]: **~енная печь** *f* → **~на**; **~ик** *m* [1] *dim*. → **дом**
**домини́ровать** [7] (pre)dominate
**домино́** *n* [*indecl*.] dominoes
**домкра́т** *m* [1] jack
**до́мна** *f* [5; *g/pl*.: -мен] blast furnace
**домовладе́лец** *m* [1; -льца] house owner
**домога́ться** [1] (Р) strive for, solicit
**домо́|й** home; **~ро́щенный** [14] homespun; crude, primitive; **~се́д** *m* [1] stay-at-home; **~хозя́йка** *f* [5; *g/pl*.: -зя́ек] housewife
**домрабо́тница** *f* [5] domestic (servant), maid
**до́мысел** *m* [1; -сла] conjecture
**донага́** *adv*.: **разде́ть ~** leave nothing on; *coll. fig*. fleece
**доне|се́ние** *n* [12] *mst. mil*. dispatch, report; **~сти́(сь)** → **доноси́ть(ся)**
**донжуа́н** *m* [1] Don Juan, philanderer
**до́н|изу** to the bottom; **~има́ть** [1], ⟨**~**я́ть⟩ [дойму́, -мёшь; → **заня́ть**] weary, exhaust (T with)
**до́нор** *m* [1] donor (*mst. of blood*)
**доно́с** *m* [1] *law* denunciation, information (**на** В against); **~и́ть** [15], ⟨донести́⟩ [24; -су́, -сёшь] **1.** carry *or* bring ([up] to); **2.** report (**о** П *s.th*., about, on); denounce, inform (against **на** В); *a*. **-ся** (**до** Р) waft (to); *о звуке* reach, (re)sound; **~чик** *m* [1] informer
**донско́й** [16] (*adj. of river* **Дон**) Don…
**доня́ть** → **донима́ть**
**допи|ва́ть** [1], ⟨**~**ть⟩ [-пью́, -пьёшь; → **пить**] drink up

**до́пинг** *m* [1] stimulant; *fig.* boost, shot in the arm; *sport* use of illicit substances
**допла́|та** *f* [5] additional payment, extra (*or* sur)charge; **~чивать** [1], **~ти́ть** [15] pay in addition
**допо́длинно** for sure
**дополн|е́ние** *n* [12] addition; supplement; *gr.* object; **~и́тельный** [14] additional; supplementary; extra; *adv. a.* in addition; more; **~я́ть** [28], ⟨**~ить**⟩ [13] add to, complete, embellish; *издание* enlarge
**допото́пный** [14] *joc.* old-fashioned, antediluvian
**допр|а́шивать** [1], ⟨**~оси́ть**⟩ [15] *law* interrogate, examine; *impf.* question; **~о́с** *m* [1] *law* interrogation, examination; *coll.* questioning; **~оси́ть** → **~а́шивать**
**до́пу|ск** *m* [1] access, admittance; *tech.* tolerance; **~ска́ть** [1], ⟨**~сти́ть**⟩ [15] admit (*a.* of), concede; *разрешать* allow; (*терпеть*) tolerate; (*предполагать*) suppose; *ошибку* make; **~сти́мый** [14 *sh.*] admissible, permissible; **~ще́ние** *n* [12] assumption
**допы́т|ываться**, ⟨**~а́ться**⟩ [1] *coll.* (try to) find out
**дораб|а́тывать**, ⟨**~о́тать**⟩ [1] complete, finish off; **-ся** exhaust o.s. with work (**до изнеможе́ния**)
**дореволюцио́нный** [14] prerevolutionary, before the revolution
**доро́г|а** *f* [5] road, way (*a. fig.*); (*путешествие*) passage; trip, journey; **желе́зная ~а** railroad, *Brt.* railway; **по ~е** on the way; **туда́ ему́ и ~а** *coll.* it serves him right; → *a.* **путь**
**дорого|ви́зна** *f* [5] dearness, expensiveness; **~́й** [16; до́рог, -á, -o; *comp.*: доро́же] dear (*a. fig.*), expensive
**доро́дный** [14; -ден, -дна] portly
**дорож|а́ть** [1], ⟨вз-, по-⟩ become dearer, rise in price; **~и́ть** [16 *e.*; -жу́, -жи́шь] (T) esteem (highly), (set a high) value (on)
**доро́ж|ка** *f* [5; *g/pl.*: -жек] path; *ковровая* runner; **бегова́я ~ка** race track; **~ный** [14] road..., travel..., traffic
**доса́|да** *f* [5] vexation; annoyance; **кака́я ~да!** how annoying!, what a pity!; **~ди́ть** → **~жда́ть**; **~дный** [14; -ден, -дна] annoying, vexatious; (*прискорбный*) deplorable; (**мне**) **~дно** it is annoying (annoys me); **~довать** [7] feel *or* be annoyed *or* vexed (**на** B at, with); **~жда́ть** [1], ⟨**~ди́ть**⟩ [15 *e.*; -ажу́, -ади́шь] vex, annoy (Д/T a p. with)
**доск|а́** *f* [5; *ac/sg*: до́ску; *pl.*: до́ски, до́сок, до́скам] board, plank; (*a.* **кла́ссная ~а́**) blackboard; *мемориальная* plate; **ша́хматная ~а́** chessboard; **поста́вить на одну́ ~́у** put on the same level
**доскона́льный** [14; -лен, -льна] thorough
**досло́вный** [14] literal, verbatim
**досм|а́тривать** [1], ⟨**~отре́ть**⟩ [9; -отрю́, -о́тришь] see up to *or* to the end (**до** P); *на таможне* examine; **~о́тр** *m* [1] (customs) examination; **~отре́ть** → **~а́тривать**
**доспе́хи** *m/pl.* [1] *hist.* armo(u)r
**досро́чный** [14] ahead of schedule, early
**дост|ава́ть** [5], ⟨**~а́ть**⟩ [-ста́ну, -ста́нешь] take (out, *etc.*); get; procure; ([**до**] P) touch; reach (to); **-ся** (Д) fall to a *p.'s* lot; **~ава́ться по насле́дству** inherit; (*быть наказанным*) catch it; **~а́вить** → **~авля́ть**; **~а́вка** *f* [5; *g/pl.*: -вок] delivery; conveyance; **с ~а́вкой** (**на́ дом**) carriage paid; free to the door; **~авля́ть** [28], ⟨**~а́вить**⟩ [14] deliver, hand; bring; *fig.* cause, give; **~а́ток** *m* [1; -тка] prosperity; sufficiency; **жить в ~а́тке** be comfortably off; **~а́точно** sufficiently; (P) (be) enough, sufficient; suffice; **~а́точный** [14; -чен, -чна] sufficient
**дости|га́ть** [1], ⟨**~́гнуть**⟩, ⟨**~́чь**⟩ [21; -г-: -сти́гну, -гнешь] (P) reach, arrive at, attain (*a. fig.*); *о ценах* amount *or* run up (to); **~же́ние** *n* [12] attainment, achievement; **~жи́мый** [14 *sh.*] attainable
**достове́рный** [14; -рен, -рна] trustworthy, reliable
**досто́|инство** *n* [9] dignity; (*положительное качество*) merit, virtue;

(*ценность, стоимость*) worth, value; **~йный** [14; -óин, -óй-на] worthy (*a.* of P); well-deserved; **~примечáтельность** *f* [8] (*mst. pl.*) place of interest; ***осмóтр ~примечáтельностей*** sight-seeing; **~я́ние** *n* [12] property (*a. fig.*); ***стать ~я́нием общéственности*** become public property

**дóступ** *m* [1] access; **~́ный** [14; -пен, -пна] accessible (*a. fig.*); approachable, affable; (*понятный*) comprehensible; *цена* moderate

**досýг** *m* [1] leisure; ***на ~е*** at leisure, during one's spare time

**дóс|уха** (quite) dry; **~́ыта** to one's fill

**дотáция** *f* [7] state subsidy

**дотлá**: utterly; ***сгорéть ~*** burn to the ground

**дотóшный** [14; -шен, -шна] meticulous

**дотр|áгиваться** [1], ⟨**~óнуться**⟩ [20] (**до** P) touch

**дóх|лый** [14] *животное* dead; P *о человеке* puny; **~ля́тина** *f* [5] carrion; feeble person; **~нуть**[1] [21], ⟨из-, по-⟩ (*of animals*) die; P (*of human beings*) *coll.* croak, kick the bucket; **~нýть**[2] → ***дышáть***

**дохóд** *m* [1] income, revenue; (*выручка*) proceeds *pl.*; **~и́ть** [15], ⟨дойти́⟩ [дойдý, -дёшь; → **идти́**] (**до** P) go *or* come (to), arrive (at), reach: *hist.* come down to; *о ценах* rise *or* run up to; **~ный** [14; -ден, -дна] profitable

**доцéнт** *m* [1] senior lecturer, assistant professor, *Brt.* reader

**дочéрн|ий** [15] daughter's; ***~яя компáния*** affiliate

**дóчиста** (quite) clean; *coll.* completely

**дочи́т|ывать**, ⟨**~áть**⟩ finish reading *or* read up to (**до** P)

**дóч|ка** *f* [5; *g/pl.*: -чек] *coll.* = **~ь** *f* [дóчери, *etc.* = 8; *pl.*: дóчери, -рéй, *etc. e.*; *instr.*: -рьми́] daughter

**дошкóльн|ик** *m* [1] child under school age; **~ый** *m* [1] preschool

**дощ|áтый** [14] of boards, plank…; **~éчка** *f* [5; *g/pl.*: -чек] *dim.* → ***доскá***

**доя́рка** *f* [5; *g/pl.*: -рок] milkmaid

**драгоцéнн|ость** *f* [8] jewel, gem (*a. fig.*); precious thing *or* possession; **~ый** [14; -цéнен, -цéнна] precious (*a.* stone), costly, valuable

**дразни́ть** [13; -ню́, дрáзнишь] **1.** ⟨по-⟩ tease, mock; **2.** ⟨раз-⟩ excite, tantalize

**дрáка** *f* [5] scuffle, fight

**дракóн** *m* [1] dragon; **~овский** [16] draconian, extremely severe

**дрáма** *f* [5] drama; *fig.* tragedy; **~ти́ческий** [16] dramatic (*a. fig.*); **~тýрг** *m* [1] playwright, dramatist

**драп|ировáть** [7], ⟨за-⟩ drape; **~́овый** [14] (of thick) woolen cloth (***драп***)

**дра|ть** [дерý, -рёшь; драл, -á, -о; …дрáнный], ⟨со-⟩ (→ ***сдирáть***) pull (off); tweak (*p.'s* ear B/***за*** B); *coll.* → ***выдирáть & раздирáть***; **-ся**, ⟨по-⟩ scuffle, fight, struggle; **~чли́вый** [14 *sh.*] pugnacious

**дребе|дéнь** *coll. f* [8] trash; **´~зг** *coll. m* [1] tinkle, jingle, rattle; **~зжáть** [4; -зжи́т], ⟨за-⟩ tinkle, jingle, rattle

**древ|еси́на** *f* [5] timber; **~éсный** [14]: ***~éсный спирт*** methyl alcohol; ***~éсный ýголь*** charcoal; **~́ко** *n* [9; *pl.*: -ки, -ков] flagpole

**дрéвн|ий** [15; -вен, -вня] ancient (*a. su.*), antique; aged, (very) old; **~ость** *f* [8] antiquity (*a. pl.* = -ties)

**дрейф** *m* [1] *naut.*, **~овáть** [7] drift

**дрем|áть** [2], ⟨за-⟩ doze (off), slumber; **~óта** *f* [5] drowsiness, sleepiness; **~ýчий** [17] dense (*a. fig.*)

**дрессировáть** [7], ⟨вы́-⟩ train

**дроб|и́ть** [14 *e.*; -блю́, -би́шь; -блённый], ⟨раз-⟩ break in pieces, crush; (*делить*) divide *or* split up; **~́ный** [14; -бен, -бна] *math.* fractional; **~ь** *f* [8] *coll.* (small) shot; *барабанная math.* [*from g/pl. e.*] fraction; ***десяти́чная ~ь*** decimal

**дров|á** *n pl.* [9] firewood; **~яни́к** *m* [1], **~янóй** [14]: ***~ сарáй*** woodshed

**дрóг|нуть** **1.** [21] (*зябнуть*) shiver *or* shake (with cold); ⟨про-⟩ be chilled to the bone; **2.** [20 *st.*] *pf. голос* quaver; (*заколебаться*) waver, falter; flinch; ***не ~нув*** without flinching; **~жáть** [4 *e.*; -жý, -жи́шь], ⟨за-⟩ tremble, shake, shiver (**от** P with); *о пламени и т. д.* flicker, glimmer; dread (s.th. ***пéред***

Т); be anxious (**за** В about); tremble (for s.o.); grudge (**над** Т); **~жжи** *f/pl.* [8; *from gen. e.*] yeast; **~жь** *f* [8] trembling, shiver; vibration

**дрозд** *m* [1 *e.*] thrush; ***чёрный ~*** blackbird

**друг** *m* [1; *pl.*: друзья́, -зе́й, -зья́м] friend (*a. address*); ***~ ~а*** each (one an)other; ***~ за ~ом*** one after another; ***~ с ~ом*** with each other; **~о́й** [16] (an)other, different; else, next, second; ***(н)и тот (н)и ~о́й*** both (neither); ***на ~о́й день*** the next day

**дру́ж|ба** *f* [5] friendship; **~елю́бный** [14; -бен, -бна] amicable, friendly; **~еский** [16], **~ественный** [14 *sh.*] friendly; *comput.* userfriendly; **~и́ть** [16; -жу́, -у́жишь] be friends, be on friendly terms (**с** Т with); **~и́ще** *m* [11] old chap *or* boy; **~ный** [14; -жен, -жна́, -о; дру́жны́] friendly, on friendly terms; (*совместный*) joint, concerted; *bot.*, *mil.*, *etc.* vigorous; *adv. a.* together; at once

**дря́|блый** [14; дрябл, -а́, -о] limp, flabby; **~зги** *coll. f/pl.* [5] squabbles; **~нно́й** P [14] wretched, worthless, trashy; **~нь** *coll. f* [8] rubbish, trash (*a. fig.*); P *вещь* rotten thing; *человек* rotter; **~хлый** [14; дряхл, -а́, -о] decrepit; *coll. дом и т. д.* dilapidated

**дуб** *m* [1; *pl. e.*] oak; **~и́на** *f* [5] club, cudgel; P boor, dolt; **~и́нка** *f* [5; *g/pl.*: -нок] (policeman's) club; **~лёр** *m* [1], **~лика́т** *m* [1] duplicate; reserve; *thea.* understudy; **~ли́ровать** [7] *impf.* duplicate; *thea.* understudy a part; *cine.* dub; **~о́вый** [14] oak(en)

**дуг|а́** *f* [5; *pl. st.*] arc (*a. el.*); ***согну́ть в ~у́*** bring under, compel; **~о́й** arched

**ду́дк|а** *f* [5; *g/pl.*: -док] pipe; *coll.* ***~и!*** not on your life!; ***пляса́ть под чью-л. ~у*** dance to s.b.'s tune

**ду́ло** *n* [9] muzzle; barrel (gun)

**ду́ма** *f* [5] **1.** *old use* thought; meditation; **2.** *pol.* duma, parliament; (*in Russia*) duma = council; elective legislative assembly; **~ть** [1], ⟨по-⟩ think (**о** П about, of); reflect (**над** Т, **о** П on); (+ *inf.*) intend to, be going to; care (**о** П about); ***как ты ~ешь?*** what do you think?; ***мно́го о себе́ ~ть*** be conceited; ***не до́лго ~я*** without hesitation; **-ся** seem, appear; ***~ется, он прав*** I think he is right; ***мне ~ется, что*** I think that …

**дун|ове́ние** *n* [12] waft, breath; **~уть** → **дуть**

**дупло́** *n* [9; *pl. st.*: ду́пла, -пел, -плам] *дерева* hollow; *в зубе* cavity (*in tooth*)

**ду́р|а** *f* [5] silly woman; **~а́к** *m* [1 *e.*] fool, simpleton; ***~а́к ~ако́м*** arrant fool; ***сваля́ть ~ака́*** do something foolish; **~а́цкий** [16] foolish, silly, idiotic; **~а́чество** *coll. n* [9] tomfoolery; **~а́чить** [16], ⟨о-⟩ fool, hoax; **-ся** play the fool; **~е́ть** *coll.* [8], ⟨о-⟩ become stupefied; **~и́ть** *coll.* [13]: ***~и́ть го́лову*** confuse, deceive; → ***~а́читься***; be naughty *or* obstinate

**дурма́н** *m* [1] *fig.* narcotic; **~ить** [13], ⟨о-⟩ stupefy

**дурн|е́ть** [8], ⟨по-⟩ grow plain *or* ugly; **~о́й** [14; ду́рен, -рна́, -о] bad; *о внешности* plain, ugly; ***мне ~о*** I feel (am) sick *or* unwell; **~ота́** *coll. f* [5] giddiness; nausea

**дурь** *coll. f* [8] folly, caprice

**ду́т|ый** [14] *fig. авторитет* inflated; *цифры* distorted; **~ь** [18], ⟨по-⟩, *once* ⟨ду́нуть⟩ [20] blow; ***ду́ет*** there is a draught (draft); **-ся**, ⟨на-⟩ swell; *coll.* sulk; be angry with (**на** В)

**дух** *m* [1] *времени* spirit; *боевой* courage; (*привидение*) ghost; ***здоро́вый ~ в здоро́вом те́ле*** a sound mind in a sound body; **(не) *в ~е*** in a good (bad) temper *or* in high (low) spirits; ***в моём ~е*** to my taste; ***па́дать ~ом*** lose heart; ***прису́тствие ~а*** presence of mind; P ***~ом*** in a jiffy *or* trice; old use ***во весь ~, что есть ~у*** at full speed; **~и́** *m/pl.* [1 *e.*] perfume

**духов|е́нство** *n* [9] *coll.* clergy; **~ка** *f* [5; *g/pl.*: -вок] oven; **~ный** [14] spiritual; *состояние* mental; ecclesiastical, clerical, religious; ***~ный мир*** inner world; **~о́й** [14] *mus.* wind (*instrument*); ***~о́й орке́стр*** *m* brass band

**духота́** *f* [5] sultriness, stuffiness

**душ** *m* [1] shower; ***приня́ть ~*** take a shower

Д

E

**душ|á** *f* [5; *ac/sg*.: дýшу; *pl. st.*] soul; *fig.* heart; *hist.* serf; ***в ~é*** at heart; ***~á в ~у*** at one; in harmony; ***в глубинé ~и́*** in one's heart of hearts; ***~и́ не чáять*** adore; ***~á óбщества*** life and soul of the party; ***не по ~é*** not to like (the idea of) *or* care; **от (всей) ~и́** from (with all) one's heart; ***~á в пя́тки ушлá*** have one's heart in one's mouth

**душ|евнобольнóй** [14] mentally ill *or* deranged (person); **~éвный** [14] sincere, heartfelt, cordial; **~ераздирáющий** [17] heart-rending

**душ|и́стый** [14 *sh.*] fragrant; *горошек* sweet (*peas*); **~и́ть** [16] **1.** ⟨за-⟩ strangle; smother (*a. fig.*); **2.** ⟨на-⟩ perfume (**-ся** o.s.); **~ный** [14; -шен, -шнá, -о] stuffy, sultry

**дуэ́|ль** *f* [8] *hist.* duel (*a. fig.*); **~т** *m* [1] duet

**ды́б|ом** (*stand*) on end (*of hair*); **~ы́**: (***встать** etc.*) ***на ~ы́*** rear (*a.* up); *fig.* resist, revolt (against)

**дым** *m* [1] smoke; **~и́ть** [14 *e.*; -млю́, -ми́шь], ⟨на-⟩ *or* **~и́ться** smoke; **~ка** *f* [5] haze; **~ный** [14] smoky; **~овóй** [14]: ***~ová труба́*** chimney; *naut.* funnel; **~óк** *m* [1; -мкá] small puff of smoke

**дымохóд** *m* [1] flue

**ды́ня** *f* [6] (musk) melon

**дыр|á** *f* [5; *pl. st.*], **~ка** *f* [5; *g/pl.*: -рок] hole; **~я́вый** [14 *sh.*] having a hole, full of holes; *coll. память* bad; ***~я́вая головá*** *coll.* forgetful person

**дыхá|ние** *n* [12] breath(ing); ***искýсственное ~ние*** artificial respiration; **~тельный** [14] respiratory; ***~тельное гóрло*** windpipe

**дышáть** [4], ⟨по-⟩, *coll.* (*a.* once) ⟨дохнýть⟩ [20] breathe (T s.th.); *a.* devote *o.s.* to; ***~ свéжим вóздухом*** take the air; ***éле ~*** *or* ***~ на лáдан*** have one foot in the grave; *о вещах* be completely worn out *or* very old

**дья́вол** *m* [1] devil; **~ьский** [16] devilish, diabolical

**дья́кон** *m* [1] deacon

**дю́жин|а** *f* [5] dozen

**дю́|йм** *m* [1] inch; **~на** *f* [5] dune

**дя́дя** *m* [6; *g/pl.*: -дей] uncle (*a. coll. as mode of address by child to any adult male*)

**дя́тел** *m* [1; -тла] woodpecker

# Е

**Евáнгелие** *n* [12] *collect.* the Gospels

**еврé|й** *m* [3] Jew; **~ка** *f* [5; *g/pl.*: -рéек] Jewess; **~ский** [16] Jewish

**европ|éец** *m* [1; -пéйца], **~éйка** *f* [5; *g/pl.*: -пéек], **~éйский** [16] European; **Ꞩéйский Союз** European Union

**éгерь** *m* [4; *pl.*: *a.* -ря́, *etc.*] hunter, huntsman; chasseur

**еги́п|етский** [16] Egyptian; **~тя́нин** *m* [1; *pl.*: -я́не, -я́н], **~тя́нка** *f* [5; *g/pl.*: -нок] Egyptian

**егó** (ji'vɔ) his; its; → ***он***

**едá** *f* [5] food, meal

**едвá** (*a.* ***~ ли***) hardly, scarcely; → *a.* ***éле***; no sooner; ***~ не*** almost, nearly; ***~ ли не*** perhaps

**един|éние** *n* [12] unity, union; **~и́ца** *f* [5] *math.* one; *часть, величина* unit; *coll. оценка* very bad; *pl.* (a) few; **~и́чный** [14; -чен, -чна] single, isolated

**еди́но|...** (→ *a.* ***однó***): **~бóрство** *n* [9] (single) combat; **~влáстие** *n* [12] autocracy; **~врéменный** [14] once only; *пособие* extraordinary; **~глáсие** *n* [12] unanimity; **~глáсный** [14; -сен, -сна] unanimous; **~глáсно** unanimously; **~дýшие** *n* [12] unanimity; **~дýшный** [14; -шен, -шна] unanimous; **~ли́чный** [14] individual, personal; **~мы́шленник** *m* [1] like-minded p., associate, confederate; **~обрáзный** [14; -зен, -зна] uniform

**еди́нствен|ный** [14 *sh.*] only, single, sole; ***~ный в своём рóде*** unique;

**~ое число́** *gr.* singular
**еди́н|ство** *n* [9] unity; *взглядов и т. д.* unanimity; **~ый** [14 *sh.*] one, single, common; (*только один*) only (one, sole); (*объединённый*) one whole; united; ***все до ~ого*** all to a man
**е́дкий** [16; -док, -дка́, -о] caustic
**едо́к** *m* [1 *e.*] (*coll.* big) eater; ***на ка́ждого ~а́*** per head; ***пять ~о́в в семье́*** five mouths to feed
**её** her; its; → ***она́***
**ёж** *m* [1 *e.*] hedgehog
**ежеви́ка** *f* [5] blackberry, -ries *pl.*
**еже|го́дный** [14] annual; **~дне́вный** [14] daily, everyday; **~ме́сячный** [14] monthly; **~мину́тный** [14] (occurring) every minute; (*непрерывный*) continual; **~неде́льник** *m* [1], **~неде́льный** [14] weekly; **~ча́сный** [14] hourly
**ёжиться** [16], ⟨съ-⟩ shiver (from cold, fever); shrink (from fear); *от смущения* be shy, hem and haw
**ежо́в|ый** [14]: ***держа́ть в ~ых рукави́цах*** rule with a rod of iron
**езд|а́** *f* [5] ride, drive; **~́ить** [15], go (T by), ride, drive; (*посещать регулярно*) come, visit; travel
**ей**: ***~-бо́гу*** *int./coll.* really, indeed
**е́ле** (*a.* **е́ле-е́ле**) hardly, scarcely, barely; *слегка* slightly; *с трудом* with (great) difficulty
**еле́йный** [14] *fig.* unctuous
**ёлка** *f* [5; *g/pl.*: ёлок] fir; ***рожде́ственская*** (***нового́дняя***) **~** Christmas (New Year's) tree *or* (children's) party (***на*** В to, for; ***на*** П at)
**ел|о́вый** [14] fir; **~ь** *f* [8] fir; **~́ьник** *m* [1] fir-grove; *collect.* firwood
**ёмк|ий** [16; ёмок, ёмка] capacious; **~ость** *f* [8] capacity; ***~ость запомина́ющего устро́йства*** storage capacity; *comput.* memory capacity
**ено́т** *m* [1] raccoon
**епи́скоп** *m* [1] bishop
**ерала́ш** *m* [1] *coll.* jumble, muddle
**е́ре|сь** *f* [8] heresy; *fig.* nonsense
**ёрзать** [1] *coll.* fidget
**еро́шить** [16] → ***взъеро́шивать***
**ерунда́** *f* [5] *coll.* nonsense; trifle(s)
**ёрш** *m* [1 *e.*] **1.** *zo.* ruff; **2.** *coll.* mixture of vodka with beer *or* wine
**е́сли** if; in case; once (*a.* **~ уж**[**е́**]); ***а*** *or* ***и ~*** if ever; whereas; ***~ и*** *or* (***да́***)***же*** even though; ***ах*** *or* **о, ~ б**(**ы**)**...** oh, could *or* would...; ***~ бы не*** but for; ***~ то́лько*** provided
**есте́ств|енно** naturally, of course; **~енный** [14 *sh.*] natural; ***~енные нау́ки*** natural sciences; **~о́** *n* [9] *человека* nature; essence; **~озна́ние** *n old use* [12] natural science
**есть**[1] [ем, ешь, ест, еди́м, еди́те, едя́т; е́шь(те)!; ел; ...е́денный] **1.** ⟨съ-, по-⟩ eat (*pf. a.* up), have; **2.** ⟨разъ-⟩ eat away (*of rust*); *chem.* corrode
**есть**[2] → ***быть*** am, is, are; there is (are); ***у меня́ ~ ...*** I have ...; ***так и ~*** I thought as much
**ефре́йтор** *m* [1] *mil.* private first class, *Brt.* lance-corporal
**е́ха|ть** [е́ду, е́дешь; поезжа́й!], ⟨по-⟩ (be) go(ing, *etc.*) (by T), ride, drive (T *or* **в, на** П in, on); (**в, на** В) leave (for), go (to); (***за*** T) go for, fetch; ***по~ли! → идти́***
**ехи́д|ный** [14; -ден, -дна] caustic, spiteful; malicious; **~ство** *n* [9] spite, malice; innuendo
**ещё** (**не**) (not) yet; (**всё**) **~** still (*a.* with *comp.*); another, more (and more ***~ и ~***); ***~ раз*** once more; again; ***кто ~?*** who else?; *о времени* as early (late, *etc.*); ***~ бы!*** (to be) sure! I should think so!, of course!; ***пока́ ~*** for the time being; ***э́то ~ ничего́*** it could have been worse; ***он ~ мо́лод*** he is still young

Е

# Ж

**ж** → **же**
**жа́б|а** *f* [5] toad; **~ра** *f* [5] gill
**жа́воронок** *m* [1; -нка] lark
**жа́дн|ичать** [1], ⟨по-⟩ be greedy *or* avaricious; **~ость** *f* [8] greed(iness), avarice; **~ый** [14; -ден, -днá, -o] greedy (**на** B, **до** P, **к** Д of), avaricious
**жа́жда** *f* [5] thirst (*a. fig.*, P *or inf.* for); **~ть** [-ду, -дешь] thirst, crave (P *or inf.* for)
**жаке́т** *m* [1] (lady's) jacket
**жале́ть** [8], ⟨по-⟩ **1.** pity, feel sorry for; (**о** П) regret; **2.** (P *or* B) spare; (*скупиться*) grudge
**жа́лить** [13], ⟨у-⟩ sting, bite
**жа́лк|ий** [16; -лок, -лкá, -o; *comp.*: жáльче] pitiable; (*несчастный*) pathetic, wretched; **~о** → **жаль**
**жа́ло** *n* [9] sting (*a. fig.*)
**жа́лоб|а** *f* [5] complaint; **~ный** [14; -бен, -бна] mournful, plaintive
**жа́лова|нье** *n* [10] *old use* pay, salary; **~ть** [7]: **не ~ть** not like; ⟨по-⟩ *mst. iro.* come (to visit, see a p. **к** Д); **-ся** (**на** B) complain (of, about)
**жа́лост|ливый** [14 *sh.*] *coll.* compassionate; **~ный** [14; -тен, -тна] mournful; (*соболезнующий*) compassionate; **~ь** *f* [8] pity, compassion
**жаль** it is a pity (**как ~** what a pity); (*as adv.*) unfortunately; (Д ~ В): **мне ~ его́** I am sorry for *or* I pity him; *a.* regret; grudge
**жанр** *m* [1] genre; **~овый** [14] genre…; **~овая жи́вопись** genrepainting
**жар** *m* [1; в ~ý] heat; *med.* fever; *fig.* ardo(u)r; **~á** *f* [5] heat, hot weather; **~еный** [14] roast, broiled; fried, grilled; → *a.* **~ко́е**; **~ить** [13], ⟨за-, из-⟩ roast; fry; *coll.* *о солнце* burn; **~кий** [16; -рок, -ркá, -o; *comp.*: жáрче] hot; *fig.* heated, ardent, vehement, intense; **мне ~ко** I am hot; **~ко́е** *n* [16] roast meat; **~опонижа́ющий** [17] *med.* febrifugal
**жасми́н** *m* [1] jasmin(e)
**жа́т|ва** *f* [5] harvest(ing); **~венный** [14] reaping
**жать¹** [жну, жнёшь; …жáтый], ⟨с-⟩ [сожнý], ⟨по-⟩ reap, cut, harvest
**жать²** [жму, жмёшь; …жáтый], ⟨с-⟩, ⟨по-⟩ press, squeeze; **~ ру́ку** shake hands (Д with); *об обуви и т. д.* pinch; **-ся** shrink (**от** P with); crowd, huddle up, snuggle; (*быть в нерешительности*) hesitate, waver
**жва́ч|ка** *f* [5] chewing, rumination; *coll.* chewing gum; **~ный** [14]: **~ные** (**живо́тные**) *n/pl.* ruminants
**жгут** *m* [1 *e.*] *med.* tourniquet
**жгу́чий** [17 *sh.*] burning; smarting
**ждать** [жду, ждёшь; ждал, -á, -o], ⟨подо-⟩ wait (for P); (*ожидать*) expect, await; **вре́мя не ждёт** time presses; **~ не дожда́ться** wait impatiently (P for)
**же 1.** *conj.* but, and; whereas, as to; **2.** → **ведь**; *a. do + vb.*; **э́то ~** the (this) very, same *место*, *время и т. д.*; **э́тот ~ челове́к** this very man; **что ~ ты молча́л?** why on earth didn't you tell me about it?; **скажи́ ~ что́-нибудь!** for goodness' sake say something!; **когда́ ~ она́ уйдёт** whenever will she leave?
**жева́|ть** [7 *e.*; жую, жуёшь] chew; **~тельный** [14] *движение мышцы* masticatory; *резинка* chewing
**жезл** *m* [1 *e.*] *маршальский* staff; rod
**жела́|ние** *n* [12] wish, desire; **по** (**согла́сно**) **~нию** at, by (as) request(ed); **~нный** [14] desired; wished for; *гость и т. д.* welcome; (*любимый*) beloved; **~тельный** [14; -лен, -льна] desirable, desired; **мне ~тельно** I am anxious to; **~ть** [1], ⟨по-⟩ wish (Д/P a p. s.th.), desire; **э́то оставля́ет ~ть лу́чшего** it leaves much to be desired; **~ющие** *pl.* [17] those interested in, those wishing to …
**желе́** *n* [*indecl.*] jelly (*a. fish, meat*)
**железа́** *f* [5; *pl.*: жéлезы, желёз, железáм] *anat.* gland

**железнодоро́жник** *m* [1] railroad (*Brt.* railway-) man; **~нодоро́жный** [14] railroad…, *Brt.* railway…; **∴ный** [14] iron; **∴ная доро́га** railway; **∴о** *n* [9] iron; **кро́вельное ∴о** sheet iron; **куй ∴о, пока́ горячо́** strike while the iron is hot; **~обето́н** *m* [1] reinforced concrete

**жёлоб** *m* [1; *pl.*: -ба́, *etc. e.*] gutter; chute

**желт|е́ть** [8], ⟨по-⟩ grow *or* turn yellow; *impf.* (*a.* **-ся**) appear yellow; **~изна́** *f* [5] yellow(ness); **~ова́тый** [14 *sh.*] yellowish; **~о́к** *m* [1; -тка́] yolk; **~у́ха** *f med.* [5] jaundice

**жёлтый** [14; жёлт, -а́, -о] yellow

**желу́до|к** *m* [1; -дка] stomach; **~чный** [14] gastric, stomach

**жёлудь** *m* [4; from *g/pl. e.*] acorn

**же́лч|ный** [14] gall…; **~ный пузы́рь** gall bladder; [жёлчен, -а́, -о] *fig.* irritable; **~ь** *f* [8] bile, gall (*a. fig.*)

**жема́н|иться** [13] *coll.* mince; be prim; behave affectedly; **~ный** [14; -а́нен, -а́нна] affected, mincing, prim; **~ство** *n* [9] primness, prudery, affectedness

**же́мч|уг** *n* [1; *pl.*: -га́, *etc. e.*] *coll.* pearls *pl.*; **~у́жина** *f* [5] pearl; **~у́жный** [14] pearly

**жен|а́** *f* [5; *pl. st.*: жёны] wife; **~а́тый** [14 *sh.*] married (*man*; **на** П to a p.); **~и́ть** [13; женю́, же́нишь] (*im*)*pf.* marry (*a man* **на** П to); **-ся** marry (*v/t.* **на** П; *of men*); **~и́тьба** *f* [5] marriage (**на** П to); **~и́х** *m* [1 *e.*] fiancé; bridegroom; **~оненави́стник** *m* [1] misogynist, woman hater; **~оподо́бный** [14; -бен, -бна] effeminate; **∴ский** [16] female, lady's, woman's, women's, girl's; *gr.* feminine; **∴ственный** [14 *sh.*] feminine, womanly; **∴щина** *f* [5] woman

**жердь** *f* [8; *from g/pl. e.*] pole

**жереб|ёнок** *m* [2] foal, colt; **~е́ц** *m* [1; -бца́] stallion

**жёрнов** *m* [1; *pl. e.*: -ва́] millstone

**же́ртв|а** *f* [5] victim; sacrifice; (*a.* = **прино́сить в ~у**); **~овать** [7], ⟨по-⟩ (Т) sacrifice (*v/t.*: o.s. **собо́й**); (В) give

**жест** *m* [1] gesture; **~икули́ровать** [7] gesticulate

**жёсткий** [16; -ток, -тка́, -о; *comp.*: -тче] hard; *слова*, *условия* harsh; *мясо* tough; *материал* stiff, rigid; *критика*, *меры* severe

**жесто́к|ий** [16; жесто́к, -а́, -о] cruel; (*ужасный*) terrible, dreadful; *мороз* fierce; *действительность* grim; **~осе́рдие** *n* [12] hard-heartedness; **~ость** *f* [8] cruelty, brutality

**жест|ь** *f* [8] tin (plate); **~яно́й** [14] tin…

**жето́н** *m* [1] counter; token

**жечь**, ⟨с-⟩ [26; г/ж: (со)жгу́, -жжёшь, -жгу́т; (с)жёг, (со)жгла́; сожжённый] burn (*a. fig.*); torment

**живи́т|ельный** [14; -лен, -льна] life-giving, vivifying; *воздух* crisp, bracing

**жи́вность** *f* [8] *coll.* small (domestic) animals, poultry and fowl

**жив|о́й** [14; жив, -а́, -о] living; alive (*pred.*); (*деятельный и т. д.*) lively, vivacious; *ум* quick; (*подвижный*) nimble; *воображение* lively, vivid; **в ~ы́х** alive; **как ~о́й** true to life; **~ и здоро́в** safe and sound; **ни ~ ни мёртв** more dead than alive; petrified with fear *or* astonishment; **заде́ть за ~о́е** cut to the quick; **принима́ть ~о́е уча́стие** take an active part; feel keen sympathy (with); **~опи́сец** *m* [1; -сца] painter; **~опи́сный** [14; -сен, -сна] picturesque; **∴опись** *f* [8] painting; **∴ость** *f* [8] liveliness, vivacity; animation

**живо́т** *m* [1 *e.*] abdomen, stomach, belly; **~во́рный** [14; -рен, -рна] vivifying; **~ново́дство** *n* [9] cattle breeding; **~ное** *n* [14] animal; **~ный** [14] animal; *fig.* bestial, brutal; **~ный мир** animal kingdom; **~ный страх** blind fear

**жив|отрепе́щущий** [17] actual, topical, of vital importance; *fig.* burning; **~у́чий** [17 *sh.*] (*выносливый*) hardy, tough; *традиция и т. д.* enduring; **~ьём** alive

**жидк|ий** [16; -док, -дка́, -о; *comp.*: жи́же] liquid, fluid; (*водянистый*) watery, weak; *каша и т. д.* thin; *волосы и т. д.* sparse, scanty; **~ость** *f* [8] liquid

**жи́жа** *f* [5] *coll.* liquid; (*грязь*) slush; (*бульон*) broth

**жи́зне|нность** *f* [8] viability; vitality; **~нный 1.** [14 *sh.*] (of) life('s), wordly; vivid; **2.** [14] (*жизненно важный*) vital;

**~ра́достный** [14; -тен, -тна] cheerful, joyful; **~спосо́бный** [14; -бен, -бна] viable

**жизн|ь** *f* [8] life; **(*никогда́*) *в ~и не …*** never (in one's life); ***о́браз ~и*** way of life; ***провести́ в ~ь*** put into practice; ***при ~и*** in *a p.'s* lifetime; alive; ***вопро́сы ~и и сме́рти*** vital question

**жи́л|а** *f* [5] *coll.* sinew, tendon; vein (*a. geol.*); **~е́т** *m* [1], **~е́тка** *f* [5; *g/pl.*: -ток] vest, *Brt.* waistcoat; **~е́ц** *m* [1; -льца́] lodger, roomer; tenant; **~истый** [14 *sh.*] sinewy, wiry; *мясо* stringy; **~и́ще** *n* [11] dwelling, lodging(s); **~и́щный** [14] housing; **~ка** *f* [5; *g/pl.*: -лок] *dim.* → **~а**; veinlet; *на листьях, мраморе* vein (*a. fig.*); **~о́й** [14]: ***~о́й дом*** dwelling, house; **~пло́щадь** *f* [8] living space; **~ьё** *n* [10] habitation; dwelling; lodging(s)

**жир** *m* [1; в -у́; *pl. e.*] fat; grease; ***ры́бий ~*** cod-liver oil; **~е́ть** [8], ⟨о-, раз-⟩ grow fat; **~ный** [14; -рен, -рна́, -о] fat; (of) grease, greasy; *земля* rich soil; *typ.* bold(faced); **~ово́й** [14] fat(ty)

**жит|е́йский** [16] wordly, (of) life('s); everyday; **~ель** *m* [4], **~ельница** *f* [5] inhabitant, resident; **~ельство** *n* [9] residence; ***вид на ~ельство*** residence permit; **~ие́** *n* [12] life, biography (*mst. of a saint*)

**жи́тница** *f* [5] *fig.* granary

**жить** [живу́, -вёшь; жил, -á, -о; нé жил(и)] live (Т, ***на*** В [up]on; Т *a.* for); (*проживать*) reside, lodge; ***как живёте?*** how are you (getting on)?; ***жи́л(и)-бы́л(и) …*** once upon a time there was (were) …; **~ся**: ***ей хорошо́ живётся*** she is well off; **~ё(-бытьё)** *coll. n* [10] life, living

**жмот** *m* [1] *coll.* skinflint, miser

**жму́рить** [13], ⟨за-⟩ screw up, tighten, narrow (one's eyes **-ся**)

**жрать** P *coarse* [жру, жрёшь, жрал, -á, -о], ⟨со-⟩ devour, gorge, gobble

**жре́бий** *m* [3] lot (*a. fig.* = destiny); ***броса́ть (тяну́ть) ~*** cast (draw) lots; ***~ бро́шен*** the die is cast

**жрец** *m* [1 *e.*] (pagan) priest (*a. fig.*)

**жужжа́|ние** *n* [12], **~ть** [4 *e.*; жужжу́, -и́шь] buzz, hum

**жу|к** *m* [1 *e.*] beetle; ***ма́йский ~к*** cockchafer; **~лик** *coll. m* [1] (*мошенник*) swindler, cheat, trickster; (*вор*) filcher, pilferer; **~льничать** [1], ⟨с-⟩ cheat, trick

**жура́вль** *m* [4 *e.*] (*zo.*, *well*) crane

**жури́ть** *coll.* [13], ⟨по-⟩ scold mildly, reprove

**журна́л** *m* [1] magazine, periodical, journal; diary; *naut.* log(book); **~и́ст** *m* [1] news(paper)man, journalist; **~и́стика** *f* [5] journalism

**журча́|ние** *n* [12], **~ть** [-чи́т] purl, murmur

**жу́т|кий** [14; -ток, -тка́, -о] weird, uncanny, sinister; ***мне ~ко*** I am terrified; *coll.* **~ь** *f* [8] horror; **(*меня́*) *пря́мо ~ь берёт*** I feel terrified

**жюри́** *n* [*indecl.*] jury (prizes)

# З

**за 1.** (В): (*direction*) behind; over, across, beyond; out of; (*distance*) at; (*time*) after; over, past; before (*a.* ***~ … до*** Р); ***ему́ ~ со́рок*** he is over forty; (with) in, for, during; (*object*[*ive*], *favo*[*u*]*r*, *reason*, *value*, *substitute*) for; ***~то́, ~ что*** because; ***~ что?*** what for? why?; **2.** (Т): (*position*) behind; across, beyond; at, over; after (*time & place*); because of; with; ***~ мной …*** *a.* I owe …; ***ко́мната ~ мной*** I'll take (*or* reserve) the room

**заба́в|а** *f* [5] amusement, entertainment; **~ля́ть** [28], ⟨(по)~ить⟩ [13] amuse (**-ся** o.s., be amused at Т); **~ный** [14; -вен, -вна] amusing, funny

**забасто́в|ка** *f* [5; *g/pl.*: -вок] strike, walkout; ***всео́бщая ~ка*** general strike; **~очный** [14] strike…; **~щик** *m* [1] striker

**забве́ние** *n* [12] oblivion

**забе́|г** *m* [1] *sport* heat, race; **~га́ть** [1], ⟨**~жа́ть**⟩ [4; забегу́, -ежи́шь, -егу́т; -еги́!] run in(to), get; *далеко* run off; *coll.* drop in (**к** Д on); ***~га́ть вперёд*** anticipate, forestall

**забере́менеть** [8] *pf.* become pregnant

**заб|ива́ть** [1], ⟨**~и́ть**⟩ [-бью́, -бьёшь; → ***бить***] drive in; *гвоздями* nail up; *гол* score; (*засорить*) block (up); *фонтан* spout forth; *тревогу* sound; *coll. голову* stuff; **-ся** *coll.* (*спрятаться*) hide, get; *pf.* begin to beat; get clogged (T with)

**заб|ира́ть** [1], ⟨**~ра́ть**⟩, [-беру́, -рёшь; → ***брать***] take (*a.*, *coll.*, away); *в плен* capture (*a. fig.*), seize; arrest; (*отклониться*) turn, steer; **-ся** climb *or* creep (in, up); *тайно* steal in, penetrate; (*спрятаться*) hide; *далеко* get

**заби́|тый** [14] browbeaten, cowed, downtrodden; **~ть** → ***~ва́ть***; **~я́ка** *m/f* [5] bully, squabbler

**заблаго|вре́менно** in good time; in advance; **~вре́менный** [14] done ahead of time; timely; **~рассу́диться** [15; *impers.* Д with] think fit

**забл|уди́ться** [15] *pf.* lose one's way, go astray; **~у́дший** [17] *fig.* gone astray; **~ужда́ться** [1] be mistaken, err; **~ужде́ние** *n* [12] error, mistake; (*ложное мнение*) delusion; ***ввести́ в ~ужде́ние*** mislead

**забол|ева́ть** [1], ⟨**~е́ть**⟩ [8] fall sick *or* ill (of T), be taken ill with; *о боли* begin to ache; *su.*: **~ева́ние** *n* [12] → ***боле́знь***

**забо́р** *m* [1] fence

**забо́т|а** *f* [5] care (**о** П about, of), concern, anxiety, worry, trouble; ***без ~*** *жизнь* carefree; **~иться** [15], ⟨по-⟩ (**о** П) care (for), take care of, look after; worry, be anxious (about); **~ливый** [14 *sh.*] *хозяин* careful, provident; *по отношению к кому-л.* attentive, thoughtful, solicitous

**забр|а́сывать** [1] **1.** ⟨**~оса́ть**⟩ (T) (*заполнить*) fill up; *вопросами и т. д.* shower (T with); *камнями* pelt; **2.** ⟨**~о́сить**⟩ [15] throw, fling (*a. fig.*), cast; *дело*, *ребёнка и т. д.* neglect; **~а́ть** → ***заби-ра́ть***; **~еда́ть** [1], ⟨**~ести́**⟩ [25] wander *or* get (in[to], far); **~оса́ть**, **~о́сить** → ***~а́сывать***; **~о́шенный** [14] neglected; deserted; *ребёнок* unkempt

**забры́згать** [1] *pf.* splash; *грязью* bespatter

**заб|ыва́ть** [1], ⟨**~ы́ть**⟩ [-бу́ду, -бу́дешь] forget (o.s. **-ся** *перейти границу дозволенного*; *a.* nap, doze); **~ы́вчивый** [14 *sh.*] forgetful; absent-minded; **~ытьё** *n* [10; в -тьи́] (*беспамятство*) unconsciousness, swoon; (*дремота*) drowsiness; (*лёгкий сон*) slumber

**зава́л** *m* [1] obstruction, blockage; **~ивать** [1], ⟨**~и́ть**⟩ [13; -алю́, -а́лишь] fill *or* heap (up); cover; *дорогу* block, obstruct, close; *работой* overburden (with T); *экзамен coll.* fail; *дело* ruin; **-ся** fall; *стена* collapse

**зава́р|ивать** [1], ⟨**~и́ть**⟩ [13; -арю́, -а́ришь] brew, make (tea); pour boiling water (over); *coll. fig.* ***~и́ть ка́шу*** stir up trouble

**зав|еде́ние** *n* [12] establishment, institution; ***вы́сшее учё́бное ~еде́ние*** higher education(al) institution; **~е́довать** [7] (T) be in charge *or* the head *or* chief of, manage; **~е́домый** [14] undoubted; ***~е́домо зна́я*** being fully aware; ***дава́ть ~е́домо ло́жные показа́ния*** commit perjury; **~е́дующий** *m* [17] (T) chief, head; director; **~ести́** → ***~ози́ть***

**зав|ере́ние** *n* [12] assurance; **~е́рить** → ***~еря́ть***; **~ерну́ть** → ***~ёртывать***; **~ерте́ть** [11; -ерчу́, -е́ртишь] *pf.* start turning (*v/i.* **-ся**); **~ёртывать** [1], ⟨**~ерну́ть**⟩ [20] wrap up; *за угол* turn (*a.* up; *кран и т. д.* off); screw up; (*зайти*) drop in; **~ерша́ть** [1], ⟨**~ерши́ть**⟩ [16 *e.*; -шу́, -ши́шь, -шённый] finish, complete; **-ся** *успехом* crown; **~ерше́ние** *n* [12] conclusion, end; completion; **~еря́ть** [28], ⟨**~е́рить**⟩ [13] assure (В/**в** П a p. of); attest, authenticate; *подпись* witness a signature

**заве́|са** *f* [5] *секретности fig.* veil; ***дымова́я ~са*** smoke screen; **~сить** → ***~шивать***; **~сти́** → ***заводи́ть***

3

**заве́т** *m* [1] *Bibl.* (**Ве́тхий** Old, **Но́вый** New) Testament; **~ный** [14]: **~ная мечта́** cherished ambition

**заве́|шивать** [1], ⟨**~сить**⟩ [15] cover, hang with, curtain

**завеща́|ние** *n* [12] testament, will; **~ть** [1] *im*(*pf.*) leave, bequeath

**завзя́тый** [14] *coll. курильщик* inveterate; incorrigible

**зав|ива́ть** [1], ⟨**~и́ть**⟩ [-вью́, -вьёшь; → **вить**] *волосы* wave, curl; wind round; **~и́вка** *f* [5; *g/pl.*: -вок] wave (*in hair*)

3

**зави́д|ный** [14; -ден, -дна] enviable; **~овать** [7], ⟨по-⟩ envy (Д/**в** П *a p. a th.*), be envious (of)

**зави́н|чивать** [1], ⟨**~ти́ть**⟩ [15 *e.*; -нчу́, -нти́шь] screw up, down *or* tight

**зави́с|еть** [11] depend (**от** Р on); **~имость** *f* [8] dependence; **в ~имости от** (Р) depending on; **~имый** [14 *sh.*] dependent

**зави́ст|ливый** [14 *sh.*] envious; **´~ь** *f* [8] envy (**к** Д of, at)

**зави|то́й** [14] curly; **~то́к** *m* [1; -тка́] curl, ringlet; **´~ть** → **~ва́ть**

**завлад|ева́ть** [1], ⟨**~е́ть**⟩ [8] (Т) take possesion *or* hold of, seize, capture (*a. fig.*)

**завл|ека́тельный** [14; -лен, -льна] enticing, tempting; **~ека́ть** [1], **~е́чь** [26] (al)lure, entice, tempt

**заво́д**[1] *m* [1] works, factory, plant, mill (**на** П/В at/to); **ко́нский ~** stud farm

**заво́д**[2] *m* [1] winding mechanism; **~и́ть** [15], ⟨**завести́**⟩ [25] **1.** (*приводить*) take, bring, lead; **2.** *дело* establish, set up, found; *привычку, дружбу и т. д.* form, contract; *машину и т. д.* get, procure, acquire; *разговор и т. д.* start (*a. мотор*), begin; *собаку и т. д.* keep; **3.** *часы* wind up; **-ся**, ⟨**завести́сь**⟩ appear; (*возбудиться*) become excited; get, have; **~но́й** [14] *tech.* starting; *игрушка* mechanical; *человек* full of beans; **~ский**, **~ско́й** [16] works…; factory…

**заво|ева́ние** *n* [12] conquest; *fig.* (*mst. pl.*) achievement(s); **~ева́тель** *m* [4] conqueror; **~ёвывать** [1], ⟨**~ева́ть**⟩ [6] conquer; (*добиться*) win, gain

**зав|ози́ть** [15], ⟨**~езти́**⟩ [24] take, bring, drive; *coll.* deliver

**завол|а́кивать** [1], ⟨**~о́чь**⟩ [26] obscure; *слезами* cloud; get cloudy

**завор|а́чивать** [1], ⟨**~оти́ть**⟩ [15] turn (up, down); roll up

**завсегда́тай** *m* [3] habitué, regular

**за́втра** tomorrow

**за́втрак** *m* [1] breakfast (**за** Т at; **на** В, **к** Д for); **~ать** [1], ⟨по-⟩ (have *or* take) breakfast

**за́втрашний** [15] tomorrow's; **~ день** tomorrow; *fig.* (near) future

**за́вуч** *m* [1; *g/pl.*: -ей] (= **заве́дующий учёбной ча́стью**) director of studies (*at school*)

**завыва́ть** [1], ⟨**завы́ть**⟩ [22] howl

**зав|яза́ть** [3], ⟨**~я́знуть**⟩ [21] sink in, stick; *coll. fig.* get involved in; **~яза́ть** → **~я́зывать**; **~я́зка** *f* [5; *g/pl.*: -зок] string, tie; *начало* beginning, starting point; *романа и т. д.* opening; **~я́зывать** [1], ⟨**~яза́ть**⟩ [3] tie (up), bind, fasten; *fig. разговор и т. д.* begin, start; **´~язь** *bot. f* [8] ovary; **~я́нуть** → **вя́нуть**

**заг|ада́ть** → **~а́дывать**; **~а́дить** → **~а́живать**; **~а́дка** *f* [5; *g/pl.*: -док] riddle, enigma; **~а́дочный** [14; -чен, -чна] enigmatic; mysterious; **~а́дывать**, ⟨**~ада́ть**⟩ [1] *загадку* propose; *coll. замыслить* plan; **~а́живать** [1], ⟨**~а́дить**⟩ [15] soil, befoul

**зага́р** *m* [1] sunburn, tan

**загво́здка** *f* [5; *g/pl.*: -док] hitch; snag

**заги́б** *m* [1] bend; *страницы* dogear; **~а́ть** [1], ⟨**загну́ть**⟩ [20] bend, fold (over), turn up; *pf. coll.* exaggerate

**загла́в|ие** *n* [12] title; **~ный** [14] title…; **~ная бу́ква** capital letter

**загла́|живать** [1], ⟨**~дить**⟩ [15] smooth; *утюгом* press, iron; *fig.* make up (*or* amends) for; expiate

**загл|о́хнуть** → **гло́хнуть 2.** **~о́хший** [17] *сад* overgrown; **~уша́ть** [1], ⟨**~уши́ть**⟩ [16] → **глуши́ть 2.**

**загля́|дывать** [1], ⟨**~ну́ть**⟩ [19] glance; peep in; *в книгу* look (through, up); look in; (*навестить*) drop in *or* call (**к** Д on); **~дываться** [1], ⟨**~де́ться**⟩ [11] (**на** В) gaze, gape *or* stare (at), feast

one's eyes *or* gloat (up[on])
**заг|на́ть** → **~оня́ть**; **~ну́ть** → **~иба́ть**; **~ова́ривать** [1], ⟨**~овори́ть**⟩ [13] **1.** *v/i.* begin *or* start to talk *or* speak; **2.** *v/t.* tire with one's talk; **3. -ся** *слишком увлечься разговором* be carried away by a conversation; ramble, be confused; **~овор** *m* [1] conspiracy, plot; **~овори́ть** → **~ова́ривать**; **~ово́рщик** *m* [1] conspirator, plotter
**заголо́вок** *m* [1; -вка] heading, headline
**заго́н** *m* [1] enclosure; **быть в ~е** *fig.* be kept down, suffer neglect
**загоня́ть** [28], ⟨**загна́ть**⟩ [-гоню́, -го́нишь; → **гнать**] drive (in, off); (*измучить*) exhaust, fatigue
**загор|а́живать** [1], ⟨**~оди́ть**⟩ [15, 15 *e.*; -рожу́, -ро́ди́шь] enclose, fence in; *дорогу* block (up); **-ся** *от ветра* protect; **~а́ть** [1], ⟨**~е́ть**⟩ [9] sunbathe; become sunburnt; **-ся** catch fire; begin to burn; *свет* light up; *от гнева* blaze up; *щёки* blush; *спор* break out; **~е́лый** [14] sunburnt; **~оди́ть** → **~а́живать**; **~о́дка** *coll. f* [5; *g/pl.*: -док] fence, enclosure; partition; **´~одный** [14] *дом и т. д.* country; out-of-town
**загот|а́вливать** [1] & **~овля́ть** [28], ⟨**~о́вить**⟩ [14] prepare; *впрок* store up; lay in; **~о́вка** *f* [5; *g/pl.*: -вок] procurement, storage, laying in
**загра|ди́тельный** [14] *mil. огонь* barrage; **~жда́ть** [1], ⟨**~ди́ть**⟩ [15 *e.*; -ажу́, -ади́шь; -аждённый] block, obstruct; **~жде́ние** *n* [12] block(ing), obstruction; **про́волочное ~жде́ние** barbed-wire entanglement
**грани́ц|а** *f* [5] *collect.* foreign countries; **жить ~ей** live abroad
**заграни́чный** [14] foreign, from abroad
**загре|ба́ть** [1], ⟨**~сти́**⟩ → **грести́**
**загро́бн|ый** [14] beyond the grave; *голос* sepulchral; **~ый мир** the other world; **~ая жизнь** the beyond
**загромо|жда́ть** [1], ⟨**~зди́ть**⟩ [15 *e.*; -зжу́, -зди́шь; -мождённый] block (up), (en)cumber, crowd; *fig.* cram, overload
**загрубе́лый** [14] callous, coarse
**загр|ужа́ть** [1], ⟨**~узи́ть**⟩ [15 *e.*; -ужу́, -у́зи́шь] (T) load; *coll. работой* keep busy, assign work to; be occupied with work; **~у́зка** *f* [5] loading; workload; **~ыза́ть** [1], ⟨**~ы́зть**⟩ [24; *pt. st.*; загры́зенный] bite (*fig.* worry) to death
**загрязн|е́ние** *n* [12] pollution, contamination; **~е́ние окружа́ющей среды́** environmental pollution; **~я́ть** [28], ⟨**~и́ть**⟩ [13] (**-ся** become) soil(ed); pollute(d), contaminate(d)
**ЗАГС**, **загс** *m* [1] (*abbr.* **отде́л за́писей а́ктов гражда́нского состоя́ния**) registry office
**зад** *m* [1; на -у́; *pl. e.*] back, rear *or* hind part; buttocks; *животного* rump; *pl.* things already known *or* learned; **~ом наперёд** back to front
**зад|а́бривать** [1], ⟨**~о́брить**⟩ [13] (B) cajole, coax, wheedle
**зад|ава́ть** [5], ⟨**~а́ть**⟩ [-да́м, -да́шь, *etc.*, → **дать**; зада́л, -а́, -о́; за́данный (за́дан, -а́, -о)] *задание* set, assign; *вопрос* ask; **~ава́ть тон** set the tone; *coll.* **я тебе́ ~а́м!** you'll catch it!; **-ся** [*pt.*: -да́лся, -ла́сь] **це́лью (мы́слью)** take it into one's head to do, set one's mind on doing
**зада́в|ливать** [1], ⟨**~и́ть**⟩ [14] crush; P *машиной* run over, knock down; (*задушить*) strangle
**зада́ние** *n* [12] assignment, task; *важное* mission; **дома́шнее ~** homework
**зада́ток** *m* [1; -тка] advance, deposit; *pl.* instincts, inclinations
**зада́|ть** → **~ва́ть**; **~ча** *f* [5] problem (*a. math.*); task; (*цель*) object(ive), aim, end; **~чник** *m* [1] book of (mathematical) problems
**задв|ига́ть** [1], ⟨**~и́нуть**⟩ [20] push (into, *etc.*); *ящик* shut; *задвижку* slide; **~и́жка** *f* [5; *g/pl.*: -жек] bolt; **~ижно́й** [14] sliding (*door*)
**зад|ева́ть** [1], ⟨**~е́ть**⟩ [-е́ну, -е́нешь; -е́тый] **1.** be caught (**за** B on), brush against, touch; *fig.* hurt, wound; *med.* affect; **~е́ть за живо́е** cut to the quick; **2.** *coll.* (*подевать*) mislay; **~е́лывать**, ⟨**~е́лать**⟩ [1] block up, close (up); wall up

З

**задёр|гать** [1] *pf. coll.* worry, harrass; **~гивать** [1], ⟨**~нуть**⟩ [20] *занавеску* draw

**задержа́ние** *n* [12] arrest

**задéрж|ивать** [1], ⟨**~áть**⟩ [4] detain, delay; arrest; *выплату и т. д.* withhold, stop; (*замедлить*) slow down; **-ся** stay; be delayed; linger; stop; be late; **~ка** *f* [5; *g/pl.*: -жек] delay; (*a. tech.*) trouble, setback

**задёрнуть** → ***задёргивать***

**задéть** → ***задевáть***

**зад|ирáть** [1], ⟨**~рáть**⟩ [-дерý, -рёшь; → ***драть***] lift or pull (up); *impf.* provoke, pick a quarrel (with); ***~(и)рáть нос*** be haughty, turn up one's nose

**зáдний** [15] back, hind; *mot.* reverse (*gear*)

**задóлго** (***до*** Р) long before

**зад|олжáть** [1] *pf.* (*наделать долгов*) run into debt; (Д) owe; **~óлженность** *f* [8] debts *pl.*

**зáдом** backward(s); → ***зад***

**задóр** *m* [1] fervo(u)r; ***ю́ношеский ~*** youthful enthusiasm; **~ный** [14; -рен, -рна] fervent, ardent

**задрáть** → ***задирáть***

**зад|увáть** [1], ⟨**~ýть**⟩ [18] blow out; *ветер* begin to blow; *impf.* blow (in)

**задý|мать** → ***~мывать***; **~мчивый** [14 *sh.*] thoughtful, pensive; **~мывать**, ⟨**~мать**⟩ [1] conceive; (*решить*) resolve, decide; (*намереваться*) plan, intend; **-ся** think (***о*** П about, of); reflect, meditate (***над*** Т on); ***глубокó ~маться*** be lost in thought; *coll.* (*колебаться*) hesitate; **~ть** → ***~вать***

**задушéвный** [14] sincere, intimate

**зад|ыхáться** [1], ⟨**~охнýться**⟩ [21] gasp, pant; choke (*a. fig.* ***от*** Р with)

**заéзд** *m* [1] *sport* lap, round

**заезжáть** [1], ⟨**заéхать**⟩ [-éду, -éдешь; -езжáй!] call on (*on the way*), drive, go *or* come (***к*** Д to [see, *etc.*] *or* ***в*** В into); pick up, fetch (***за*** Т)

**заём** *m* [1; зáйма] loan

**за|éхать** → ***~езжáть***; ***~жáть*** → ***~жимáть***; ***~жéчь*** → ***~жигáть***

**заж|ивáть** [1], ⟨**~и́ть**⟩ [-ивý; -вёшь; зáжил, -á, -о] **1.** heal, (*затягиваться*) close up; **2.** begin to live

**зáживо** alive

**зажигá|лка** *f* [5; *g/pl.*: -лок] (cigarette) lighter; **~ние** *n* [12] ignition; ***~тельный*** [14] incendiary; *fig.* stirring, rousing; **~ть** [1], ⟨**зажéчь**⟩ [26 г/ж: -жгý, -жжёшь; → ***жечь***] light, kindle (*a. fig.*); *спичку* strike; *свет* turn on; **-ся** light (up); catch fire; become enthusiastic (Т about)

**заж**и́**м** *m* [1] clamp; *tech.* terminal; *fig.* suppression; **~áть** [1], ⟨**зажáть**⟩ [-жмý, -жмёшь; -жáтый] press, squeeze; clutch; *fig. критику* suppress; *рот* stop; *нос* hold; *уши* close

**зажи́|точный** [14; -чен, -чна] prosperous; **~точность** *f* [8] prosperity; **~ть** → ***~вáть***

**зазевáться** [1] stand gaping at

**зазем|лéние** *n* [12], **~ля́ть** [28], ⟨**~ли́ть**⟩ [13] *el.* ground, *Brt.* earth

**зазна|вáться** [5], ⟨**~ться**⟩ [1] be(come) conceited; put on airs

**зазóр** *m* [1] *tech.* clearance, gap

**заз|óрный** [14; -рен, -рна] shameful, scandalous; **~рéние** *n* [12]: ***без ~рéния*** (***сóвести***) without remorse *or* shame

**зазýбр|ивать** [1] → ***зубри́ть***; **~ина** *f* [5] notch

**заи́грывать** *coll.* [1] (**с** Т) flirt, make advances (to); (*заискивать*) ingratiate o.s. (with)

**зáйк|а** *m/f* [5] stutterer; **~áние** *n* [12] stuttering, stammering; **~áться** [1], *once* ⟨**~нýться**⟩ [20] stutter; stammer; *coll.* (give a) hint (**о** П at), suggest, mention in passing

**заи́мствова|ние** *n* [12] borrowing; loan word (*a.* ***~нное слóво***); **~ть** [7] *impf.*, *a.* ⟨**по-**⟩ borrow, adopt

**заиндевéлый** [14] frosty, covered with hoar-frost

**заинтересóв|ывать(ся)** [1], ⟨**~áть(ся)**⟩ [7] (be[come]) interest(ed in Т), rouse a p.'s interest (***в*** П in); ***я ~ан*(а)** I am interested (***в*** П in)

**заи́скивать** [1] ingratiate o.s. (***у*** Р with)

**зайти́** → ***заходи́ть***

**закавкáзский** [16] Transcaucasian

**закады́чный** [14] bosom (friend)

**зака́з** *m* [1] order; ***дать, сде́лать ~*** (***на*** В/Д) place an order (for… with); ***на ~*** to order; *об одежде* (made) to measure; **~а́ть → ~ывать**; **~но́й** [14]: ***~но́е*** (***пись-мо́***) registered (letter); **~чик** *m* [1] customer; **~ывать** [1], ⟨**~а́ть**⟩ [3] order (***се-бе́*** o.s.)

**зака́л|ка** *f* [5] tempering; *fig.* hardening; (*выносливость*) endurance, hardiness; **~я́ть** [28], ⟨**~и́ть**⟩ [13] temper; *fig.* harden; **~ённый** *металл* tempered (*metal*); *fig.* hardened

**зак|а́лывать** [1], ⟨**~оло́ть**⟩ [17] kill, slaugter; *штыком и т. д.* stab; *булавкой* pin (up); ***у меня́ ~оло́ло в боку́*** I have a stitch in one's side; **~а́нчивать** [1], ⟨**~о́нчить**⟩ [16] finish, conclude; **~а́пывать** [1], ⟨**~опа́ть**⟩ [1] bury; *яму* fill up

**зака́т** *m* [1] sunset; *fig.* decline; **~ывать** [1] **1.** ⟨**~а́ть**⟩ roll up; **2.** ⟨**~и́ть**⟩ [15] roll (***в, под*** В into, under, *etc.*); *глаза* screw up; ***~и́ть истéрику*** go into hysterics; **-ся** roll; *о солнце* set (*of sun etc.*); *fig.* end; *смехом, слезами* burst (out laughing *or* into tears)

**зака́шлять** [28] *pf.* start coughing; **-ся** have a fit of coughing

**заква́ска** *f* [5] ferment; leaven; *fig.* breed

**заки́|дывать** [1] **1.** ⟨**~да́ть**⟩ [1] *coll. яму* fill up, cover; *fig. вопросами* ply; *камнями* pelt; **2.** ⟨**~нуть**⟩ [20] throw (***в, на, за*** В in[to], on, over, behind, *etc.*); *сеть* throw out; *голову* throw back; fling, cast; ***~нуть у́дочку*** *fig.* put out feelers

**зак|ипа́ть** [1], ⟨**~ипе́ть**⟩ [10; -пи́т] begin to boil; → ***кипе́ть***; **~иса́ть** [1], ⟨**~и́с-нуть**⟩ [21] turn sour

**закла́д|ка** *f* [5; *g/pl.*: -док] bookmark; **~ывать** [1], ⟨**заложи́ть**⟩ [16] put (*a.* in, *etc.*), lay (*a.* out [*сад*], the foundation [*фундамент*] of, found), place; (*задеть*) mislay; (*загромоздить*) heap, pile (T with); wall up; *в ломбард* pawn; *страницу* mark, put in; *impers. нос, уши* stuff

**закл|ёвывать** [1], ⟨**~ева́ть**⟩ [6 *e.*; -клюю́, -юёшь] *fig. coll.* bait, hector, torment; **~е́ивать** [1], ⟨**~е́ить**⟩ [13] glue *or* paste up (over); *конверт* seal; **~ёпка** *f* [5; *g/pl.*: -пок], **~ёпывать**, ⟨**~епа́ть**⟩ [1] rivet

**заклина́|ние** *n* [12] entreaty *mst. pl.*; **~ть** [1] entreat

**заключ|а́ть** [1], ⟨**~и́ть**⟩ [16 *e.*; -чу́, -чи́шь; -чённый] enclose, put; *в тюрьму* confine, imprison; conclude (= finish, with T; = infer, from ***из*** P, ***по*** Д – ***что***; *v/t.*: *договор* [= make] *мир и т. д.*); *impf.* (*a.* ***в себе́***) contain; **~а́ться** [1] consist (***в*** П in); (*заканчиваться*) end (T with); **~е́ние** *n* [12] confinement, imprisonment (*a. тюремное*); (*вывод*) conclusion; **~ённый** [14] prisoner; **~и́тель-ный** [14] final, concluding

**закля́тый** [14] sworn; ***~ враг*** enemy

**закол|а́чивать** [1], ⟨**~оти́ть**⟩ [15] drive in; *гвоздями* nail up; *досками* board up; **~до́вывать** [1], ⟨**~дова́ть**⟩ bewitch, charm; ***~до́ванный круг*** vicious circle; **~оти́ть → ~а́чивать**; **~о́ть → *зака́лы-вать***

**зако́лка** *f* [5; *g/pl.*: -лок] hairpin

**зако́н** *m* [1] law; (*правило*) rule; ***на-ру́шить ~*** break the law; ***по*** (***вопреки́***) ***~у*** according (contrary) to law; **~ность** *f* [8] legality, lawfulness; **~ный** [14; -о́нен, -о́нна] legal, lawful, legitimate

**законо|да́тель** *m* [4] legislator; **~да́-тельный** [14] legislative; **~да́тельство** *n* [9] legislation; **~ме́рность** *f* [8] regularity; **~ме́рный** [14; -рен, -рна] regular; normal; **~прое́кт** *m* [1] bill, draft

**зако́|нчить → *зака́нчивать***; **~па́ть → *зака́пывать***; **~пте́лый** [14] sooty; **~ре-не́лый** [14] deeprooted, inveterate, ingrained; **~рю́чка** *f* [5; *g/pl.*: -чек] *на письме* flourish; *fig.* hitch; **~у́лок** *m* [1; -лка] alleyway, (*Brt.*) (narrow) lane; *coll. уголок* nook; **~чене́лый** [14] numb with cold

**закра́|дываться** [1], ⟨**~сться**⟩ [25; *pt. st.*] creep in *mst. fig.*; **~шивать** [1], ⟨**~сить**⟩ [15] paint over

**закреп|ля́ть** [28], ⟨**~и́ть**⟩ [14 *e.*; -плю́, -пи́шь; -плённый] secure, fasten, (*a. phot.*) fix; *успехи* consolidate; assign (***за*** T to)

**закрепо|щáть** [1], ⟨**~стúть**⟩ [15 *e.*; -ощý, -остúшь; -ощённый] enserf
**закрóйщи|к** *m* [1], **~ца** *f* [5] cutter
**закругл|éние** *n* [12] rounding (off); curve; **~я́ть** [28], ⟨**~úть**⟩ [13] round (off); **-ся** *coll. joc.* round off
**закрý|чивать** [1], ⟨**~тúть**⟩ [15] turn (round, off, up); twist
**закр|ывáть** [1], ⟨**~ы́ть**⟩ [22] shut, close; *на замок* lock (up); *крышкой и т. д.* cover, hide; *кран* turn off; ***~ывáть глазá* (на** B) shut one's eyes (to); **~ы́тие** *n* [12] closing, shutting; ***врéмя ~ы́тия*** closing time; **~ы́ть** → ***~ывáть***; **~ы́тый** [14] closed; (*тайный*) secret; *платье* high-necked; ***в ~ы́том помещéнии*** indoor(s)
**закулúсный** [14] occuring behind the scenes; secret
**закуп|áть** [1], ⟨**~úть**⟩ [14] buy (*a.* in), purchase; **´~ка** *f* [5; *g/pl.*: -пок] purchase
**закупóр|ивать** [1], ⟨**~ить**⟩ [13] *бутылку* cork (up); *бочку* bung (up); **´~ка** *f* [5; *g/pl.*: -рок] corking; *med.* embolism
**закýпочн|ый** [14]: ***~ая ценá*** purchase price
**закýпщик** *m* [1] purchasing agent, buyer
**закýр|ивать** [1], ⟨**~úть**⟩ [13; -урю́, -ýришь] light a cigarette *etc.*; ***~ú(те)!*** have a cigar(ette)!
**закýс|ка** *f* [5; *g/pl.*: -сок] hors d'œuvres; ***на ~ку*** *a.* for the last bit; *coll.* as a special treat; **~очная** *f* [14] snackbar; **~ывать** [1], ⟨**~úть**⟩ [15] bite (*a.* one's lip[s]); take *or* have a snack; eat (s.th. [*with, after a drink*] T); ***~úть удилá*** *fig.* get the bit between one's teeth
**закýт|ывать**, ⟨**~ать**⟩ [1] wrap up
**зал** *m* [1] hall; room; ***спортúвный ~*** gymnasium
**зал|егáние** *n* [12] *geol.* deposit(ion); **~егáть** [1], ⟨**~éчь**⟩ [26; -ля́гу, -ля́жешь] *geol.* lie; *в засаду* hide; (*заболеть*) take to one's bed
**заледенéлый** [14] icy, ice cold; covered with ice
**зал|ежáлый** [14] stale, spoiled (by long storage); **~ёживаться** [1], ⟨**~ежáться**⟩ [4 *e.*; -жýсь, -жúшься] lie (too) long (*a.* goods, & spoil thus); **´~ежь** *f* [8] *geol.* deposit
**зал|езáть** [1], ⟨**~éзть**⟩ [24 *st.*] climb up, in(to) *etc.*; hide; (*проникнуть*) steal *or* get in(to); ***~éзть в кармáн*** pick s.o.'s pocket; ***~éзть в долгú*** run into debt; **~епля́ть** [28], ⟨**~епúть**⟩ [14] stop, close; (*заклеить*) glue *or* paste up; stick over; **~етáть** [1], ⟨**~етéть**⟩ [11] fly in(to), up, far, off, beyond; ***~етéть высокó*** rise in the world
**залé|чивать** [1], ⟨**~чúть**⟩ [16] heal; *coll.* doctor to death; **~чь** → ***~гáть***
**зал|úв** *m* [1] gulf, bay; **~ивáть** [1], ⟨**~úть**⟩ [-лью́, -льёшь; зáлúл, -á, -о; зáлúтый] (T) flood, overflow; pour (all) over, cover; (*вливать*) fill; *огонь* extinguish; **-ся** break into *or* shed (tears ***слезáми***), burst out (laughing ***смéхом***); *о птице* trill, warble; **~ивнóе** *n* [14] *su.* fish *or* meat in aspic; **~ивнóй** [14]: ***~ивнóй луг*** water-meadow; **~úть** → ***~ивáть***
**зал|óг** *m* [1] pledge (*a. fig.*); security; *gr.* voice; *fig.* guarantee; ***отдáть в ~óг*** pawn; ***под ~óг*** on the security; **~ожúть** → ***заклáдывать***, **~óжник** *m* [1], **~óжница** *f* [5] hostage
**залп** *m* [1] volley; salvo; ***вы́пить ´~ом*** at one draught; *прочитать* at one sitting; *произнести* without pausing for breath
**замá|зка** *f* [5] putty; **~зывать** [1], ⟨**~зать**⟩ [3] (*запачкать*) smear, soil; *краской* paint over; *щели* putty; *coll. fig.* veil, hush up; **~лчивать** [1], ⟨**замолчáть**⟩ [4 *e.*; -чý, -чúшь] conceal, keep secret; **~нивать** [1], ⟨**~нúть**⟩ [13; -маню́, -мáнишь] lure, decoy, entice; **~нчивый** [14 *sh.*] alluring, tempting; **~хиваться** [1], *once* ⟨**~хнýться**⟩ [20] lift one's arm (*etc.* T/**на** B against), threaten (with); **~шка** *coll. f* [5; *g/pl.*: -шек] *mst. pl.* habit, manner
**замедл|éние** *n* [12] slowing down, delay; **~я́ть** [28], ⟨**´~ить**⟩ [13] slow down, reduce; *скорость* decelerate; *развитие* retard
**замé|на** *f* [5] substitution (T/P of/for), replacement (T by); *law* commutation; substitute; **~нúмый** [14 *sh.*] replacea-

ble, exchangeable; **~нитель** *m* [4] substitute; **~нять** [28], ⟨**~нить**⟩ [13; -меню, -мéнишь; -менённый] replace (T by), substitute (T/B *p.*, *th.* for); *law* commute (for, into)

**замерéть** → ***замирáть***

**замерзá|ние** *n* [12] freezing; ***тóчка ~ния*** freezing point; ***на тóчке ~ния*** *fig.* at a standstill; **~ть** [1], ⟨замёрзнуть⟩ [21] freeze (up); be frozen (to death, *a. coll.* = feel very cold)

**зáмертво** (as, if) dead, unconscious

**замести́** → ***заметáть***

**замести́|тель** *m* [4] deputy; vice…; **~ть** → ***замещáть***

**заме|тáть** [1], ⟨**~сти́**⟩ [25; -т-: -метý] sweep (up); *снегом* drift, cover; *дорогу* block up; *следы* wipe out

**замé|тить** → ***~чáть***; **~тка** *f* [5; *g/pl.*: -ток] mark; (*запись*) note; *в газете* paragraph, short article, item; ***взять на ~тку*** make a note (of); **~тный** [14; -тен, -тна] noticeable, perceptible; marked, appreciable; *успех*, *человек* outstanding, remarkable; **~тно** *a.* one (it) can (be) see(n), notice(d); **~чáние** *n* [12] remark, observation; *pl.* criticism; *выговор* reproof, rebuke; **~чáтельный** [14; -лен, -льна] remarkable, outstanding; wonderful; noted (T for); **~чáть** [1], ⟨**~тить**⟩ [15] notice, mark; (*сказать*) observe, remark

**замешáтельств|о** *n* [9] confusion, embarrassment; ***в ~е*** confused, disconcerted, embarrased; ***привести́ в ~о*** throw into confusion

**зам|éшивать**, ⟨**~ешáть**⟩ [1] involve, entangle; ***~éшан(а) в*** (П) *a.* mixed up with; **~éшкаться** [1] *pf.* linger, tarry; **~ещáть** [1], ⟨**~ести́ть**⟩ [15 *e.*; -ещý, -ести́шь; -ещённый] replace; substitute; act for, deputize; *вакансию* fill; **~ещéние** *n* [12] substitution (*a. math.*, *chem.*); replacement; deputizing; filling

**зам|инáть** *coll.* [1], ⟨**~я́ть**⟩ [-мнý, -мнёшь; -мя́тый] put a stop to; ***~я́ть разговóр*** change the subject; **-ся** falter, halt; be(come) confused; **~и́нка** *f* [5; *g/pl.*: -нок] hesitation (*in speech*); hitch; **~ирáть** [1], ⟨**~ерéть**⟩ [12; зáмер, -рлá, -о] be(come) *or* stand stockstill, transfixed (**от** P with); stop; *о звуках* fade, die away; ***у меня́ сéрдце ~ерло*** my heart stood still

**зáмкнутый** [14 *sh.*] exclusive; *жизнь* unsociable; *человек* reserved; → ***замыкáть***

**зáм|ок**[1] *m* [1; -мка] castle; ***воздýшные ~ки*** castles in the air

**зам|óк**[2] *m* [1; -мкá] lock; *на ожерелье* clasp; ***на ~кé*** *or* ***под ~кóм*** under lock and key

**замóл|вить** [14] *pf.*: ***~вить слóв(éчк)о*** *coll.* put in a word (**за** В, **о** П for a *p.*); **~кáть** [1], ⟨**~кнуть**⟩ [21] fall silent, stop (speaking *etc.*), cease, break off; *шаги и т. д.* die away *or* off; **~чáть** [4 *e.*; -чý, -чи́шь] *pf.* **1.** *v/i.* → ***~кáть***; **2.** *v/t.* → ***замáлчивать***

**замор|áживать** [1], ⟨**~óзить**⟩ [15] freeze, ice; **~óзки** *m/pl.* [1] (light morning *or* night) frost; **~ский** [16] oversea(s)

**зáмуж** → ***выдавáть & выходи́ть***; **~ем** married (***за*** T to, *of women*); **~ество** *n* [9] marriage (*of women*); **~ний** [15]: ***~няя*** (***жéнщина***) married (woman)

**замурóв|ывать** [1], ⟨**~áть**⟩ [7] immure; wall up

**замýч|ивать** [1], ⟨**~ить**⟩ [16] torment the life out of; bore to death; *измотать* fatigue, exhaust

**зáмш|а** *f* [5], **~евый** [14] chamois, suede

**замыкá|ние** *n* [12]: ***корóткое ~ние*** *el.* short circuit; **~ть** [1], ⟨замкнýть⟩ [20] (en)close; **-ся** isolate o.s. (**в** В *or* T in); ***-ся в себé*** become unsociable

**зáм|ысел** *m* [1; -сла] project, plan, design; scheme, idea; **~ы́слить** → ***~ышля́ть***; **~ыслова́тый** [14 *sh.*] intricate, ingenious; fanciful; **~ышля́ть** [28], ⟨**~ы́слить**⟩ [15] plan, intend; contemplate; *план и т. д.* conceive

**замя́ть(ся)** → ***заминáть(ся)***

**зáнав|ес** *m* [1] curtain (*a. thea.*); **~éсить** → ***~éшивать***; **~éска** *f* [5; *g/pl.*: -сок] (*window*) curtain; **~éшивать** [1], ⟨**~éсить**⟩ [15] curtain

**зан|áшивать** [1], ⟨**~оси́ть**⟩ [15] wear out; **~ести́** → ***~оси́ть***

**занимá|тельный** [14; -лен, -льна] inter-

З

esting, entertaining, amusing; *человек* engaging; **~ть** [1], ⟨заня́ть⟩ [займу́, -мёшь; за́нял, -а́, -о; заня́вший; за́нятый (за́нят, -а́, -о)] **1.** borrow (**у** P from); **2.** (T) occupy, (*a. time*) take; *место, пост* fill, take up; interest, engross, absorb; *развлекать* entertain; **-ся** [заня́лся́, -ла́сь] **1.** occupy *or* busy o.s. (with); (*a.* sport) engage in; *кем-то* attend (to); *учиться* learn, study; set about, begin to; **2.** *v/i. огонь* blaze *or* flare up; *заря* break, dawn; → *a.* ***заря́***

**за́ново** anew, afresh

3

**зано́|за** *f* [5] splinter; **~зи́ть** [15 *e.*; -ожу́, -ози́шь] *pf.* get a splinter (in)

**зано́с** *m* [1] drift; **~и́ть** [15] **1.** ⟨занести́⟩ [24; -с-: -су́, -сёшь] bring, carry; *в протокол и т. д.* note down, enter, register; (*a. impers.*) (be) cast, get; *дороги* drift, cover, block up; *руку* lift, raise; ***куда́ её занесло́?*** where on earth has she got to?; **2.** *pf.*, → ***зана́шивать***; **~чивый** [14 *sh.*] arrogant, haughty

**зану́д|а** *coll. m/f* [5] bore; **~ливый** [14 *sh.*] boring, tiresome

**заня́т|ие** *n* [12] occupation, work, business; excercise (T of); *pl.* studies, lessons; **~ный** [14; -тен, -тна] → *coll.* ***занима́тельный***; **~ь(ся)** → ***занима́ть(ся)***; **~о́й** [14] busy; **~ый** [14; за́нят, -а́, -о] occupied, busy, engaged

**заодно́** together; at one; (*попутно*) at the same time, besides, too

**заостр|я́ть** [28], ⟨~и́ть⟩ [13] sharpen; *fig.* stress; **-ся** become pointed *or* sharp

**зао́чн|ик** [1] *univ.* student taking a correspondence course; **~ый** [14] in a *p.'s* absence; ***~ое обуче́ние*** instruction by correspondence; ***~ое реше́ние*** *n law* judg(e)ment by default

**за́пад** *m* [1] west; ♀ the West; → ***восто́к***; **~а́ть** [1], ⟨запа́сть⟩ [25; -па́л, -а] fall behind; *в память и т. д.* impress (*a.* **на** *or* **в** B on); **~ный** [14] west(ern, -erly)

**западн|я́** *f* [6; *g/pl.*: -не́й] trap; ***попа́сть в ~ю́*** *mst. fig.* fall into a trap

**запа́|здывать**, ⟨запозда́ть⟩ [1] be late (**на** B for), be slow (**с** T with); **~ивать** [1], ⟨~я́ть⟩ [28] solder (up); **~ко́вывать** [1], ⟨~кова́ть⟩ [7] pack (up), wrap up

**запа́л** *m* [1] *mil., mining* touchhole, fuse; impulse; fit of passion; **~ьчивый** [14 *sh.*] quick-tempered, irascible

**запа́с** *m* [1] stock (*a. fig., слов и т. д.* = store, supply, (*a. mil.*) reserve); ***у нас два часа́ в ~е*** we have two hours in hand; ***про ~*** in store *or* reserve; **~а́ть** [1], ⟨~ти́⟩ [24 -с-: -су́, -сёшь]; **-ся**, ⟨~ти́сь⟩ provide o.s. (with T); **~ливый** [14 *sh.*] provident; **~но́й**, **~ный** [14] spare (*a. tech.*); reserve… (*a. mil.*); ***~ный вы́ход*** emergency exit; **~ть** → ***запада́ть***

**за́п|ах** *m* [1] smell, odo(u)r, scent; **~ахивать** [1] **1.** ⟨~аха́ть⟩ [3] plow (*Brt.* plough) *or* turn up; **2.** ⟨~ахну́ть⟩ [20] wrap (**-ся** o.s.) (**в** B, T in); *дверь* slam; **~ая́ть** → ***~а́ивать***

**запе|ва́ла** *m/f* [5] leader (of choir); *coll.* initiator, leader; **~ва́ть** [1], ⟨~́ть⟩ [-пою́, -поёшь; -пе́тый] start singing; *impf.*: lead a choir; **~ка́нка** *f* [5; *g/pl.*: -нок] baked pudding; **~ка́ть** [1], ⟨~́чь⟩ [26] bake; **-ся** *кровь* clot, coagulate; *губы* crack; **~ре́ть** → ***запира́ть***

**запеча́т|ать** → ***~ывать***; **~лева́ть** [1], ⟨~ле́ть⟩ [8] embody, render; *в памяти* imprint, impress (**в** П on), retain; **~ывать**, ⟨~ать⟩ [1] seal (up)

**запе́чь** → ***запека́ть***

**запи|ва́ть**, ⟨~́ть⟩ [1 -пью́, -пьёшь; → ***пить***] wash down (T with), drink *or* take (with, after); *pf.* take to drink

**зап|ина́ться** [1], ⟨~ну́ться⟩ [20] *rare* stumble (***за*** *or* **о** B over, against); *о речи* falter, pause, hesitate; **~и́нка** *f* [5]: ***без ~и́нки*** fluently, smoothly

**запира́|тельство** *n* [9] disavowal, denial; **~ть** [1], ⟨запере́ть⟩ [12; за́пер, -ла́, -о; за́пертый (за́перт, -а́, -о)] lock (up; *a.* ***~ть на ключ, замо́к***); **-ся** lock o.s. in

**запис|а́ть** → ***~ывать***; **~ка** *f* [5; *g/pl.*: -сок] note, short letter; *докладная* memorandum; *pl.* *воспоминания* notes, memoirs; *труды* transactions, proceedings; **~но́й** [14]: ***~на́я кни́жка*** notebook; **~ывать** [1], ⟨~а́ть⟩ [3] write down, note (down); record (*тж. на плёнку и т. д.*); *в члены и т. д.* enter,

enrol(l), register; **-ся** enrol(l), register, enter one's name; make an appointment (***к врачу́*** with a doctor); **´~ь** *f* [8] entry; enrol(l)ment; registration; record(ing)
**запи́ть** → ***запива́ть***
**запи́х|ивать** *coll.* [1], ⟨**~а́ть**⟩ [1], *once* ⟨**~ну́ть**⟩ [20] cram, stuff
**запла́ка|нный** [14 *sh.*] tearful, in tears, tear-stained; **~ть** [3] *pf.* begin to cry
**запла́та** *f* [5] patch
**запле́сневелый** [14] mo(u)ldy
**запле|та́ть** [1], ⟨**~сти́**⟩ [25 -т-: -плету́, -тёшь] braid, plait; **-ся**: ***но́ги ~та́ются*** be unsteady on one's legs; ***язы́к ~та́ется*** slur, falter
**заплы́|в** *m* [1] *water sports* round, heat; **~ва́ть¹** [1], ⟨**~ть**⟩ [23] swim far out
**заплы|ва́ть²** [23], ⟨**~ть**⟩ *об отёке* swell, puff up
**запну́ться** → ***запина́ться***
**запове́д|ник** *m* [1] reserve, preserve; ***госуда́рственный ~ник*** national park; sanctuary; **~ный** [14] prohibited, reserved; *мечта и т. д.* secret, precious; **~ь** ('za-) *f* [8] *Bibl.* commandment
**запод|а́зривать** [1], ⟨**~о́зрить**⟩ [13] suspect (**в** П of)
**запозда́|лый** [14] (be) late(d), tardy; **~ть** → ***запа́здывать***
**запо́|й** *m* [3] periodic hard drinking
**заполз|а́ть** [1], ⟨**~ти́**⟩ [24] creep into, under
**заполн|я́ть** [28], ⟨**~ить**⟩ [13] fill (up); *бланк* fill out (*Brt.* in)
**заполя́р|ный** [14] polar, transpolar; **~ье** *n* [10; *g/pl.*: -ий] polar regions
**запом|ина́ть** [1], ⟨**~нить**⟩ [13] remember, keep in mind; *стихи и т. д.* memorize; **~ина́ющий** [17]: ***~ина́ющее устро́йство*** computer memory, storage; **-ся** (Д) remember, stick in one's mind
**за́понка** *f* [5; *g/pl.*: -нок] cuff link; collar button (*Brt.* stud)
**запо́р** *m* [1] bar, bolt; lock; *med.* constipation; ***на ~е*** bolted, locked
**запороши́ть** [16 *e.*; *3rd p. only*] powder *or* cover (with snow Т)
**запоте́лый** *coll.* [14] moist, sweaty; *о стекле* misted
**заправ|и́ла** *m* [5] *coll.* boss, leader; **~ля́ть** [28], ⟨**~ить**⟩ [14] put, tuck (in); *блюдо* (Т) dress, season; *горючим* tank (up), refuel; **~ка** *f* [5; *g/pl.*: -вок] refuel(l)ing; seasoning, condiment; **~очный** [14]: ***~очная ста́нция*** *f* filling (gas) station; **~ский** [16] true, real
**запр|а́шивать** [1], ⟨**~оси́ть**⟩ [15] ask, inquire (**у** Р/**о** П for/about); (*a.* Р) request; *coll. цену* charge, ask (**с** Р)
**запре́|т** *m* [1] → ***~ще́ние***; ***наложи́ть ~т*** place a ban (**на** В on); **~ти́тельный** [14] prohibitive; **~ти́ть** → ***~щა́ть***; **~тный** [14] forbidden; ***~тная зо́на*** *mil.* restricted area; **~ща́ть** [1], ⟨**~ти́ть**⟩ [15 *e.*; -ещу́, -ети́шь; -ещённый] forbid, prohibit, ban; **~ще́ние** *n* [12] prohibition; *law* injunction
**заприхо́довать** [7] *pf.* enter, book
**запроки́|дывать** [1], ⟨**~нуть**⟩ [20] throw back
**запро́с** *m* [1] inquiry (**о** П about); *pl. потребности* needs, interests; **~и́ть** → ***запра́шивать***; **´~то** without formality
**запру́|да** *f* [5] dam, weir; **~живать** [1], ⟨**~ди́ть**⟩ **1.** [15 & 15 *e.*; -ужу́, -у́ди́шь] dam up; **2.** [15 *e.*; -ужу́, -у́ди́шь] *coll.* block up, crowd
**запр|яга́ть** [1], ⟨**~я́чь**⟩ [26 г/ж: -ягу́, -я́жешь; → ***напря́чь***] harness; **~я́тывать** [1], ⟨**~я́тать**⟩ [3] hide, conceal; put (away); **~я́чь** → ***запряга́ть***
**запу́г|ивать**, ⟨**~а́ть**⟩ [1] intimidate; **~анный** (in)timid(ated)
**за́пус|к** *m* [1] start; *ракеты* launching; **~ка́ть** [1], ⟨**~ти́ть**⟩ [15] **1.** neglect; **2.** *tech.* start, set going; *змея* fly; *ракету* launch; *coll.* (*a.* Т/**в** В) fling, hurl (s.th. at) put, thrust; **~те́лый** [14] desolate; **~ти́ть** → ***~ка́ть***
**запу́|тывать**, ⟨**~тать**⟩ [1] (**-ся** become, get) tangle(d, *etc.*); *fig.* confuse, perplex; complicate; *coll.* ***~таться в долга́х*** be deep in debt; **~танный** *тж.* intricate; ***~танный вопро́с*** knotty question; **~щенный** [14] deserted, desolate; neglected, uncared-for, unkempt
**запыха́ться** *coll.* [1] *pf.* pant, be out of breath

З

**запя́стье** *n* [10] wrist; *poet.* bracelet
**запята́я** *f* [14] comma; *coll.* snag
**зараб|а́тывать**, ⟨**~о́тать**⟩ [1] earn; ***~а́тывать на жи́знь*** earn one's living; **-ся** *coll.* overwork; work late *or* long; **´~отный** [14]: ***´~отная пла́та*** wages *pl.*; *служащего* salary; pay; **´~оток** [1; -тка] earnings *pl.*
**зара|жа́ть** [1], ⟨**~зи́ть**⟩ [15 *e.*; -ражу́, -рази́шь; -ражённый] infect (*a. fig.*); **-ся** become infected (T with), catch; **~же́ние** *n* [12] infection; ***~же́ние кро́ви*** blood poisoning
**зара́з** *coll.* at once; at one sitting
**зара́|за** *f* [5] infection; contagion; **~зи́тельный** [14; -лен, -льна] *mst. fig.* infectious; **~зи́ть** → ***~жа́ть***; **~зный** [14; -зен, -зна] infectious, contagious
**зара́нее** beforehand, in advance; ***~ ра́доваться*** (Д) look forward to
**зара|ста́ть** [1], ⟨**~сти́**⟩ [24; -сту́, -стёшь; → ***расти́***] be overgrown (with)
**за́рево** *n* [9] blaze, glow, gleam
**заре́з** *m* [1] *coll.* disaster; ***до ~у, по ~*** *coll.* (*need s.th.*) very badly
**заре|ка́ться** [1], ⟨**~́чься**⟩ [26] forswear, promise to give up; **~комендова́ть** [7]: ***~комендова́ть себя́*** (T) show o.s., prove o.s. (to be)
**заржа́вленный** [14] rusty
**зарисо́вка** *f* [5; *g/pl.*: -вок] drawing, sketch
**зарни́ца** *f* [5] summer (heat) lightning
**зар|оди́ть(ся)** → ***~ожда́ть(ся)***; **~о́дыш** *m* [1] embryo, f(o)etus, germ (*a. fig.*); ***подави́ть в ~о́дыше*** nip in the bud; **~ожда́ть** [1], ⟨**~оди́ть**⟩ [15 *e.*; -ожу́, -оди́шь; -ождённый] generate, engender; **-ся** arise; conception
**заро́к** *m* [1] vow, pledge, promise
**зарони́ть** [13; -роню́, -ро́нишь] *pf. fig.* rouse; infuse
**за́росль** *f* [8] underbrush; thicket
**зар|пла́та** *f* [5] *coll.* → ***~́аботный***
**заруб|а́ть** [1], ⟨**~и́ть**⟩ [14] kill; ***~и́(те) на носу́ (на лбу́, в па́мяти)!*** mark it well!
**зарубе́жный** [14] foreign
**зар|уби́ть** → ***~уба́ть***; **~у́бка** *f* [5; *g/pl.*: -бок] incision, notch; **~убцева́ться** [7] *pf.* cicatrize
**заруч|а́ться** [1], ⟨**~и́ться**⟩ [16 *e.*; -учу́сь, -учи́шься] (T) secure; ***~и́ться согла́сием*** obtain consent
**зар|ыва́ть** [1], ⟨**~ы́ть**⟩ [22] bury; ***~ы́ть тала́нт в зе́млю*** bury one's talent
**зар|я́** *f* [6; *pl.*: зо́ри, зорь, заря́м, зо́рям] (***у́тренняя***) ***~я́*** (*a. fig.*) dawn; ***вече́рняя ~я́*** evening glow; ***на ~е́*** at dawn *or* daybreak (*a.* ***с ~е́й***); *fig.* at the earliest stage *or* beginning; ***от ~и́ до ~и́*** from morning to night, all day (night); ***~я́ занима́ется*** dawn is breaking
**заря́|д** *m* [1] charge (*mil.*, *el.*); *fig. бодрости* store; **~ди́ть** → ***~жа́ть***; **~дка** *f* [5] *el.* charge, charging; *sport*: gymnastics *pl.*, exercises; **~жа́ть** [1], ⟨**~ди́ть**⟩ [15 & 15 *e.*; -яжу́, -я́ди́шь; -я́женный & -яжённый] *mil.*, *phot.* load; *el.* charge; *pl. coll.* set in, go on & on
**заса́|да** *f* [5] ambush; ***попа́сть в ~ду*** be ambushed; **~живать** [1], ⟨**~ди́ть**⟩ [15] plant (T with); *coll. в тюрьму* confine; *за работу и т. д.* compel (*to do s.th.*); **-ся**, *coll.* ⟨**засе́сть**⟩ [25; -ся́ду, -дешь; -се́л] sit down; *в засаде* hide, lie in ambush; (***за*** B) begin to, bury *o.s.* in
**заса́л|ивать** [1], ⟨**засоли́ть**⟩ [13; -олю́, -о́ли́шь, -о́ленный] salt; *мясо* corn
**зас|а́ривать** [1] & **засоря́ть** [28], ⟨**~ори́ть**⟩ [13] litter; *трубу и т. д.* clog; *сорняками* become weedy; ***~ори́ть глаз(а́)*** have (get) s.th. in one's eye(s)
**зас|а́сывать** [1], ⟨**~оса́ть**⟩ [-су́, -сёшь, -о́санный] suck in; *о болоте* engulf, swallow up
**заса́харенный** [14] candied, crystallized
**засвет|и́ть(ся)** [13; -све́тится] *pf.* light (up); **´~ло** by daylight; before dark
**засвиде́тельствовать** [7] *pf.* testify; attest, authenticate
**засе́|в** *m* [1] sowing; **~ва́ть** [1], ⟨**~ять**⟩ [27] sow
**заседа́|ние** *n* [12] *law, parl.* session; meeting; (*prp.*: in, at ***на*** П); **~тель** *m* [4]: ***наро́дный ~тель*** *approx.* juryman; **~ть** [1] **1.** be in session; sit; meet; **2.** ⟨**засе́сть**⟩ [-ся́ду, -дешь; -се́л] stick
**засе|ка́ть** [1], ⟨**~́чь**⟩ [26] **1.** [-сёк, -ла́; -сечённый] notch; *время* mark, note;

***∴чь на ме́сте преступле́ния*** catch red-handed
**засел|е́ние** *n* [12] settlement, colonization; **~я́ть** [28], ⟨**~и́ть**⟩ [13] people, populate; *дом* occupy, inhabit
**засе́|сть** → ***заса́живаться & ~да́ть* 2.**; **~чь** → ***~ка́ть***; **~ять** → ***~ва́ть***
**заси́|живать** [11], ⟨**~де́ть**⟩ [11] ***~женный*** [**му́хами**] flyblow(n); **-ся** sit *or* stay (too) long; sit up late
**заскору́злый** [14] hardened, calloused
**засло́н|ка** *f* [5; *g/pl.*: -нок] (stove) damper; *tech.* slide valve; **~я́ть** [28], ⟨**~и́ть**⟩ [13] shield, screen; *свет* shut off; stand in s.o.'s light; *fig.* put into the background
**заслу́|га** *f* [8] merit, desert; ***он получи́л по ~гам*** (it) serves him right; **~женный** [14] merited, (well-)deserved, just; *человек* worthy, hono(u)red (*a. in titles*); **~живать** [1], ⟨**~жи́ть**⟩ [16] merit, deserve (*impf. a.* P); *coll.* earn
**заслу́ш|ивать**, ⟨**~ать**⟩ [1] hear; **-ся** listen (T, P to) with delight
**засм|а́триваться** [1], ⟨**~отре́ться**⟩ [9; -отрю́сь, -о́тришься] (**на** B) feast one's eyes ([up]on), look (at) with delight
**засме́|ивать** [1; -ею́, -ёшь], ⟨**~я́ть**⟩ [27 *e.*] ridicule
**засну́ть** → ***засыпа́ть*** *2*
**зас|о́в** *m* [1] bar, bolt; **~о́вывать** [1], ⟨**~у́нуть**⟩ [20] put, slip, tuck; (*задеть куда-то*) mislay; **~оли́ть** → ***~а́ливать*** *2*
**засор|е́ние** *n* [12] littering, obstruction, clogging up; **~и́ть**, **~я́ть** → ***заса́ривать***
**засоса́ть** → ***заса́сывать***
**засо́х|ший** [17] dry, dried up; *bot.* dead; **~нуть** → ***засыха́ть***
**за́спанный** *coll.* [14] looking sleepy
**заста́|ва** *f* [5]: ***пограни́чная ~ва*** frontier post; **~ва́ть** [5], ⟨**~ть**⟩ [-а́ну, -а́нешь] *дома и т. д.* find; *неожиданно* surprise; ***~ть на ме́сте преступле́ния*** catch red-handed; **~вля́ть** [28], ⟨**~вить**⟩ [14] **1.** compel, force, make; ***~вить ждать*** keep waiting; ***~вить замолча́ть*** silence; **2.** (T) block (up); fill; **~ре́лый** [14] inveterate; *med.* chronic; **~ть** → ***~ва́ть***
**заст|ёгивать** [1], ⟨**~егну́ть**⟩ [20; -ёгнутый] button up (*a.* **-ся** o.s. up); *пряжкой, крючками* buckle, clasp, hook (up); **~ёжка** *f* [5; *g/pl.*: -жек] fastener; clasp, buckle
**застекл|я́ть** [28], ⟨**~и́ть**⟩ [13] glaze, fit with glass
**засте́нчивый** [14 *sh.*] shy, bashful
**засти|га́ть** [1], ⟨**∴гнуть**⟩, ⟨**∴чь**⟩ [21 -г-: -и́гну, -и́гнешь; -и́г, -и́гла; -и́гнутый] surprise, catch; ***∴гнуть врасплo̸х*** take unawares
**заст|ила́ть** [1], ⟨**~ла́ть**⟩ [-телю́, -те́лешь; за́стланный] cover; *глаза, небо* cloud
**засто́|й** *m* [3] stagnation; *econ.* depression; **~йный** [14] stagnant, chronic; **~льный** [14] table…; drinking; **~я́ться** [-ою́сь, -ои́шься] *pf. перед картиной и т. д.* stand *or* stay too long; *о воде и т. д.* be(come) stagnant *or* stale
**застр|а́ивать** [1], ⟨**~о́ить**⟩ [13] build on (up, over); **~aхо́вывать** [1], ⟨**~ахова́ть**⟩ [7] insure; *fig.* safeguard; **~ева́ть** [1], ⟨**~я́ть**⟩ [-я́ну, -я́нешь] stick; *coll.* (*задержаться*) be delayed; **~е́ливать** [1], ⟨**~ели́ть**⟩ [13; -елю́, -е́лишь; -е́ленный] shoot, kill; **~е́льщик** *m* [1] skirmisher; *fig.* instigator; initiator; **~о́ить** → ***~а́ивать***; **~о́йка** *f* [5; *g/pl.*: -о́ек] building (on); ***пра́во на ~о́йку*** building permit; **~я́ть** → ***~ева́ть***
**за́ступ** *m* [1] spade
**заступ|а́ться** [1], ⟨**~и́ться**⟩ [14] (***за*** B) take s.b.'s side; protect; intercede for; **∴ник** *m* [1], **∴ница** *f* [5] defender, protector; **∴ничество** *n* [9] intercession
**засты|ва́ть** [1], ⟨**∴ть**⟩ [-ы́ну, -ы́нешь] cool down; *жир и т. д.* congeal; *на месте* stiffen, stand stockstill; ***кровь ∴ла у него в жи́лах*** his blood ran cold
**засу́нуть** → ***засо́вывать***
**за́суха** *f* [5] drought
**засу́ч|ивать** [1], ⟨**~и́ть**⟩ [16] turn *or* roll up
**засу́ш|ивать** [1], ⟨**~и́ть**⟩ [16] dry (up); **~ливый** [14 *sh.*] dry
**засчи́т|ывать**, ⟨**~а́ть**⟩ [1] take into account; include, reckon
**зас|ыпа́ть** [1] **1.** ⟨**~ы́пать**⟩ [2] (T) fill up; (*покрыть*) cover; *fig.* heap, ply, over-

З

whelm; *цветами и т. д.* strew; **2.** ⟨**~нуть**⟩ [20] fall asleep; **~ыхать** [1], ⟨**~óхнуть**⟩ [21] dry up; wither

**затá|ивать** [1], ⟨**~ить**⟩ [13] conceal, hide; *дыхание* hold; *обиду* bear; **~ённый** *a.* secret

**зат|áпливать** [1] **~опля́ть** [28], ⟨**~опи́ть**⟩ [14] **1.** *печь* light; **2.** flood; *судно* sink; **~áптывать** [1], ⟨**~оптáть**⟩ [3] trample, tread (down); **~áскивать** [1] **1.** ⟨**~аскáть**⟩ [1] wear out; **~áсканный** worn, shabby; *выражение* hackneyed; **2.** ⟨**~ащи́ть**⟩ [16] drag, pull (off, away); (*задеть куда-л.*) mislay; *в гости* take s.o. to one's (*or* somebody's) place

**затв|ердевáть** [1], ⟨**~ердéть**⟩ [8] harden

**затвóр** *m* [1] *винтовки* lock, bolt; *phot.* shutter; **~я́ть** [28], ⟨**~и́ть**⟩ [13; -орю́, -óришь; -óренный] shut, close; **-ся** shut o.s. up

**зат|евáть** *coll.* [1], ⟨**~éять**⟩ [27] start, undertake; ***что он ~éял?*** what is he up to?; **~éйливый** [14 *sh.*] ingenious, intricate; **~екáть** [1], ⟨**~éчь**⟩ [26] flow (in, *etc.*); (*распухнуть*) swell up; *ноги* be(-come) numb, be asleep

**затéм** then; *по этой причине* for that reason, that is why; ***~ чтóбы*** in order to (*or* that)

**затемн|éние** *n* [12] darkening; *mil.* blackout; *med. в лёгких* dark patch; **~я́ть** [28], ⟨**~и́ть**⟩ [13] darken, overshadow, (*a. fig.*) obscure

**затер|éть** → ***затирáть***; **~я́ть** [28] *pf.* lose; **-ся** get *or* be lost; *о вещи* disappear; *селение и т. д.* lost *or* inconspicuous in the midst of

**затесáться** [3] (**в** В) worm o.s. into

**затé|чь** → ***затекáть***; **~я** *f* [6] plan, undertaking; escapade; **~ять** → ***~вáть***

**зат|ирáть** *coll.* [1], ⟨**~ерéть**⟩ [12] *mst. fig.* impede, give no chance to get on; **~ихáть** [1], ⟨**~и́хнуть**⟩ [21] become silent *or* quiet, stop (speaking, *etc.*); *звук* die away, fade; (*успокоиться*) calm down, abate; **~и́шье** *n* [10] lull, calm

**заткнýть** → ***затыкáть***

**затм|евáть** [1], ⟨**~и́ть**⟩ [14 *e.*; *no* 1st *p. sg.*; -ми́шь], **~éние** *n* [12] eclipse; ***на негó нашлó ~éние*** his mind went blank

**затó** but (then, at the same time), but on the other hand

**затовáривание** *comm. n* [12] glut

**затоп|и́ть**, **~ля́ть** → ***затáпливать***; **~тáть** → ***затáптывать***

**затóр** *m* [1] obstruction; ***~ ýличного движéния*** traffic jam

**заточ|áть** [1], ⟨**~и́ть**⟩ [16 *e.*; -чý, -чи́шь, -чённый] *old use* confine, imprison; **~éние** *n* [12] confinement, imprisonment

**затрá|вливать** [1], ⟨**~ви́ть**⟩ [14] hunt *or* chase down; *fig.* persecute; bait; **~гивать** [1], ⟨**затрóнуть**⟩ [20] touch (*a. fig.*, [up]on); affect; ***затрóнуть чьё-л. самолю́бие*** wound s.o.'s pride

**затрá|та** *f* [5] expense, outlay; **~чивать** [1], ⟨**~тить**⟩ [15] spend

**затрóнуть** → ***затрáгивать***

**затрудн|éние** *n* [12] difficulty, trouble; embarrassment; ***в ~éнии*** *a.* at a loss; **~и́тельный** [14; -лен, -льна] difficult, hard; embarrassing; ***~и́тельное положéние*** predicament; **~я́ть** [28], ⟨**~и́ть**⟩ [13] embarrass, (cause) trouble; *что-л.* render (more) difficult; *кого-л.* inconvenience; *что-л.* aggravate, complicate; **-ся** *a.* be at a loss (**в** П, Т for)

**зату|мáнивать(ся)** [1], ⟨**~мáнить(ся)**⟩ [13] fog, dim, cloud; **~хáть** [1], ⟨**~́хнуть**⟩ [21] die away, fade; *огонь* go out; **~шёвывать** [1], ⟨**~шевáть**⟩ [6] shade; *fig. coll.* veil; gloss over; **~ши́ть** [16] → ***туши́ть***

**зáтхлый** [14] musty, fusty

**зат|ыкáть** [1], ⟨**~кнýть**⟩ [20] stop up, plug, (*пробкой*) cork; ***~кнýть когó-л. за пóяс*** *coll.* outdo s.o.; **~ы́лок** *m* [1; -лка] back of the head

**заты́чка** *f* [5; *g/pl.*: -чек] stopper, plug

**затя́|гивать** [1], ⟨**~нýть**⟩ [19] tighten, draw tight; (*засосать*) draw in, *etc.*; (*покрыть*) cover; *рану* close; *время* protract, delay; ***~гивать пéсню*** *coll.* strike up a song; **~жка** *f* [5; *g/pl.*: -жек] protraction, delaying; ***сдéлать ~жку*** draw, inhale, take a whiff; **~жнóй** [14] long, lengthy, protracted

**зау|ны́вный** [14; -вен, -вна] doleful, mournful; **~ря́дный** [14; -ден, -дна] common(place), ordinary, mediocre; **~се́ница** *f* [5] hangnail

**зау́треня** *f* [6] matins *pl.*

**зау́ч|ивать** [1], ⟨**~и́ть**⟩ [16] memorize

**захва́т** *m* [1] seizure, capture; usurpation; **~ывать** [1], ⟨**~и́ть**⟩ [15] grasp; take (along with one, *a.* **с собо́й**); (*завладеть*) seize, capture; usurp; *fig.* absorb, captivate, thrill; (*застигнуть*) catch; *дух* take (away [*breath*], by [*surprise*], *etc.*); **~нический** [16] aggressive; **~чик** *m* [1] invader, aggressor; **~ывать** → **~и́ть**

**захвора́ть** [1] *pf.* fall sick *or* ill

**захл|ёбываться** [1], ⟨**~ебну́ться**⟩ [20] choke, stifle (Т, **от** Р with); *fig. от гнева* be beside o.s.; **~ёстывать** [1], ⟨**~естну́ть**⟩ [20; -хлёснутый] swamp, overwhelm; flow over; **~о́пывать(ся)** [1], ⟨**~о́пнуть(ся)**⟩ [20] slam, bang

**захо́д** *m* [1] (**со́лнца** sun)set; *в порт* call; *ae.* approach; **~и́ть** [5], ⟨**зайти́**⟩ [зайду́, -дёшь; *g. pt.*: зайдя́; → **идти́**] go *or* come in *or* to (see, *etc.*), call *or* drop in (**к** Д, **в** В on, at); pick up, fetch (**за** Т); *naut.* call, enter; *куда-то* get; *за угол* turn, *ширму и т. д.* go behind (**за** В); *astr.* set; **речь зашла́ о** (П) (we, *etc.*) began (came) to (*or* had a) talk (about)

**захолу́ст|ный** [14] remote, provincial; **~ье** *n* [10] out-of-the-way place

**захуда́лый** [14] *coll.* shabby, impoverished

**зацеп|ля́ть** [28], ⟨**~и́ть**⟩ [14] (*a.* **за** В) catch, hook on, grapple; (*соединить*) fasten; **-ся** → **задева́ть**

**зачаро́в|ывать** [1], ⟨**~а́ть**⟩ [7] charm, enchant

**зачасти́|ть** [15; -щу́, -сти́шь; -и́вший] *pf.* take to doing; begin to visit often (**в го́сти и т. д.**); **~л дождь** it began to rain heavily

**зачасту́ю** *coll.* often, frequently

**зача́|тие** *n* [12] conception; **~ток** *m* [1; -тка] embryo; rudiment; **~точный** [14] rudimentary; **~ть** [-чну́, -чнёшь; зача́л, -á, -o; зача́тый (зача́т, -á, -o)] *pf.* conceive

**заче́м** why, wherefore, what for; **~то** for some reason or other

**зач|ёркивать** [1], ⟨**~еркну́ть**⟩ [20; -чёркнутый] cross out, strike out; **~ёрпывать** [1], ⟨**~ерпну́ть**⟩ [20; -че́рпнутый] scoop, draw up; *суп* ladle; **~ерстве́лый** [14] stale; **~е́сть** → **~и́тывать**; **~ёсывать** [1], ⟨**~еса́ть**⟩ [3] comb (back); **~ёт** *m* [1] reckoning; *educ.* test; credit; *coll.* **э́то не в ~ёт** this does not count

**зач|и́нщик** *m* [1] instigator; **~исля́ть** [28], ⟨**~и́слить**⟩ [13] enrol(l), enlist; *в штат* take on the staff; *comm.* enter; **~и́тывать** [1], ⟨**~е́сть**⟩ [25 -т-: -чту́, -чтёшь; → **проче́сть**] reckon, charge, account; *educ.* credit; **~и́тывать**, ⟨**~ита́ть**⟩ [1] read (to, aloud); *coll. взятую книгу* not return; **-ся** (*увлечься*) be(come) absorbed (Т in); go on reading for too long

**заш|ива́ть** [1], ⟨**~и́ть**⟩ [-шью́, -шьёшь; → **шить**] sew up; **~нуро́вывать** [1], ⟨**~нурова́ть**⟩ [7] lace (up); **~то́панный** [14] darned

**защёлк|а** *f* [5; *g/pl.*: -лок] latch; **~ивать** [1], ⟨**~нуть**⟩ [20] snap, latch

**защем|ля́ть** [28], ⟨**~и́ть**⟩ [14 *e.*; - емлю́, -еми́шь; -емлённый] pinch, jam; *impers. fig.* ache

**защи́|та** *f* [5] defense (*Brt.* -nce), protection, cover; *sport*, *law* the defense (-nce); **~ти́ть** → **~ща́ть**; **~тник** *m* [1] defender; protector; *law* advocate (*a. fig.*), counsel for the defense (-nce); *sport* (full)back; **~тный** [14] protective, safety…; *цвет* khaki…; *шлем* crash; **~ща́ть** [1], ⟨**~ти́ть**⟩ [15; -ищу́, -ити́шь; -ищённый] (**от** Р) defend (from, against); *от дождя и т. д.* protect (from); uphold, back, stand up for; advocate; *диссертацию* maintain, support; *impf. law* defend, plead (for)

**заяв|и́ть** → **~ля́ть**; **~ка** *f* [5; *g/pl.*: -вок] application (for **на** В); claim; request; **~ле́ние** *n* [12] declaration, statement; (*просьба*) petition, application (for **о** П); **~ля́ть** [28], ⟨**~и́ть**⟩ [14] (*a.* о П) declare, announce, state; *права* claim; (*сообщить*) notify, inform

З

**зая́длый** *coll.* [14] → ***завзя́тый***

**зая́|ц** *m* [1; за́йца] hare; *coll.* stowaway; *в автобусе и т. д.* bilker; **~чий** [18] hare('s)…; ***~чья губа́*** harelip

**зва́|ние** *n* [12] *mil.* rank (*тж. академическое*); *чемпиона и т. д.* title; standing; **~ный** [14] invited; **~ть** [зову́, зовёшь; звал, -а́, -о; (…) зва́нный (зван, -а́, -о)] **1.** 〈по-〉 call; invite ([*a.* ***~ть в го́сти***] **к** Д, **на** В to); **2.** 〈на-〉 (Т) (be) called; ***как Вас зову́т?*** what is your (first) name?; ***меня́ зову́т Петро́м*** or ***Пётр*** my name is Peter

З

**звезда́** *f* [5; *pl.* звёзды, *etc. st.*] star (*a. fig.*); ***морска́я ~*** *zo.* starfish

**звёзд|ный** [14] star…, stellar; *небо* starry; *ночь* starlit; **~очка** *f* [5; *g/pl.*: -чек] starlet; asterisk

**звен|е́ть** [9], 〈за-, про-〉 ring, jingle, clink; ***у меня́ ~и́т в уша́х*** my ears are ringing

**звено́** *n* [9; *pl.*: зве́нья, -ьев] link; *fig.* team, section, *производства* branch

**звери́н|ец** *m* [1; -нца] menagerie; **~ый** [14] animal; *fig.* savage, brutal; → ***зве́рский***

**звerово́дство** *n* [9] fur-farming

**звéр|ский** [16] → ***звери́ный***; *fig.* brutal; *coll. mst. adv.* (*очень*) awful(ly), dog(-tired); **~ство** [9] brutality; *pl.* atrocities; **~ь** *m* [4; *from g/pl. e.*] (wild) animal, beast; *fig.* brute

**звон** *m* [1] ring, jingle, peal, chime; **~а́рь** *m* [4 *e.*] bell ringer; rumo(u)rmonger; **~и́ть** [13], 〈по-〉 ring (*v/t.* **в** В), chime, peal; (Д) telephone, call up; ***вы не туда́ звони́те*** you've got the wrong number; **~кий** [16; зво́нок, -нка́, -о; *comp.*: зво́нче] sonorous, clear; resonant; *gr.* voiced; **~о́к** *m* [1; -нка́] bell; (*звук*) ring

**звук** *m* [1] sound; ***пусто́й ~*** empty words; **~ово́й** [14] sound…; **~оза́пись** *f* [8] sound recording; **~онепроница́емый** [14] soundproof; **~оопера́тор** *m* [1] *cine.* sound producer

**звуч|а́ние** *n* [12] sounding; **~а́ть** [4 *e.*; 3rd *p. only*], 〈про-〉 (re)sound; *звонок* bell, ring; **~ный** [14; -чен, -чна́, -о] sonorous, clear; resonant

**звя́к|ать** [1], 〈~нуть〉 [20] jingle, tinkle

**зги**: (*only in phr.*) ***ни зги не ви́дно*** it is pitch-dark

**зда́ние** *n* [12] building

**зде|сь** (*of place*) here; (*on mail*) local; ***~сь нет ничего́ удиви́тельного*** there is nothing surprising in this; **~шний** [15] local; ***я не ~шний*** I am a stranger here

**здоро́в|аться** [1], 〈по-〉 (**с** Т) greet *or* salute (o.a.); wish good morning, *etc.*; ***~аться за́ руку*** shake hands; **~о!**[1] hi!, hello!; **´~о**[2] awfully; well done; **~ый** [14 *sh.*] *com.* healthy (*a. su.*), sound (*a. fig.*); *пища* wholesome; *климат* salubrious; P strong; in good health; **бу́дь(те) ~(ы)!** good-by(e)!, good luck!; (*ваше здоровье!*) your health!; **~ье** *n* [10] health; ***как ва́ше ~ье?*** how are you?; ***за ва́ше ~ье!*** your health!, here's to you!; ***на ~ье!*** good luck (health)!; **е́шь(те) на ~ье!** help yourself, please!

**здра́в|ница** *f* [5] health resort, sanatorium; **~омы́слящий** [17] sane, sensible; **~оохране́ние** *n* [12] public health service; **~ствовать** [7] be in good health; **~ствуй(те)!** hello!, hi!, good morning! (*etc.*); *при знакомстве* how do you do?; **~ый** [14 *sh.*] → ***здоро́вый***; *fig.* sound, sane, sensible; ***~ый смысл*** common sense; ***в ~ом уме́*** in one's senses; ***~ и невреди́м*** safe and sound

**зе́бра** *f* [5] zebra

**зев** *m* [1] *anat.* pharynx; **~а́ка** *m/f* [5] gaper; **~а́ть** [1], *once* 〈~ну́ть〉 [20] yawn; ***~а́ть по сторона́м*** stand about gaping; ***не ~а́й!*** look out!; **~о́к** *m* [1; -вка́] yawn; **~о́та** *f* [5] yawning

**зелен|е́ть** [8], 〈за-, по-〉 grow, turn *or* be green; *impf.* (*a.* **-ся**) appear *or* show green; **~ова́тый** [14 *sh.*] greenish

**зелён|ый** [14; зе́лен, -а́, -о] green (*a. fig.*), verdant; ***~ая у́лица*** *fig.* green light; ***~ юне́ц*** *coll.* greenhorn

**зе́л|ень** *f* [8] verdure; green; *cul.* potherbs, greens *pl.*; **~ье** *n* [10] *coll.* potion, alcoholic drink

**земе́льный** [14] land…; ***~ уча́сток*** plot of land

**землевладе́|лец** *m* [1; -льца] landowner; **~ние** *n* [12] land ownership

**земледе́л|ец** *m* [1; -льца] farmer; **~ие** *n*

[12] agriculture, farming; **~ьческий** [16] agricultural

**земле|мéр** *m* [1] (land)surveyor; **~пóльзование** *n* [12] land tenure; **~трясéние** *n* [12] earthquake; **~черпáлка** *f* [5; *g/pl.*: -лок] dredger, excavator

**землúстый** [14 *sh.*] earthy; *цвет лица* ashy, sallow

**земл|я́** *f* [6; *ac/sg.*: зéмлю; *pl.*: зéмли, земéль, зéмлям] earth (as planet **2я́**); land; (*поверхность, почва*) ground, soil; **на ~ю** to the ground; **~я́к** *m* [1 *e.*] (fellow) countryman; **~янúка** *f* [5] (wild) strawberry, -ries *pl.*; **~я́нка** *f* [5; *g/pl.*: -нок] *mil.* dugout; **~янóй** [14] earth(en); **~яны́е рабóты** excavations

**земновóдный** [14] amphibious

**земнóй** [14] (of the) earth, terrestrial; earthly; *fig.* earthy, mundane

**зенúт** *m* [1] zenith (*a. fig.*); **~ный** [14] *mil.* anti-aircraft…

**зенúц|а** *f* [5]: **беречь как ~у óка** cherish

**зéркал|о** *n* [9; *pl. e.*] looking glass, mirror (*a. fig.*); **~ьный** [14] *fig.* (dead-)smooth; **~ьное стеклó** plate glass

**зерн|úстый** [14 *sh.*] grainy, granular; **~ó** *n* [9; *pl.*: зёрна, зёрен, зёрнам] grain (*a. coll.*), corn (*a. fig.*), seed; **~ó úстины** grain of truth; **кóфе в зёрнах** coffee beans; **~овóй** [14] grain…; *su. pl.* cereals

**зефúр** *m* [1] sweetmeat (*of egg-white, sugar and gelatin(e)*)

**зигзáг** *m* [1], **~ообрáзный** [14; -зен, -зна] zigzag

**зим|á** *f* [5; *ac/sg.*: зúму; *pl. st.*] winter (T in [the]; **на** B for the); **~ний** [15] winter…, wintry; **~овáть** [7], ⟨за-, пере-⟩ winter, hibernate

**зия́ть** [28] gape

**злак** *m* [1] *pl.* gramineous plants; **хлéбные ~и** *pl.* cereals

**злáто…** *obs. or poet.* gold(en)

**злить** [13], ⟨обо-, разо-⟩ anger, make angry; (*раздражать*) vex, irritate; **~ся** be(come) *or* feel angry (**на** B with); be in a bad temper

**зло** *n* [9; *pl. gen.* зол *only*] evil; (**меня́**) **~ берёт** it annoys me

**злóб|а** *f* [5] malice, spite; rage; **~а дня** topic of the day; **~ный** [14; -бен, -бна] spiteful, malicious; **~однéвный** [14; -вен, -вна] topical, burning; **~ствовать** [7] → **злúться**

**злов|éщий** [17 *sh.*] ominous; **~óние** *n* [12] stench; **~óнный** [14; -óнен, -óнна] stinking, fetid; **~рéдный** [14; -ден, -дна] pernicious, noxious

**злодé|й** *m* [3] villian; **~йский** [16] *преступление* vile, outrageous; *замысел и т. д.* malicious; **~йство** *n* [9], **~я́ние** *n* [12] outrage, villainy, crime

**злой** [14; зол, зла, зло] wicked, evil; *язык, действие* malicious, spiteful; angry (with **на** B); *собака* fierce; *нрав* severe; **~ гéний** evil genius

**зло|кáчественный** [14 *sh.*] *med.* malignant; **~ключéние** *n* [12] misfortune; **~намéренный** [14 *sh.*] malevolent; **~пáмятный** [14; -тен, -тна] rancorous; **~полýчный** [14; -чен, -чна] unfortunate, ill-fated; **~рáдный** [14; -ден, -дна] gloating

**злословú|е** *n* [12], **~ть** [14] malicious gossip, backbiting

**злóст|ный** [14; -тен, -тна] malicious, spiteful; malevolent; *закоренелый* inveterate; **~ь** *f* [8] spite, rage

**зло|счáстный** [14; -тен, -тна] → **~полýчный**

**злоумы́шленник** *m* [1] plotter; malefactor

**злоупотреб|лéние** *n* [12], **~ля́ть** [28], ⟨**~úть**⟩ [14 *e.*; -блю́, -бúшь] (T) *властью, доверием* abuse; *спиртным* drink too much

**зме|úный** [14] snake('s), serpent('s), serpentine; **~úться** [13] meander, wind (o.s.); **~й** *m* [3]: **воздýшный ~й** kite; **~я́** *f* [6; *pl. st.*: змéи, змей] snake, serpent (*a. fig.*)

**знак** *m* [1] sign, mark; *дружбы и т. д.* token; symbol; (*предзнаменование*) omen; (*значок*) badge; signal; **дорóжный ~** road sign; **~и** *pl.* **препинáния** punctuation marks; **в ~** (P) in token *or* as a sign of

**знакóм|ить** [14], ⟨по-⟩ introduce (B/**с** T a *p.* to); *a.* ⟨о-⟩ acquaint (**с** T with); **-ся** (**с** T) *p.*: meet, make the acquaintance

of, (*a. th.*) become acquainted with; *th.*: familiarize o.s. with, go into; **~ство** *n* [9] acquaintance (-ces *pl.*); **~ый** [14 *sh.*] familiar, acquainted (**с** T with); know; *su.* acquaintance; **~ьтесь, ...,** meet…
**знамена́тель** *m* [4] denominator; **~ный** [14; -лен, -льна] memorable, remarkable; (*важный*) significant, important
**знаме́н|ие** *n* [12]: ***~ие вре́мени*** sign of the times; **~и́тость** *f* [8] fame, renown; *p.*: celebrity; **~и́тый** [14 *sh.*] famous, renowned, celebrated (T by, for); **~ова́ть** [7] *impf.* mark, signify
**зна́мя** *n* [13; *pl.*: -мёна, -мён] banner, flag; *mil.* standard; colo(u)rs
**зна́ни|е** *n* [12] (*a. pl.* ~я) knowledge; ***со ~ем де́ла*** capable, competently
**зна́т|ный** [14; -тен, -тна́, -о] *род и т. д.* noble; **~о́к** *m* [1 *e.*] expert; *ценитель* connoisseur
**знать**¹ [1] know; ***дать ~*** (Д) let know; ***дать себя́ (о себе́) ~*** make itself felt (send news); ***кто его́ зна́ет*** goodness knows
**знать**² *f* [8] *hist.* nobility, notables *pl.*
**знач|е́ние** *n* [12] meaning, sense; *math.* value; significance, importance (*vb.*: ***име́ть*** be of); **~и́тельный** [14; -лен, -льна] considerable; large; (*важный*) important, significant; **~и́ть** [16] mean, signify; (*иметь значение*) matter; ***~и́т*** consequently, so; well (then); **-ся** be mentioned, be registered; *impers.* (it) say(s); **~о́к** *m* [1; -чка́] badge; (*пометка*) sign
**зноби́т|ь**: ***меня́ ~*** I feel shivery
**зной** *m* [3] heat, sultriness; **~ный** [14; зно́ен, зно́йна] sultry, hot
**зоб** *m* [1] crop, craw (*of birds*); *med.* goiter (-tre)
**зов** *m* [1] call
**зо́дчество** *n* [9] architecture
**зола́** *f* [5] ashes *pl.*
**золо́вка** *f* [5; *g/pl.*: -вок] sister-in-law (*husband's sister*)
**золоти́|стый** [14 *sh.*] golden; **~ть** [15 *e.*; -очу́, -оти́шь], ⟨по-, вы́-⟩ gild
**зо́лот|о** *n* [9] gold; ***на вес ~а*** worth its weight in gold; **~о́й** [14] gold(en) (*a. fig.*); ***~о́е дно*** gold mine; ***~о́й запа́с*** *econ.* gold reserves; ***~ы́е ру́ки*** golden hands; ***~а́я середи́на*** golden mean
**золочёный** [14] gilt, gilded
**Зо́лушка** *f* [5; *g/pl.*: -шек] Cinderella
**зо́н|а** *f* [5] zone; **~а́льный** [14] zonal, regional
**зонд** *m* [1] probe, sound; **~и́ровать** [7] sound; ***~и́ровать по́чву*** *fig.* explore the ground
**зонт**, **~ик** *m* [1] umbrella; sunshade; ***складно́й ~ик*** telescopic umbrella
**зоо́|лог** *m* [1] zoologist; **~логи́ческий** [16] zoological; **~ло́гия** *f* [7] zoology; **~па́рк** *m* [1] zoo(logical garden)
**зо́ркий** [16; зо́рок, -рка́, -о; *comp.*: зо́рче] sharp-sighted (*a. fig.*); observant, watchful, vigilant
**зрачо́к** *m* [1; -чка́] *anat.* pupil
**зре́л|ище** *n* [11] sight; spectacle; show; **~ость** *f* [8] ripeness; *о человеке* maturity; **~ый** [14; зрел, -а́, -о] ripe, mature; ***по ~ому размышле́нию*** on reflection
**зре́ни|е** *n* [12] (eye)sight; ***по́ле ~я*** field of vision, eyeshot; *fig.* horizon; ***обма́н ~я*** optical illusion; ***то́чка ~я*** point of view; standpoint, angle (*prp.*: ***с то́чки ~я = под угло́м ~я*** from …)
**зреть** [8], ⟨со-, вы́-⟩ ripen, mature
**зри́тель** *m* [4] spectator, onlooker, observer; **~ный** [14] visual, optic; ***~ный зал*** hall, auditorium; ***~ная па́мять*** visual memory
**зря** *coll.* in vain, to no purpose, (all) for nothing; ***~ ты э́то сде́лал*** you should not have done it
**зря́чий** [17] sighted (*opp. blind*)
**зуб** *m* [1; *from g/pl. e.*; зу́бья, зу́бьев] tooth; *tech. a.* cog; ***до ~о́в*** to the teeth; ***не по ~а́м*** too tough (*a. fig.*); ***сквозь ~ы*** through clenched teeth; ***име́ть ~ (на*** B) have a grudge against; **~а́стый** [14 *sh.*] *fig.* sharptongued; **~е́ц** *m* [1; -бца́] *tech.* → ***зуб***; **~и́ло** *n* [9] chisel; **~но́й** [14] tooth, dental; ***~но́й врач*** *m* dentist; ***~на́я боль*** toothache; ***~на́я щётка*** toothbrush; **~овраче́бный** [14]: ***~овраче́бный кабине́т*** dental surgery
**зу́бр** *m* [1] European bison; *fig.* diehard; *coll.* pundit
**зубр|ёжка** *f* [5] cramming; **~и́ть 1.** [13],

⟨за-⟩ notch; ***зазу́бренный*** jagged; **2.** [13; зубрю́, зубри́шь], ⟨вы́-, за-⟩ [зазу́бренный] cram, learn by rote
**зу́бчатый** [14] *tech.* cog (wheel)…, gear…; jagged
**зуд** *m* [1], **~е́ть** *coll.* [9] itch; urge; *fig.* complain constantly, talk boringly
**зу́ммер** *m* [1] buzzer
**зы́б|кий** [16; зы́бок, -бка́, -о; *comp.*: зы́бче] unsteady, unstable (*a. fig.*) vague; **~ь** *f* [8] ripples *pl.*
**зы́чный** [14; -чен, -чна; *comp.*: -чнее] loud, shrill
**зя́б|нуть** [21], ⟨(пр)о-⟩ feel chilly; **~ь** *f* [8] winter tillage *or* cold
**зять** *m* [4; *pl. e.*: зятья́, -ьёв] son- *or* brother-in-law (*daughter's or sister's husband*)

# И



**и 1.** *cj.* and; and then, and so; but; (even) though, much as; (that's) just (what… is *etc.*), (this) very *or* same; **2.** *part.* oh; too, (n)either; even; ***и … и …*** both … and
**и́бо** *c.j.* for
**и́ва** *f* [5; *pl.st.*] willow; ***плаку́чая ~*** weeping willow
**и́волга** *f* [5] oriole
**игл|а́** *f* [5] needle (*a. tech.*); *bot.* thorn, prickle; *zo.* quill, spine, bristle; **~отерапи́я** *f* [7], **~ука́лывание** *n* [12] acupuncture
**игнори́ровать** [7] (*im*)*pf.* ignore
**и́го** *n* [9] *fig.* yoke
**иго́л|ка** *f* [5; *g/pl.*: -лок] → ***игла́***; ***как на ~ках*** on tenterhooks; ***с ~(оч)ки*** brand-new, spick-and-span; **~ьный** [14] needle('s)…; ***~ьное у́шко*** eye of a needle
**иго́рный** [14] gambling; card…
**игра́** *f* [5; *pl. st.*] play; game (***в*** В of); sparkle; ***~ слов*** play on words, pun; ***~ не сто́ит свеч*** it isn't worth while; ***~ воображе́ния*** pure fantasy; **~льный** [14] *карта* playing; **~ть** [1], ⟨по-, сыгра́ть⟩ play (***в*** В, ***на*** П); *в азартные игры* gamble; sparkle (wine, *etc.*); *thea. a.* act; ***~ть свое́й жи́знью*** risk one's life; ***э́то не ~ет ро́ли*** it does not matter
**игри́|вый** [14 *sh.*] playful; **~стый** [14 *sh.*] sparkling
**игро́к** *m* [1 *e.*] player; gambler
**игру́шка** *f* [5; *g/pl.*: -шек] toy; *fig.* plaything
**идеа́л** *m* [1] ideal; **~изи́ровать** [7] (*im*)*pf.* idealize; **~и́зм** *m* [1] idealism; **~и́ст** *m* [1] idealist; **~исти́ческий** [16] idealistic; **~ьный** [14; -лен, -льна] ideal
**идентифика́тор** *m* [1] *comput.* name
**идео́лог** *m* [1] ideologist; **~и́ческий** [16] ideologic(al); **~ия** *f* [7] ideology
**иде́я** *f* [6] idea
**иди́лл|ия** *f* [7] idyl(l); **~и́ческий** [16] idyllic
**идио́ма** *f* [5] idiom
**идио́т** *m* [1] idiot; **~и́зм** *m* [1] idiocy; **~ский** [16] idiotic
**и́дол** *m* [1] idol (*a. fig.*)
**идти́** [иду́, идёшь; шёл, шла; ше́дший; идя́, *coll.* и́дучи], ⟨пойти́⟩ [пойду́, -дёшь; пошёл, -шла́] (be) go(ing, *etc.*; *a. fig.*), walk; come; (***за*** Т) follow, *a.* go for, fetch; leave; (*двигать*[*ся*]) move (*a.* chess, T), flow, drift (***в, на*** В); *школу и т. д.* enter; *армию и т. д.* join, become; (*происходить*) proceed, be in progress, take place; *thea. фильм* be on; *дорога* lead (*о карте* ***с*** Р); (***на*** В) attack; *о товаре* sell; (***в, на, под*** В) be used, spent (for); (***к*** Д) suit; (***за*** В) marry; ***~ в счёт*** count; ***~ на вёслах*** row; ***пойти́ в отца́*** take after one's father; ***идёт!*** all right!, done!; ***пошёл (пошли́)!*** (let's) go!; ***де́ло (речь) идёт о*** (П) the question *or* matter is (whether), it is a question *or* matter of; … is at stake; ***ему́ идёт*** *or* ***пошёл шесто́й год (деся́ток)*** he is over five (fifty)
**иезуи́т** *m* [1] Jesuit (*a. fig.*)
**иера́рхия** *f* [7] hierarchy

**иеро́глиф** *m* [1] hieroglyph(ic)
**иждиве́н|ец** *m* [1; -нца] dependent (-dant); **~ие** *n* [12]: ***быть на ~ии*** (P) be s.o.'s dependent (-dant)
**из, ~о** (P) from, out of; of; for, through; with; in; by; ***что ж ~ э́того?*** what does that matter?
**изба́** *f* [5; *pl. st.*] (peasant's) house, cottage
**избав|и́тель** *m* [4] rescuer, deliverer; **∠ить → *~ля́ть***; **~ле́ние** *n* [12] deliverance, rescue; **~ля́ть** [28], ⟨**∠ить**⟩ [14] (**от** P from) (*освободить*) deliver, free; (*спасти*) save; *от боли* relieve; **-ся** (**от** P) get rid of
**избало́ванный** [14 *sh.*] spoilt
**избе|га́ть** [1], ⟨**~жа́ть**⟩ [4; -егу́, -ежи́шь, -егу́т], ⟨**∠гнуть**⟩ [21] (P) avoid, shun; *смерти* escape; (*уклониться*) evade; **~жа́ние** *n* [12]: ***во ~жа́ние*** (P) (in order) to avoid
**изб|ива́ть** [1], ⟨**~и́ть**⟩ [изобью́, -бьёшь; → ***бить***] beat unmercifully; **~ие́ние** *n* [12] beating; massacre
**избира́тель** *m* [4] voter, elector; *pl. a.* electorate; constituency; **~ный** [14] electoral; ballot…, election; ***~ный уча́сток*** polling station; ***~ный о́круг*** constituency
**изб|ира́ть** [1], ⟨**~ра́ть**⟩ [-беру́, -рёшь; → ***брать***] choose; elect (В/**в** И *pl. or*/Т); **∠ранный** *a.* select(ed); ***∠ранные сочине́ния*** selected works
**изби́|тый** [14 *sh.*] *fig.* hackneyed, trite; **~ть → *~ва́ть***
**избра́|ние** *n* [12] election; **~нник** *m* [1] (young) man of her choice; **~ть → *избира́ть***
**избы́т|ок** *m* [1; -тка] surplus; abundance, plenty; ***в ~ке, с ~ком*** in plenty, plentiful(ly); ***в ~ке чу́вств*** *fig.* overcome by emotion; **~очный** [14; -чен, -чна] superfluous, surplus…
**и́звер|г** *m* [1] monster, cruel person; **~же́ние** *n* [12] eruption
**изверну́ться → *извора́чиваться***
**извести́ → *изводи́ть***
**изве́ст|ие** *n* [12] news *sg.*; information; *pl. a.* bulletin; ***после́дние ~ия*** *rad.* news(cast), the latest news; **извести́ть → *извеща́ть***
**извёстк|а** *f* [5], **~о́вый** [14] lime
**изве́стн|ость** *f* [8] reputation, fame; ***по́льзоваться*** (***мирово́й***) ***~остью*** be (world-)renowned *or* famous *or* well-known; ***ста́вить*** (В) ***в ~ость*** bring s.th. to a p.'s notice (**о** П); **~ый** [14; -тен, -тна] known (for Т; as ***как, за*** В), familiar; well-known, renowned, famous; notorious; (*некоторый*) certain; ***наско́лько мне ~о*** as far as I know; (***мне***) **~о** it is known (I know); ***ему́ э́то хорошо́ ~о*** he is well aware of this
**извест|ня́к** *m* [1 *e.*] limestone; **ʹ~ь** *f* [8] lime
**изве|ща́ть** [1], ⟨**~сти́ть**⟩ [15 *e.*; -ещу́, -ести́шь; -ещённый] inform (**о** П of); notify; *comm. a.* advise; **~ще́ние** *n* [12] notification, notice; *comm.* advice
**изви|ва́ться** [1] wind, meander, twist; *о теле, змее и т. д.* wriggle; **∠лина** *f* [5] bend, curve; turn; *мозга* convolution; **∠листый** [14 *sh.*] winding, tortuous
**извин|е́ние** *n* [12] apology, excuse; **~и́тельный** [14; -лен, -льна] pardonable; [*no sh.*] apologetic; **~я́ть** [28], ⟨**~и́ть**⟩ [13] excuse, pardon; forgive (Д/В a p. a th.); ***~и́(те)!*** excuse me!, I am sorry!; ***нет, уж ~и́(те)!*** oh no!, on no account!; **-ся** apologize (***пе́ред*** Т, ***за*** В to/for); **~я́юсь!** *coll.* → ***~и́(те)!***
**извле|ка́ть** [1], ⟨**∠чь**⟩ [26] take *or* draw out; extract (*a. math.*); *выгоду* derive; **~че́ние** *n* [12] extract(ion)
**извне́** from outside
**изводи́ть** *coll.* [15], ⟨**извести́**⟩ [25] (*израсходовать*) use up; (*измучить*) exhaust, torment
**изво́л|ить** [13] *iro.* please, deign; **~ь(те)** + *inf.* (would you) please + *vb*
**извор|а́чиваться** [1], ⟨**изверну́ться**⟩ [20] *coll.* dodge; (try to) wriggle out; **~о́тливый** [14 *sh.*] resourceful; shrewd
**извра|ща́ть** [1], ⟨**~ти́ть**⟩ [15 *e.*; -ащу́, -ати́шь; -ащённый] *факты* misconstrue, distort; *о человеке* pervert
**изги́б** *m* [1] bend, curve, turn; *fig.* shade; **~а́ть** [1], ⟨**изогну́ть**⟩ [20] bend, curve, crook (*v/i.* **-ся**)

**изгла́|живать** [1], ⟨**~дить**⟩ [15] (**-ся** be[-come]) efface(d), erase(d); **~дить из па́мяти** blot out of one's memory

**изгна́|ние** *n* [12] *old use, lit.* banishment; exile; **~нник** *m* [1] exile; **~ть** → **изгоня́ть**

**изголо́вье** *n* [10] *кровати* head

**изг|оня́ть** [28], ⟨**~на́ть**⟩ [-гоню́, -го́нишь; -гна́л, -ла́] drive out; oust; expel; exile, banish

**и́згородь** *f* [8] fence; *зелёная* hedge(-row)

**изгот|а́вливать** [1], **~овля́ть** [28], ⟨**~о́вить**⟩ [14] make, produce, manufacture; **~овле́ние** *n* [12] manufacture; making; *mil.* preparation

**изда|ва́ть** [5], ⟨**~ть**⟩ [-да́м, -да́шь, *etc.*, → **дать**; и́зданный (и́здан, -á, -o)] publish; *приказ* issue; *запах* exhale; *звук* utter, emit; *law* promulgate

**и́зда|вна** for a long time; from time immemorial; **~лека́, ~лёка ~ли** from afar; from a distance

**изда́|ние** *n* [12] publication; edition; issue; **~тель** *m* [4] publisher; **~тельство** *n* [9] publishing house, publishers *pl.*; **~ть** → **издава́ть**

**издева́т|ельство** *n* [9] jeering, scoffing, sneering (**над** T at); **~ься** [1] jeer, sneer, mock (**над** T at); bully

**изде́лие** *n* [12] product, article; (needle)work; *pl. a.* goods

**издёргать** [1] harass, harry; **-ся** overstrain one's nerves; worry one's head off

**издерж|а́ться** [4] *pf. coll.* spend a lot of (*or* run short of) money; **∠ки** *f/pl.* [5; *gen*: -жек] expenses; *law* costs

**издыха́ть** [1] → **до́хнуть**

**изж|ива́ть** [1], ⟨**~и́ть**⟩ [-живу́, -вёшь; -жи́тый, *coll.* -то́й (изжи́т, -á, -o)] (gradually) overcome; **~и́ть себя́** be(come) outdated, have had one's day; **~о́га** *f* [5] heartburn

**и́з-за** (P) from behind; from; because of; over; for (the sake of); **~ чего́?** why?, for what reason?; **~ э́того** for that reason

**излага́ть** [1], ⟨изложить⟩ [16] state, set forth, expound, word

**излеч|е́ние** *n* [12] cure, (medical) treatment; (*выздоровление*) recovery; **∠ивать** [1], ⟨**~и́ть**⟩ [16] cure; **~и́мый** [14 *sh.*] curable

**изл|ива́ть** [1], ⟨**~и́ть**⟩ [изолью́, -льёшь; → **лить**]: **~и́ть ду́шу** unbosom o.s.; *гнев* give vent (*to anger*)

**изли́ш|ек** *m* [1; -шка] surplus, *a.* **~ество** *n* [9] excess; **~не** unnecessarily; **~ний** [15; -шен, -шня, -не] superfluous, excessive; (*ненужный*) needless

**изл|ия́ние** *n* [12] outpouring, effusion; **~и́ть** [28] → **~ива́ть**

**изловчи́ться** *coll.* [16 *e.*; -чу́сь, -чи́шься] *pf.* contrive

**излож|е́ние** *n* [12] exposition, account; **~и́ть** → **излага́ть**

**изло́манный** [14] broken; warped; *жизнь, характер* spoilt, deformed

**излуч|а́ть** [1] radiate; **~е́ние** *n* [12] radiation

**излу́чина** *f* [5] *реки* → **изги́б**

**излю́бленный** [14] favo(u)rite

**изме́н|а** *f* [5] treason (Д to); *супружеская* unfaithfulness; **~е́ние** *n* [12] change, alteration, modification; **~и́ть** → **~я́ть**; **~ник** *m* [1] traitor; **~чивый** [14 *sh.*] changeable, variable; *о человеке, настроении* fickle; **~я́ть** [28], ⟨**~и́ть**⟩ [13; -еню́, -е́нишь] **1.** *v/i.* change (*v/i.* **-ся**) alter; modify; vary; **2.** *v/i.* (Д) betray; be(come) unfaithful (to); *клятве и т. д.* break, violate; *память* fail

**измер|е́ние** *n* [12] measurement; *math.* dimension; **~и́мый** [14 *sh.*] measurable; **~и́тельный** [14]: **~и́тельный прибо́р** measuring instrument, gauge; **~я́ть** [28], ⟨**∠ить**⟩ [13 *st.*] measure; *температуру* take; *глубину* fathom (*a. fig.*)

**изможде́нный** [14 *sh.*] *вид* emaciated; (*изнурённый*) exhausted

**измо́р**: **взять кого́-нибудь ~ом** *fig.* worry s.o. into doing s.th

**и́зморозь** *f* [8] rime, hoar-frost

**и́зморось** *f* [8] drizzle

**изму́чи|вать** [1], ⟨**~ть**⟩ [16] (**-ся** be[-come]) fatigue(d), exhaust(ed), wear (worn) out

**измышле́ние** *n* [12] fabrication, invention

И

**изна́нка** *f* [5] back, inside; *ткани* wrong side; *fig.* seamy side
**изнаси́лов|ание** *n* [12], **~ать** [7] *pf.* rape, assault, violation
**изна́шивать** [1], ⟨**износи́ть**⟩ [15] wear out; *v/i.* **-ся**
**изне́женный** [14] coddled
**изнем|ога́ть** [1], ⟨**~о́чь**⟩ [26; г/ж: -огу́, -о́жешь, -о́гут] be(come) exhausted *or* enervated; ***~ога́ть от уста́лости*** feel dead tired; **~оже́ние** *n* [12] exhaustion, weariness
**изно́с** *m* [1] wear (and tear); ***рабо́тать на ~*** wear o.s. out with work; **~и́ть** → ***изна́шивать***
**изно́шенный** [14 *sh.*] worn (out); threadbare
**изнур|е́ние** *n* [12] exhaustion, fatigue; **~и́тельный** [14; -лен, -льна] *труд* hard, exhausting; *болезнь* wasting; **~я́ть** [28], ⟨**~и́ть**⟩ (**-ся** be[come]) fatigue(d), exhauste(d)
**изнутри́** from within; on the inside
**изны|ва́ть** [1] *impf.* (**от** P); ***~ва́ть от жа́жды*** be dying of thirst; ***~ва́ть от ску́ки*** be bored to death
**изоби́л|ие** *n* [12] abundance, plenty (P *a.* **в** П of); **~овать** [7] abound (T in); **~ьный** [14; -лен, -льна] rich, abundant (T in)
**изоблич|а́ть** [1], ⟨**~и́ть**⟩ [16 *e.*; -чу́, -чи́шь; -чённый] unmask; *impf.* reveal, show
**изобра|жа́ть** [1], ⟨**~зи́ть**⟩ [15 *e.*; -ажу́, -ази́шь; -ажённый] represent, portray, depict; describe; express; ***~жа́ть из себя́*** (B) make o.s. out to be; **~же́ние** *n* [12] representation; description; *образ* image, picture; **~зи́тельный** [14]: ***~зи́тельное иску́сство*** fine arts
**изобре|сти́** → ***~та́ть***; **~та́тель** *m* [4] inventor; **~та́тельный** [14; -лен, -льна] inventive, resourceful; **~та́ть** [1], ⟨**~сти́**⟩ [25 -т-: -брету́, -тёшь] invent; **~те́ние** *n* [12] invention
**изо́гнут|ый** [14 *sh.*] bent, curved; **~ь** → ***изгиба́ть***
**изо́дранный** [14] *coll.* → ***изо́рванный***
**изол|и́ровать** [7] (*im*)*pf.* isolate; *el. a.* insulate; **~я́тор** *m* [1] *el.* insulator; *med.* isolation ward; *в тюрьме* cell, jail for imprisonment during investigation; **~я́ция** *f* [7] isolation; *el.* insulation
**изо́рванный** [14] torn, tattered
**изощр|ённый** [14] refine, subtle; **~я́ться** [28], ⟨**~и́ться**⟩ [13] exert o.s., excel (**в** П *or* T in); ***~я́ться в остроу́мии*** sparkle with wit
**из-под** (P) from under; from; from the vicinity of; ***буты́лка ~ молока́*** milk bottle
**изразе́ц** *m* [1; -зца́] (Dutch) tile
**и́зредка** occasionally; *местами* here and there
**изре́з|ывать** [1], ⟨**~ать**⟩ [3] cut up
**изре|ка́ть** [1], ⟨**~́чь**⟩ *iro.* pronounce; **~че́ние** *n* [12] aphorism, maxim
**изруб|а́ть** [1], ⟨**~и́ть**⟩ [14] chop, mince; cut (up)
**изря́дный** [14; -ден, -дна] *сумма* large, fair; *мороз* rather severe; *подлец* real scoundrel
**изуве́ч|ивать**, [1], ⟨**~ить**⟩ [16] mutilate
**изум|и́тельный** [14; -лен, -льна] amazing, wonderful; **~и́ть(ся)** → ***~ля́ть(ся)***; **~ле́ние** *n* [12] amazement; **~ля́ть** [28], ⟨**~и́ть**⟩ [14 *e.*; -млю́, -ми́шь, -млённый] (**-ся** Д be) amaze(d), astonish(ed), surprise(d at)
**изумру́д** *m* [1] emerald
**изуч|а́ть** [1], ⟨**~и́ть**⟩ [16] study, learn; (*ознакомиться*) familiarize o.s. with; (*овладеть*) master; *тщательно* scrutinize; **~е́ние** *n* [12] study
**изъе́здить** [15] *pf.* travel all over
**изъяв|и́тельный** [14] *gr.* indicative; **~ля́ть** [28], ⟨**~и́ть**⟩ [14] express, show; *согласие* give
**изъя́н** *m* [1] defect, flaw
**изыма́ть** [1], ⟨**изъя́ть**⟩ [изыму́, изы́мешь] withdraw, confiscate
**изыска́ние** *n* [12] *mst. mining* prospecting
**изы́сканный** [14 *sh.*] refined, elegant; *еда и т. д.* choice, exquisite
**изы́ск|ивать** [1], ⟨**~а́ть**⟩ [3] find
**изю́м** *m* [1] *coll.* raisins *pl.*; sultanas; **~инка** *f* [5]: **с *~инкой*** piquant
**изя́щн|ый** [14; -щен, -щна] graceful, elegant

**ик|а́ть** [1], ⟨**~ну́ть**⟩ [20] hiccup

**ико́н|а** *f* [5] icon; **´~опись** *f* [8] icon painting

**ико́та** *f* [5] hiccup

**икра́¹** *f* [5] (hard) roe, spawn, caviar; ***зерни́стая ~*** soft caviar; ***па́юсная ~*** pressed caviar

**икра́²** *f* [5] *mst. pl.* [*st.*] calf (*of leg*)

**ил** *m* [1] silt

**и́ли** or; or else; **~ … ~ …** either… or

**иллю|зия** *f* [7] illusion; **~мина́ция** *f* [7] illumination; **~мини́ровать** [7] (*im*)*pf.* illuminate; **~стра́ция** *f* [7] illustration; **~стри́ровать** [7] (*im*)*pf.* illustrate

**имби́рь** *m* [4 *e.*] ginger

**име́ние** *n* [12] estate, landed property

**имени́|ны** *f/pl.* [5] name day; nameday party; **~тельный** [14] *gr.* nominative; **~тый** [14 *sh.*] eminent, distinguished

**и́менно** just, very (*adj.*), exactly, in particular; (*a.* **а ~, и ~**) namely, to wit, that is to say; (*a.* **вот ~**) *coll.* indeed

**именова́ть** [7], ⟨на-⟩ call, name

**име́ть** [8] have, possess; ***~ де́ло с*** (T) have to do with; ***~ ме́сто*** take place; ***~ в виду́*** have in mind, mean, intend; (*не забывать*) remember, bear in mind; **-ся** *под рукой* be at, in *or* on hand; (**у** P) have there is, are, *etc.*

**имита́ция** *f* [7] imitation

**иммигра́нт** *m* [1] immigrant

**иммуните́т** *m* [1] immunity

**императ|ор** *m* [1] emperor; **~ри́ца** *f* [5] empress

**импе́р|ия** *f* [7] empire; **~ский** [16] imperial

**и́мпорт** *m* [1], **~и́ровать** [7] (*im*)*pf.* import; **~ный** [14] imported

**импоте́нция** *f* [7] sexual impotence

**импровизи́ровать** [7] (*im*)*pf.* ⟨сымпровизи́ровать⟩ improvise

**и́мпульс** *m* [1] impulse; *el.* pulse; **~и́вный** [14; -вен, -вна] impulsive

**иму́щ|ество** *n* [9] property; belongings *pl.*; ***недви́жимое ~ество*** real estate; **~ий** [17] well-to-do; ***власть ~ие*** the powers that be

**и́мя** *n* [13] (*esp.* first, Christian) name (*a. fig. gr.*; parts of speech = *Lat.* nomen); ***и́мени: шко́ла им. Че́хова*** Chekhov school; ***во ~*** for the sake of; ***от и́мени*** in the name of (P); ***на ~*** addressed to, for; ***по и́мени*** named; in name (only); (know) by name; ***называ́ть ве́щи свои́ми имена́ми*** call a spade a spade

**и́на́че** differently; otherwise, (or) else; ***так и́ли ~*** one way *or* another, anyhow

**инвали́д** *m* [1] invalid; ***~ труда́*** (***войны́***) disabled worker (veteran, *Brt.* ex-serviceman)

**инвент|аризáция** *f* [7] stock-taking; **~а́рь** *m* [4 *e.*] *список* inventory; stock, equipment; implements

**инд|е́ец** *m* [1; -е́йца] (American) Indian; **~е́йка** *f* [5; *g/pl.*: -е́ек] turkey; **~е́йский** [16] (American) Indian; **~иа́нка** *f* [5; *g/pl.*: -нок] *fem.* of **~е́ец, ~и́ец**

**индиви́д** *m* [1] individual; **~уа́льность** *f* [8] individuality; **~уа́льный** [14; -лен, -льна] individual

**инди́|ец** *m* [1; -йца] Indian; **~йский** [16] Indian

**инду́с** *m* [1], **~ка** *f* [5; *g/pl.*: -сок], **~ский** [16] Hindu

**инд|устриа́льный** [14] industrial; **~у́стрия** *f* [7] industry

**индю́к** *m* [1 *e.*] turkey (cock)

**и́ней** *m* [3] hoar-frost

**ине́р|тность** *f* [8] inertness, inaction; **~тный** [14; -тен, -тна] inert; **~ция** *f* [7] inertia; *phys.* ***по ~ции*** under one's own momentum; *fig.* mechanically

**инжене́р** *m* [1] engineer; **´~-строи́тель** *m* [1/4] civil engineer

**инициа́|лы** *m/pl.* [1] initials; **~ти́ва** *f* [5] initiative; **~ти́вный** [14; -вен, -вна] enterprising, full of initiative; **~тор** *m* [1] initiator, organizer

**инкруста́ция** *f* [7] inlay, incrustation

**иногда́** sometimes, now and then

**иногоро́дний** [15] nonresident, person from another town

**ино́|й** [14] (an)other, different; (*некоторый и т. д.*) some, many a; ***~й раз*** sometimes; ***не кто ~й*** (***не что ~е***), ***как …*** none other than

**иноро́дн|ый** [14], heterogeneous; ***~ое те́ло*** *med.* foreign body

**иносказа́тельный** [14; -лен, -льна] allegorical

**иностра́н|ец** *m* [1; -нца], **~ка** *f* [5; *g/pl.*: -нок] foreigner; **~ный** [14] foreign; → *a.* ***министе́рство***
**инсинуа́ция** *f* [7] insinuation
**инспе́к|тор** *m* [1] inspector; **~ция** *f* [7] inspection
**инста́нция** *f* [7] *pl.* (official) channels; *pol.* level of authority; *law* instance
**инсти́нкт** *m* [1] instinct; **~и́вный** [14; -вен, -вна] instinctive
**институ́т** *m* [1] institute; *брака и т. д.* institution
**инстру́кция** *f* [7] instruction, direction; ***~ по эксплуата́ции*** manual
**инструме́нт** *m* [1] *mus. etc.* instrument; *рабочий* tool
**инсу́льт** *m* [1] *med.* stroke
**инсцени́р|овать** [7] *(im)pf.* adapt for the stage *or* screen; *fig.* feign; **~о́вка** *f* [5; *g/pl.*: -вок] dramatization
**интегра́ция** *f* [7] integration
**интелле́кт** *m* [1] intellect; **~уа́льный** [14; -лен, -льна] intellectual
**интеллиге́н|т** *m* [1] intellectual; **~тность** *f* [8] intelligence and good breeding; **~тный** [14; -тен, -тна] cultured, well-educated; **~ция** *f* [7] intelligentsia, intellectuals *pl.*
**интенси́вный** (-tɛn-) [14; -вен, -вна] intense, (*a. econ.*) intensive
**интерва́л** *m* [1] interval; *typ.* space
**интервью́** (-tɛr-) *n* [*indecl.*], ***брать, взять ~***, **~и́ровать** (-tɛr-) [7] *(im)pl.* interview
**интере́с** *m* [1] interest (***к*** Д in; ***име́ть ~ для*** P be of/to; ***в ~ах*** P in the/of); use; **~ный** [14; -сен, -сна] interesting; *о внешности* handsome, attractive; ***~но, кто э́то сказа́л?*** I wonder who said this?; **~ова́ть** [7], ⟨за-⟩ (**-ся** be[-come]) interest(ed), take an interest (T in)
**интерна́т** *m* [1]: ***шко́ла-~*** boarding school
**интернациона́льный** [14; -лен, -льна] international
**интерпрета́ция** *f* [7] interpretation
**интерфе́йс** *m* [1] *comput.* interface
**интерье́р** *m* [1] *art* interior
**инти́мн|ость** *f* [8] intimacy; **~ый** [14; -мен, -мна] intimate
**интона́ция** *f* [7] intonation
**интри́г|а** *f* [5] intrigue; **~а́н** *m* [1] intriguer; **~а́нка** *f* [5; *g/pl.*: -нок] intrigante; **~ова́ть** [7], ⟨за-⟩ intrigue
**интуи|ти́вный** [14; -вен, -вна] intuitive; **~́ция** *f* [7] intuition
**интури́ст** *m* [1] foreign tourist
**инфа́ркт** *m* [1] infarction
**инфе́кция** *f* [7] infection
**инфля́ция** *f* [7] inflation
**информ|а́ция** *f* [7] information; **~и́ровать** [7] *(im)pf.*, ⟨про-⟩ inform
**инциде́нт** *m* [1] *mst. mil.*, *pol.* incident
**ипподро́м** *m* [1] racetrack (course)
**и́рис**[1] *m* [1] *bot.* iris
**ири́с**[2] *m* [1], **~ка** *f* [5; *g/pl.*: -сок] toffee
**ирла́нд|ец** *m* [1; -дца] Irishman; **~ка** *f* [5; *g/pl.*: -док] Irishwoman; **~ский** [16] Irish
**ирон|изи́ровать** [7] speak ironically (about ***над*** T); **~и́ческий** [16] ironic(al); **~́ия** *f* [7] irony
**иск** *m* [1] *law* suit, action
**иска|жа́ть** [1], ⟨**~зи́ть**⟩ [15 *e.*; -ажу́, -ази́шь; -ажённый] distort, twist; misrepresent; **~же́ние** *n* [12] distortion
**иска́ть** [3], ⟨по-⟩ (B) look for; (*mst.* P) seek
**исключ|а́ть** [1], ⟨**~и́ть**⟩ [16 *e.*; -чу́, -чи́шь; -чённый] exclude, leave out; *из школы* expel; **~а́я** (P) except(ing); ***~ено́*** ruled out; **~е́ние** *n* [12] exclusion; expulsion; exception (***за*** T with the; ***в ви́де*** P as an); **~и́тельный** [14; -лен, -льна] exceptional; ***~и́тельная ме́ра наказа́ния*** capital punishment; *coll.* excellent; *adv. a.* solely, only; **~и́ть** → ***~а́ть***
**иско́мый** [14] sought-after, looked-for
**иско́нный** [14] primordial
**ископа́ем|ый** [14] (*a. fig. su. n*) fossilized; *pl. su.* minerals; ***поле́зные ~ые*** mineral resources
**искорен|я́ть** [28], ⟨**~и́ть**⟩ [13] eradicate, extirpate
**и́скоса** askance; sideways; ***взгляд ~*** sidelong glance
**и́скра** *f* [5] spark(le); flash; ***~ наде́жды*** glimmer of hope
**и́скренн|ий** [15; -ренен, -ренна, -е/о,

-и/ы] sincere, frank, candid; **~е *Ваш*** yours sincerely; **~ость** *f* [8] sincerity, frankness
**искр|и́стый** [14 *sh.*] spark(l)ing; **~и́ться** [13] sparkle, scintillate
**искуп|а́ть** [1], ⟨**~и́ть**⟩ (B) atone for; make up for; **~ле́ние** *n* [12] atonement
**искуси́ть** → ***искуша́ть***
**иску́с|ный** [14; -сен, -сна] skil(l)ful; expert; skilled; **~ственный** [14 *sh.*] artificial; *зубы и т. д.* false; *жемчуг и т. д.* imitation; **~ство** *n* [9] fine arts; *мастерство* skill, trade, craft
**иску|ша́ть** [1], ⟨**~си́ть**⟩ [15 *e.*; -ушу́, -уси́шь] tempt; ***~ша́ть судьбу́*** tempt fate; **~ше́ние** *n* [12] temptation; ***поддава́ться ~ше́нию*** yield to temptation; **~шённый** [14 *sh.*] experienced
**исла́м** *m* [1] Islam
**испа́н|ец** *m* [1; -нца], **~ка** *f* [5; *g/pl.*: -нок] Spaniard; **~ский** [16] Spanish
**испар|е́ние** *n* [12] evaporation; *pl. a.* vapo(u)r(s); **~я́ть** [28], ⟨**~и́ть**⟩ [13] evaporate (*v/i.* **-ся**, *a. fig.*)
**испе|пеля́ть** [28], ⟨**~пели́ть**⟩ [13] *lit.* burn to ashes; ***~пеля́ющий взгляд*** annihilating look; **~щря́ть** [28], ⟨**~щри́ть**⟩ [13] mottle, spot (with), cover all over (with)
**испи́с|ывать** [1], ⟨**~а́ть**⟩ [3] write on, cover with writing; *тетрадь* fill (up); **~ан** full of notes, *etc.*
**испове́доваться** [7] (*im*)*pf.* confess (***пе́ред*** Т to a p.; **в** П *s.th.*)
**и́споведь** *f* [8] confession (*eccl.* [*prp.*: **на** В/П to/at] *a. fig.*)
**и́спод|воль** *coll.* gradually; **~ло́бья** (*недоверчиво*) distrustfully; (*нахмурившись*) frowningly; **~тишка́** *coll.* in an underhand way
**испоко́н**: ***~ ве́ку*** (**веко́в**) → ***и́здавна***
**исполи́н** *m* [1] giant; **~ский** [16] gigantic
**исполн|е́ние** *n* [12] execution; fulfil(l)ment, performance; *обязанности* discharge; **~и́мый** [14 *sh.*] realizable; practicable; **~и́тель** *m* [4] executor; *thea., mus.* performer; *law* bailiff; ***соста́в ~и́телей*** *thea.* cast; **~и́тельный** [14] executive; [-лен, -льна] efficient and reliable; **~я́ть** [28], ⟨**~ить**⟩ [13] carry out, execute; *долг* fulfil(l), do; *обещание* keep; *thea., mus.* perform; **-ся** come true; *лет* be: ***ей ~илось пять лет*** she is five; *прошло* pass (since [***с тех пор***] ***как***)
**испо́льзова|ние** *n* [12] use, utilization; **~ть** [7] (*im*)*pf.* use, utilize
**испо́р|тить** → ***по́ртить***; **~ченный** [14 *sh.*] spoilt; (*тж. ребёнок*) broken; *о человеке* depraved
**исправ|и́тельно-трудово́й** [1]: ***~и́тельно-трудова́я коло́ния*** *approx.* reformatory; **~ле́ние** *n* [12] correction; repair; *человека* reform; **~ля́ть** [28], ⟨**~ить**⟩ [14] correct; improve; reform; repair; **-ся** reform
**испра́вн|ость** *f* [8] good (working) order; ***в ~ости*** = **~ый** [14; -вен, -вна] intact, in good working order
**испражн|е́ние** *n* [12] *med.* defecation; *pl.* f(a)eces; **~я́ться** [28], ⟨**~и́ться**⟩ [13] defecate
**испу́г** *m* [1] fright; **~а́ть** → ***пуга́ть***
**испус|ка́ть** [1], ⟨**~ти́ть**⟩ [15] *звуки* utter; *запах* emit; ***~ти́ть дух*** give up the ghost
**испыт|а́ние** *n* [12] test, trial; (*a. fig.*) ordeal; examination (***на*** П at); **~анный** [14] tried; **~а́тельный** [14] test; *срок* probationary; **~у́ющий** [17] *взгляд* searching; **~ывать**, ⟨**~а́ть**⟩ [1] try (*a. fig.*), test; (*подвергнуться*) experience, undergo; *боль и т. д.* feel
**иссле́дова|ние** *n* [12] investigation, research; *geogr.* exploration; *med.* examination; *chem.* analysis; *научное* treatise, paper, essay (***по*** Д on); **~тель** *m* [4] research worker, researcher; explorer; **~тельский** [16] research… (*a.* ***нау́чно-~тельский***); **~ть** [7] (*im*)*pf.* investigate; explore; do research into; examine (*a. med.*); *chem.* analyze (*Brt.* -yse)
**исступл|е́ние** *n* [12] *о слушателях и т. д.* ecstasy, frenzy; (*ярость*) rage; **~ённый** [14] frantic
**исс|яка́ть** [1], ⟨**~я́кнуть**⟩ [21] *v/i.* dry (*v/i.* up); *fig. a.* exhaust, wear out (*v/i.* o.s. *or* become …)
**ист|ека́ть** [1], ⟨**~е́чь**⟩ [26] *время* elapse; *срок* expire, become due; ***~ека́ть кро́вью*** bleed to death; **~е́кший** [17]

past, last

**истéр|ика** *f* [5] hysterics *pl.*; **~úческий** [16], **~úчный** [14; -чен, -чна] hysterical; **~úя** *f* [7] hysteria

**истéц** *m* [1; -тцá] plaintiff; *в бракоразводном процессе* petitioner

**истечéни|е** *n* [12] *срока* expiration; *времени* lapse; **по ~и** (P) at the end of

**истéчь** → ***истекáть***

**úстин|а** *f* [5] truth; ***избúтая ~а*** truism; **~ный** [14; -инен, -инна] true, genuine; *правда* plain

**истл|евáть** [1], 〈**~éть**〉 [8] rot, decay; *об углях* die away

**истóк** *m* [1] source (*a. fig.*)

**истолк|овáние** *n* [12] interpretation; commentary; **~óвывать** [1], 〈**~овáть**〉 [7] interpret, expound

**истóм|а** *m* [5] languor; **~úться** [14 *e.*; -млюсь, -мúшься] (be[come]) tire(d), weary (-ied)

**истоптáть** [3] *pf.* trample; *обувь* wear out

**истóр|ик** *m* [1] historian; **~úческий** [16] historical; *событие и т. д.* historic; **~úя** *f* [7] history; *рассказ* story; *coll.* event, affair, thing; ***вéчная ~úя!*** the same old story!; ***~úя болéзни*** case history

**источ|áть** [1], 〈**~úть**〉 [16 *e.*; -чý, -чúшь] give off, impart; *запах* emit; **~́ник** *m* [1] spring; (*a. fig.*) source

**истощ|áть** [1], 〈**~úть**〉 [16 *e.*; -щý, -щúшь; -щённый] (**-ся** be[come]) exhaust(ed); *запасы* use(d) up; *ресурсы* deplete; **~ённый** [14 *sh.*] *человек* emaciated

**истрáчивать** [1] → ***трáтить***

**истреб|úтель** *m* [4] destroyer; *ае.* fighter plane; **~úтельный** [14] *война* destructive; fighter…; **~úть** → ***~лять***; **~лéние** *n* [12] destruction; *тараканов и т. д.* extermination; **~лять** [28], 〈**~úть**〉 [14 *e.*; -блю, -бúшь; -блённый] destroy, annihilate; exterminate

**úстый** [14] true, genuine

**истязá|ние** *n* [12], **~ть** [1] torture

**исхóд** *m* [1] end, outcome, result; *Bibl.* Exodus; ***быть на ~е*** be coming to an end; *о продуктах и т. д.* be running short of; **~úть** [15] (***из*** P) come, emanate (from); (*происходить*) originate; (*основываться*) proceed (from); **~ный** [14] initial; ***~ное положéние*** (***~ная тóчка***) point of departure

**исхудáлый** [14] emaciated, thin

**исцарáпать** [1] *pf.* scratch (all over)

**исцел|éние** *n* [12] healing; (*выздоровление*) recovery; **~ять** [28], 〈**~úть**〉 [13] heal, cure; **-ся** recover

**исчез|áть** [1], 〈**~́нуть**〉 [21] disappear, vanish; **~новéние** *n* [12] disappearance; **~́нуть** → ***~áть***

**исчéрп|ывать**, 〈**~ать**〉 [1] exhaust, use up; *вопрос и т. д.* settle; **~ывающий** exhaustive

**исчисл|éние** *n* [12] calculation; calculus; **~ять** [28], 〈**~́ить**〉 [13] calculate

**итáк** thus, so; well, then, now

**итальян|ец** *m* [1; -нца], **~ка** *f* [5; *g/pl.*: -нок], **~ский** [16] Italian

**итóг** *m* [1] sum, total; result; ***в ~е*** in the end; *подвести* sum up; **~ó** (-'vɔ) altogether; in all; total

**их** → ***онú***, (*a. possessive adj.*) their(s)

**ишь** *int. coll.* P (just) look!; listen!

**ищéйка** *f* [5; *g/pl.*: -еек] bloodhound

**ию|ль** *m* [4] July; **~нь** *m* [4] June

# Й

**йог** *m* [1] yogi; **~́а** yoga

**йод** *m* [1] iodine; **~́ный** [14]; ***~́ный раствóр*** tincture of iodine

**йó|та** *f* [5]: ***ни на ~́ту*** not a jot

# К

**к, ко** (Д) to, toward(s); *о времени тж.* by; for; **~ *тому́ же*** besides
**-ка** *coll.* (*after vb.*) just, will you
**каба́к** *m* [1 *e.*] *hist.* tavern *fig. coll.* hubbub and disorder
**кабала́** *f* [5] *hist.* debt-slavery; *fig.* bondage
**каба́н** *m* [1 *e.*] (*a.* wild) boar
**кабачо́к** *m* [1; *g/pl.*: -чков] vegetable marrow
**ка́бель** *m* [4] cable
**каби́н|а** *f* [5] cabin, booth; *ae.* cockpit; *водителя* cab; **~е́т** *m* [1] study, office; *med.* (consulting) room; *pol.* cabinet
**каблу́к** *m* [1 *e.*] heel (*of shoe*); ***быть под ~о́м*** *fig.* be under s.o.'s thumb
**кабота́ж** *m* [1] coastal trade
**кавале́р** *m* [1] bearer of an order; *old use* boyfriend; *в танце* partner
**кавале|ри́йский** [16] cavalry…; **~ри́ст** *m* cavalryman; **~́рия** *f* [7] cavalry
**ка́верзный** *coll.* [14] tricky
**кавка́з|ец** *m* [1; -зца] Caucasian; **~ский** [16] Caucasian
**кавы́чк|и** *f/pl.* [5; *gen.*: -чек] quotation marks; ***в ~ах*** *fig. coll.* socalled
**ка́дка** *f* [5; *g/pl.*: -док] tub, vat
**ка́дмий** *m* [3] cadmium
**кадр** *m* [1] *cine.* frame, still; close-up
**ка́др|овый** [14] *mil.* regular; *рабочий* skilled; **~ы** *pl.* skilled workers; experienced personnel
**кады́к** *m* [1 *e.*] Adam's apple
**каждодне́вный** [14] daily
**ка́ждый** [14] every, each; *su.* everybody, everyone
**ка́ж|ется**, **~ущийся**, → ***каза́ться***
**каза́к** *m* [1 *e.*; *pl. a.* 1] Cossack
**каза́рма** *f* [5] *mil.* barracks *pl.*
**каза́|ться** [3], ⟨по-⟩ (T) seem, appear, look; ***мне ка́жется (~лось), что …*** it seems (seemed) to me that; ***он, ка́жется, прав*** he seems to be right; *тж.* apparently; ***ка́жущийся*** seeming; ***~лось бы*** one would think; it would seem
**каза́х** *m* [1], **~ский** [16] Kazak(h)
**каза́|цкий** [16], **~чий** [18] Cossack('s)…
**каза́шка** *f* [5; *g/pl.*: -шек] Kazak(h) woman
**каз|ённый** [14] *подход и т. д.* formal; bureaucratic; *банальный* commonplace; ***на ~ённый счёт*** at public expense; **~на́** *f* [5] treasury, exchequer; **~начéй** *m* [3] treasurer
**казн|и́ть** [13] (*im*)*pf.* execute, put to death; *impf. fig.* ***~и́ть себя́, -ся*** torment o.s. with remorse; **~ь** *f* [8] execution
**кайма́** *f* [5; *g/pl.*: каём] border; hem
**как** how; as; like; what; since; *coll.* when, if; (+ *su.*, *adv.*) very (much), awfully; (+ *pf.*, *vb.*) suddenly; ***я ви́дела, как он шёл …*** I saw him going …; ***~ бу́дто, ~ бы*** as if, as it were; ***~ бы мне*** (+ *inf.*) how am I to …; ***~ ни*** however; ***~ же!*** sure!; ***~ (же) так?*** you don't say !; ***~ …, так и …*** both … and …; ***~ когда́*** *etc.* that depends; ***~ не*** (+ *inf.*) of course …; ***~ мо́жно скоре́е (лу́чше)*** as soon as (in the best way) possible
**кака́о** *n* [*indecl.*] cocoa
**ка́к-нибудь** somehow (or other); anyhow; sometime
**како́в** [-ва́, -о́] how; what; what sort of; (such) as; ***~!*** just look (at him)!; ***~о́?*** what do you say?; **~о́й** [14] which
**како́й** [16] what, which; *тж.* how; such as; *coll.* any; that; ***ещё ~!*** and what … (*su.*)!; ***како́е там!*** not at all!; **~-либо, ~-нибудь** any, some; *coll.* no more than, (only) about **~-то** some, a
**ка́к-то** *adv.* somehow; somewhat; *coll.* (*тж.* ***~ раз***) once, one day
**каламбу́р** *m* [1] pun
**каланча́** *f* [5; *g/pl.*: -че́й] watchtower; *fig. coll. о человеке* beanpole
**кала́ч** *m* [1 *e.*] small (*padlock-shaped*)

white loaf; ***тёртый ~*** *fig. coll.* cunning, fellow

**кале́ка** *m/f* [5] cripple

**календа́рь** *m* [4 *e.*] calendar

**калёный** [14] red-hot; *орехи* roasted

**кале́чить** [16], ⟨ис-⟩ cripple, maim

**кали́бр** *m* [1] caliber (-bre); *tech.* gauge

**ка́лий** *m* [3] potassium

**кали́на** *f* [5] snowball tree

**кали́тка** *f* [5; *g/pl.*: -ток] wicket-gate

**кали́ть** [13] **1.** ⟨на-, рас-⟩ heat *орехи*; roast; **2.** ⟨за-⟩ *tech.* temper

**кало́рия** *f* [7] calorie

**ка́лька** *f* [5; *g/pl.*: -лек] tracing paper; *fig. ling.* loan translation, calque

**калькул|я́тор** *m* [1] calculator; **~я́ция** *f* [7] calculation

**кальсо́ны** *f/pl.* [5] long underpants

**ка́льций** *m* [3] calcium

**ка́мбала** *f* [5] flounder

**камен|е́ть** [8], ⟨о-⟩ turn (in)to stone, petrify; **~и́стый** [14 *sh.*] stony; **~ноу́гольный** [14]: ***~ноу́гольный бассе́йн*** coalfield; **´~ный** [14] stone…; *fig.* stony; *соль* rock; ***´~ный у́голь*** coal; **~оло́мня** *f* [6; *g/pl.*: -мен] quarry; **´~щик** *m* [1] bricklayer; **´~ь** *m* [4; -мня; *from g/pl. e.*] stone; rock; *fig.* weight; ка́мнем like a stone; ***´~ь преткнове́ния*** stumbling block

**ка́мер|а** *f* [5] *тюремная*; cell; *tech.* chamber; *phot.* camera; *mot.* inner tube; ***~а хране́ния*** left luggage office; **~ный** [14] *mus.* chamber…

**ками́н** *m* [1] fireplace

**камо́рка** *f* [5; *g/pl.*: -рок] closet, small room

**кампа́ния** *f* [7] *mil., pol.* campaign

**камфара́** *f* [5] camphor

**камы́ш** *m* [1 *e.*], **~о́вый** [14] reed

**кана́ва** *f* [5] ditch; *сточная* gutter

**кана́д|ец** *m* [1; -ца], **~ка** [5; *g/pl.*: -ок], **~ский** [16] Canadian

**кана́л** *m* [1] canal; *radio, TV, fig.* channel; **~иза́ция** *f* [7] *городская* sewerage

**канаре́йка** *f* [5; *g/pl.*: -е́ек] canary

**кана́т** *m* [1], **~ный** [14] rope; cable

**канва́** *f* [5] canvas; *fig.* basis; outline

**кандида́т** *m* [1] candidate; kandidat (*in former USSR, holder of postgraduate higher degree before doctorate*); **~у́ра** *f* [5] candidature

**кани́кулы** *f/pl.* [5] vacation, *Brt. a.* holidays (***на*** П, ***в*** В during)

**канит́ель** *coll. f* [8] tedious and drawn-out procedure

**канона́да** *f* [5] cannonade

**кано́э** *n* [*indecl.*] canoe

**кант** *m* [1] edging, piping

**кану́н** *m* [1] eve

**ка́нуть** [20] *pf.*: ***как в во́ду ~*** disappear without trace; ***~ в ве́чность*** (***в Ле́ту***) sink into oblivion

**канцеля́р|ия** *f* [7] office; **~ский** [16] office…; ***~ские това́ры*** stationery

**ка́нцлер** *m* [1] chancellor

**ка́п|ать** [1 & 2], *once* ⟨~нуть⟩ [20] drip, drop, trickle; *дождь* fall; **~елька** [5; *g/pl.*: -лек] droplet; *sg. coll.* bit, grain

**капита́л** *m* [1] *fin.* capital; *акционерный* stock; *оборотный* working capital; **~и́зм** *m* [1] capitalism; **~и́ст** *m* [1] capitalist; **~исти́ческий** [16] capitalist(ic); **~овложе́ние** *n* [12] investment; **~ьный** [14] fundamental, main; ***~ьный ремо́нт*** major repairs

**капита́н** *m* [1] *naut., mil., sport* captain; *торгового судна* skipper

**капитул|и́ровать** *f* [7] *(im)pf.* capitulate; **~я́ция** *f* [7] capitulation

**капка́н** *m* [1] trap (*a. fig.*)

**ка́пл|я** *f* [6; *g/pl.*: -пель] drop; *sg. coll.* bit, grain; **~ями** drops by; ***как две ~и воды́*** as like as two peas

**капо́т** *m* [1] *mot.* hood, *Brt.* bonnet

**капри́з** *m* [1] whim, caprice; **~ничать** *coll.* [1] be capricious; *о ребёнке* play up; **~ный** [14; -зен, -зна] capricious, whimsical; wil(l)ful

**ка́псула** *f* [5] capsule

**капу́ста** *f* [5] cabbage; ***ки́слая ~*** sauerkraut; ***цветна́я ~*** cauliflower

**капюшо́н** *m* [1] hood

**ка́ра** *f* [5] punishment

**караби́н** *m* [1] carbine

**кара́бкаться** [1], ⟨вс-⟩ climb

**карава́й** *m* [3] (big) loaf

**карава́н** *m* [1] caravan; *кораблей и т. д.* convoy

**кара́емый** [14 *sh.*] *law.* punishable

**кара́куля** *f* [6] *f* scribble
**кара́куль|ь** *m* [4], **~евый** [14] astrakhan
**караме́ль** *f* [8] caramel(s)
**каран|да́ш** *m* [1 *e.*] pencil; **~ти́н** *m* [1] quarantine
**карапу́з** *coll. m* [1] chubby tot
**кара́сь** *m* [4 *e.*] crucian
**карате́** *n* [*indecl.*] karate
**кара́|тельный** [14] punitive; **~ть** [1], ⟨по-⟩ punish
**карау́л** *m* [1] sentry, guard; ***стоять на ~е*** be on guard; *int.* **~!** help!; **~ить** [13], ⟨по-⟩ guard, watch (*coll.* ...out, for); **~ьный** [14] sentry... (*a. su.*); ***~ьное помеще́ние*** guardroom
**карбу́нкул** *m* [1] carbuncle
**карбюра́тор** *m* [1] carburet(t)or
**каре́л** *m* [1] Karelian; **~ка** [5; *g/pl.*: -ок] Karelian
**каре́та** *f* [5] *hist.* carriage, coach
**ка́рий** [15] (dark) brown
**карикату́р|а** *f* [5] caricature, cartoon; **~ный** [14] caricature...; [-рен, -рна] comic(al), funny
**карка́с** *m* [1] frame(work), skeleton
**ка́рк|ать** [1], *once* ⟨-нуть⟩ [20] croak (*coll., fig.*), caw
**ка́рлик** *m* [1] dwarf; **~овый** [14] dwarf...; dwarfish
**карма́н** *m* [1] pocket; ***э́то мне не по ~у*** *coll.* I can't afford that; ***э́то бьёт по ~у*** that costs a pretty penny; ***держи́ ~ (ши́ре)*** that's a vain hope; ***она́ за сло́вом в ~е ле́зет*** she has a ready tongue; **~ный** [14] pocket...; ***~ный вор*** pickpocket
**карнава́л** *m* [1] carnival
**карни́з** *m* [1] cornice; *для штор* curtain fixture
**ка́рт|а** *f* [5] map; *naut.* chart; (playing) card; ***ста́вить (всё) на ~у*** stake (have all one's eggs in one basket); **~а́вить** [14] mispronounce *Russ. r or l* (*esp. as uvular* r *or* u, v); **~ёжник** *m* [1] gambler (*at cards*)
**карти́н|а** *f* [5] picture (**на** П in); *cine.* movie; *art* painting; scene (*a. thea.*); **~ка** [5; *g/pl.*: -нок] (small) picture, illustration; **~ный** [14] picture...
**карто́н** *m* [1] cardboard; **~ка** [5; *g/pl.*: -нок] (cardboard) box
**картоте́ка** *f* [5] card index
**карто́фель** *m* [4] *collect.* potatoes *pl.*
**ка́рточ|ка** *f* [5; *g/pl.*: -чек] card; *coll.* photo; season ticket; **~ный** [14] card(s)...; ***~ный до́мик*** house of cards
**карто́шка** *coll. f* [5; *g/pl.*: -шек] potato(es)
**карусе́ль** *f* [8] merry-go-round
**ка́рцер** *m* [1] cell, lockup
**карье́р** *m* [1] full gallop (at T); ***с ме́ста в ~*** at once; **~а** *f* [5] career; **~и́ст** *m* [1] careerist
**каса́|тельная** *f* [14] *math.* tangent; **~ться** [1], ⟨косну́ться⟩ [20] touch (*a. fig.*); concern; *coll.* be about, deal *or* be concerned with; ***де́ло ~ется = де́ло идёт о → идти́***; ***что ~ется ...*** as regards, as to
**ка́ска** *f* [5; *g/pl.*: -сок] helmet
**каска́д** *m* [1] cascade
**каспи́йский** [16] Caspian
**ка́сса** *f* [5] pay desk *or* office; (*a.* ***биле́тная ~***) *rail.* ticket window, *Brt.* booking office; *thea.* box office; *деньги* cash; *в магазине* cash register; ***сберега́тельная ~*** savings bank
**кассац|ио́нный** [14] → ***апелляцио́нный***; **~ия** *law* [7] cassation
**кассе́т|а** *f* [5], **~ный** [14] cassette
**касси́р** *m* [1], **~ша** *f* [5] cashier
**ка́ста** *f* [5] caste (*a. fig.*)
**касто́ровый** [14] castor
**кастри́ровать** [7] (*im*)*pf.* castrate
**кастрю́ля** *f* [6] saucepan; pot
**катакли́зм** *m* [1] cataclysm
**катализа́тор** *m* [1] catalyst
**катало́г** *m* [1] catalogue
**ката́ние** *n* [10] driving, riding, skating, *etc.* (→ ***ката́ть[ся]***)
**катастро́ф|а** *f* [5] catastrophe; **~и́ческий** [16] catastrophic
**ката́ть** [1] roll (*a. tech.*); ⟨по-⟩ (take for a) drive, ride, row, *etc.*; **-ся** (go for a) drive, ride (*a. верхом, etc.*), row (*на лодке*); skate (*на коньках*); sled(ge) (*на санях*), *etc.*; roll
**катег|ори́ческий** [16], **~ори́чный** [14; -чен, -чна] categorical; **~о́рия** *f* [7] category
**ка́тер** *m* [1; *pl., etc. e.*] *naut.* cutter; **мо-**

***тóрный*** **~** motor-launch
**катúть** [15], ⟨по-⟩ roll, wheel (*v/i* **-ся**; sweep; *слёзы* flow; *волны* roll; → ***ка-тáться***)
**катóк** *m* [1; -тка] (skating) rink
**катóл|ик** *m* [1], **~ичка** *f* [5; *g/pl.*: -чек], **~ический** [16] (Roman) Catholic
**кáтор|га** *f* [5] penal servitude, hard labo(u)r; *fig.* very hard work, drudgery, **~жный** [14] hard, arduous
**катýшка** *f* [5; *g/pl.*: -шек] spool; *el.* coil
**каучýк** *m* [1] caoutchouc, india rubber
**кафé** *n* [*indecl.*] café
**кáфедра** *f* [5] *в церкви* pulpit; department (*of English, etc.*); *univ.* chair
**кáфель** *m* [4] (Dutch) tile
**качá|лка** *f* [5; *g/pl.*: -лок] rocking chair; **~ние** *n* [12] rocking; swing(ing); *нефти, воды* pumping; **~ть** [1] **1.** ⟨по-⟩, *once* ⟨качнýть⟩ [20] rock; swing; shake (*a.* one's head ***головóй***), toss; *naut.* roll, pitch; (**-ся** *v/i.*; stagger, lurch); **2.** ⟨на-⟩ pump
**качéли** *f/pl.* [8] swing; seesaw
**кáчеств|енный** [14] qualitative; high-quality; **~о** *n* [9] quality; ***в ~е*** (P) in one's capacity as, in the capacity of
**кáч|ка** *f* [5] rolling *naut.* (***бортовáя*** *or* ***боковáя ~ка***); pitching (***килевáя ~ка***); ~нýть(ся) → ***~áть*(ся)**
**кáш|а** *f* [5] ***грéчневая ~а*** buckwheat gruel; ***мáнная ~а*** semolina; ***овсяная ~а*** porridge; ***рисовая ~а*** boiled rice; *coll. fig.* mess, jumble; ***заварúть ~у*** stir up trouble
**кашалóт** *m* [1] sperm whale
**кáш|ель** *m* [4; -шля], **~лять** [28], *once* ⟨~лянуть⟩ [20] cough
**каштáн** *m* [1], **~овый** [14] chestnut
**каюта** *f* [5] *naut.* cabin, stateroom
**кáяться** [27], ⟨по-⟩ (**в** П) repent
**квадрáт** *m* [1], **~ный** [14] square
**квáк|ать** [1], *once* ⟨~нуть⟩ [20] croak
**квалифи|кáция** *f* [7] qualification(s); **~цúрованный** [14] qualified, competent; *рабочий* skilled, trained
**квартáл** *m* [1] quarter (= 3 months); block, *coll.* building (*betw. 2 cross streets*); **~ьный** [14] quarter(ly)
**квартúр|а** *f* [5] apartment, *Brt.* flat; ***двухкóмнатная ~а*** two-room apt./flat; **~áнт** *m* [1], **~áнтка** *f* [5; *g/pl.*: -ток] lodger; **~ный** [14] housing, house-…; ***~ная плáта*** = **квартплáта** *f* [5] rent; **~осъёмщик** *m* [1] tenant
**квас** *m* [1; -а, -у; *pl. e.*] kvass (*Russ. drink*); **~úть** [15], ⟨за-⟩ sour
**квáшеный** [14] sour, fermented
**квéрху** up, upward(s)
**квит|áнция** *f* [7] receipt; ***багáжная ~áнция*** (luggage) ticket; **~**(ы) *coll.* quits, even, square
**квóрум** *m* [1] *parl.* quorum
**квóта** *f* [5] quota, share
**кедр** *m* [1] cedar; ***сибúрский ~*** Siberian pine; **~óвый** [14]: ***~óвый орéх*** cedar nut
**кекс** *m* [1] cake
**келéйно** privately; in camera
**кельт** *m* [1] Celt; **~ский** [16] Celtic
**кéлья** *f* [6] *eccl.* cell
**кем** T → ***кто***
**кéмпинг** *m* [1] campsite
**кенгурý** *m* [*indecl.*] kangaroo
**кéпка** *f* [5; *g/pl.*: -ок] (peaked) cap
**керáм|ика** *f* [5] ceramics; **~úческий** [16] ceramic
**керосúн** *m* [1], **~овый** [14] kerosene
**кетá** *f* [5] Siberian salmon
**кефáль** *f* [8] grey mullet
**кефúр** *m* [1] kefir
**кибернéтика** *f* [5] cybernetics
**кив|áть** [1], *once* ⟨~нýть⟩ [20] nod; point (to ***на*** В); **~óк** [1; -вкá] nod
**кидá|ть(ся)** [1], *once* ⟨кúнуть(ся)⟩ [20] → ***бросáть*(ся)**; ***менá ~ет в жар и хóлод*** I'm hot and cold all over
**киев|лянин** *m* [1; *pl.*: -яне, -ян], **~лянка** *f* [5; *g/pl.*: -нок] person from Kiev; **´~ский** [16] Kiev…
**кий** *m* [3; кия; *pl.*: кий, киёв] cue
**килó** *n* [*indecl.*] → ***~грáмм***; **~вáтт (-чáс)** *m* [1; *g/pl.*] kilowatt(-hour); **~грáмм** *m* [1] kilogram(me); **~мéтр** *m* [1] kilometer (*Brt.* -tre)
**киль** *m* [4] keel; **~вáтер** (-tɛr) *m* [1] wake
**кúлька** *f* [5; *g/pl.*: -лек] sprat
**кинематóгр|аф** *m* [1], **~áфия** *f* [7] cinematography
**кинескóп** *m* [1] television tube

**кинжа́л** *m* [1] dagger
**кино́** *n* [*indecl.*] movie, motion picture, *Brt.* the pictures, cinema (**в** В/П to/at); *coll.* screen, film; **~актёр** *m* [1] screen (*or* film) actor; **~актри́са** *f* [5] screen (*or* film) actress; **~журна́л** *m* [1] newsreel; **~звезда́** *coll. f* [5; *pl.* -звёзды] filmstar; **~карти́на** *f* [5] film; **~ле́нта** *f* [5] reel, film (copy); **~опера́тор** *m* [1] cameraman; **~плёнка** *f* [5; *g/pl.*: -нок] film (strip); **~режиссёр** *m* [1] film director; **~сеа́нс** *m* [1] show, performance; **~сту́дия** *f* [7] film studio; **~сцена́рий** *m* [3] scenario; **~съёмка** *f* [5; *g/pl.*: -мок] shooting (*of a film*), filming; **~теа́тр** *m* [1] movie theater, cinema; **~хро́ника** *f* [5] newsreel
**ки́нуть(ся)** → ***кида́ть(ся)***
**кио́ск** *m* [1] kiosk, stand; ***газе́тый ~*** newsstand
**ки́па** *f* [5] pile, stack; *товаров* bale, pack
**кипари́с** *m* [1] cypress
**кипе́|ние** *n* [12] boiling; ***то́чка ~ния*** boiling point; **~ть** [10 *e.*; -плю́, -пи́шь], ⟨за-, вс-⟩ boil; *от возмущения* seethe; be in full swing (*о работе и т. д.*)
**кипу́ч|ий** [17 *sh.*] *жизнь* busy, lively, vigorous, exuberant, vehement, seething; *деятельность* tireless
**кипят|и́льник** *m* [1] boiler; **~и́ть** [15 *e.*; -ячу́, -яти́шь], ⟨вс-⟩ boil (up; *v/i.* **-ся**); *coll.* be(come) excited; **~о́к** *m* [1; -тка́] boiling (hot) water
**кирги́з** *m* [1], **~ский** [16] Kirghiz
**кири́ллица** *f* [5] Cyrillic alphabet
**кирка́** *f* [5; *g/pl.*: -рок] pick(ax[e])
**кирпи́ч** *m* [1 *e.*], **~ный** [14] brick
**кисе́ль** *m* [4 *e.*] (kind of) blancmange
**кисл|ова́тый** [14 *sh.*] sourish; **~оро́д** *m* [1] oxygen; **~ота́** [5; *pl. st.*: -о́ты] sourness, acidity; **~о́тный** [14] acid; **~ый** [14; -сел, -сла́, -о] sour, acid…
**ки́снуть** [21], ⟨с-, про-⟩ turn sour; *coll. fig.* mope
**ки́ст|очка** *f* [5; *g/pl.*: -чек] brush; *dim. of* **~ь** *f* [8; *from g/pl. e.*] brush; *винограда* cluster, bunch; *руки* hand
**кит** *m* [1 *e.*] whale
**кита́|ец** *m* [1; -тайца] Chinese; **~йский** [16] Chinese; **~я́нка** *f* [5; *g/pl.*: -нок] Chinese
**ки́тель** *m* [4; *pl.* -ля, *etc. e.*] *mil.* jacket
**кич|и́ться** [16 *e*; -чу́сь, -чи́шься] put on airs; *хвастаться* boast (of T); **~ли́вый** [14 *sh.*] haughty, conceited
**кише́ть** [киши́т] teem, swarm (with T; *тж.* ***кишмя́ ~***)
**киш|е́чник** [1] bowels, intestines *pl.*; **~е́чный** [14] intestinal, enteric; **~ка́** *f* [5; *g/pl.*: -о́к] intestine (small ***то́нкая***, large ***то́лстая***), gut; *pl. coll.* bowels; *для воды* hose
**клавиату́ра** *f* [5] keyboard (*тж. tech.*)
**кла́виш** *m* [1], **~а** *f* [5] *mus.*, *tech.* key
**клад** *m* [1] treasure (*a. fig.*); **~бище** *n* [11] cemetery; **~ка** *f* [5] laying, (*brick-, stone*)work; **~ова́я** *f* [14] *в доме* pantry, larder; stock- *or* storeroom; **~овщи́к** *m* [1 *e.*] storekeeper
**кла́ня|ться** [28], ⟨поклони́ться⟩ [13; -оню́сь, -о́нишься] (Д) bow (to); *old use приветствовать* greet
**кла́пан** *m* [1] *tech.* valve; *на одежде* flap
**класс** *m* [1] class; *школы* grade, *Brt.* form; classroom; **~ик** *m* [1] classic; **~ифици́ровать** [7] (*im*)*pf.* class(ify); **~и́ческий** [16] classic(al); **~ный** [14] class; *coll.* classy; **~овый** [14] *pol. soc.* class
**класть** [кладу́, -дёшь; клал] **1.** ⟨положи́ть⟩ [16] (**в, на**, *etc.*, В) put, lay (down, on, *etc.*); *в банк* deposit; **в осно́ву** (**в** В take as basis); ***положи́ть коне́ц*** put an end (to Д); ***положи́ть под сукно́*** shelve; **2.** ⟨сложи́ть⟩ [16] *оружие* lay (down)
**клева́ть** [6 *e.*; клюю́, клюёшь], *once* ⟨клю́нуть⟩ [20] peck, pick; *о рыбе* bite; ***~ но́сом*** *coll.* nod
**кле́вер** *m* [1] clover, trefoil
**клевет|а́** *f* [5], **~а́ть** [3; -вещу́, -ве́щешь], ⟨о-⟩ *v/t.*, ⟨на-⟩ (**на** В) slander; **~ни́к** *m* [1 *e.*] slanderer; **~ни́ческий** 16] slanderous
**клеёнка** *f* [5] oilcloth
**кле́|ить** [13], ⟨с-⟩ glue, paste; **-ся** stick; *coll.* work, get on *or* along; **~й** *m* [3; на клею́] glue, paste; **~йкий** [16; кле́ек, кле́йка] sticky, adhesive

К

**клейм|и́ть** [14 *e.*; -млю́, -ми́шь], ⟨за-⟩ brand; *fig. a.* stigmatize; **~о́** *n* [9; *pl. st.*] brand; *fig.* stigma, stain; ***фабри́чное ~о́*** trademark
**клён** *m* [1] maple
**клепа́ть** [1], ⟨за-⟩ rivet
**клёпка** *f* [5; *g/pl.*: -пок] riveting
**кле́т|ка** *f* [5; *g/pl.*: -ток] cage; square, check; *biol.* (*a.* **~очка**) cell; ***в ~(оч)ку*** check(er)ed; *Brt.* chequered; ***грудна́я ~ка*** thorax; **~ча́тка** *f* [5] cellulose; **~чатый** [14] checkered (*Brt.* chequered)
**кле|шня́** *f* [6; *g/pl.*: -не́й] claw; **~щ** *m* [1; *g/pl.*: -ще́й] tick; **~щи** *f/pl.* [5; *gen.*: -ще́й, *etc. e.*] pincers
**клие́нт** *m* [1] client; **~у́ра** *f* [5] *collect.* clientele
**кли́зма** *f* [5] enema
**кли́ка** *f* [5] clique
**кли́макс** *m* [1] climacteric, menopause
**кли́мат** *m* [1] climate; **~и́ческий** [16] climatic
**клин** *m* [3; *pl.*: кли́нья, -ьев] wedge; gusset; **~ом** (*борода и т. д.*) pointed; ***свет не ~ом сошёлся*** the world is large; there is always a way out
**кли́ника** *f* [5] clinic
**клино́к** *m* [1; -нка] blade
**кли́ренс** *m* [1] *tech.* clearance
**кли́ринг** *m* [1] *fin.* clearing
**клич** *m* [1] call; cry; **~ка** *f* [5; *g/pl.*: -чек] *животного* name; (*прозвище*) nickname
**клише́** *n* [*indecl.*] cliché (*a. fig.*)
**клок** *m* [1 *e. pl.*: -о́чья, -ьев; клоки́, -ко́в] *волос* tuft; shred, rag, tatter
**клокота́ть** [3] seethe (*тж. fig.*), bubble
**клон|и́ть** [13; -оню́, -о́нишь], ⟨на-, с-⟩ bend, bow; *fig.* incline; drive (*or* aim) at (**к** Д); ***меня́ ~и́т ко сну*** I am nodding off; (**-ся** *v/i.*; *a.* decline; approach)
**клоп** *m* [1 *e.*] bedbug
**кло́ун** *m* [1] clown
**клочо́к** *m* [1; -чка] *бумаги* scrap; *земли* patch
**клуб**[1] *m* [1; *pl. e.*] *дыма* cloud, puff; *a.* **~о́к**; **~**[2] *m* [1] club(house); **~ень** *m* [4; -бня] tuber, bulb; **~и́ться** [14 *e.*; 3[rd] *p. only*] *дым* wreathe, puff (up); *пыль* whirl
**клубни́ка** *f* [5] (*cultivated*) strawberry, -ries *pl.*
**клубо́к** *m* [1; -бка́] *шерсти* ball; *противоречий* tangle
**клу́мба** *f* [5] (flower) bed
**клык** *m* [1 *e.*] *моржа* tusk; *человека* canine (tooth); *животного* fang
**клюв** *m* [1] beak, bill
**клю́ква** *f* [5] cranberry, -ries *pl.*; ***разве́систая ~*** *mythology* s.th. improbable, nonsensical
**клю́нуть** → ***клева́ть***
**ключ** *m* [1 *e.*] key (*a. fig.*, clue); *tech.* [***га́ечный ~***] = wrench, spanner; *mus.* clef; (*родник*) spring; **~и́ца** *f* [5] clavicle, collarbone
**клю́шка** *f* [5; *g/pl.*: -шек] (golf) club; (hockey) stick
**кля́нчить** *coll.* [16] beg for
**кляп** *m* [1] gag
**кля|сть** [-яну́, -нёшь, -ял, -а́, -о] → ***прокли́нать***; **-ся** ⟨покля́сться⟩ swear (**в** П s.th.; Т by); **~тва** *f* [5] oath; ***дать ~тву***; (*or* ***~твенное обеща́ние***) take an oath, swear
**кля́уза** *f* [5] intrigue; cavil; slander
**кля́ча** *f* [5] *pej.* (*horse*) jade
**кни́г|а** *f* [5] book; **~опеча́тание** *n* [12] (book-)printing, typography; **~охрани́лище** *n* [11] book depository; library
**кни́ж|ка** *f* [5; *g/pl.*: -жек] book(let); *записная* notebook; *чековая* check (*Brt.* cheque)book; ***сберега́тельная ~ка*** savings bank book; **~ный** [14] book…; *о слове* bookish; **~о́нка** *f* [5; *g/pl.*: -нок] trashy book
**кни́зу** down, downward(s)
**кно́пк|а** *f* [5; *g/pl.*: -пок] thumbtack, *Brt.* drawing pin; *el.* (push) button; (snap), fastener; ***нажа́ть на все ~и*** *fig.* pull all wires
**кнут** *m* [1 *e.*] whip
**кня|ги́ня** *f* [6] princess (*prince's consort*); **~жна́** *f* [5; *g/pl.*: -жо́н]) princess (*prince's unmarried daughter*); **~зь** *m* [4; *pl.*: -зья́; -зе́й] prince; ***вели́кий ~зь*** grand duke
**коа|лицио́нный** [14] coalition…; **~ли́ция** *f* [7] coalition

**кобе́ль** *m* [4 *e.*] (male) dog
**кобура́** *f* [5] holster
**кобы́ла** *f* [5] mare; *sport* horse
**ко́ваный** [14] wrought (*iron*.)
**кова́р|ный** [14; -рен, -рна] crafty, guileful, insidious; **~ство** *n* [9] craftiness, guile, wile
**кова́ть** [7 *e.*; кую́, куёшь] **1.** 〈вы́-〉 forge; **2.** 〈под-〉 shoe (*horse*)
**ковёр** *m* [1; -вра́] carpet, rug
**кове́ркать** [1], 〈ис-〉 distort; *слова* mispronounce; *жизнь* spoil, ruin
**коври́жка** *f* [5; *g/pl.*: -жек] gingerbread
**ковче́г** *m* [1]: ***Но́ев ~*** Noah's Ark
**ковш** *m* [1 *e.*] scoop; *землечерпалки* bucket
**ковы́ль** *m* [4 *e.*] feather grass
**ковыля́ть** [28] hobble; *о ребёнке* toddle
**ковыря́ть** [28], 〈по-〉 pick, poke
**когда́** when; while, as; *coll.* if; ever; sometimes; → ***ни***; ***~ как*** it depends; **~-либо**; **~-нибудь** (at) some time (or other), one day; *interr.* ever; **~-то** once, one day, sometime
**ко́|готь** *m* [4; -гтя; *from g/pl. e.*] claw
**код** *m* [1], **~и́ровать** [7], 〈за-〉 code
**ко́е|-где́** here and there, in some places; **´~-ка́к** anyhow, somehow; with (great) difficulty; **´~-како́й** [16] some; any; **´~-когда́** off and on; **´~-кто́** [23] some(-body); **´~-куда́** here and there, (in)to some place(s), somewhere; **´~-что́** [23] something; a little
**ко́ж|а** *f* [5] skin; *материал* leather; ***из ~и (во́н) лезть*** *coll.* do one's utmost; ***~а да ко́сти*** skin and bone; **~аный** [14] leather…; **~ица** *f* [5] skin, peel; rind; (*a.* **~ура́** *f* [5]); cuticle
**коз|а́** *f* [5; *pl. st.*] (she-)goat; **~ёл** [1; -зла́] (he-)goat; ***~ёл отпуще́ния*** scapegoat; **~и́й** [18] goat…; **~лёнок** *m* [2] kid; **~лы** *f/pl.* [5; *gen.*: -зел] *для пилки* trestle
**ко́зни** *f/pl.* [8] intrigues, plots
**коз|ырёк** *m* [1; -рька́] peak (*of cap*); **~ырь** *m* [4; *from g/pl. e.*] trump; **~ыря́ть** *coll.* [28], *once* 〈**~ырну́ть**〉 [20] (*хвастаться*) boast
**ко́йка** *f* [5; *g/pl.*: ко́ек] bed, bunkbed; *naut.* berth
**коке́т|ка** *f* [5; *g/pl.*: -ток] coquette; **~ливый** [14 *sh.*] coquettish; **~ничать** [1] flirt (with); **~ство** *n* [9] coquetry
**коклю́ш** *m* [1] whooping cough
**ко́кон** *m* [1] cocoon
**кок|о́с** *m* [1] coco; *плод* coconut; **~о́совый** [14] coco(nut)…
**кокс** *m* [1] coke
**кол 1.** [1 *e.*; ко́лья, -ев] stake, picket; **2.** [*pl.* 1 *e.*] ***ни ~а́ ни двора́*** neither house nor home
**колбаса́** *f* [5; *pl. st.*: -а́сы] sausage
**колго́тки** *f* [5; *g/pl.*: -ток] *pl.* panty hose, *Brt.* tights *pl.*
**колдо́бина** *f* [5] rut, pothole
**колд|ова́ть** [7] practice (-ise) witchcraft; conjure; **~овство́** *n* [9] magic, sorcery; **~у́н** *m* [1 *e.*] sorcerer, wizard; **~у́нья** *f* [6] sorceress, witch, enchantress
**колеб|а́ние** *n* [12] oscillation; vibration; *fig.* (*сомнение*) hesitation; (*a. comm.*) fluctuation; **~а́ть** [2 *st.*: -е́блю, *etc.*; -е́бли(те); -е́бля], 〈по-〉, *once* 〈**~ну́ть**〉 [20] shake (*a. fig.*); **-ся** shake; (*a. comm.*) fluctuate; waver, hesitate; oscillate, vibrate
**коле́н|о** *n* [*sg.*: 9; *pl.*: 4] knee; ***стать на ~и*** kneel; ***по ~и*** knee-deep; ***ему́ мо́ре по ~о*** he doesn't care a damn; [*pl.*: -нья, -ев; *pl. a.* 9] *tech.* bend, crank; **~чатый** [14] *tech. вал* crank (shaft)
**колес|и́ть** *coll.* [15 *e.*; -ешу́, -еси́шь] travel about, rove; **~ни́ца** *f* [5] chariot; **~о́** *n* [9; *pl. st.*: -лёса] wheel; ***кружи́ться, как бе́лка в ~е́*** run round in circles; ***вставля́ть кому́-нибудь па́лки в колёса*** put a spoke in a p.'s wheel
**коле|я́** *f* [6; *g/pl.*: -ле́й] rut, (*a. rail*) track (*both a. fig.*); ***вы́битый из ~и́*** unsettled
**коли́бри** *m/f* [*indecl.*] hummingbird
**ко́лики** *f/pl.* [5] colic
**коли́честв|енный** [14] quantitative; *gr.* cardinal (*number*); **~о** *n* [9] quantity; number; amount
**ко́лка** *f* [5] splitting, chopping
**ко́лк|ий** [16; ко́лок, колка́, ~о] prickly; *fig.* biting; **~ость** *f* [8] sharpness
**колле́г|а** *m/f* [5] colleague; **~ия** *f* [7] board, collegium; ***~ия адвока́тов*** the

К

Bar

**коллекти́в** *m* [1] group, body; **~иза́ция** *f* [7] *hist.* collectivization; **~ный** [14] collective, joint

**коллек|ционе́р** *m* [1] collector; **~ция** [7] collection

**коло́д|а** *f* [5] block; *карт* pack, deck; **~ец** [1; -дца] well; **~ка** *f* [5; *g/pl.*: -док] last; *tech.* (*brake*) shoe

**ко́локол** *m* [1; *pl.*: -ла́, *etc. e.*] bell; **~о́льня** *f* [6; *g/pl.*: -лен] bell tower, belfry; **~о́льчик** *m* [1] (little) bell; *bot.* bluebell

**коло́ния** *f* [7] colony

**коло́н|ка** *f* [5; *g/pl.*: -нок] *typ.* column; (*apparatus*) water heater, *Brt.* geyser; *a. dim. of* **~на** *f* [5] column (*arch. a.* pillar)



**колори́т** *m* [1] colo(u)ring; colo(u)r; **~ный** [14; -тен, -тна] colo(u)rful, picturesque

**ко́лос** *m* [1; *pl.*: -ло́сья, -ьев], (*agric.*) ear, spike; **~и́ться** [15 *e.*; *3rd p. only*] form ears

**колосса́льный** [14; -лен, льна] colossal, fantastic

**колоти́ть** [15] knock (***в*** В, ***по*** Д at, on)

**коло́ть** [17] **1.** ⟨рас-⟩ split, cleave; *орехи* crack; **2.** ⟨на-⟩ (Р) chop; **3.** ⟨у-⟩, *once* ⟨кольну́ть⟩ [20] prick; *fig. coll.* taunt; **4.** ⟨за-⟩ stab; *животное* kill, slaughter (*animals*); *impers.* have a stitch in one's side

**колпа́к** *m* [1 *e.*] cap; shade; bell glass

**колхо́з** *m* [1] collective farm, kolkhoz; **~ный** [14] kolkhoz…; **~ник** *m* [1], **~ница** *f* [5] collective farmer

**колыбе́ль** *f* [8] cradle; **~ный** [14]: ***~ная*** (***пе́сня***) *f* lullaby

**колых|а́ть** [3 *st.*: -ы́шу, *etc.*, *or* 1], ⟨вс-⟩, *once* ⟨**~ну́ть**⟩ [20] sway, swing; *листья* stir; *пламя* flicker; **-ся** *v/i.*

**ко́лышек** *m* [1; -шка] peg

**кольну́ть** → ***коло́ть*** *3. & impers.*

**коль|цево́й** [14] ring…; circular; **~цо́** *n* [9; *pl. st., gen.*: коле́ц] ring; circle; ***обруча́льное ~цо́*** wedding ring; *hist.* **~чу́га** *f* [5] shirt of mail

**колю́ч|ий** [17 *sh.*] thorny, prickly; *проволока* barbed; *fig.* → ***ко́лкий***; **~ка** *f* [5; *g/pl.*: -чек] thorn, prickle; barb

**коля́ска** *f* [5; *g/pl.*: -сок] *мотоцикла* side-car; *детская* baby carriage, *Brt.* pram; *инвалидная* wheelchair

**ком** *m* [1; *pl.*: ко́мья, -ьев] lump, clod

**кома́нда** *f* [5] command, order; *naut.* crew; *sport* team; ***пожа́рная ~*** fire brigade

**команди́р** *m* [1] commander; **~ова́ть** [7] (*im*)*pf.*, *a.* ⟨от-⟩ send (on a mission); **~о́вка** *f* [5; *g/pl.*: -вок] business trip; ***она́ в ~о́вке*** she is away on business

**кома́нд|ный** [14] command(ing); **~ование** *n* [12] command; **~овать** [7] ([***над***] Т) command (*a.* [give] order[s], ⟨с-⟩); *coll.* order about **~ующий** [17] (Т) commander

**кома́р** *m* [1 *e.*] mosquito, gnat

**комба́йн** *m* [1] *agric.* combine

**комбин|а́т** *m* [1] industrial complex; group of complementary enterprises; ***~а́т бытово́го обслу́живания*** multiple (consumer-)services establishment; **~а́ция** *f* [7] combination; *econ.* merger; **~и́ровать** [7], ⟨с-⟩ combine

**коме́дия** *f* [7] comedy; farce

**коменда́|нт** *m* [1] *mil.* commandant; superintendent; *общежития* warden; **~нтский** [16]: ***~нтский час*** curfew; **~ту́ра** *f* [5] commandant's office

**коме́та** *f* [5] comet

**ком|и́зм** *m* [1] comic side; **~ик** *m* [1] comedian, comic (actor)

**комисса́р** *m* [1] commissar; commissioner; **~иа́т** *m* [1] commissariat

**коми|ссио́нный** [14] commission (*a. comm.*; *pl. su.* = sum); **~ссия** *f* [7] commission (*a. comm.*), committee; **~те́т** *m* [1] committee

**коми́ч|еский** [16], **~ный** [14; -чен, -чна] comic(al), funny

**ко́мкать** [1], ⟨ис-, с-⟩ crumple

**коммент|а́рий** *m* [3] comment(ary); **~а́тор** *m* [1] commentator; **~и́ровать** [7] (*im*)*pf.* comment (on)

**коммер|са́нт** *m* [1] merchant; businessman; **~ческий** [16] commercial

**комму́н|а** *f* [5] commune; **~а́льный** [14] communal; municipal; ***~а́льная кварти́ра*** (*coll.* ***~а́лка***) communal flat;

**~и́зм** *m* [1] communism; **~ика́ция** *f* [7] communication (*pl. mil.*); **~и́ст** *m* [1], **~и́стка** *f* [5; *g/pl.*: -ток], **~исти́ческий** [14] communist
**коммута́тор** *m* [1] *el.* switchboard
**ко́мнат|а** *f* [5] room; **~ный** [14] room…; *bot.* house…
**комо́к** *m* [1; -мка́] lump, clod
**компа́н|ия** *f* [7] company (*a. comm*); ***води́ть ~ию с*** (T) associate with; **~ьо́н** *m* [1] *comm.* partner; companion
**компа́ртия** *f* [7] Communist Party
**ко́мпас** *m* [1] compass
**компенс|а́ция** *f* [7] compensation; **~и́ровать** [7] (*im*)*pf.* compensate
**компете́н|тный** [14; -тен, -тна] competent; **~ция** [7] competence; scope
**ко́мплек|с** *m* [1], **~сный** [14] complex; **~т** *m* [1] (complete) set; **~тный** [14], **~това́ть** [7], ⟨у-⟩ complete
**комплиме́нт** *m* [1] compliment
**компози́тор** *m* [1] *mus.* composer
**компости́ровать** [7], ⟨про-⟩ punch
**компо́т** *m* [1] compote, stewed fruit
**компре́сс** *m* [1] compress
**компром|ети́ровать** [7], ⟨с-⟩, **~и́сс** *m* [1] compromise (*v/i. a.* ***идти́ на ~и́сс***)
**компью́тер** *m* [1] computer
**комсомо́л** *m* [1] *hist.* Komsomol (Young Communist League); **~ец** *m* [1; -льца], **~ка** *f* [5; *g/pl.*: -лок], **~ьский** [16] Komsomol
**комфо́рт** *m* [1] comfort, convenience; **~а́бельный** [14; -лен, -льна] comfortable, convenient
**конве́йер** *m* [1] (belt) conveyor; assembly line
**конве́нция** *f* [7] convention, agreement
**конве́рсия** *f* [7] *econ.* conversion
**конве́рт** *m* [1] envelope
**конв|ои́р** *m* [1], **~ои́ровать** [7], **~о́й** *m* [3], **~о́йный** [14] convoy, escort
**конгре́сс** *m* [1] congress
**конденс|а́тор** (-dɛ-) *m* [1] *пара* condenser; *el.* capacitor; **~и́ровать** [7] (*im*)*pf.* condense; evaporate (*milk*)
**конди́тер|ская** *f* [16]: ***~ский магази́н*** confectioner's shop; ***~ские изде́лия*** *pl.* confectionery
**кондиционе́р** *m* [1] air conditioner
**коневóдство** *n* [9] horse-breeding
**конёк** *m* [1; -нька́] skate; *coll.* hobby
**кон|е́ц** *m* [1; -нца́] end; close; point; *naut.* rope; ***без ~ца́*** endless(ly); ***в ~е́ц (до ~ца́)*** completely; ***в ~це́*** (P) at the end of; ***в ~це́ ~цо́в*** at long last; ***в оди́н ~е́ц*** one way; ***в о́ба ~ца́*** there and back; ***на худо́й ~е́ц*** at (the) worst; ***под ~е́ц*** in the end; ***тре́тий с ~ца́*** last but two
**коне́чно** (-ʃnə-) of course, certainly
**коне́чности** *f/pl.* [8] extremities
**коне́чн|ый** [14; -чен, -чна] *philos., math.* finite; final, terminal; *цель и т. д.* ultimate
**конкре́тный** [14; -тен, -тна] concrete, specific
**конкур|е́нт** *m* [1] competitor; rival; **~ентноспосо́бный** [14; -бен, -бна] competitive; **~е́нция** *coll. f* [7] competition; **~и́ровать** [7] compete; **´~с** *m* [1] competition
**ко́нн|ица** *f* [5] *hist.* cavalry; **~ый** [14] horse…; (of) cavalry
**конопля́** *f* [6] hemp; **~ный** [14] hempen
**коносаме́нт** *m* [1] bill of lading
**консерв|ати́вный** [14; -вен, -вна] conservative; **~ато́рия** *f* [7] conservatory, *Brt.* school of music, conservatoire; **~и́ровать** [7] (*im*)*pf., a.* ⟨за-⟩ conserve, preserve; can, *Brt.* tin; **~́ный** [14], **~́ы** *m/pl.* [1] canned (*Brt.* tinned) food
**ко́нский** [16] horse (*hair, etc.*)
**консолида́ция** *f* [7] consolidation
**конспе́кт** *m* [1] summary, abstract; synopsis; notes made at a lecture; **~и́ровать** [7] make an abstract (of P); make notes at a lecture
**конспир|ати́вный** [14; -вен, -вна] secret; **~а́ция** *f* [7], conspiracy
**конст|ати́ровать** [7] (*im*)*pf.* establish, ascertain; **~иту́ция** *f* [7] constitution
**констр|уи́ровать** [7] (*im*)*pf. a.* ⟨с-⟩ design; **~ukти́вный** [14; -вен, -вна] constructive; **~у́ктор** *m* [1] designer; constructor; **~у́кция** *f* [7] design; construction, structure
**ко́нсул** *m* [1] consul; **~ьский** [16] consular; **~ьство** *n* [9] consulate; **~ьта́ция** *f* [7] consultation; advice; ***юриди́ческая консульта́ция*** legal advice office;

K

**~ьти́ровать** [7], ⟨про-⟩ advise; **-ся** consult (with **с** T)
**конта́кт** *m* [1] contact; **~ный** [14] *tech.* contact…; [-тен, -тна] *coll.* sociable
**континге́нт** *m* [1] quota, contingent
**контине́нт** *m* [1] continent
**конто́ра** *f* [5] office
**контраба́нд|а** *f* [5] contraband, smuggling; ***занима́ться ~ой*** smuggle; **~и́ст** *m* [1] smuggler
**контр|аге́нт** *m* [1] contractor; **~адмира́л** *m* [1] rear admiral
**контра́кт** *m* [1] contract
**контра́льто** *n* [9] contralto
**контра́ст** *m* [1], **~и́ровать** [7] contrast
**контрата́ка** *f* [5] counterattack
**контрибу́ция** *f* [7] contribution
**контрол|ёр** *m* [1] inspector (*rail. a.* ticket collector); **~и́ровать** [7], ⟨про-⟩ control, check; **~ь** *m* [4] control, checking; **~ьный** [14] control…, check…; ***~ьная рабо́та*** test (*in school*, *etc.*)
**контр|разве́дка** *f* [5] counterespionage, counterintelligence; **~револю́ция** *f* [7] counterrevolution
**конту́з|ить** [15] *pf.*; **~ия** *f* [7] contusion; shell-shock
**ко́нтур** *m* [1] contour, outline
**конура́** *f* [5] kennel
**ко́нус** *m* [1] cone; **~oобра́зный** [14; -зен, -зна] conic(al)
**конфедера|ти́вный** [14] confederative; **~ция** *f* [7] confederation
**конфере́нция** *f* [7] conference (at ***на*** П)
**конфе́та** *f* [5] candy, *Brt.* sweet(s)
**конфи|денциа́льный** [14; -лен, -льна] confidential; **~скова́ть** [7] (*im*)*pf.* confiscate
**конфли́кт** *m* [1] conflict
**конфу́з|ить** [15], ⟨с-⟩ (**-ся** be[come]) embarrass(ed), confuse(d); **~ливый** *coll.* [14 *sh.*] bashful, shy
**конц|ентрат** *m* [1] concentrated product; **~ентрацио́нный** [14] *coll.*, → ***~ла́герь***; **~ентри́ровать** [7], ⟨с-⟩ concentrate (**-ся** *v/i.*); **~е́рт** *m* [1] concert (***на*** П at); *mus.* concerto; **~ла́герь** *m* [4] concentration camp
**конч|а́ть** [1], ⟨**~ить**⟩ [16] finish, end, (**-ся** *v/i.*); *univ.*, *etc.* graduate from; **-ся** *срок* terminate, expire; **~ено!** enough!; **~ик** *m* [1] tip; point; **~и́на** *f* [5] decease
**коньюнкту́р|а** *f* [5] *comm.* state of the market; **~щик** *m* [1] timeserver
**конь** *m* [4 *e.*; *nom/pl. st.*] horse; *poet.* steed; *chess* knight; **~ки́** *m/pl.* [1] (***ро́ликовые*** roller) skates; **~кобе́жец** *m* [1; -жца] skater; **~кобе́жный** [14] skating
**конья́к** *m* [1 *e.*; *part.g.*: -у́] cognac
**ко́н|юх** *m* [1] groom; **~ю́шня** *f* [6; *g/pl.*: -шен] stable
**коопер|ати́в** *m* [1] cooperative (store, society); **~а́ция** *f* [7] cooperation; ***потреби́тельская ~а́ция*** consumers' society
**координа́ты** *f/pl.* [5] *math.* coordinates; *coll.* particulars for making contact (*address*, *telephone and fax numbers etc.*)
**координи́ровать** [7] (*im*)*pf.* coordinate
**копа́ть** [1], ⟨вы́-⟩ dig (up); **-ся** *impf.* dig, root; *в вещах* rummage (about); *в саду и т. д.* putter about; (*медленно делать*) dawdle
**копе́йка** *f* [5; *g/pl.*: -е́ек] kopeck
**копи́лка** *f* [5; *g/pl.*: -лок] money box
**копир|ова́льный** [14]: ***~ова́льная бума́га*** *f* (*coll.* **~ка**) carbon paper; **~ова́ть** [7], ⟨с-⟩ copy; **~о́вщик** *m* [1] copyist
**копи́ть** [14], ⟨на-⟩ accumulate, save; store up
**ко́п|ия** *f* [7] copy (*vb.* **снять ~ию с** P); **~на́** *f* [5; *pl.*: ко́пны, -пён, -пна́м] stack; *волос* shock
**ко́поть** *f* [8] lampblack; soot
**копоши́ться** [16 *e.*; -шу́сь, -ши́шься], ⟨за-⟩ *coll. о людях* putter about, mess around
**копти́ть** [15 *e.*; -пчу́, -пти́шь, -пчённый], ⟨за-⟩ smoke
**копы́то** *n* [9] hoof
**копьё** *n* [10; *pl. st.*] spear; lance
**кора́** *f* [5] bark; *земли и т. д.* crust
**кораб|лекруше́ние** *n* [12] shipwreck; **~лестрое́ние** *n* [12] shipbuilding; **~ль** *m* [4 *e.*] ship
**кора́лл** *m* [1] coral; **~овый** [14] coral…, coralline
**Кора́н** *m* [1] Koran

**коре́|ец** *m* [1; -е́йца], **~йский** [16] Korean

**корен|а́стый** [14 *sh.*] thickset, stocky; **~и́ться** [13] be rooted in; **~но́й** [14] native; (*основной*) fundamental; *зуб* molar; **ˊ~ь** *m* [4; -рня; *from g/pl. e.*] root; ***в ко́рне*** radically; ***пусти́ть ко́рни*** take root; ***вы́рвать с ко́рнем*** pull up by the roots; **ˊ~ья** *n/pl.* [*gen.*: -ьев] roots

**корешо́к** *m* [1; -шка́] rootlet; *книги* spine; *квитанции* stub, counterfoil

**корея́нка** *f* [5; (*g/pl.*: -нок)] Korean

**корзи́н(к)а** *f* [5 (*g/pl.*: -нок)] basket

**коридо́р** *m* [1] corridor, passage

**кори́нка** *f* [5; *no pl.*] currant(s)

**корифе́й** *m* [3] *fig.* luminary

**кори́ца** *f* [5] cinnamon

**кори́чневый** [14] brown

**ко́рка** *f* [5; *g/pl.*: -рок] *хлеба и т. д.* crust; *кожура* rind, peel

**корм** *m* [1; *pl.*: -ма́ *etc. e.*] fodder

**корма́** *f* [5] *naut.* stern

**корм|и́лец** *m* [1; льца] breadwinner; **~и́ть** [14], ⟨на-, по-⟩ feed; ***~и́ть гру́дью*** nurse; ⟨про-⟩ *fig.* maintain, support; **-ся** live on (T); **~ле́ние** *n* [12] feeding; nursing

**корнеплóды** *m/pl.* [1] root crops

**коро́б|ить** [14], ⟨по-⟩ warp (*a. fig.*); jar upon, grate upon: **~ка** *f* [5; *g/pl.*: -бок] box, case

**коро́в|а** *f* [5] cow; ***до́йная ~а*** milch cow; **~ий** [18] cow…; **~ка** *f* [5; *g/pl.*: -вок]: ***бо́жья ~ка*** ladybird; **~ник** *m* [1] cowshed

**короле́в|а** *f* [5] queen; **~ский** [16] royal, regal; **~ство** *n* [9] kingdom

**коро́ль** *m* [4 *e.*] king

**коромы́сло** *n* [9; *g/pl.*: -сел] yoke; (*a. scale*) beam

**коро́н|а** *f* [5] crown; **~а́ция** coronation; **~ка** *f* [5; *g/pl.*: -нок] (*of tooth*) crown; **~ова́ние** *n* [12] coronation; **~ова́ть** [7] (*im*)*pf.* crown

**корот|а́ть** *coll.* [1], ⟨с-⟩ while away; **ˊ~кий** [16; ко́роток, -тка́, ко́ро́тко́, ко́ро́тки́; *comp.*: коро́че] short, brief; ***на ˊ~кой ноге́*** on close terms; ***коро́че*** (***говоря́***) in a word, in short, in brief; ***ˊ~ко и я́сно*** (quite) plainly; ***ру́ки ~ки́!*** just try!

**ко́рпус** *m* [1] body; [*pl.*: -са́, *etc. c.*] frame, case; building; (*a. mil.*, *dipl.*) corps; *судна* hull

**коррект|и́ва** *f* [5] correction; **~и́ровать** [7], ⟨про-⟩ correct; *typ.* proofread; **ˊ~ный** [14; -тен, -тна] correct, proper; **ˊ~ор** *m* [1] proofreader; **~у́ра** *f* [5] proof(-reading)

**корреспонд|е́нт** *m* [1] correspondent; **~е́нция** *f* [7] correspondence

**корсе́т** *m* [1] corset, *Brt. a.* stays *pl.*

**корт** *m* [1] (tennis) court

**корте́ж** *f* [5; *g/pl.*: -же́й] cortège; motorcade

**ко́ртик** *m* [1] dagger

**ко́рточк|и** *f/pl.* [5; *gen.*: -чек]: **сесть** (**сиде́ть**) ***на ~и*** (***~ах***) squat

**корчева́|ние** *n* [12] rooting out; **~ть** [7], ⟨вы́-, рас-⟩ root out

**ко́рчить** [16], ⟨с-⟩ *impers.* (**-ся**) writhe (***от бо́ли*** with pain); convulse; (*no pf.*) *coll. рожи* make faces; (*a.* ***~ из себя́***) pose as

**ко́ршун** *m* [1] kite

**коры́ст|ный** [14; -тен, -тна] selfish, self-interested; *a.* = **~олюби́вый** [14 *sh.*] greedy, mercenary; **~олю́бие** *n* [12] self-interest, cupidity; **~ь** *f* [8] gain, profit; cupidity

**коры́то** *n* [9] through

**корь** *f* [8] measles

**ко́рюшка** *f* [5; *g/pl.*: -шек] smelt

**коря́вый** [14 *sh.*] knotty, gnarled; rugged, rough; *почерк* crooked; *речь* clumsy

**коса́** *f* [5; *ac/sg.*: ко́су; *pl. st.*] **1.** plait, braid; **2.** [*ac/sg. a.* косу́] scythe; spit (*of land*)

**ко́свенный** [14] oblique, indirect (*a. gr.*); *law.* circumstantial

**коси́|лка** *f* [5; *g/pl.*: -лок] mower machine; **~ть**, ⟨с-⟩ **1.** [15; кошу́, ко́сишь] mow; **2.** [15 *e.*; кошу́, коси́шь] squint; **-ся**, ⟨по-⟩ *v/i.*; *a.* look askance (**на** В at); **~чка** *f* [5; *g/pl.*: -чек] *dim.* → ***коса́*** *1*

**косма́тый** [14 *sh.*] shaggy

**косм|е́тика** *f* [5] cosmetics *pl.*: **~ети́ческий** [16] cosmetic; **~и́ческий** [16] cosmic; *корабль* spaceship, space-

craft; **~она́вт** *m* [1] cosmonaut, astronaut
**ко́сн|ость** *f* [8] sluggishness, inertness, stagnation; **~уться** [14] → ***каса́ться***; **~ый** [14; -сен, -сна] sluggish, inert, stagnant
**косо|гла́зый** [14 *sh.*] cross- *or* squint-eyed; **~й** [14; кос, -á, -о] slanting, oblique; sloping; *coll. улыбка* wry; **~ла́пый** [14 *sh.*] pigeon-toed; *coll.* неуклюжий clumsy
**костёр** *m* [1; -тра́] (camp)fire, bonfire
**кост|и́стый** [14 *sh.*] bony; **~ля́вый** [14 *sh.*] scrawny, raw-boned; *рыба*; **~очка** *f* [5; *g/pl.*: -чек] bone; *bot.* pit, stone; ***перемыва́ть ~очки*** gossip (Д about)
**косты́ль** [4 *e.*] crutch
**кост|ь** *f* [8; в -ти́; *from g/pl. e.*] bone; ***промо́кнуть до ~е́й*** get soaked to the skin
**костю́м** *m* [1] suit; dress; costume
**костя́|к** *m* [1 *e.*] skeleton; *fig.* backbone; **~но́й** [14] bone…
**косу́ля** *f* [6] roe deer
**косы́нка** *f* [5; *g/pl.*: -нок] kerchief
**кося́к** *m* [1 *e.*] (door)post; *птиц* flock; *рыбы* school
**кот** *m* [1 *e.*] tomcat; → *a.* ***ко́тик***; ***купи́ть ~а́ в мешке́*** buy a pig in a poke; ***~ напла́кал*** *coll.* very little
**кот|ёл** *m* [1; -тла́] boiler, cauldron; **~ело́к** *m* [1; -лка́] kettle, pot; *mil.* mess tin; *шляпа* bowler
**котёнок** *m* [2] kitten
**ко́тик** *m* [1] *dim.* → ***кот***; fur seal; *мех* sealskin; *adj.*: **~овый** [14]
**котле́та** *f* [5] cutlet; burger; rissole chop
**котлови́на** *f* [5] *geogr.* hollow, basin
**кото́р|ый** [14] which; who; that; what; many a; one; ***~ый раз*** how many times; ***~ый час?*** what time is it?; ***в ~ом часу́?*** (at) what time?
**котте́дж** *n* [1; *g/pl.* -ей] small detached house
**ко́фе** *m* [*indecl.*] coffee; ***раствори́мый ~*** instant coffee; **~ва́рка** *f* [5; *g/pl.*: -рок] coffeemaker; **~йник** *m* [1] coffeepot; **~мо́лка** *f* [5; *g/pl.*: -лок] coffee mill; **~йный** [14] coffee…
**ко́фт|а** *f* [5] (woman's) jacket; (***вя́заная ~а***) jersey, cardigan; **~очка** *f* [5; *g/pl.*: -чек] blouse
**коча́н** *m* [1 *e.*] head (*of cabbage*)
**кочев|а́ть** [7] be a nomad; wander, roam; move from place to place; **~ник** *m* [1] nomad
**кочене́ть** [8], ⟨за-, о-⟩ grow numb (**от** P with), stiffen
**кочерга́** *f* [5; *g/pl.*: -рёг] poker
**ко́чка** *f* [5; *g/pl.*: -ек] hummock; tussock
**коша́чий** [18] cat('s); feline
**кошелёк** *m* [1; -лька́] purse
**ко́шка** *f* [5; *g/pl.*: -шек] cat
**кошма́р** *m* [1] nightmare; **~ный** [14; -рен, -рна] nightmarish; horrible, awful
**кощу́нств|енный** [14 *sh.*] blasphemous; **~о** *n* [9] blasphemy; **~овать** [7] blaspheme
**коэффицие́нт** *m* [1] *math.*, *el.* coefficient; factor; ***~ поле́зного де́йствия*** efficiency
**краб** *m* [1] *zo.* crab
**кра́деный** [14] stolen (goods *n su.*)
**краеуго́льный** [14] basic; *fig. камень* corner(stone)
**кра́жа** *f* [5] theft; ***~ со взло́мом*** burglary
**край** *m* [3; с кра́ю; в краю́: *pl.*: -а́я, -аёв, *etc. e.*] edge; (b)rim; brink (*a. fig.* = edge); end; fringe, border, outskirt; region, land, country; **~ний** [15] outermost, (*a. fig.*) utmost, extreme(ly, utterly, most, very, badly **~не**); ***в ~нем слу́чае*** as a last resort; in case of emergency; **~ность** *f* [8] extreme; (*о положении*) extremity; ***до ~ности*** = **~не**; ***впада́ть в*** (***доходи́ть до***) ***~ности*** go to extremes
**крамо́ла** *f* [5] *obs.* sedition
**кран** *m* [1] *tech.* tap; (stop)cock; crane
**кра́пать** [1 *or* 2 *st.*] drip, trickle
**крапи́в|а** *f* [5] (stinging) nettle; **~ница** *f* [5] nettle rash
**кра́пинка** *f* [5; *g/pl.*: -нок] speck, spot
**крас|а́** *f* [5] → **~ота́**; **~а́вец** *m* [1; -вца] handsome man; **~а́вица** *f* [5] beautiful woman; **~и́вый** [14 *sh.*] beautiful; handsome; *a. слова и т. д. iro.* pretty
**крас|и́тель** *m* [4] dye(stuff); **~ить** [15], ⟨(п)о-, вы́-, рас-⟩ paint, colo(u)r, dye; *coll.* ⟨на-⟩ paint, makeup; **~ка** *f* [5; *g/pl.*: -сок] colo(u)r, paint, dye

**красне́ть** [8], ⟨по-⟩ redden, grow *or* turn red; *от стыда* blush; *impf.* be ashamed; (*a.* **-ся**) appear *or* show red

**красно|арме́ец** *m* [1; -ме́йца] *hist.* Red Army man; **~ба́й** *m* [3] *coll.* phrasemaker; rhetorician; glib talker; **~ва́тый** [14 *sh.*] reddish; **~речи́вый** [14 *sh.*] eloquent; **~ре́чие** *n* [12] eloquence; **~та́** *f* [5] redness; **~щёкий** [16 *sh.*] ruddy

**красну́ха** *f* [5] German measles

**кра́с|ный** [14; -сен, -сна́, -о] red (*a. fig.*); ***~ная строка́*** *f typ.* (*first line of*) new paragraph, new line; ***~ная цена́*** *f coll.* outside price; ***~ное словцо́*** *n coll.* witticism; ***проходи́ть ~ной ни́тью*** run through (*of motif, theme, etc.*)

**красова́ться** [7] stand out *or* impress because of beauty; *coll.* flaunt, show off

**красота́** *f* [5; *pl. st.*: -со́ты] beauty

**кра́сочный** [14; -чен, -чна] colo(u)rful

**красть** [25 *pt. st.*; кра́денный], ⟨у-⟩ steal (**-ся** *v/i., impf.*; *a.* prowl, slink)

**кра́тер** *m* [1] crater

**кра́тк|ий** [16; -ток, -тка́, -о; *comp.*: кра́тче] short, brief, concise; ***и́ ~ое*** *the letter* й; → *a.* ***коро́ткий***; **~овре́менный** [14; -енен, -енна] of short duration; (*преходящий*) transitory; **~осро́чный** [14; -чен, -чна] short; *ссуда и т. д.* shortterm; **~ость** *f* [8] brevity

**кра́тный** [14; -тен, -тна] divisible without remainder

**крах** *m* [1] failure, crash, ruin

**крахма́л** *m* [1], **~ить** [13], ⟨на-⟩ starch; **~ьный** [14] starch(ed)

**кра́шеный** [14] painted; dyed

**креве́тка** *f* [5; *g/pl.*: -ток] *zo.* shrimp

**креди́т** *m* [1] credit; **в ~** on credit; **~ный** [14], **~ова́ть** [7] (*im*)*pf.* credit; **~о́р** *m* [1] creditor; **~оспосо́бный** [14; -бен, -бна] creditworthy; solvent

**кре́йс|ер** *m* [1] cruiser; **~и́ровать** [7] cruise; ply

**крем** *m* [1] cream; ***~ для лица́*** face cream; ***~ для о́буви*** shoe polish

**крем|ато́рий** *m* [3] crematorium; **~а́ция** *f* [7] cremation; **~и́ровать** [7] cremate

**кремл|ёвский** [16], **℮ь** *m* [4 *e.*] Kremlin

**кре́мний** [3] *chem.* silicon

**крен** *m* [1] *naut.* list, heel; *ae.* bank

**кре́ндель** *m* [4 *from g/pl. e.*] pretzel

**крени́ть** [13], ⟨на-⟩ list (**-ся** *v/i.*)

**креп** *m* [1] crepe, crape

**креп|и́ть** [14 *e.*; -плю́, -пи́шь] fix, secure; *fig.* strengthen; **-ся** hold out, bear up; **´~кий** [16; -пок, -пка́, -о; *comp.*: кре́пче] strong; sturdy; *здоровье* sound, robust; ***´~кий оре́шек*** hard nut to crack; **´~ко** *a.* strongly, firmly; **´~нуть** [21], ⟨о-⟩ grow strong(er)

**крепост|но́й** [14] *hist. su.* serf; ***~но́е пра́во*** serfdom; **´~ь** *f* [8; *from g/pl. e.*] fortress; → ***кре́пкий*** strength; firmness, *etc.*

**кре́сло** *n* [9; *g/pl.*: -сел] armchair

**крест** *m* [1 *e.*] cross (*a. fig.*); **~-на́-~** crosswise; **~и́ны** *f/pl.* [5] baptism, christening; **~и́ть** [15; -щённый] (*im*)*pf.*, ⟨о-⟩ baptize, christen; ⟨пере-⟩ cross (**-ся** o.s.); **´~ник** *m* [1] godson; **´~ница** *f* [5] goddaughter; **´~ный** [14] **1.** (of the) cross; **2.** ***´~ный*** (***оте́ц***) godfather; ***´~ная*** (***мать***) godmother

**крестья́н|ин** *m* [1; *pl.*: -я́не, -я́н] peasant; **~ка** *f* [5; *g/pl.*: -нок] peasant woman; **~ский** [16] farm(er['s]), peasant…; country…; **~ство** *n* [9] *collect.* peasants; peasantry

**крети́н** *m* [1] cretin; *fig. coll.* idiot

**креще́ние** *n* [12] baptism, christening; ℮ Epiphany

**крив|а́я** *f* [14] *math.* curve; **~изна́** *f* [5] crookedness, curvature; **~и́ть** [14 *e.*; -влю́, -ви́шь, -влённый], ⟨по-, с-⟩ (**-ся** be[come]) crook(ed), (bent); ⟨с-⟩ (**-ся**) make a wry face; ***~и́ть душо́й*** act against one's conscience *or* convictions; **~ля́нье** *n* [12] affectation; **~ля́ться** [18] (make) grimace(s); mince; **~о́й** [14; крив, -а́, -о] crooked (*a. fig.*), wry; curve(d); P one-eyed; **~оно́гий** [16 *sh.*] bandy-legged, bowlegged; **~ото́лки** *coll. m/pl.* [1] rumo(u)rs, gossip

**кри́зис** *m* [1] crisis

**крик** *m* [1] cry, shout; outcry; ***после́дний ~ мо́ды*** the latest word in fashion; **~ли́вый** [14 *sh.*] shrill; clamorous; loud; **´~нуть** → ***крича́ть***

**кри|мина́льный** [14] criminal; **~ста́лл**

*m* [1] crystal; ~**ста́льный** [14; -лен, -льна] crystalline; *fig.* crystal-clear

**крите́рий** *m* [3] criterion

**кри́ти|к** *m* [1] critic; ~**ка** *f* [5] criticism; *lit., art* critique, review; ~**кова́ть** [7] criticize; **∠ческий** [16], **∠чный** [14; -чен, -чна] critical

**крича́ть** [4 *e.*; -чу́, -чи́шь], ⟨за-⟩, *once* ⟨кри́кнуть⟩ [20] cry (out), shout (***на*** В at); scream

**кров** *m* [1] roof; shelter

**крова́|вый** [14 *sh.*] bloody; ~**ть** *f* [8] bed

**кро́вельщик** *m* [1] roofer

**кровено́сный** [14] blood (*vessel*)

**кро́вля** *f* [6; *g/pl.*: -вель] roof(ing)

**кро́вный** [14] (*adv.* by) blood; (*жизненно важный*) vital

К

**крово|жа́дный** [14; -ден, -дна] bloodthirsty; ~**излия́ние** *n* [12] *med.* h(a)emorrhage; ~**обраще́ние** *n* [12] circulation of the blood; ~**пи́йца** *m/f* [5] bloodsucker; ~**подтёк** *m* [1] bruise; ~**проли́тие** *n* [12] bloodshed; ~**проли́тный** [14; -тен, -тна] → ***крова́вый***; ~**смеше́ние** *n* [12] incest; ~**тече́ние** *n* [12] bleeding; → ***~излия́ние***; ~**точи́ть** [16 *e.*; -чи́т] bleed

**кров|ь** *f* [8; -ви] blood (*a. fig.*); ~**яно́й** [14] blood…

**кро|и́ть** [13; кро́енный], ⟨вы́-, с-⟩ cut (out); **∠йка** *f* [5] cutting (out)

**крокоди́л** *m* [1] crocodile

**кро́лик** *m* [1] rabbit

**кро́ме** (Р) except, besides (*a.* ~ ***того́***), apart (*or* aside) from; but

**кромса́ть** [1], ⟨ис-⟩ hack

**кро́на** *f* [5] crown (*of tree*); (*unit of currency*) crown, krone, krona

**кропи́ть** [14 *e.*; -плю́, -пи́шь, -плённый], ⟨о-⟩ sprinkle

**кропотли́вый** [14 *sh.*] laborious, toilsome; painstaking, assiduous

**кроссво́рд** *m* [1] crossword puzzle

**кроссо́вки** *f* [5; *g/pl.*: -вок] running shoes; *Brt.* trainers

**крот** *m* [1 *e.*] *zo.* mole

**кро́ткий** [16; -ток, -тка́, -о; *comp.*: кро́тче] gentle, meek

**кро́|ха** *f* [5; *ac/sg.*: кро́ху; *from dat/pl. e.*] crumb; *о количестве* bit; **∠хотный** *coll.* [14; -тен, -тна], **∠шечный** *coll.* [14] tiny; ~**ши́ть** [16], ⟨на-, по-, из-⟩ crumb(le); (*мелко рубить*) chop; **∠шка** *f* [5; *g/pl.*: -шек] crumb; *coll.* little one; ***ни ∠шки*** not a bit

**круг** *m* [1; в, на -у́; *pl. e.*] circle (*a. fig.*); *интересов и т. д.* sphere, range; ~**лова́тый** [14 *sh.*] roundish; ~**лоли́цый** [14 *sh.*] chubbyfaced; **∠лый** [14; кругл, -á, -о] round; *coll. дурак* perfect; ***∠лая су́мма*** round sum; ***∠лые су́тки*** day and night; ~**ово́й** [14] circular; *порука* mutual; ~**оборо́т** *m* [1] circulation; *событий* succession; ~**озо́р** *m* [1] prospect; range of interests; ~**о́м** round; *вокруг* around, (round) about; ~**осве́тный** [14] round-the-world

**кру́ж|ево** *n* [9; *pl. e.*; *g/pl.*: кру́жев] lace; ~**и́ть** [16 & 16 *e.*; кружу́, кру́жишь], ⟨за-, вс-⟩ turn (round), whirl; circle; spin; *плутать* stray about; (**-ся** *v/i.*); ***вскружи́ть го́лову*** (Д) turn s.o.'s head; ***голова́ ~ится*** (***у*** Р) feel giddy; ~**ка** *f* [5; *g/pl.*: -жек] mug; tankard; *пива* glass

**кру́жный** *coll.* [14] traffic circle, *Brt.* roundabout

**кружо́к** *m* [1; -жка́] (small) circle; *lit. pol.* study group

**круп** *m* [1] *лошади* croup

**круп|а́** *f* [5] groats *pl.*; *fig. снег* sleet; ~**и́нка** *f* [5; *g/pl.*: -нок] grain (*a. fig.* = ***~и́ца*** *f* [5])

**кру́пный** [14; -пен, -пна́, -о] big, large(-scale), great; (*выдающийся*) outstanding; (*важный*) important, serious; *cine.* close (up); *fig.* ~ ***разгово́р*** high words

**крутизна́** *f* [5] steep(ness)

**крути́ть** [15], ⟨за-, с-⟩ twist; twirl; roll (up); turn; whirl; Р *impf.* be insincere *or* evasive; trick; *любовь* have a love affair (with)

**круто́|й** [14; крут, -á, -о; *comp.*: кру́че] steep, (*резкий*) sharp, abrupt; (*неожиданный*) sudden; *яйцо* hard (*a.* -boiled); *мера и т. д.* harsh; ′~**сть** *f* [8] harshness

**круше́ние** *n* [12] wreck; *надежд* ruin; collapse; *a. rail.* derailment

**крыжо́вник** *m* [1] gooseberry bush; *collect.* gooseberries

**крыл|а́тый** [14 *sh.*] winged (*a. fig.*); **~о́** *n* [9; *pl.*: кры́лья; -льев] wing (*a. arch., ae., pol.*); **~ьцо́** *n* [9; *pl.* кры́льца, -ле́ц, -льца́м] steps *pl.*; porch
**кры́мский** [16] Crimean
**кры́са** *f* [5] rat
**крыть** [22], ⟨по-⟩ cover, roof; *краской* coat; *в картах* trump; **-ся** *impf.* (**в** П) lie *or* be in; be concealed
**кры́ш|а** *f* [5] roof; **~ка** *f* [5; *g/pl.*: -шек] lid, cover; P (Д p.'s) end
**крюк** *m* [1 *e.*; *pl. a.*: крю́чья, -ев] hook; *coll.* detour
**крюч|кова́тый** [14 *sh.*] hooked; **~котво́рство** *n* [9] chicanery; pettifoggery; **~о́к** *m* [1; -чка́] hook; ***~о́к для вяза́ния*** crochet hook
**кряж** *m* [1] mountain range; chain of hills
**кря́к|ать** [1], *once* ⟨~нуть⟩ [20] quack
**кряхте́ть** [11] groan, grunt
**кста́ти** to the point (*or* purpose); opportune(ly), in the nick of time; apropos; besides, too, as well; incidentally, by the way
**кто** [23] who; **~ …, ~ …** some…, others …; ***~ бы ни*** whoever; ***~ бы то ни́ был*** who(so)ever it may be; **~** *coll.* = **~-либо**, **~-нибудь**, **~-то** [23] anyone; someone
**куб** *m* [1] *math.* cube
**ку́барем** *coll.* head over heels
**ку́б|ик** *m* [1] (small) cube; *игрушка* brick, block (*toy*); **~и́ческий** [16] cubic
**ку́бок** *m* [1; -бка] goblet; *приз* cup
**кубоме́тр** *m* [1] cubic meter (-tre)
**кувши́н** *m* [1] jug; pitcher
**кувши́нка** *f* [5; *g/pl.*: -нок] water lily
**кувырк|а́ться** [1], *once* ⟨~ну́ться⟩ [20] somersault, tumble; **~о́м** → ***ку́барем***
**куда́** where (… to); what … for; *coll.* (*a.* ***~ как[о́й]***, *etc.*) very, awfully, how; at all; by far, much; (*a.* + Д [& *inf.*]) how can …; ***~ ни*** wherever; (*a.* ***~ тут, там***) (that's) impossible!, certainly not!, what an idea!, (*esp.* ***~ тебе́!***) rats!; **~ …, ~ …** to some places …, to others …; ***~ вы*** (*i. e.* ***идёте***)**?**; where are you going?; ***хоть ~*** P fine; couldn't be better; → ***ни ~*** = **~-либо**, **~-нибудь**, **~-то** any-, somewhere
**куда́хтать** [3] cackle, cluck
**куде́сник** *m* [1] magician, sorcerer
**ку́др|и** *f/pl.* [-е́й, *etc. e.*] curls; **~я́вый** [14 *sh.*] curly(-headed); *дерево* bushy
**кузн|е́ц** *m* [1 *e.*] (black)smith; **~е́чик** *m* [1] *zo.* grasshopper; **~ица** *f* [5] smithy
**ку́зов** *m* [1; *pl.*: -ва́, *etc. e.*] body (*of car, etc.*)
**кукаре́кать** [1] crow
**ку́киш** P *m* [1] *coll.* (*gesture of derision*) fig, fico
**ку́к|ла** *f* [5; *g/pl.*: -кол] doll; **~олка** *f* [5; *g/pl.*: -лок] **1.** *dim.* → **~ла**; **2.** *zo.* chrysalis; **~ольный** [14] doll('s); ***~ольный теа́тр*** puppet show
**кукуру́з|а** *f* [5] corn, *Brt.* maize; **~ный** [14] corn…; ***~ные хло́пья*** cornflakes
**куку́шка** *f* [5; *g/pl.*: -шек] cuckoo
**кула́к** *m* [1 *e.*] fist; *hist.* kulak (*prosperous farmer or peasant*)
**кулёк** *m* [1; -лька́] (paper) bag
**кули́к** *m* [1 *e.*] curlew; snipe
**кулина́р|ия** *f* [7] cookery; **~ный** [14] culinary
**кули́са** *f* [5] *thea.* wing, side; ***за ~ми*** behind the scenes
**кули́ч** *m* [1 *e.*] Easter cake
**куло́н** *m* [1] pendant
**кулуа́ры** *m/pl.* [1] *sg. not used* lobbies
**куль** *m* [4 *e.*] sack, bag
**культ** *m* [1] cult; **~иви́ровать** [7] cultivate; **~у́ра** *f* [5] culture; standard (***земледе́лия*** of farming); ***зерновы́е ~у́ры*** cereals; **~у́рный** [14; -рен, -рна] cultural; cultured, well-bred
**культя́** *f* [7 *e.*] *med.* stump
**кума́ч** *m* [1 *e.*] red calico
**куми́р** *m* [1] idol
**кумовство́** *n* [9] *fig.* favo(u)ritism; nepotism
**куни́ца** *f* [5] marten
**купа́|льный** [14] bathing; ***~льный костю́м*** bathing suit, *Brt.* bathing costume; **~льщик** *m* [1] bather; **~ть(ся)** [1], ⟨вы́-, ис-⟩ (take a) bath; bathe
**купе́** (-'pɛ) *n* [*indecl.*] *rail.* compartment
**купе́|ц** *m* [1; -пца́] merchant; **~ческий** [16] merchant('s); **~чество** *n* [9] *collect.* merchants

К

**купи́ть** → ***покупа́ть***
**купле́т** *m* [1] couplet, stanza; song
**ку́пля** *f* [6] purchase
**ку́пол** *m* [1; *pl.*: -ла] cupola, dome
**ку́пчая** *f* [14] *hist.* deed of purchase
**купю́ра** *f* [5] bill, banknote; *в тексте* cut, excision
**курга́н** *m* [1] burial mound, barrow
**ку́р|ево** *coll. n* [9] tobacco, cigarettes; **~е́ние** *n* [12] smoking; **~и́льщик** *m* [1] smoker
**кури́ный** [14] chicken…; hen's; *coll. память* short; *med.* night (*слепота* blindness)
**кури́|тельный** [14] smoking; **~ть** [13; курю́, ку́ришь], ⟨по-, вы-⟩ smoke (**-ся** *v/i.*)
**ку́рица** *f* [5; *pl.*: ку́ры, *etc. st.*] hen; *cul.* chicken
**курно́сый** [14 *sh.*] snub-nosed
**куро́к** *m* [1; -рка́] cock (*of weapon*)
**куропа́тка** *f* [5; *g/pl.*: -ток] partridge
**куро́рт** *m* [1] health resort
**курс** *m* [1] course (*naut., ae., med., educ.*; ***держа́ть ~ на*** (В) head for; *a. univ.* year); *fin.* rate of exchange; *fig.* line, policy; ***держа́ть (быть) в ~е*** (P) keep (be) (well) posted on; **~а́нт** *m* [1] *mil.* cadet; **~и́в** *m* [1] *typ.* italics; **~и́ровать** [7] ply; **~о́р** *m* [1] *computer* cursor
**ку́ртка** *f* [5; *g/pl.*: -ток] jacket
**курча́вый** [14 *sh.*] curly(-headed)
**курь|ёз** *m* [1] curious; amusing; **~е́р** *m* [1] messenger; courier
**куря́щий** *m* [17] smoker
**кус|а́ть** [1], ⟨укуси́ть⟩ [15] bite (**-ся** *v/i., impf.*), sting; **~о́к** *m* [1; -ска́] piece, bit, morsel; scrap; *мыла* cake; *пирога и т. д.* slice; ***на ~ки́*** to pieces; ***зараба́тывать на ~о́к хле́ба*** earn one's bread and butter; **~о́чек** *m* [1; -чка] *dim.* → ***~о́к***
**куст** *m* [1 *e.*] bush, shrub; **~а́рник** *m* [1] *collect.* bush(es), shrub(s)
**куста́р|ный** [14] handicraft…; hand(-made); *fig.* primitive, crude; **~ь** *m* [4 *e.*] craftsman
**ку́тать(ся)** [1], ⟨за-⟩ muffle *or* wrap o.s. (up, in)
**кут|ёж** *m* [1 *e.*], **~и́ть** [15] carouse
**ку́х|ня** *f* [6; *g/pl.*: ку́хонь] kitchen; *русская и т. д.* cuisine, cookery; **~онный** [14] kitchen…
**ку́цый** [14 *sh.*] dock-tailed; short
**ку́ч|а** *f* [5] heap, pile; a lot of; **~ами** in heaps, in crowds; ***вали́ть всё в одну́ ~у*** lump everything together; ***класть в ~у*** pile up; **~ер** *m* [1; *pl.*: -ра, *etc. e.*] coachman; **~ка** *f* [5; *g/pl.*: -чек] *dim.* → **~а**; small group
**куша́к** *m* [1 *e.*] belt, girdle, sash
**ку́ша|нье** *n* [10] dish; food; **~ть** [1], ⟨по-⟩ eat (up ⟨с-⟩)
**куше́тка** *f* [5; *g/pl.*: -ток] couch
**кюве́т** *m* [1] drainage ditch

# Л

**лабири́нт** *m* [1] labyrinth, maze
**лабор|а́нт** *m* [1], **~а́нтка** *f* [5; *g/pl.*: -ток] laboratory assistant; **~ато́рия** *f* [7] laboratory
**ла́ва** *f* [5] lava
**лави́на** *f* [5] avalanche
**лави́ровать** [7] *naut.* tack; (*fig.*) maneuver (-noeuvre)
**лавр** *m* [1] laurel; **~о́вый** [14] (of) laurel(s)
**ла́гер|ь 1.** [4; *pl.*: -ря́, *etc. e.*] camp (*a., pl.*: -ри, *etc. st., fig.*); ***располага́ться (стоя́ть) ~ем*** camp (out), be encamped; **~ный** [14] camp…
**лад** *m* [1; в ~у́; *pl. e.*]: **(не) в ~у́ (~а́х)** → **(не) ~ить**; **идти на ~** work (well), get on *or* along; **~а́н** *m* [1] incense; **дыша́ть на ~а́н** have one foot in the grave; **~ить** *coll.* [15], ⟨по-, с-⟩ get along *or* on (well), *pf. a.* make it up; (*справиться*) manage; **не ~ить** *a.* be at odds *or* variance; **-ся** *coll. impf.* → **идти́ на ~, ~ить**; **~но**

*coll.* all right, O.K.; **~ный** [14; -ден, -дна́, -о] *coll.* fine, excellent
**ладо́|нь** *f* [8], P *f* [5] palm; ***как на ~ни*** spread before the eyes; ***бить в ~ши*** clap (one's hands)
**ладья́** *f* [6] *obs.* boat; *chess*: rook
**лаз|е́йка** *f* [5; *g/pl.*: -е́ек] loophole; **~ить** [15] climb (*v/t.* ***на*** B); clamber
**лазу́р|ный** [14; -рен, -рна], **~ь** *f* [8] azure
**лай** *m* [3] bark(ing), yelp; **~ка** *f* [5; *g/pl.*: ла́ек] **1.** Eskimo dog; **2.** *кожа* kid; **~ковый** [14] kid…
**лак** *m* [1] varnish, lacquer; **~овый** [14] varnish(ed), lacquer(ed); *кожа* patent leather…
**лака́ть** [1], 〈вы́-〉 lap
**лаке́й** *m* [3] *fig.* flunk(e)y; **~ский** [16] *fig.* servile
**лакирова́ть** [7], 〈от-〉 lacquer, varnish
**ла́ком|иться** [14], 〈по-〉 (T) enjoy, relish (*a. fig.*), eat with delight; **~ка** *coll. m/f* [5] lover of dainties; ***быть ~кой*** *a.* have a sweet tooth; **~ство** *n* [9] dainty, delicacy; *pl.* sweetmeats; **~ый** [14 *sh.*] dainty; ***~ый кусо́(че)к*** *m* tidbit, *Brt.* titbit
**лакони́ч|еский** [16], **~ный** [14; -чен, -чна] laconic(al)
**ла́мп|а** *f* [5] lamp; **~а́да** *f* [5 (*g/pl.*:] lamp (*for icon*); **~овый** [14] lamp…; **~очка** *f* [5; *g/pl.*: -чек] bulb
**ландша́фт** *m* [1] landscape
**ла́ндыш** *m* [1] lily of the valley
**лань** *f* [8] fallow deer; hind, doe
**ла́па** *f* [5] paw; *fig.* clutch
**лапша́** *f* [5] noodles *pl.*; noodle soup
**ларёк** *m* [1; -рька́] kiosk, stand
**ла́ск|а** *f* [5] caress; **~а́тельный** [14] endearing, pet; *a.* **~овый**; **~а́ть** [1], 〈при-〉 caress; pet, fondle; **-ся** endear o.s. (**к** Д to); *о собаке* fawn (*of dog*); **~овый** [14 *sh.*] affectionate, tender; caressing; *ветер* soft
**ла́сточка** *f* [5; *g/pl.*: -чек] swallow
**лата́ть** *coll.* [1], 〈за-〉 patch, mend
**латви́йский** [16] Latvian
**лати́нский** [16] Latin
**лату́нь** *f* [8] brass
**ла́ты** *f/pl.* [5] *hist.* armo(u)r
**латы́нь** *f* [8] Latin
**латы́ш** *m* [1 *e.*], **~ка** *f* [5; *g/pl.*: -шек] Lett; **~ский** [16] Lettish
**лауреа́т** *m* [1] prizewinner
**ла́цкан** *m* [1] lapel
**лачу́га** *f* [5] hovel, shack
**ла́ять** [27], 〈за-〉 bark
**лгать** [лгу, лжёшь, лгут; лгал, -а́, -о], 〈со-〉 lie, tell lies
**лгун** *m* [1 *e.*], **~ья** *f* [6] liar
**лебёдка** *f* [5; *g/pl.*: -док] winch
**лебе|ди́ный** [14] swan…; **´~дь** *m* [4; *from g/pl.*: *e.*] (*poet. a. f*) swan; **~зи́ть** *coll.* [15 *e.*; -бежу́, -бези́шь] fawn (***перед*** T upon)
**лев** *m* [1; льва́] lion; ♌ Leo
**лев|ша́** *m/f* [5; *g/pl.*: -ше́й] left-hander; **~ый** [14] left (*a. fig.*), left-hand; *ткани* wrong (*side*; on **с** P)
**лега́льный** [14; -лен, -льна] legal
**леге́нд|а** *f* [5] legend; **~а́рный** [14; -рен, -рна] legendary
**легио́н** *m* [1] legion (*mst. fig = a great number of people*)
**лёгкий** (-xk-) [16; лёгок, легка́; *a.* лёгки; *comp.*: ле́гче] light (*a. fig.*); *нетрудный* easy; *прикосновение* slight; (Д) ***легко́*** + *inf.* it is very well for … + *inf.*; ***лёгок на поми́не*** *coll.* talk of the devil!
**легкоатле́т** *m* [1] track and field athlete
**легко|ве́рный** (-xk-) [14; -рен, -рна] credulous; **~ве́сный** [14; -сен, -сна] lightweight; *fig.* shallow; **~во́й** [14]: ***легково́й автомоби́ль*** *a.* ***~ва́я (а́вто)маши́на*** auto(mobile), car
**лёгкое** *n* [16] lung
**легкомы́сл|енный** (-xk-) [14 *sh.*] light-minded, frivolous; thoughtless; **~ие** *n* [12] levity; frivolity; flippancy
**лёгкость** (-xk-) *f* [8] lightness; easiness; ease
**лёд** *m* [1; льда́, на льду́] ice
**лед|ене́ть** [8], 〈за-, о-〉 freeze, ice (up, over); grow numb (*with cold*); **~ене́ц** *m* [1; -нца́] (sugar) candy; **~ени́ть** [13], 〈о(б)-〉 freeze, ice; *сердце* chill; **~ни́к** *m* [1 *e.*] glacier; **~нико́вый** [14] glacial; ice…; **~око́л** *m* [1] icebreaker; **~охо́д** *m* [1] pack ice; **~яно́й** [14] ice…; ice-cold; icy (*a. fig.*)
**лежа́|ть** [4 *e.*; лёжа] lie; (*быть располо-*

Л

*ложенным*) be (situated); rest, be incumbent; **~ть в осно́ве** (**в** П form the basis); **~чий** [17] lying; **~чий больно́й** (in)patient
**ле́звие** *n* [12] edge; razor blade
**лезть** [24 *st*.: ле́зу; лезь!; лез, -ла], ‹по-› (be) climb(ing, *etc*.; *v/t*.); creep; (*проникнуть*) penetrate; *coll*. reach into; (**к** Д [**с** Т]) importune, press; *о волосах* fall out; (**на** В) fit (*v/t*); P *не в своё дело* meddle
**лейбори́ст** *m* [1] *pol*. Labo(u)rite
**ле́й|ка** *f* [5; *g/pl*.: ле́ек] watering can; **~копла́стырь** *m* [4] adhesive plaster; **~тена́нт** *m* [1] (second) lieutenant; **~тмоти́в** *m* [1] leitmotif
**лека́р|ственный** [14] medicinal; **~ство** *n* [9] drug, medicine, remedy (**против** Р for)
**ле́ксика** *f* [5] vocabulary
**ле́к|тор** *m* [1] lecturer; **~то́рий** *m* [3] lecture hall; **~ция** *f* [7] lecture (at **на** П; *vb*.: **слу́шать** [**чита́ть**] attend [give, deliver])
**леле́ять** [27] pamper; *fig*. cherish
**лён** *m* [1; льна́] flax
**лени́в|ец** *m* [1; -вца] → **лентя́й**; **~ица** *f* [5] → **лентя́йка**; **~ый** [14 *sh*.] lazy, idle; *вялый* sluggish
**лени́ться** [13; леню́сь, ле́нишься], be lazy
**ле́нта** *f* [5] ribbon; band; *tech*. tape
**лентя́й** *m* [3], **~ка** *f* [5; *g/pl*.: -я́ек] lazybones; sluggard; **~ничать** *coll*. [1] idle
**лень** *f* [8] laziness, idleness; *coll*. (**мне**) **~** I am too lazy to …
**леопа́рд** *m* [1] leopard
**лепе|сто́к** *m* [1; -тка́] petal; **~т** *m* [1], **~та́ть** [4], ‹про-› babble, prattle
**лепёшка** *f* [5; *g/pl*.: -шек] scone
**леп|и́ть** [14], ‹вы́-, с-› sculpture, model, mo(u)ld; *coll*. ‹на-› stick (**на** В to); **~ка** model(l)ing; **~но́й** [14] mo(u)lded; **~но́е украше́ние** stucco mo(u)lding
**ле́пт|а** *f* [5]: **внести́ свою́ ~у** make one's own contribution to s.th
**лес** *m* [1] [и́з лесу, из ле́са; в лесу́: *pl*.: леса́, *etc*. *e*.] wood, forest; *материал* lumber, *Brt*. timber; *pl*. scaffolding; **~ом** through a (the) wood

**леса́** *f* [5; *pl*.: лёсы, *etc*. *st*.] (fishing) line
**леси́стый** [14 *sh*.] woody, wooded
**ле́ска** *f* [5; *g/pl*.: -сок] → **леса́**
**лес|ни́к** *m* [1 *e*.] ranger, forester; **~ни́чество** *n* [9] forest district; **~ни́чий** *m* [17] forest warden; **~но́й** [14] forest…; wood(y); lumber…; timber…
**лесо|во́дство** *n* [9] forestry; **~насажде́ние** *n* [12] afforestation; wood; **~пи́льный** [14]: **~пи́льный заво́д** = **~пи́льня** *f* [6; *g/pl*.: -лен] sawmill; **~ру́б** *m* [1] lumberman, woodcutter
**ле́стница** (-sn-) *f* [5] (flight of) stairs *pl*., staircase; *приставная* ladder; **пожа́рная ~** fire escape
**ле́ст|ный** [14; -тен, -тна] flattering; **~ь** *f* [8] flattery
**лёт** *m* [1]: **хвата́ть на лету́** grasp quickly, be quick on the uptake
**лета́**, **лет** → **ле́то**; → *a*. **год**
**лета́тельный** [14] flying
**лета́ть** [1] fly
**лете́ть** [1], ‹по-› (be) fly(ing)
**ле́тний** [15] summer…
**лётный** [14] *погода* flying; **~ соста́в** aircrew
**ле́т|о** *n* [9; *pl*. *e*.] summer (T in [the]; **на** В for the); *pl*. years, age (**в** В at); **ско́лько вам ~?** how old are you? (→ **быть**); **в ~а́х** elderly, advanced in years; **~опись** *f* [8] chronicle; **~осчисле́ние** *n* [12] chronology; era
**лету́ч|ий** [17 *sh*.] *chem*. volatile; **~ая мышь** *zo*. bat
**лётчи|к** *m* [1], **~ца** *f* [5] pilot, aviator, flier, air(wo)man; **лётчик-испыта́тель** test pilot
**лечéбн|ица** *f* [5] clinic, hospital; **~ый** [14] medic(in)al
**леч|е́ние** *n* [12] *med*. treatment; **~и́ть** [16] treat; **-ся** undergo treatment, be treated; treat (one's … **от** Р)
**лечь** → **ложи́ться**; → *a*. **лежа́ть**
**ле́ший** *m* [17] *Russian mythology* wood goblin; P Old Nick
**лещ** *m* [1 *e*.] *zo*. bream
**лж|е…** false; pseudo…; **~е́ц** *m* [1 *e*.] mock…; liar; **~и́вость** *f* [8] mendacity; **~и́вый** [14 *sh*.] false, lying; mendacious
**ли**, (*short*, *after vowels*, *a*.) **ль 1.** (*interr*,

*part.*) ***знáет ~ онá …?*** (= ***онá знáет …?***) does she know…?; **2.** (*cj.*) whether, if; **…, ~, … ~** whether …, or…
**либерáл** *m* [1], **~ьный** [14; -лен, -льна] liberal
**ли́бо** or; **~ …, ~ …** either … or …
**либрéтто** *n* [*indecl.*] libretto
**ли́вень** *m* [4; -вня] downpour, cloudburst
**ливрéя** *f* [6; *g/pl.*: -рéй] livery
**ли́га** *f* [5] league
**ли́дер** *m* [1] *pol.*, *sport* leader
**лиз|áть** [3], *once* ⟨~нýть⟩ lick
**лик** *m* [1] face; countenance; *образ* image; *eccl.* assembly; ***причи́слить к ∠у святы́х*** canonize
**ликвиди́ровать** [7] (*im*)*pf.* liquidate
**ликёр** *m* [1] liqueur
**ликовáть** [7], ⟨воз-⟩ exult
**ли́лия** *f* [7] lily
**лилóвый** [14] lilac(-colo[u]red)
**лими́т** *m* [1] quota, limit; **~и́ровать** [7] (*im*)*pf.* limit
**лимóн** *m* [1] lemon; **~áд** *m* [1] lemonade; **~ный** [14] lemon; ***~ная кислотá*** citric acid
**ли́мфа** *f* [5] lymph
**лингви́стика** *f* [5] → ***языкознáние***
**линéй|ка** *f* [5; *g/pl.*: -éек] line, ruler; **~ный** [14] linear
**ли́н|за** *f* [5] lens; ***контáктные ~зы*** contact lenses; **~ия** *f* [7] line (*a. fig.*; ***по*** Д in); **~кóр** *m* [1] battleship; **~овáть** [7], ⟨на-⟩ rule; **~óлеум** *m* [1] linoleum
**линчевáть** [7] (*im*)*pf.* lynch
**линь** *m* [4 *e.*] *zo.* tench
**ли́н|ька** *f* [5] mo(u)lt(ing); **~я́лый** *coll.* [14] *о ткани* faded; mo(u)lted; **~я́ть** [28], ⟨вы́-, по-⟩ fade; mo(u)lt
**ли́па** *f* [5] linden, lime tree
**ли́п|кий** [16; -пок, -пкá, -о] sticky, adhesive; *пластырь* sticking; **~нуть** [21], ⟨при-⟩ stick
**ли́р|а** *f* [5] lyre; **~ик** *m* [1] lyric poet; **~ика** *f* [5] lyric poetry; **~и́ческий** [16], **~и́чный** [14; -чен, -чна] lyric(al)
**лис|(и́ц)á** *f* [5; *pl. st.*] fox (silver… ***черно-бýрая***); **∠ий** [18] fox…; foxy
**лист** *m* **1.** [1 *e.*] sheet; (*исполнительный*) writ; **2.** [1 *e.*; *pl. st.*: ли́стья, -ев] *bot.* leaf; *coll. a.* → **~вá**; **~áть** *coll.* [1] leaf *or* thumb through; **~вá** *f* [5] *collec.* foliage, leaves *pl.*; **∠венница** *f* [5] larch; **∠венный** [14] deciduous; **∠ик** *m* [1] *dim.* → ~; **~óвка** *f* [5 *g/pl.*: -вок] leaflet; **~óк** *m* [1; -ткá] *dim.* → ~; slip; **~овóй** [14] sheet…; *железо и т. д.*
**литéйный** [14]: **~ цех** foundry
**литер|áтор** *m* [1] man of letters; writer; **~атýра** *f* [5] literature; **~атýрный** [14; -рен, -рна] literary
**литóв|ец** *m* [1; -вца], **~ка** *f* [5; *g/pl.*: -вок], **~ский** [16] Lithuanian
**литóй** [14] cast
**литр** *m* [1] liter (*Brt.* -tre)
**лить** [лью, льёшь; лил, -á, -о; лей(те)! ли́тый (лит, -á, -о)] pour; *слёзы* shed; *tech.* cast; ***дождь льёт как из ведрá*** it's raining cats and dogs; **-ся** flow, pour; *песня* sound; *слёзы и т. д.* stream; **~ён** [10] founding, cast(ing)
**лифт** *m* [1] elevator, *Brt.* lift; **~ёр** *m* [1] lift operator
**ли́фчик** *m* [1] bra(ssière)
**лих|óй** [14; лих, -á, -о] *coll.* bold, daring; dashing; **~орáдка** *f* [5] fever; **~орáдочный** [14; -чен, -чна] feverish; **∠ость** *f* [8] *coll.* swagger; spirit; dash
**лицев|áть** [7], ⟨пере-⟩ face; turn; **~óй** [14] face…; front…; *сторона* right; ***~óй счёт*** personal account
**лицемéр** *m* [1] hypocrite; **~ие** *n* [12] hypocrisy; **~ный** [14; -рен, -рна] hypocritical; **~ить** [13] dissemble
**лицéнзия** *f* [7] license (*Brt.* -ce) (В for ***на***)
**лиц|ó** *n* [9; *pl. st.*] face; countenance (*change v/t.* ***в*** П); front; person, individual(ity); ***в ~ó*** by sight; to s.b.'s face; ***от ~á*** (Р) in the name of; ***~óм к ~ý*** face to face; ***быть*** (Д) ***к ~ý*** suit *or* become a p.; ***нет ~á*** be bewildered; ***должностнóе ~ó*** official
**личи́нка** *f* [5; *g/pl.*: -нок] larva; maggot
**ли́чн|ость** *f* [8] personality; person, individual; **~ый** [14] personal; private
**лишáй** *m* [3 *e.*] *bot.* lichen (*a.* **~ник**); *med.* herpes
**лиш|áть** [1], ⟨~и́ть⟩ [16 *e.*; -шý, -ши́шь, -шённый] deprive; strip (of Р); *на-*

Л

*следства* disinherit; **~а́ть себя́ жи́зни** commit (*suicide*); **~ённый** *a.* devoid of, lacking; **-ся** (P) lose; **~и́ться чу́вств** faint; **~е́ние** *n* [12] (de)privation; loss; *pl.* privations, hardships; **~е́ние прав** disfranchisement; **~е́ние свобо́ды** imprisonment; **~и́ть(ся)** → **~а́ть(ся)**
**ли́шн|ий** [15] superfluous, odd, excessive, over…; sur…; *запасной* spare; extra; *ненужный* needless, unnecessary; *su.* outsider; **~ее** undue (*things*, *etc.*); *выпить* (*a.* a glass) too much; **… с ~им** over …; **~ий раз** once again; **не ~е** + *inf.* (p.) had better
**лишь** (*a.* + **то́лько**) only; merely, just; as soon as, no sooner … than, hardly; **~ бы** if only, provided that
**лоб** *m* [1; лба; во, на лбу́] forehead
**лови́ть** [14], ⟨пойма́ть⟩ [1] catch; *в западню* (en)trap; *случай* seize; **~ на сло́ве** take at one's word; *по радио* pick up
**ло́вк|ий** [16; ло́вок, ловка́, -о; *comp.*: ло́вче] dexterous, adroit, deft; **~ость** *f* [8] adroitness, dexterity
**ло́в|ля** *f* [6] catching; *рыбы* fishing; **~у́шка** *f* [5; *g/pl.*: -шек] trap; (*силок*) snare
**логари́фм** *m* [1] *math.* logarithm
**ло́г|ика** *f* [5] logic; **~и́ческий** [16], **~и́чный** [11; -чен, -чна] logical
**ло́гов|ище** *n* [11], **~о** *n* [9] lair, den
**ло́д|ка** *f* [5; *g/pl.*: -док] boat; **подво́дная ~ка** submarine
**лоды́жка** *f* [5; *g/pl.*: -жек] ankle
**ло́дырь** *coll. m* [4] idler, loafer
**ло́жа** *f* [5] *thea.* box
**ложби́на** *f* [5] narrow, shallow gully; *fig. coll.* cleavage
**ло́же** *n* [11] channel, bed (*a. of. river*)
**ложи́ться** [16 *e.*; -жу́сь, -жи́шься], ⟨лечь⟩ [26] [г/ж: ля́гу, лгут; ля́г(те)!; лёг, легла́] lie down; **~ в** (B) go to (*bed*, *a.* **~** [**спать**]); **~ в больни́цу** go to hospital
**ло́жка** *f* [5; *g/pl.*: -жек] spoon; **ча́йная ~** teaspon; **столо́вая ~** tablespoon
**ло́ж|ный** [14; -жен, -жна] false; **~ный шаг** false step; **~ь** *f* [8; лжи; ло́жью] lie, falsehood
**лоза́** *f* [5; *pl. st.*] *виноградная* vine
**ло́зунг** *m* [1] slogan
**локализова́ть** [7] (*im*)*pf.* localize
**локо|моти́в** *m* [1] locomotive, railway engine; **´~н** *m* [1] curl, lock; **´~ть** *m* [4; -ктя; *from g/pl. e.*] elbow
**лом** *m* [1; *from g/pl.*: *e.*] crowbar; *металлолом* scrap (metal); **´~аный** [14] broken; **~а́ть** [1], ⟨по-, с-⟩ break (*a.* up); *дом* pull down; **~а́ть себе́ го́лову** rack one's brains (**над** T over); **-ся** break; ⟨по-⟩ P clown, jest; put on airs
**ломба́рд** *m* [1] pawnshop
**лом|и́ть** [14] *coll.* → **~а́ть**; *impers.* ache, feel a pain in; **-ся** bend, burst; *в дверь и т. д.* force (*v/t.* **в** B), break (into); **´~ка** *f* [15] breaking (up); **´~кий** [16; ло́мок, ломка́, -о] brittle, fragile; **~о́та** *f* [5] rheumatic pain, ache *pl.*; **~о́ть** *m* [4; -мтя́] slice; **´~тик** *m* [1] *dim.* → **~о́ть**
**ло́н|о** *n* [9] *семьи* bosom; **на ~е приро́ды** in the open air
**ло́па|сть** *f* [8; *from g/pl. e.*] blade; *ae.* vane; **´~та** *f* [8] shovel, spade; **´~тка** *f* [5; *g/pl.*: -ток] **1.** *dim.* → **~та**; **2.** *anat.* shoulder blade
**ло́паться** [1], ⟨-нуть⟩ [20] break, burst; split, crack; **чуть не ~ от сме́ха** split one's sides with laughter
**лопу́х** *m* [1 *e.*] *bot.* burdock; *coll.* fool
**лоск** *m* [1] luster (-tre), gloss, polish
**лоску́т** *m* [1 *e.*; pl. *a.*: -ку́тья, -ьев] rag, shred, scrap
**лос|ни́ться** [13] be glossy, shine; **~оси́на** *f* [5] *cul.* **~о́сь** *m* [1] salmon
**лось** *m* [4; *from g/pl. e.*] elk
**лотере́я** *f* [6] lottery
**лото́к** *m* [1; -тка́] street vendor's tray *or* stall; **продава́ть с лотка́** sell in the street
**лохм|а́тый** [14 *sh.*] shaggy, dishevel(l)ed; **~о́тья** *n/pl.* [*gen.*: -ьев] rags
**ло́цман** *m* [1] *naut.* pilot
**лошад|и́ный** [14] horse…; **~и́ная си́ла** horsepower; **´~ь** *f* [8; *from g/pl. e.*, *instr.*: -дьми́ & -дя́ми] horse
**лощи́на** *f* [5] hollow, depression
**лоя́льн|ость** *f* [8] loyalty; **~ый** [14; -лен, -льна] loyal
**лу|бо́к** *m* [1; -бка́] cheap popular print;

**~г** *m* [1; на -ý; *pl.* -á, *etc. e.*] meadow
**лу́ж|а** *f* [5] puddle, pool; ***сесть в ~у*** *coll.* get into a mess
**лужа́йка** *f* [5; *g/pl.*: -áек] (small) glade
**лук** *m* [1] **1.** *collect.* onion(s); **2.** bow (*weapon*)
**лука́в|ить** [14], ⟨с-⟩ dissemble, be cunning; **~ство** *n* [9] cunning, slyness, ruse; **~ый** [14 *sh.*] crafty, wily; (*игривый*) saucy, playful
**лу́ковица** *f* [5] onion; *bot.* bulb
**лун|á** *f* [5] moon; **~áтик** *m* [1] sleepwalker, somnambulist; **∻ный** [14] moon(lit); *astr.* lunar
**лу́па** *f* [5] magnifying glass
**лупи́ть** [14] thrash, flog
**лупи́ться** [14], ⟨об-⟩ peel, scale (off)
**луч** *m* [1 *e.*] ray, beam; **~ево́й** [14] radial; radiation (***боле́знь*** sickness); **~еза́рный** [14; -рен, -рна] resplendent; **~и́стый** [14 *sh.*] radiant
**лу́чш|е** *adv.*, *comp.* → ***хорошо́***; **~ий** [17] better; best (***в ~ем слу́чае*** at …)
**лущи́ть** [16 *e.*; -щу́, -щи́шь], ⟨вы́-⟩ shell, husk
**лы́ж|а** *f* [5] ski; snowshoe (*vb.*: ***ходи́ть***, *etc.*, ***на ~ах***); **~ник** *m* [1], **~ница** *f* [5] skier; **~ный** [14] ski…
**лы́с|ый** [14 *sh.*] bald; **~ина** *f* [5] bald spot, bald patch
**ль** → ***ли***
**льви́|ный** [14] lion's; ***~ный зев*** *bot.* snapdragon; **~ца** *f* [5] lioness
**льго́т|а** *f* [5] privilege; **~ный** [14; -тен, -тна] privileged; (*сниженный*) reduced; preferential; favo(u)rable
**льди́на** *f* [5] ice floe
**льну́ть** [20], ⟨при-⟩ cling, stick (to); *fig. coll.* have a weakness (for)
**льняно́й** [14] flax(en); *ткань* linen…
**льст|е́ц** *m* [1 *e.*] flatterer; **~и́вый** [14 *sh.*] flattering; **~и́ть** [15], ⟨по-⟩ flatter; delude (o.s. ***себя́*** with T)
**любе́зн|ичать** *coll.* [1] (**с** T) pay court (**с** T to), flirt, pay compliments (**с** T to); **~ость** *f* [8] courtesy; kindness; (*услуга*) favo(u)r; *pl.* compliments; **~ый** [14; -зен, -зна] polite, amiable, kind; obliging
**люби́м|ец** *m* [1; -мца], **~ица** *f* [5] favo(u)rite, pet; **~ый** [14] beloved, darling; favo(u)rite, pet
**люби́тель** *m* [4], **~ница** *f* [5] lover, fan; amateur; **~ский** [16] amateur
**люби́ть** [14] love; like, be (⟨по-⟩ grow) fond of; *pf.* fall in love with
**любов|а́ться** [7], ⟨по-⟩ (T *or* **на** B) admire, (be) delight(ed) (in); **∻ник** *m* [1] lover; **∻ница** *f* [5] mistress; **∻ный** [14] love…; *отношение* loving, affectionate; ***∻ная связь*** love affair; **∻ь** *f* [8; -бви́, -бо́вью] love (**к** Д of, for)
**любо|зна́тельный** [14; -лен, -льна] inquisitive, curious; *ум* inquiring; **∻й** [14] either, any(one *su.*); **~пы́тный** [14; -тен, -тна] curious, inquisitive; interesting; ***мне ~пы́тно …*** I wonder …; **~пы́тство** *n* [9] curiosity; interest; ***пра́здное ~пы́тство*** idle curiosity
**лю́бящий** [17] loving, affectionate
**люд** *m* [1] *collect. coll.*, **∻и** [-е́й, -ям, -ьми́, -ях] people; ***вы́йти в ∻и*** get on in life; ***на ∻ях*** in the presence of others, in company; **∻ный** [14; -ден, -дна] crowded; **~о́ед** *m* [1] cannibal; *в сказках* ogre
**люк** *m* [1] hatch(way); manhole
**лю́стра** *f* [5] chandelier, luster (*Brt.* -tre)
**лютера́н|ин** *m* [1; *nom./pl.* -ра́не, g. -ра́н], **~ка** *f* [5; *g/pl.*: -нок], **~ский** [16] Lutheran
**лю́тик** *m* [1] buttercup
**лю́тый** [14; лют, -á, -о; *comp.*: -те́е] fierce, cruel
**люце́рна** *f* [5] alfalfa, lucerne
**ляг|а́ть(ся)** [1], ⟨~ну́ть⟩ [20] kick
**лягуш|а́тник** *m* [1] wading pool for children; **∻ка** *f* [5; *g/pl.*: -шек] frog
**ля́жка** *f* [5; *g/pl.*: -жек] *coll.* thigh, haunch
**лязг** *m* [1], **∻ать** [1] clank, clang; *зубами* clack
**ля́мк|а** *f* [5; *g/pl.*: -мок] strap; ***тяну́ть ~у*** *fig. coll.* drudge, toil

# M

**мавзоле́й** *m* [3] mausoleum
**магази́н** *m* [1] store, shop
**магистра́ль** *f* [8] main; *rail.* main line; *водная* waterway; thoroughfare; trunk (line)
**маги́ческий** [16] magic(al)
**ма́гний** *m* [3] *chem.* magnesium
**магни́т** *m* [1] magnet; **~офо́н** *m* [1] tape recorder
**магомета́н|ин** *m* [1; *pl.*: -а́не, -а́н], **~ка** *f* [5; *g/pl.*: -нок] Mohammedan
**ма́з|ать** [3] **1.** ⟨по-, на-⟩ (*пачкать*) smear; *esp. eccl.* anoint; *маслом и т. д.* spread, butter; **2.** ⟨с-⟩ oil, lubricate; **3.** *coll.* ⟨за-⟩ soil; *impf.* daub; **~ня́** *coll. f* [6] daub(ing); **~о́к** *m* [1; -зка́] daub; stroke; *med.* smear; swab; **~у́т** *m* [1] heavy fuel oil; **~ь** *f* [8] ointment
**май** *m* [3] May
**ма́й|ка** *f* [5; *g/pl.*: ма́ек] undershirt, T-shirt; sports shirt; **~оне́з** *m* [1] mayonnaise; **~о́р** *m* [1] major; **~ский** [16] May(-Day)…
**мак** *m* [1] poppy
**макаро́ны** *m* [1] macaroni
**мак|а́ть** [1], *once* ⟨**~ну́ть**⟩ [20] dip
**маке́т** *m* [1] model; *mil.* dummy
**ма́клер** *m* [1] *comm.* broker
**макну́ть** → ***мака́ть***
**максим|а́льный** [14; -лен, -льна] maximum; **´~ум** *m* [1] maximum; at most
**маку́шка** *f* [5; *g/pl.*: -шек] top; *головы* crown
**малева́ть** [6], ⟨на-⟩ *coll.* paint, daub
**мале́йший** [17] least, slightest
**ма́ленький** [16] little, small; (*низкий*) short; trifling, petty
**мали́н|а** *f* [5] raspberry, -ries *pl.*; **~овка** *f* [5; *g/pl.*: -вок] robin (redbreast); **~овый** [14] raspberry-…; crimson
**ма́ло** little (*a.* **~ что**); few (*a.* **~ кто**); a little; not enough; less; **~ где** in few places; **~ *когда́*** seldom; *coll.* **~ *ли что*** much, many things, anything; (*a.*) yes, but …; that doesn't matter, even though; **~ *того́*** besides, and what is more; **~ *то-го́, что*** not only (that)
**мало|ва́жный** [14; -жен, -жна] insignificant, trifling; **~ва́то** *coll.* little, not (quite) enough; **~вероя́тный** [14; -тен, -тна] unlikely; **~габари́тный** [14; -тен, -тна] small; **~гра́мотный** [14; -тен, -тна] uneducated, ignorant; *подход и т. д.* crude, faulty; **~доказа́тельный** [14; -лен, -льна] unconvincing; **~ду́шный** [14; -шен, -шна] pusillanimous; **~зна́чащий** [17 *sh.*] → ***~ва́жный***; **~иму́щий** [17 *sh.*] poor; **~кро́вие** *n* [12] an(a)emia; **~ле́тний** [15] minor, underage; little (one); **~литра́жка** *f* [5; *g/pl.*: -жек] *coll.* compact (car); mini car; **~лю́дный** [14; -ден, -дна] poorly populated (*or* attended); **~-ма́льски** *coll.* in the slightest degree; at all; **~общи́тельный** [14; -лен, -льна] unsociable; **~о́пытный** [14; -тен, -тна] inexperienced; **~-пома́лу** *coll.* gradually, little by little; **~приго́дный** [14; -ден, -дна] of little use; **~ро́слый** [14 *sh.*] undersized; **~содержа́тельный** [14; -лен, льна] uninteresting, shallow, empty
**ма́л|ость** *f* [8] *coll.* trifle; a bit; **~оце́нный** [14; -е́нен, -е́нна] of little value, inferior; **~очи́сленный** [14 *sh.*] small (in number), few; **~ый** [14; мал, -а́; *comp.*: ме́ньше] small, little; *ростом* short; → ***~енький***; *su.* fellow, guy; ***без ~ого*** almost, all but; ***от ~а до вели́ка*** young and old; ***с ~ых лет*** from childhood; **~ы́ш** *coll. m* [1 *e.*] kid(dy), little boy
**ма́льч|ик** *m* [1] boy, lad; **~и́шеский** [16] boyish; mischievous; **~и́шка** *coll. m* [5; *g/pl.*: -шек] urchin; greenhorn; **~уга́н** *coll. m* [1] → ***малы́ш***; *a.* → ***~и́шка***
**малю́тка** *m/f* [5; *g/pl.*: -ток] baby, tot
**маля́р** *m* [1 *e.*] (house) painter
**маляри́я** *f* [7] *med.* malaria
**ма́м|а** *f* [5] mam(m)a, mother; **~а́ша** *coll. f* [5], *coll. f* **~очка** *f* [5; *g/pl.*: -чек] mommy, mummy
**ма́нго** *n* [*indecl.*] mango

**мандари́н** *m* [1] mandarin(e), tangerine
**манда́т** *m* [1] mandate
**ман|ёвр** *m* [1], **~еври́ровать** [7] maneuver, *Brt.* manoeuvre; **~е́ж** *m* [1] riding school; *цирк* arena; **~еке́н** *m* [1] mannequin (*dummy*)
**мане́р|а** *f* [5] manner; **~ный** [14; -рен, -рна] affected
**манже́т(к)а** *f* [(5; *g/pl.*: -ток)] cuff
**манипули́ровать** [7] manipulate
**мани́ть** [13; маню́, ма́нишь], ⟨по-⟩ (T) beckon; *fig.* entice, tempt
**ма́н|ия** *f* [7] (**вели́чия** megalo)mania; **~ки́ровать** [7] (*im*)*pf.* (T) neglect
**ма́нная** [14]: **~ *крупа́*** semolina
**мара́зм** *m* [1] *med.* senility; *fig.* nonsense, absurdity
**мара́ть** *coll.* [1], ⟨за-⟩ soil, stain; ⟨на-⟩ scribble, daub; ⟨вы́-⟩ delete
**марганцо́вка** *f* [5; -вок] *chem.* potassium manganate
**маргари́н** *m* [1] margarine
**маргари́тка** *f* [5; *g/pl.*: -ток] daisy
**маринова́ть** [7], ⟨за-⟩ pickle
**ма́рк|а** *f* [5; *g/pl.*: -рок] (postage) stamp; make; grade, brand, trademark; **~е́тинг** *m* [1] marketing; **~си́стский** [16] Marxist
**ма́рля** *f* [6] gauze
**мармела́д** *m* [1] fruit jelly (*candied*)
**ма́рочный** [14] *вино* vintage
**март** *m* [1], **≈овский** [16] March
**марты́шка** *f* [5; *g/pl.*: -шек] marmoset
**марш** *m* [1], **~ирова́ть** [7] march; **~ру́т** *m* [1] route, itinerary; **~ру́тный** [14]: ***~ру́тное такси́*** fixedroute taxi
**ма́ск|а** *f* [5; *g/pl.*: -сок] mask; **~ара́д** *m* [1] (*a.* ***бал-~ара́д***) masked ball, masquerade; **~ирова́ть** [7], ⟨за-⟩, **~иро́вка** *f* [5; *g/pl.*: -вок] mask; disguise, camouflage
**ма́сл|еница** *f* [5] Shrovetide; **~ёнка** *f* [5; *g/pl.*: -нок] butter dish; **~еный** [14] → ***~яный***; **~и́на** *f* [5] olive; **~и́чный** [14] olive…; oil …; **~о** *n* [9; *pl.*: -сла́, -сел, -сла́м] (*a.* ***сли́вочное ~о***) butter; (*a.* ***расти́тельное ~о***) oil; ***как по ~у*** *fig.* swimmingly; **~озаво́д** creamery; **~яный** [14] oil(y); butter(y); greasy; *fig.* unctuous
**ма́сс|а** *f* [5] mass; bulk; *людей* multitude; *coll.* a lot; **~а́ж** *m* [1], **~и́ровать** [7] (*pt. a. pf.*) massage; **~и́в** *m* [1] *горный* massif; **~и́вный** [14; -вен, -вна] massive; **~овый** [14] mass…; popular…
**ма́стер** *m* [1; *pl.*: -pá, *etc. e.*] master; (*бригадир*) foreman; (*умелец*) craftsman; (*знаток*) expert; ***~ на все ру́ки*** jack-of-all-trades; **~и́ть** *coll.* [13], ⟨с-⟩ work; make; **~ска́я** *f* [16] workshop; *художник и т. д.* atelier, studio; **~ско́й** [16] masterly (*adv.* ***~ски́***); **~ство́** *n* [9] trade, craft; skill, craftsmanship
**масти́тый** [14 *sh.*] venerable; eminent
**масть** *f* [8; *from g/pl. e.*] colo(u)r (*of animal's coat*); *карты* suit
**масшта́б** *m* [1] scale (on **в** П); *fig.* scope; caliber (-bre); repute
**мат** *m* [1] **1.** *sport* mat; **2.** *chess* checkmate; **3.** foul language
**матема́ти|к** *m* [1] mathematician; **~ка** *f* [5] mathematics; **≈ческий** [16] mathematical
**материа́л** *m* [1] material; **~и́зм** *m* [1] materialism; **~и́ст** *m* [1] materialist; **~исти́ческий** [16] materialistic; **~ьный** [14; -лен, -льна] material; economic; financial
**матери́к** *m* [1 *e.*] continent
**матери́|нский** [16] mother('s), motherly, maternal; **~нство** *n* [9] maternity; **′~я** *f* [7] matter; *ткань* fabric, material
**ма́тка** *f* [5; *g/pl.*: -ток] *anat.* uterus
**ма́товый** [14] dull, dim, mat
**матра́с** *m* [1] mattress
**ма́трица** *f* [5] *typ.* matrix; die, mo(u)ld; *math.* array of elements
**матро́с** *m* [1] sailor, seaman
**матч** *m* [1] *sport* match
**мать** *f* [ма́тери, *etc.* = 8; *pl.*: ма́тери, -ре́й, *etc. e.*] mother
**мах** *m* [1] stroke, swing; **с** (**одного́**) ***≈у*** at one stroke *or* stretch; at once; ***дать ≈у*** miss one's mark, make a blunder; **~а́ть** [3, *coll.* 1], *once* ⟨**~ну́ть**⟩ [20] (T) wave; *хвостом* wag; *крыльями* flap; *pf. coll.* go; ***~ну́ть руко́й на*** (B) give up; **~ови́к** *m* [1 *e.*], **~ово́й** [14]: ***~ово́е колесо́*** flywheel
**махо́рка** *f* [5] coarse tobacco

**махро́вый** [14] *bot.* double; Turkish *or* terry-cloth (*полотенце* towel); *fig.* dyed-in-the-wool
**ма́чеха** *f* [5] stepmother
**ма́чта** *f* [5] mast
**маши́н|а** *f* [5] machine; engine; *coll.* car; ***стира́льная ~а*** washing machine; ***шве́йная ~а*** sewing-machine; **~а́льный** [14; -лен, -льна] mechanical, perfunctory; **~и́ст** *m* [1] *rail.* engineer, *Brt.* engine driver; **~и́стка** *f* [5; *g/pl.*: -ток] (girl) typist; **~ка** *f* [5; *g/pl.*: -нок] (*пишущая*) typewriter; **~ный** [14] machine…, engine…; **~опись** *f* [8] typewriting; **~острое́ние** *n* [12] mechanical engineering
**мая́к** *m* [1 *e.*] lighthouse; beacon; leading light
**ма́я|тник** *m* [1] pendulum; **~ться** P [27] drudge; *от боли* suffer; **~чить** *coll.* [16] loom
**мгла** *f* [5] gloom, darkness; heat mist
**мгнове́н|ие** *n* [12] moment; instant; ***в ~ие о́ка*** in the twinkling of an eye; **~ный** [14; -е́нен, -е́нна] momentary, instantaneous
**ме́б|ель** *f* [8] furniture; **~лиро́вка** *f* [5] furnishing(s)
**мёд** *m* [1; *part. g.*: мёду; в меду́; *pl. e.*] honey
**меда́ль** *f* [8] medal; **~о́н** *m* [1] locket, medallion
**медве́|дица** *f* [5] she-bear; *astr.* **2дица** Bear; **~дь** *m* [4] bear (*coll. a. fig.*); **~жий** [18] bear('s)…; *услуга* bad (*service*); **~жо́нок** *m* [2] bear cub
**ме́ди|к** *m* [1] physician, doctor; medical student; **~каме́нты** *m/pl.* [1] medication, medical supplies; **~ци́на** *f* [5] medicine; **~ци́нский** [16] medical
**ме́дл|енный** [14 *sh.*] slow; **~и́тельный** [14; -лен, -льна] sluggish, slow, tardy; **~ить** [14], ⟨про-⟩ delay, linger; be slow, tarry; hesitate
**ме́дный** [14] copper…
**мед|осмо́тр** *m* [1] medical examination; **~пу́нкт** *m* [1] first-aid station; **~сестра́** *f* [5; *pl. st.*: -сёстры, -сестёр, -сёстрам] (*medical*) nurse
**меду́за** *f* [5] jellyfish
**медь** *f* [8] copper; *coll.* copper (*coin*)
**меж** → **~ду**; **~а́** *f* [5; *pl.*: ме́жи, меж, межа́м] boundary; **~доме́тие** *n* [12] *gr.* interjection; ***~континента́льный*** intercontinental
**ме́жду** (T) between; among(st); ***~ тем*** meanwhile, (in the) meantime; ***~ тем как*** whereas, while; **~горо́дный** [14] *tel.* long-distance…, *Brt.* trunk…; interurban; **~наро́дный** [14] international
**межплане́тный** [14] interplanetary
**мексик|а́нец** *m* [1; -нца], **~а́нка** *f* [5; *g/pl.*: -нок], **~а́нский** [16] Mexican
**мел** *m* [1; в ~у́] chalk; *для побелки* whitewash
**меланхо́л|ик** *m* [1] melancholic; **~и́ческий** [16], **~и́чный** [14; -чен, -чна] melancholy, melancholic; **~ия** *f* [7] melancholy
**меле́ть** [8], ⟨об-⟩ grow shallow
**ме́лк|ий** [16; -лок, -лка́, -о; *comp.*: ме́льче] small, little; *интересы* petty; *песок* fine; *река* shallow; *тарелка* flat; ***~ий дождь*** drizzle; **~ота́** *f* [8] small fry
**мелоди́|ческий** [16] melodic; melodious; **~чный** [14; -чен, -чна] melodious; **´~я** *f* [7] melody
**ме́лоч|ность** *f* [8] pettiness, smallmindedness, paltriness; **~ный** [14; -чен, -чна] petty, paltry; **~ь** *f* [8; *from g/pl. e.*] trifle; trinket; *coll.* small fry; *деньги* (small) change; *pl.* details, particulars
**мел|ь** *f* [8] shoal, sandbank; ***на ~и́*** aground; *coll.* in a fix
**мельк|а́ть** [1], ⟨~ну́ть⟩ [20] flash; gleam; flit; fly (past); pass by fleetingly; **~ом** for a brief moment; ***взгляну́ть ~ом*** cast a cursory glance
**ме́льни|к** *m* [1] miller; **~ца** *f* [5] mill
**мельхио́р** *m* [1] cupronickel, German silver
**мельч|а́ть** [1], ⟨из-⟩ become (**~и́ть** [16 *e.*; -чу́, -чи́шь] make) small(er) *or* shallow(er); become petty
**мелюзга́** *coll.* *f* [5] → ***ме́лочь*** *coll.*
**мемориа́л** *m* [1], **~ный** [14] memorial; ***~ная доска́*** memorial plaque
**мему́ары** *m/pl.* [1] memoirs
**ме́нее** less; ***~ всего́*** least of all; ***тем не ~*** nevertheless

**ме́ньш|е** less; smaller; *a.* ***ме́нее***; **~ий** [17] smaller, lesser; younger; least; **~инство́** *n* [9] minority
**меню́** *n* [*indecl.*] menu, bill of fare
**меня́ть** [28], ⟨по-, об-⟩ exchange, barter (**на** B for); change (→ ***пере~***); **-ся** *v/i.* (*T*/**с** T s.th. with)
**ме́р|а** *f* [5] measure; degree, way; ***по ~е*** (P) *or* ***того́ как*** according to (*a.* ***в ~у*** P); as far as; while the …, the … (+ *comp.*); ***по кра́йней*** (***ме́ньшей***) ***~е*** at least
**мере́нга** *f* [5] meringue
**мере́щиться** [16], ⟨по-⟩ (Д) seem (*to hear, etc.*); appear (to), imagine
**мерз|а́вец** *coll. m* [1; -вца] swine, scoundrel; **~кий** [16; -зок, -зка́, -о] vile, disgusting, loathsome, foul
**мёрз|лый** [14] frozen; **~нуть** [21], ⟨за-⟩ freeze; feel cold
**ме́рзость** *f* [8] vileness, loathsomeness
**ме́рин** *m* [1] gelding; ***врать как си́вый ~*** lie in one's teeth
**ме́р|ить** [13], ⟨с-⟩ measure; ⟨при-, по-⟩ *coll.* try on; **~ка** *f* [5; *g*/*pl.*: -рок]: ***снять ~ку*** take s.o.'s measure
**ме́ркнуть** [21], ⟨по-⟩ fade, darken
**мерлу́шка** *f* [5; *g*/*pl.*: -шек] lambskin
**ме́р|ный** [14; -рен, -рна] measured; rhythmical; **~оприя́тие** *n* [12] measure; action
**ме́ртв|енный** [14 *sh.*] deathly (pale); **~е́ть** [8], ⟨о-⟩ deaden; *med.* mortify; grow *or* turn numb (pale, desolate); **~е́ц** *m* [1 *e.*] corpse
**мёртв|ый** [14; мёртв, мертва́, мёртво; *fig.*: мертво́, мертвы́] dead; ***~ая то́чка*** dead point, dead center (-tre) *fig.*; ***на ~ой то́чке*** at a standstill
**мерца́|ние** *n* [12], **~ть** [1] twinkle
**меси́ть** [15], ⟨за-, с-⟩ knead
**ме́сса** *f* [5] *mus.* mass
**мести́** [25 -т-; мету́, метёшь; мётший], ⟨под-⟩ sweep, whirl
**ме́стн|ость** *f* [8] region, district, locality, place; **~ый** [14] local; ***~ый жи́тель*** local inhabitant
**ме́ст|о** *n* [9; *pl. e.*] place, site; *сидение* seat; *coll. old use* job, post; *в тексте* passage *pl. a.*; → **~ность**; ***о́бщее*** (*or* ***изби́тое***) ***~о*** platitude, commonplace; (***заде́ть за***) ***больно́е ~о*** tender spot (touch on the raw); (***не***) ***к ~у*** in (out of) place; ***не на ~е*** in the wrong place; ***~а́ми*** in (some) places, here and there; ***спа́льное ~о*** berth; **~ожи́тельство** *n* [9] residence; **~оиме́ние** *n* [12] *gr.* pronoun; **~онахожде́ние**, **~оположе́ние** *n* [12] location, position; **~опребыва́ние** *n* [12] whereabouts; residence; **~орожде́ние** *n* [12] deposit; *нефтяное* field
**месть** *f* [8] revenge
**ме́ся|ц** *m* [1] month; moon; ***в ~ц*** a month, per month; ***медо́вый ~ц*** honeymoon; **~чный** [14] month's; monthly
**мета́лл** *m* [1] metal; **~и́ст** *m* [1] metalworker; **~и́ческий** [16] metal(lic); **~урги́я** *f* [7] metallurgy
**метаморфо́за** *f* [5] metamorphosis; change in s.o.'s behavio(u)r, outlook, etc.
**мет|а́ть** [3] **1.** ⟨на-, с-⟩ baste, tack; **2.** [3], *once* ⟨~ну́ть⟩ [20] throw; ***~а́ть икру́*** spawn; **-ся** toss (*in bed*); rush about
**мете́ль** [8] snowstorm, blizzard
**метеоро́лог** *m* [1] meteorologist; **~и́ческий** [16] meteorological; **~и́я** *f* [7] meteorology
**ме́т|ить** [15], ⟨по-⟩ mark; (**в, на** B) aim, drive at, mean; **~ка** [5; *g*/*pl.*: -ток] mark(ing); **~кий** [16; -ток, -тка́, -о] well-aimed; *стрелок* good; keen, accurate, steady; pointed; (*выражение*) apt, to the point
**мет|ла́** *f* [5; *pl. st.*: мётлы, мётел; мётлам] broom; **~ну́ть** → ***мета́ть***
**ме́тод** *m* [1] method; **~и́ческий** [16], **~и́чный** [14; -чен, -чна] methodic(al), systematic(al)
**метр** *m* [1] meter, *Brt.* metre
**ме́трика** *f* [5] *obs.* birth certificate
**метри́ческ|ий** [16]: ***~ая систе́ма*** metric system
**метро́** *n* [*indecl.*], **~полите́н** *m* [1] subway, *Brt.* tube, underground
**мех** *m* [1; *pl.*: -ха́, *etc.*, *e.*] fur; ***на ~у́*** fur-lined
**механ|и́зм** *m* [1] mechanism, gear; **~ик** *m* [1] mechanic; *naut.* engineer; **~ика** *f* [5] mechanics; **~и́ческий** [16] mechan-

М

ical

**мехов|о́й** [14] fur…; **~щи́к** *m* [1 *e.*] furrier

**меч** *m* [1 *e.*] sword; ***Damо́клов ~*** sword of Damocles

**мече́ть** *f* [8] mosque

**мечта́** *f* [5] dream, daydream, reverie; **~тель** *m* [4] (day)dreamer; **~тельный** [14; -лен, -льна] dreamy; **~ть** [1] dream (**о** П of)

**меша́|ть** [1], ⟨раз-⟩ stir; ⟨с-, пере-⟩ mix; *о чувствах* mingle; ⟨по-⟩ disturb; (*препятствовать*) hinder, impede, prevent; ***вам не ~ет*** (***~ло бы***) you'd better; **-ся** meddle, interfere (**в** В with); ***не ~йтесь не в своё дело!*** mind your own business!

**ме́шк|ать** *coll.* [1], ⟨про-⟩ → ***ме́длить***; **~ова́тый** [14 *sh.*] (*clothing*) baggy

**мешо́к** *m* [1; -шка́] sack, bag

**мещан|и́н** *m* [1; *pl.*: -а́не, -а́н], **~ский** [16] *hist.* (petty) bourgeois, Philistine; narrow-minded

**мзда** *f* [5] *archaic, now joc.* recompense, payment; *iro.* bribe

**миг** *m* [1] moment, instant; **~ом** *coll.* in a trice (*or* flash); **~а́ть** [1], *once* ⟨~ну́ть⟩ [20] blink, wink; *звёзды* twinkle; *огоньки* glimmer

**мигре́нь** *f* [8] migraine

**ми́зерный** [14; -рен, -рна] scanty, paltry

**мизи́нец** [1; -нца] little finger

**микро́б** *m* [1] microbe

**микроско́п** *m* [1] microscope

**микрофо́н** *m* [1] microphone

**миксту́ра** *f* [5] medicine (*liquid*), mixture

**ми́ленький** *coll.* [16] lovely; dear; (*as form of address*) darling

**милици|оне́р** *m* [1] policeman; militiaman; **ˊ~я** *f* [7] police; militia

**милли|а́рд** *m* [1] billion; **~ме́тр** *m* [1] millimeter (*Brt.* -tre); **~о́н** *m* [1] million

**мило|ви́дный** [14; -ден, -дна] nice-looking; **~се́рдие** *n* [12] charity, mercy; **~се́рдный** [14; -ден, -дна] charitable, merciful; **ˊ~стыня** *f* [6] alms; **ˊ~сть** *f* [8] mercy; (*одолжение*) favo(u)r; ***ˊ~сти про́сим!*** welcome!; *iro., coll.* ***по твое́й*** (***ва́шей***) ***ми́лости*** because of you

**ми́лый** [14; мил, -а́, -о] nice, lovable, sweet; (my) dear, darling

**ми́ля** *f* [6] mile

**ми́мо** (Р) past, by; ***бить ~*** miss; **~лётный** [14; -тен, -тна] fleeting, transient; **~хо́дом** in passing; incidentally

**ми́на** *f* [5] **1.** *mil.* mine; **2.** mien, expression

**минда́|лина** *f* [5] almond; *anat.* tonsil; **~ль** *m* [4 *e.*] *collect.* almond(s); **~льничать** *coll.* [1] be too soft (towards **с** Т)

**миниатю́р|а** *f* [5], **~ный** [14; -рен, -рна] miniature…; *fig.* tiny, diminutive

**ми́нимум** *m* [1] minimum; ***прожи́точный ~*** living wage; *adv.* at the least

**министе́р|ство** *n* [9] *pol.* ministry; ***~е́рство иностра́нных*** (***вну́тренних***) ***дел*** Ministry of Foreign (Internal) Affairs; **~р** *m* [1] minister, secretary

**мин|ова́ть** [7] (*im*)*pf.*, ⟨~у́ть⟩ [20] pass (by); *pf.* be over; escape; (Д) **~уло** (*о возрасте*) → ***испо́лниться***; **~у́вший**, **~у́вшее** *su.* past

**мино́рный** [14] *mus.* minor; *fig.* gloomy, depressed

**ми́нус** *m* [1] *math.* minus; *fig.* shortcoming

**мину́т|а** *f* [5] minute; moment, instant (**в** В at; ***на*** В for); ***сию́ ~у*** at once, immediately; at this moment; ***с ~ы на ~у*** (at) any moment; → ***пя́тый***, ***пять***; **~ный** [14] minute('s); moment('s), momentary

**ми́нуть** → ***минова́ть***

**мир** *m* [1] **1.** peace; **2.** [*pl. e.*] world; *fig.* universe, planet; ***не от ~а сего́*** otherworldly

**мир|и́ть** [13], ⟨по-, при-⟩ reconcile (to **с** Т); **-ся** make it up, be(come) reconciled; ⟨при-⟩ resign o.s. to; put up with; **~ный** [14; -рен, -рна] peace…; peaceful

**мировоззре́ние** *n* [12] weltanschauung, world view; ideology

**мирово́й** [14] world('s); worldwide, universal; *coll.* first-class

**миро|люби́вый** [14 *sh.*] peaceable; peaceloving; **~тво́рческий** [16] peacemaking

**ми́ска** *f* [5; *g/pl.*: -сок] dish, tureen; bowl
**ми́ссия** *f* [7] mission; *dipl.* legation
**ми́стика** *f* [5] mysticism
**мистифика́ция** *f* [7] mystification; hoax
**ми́тинг** *m* [1] *pol.* mass meeting; **~ова́ть** [7] *impf. coll.* hold (*or* take part in) a mass meeting
**митрополи́т** *m* [1] *eccl.* metropolitan
**миф** *m* [1] myth; **~и́ческий** [16] mythic(al); **~оло́гия** *f* [7] mythology
**ми́чман** *m* [1] warrant officer
**мише́нь** *f* [8] target
**ми́шка** *coll. m* [5; *g/pl.*: -шек] (*pet name used for*) bear; (***плю́шевый***) teddy bear
**мишура́** *f* [5] tinsel
**младе́н|ец** *m* [1; -нца] infant, baby; **~чество** *n* [9] infancy
**мла́дший** [17] younger, youngest; junior
**млекопита́ющее** *n* [17] *zo.* mammal
**мле́чный** [14] milk…, milky (*a.* ♌, *ast.*); **~ сок** latex
**мне́ни|е** *n* [12] opinion (***по*** Д in); ***общественное ~е*** public opinion; ***по моему́ ~ю*** to my mind
**мни́|мый** [14 *sh.*, *no m*] imaginary; (*ложный*) sham; **~тельный** [14; -лен, -льна] (*подозрительный*) hypochondriac(al); suspicious
**мно́гие** *pl.* [16] many (people, *su.*)
**мно́го** (Р) much, many; a lot (*or* plenty) of; ***ни ~ ни ма́ло*** *coll.* neither more nor less; **~ва́то** *coll.* rather too much (many); **~вeково́й** [14] centuries-old; **~гра́нный** [14; -а́нен, -а́нна] many-sided; **~де́тный** [14; -тен, -тна] having many children; **~значи́тельный** [14; -лен, -льна] significant; **~кра́тный** [14; -тен, -тна] repeated; *gr.* frequentative; **~ле́тний** [15] longstanding, of many years; *план и т. д.* long-term…; *bot.* perennial **~лю́дный** [14; -ден, -дна] crowded, populous; *митинг* mass…; **~национа́льный** [14; -лен, -льна] multinational; **~обеща́ющий** [17] (very) promising; **~обра́зный** [14; -зен; -зна] varied, manifold; **~сло́вный** [14; -вен, -вна] wordy; **~сторо́нний** [15; -о́нен, -о́ння] many-sided; **~страда́льный** [14; -лен, -льна] long-suffering; **~то́чие** *n* [12] ellipsis; **~уважа́емый** [14] dear (*address*); **~цве́тный** [14; -тен, -тна] multicolo(u)red; **~чи́сленный** [14 *sh.*] numerous; **~эта́жный** [14] manystoried (*Brt.* -reyed)
**мно́ж|ественный** [14. *sh.*] *gr.* plural; **~ество** *n* [9] multitude; a great number; **~имое** *n* [14] *math.* multiplicand; **~итель** *m* [4] multiplier, factor; **~ить** ⟨по-⟩ → ***умножа́ть***
**мобилизова́ть** [7] (*im*)*pf.* mobilize
**моби́льный** [14; -лен, -льна] mobile
**моги́л|а** *f* [5] grave; **~ьный** [14] tomb…
**могу́|чий** [17 *sh.*], **~щественный** [14 *sh.*] mighty, powerful; **~щество** *n* [9] might, power
**мо́д|а** *f* [5] fashion, vogue; **~ели́рование** *n* [12] *tech.* simulation; **~е́ль** (-dɛl) *f* [8] model; **~елье́р** *m* [1] fashion designer; **~е́м** (-dɛ-) *m* [1] *comput.* modem; **~ернизи́ровать** (-dɛr-) [7] (*im*)*pf.* modernize; **~ифици́ровать** [7] (*im*)*pf.* modify; **~ный** [14; -ден, -дна́, -о] fashionable, stylish; *песня* popular
**мо́ж|ет быть** perhaps, maybe; **~но** (***мне***, *etc.*) one (I, *etc.*) can *or* may; it is possible; → ***как***
**можжеве́льник** *m* [1] juniper
**моза́ика** *f* [5] mosaic
**мозг** *m* [1; -а (-у); в ~у́; *pl. e.*] brain; *костный* marrow; *спинной* cord; ***шевели́ть ~а́ми*** *coll.* use one's brains; ***уте́чка ~о́в*** brain drain; **~ово́й** [14] cerebral
**мозо́|листый** [14 *sh.*] horny, calloused; **~лить** [13]: ***~лить глаза́*** Д *coll.* be an eyesore to; **~ль** *f* [8] callus; corn
**мо|й** *m*, **~я́** *f*, **~ё** *n*, **~и́** *pl.* [24] my; mine; *pl. su. coll.* my folks; → ***ваш***
**мо́к|нуть** [21], ⟨про-⟩ become wet; soak; **~ро́та** *f* [5] *med.* phlegm; **~рый** [14; мокр, -á, -о] wet
**мол** *m* [1] jetty, pier, mole
**молв|а́** *f* [5] rumo(u)r; talk; **~ить** [14] (*im*)*pf. obs.*, ⟨про-⟩ say, utter
**молдава́н|ин** *m* [1; *pl.*: -ва́не, -а́н], **~ка** *f* [5; *g/pl.*: -нок] Moldavian
**моле́бен** *m* [1; -бна] *eccl.* service; public prayer
**моле́кул|а** *f* [5] molecule; **~я́рный** [14]

molecular

**моли́т|ва** *f* [5] prayer; **~венник** *m* [1] prayer book; **~ь** [13; молю́, мо́лишь] (**о** П) implore, entreat, beseech (for); **~ься**, ⟨по-⟩ pray (Д to; **о** П for); *fig.* idolize (***на*** В)

**молни|ено́сный** [14; -сен, сна] instantaneous; **´~я** *f* [7] lightning; (*застёжка*) zipper, zip fastener

**молод|ёжь** *f* [8] *collect.* youth, young people *pl.*; **~е́ть** [8], ⟨по-⟩ grow (look) younger; **~е́ц** *coll.* *m* [1; -дца́] fine fellow, brick; (*оценка*) *as int.* well done!; **~и́ть** [15 *e.*; -ложу́, -лоди́шь] make look younger; **~ня́к** *m* [1 *e.*] *о животных* offspring; *о лесе* undergrowth; **~ожёны** *m/pl.* [1] newly wedded couple; **~о́й** [14; мо́лод, -а́, -о; *comp.*: моло́же] young; *картофель, месяц* new: *pl. a.* = ***~ожёны***; **´~ость** *f* [8] youth, adolescence; **~цева́тый** [14 *sh.*] smart; *шаг* sprightly

М

**молоժа́вый** [14 *sh.*] youthful, young-looking

**моло́к|и** *f/pl.* [5] milt, soft roe; **~о́** *n* [9] milk; **сгущённое ~о́** condensed milk; **~осо́с** *coll.* *m* [1] greenhorn

**мо́лот** *m* [1] sledgehammer; **~о́к** *m* [1; -тка́] hammer; **с *~ка́*** by auction; **~́ь** [17; мелю́, ме́лешь, меля́], ⟨пере-, с-⟩ grind; *coll.* talk (*вздор* nonsense); **~ьба́** *f* [5] threshing (time)

**моло́чн|ик** *m* [1] milk jug; **~ый** [14] milk…; dairy…

**мо́лча** silently, tacitly; in silence; **~ли́вый** [14 *sh.*] taciturn; *согласие* tacit; **~́ние** *n* [12] silence; **~́ть** [4 *e.*; мо́лча] be (*or* keep) silent; **(за)*молчи́!*** shut up!

**моль** *f* [8] (clothes) moth

**мольба́** *f* [5] entreaty; (*молитва*) prayer

**моме́нт** *m* [1] moment, instant (**в** В at); (*черта, сторона*) feature, aspect; **~а́льный** [14] momentary, instantaneous

**мона́рхия** *f* [7] monarchy

**мона|сты́рь** *m* [4 *e.*] monastery; *женский* convent; **~́х** *m* [1] monk; **~́хиня** *f* [6] nun (*a.*, *F*, **~́шенка** *f* [5; *g/pl.*: -нок]); **~́шеский** [16] monastic; monk's

**монго́льский** [16] Mongolian

**моне́т|а** *f* [5] coin; ***той же ~ой*** in a p.'s own coin; ***за чи́стую ~у*** in good faith; ***зво́нкая ~а*** hard cash; **~ный** [14] monetary; ***~ный двор*** mint

**монито́р** *m* [1] *tech.* monitor

**моно|ло́г** *m* [1] monologue; **~полизи́ровать** [7] (*im*)*pf.* monopolize; **~по́лия** *f* [7] monopoly; **~то́нный** [14; -то́нен, -то́нна] monotonous

**монт|а́ж** *m* [1] assembly, installation, montage; **~ёр** *m* [1] fitter; electrician; **~и́ровать** [7], ⟨с-⟩ *tech.* assemble, mount, fit; *cine.* arrange

**монуме́нт** *m* [1] monument; ***~а́льный*** [14; -лен, -льна] monumental (*a. fig.*)

**мопе́д** *m* [1] moped

**мора́ль** *f* [8] morals, ethics *pl.*; morality; moral; **чита́ть ~** *coll.* lecture, moralize; **~ный** [14; -лен, -льна] moral; ***~ное состоя́ние*** morale

**морг** *m* [1] morgue

**морг|а́ть** [1], ⟨**~ну́ть**⟩ [20] blink (Т); ***и гла́зом не ~ну́в*** *coll.* without batting an eyelid

**мо́рда** *f* [5] muzzle, snout

**мо́ре** *n* [10; *pl. e.*] sea; seaside (***на*** П at); ***~м*** by sea; **~пла́вание** *n* [12] navigation; **~пла́ватель** *m* [4] navigator, seafarer

**морж** *m* [1 *e.*], ***~о́вый*** [14] walrus; *coll.* out-of-doors winter bather

**мори́ть** [13], ⟨за-, у-⟩ exterminate; ***~ го́лодом*** starve; exhaust

**морко́в|ь** *f* [8], *coll.* ***~ка*** *f* [5; *g/pl.*: -вок] carrot(s)

**моро́женое** *n* [14] ice cream

**моро́з** *m* [1] frost; **~и́льник** *m* [1] deep-freeze; **~ить** [15], ⟨за-⟩ freeze; **~ный** [14; -зен, -зна] frosty

**мороси́ть** [15; -си́т] drizzle

**моро́чить** *coll.* [16] fool, pull the wool over the eyes of

**морс** *m* [1]: fruit drink; ***клю́квенный ~*** cranberry juice

**морско́й** [14] sea…, maritime; naval; nautical; seaside…; ***~ волк*** sea dog, old salt

**мо́рфий** *m* [3] morphine, morphia

**морфоло́гия** *f* [7] morphology

**морщи́|на** *f* [5] wrinkle; **~нистый** [14

*sh.*] wrinkled; ⁓ть [16], ⟨на-, с-⟩ wrinkle, frown (*v/i.* **⁓ться**); *ткань* crease
**моря́к** *m* [1 *e.*] seaman, sailor
**моск|ви́ч** *m* [1 *e.*], **⁓ви́чка** *f* [5; *g/pl.*: -чек] Muscovite; **⁓о́вский** [16] Moscow…
**моски́т** *m* [1] mosquito
**мост** *m* [1 & 1 *e.*; на⁓у́; *pl. e.*] bridge; **⁓и́ть** [15 *e.*; мощу́, мости́шь, мощённый], ⟨вы́-⟩ pave; **⁓ки́** *m/pl.* [1 *e.*] footbridge; **⁓ова́я** *f* [14] *old use* carriage way
**мот** *m* [1] spendthrift, prodigal
**мот|а́ть** [1], ⟨на-, с-⟩ reel, wind; *coll.* ⟨по-⟩, *once* ⟨⁓ну́ть⟩ shake, wag; (*трясти*) jerk; *coll.* ⟨про-⟩ squander; ***⁓а́й отсю́да!*** scram!; **-ся** *impf.* dangle; P knock about
**моти́в**[1] *m* [1] *mus.* tune; motif
**моти́в**[2] *m* [1] motive, reason; **⁓и́ровать** [7] (*im*)*pf.* give a reason (for), justify
**мото́к** *m* [1; -тка] skein, hank
**мото́р** *m* [1] motor, engine
**мото|ро́ллер** *m* [1] motor scooter; **⁓ци́кл** [1], **-е́т** *m* [1] motorcycle; **⁓цикли́ст** *m* [1] motorcyclist
**мотылёк** *m* [1; -лька́] moth
**мох** *m* [1; мха & мо́ха, во (на) мху́: *pl.*: мхи, мхов] moss
**мохна́тый** [14 *sh.*] shaggy, hairy
**моч|а́** *f* [5] urine; **⁓а́лка** *f* [5; *g/pl.*: -лок] washing-up mop; loofah; bath sponge; **⁓ево́й** [14]: ***⁓ево́й пузы́рь*** *anat.* bladder; **⁓и́ть** [16], ⟨на-, за-⟩ wet, moisten; soak, steep (*v/i.* **-ся**; *a.* urinate); **⁓ка** *f* [5; -чек] lobe (*of the ear*)
**мочь**[1] [26 г/ж: могу́, мо́жешь, мо́гут; мог, -ла́; могу́щий], ⟨с-⟩ can, be able; may; ***я не могу́ не*** + *inf.* I can't help …ing; ***мо́жет быть*** maybe, perhaps; ***не мо́жет быть!*** that's impossible!
**моч|ь**[2] P *f* [8]: ***во всю ⁓ь, изо всей ⁓и, что есть ⁓и*** with all one's might; ***⁓и нет*** it's unbearable
**моше́нни|к** *m* [1] swindler, cheat; **⁓чать** [1], ⟨с-⟩ swindle; **⁓чество** *n* [9] swindling, cheating
**мо́шка** *f* [5; *g/pl.*: -шек] midge
**мо́щи** *f/pl.* [*gen.*: -щей, *etc. e.*] relics
**мо́щ|ность** *f* [8] power; *tech.* capacity; *предприятия* output; **⁓ный** [14; мо́щен, -щна́, -о] powerful, mighty; **⁓ь** *f* [8] power, might; strength
**мрак** *m* [1] dark(ness); gloom
**мра́мор** *m* [1] marble
**мрачн|е́ть** [8], ⟨по-⟩ darken; become gloomy; **⁓ый** [14; -чен, -чна́, -о] dark; gloomy, somber (*Brt.* -bre)
**мсти́|тель** *m* [4] avenger; **⁓тельный** [14; -лен, -льна] revengeful; **⁓ть** [15], ⟨ото-⟩ revenge o.s., take revenge (Д on); (**за** В) avenge a p.
**мудр|ёный** *coll.* [14; -ён, -ена́; -енée] difficult, hard, intricate; (*замысловатый*) fanciful; ***не ⁓ено́, что*** (it's) no wonder; **⁓е́ц** *m* [1 *e.*] sage; **⁓и́ть** *coll.* [13], ⟨на-⟩ complicate matters unnecessarily; **⁓ость** *f* [8] wisdom; ***зуб ⁓ости*** wisdom tooth; **⁓ствовать** *coll.* [7] → ***⁓и́ть***; **⁓ый** [14; мудр, -á, -о] wise
**муж** *m* **1.** [1; *pl.*: -жья́, -жéй, -жья́м] husband; **2.** *rare* [1; *pl.*: -жи́, -жéй, -жа́м] man; **⁓а́ть** [1], ⟨воз-⟩ mature, grow; **-ся** *impf.* take courage; **⁓ественный** [14 *sh.*] steadfast; manly; **⁓ество** *n* [9] courage, fortitude; **⁓и́к** *m* [1 *e.*] peasant; P man; **⁓ско́й** [16] male, masculine (*a. gr.*); (gentle)man('s); **⁓чи́на** *m* [5] man
**музе́й** *m* [3] museum
**му́зык|а** *f* [5] music; **⁓а́льный** [14; -лен, -льна] musical; **⁓а́нт** *m* [1] musician
**му́ка**[1] *f* [5] pain, torment, suffering, torture(s); *coll.* trouble
**мука́**[2] *f* [5] flour
**мультфи́льм** *m* [1] animated cartoon
**му́мия** *f* [7] mummy
**мунди́р** *m* [1] full-dress uniform; ***карто́фель в ⁓е*** *coll.* potatoes cooked in their jackets *or* skin
**мундшту́к** (-nʃ-) *m* [1 *e.*] cigarette holder; *mus.* mouthpiece
**муниципалите́т** *m* [1] municipality; town council
**мурав|е́й** *m* [3; -вья́; *pl.*: -вьи́, -вьёв] ant; **⁓е́йник** *m* [1] ant hill
**мура́шки**: **⁓** (**от** Р) ***бе́гают по спине́*** (**у** Р F) (s.th.) gives (a p.) the creeps
**мурлы́кать** [3 & 1] purr; *coll. песню* hum
**муска́т** *m* [1] nutmeg; *вино* muscat; **⁓ный** [14]: ***⁓ный оре́х*** nutmeg

М

**му́скул** *m* [1] muscle; **~ату́ра** *f* [5] *collect.* muscles; muscular system; **~и́стый** [14 *sh.*] muscular
**му́сор** *m* [1] rubbish, refuse; sweepings; **~ить** [13], ⟨за-, на-⟩ *coll.* litter; **~опро́вод** *m* [1] refuse chute
**муссо́н** *m* [1] monsoon
**мусульма́н|ин** *m* [1; *pl.*: -а́не, -а́н], **~ка** *f* [5; *g*/*pl.*: -нок] Muslim
**мут|и́ть** [15; мучу́, му́ти́шь], ⟨вз-, по-⟩ make muddy; *fig.* trouble; fog; ***меня́ ~и́т*** *coll.* I feel sick; **-ся** = **~не́ть** [8], ⟨по-⟩ grow turbid; blur; **∠ный** [14; -тен, -тна́, -о] muddy (*a. fig.*); troubled (*waters*); dull; blurred; foggy; **~о́вка** *f* [5; *g*/*pl.*: -вок] whisk; **~ь** *f* [8] dregs *pl.*; murk
**му́фта** *f* [5] muff; *tech.* (*~ сцепления*) clutch sleeve, coupling sleeve
**му́фтий** *m* [3] *eccl.* Mufti
**му́х|а** *f* [5] fly; **~омо́р** *m* [1] fly agaric (*mushroom*); *coll.* decrepit old person
**муч|е́ние** *n* [12] → ***му́ка***; **∠еник** *m* [1] martyr; **~и́тель** *m* [4] tormentor; **~и́тельный** [14; -лен, -льна] painful, agonizing; **∠ить** [16], P **∠ать** [1], ⟨за-, из-⟩ torment, torture; *fig.* vex, worry; **-ся** suffer (*pain*); *fig.* suffer torments; *над задачей и т. д.* take great pains (over), toil
**му́шк|а** *f* [5; *g*/*pl.*: -шек] *ружья* (fore)-sight; ***взять на ~у*** take aim (at)
**мчать(ся)** [4], ⟨по-⟩ rush *or* speed (along)
**мши́стый** [14 *sh.*] mossy
**мще́ние** *n* [12] vengeance
**мы** [20] we; ***~ с ним*** he and I
**мы́л|ить** [13], ⟨на-⟩ soap; ***~ить го́лову*** (Д) *coll.* give s.o. a dressingdown, scold; **~о** *n* [9; *pl. e.*] soap; **~ьница** *f* [5] soap dish; **~ьный** [14] soap(y); ***~ьная пе́на*** lather, suds
**мыс** *m* [1] *geogr.* cape, promontory
**мы́сл|енный** [14] mental; **~имый** [14 *sh.*] conceivable; **~и́тель** *m* [4] thinker; **~ить** [13] think (**о** of, about); reason; (*представлять*) imagine; **~ь** *f* [8] thought, idea (**о** П of); ***за́дняя ~ь*** ulterior motive
**мыта́рство** *n* [9] hardship, ordeal
**мы́ть(ся)** [22], ⟨по-, у-, вы́-⟩ wash (o.s.)
**мыча́ть** [4 *e.*; -чу́, -чи́шь] moo, low; *coll.* mumble
**мышело́вка** *f* [5; *g*/*pl.*: -вок] mouse-trap
**мы́шечный** [14] muscular
**мы́шк|а** *f* [5; *g*/*pl.*: -шек]: ***под ~ой*** under one's arm
**мышле́ние** *n* [12] thinking, thought
**мы́шца** *f* [5] muscle
**мышь** *f* [8; *from g*/*pl. e.*] mouse
**мышья́к** *m* [1 *e.*] *chem.* arsenic
**мэр** *m* [1] mayor
**мя́гк|ий** (-xk-) [16; -гок, -гка́, -о; *comp.*: мя́гче] soft; *движение* smooth; *мясо и т. д.* tender; *fig.* mild, gentle; lenient; ***~ое кре́сло*** easy chair; ***~ий ваго́н*** *rail.* first-class coach *or* car(riage); **~осерде́чный** [14; -чен, -чна] soft-hearted; **~ость** *f* [8] softness; *fig.* mildness **~оте́лый** [14] *fig.* flabby, spineless
**мя́к|иш** *m* [1] soft part (*of loaf*); **∠нуть** [21], ⟨на-, раз-⟩ become soft; **∠оть** *f* [8] flesh; *плода* pulp
**мя́мл|ить** P [13] mumble; **~я** *m* & *f* [6] *coll.* mumbler; irresolute person; milksop
**мяс|и́стый** [14 *sh.*] fleshy; pulpy; **~ни́к** *m* [1 *e.*] butcher; **~но́й** [14] meat…; butcher's; **∠о** *n* [9] meat; flesh **~ору́бка** *f* [5; *g*/*pl.*: -бок] mincer
**мя́та** *f* [8] mint
**мяте́ж** *m* [1 *e.*] rebellion, mutiny; **~ник** *m* [1] rebel, mutineer
**мять** [мну, мнёшь; мя́тый], ⟨с-, по-, из-⟩ [сомну́; изомну́] (c)rumple, press; knead; *траву и т. д.* trample; **-ся** be easily crumpled; *fig. coll.* waver, vacillate
**мяу́к|ать** [1], *once* ⟨**~нуть**⟩ mew
**мяч** *m* [1 *e.*] ball; **∠ик** [1] *dim.* → ***мяч***

# Н

**на**[1] **1.** (В): (*направление*) on, onto; to, toward(s); into, in; (*длительность, назначение и т. д.*) for; till; *math.* by; **~ что?** what for?; **2.** (П): (*расположение*) on, upon; in, at; with; for; **~ ней ...** she has ... on

**на**[2] *int. coll.* there, here (you are); *a.* **вот тебе́ на!** well, I never!

**набав|ля́ть** [28], ⟨**~ить**⟩ [14] raise, add to, increase

**наба́т** *m* [1]: **бить в ~** *mst. fig.* sound the alarm

**набе́|г** *m* [1] incursion, raid; **~га́ть** [1], ⟨**~жа́ть**⟩ [4; -егу́, -ежи́шь, -егу́т; -еги́(-те)!] run (into **на** В); (*покрывать*) cover; **~гаться** [1] *pf. be* exhausted with running about

**набекре́нь** *coll.* aslant, cocked

**на́бережная** *f* [14] embankment, quay

**наби|ва́ть** [1], ⟨**~ть**⟩ [-бью, -бьёшь; → **бить**] stuff, fill; **~вка** *f* [5; *g/pl.*: -вок] stuffing, padding

**набира́ть** [1], ⟨**набра́ть**⟩ [-беру́, -рёшь; → **брать**] gather; *на работу* recruit; *tel.* dial; *typ.* set; take (many, much); *высоту, скорость* gain; **-ся** (*набиться*) become crowded; P (*напиться*) get soused; **-ся сме́лости** pluck up one's courage

**наби́|тый** [14 *sh.*] (Т) packed; P **~тый дура́к** arrant fool; **битко́м ~тый**; *coll.* crammed full; **~ть** → **~ва́ть**

**наблюд|а́тель** *m* [4] observer; **~а́тельный** [14; -лен, -льна] observant, alert; *пост* observation; **~а́ть** [1] (*v/t.* & **за** Т) observe; watch; (*a.* **про-**); see to (it that); **-ся** be observed *or* noted; **~е́ние** *n* [12] observation; supervison

**набо́йк|а** *f* [5; *g/pl.*: -бо́ек] heel (*of shoe*); **набива́ть** ⟨-би́ть⟩ **~у** put a heel on, heel

**на́бок** to *or* on one side, awry

**наболе́вший** [16] sore, painful (*a. fig.*)

**набо́р** *m* [1] *на курсы и т. д.* enrol(l)ment; (**компле́кт**) set, kit; typesetting

**набр|а́сывать** [1] **1.** ⟨**~оса́ть**⟩ [1] sketch, design, draft; **2.** ⟨**~о́сить**⟩ [15] throw over *or* on (**на** В); **-ся** fall (up)on

**набра́ть** → **набира́ть**

**набрести́** [25] *pf. coll.* come across (**на** В); happen upon

**набро́сок** *m* [1; -ска] sketch, draft

**набух|а́ть** [1], ⟨**~нуть**⟩ [21] swell

**нава́л|ивать** [1], ⟨**~и́ть**⟩ [13; -алю́, -а́лишь, -а́ленный] heap; *работу* load (with); **-ся** fall (up)on

**нава́лом** *adv.* in bulk; *coll.* loads of

**наве́д|ываться**, ⟨**~аться**⟩ [1] *coll.* call on (**к** Д)

**наве́к**, **~и** forever, for good

**наве́рн|о(е)** probably; for certain, definitely; (*a.*, *coll.* **~яка́**) for sure, without fail

**навёрстывать**, ⟨наверста́ть⟩ [1] make up for

**наве́рх** up(ward[s]); *по лестнице* upstairs; **~у́** above; upstairs

**наве́с** *m* [1] awning; annex (*with sloping roof*); shed, carport

**навеселе́** *coll.* tipsy, drunk

**навести́** → **наводи́ть**

**навести́ть** → **навеща́ть**

**наве́тренный** [14] windward

**наве́чно** forever, for good

**наве|ща́ть** [1], ⟨**~сти́ть**⟩ [15 *e.*; -ещу́, -ести́шь; -ещённый] call on

**на́взничь** backwards, on one's back

**навзры́д**: **пла́кать ~** sob

**навига́ция** *f* [7] navigation

**навис|а́ть** [1], ⟨**~нуть**⟩ [21] hang (over); *опасность и т. д.* impend, threaten

**навле|ка́ть** [1], ⟨**~чь**⟩ [26] (**на** В) bring on, incur

**наводи́ть** [15], ⟨навести́⟩ [25] (**на** В) direct (at); point (at), turn (to); lead (to), bring on *or* about, cause, raise (→ **нагоня́ть**); make; construct; **~ на мысль** come up with an idea; **~ поря́док** put in order; **~ ску́ку** bore; **~ спра́вки** inquire (**о** П after)

**наводн|е́ние** *n* [12] flood, inundation; **~я́ть** [28], ⟨**~и́ть**⟩ [13] flood with (*a. fig.*), inundate with

**наво́з** *m* [1], **~ить** [15], ⟨у-⟩ dung, manure
**на́волочка** *f* [5; *g*/*pl*.: -чек] pillowcase
**навостри́ть** [13] *pf*. *уши* prick up
**навря́д (ли)** hardly, scarcely
**навсегда́** forever; ***раз и ~*** once and for all
**навстре́чу** toward(s); ***идти́ ~*** (Д) go to meet; *fig*. meet halfway
**навы́ворот** P (*наизнанку*) inside out; ***де́лать ши́ворот-~*** put the cart before the horse
**на́вык** *m* [1] experience, skill (**в** П in)
**навя́з|ывать** [1], ⟨**~а́ть**⟩ [3] *мнение*, *волю* impose, foist ([up]on; Д *v*/*i*. **-ся**); **~чивый** [14 *sh*.] obtrusive; ***~чивая иде́я*** idée fixe
**наг|иба́ть** [1], ⟨**~ну́ть**⟩ [20] bend, bow, stoop (*v*/*i*. **-ся**)
**нагишо́м** *coll*. stark naked
**нагл|е́ть** [8], ⟨об-⟩ become impudent; **~е́ц** *m* [1 *e*.] impudent fellow; **~ость** *f* [8] impudence, insolence; ***верх ~ости*** the height of impudence; ***~ухо*** tightly; **~ый** [14; нагл, -á, -o] impudent, insolent, *coll*. cheeky
**нагляд|е́ться** [11]: ***не ~е́ться*** never get tired of looking (at); **~ный** [14; -ден, -дна] clear, graphic; (*очевидный*) obvious; *пособие* visual; ***~ный уро́к*** object lesson
**нагна́ть** → ***нагоня́ть***
**нагнета́ть** [1]: ***~ стра́сти*** stir up passions
**нагное́ние** *n* [12] suppuration
**нагну́ть** → ***нагиба́ть***
**нагов|а́ривать** [1], ⟨**~ори́ть**⟩ [13] say, tell, talk ([too] much *or* a lot of …); *coll*. slander (a p. **на** B, **о** П); (*записать*) record; **~ори́ться** *pf*. talk o.s. out; ***не ~ори́ться*** never get tired of talking
**наго́й** [14; наг, -á, -o] nude, naked, bare
**нагон|я́й** *coll*. *m* [3] scolding, upbraiding; **~я́ть** [28], ⟨нагна́ть⟩ [-гоню́, -го́нишь; → ***гнать***] overtake, catch up (with); (*навёрстывать*) make up (for); ***~я́ть страх, ску́ку***, *etc*. **на** (B) frighten, bore, *etc*.
**нагота́** *f* [5] nudity; nakedness
**нагот|а́вливать** [1], ⟨**~о́вить**⟩ [14] prepare; (*запастись*) lay in; **~о́ве** in readiness, on call

**награ́бить** [14] *pf*. amass by robbery, plunder (a lot of)
**награ́|да** *f* [5] reward (**в** B as a); (*знак отличия*) decoration; **~жда́ть** [1], ⟨**~ди́ть**⟩ [15 *e*.; -ажу́, -ади́шь; -аждённый] (T) reward; decorate; *fig*. endow with
**нагрева́т|ельный** [14] heating; **~ь** [1] → ***греть***
**нагромо|жда́ть** [1], ⟨**~зди́ть**⟩ [15 *e*.; -зжу́, зди́шь; -ождённый] pile up, heap up
**нагру́дник** *m* [1] bib, breastplate
**нагру|жа́ть** [1], ⟨**~зи́ть**⟩ [15 & 15 *e*.; -ужу́, -у́зи́шь; -у́жённый] load (with T); *coll*. *работой a*. burden, assign; **~зка** *f* [5; *g*/*pl*.: -зок] load(ing); *coll*. *a* burden, job, assignment; *преподавателя* teaching load
**нагря́нуть** [20] *pf*. *о гостях* appear unexpectedly, descend (on)
**над, ~о** (T) over, above; *смеяться* at; about; *трудиться* at, on
**нада́в|ливать** [1], ⟨**~и́ть**⟩ [14] (*a*. **на** B) press; squeeze; *соку* press out
**надба́в|ка** *f* [5; *g*/*pl*.: -вок] addition; extra charge; *к зарплате* increment, rise; **~ля́ть** [28], ⟨**~ить**⟩ [14] *coll*. → ***набавля́ть***
**надви|га́ть** [1], ⟨**~нуть**⟩ [20] move, push, pull (up to, over); ***~га́ть ша́пку*** pull one's hat over one's eyes; **-ся** approach, draw near; (*закрыть*) cover
**на́двое** in two (parts *or* halves); ambiguously; ***ба́бушка ~ сказа́ла*** it remains to be seen
**надгро́бие** *n* [12] tombstone
**наде|ва́ть** [1], ⟨**~ть**⟩ [-е́ну, -е́нешь; -е́тый] put on (*clothes*, *etc*.)
**наде́жд|а** *f* [5] hope (**на** B of); ***подава́ть ~ы*** show promise
**надёжный** [14; -жен, -жна] reliable, dependable; (*прочный*) firm; (*безопасный*) safe
**наде́л|ать** [1] *pf*. make (a lot of); (*причинять*) do, cause, inflict; **~я́ть** [28], ⟨**~и́ть**⟩ [13] *умом и т. д*. endow with
**наде́ть** → ***надева́ть***
**наде́яться** [27] (**на** B) hope (for); (*по-*

*лагаться*) rely (on)
**надзо́р** *m* [1] supervision; *милиции и т. д.* surveillance
**надл|а́мывать**, ⟨**~ома́ть**⟩ [1] *coll.*, ⟨**~оми́ть**⟩ [14] crack; *fig.* overtax, break down
**надлежа́|ть** [4; *impers.* + *dat. and inf.*] it is necessary; **~щий** [17] appropriate, suitable; ***~щим о́бразом*** properly, duly
**надлома́ть** → ***надла́мывать***
**надме́нный** [14; -е́нен, -е́нна] haughty
**на́до** it is necessary (for Д); (Д) (one) must (*go*, *etc.*); need; want; ***так ему́ и ~*** it serves him right; **~бность** *f* [8] need (***в*** П for), necessity; affair, matter (***по*** Д in); ***по ме́ре ~бности*** when necessary
**надо|еда́ть** [1], ⟨**~е́сть**⟩ [-е́м, -е́шь, *etc.*, → ***е́сть***[1]] (Д, Т) tire; *вопросами и т. д.* bother, pester; ***мне ~е́л…*** I'm tired (of) fed up (with); **~е́дливый** [14 *sh.*] tiresome; *человек* troublesome, annoying
**надо́лго** for (a) long (time)
**надорва́ть** → ***надрыва́ть***
**надпи́|сывать** [1], ⟨**~са́ть**⟩ [3] inscribe; *конверт и т. д.* superscribe; **´~сь** *f* [8] inscription
**надре́з** *m* [1] cut, incision; **~а́ть** *and* **~ывать** [1], ⟨**~ать**⟩ [3] cut, incise
**надруга́тельство** *n* [9] outrage
**надры́в** *m* [1] rent, tear; *fig.* strain; **~а́ть** [1], ⟨**надорва́ть**⟩ [-ву́, -вёшь; надорва́л, -а́, -о; -о́рванный] tear; *здоровье* undermine; (over)strain (o.s. себя́, **-ся**; be[come] worn out *or* exhausted; let o.s. go; ***~а́ть живо́т от сме́ха, ~а́ться*** (***со́ смеху***) split one's sides (with laughter)
**надстр|а́ивать** [1], ⟨**~о́ить**⟩ [13] build on; raise the height of; **~о́йка** [5; *g/pl.*: -ро́ек] superstructure
**наду|ва́ть** [1], ⟨**~ть**⟩ [18] inflate; (*обманывать*) dupe; ***~ть гу́бы*** pout; **-ся** *v/i. coll.* (*обидеться*) be sulky (***на*** В with); **~вно́й** [14] inflatable, air…; **~ть** → ***~ва́ть***
**наду́м|анный** [14] far-fetched, strained; **~ать** *coll.* [1] *pf.* think (of), make up one's mind
**наду́тый** [1] (*обиженный*) sulky
**наеда́ться** [1], ⟨**нае́сться**⟩ [-е́мся, -е́шься, *etc.*, → ***есть***[1]] eat one's fill
**наедине́** alone, in private
**нае́зд** *m* [1] (***~ом*** on) short *or* flying visit(s); **~ник** *m* [1] rider
**нае|зжа́ть** [1], ⟨**~хать**⟩ [нае́ду, -е́дешь] (***на*** В) run into *or* over; *coll.* come (occasionally), call on (***к*** Д)
**наём** *m* [1; на́йма] *работника* hire; *квартиры* rent; **~ник** *m* [1] *солдат* mercenary; **~ный** [14] hired
**нае́|сться** → ***~да́ться***; **~хать** → ***~зжа́ть***
**нажа́ть** → ***нажима́ть***
**нажда́|к** *m* [1 *e.*], **~чный** [14] emery
**нажи́|ва** *f* [5] gain, profit; **~ва́ть** [1], ⟨**~ть**⟩ [-живу́, -вёшь; на́жил, -а́, -о; нажи́вший; на́житый (на́жит, -а́, -о)] earn, gain; *добро* amass; *состояние*, *врагов* make; *ревматизм* get; **~вка** *f* [5; *g/pl.*: -вок] bait
**нажи́м** *m* [1] pressure (*a. fig.*); **~а́ть** [1], ⟨**нажа́ть**⟩ [-жму́, -жмёшь; -жа́тый] (*a.* ***на*** В) press, push (*a. coll. fig.* = urge, impel; influence)
**нажи́ть** → ***нажива́ть***
**наза́д** back(ward[s]); ***~!*** get back!; ***тому́ ~*** ago
**назва́|ние** *n* [12] name; title; **~ть** → ***называ́ть***
**назе́мный** [14]: ***~ тра́нспорт*** overland transport
**назида́|ние** *n* [12] edification (for p.'s ***в*** В/Д); **~тельный** [14; -лен, -льна] edifying
**на́зло́** Д out of spite, to spite (s.b.)
**назнач|а́ть** [1], ⟨**~ить**⟩ [16] appoint (p. s.th. В/Т), designate; *время и т. д.* fix, settle; *лекарство* prescribe; *день и т. д.* assign; **~е́ние** *n* [12] appointment; assignment; (*цель*) purpose; prescription; (*место ~ения*) destination
**назо́йливый** [14 *sh.*] importunate
**назре|ва́ть** [1], ⟨**~ть**⟩ [8] ripen, mature; *fig.* be imminent *or* impending; ***~ло вре́мя*** the time is ripe
**назубо́к** *coll.* by heart, thoroughly
**называ́|ть** [1], ⟨**назва́ть**⟩ [-зову́, -зовёшь; -зва́л, -а́, -о; на́званный (на́зван, -а́, -о)] call, name; (*упомянуть*) mention; ***~ть себя́*** introduce o.s.; ***~ть ве́щи свои́ми имена́ми*** call a spade a spade;

***так ~емый*** so-called; **-ся** call o.s., be called; ***как ~ется …?*** what is (*or* do you call) …?
**наи…** *in compds.* of all, very; **~бóлее** most, …est of all
**наи́вн|ость** *f* [8] naiveté; **~ый** [14; -вен, -вна] naive, ingenuous
**наизна́нку** inside out
**наизу́сть** by heart
**наиме́нее** least … of all
**наименова́ние** *n* [12] name; title
**наискосо́к** obliquely
**найти́|е** *n* [12]: ***по ~ю*** by intuition
**найти́** → ***находи́ть***
**наказ|а́ние** *n* [12] punishment (***в*** B as a); penalty; *coll.* nuisance; **~у́емый** [14 *sh.*] punishable; **~ывать** [1], ⟨**~а́ть**⟩ [3] punish
**нака́л** *m* [1] incandescence; **~ивать** [1], ⟨**~и́ть**⟩ [13] incandesce; ***стра́сти ~ились*** passions ran high; ***~ённый*** incandescent, red-hot; *атмосфера* tense
**нак|а́лывать** [1], ⟨**~оло́ть**⟩ [17] *дров* chop
**накану́не** the day before; **~** (P) on the eve (of)
**нака́п|ливать** [1] **& ~опля́ть** [28], ⟨**~опи́ть**⟩ [14] accumulate, amass; *деньги* save up
**наки́|дка** *f* [5; *g/pl.*: -док] cape, cloak; **~дывать** [1] **1.** ⟨**~да́ть**⟩ [1] throw about; **2.** ⟨**~нуть**⟩ [20] throw on; *coll.* (*набавить*) add; raise; **-ся** (***на*** B) *coll.* fall (up)on
**на́кипь** *f* [8] *пена* scum (*a. fig.*); *осадок* scale
**наклад|на́я** *f* [14] invoice, waybill; **~но́й** [14]: ***~ные расхо́ды*** overhead, expenses, overheads; **~ывать** *and* **налага́ть** [1], ⟨**наложи́ть**⟩ [16] (***на*** B) lay (on), apply (to); put (on), set (to); *взыскание, штраф* impose; *отпечаток* leave; (*наполнить*) fill, pack, load
**накле́|ивать** [1], ⟨**~ить**⟩ [13; -е́ю] glue *or* paste on; *марку* stick on; **~йка** *f* [5; *g/pl.*: -е́ек] label
**накло́н** *m* [1] incline; slope; **~е́ние** *n* [12] *gr.* inclination; mood; **~и́ть** → ***~я́ть***; **~ный** [14] inclined, slanting; **~я́ть** [28], ⟨**~и́ть**⟩ [13; -оню́, -о́нишь; -онённый] bend, tilt; bow, stoop; incline; **-ся** *v/i.*
**накова́льня** *f* [6; *g/pl.*: -лен] anvil
**наколо́ть** → ***нака́лывать***
**наконе́|ц** (***~ц-то*** oh) at last, finally; at length; **~чник** *m* [1] tip, point
**накоп|ле́ние** *n* [12] accumulation; **~ля́ть**, **~и́ть** → ***нака́пливать***
**накрахма́ленный** [14] starched
**на́крепко** fast, tight
**накры|ва́ть** [1], ⟨**~ть**⟩ [22] cover; *стол* (*a.* B) lay (*the table*); P *преступника* catch, trap
**накуп|а́ть** [1], ⟨**~и́ть**⟩ [14] (P) buy up (a lot)
**наку́р|ивать** [1], ⟨**~и́ть**⟩ [13; -урю́, -у́ришь; -у́ренный] fill with smoke *or* fumes
**налага́ть** → ***накла́дывать***
**нала́|живать** [1], ⟨**~дить**⟩ [15] put right *or* in order, get straight, fix; *дела* get things going; *отношения* establish
**нале́во** to *or* on the left of; → ***напра́во***
**нале|га́ть** [1], ⟨**~чь**⟩; [26; г/ж: -ля́гу, -ля́жешь, -ля́гут; -лёг, -гла́; -ля́г(те)!] (***на*** B) lean (on); press (against, down); *fig. на работу и т. д.* apply o.s. (to)
**налегке́** *coll.* with no baggage (*Brt.* luggage)
**нал|ёт** *m* [1] *mil., ae.* raid, attack; *med.* fur; (*a. fig.*) touch; **~ета́ть** [1], ⟨**~ете́ть**⟩ [11] (***на*** B) fly (at, [*a.* knock, strike] against); swoop down; raid, attack; (*наброситься*) fall ([up]on); *о ветре, буре* spring up; **~ётчик** *m* [1] bandit
**нале́чь** → ***налега́ть***
**нали|ва́ть** [1], ⟨**~ть**⟩ [-лью́, -льёшь; -ле́й(те)!; нали́л, -а́, -о; -ли́вший; нали́тый (нали́т, -а́, -о)] pour (out); fill; *p. pt. p.* (*a.* ***~то́й***) ripe, jucy; *о теле* firm; (**-ся** *v/i.*; *a.* ripen); **~вка** *f* [5; *g/pl.*: -вок] (fruit) liqueur; **~м** *m* [1] burbot
**налито́й, нали́ть** → ***налива́ть***
**налицо́** present, on hand
**нали́ч|ие** *n* [12] presence; **~ность** *f* [8] cash-in-hand; *a* → ***~ие***; ***в ~ности*** → ***налицо́***; **~ный** [14] (*a. pl., su.*); *деньги* ready cash (*a.* down T); (*имеющийся*) present, on hand; ***за ~ные*** for cash
**нало́г** *m* [1] tax; *на товары* duty;

Н

**~оплате́льщик** *m* [1] taxpayer
**нало́ж|енный** [14]: ***~енным платежо́м*** cash (*or* collect) on delivery; **~и́ть** → ***накла́дывать***
**налюбова́ться** [7] *pf.* (T) gaze to one's heart's content; ***не ~*** never get tired of admiring (o.s. ***собо́й***)
**нама́|зывать** [1] → *мазать*; **~тывать** [1] → ***мота́ть***
**нам|ёк** *m* [1] (***на*** B) allusion (to), hint (at); **~ека́ть** [1], ⟨**~екну́ть**⟩ [20] (***на*** B) allude (to), hint (at)
**намер|ева́ться** [1] intend → (***я*** I, *etc.*) **~ен(а)**; **~ение** *n* [12] intention, design; purpose (**с** T on); **~енный** [14] intentional, deliberate
**намета́ть** → ***намётывать***
**наме́тить** → ***намеча́ть***
**нам|ётка** *f* [5; *g/pl.*: -ток], **~ётывать** [1], ⟨**~ета́ть**⟩ [3] *sew.* baste, tack
**наме|ча́ть** [1], ⟨**~тить**⟩ [15] (*планировать*) plan, have in view; (*отбирать*) nominate, select
**намно́го** much, (by) far
**намок|а́ть** [1], ⟨**~нуть**⟩ [21] get wet
**намо́рдник** *m* [1] muzzle
**нанести́** → ***наноси́ть***
**нани́з|ывать** [1], ⟨**~а́ть**⟩ [3] string, thread
**нан|има́ть** [1], ⟨**~я́ть**⟩ [найму́, -мёшь; на́нял, -а́, -о; -я́вший; на́нятый (на́нят, -а́, -о)] rent, hire; *рабочего* take on, engage; **-ся** *coll.* take a job
**на́ново** anew, (over) again
**наноси́ть** [15], ⟨**нанести́**⟩ [24 -с-: несу́, -сёшь; -нёс, -несла́] bring (much, many); *водой* carry, waft, deposit, wash ashore; *краску и т. д.* lay on, apply; *на карту и т. д.* plot, draw; (*причинять*) inflict (on Д), cause; *визит* pay; *удар* deal
**наня́ть(ся)** → ***нанима́ть(ся)***
**наоборо́т** the other way round, vice versa, conversely; on the contrary
**наобу́м** *coll.* at random, haphazardly; without thinking
**наотре́з** bluntly, categorically
**напа|да́ть** [1], ⟨**~сть**⟩ [25; *pt. st.*: -па́л, -а; -па́вший] (***на*** B) attack, fall (up)on; (*случайно обнаружить*) come across or upon; hit on; *страх* come over, seize, grip; **~да́ющий** *m* [17] assailant; *sport* forward; **~де́ние** *n* [12] attack; assault; **~дки** *f/pl.* [5; *gen.*: -док] accusations; (*придирки*) carping, faultfinding *sg.*
**нап|а́ивать** [1], ⟨**~ои́ть**⟩ [13] *водой и т. д.* give to drink; *спиртным* make drunk
**напа́|сть** **1.** *coll. f* [8] misfortune, bad luck; **2.** → ***~да́ть***
**напе́|в** *m* [1] melody, tune; **~ва́ть** [1] hum, croon
**напере|бо́й** *coll.* vying with one another; **~гонки́** *coll.*: ***бежа́ть ~гонки́*** racing one another; **~ко́р** (Д) in spite *or* defiance (of), counter (to); **~ре́з** cutting (across s.b.'s way Д, Р); **~чёт** each and every; *as pred.* not many, very few
**напёрсток** *m* [1; -тка] thimble
**напи|ва́ться** [1], ⟨**~ться**⟩ [-пью́сь, -пьёшься; -пи́лся, -пила́сь; пе́йся, -пе́йтесь!] drink, quench one's thirst; (*опьянеть*) get drunk
**напи́льник** *m* [1] (*tool*) file
**напи́|ток** *m* [1; -тка] drink, beverage; ***прохлади́тельные*** (***спиртны́е***) ***~тки*** soft (alcoholic) drinks; **~ться** → ***~ва́ться***
**напи́х|ивать**, ⟨**~а́ть**⟩ [1] cram into, stuff into
**наплы́в** *m* [1] *покупателей и т. д.* influx
**напова́л** outright, on the spot
**наподо́бие** (P) like, resembling
**напои́ть** → ***напа́ивать***
**напока́з** for show; → ***выставля́ть***
**наполн|я́ть** [28], ⟨**~ить**⟩ [13] (T) fill; crowd; *p. pt. p. a.* full
**наполови́ну** half; (*do*) by halves
**напом|ина́ние** *n* [12] reminding, reminder; **~ина́ть** [1], ⟨**~нить**⟩ [13] remind (a. p. of Д/**о** П)
**напо́р** *m* [1] pressure (*a. fig.*); **~истость** [8] push, vigo(u)r
**напосле́док** *coll.* in the end, finally
**напра́в|ить(ся)** → ***~ля́ть(ся)***; **~ле́ние** *n* [12] direction (***в*** П, ***по*** Д in); *fig.* trend, tendency; **~ля́ть** [28], ⟨**~ить**⟩ [14] direct, aim; send, refer to; assign, detach; **-ся**

Н

head for; (*coll.*) get going, get under way; turn (***на*** В to)
**напра́во** (**от** Р) to the right, on the right
**напра́сн|ый** [14; -сен, -сна] vain; (*необоснованный*) groundless, idle; **~о** in vain; (*незаслуженно*) wrongly
**напр|а́шиваться** [1], ⟨**~оси́ться**⟩ [15] (***на*** В) (pr)offer (o.s. for), solicit; *на оскорбления* provoke; *на комплименты* fish (for); *impf. выводы и т. д.* suggest itself
**наприме́р** for example, for instance
**напро|ка́т** for hire; ***взять*** (***дать***) ***~ка́т*** hire (out); **~лёт** *coll.* (all)… through(-out); without a break; **~ло́м** *coll.*: ***идти́ ~ло́м*** force one's way; (*act*) regardless of obstacles
**напроси́ться** → ***напра́шиваться***
**напро́тив** (Р) opposite; on the contrary; → *a.* ***наперекóр*** *and* ***наоборо́т***
**напря|га́ть** [1], ⟨**~чь**⟩ [26; г/ж: -ягу́, -яжёшь; -пря́г] strain (*a. fig.*); exert; *мускулы* tense; **~же́ние** *n* [12] tension (*a. el.* voltage), strain, exertion, effort; close attention; **~жённый** [14 *sh.*] *отношения* strained; *труд и т. д.* (in)tense; *внимание* keen, close
**напрями́к** *coll.* straight out; outright
**напря́чь** → ***напряга́ть***
**напу́ганный** [14] scared, frightened
**напус|ка́ть** [1], ⟨**~ти́ть**⟩ [15] let in, fill; set on (**на** В); *coll.* (***~ка́ть на себя́***) put on (*airs*); Р *страху* cause; **-ся** *coll.* fly at, go for (***на*** В); **~кно́й** [14] affected, assumed, put-on
**напу́тств|енный** [14] farewell…, parting; **~ие** *n* [12] parting words
**напы́щенный** [14 *sh.*] pompous; *стиль* high-flown
**наравне́** (**с** Т) on a level with; equally; together (*or* along) with
**нараспа́шку** *coll.* unbuttoned; (***душа́***) **~** frank, candid
**нараспе́в** with a singsong voice
**нараст|а́ть** [1], ⟨**~и́**⟩ [24; -стёт; → ***расти́***] grow; *о процентах* accrue; increase; *о звуке* swell
**нарасхва́т** *coll.* like hot cakes
**нарез|а́ть** [1], ⟨**~ать**⟩ [3] cut; *мясо* carve; *ломтиками* slice; **~ывать** → ***~а́ть***
**нарека́ние** *n* [12] reprimand, censure
**наре́чие**[1] *n* [12] dialect
**наре́чие**[2] *gr.* adverb
**нарица́тельный** [14] *econ.* nominal; *gr.* common
**нарко́|з** *m* [1] narcosis, an(a)esthesia; **~ма́н** *m* [1] drug addict; **~тик** *m* [1] narcotic
**наро́д** *m* [1] people, nation; **~ность** *f* [8] nationality; **~ный** [14] people's, popular, folk…; national; ***~ное хозя́йство*** national economy
**наро́ст** *m* [1] (out)growth
**нароч|и́тый** [14 *sh.*] deliberate, intentional; *adv.* = **~но** *a.* on purpose; *coll.* in fun; *coll. a.* → ***на́зло́***; **´~ный** [14] courier
**на́рты** *f/pl.* [5] sledge (*drawn by dogs or reindeer*)
**нару́ж|ность** *f* [8] exterior; outward appearance; **~ный** [14], external; *спокойствие и т. д.* outward(s); **~у** outside, outward(s); ***вы́йти ~у*** *fig.* come to light
**наруш|а́ть** [1], ⟨**~ить**⟩ [16] disturb; *правило и т. д.* infringe, violate; *тишину и т. д.* break; **~е́ние** *n* [12] violation, transgression, breach; disturbance; **~и́тель** *m* [4] *границы* trespasser; *спокойствия* disturber; *закона* infringer; **~ить** → ***~а́ть***
**нарци́сс** *m* [1] daffodil
**на́ры** *f/pl.* [5] plank bed
**нары́в** *m* [1] abcess; → ***гнои́ть***; **~а́ть** [1], ⟨нарва́ть⟩ *med.* come to a head
**наря́|д** *m* [1] *одежда* attire, dress; **~ди́ть** → ***~жа́ть***; **~дный** [14; -ден, -дна] well-dressed; elegant; smart
**наряду́** (**с** Т) together (*or* along) with, side by side; at the same time; *a.* → ***наравне́***
**наря|жа́ть** [1], ⟨**~ди́ть**⟩ [15 & 15 *e.*; -яжу́, -я́дишь; -я́женный & -яжённый] dress up (as) (*v/i.* **-ся**)
**наса|жда́ть** [1], ⟨**~ди́ть**⟩ [15] (im)plant (*a. fig.*); → *a.* ***~живать***; **~жде́ние** *n* [12] *mst. pl.* specially planted trees, bushes; **~живать** [1], ⟨**~жа́ть**⟩, ⟨**~ди́ть**⟩ [15] plant (many); *на ручку* haft
**насви́стывать** [1] whistle

**наседа́ть** [1] *impf.* press (*of crowds, etc.*)
**насеко́мое** *n* [14] insect
**насел|е́ние** *n* [12] population; *города* inhabitants; **~ённый** [14; -лён, -лена́, -лено́] populated; **~ённый пункт** (*official designation*) locality, built-up area; **~я́ть** [28], 〈**~и́ть**〉 [13] people, settle; *impf.* inhabit, live in
**наси́женный** [14] snug; familiar, comfortable
**наси́|лие** *n* [12] violence, force; (*принуждение*) coercion; **~ловать** [7] violate, force; rape; (*a.* **из-**); **~лу** *coll.* → **е́ле**; **~льно** by force; forcibly; **~льственный** [14] forcible; *смерть* violent
**наск|а́кивать** [1], 〈**~очи́ть**〉 [16] (**на** В) *fig. coll.* fly at, fall (up)on; *камень и т. д.* run *or* strike against; (*столкнуться*) collide (with)
**наскво́зь** throughout; *coll.* through and through
**наско́лько** as (far as); how (much); to what extent
**на́скоро** *coll.* hastily, in a hurry
**наскочи́ть** → **наска́кивать**
**наску́чить** *coll.* [16] *pf.*, → **надоеда́ть**
**насла|жда́ться** [1], 〈**~ди́ться**〉 [15 *е.*; -ажу́сь, -ади́шься] (T) enjoy (o.s.), (be) delight(ed); **~жде́ние** *n* [12] enjoyment; delight; pleasure
**насле́д|ие** *n* [12] heritage, legacy; → *a.* **~ство**; **~ник** *m* [1] heir; **~ница** *f* [5] heiress; **~ный** [14] *принц* crown…; **~овать** [7] (*im*)*pf.*, 〈у-〉 inherit; (Д) succeed to; **~ственность** *f* [8] heredity; **~ственный** [14] hereditary; *имущество* inherited; **~ство** *n* [9] inheritance; → *a.* **~ие**; *vb.* + **в ~ство** (*or* **по ~ству**) inherit
**наслое́ние** *n* [12] stratification
**насл|у́шаться** [1] *pf.* (P) listen to one's heart's content; **не мочь ~у́шаться** never get tired of listening to; *a.* = **~ы́шаться** [4] (P) hear a lot (of) *or* much; → **понаслы́шке**
**насма́рку**: **пойти́ ~** come to nothing
**на́смерть** to death (*a. fig.*), mortally; **стоя́ть ~** fight to the last ditch
**насме|ха́ться** [1] mock, jeer; sneer (at **над** T); **~шка** *f* [5; *g/pl.*: -шек] mockery, ridicule; **~шливый** [14 *sh.*] derisive, mocking; **~шник** *m* [1], **~шница** *f* [5] scoffer, mocker
**на́сморк** *m* [1] cold (*in the head*); **подхвати́ть ~** catch a cold
**насмотре́ться** [9; -отрю́сь, -о́тришься] *pf.* → **нагляде́ться**
**насо́с** *m* [1] pump
**на́спех** hastily, carelessly
**наста|ва́ть** [5], 〈**~ть**〉 [-ста́нет] come; **~вить** → **~вля́ть**; **~вле́ние** *n* [12] (*поучение*) admonition, guidance; **~вля́ть** [28], 〈**~вить**〉 [14] **1.** put, place, set (many P); **2.** (*поучать*) instruct; teach (Д, **в** П s.th.) **~ивать** [1], 〈настоя́ть〉 [-стою́, -стои́шь] insist (**на** П on); *чай и т. д.* draw, extract; **настоя́ть на своём** insist on having it one's own way; **~ть** → **~ва́ть**
**на́стежь** wide open
**насти|га́ть** [1], 〈**~гнуть**〉 & 〈**~чь**〉 [21; -г-: -и́гну] overtake; catch (up with)
**наст|ила́ть** [1], 〈**~ла́ть**〉 [-телю́, -те́лешь; на́стланный] lay, spread; *досками* plank; *пол* lay
**насто́й** *m* [3] infusion, extract; **~ка** *f* [5; *g/pl.*: -оек] liqueur; *a.* → **~**
**насто́йчивый** [14 *sh.*] persevering; *требование* urgent, insistent, persistent; (*упорный*) obstinate
**насто́ль|ко** so (*or* as [much]); **~ный** [14] table…
**настор|а́живаться** [1], 〈**~ожи́ться**〉 [16 *е.*; -жу́сь, -жи́шься] prick up one's ears; become suspicious; **~оже́** on the alert, on one's guard
**настоя́|ние** *n* [12] insistence, urgent request (**по** Д at); **~тельный** [14; -лен, -льна] urgent, pressing, insistent; **~ть** → **наста́ивать**
**настоя́щ|ий** [17] present (*time*) (**в** В at); *a. gr.* **~ее время** present tense; true, real, genuine; **по-~ему** properly
**настр|а́ивать** [1], 〈**~о́ить**〉 [13] build (many P); *инструмент, оркестр, радио* tune (up, in); *против* set against; *a.* **нала́живать** adjust; **~ого** strictly; **~ое́ние** *n* [12] mood, spirits *pl.*, frame (of mind); **~о́ить** → **~а́ивать**; **~о́йка** *f* [5; *g/pl.*: -оек] tuning

Н

**наступ|áтельный** [14] offensive; **~áть** [1], 〈**~и́ть**〉 [14] tread *or* step (**на** B on); (*начаться*) come, set in; *impf. mil.* attack, advance; (*приближаться*) approach; **~лéние** *n* [12] offensive, attack, advance; coming, approach; *дня* daybreak; *сумерек* nightfall (**с** T at)
**настýрция** [7] nasturtium
**насýпить(ся)** [14] *pf.* frown
**нáсухо** dry
**насýщный** [14; -щен, -щна] vital; **~ хлеб** daily bread
**насчёт** (P) *coll.* concerning, about
**насчи́т|ывать**, 〈**~áть**〉 [1] number (= *to have or contain*); **-ся** *impf.* there is (are)
**насып|áть** [1], 〈**´~ать**〉 [2] pour; fill; **´~ь** *f* [8] embankment
**насы|щáть** [1], 〈**´~тить**〉 [15] satisfy; *влагой* saturate; **~щéние** *n* [12] satiation; saturation
**нат|áлкивать** [1], 〈**~олкнýть**〉 [20] (**на** B) push (against, on); *coll.* prompt, suggest; **-ся** strike against; (*случайно встретить*) run across
**натвори́ть** *coll.* [13] *pf.* do, get up to
**нат|ирáть** [1], 〈**~ерéть**〉 [12] (T) rub; *мозоль* get; *пол* wax, polish
**нáтиск** *m* [1] pressure; *mil.* onslaught, charge
**наткнýться** → **натыкáться**
**натолкнýть(ся)** → **натáлкиваться**
**натощáк** on an empty stomach
**натрáв|ливать** [1], 〈**~и́ть**〉 [14] set (**на** B on), incite
**нáтрий** *m* [3] *chem.* sodium
**натý|га** *coll. f* [5] strain, effort; **´~го** *coll.* tight(ly)
**натýр|а** *f* [5] (*характер*) nature; (artist's) model (= **~щик** *m* [1], **~щица** [5]): **с ~ы** from nature *or* life; **~áльный** [14; -лен, -льна] natural
**нат|ыкáться** [1], 〈**~кнýться**〉 [20] (**на** B) run *or* come across
**натя́|гивать** [1], 〈**~нýть**〉 [19] stretch, draw tight; pull (**на** B on); draw in (*reins*); **~жка** *f* [5; *g/pl.*: -жек] forced *or* strained interpretation; **допусти́ть ~жку** stretch a point; **с ~жкой** *a.* at a stretch; **~нутый** [14] tight; *отношения* strained; *улыбка* forced; **~нýть** → **~гивать**
**наугáд** at random, by guessing
**наýка** *f* [5] science; *coll.* lesson
**наутёк**: *coll.* **пусти́ться ~** take to one's heels
**наýтро** the next morning
**научи́ть** [16] teach (B/Д a p. s.th.); **-ся** learn (Д s.th.)
**наýчный** [14; -чен, -чна] scientific
**наýшники** *m/pl.* [1] ear- *or* headphones; earmuffs
**нахá|л** *m* [1] impudent fellow; **~льный** [14; -лен, -льна] impudent, insolent; **~льство** *n* [12] impudence, insolence
**нахвáт|ывать** 〈**~áть**〉 *coll.* [1] (P) pick up, come by, get hold of; hoard; *a.* **-ся**
**нахлы́нуть** [20] *pf.* flow; gush (over, into); *чувства* sweep over
**нахмýривать** [1] → **хмýрить**
**наход|и́ть** [15], 〈найти́〉 [найдý, -дёшь; нашёл, -шлá; -шéдший; нáйденный; *g. pt.*: найдя́] **1.** find (*a. fig.* = think, consider).; *impf. удовольствие* take; **2.** come (over **на** B); (*закрыть*) cover; *тоска и т. д.*; be seized with; (**-ся**, 〈найти́сь〉) be (found, there, [*impf.*] situated, located); (*иметься*) happen to have; (*не растеряться*) not be at a loss; **´~ка** *f* [5; *g/pl.*: -док] find; *coll.* discovery; *coll. fig.* godsend; **стол ´~ок** lost-property office; **´~чивый** [14 *sh.*] resourceful; quick-witted, smart
**нацéнка** *f* [5; *g/pl.*: -нок] markup
**национал|из(и́р)овáть** [7] *(im)pf.* nationalize; **~и́зм** *m* [1] nationalism; **´~ьность** *f* [8] nationality; **´~ьный** [14; -лен, -льна] national
**нáция** *f* [7] nation
**начá|ло** *n* [9] beginning (at a П); (*источник*) source, origin; (*основа*) basis; principle; **~льник** *m* [1] head, chief, superior; **~льный** [14] initial, first; *строки* opening; **~льство** *n* [9] (the) authorities; command(er[s], chief[s], superior[s]); (*администрация*) administration, management; **~тки** *m/pl.* [1] elements; **~ть(ся)** → **начинáть(ся)**
**начекý** on the alert, on the qui vive

**на́черно** roughly, in draft form
**начина́|ние** *n* [12] undertaking; **~ть** [1], ⟨**нача́ть**⟩ [-чну́, -чнёшь; на́чал, -а́, -о; нача́вший; на́чатый (на́чат, -а́, -о)] begin, start (**с** P *or* T with); **-ся** *v/i.*; **~ющий** [17] beginner
**начина́я** *as prep.* (**с** P) as (from), beginning (with)
**начи́н|ка** [5; *g/pl.*: -нок] *mst. cul.* filling, stuffing; **~я́ть** [28] ⟨**~и́ть**⟩ [13] fill, stuff (with T)
**начисле́ние** *n* [12] additional sum, extra charge
**на́чисто** clean; → ***на́бело***; (*полностью*) fully
**начи́т|анный** [14 *sh.*] well-read; **~а́ться** [1] (P) read (a lot of); *достаточно* read enough (of); ***не мочь ~а́ться*** never get tired of reading
**наш** *m*, **~а** *f*, **~е** *n*, **~и** *pl.* [25] our; ours; ***по ~ему*** to our way of thinking; ***~а взяла́!*** we've won!
**нашаты́р|ный** [14]: ***~ный спирт*** *m* liquid ammonia; *coll. a.* **~ь** *m* [4 *e.*] *chem.* ammonium chloride
**наше́ствие** *n* [12] invasion, inroad
**наши|ва́ть** [1], ⟨**~ть**⟩ [-шью́, -шьёшь; → ***шить***] sew on (***на*** B *or* П) *or* many…; **~вка** *f* [5; *g/pl.*: -вок] *mil.* stripe, chevron
**нащу́п|ывать**, ⟨**~ать**⟩ [1] find by feeling *or* groping; *fig.* discover; detect
**наяву́** while awake, in reality
**не** not; no; **~ *то*** *coll.* or else, otherwise
**неаккура́тный** [14; -тен, -тна] (*небрежный*) careless; (*неряшливый*) untidy; *в работе* inaccurate; unpunctual
**небе́сный** [14] celestial, heavenly; *цвет* sky-blue; (*божественный*) divine; → ***небосво́д***
**неблаго|ви́дный** [14; -ден, -дна] unseemly; **~да́рность** *f* [8] ingratitude; **~да́рный** [14; -рен, -рна] ungrateful; **~полу́чный** [14; -чен, чна] unfavorable, adverse, bad; *adv.* not successfully, not favo(u)rably; **~прия́тный** [14; -тен, -тна] unfavo(u)rable, inauspicious; **~разу́мный** [14; -мен, -мна] imprudent; unreasonable; **~ро́дный** [14; -ден, -дна] ignoble; **~скло́нный** [14; -о́нен, -о́нна] unkindly; ill-disposed; ***судьба́ ко мне ~скло́нна*** fate has not treated me too kindly
**не́бо**[1] *n* [9; *pl.*: небеса́, -е́с] sky (in ***на*** П); heaven(s); ***под откры́тым ~м*** in the open air
**нёбо**[2] *n* [9] *anat.* palate
**небога́тый** [14 *sh.*] of modest means; poor
**небольш|о́й** [17] small; short; ***… с ~и́м*** … odd
**небо|сво́д** *m* [1] firmament; *a.* **~скло́н** *m* [1] horizon; **~скрёб** *m* [1] skyscraper
**небре́жный** [14; -жен, -жна] careless, negligent; slipshod
**небы|ва́лый** [14] unheard-of, unprecedented; **~ли́ца** *f* [5] fable, invention
**нева́жн|ый** [14; -жен, -жна, -о] unimportant, trifling; *coll.* poor, bad; ***э́то ~о*** it does not matter
**невдалеке́** not far off *or* from (**от** P)
**невдомёк**: ***мне бы́ло ~*** it never occurred to me
**неве́|дение** *n* [12] ignorance; **~домый** [14 *sh.*] unknown; **~жа** *m/f* [5] boor; **~жда** *m/f* [5] ignoramus; **~жество** *n* [9] ignorance; **~жливость** *f* [8] incivility; **~жливый** [14 *sh.*] impolite, rude
**неве́р|ие** *n* [12] *в свои силы* lack of self-confidence; **~ный** [14; -рен, -рна, -о] incorrect; *fig.* false; *друг* unfaithful; *походка и т. д.* unsteady; *su.* infidel; **~оя́тный** [14; -тен, -тна] improbable; incredible
**невесо́мый** [14 *sh.*] imponderable; weightless (*a. fig.*)
**неве́ст|а** *f* [5] fiancée, bride; *coll.* marriageable girl; **~ка** *f* [5; *g/pl.*: -ток] daughter-in-law; sister-in-law (*brother's wife*)
**невз|го́да** *f* [5] adversity, misfortune; **~ира́я** (***на*** B) in spite of, despite; without respect (of p.'s); **~нача́й** *coll.* unexpectedly, by chance; **~ра́чный** [14; -чен, -чна] plain, unattractive; **~ыска́тельный** [14] unpretentious, undemanding
**неви́д|анный** [14] singular, unprecedented; **~имый** [14 *sh.*] invisible
**неви́нный** [14; -и́нен, -и́нна] innocent, virginal

**невку́сный** [14; -сен, -сна] unpalatable
**невме|ня́емый** [14 *sh.*] *law* irresponsible; *coll.* beside o.s. **~ша́тельство** *n* [9] nonintervention
**невнима́тельный** [14; -лен, -льна] inattentive
**невня́тный** [14; -тен, -тна] indistinct, inarticulate
**не́вод** *m* [1] seine, sweep-net
**невоз|врати́мый** [14 *sh.*], **~вра́тный** [14; -тен, -тна] irretrievable, irreparable, irrevocable; **~мо́жный** [14; -жен, -жна] impossible; **~мути́мый** [14 *sh.*] imperturbable
**нево́л|ить** [13] force, compel; **~ьный** [14; -лен, -льна] involuntary; (*вынужденный*) forced; **~я** *f* [6] captivity; *coll.* *необходимость* need, necessity; ***охо́та пу́ще ~и*** where there's a will, there's a way
**невоо|брази́мый** [14 *sh.*] unimaginable; **~ружённый** [14] unarmed; ***~ружённым гла́зом*** with the naked eye
**невоспи́танный** [14 *sh.*] ill-bred
**Н**
**невосполни́мый** [14 *sh.*] irreplaceable
**невпопа́д** *coll.* → ***некста́ти***
**невреди́мый** [14 *sh.*] unharmed, sound
**невы́|годный** [14; -ден, -дна] unprofitable; *положение* disadvantageous; **~держанный** [14 *sh.*] inconsistent, uneven; *сыр и т. д.* unripe; **~носи́мый** [14 *sh.*] unbearable, intolerable; **~полне́ние** *n* [12] nonfulfil(l)ment; **~полни́мый** → ***неисполни́мый***; **~рази́мый** [14 *sh.*] inexpressible, ineffable; **~рази́тельный** [14; -лен, -льна] inexpressive; **~со́кий** [16; -со́к, -á, -со́ко́] low, small; *человек* short; *качество* inferior
**не́где** there is nowhere (+ *inf.*); ***~ сесть*** there is nowhere to sit
**негла́сный** [14; -сен, -сна] secret; *расследование* private
**него́д|ный** [14; -ден, -дна, -о] unsuitable; unfit; *coll.* worthless; **~ова́ние** *n* [12] indignation; **~ова́ть** [7] be indignant (***на*** В with); **~я́й** *m* [3] scoundrel, rascal
**негр** *m* [1] Negro
**негра́мотн|ость** → ***безгра́мотность***; **~ый** → ***безгра́мотный***
**негритя́н|ка** *f* [5; *g/pl.*: -нок] Negress; **~ский** [16] Negro…
**неда́|вний** [15] recent; ***с ~вних*** (***~вней***) ***пор***(***ы́***) of late; **~вно** recently; **~лёкий** [16; -ёк, -ека́, -еко́ *and* -ёко] near(by), close; short; not far (off); (*недавний*) recent; (*глуповатый*) dull, stupid; **~льнови́дный** [14] lacking foresight, shortsighted; **~ром** not in vain, not without reason; justly
**недви́жимость** *f* [8] *law* real estate
**неде|йстви́тельный** [14; -лен, -льна] invalid, void; **~ли́мый** [14] indivisible
**неде́л|ьный** [14] a week's, weekly; **~я** *f* [6] week; ***в ~ю*** a *or* per week; ***на э́той*** (***про́шлой, бу́дущей***) ***~е*** this (last, next) week; ***че́рез ~ю*** in a week's time
**недобро|жела́тельный** [14; -лен, -льна] malevolent, ill-disposed; **~ка́чественный** [14 *sh.*] inferior, low-grade; **~со́вестный** [14; -тен, -тна] *конкуренция* unscrupulous, unfair; *работа* careless
**недо́брый** [14; -до́бр, -á, -о] unkind(ly), hostile; *предзнаменование* evil, bad
**недове́р|ие** *n* [12] distrust; **~чивый** [14 *sh.*] distrustful (***к*** Д of)
**недово́ль|ный** [14; -лен, -льна] (Т) dissatisfied, discontented; **~ство** *n* [9] discontent, dissatisfaction
**недога́дливый** [14 *sh.*] slowwitted
**недоеда́|ние** *n* [12] malnutrition; **~ть** [1] be underfed *or* undernourished
**недо́лго** not long, short; ***~ и*** (+ *inf.*) one can easily; ***~ ду́мая*** without hesitation
**недомога́ть** [1] be unwell *or* sick
**недомо́лвка** *f* [5; *g/pl.*: -вок] reservation, innuendo
**недооце́н|ивать** [1], 〈**~и́ть**〉 [13] underestimate, undervalue
**недо|пусти́мый** [14 *sh.*] inadmisible, intolerable; **~ра́звитый** [14 *sh.*] underdeveloped; **~разуме́ние** *n* [12] misunderstanding (***по*** Д through); **~рого́й** [16; -до́рог, -á, -о] inexpensive
**недослы́шать** [1] *pf.* fail to hear all of
**недосмо́тр** *m* [1] oversight, inadvertence (***по*** Д through); **~е́ть** [9; -отрю́,

-о́тришь; -о́тренный] *pf.* overlook (*s.th.*)
**недост|ава́ть** [5], ⟨**~а́ть**⟩ [-ста́нет] *impers.*: (Д) (be) lack(ing), want(ing), be short *or* in need of (Р) *кого-л.*; miss; ***э́того ещё ~ава́ло!***; and that too!; **~а́ток** *m* [1; -тка] lack, shortage (Р, **в** П of); deficiency; defect, shortcoming; ***физи́ческий ~а́ток*** deformity; **~а́точный** [14; -чен, -чна] insufficient, deficient, inadequate; *gr.* defective; **~а́ть** → ***~ава́ть***
**недо|стижи́мый** [14 *sh.*] unattainable; **~сто́йный** [14; -о́ин, -о́йна] unworthy; **~сту́пный** [14; -пен, -пна] inaccessible
**недосу́г** *coll. m* [1] lack of time (***за*** Т, ***по*** Д for); ***мне ~*** I have no time
**недосяга́емый** [14 *sh.*] unattainable
**недоум|ева́ть** [1] be puzzled, be perplexed; **~е́ние** *n* [12] bewilderment; ***в ~е́нии*** in a quandary
**недочёт** *m* [1] deficit; *изъян* defect
**не́дра** *n/pl.* [9] *земли* bowels, depths (*a. fig.*)
**не́друг** *m* [1] enemy, foe
**недружелю́бный** [14; -бен, -бна] unfriendly
**неду́г** *m* [1] ailment
**недурно́й** [14; -ду́рен & -рён, -рна́, -о] not bad; *собой* not bad-looking
**недю́жинный** [14] out of the ordinary, uncommon
**неесте́ственный** [14 *sh.*] unnatural; *смех* affected; *улыбка* forced
**нежела́|ние** *n* [12] unwillingness; **~тельный** [14; -лен, -льна] undesirable
**не́жели** *lit.* → **чем** than
**нежена́тый** [14] single, unmarried
**нежило́й** [14] not fit for habitation
**не́ж|ить** [16] luxuriate; **~ничать** *coll.* [1] caress, spoon; **~ность** *f* [8] tenderness; *pl.* display of affection **~ный** [14; -жен, -жна́, -о] tender, affectionate; *о коже, вкусе* delicate
**незаб|ве́нный** [14 *sh.*], **~ыва́емый** [14 *sh.*] unforgettable; **~у́дка** *f* [5; *g/pl.*: -док] *bot.* forget-me-not
**незави́сим|ость** *f* [8] independence; **~ый** [14 *sh.*] independent
**незада́чливый** *coll.* [14 *sh.*] unlucky
**незадо́лго** shortly (***до*** Р before)
**незако́нный** [14; -о́нен, -о́нна] illegal, unlawful, illicit; *ребёнок и т. д.* illegitimate
**незаме|ни́мый** [14 *sh.*] irreplaceable; **~тный** [14; -тен, -тна] imperceptible, inconspicuous; *человек* plain, ordinary; **~ченный** [14] unnoticed
**неза|мыслова́тый** *coll.* [14 *sh.*] simple, uncomplicated; **~па́мятный** [14]: **с *~па́мятных времён*** from time immemorial; **~те́йливый** [14 *sh.*] plain, simple; **~уря́дный** [14; -ден, -дна] outstanding, exceptional
**не́зачем** there is no need *or* point
**незва́ный** [14] uninvited
**нездоро́в|иться** [14]: ***мне ~ится*** I feel (am) unwell; **~ый** [14 *sh.*] sick; morbid (*a. fig.*); *климат и т. д.* unhealthy
**незло́бивый** [14 *sh.*] forgiving
**незнако́м|ец** *m* [1; -мца], **~ка** *f* [5; *g/pl.*: -мок] stranger; **~ый** [14] unknown, unfamiliar
**незна́|ние** *n* [12] ignorance; **~чи́тельный** [14; -лен, -льна] insignificant
**незр|е́лый** [14 *sh.*] unripe; *fig.* immature; **~и́мый** [14 *sh.*] invisible
**незы́блемый** [14 *sh.*] firm, stable, unshak(e)able
**неиз|бе́жный** [14; -жен, -жна] inevitable; **~ве́стный** [14; -тен, -тна] unknown; *su. a.* stranger; **~глади́мый** [14 *sh.*] indelible; **~лечи́мый** [14 *sh.*] incurable; **~ме́нный** [14; -е́нен, -е́нна] invariable; immutable; **~мери́мый** [14 *sh.*] immeasurable, immense; **~ъясни́мый** [14 *sh.*] inexplicable
**неим|е́ние** *n* [12]: ***за ~е́нием*** (Р) for want of; **~ове́рный** [14; -рен, -рна] incredible; **~у́щий** [17] poor
**нейс|кренний** [15; -енен, -енна] insincere; **~кушённый** [14; -шён, -шена́] inexperienced, innocent; **~полне́ние** *n* [12] *закона* failure to observe (*the law*); **~полни́мый** [14 *sh.*] impracticable
**неиспр|ави́мый** [14 *sh.*] incorrigible; **~а́вность** *f* [8] disrepair; carelessness; **~а́вный** [14; -вен, -вна] out of order, broken, defective; *плательщик* un-

Н

punctual
**неиссяка́емый** [14 *sh.*] inexhaustible
**нейстов|ство** *n* [9] rage, frenzy; **~ствовать** [7] rage; **~ый** [14 *sh.*] frantic, furious
**неис|тощи́мый** [14 *sh.*] inexhaustible; **~треби́мый** [14 *sh.*] ineradicable; **~цели́мый** [14 *sh.*] incurable; **~черпа́емый** [14 *sh.*] → **~тощи́мый**; **~числи́мый** [14 *sh.*] innumerable
**нейло́н** *m* [1], **~овый** [14] nylon (…)
**нейтрал|ите́т** *m* [1] neutrality; **~ьный** [14; -лен, -льна] neutral
**некази́стый** *coll.* [14 *sh.*] → **невзра́чный**
**не́|кий** [24 *st.*] a certain, some; **~когда** there is (**мне ~когда** I have) no time; once; **~кого** [23] there is (**мне ~кого** I have) nobody *or* no one (to *inf.*); **~компете́нтный** [14; -тен, -тна] incompetent; **~корре́ктный** [-тен, -тна] impolite, discourteous; **~который** [14] some (*pl.* **из** Р of); **~краси́вый** [14 *sh.*] plain, unattrative; *поведение* unseemly, indecorous
**некроло́г** *m* [1] obituary
**некста́ти** inopportunely; (*неуместно*) inappropriately
**не́кто** somebody, someone; a certain
**не́куда** there is nowhere (+ *inf.*); **мне ~ пойти́** I have nowhere to go; *coll.* **ху́же** *и т. д.* **~** could not be worse, *etc.*
**некуря́щий** [17] nonsmoker, nonsmoking
**нел|а́дный** *coll.* [14; -ден, -дна] wrong, bad; **будь он ~а́ден!** blast him!; **~ега́льный** [14; -лен, -льна] illegal; **~е́пый** [14 *sh.*] absurd
**нело́вкий** [16; -вок, -вка́, -о] awkward, clumsy; *ситуация* embarrassing
**нело́вко** *adv.* → **нело́вкий**; **чу́вствовать себя́ ~** feel ill at ease
**нелоги́чный** [14; -чен, -чна] illogical
**нельзя́** (it is) impossible, one (**мне** I) cannot *or* must not; **~!** no!; **как ~ лу́чше** in the best way possible, excellently; **~ не → не** (**мочь**)
**нелюди́мый** [14 *sh.*] unsociable
**нема́ло** (Р) a lot, a great deal (of)
**неме́дленный** [14] immediate
**неме́ть** [8], ⟨о-⟩ grow dumb, numb
**не́м|ец** *m* [1; -мца], **~е́цкий** [16], **~ка** *f* [5; *g/pl.*: -мок] German
**неми́лость** *f* [8] disgrace, disfavour
**немину́емый** [14 *sh.*] inevitable
**немно́|гие** *pl.* [16] (a) few, some; **~го** a little; *слегка* slightly, somewhat; **~гое** *n* [16] few things, little; **~гим** a little; **~ж(еч)ко** *coll.* a (little) bit, a trifle
**немо́й** [14; нем, -а́, -о] dumb, mute
**немо|лодо́й** [14; -мо́лод, -а́, -о] elderly; **~та́** *f* [5] dumbness, muteness
**не́мощный** [14; -щен, -щна] infirm
**немы́слимый** [14 *sh.*] inconceivable, unthinkable
**ненави́|деть** [11], ⟨воз-⟩ hate; **~стный** [14; -тен, -тна] hateful, odious; **~сть** (ˈne-) *f* [8] hatred (**к** Д of)
**нена|гля́дный** [14] *coll.* beloved; **~дёжный** [14; -жен, -жна] unreliable; (*непрочный*) unsafe, insecure; **~до́лго** for a short while; **~ме́ренный** [14] unintentional; **~паде́ние** *n* [12] nonaggression; **~́стный** [14; -тен, -тна] rainy, foul; **~́стье** *n* [10] foul weather; **~сы́тный** [14; -тен, -тна] insatiable
**нен|орма́льный** [14; -лен, -льна] abnormal; *coll.* crazy; **~у́жный** [14; -жен, -жна́, -о] unnecessary
**необ|ду́манный** [14 *sh.*] rash, hasty; **~ита́емый** [14 *sh.*] uninhabited; *остров* desert; **~озри́мый** [14 *sh.*] immense, boundless; **~осно́ванный** [14 *sh.*] unfounded; **~рабо́танный** [14] *земля* uncultivated; **~у́зданный** [14 *sh.*] unbridled, ungovernable
**необходи́м|ость** *f* [8] necessity (**по** П of), need (Р, **в** П for); **~ый** [14 *sh.*] necessary (П; **для** Р for), essential; **→ ну́жный**
**необ|щи́тельный** [14; -лен, -льна] unsociable, reserved; **~ъясни́мый** [14 *sh.*] inexplicable; **~ъя́тный** [14; -тен, -тна] immense, unbounded; **~ыкнове́нный** [14; -е́нен, -е́нна] unusual, uncommon; **~ы́ч(а́й)ный** [14; -ч(а́)ен, -ч(а́й)на] extraordinary, exceptional; **~яза́тельный** [14; -лен, -льна] optional; *человек* unreliable
**неограни́ченный** [14 *sh.*] unrestricted

Н

**неод|нокра́тный** [14] repeated; **~обре́ние** *n* [12] disapproval; **~обри́тельный** [14; -лен, -льна] disapproving; **~оли́мый** → ***непреодоли́мый***; **~ушевлённый** [14] inanimate

**неожи́данн|ость** *f* [8] unexpectedness, surprise; **~ый** [14 *sh.*] unexpected, sudden

**нео́н** *m* [1] *chem.* neon; **~овый** [14] neon…

**неоп|ису́емый** [14 *sh.*] indescribable; **~ла́ченный** [14 *sh.*] unpaid, unsettled; **~ра́вданный** [14] unjustified; **~ределённый** [14; -ёнен, -ённа] indefinite (*a. gr.*), uncertain, vague; **~ровержи́мый** [14 *sh.*] irrefutable; **~ытный** [14; -тен, -тна] inexperienced

**неос|ведомлённый** [14; -лён, -лена́, -лены́] ill-informed; **~ла́бный** [14; -бен, -бна] unremitting, unabated; **~мотри́тельный** [14; -лен, -льна] imprudent; **~пори́мый** [14 *sh.*] undisputable; **~торо́жный** [14; -жен, -жна] careless, incautious; imprudent; **~уществи́мый** [14 *sh.*] impracticable; **~яза́емый** [14 *sh.*] intangible

**неот|врати́мый** [14 *sh.*] inevitable; **~ёсанный** [14 *sh.*] unpolished; *coll.* *человек* uncouth; **~куда** → ***не́где***; **~ло́жный** [14; -жен, -жна] pressing, urgent; **~лу́чный** ever-present → ***постоя́нный***; **~рази́мый** [14 *sh.*] irresistible; *довод* irrefutable; **~сту́пный** [14; -пен, -пна] persistent; importunate; **~чётливый** [14 *sh.*] indistinct, vague; **~ъе́млемый** [14 *sh.*] *часть* integral; *право* inalienable

**неохо́т|а** *f* [5] reluctance; (***мне***) **~а** *coll.* I (*etc.*) am not in the mood; **~но** unwillingly

**не|оцени́мый** [14 *sh.*] inestimable; invaluable; **~перехо́дный** [14] *gr.* intransitive

**неплатёжеспосо́бный** [14; -бен, -бна] insolvent

**непо|беди́мый** [14 *sh.*] invincible; **~воро́тливый** [14 *sh.*] clumsy, slow; **~го́да** *f* [5] foul weather; **~греши́мый** [14 *sh.*] infallible; **~далёку** not far (away *or* off); **~да́тливый** [14 *sh.*] unyielding, intractable

**непод|ви́жный** [14; -жен, -жна] motionless, fixed, stationary; **~де́льный** [14; -лен, -льна] genuine, unfeigned; *искренний* sincere; **~ку́пный** [14; -пен, -пна] incorruptible; **~оба́ющий** [17] improper, unbecoming; **~ража́емый** [14 *sh.*] inimitable; **~ходя́щий** [17] unsuitable; **~чине́ние** *n* [12] insubordination

**непо|зволи́тельный** [14; -лен, -льна] not permissible; **~колеби́мый** [14 *sh.*] (*надёжный*) firm, steadfast; (*стойкий*) unflinching; **~ко́рный** [14; -рен, -рна] refractory; **~ла́дка** *coll.* *f* [5; *g/pl.*: -док] *tech.* defect, fault; **~лный** [14; -лон, -лна́, -о] incomplete; *рабочий день* short; **~ме́рный** [14; -рен, -рна] excessive, inordinate

**непоня́т|ливый** [14 *sh.*] slow-witted; **~ный** [14; -тен, -тна] unintelligible, incomprehensible; *явление* strange, odd

**непо|прави́мый** [14 *sh.*] irreparable, irremediable; **~ря́дочный** [14; -чен, -чна] dishono(u)rable; disreputable; **~се́дливый** [14 *sh.*] fidgety; **~си́льный** [14; -лен, -льна] beyond one's strength; **~сле́довательный** [14; -лен, -льна] inconsistent; **~слу́шный** [14; -шен, -шна] disobedient

**непо|сре́дственный** [14 *sh.*] immediate, direct; (*естественный*) spontaneous; **~стижи́мый** [14 *sh.*] inconceivable; **~стоя́нный** [14; -я́нен, -я́нна] inconstant, changeable, fickle; **~хо́жий** [17 *sh.*] unlike, different (***на*** B from)

**непра́в|да** *f* [5] untruth, lie; (it is) not true; ***все́ми пра́вдами и ~дами*** by hook or by crook; **~доподо́бный** [14; -бен, -бна] improbable; implausible; **~ильный** [14; -лен, -льна] incorrect, wrong; irregular (*a. gr.*); improper (*a. math.*); **~ый** [14; непра́в, -á, -о] mistaken; (*несправедливый*) unjust

**непре|взойдённый** [14 *sh.*] unsurpassed; **~дви́денный** [14] unforeseen; **~дубеждённый** [14] unbiased; **~кло́нный** [14; -о́нен, -о́нна] inflexible; obdurate, inexorable; **~ло́жный** [14; -жен, жна] *истина* indisputable; **~ме́нный**

Н

[14; -е́нен, -е́нна] indispensable, necessary; **~ме́нно** → ***обяза́тельно***; **~одоли́мый** [14 *sh.*] insuperable; *стремление* irresistible; **~река́емый** [14 *sh.*] indisputable; **~ры́вный** [14; -вен, -вна] uninterrupted, continuous; **~ста́нный** [14; -а́нен, -а́нна] incessant

**непри|вы́чный** [14; -чен, -чна] unaccustomed; (*необычный*) unusual; **~гля́дный** [14; -ден, -дна] *внешность* homely; unattractive; ungainly; **~го́дный** [14; -ден, -дна] unfit; useless; **~е́млемый** [14 *sh.*] unacceptable; **~косновéнный** [14; -е́нен, -е́нна] inviolable; *mil. запас* emergency; **~кра́шенный** [14] unvarnished; **~ли́чный** [14; -чен, -чна] indecent, unseemly; **~ме́тный** [14; -тен, -тна] imperceptible; *человек* unremarkable; **~мири́мый** [14 *sh.*] irreconcilable; **~нуждённый** [14 *sh.*] unconstrained; relaxed, laid-back; **~сто́йный** [14; -о́ен, -о́йна] obscene, indecent; **~сту́пный** [14; -пен, -пна] inaccessible; *крепость* impregnable; *человек* unapproachable, haughty; **~тво́рный** [14; -рен, -рна] genuine, unfeigned; **~тяза́тельный** [14; -лен, -льна] modest, unassuming

**неприя́|зненный** [14 *sh.*] inimical, unfriendly; **~знь** *f* [8] hostility

**неприя́|тель** *m* [4] enemy; **~тельский** [16] hostile, enemy('s); **~тность** *f* [8] unpleasantness; trouble; **~тный** [14; -тен, -тна] disagreeable, unpleasant

**непро|гля́дный** [14; -ден, -дна] *тьма* pitch-dark; **~должи́тельный** [14; -лен, -льна] short, brief; **~е́зжий** [17] impassable; **~зра́чный** [14; -чен, -чна] opaque; **~изводи́тельный** [14; -лен, -льна] unproductive; **~изво́льный** [14; -лен, -льна] involuntary; **~мока́емый** [14 *sh.*] waterproof; **~ница́емый** [14 *sh.*] impenetrable, impermeable; *улыбка и т. д.* inscrutable; **~сти́тельный** [14; -лен, -льна] unpardonable; **~ходи́мый** [14 *sh.*] impassable; *coll.* complete; **~́чный** [14; -чен, -чна, -о] flimsy; *мир* unstable

**нерабо́чий** [17] nonworking, free, off (*day*)

**нера́в|енство** *n* [9] inequality; **~номе́рный** [14; -рен, -рна] uneven; **~ный** [14; -вен, -вна́, -о] unequal

**неради́вый** [14 *sh.*] careless, negligent

**нераз|бери́ха** *coll. f* [5] muddle, confusion; **~бо́рчивый** [14 *sh.*] illegible; *fig.* undiscriminating; *в средствах* unscrupulous; **~вито́й** [14; -ра́звит, -а́, -о] undeveloped; *ребёнок* backward; **~личи́мый** [14 *sh.*] indistinguishable; **~лу́чный** [14; -чен, -чна] inseparable; **~реши́мый** [14 *sh.*] insoluable; **~ры́вный** [14; -вен, -вна] indissoluble; **~у́мный** [14; -мен, -мна] injudicious

**нерасположе́ние** *n* [12] *к человеку* dislike; disinclination (to, for)

**нерациона́льный** [14; -лен, -льна] unpractical

**нерв** *m* [1] nerve; **~и́ровать** [7], **~́ничать** [1] to get on one's nerves; become fidgety *or* irritated; **~́(о́з)ный** [14; -вен, -вна́, -о (-зен, -зна)] nervous; high-strung

**нереа́льный** [14; -лен, -льна] unreal; (*невыполнимый*) impracticable

**нереши́тельн|ость** *f* [8] indecision; ***в ~ости*** undecided; **~ый** [14; -лен, -льна] indecisive, irresolute

**нержаве́ющ|ий** [15] rust-free; ***~ая сталь*** stainless steel

**неро́|бкий** [16; -бок, -бка́, -о] not timid; brave; **~вный** [14; -вен, -вна́, -о] uneven, rough; *пульс* irregular

**неря́|ха** *m/f* [5] sloven; **~шливый** [14 *sh.*] slovenly; *в работе* careless, slipshod

**несамостоя́тельный** [14; -лен, -льна] not independent

**несбы́точный** [14; -чен, -чна] unrealizable

**не|своевре́менный** [14; -енен, -енна] inopportune, untimely; tardy; **~свя́зный** [14; зен, зна] incoherent; **~сгора́емый** [14] fireproof; **~сде́ржанный** [14 *sh.*] unrestrained; **~серьёзный** [14; -зен, -зна] not serious, frivolous; **~сказа́нный** *lit.* [14 *sh.*, *no m*] indescribable; **~скла́дный** [14; -ден, -дна] *человек* ungainly; *речь* incoherent; **~склоня́емый** [14 *sh.*] *gr.* indeclin-

Н

able
**нéсколько** [32] a few; some, several; *adv.* somewhat
**не|скрóмный** [14; -мен, -мнá, -о] immodest; **~слы́ханный** [14 *sh.*] unheard-of; (*беспримерный*) unprecedented; **~смéтный** [14; -тен, -тна] innumerable, incalculable
**несмотря́** (**на** В) in spite of, despite, notwithstanding; (al)though
**неснóсный** [14; -сен, -сна] intolerable
**несо|блюдéние** *n* [12] nonobservance; **~вершеннолéтие** *n* [12] minority; **~вершéнный** [14; -éнен, -éнна] *gr.* imperfective; **~вершéнство** *n* [9] imperfection; **~вмести́мый** [14 *sh.*] incompatible; **~глáсие** *n* [12] disagreement; **~измери́мый** [14 *sh.*] incommensurable; **~круши́мый** [14 *sh.*] indestructible; **~мнéнный** [14; -éнен, -éнна] undoubted; ***~мнéнно*** *a.* undoubtedly, without doubt; ***~отвéтствие*** *n* [12] discrepancy; **~размéрный** [14; -éрен, -éрна] disproportionate; **~стоя́тельный** [14; -лен, -льна] *должник* insolvent; (*необоснованный*) groundless, unsupported
**несп|окóйный** [14; -óен, -óйна] restless, uneasy; **~осóбный** [14; -бен, -бна] incapable (**к** Д, **на** В of); **~раведли́вость** *f* [8] injustice, unfairness; **~раведли́вый** [14 *sh.*] unjust, unfair; **~ростá** *coll.* → ***недáром***
**несрав|нéнный** [14; -éнен, -éнна] *and* **~ни́мый** [14 *sh.*] incomparable, matchless
**нестерпи́мый** [14 *sh.*] intolerable
**нести́** [24; -с-: -сý], ⟨по-⟩ (be) carry(ing, *etc.*); bear; bring; *убытки и т. д.* suffer; *о запахе и т. д.* smell (of T); drift, waft; (**-сь** *v/i.*; *a.* be heard; spread); ⟨с-⟩ lay (eggs **-сь**); talk *чушь*; ***несёт*** (*сквозит*) there's a draft (*Brt.* draught)
**не|стрóйный** [14; -óен, -óйна, -о] *звуки* discordant; *ряды* disorderly; **~сурáзный** *coll.* [14; -зен, -зна] senseless, absurd; **~сусвéтный** [14] unimaginable; *чушь* sheer
**несчáст|ный** [14; -тен, -тна] unhappy, unfortunate; ***~ный слýчай*** accident; **~ье** *n* [12] misfortune; disaster; accident; ***к ~ью*** unfortunately
**несчётный** [14; -тен, -тна] innumerable
**нет 1.** *part.*: no; **~ ещё** not yet; **2.** *impers. vb.* [*pt.* нé было, *ft.* не бýдет] (P) there is (are) no; ***у меня́*** (*etc.*) **~** I (*etc.*) have no(ne); ***егó*** (***её***) **~** (s)he is not (t)here *or* in; ***на ~ и судá нет*** well, it can't be helped
**нетакти́чный** [14; -чен, -чна] tactless
**нетвёрдый** [14; -вёрд, -вердá] unsteady; shaky (*a. fig.*)
**нетерп|ели́вый** [14 *sh.*] impatient; **~éние** *n* [12] impatience; **~и́мый** [14 *sh.*] intolerant; (*невыносимый*) intolerable
**не|тлéнный** [14; -éнен, -éнна] imperishable; **~трéзвый** [14; трезв, -á, -о] drunk (*a.* ***в ~трéзвом ви́де***); **~трóнутый** [14 *sh.*] untouched; *fig.* chaste, virgin; **~трудоспосóбный** [14; -бен, -бна] disabled
**нéт|то** [*indecl.*] *comm.* net; **~у** *coll.* → ***нет*** *2*
**неу|важéние** *n* [12] disrespect (**к** Д for); **~вéренный** [14 *sh.*] uncertain; **~вядáемый** [14 *sh.*] *rhet.* unfading; everlasting; **~вя́зка** [5; *g/pl.*: -зок] *coll.* misunderstanding; (*несогласованность*) discrepancy, lack of coordination; **~гаси́мый** [14 *sh.*] inextinguishable; **~гомóнный** [14; -óнен, -óнна] restless, untiring
**неудáч|а** *f* [5] misfortune; failure; ***потерпéть ~у*** fail; **~ливый** [14 *sh.*] unlucky; **~ник** *m* [1] unlucky person, failure; **~ный** [14; -чен, -чна] unsuccessful, unfortunate
**неуд|ержи́мый** [14 *sh.*] irrepressible; **~иви́тельно** (it is) no wonder
**неудóб|ный** [14; -бен, -бна] uncomfortable; *время* inconvenient; *положение* awkward, embarrassing; **~ство** *n* [9] inconvenience
**неудов|летвори́тельный** [14; -лен, -льна] unsatisfactory; **~летворённость** *f* [8] dissatisfaction, discontent; **~óльствие** *n* [12] displeasure
**неужéли** *interr. part.* really?, is it possible?
**неу|жи́вчивый** [14 *sh.*] unsociable, unaccommodating; **~клóнный** [14;

-óнен, -óнна] steady; **~клю́жий** [17 *sh.*] clumsy, awkward; **~кроти́мый** [14 *sh.*] indomitable; **~лови́мый** [14 *sh.*] elusive; (*еле заметный*) imperceptible; **~мéлый** [14 *sh.*] unskil(l)ful, awkward; **~мéние** *n* [12] inability; **~мéренный** [14 *sh.*] intemperate, immoderate; **~мéстный** [14; -тен, -тна] inappropriate; **~моли́мый** [14 *sh.*] inexorable; **~мы́шленный** [14 *sh.*] unintentional; **~потреби́тельный** [14; -лен, -льна] not in use, not current; **~рожáй** *m* [3] bad harvest; **~стáнный** [14; -áнен, -áнна] tireless, unwearying; *a.* → **~томи́мый**; **~стóйка** [5; *g/pl.*: -оек] forfeit; **~стóйчивый** [14 *sh.*] unstable; unsteady; *погода* changeable; **~страши́мый** [14 *sh.*] intrepid, dauntless; **~сту́пчивый** [14 *sh.*] unyielding, tenacious; **~толи́мый** [14 *sh.*] unquenchable; **~томи́мый** [14 *sh.*] tireless, indefatigable

**нéуч** *coll. m* [1] ignoramus

**неу|чти́вый** [14 *sh.*] uncivil; **~ю́тный**; [14; -тен, -тна] comfortless; **~язви́мый** [14 *sh.*] invulnerable

**Н**

**нефт|епровóд** *m* [1] pipeline; **~ь** *f* [8] (mineral) oil, petroleum; **~янóй** [14] oil…

**не|хвáтка** *f* [5; *g/pl.*: -ток] shortage; **~хорóший** [17; -рóш, -á] bad; **~хотя** unwillingly; **~цензу́рный** [14; -рен, -рна] unprintable; **~цензу́рное слóво** swear-word; **~чáянный** [14] *встреча* unexpected; (*случайный*) accidental; (*неумышленный*) unintentional

**нéчего** [23]: (**мне**, *etc.*) + *inf.* (there is *or* one can), (I have) nothing to…; (one) need not, (there is) no need; (it is) no use; stop …ing

**не|человéческий** [16] inhuman; *усилия* superhuman; **~чéстный** [14; -тен, -тнá, -о] dishonest; **~чётный** [14] odd (*number*)

**нечист|оплóтный** [14; -тен, -тна] dirty; *fig.* unscrupulous; **~отá** *f* [5; *pl. st.*: -óты] dirtiness; *pl.* sewage; **~ый** [14; -чи́ст, -á, -о] unclean, dirty; impure; *помыслы и т. д.* evil, vile, bad, foul

**нéчто** something

**не|чувстви́тельный** [14; -лен, -льна] insensitive, insensible (**к** Д to); **~щáдный** [14; -ден, -дна] merciless; **~я́вка** *f* [5] nonappearance; **~я́ркий** [16; -я́рок, -яркá, -о] dull, dim; *fig.* mediocre; **~я́сный** [14; -сен, -снá, -о] not clear; *fig.* vague

**ни** not a (single **оди́н**); **~ …, ~** neither … nor; … ever (*e. g.* **кто** [**бы**] **~** whoever); ***кто* (*что, когдá, где, кудá*) *бы то ~ был*(*о*)** whosoever (what-, when-, wheresoever); ***как ~*** + *vb. a.* in spite of *or* for all + *su.*; ***как бы* (*то*) *~ бы́ло*** anyway, whatever happens; ***~ за что ~ про что***, for no apparent reason

**нигдé** nowhere

**ни́ж|е** below, beneath; *ростом* shorter; **~еподписáвшийся** *m* [17] (the) undersigned; **~ний** [15] lower; under…; *этаж* first, *Brt.* ground

**низ** *m* [1; *pl. e.*] bottom, lower part; **~áть** [3], ⟨на-⟩ string, thread

**низи́на** *f* [5] hollow, lowland

**ни́зк|ий** [16; -зок, -зкá, -о; *comp.*: ни́же] low; *fig.* mean, base; *рост* short; **~oрóслый** [14 *sh.*] undersized, stunted; *кустарник* low; **~осóртный** [14; -тен, -тна] lowgrade; *товар* of inferior quality

**ни́зменн|ость** *f* [8] *geogr.* lowland, plain; **~ый** [14 *sh.*] low-lying

**низó|вье** *n* [10; *g/pl.*: -вьев] lower reaches (*of a river*); **~сть** *f* [8] meanness

**никáк** by no means, not at all; **~óй** [16] no … (at all *coll.*)

**ни́кел|ь** *m* [4] nickel; **~ирóванный** [14 *sh.*] nickel-plated

**никогдá** never

**ни|кóй**: *now only in* ***~кóим óбразом*** by no means *and* **ни в кóем слу́чае** on no account; **~ктó** [23] nobody, no one, none; **~кудá** nowhere; → *a.* ***годи́ться, гóдный***; **~кчёмный** *coll.* [14] good-for-nothing; **~мáло** → **скóлько**; **~откýда** from nowhere; **~почём** *coll.* very cheap, easy, *etc.*; **~скóлько** not in the least, not at all

**нисходя́щий** [17] descending

**ни́т|ка** *f* [5; *g/pl.*: -ток], **~ь** [8] thread; *жемчуга* string; *хлопчатобумажная* cotton; **~ь** *a.* filament; **до ~ки** *coll.* to the skin; ***шито белыми ~ками*** be transparent; ***на живую ~ку*** carelessly, superficially

**ничего** nothing; not bad; so-so; no(t) matter; ***~!*** never mind!, that's all right!; ***~ себе!*** well (I never)!

**нич|ей** *m*, **~ья** *f*, **~ьё** *n*, **~ьи** *pl*. [26] nobody's; *su. f в игре* draw

**ничком** prone

**ничто** [23] nothing → ***ничего***; **~жество** *n* [9] nonentity; **~жный** [14; -жен, -жна] insignificant, tiny; *причина* paltry

**нич|уть** *coll*. → ***нисколько***; **~ья** → ***~ей***

**ниша** *f* [5] niche

**нищ|ая** *f* [17], **~енка** *coll*. [5; *g/pl*.: -нок] beggar woman; **~енский** [16] beggarly; **~ета** *f* [5] poverty, destitution; **~ий** **1.** [17; нищ, -а, -е] beggarly; **2.** *m* [17] beggar

**но** but, yet, still, nevertheless

**новатор** *m* [1] innovator

**новелла** *f* [5] short story

**нов|енький** [16; -нек] (brand-) new; **~изна** *f* [5], **~инка** [5; *g/pl*.: -нок] novelty; **~ичок** *m* [1; -чка] novice, tyro

**ново|брачный** [14] newly married; **~введение** *n* [12] innovation; **~годний** [15] New Year's (Eve ***~годний вечер***); **~луние** *n* [12] new moon; **~рождённый** [14] newborn (child); **~селье** *n* [10] house-warming; ***справлять*** ⟨справить⟩ ***~селье*** give a house-warming party

**нов|ость** *f* [8] (piece of) news; novelty; **~шество** *n* [9] innovation, novelty; **~ый** [14; нов, -а, -о] new; novel; (*последний*) fresh; ***2ый год*** *m* New Year's Day; ***с 2ым годом!*** Happy New Year!; ***что ~ого?*** what's (the) new(s)?

**ног|а** *f* [5; *ac/sg*.: ногу; *pl*.: ноги, ног, ногам, *etc. e*.] foot, leg; ***идти в ~у со временем*** keep abreast of the times; ***со всех ~*** as fast as one's legs will carry one; ***стать на ~и*** *выздороветь* recover; become independent; ***положить ~у на ~у*** cross one's legs; ***ни ~ой*** (***к*** Д) never set foot (*in s.o.'s house*); ***~и унести*** (have a narrow) escape; ***под ~ами*** underfoot

**ноготь** *m* [4; -гтя; *from g/pl*.: *e*.] (finger-, toe-) nail

**нож** *m* [1 *e*.] knife; ***на ~ах*** at daggers drawn; **~ик** *m* [1] *coll*. → **нож**; **~ка** *f* [5; *g/pl*.: -жек] *dim*. → **нога**; *стула и т. д.* leg; **~ницы** *f/pl*. [5] (pair of) scissors; *econ*. discrepancy; **~ной** [14] foot…; **~ны** *f/pl*. [5; *gen*.: -жен] sheath

**ноздря** [6; *pl*.: ноздри, ноздрей, *etc. e*.] nostril

**ноль** *m*. = **нуль** *m* [4] naught; zero

**номер** *m* [1; *pl*.: -ра, *etc. e*.] number ([with] **за** T); (*размер*) size; *в отеле* room; *программы* item, turn; trick; ***выкинуть ~*** do an odd *or* unexpected thing; (*a*., *dim*., **~ок** *m* [1; -рка]) cloakroom ticket

**номинальный** [14; -лен, -льна] nominal

**нора** *f* [5; *ac/sg*.: -ру; *pl. st*.] hole, burrow, lair

**норве|жец** *m* [1; -жца], **~жка** *f* [5; *g/pl*.: -жек], **~жский** [16] Norwegian

**норка** *f* [5; *g/pl*.: -рок] *zo*. mink

**норм|а** *f* [5] norm, standard; *выработки и т. д.* rate; **~ализовать** [7] (*im*)*pf*. standardize; **~альный** [14; -лен, -льна] normal

**нос** *m* [1; в, на носу; *pl. e*.] nose; *птицы* beak; *лодки*, bow, prow; ***водить за ~*** lead by the nose; (*вскоре*) ***на ~у*** at hand; ***у меня идёт кровь ~ом*** my nose is bleeding; **~ик** *m* [1] *dim*. → **нос**; spout

**носи|лки** *f/pl*. [5; -лок] stretcher; **~льщик** *m* [1] porter; **~тель** *m med*. [4] carrier; **~ть** [15] carry, bear, *etc*.; → ***нести***; wear (*v/i*. **-ся**); *coll*. **-ся** run about; (**с** T) *a*. have one's mind occupied with

**носовой** [14] *звук* nasal; *naut*. bow; ***~ платок*** handkerchief

**носок** *m* [1; -ска] sock; *ботинка* toe

**носорог** *m* [1] rhinoceros

**нот|а** *f* [5] note; *pl. a*. music; ***как по ~ам*** without a hitch

**нотариус** *m* [1] notary (public)

**нотация** *f* [7] reprimand, lecture

**ноч|евать** [7], ⟨пере-⟩ pass (*or* spend) the night; **~ёвка** *f* [5; *g/pl*.: -вок] overnight stop (*or* stay *or* rest); *a*. → ***~лег***; **~лег** *m* [1] night's lodging, night quarters; *a*. → ***~ёвка***; **~ной** [14] night(ly), (*a. bot*., *zo*.) nocturnal; **~ь** *f* [8; в ночи;

*from g/pl. e.*] night; **⁓ью** at (*or* by) night (= *a.* ***в ⁓ь, по ⁓áм***); ***⁓ь под …*** (В) … night
**нóша** *f* [5] load, burden
**ноя́брь** *m* [4 *e.*] November
**нрав** *m* [1] disposition, temper; *pl.* ways, customs; ***(не) по ⁓у*** (Д) (not) to one's liking; **⁓иться** [14], ⟨по-⟩ please (a p. Д); ***онá мне ⁓ится*** I like her; **⁓оучéние** *n* [12] moral admonition; **⁓ственность** *f* [8] morals *pl.*, morality; **⁓ственный** [14 *sh.*] moral
**ну** (*a.* **⁓-ка**) well *or* now (then ***же***)***!*** come (on)!, why!, what!; the deuce (take him *or* it ***⁓ егó***)***!***; (*a.* ***да ⁓?***) indeed?, really?, you don't say!; ha?; ***⁓ да*** of course, sure; ***⁓ так чтó же?*** what about it?
**нýдный** [14; нýден, -á, -о] tedious, boring
**нужд|á** *f* [5; *pl. st.*] need, want (**в** П of); ***в слýчае ⁓ы́*** if necessary; ***в э́том нет ⁓ы́*** there is no need for this; **⁓áться** [1] (**в** П) (be in) need (of); *в деньгах* be hard up, needy
**нýжн|ый** [14; нýжен, -жнá, -о, нýжны́] necessary (Д for); (Д) **⁓о** + *inf.* must (→ ***нáдо***)
**нуль** → ***ноль***
**нумер|áция** *f* [7] numeration; numbering; **⁓овáть** [7], ⟨за-, про-⟩ number
**нýтрия** *f* [7] *zo.* coypu; *мех* nutria
**ны́н|е** *obs.* now(adays), today; **⁓ешний** *coll.* [15] present *coll.* today's; **⁓че** *coll.* → ***⁓е***
**ныр|я́ть** [28], *once* ⟨⁓нýть⟩ [20] dive
**ныть** [22] ache; *coll.* whine, make a fuss
**нюх** [1], **⁓ать** [1], ⟨по-⟩ *о животном* smell, scent
**ня́н|чить** [16] nurse, tend; **-ся** *coll.* fuss over, busy o.s. (**с** T with); **⁓я** *f* [6] (**⁓ька** [5; -нек]) nurse, *Brt. a.* nanny

# О

**о**, **об**, **обо 1.** (П) about, of; on; **2.** (В) against, (up)on; ***бок ó бок*** side by side; ***рукá óб руку*** hand in hand
**о!** *int.* oh!, o!
**óб|а** *m & n*, **⁓е** *f* [37] both
**обагр|я́ть** [28], ⟨⁓и́ть⟩ [13]: ***⁓и́ть рýки в крови́*** steep one's hands in blood
**обанкрóтиться** → ***банкрóтиться***
**обая́|ние** *n* [12] spell, charm; **⁓тельный** [14; -лен, -льна] charming
**обвáл** *m* [1] collapse; landslide; *снежный* avalanche; **⁓иваться** [1], ⟨⁓и́ться⟩ [13; обвáлится] fall in *or* off; **⁓я́ть** [1] *pf.* roll
**обвари́ть** [13; -арю́, -áришь] scald; pour boiling water over
**обвé|сить** [15] *coll.* → ***⁓шивать***
**обвести́** → ***обводи́ть***
**обвéтренный** [14 *sh.*] weatherbeaten; *губы* chapped
**обветшáлый** [14] decayed
**обвéш|ивать**, ⟨⁓ать⟩ [1] **1.** hang, cover (T with); **2.** *pf.* ⟨обвéсить⟩ [1] give short weight to; cheat
**обви|вáть** [1], ⟨⁓ть⟩ [обовью́, -вьёшь; → ***вить***] wind round; ***⁓ть шéю рукáми*** throw one's arms round s.o.'s neck
**обвин|éние** *n* [12] accusation, charge; *law* indictment; the prosecution; **⁓и́тель** *m* [4] accuser; *law* prosecutor; **⁓и́тельный** [14] accusatory; *заключение* of 'guilty'; **⁓я́ть** [28] ⟨⁓и́ть⟩ [13] (**в** П) accuse (of), charge (with); **⁓я́емый** accused; (*ответчик*) defendant
**обви́слый** *coll.* [14] flabby
**обви́|ть** → ***⁓вáть***
**обводи́ть** [13], ⟨обвести́⟩ [25] lead, see *or* look (round, about); enclose, encircle *or* border (T with); ***⁓ вокрýг пáльца*** twist round one's little finger
**обвор|áживать** [1], ⟨⁓ожи́ть⟩ [16 *e.*; -жý, -жи́шь, -жённый] charm, fascinate; **⁓ожи́тельный** [14; -лен, -льна] charming, fascinating; **⁓ожи́ть** → ***⁓áживать***
**обвя́з|ывать** [1], ⟨⁓áть⟩ [3] *верёвкой* tie up *or* round

**обгоня́ть** [28], 〈**обогна́ть**〉 [обгоню́, -о́нишь; обо́гнанный] (out) distance, outstrip (*a. fig.*); pass, leave behind
**обгрыз|а́ть** [1], 〈**~̷ть**〉 [24; *pt. st.*] gnaw (at, round, away)
**обд|ава́ть** [5], 〈**~а́ть**〉 [-а́м, -а́шь; → ***дать***; о́бдал, -а́, -о; о́бданный (о́бдан, -а́, -о)] pour over; ***~а́ть кипятко́м*** scald; ***~а́ть гря́зью*** bespatter with mud
**обдел|я́ть** [28], 〈**~и́ть**〉 [13; -елю́, -е́лишь] deprive of one's due share (of T)
**обдира́ть** [1], 〈**ободра́ть**〉 [обдеру́, -рёшь; ободра́л, -а́, -о; обо́дранный] *кору* bark, *обои и т. д.* tear (off); *тушу* skin; *колено* scrape; *fig. coll.* fleece
**обду́м|ать** → ***~ывать***; **~анный** [14 *sh.*] well considered; **~ывать**, 〈**~ать**〉 [1] consider, think over
**обе́д** *m* [1] dinner (***за*** T at, ***на*** В, ***к*** Д for), lunch; ***до*** (***по́сле***) ***~а*** in the morning (afternoon); **~ать** [1], 〈**по-**〉 have dinner (lunch), dine; **~енный** [14] dinner…, lunch…
**обедне́вший** [17] impoverished
**обез|бо́ливание** *n* [12] an(a)esthetization; **~вре́живать** [1], 〈**~вре́дить**〉 [15] render harmless; neutralize; **~до́ленный** [14] unfortunate, hapless; **~зара́живание** *n* [12] disinfection; **~лю́деть** [8] *pf.* become depopulated, deserted; **~обра́живать** [1], 〈**~обра́зить**〉 [15] disfigure; **~опа́сить** [15] *pf.* secure (**от** P against); **~ору́живать** [1], 〈**~ору́жить**〉 [16] disarm (*a. fig.*); **~у́меть** [8] *pf.* lose one's mind, go mad
**обезья́н|а** *f* [5] monkey; ape; **~ий** [18] monkey('s); apish, apelike; **~ичать** *coll.* [1] ape
**обели́ск** *m* [1] obelisk
**обер|ега́ть** [1], 〈**~е́чь**〉 [26; г/ж: -гу, -жёшь] guard, *v/i.* **-ся**, protect o.s.; (against, from **от** P)
**оберну́ть(ся)** → ***обёртывать***(***ся***)
**обёрт|ка** *f* [5; *g/pl.*: -ток] *книги* cover; **~очный** [14] wrapping (*or* brown) paper; **~ывать** [1], 〈**оберну́ть**〉 [20] wrap (up); wind; ***~ывать лицо́*** turn one's face toward(s); **-ся** turn (round, *coll.* back)
**обескура́ж|ивать** [1], 〈**~ить**〉 [16] discourage, dishearten
**обеспе́ч|ение** *n* [12] securing; *о займе* (***под*** В on) security, guarantee; *порядка* maintenance; *социальное* security; **~енность** *f* [8] (adequate) provision; *зажиточность* prosperity; **~енный** [14] well-to-do; well provided for; **~ивать** [1], 〈**~ить**〉 [16] (*снабжать*) provide (for; with T); *мир и т. д.* secure, guarantee; ensure
**обесси́л|еть** [8] *pf.* become enervated, exhausted; **~ивать** [1], 〈**~ить**〉 [13] enervate, weaken
**обесцве́|чивать** [1], 〈**~тить**〉 [15] discolo(u)r, make colo(u)rless
**обесце́н|ивать** [1], 〈**~ить**〉 [13] depreciate
**обесче́стить** [15] *pf.* dishono(u)r; *себя* disgrace o.s
**обе́т** *m* [1] vow, promise; **~ова́нный** [14]: ***~ова́нная земля́*** the Promised Land
**обеща́|ние** *n* [12], **~ть** [1] (*im*)*pf.*, *coll. a.* 〈**по-**〉 promise
**обжа́лование** *n* [12] *law* appeal
**обж|ига́ть** [1], 〈**~е́чь**〉 [26; г/ж: обожгу́, -жжёшь, обжёг, обожгла́; обожжённый] burn; scorch; *глину* bake; **-ся** burn o.s. (*coll.* one's fingers)
**обжо́р|а** *coll. m/f* [5] glutton; **~ливый** *coll.* [14 *sh.*] gluttonous; **~ство** *coll. n* [9] gluttony
**обзав|оди́ться** [15], 〈**~ести́сь**〉 [25] provide o.s. (T with), acquire, set up
**обзо́р** *m* [1] survey; review
**обзыва́ть** [1], 〈**обозва́ть**〉 [обзову́, -ёшь; обозва́л, -а́, -о; обо́званный] call (*names* T)
**оби|ва́ть** [1], 〈**~̷ть**〉 [обобью́, обобьёшь; → ***бить***] upholster; **~̷вка** *f* [5] upholstery
**оби́|да** *f* [5] insult; ***не в ~ду будь сказа́но*** no offense (-nce) meant; ***не дать в ~ду*** let not be offended; **~деть(ся)** → ***~жа́ть***(***ся***); **~дный** [14; -ден, -дна] offensive, insulting; ***мне ~дно*** it is a shame *or* vexing; it offends *or* vexes me; I am sorry (for ***за*** В); **~дчивый** [14 *sh.*] touchy; **~дчик** *coll. m* [1] of-

О

fender; **~жа́ть** [1], ⟨~деть⟩ [11] (**-ся** be), offend(ed), (*a.* be angry with *or* at **на** B); wrong; overreach (→ *a.* **обделя́ть**); **~женный** [14 *sh.*] offended (*a.* → **~жа́ть(ся)**)
**оби́лие** *n* [12] abundance, plenty
**оби́льный** [14; -лен, -льна] abundant (T in), plentiful, rich (in)
**обиня́к** *m* [1 *e.*] *only in phrr.* **говори́ть ~а́ми** beat about the bush; **говори́ть без ~о́в** speak plainly
**обира́ть** *coll.* [1], ⟨обобра́ть⟩ [оберу́, -ёшь; обобра́л, -а́, -о; обо́бранный] rob
**обита́|емый** [14 *sh.*] inhabited; **~тель** *m* [4] inhabitant; **~ть** [1] live, dwell, reside
**оби́ть** → **обива́ть**
**обихо́д** *m* [1] use, custom, practice; **предме́ты дома́шнего ~а** household articles; **~ный** [14; -ден, -дна] everyday; *язык* colloquial
**обкла́дывать** [1], ⟨обложи́ть⟩ [16] *подушками* lay round; *тучами* cover; *med.* fur; → **облага́ть**
**обкра́дывать** [1], ⟨обокра́сть⟩ [25; обкраду́, -дёшь; *pt. st.*: обкра́денный] rob
**обла́ва** *f* [5] *на охоте* battue; *полиции* raid; roundup
**облага́|емый** [14 *sh.*] taxable; **~ть** [1], ⟨обложи́ть⟩ [16] *налогом* impose (*tax* T)
**облагор|а́живать** [1], ⟨~о́дить⟩ [15] ennoble, refine
**облада́|ние** *n* [12] possession (of T); **~тель** *m* [4] possessor; **~ть** [1] (T) possess, have; be in (**хоро́шим здоро́вьем**) good health
**о́блак|о** *n* [9; *pl.*: -ка́, -ко́в] cloud; **вита́ть в ~а́х** be up in the clouds
**обл|а́мывать** [1], ⟨~ома́ть⟩ [1] & ⟨~оми́ть⟩ [14] break off
**обласка́ть** [1] *pf.* treat kindly
**област|но́й** [14] regional; **´~ь** *f* [8; *from g/pl. e.*] region; *fig.* province, sphere, field
**облач|а́ться** [1], ⟨~и́ться⟩ [16] *eccl.* put on one's robes; *coll. joc.* array oneself
**облачи́ться** → **облача́ться**
**о́блачный** [14; -чен, -чна] cloudy
**обле|га́ть** [1], ⟨´~чь⟩ [26; г/ж: → **лечь**] fit closely
**облегч|а́ть** [1], ⟨~и́ть⟩ [16 *e.*; -чу́, -чи́шь, -чённый] lighten; (*упростить*) facilitate; *боль* ease, relieve
**обледене́лый** [14] ice-covered
**облёзлый** *coll.* [14] mangy, shabby
**обле|ка́ть** [1], ⟨´~чь⟩ [26] *полномочиями* invest (T with); (*выразить*) put, express
**облеп|ля́ть** [28], ⟨~и́ть⟩ [14] stick all over (*or* round); (*окружить*) surround; *о мухах и т. д.* cover
**облет|а́ть** [1], ⟨~е́ть⟩ [11] fly round (*or* all over, past, in); *листья* fall; *о слухах и т. д.* spread
**обле́чь** [1] → **облега́ть & облека́ть**
**обли|ва́ть** [1], ⟨´~ть⟩ [оболью́, -льёшь; обле́й!; о́бли́л, -а́, -о; о́бли́тый (о́бли́т, -а́, -о)] pour (s.th. T) over; **´~ть гря́зью** *coll.* fling mud (at); **-ся** [*pf.*: -и́лся, -ила́сь, -и́лось] (T) pour over o.s.; *слезами* shed; *потом* be dripping; *or кровью* covered; *сердце* bleed
**облига́ция** *f* [7] *fin.* bond, debenture
**обли́з|ывать** [1], ⟨~а́ть⟩ [3] lick (off); **-ся** lick one's lips (*or* o.s.)
**о́блик** *m* [1] aspect, look; appearance
**обли́|ть(ся)** → **~ва́ть(ся)**; **~цо́вывать** [1], ⟨~цева́ть⟩ [7] face (with), revet
**облич|а́ть** [1], ⟨~и́ть⟩ [16 *e.*; -чу́, -чи́шь, -чённый] unmask; (*раскрывать*) reveal; (*обвинять*) accuse (**в** П of); **~и́тельный** [14; -лен, -льна] accusatory, incriminating; **~и́ть** → **~а́ть**
**облож|е́ние** *n* [12] taxation; **~и́ть** → **обкла́дывать** *and* **облага́ть**; **´~ка** [5; *g/pl.*: -жек] cover; (*супер´~ка*) dustcover, folder
**облок|а́чиваться** [1], ⟨~оти́ться⟩ [15 & 15 *e.*; -кочу́сь, -ко́ти́шься] lean one's elbow (**на** B on)
**облом|а́ть, ~и́ть** → **обла́мывать**; **´~ок** *m* [1; -мка] fragment; *pl.* debris, wreckage
**облуч|а́ть** [1], ⟨~и́ть⟩ [16 *e.*; -чу́, -чи́шь, -чённый] irradiate
**облюбова́ть** [7] *pf.* take a fancy to, choose
**обма́з|ывать** [1], ⟨~ать⟩ [3] besmear; plaster, putty, coat, cement
**обма́к|ивать** [1], ⟨~ну́ть⟩ [20] dip

О

**обма́н** *m* [1] deception; deceit, *mst. law* fraud; **~ зре́ния** optical illusion; **~ный** [14] deceitful, fraudulent; **~у́ть(ся)** → **~ывать(ся)**; **~чивый** [14 *sh.*] deceptive; **~щик** *m* [1], **~щица** *f* [5] cheat, deceiver; **~ывать** [1], ⟨**~у́ть**⟩ [20] (**-ся** be) deceive(d), cheat; be mistaken (in **в** П)

**обм|а́тывать**, ⟨**~ота́ть**⟩ [1] wind (round); **~а́хивать** [1], ⟨**~ахну́ть**⟩ [20] *пыль* wipe, dust; *веером* fan

**обме́н** *m* [1] exchange (in/for в/**на** В); interchange (Т, Р of); **~ивать** [1], ⟨**~я́ть**⟩ [28] exchange (**на** В for; **-ся** Т s.th.)

**обм|е́ривать** → **ме́рить**; **~ета́ть** [1], ⟨**~ести́**⟩ [25 -т-: обмету́] sweep (off), dust; **~озго́вывать** [1], ⟨**~озгова́ть**⟩ [7] *coll.* think over

**обмо́лв|иться** [14] *pf.* make a slip of the tongue; (*упомянуть*) mention, say; **~ка** *f* [5; *g/pl.*: -вок] slip of the tongue

**обморо́зить** [15] *pf.* frostbite

**о́бморок** *m* [1] fainting spell, swoon

**обмот|а́ть** → **обма́тывать**; **~ка** *f* [5; *g/pl.*: -ток] *el.* winding

**обмундирова́|ние** *n* [12], **~ть** [7] *pf.* fit out with uniform

**обмы|ва́ть** [1], ⟨**~ть**⟩ [22] bathe, wash (off); *coll. покупку и т. д.* celebrate

**обнадёж|ивать** [1], ⟨**~ить**⟩ [16] (re)assure, encourage, give hope to

**обнаж|а́ть** [1], ⟨**~и́ть**⟩ [16 *e.*; -жу́, -жи́шь; -жённый] *голову* bare, uncover; *fig.* lay bare; *шпагу* draw, unsheathe; **~ённый** [14; -жён, -жена́] naked, bare; nude (*a. su*)

**обнаро́довать** [7] *pf.* promulgate

**обнару́ж|ивать** [1], ⟨**~ить**⟩ [16] (*выявить*) disclose, show, reveal; (*найти*) discover, detect; **-ся** appear, show; come to light; be found, discovered

**обнести́** → **обноси́ть**

**обн|има́ть** [1], ⟨**~я́ть**⟩ [обниму́, обни́мешь; о́бнял, -а́, -о; о́бнятый (о́бнят, -а́, -о)] embrace, hug, clasp in one's arms

**обно́в|(к)а** *f* [5; (*g/pl.*: -вок)] *coll.* new; article of clothing; **~и́ть** → **~ля́ть**; **~ле́ние** *n* [12] *репертуара и т. д.* renewal; (*ремонт и т. д.*) renovation; **~ля́ть** [28], ⟨**~и́ть**⟩ [14 *e.*; -влю́, -ви́шь; -влённый] renew; renovate; update; repair

**обн|оси́ть** [15], ⟨**~ести́**⟩ [24; -с-: -су́] pass (round); *coll.* serve; (Т) fence in, enclose; **-ся** *coll. impf.* wear out one's clothes

**обню́х|ивать**, ⟨**~ать**⟩ [1] sniff around

**обня́ть** → **обнима́ть**

**обобра́ть** → **обира́ть**

**обобщ|а́ть** [1], ⟨**~и́ть**⟩ [16 *e.*; -щу́, -щи́шь; -щённый] generalize; **~и́ть** → **~а́ть**

**обога|ща́ть** [1], ⟨**~ти́ть**⟩ [15 *e.*; -ащу́, -ти́шь; -ащённый] enrich; *руду* concentrate

**обогна́ть** → **обгоня́ть**

**обогну́ть** → **огиба́ть**

**обоготворя́ть** [28] → **боготвори́ть**

**обогрева́ть** [1] → **греть**

**о́бод** *m* [1; *pl.*: обо́дья, -дьев] rim, felloe; **~о́к** *m* [1; -дка́] rim

**обо́др|анный** [14 *sh.*] *coll.* ragged, shabby; **~а́ть** → **обдира́ть**; **~е́ние** *n* [12] encouragement; **~я́ть** [28], ⟨**~и́ть**⟩ [13] cheer up, reassure; **-ся** take heart, cheer up

**обожа́ть** [1] adore, worship

**обожеств|ля́ть** [28], ⟨**~и́ть**⟩ [14 *e.*; -влю́, -ви́шь; -влённый] deify

**обожжённый** [14; -ён, -ена́] burnt

**обозва́ть** → **обзыва́ть**

**обознач|а́ть** [1], ⟨**~ить**⟩ [16] denote, designate, mark; **-ся** appear; **~е́ние** *n* [12] designation; *знак* sign, symbol

**обозр|ева́ть** [1], ⟨**~е́ть**⟩ [9], **~е́ние** *n* [12] survey; *mst. lit.* review

**обо́|и** *m/pl.* [3] wallpaper; **~йти́(сь)** → **обходи́ть(ся)**; **~кра́сть** → **обкра́дывать**

**оболо́чка** *f* [5; *g/pl.*: -чек] cover(ing), envelope; *anat. слизистая и т. д.* membrane; **ра́дужная** (**рогова́я**) **~** iris (cornea)

**оболь|сти́тель** *m* [4] seducer; **~сти́тельный** [14; -лен, -льна] seductive; **~ща́ть** [1], ⟨**~сти́ть**⟩ [15 *e.*; -льщу́, льсти́шь; -льщённый] seduce; (**-ся** be) delude(d; flatter o.s.)

**обомле́ть** [8] *pf. coll.* be stupefied

**обоня́ние** *n* [12] (sense of) smell

**обора́чивать(ся)** → **обёртывать(ся)**

**оборв|áнец** *coll. m* [1; -нца] ragamuffin; **ᷝанный** [14 *sh.*] ragged; **~áть** → **обрывáть**

**обóрка** *f* [5; *g/pl.*: -рок] frill, ruffle

**оборóн|а** *f* [5] defense (*Brt.* defence); **~ительный** [14] defensive; **~ный** [14] defense…, armament…; **~ная промы́шленность** defense industry; **~оспосóбность** *f* [8] defensive capability; **~я́ть** [28] defend

**оборóт** *m* [1] turn; *tech.* revolution, rotation; *fin.* circulation; *comm.* turnover; *сторона* back, reverse; **(см.) на ~е** please turn over (PTO); **ввести́ в ~** put into circulation; **взять когó-нибудь в ~** *fig. coll.* get at s.o.; take s.o. to task; **~и́ть(ся)** P [15] *pf.* → **оберну́ть(ся)**; **~ливый** [14 *sh.*] *coll.* resourceful; **~ный** [14] *сторона* back, reverse; *fig.* seamy (*side*); **~ный капитáл** working capital

**обору́дова|ние** *n* [12] equipment; **вспомогáтельное ~ние** *comput.* peripherals, add-ons; **~ть** [7] (*im*)*pf.* equip, fit out

**обосн|овáние** *n* [12] substantiation; ground(s); **~óвывать** [1], ⟨**~овáть**⟩ [7] prove, substantiate; **-ся** settle down

**обос|обля́ть** [28], ⟨**~óбить**⟩ [14] isolate; **-ся** keep aloof, stand apart

**обостр|я́ть** [28], ⟨**~и́ть**⟩ [13] (**-ся** become); (*ухудшить*) aggravate(d), strain(ed); *о чувствах* become keener; *med.* become acute

**обою́дный** [14; -ден, -дна] mutual, reciprocal

**обраб|áтывать**, ⟨**~óтать**⟩ [1] work, process; *agr.* till; *текст и т. д.* elaborate, finish, polish; *chem. etc.* treat; (*адаптировать*) adapt; *coll.* work upon, win round **когó-л.**; *p. pr. a. промышленность* manufacturing; **~óтка** *f* [5; *g/pl.*: -ток] processing; *agric.* cultivation; elaboration; adaptation

**óбраз** *m* [1] manner, way (T in), mode; shape, form; *lit.* figure, character; image; [*pl.*: -á, *etc. e.*] icon; **каки́м (таки́м) ~ом** how (thus); **никóим ~ом** by no means; **~ жи́зни** way of life; **~éц** *m* [1; -зцá] specimen, sample; (*пример*) model, example; *материала* pattern; **~ный** [14; -зен, -зна] graphic, picturesque, vivid; **~овáние** *n* [12] *слова и т. д.* formation; education **~óванный** [14 *sh.*] educated; **~овáтельный** [14; -лен, -льна] educational (*qualification*); **~óвывать** [1], ⟨**~овáть**⟩ [7] form; **-ся** (*v/i.*) arise; constitute; **~у́мить(ся)** [14] *pf. coll.* bring (come) to one's senses; **~цóвый** [14] exemplary, model…; **ᷝчик** *m* [1] → **~éц**

**обрам|ля́ть** [28], ⟨**ᷝить**⟩ [14 *st.*], *fig.* ⟨**~и́ть**⟩ [14 *e.*; -млю́, -ми́шь; -млённый] frame

**обраст|áть** [1], ⟨**~и́**⟩ [24; -ст-: -сту́; обрóс, -лá] *мхом и т. д.* become overgrown with, covered with

**обра|ти́ть** → **~щáть**; **ᷝтный** [14] back, return…; reverse, (*a. math.* inverse; *law* retroactive; **ᷝтная связь** *tech.* feedback (*a. fig.*); **ᷝтно** back; **~щáть** [1], ⟨**~ти́ть**⟩ [15 *e.*; -ащу́, -ати́шь; -ащённый] turn; *взор* direct; *eccl.* convert; draw *or* pay *or* (**на себя́**) attract (*attention*; to **на** В); **не ~щáть внимáния (на** В) disregard; **-ся** turn (**в** В to); address o.s. (**к** Д to); apply (to; for **за** Т); appeal; **~щáться в бéгство** take to flight; *impf.* (**с** Т) treat, handle; *двигаться* circulate; **~щéние** *n* [12] address, appeal; *оборот* circulation; (**с** Т) treatment (of), management; manners

**обрéз** *m* [1] edge; **дéнег в ~** just enough money; **~áть** [1], ⟨**~ать**⟩ [3] cut (off); cut short; *ногти и т. д.* pare; *ветки* prune; *coll.* (*прервать*) snub, cut short; **~ок** *m* [1; -зка] scrap; *pl.* clippings **~ывать** [1] → **~áть**

**обре|кáть** [1], ⟨**ᷝчь**⟩ [26] condemn, doom (to **на** В, Д)

**обремен|и́тельный** [14; -лен, -льна] burdensome; **~я́ть** [28], ⟨**~и́ть**⟩ [13] burden

**обре|чённый** [14] doomed (to **на** В); **ᷝчь** → **~кáть**

**обрисóв|ывать** [1], ⟨**~áть**⟩ [7] outline, sketch; **-ся** loom, appear

**обрóсший** [17] covered with

**обруб|áть** [1], ⟨**~и́ть**⟩ [14] chop (off), lop; **ᷝок** *m* [1; -бка] stump, block

**о́бруч** *m* [1; *from g/pl.: e.*] hoop; **~а́льный** [14] wedding…; **~а́ться** [1], ⟨**~и́ться**⟩ [16 *e.*; -чу́сь, -чи́шься] be(-come) engaged (to **с** T); **~е́ние** *n* [12] betrothal

**обру́ш|ивать** [1], ⟨**~ить**⟩ [16] bring down; **-ся** fall in, collapse; fall (up)on (***на*** B)

**обры́в** *m* [1] precipice; *tech.* break; **~а́ть** [1], ⟨оборва́ть⟩ [-ву́, -вёшь; -ва́л, -вала́, -о; обо́рванный] tear *or* pluck (off); break off, cut short; **-ся** *a.* fall (from **с** P); **~истый** [14 *sh.*] steep; abrupt; **~ок** *m* [1; -вка] scrap, shred; **~очный** [14; -чен, -чна] scrappy

**обры́зг|ивать**, ⟨**~ать**⟩ [1] sprinkle

**обрю́зглый** [14] flabby, bloated

**обря́д** *m* [1] ceremony, rite

**обса́живать** [1], ⟨обсади́ть⟩ [15] plant round (T with)

**обсервато́рия** *f* [7] observatory

**обсле́дова|ние** *n* [12] (P) inspection (of), inquiry (into), investigation (of); medical examination; **~ть** [7] *(im)pf.* inspect, examine, investigate

**обслу́ж|ивание** *n* [12] service; *tech.* servicing, maintenance; operation; **~ивать** [1], ⟨**~и́ть**⟩ [16] serve, attend; *tech.* service

**обсо́хнуть** → ***обсыха́ть***

**обста|вля́ть** [28], ⟨**~́вить**⟩ [14] surround (with); furnish (T with); *coll.* outwit, deceive **~но́вка** *f* [5; *g/pl.*: -вок] furniture; (*обстоятельства*) situation, conditions *pl.*

**обстоя́тель|ный** [14; -лен, -льна] detailed, circumstantial; *coll.* *человек и т. д.* thorough; **~ство** *n* [9] circumstance (***при*** П, **в** П under, in); ***по ~ствам*** depending on circumstances

**обстоя́ть** [-ои́т] be, get on; stand; ***как обсто́ит де́ло с*** (T)? how are things going?

**обстре́л** *m* [1] bombardment, firing; **~ивать** [1], ⟨**~я́ть**⟩ [28] fire at, on; shell

**обстру́кция** *f* [7] *pol.* obstruction, filibustering

**обступ|а́ть** [1], ⟨**~и́ть**⟩ [14] surround

**об|сужда́ть** [1], ⟨**~суди́ть**⟩ [15; -ждённый] discuss; **~сужде́ние** *n* [12] discussion; **~суши́ться** [16] *pf.* dry o.s.; **~счита́ть** [1] *pf.* cheat; **-ся** miscalculate

**обсып|а́ть** [1], ⟨**~́ать**⟩ [2] strew, sprinkle

**обс|ыха́ть** [1], ⟨**~о́хнуть**⟩ [21] dry

**обт|а́чивать** [1], ⟨**~очи́ть**⟩ [16] turn; **~ека́емый** [14] streamlined; *ответ* vague; **~ере́ть** → ***~ира́ть***; **~ёсывать** [1], ⟨**~еса́ть**⟩ [3] hew; **~ира́ть** [1], ⟨**~ере́ть**⟩ [12; оботру́; обтёр; *g. pt. a.*: -тёрши & -терёв] rub off *or* down, wipe (off), dry; *coll.* wear thin

**обточи́ть** → ***обта́чивать***

**обтрёпанный** [14] shabby, *обшлага* frayed

**обтя́|гивать** [1], ⟨**~ну́ть**⟩ [19] *мебель* cover (T with); *impf.* be closefitting; **~жка** *f* [5]: ***в ~жку*** closefitting dress

**обу|ва́ть** [1], ⟨**~́ть**⟩ [18] put (**-ся** one's) shoes on; **´~вь** *f* [8] footwear, shoes *pl.*

**обу́гл|иваться** [1], ⟨**~иться**⟩ [13] char; carbonize

**обу́за** *f* [5] *fig.* burden

**обу́зд|ывать** [1], ⟨**~а́ть**⟩ [1] bridle, curb

**обусло́в|ливать** [1], ⟨**~ить**⟩ [14] make conditional (T on); cause

**обу́ть(ся)** → ***обува́ть(ся)***

**о́бух** *m* [1] *топора* head; ***его́ как ~ом по голове́*** he was thunderstruck

**обуч|а́ть** [1], ⟨**~и́ть**⟩ [16] teach (Д s.th.), train; **-ся** (Д) learn, be taught; **~е́ние** *n* [12] instruction, training; education

**обхва́т** *m* [1] arm's span; circumference; **~ывать** [1], ⟨**~и́ть**⟩ [15] clasp (T in), embrace, enfold

**обхо́д** *m* [1] round; *полицейского* beat; ***де́лать ~*** make one's round(s); ***пойти́ в ~*** make a detour; **~и́тельный** [14; -лен, -льна] affable, amiable; **~и́ть** [15], ⟨обойти́⟩ [обойду́, -дёшь; → ***идти́***] go round; visit (all [one's]); (*вопрос*) avoid, evade; *закон* circumvent; pass over (T in); (**-ся**, ⟨-сь⟩) cost (***мне*** me); (*справиться*) manage, make, do with(out) (***без*** P); there is (*no … without*); treat (**с** T s.b.); **~ный** [14] roundabout

**обш|а́ривать** [1], ⟨**~а́рить**⟩ [13] rummage (around); **~ива́ть** [1], ⟨**~и́ть**⟩ [обошью́, -шьёшь; → ***шить***] sew round,

О

border (T with); *досками и т. д.* plank, face, *coll.* clothe; **~и́вка** *f* [5] trimming, *etc.* (*vb.*)

**обши́|рный** [14; -рен, -рна] vast, extensive; (*многочисленный*) numerous; **~ть** → **~ва́ть**

**общаться** [1] associate (**с** T with)

**обще|досту́пный** [14; -пен, -пна] popular; *a.* → **досту́пный**; **~жи́тие** *n* [12] hostel; society, community; communal life; **~изве́стный** [14; -тен, -тна] well-known

**обще́ние** *n* [12] intercourse; relations

**общепри́нятый** [14 *sh.*] generally accepted, common

**обще́ств|енность** *f* [8] community, public; **~енный** [14] social, public; **~енное мне́ние** public opinion; **´~о** *n* [9] society; company (*a. econ*); association; community; **акционе́рное ´~о** joint-stock company; **~ове́дение** *n* [12] social science

**общеупотреби́тельный** [14; -лен, -льна] current, in general use

**о́бщ|ий** [17; общ, -á, -е] general; common (in **~его**); public; total, (**в ~ем** on the) whole; **~ина** *f* [5] *eccl. pol., etc.* group, community; **~и́тельный** [14; -лен, -льна] sociable, affable; **~ность** *f* [8] community

**объе|да́ть** [1], 〈**~́сть**〉 [-е́м, -е́шь, *etc.* → **есть**] eat *or* gnaw round, away; **-ся** overeat

**объедин|е́ние** *n* [12] association, union; *действие* unification; **~я́ть** [28], 〈**~и́ть**〉 [13] unite, join; **-ся** (*v/i.*) join, unite (with)

**объе́дки** *coll. m/pl.* [1] leftovers

**объе́|зд** *m* [1] detour, by-pass; *vb.* + **в ~зд** = **~зжа́ть** [1] **1.** 〈**~хать**〉 [-е́ду, -е́дешь] go, drive round; travel through *or* over; visit (all [one's]); **2.** 〈**~здить**〉 [15] break in (*horses*); **~кт** *m* [1] object; **~кти́вный** [14; -вен, -вна] objective

**объём** *m* [1] volume; (*величина*) size; *знаний и т. д.* extent, range; **~истый** [14 *sh.*] *coll.* voluminous, bulky

**объе́сть(ся)** → **объеда́ть(ся)**

**объе́хать** → **объезжа́ть** *1*

**объяв|и́ть** → **~ля́ть**; **~ле́ние** *n* [12] announcement, notice; *реклама* advertisement; *войны* declaration; **~ля́ть** [28], 〈**~и́ть**〉 [14] declare (s.th. *a.* **о** П; s.b. [to be] s.th. В/Т), tell, anounce, proclaim; *благодарность* express

**объясн|е́ние** *n* [12] explanation; declaration (of love **в любви́**); **~и́мый** [14 *sh.*] explicable, accountable; **~и́тельный** [14] explanatory; **~я́ть** [28], 〈**~и́ть**〉 [13] explain, illustrate; account for; **-ся** explain o.s.; be accounted for; have it out (**с** T with); *impf.* make o.s. understood (T by)

**объя́тия** *n/pl.* [12] embrace (*vb.*: **заключи́ть в ~**); **с распростёртыми ~ми** with open arms

**обыва́тель** *m* [4] philistine; **~ский** [16] narrow-minded; philistine…

**обы́гр|ывать**, 〈**~а́ть**〉 [1] beat (*at a game*); win

**обы́денный** [14] everyday, ordinary

**обыкнове́н|ие** *n* [12] habit; **по ~ию** as usual; **~ный** [14; -е́нен, -е́нна] ordinary; *действия* usual, habitual

**о́быск** *m* [1], **~́ивать** [1], 〈**~а́ть**〉 [3] search

**обы́ч|ай** *m* [3] custom; *coll.* habit; **~ный** [14; -чен, -чна] customary, usual, habitual

**обя́занн|ость** *f* [8] duty; **во́инская ~ость** military service; **исполня́ющий ~ости** (P) acting; **~ый** [14 *sh.*] obliged; indebted; **он вам обя́зан жи́знью** he owes you his life

**обяза́тель|ный** [14; -лен, -льна] obligatory, compulsory; **~но** without fail, certainly; **~ство** *n* [9] obligation; *law* liability; engagement; **вы́полнить свои́ ~ства** meet one's obligations

**обя́з|ывать** [1], 〈**~а́ть**〉 [3] oblige; bind, commit; **-ся** engage, undertake, pledge o. s

**овдове́вший** [17] widowed

**овёс** *m* [1; овса́] oats *pl*

**ове́чий** [18] sheep('s)

**овлад|ева́ть** [1], 〈**~е́ть**〉 [8] (T) seize, take possession of; get control over; *знаниями* master; **~е́ть собо́й** regain one's self-control

**о́вощ|и** *m/pl.* [1; *gen.*: -щей, *etc. e.*] veg-

etables; **~но́й** [14]: ***~но́й магази́н*** place selling fresh fruits and vegetables; (*chiefly Brt.*) greengrocer's
**овра́г** *m* [1] ravine
**овся́нка** *f* [5; *g/pl.*: -нок] oatmeal
**овц|а́** *f* [5; *pl. st.*; *g/pl.*: ове́ц] sheep; **~ево́дство** *n* [9] sheepbreeding
**овча́рка** *f* [5; *g/pl.*: -рок] sheepdog; ***неме́цкая ~*** Alsation (dog)
**овчи́на** *f* [5] sheepskin
**огиба́ть** [1], ⟨обогну́ть⟩ [20] turn *or* bend (round)
**оглавле́ние** *n* [12] table of contents
**огла́|ска** *f* [5] publicity; **~ша́ть** [1], ⟨~си́ть⟩ [15 *e.*; -ашу́, -аси́шь, -ашённый] announce, make public; **-ся** *криками и т. д.* fill; resound; ring; **~ше́ние** *n* [12] proclamation; publication
**оглуш|а́ть** [1], ⟨~и́ть⟩ [16 *e.*; -шу́, -ши́шь, -шённый] deafen; stun; **~и́тельный** [14; -лен, -льна] deafening; stunning
**огля́|дка** *coll.* *f* [5] looking back; ***без ~дки*** without turning one's head; ***с ~дкой*** carefully; **~дывать** [1], ⟨~де́ть⟩ [11] examine, look around; **-ся 1.** look round; *fig.* to adapt o.s.; **2.** *pf.*: ⟨~ну́ться⟩ [20] look back (***на*** В at)
**о́гне|нный** [14] fiery; **~опа́сный** [14; -сен, -сна] inflammable; **~сто́йкий** [16; -о́ек, -о́йка] → ***~упо́рный***; **~стре́льный** [14] fire (*arm*); **~туши́тель** *m* [4] fire extinguisher; **~упо́рный** [14; -рен, -рна] fireproof
**огов|а́ривать** [1], ⟨~ори́ть⟩ [13] (*оклеветать*) slander; *условия* stipulate; **-ся** make a slip of the tongue; → ***обмо́лвиться***; **~о́рка** *f* [5; *g/pl.*: -рок] slip of the tongue; reservation, proviso
**огол|я́ть** [28], ⟨~и́ть⟩ [13] bare
**огонёк** *m* [1; -нька́] (small) light; *fig.* zest, spirit
**ого́нь** *m* [4; огня́] fire (*a. fig.*); light; ***из огня́ да в по́лымя*** out of the frying pan into the fire; ***пойти́ в ~ и во́ду*** through thick and thin; ***тако́го днём с огнём не найдёшь*** impossible to find another like it
**огор|а́живать** [1], ⟨~оди́ть⟩ [15 & 15 *e.*; -ожу́, -о́ди́шь; -о́женный] enclose, fence (in); **~о́д** *m* [1] kitchen garden; **~о́дник** *m* [1] market *or* kitchen gardener; **~о́дничество** *n* [9] market gardening
**огорч|а́ть** [1], ⟨~и́ть⟩ [16 *e.*; -чу́, -чи́шь; -чённый] grieve (**-ся** *v/i.*), (be) vex(ed), distress(ed Т); **~е́ние** *n* [9] grief, affliction; **~и́тельный** [14; -лен, -льна] grievous; distressing
**огра|бле́ние** *n* [12] burglary, robbery; **~́да** *f* [5] fence; *каменная* wall; **~жда́ть** [1], ⟨~ди́ть⟩ [15 *e.*; -ажу́, -ади́шь; -аждённый] *обречь* guard, protect; **~жде́ние** *n* [12] barrier; railing
**огранич|е́ние** *n* [12] limitation; restriction; **~́енный** [14 *sh.*] confined; *средства* limited; *человек* narrow(-minded); **~́ивать** [1], ⟨~́ить⟩ [16] confine, limit, restrict (o.s. **-ся**; to Т); content o.s. with; not go beyond; **~и́тельный** [14; -лен, -льна] restrictive, limiting
**огро́мный** [14; -мен, -мна] huge, vast; *интерес и т. д.* enormous, tremendous
**огрубе́лый** [14] coarse, hardened
**огрыз|а́ться** *coll.* [1], *once* ⟨~ну́ться⟩ [20] snap (at); **~́ок** *m* [1; -зка] bit, end; *карандаша* stump, stub
**огу́льный** *coll.* [14; -лен, -льна] wholesale, indiscriminate; (*необоснованный*) unfounded
**огуре́ц** *m* [1; -рца́] cucumber
**ода́лживать** [1], ⟨одолжи́ть⟩ [16 *e.*; -жу́, -жи́шь] lend (Д/В a. p. s.th.); *coll.* *взять* borrow
**одар|ённый** [14 *sh.*] gifted; talented; **~́ивать** [1], ⟨~и́ть⟩ [13] give (presents) to (Т); *fig.* (*impf.* **~я́ть** [28]) endow (Т with)
**оде|ва́ть** [1], ⟨~́ть⟩ [-е́ну, -е́нешь; -е́тый] dress in; clothe in (**-ся** *v/i.* dress o.s., clothe o.s.); **~́жда** *f* [5] clothes *pl.*, clothing
**одеколо́н** *m* [1] eau de cologne
**одеревене́лый** [14] numb
**оде́рж|ивать** [1], ⟨~а́ть⟩ [4] gain, win; ***~а́ть верх над*** (Т) gain the upper hand (over); **~и́мый** [14 *sh.*] (Т) obsessed (by); *страхом* ridden (by)
**оде́ть(ся)** → ***одева́ть(ся)***

О

**одея́ло** *n* [9] blanket, cover(let); *стёганое* quilt

**оди́н** *m*, **одна́** *f*, **одно́** *n*, **одни́** *pl*. [33] one; alone; only; a, a certain; some; **~ мой друг** a friend of mine; **одно́** *su*. one thing, thought, *etc*.; **~ на ~** tête-à-tête; **все до одного́** (*or* **все как ~**) all to a (*or* the last) man

**один|а́ковый** [14 *sh*.] identical (with), the same (as); **~надцатый** [14] eleventh; → **пятый**; **~надцать** [35] eleven; → **пять**; **~о́кий** [16 *sh*.] lonely, lonesome; (*незамужняя и т. д.*) single; **~о́чество** *n* [9] solitude, loneliness; **~о́чка** *m/f* [5; *g/pl*.: -чек] lone person; one-man boat (*or coll*. cell); **~о́чкой, в ~о́чку** alone; **~о́чный** [14] single; *заключение* solitary; individual; one-man…

**одио́зный** [14; -зен, -зна] odious, offensive

**одича́лый** [14] (having gone) wild

**одна́жды** once, one day

**одна́ко**, (*a*. **~ж[е]**) however; yet, still; but, though

**одно|…**: **~бо́кий** [16 *sh*.] *mst. fig*. one-sided; **~бо́ртный** [14] singlebreasted; **~вре́ме́нный** [14] simultaneous; **~зву́чный** [14; -чен, -чна] monotonous; **~зна́чный** [14; -чен, -чна] synonymous; *math*. simple; **~имённый** [14; -ёнен, -ённа] of the same name; **~кла́ссник** *m* [1] classmate; **~коле́йный** [14] single-track; **~кра́тный** [14; -тен, -тна] occurring once, single; **~ле́тний** [15] one-year(-old); *bot*. annual; **~ле́ток** *m* [1; -тка] of the same age (as); **~ме́стный** [14] singleseater; **~обра́зный** [14; -зен, -зна] monotonous; **~ро́дный** [14; -ден, -дна] homogeneous; **~сло́жный** [14; -жен, -жна] monosyllabic; *fig*. terse, abrupt; **~сторо́нний** [15; -о́нен, -о́ння] one-sided (*a. fig*.); unilateral; *движение* oneway; **~фами́лец** *m* [1; -льца́] namesake; **~цве́тный** [14; -тен, -тна] monochromatic; **~эта́жный** [14] one-storied (*Brt*. -reyed)

**одобр|е́ние** *n* [12] approval; **~и́тельный** [14; -лен, -льна] approving; **~я́ть** [28], 〈**~ить**〉 [13] approve (of)

**одол|ева́ть** [1], 〈**~е́ть**〉 [8] overcome, defeat; *fig*. master; cope with; *страх и т. д*. (be) overcome (by)

**одолж|е́ние** *n* [12] favo(u)r, service; **~и́ть** → **ода́лживать**

**одува́нчик** *m* [1] dandelion

**оду́м|ываться**, 〈**~аться**〉 [1] change one's mind

**одура́чивать** → **дура́чить**

**одур|ма́нивать** [1], 〈**~ма́нить**〉 [13] stupefy

**одутлова́тый** [14 *sh*.] puffy

**одухотворённый** [14 *sh*.] inspired

**одушев|лённый** [14] *gr*. animate; **~ля́ть** [28], 〈**~и́ть**〉 [14 *e*.; -влю́, -ви́шь; -влённый] animate; (*воодушевить*) inspire

**оды́шка** *f* [5] short breath

**ожере́лье** *n* [10] necklace

**ожесточ|а́ть** [1], 〈**~и́ть**〉 [16 *e*.; -чу́, -чи́шь; -чённый] harden; embitter **~е́ние** [12] bitterness; **~ённый** [14 *sh*.] *a*. hardened, fierce, bitter

**ожи|ва́ть** [1], 〈**~ть**〉 [-иву́, -ивёшь; о́жил, -а́, -о] revive; **~ви́ть(ся)** → **~вля́ть(ся)**; **~вле́ние** *n* [12] animation; **~влённый** [14 *sh*.] animated, lively; **~вля́ть** [28], 〈**~ви́ть**〉 [14 *e*.; -влю́, -ви́шь, -влённый] revive; enliven, animate; **-ся** quicken, revive; brighten

**ожида́|ние** *n* [12] expectation; ***зал ~ния*** waiting room; **обману́ть ~ния** disappoint; **~ть** [1] wait (for P); expect; ***как мы и ~ли*** just as we expected

**ожи́ть** → ***ожива́ть***

**ожо́г** *m* [1] burn; *кипятком* scald

**озабо́|чивать** [1], 〈**~тить**〉 [15] disquiet, alarm; **~ченный** [14 *sh*.] anxious, worried (T about); (*поглощённый*) preoccupied

**озагла́в|ливать** [1], 〈**~ить**〉 [14] give a title to; head (*a chapter*)

**озада́ч|ивать** [1], 〈**~ить**〉 [16] puzzle, perplex

**озар|я́ть** [28], 〈**~и́ть**〉 [13] (**-ся** be[-come]) illuminate(d), light (lit) up; brighten, lighten

**озвере́ть** [8] *pf*. become furious

**оздоров|ля́ть** [1], 〈**~и́ть**〉 [14] *обста-*

*новку и т. д.* improve
**о́зеро** *n* [9; *pl.*: озёра, -ёр] lake
**ози́мый** [14] winter (*crops*)
**озира́ться** [1] look round
**озлоб|ля́ть** [28], ⟨**ʹ~ить**⟩ [14] (**-ся** become) embitter(ed); **~ле́ние** *n* [12] bitterness, animosity
**ознак|омля́ть** [28], ⟨**~о́мить**⟩ [14] familiarize (**-ся** o.s., **с** T with)
**ознамен|ова́ние** *n* [12] marking, commemoration (**в** B in); **~о́вывать** [1], ⟨**~ова́ть**⟩ [7] mark, commemorate, celebrate
**означа́ть** [1] signify, mean
**озно́б** *m* [1] chill; shivering; **чу́вствовать ~** feel shivery
**озор|ни́к** *m* [1 *e.*], **~ни́ца** *f* [5] *coll.* → **шалу́н(ья)**; *coll.* **~нича́ть** [1] → **шали́ть**; **~но́й** *coll.* [14] mischievous, naughty; **~ство́** *coll. n* [9] mischief, naughtiness
**ой** *int.* oh! o dear!
**ока́з|ывать** [1], ⟨**~а́ть**⟩ [3] show; render, do; *влияние* exert; *предпочтение* give; **-ся** (T) turn out (to be), be found; find o.s
**окайм|ля́ть** [28], ⟨**~и́ть**⟩ [14 *e.*; -млю́, -ми́шь, -млённый] border
**окамене́лый** [14] petrified
**ока́нчивать** [1], ⟨**око́нчить**⟩ [16] finish, end (**-ся** *v/i.*)
**ока́пывать** [1], ⟨**окопа́ть**⟩ [1] dig round; entrench (**-ся** o.s.)
**океа́н** *m* [1], **~ский** [16] ocean
**оки́|дывать** [1], ⟨**~нуть**⟩ [20] (**взгля́дом**) take in at a glance
**окис|ля́ть** [28], ⟨**~ли́ть**⟩ [13] oxidize; **ʹ~ь** *f* [8] *chem.* oxide
**оккуп|ацио́нный** [14] occupation…; **~и́ровать** [7] (*im*)*pf.* occupy
**окла́д** *m* [1] salary; salary scale
**окла́дистый** [14 *sh.*] (*of a beard*) full
**окле́и|вать** [1], ⟨**~ть**⟩ [13] paste over (with); *обоями* paper
**о́клик** *m* [1], **~а́ть** [1], ⟨**ʹ~нуть**⟩ [20] call, hail
**окно́** *n* [9; *pl. st*: о́кна, о́кон, о́кнам] window (*look* through **в** B); *school sl.* free period
**о́ко** *n* [9; *pl.*: о́чи, оче́й, *etc. e.*] *mst. poet.* eye
**око́вы** *f/pl.*: [5] fetters (*mst. fig.*)
**околдова́ть** [7] *pf.* bewitch
**окол|ева́ть** [1], ⟨**~е́ть**⟩ [8] die (*of animals*)
**о́кол|о** (P) (*приблизительно*) about, around, nearly; (*рядом*) by, at, near; nearby
**око́нный** [14] window…
**оконч|а́ние** *n* [12] end(ing *gr.*) close, termination; *работы* completion ([up]on **по** П); *univ.* graduation; **~а́тельный** [14; -лен; -льна] final, definitive; **ʹ~ить** → **ока́нчивать**
**око́п** *m* [1] *mil.* trench; **~а́ть(ся)** → **ока́пывать(ся)**
**о́корок** *m* [1; *pl.*: -ка́, *etc. e.*] ham
**око|стене́лый** [14] ossified (*a. fig.*); **~чене́лый** [14] numb (with cold)
**око́ш|ечко** *n* [9; *g/pl.*: -чек], **~ко** [9; *g/pl.*: -шек] *dim.* → **окно́**
**окра́ина** *f* [5] outskirts *pl.*
**окра́|ска** *f* [5] painting; dyeing; colo(u)ring; *fig.* tinge; **~шивать** [1], ⟨**~сить**⟩ [15] paint; dye; stain; tint
**окре́стн|ость** (*often pl.*) *f* [8] environs *pl.*, neighbo(u)rhood; **~ый** [14] surrounding; in the vicinity
**окрова́вленный** [14] bloodstained, bloody
**о́круг** *m* [1; *pl.*: -га́, *etc. e.*] region, district; circuit
**округл|я́ть** [28], ⟨**~и́ть**⟩ [13] round (off); **ʹ~ый** [14 *sh.*] rounded
**окруж|а́ть** [1], ⟨**~и́ть**⟩ [16 *e.*; -жу́, -жи́шь; -жённый] surround; **~а́ющий** [17] surrounding; **~е́ние** *n* [12] *среда* environment; *mil.* encirclement; *люди* milieu, circle, company; **~и́ть** → **~а́ть**; **~но́й** [14] district…; circular; **ʹ~ность** *f* [8] circumference
**окрыл|я́ть** [28], ⟨**~и́ть**⟩ [13] *fig.* encourage, lend wings, inspire
**октя́брь** *m* [4 *e.*], **~ский** [16] October; *fig.* Russian revolution of October 1917
**окун|а́ть** [1], ⟨**~у́ть**⟩ [20] dip, plunge (*v/i.* **-ся**; dive, *a. fig.*)
**о́кунь** *m* [4; *from g/pl. e.*] perch (*fish*)
**окуп|а́ть** [1], ⟨**~и́ть**⟩ [14], (**-ся** be) offset, recompense(d), compensate(d)
**оку́рок** *m* [1; -рка] cigarette end, stub,

О

butt
**оку́т|ывать**, ⟨**~ать**⟩ [1] wrap (up); *fig.* shroud, cloak
**ола́дья** *f* [6; *g/pl.*: -дий] *cul.* fritter
**оледене́лый** [14] frozen, iced
**оле́нь** *m* [4] deer; ***се́верный ~*** reindeer
**оли́в|а** *f* [5], **~ка** *f* [5; *g/pl.*: -вок], olive (tree); **~ковый** [14] olive…
**олимп|иа́да** *f* [5] Olympiad, Olympics; **~и́йский** [16] Olympic; ***~и́йские и́гры*** Olympic Games
**олицетвор|е́ние** *n* [12] personification, embodiment; **~я́ть** [28], ⟨**~и́ть**⟩ [13] personify, embody
**о́лов|о** *n* [9], tin; **~я́нный** [14] tin, tin--bearing, stannic
**о́лух** *m* [1] *coll.* blockhead, dolt
**ольх|а́** *f* [5], **~о́вый** [14] alder (tree)
**ома́р** *m* [1] lobster
**оме́ла** *f* [5] mistletoe
**омерз|е́ние** *n* [12] loathing; **~и́тельный** [14; -лен, -льна] sickening, loathsome
**омертве́лый** [14] stiff, numb; *med.* necrotic
**омле́т** *m* [1] omelet(te)
**омоложе́ние** *n* [12] rejuvenation
**омо́ним** *m* [1] *ling.* homonym
**омрач|а́ть** [1], ⟨**~и́ть**⟩ [16 *e.*; -чу́, -чи́шь; -чённый] darken, sadden (*v/i.* **-ся**)
**о́мут** *m* [1] whirlpool; deep place (*in river or lake*); ***в ти́хом ~е че́рти во́дятся*** still waters run deep
**омы|ва́ть** [1], ⟨**~ть**⟩ [22] wash (*of seas*)
**он** *m*, **~а́** *f*, **~о́** *n*, **~и́** *pl.* [22] he, she, it, they
**онда́тра** [5] muskrat; *мех* musquash
**онеме́лый** [14] dump; numb
**опа|да́ть** [1], ⟨**~сть**⟩ [25; *pt. st.*] fall (off); (*уменьшаться*) diminish, subside
**опа́здывать**, ⟨**опозда́ть**⟩ [1] be late (***на*** В, ***к*** Д for); ***на пять мину́т*** arrive 5 min, late; *на поезд* miss; *impf. only* be slow (*of timepieces*)
**опал|я́ть** [28], ⟨**~и́ть**⟩ [13] singe
**опас|а́ться** [1] (P) fear, apprehend; beware (of); **~е́ние** *n* [12] fear, apprehension, anxiety; **~ка** *f* [5; *g/pl.*: -сок]: **с *~кой*** cautiously, warily; **~ливый** [14 *sh.*] wary; anxious; **~ность** [8] danger, peril; risk (**с** Т/ ***для*** Р at/of); **с *~ностью для себя́*** at a risk to himself; **~ный** [14; -сен, -сна] dangerous (***для*** Р to); **~ть** → ***опада́ть***
**опе́к|а** *f* [5] guardianship, (*a. fig.*) tutelage; *над имуществом* trusteeship; **~а́ть** [1] be guardian (trustee) of; patronize; **~а́емый** [14] ward; **~у́н** *m* [1 *e.*], **~у́нша** *f* [5] guardian; trustee
**о́пера** *f* [5] opera
**опер|ати́вный** [14] *руководство* efficient; *med.* surgical; **~а́тор** *m* [1] operator; **~ацио́нный** [14] operating; ***~ацио́нная*** *su.* operating room; **~а́ция** *f* [7] operation; ***перенести́ ~а́цию*** be operated on
**опер|ежа́ть** [1], ⟨**~ди́ть**⟩ [15] outstrip (*a. fig.* = outdo, surpass); **~ние** *n* [12] plumage; **~ться** → ***опира́ться***
**опери́ровать** [7] (*im*)*pf.* operate
**о́перный** [14] opera(tic); ***~ теа́тр*** opera house
**опер|я́ться** [28], ⟨**~и́ться**⟩ [13] fledge
**опеча́т|ка** *f* [5; *g/pl.*: -ток] misprint, erratum; **~ывать**, ⟨**~ать**⟩ [1] seal (up)
**опе́шить** *coll.* [16] *pf.* be taken aback
**опи́лки** *f/pl.* [5; *gen.*: -лок] sawdust
**опира́ться** [1], ⟨**опере́ться**⟩ [12; обопру́сь, -рёшься, опёрся, оперла́сь] lean (***на*** В against, on), *a. fig.* = rest, rely ([up]on)
**опис|а́ние** *n* [12] description; **~а́тельный** [14] descriptive; **~а́ть** → ***~ывать***; **~ка** *f* [5; *g/pl.*: -сок] slip of the pen; **~ывать** [1], ⟨**~а́ть**⟩ [3] describe (*a. math.*); list, make an inventory (of); *имущество* distrain; **-ся** make a slip of the pen; **'~ь** *f* [8] list, inventory; distraint
**опла́к|ивать** [1], ⟨**~ать**⟩ [3] bewail, mourn (over)
**опла́|та** *f* [5] pay(ment); (*вознаграждение*) remuneration, settlement; **~чивать** [1], ⟨**~ти́ть**⟩ [15] pay (for); *счёт* settle; ***~ти́ть убы́тки*** pay damages
**оплеу́ха** *coll. f* [5] slap in the face
**оплодотвор|е́ние** *n* [12] impregnation; fertilization; **~я́ть** [28], ⟨**~и́ть**⟩ [13] impregnate; fertilize, fecundate
**опло́т** *m* [1] bulwark, stronghold
**оплошность** *f* [8] blunder
**опове|ща́ть** [1], ⟨**~сти́ть**⟩ [15 *e.*; -ещу́,

-ести́шь; -ещённый] notify; inform
**опозда́|ние** *n* [12] lateness; delay; *vb.* + **с ~нием** = **~ть** → ***опа́здывать***
**опозн|ава́тельный** [14] distinguishing; **~ава́ть** [5], ⟨**~а́ть**⟩ [1] identify
**о́ползень** *m* [4; -зня] landslide
**ополч|а́ться** [1], ⟨**~и́ться**⟩ [16 *e.*; -чу́сь, -чи́шься] take up arms (against); *fig.* turn (against)
**опо́мниться** [13] *pf.* come to *or* recover one's senses
**опо́р** *m* [1]: ***во весь ~*** at full speed, at a gallop
**опо́р|а** *f* [5] support, prop, rest; **~ный** [14] *tech.* bearing, supporting
**опоро́|жнить** [13] *pf.* empty; **~чивать** [1], ⟨**~чить**⟩ [16] defile
**опошл|я́ть** [28], ⟨**~ить**⟩ [13] vulgarize
**опоя́с|ывать** [1], ⟨**~ать**⟩ [3] gird
**оппозици|о́нный** [14], **´~я** *f* [7] opposition…
**оппон|е́нт** *m* [1] opponent; **~и́ровать** [7] (Д) oppose; *univ.* act as opponent at defense of dissertation, *etc.*
**опра́ва** *f* [5] *камня* setting; *очков и т. д.* rim, frame
**оправд|а́ние** *n* [12] justification, excuse; *law* acquittal; **~а́тельный** [14] justificatory; *приговор* 'not guilty'; **~ывать** [1], ⟨**~а́ть**⟩ [1] justify, excuse; *law* acquit; ***~а́ть дове́рие*** come up to expectations; **-ся** *a.* prove (*or* come) true
**оправ|ля́ть** [28], ⟨**~ить**⟩ [14] ***ка́мень*** set; **-ся** recover (*a.* o.s.)
**опра́шивать** [1], ⟨**опроси́ть**⟩ [15] interrogate, cross-examine
**определ|е́ние** *n* [12] determination; *ling.*, *etc.* definition; decision; *gr.* attribute; **~ённый** [14; -ёнен, -ённа] definite; certain; ***в ~ённых слу́чаях*** in certain cases; **~я́ть** [28], ⟨**~и́ть**⟩ [13] determine; define; **-ся** take shape; (*проясниться*) become clearer
**опров|ерга́ть** [1], ⟨**~е́ргнуть**⟩ [21] refute; disprove; **~ерже́ние** *n* [12] refutation; denial
**опроки́|дывать** [1], ⟨**~нуть**⟩ [20] overturn, upset, *о лодке* capsize (**-ся** *v/i.*); *планы* upset
**опро|ме́тчивый** [14 *sh.*] rash, precipitate; **~метью**: ***вы́бежать ~метью*** rush out headlong
**опро́с** *m* [1]: interrogation; cross-examination; referendum; ***~ обще́ственного мне́ния*** opinion poll; **~и́ть** → ***опра́шивать***; **~ный** [14] *adj. of* ~; ***~ный лист*** questionnaire
**опры́с|кивать**, ⟨**~ать**⟩ [1] sprinkle, spray
**опря́тный** [14; -тен, -тна] tidy
**о́птика** *f* [5] optics
**опто́|вый** [14], **´~м** *adv.* wholesale
**опубликов|а́ние** *n* [12] publication; **~ывать** [1] → ***публикова́ть***
**опус|ка́ть** [1], ⟨**~ти́ть**⟩ [15] lower; let down; *голову* hang; *глаза* look down; (*исключить*) omit; ***~ти́ть ру́ки*** lose heart; **-ся** sink; *о температуре* fall; *о солнце, температуре* go down; *fig.* come down (in the world); *p. pt. a.* down and out
**опуст|е́лый** [14] deserted; **~и́ть(ся)** → ***опуска́ть(ся)***; **~оша́ть** [1], ⟨**~оши́ть**⟩ [16 *e.*; -шу́, -ши́шь; -шённый] devastate; **~оше́ние** *n* [12] devastation; **~оши́тельный** [14; -лен, -льна] devastating
**опу́т|ывать**, ⟨**~ать**⟩ [1] entangle (*a. fig.*); ensnare
**опух|а́ть** [1], ⟨**~нуть**⟩ [21] swell; **´~оль** *f* [8] swelling; tumo(u)r
**опу́шка** *f* [5; *g/pl.*: -шек] edge (*of a forest*)
**опыл|я́ть** [28], ⟨**~и́ть**⟩ [13] pollinate
**о́пыт** *m* [1] *жизненный и т. д.* experience; experiment; **~ный** [14] [-тен, -тна] experienced; experiment(al); empirical
**опьяне́ние** *n* [12] intoxication
**опя́ть** again; *a. coll.*, ***~-таки*** (and) what is more; but again; however
**ора́ва** *coll. f* [5] gang, horde, mob
**ора́кул** *m* [1] oracle
**ора́нже|вый** [14] orange…; **~ре́я** *f* [6] greenhouse
**ора́ть** *coll.* [ору́, орёшь] yell, bawl
**орби́т|а** *f* [5] orbit; ***вы́вести на ~у*** put into orbit
**о́рган**[1] *m* [1] *biol.*, *pol.* organ
**орга́н**[2] *m* [1] *mus.* organ
**организ|а́тор** *m* [1] organizer; **~м** *m* [1] organism; **~ова́ть** [7] (*im*)*pf.* (*impf. a.* **~о́вывать** [1]) arrange, organize (*v/i.*

О

**-ся**)
**органи́ч|еский** [16] organic; **~ный** [14; -чен, -чна]: ***~ное це́лое*** integral whole
**о́ргия** *f* [7] orgy
**орда́** *f* [5; *pl. st.*] horde
**о́рден** *m* [1; *pl.*: -на́, *etc. e.*] order, decoration
**о́рдер** *m* [1; *pl.*: -ра́, *etc. e.*] *law* warrant, writ
**орёл** *m* [1; орла́] eagle; ***~ или ре́шка?*** heads or tails?
**орео́л** *m* [1] halo, aureole
**оре́х** *m* [1] nut; ***гре́цкий ~*** walnut; ***лесно́й ~*** hazelnut; ***муска́тный ~*** nutmeg; **~овый** [14] nut…; (*wood*) walnut
**оригина́льный** [14; -лен, -льна] original
**ориенти́р|оваться** [7] (*im*)*pf.* orient o.s. (***на*** В by), take one's bearings; **~о́вка** *f* [5; *g/pl.*: -вок] orientation, bearings *pl.*; **~о́вочный** [14; -чен, -чна] approximate
**орке́стр** *m* [1] orchestra; band
**орли́ный** [14] aquiline
**орна́мент** *m* [1] ornament, ornamental design
**оро|ша́ть** [1], ⟨**~си́ть**⟩ [15; -ошу́, -оси́шь; -ошённый] irrigate; **~ше́ние** *n* [12] irrigation
**ору́д|ие** *n* [12] tool (*a. fig.*); instrument, implement; *mil.* gun; **~ийный** [14] gun…; **~овать** *coll.* [7] (Т) handle, operate
**оруж|е́йный** [14] arms…; **~ие** *n* [12] weapon(s), arm(s); *холодное* (*cold*) steel
**орфогра́ф|ия** *f* [7] spelling; **~и́ческий** [16] orthographic(al)
**орхиде́я** *f* [6] *bot.* orchid
**оса́** *f* [5; *pl. st.*] wasp
**оса́|да** *f* [5] siege; **~ди́ть** → ***~жда́ть*** *and* ***~живать***; **~док** *m* [1; -дка] precipitation, sediment; *fig.* aftertaste; **~жда́ть** [1], ⟨**~ди́ть**⟩ [15 & 15 *e.*; -ажу́, -а́дишь; -аждённый] besiege; ***~жда́ть вопро́сами*** ply with questions; **~живать** [1], ⟨**~ди́ть**⟩ [15] check, snub
**оса́н|истый** [14 *sh.*] dignified, stately; **~ка** *f* [5] carriage, bearing
**осв|а́ивать** [1], ⟨**~о́ить**⟩ [13] (*овладевать*) assimilate, master; *новые земли и т. д.* open up; **-ся** accustom o.s. (**в** П to); familiarize o.s. (**с** Т with)
**осведом|ля́ть** [28], ⟨**~ить**⟩ [14] inform (**о** П of); **-ся** inquire (**о** П after, for; about); **~лённый** [14] informed; versed (in)
**освеж|а́ть** [1], ⟨**~и́ть**⟩ [16 *e.*; -жу́, -жи́шь; -жённый] refresh; freshen *or* touch up; *fig.* brush up; **~а́ющий** [17 *sh.*] refreshing
**осве|ща́ть** [1], ⟨**~ти́ть**⟩ [15 *e.*; -ещу́, -ети́шь; -ещённый] light (up), illuminate; *fig.* elucidate, cast light on; cover, report on (*in the press*)
**освиде́тельствова|ние** *n* [12] examination; **~ть** [7] *pf.* examine
**осви́ст|ывать** [1], ⟨**~а́ть**⟩ [3] hiss (off)
**освобо|ди́тель** *m* [4] liberator; **~ди́тельный** [14] emancipatory, liberation; **~жда́ть** [1], ⟨**~ди́ть**⟩ [15 *e.*; -ожу́, -оди́шь; -ождённый] (set) free, release; liberate, *рабов и т. д.* emancipate; *от уплаты* exempt; *место* clear; ***~ди́ть от до́лжности*** relieve of one's post; **~жде́ние** *n* [12] liberation; release, emancipation; exemption
**осво|е́ние** *n* [12] assimilation; mastering; *земель* opening up; **~ить(ся)** → ***осва́ивать*(ся)**
**освя|ща́ть** [1], ⟨**~ти́ть**⟩ [15 *e.*; -ящу́, -яти́шь; -ящённый] *eccl.* consecrate
**осе|да́ть** [1], ⟨**~сть**⟩ [25; ося́дет; осе́л; → ***сесть***] subside, settle; **~длый** [14] settled
**осёл** *m* [1; осла́] donkey, ass (*a. fig.*)
**осени́ть** → ***осеня́ть***
**осе́н|ний** [15] autumnal, fall…; **~ь** *f* [8] fall, autumn (in [the] Т)
**осен|я́ть** [28], ⟨**~и́ть**⟩ [13] overshadow; ***~и́ть кресто́м*** make the sign of the cross; ***меня́ ~и́ла мысль*** it dawned on me, it occurred to me
**осе́сть** → ***оседа́ть***
**осётр** *m* [1 *e.*] sturgeon
**осетри́на** *f* [5] *cul.* sturgeon
**осе́чка** *f* [5; *g/pl.*: -чек] misfire
**оси́ли|вать** [1], ⟨**~ть**⟩ [13] → ***одолева́ть***
**оси́н|а** *f* [5] asp; **~овый** [14] asp
**оси́пнуть** [21] *pf.* grow hoarse

О

**осироте́лый** [14] orphan(ed); *fig.* deserted
**оска́ли|вать** [1], 〈**~ть**〉 [13]: ***~ть зу́бы*** bare one's teeth
**оскандáли|ваться** [1], 〈**-иться**〉 [13] *coll.* disgrace o.s.; make a mess of s. th.
**осквер|ня́ть** [28], 〈**~и́ть**〉 [13] profane, desecrate, defile
**оско́лок** *m* [1; -лка] splinter, fragment
**оскорб|и́тельный** [14; -лен, -льна] offensive, insulting; **~ле́ние** *n* [12] insult, offence; **~ля́ть** [28], 〈**~и́ть**〉 [14 *e.*; -блю́, -би́шь; -блённый] (**-ся** feel) offend(ed), insult(ed)
**оскуд|ева́ть** [1], 〈**~е́ть**〉 [8] grow scarce
**ослаб|ева́ть** [1], 〈**~е́ть**〉 [8] grow weak *or* feeble; *натяжение* slacken; *ветер и т. д.* abate; **~ить** → ***~ля́ть***; **~ле́ние** *n* [12] weakening; slackening; relaxation; **~ля́ть** [28], 〈**~ить**〉 [14] weaken, slacken; *внимание и т. д.* relax, loosen
**ослеп|и́тельный** [14; -лен, -льна] dazzling; **~ля́ть** [28], 〈**~и́ть**〉 [14 *e.*; -плю́, -пи́шь; -плённый] blind; dazzle; **~нуть** [21] *pf.* go blind
**осложн|е́ние** *n* [12 complication; **~я́ть** [28], 〈**~и́ть**〉 [13] (**-ся** be[come]) complicate(d)
**ослу́ш|иваться**, 〈**~аться**〉 [1] disobey
**ослы́шаться** [4] *pf.* mishear
**осм|а́тривать** [1], 〈**~отре́ть**〉 [9; -отрю́, -о́тришь; -о́треный] view, look around; examine, inspect; see; **-ся** look round; *fig.* take one's bearings; see how the land lies
**осме́|ивать** [1], 〈**~я́ть**〉 [27 *e.*; -ею́, -еёшь; -е́янный] mock, ridicule, deride
**осме́ли|ваться** [1], 〈**~ться**〉 [13] dare, take the liberty (of), venture
**осмея́|ние** *n* [12] ridicule, derision; **~ть** → ***осме́ивать***
**осмо́тр** *m* [1] examination, inspection; *достопримечательностей* sight-seeing; **~е́ть(ся)** → ***осма́тривать(ся)***; **~и́тельность** *f* [8] circumspection; **~и́тельный** [14; -лен, -льна] circumspect
**осмы́сл|енный** [14 *sh.*] sensible; intelligent; **~ивать** [1] *and* **~я́ть** [28], 〈**~ить**〉 [13] comprehend, grasp, make sense of
**оснá|стка** *f* [5] *naut.* rigging (out, up); **~щáть** [1], 〈**~сти́ть**〉 [15 *e.*; -ащу́, -асти́шь; -ащённый] rig; equip; **~ще́ние** *n* [12] rigging, fitting out; equipment
**осно́в|а** *f* [5] basis, foundation, fundamentals; *gr.* stem; **~а́ние** *n* [12] foundation, basis; *math., chem.* base; (*причина*) ground(s), reason; argument; **~а́тель** *m* [4] founder; **~а́тельный** [14; -лен, -льна] wellfounded, sound, solid; (*тщательный*) thorough; **~а́ть** → ***~ывать***; **~но́й** [14] fundamental, basic, principal, primary; ***в ~но́м*** on the whole; **~опол́ожник** *m* [1] founder; **~ывать**, 〈**~а́ть**〉 [7] found; establish; **-ся** be based, rest (on)
**осо́ба** *f* [5] person; personage; ***ва́жная ~*** bigwig
**осо́бенн|ость** *f* [8] peculiarity; feature; **~ый** [14] (e)special, particular, peculiar
**особня́к** *m* [1 *e.*] private residence, detached house
**особняко́м** by o.s., separate(ly); ***держа́ться ~*** keep aloof
**осо́б|ый** [14] → ***~енный***
**осозн|ава́ть** [5], 〈**~а́ть**〉 [1] realize
**осо́ка** *f* [5] *bot.* sedge
**о́сп|а** *f* [5] smallpox; ***ветряна́я ~а*** chickenpox
**осп|а́ривать** [1], 〈**~о́рить**〉 [13] contest, dispute; *звание чемпиона и т. д.* contend (for)
**остава́ться** [5], 〈**оста́ться**〉 [-а́нусь, -а́нешься] (Т) remain, stay; be left; keep, stick (to); be(come); have to; go, get off; (***за*** Т) get, win; *право и т. д.* reserve; *долг* owe; ***~ без*** (Р) lose, have no (left); ***~ с но́сом*** *coll.* get nothing
**остав|ля́ть** [28], 〈**~ить**〉 [14] leave; abandon; (*отказаться*) give up; drop, stop; *в покое* leave (*alone*); keep; ***~ля́ть за собо́й*** reserve
**остально́|й** [14] remaining; *pl. a.* the others; *n & pl. a. su.* the rest (***в ~м*** in other respects; as for the rest)
**остан|а́вливать** [1], 〈**~ови́ть**〉 [14] stop, bring to a stop; *взгляд* rest, fix; **-ся** stop; *в отеле и т. д.* put up (***в*** П at); *в речи* dwell (***на*** П on); **~ки**

О

*m/pl.* [1] remains; ~**ови́ть(ся)** → ***~а́вливать(ся)***; ~**о́вка** *f* [5; *g/p.*: -вок] stop(-page); *автобусная* bus stop; ***~о́вка за ...*** (T) (*only*) ... is holding up

**оста́|ток** *m* [1; -тка] remainder (*a. math*), rest; *ткани* remnant; *pl.* remains; ~**ться** → ***~ва́ться***

**остекл|я́ть** [28], ⟨~**и́ть**⟩ [13] glaze

**остервене́лый** [14] frenzied

**остер|ега́ться** [1], ⟨~**е́чься**⟩ [26 г/ж: -егу́сь, -ежёшься, -егу́тся] (P) beware of, be careful of

**о́стов** *m* [1] frame, framework; *anat.* skeleton

**остолбене́лый** *coll.* [14] dumbfounded

**осторо́жн|ость** *f* [8] care; caution; ***обраща́ться с ~остью!*** handle with care!; ~**ый** [14; -жен, -жна] cautious, careful; (*благоразумный*) prudent; ***~о!*** look out!

**остри|га́ть** [1], ⟨~́**чь**⟩ [26; г/ж: -игу́, -ижёшь, -игу́т] cut; *овец* shear; *ногти* pare; ~**ё**; *n* [12; *g/pl.*: -иёв] point; spike; ~́**ть** [13], ⟨за-⟩ sharpen; ⟨с-⟩ joke; be witty; ~́**чь** → ***~га́ть***

**о́стров** *m* [1; *pl.*: -ва́, *etc. e.*] island; isle; ~**итя́нин** *m* [1; -я́не, -я́н] islander; ***~о́к*** *m* [1; -вка́] islet

**остро|гла́зый** *coll.* [14 *sh.*] sharp-sighted; ~**коне́чный** [14; -чен, -чна] pointed; ~**та́**[1] *f* [5; *pl. st*; -о́ты] sharpness, keenness, acuteness; ~́**та**[2] *f* [5] witticism; joke; ~**у́мие** *n* [12] wit; ~**у́мный** [14; -мен, -мна] witty; *решение* ingenious

**о́стр|ый** [14; остр, (*coll. a.* остёр), -а́, -о] sharp, pointed; *интерес* keen; *угол и т. д.* acute; critical; ~**я́к** *m* [1 *e.*] wit(ty fellow)

**оступ|а́ться** [1], ⟨~**и́ться**⟩ [14] stumble

**остыва́ть** [1] → ***сты́нуть***

**осу|жда́ть** [1], ⟨~**ди́ть**⟩ [15; -уждённый] censure, condemn; *law* convict; ***~жде́ние*** *n* [12] condemnation; *law* conviction

**осу́нуться** [20] *pf.* grow thin

**осуш|а́ть** [1], ⟨~**и́ть**⟩ [16] drain; dry (up); (*опорожнить*) empty

**осуществ|и́мый** [14 *sh.*] feasible; practicable; ~**ля́ть** [28], ⟨~**и́ть**⟩ [14 *e.*; -влю́, -ви́шь; -влённый] bring about, realize; **-ся** be realized, fulfilled, implemented; *мечта* come true; ~**ле́ние** *n* [12] realization

**осчастли́вить** [14] *pf.* make happy

**осып|а́ть** [1], ⟨~́**ать**⟩ [2] strew (with); shower (on); *звёздами* stud (with); *fig.* heap (on); **-ся** crumble; fall

**ось** *f* [8; *from g/pl. e.*] axis; axle

**осяза́|емый** [14 *sh.*] tangible; ~**ние** *n* [12] sense of touch; ~**тельный** [14] tactile; [-лен, -льна] palpable; ~**ть** [1] touch, feel

**от, ото** (P) from; of; off; against; for, with; in; *имени* on behalf of

**ота́пливать** [1], ⟨отопи́ть⟩ [14] heat

**отбав|ля́ть** [28], ⟨~́**ить**⟩ [14]: *coll.* ***хоть ~ля́й*** more than enough, in plenty

**отбе|га́ть** [1], ⟨~**жа́ть**⟩ [4; -бегу́, -бежи́шь, -бегу́т] run off

**отби|ва́ть** [1], ⟨~́**ть**⟩ [отобью́, -бьёшь; → ***бить***] beat, strike (*or* kick) off; *mil.* repel; *coll. девушку* take away (**у** P from;) *край* break away; *охоту* discourage s.o. from sth.; **-ся** ward off (**от** P); *от группы* get lost; drop behind; break off; *coll.*; (*избавиться*) get rid of

**отбивна́я** *f* [14]: *cul.* ***~ котле́та*** *su.* chop

**отбира́ть** [1], ⟨отобра́ть⟩ [отберу́, -рёшь; отобра́л, -а́, -о; ото́бранный] (*забрать*) take (away); seize; (*выбрать*) select, pick out; *билеты* collect

**отби́ть(ся)** → ***отбива́ть(ся)***

**о́тблеск** *m* [1] reflection, gleam

**отбо́й** *m* [3]: ***нет отбо́ю от*** (P) have very many

**отбо́р** *m* [1] selection, choice; ~**ный** [14] select, choice; ~**очный** [14]: ***~очное соревнова́ние*** *sport* knock-out competition

**отбр|а́сывать** [1], ⟨~**о́сить**⟩ [15] throw off *or* away; *mil.* throw back; *идею* reject; *тень* cast; ~**о́сы** *m/pl.* [1] refuse, waste

**отбы|ва́ть** [1], ⟨~́**ть**⟩ [-бу́ду, -бу́дешь; о́тбыл, -а́, -о] **1.** *v/i.* leave, depart (**в** B for); **2.** *v/t. срок и т. д.* serve, do (time); ~́**тие** *n* [12] departure

**отва́|га** *f* [5] bravery, courage; ~**жи-**

**ваться** [1], ⟨**~житься**⟩ [16] have the courage to, venture to, dare to; **~жный** [14; -жен, -жна] valiant, brave

**отва́л**: ***до ~а*** *coll.* one's fill; **~иваться** [1], ⟨**~и́ться**⟩ [13; -али́тся] fall off; slip

**отварно́й** [14] *cul.* boiled

**отвезти́** → ***отвози́ть***

**отверг|а́ть** [1], ⟨**~нуть**⟩ [21] reject, turn down; repudiate, spurn

**отвердева́ть** [1] → ***тверде́ть***

**отверну́ть(ся)** → ***отвёртывать*** *and* ***отвора́чивать(ся)***

**отвёрт|ка** [5; *g/pl.*: -ток] screwdriver; **~ывать** [1], ⟨отверну́ть⟩ [20; отвёрнутый], ⟨отверте́ть⟩ *coll.* [11] unscrew

**отве́с|ный** [14; -сен, -сна] precipitous, steep, sheer; **~ти́** → ***отводи́ть***

**отве́т** *m* [1] answer, reply (***в ~ на*** В in reply to); ***быть в ~е*** be answerable (***за*** for)

**ответвл|е́ние** *n* [12] branch, offshoot; **~я́ться** [28] branch off

**отве́|тить** → ***~ча́ть***; **~тственность** *f* [8] responsibility; **~тственный** [14 *sh.*] responsible (to ***пе́ред*** Т); **~тчик** *m* [1] defendant; **~ча́ть** [1], ⟨**~тить**⟩ [15] (**на** В) answer, reply (to); (**за** В) answer, account (for); (*соответствовать*) (Д) answer, suit, meet

**отви́н|чивать** [1], ⟨**~ти́ть**⟩ [15 *e.*; -нчу́, -нти́шь; -и́нченный] unscrew

**отвис|а́ть** [1], ⟨**~нуть**⟩ [21] hang down, flop, sag; **~лый** [14] loose, flopping, sagging

**отвле|ка́ть** [1], ⟨**~чь**⟩ [26] divert, distract; **~чённый** [14 *sh.*] abstract

**отвод|и́ть** [15], ⟨отвести́⟩ [25] lead, take; *глаза* avert; *удар* parry; *кандидатуру* reject; *землю* allot; ***~и́ть ду́шу*** *coll.* unburden one's heart

**отво|ёвывать** [1], ⟨**~ева́ть**⟩ [6] (re)conquer, win back; **~зи́ть** [15], ⟨отвезти́⟩ [24] take, drive away

**отвора́чивать** [1], ⟨отверну́ть⟩ [20] turn off; **-ся** turn away

**отвори́ть(ся)** → ***отворя́ть(ся)***

**отворо́т** *m* [1] lapel

**отвор|я́ть** [28], ⟨**~и́ть**⟩ [13; -орю́, -о́ришь; -о́ренный] open (*v/i.* **-ся**)

**отвра|ти́тельный** [14; -лен, -льна] disgusting, abominable; **~ща́ть** [1], ⟨**~ти́ть**⟩ [15 *e.*; -ащу́, -ати́шь; -ащённый] avert; **~ще́ние** *n* [12] aversion, disgust (**к** Д for, at)

**отвык|а́ть** [1], ⟨**~нуть**⟩ [21] (**от** Р) get out of the habit of, grow out of, give up

**отвя́з|ывать** [1], ⟨**~а́ть**⟩ [3] (**-ся** [become) untie(d), undo(ne); *coll.* (*отделываться*) get rid of (**от** Р); ***отвяжи́сь!*** leave me alone!

**отга́д|ывать** [1], ⟨**~а́ть**⟩ guess; **~ка** *f* [5; *g/pl.*: -док] solution (to a riddle)

**отгиба́ть** [1], ⟨отогну́ть⟩ [20] unbend; turn up (*or* back)

**отгов|а́ривать** [1], ⟨**~ори́ть**⟩ [13] dissuade (**от** Р from); **~о́рка** *f* [5; *g/pl.*: -рок] excuse, pretext

**отголо́сок** *m* [1; -ска] → ***о́тзвук***

**отгоня́ть** [28], ⟨отогна́ть⟩ [отгоню́, -о́нишь; ото́гнанный; → ***гнать***] drive (*or* frighten) away; *fig. мысль* banish, suppress

**отгор|а́живать** [1], ⟨**~оди́ть**⟩ [15 & 15 *e.*; -ожу́, -о́ди́шь; -о́женный] fence in; *в доме* partition off

**отгру|жа́ть** [1], ⟨**~зи́ть**⟩ [15 & 15; *e.*; -ужу́, -у́зишь; -у́женный & -ужённый] ship, dispatch

**отгрыз|а́ть** [1], ⟨**~ть**⟩ [24; *pt. st.*] bite off, gnaw off

**отда|ва́ть** [5], ⟨**~ть**⟩ [-да́м, -да́шь, *etc.*, → ***дать***; о́тдал, -а́, -о] give back, return; give (away); *в школу* send (**в** В to); *долг* pay; ***~ва́ть честь*** (Д) *mil.* salute; *coll.* sell; ***~ва́ть до́лжное*** give s.o. his due; ***~ва́ть прика́з*** give an order; *impf.* smell or taste (Т of); **-ся** devote o.s. to; *чувство* surrender, give o.s. to; *о звуке* resound

**отда́в|ливать** [1], ⟨**~и́ть**⟩ [14] crush; (*наступить*) tread on

**отдал|е́ние** *n* [12]: ***в ~е́нии*** in the distance; **~ённый** [14 *sh.*] remote; **~я́ть** [28], ⟨**~и́ть**⟩ [13] move away; *встречу* put off, postpone; *fig.* alienate; **-ся** move away (**от** Р from); *fig.* become estranged; digress

**отда́|ть(ся)** → ***отдава́ть(ся)***; **~ча** *f* [5] return; *mil.* recoil; *tech.* output, efficiency

**отде́л** *m* [1] department; *в газете* sec-

O

tion; ~ **ка́дров** personnel department; **~ать(ся)** → **~ывать(ся)**; **~е́ние** *n* [12] separation; department, division; branch (office); *mil.* squad; *в столе и т. д.* compartment; *в больнице* ward; *концерта* part; *coll.* (police) station; **~е́ние свя́зи** post office; **~и́мый** [14 *sh.*] separable; **~и́ть(ся)** → **~я́ть(ся)**; **~ка** *f* [5; *g/pl.*: -лок] finishing; *одежды* trimming; **~ывать**, ⟨**~ать**⟩ [1] finish, put the final touches to; decorate; **-ся** get rid of (**от** Р); get off, escape (Т with); **~ьность** *f* [8]: **в ~ьности** individually; **~ьный** [14] separate; individual; **~я́ть** [28], ⟨**~и́ть**⟩ [13; -елю́, -е́лишь] separate (*v/i.* **-ся от** Р from; come off)

**отдёр|гивать** [1], ⟨**~нуть**⟩ [20] draw back; pull aside

**отдира́ть** [1], ⟨**отодра́ть**⟩ [отдеру́, -рёшь; отодра́л, -а́, -о; ото́дранный] tear *or* rip (off); *pf. coll.* thrash

**отдохну́ть** → **отдыха́ть**

**отду́шина** *f* [5] (air) vent (*a. fig.*)

**о́тдых** *m* [1] rest, relaxation; holiday; **~а́ть** [1], ⟨**отдохну́ть**⟩ [20] rest, relax

**отдыша́ться** [4] *pf.* get one's breath back

**О**

**отёк** *m* [1] swelling, edema

**оте|ка́ть** [1], ⟨**~чь**⟩ [26] swell

**оте́ль** *m* [4] hotel

**оте́ц** *m* [1; отца́] father

**оте́че|ский** [16] fatherly; paternal; **~ственный** [14] native, home…; *война* patriotic; **~ство** *n* [9] motherland, fatherland, one's (native) country

**оте́чь** → **отека́ть**

**отжи|ва́ть** [1], ⟨**~ть**⟩ [-живу́; -вёшь; о́тжил, -а́, -о; о́тжи́тый (о́тжи́т, -а́, -о)] (have) live(d, had) (one's time *or* day); *о традиции и т. д.* become obsolete, outmoded; die out

**о́тзвук** *m* [1] echo, repercussion; *чувство* response

**о́тзыв** *m* [1] opinion, judg(e)ment (**по** Д on *or* about), reference; comment, review; *дипломата* recall; **~а́ть** [1], ⟨**отозва́ть**⟩ [отзову́, -вёшь; ото́званный] take aside; recall; **-ся** respond, answer; speak (**о** П of *or* to); (re)sound; (*вызвать*) call forth (T s.th.); (*влиять*) affect (**на** В s.th.); **~чивый** [14 *sh.*] responsive

**отка́з** *m* [1] refusal, denial, rejection (**в** П, Р of); renunciation (**от** Р of); *tech.* failure; **без ~а** smoothly; **по́лный до ~а** cram-full; **получи́ть ~** be refused; **~ывать** [1], ⟨**~а́ть**⟩ [3] refuse, deny (a p. s.th. Д/**в** П); *tech.* fail; **-ся** (**от** Р) refuse, decline, reject; renounce, give up; (**я**) **не откажу́сь** *coll.* I wouldn't mind

**отка́|лывать** [1], ⟨**отколо́ть**⟩ [17] break *or* chop off; *булавку* unpin, unfasten; **-ся** break off; come undone; *fig.* break away; **~пывать**, ⟨**откопа́ть**⟩ [1] dig up, unearth; **~рмливать** [1], ⟨**откорми́ть**⟩ [14] fatten up; **~тывать** [1], ⟨**~ти́ть**⟩ [15] roll, haul (away) (**-ся** *v/i.*); **~чивать**, ⟨**~ча́ть**⟩ [1] pump out; resuscitate; **~шливаться** [1], ⟨**~шляться**⟩ [28] clear one's throat

**отки|дно́й** [14] *сидение* tip-up; **~дывать** [1], ⟨**~нуть**⟩ [20] throw away; turn back, fold back; **-ся** lean back recline

**откла́дывать** [1], ⟨**отложи́ть**⟩ [16] lay aside; *деньги* save; (*отсрочить*) put off, defer, postpone

**откле́|ивать** [1], ⟨**~ить**⟩ [13] unstick; **-ся** come unstuck

**о́тклик** *m* [1] response; comment; → *a.* **о́тзвук**; **~а́ться** [1], ⟨**~нуться**⟩ [20] (**на** В) respond (to), answer; comment (on)

**отклон|е́ние** *n* [12] deviation; *от темы* digression; *предложения* rejection; **~я́ть** [28], ⟨**~и́ть**⟩ [13; -оню́, -о́нишь] decline, reject; **-ся** deviate; digress

**отклю|ча́ть** [4], ⟨**~чи́ть**⟩ [16] *el.* cut off, disconnect; *p. p. p.* dead

**отк|оло́ть** → **~а́лывать**; **~опа́ть** → **~а́пывать**; **~орми́ть** → **~а́рмливать**

**отко́с** *m* [1] slope, slant, escarp

**открове́н|ие** *n* [12] revelation; **~ный** [14; -е́нен, -е́нна] frank, candid, blunt, outspoken

**откры|ва́ть** [1], ⟨**~ть**⟩ [22] open; *кран* turn on; *новую планету* discover; *тайну* disclose, reveal; *памятник* unveil; *учреждение* inaugurate; **-ся** open; *кому-л.* unbosom o.s.; **~тие** *n* [12]

opening; discovery; revelation; inauguration; unveiling; ∴тка *f* [5; *g/pl.*: -ток] (*с видом* picture) post card; ∴тый [14] open; *слушания и т. д.* public; ∴ть(ся) → **~ва́ться**
**отку́да** where from?; whence; **~ вы?** where do you come from? **~ вы зна́ете?** how do you know …?; **~-нибудь, ~-то** (from) somewhere or other
**откуп|а́ться** [1], ⟨~и́ться⟩ [14] pay off
**откупо́ри|вать** [1], ⟨~ть⟩ [13] uncork; open
**отку́с|ывать** [1], ⟨~и́ть⟩ [15] bite off
**отлага́тельств|о** *n* [9]: **де́ло не те́рпит ~а** the matter is urgent
**отлага́ться** [1], ⟨отложи́ться⟩ [16] *geol.* be deposited
**отла́мывать**, ⟨отлома́ть⟩ [1], ⟨отломи́ть⟩ [14] break off (*v/i.* **-ся**)
**отл|ёт** *m* [1] *птиц* flying away; ~ета́ть [1], ⟨~ете́ть⟩ [11] fly away *or* off; *coll.* come off
**отли́в**[1] *m* [1] ebb (tide)
**отли́в**[2] *m* [1] play of colo(u)rs, shimmer
**отли|ва́ть**[1] [1], ⟨~ть⟩ [отолью́, -льёшь; о́тли́л, -а́, -о; → **лить**] pour off, in, out (some… Р); *tech.* found, cast
**отлива́ть**[2] *impf.* (Т) shimmer, play
**отлич|а́ть** [1], ⟨~и́ть⟩ [16 *e.*; -чу́, -чи́шь; -чённый] distinguish (**от** Р from); **-ся** *a. impf.* differ; be noted (Т for); ∴ие *n* [12] distinction, difference; **в ∴ие от** (Р) as against; **зна́ки ∴ия** decorations; ~и́тельный [14] distinctive; ∴ник *m* [1], **∴ница** *f* [5] excellent pupil, *etc.*; ∴ный [14; -чен, -чна] excellent, perfect; *от чего-л.* different; *adv. a.* very good (*as su. a mark* → **пятёрка**)
**отло́гий** [16 *sh.*] sloping
**отлож|е́ние** *n* [12] deposit; ~и́ть(ся) → **откла́дывать & отлага́ться**; ~но́й [14] *воротник* turndown
**отлом|а́ть** ⟨~и́ть⟩ → **отла́мывать**
**отлуч|а́ться** [1], ⟨~и́ться⟩ [16 *e.*; -чу́сь, -чи́шься] (**из** Р) leave, absent o.s. (from); ∴ка *f* [5] absence
**отма́лчиваться** [1] keep silent
**отма́|тывать** [1], ⟨отмота́ть⟩ [1] wind *or* reel off, unwind; ~хиваться [1], ⟨~хну́ться⟩ [20] disregard, brush aside

**о́тмель** *f* [8] shoal, sandbank
**отме́н|а** *f* [5] *закона* abolition; *спектакля* cancellation; *приказа* countermand; ~ный [14; -е́нен, -е́нна] → **отли́чный**; ~я́ть [28], ⟨~и́ть⟩ [14; -еню́, -е́нишь] abolish; cancel; countermand
**отмер|е́ть** → **отмира́ть**; ~за́ть [1], ⟨отмёрзнуть⟩ [21] be frostbitten
**отме́р|ивать** [1] & **~я́ть** [28], ⟨~ить⟩ [13] measure (off)
**отме́стк|а** *coll. f* [5]: **в ∴у** in revenge
**отме́|тка** *f* [5; *g/pl.*: -ток] mark, *школьная тж.* grade; ~ча́ть [1], ⟨~тить⟩ [15] mark, note
**отмира́ть** [1], ⟨отмере́ть⟩ [12; отомрёт; о́тмер, -рла́, -о; отме́рший] *об обычае* die away *or* out
**отмор|а́живать** [1], ⟨~о́зить⟩ [15] frostbite
**отмота́ть** → **отма́тывать**
**отмы|ва́ть** [1], ⟨∴ть⟩ [22] clean; wash (off); ~ка́ть [1], ⟨отомкну́ть⟩ [20] unlock, open; ∴чка *f* [5; *g/pl.*: -чек] master key; picklock
**отне́киваться** *coll.* [1] deny, disavow
**отнести́(сь)** → **относи́ть(ся)**
**отнима́ть** [1], ⟨отня́ть⟩ [-ниму́, -ни́мешь; о́тнял, -а́, -о; о́тнятый (о́тнят, -а́, -о)] take away (**у** Р from); *время* take; amputate; **~ от гру́ди** wean; **-ся** *coll.* be paralyzed
**относи́тельн|ый** [14; -лен, -льна] relative; **~о** (Р) concerning, about
**отно|си́ть** [15], ⟨отнести́⟩ [24; -с-, -есу́; -ёс, -есла́] take (Д, **в** В, **к** Д to); *ветром и т. д.* carry (off, away); *на место* put; *fig.* refer to; ascribe; **-ся**, ⟨отнести́сь⟩ (**к** Д) treat, be; *impf.* concern; refer; belong; date from; be relevant; **э́то к де́лу не ∴сится** that's irrelevant; ~ше́ние *n* [12] attitude (toward[s] **к** Д); treatment; relation; *math.* ratio; respect (**в** П, **по** Д in, with); **по ~ше́нию** (**к** Д) as regards, to(ward[s]); **име́ть ~ше́ние** (**к** Д) concern, bear a relation to
**отны́не** *old use* henceforth
**отню́дь**: **~ не** by no means
**отня́ть(ся)** → **отнима́ть(ся)**
**отобра|жа́ть** [1], ⟨~зи́ть⟩ [15 *e.*; -ажу́, -ази́шь; -ажённый] represent; reflect

О

**ото|бра́ть** → ***отбира́ть***; **~всю́ду** from everywhere; **~гна́ть** → ***отгоня́ть***; **~гну́ть** → ***отгиба́ть***; **~грева́ть** [1], ⟨**~гре́ть**⟩ [8; -гре́тый] warm (up); **~двига́ть**[1], ⟨**~дви́нуть**⟩ [20 *st.*] move aside, away (*v/i.* **-ся**)

**отодра́ть** → ***отдира́ть***

**отож(д)еств|ля́ть** [28], ⟨**~и́ть**⟩ [14; -влю́, -ви́шь; -влённый] identify

**ото|зва́ть(ся)** → ***отзыва́ть(ся)***; **~йти́** → ***отходи́ть***; **~мкну́ть** → ***отмыка́ть***; **~мсти́ть** → ***мстить***

**отоп|и́ть**[28] → ***ота́пливать***; **~ле́ние** *n* [12] heating

**оторва́ть(ся)** → ***отрыва́ть(ся)***

**отороп́еть** [8] *pf. coll.* be struck dumb

**отосла́ть** → ***отсыла́ть***

**отпа|да́ть** [1], ⟨**~́сть**⟩ [25; *pt. st.*] (**от** Р) fall off *or* away; *fig.* (*миновать*) pass

**отпе|ва́ние** *n* [12] funeral service; **~́тый** [14] *coll.* inveterate, out-and-out; **~ре́ть(ся)** → ***отпира́ть(ся)***

**отпеча́т|ок** *m* [1; -тка] (im)print; impress; *a. fig.* ***~ок па́льца*** fingerprint; **~ывать**, ⟨**~а́ть**⟩ [1] print; type; **-ся** imprint, impress

**отпи|ва́ть** [1], ⟨**~́ть**⟩ [отопью́, -пьёшь; о́тпил, -а́, -о; -пе́й(те)!] drink (some… Р); **~́ливать** [1], ⟨**~ли́ть**⟩ [13] saw off

**отпира́ть** [1], ⟨**отпере́ть**⟩ [12; отопру́, -прёшь; о́тпер, -рла́, -о; отперший; о́тпертый (-ерт, -а́, -о)] unlock, unbar, open; **-ся**[1] open

**отпира́ться**[2] deny; disown

**отпи́ть** → ***отпива́ть***

**отпи́х|ивать** *coll.* [1], *once* ⟨**~ну́ть**⟩ [20] push off; shove aside

**отпла́|та** *f* [5] repayment, requital; **~чивать** [1], ⟨**~ти́ть**⟩ [15] (re)pay, requite

**отплы|ва́ть** [1], ⟨**~́ть**⟩ [23] sail, leave; swim (off); **~́тие** *n* [12] sailing off, departure

**о́тповедь** *f* [8] rebuff, rebuke

**отпо́р** *m* [1] repulse, rebuff

**отпоро́ть** [17] *pf.* rip (off)

**отправ|и́тель** *m* [4] sender; **~́ить(ся)** → ***~ля́ть(ся)***; **~́ка** *coll. f* [5] sending off, dispatch; **~ле́ние** *n* [12] dispatch; departure; **~ля́ть** [28], ⟨**~́ить**⟩ [14] send, dispatch, forward; mail; *impf. only* exercise, perform (*duties*, *functions*, *etc.*); **-ся** set out; go; leave, depart (**в, на** В for); **~но́й** [14] starting…

**отпра́шиваться**[1], ⟨**отпроси́ться**⟩ [15] ask for leave; *pf.* ask for and obtain leave

**отпры́г|ивать** [1], *once* ⟨**~нуть**⟩ [20] jump, spring back (*or* aside)

**о́тпрыск** *m* [1] *bot. and fig.* offshoot, scion

**отпря́нуть** [20 *st.*] *pf.* recoil

**отпу́г|ивать**[1], ⟨**~ну́ть**⟩ [20] scare away

**о́тпуск** *m* [**1**; *pl.* -ка́, *etc. e.*] holiday(s), leave (*a. mil.*), vacation (on: *go* **в** В; *be* **в** П); ***~ по боле́зни*** sick leave; **~а́ть** [1], ⟨**отпусти́ть**⟩ [15] **1.** let go; release, set free; dismiss; slacken; *бороду* grow; *coll. шутку* crack; **2.** *товар* serve; **~ни́к** *m* [1 *e.*] vacationer, holiday maker; **~но́й** [14] **1.** vacation…, holiday…; **2.** *econ. цена* selling

**отпуще́н|ие** *n* [12] ***козёл ~ия*** scapegoat

**отраб|а́тывать**, ⟨**~о́тать**⟩ [1] *долг и т. д.* work off; finish work; *p. pt. p. a. tech.* waste, exhaust

**отра́в|а** *f* [5] poison; *fig.* bane; **~ле́ние** *n* [12] poisoning; **~ля́ть** [28], ⟨**~и́ть**⟩ [14] poison; *fig.* spoil

**отра́д|а** *f* [5] comfort, joy, pleasure; **~ный** [14; -ден, -дна] pleasant, gratifying, comforting

**отра|жа́ть** [1], ⟨**~зи́ть**⟩ [15 *e.*; -ажу́, -ази́шь; -ажённый] repel, ward off; *в зеркале, образе* reflect, mirror; **-ся** (*v/i.*) (**на** П) affect; show

**о́трасль** *f* [8] branch

**отра|ста́ть** [1], ⟨**~сти́**⟩ [24; -ст-: -сту́; → ***расти́***] grow; **~́щивать** [1], ⟨**~сти́ть**⟩ [15 *e.*; -ащу́, -асти́шь; -ащённый] (let) grow

**отре́бье** *n* [10] *obs.* waste; *fig.* rabble

**отре́з** *m* [1] length (*of cloth*); **~а́ть**, **~ывать** [1], ⟨**~ать**⟩ [3] cut off; *coll.* give a curt answer

**отрезв|ля́ть** [28], ⟨**~и́ть**⟩ [14 *e.*; -влю́, -ви́шь; -влённый] sober

**отре́з|ок** *m* [1; -зка] piece; *дороги* stretch; *времени* space; *math.* segment; **~ывать** → ***~а́ть***

**отре|ка́ться** [1], ⟨**҇чься**⟩ [26] (**от** P) disown, disavow; *от убеждений и т. д.* renounce; **҇чься от престо́ла** abdicate

**отре|че́ние** *n* [12] renunciation; abdication; **҇чься → ~ка́ться**; **~шённый** [14] estranged, aloof

**отрица́|ние** *n* [12] negation, denial; **~тельный** [14; -лен, -льна] negative; **~ть** [1] deny; (*law*) **~ть вино́вность** plead not guilty

**отро́|г** *m* [1] *geogr.* spur; **ʹ~ду** *coll.* in age; from birth; in one's life; **~дье** *n* [10] *coll. pej.* spawn; **~сток** *m* [1; -тка] *bot.* shoot; *anat.* appendix; **҇чество** *n* [9] boyhood; adolescence

**отруб|а́ть** [1], ⟨**~и́ть**⟩ [14] chop off

**о́труби** *f/pl.* [8; *from g/pl. e.*] bran

**отры́в** *m* [1]: **в ~е** (**от** P) out of touch (with); **~а́ть** [1] **1.** ⟨оторва́ть⟩ [-рву́, -вёшь; -ва́л, -а́, -о; ото́рванный] tear off; *от работы* tear away; separate; **-ся** (**от** P) come off; tear o.s. away; *от друзей* lose contact (with); **не ~а́ясь** without rest; **2.** ⟨отры́ть⟩ [22] dig up, out; **~истый** [14 *sh.*] abrupt; **~но́й** [14] perforated; tearoff (*sheet, block, calendar etc.*); **~ок** *m* [1; -вка] fragment; extract, passage; **~очный** [14; -чен, -чна] fragmentary, scrappy

**отры́жка** *f* [5; *g/pl.*: -жек] belch(ing), eructation

**отры́ть → отрыва́ть**

**отря́|д** *m* [1] detachment; *biol.* class; **~хивать** [1], *once* ⟨**~хну́ть**⟩ [20] shake off

**отсве́чивать** [1] be reflected; shine (with T)

**отсе́|ивать** [1], ⟨**~ять**⟩ [27] sift, screen; *fig.* eliminate; **~ка́ть** [1], ⟨**~чь**⟩ [26; *pt.*: -се́к, -секла́; -сечённый] sever; cut off; **~че́ние** *n* [12]: **дава́ть го́лову на ~че́ние** *coll.* stake one's life

**отси́|живать** [1], ⟨**~де́ть**⟩ [11; -жу́, -ди́шь] sit out; *в тюрьме* serve; *ногу* have pins and needles (in one's leg)

**отск|а́кивать** [1], ⟨**~очи́ть**⟩ [16] jump aside, away; *мяч* rebound; *coll.* break off, come off

**отслу́ж|ивать** [1], ⟨**~и́ть**⟩ [16] *в армии* serve (one's time); *одежда и т. д.* be worn out

**отсове́товать** [7] *pf.* dissuade (from)

**отсо́хнуть → отсыха́ть**

**отсро́ч|ивать** [1], ⟨**~ить**⟩ [16] postpone; **~ка** *f* [5; *g/pl.*: -чек] postponement, delay; *law* adjournment

**отста|ва́ть** [5], ⟨**҇ть**⟩ [-а́ну, -а́нешь] (**от** P) lag *or* fall behind; be slow (**на пять мину́т** 5 min.); *обои и т. д.* come off; *coll. pf.* leave alone

**отста́в|ка** *f* [5] resignation; retirement; (*увольнение*) dimissal; **в ~ке** = **~но́й**; **~ля́ть** [28], ⟨**~ить**⟩ [14] remove, set aside; **~но́й** [14] *mil.* retired

**отст|а́ивать**[1] [1], ⟨**~оя́ть**⟩ [-ою́, -ои́шь] defend; *права и т. д.* uphold, maintain; stand up for

**отст|а́ивать**[2] [1], ⟨**~оя́ть**⟩ stand (through), remain standing

**отста́|лость** *f* [8] backwardness; **~лый** [14] backward; **~ть → ~ва́ть**

**отстёгивать** [1], ⟨отстегну́ть⟩ [20; -ёгнутый] unbutton, unfasten

**отстоя́ть** [1] *pf.* be at a distance (of P)

**отстоя́ть(ся) → отста́ивать(ся)**

**отстр|а́ивать** [1], ⟨**~о́ить**⟩ [13] finish building; build (up); **~аня́ть** [28], ⟨**~ани́ть**⟩ [13] push aside, remove; *от должности* dismiss; **-ся** (**от** P) dodge; shirk; keep aloof; **~о́ить → ~а́ивать**

**отступ|а́ть** [1], ⟨**~и́ть**⟩ [14] step back; *mil.* retreat, fall back; *в ужасе* recoil; *fig.* back down; go back on; *от правила* deviate; **~ле́ние** *n* [12] retreat; deviation; *в изложении* digression

**отсу́тств|ие** *n* [12] absence; **в её ~ие** in her absence; **за ~ием** for lack of; **находи́ться в ~ии** be absent; **~овать** [7] be absent; be lacking

**отсчи́т|ывать**, ⟨**~а́ть**⟩ [1] count (out); count (off)

**отсыл|а́ть** [1], ⟨отосла́ть⟩ [-ошлю́, -шлёшь; ото́сланный] send (off, back); refer (**к** Д to); **҇ка** *f* [5; *g/pl.*: -лок] → **ссы́лка**

**отсып|а́ть** [1], ⟨**҇ать**⟩ [2] pour (out); measure (out)

**отсы|ре́лый** [14] damp; **~ха́ть** [1], ⟨отсо́хнуть⟩ [21] dry up; wither

**отсю́да** from here; (*следовательно*)

hence; (*fig.*) from this

**отта́|ивать** [1], ⟨**~ять**⟩ [27] thaw out; **~лкивать** [1], ⟨**оттолкну́ть**⟩ [20] push away, aside; *fig.* antagonize; *друзей* alienate; **~лкивающий** [17] repulsive, repellent; **~скивать** [1], ⟨**~щи́ть**⟩ [16] drag away, aside; **~чивать** [1], ⟨**отточи́ть**⟩ [16] whet, sharpen; *стиль и т. д.* perfect; **~ять** → ***~ивать***

**отте́н|ок** *m* [1; -нка] shade, nuance (*a. fig.*); tinge; **~я́ть** [28], ⟨**~и́ть**⟩ [13] shade; (*подчеркнуть*) set off, emphasize

**о́ттепель** *f* [8] thaw

**оттесн|я́ть** [28], ⟨**~и́ть**⟩ [13] push back, aside; *mil.* drive back

**о́ттиск** *m* [1] impression, offprint

**отто|го́** therefore, (*a.* ***~го́ и***) that's why; ***~го́ что*** because; **~лкну́ть** → ***отта́лкивать***; **~пы́рить** *coll.* [13] *pf.* bulge, protrude, stick out (*v/i.* **-ся**); **~чи́ть** → ***отта́чивать***

**отту́да** from there

**оття́|гивать** [1], ⟨**~ну́ть**⟩ [20; -я́нутый] draw out, pull away (*mil.*) draw off (back); *coll. решение* delay; ***он хо́чет ~ну́ть вре́мя*** he wants to gain time

**отуч|а́ть** [1], ⟨**~и́ть**⟩ [16] break (**от** P of), cure (of); wean; **-ся** break o.s. (of)

**отхлы́нуть** [20] *pf.* flood back, rush back

**отхо́д** *m* [1] departure; withdrawal; *fig.* deviation; **~и́ть** [15], ⟨**отойти́**⟩ [-ойду́, -дёшь; отошёл, -шла́; отойдя́] move (away, off); leave, depart; deviate; *mil.* withdraw; (*успокоиться*) recover; **~ы** *m/pl.* [1] waste

**отцве|та́ть** [1], ⟨**~сти́**⟩ [25; -т-: -ету́] finish blooming, fade (*a. fig.*)

**отцеп|ля́ть** [28], ⟨**~и́ть**⟩ [14] unhook; uncouple; *coll.* ***~и́сь!*** leave me alone!

**отцо́в|ский** [16] paternal; fatherly; **~ство** *n* [9] paternity

**отча́|иваться** [1], ⟨**~яться**⟩ [27] despair (of **в** П); be despondent

**отча́ли|вать** [1], ⟨**~ть**⟩ [13] cast off, push off; *coll.* ***~вай!*** beat it!; scram!

**отча́сти** partly, in part

**отчая|ние** *n* [12] despair; **~нный** [14 *sh.*] desperate; **~ться** → ***отча́иваться***

**о́тче**: ***♀ наш*** Our Father; Lord's Prayer

**отчего́** why; ***~-то*** that's why

**отчека́н|ивать** [1], ⟨**~ить**⟩ [13] mint, coin; say distinctly

**о́тчество** *n* [9] patronymic

**отчёт** *m* [1] account (**о, в** П of), report (on); ***(от)дава́ть себе́ ~ в*** (П) realize *v/t.*; **~ливый** [14 *sh.*] distinct, clear; **~ность** *f* [8] accounting

**отчи́|зна** *f* [5] fatherland; **´~й** [17]: ***´~й дом*** family home; **´~м** *m* [1] stepfather

**отчисл|е́ние** *n* [12] (*вычет денег*) deduction; *студента* expulsion; **~я́ть** [28], ⟨**~ить**⟩ [13] deduct; dismiss

**отчи́т|ывать** *coll.*, ⟨**~а́ть**⟩ [1] *coll.* read a lecture to; tell off; **-ся** give *or* render an account (to ***пе́ред*** Т)

**от|чужда́ть** [1] *law.* alienate; estrange; **~шатну́ться** [20] *pf.* start *or* shrink back; recoil; **~швырну́ть** *coll.* [20] *pf.* fling (away); throw off; **~ше́льник** *m* [1] hermit; *fig.* recluse

**отъе́|зд** *m* [1] departure; **~зжа́ть** [1], ⟨**~хать**⟩ [-е́ду, -е́дешь] drive (off), depart

**отъя́вленный** [14] inveterate, thorough, out-and-out

**оты́гр|ывать**, ⟨**~а́ть**⟩ [1] win back, regain; **-ся** regain one's lost money

**оты́ск|ивать** [1], ⟨**~а́ть**⟩ [3] find; track down; **-ся** turn up; appear

**отяго|ща́ть** [1], ⟨**~ти́ть**⟩ [15 *e.*; -щу́, -оти́шь; -още́нный] burden

**отягч|а́ть** [4], ⟨**~и́ть**⟩ [16] make worse, aggravate

**офиц|е́р** *m* [1] officer; **~е́рский** [16] office(r's, -s'); **~иа́льный** [14; -лен, -льна] official; **~иа́нт** *m* [1] waiter; **~иа́нтка** *f* [5] waitress

**оформ|ля́ть** [28], ⟨**~ить**⟩ [14] *книгу* design; *документы* draw up; *витрину* dress; *брак* register; ***~ить на рабо́ту*** take on the staff

**офо́рт** *m* [1] etching

**ох** *int.* oh!, ah!; **~анье** *n* [10] *col.* moaning, groaning

**оха́пка** *f* [5; *g/pl.*: -пок] armful

**о́х|ать** [1], *once* ⟨**~нуть**⟩ [20] groan

**охва́т|ывать** [1], ⟨**~и́ть**⟩ [15] enclose; *о чувстве* seize, grip; *вопросы* embrace; *пламенем* envelop; *fig.* comprehend

**охла|дева́ть**, ⟨**~де́ть**⟩ [8] grow cold (toward); *a. fig.* lose interest in; **~жда́ть** [1], ⟨**~ди́ть**⟩ [15 *e.*; -ажу́, -ади́шь; -аждённый] cool; **~жде́ние** *n* [12] cooling

**охмеле́ть** [8] *coll.* get tipsy

**о́хнуть** → ***о́хать***

**охо́та**[1] *f* [5] *coll.* desire (for), mind (to)

**охо́т|а**[2] *f* [5] (***на*** В, ***за*** Т) hunt(ing) (of, for); chase (after); **~иться** [15] (***на*** В, ***за*** Т) hunt; chase (after); **~ник**[1] *m* [1] hunter

**охо́тник**[2] *m* [1] volunteer; lover (of ***до*** Р)

**охо́тничий** [18] hunting, shooting; hunter's

**охо́тн|о** willingly, gladly, with pleasure; ***~нее*** rather; ***~нее всего́*** best of all

**охра́н|а** *f* [5] guard(s); *прав* protection; ***ли́чная ~а*** bodyguard; **~я́ть** [28], ⟨**~и́ть**⟩ [13] guard, protect (***от*** Р from, against)

**охри́п|лый** *coll.* [14], **~ший** [17] hoarse

**оце́н|ивать** [1], ⟨**~и́ть**⟩ [13; -еню́, -е́нишь] value (***в*** В at); estimate; *ситуацию* appraise; (*по достоинству*) appreciate; **~ка** *f* [5; *g/pl.*: -нок] evaluation, estimation; appraisal; appreciation; *школьная* mark

**оцепене́|лый** [14] torpid, benumbed; *fig.* petrified, stupefied; **~ние** *n* [12]: ***в ~нии*** petrified

**оцеп|ля́ть** [28], ⟨**~и́ть**⟩ [14] encircle, cordon off

**оча́г** *m* [1 *e.*] hearth (*a. fig.*); *fig.* center (-tre), seat

**очаров|а́ние** *n* [12] charm, fascination; **~а́тельный** [14; -лен, -льна] charming; **~ывать** [1], ⟨**~а́ть**⟩ [7] charm, fascinate, enchant

**очеви́д|ец** *m* [1; -дца] eyewitness; **~ный** [14; -ден, -дна] evident, obvious

**о́чень** very; (very) much

**очередно́й** [14] next (in turn); yet another; latest

**о́черед|ь** *f* [8; *from g/pl. e.*] turn (***по ~и*** in turns); order, succession; line (*Brt.* queue); *mil.* volley; ***ва́ша ~ь*** *or* ***~ь за ва́ми*** it is your turn; ***на ~и*** next; ***в свою́ ~ь*** in (for) my, *etc.*, turn (part)

**о́черк** *m* [1] sketch; essay

**очерня́ть** [28] → ***черни́ть***

**очерстве́лый** [14] hardened, callous

**очер|та́ние** *n* [12] outline, contour; **~чивать** [1], ⟨**~ти́ть**⟩ [15] outline, sketch; ***~тя́ го́лову*** *coll.* headlong

**очи́|стка** *f* [5; *g/pl.*: -ток] clean(s)ing; *tech.* refinement; *pl.* peelings; ***для ~стки со́вести*** clear one's conscience; **~ща́ть** [1], ⟨**~стить**⟩ [15] clean(se); clear; peel; purify; *tech.* refine

**очк|и́** *n/pl.* [1] spectacles, eyeglasses; ***защи́тные ~и́*** protective goggles; **~о́** *n* [9; *pl.*: -ки́, -ко́в] *sport*: point; *cards*: spot, *Brt.* pip; **~овтира́тельство** *coll. n* [9] eyewash, deception

**очну́ться** [20] *pf.* → ***опо́мниться***

**очути́ться** [15; *1 st. p. sg. not used*] find o.s.; come to be

**ошале́лый** *coll.* [14] crazy, mad

**оше́йник** *m* [1] collar (*on a dog only*)

**ошелом|ля́ть** [28], ⟨**~и́ть**⟩ [14 *e.*; -млю́, -ми́шь; -млённый] stun, stupefy

**ошиб|а́ться** [1], ⟨**~и́ться**⟩ [-бу́сь, -бёшься; -и́бся, -и́блась] be mistaken, make a mistake, err; be wrong *or* at fault; **~ка** *f* [5; *g/pl.*: -бок] mistake (***по*** Д by), error, fault; **~очный** [14; -чен, -чна] erroneous, mistaken

**ошпа́р|ивать** [1], ⟨**~ить**⟩ [13] scald

**ощу́п|ывать**, ⟨**~ать**⟩ [1] feel, grope about; touch; **´~ь** *f* [8]: ***на ´~ь*** to the touch; ***дви́гаться на ´~ь*** grope one's way; **´~ью** *adv.* gropingly; *fig.* blindly

**ощу|ти́мый** [14 *sh.*], **~ти́тельный** [14; -лен, -льна] palpable, tangible; felt; (*заметный*) appreciable; **~ща́ть** [1], ⟨**~ти́ть**⟩ [15 *e.*; -ущу́, -ути́шь; -ущённый] feel, sense; experience; **-ся** be felt; **~ще́ние** *n* [12] sensation; feeling

О

# П

**павиа́н** *m* [1] baboon
**павильо́н** *m* [1] pavilion; exhibition hall
**павли́н** *m* [1], **~ий** [18] peacock
**па́водок** *m* [1; -дка] flood, freshet
**па́|губный** [14; -бен, -бна] ruinous, pernicious; **~даль** *f* [8] carrion
**па́да|ть** [1] **1.** ⟨упа́сть⟩ [25; *pt. st.*] fall; *цена* drop; **2.** ⟨пасть⟩ [15] *fig.* fall; ***~ть ду́хом*** lose heart
**пад|е́ж**[1] *m* [1 *e.*] *gr.* case; **~ёж**[2] *m* [1 *e.*] *скота* murrain; epizootic; **~е́ние** *n* [12] fall; *fig.* downfall; **~кий** [16; -док, -дка] (***на*** B) greedy (for), having a weakness (for)
**па́дчерица** *f* [5] stepdaughter
**паёк** *m* [1; пайка́] ration
**па́зух|а** *f* [5] bosom (***за*** B, ***за*** T in); *anat.* sinus; ***держа́ть ка́мень за ~ой*** harbo(u)r a grudge (against)
**пай** *m* [3; *pl. e.*: пай, паёв] share; **~щик** *m* [1] shareholder
**паке́т** *m* [1] parcel, package, packet; paper bag
**па́кля** *f* [6] (*material*) tow, oakum
**пакова́ть** [7], ⟨у-, за-⟩ pack
**па́кость** *f* [8] filth, smut; dirty trick; **пакт** *m* [1] pact, treaty
**пала́т|а** *f* [5] chamber (*often used in names of state institutions*); *parl.* house; *больничная* ward; ***оруже́йная ~а*** armo(u)ry; **~ка** *f* [5; *g/pl.*: -ток] tent; ***в ~ках*** under canvas
**пала́ч** *m* [1 *e.*] hangman, executioner; *fig.* butcher
**па́л|ец** *m* [1; -льца] finger; *ноги* toe; ***смотре́ть сквозь па́льцы*** connive (***на*** B at); ***знать как свой пять ~ьцев*** have at one's fingertips; **~иса́дник** *m* [1] (small) front garden
**пали́тра** *f* [5] palette
**пали́ть** [13] **1.** ⟨c-⟩ burn, scorch; **2.** ⟨o-⟩ singe; **3.** ⟨вы́-⟩ fire, shoot
**па́л|ка** *f* [5; *g/pl.*: -лок] stick; *трость* cane; ***из-под ~ки*** *coll.* under constraint; ***э́то ~ка о двух конца́х*** it cuts both ways; **~очка** *f* [5; *g/pl.*: -чек] (small) stick; *mus.* baton; *волшебная* wand; *med.* bacillus
**паломни|к** *m* [1] pilgrim; **~чество** *n* [9] pilgrimage
**па́лтус** *m* [1] halibut
**па́луба** *f* [5] deck
**пальба́** *f* [5] firing; fire
**па́льма** *f* [5] palm (tree)
**пальто́** *n* [*indecl.*] (over)coat
**па́мят|ник** *m* [1] monument, memorial; **~ный** [14; -тен, -тна] memorable, unforgettable; **~ь** *f* [8] memory (***на, о*** П in/of); remembrance; recollection (***о*** П of); ***на ~ь*** *a.* by heart; ***бымь без ~и*** *coll.* be crazy (**от** P about s.o.)
**пане́ль** *f* [8] panel; panel(l)ing
**па́ника** *f* [5] panic
**панихи́да** *f* [5] funeral service; ***гражда́нская ~*** civil funeral
**пансиона́т** *m* [1] boardinghouse
**панте́ра** *f* [5] panther
**па́нты** *f/pl.* [5] antlers of young Siberian stag
**па́нцирь** *m* [4] coat of mail
**па́па**[1] *coll. m* [5] papa, dad(dy)
**па́па**[2] *m* [5] pope
**па́перть** *f* [8] porch (*of a church*)
**папиро́са** *f* [5] *Russian cigarette*
**па́пка** *f* [5; *g/pl.*: -пок] folder; file
**па́поротник** *m* [1] fern
**пар** [1; в -у; *pl. e.*] **1.** steam; **2.** fallow
**па́ра** *f* [5] pair, couple
**пара́граф** *m* [1] *текста* section; *договора и т. д.* article
**пара́д** *m* [1] parade; **~ный** [14] *форма* full; *дверь* front
**парадо́кс** *m* [1] paradox; **~а́льный** [14; -лен, -льна] paradoxical
**парали|зова́ть** [7] (*im*)*pf.* paralyze (*a. fig.*); **~ч** *m* [1] paralysis
**паралле́ль** *f* [8] parallel; ***провести́ ~*** draw a parallel; (*между*) between
**парашю́т** (-'ʃut) *m* [1] parachute; **~и́ст** [1] parachutist
**паре́ние** *n* [12] soar(ing), hover(ing)
**па́рень** *m* [4; -рня; *from g/pl. e.*] lad, boy;

*coll.* chap
**пари́** *n* [*indecl.*] bet, wager (*vb.*: **держа́ть ~**)
**париж|а́нин** *m* [1; *pl.*: -а́не, -а́н], **~а́нка** *f* [5; *g/pl.*: -нок] Parisian
**пари́к** *m* [1 *e.*] wig; **~ма́хер** *m* [1] hairdresser, barber; **~ма́херская** *f* [16] hairdressing salon, barber's (shop)
**пари́|ровать** [7] (*im*)*pf.*, *a.* ⟨от-⟩ parry; **~ть**¹ [13] soar, hover
**па́рить**² [13] steam (*in a bath*: **-ся**)
**парке́т** *m* [1], **~ный** [14] parquet
**парла́мент** *m* [1] parliament; **~а́рий** *m* [3] parliamentarian; **~ский** [16] parliamentary
**парни́к** *m* [1 *e.*], **~о́вый** [14] hotbed; **~о́вый эффе́кт** greenhouse effect
**парни́шка** *m* [5; *g/pl.*: -шек] *coll.* boy, lad, youngster
**па́рный** [14] paired; twin…
**паро|во́з** *m* [1] steam locomotive; **~во́й** [14] steam…; **~ди́ровать** [7] (*im*)*pf.*, **~́дия** *f* [7] parody
**паро́ль** *m* [4] password, parole
**паро́м** *m* [1] ferry(boat); **переправля́ть на ~е** ferry; **~щик** *m* [1] ferryman
**парохо́д** *m* [1] steamer; **~ный** [14] steamship…; **~ство** *n* [9] steamship line
**па́рт|а** *f* [5] school desk; **~е́р** (-'tɛr) *m* [1] *thea.* stalls; **~иза́н** *m* [1] guerilla, partisan; **~иту́ра** *f* [5] *mus.* score; **~ия** *f* [7] party; *comm.* lot, consignment, batch; *sport* game; set; match; *mus.* part; **~нёр** *m* [1], **~нёрша** *f* [5] partner
**па́рус** *m* [1; *pl.*: -са́, *etc. e.*] sail; **на всех ~а́х** under full sail; **~и́на** *f* [5] sailcloth, canvas, duck; **~и́новый** [14] canvas…; **~ник** *m* [1] = **~ное су́дно** *n* [14/9] sailing ship
**парфюме́рия** *f* [7] perfumery
**парч|а́** *f* [5], **~о́вый** brocade
**парши́вый** [14 *sh.*] mangy; *coll. настроение* bad
**пас** *m* [1] pass (*sport*, *cards*); **я ~** count me out
**па́сека** *f* [5] apiary
**па́сквиль** *m* [4] lampoon
**па́смурный** [14; -рен, -рна] dull, cloudy; *вид* gloomy
**пасова́ть** [7] pass (*sport*; *cards*, ⟨с-⟩; *coll.* give in, yield (**пе́ред** T to)
**па́спорт** *m* [1; *pl.*: -та́, *etc. e.*], **~ный** [14] passport
**пассажи́р** *m* [1], **~ка** *f* [5; *g/pl.*: -рок], **~ский** [16] passenger
**пасси́в** *m* [1] *comm.* liabilities *pl.*; **~ный** [14; -вен, -вна] passive
**па́ста** *f* [5] paste; **зубна́я ~** toothpaste
**па́ст|бище** *n* [11] pasture; **~ва** *f* [5] *eccl.* flock; **~и́** [24 -с-] graze (*v/i.* **-сь**), pasture; **~у́х** *m* [1 *e.*] herdsman, shepherd; **~ь 1.** → **па́дать**; **2.** *f* [8] jaws *pl.*, mouth
**Па́сха** *f* [5] Easter (**на** B for); Easter pudding (*sweet dish of cottage cheese*); **~́льный** [14] Easter…
**па́сынок** *m* [1; -нка] stepson
**пате́нт** *m* [1], **~ова́ть** [7] (*im*)*pf.*, *a.* ⟨за-⟩ patent
**па́тока** *f* [5] molasses, *Brt. a.* treacle
**патр|ио́т** *m* [1] patriot; **~иоти́ческий** [16] patriotic; **~о́н** *m* [1] cartridge, shell; (lamp) socket; **~онта́ш** *m* [1] cartridge belt, pouch; **~ули́ровать** [7], **~у́ль** *m* [4 *e.*] *mil.* patrol
**па́уза** *f* [5] pause
**пау́к** *m* [1 *e.*] spider
**паути́на** *f* [5] cobweb
**па́фос** *m* [1] pathos; enthusiasm, zeal (for)
**пах** *m* [1; в -у́] *anat.* groin
**паха́ть** [3], ⟨вс-⟩ plow (*Brt.* plough), till
**па́хн|уть**¹ [20] smell (T of); **~у́ть**² [20] *pf. coll.* puff, blow
**па́хот|а** *f* [5] tillage; **~ный** [14] arable
**паху́чий** [17 *sh.*] odorous, strongsmelling
**пацие́нт** *m* [1], **~ка** *f* [5; *g/pl.*: -ток] patient
**па́чка** *f* [5; *g/pl.*: -чек] pack(et), package; *писем* batch
**па́чкать** [1], ⟨за-, ис-, вы-⟩ soil
**па́шня** *f* [6; *g/pl.*: -шен] tillage, field
**паште́т** *m* [1] pâté
**пая́льник** *m* [1] soldering iron
**пая́ть** [28], ⟨за-⟩ solder
**пев|е́ц** *m* [1; -вца], **~и́ца** *f* [5] singer; **~у́чий** [17 *sh.*] melodious; **~́чий** [17] singing; **~́чая пти́ца** songbird; *su. eccl.* choirboy
**педаго́г** *m* [1] pedagogue, teacher; **~ика**

П

*f* [5] pedagogics; **~и́ческий** [16]: **~и́ческий институ́т** teachers' training college; **~и́чный** [14; -чен, -чна] sensible

**педа́ль** *f* [8] treadle, pedal

**педа́нт** *m* [1] pedant; **~и́чный** [14; -чен, -чна] pedantic

**педиа́тр** *m* [1] p(a)ediatrician

**пейза́ж** *m* [1] landscape

**пека́р|ня** *f* [6; *g/pl.*: -рен] bakery; **~ь** *m* [4; *a.* -ря́, *etc. e.*] baker

**пелен|а́** *f* [5] shroud; **~а́ть** [1], ⟨за-, с-⟩ swaddle

**пелён|ка** *f* [5; *g/pl.*: -нок] diaper, *Brt. a.* nappy; **с ~ок** *fig.* from the cradle

**пельме́ни** *m/pl.* [-ней] *cul.* kind of ravioli

**пе́на** *f* [5] foam, froth; *мыльная* lather, soapsuds

**пе́ние** *n* [12] singing; *петуха* crow

**пе́н|истый** [14 *sh.*] foamy, frothy; **~иться** [13], ⟨вс-⟩ foam, froth; **~ка** *f* [5; *g/pl.*: -нок] *на молоке и т. д.* skin; **снять ~ки** skim (**с** P); *fig.* take the pickings (of)

**пенси|оне́р** *m* [1] pensioner; **~о́нный** [14], **´~я** *f* [7] pension

**пень** *m* [4; пня] stump

**пеньк|а́** *f* [5] hemp; **~о́вый** [14] hemp(en)

**пе́ня** *f* [6; *g/pl.*: -ней] fine (*penalty*)

**пеня́|ть** *coll.* [28]: blame; **~й на себя́!** it's your own fault!

**пе́пел** [1; -пла] ashes *pl.*; **~и́ще** *n* [11] site of a fire; **~ьница** *f* [5] ashtray; **~ьный** [14] ashy; *цвет* ashgrey

**пе́рвен|ец** *m* [1; -нца] first-born; **~ство** *n* [9] first place; *sport* championship

**перви́чный** [14; -чен, -чна] primary

**перво|бы́тный** [14; -тен, -тна] primitive, primeval; **~исто́чник** *m* [1] primary source; origin; **~кла́ссный** [14] first-rate *or* -class; **~ку́рсник** *m* [1] freshman; **´~-на́перво** P *coll.* first of all; **~нача́льный** [14; -лен, -льна] original; primary; **~очередно́й** [14] first and foremost; immediate; **~со́ртный** → **~кла́ссный**; **~степе́нный** [14; -е́нен, -е́нна] paramount, of the first order

**пе́рв|ый** [14] first; former; earliest; **~ый эта́ж** first (*Brt.* ground) floor; **~ое вре́мя** at first; **~ая по́мощь** first aid; **~ый рейс** maiden voyage; **из ~ых рук** firsthand; **на ~ый взгляд** at first sight; **~ое** *n* first course (*meal*; **на** B for); **~ым де́лом** (**до́лгом**) *or* **в ~ую о́чередь** first of all, first thing; *coll.* **~е́йший** the very first; → **пя́тый**

**перга́мент** *m* [1] parchment

**переб|ега́ть** [1], ⟨**~ежа́ть**⟩ [4; -егу́, -ежи́шь, -егу́т] run over (*or* across); **~е́жчик** *m* [1] traitor, turncoat; **~ива́ть** [1], ⟨**~и́ть**⟩ [-бью, -бьёшь, → **би́ть**] interrupt

**переб|ива́ться** ⟨**~и́ться**⟩ *coll.* make ends meet

**переб|ира́ть** [1], ⟨**~ра́ть**⟩ [-беру́, -рёшь; -бра́л, -а́, -о; -е́бранный] look through; sort out (*a. fig.*); turn over, think over; *impf. mus.* finger; **-ся** move (**на, в** B into); cross (*v/t.* **че́рез** B)

**переб|и́ть 1.** → **~ива́ть**; **2.** *pf.* kill, slay; *посуду* break; **~о́й** *m* [3] interruption, intermission; **~оро́ть** [17] *pf.* overcome, master

**пребр|а́нка** F *f* [5; *g/pl.*: -нок] wrangle; **~а́сывать** [1], ⟨**~о́сить**⟩ [15] throw over; *mil., comm.* transfer, shift; **-ся**; *словами* exchange (*v/t.* T); **~а́ть(ся)** → **перебира́ть(ся)**; **~о́ска** *f* [5; *g/pl.*: -сок] transfer

**перева́л** *m* [1] pass; **~ивать** [1], ⟨**~и́ть**⟩ [13; -алю́, -а́лишь; -а́ленный] transfer, shift (*v/i.* **-ся**; *impf.* waddle); *coll.* cross, pass; *impers.* **ему́ ~и́ло за 40** he is past 40

**перева́р|ивать** [1], ⟨**~и́ть**⟩ [13; -арю́, -а́ришь; -а́ренный] digest; *coll. fig.* **она́ его́ не ~ивает** she can't stand him

**пере|везти́** → **~вози́ть**; **~вёртывать** [1], ⟨**~верну́ть**⟩ [20; -вёрнутый] turn over (*v/i.* **-ся**); **~ве́с** *m* [1] preponderance; **~вести́(сь)** → **переводи́ть(ся)**; **~ве́шивать** [1], ⟨**~ве́сить**⟩ [15] hang (elsewhere); reweigh; *fig.* outweigh; **-ся** lean over; **~вира́ть** [1], ⟨**~вра́ть**⟩ [-вру́, -врёшь; -е́вранный] *coll.* garble; misquote; misinterpret

**перево́д** *m* [1] transfer; translation (**с** P/**на** B from/into); *денег* remittance; *почтовый* (money *or* postal) order;

П

**~и́ть** [15], ⟨перевести́⟩ [25] lead; transfer; translate (с/**на** В from/into) interpret; remit; set (*watch, clock; usu.* **стре́лку**); ***~и́ть дух*** take a breath; **-ся**, ⟨-сь⟩ be transferred, move; **~ный** [14] translated; (*a. comm.*) transfer…; **~чик** *m* [1], **~чица** *f* [5] translator; interpreter

**перевоз|и́ть** [15], ⟨перевезти́⟩ [24] transport, convey; *мебель* remove; *через реку и т. д.* ferry (over); **~ка** *f* [5; *g/pl.*: -зок] transportation, conveyance, ferrying, *etc.*

**пере|вооруже́ние** *n* [12] rearmament; **~вора́чивать** [1] → ***~вёртывать***; **~воро́т** *m* [1] revolution; *государственный* coup d'état; **~воспита́ние** *n* [12] reeducation; **~вра́ть** → ***~вира́ть***; **~вы́боры** *m/pl.* [1] reelection

**перевя́з|ка** *f* [5; *g/pl.*: -зок] dressing, bandage; **~очный** [14] dressing…; **~ывать** [1], ⟨**~а́ть**⟩ [3] tie up; *рану и т. д.* dress, bandage

**переги́б** *m* [1] bend, fold; *fig.* exaggeration; **~а́ть** [1], ⟨перегну́ть⟩ [20] bend; ***~а́ть па́лку*** go too far; **-ся** lean over

**перегля́|дываться** [1], *once* ⟨**~ну́ться**⟩ [19] exchange glances

**пере|гна́ть** → ***~гоня́ть***; **~гно́й** *m* [3] humus; **~гну́ть(ся)** → ***~гиба́ть*(ся)**

**перегов|а́ривать** [1], ⟨**~ори́ть**⟩ [13] talk (s. th) over (***о*** T), discuss; **~о́ры** *m/pl.* [1] negotiations; ***вести́ ~о́ры*** (**с** T) negotiate (with)

**перег|о́нка** *f* [5] distillation; **~оня́ть** [28], ⟨**~на́ть**⟩ [-гоню́, -го́нишь; -гна́л, -а́, -ой; -е́гнанный] **1.** outdistance, leave behind; *fig.* overtake, outstrip, surpass, outdo; **2.** *chem.* distil

**перегор|а́живать** [1], ⟨**~оди́ть**⟩ [15 & 15 *e.*; -рожу́, -роди́шь] partition (off); **~а́ть** [1], ⟨**~е́ть**⟩ [9] *лампочка, пробка* burn out; **~о́дка** *f* [5; *g/pl.*: -док] partition

**перегр|ева́ть** [1], ⟨**~е́ть**⟩ [8; -е́тый] overheat; **~ужа́ть** [1], ⟨**~узи́ть**⟩ [15 & 15 *e.*; -ужу́, -у́зишь], overload; **~у́зка** *f* [5; *g/pl.*: -зок] *двигателя* overload; *о работе* overwork; **~уппирова́ть** [7] *pf.* regroup; **~уппиро́вка** *f* [5; -вок] regrouping; **~ыза́ть** [1], ⟨**~ы́зть**⟩ [24; *pt. st.*: -ы́зенный] gnaw through

**пе́ред**¹, **~о** (T) before; in front of; ***извини́ться ~ кем-л.*** apologize to s.o.

**перёд**² *m* [1; пе́реда; *pl.*: -да́, *etc. e.*] front

**перед|ава́ть** [5], ⟨**~а́ть**⟩ [-да́м, -да́шь, *etc.* → ***да́ть***; *pt.* пе́редал, -а́, -о] pass, hand (over), deliver; give (*a. привет*); *radio, TV* broadcast, transmit; *содержание* render; tell; *по телефону* take a message (for Д, *on the phone*); **-ся** *med.* be transmitted, communicated; **~а́тчик** *m* [1] transmitter; **~а́ть(ся)** → ***~ава́ть*(ся)**; **~а́ча** *f* [5] delivery, handing over; transfer; broadcast, (*a. tech.*) transmission; *mot.* gear

**передв|ига́ть** [1], ⟨**~и́нуть**⟩ [20] move, shift; **~иже́ние** *n* [12] movement; *грузов* transportation; **~ижно́й** [14] travel(l)ing, mobile

**переде́л|ка** [5; *g/pl.*: -лок] alteration; *coll.* ***попа́сть в ~ку*** get into a pretty mess; **~ывать**, ⟨**~ать**⟩ [1] do again; alter; ***~ать мно́го дел*** do a lot

**пере́дн|ий** [15] front…, fore…; **~ик** *m* [1] apron; **~яя** *f* [15] (entrance) hall, lobby

**передов|и́ца** *f* [5] leading article, editorial; **~о́й** [14] foremost; *mil.* frontline; ***~а́я статья́ → передови́ца***

**пере|дохну́ть** [20] *pf.* pause for breath *or* a rest; **~дра́знивать** [1], ⟨дразни́ть⟩ [13; -азню́, -а́знишь] mimic; **~дря́га** *coll. f* [5] fix, scrape; **~ду́мывать**, ⟨**~ду́мать**⟩ [1] change one's mind; *coll.* → ***обду́мать***; **~ды́шка** *f* [5; *g/pl.*: -шек] breathing space, respite

**пере|е́зд** *m* [1] *rail., etc.* crossing; *в другое место* move (**в, на** В [in]to); **~езжа́ть** [1], ⟨**~е́хать**⟩ [-е́ду, -е́дешь; -езжа́й!] **1.** *v/i.* cross (*v/t.* ***че́рез*** B); move (B, ***на*** B [in]to); **2.** *v/t. машиной* run over

**переж|да́ть** → ***~ида́ть***; **~ёвывать** [1], ⟨**~ева́ть**⟩ [7 *e.*; -жую́, -жуёшь] masticate, chew; *fig.* repeat over and over again; **~ива́ние** *n* [12] emotional experience; worry *etc.*; **~ива́ть**, ⟨**~и́ть**⟩ [-живу́, -вёшь; пе́режи́л, -а́, -о; пе́режи́тый (пе́режи́т, -а́, -о)] experience; live through, endure; *жить дольше* survive, outlive; **~идать** [1], ⟨**~дать**⟩ [-жду́, -ждёшь; -ждал, -а́, -о] wait (till s.th. is over); **~иток** *m* [1; -тка] survival

**перезаклю|чать** [1], ⟨**~чить**⟩ [16 *e*.; -чу́, -чи́шь; -чённый]: ***~чить догово́р* (*контра́кт*)** renew a contract

**перезре́лый** [14] overripe; *fig.* past one's prime

**переиз|бира́ть** [1], ⟨**~бра́ть**⟩ [-беру́, -рёшь; -бра́л, -а́, -о; -и́збранный] reelect; **~бра́ние** *n* [12] reelection; **~дава́ть** [5], ⟨**~да́ть**⟩ [-да́м, -да́шь, *etc.* → ***дать***; -да́л, -а́, -о] reprint, republish; **~да́ние** *n* [12] republication; new edition, reprint; **~да́ть** → ***~дава́ть***

**переименова́ть** [7] *pf.* rename

**переина́чи|вать** *coll.* [1], ⟨**~ть**⟩ [16] alter, modify; (*исказить*) distort

**перейти́** → ***переходи́ть***

**переки́|дывать** [1], ⟨**~нуть**⟩ [20] throw over (че́рез B); **-ся** exchange (*v/t.* T); *огонь* spread

**переки|па́ть** [1], ⟨**~пе́ть**⟩ [10 *e*.; 3rd *p. only*] boil over

**пе́рекись** *f* [8] *chem.* peroxide; ***~ водоро́да*** hydrogen peroxide

**перекла́д|ина** *f* [5] crossbar, crossbeam; **~ывать** [1], ⟨**переложи́ть**⟩ [16] put, lay (elsewhere); move, shift; interlay (T with); → ***перелага́ть***

**перекл|ика́ться** [1], ⟨**~и́кнуться**⟩ [20] call to o.a.; have s.th. in common (**с** T with); reecho (*v/t.* **с** T)

**переключ|а́тель** *m* [4] switch; **~а́ть** [1], ⟨**~и́ть**⟩ [16; -чу́, -чи́шь; -чённый] switch over (*v/i.* **-ся**); *внимание* switch; **~е́ние** *n* [12] switching over; **~и́ть** → ***~а́ть***

**переко́шенный** [14] twisted, distorted; *дверь и т. д.* warped; wry

**перекрёст|ный** [14] cross...; ***~ный ого́нь*** cross-fire; ***~ный допро́с*** cross-examination; **~ок** *m* [1; -тка] crossroads, crossing

**перекр|ыва́ть** [1], ⟨**~ы́ть**⟩ [22] cover again; *рекорд и т. д.* exceed, surpass; *закрыть* close; *реку* dam; **~ы́тие** *n* [12] *arch.* ceiling; floor

**перекý́с|ывать** [1], ⟨**~и́ть**⟩ [15] bite through; *coll.* have a bite *or* snack

**перел|ага́ть** [1], ⟨**~ожи́ть**⟩ [16]: ***~ожи́ть на му́зыку*** set to music

**перел|а́мывать** [1] **1.** ⟨**~оми́ть**⟩ [14] break in two; *fig.* overcome; change; **2.** ⟨**~ома́ть**⟩ [1] break

**перел|еза́ть** [1], ⟨**~е́зть**⟩ [24 *st.*; -ле́з] climb over, get over (***че́рез*** B)

**перел|ёт** *m* [1] *птиц* passage; *ae.* flight; **~ета́ть** [1], ⟨**~ете́ть**⟩ [11] fly over (across); migrate; overshoot; **~ётный** [14]: ***~ётная пти́ца*** bird of passage *a. fig.*, migratory bird

**перели́|в** *m* [1] *голоса* modulation; *цвета* play; **~ва́ние** *n* [12] *med.* transfusion; **~ва́ть** [1], ⟨**~ть**⟩ [-пью́, -льёшь, *etc.*, → **лить**] decant, pour from one vessel into another; *med.* transfuse; ***~ва́ть из пусто́го в поро́жнее*** mill the wind; **-ся** overflow; *impf. о цвете* play, shimmer

**перели́ст|ывать**, ⟨**~а́ть**⟩ [1] *страницы* turn over; *книгу* look *or* leaf through

**перели́ть** → ***перелива́ть***

**перелицева́ть** [7] *pf.* turn, make over

**перелож|е́ние** *n* [12] transposition; arrangement; *на музыку* setting to music; **~и́ть** → ***перекла́дывать***, ***перелага́ть***

**перело́м** *m* [1] break, fracture; *fig.* crisis, turning point; **~а́ть**, **~и́ть** → ***перела́мывать***

**перем|а́лывать** [1], ⟨**~оло́ть**⟩ [17; -мелю́, -ме́лешь; -меля́] grind, mill; **~ежа́ть(ся)** [1] alternate

**переме́н|а** *f* [5] change; *в школе* break; **~и́ть(ся)** → ***~я́ть(ся)***; **~ный** [14] variable; *el.* alternating; **~чивый** *coll.* [14] changeable; **~я́ть** [28], ⟨**~и́ть**⟩ [13; -еню́, -е́нишь] change (*v/i.* **-ся**)

**переме|сти́ть(ся)** → ***~ща́ть(ся)***; **~шивать**, ⟨**~ша́ть**⟩ [1] intermingle, intermix; *coll.* mix (up); **-ся**: ***у меня́ в голове́ всё ~ша́лось*** I feel confused; **~ща́ть** [1], ⟨**~сти́ть**⟩ [15 *e*.; -ещу́, -ести́шь; -ещённый] move, shift (*v/i.* **-ся**)

**переми́рие** *n* [12] armistice, truce

**перемоло́ть** → ***перема́лывать***

**перенаселе́ние** *n* [12] overpopulation

**перенести́** → ***переноси́ть***

**перен|има́ть** [1], ⟨**~я́ть**⟩ [-ейму́, -мёшь; перен́ял, -а́, -о; пе́ренятый (пе́ренят, -а́, -о)] adopt; *манеру и т. д.* imitate
**перено́с** *m* [1] *typ*. word division; ***знак ~а*** hyphen; **~и́ть**, ⟨**перенести́**⟩ [24 -с-] transfer, carry over; (*испытать*) bear, endure, stand; (*отложить*) postpone, put off (till ***на*** В); **~ица** *f* [5] bridge (*of nose*)
**перено́с|ка** *f* [5; *g/pl*.: -сок] carrying over; **~ный** [14] portable; figurative
**переня́ть** → ***перенима́ть***
**переобору́дова|ть** [7] (*im*)*pf*; refit, reequip; **~ние** *n* [12] reequipment
**переод|ева́ться** [1], ⟨**~е́ться**⟩ [-е́нусь, -нешься] change (one's clothes); **~е́тый** [14 *sh*.] *a*. disguised
**переоце́н|ивать** [1], ⟨**~и́ть**⟩ [13; -еню́, -е́нишь] overestimate, overrate; (*оценить заново*) revalue; **~ка** *f* [5; *g/pl*.: -нок] overestimation; revaluation
**пе́репел** *m* [1; *pl*.: -ла́, *etc. e*.] *zo*. quail
**перепеча́т|ка** *f* [5; *g/pl*.: -ток] reprint; **~ывать**, ⟨**~ать**⟩ [1] reprint; *на машинке* type
**перепи́с|ка** *f* [5; *g/pl*.: -сок] correspondence; **~ывать** [1], ⟨**~а́ть**⟩ [3] rewrite, copy; ***~а́ть на́бело*** make a fair copy; **-ся** *impf*. correspond (**с** Т with); **~ь** ('pe-) *f* [8] census
**перепла́|чивать** [1], ⟨**~ти́ть**⟩ [15] overpay
**перепл|ета́ть** [1], ⟨**~ести́**⟩ [25 -т-] *книгу* bind; interlace, intertwine (*v/i*. **-ся** ⟨-сь⟩); **~ёт** *m* [1] binding, book cover; **~ётчик** *m* [1] bookbinder; **~ыва́ть** [1], ⟨**~ы́ть**⟩ [23] swim *or* sail (***че́рез*** В across)
**переполз|а́ть** [1], ⟨**~ти́**⟩ [24] creep, crawl
**перепо́лн|енный** [14 *sh*.] overcrowded; *жидкостью* overflowing; overfull; **~я́ть** [28], ⟨**~ить**⟩ [13] overfill; **-ся** (*v/i*.) be overcrowded
**переполо́|х** *m* [1] commotion, alarm, flurry; **~ши́ть** *coll*. [16 *e*.; -шу́, -ши́шь; -шённый] *pf*. (**-ся** get) alarm(ed)
**перепо́нка** [5; *g/pl*. -нок] membrane; *птицы* web; ***бараба́нная ~*** eardrum
**перепра́в|а** *f* [5] crossing, passage; *брод* ford; temporary bridge; **~ля́ть** [28], ⟨**~ить**⟩ [14] carry (over), convey, take across; transport (to); *mail* forward; **-ся** cross, get across
**перепрод|ава́ть** [5], ⟨**~а́ть**⟩ [-да́м, -да́шь, *etc*. → ***дать***; *pt*.: -о́да́л, -да́, -о] resell; **~а́жа** *f* [5] resale
**перепры́г|ивать** [1], ⟨**~нуть**⟩ [20] jump (over)
**перепу́г** *coll*. *m* [1] fright (of **с ~у**); **~а́ть** [1] *pf*. (**-ся** get) frighten(ed)
**перепу́тывать** [1] → ***пу́тать***
**перепу́тье** *n* [10] *fig*. crossroad(s)
**перераб|а́тывать**, ⟨**~о́тать**⟩ [1] work into; remake; *книгу* revise; **~о́тка** *f* [5; *g/pl*.: -ток] processing; remaking; revision; ***~о́тка втори́чного сырья́*** recycling
**перерас|та́ть** [1], ⟨**~ти́**⟩ [24; -ст-; -ро́с, -сла́] (*видоизмениться*) grow, develop; *о росте* outstrip; **~хо́д** *m* [1] excess expenditure
**перерез|а́ть** *and* **~ывать** [1], ⟨**~а́ть**⟩ [3] cut (through); cut off, intercept; kill (all *or* many of)
**переро|жда́ться** [1], ⟨**~ди́ться**⟩ [15 *e*.; -ожу́сь, -оди́шься; -ождённый] *coll*. be reborn; *fig*. regenerate; *biol*. degenerate
**переруб|а́ть** [1], ⟨**~и́ть**⟩ [14] hew *or* cut through
**переры́в** *m* [1] interruption; break; interval; ***~ на обе́д*** lunch time
**переса́|дка** *f* [5; *g/pl*.: -док] *bot*., *med*. transplanting; *med*. grafting; *rail*. change; **~живать** [1], ⟨**~ди́ть**⟩ [15] transplant; graft; make change seats; **-ся**, ⟨**пересе́сть**⟩ [25; -ся́ду, -ся́дешь, -се́л] take another seat, change seats; *rail*. change (*trains*)
**пересд|ава́ть** [5], ⟨**~а́ть**⟩ [-да́м, -да́шь, *etc*., → ***дать***] repeat (*exam*.)
**пересе|ка́ть** [1], ⟨**~чь**⟩ [26; *pt*. -се́к, -секла́] traverse; intersect, cross (*v/i*. **-ся**)
**пересел|е́нец** *m* [1; -нца] migrant; (re)settler; **~е́ние** *n* [12] (e)migration; **~я́ть** [28], ⟨**~и́ть**⟩ [13] (re)move (*v/i*. **-ся**; [e]migrate)
**пересе́сть** → ***переса́живаться***
**пересе|че́ние** *n* [12] crossing; intersec-

П

tion; ˷чь → ***~кáть***
**переси́ли|вать** [1], ⟨~ть⟩ [13] overpower; *fig.* master, subdue
**переска́з** *m* [1] retelling; **~ывать** [1], ⟨~áть⟩ [3] retell
**переск|áкивать** [1], ⟨~очи́ть⟩ [16] jump (over ***чéрез*** В); *при чтении* skip over
**переслáть** → ***пересылáть***
**пересм|áтривать** [1], ⟨~отрéть⟩ [9; -отрю́, -óтришь; -óтренный] reconsider, *планы* revise; *law* review; **~óтр** *m* [1] reconsideration, revision; *law* review
**пересо|ли́ть** [13; -солю́, -óли́шь] *pf.* put too much salt (**в** В in); *coll. fig.* go too far; ˷**хнуть** → ***пересыхáть***
**переспáть** → ***спать***; oversleep; *coll.* spend the night; sleep with s.o.
**переспр|áшивать** [1], ⟨~оси́ть⟩ [15] repeat one's question
**пересcóриться** [13] *pf.* quarrel (*mst. with everybody*)
**перест|авáть** [5], ⟨~áть⟩ [-áну, -áнешь] stop, cease, quit; **~авля́ть** [28], ⟨~áвить⟩ [14] put (elsewhere), (*тж. часы*) set, move; *мебель* rearrange; **~анóвка** *f* [5; *g/pl.*: -вок] transposition; rearrangement; *math.* permutation; **~áть** → ***~авáть***
**перестр|áивать** [1], ⟨~óить⟩ [13] rebuild, reconstruct; *работу* reorganize; *силы* regroup; **-ся** (*v/i.*) adapt, change one's views; **~éливаться** [1], **~éлка** *f* [5; *g/pl.*: -лок] firing; skirmish; **~óить** → ***~áивать***; **~óйка** *f* [5; *g/pl.*: -óек] rebuilding, reconstruction; reorganization; perestroika
**переступ|áть** [1], ⟨~и́ть⟩ [14] step over, cross; *fig.* transgress
**пересчи́т|ывать**, ⟨~áть⟩ [1] (re)count; count up
**перес|ылáть** [1], ⟨~лáть⟩ [-ешлю́, -шлёшь; -éсланный] send (over), *деньги* remit; *письмо* forward; **~ы́лка** *f* [5; *g/pl.*: -лок] remittance; ***стóимость ~ы́лки*** postage; carriage; **~ыхáть** [1], ⟨~óхнуть⟩ [21] dry up; *горло* be parched
**перетá|скивать** [1], ⟨~щи́ть⟩ [16] drag *or* carry (***чéрез*** В over, across)
**перет|я́гивать** [1], ⟨~яну́ть⟩ [19] draw (*fig. на свою сторону* win) over; *верёвкой* cord
**переубе|ждáть** [1], ⟨~ди́ть⟩ [15 *e.*; *no 1st. p. sg.*; -ди́шь, -еждённый] make s.o. change his mind
**переу́лок** *m* [1; -лка] lane, alleyway; side street
**переутомл|éние** *n* [12] overstrain; overwork; **~ённый** [14 *sh.*] overtired
**переучёт** *m* [1] stock-taking
**перехвáт|ывать** [1], ⟨~и́ть⟩ [15] intercept, catch; *coll. денег* borrow; *перекусить* have a quick snack
**перехитри́ть** [13] *pf.* outwit
**перехóд** *m* [1] passage; crossing; *fig.* transition; **~и́ть** [15], ⟨перейти́⟩ [-йду́, -дёшь; -шёл, -шлá; → ***идти́***] cross, go over; pass (on), proceed; (**к** Д to); turn (**в** В [in]to); *границы* exceed, transgress; **~ный** [14] transitional; *gr.* transitive; intermittent; **~я́щий** [17] *sport* challenge (*cup, etc.*)
**пéрец** *m* [1; -рца] pepper; ***стручкóвый ~*** paprika
**пéречень** *m* [4; -чня] list; enumeration
**пере|чёркивать** [1], ⟨~черкну́ть⟩ [20] cross out; **~чéсть** → ***~счи́тывать & ~чи́тывать***; **~числя́ть** [28], ⟨~чи́слить⟩ [13] enumerate; *деньги* transfer; **~чи́тывать**, ⟨~читáть⟩ [1] & ⟨~чéсть⟩ [-чту́, -чтёшь, -чёл, -члá] reread; read (many, all ...); ˷**чить** *coll.* [16] contradict; oppose; ´**~чница** *f* [5] pepper-pot; **~шагну́ть** [20] *pf.* step over; cross; **~шéек** *m* [1; -шéйка] isthmus; **~шёптываться** [1] whisper (to one another); **~шивáть** [1], ⟨~ши́ть⟩ [-шью́, -шьёшь, *etc.* → ***шить***] *sew* alter; **~щеголя́ть** *coll.* [28] *pf.* outdo
**пери́ла** *n/pl.* [9] railing; banisters
**пери́на** *f* [5] feather bed
**пери́од** *m* [1] period; *geol.* age; ˷**ика** *f* [5] *collect.* periodicals; **~и́ческий** [16] periodic(al); *math.* recurring
**перифери́я** *f* [7] periphery; outskirts *pl.* (**на** П in); the provinces
**перламу́тр** *m* [1] mother-of-pearl
**перлóвый** [14] pearl (*крупа* barley)
**пернáтые** *pl.* [14] *su.* feathered, feathery (*birds*)

**перó** *n* [9; *pl.*: пéрья, -ьев] feather, plume; pen; ***ни пýха ни перá!*** good-luck!; **~чúнный** [14]: ***~чúнный нó-ж(ик)*** penknife
**перрóн** *m* [1] *rail.* platform
**перс|úдский** [16] Persian; **˜ик** *m* [1] peach; **~óна** *f* [5] person; **~онáл** *m* [1] personnel; staff; **~пектúва** *f* [5] perspective; *fig.* prospect, outlook; **~пектúвный** [14; -вен, -вна] with prospects; forward-looking, promising
**пéрстень** *m* [4; -тня] ring (*with a precious stone*, *etc.*)
**пéрхоть** *f* [8] dandruff
**перчáтка** *f* [5; *g/pl.*: -ток] glove
**пёс** *m* [1; пса] dog
**пéсенка** *f* [5; *g/pl.*: -нок] song
**песéц** *m* [1; песцá] Arctic fox; ***бéлый*** (***голубóй***) **~** white (blue) fox (fur)
**пéсн|ь** *f* [8] (*poet.*, *eccl.*), **~я** *f* [6; *g/pl.*: -сен] song; *coll.* ***дóлгая ~я*** long story; ***стáрая ~я*** it's the same old story
**песó|к** *m* [1; -скá] sand; *сахарный* granulated sugar; **~чный** [14] sand(y); ***~чное печéнье*** shortbread
**пессимистúч|еский** [16], **~ный** [14; -чен, -чна] pessimistic
**пестр|éть** [8] *ошибками* be full (of); **~úть** [13], **пёстрый** [14; пёстр, пестрá, пёстро & пестрó] variegated, parti-colo(u)red, motley (*a. fig.*); gay
**песч|áный** [14] sand(y); **~úнка** *f* [5; *g/pl.*: -нок] grain (of sand)
**петлúца** *f* [5] buttonhole; tab
**пéтля** *f* [6; *g/pl.*: -тель] loop (*a.*, *ae.*, ***мёртвая ~***); *для крючка* eye; stitch; *дверная* hinge; ***спустúть пéтлю*** drop a stitch
**петрýшка** *f* [5] parsley
**петý|х** *m* [1 *e.*] rooster, cock; **~шúный** [14] cock(s)…
**петь** [пою́, поёшь; пéтый] **1.** ⟨с-, про-⟩ sing; **2.** ⟨про-⟩ *петух* crow
**пехóт|а** *f* [5], **~ный** [14] infantry; **~úнец** *m* [1; -нца] infantryman
**печáл|ить** [13], ⟨о-⟩ grieve (*v/i.* **-ся**); **~ь** *f* [8] grief, sorrow; **~ьный** [14; -лен, -льна] sad, mournful, sorrowful
**печáт|ать** [1], ⟨на-⟩ print; *на машинке* type; **-ся** *impf.* be in the press; appear in (**в** П); **~ник** *m* [1] printer; **~ный** [14] printed; printing; **~ь** *f* [8] seal, stamp (*a. fig.*); *пресса* press; *мелкая, чёткая* print, type; ***вы́йти из ~и*** be published
**печён|ка** *f* [5; *g/pl.*: -нок] *cul.* liver; **~ый** [14] baked
**пéчень** *f* [8] *anat.* liver
**печéнье** *n* [10] cookie, biscuit
**пéчка** *f* [5; *g/pl.*: -чек] → ***печь***[1]
**печь**[1] *f* [8; в -чú; *from g/pl. e.*] stove; oven; *tech.* furnace; kiln
**печь**[2] [26], ⟨ис-⟩ bake; *солнце* scorch
**пеш|ехóд** *m* [1], **~ехóдный** [14] pedestrian; **˜ка** *f* [5; *g/pl.*: -шек] *in chess* pawn (*a. fig.*); **~кóм** on foot
**пещéра** *f* [5] cave
**пиан|úно** *n* [*indecl.*] upright (piano); **~úст** *m* [1] pianist
**пивнáя** *f* [14] pub, saloon
**пи́во** *n* [9] beer; ***свéтлое ~*** pale ale; **~вáр** *m* [1] brewer; **~вáренный** [14]: ***~вáренный завóд*** brewery
**пигмéнт** *m* [1] pigment
**пиджáк** *m* [1 *e.*] coat, jacket
**пижáма** *f* [5] pajamas (*Brt.* py-) *pl.*
**пик** *m* [1] peak; ***часы́ ~*** rush hour
**пикáнтный** [14; -тен, -тна] piquant, spicy (*a. fig.*)
**пикáп** *m* [1] pickup (van)
**пикéт** *m* [1], **~úровать** [7] (*im*)*pf.* picket
**пи́ки** *f/pl.* [5] spades (*cards*)
**пикúровать** *ae.* [7] (*im*)*pf.* dive
**пи́кнуть** [20] *pf.* peep; ***он и ~ не успéл*** before he could say knife; ***тóлько пи́кни!*** (*threat implied*) just one peep out of you!
**пил|á** *f* [5; *pl. st.*], **~úть** [13; пилю́, пи́лишь] saw; **~óт** *m* [1] pilot
**пилю́ля** *f* [6] pill
**пингвúн** *m* [1] penguin
**пинóк** *m* [1; -нкá] *coll.* kick
**пинцéт** *m* [1] pincers, tweezers *pl.*
**пиóн** *m* [1] peony
**пионéр** *m* [1] pioneer
**пипéтка** [5; *g/pl.*: -ток] *med.* dropper
**пир** [1; в ~ý; *pl. e.*] feast
**пирамúда** *f* [5] pyramid
**пирáт** *m* [1] pirate
**пирó|г** *m* [1 *e.*] pie; **~жное** *n* [14] pastry; (fancy) cake; **~жóк** *m* [1; -жкá] pastry;

П

patty
**пир|ýшка** *f* [5; *g/pl.*: -шек] carousal, binge, revelry; **⁓шество** *n* [9] feast, banquet
**писá|ние** *n* [12] writing; (*священное*) Holy Scripture; **⁓тель** *m* [4] writer, author; **⁓тельница** *f* [5] authoress; **⁓ть** [3], ⟨на-⟩ write; *картину* paint
**писк** *m* [1] chirp, squeak; **⁓ли́вый** [14 *sh.*] squeaky; **⁓нуть** → ***пищáть***
**пистолéт** *m* [1] pistol
**пи́сч|ий** [17]: ***⁓ая бумáга*** writing paper, note paper
**пи́сьмен|ность** *f* [8] *collect.* literary texts; written language; **⁓ный** [14] written; in writing; *стол и т. д.* writing
**письмó** *n* [9; *pl. st., gen.*: пи́сем] letter; writing (**на** П in); ***деловóе ⁓*** business letter; ***заказнóе ⁓*** registered letter
**питá|ние** *n* [12] nutrition; nourishment; feeding; **⁓тельный** [14; -лен, -льна] nutritious, nourishing; **⁓ть** [1] nourish (*a. fig.*), feed (*a. tech.*); *надежду и т. д.* cherish; *ненависть* bear against (**к** Д); **-ся** feed *or* live (Т on)
**питóм|ец** *m* [1; -мца], **⁓ица** *f* [5] foster child; charge; pupil; alumnus; **⁓ник** *m* [1] nursery
**пить** [пью, пьёшь; пил, -á, -о; пéй(те)!; пи́тый; пит, питá, пи́то], ⟨вы-⟩ drink (*pf. a.* up; **за** В to); have, take; ***мне хóчется ⁓*** I feel thirsty; **⁓ё** *n* [10] drink(-ing); **⁓евóй** [14] *вода* drinking
**пи́хта** *f* [5] fir tree
**пи́цц|а** *f* [5] pizza; **⁓ери́я** *f* [7] pizzeria
**пи́чкать** *coll.* [1], ⟨на-⟩ *coll.* stuff, cram (with Т)
**пи́шущ|ий** [17]: ***⁓ая маши́нка*** typewriter
**пи́ща** *f* [5] food (*a. fig.*)
**пищáть** [4 *e.*; -щý, -щи́шь], ⟨за-⟩, *once* ⟨пи́скнуть⟩ [20] peep, squeak, cheep
**пище|варéние** *n* [12] digestion; **⁓вóд** *m* [1] *anat.* (o)esophagus, gullet; **⁓вóй** [14]: ***⁓вые продýкты*** foodstuffs
**пия́вка** *f* [5; *g/pl.*: -вок] leech
**плáва|ние** *n* [12] swimming; *naut.* navigation; (*путешествие*) voyage, trip; **⁓ть** [1] swim; float; sail, navigate
**плáв|ить** [14], ⟨рас-⟩ smelt; **⁓ки** *pl.* [5; *g/pl.*: -вок] swimming trunks; **⁓кий** [16]: ***⁓кий предохрани́тель*** fuse; **⁓ни́к** *m* [1 *e.*] fin, flipper
**плáвный** [14; -вен, -вна] *речь и т. д.* fluent; *движение и т. д.* smooth
**плавýч|есть** *f* [8] buoyancy; **⁓ий** [17] *док* floating
**плагиáт** *m* [1] plagiarism
**плакáт** *m* [1] poster
**плáк|ать** [3] weep, cry (**от** Р for; **о** П); **-ся** *coll.* complain (**на** В of); **⁓са** *coll. m/f* [5] crybaby; **⁓си́вый** *coll.* [14 *sh.*] *голос* whining
**плам|енéть** [8] blaze, flame; **⁓енный** [14] flaming, fiery; *fig. a.* ardent; **⁓я** *n* [13] flame; blaze
**план** [1] plan; scheme; plane; ***учéбный ⁓*** curriculum; ***перéдний ⁓*** foreground; ***зáдний ⁓*** background
**планёр**, **плáнер** *ae. m* [1] *ae.* glider
**планéта** *f* [5] planet
**плани́ров|ать** [7] **1.** ⟨за-⟩ plan; **2.** ⟨с-⟩ *ae.* glide; **⁓ка** *f* [5; *g/pl.*: -вок] planning; *парка и т. д.* lay(ing)-out
**плáнка** *f* [5; *g/pl.*: -нок] plank; *sport* (cross)bar
**плáно|вый** [14] planned; plan(ning); **⁓мéрный** [14; -рен, -рна] systematic, planned
**плантáция** *f* [7] plantation
**пласт** *m* [1 *e.*] layer, stratum
**плáст|ика** *f* [5] plastic arts *pl.*; eurhythmics; **⁓и́нка** *f* [5; *g/pl.*: -нок] plate; record, disc; **⁓и́ческий** [16]: ***⁓и́ческая хирурги́я*** plastic surgery; **⁓мáсса** *f* [5] plastic; **⁓ырь** *m* [4] plaster
**плáт|а** *f* [5] pay(ment); fee; wages *pl.*; *за проезд* fare; *за квартиру* rent; **⁓ёж** *m* [1 *e.*] payment; **⁓ёжеспосóбный** [14; -бен, -бна] solvent; **⁓ёжный** [14] of payment; **⁓ина** *f* [5] platinum; **⁓и́ть** [15], ⟨за-, у-⟩ pay (Т in; **за** В for); settle (*account* **по** Д); **-ся**, ⟨по-⟩ *fig.* pay (Т with, **за** В for); **⁓ный** [14] paid; be paid for
**платóк** *m* [1; -ткá] handkerchief
**платфóрма** *f* [5] platform (*a. fig.*)
**плáт|ье** *n* [10; *g/pl.*: -ьев] dress, gown; **⁓янóй** [14] clothes…; ***⁓янóй шкаф*** wardrobe
**плáха** *f* [5] (*hist.* executioner's) block

П

**плац|да́рм** *m* [1] base; *mil.* bridgehead; **~ка́рта** *f* [5] ticket for a reserved seat *or* berth

**пла|ч** *m* [1] weeping; **~че́вный** [14; -вен, -вна] deplorable, pitiable, lamentable; **~шмя́** flat, prone

**плащ** *m* [1 *e.*] raincoat; cloak

**плебисци́т** *m* [1] plebiscite

**плева́ть** [6 *e.*; плюю́, плюёшь], *once* ⟨плю́нуть⟩ [20] spit (out); not care (***на*** В for)

**плево́к** [1; -вка] spit(tle)

**плеври́т** *m* [1] pleurisy

**плед** *m* [1] plaid, blanket

**плем|енно́й** [14] tribal; *скот* brood…, *лошадь* stud…; **~́я** *n* [13] tribe; breed; *coll.* brood; ***на ~́я*** for breeding

**племя́нни|к** *m* [1] nephew; **~ца** *f* [5] niece

**плен** *m* [1; в ~у́] captivity; ***взять (по-па́сть) в ~*** (be) take(n) prisoner

**плен|а́рный** [14] plenary; **~и́тельный** [14; -лен, -льна] captivating, fascinating; **~и́ть(ся)** → ***~я́ть(ся)***

**плёнка** *f* [5; *g/pl.*: -нок] film; *для записи* tape

**пле́н|ник** *m* [1], **~ный** *m* [14] captive, prisoner; **~я́ть** [28], ⟨**~и́ть**⟩ [13] (**-ся** be) captivate(d)

**пле́нум** *m* [1] plenary session

**пле́сень** *f* [8] mo(u)ld

**плеск** *m* [1], **~а́ть** [3], *once* ⟨плесну́ть⟩ [20], **-а́ться** *impf.* splash

**пле́сневеть** [8], ⟨за-⟩ grow mo(u)ldy, musty

**пле|сти́** [25 -т-: плету́], ⟨с-, за-⟩ braind, plait; weave; *coll.* ***~сти́ небыли́цы*** spin yarns; ***~сти́ интри́ги*** intrigue (against); *coll.* ***что ты ~тёшь?*** what on earth are you talking about?; **-сь** drag, lag; **~тёный** [14] wattled; wicker…; **~те́нь** *m* [4; -тня́] wattle fence

**плётка** *f* [5; *g/pl.*: -ток], **плеть** *f* [8; *from g/pl. e.*] lash

**плеч|о́** *n* [9; *pl.*: пле́чи, плеч, -ча́м] shoulder; *tech.* arm; ***с (о всего́) ~а́*** with all one's might; (И) ***не по ~у́*** (Д) not be equal to a th.; → *a.* ***гора́*** *coll.*

**плешь** *f* [8] bald patch

**плит|а́** *f* [5; *pl. st.*] slab, (flag-, grave-) stone; *металлическая* plate; (*kitchen*) range; (*gas*) cooker, stove; **~́ка** *f* [5; *g/pl.*: -ток] tile; *шоколада* bar; cooker, stove; electric hotplate

**плов|е́ц** *m* [1; -вца́] swimmer

**плод** *m* [1 *e.*] fruit; **~и́ть** [15 *e.*; пложу́, -ди́шь], ⟨рас-⟩ propagate, multiply (*v/i.* **-ся**); **~ови́тый** [14 *sh.*] fruitful, prolific (*a. fig.*); **~ово́дство** *n* [9] fruit growing; **~о́вый** [14] fruit…; ***~о́вый сад*** orchard; **~оно́сный** [14; -сен, -сна] fruit-bearing; **~оро́дие** *n* [12] fertility; **~оро́дный** [14; -ден, -дна] fertile; **~отво́рный** [14; -рен, -рна] fruitful, productive; *влияние* good, positive

**пло́мб|а** *f* [5] (lead) seal; *зубная* filling; **~и́ровать** [7], ⟨о-⟩ seal; ⟨за-⟩ fill, stop

**пло́ск|ий** [16; -сок, -ска́, -о; *comp.*: пло́ще] flat (*a. fig.* = stale, trite), level; **~ого́рье** *n* [10] plateau, tableland; **~огу́бцы** *pl.* [1; *g/pl.*: -цев] pliers; **~ость** *f* [8; *from g/pl. e.*] flatness; plane (*a. math.*); platitude

**плот** *m* [1 *e.*] raft; **~и́на** *f* [5] dam, dike; **~́ник** *m* [1] carpenter

**пло́тн|ость** *f* [8] density (*a. fig.*); solidity; **~ый** [14; -тен, -тна́, -о] compact, solid; *ткань* dense, close, thick; *о сложении* thickset

**плот|оя́дный** [14; -ден, -дна] carnivorous; *взгляд* lascivious; **~́ский** [16] carnal; **~ь** *f* [8] flesh

**плох|о́й** [16; плох, -а́, -о; *comp.*: ху́же] bad; **~́о** bad(ly); *coll.* bad mark; → ***дво́йка & едини́ца***

**площа́д|ка** *f* [5; *g/pl.*: -док] ground, area; *детская* playground; *sport* court; platform; *лестничная* landing; ***пускова́я ~ка*** launching pad; ***стро́ительная ~ка*** building site; **´~ь** *f* [8; *from g/pl. e.*] square; area (*a. math.*); space; ***жила́я ´~ь*** → ***жилпло́щадь***

**плуг** *m* [1; *pl. e.*] plow, *Brt.* plough

**плут** *m* [1 *e.*] rogue; trickster, cheat; **~а́ть** [1] *coll.* stray; **~ова́ть** [7], ⟨с-⟩ trick, cheat; **~овство́** *n* [9] trickery, cheating

**плыть** [23] (be) swim(ming); float(ing); *на корабле* sail(ing); ***~ по тече́нию*** *fig.* swim with the tide; → ***пла́вать***

**плю́нуть** → ***плева́ть***

П

**плюс** (*su. m* [1]) plus; *coll.* advantage
**плюш** *m* [1] plush
**плющ** *m* [1 *e.*] ivy
**пляж** *m* [1] beach
**пляс|áть** [3], ⟨с-⟩ dance; **˷ка** *f* [5; *g/pl.*: -сок] (folk) dance; dancing
**пневмати́ческий** [16] pneumatic
**пневмони́я** *f* [7] pneumonia
**по 1.** (Д); on, along; through; all over; in; by; according to, after; through; owing to; for; over; across; upon; each, at a time (*2, 3, 4, with* В; ***по два***); **2.** (В) to, up to; till, through; for; **3.** (П) (up)-on; ***~ мне*** for all I care; ***~ ча́су в день*** an hour a day
**по-** (in *compds.*); → ***ру́сский***, ***ваш***
**поба́иваться** [1] be a little afraid of (Р)
**побе́г** *m* [1] escape, flight; *bot.* shoot, sprout
**побег|у́шки**: ***быть на ~у́шках*** *coll.* run errands (***у*** Р for)
**побе́|да** *f* [5] victory; **~ди́тель** *m* [4] victor; winner; **~ди́ть** → ***~жда́ть***; **~дный** [14], **~доно́сный** [14; -сен, -сна] victorious; **~жда́ть** [1], ⟨~ди́ть⟩ [15 *e.*; *1st p. sg. not used*; -ди́шь, -еждённый] be victorious (В over), win (*a.* victory), conquer, defeat; beat; *страх, сомнения* overcome
**побере́жье** *n* [10] coast, seaboard, littoral
**побла́жка** *coll. f* [5; *g/pl.*: -жек] indulgence
**побли́зости** close by; (***от*** Р) near
**побо́и** *m/pl.* [3] beating; **~ще** *n* [11] bloody battle
**побо́р|ник** *m* [1] advocate; **~о́ть** [17] *pf.* conquer; overcome; beat
**побо́чный** [14] *эффект* side; *продукт* by-(*product*); *old use сын, дочь* illegitimate
**побу|ди́тельный** [14]: ***~ди́тельная причи́на*** motive; **~жда́ть** [1], ⟨~ди́ть⟩ [15 *e.*; -ужу́, -уди́шь; -уждённый] induce, prompt, impel; **~жде́ние** *n* [12] motive, impulse, incentive
**пова́д|иться** *coll.* [15] *pf.* fall into the habit (of [visiting] *inf.*); **~ка** [5; *g/pl.*: -док] *coll.* habit
**пова́льный** [14] indiscriminate; *увлечение* general
**по́вар** *m* [1; *pl.*: -рá, *etc. e.*] culinary; cook; **˷енный** [14] *книга* cook (*book*, *Brt.* cookery book); *соль* (*salt*) table
**пове|де́ние** *n* [12] behavio(u)r, conduct; **~ли́тельный** [14; -лен, -льна] *тон* peremptory; *gr.* imperative
**поверг|а́ть** [1], ⟨˷нуть⟩ [21] *в отчаяние* plunge into (***в*** В)
**пове́р|енный** [14]: ***~енный в дела́х*** chargé d'affaires; **~ить** → ***ве́рить***; **~ну́ть(ся)** → ***повора́чивать(ся)***
**пове́рх** (Р) over, above; **~ностный** [14; -тен, -тна] *fig.* superficial; surface…; **~ность** *f* [8] superficiality
**пове́рье** *n* [10] popular belief, superstition
**пове́сить(ся)** → ***ве́шать(ся)***
**повествова́|ние** *n* [12] narration, narrative; **~тельный** [14] *стиль* narrative; ***~тельное предложе́ние*** *gr.* sentence; **~ть** [7] narrate (*v/t.* ***о*** П)
**пове́ст|ка** *f* [5; *g/pl.*: -ток] *law* summons; (*уведомление*) notice; ***~ка дня*** agenda; **´~ь** *f* [8; *from g/pl. e.*] story, tale
**по-ви́димому** apparently
**пови́дло** *n* [9] jam
**пови́н|ность** *f* [8] duty; **~ный** [14; -и́нен, -и́нна] guilty; **~ова́ться** [7] (*pt. a. pf.*) (Д) obey; comply with; **~ове́ние** *n* [12] obedience
**по́вод** *m* **1.** [1] ground, cause; occasion (on ***по*** Д); ***по ~у*** (Р) as regards, concerning; **2.** [1; в -ду́: *pl.*: -о́дья, -о́дьев] rein; ***на ~у́*** (***у*** Р) be under s.b.'s thumb; **~о́к** *m* [1; -дкá и т. д.; *pl.* -дки́ и т. д.] (dog's) lead
**пово́зка** *f* [5; *g/pl.*: -зок] vehicle, conveyance; (*not equipped with springs*) carriage; cart
**повор|а́чивать** [1], ⟨поверну́ть⟩ [20] turn (*v/i.* **-ся**; ***~а́чивайся!*** come on!); **~о́т** *m* [1] turn; **~о́тливый** [14 *sh.*] nimble, agile; **~о́тный** [14] turning (*a. fig.*)
**повре|жда́ть** [1], ⟨~ди́ть⟩ [15 *e.*; -ежу́, -еди́шь; -еждённый] damage; *ногу и т. д.* injure, hurt; **~жде́ние** *n* [12] damage; injury
**поврем|ени́ть** [13] *pf.* wait a little; **~ённый** [14] *оплата* payment on time ba-

sis (*by the hour, etc.*)

**повсе|днéвный** [14; -вен, -вна] everyday, daily; **~мéстный** [14; -тен, -тна] general, universal; **~мéстно** everywhere

**повстáн|ец** *m* [1; -нца] rebel, insurgent; **~ческий** [16] rebel(lious)

**повсю́ду** everywhere

**повтор|éние** *n* [12] repetition; *материала* review; *событий* recurrence; **~́ный** [14] repeated, recurring; **~я́ть** [28], ⟨**~и́ть**⟩ [13] repeat (**-ся** o.s.); review

**повы|шáть** [1], ⟨**~́сить**⟩ [15] raise, increase; *по службе* promote; **-ся** rise; *в звании* advance; **~шéние** *n* [12] rise; promotion; **~́шенный** [14] increased, higher; *температура* high

**повя́з|ка** *f* [5; *g/pl.*: -зок] *med.* bandage; band, armlet

**пога|шáть** [1], ⟨**~си́ть**⟩ [15] put out, extinguish; *долг* pay; *марку* cancel

**погиб|áть** [1], ⟨**~́нуть**⟩ [21] perish; be killed, fall; **~́ший** [17] lost, killed

**погло|щáть** [1], ⟨**~ти́ть**⟩ [15; -ощу́; -ощённый] swallow up, devour; (*впитывать*) absorb (*a. fig.*)

**погля́дывать** [1] cast looks (**на** В at)

**погов|áривать** [1]: **~áривают** there is talk (**о** П of); **~óрка** [5; *g/pl.*: -рок] saying, proverb

**погó|да** *f* [5] weather (**в** В, **при** П in); **э́то ~ды не дéлает** this does not change anything; **~ди́ть** *coll.* [15 *e.*; -гожу́, -годи́шь] *pf.* wait a little; **~дя́** later; **~лóвный** [14] general, universal; **~лóвно** without exception; **~лóвье** *n* [10] livestock

**погóн** *m* [1] *mil.* shoulder strap

**погóн|я** *f* [6] pursuit (**за** T of); pursuers *pl.*; **~я́ть** [28] drive *or* urge (on); drive (*for a certain time*)

**пограни́чн|ый** [14] border…; **~ик** *m* [1] border guard

**пóгре|б** [1; *pl.*: -бá, *etc. e.*] cellar; **~бáльный** [14] funeral; **~бéние** *n* [12] burial; funeral; **~му́шка** *f* [5; *g/pl.*: -шек] rattle; **~́шность** *f* [8] error, mistake

**погру|жáть** [1], ⟨**~зи́ть**⟩ [15 & 15 *e.*; -ужу́, -у́зи́шь; -у́женный & -ужённый] immerse; sink, plunge, submerge (*v/i.* **-ся**); **~жённый** *a.* absorbed, lost (**в** В in); load, ship; **~жéние** *n* [12] *подлодки* diving; *аппарата* submersion; **~́зка** [5; *g/pl.*: -зок] loading, shipment

**погряз|áть** [1], ⟨**~́нуть**⟩ [21] get stuck (**в** T in)

**под, ~о 1.** (B) (*направление*) under; toward(s), to; (*возраст, время*) about; on the eve of; à la, in imitation of; for, suitable as; **2.** (T) (*расположение*) under, below, beneath; near, by; *сражение* of; *для* (used) for; **пóле ~ рóжью** rye field

**пода|вáть** [5], ⟨**~́ть**⟩ [-дáм, -дáшь, *etc.*, → **дать**] give; serve (*a. sport*); *заявление* hand (*or* send) in; *жалобу* lodge; *пример* set; *руку помощи* render; **~́ть в суд** (**на** B) bring an action against; **не ~вáть ви́ду** give no sign; **-ся** move; yield

**подав|и́ть** → **~ля́ть**; **~и́ться** *pf.* [14] choke; **~лéние** *n* [12] suppression; **~ля́ть** [28], ⟨**~и́ть**⟩ [14] suppress; repress; depress; crush; **~ля́ющий** *a.* overwhelming

**подáвно** *coll.* so much *or* all the more

**подáгра** *f* [5] gout; podagra

**подáльше** *coll.* a little farther

**подá|рок** *m* [1; -рка] present, gift; **~тливый** [14 *sh.*] (com)pliant; **~ть(ся)** → **~вáть(ся)**; **~ча** *f* [5] serve; *sport* service; *материала* presentation; *воды, газа* supply; *tech.* feed(ing); **~чка** *f* [5; *g/pl.*: -чек] sop; *fig.* tip

**подбе|гáть** [1], ⟨**~жáть**⟩ [4; -бегу́, -бежи́шь, -бегу́т] run up (**к** Д to)

**подби|вáть** [1], ⟨**~́ть**⟩ [подобью́, -бьёшь, *etc.*, → **бить**] line (Twith); *подмётку* (re)sole; hit, injure; *coll.* instigate, incite; **~́тый** *coll.* *глаз* black

**под|бирáть** [1], ⟨**~обрáть**⟩ [подберу́, -рёшь; подобрáл, -á, -о; подóбранный] pick up; *юбку* tuck up; *живот* draw in; (*отбирать*) pick out, select; **-ся** sneak up (**к** Д to); **~би́ть** → **~бивáть**; **~бóр** *m* [1] selection; assortment; **на ~бóр** choice, well-matched, select

**подборóдок** *m* [1; -дка] chin

**подбр|áсывать** [1], ⟨**~óсить**⟩ [15] throw *or* toss (up); jolt; *в огонь* add; (*подвез-*

*ти*) give a lift

**подва́л** *m* [1] basement; cellar

**подвезти́** → ***подвози́ть***

**подвер|га́ть** [1], 〈∠гнуть〉 [21] subject, expose; ***∠гнуть испыта́нию*** put to the test; ***∠гнуть сомне́нию*** call into question; **-ся** undergo; **∠женный** [14 *sh.*] subject to

**подве́с|ить** → ***подве́шивать***; **~но́й** [14] hanging, pendant; *мост* suspension; *мотор* outboard

**подвести́** → ***подводи́ть***

**подве́тренный** [14] *naut.* leeward; sheltered side

**подве́|шивать** [1], 〈~сить〉 [15] hang (under; on); suspend (from)

**по́двиг** *m* [1] feat, exploit, deed

**подви|га́ть** [1], 〈∠нуть〉 [20] move little (*v/i.* **-ся**); **~жно́й** [14] *mil.* mobile; *rail.* rolling; **∠жность** *f* [8] mobility; *человека* agility; **∠нуть(ся)** → ***~га́ть(ся)***

**подвла́стный** [14; -тен, -тна] subject to, dependent on

**подводи́ть** [15], 〈подвести́〉 [25] lead ([up] to); *фундамент* lay; build; *coll.* let a p. down (*обмануть и т. д.*); ***~ ито́ги*** sum up

**подво́дн|ый** [14] underwater; submarine; ***~ая ло́дка*** submarine; ***~ый ка́мень*** reef; *fig.* unexpected obstacle

**подво́з** *m* [1] supply; **~и́ть** [15], 〈подвезти́〉 [24] bring, transport; *кого-л.* give a p. a lift

**подвы́пивший** *coll.* [17] tipsy, slightly drunk

**подвя́з|ывать** [1], 〈~а́ть〉 [3] tie (up)

**под|гиба́ть** [1], 〈~огну́ть〉 [20] tuck (under); bend (*a.* **-ся**); ***но́ги ~гиба́ются от уста́лости*** I am barely able to stand (*with tiredness*)

**подгля́д|ывать** [1], 〈~е́ть〉 [11] peep at, spy on

**подгов|а́ривать** [1], 〈~ори́ть〉 [13] instigate, put a p. up to

**под|гоня́ть** [28], 〈~огна́ть〉 [подгоню́, -го́нишь, → ***гнать***] drive to *or* urge on, hurry; *к фигуре и т. д.* fit, adapt (to)

**подгор|а́ть** [1], 〈~е́ть〉 [9] burn slightly

**подготов|и́тельный** [14] preparatory; *работа* spadework; **∠ка** *f* [5; *g/pl.*: -вок] preparation, training (**к** Д for); **~ля́ть** [28], 〈∠ить〉 [14] prepare; ***∠ить по́чву*** *fig.* pave the way

**подда|ва́ться** [5], 〈∠ться〉 [-да́мся, -да́шься, *etc.*, → ***дать***] yield; ***не ~ва́ться описа́нию*** defy *or* beggar description

**подда́к|ивать** [1], 〈~нуть〉 [20] say yes (to everything), consent

**по́дда|нный** *m* [14] subject; **~нство** *n* [9] nationality, citizenship; **∠ться** → ***~ва́ться***

**подде́л|ка** [5; *g/pl.*: -лок] *бумаг, подписи, денег и т. д.* forgery, counterfeit; **~ывать**, 〈~ать〉 [1] forge; **~ьный** [14] counterfeit…; sham…

**подде́рж|ивать** [1], 〈~а́ть〉 [4] support; back (up); *порядок* maintain; *разговор и т. д.* keep up; **~ка** *f* [5; *g/pl.*: -жек] support; backing

**поде́л|ать** *coll.* [1] *pf.* do; ***ничего́ не ~аешь*** there's nothing to be done; → *a.* ***де́лать***; *coll.* ***~о́м***: ***~о́м ему́*** it serves him right

**поде́ржанный** [14] secondhand; worn, used

**поджа́р|ивать** [1], 〈~ить〉 [13] fry, roast, grill slightly; brown; *хлеб* toast

**поджа́рый** [14 *sh.*] lean

**поджа́ть** → ***поджима́ть***

**под|же́чь** → ***~жига́ть***; **~жига́ть** [1], 〈~же́чь〉 [26; подожгу́; -ожжёшь; поджёг, подожгла́; подожжённый] set on fire (*or* fire to)

**под|жида́ть** [1], 〈~ожда́ть〉 [-ду́, -дёшь; -а́л, -а́, -о] wait (for Р, В)

**под|жима́ть** [1], 〈~жа́ть〉 [подожму́, -мёшь; поджа́тый] draw in; *ноги* cross (one's legs); *губы* purse (one's lips); ***~жа́ть хвост*** have one's tail between one's legs; ***вре́мя ~жима́ет*** time is pressing

**поджо́г** *m* [1] arson

**подзаголо́вок** *m* [1; -вка] subtitle

**подзадо́р|ивать** *coll.* [1], 〈~ить〉 [13] egg on, incite (**на** В, **к** Д to)

**подза|ты́льник** *m* [1] cuff on the back of the head; **~щи́тный** *m* [14] *law* client

**подзе́мный** [14] underground, subterranean; **~ толчо́к** tremor
**под|зыва́ть** [1], ⟨**~озва́ть**⟩ [подзову́, -ёшь; подозва́л, -á, -о; подо́званный] call, beckon
**под|карау́ливать** *coll.* [1], ⟨**~карау́лить**⟩ [13] → ***подстерега́ть***; **~ка́рмливать** [1], ⟨**~корми́ть**⟩ [14] *скот* feed up, fatten; *растения* give extra fertilizer; **~ка́тывать** [1], ⟨**~кати́ть**⟩ [15] roll *or* drive up; **~ка́шиваться** [1], ⟨**~коси́ться**⟩ [15] give way
**подки́|дывать** [1], ⟨**~нуть**⟩ [20] → ***подбра́сывать***; **~дыш** *m* [1] foundling
**подкла́д|ка** [5; *g/pl.*: -док] lining; **~ывать** [1], ⟨подложи́ть⟩ [16] lay (under); (*добавить*) add; ***подложи́ть свинью́*** *approx.* play a dirty trick on s.o
**подкле́|ивать** [1], ⟨**~ить**⟩ [13] glue, paste
**подключ|а́ть** [4], ⟨**~и́ть**⟩ [16] *tech.* connect, link up; *fig.* include, attach
**подко́в|а** *f* [5] horseshoe; **~ывать** [1], ⟨**~а́ть**⟩ [7 *e.*; -кую́, -куёшь] shoe; give a grounding in; **~анный** [14] *a.* versed in
**подко́жный** [14] hypodermic
**подкоси́ть|ся** → ***подка́шиваться***
**подкра́|дываться** [1], ⟨**~сться**⟩ [25] steal *or* sneak up (**к** Д to); **~шивать** [1], ⟨**~сить**⟩ [15] touch up one's make-up (*a.* **-ся**)
**подкреп|ля́ть** [28], ⟨**~и́ть**⟩ [14 *e.*; -плю́, -пи́шь, -плённый] reinforce, support; *fig.* corroborate; **-ся** fortify o.s.; **~ле́ние** *n* [12] *mil.* reinforcement
**по́дкуп** *m* [1], **~а́ть** [1], ⟨**~и́ть**⟩ [14] suborn; bribe; *улыбкой и т. д.* win over, charm
**подла́|живаться** [1], ⟨**~диться**⟩ [15] adapt o.s. to, fit in with; humo(u)r, make up to
**по́дле** (Р) beside, by (the side of); nearby
**подлеж|а́ть** [4 *e.*; -жу́, -жи́шь] be subject to; be liable to; (И) ***не ~и́т сомне́нию*** there can be no doubt (about); **~а́щий** [17] subject (Д to); liable to; **~а́щее** *n* *gr.* subject
**подле|за́ть** [1], ⟨**~́зть**⟩ [24 *st.*] creep (under; up); **~́сок** *m* [1; -ска и т. д.] undergrowth; **~та́ть** [1], ⟨**~те́ть**⟩ [11] fly up (to)
**подле́ц** *m* [1 *e.*] scoundrel, rascal
**подли|ва́ть** [1], ⟨**~́ть**⟩ [подолью́, -льёшь; подле́й! подли́л, -а, -о; подли́тый (-ли́т, -á, -о)] add to, pour on; **~́вка** *f* [5; *g/pl.*: -вок] gravy; sauce
**подли́з|а** *coll. m/f* [5] toady; **~ываться** *coll.* [1], ⟨**~а́ться**⟩ [3] flatter, insinuate o.s. (**к** Д with), toady (to)
**по́длинн|ик** *m* [1] original; **~ый** [14; -инен, -инна] original; authentic, genuine; true, real
**подли́ть** → ***подлива́ть***
**подло́|г** *m* [1] forgery; **~жи́ть** → ***подкла́дывать***; **~жный** [14; -жен, -жна] spurious, false
**по́дл|ость** *f* [8] meanness; baseness; low-down trick; **~ый** [14; подл, -á, -о] mean, base, contemptible
**подма́з|ывать** [1], ⟨**~ать**⟩ [3] grease (*a.*, *coll. fig.*); **-ся** *coll.* insinuate o.s., curry favo(u)r (**к** Д with)
**подма́н|ивать** [1], ⟨**~и́ть**⟩ [13; -аню́, -а́нишь] beckon, call to
**подме́н|а** *f* [5] substitution (*of s.th. false for s.th. real*), exchange; **~ивать** [1], ⟨**~и́ть**⟩ [13; -еню́, -е́нишь] substitute (Т/В s.th./for), (ex)change
**подме|та́ть** [1], ⟨**~сти́**⟩ [25; -т-: -мету́] sweep; **~́тить** → ***подмеча́ть***
**подмётка** *f* [5; *g/pl.*: -ток] sole
**подме|ча́ть** [1], ⟨**~́тить**⟩ [15] notice, observe, perceive
**подме́ш|ивать**, ⟨**~а́ть**⟩ [1] mix *or* stir (into), add
**подми́г|ивать** [1], ⟨**~ну́ть**⟩ [20] wink (Д at)
**подмо́га** *coll. f* [5] help, assistance
**подмок|а́ть** [1], ⟨**~́нуть**⟩ get slightly wet
**подмо́стки** *m/pl.* [1] *thea.* stage
**подмо́ченный** [14] slightly wet; *coll. fig.* tarnished
**подмы|ва́ть** [1], ⟨**~́ть**⟩ [22] wash (*a.* out, away); undermine; *impf. coll.* (*impers.*) ***меня́ так и ~ва́ет…*** I can hardly keep myself from…
**поднести́** → ***подноси́ть***
**поднима́ть** [1], ⟨подня́ть⟩ [-ниму́, -ни́мешь; по́днятый (-нят, -á, -о)] lift; pick

П

up (**с** Р from); hoist; *тревогу, плату* raise; *оружие* take up; *флаг* hoist; *якорь* weigh; *паруса* set; *шум* make; **~ нос** put on airs; **~ на́ ноги** rouse; **~ на́ смех** ridicule; **-ся** [*pt*.: -ня́лся́, -ла́сь] (**с** Р from) rise; go up (stairs **по ле́стнице**); *coll*. climb (hill **на холм**); *спор и т. д.* arise; develop

**подного́тная** *coll. f* [14] all there is to know; the ins and outs *pl*.

**подно́ж|ие** *n* [12] foot, bottom (*of a hill, etc*.) (at **у** Р); pedestal; **~ка** *f* [5; *g/pl*.: -жек] footboard; *mot*. running board; (*wrestling*) tripping up one's opponent

**подно́|с** *m* [1] tray; **~си́ть** [15], ⟨поднести́⟩ [24 -с-] bring, carry, take; present (Д); **~ше́ние** *n* [12] gift, present

**подня́т|ие** *n* [12] lifting; raising, hoisting, *etc*., →; **поднима́ть(ся)**; **~ь(ся)** → **поднима́ть(ся)**

**подоб|а́ть**: *impf*. (*impers*.) **~а́ет** it becomes; befits; **ˊ~ие** *n* 12] resemblance; image (*a. eccl*.); *math*. similarity; **ˊ~ный** [14; -бен, -бна] similar (Д to); such; **и тому́ ˊ~ное** and the like; **ничего́ ˊ~ного** nothing of the kind; **ˊ~но тому́ как** just as; **~остра́стный** [14; -тен, -тна] servile

**подо|бра́ть(ся)** → **подбира́ть(ся)**; **~гна́ть** → **подгоня́ть**; **~гну́ть(ся)** → **подгиба́ть(ся)**; **~грева́ть** [1], ⟨-греть⟩ [8; -етый] warm up, heat up; rouse; **~двига́ть** [1], ⟨-дви́нуть⟩ [20] move (**к** Д [up] to) (*v/i*. **-ся**); **~жда́ть** → **поджида́ть & ждать**; **~зва́ть** → **подзыва́ть**

**подозр|ева́ть** [1], ⟨заподо́зрить⟩ [13] suspect (**в** П of); **~е́ние** *n* [12] suspicion; **~и́тельный** [14; -лен, -льна] suspicious

**подойти́** → **подходи́ть**

**подоко́нник** *m* [1] window sill

**подо́л** *m* [1] hem (*of skirt*)

**подо́лгу** (for a) long (time)

**подо́нки** *pl*. [*sg*. 1; -нка] dregs; *fig*. scum, riffraff

**подо́пытный** [14; -тен, -тна] experimental; **~ кро́лик** *fig*. guineapig

**подорва́ть** → **подрыва́ть**

**подоро́жник** *m* [1] *bot*. plantain

**подо|сла́ть** → **подсыла́ть**; **~спе́ть** [8] *pf*. come (in time); **~стла́ть** → **подстила́ть**

**подотчётный** [14; -тен, -тна] accountable to

**подохо́дный** [14]; **~ нало́г** income tax

**подо́шва** *f* [5] sole (*of foot or boot*); *холма и т. д.* foot, bottom

**подпа|да́ть** [1], ⟨ˊ~сть⟩ [25; *pt. st*.] fall (under); **~ли́ть** [13] *pf. coll*. → **подже́чь**; singe; *coll*. **ˊ~сть** → **~да́ть**

**подпира́ть** [1], ⟨подпере́ть⟩ [12; подопру́, -прёшь] support, prop up

**подпис|а́ть(ся)** → **ˊ~ывать(ся)**; **ˊ~ка** *f* [5; *g/pl*.: -сок] subscription (**на** В to; for); signed statement; **~но́й** [14] subscription…; **ˊ~чик** *m* [1] subscriber; **ˊ~ывать(ся)** [1], ⟨**~а́ть(ся)**⟩ [3] sign; subscribe (**на** В to; for); **ˊ~ь** *f* [8] signature (for **на** В); **за ˊ~ью** (Р) signed by

**подплы|ва́ть** [1], ⟨ˊ~ть⟩ [23] swim up to; sail up to [**к** Д]

**подпо|лза́ть** [1], ⟨~лзти́⟩ [24] creep *or* crawl (**под** В under; **к** Д up to); **~лко́вник** *m* [1] lieutenant colonel; **ˊ~лье** [10; *g/pl*.: -ьев] cellar; (*fig*.) underground work *or* organization; **ˊ~льный** [14] underground…; **ˊ~р(к)а** *f* [5 (*g/pl*.: -рок)] prop; **ˊ~чва** *f* [5] subsoil; **~я́сывать** [1], ⟨~я́сать⟩ [3] belt; gird

**подпр|ы́гивать** [1], *once* ⟨~ы́гнуть⟩ [20] jump up

**подпус|ка́ть** [1], ⟨~ти́ть⟩ [15] allow to approach

**подра|ба́тывать** [1], ⟨~бо́тать⟩ [1] earn additionally; put the finishing touches to

**подр|а́внивать** [1], ⟨~овня́ть⟩ [28] straighten; level; *изгородь* clip; *волосы* trim

**подража́|ние** *n* [12] imitation (in/of **в** В/Д); **~тель** *m* [4] imitator (of Д); **~ть** [1] imitate, copy (*v/t*. Д)

**подраздел|е́ние** *n* [12] subdivision; subunit; **~я́ть** [28], ⟨~и́ть⟩ [13] (**-ся** be) subdivide(d) (into **на** В)

**подра|зумева́ть** [1] mean (**под** Т by), imply; **-ся** be implied; be meant, be understood; **~ста́ть** [1], ⟨~сти́⟩ [24 -ст-; -ро́с, -ла́] grow (up); grow a little older; **~ста́ющее поколе́ние** the rising generation

**подрез|а́ть &; ∼ывать** [1], ⟨∼ать⟩ [3] cut; clip, trim

**подро́бн|ость** *f* [8] detail; ***вдава́ться в ∼ости*** go into details; **∼ый** [14; -бен, -бна] detailed, minute; **∼о** in detail, in full

**подровня́ть** → ***подра́внивать***

**подро́сток** *m* [1; -стка] juvenile, teenager; youth; young girl

**подруб|а́ть** [1], ⟨∼и́ть⟩ [14] **1.** cut; **2.** *sew.* hem

**подру́га** [5] (girl) friend

**по-дру́жески** (in a) friendly (way)

**подружи́ться** [16 *e.*; -жу́сь, -жи́шься] *pf.* make friends (**с** T with)

**подрумя́ниться** [13] *pf.* rouge; *cul.* brown

**подру́чный** [14] improvised; *su.* assistant; mate

**подры́|в** *m* [1] undermining; blowing up; **∼ва́ть** [1] **1.** ⟨∼ть⟩ [22] *здоровье и т. д.* sap, undermine; **2.** ⟨подорва́ть⟩ [-рву́, -рвёшь; -рва́л, -а́, -о; подо́рванный] blow up, blast, *fig.* undermine; **∼вно́й** [14] *деятельность* subversive; ***∼вно́й заря́д*** charge

**подря́д** **1.** *adv.* successive(ly), running; one after another; **2.** *m* [1] contract; **∼чик** *m* [1], contractor

**подс|а́живать** [1], ⟨∼ади́ть⟩ [15] help sit down; *растения* plant additionally; **-ся**, ⟨∼е́сть⟩ [25; -ся́ду, -ся́дешь; -сел] sit down ( **к** Д near, next to)

**подсве́чник** *m* [1] candlestick

**подсе́сть** → ***подса́живаться***

**подска́з|ывать** [1], ⟨∼а́ть⟩ [3] prompt; **∼ка** *coll. f* [5] prompting

**подскак|а́ть** [3] *pf.* gallop (**к** Д up to); **∼ивать** [1], ⟨подскочи́ть⟩ [16] run (**к** Д [up] to); jump up

**под|сла́щивать** [1], ⟨∼сласти́ть⟩ [15 *e.*; -ащу́, -асти́шь; -ащённый] sweeten; **∼сле́дственный** *m* [14] law under investigation; **∼слепова́тый** [14 *sh.*] weak-sighted; **∼слу́шивать**, ⟨∼слу́шать⟩ [1] eavesdrop, overhear; **∼сма́тривать** [1], ⟨∼смотре́ть⟩ [9; -отрю́, -о́тришь] spy, peep; **∼сме́иваться** [1] laugh (**над** T at); **∼смотре́ть** → ***сма́тривать***

**подсне́жник** *m* [1] *bot.* snowdrop

**подсо́|бный** [14] subsidiary, by-…, side…; *рабочий* auxiliary; **∼вывать** [1], ⟨подсу́нуть⟩ [20] shove under; *coll.* palm (Д [off] on); **∼зна́тельный** [14; -лен, -льна] subconscious; **∼лнечник** *m* [1] sunflower; **∼хнуть** → ***подсыха́ть***

**подспо́рье** *coll. n* [10] help, support; ***быть хоро́шим ∼м*** be a great help

**подста́в|ить** → ***∼ля́ть***; **∼ка** *f* [5; *g/pl.*: -вок] support, prop, stand; **∼ля́ть** [28], ⟨∼ить⟩ [14] put, place, set (**под** B under); *math.* substitute; (*подвести*) *coll.* let down; ***∼ля́ть но́гу*** *or* (***но́жку***) (Д) trip (a p.) up; **∼но́й** [14] false; substitute; ***∼но́е лицо́*** figurehead

**подстан|о́вка** *f* [5; *g/pl.*: -вок] *math.* substitution; **∼ция** *f* [7] *el.* substation

**подстер|ега́ть** [1], ⟨∼е́чь⟩ [26 г/ж: -регу́, -режёшь; -рёг, -регла́] lie in wait for, be on the watch for; ***его́ ∼ега́ла опа́сность*** he was in danger

**подстил|а́ть** [1], ⟨подостла́ть⟩ [подстелю́, -е́лешь; подо́стланный & подстеленный] spread (**под** B under)

**подстр|а́ивать** [1], ⟨∼о́ить⟩ [13] build on to; *coll. fig.* bring about by secret plotting; connive against

**подстрек|а́тель** *m* [4] instigator; **∼а́тельство** *n* [9] instigation; **∼а́ть** [1], ⟨∼ну́ть⟩ [20] incite (**на** B to); stir up, provoke

**подстр|е́ливать** [1], ⟨∼ели́ть⟩ [13; -елю́, -е́лишь] hit, wound; **∼ига́ть** [1], ⟨∼и́чь⟩ [26 г/ж: -игу́, -ижёшь; -и́г, -и́гла; -и́женный] cut, crop, clip; trim, lop; **∼о́ить** → ***подстра́ивать***; **∼о́чный** [14] interlinear; foot(*note*)

**по́дступ** *m* [1] approach (*a. mil.*); **∼а́ть** [1], ⟨∼и́ть⟩ [14] approach (*v/t.* **к** Д); rise; press

**подсуд|и́мый** *m* [14] defendant; **∼ность** *f* [8] jurisdiction

**подсу́нуть** → ***подсо́вывать***

**подсч|ёт** *m* [1] calculation, computation, cast; **∼и́тывать**, ⟨∼ита́ть⟩ [1] count (up), compute

**подсы|ла́ть** [1], ⟨подосла́ть⟩ [-шлю́, -шлёшь; -о́сланный] send (secretly); **∼па́ть** [1], ⟨∼пать⟩ [2] add, pour; **∼ха́ть**

П

[1], ⟨подсо́хнуть⟩ [21] dry (up)

**подта́|лкивать** [1], ⟨подтолкну́ть⟩ [20] push; nudge; **~со́вывать** [1], ⟨~сова́ть⟩ [7] shuffle garble; **~чивать** [1], ⟨подточи́ть⟩ [16] eat (away); wash (out); sharpen; *fig.* undermine

**подтвер|жда́ть** [1], ⟨~ди́ть⟩ [15 *e.*; -ржу́, -рди́шь; -ржде́нный] confirm, corroborate; acknowledge; **-ся** prove (to be) true; **~жде́ние** [12] confirmation; acknowledg(e)ment

**под|тере́ть** → ***~тира́ть***; **~тёк** *m* [1] bloodshot spot; **~тира́ть** [1], ⟨~тере́ть⟩ [12; подотру́; подтёр] wipe (*up*); **~толкну́ть** → ***~та́лкивать***; **~точи́ть** → ***~та́чивать***

**подтру́н|ивать** [1], ⟨~и́ть⟩ [13] tease, banter, chaff (*v/t.* **над** Т)

**подтя́|гивать** [1], ⟨~ну́ть⟩ [19] pull (up); draw (in *reins*); tighten; raise (*wages*); wind *or* key up; egg on; join in (*song*); **-ся** chin; brace up; improve, pick up; **~жки** *f/pl.* [5; *gen.*: -жек] suspenders, *Brt.* braces

**поду́мывать** [1] think (о П about)

**подуч|а́ть** [1], ⟨~и́ть⟩ [16] → ***учи́ть***

**поду́шка** *f* [5; *g/pl.*: -шек] pillow; cushion, pad

**подхали́м** *m* [1] toady, lickspittle

**подхва́т|ывать** [1], ⟨~и́ть⟩ [15] catch; pick up; take up; join in

**подхо́д** *m* [1] approach (*a. fig.*); **~и́ть** [15], ⟨подойти́⟩ [-ойду́, -дёшь; -ошёл; -шла́; *g. pt.* -ойдя́] (***к*** Д) approach, go (up to); arrive, come; (Д) suit, fit; **~я́щий** [17] suitable, fit(ting), appropriate; convenient

**подцеп|ля́ть** [28], ⟨~и́ть⟩ [14] hook on; couple; *fig.* pick up; *насморк* catch (a cold)

**подча́с** at times, sometimes

**подч|ёркивать** [1], ⟨~еркну́ть⟩ [20; -ёркнутый] underline; stress

**подчин|е́ние** *n* [12] subordination (*a. gr.*); submission; subjection; **~ённый** [14] subordinate; **~я́ть** [28], ⟨~и́ть⟩ [13] subject, subordinate; put under (Д s.b.'s) command; **-ся** (Д) submit (to); прика́зу obey

**под|шива́ть** [1], ⟨~ши́ть⟩ [подошью́, -шьёшь; → ***шить***] sew on (***к*** Д to); hem; file (*papers*); **~ши́пник** *m* [1] *tech.* bearing; **~ши́ть** → ***~шива́ть***; **~шу́чивать** [1], ⟨~шути́ть⟩ [15] play a trick (***над*** T on); chaff, mock (***над*** T at)

**подъе́|зд** *m* [1] entrance, porch; *дорога* drive; approach; **~зжа́ть** [1], ⟨~хать⟩ [-е́ду, -е́дешь] (***к*** Д) drive or ride up (to); approach; *coll.* drop in (on); *fig.* get round s.o., make up to s.o.

**подъём** *m* [1] lift(ing); ascent, rise (*a. fig.*); enthusiasm; *ноги* instep; ***лёгок*** (***тяжёл***) ***на ~*** nimble (slow); **~ник** *m* [1] elevator, lift, hoist; **~ный** [14]: ***~ный мост*** drawbridge

**подъе́|хать** → ***~зжа́ть***

**под|ыма́ть(ся)** → ***~нима́ть(ся)***

**поды́ск|ивать** [1], ⟨~а́ть⟩ [3] *impf.* seek, look for; *pf.* seek out, find; (*выбрать*) choose

**подыто́ж|ывать** [1], ⟨~ить⟩ [16] sum up

**поеда́ть** [1], ⟨пое́сть⟩ → ***есть***[1]

**поеди́нок** *m* [1; -нка] duel (with weapons ***на*** П) (*mst. fig.*)

**по́езд** *m* [1; *pl.*: -да́, *etc. e.*] train; **~́ка** *f* [5; *g/pl.*: -док] trip, journey; tour

**пожа́луй** maybe, perhaps; I suppose; **~ста** please; certainly, by all means; *в ответ на благодарность* don't mention it; → *a.* (***не́ за***) ***что***

**пожа́р** *m* [1] fire (***на*** В/П to/at); conflagration; **~ище** *n* [11] scene of a fire; *coll.* big fire; **~ник** *m* [1] fireman; **~ный** [14] fire…; *su.* → ***~ник***; → ***кома́нда***

**пожа́ть** → ***пожима́ть*** & ***пожина́ть***

**пожела́ни|е** *n* [12] wish, desire; ***наилу́чшие ~я*** best wishes

**пожелте́лый** [14] yellowed

**поже́ртвование** *n* [12] donation

**пожи|ва́ть** [1]: ***как*** (***вы***) ***~ва́ете?*** how are you (getting on)?; **~ви́ться** [14 *e.*; -влю́сь, -ви́шься] *pf. coll.* get s.th. at another's expense; live off; **~́зненный** [14] life…; **~ло́й** [14] elderly

**пожи|ма́ть** [1], ⟨пожа́ть⟩ [-жму́, -жмёшь; -жа́тый] → ***жать***[1]; press, squeeze; ***~ма́ть ру́ку*** shake hands; ***~ма́ть плеча́ми*** shrug one's shoulders; **~на́ть** [1], ⟨пожа́ть⟩ [-жну́, -жнёшь; -жа́тый] → ***жать***[2]; **~ра́ть** P [1], ⟨по-

**жра́ть**〉 [-жру́, -рёшь; -а́л, -а́, -о] eat up, devour; **∴тки** *coll. m/pl.* [1] belongings, (one's) things
**по́за** *f* [5] pose, posture, attitude
**поза|вчера́** the day before yesterday; **~ди́** (Р) behind; past; **~про́шлый** [14] the … before last
**позвол|е́ние** *n* [12] permission (с Р with), leave (by); **~и́тельный** [14; -лен, -льна] permissible; **~я́ть** [28], 〈**∴ить**〉 [13] allow (*a.* of), permit (Д); **~я́ть себе́** allow o.s.; venture; *расходы* afford; **∴ь(те)** may I? let me
**позвоно́|к** *m* [1; -нка́] *anat.* vertebra; **~чник** *m* [1] spinal (*or* vertebral) column, spine, backbone; **~чный** [14] vertebral; vertebrate
**по́здн|ий** [15] (-zn-) (**~о** *a.* it is) late
**поздоро́вит|ься** *coll. pf.*: **ему́ не ~ся** it won't do him much good
**поздрав|и́тель** *m* [4] congratulator; **~и́тельный** [14] congratulatory; **∴ить** → **~ля́ть**; **~ле́ние** *n* [12] congratulation; *pl.* compliments of … (**с** Т); **~ля́ть** [28], 〈**∴ить**〉 [14] (**с** Т) congratulate (on), wish many happy returns of … (*the day, occasion, event, etc.*); send (*or* give) one's compliments (of the season)
**по́зже** later; **не ~** (Р) … at the latest
**позити́вный** [14; -вен, -вна] positive
**пози́ци|я** *f* [7] *fig.* stand, position, attitude (**по** Д on); **заня́ть твёрдую ~ю** take a firm stand
**позна|ва́ть** [5], 〈**∴ть**〉 [1] perceive; (come to) know; **∴ние** *n* [12] perception; *pl.* knowledge; *philos.* cognition
**позоло́та** *f* [5] gilding
**позо́р** *m* [1] shame, disgrace, infamy; **~ить** [13], 〈о-〉 dishono(u)r, disgrace; **~ный** [14; -рен, -рна] shameful, disgraceful, infamous, ignominious
**поимённый** [14] of names; nominal; by (roll) call
**по́ис|ки** *m/pl.* [1] search (**в** П in), quest; **∴тине** truly, really
**по|и́ть** [13], 〈на-〉 *скот* water; give to drink (s.th. Т)
**пой|ма́ть** → **лови́ть**; **~ти́** → **идти́**
**пока́** for the time being (*a.* **~ что**); meanwhile; *cj.* while; **~ (не)** until; **~!** *coll.* so long!, (I'll) see you later!
**пока́з** *m* [1] demonstration; showing; **~а́ние** (*usu. pl.*) *n* [12] evidence; *law* deposition; *techn.* reading (*on a meter, etc.*); **~а́тель** *m* [4] *math.* exponent; index; *выпуска продукции и т. д.* figure; **~а́тельный** [14; -лен, -льна] significant; revealing; **~а́ть(ся)** → **~ывать(ся)**; **~но́й** [14] ostentatious; for show; **~ывать** [1], 〈**~а́ть**〉 [3] *фильм и т. д.* show; demonstrate; point; (**на** В at); *tech.* indicate, read; **~а́ть себя́** (Т) prove o.s. *or* one's worth; ***и ви́ду не ~ывать*** seem to know nothing; look unconcerned; **-ся** appear, seem (Т); come in sight; **~ываться врачу́** see a doctor
**пока́т|ость** *f* [8] declivity; slope, incline; **~ый** [14 *sh.*] slanting, sloping; *лоб* retreating
**покая́ние** *n* [12] confession; repentance
**поки|да́ть** [1], 〈**∴нуть**〉 [20] leave, quit; (*бросить*) abandon, desert
**покла|да́я**: ***не ~да́я рук*** indefatigably; **∴дистый** [14 *sh.*] complaisant; accommodating; **∴жа** *f* [5] load; luggage
**покло́н** *m* [1] bow (*in greeting*); *fig.* **посла́ть ~ы** send regards *pl.*; **~е́ние** *n* [12] (Д) worship; **~и́ться** → **кла́няться**; **~ник** *m* [1] admirer; **~я́ться** [28] (Д) worship
**поко́иться** [13] rest, lie on; (осно́вываться) be based on
**поко́|й** *m* [3] rest, peace; calm; **оста́вить в ~е** leave alone; **приёмный ~й**; casualty ward; **~йник** *m* [1], **~йница** *f* [5] the deceased; **~йный** [14; -о́ен, -о́йна] the late; *su.* → **~йник**, **~йница**
**поколе́ние** [12] generation
**поко́нчить** [16] *pf.* ([с] Т) finish; (**с** Т) do away with; *дурной привычкой* give up; **~ с собо́й** commit suicide
**покор|е́ние** *n* [12] *природы* subjugation; **~и́тель** *m* [4] subjugator; **~и́ть(ся)** → **~я́ть(ся)**; **∴ность** *f* [8] submissiveness, obedience; **∴ный** [14; -рен, -рна] obedient, submissive; **~я́ть** [28], 〈**~и́ть**〉 [13] subjugate; subdue; *сердце* win; **-ся** submit; *необходимости и т. д.* resign o.s.

П

**поко́с** *m* [1] (hay)mowing; meadow (-land)
**покри́кивать** *coll.* [1] shout (**на** В at)
**покро́в** *m* [1] cover
**покрови́тель** *m* [4] patron, protector; **~ница** *f* [5] patroness, protectress; **~ственный** [14] protective; patronizing; *тон* condescending; **~ство** *n* [9] protection (of Д); patronage; **~ствовать** [7] (Д) protect; patronize
**покро́й** *m* [3] оде́жды cut
**покры|ва́ло** *n* [9] coverlet; **~ва́ть** [1], ⟨**~́ть**⟩ [22] (Т) cover (*a.* = defray); *краской* coat; *cards* beat, trump; **-ся** cover o.s.; *сыпью* be(come) covered; **~́тие** *n* [12] cover(ing); coat(ing); defrayal; **~́шка** *f* [5; -шек] *mot.* tire (*Brt. tyre*)
**покуп|а́тель** *m* [4], **~а́тельница** *f* [5] buyer; customer; **~а́тельный** [14] purchasing; **~а́ть**[1], ⟨купи́ть⟩ [14] buy, purchase (from **у** Р); **~́ка** *f* [5; *g/pl.*: -пок] purchase; ***идти́ за ~́ками*** go shopping; **~но́й** [14] bought, purchased
**поку|ша́ться** [1], ⟨**~си́ться**⟩ [15 *e.*; -ушу́сь, -уси́шься] attempt (*v/t.* **на** В); *на чьи-л. права* encroach ([up]on); **~ше́ние** *n* [12] attempt (**на** В [up]on)
**пол**[1] *m* [1; на́ ~; на ~́; *pl. e.*] floor
**пол**[2] *m* [1; *from g/pl. e.*] sex
**пол**[3](**...**) [*g/sg., etc.*: ~(у)...] half (...)
**полага́|ть** [1], ⟨положи́ть⟩ [16] think, suppose, guess; ***на́до ~ть*** probably; ***поло́жим, что ...*** suppose, let's assume that; **-ся** rely (on **на** В); (Д) ***~ется*** must; be due *or* proper; ***как ~ется*** properly
**по́л|день** *m* [*gen.*: -(у́)дня: *g/pl.*: -дён] noon (**в** В at); → ***обе́д***; ***по́сле ~у́дня*** in the afternoon; **~доро́ги** → ***~пути́***; **~дю́жины** [gen.: -удю́жины] half (a) dozen
**по́ле** *n* [10; *pl. e.*] field (a. *fig.*; **на, в** П in, **по** Д, Т across); ground; (*край листа*) *mst. pl.* margin; **~во́й** [14] field...; *цветы* wild
**поле́зный** [14; -зен, -зна] useful, of use; *совет и т. д.* helpful; *для здоровья* wholesome, healthy
**полем|изи́ровать** [7] engage in polemics; **~́ика** *f* [5], **~и́ческий** [16] polemic
**поле́но** *n* [9; *pl.*: -нья, -ньев] log

**полёт** *m* [1] flight; ***бре́ющий ~*** lowlevel flight
**по́лз|ать** [1], **~ти́** [24] creep, crawl; **~ко́м** on all fours; **~у́чий** [17]: ***~у́чее расте́ние*** creeper, climber
**поли|ва́ть** [1], ⟨**~́ть**⟩ [-лью́, -льёшь, → ***лить***] water; *pf.* start raining (*or* pouring); **~́вка** *f* [5] watering
**полиго́н** *m* [1] *mil.* firing range
**поликли́ника** *f* [5] polyclinic; *больничная* outpatient's department
**полиня́лый** [14] faded
**поли|рова́ть** [7], ⟨от-⟩ polish; **~ро́вка** *f* [5; *g/pl.*: -вок] polish(ing)
**по́лис** *m* [1]: ***страхово́й ~*** insurance policy
**политехни́ческий** [16]: ***~ институ́т*** polytechnic
**политзаключённый** *m* [14] political prisoner
**поли́т|ик** *m* [1] politician; **~ика** *f* [5] policy; politics *pl.*; **~и́ческий** [16] political
**поли́ть** → ***полива́ть***
**полиц|е́йский** [16] police(man *su.*); **~́ия** *f* [7] police
**поли́чн|ое** *n* [14]: ***пойма́ть с ~ым*** catch red-handed
**полиэтиле́н** *m* [1], **~овый** [14] polyethylene (*Brt.* polythene)
**полк** *m* [1 *e.*: в ~у́] regiment
**по́лка** *f* [5; *g/pl.*: -лок] shelf
**полко́в|ник** *m* [1] colonel; **~о́дец** *m* [1; -дца] (*not a designation of military rank*) commander, military leader, warlord; one who leads and supervises; **~о́й** [14] regimental
**полне́йший** [17] utter, sheer
**полне́ть** [8], ⟨по-⟩ grow stout
**полно|ве́сный** [14; -сен, -сна] of full weight; weighty; **~вла́стный** [14; -тен, -тна] sovereign; **~во́дный** [14; -ден, -дна] deep; **~кро́вный** [14; -вен, -вна] fullblooded; **~лу́ние** *n* [12] full moon; **~мо́чие** *n* [12] authority, (full) power; **~мо́чный** [14; -чен, -чна] plenipotentiary; → ***полпре́д***; **~пра́вный** [14; -вен, -вна]: ***~пра́вный член*** full member; **´~стью** completely, entirely; **~та́** *f* [5] fullness; *информации* completness; (*тучность*) corpulence;

***для ~ты́ карти́ны*** to complete the picture; **~це́нный** [14; -е́нен, -е́нна] full (value)…; *fig. специалист* fullfledged

**по́лночь** *f* [8; -(у́)ночи] midnight

**по́лн|ый** [14; по́лон, полна́, по́лно́; полне́е] full (of P *or* T); (*набитый*) packed; complete, absolute; perfect (*a. right*); (*тучный*) stout; ***~ое собра́ние сочине́ний*** complete works; ***~ы́м-~о́*** *coll.* chock-full, packed (with P); lots of

**полови́к** *m* [1 *e.*] mat

**полови́н|а** *f* [5] half (***на*** B by); ***~а (в ~е) пя́того*** (at) half past four; ***два с ~ой*** two and a half; **~ка** *f* [5; *g/pl.*: -нок] half; **~чатый** [14] *fig.* indeterminate

**полови́ца** *f* [5] floor; board

**полово́дье** *n* [10] high tide (*in spring*)

**полов|о́й**[1] [14] floor…; ***~а́я тря́пка*** floor cloth; **~о́й**[2] [14] sexual; ***~а́я зре́лость*** puberty; ***~ы́е о́рганы*** *m/pl.* genitals

**поло́гий** [16; *comp.*: поло́же] gently sloping

**полож|е́ние** *n* [12] position, location; situation; (*состояние*) state, condition; *социальное* standing; (*правила*) regulations *pl.*; thesis; ***семе́йное ~е́ние*** marital status; **~и́тельный** [14; -лен, -льна] positive; *ответ* affirmative; **~и́ть(ся)** → ***класть 1. & полага́ть*(ся)**

**поло́мка** *f* [5; *g/pl.*: -мок] breakage; breakdown

**полоса́** [5; *ac/sg.*: по́лосу́; *pl.*: по́лосы, поло́с, -са́м] stripe, streak; strip; belt, zone; field; period; ***~ неуда́ч*** a run of bad luck; **~тый** [14 *sh.*] striped

**полоска́ть** [3], ⟨про-⟩ rinse; gargle; **-ся** paddle; *о флаге* flap

**по́лость** *f* [8; *from g/pl. e.*] *anat.* cavity; ***брюшна́я ~*** abdominal cavity

**полоте́нце** *n* [11; *g/pl.*: -нец] towel (T on); ***ку́хонное ~*** dish towel; ***махро́вое ~*** Turkish towel

**поло́тн|ище** *n* [11] width; **~о́** *n* [9; *pl.*: -о́тна, -о́тен, -о́тнам], **~я́ный** [14] linen(…)

**поло́ть** [17], ⟨вы-, про-⟩ weed

**пол|пре́д** *m* [1] plenipotentiary; **~пути́** halfway (*a.* ***на ~пути́***); **~сло́ва** [9; *gen.*: -(у)сло́ва] ***ни ~сло́ва*** not a word; (a few) word(s); ***останови́ться на ~(у)сло́ве*** stop short; **~со́тни** [6; *g/sg.*: -(у)со́тни; *g/pl.*: -лусотен] fifty

**полтор|а́** *m & n*, **~ы́** *f* [*gen.*: -у́тора, -ры (*f*)] one and a half; **~а́ста** [*obl. cases*; -у́тораста] a hundred and fifty

**полу|боти́нки** *old use m/pl.* [1; *g/pl.*: -нок] (low) shoes; **~го́дие** *n* [12] half year, six months; **~годи́чный**, **~годово́й** [14] half-yearly; **~гра́мотный** [14; -тен, -тна] semiliterate; **∠денный** [14] midday…; **~живой** [14; -жи́в, -а́, -о] half dead; **~защи́тник** *m* [1] *sport* halfback; **~кру́г** *m* [1] semicircle; **~ме́сяц** *m* [1] half moon, crescent; **~мра́к** *m* [1] twilight, semidarkness; **∠ночный** [14] midnight…; **~оборо́т** *m* [1] half-turn; **~о́стров** *m* [1; *pl.*: -ва́, *etc. e.*] peninsula; **~проводни́к** *m* [1] semiconductor, transistor; **~стано́к** *m* [1; -нка] *rail.* stop; **~тьма́** *f* [5] → ***~мра́к***; **~фабрика́т** *m* [1] semifinished product *or* foodstuff

**получ|а́тель** *m* [4] addressee, recipient; **~а́ть** [1], ⟨~и́ть⟩ [16] receive, get; *разрешение и т. д.* obtain; *удовольствие* derive; **-ся**; (*оказаться*) result; prove, turn out; **~е́ние** *n* [12] receipt; **∠чка** *coll. f* [5; *g/pl.*: -чек] pay(day)

**полу|ша́рие** *n* [12] hemisphere; **~шу́бок** *m* [1; -бка] knee-length sheepskin coat

**пол|цены́**: ***за ~цены́*** at half price; **~часа́** *m* [1; *g/sg.*: -уча́са] half (an) hour

**по́лчище** *n* [11] horde; *fig.* mass

**по́лый** [14] hollow

**полы́нь** *f* [8] wormwood

**полынья́** *f* [6] polnya, patch of open water in sea ice

**по́льз|а** *f* [5] use; benefit (***на, в*** B, ***для*** P for), profit, advantage; ***в ~у*** (P) in favo(u)r of; **~ователь** *m* [4] user; **~оваться** [7], ⟨вос~оваться⟩ (T) use, make use of; avail o.s. of; *репутацией и т. д.* enjoy, have; *случаем* take

**по́ль|ка** *f* [5; *g/pl.*: -лек] **1.** Pole, Polish woman; **2.** polka; **~ский** [16] Polish

**полюбо́вный** [14] amicable

**по́люс** *m* [1] pole (*a. el*)

**поля́|к** *m* [1] Pole; **~на** *f* [5] *лесная* glade; clearing; **~рный** [14] polar

**пома́да** *f* [5] pomade; ***губна́я ~*** lipstick

**помале́ньку** *coll.* so-so; in a small way; (постепе́нно) little by little
**пома́лкивать** *coll.* [1] keep silent *or* mum
**пома́|рка** [5; *g/pl.*: -рок] blot; correction
**поместить(ся)** → ***помеща́ть(ся)***
**поме́стье** *n* [10] *hist.* estate
**по́месь** *f* [8] crossbreed, mongrel
**помёт** *m* [1] dung; (*приплод*) litter, brood
**поме́|тить** → **~ча́ть**; **~тка** *f* [5; *g/pl.*: -ток] mark, note; **~ха** *f* [5] hindrance; obstacle; *pl. only radio* interference; **~ча́ть** [1], 〈**~тить**〉 [15] mark, note
**поме́ш|анный** *coll.* [14 *sh.*] crazy; mad (about ***на*** П); **~а́тельство** *n* [9] insanity; **~а́ть** → ***меша́ть***; **-ся** *pf.* go mad; be mad (***на*** П about)
**поме|ща́ть** [1], 〈**~сти́ть**〉 [15 *e.*; -ещу́, -ести́шь; -ещённый] place; (*поселить*) lodge, accommodate; *капитал* invest; insert, publish; **-ся** locate; lodge; find room; (*вмещать*) hold; be placed *or* invested; *impf.* be (located); **~ще́ние** *n* [12] premise(s), room; investment; **~́щик** *m* [1] *hist.* landowner, landlord
**помидо́р** *m* [1] tomato
**поми́л|ование** *n* [12], **~овать** [7] *pf. law* pardon; forgiveness; ***~уй бог!*** God forbid!
**поми́мо** (Р) besides, apart from
**поми́н** *m* [1]: ***лёгок на ~е*** talk of the devil; **~а́ть** [1], 〈помяну́ть〉 [19] speak about, mention; commemorate; ***не ~а́ть ли́хом*** bear no ill will (toward[s] a p. В); **~ки** *f/pl.* [5; *gen.*: -нок] commemoration (for the dead); **~у́тно** every minute; constantly
**по́мнит|ь** [13], 〈вс-〉 remember (о П); ***мне ~ся*** (as far as) I remember; ***не ~ь себя́ от ра́дости*** be beside o.s. with joy
**помо|га́ть** [1], 〈**~́чь**〉 [26; г/ж: -огу́, -о́жешь, -о́гут, -о́г, -огла́] (Д) help; aid, assist; *о лекарстве* relieve, bring relief
**помо́|и** *m/pl.* [3] slops; *coll.* **~йка** *f* [5; *g/pl.*: -о́ек] rubbish heap
**помо́л** *m* [1] grind(ing)
**помо́лвка** *f* [5; *g/pl.*: -вок] betrothal, engagement
**помо́ст** *m* [1] dais; rostrum; scaffold
**помо́чь** → ***помога́ть***
**помо́щ|ник** *m* [1], **~ница** *f* [5] assistant; helper, aide; **´~ь** *f* [8] help, aid, assistance (***с*** Т, ***при*** П with, ***на*** В/Д to one's); relief; ***маши́на ско́рой ´~и*** ambulance; ***пе́рвая ´~ь*** first aid
**по́мпа** *f* [5] pomp
**помутне́ние** *n* [12] dimness; turbidity
**по́мы|сел** *m* [1; -сла] thought; (*намерение*) design; **~шля́ть** [28], 〈**~́слить**〉 [13], think (***о*** П of), contemplate
**помяну́ть** → ***помина́ть***
**помя́тый** [14] (c)rumpled; *трава* trodden
**пона́|добиться** [14] *pf.* (Д) be, become necessary; **~слы́шке** *coll.* by hearsay
**поне|во́ле** *coll.* willy-nilly; against one's will; **~де́льник** *m* [1] Monday (***в*** В, *pl.* ***по*** Д on)
**понемно́|гу**, *coll.* **~жку** (a) little; little by little, gradually; *coll. a.* (*так себе*) so-so
**пони|жа́ть** [1], 〈**~́зить**〉 [15] lower; (*ослабить, уменьшить*) reduce (*v/i.* **-ся**; fall, sink); **~же́ние** *n* [12] fall; reduction; drop
**поник|а́ть** [1], 〈**~́нуть**〉 [21] droop, hang (one's head голово́й); *цветы* wilt
**понима́|ние** *n* [12] comprehension, understanding; conception; ***в моём ~нии*** as I see it; **~ть** [1], 〈поня́ть〉 [пойму́, ~мёшь; по́нял, -а́, -о; по́нятый (по́нят, -а́, -о)] understand, comprehend; realize; (*ценить*) appreciate; ***~ю*** (***~ешь, ~ете*** [***ли***]) I (you) see
**поно́с** *m* [1] diarrh(o)ea
**поноси́ть** [15] revile, abuse
**поно́шенный** [14 *sh.*] worn, shabby
**понто́н** [1], **~ный** [14] pontoon
**пону|жда́ть** [1], 〈**~ди́ть**〉 [15; -у-, -ждённый] force, compel
**понука́ть** [1] *coll.* urge on, spur
**пону́р|ить** [13] hang; **~ый** [14 *sh.*] downcast
**по́нчик** *m* [1] doughnut
**поны́не** *obs.* until now
**поня́т|ие** *n* [12] idea, notion; concept(ion); (***я***) ***не име́ю ни мале́йшего ~ия*** I haven't the faintest idea; **~ливый**

П

[14 *sh.*] quick-witted; **~ный** [14; -тен, -тна] understandable; intelligible; clear, plain; **~ь** → ***понима́ть***

**поо́|даль** at some distance; **~дино́чке** one by one; **~черёдный** [14] taken in turns

**поощр|е́ние** *n* [12] encouragement; ***материа́льное ~е́ние*** bonus; **~я́ть** [28], ⟨**~и́ть**⟩ [13] encourage

**попа|да́ние** *n* [12] hit; **~да́ть** [1], ⟨**~сть**⟩ [25; *pt. st.*] (**в, на** В) (*оказаться*) get; fall; find o.s.; *в* цель hit; *на поезд* catch; *coll.* (Д *impers.*) catch it; ***не ~сть*** miss; ***как ~ло*** anyhow, at random, haphazard; ***кому́ ~ло*** to the first comer (= ***пе́рвому ~вшемуся***); **-ся** (**в** В) be caught; fall (into a trap ***на у́дочку***); *coll.* (Д + *vb.* + И) *статья и т. д.* come across, chance (up)on, meet; (быва́ть) occur, there is (are); strike (Д ***на глаза́*** a p.'s eye); ***вам не ~да́лась моя́ кни́га?*** did you happen to see my book?

**попа́рно** in pairs, two by two

**попа́сть** → ***попада́ть*(ся)**

**попер|ёк** (Р) across, crosswise; *дороги* in (*a p. 's way*); **~еме́нно** in turns; **~е́чный** [14] transverse; diametrical

**попеч|е́ние** *n* [12] care, charge (in ***на*** П); **~и́тель** *m* [4] guardian, trustee

**попира́ть** [1] trample (on); (*fig.*) flout

**поплаво́к** *m* [1; -вка́] float (*a. tech*)

**попо́йка** *coll. f* [5; *g/pl.*: -о́ек] booze

**попол|а́м** in half; half-and-half; fifty-fifty; **~знове́ние** *n* [12]: ***у меня́ бы́ло ~знове́ние*** I had half a mind to …; **~ня́ть** [28], ⟨**~нить**⟩ [13] replenish, supplement; зна́ния enrich

**пополу́дни** in the afternoon, p. m.

**попра́в|ить(ся)** → ***~ля́ть*(ся)**; **~ка** *f* [5; *g/pl.*: -вок] correction; *parl.* amendment; (*улучшение*) improvement; recovery; **~ля́ть** [28], ⟨**~ить**⟩ [14] adjust; correct, (a)mend; improve; *здоровье* recover (*v/i.* **-ся**); put on weight

**по-пре́жнему** as before

**попрек|а́ть** [1], ⟨**~ну́ть**⟩ [20] reproach (with T)

**по́прище** *n* [11] field (***на*** П in); walk of life, profession

**по́про|сту** plainly, unceremoniously; ***~сту говоря́*** to put it plainly; **~ша́йка** *coll. m/f* [5; *g/pl.*: -а́ек] beggar; cadger

**попуга́й** *m* [3] parrot

**популя́рн|ость** *f* [8] popularity; **~ый** [14; -рен, -рна] popular

**попус|ти́тельство** *n* [9] tolerance; connivance; **´~ту** *coll.* in vain, to no avail

**попу́т|ный** [14] accompanying; *ветер* fair, favo(u)rable; (***~но*** in) passing, incidental(ly); **~чик** *m* [1] travel(l)ing companion; *fig. pol.* fellow-travel(l)er

**попыт|а́ть** *coll.* [1] *pf.* try (one's luck ***сча́стья***); **~ка** [5; *g/pl.*: -ток] attempt

**пор|а́**[1] *f* [5; *ac/sg.*: по́ру; *pl. st.*] time; season; ***в зи́мнюю ~у*** in winter (time); (***давно́***) ***~а́*** it's (high) time (for Д); ***до ~ы́, до вре́мени*** for the time being; not forever; ***до*** (**с**) ***каки́х ~?*** how long (since when)?; ***до сих ~*** so far, up to now (here); ***до тех ~***(, ***пока́***) so (*or* as) long (as); ***с тех ~*** (***как***) since then (since); ***на пе́рвых ~а́х*** at first, in the beginning; ***~о́й*** at times; ***вече́рней ~о́й*** → ***ве́чером***

**по́ра**[2] *f* [5] pore

**пора|боща́ть** [1], ⟨**~ти́ть**⟩ [15 *e.*; -ощу́, -оти́шь; -ощённый] enslave, enthrall

**поравня́ться** [28] *pf.* draw level ( **с** T with), come up (to), come alongside (of)

**пора|жа́ть** [1], ⟨**~зи́ть**⟩ [15 *e.*; -ажу́, -ази́шь; -ажённый] strike (*a. fig.* = amaze; *med.* affect); defeat; **~же́ние** *n* [12] defeat; *law* disenfranchisement; **~зи́тельный** [14; -лен, -льна] striking; **~зи́ть** → ***~жа́ть***; **~нить** [13] *pf.* wound, injure

**порва́ть(ся)** → ***порыва́ть*(ся)**

**поре́з** [1], **~ать** [3] *pf.* cut

**поре́й** *m* [3] leek

**по́ристый** [14 *sh.*] porous

**порица́|ние** [12], **~ть** [1] blame, censure

**по́ровну** in equal parts, equally

**поро́г** *m* [1] threshold; *pl.* rapids

**поро́|да** *f* [5] breed, species, race; о *человеке* stock; *geol.* rock; **~дистый** [14 *sh.*] thoroughbred; **~жда́ть** [1], ⟨**~ди́ть**⟩ [15 *e.*; -ожу́, -оди́шь; -ождённый] engender, give rise to, entail

**поро́жний** *coll.* [15] empty; idling

П

**по́рознь** *coll.* separately; one by one
**поро́к** *m* [1] vice; *речи* defect; *сердца* disease
**поро́лон** *m* [1] foam rubber
**поросёнок** *m* [2] piglet
**поро́|ть** [17] **1.** ⟨рас-⟩ undo, unpick; *impf. coll.* talk (***вздор*** nonsense); **2.** *coll.* ⟨вы-⟩ whip, flog; **´~х** *m* [1] gunpowder; **~хово́й** [14] gunpowder …
**поро́ч|ить** [16], ⟨о-⟩ discredit; *репутацию* blacken, defame; **~ный** [14; -чен, -чна] *круг* vicious; *идея и т. д.* faulty; *человек* depraved
**порошо́к** *m* [1; -шка́] powder
**порт** *m* [1; в ~у́; *from g/pl. e.*] port; harbo(u)r
**порт|ати́вный** [14; -вен, -вна] portable; **´~ить** [15], ⟨ис-⟩ spoil; **-ся** (*v/i.*) break down
**порт|ни́ха** *f* [5] dressmaker; **~но́й** *m* [14] tailor
**порто́в|ый** [14] port…, dock…; ***~ый го́род*** seaport
**портре́т** *m* [1] portrait; (похо́жесть) likeness
**портсига́р** *m* [1] cigar(ette) case
**португа́л|ец** *m* [1; -льца] Portuguese; **~ка** *f* [5; *g/pl.*: -лок], **~ьский** [16] Portuguese
**порт|упе́я** *f* [6] *mil.* sword belt; shoulder belt; **~фе́ль** *m* [4] brief case; *министра* (*functions and office*) portfolio
**пору́|ка** *f* [5] bail (***на*** В *pl.* on), security; guarantee; ***кругова́я ~ка*** collective guarantee; **~ча́ть** [1], ⟨~чи́ть⟩ [16] charge (Д/В a p. with); commission, bid, instruct (+ *inf.*); entrust; **~че́ние** *n* [12] commission; instruction; *dipl.* mission; (*a. comm.*) order (***по*** Д by, on behalf of); **~чик** *m* [1] *obs.* (first) lieutenant; **~чи́тель** *m* [4] guarantor; **~чи́тельство** *n* [9] (*залог*) bail, surety, guarantee; **~чи́ть** → ***~ча́ть***
**порх|а́ть** [1], *once* ⟨~ну́ть⟩ [20] flit
**по́рция** *f* [7] (*of food*) portion, helping
**по́р|ча** *f* [5] spoiling; damage; **~шень** *m* [4; -шня] (*tech.*) piston
**поры́в** *m* [1] gust, squall; *гнева и т. д.* fit, outburst; *благородный* impulse; **~а́ть** [1], ⟨порва́ть⟩ [-ву́, -вёшь; -а́л, -а́, -о; по́рванный] tear; break off (**с** Т with); **-ся** *v/i.*; *impf.* strive; *a.* → ***рва́ть(ся)***; **~истый** [14 *sh.*] gusty; *fig.* impetuous, fitful
**поря́дко|вый** [14] *gr.* ordinal; **~м** *coll.* rather
**поря́д|ок** *m* [1; -дка] order; (*последовательность*) sequence; *pl.* conditions; ***~ок дня*** agenda; ***в ~ке исключе́ния*** by way of an exception; ***это в ~ке веще́й*** it's quite natural; ***по ~ку*** one after another; **~очный** [14; -чен, -чна] *человек* decent; fair(ly large *or* great)
**посад|и́ть** → ***сажа́ть & сади́ть***; **´~ка** *f* [5; *g/pl.*: -док] planting; *naut.* embarkation, (*a. rail.*) boarding; *ae.* landing; ***вы́нужденная ´~ка*** forced landing; **´~очный** [14] landing…
**по-сво́ему** in one's own way
**посвя|ща́ть** [1], ⟨~ти́ть⟩ [15 *e.*; -ящу́, -яти́шь; -ящённый] devote ([o.s.] to [**себя́**] Д); *кому-л.* dedicate; *в тайну* let, initiate (***в*** В into); **~ще́ние** *n* [12] initiation; dedication
**посе́в** *m* [1] sowing; crop; **~но́й** [14] sowing; ***~на́я пло́щадь*** area under crops
**поседе́вший** [14] (turned) gray, *Brt.* grey
**поселе́нец** [1; -нца] settler
**пос|ёлок** *m* [1; -лка] urban settlement; **~еля́ть** [28], ⟨~ели́ть⟩ [13] settle; **-ся** (*v/i.*) put up (***в*** П at)
**посереди́не** in the middle *or* midst of
**посе|ти́тель** [4], **~ти́тельница** *f* [5] visitor, caller; **~ти́ть** → ***~ща́ть***; **~ща́емость** *f* [8] attendance; **~ща́ть** [1], ⟨~ти́ть⟩ [15 *e.*; -ещу́, -ети́шь; -ещённый] visit, call on; *impf. занятия и т. д.* attend; **~ще́ние** *n* [12] visit (Р to), call
**поси́льный** [14; -лен, -льна] one's strength *or* possibilities; feasible
**поскользну́ться** [20] *pf.* slip
**поско́льку** so far as, as far as
**посла́|ние** *n* [12] message; *lit.* epistle; **ºния** *Bibl.* the Epistles; **~нник** *m* [1] *dipl.* envoy; **~ть** → ***посыла́ть***
**по́сле 1.** (Р) after (*a.* ***~ того́ как*** + *vb.*); ***~ чего́*** whereupon; **2.** *adv.* after(ward[s]), later (on); **~вое́нный** [14] postwar

**после́дний** [15] last; *известия, мода* latest; (*окончательный*) last, final; *из двух* latter; worst
**после́д|ователь** *m* [4] follower; **~ова-тельный** [14; -лен, -льна] consistent; successive; **~ствие** *n* [12] consequence; **~ующий** [17] subsequent, succeeding, following
**после|за́втра** the day after tomorrow; **~сло́вие** *n* [12] epilogue
**посло́вица** *f* [5] proverb
**послуш|а́ние** *n* [12] obedience; **∠ник** *m* [1] novice; **∠ный** [14; -шен, -шна] obedient
**посм|а́тривать** [1] look (at) from time to time; **~е́иваться** [1] chuckle; laugh (***над*** T at); **~е́ртный** [14] posthumous; **~е́шище** *n* [11] laughingstock, butt; **~ея́ние** *n* [12] ridicule
**посо́б|ие** *n* [12] relief, benefit; textbook, manual; ***нагля́дные ~ия*** visual aids; ***~ие по безрабо́тице*** unemployment benefit
**посо́л** *m* [1; -сла́] ambassador; **~ьство** *n* [9] embassy
**поспа́ть** [-сплю́, -спи́шь; -спа́л, -а́, -о] *pf.* (have a) nap
**поспе|ва́ть** [1], ⟨**∠ть**⟩ [8] (*созревать*) ripen; (*of food being cooked or prepared*) be done; *coll.* → ***успева́ть***
**поспе́шн|ость** *f* [8] haste; **~ый** [14; -шен, -шна] hasty, hurried; (*необдуманный*) rash
**посред|и́(не)** (P) amid(st), in the middle (of); **∠ник** *m* [1] mediator, intermediary, *comm.* middleman; **∠ничество** *n* [9] mediation; **∠ственность** *f* [8] mediocrity; **∠ственный** [14 *sh.*] middling; mediocre; ***∠ственно*** *a.* fair, so-so, satisfactory, C (mark; → ***тро́йка***); **∠ством** (P) by means of
**пост**[1] *m* [1 *e.*] post; ***~ управле́ния*** *tech.* control station
**пост**[2] *m* [1 *e.*] fasting; *eccl.* ***Вели́кий ~*** Lent
**поста́в|ить** → ***~ля́ть & ста́вить***; **~ка** *f* [5; *g/pl.*: -вок] delivery (on при); supply; **~ля́ть** [28], ⟨**~ить**⟩ [14] deliver (*v/t.*; Д p.); supply, furnish; **~щи́к** *m* [1 *e.*] supplier
**постан|ови́ть** → ***~овля́ть***; **~о́вка** *f* [5; *g/pl.*: -вок] *thea.* staging, production; *дела* organization; ***~о́вка вопро́са*** the way a question is put; **~овле́ние** *n* [12] resolution, decision; *parl., etc.* decree; **~овля́ть** [28], ⟨**~ови́ть**⟩ [14] decide; decree; **~о́вщик** *m* [1] stage manager; director (of film); producer (of play)
**посте|ли́ть** → ***стлать***; **∠ль** *f* [8] bed; **~пе́нный** [14; -е́нен, -е́нна] gradual
**пости|га́ть** [1], ⟨**∠гнуть**⟩ & ⟨**∠чь**⟩ [21] comprehend, grasp; *несчастье* befall; **~жи́мый** [14 *sh.*] understandable; conceivable
**пост|ила́ть** [1] → ***стлать***; **~и́ться** [15 *e.*; пощу́сь, пости́шься] fast; **~и́чь** → ***~ига́ть***; **∠ный** [14; -тен, -тна́, -о] *coll.* *мясо* lean; *fig.* sour; (*ханжеский*) sanctimonious
**посто́льку**: ***~ поско́льку*** to that extent, insofar as
**посторо́нни|й** [15] strange(r *su.*), outside(r), foreign (*тж. предмет*); unauthorized; ***~м вход воспрещён*** unauthorized persons not admitted
**постоя́н|ный** [14; -я́нен, -я́нна] constant, permanent; (*непрерывный*) continual, continuous; *работа* steady; *el.* direct; **~ство** *n* [9] constancy
**пострада́вший** [17] victim; *при аварии* injured
**постре́л** *coll.* *m* [1] little imp, rascal
**постри|га́ть** [1], ⟨**∠чь**⟩ [26 г/ж: -игу́, -ижёшь, -игу́т] (**-ся** have one's hair) cut; become a monk *or* nun
**постро́йка** *f* [5; *g/pl.*: -о́ек] construction; *здание* building; building site
**поступ|а́тельный** [14] forward, progressive; **~а́ть** [1], ⟨**~и́ть**⟩ [14] act; (***с*** T) treat, deal (with), handle; (***в, на*** B) enter, join; *univ.* matriculate; *заявление* come in, be received (***на*** B for); ***~и́ть в прода́жу*** be on sale; **-ся** (T) waive; **~ле́ние** *n* [12] entry; matriculation; receipt; ***~ле́ние дохо́дов*** revenue return; **∠ок** *m* [1; -пка] act; (*поведение*) behavio(u)r, conduct; **′~ь** [8] gait, step
**посты́|дный** [14; -ден, -дна] shameful;

**~лый** [14 *sh.*] *coll.* hateful; repellent

**посу́да** *f* [5] crockery; plates and dishes; ***фая́нсовая*** (*фарфоровая*) **~** earthenware (china)

**посчастли́ви|ться** [14; *impers.*] *pf.*: ***ей ~лось*** she succeeded (in *inf.*) *or* was lucky enough (to)

**посыл|а́ть** [1], ⟨посла́ть⟩ [пошлю́, -шлёшь; по́сланный] send (for ***за*** T); dispatch; **~́ка**[1] *f* [5; *g/pl.*: -лок] package, parcel

**посы́лка**[2] *f* [5; *g/pl.*: -лок] *philos.* premise

**посып|а́ть** [1], ⟨**~́ать**⟩ [2] (be-) strew (T over; with); sprinkle (with); **~́аться** *pf.* begin to fall; *fig.* rain; *coll. о вопросах* shower (with)

**посяг|а́тельство** *n* [9] encroachment; infringement; **~а́ть** [1], ⟨**~ну́ть**⟩ [20] encroach, infringe (***на*** B on); attempt

**пот** *m* [1] sweat; ***весь в ~у́*** sweating all over

**пота|йно́й** [14] secret; **~ка́ть** *coll.* [1] indulge; **~со́вка** *coll. f* [5; *g/pl.*: -вок] scuffle

**по-тво́ему** in your opinion; as you wish; ***пусть бу́дет ~*** have it your own way

**потво́рство** *n* [9] indulgence, connivance; **~вать** [7] indulge, connive (Д at)

**потёмки** *f/pl.* [5; *gen.*: -мок] darkness

**потенциа́л** *m* [1] potential

**потерпе́вший** [17] victim

**потёртый** [14 *sh.*] shabby, threadbare, worn

**поте́ря** *f* [6] loss; *времени, денег* waste

**потесни́ть** → ***тесни́ть***; **-ся** squeeze up (*to make room for others*)

**поте́ть** [8], ⟨вс-⟩ sweat, *coll.* toil; *стекло* ⟨*за-*⟩ mist over

**поте́|ха** *f* [5] fun, *coll.* lark; **~шный** [14; -шен, -шна] funny, amusing

**поти|ра́ть** *coll.* [1] rub; **~хо́ньку** *coll.* slowly; silently; secretly, on the sly

**по́тный** [14; -тен, -тна; -о] sweaty

**пото́к** *m* [1] stream; torrent; flow

**пото|ло́к** *m* [1; -лка́] ceiling; ***взять что́-л. с ~лка́*** spin s.th. out of thin air

**пото́м** afterward(s); then; ***~ок*** *m* [1; -мка] descendant, offspring; **~ственный** [14] hereditary; **~ство** *n* [9] posterity, descendants *pl.*

**потому́** that is why; ***~ что*** because

**пото́п** *m* [1] flood, deluge

**потреб|и́тель** *m* [4] consumer; **~и́ть** → ***~ля́ть***; **~ле́ние** *n* [12] consumption; use; **~ля́ть** [28], ⟨**~и́ть**⟩ [14 *e.*; -блю́, -би́шь; -блённый] consume; use; **~́ность** *f* [8] need, want (***в*** П of), requirement

**потрёпанный** *coll.* [14] shabby, tattered, worn

**потро|ха́** *m/pl.* [1 *e.*] pluck; giblets; **~ши́ть** [16 *e.*; -шу́, -ши́шь; -шённый], ⟨вы-⟩ draw, disembowel

**потряс|а́ть** [1], ⟨**~ти́**⟩ [24; -с-] shake (*a. fig.*); **~а́ющий** [17] tremendous; **~е́ние** *n* [12] shock; **~ти́** → ***~а́ть***

**поту́|ги** *f/pl.* [5] *fig.* (vain) attempt; **~пля́ть** [28], ⟨**~пи́ть**⟩ [14] *взгляд* cast down; *голову* hang; **~ха́ть** [1] → ***ту́хнуть***

**потя́гивать(ся)** → ***тяну́ть(ся)***

**поуч|а́ть** [1] *coll.* preach at, lecture; **~и́тельный** [14; -лен, -льна] instructive

**поха́бный** P [14; -бен, -бна] *coll.* obscene, smutty

**похвал|а́** *f* [5] praise; commendation; **~́ьный** [14; -лен, -льна] commendable, praiseworthy

**похи|ща́ть** [1], ⟨**~́тить**⟩ [15; -и́щу; -и́щенный] purloin; *человека* kidnap; **~ще́ние** *n* [12] theft; kidnap(p)ing, abduction

**похлёбка** *f* [5; *g/pl.*: -бок] soup

**похме́лье** *n* [10] hangover

**похо́д** *m* [1] march; *mil. fig.*, campaign; *туристский* hike; ***кресто́вый ~*** crusade

**походи́ть** [15] (***на*** B) be like, resemble

**похо́д|ка** *f* [5] gait; **~ный** [14] *песня* marching

**похожде́ние** *n* [12] adventure

**похо́ж|ий** [17 *sh.*] (***на*** B) like, resembling; similar (to); ***быть ~им*** look like; ***ни на что не ~е*** *coll.* like nothing else; unheard of

**по-хозя́йски** thriftily; wisely

**похо|ро́нный** [14] funeral...; *марш* dead; ***~ро́нное бюро́*** undertaker's office; **~́роны** *f/pl.* [5; -о́н, -она́м] funeral,

burial (**на** П at);**~тли́вый** [14 *sh.*] lustful, lewd; **´~ть** *f* [8] lust
**поцелу́й** *m* [3] kiss (**в** В on)
**по́чва** *f* [5] soil, (*a. fig.*) ground
**почём** *coll.* how much (is/are)…; (*only used with parts of verb знать*) **~ я зна́ю, что …** how should I know that
**почему́** why; **~-то** for some reason
**по́черк** *m* [1] handwriting
**почерпну́ть** [20; -е́рпнутый] get, obtain
**по́честь** *f* [8] hono(u)r
**почёт** *m* [1] hono(u)r, esteem; hono(u)rable; (*караул* guard) of hono(u)r
**почи́н** *m* [1] initiative; **по со́бственному ~у** on his own initiative
**почи́н|ка** *f* [5; *g/pl.*: -нок] repair; **отдава́ть в ~ку** have s.th. repaired; **~я́ть** [28] → **чини́ть** *1a*
**поч|ита́ть**[1] [1], ⟨**~ти́ть**⟩ [-чту́, -ти́шь; -чтённый] esteem, respect, hono(u)r; **~ти́ть па́мять встава́нием** stand in s.o.'s memory; **~ита́ть**[2] [1] *pf.* read (a while)
**по́чка** *f* [5; *g/pl.*: -чек] **1.** *bot.* bud; **2.** *anat.* kidney
**по́чт|а** *f* [5] mail, *Brt.* post (**по** Д by); **~альо́н** *m* [1] mailman, *Brt.* postman; **~а́мт** *m* [1] main post office (**на** П at)
**почте́н|ие** *n* [12] respect (**к** Д for), esteem; **~ный** [14; -е́нен, -е́нна] respectable; *возраст* venerable
**почти́** almost, nearly, all but; **~тельность** *f* [8] respect; **~тельный** [14; -лен, -льна] respectful; *coll. о расстоянии и т. д.* considerable; **~ть** → **почита́ть**
**почто́в|ый** [14] post(al), mail…; post-office; **~ый я́щик** mail (*Brt.* letter) box; **~ый и́ндекс** zip (*Brt.* post) code; **~ое отделе́ние** post office
**по́шл|ина** *f* [5] customs, duty; **~ость** [8] vulgarity; **~ый** [14; -пошл, -á, -o] vulgar
**пошту́чный** [14] by the piece
**поща́да** *f* [5] mercy
**поэ́|зия** *f* [7] poetry; **~т** *m* [1] poet; **~ти́ческий** [16] poetic(al)
**поэ́тому** therefore; and so
**появ|и́ться** → **~ля́ться**; **~ле́ние** *n* [12] appearance; **~ля́ться** [28], ⟨**~и́ться**⟩ [14] appear; emerge
**по́яс** *m* [1; *pl.*: -cá, *etc. e.*] belt; zone
**поясн|е́ние** *n* [12] explanation; **~и́тельный** [14] explanatory; **~и́ть** → **~я́ть**; **~и́ца** *f* [5] small of the back; **~о́й** [14] waist…; zonal; *портрет* half-length; **~я́ть** [28], ⟨**~и́ть**⟩ [13] explain
**праба́бушка** *f* [5; *g/pl.*: -шек] great-grandmother
**пра́вд|а** *f* [5] truth; (**э́то**) **~а** it is true; **ва́ша ~а** you are right; **не ~а ли?** isn't it, (s)he?, aren't you, they?, do(es)n't … (*etc.*)⟩?; **~и́вый** [14 *sh.*] true, truthful; **~оподо́бный** [14; -бен, -бна] (*вероятный*) likely, probable; (*похожий на правду*) probable, likely
**пра́ведн|ик** *m* [1] righteous person; **~ый** [14; -ден, -дна] just, righteous, upright
**пра́вил|о** *n* [9] rule; principle; *pl.* regulations; **как ~о** as a rule; **~а у́личного движе́ния** traffic regulations; **~ьный** [14; -лен, -льна] correct, right; *черты лица и т. д.* regular
**прави́тель** *m* [4] ruler; **~ственный** [14] governmental; **~ство** *n* [9] government
**пра́в|ить** [14] (T) govern, rule; *mot.* drive; *гранки* (proof) read; **~ка** *f* [5] proofreading; **~ле́ние** *n* [12] governing; board of directors; managing *or* governing body
**пра́внук** *m* [1] great-grandson
**пра́во**[1] *n* [9; *pl. e.*] right (**на** В to; **по** Д of, by); law; **води́тельские права́** driving license (*Brt.* licence); **~**[2] *adv. coll.* indeed, really; **~во́й** [14] legal; **~мо́чный** [14; -чен, -чна] competent; authorized; (*оправданный*) justifiable; **~наруши́тель** *m* [1] offender; **~писа́ние** *n* [12] orthography, spelling; **~сла́вие** *n* [12] Orthodoxy; **~сла́вный** [14] Orthodox; **~су́дие** *n* [12] administration of the law; **~та́** *f* [5] rightness
**пра́вый** [14; *fig.* прав, -á, -o] right, correct (*a. fig.*; *a. side*, on *a.* **с** P), right-hand
**пра́вящий** [17] ruling
**пра́дед** *m* [1] great-grandfather
**пра́здн|ик** *m* [1] (public) holiday; (religious) feast; festival; **с ~иком!** compliments *pl.* (of the season)!; **~ичный** [14] festive, holiday…; **~ование** *n* [12] cele-

bration; **~овать** [7], ⟨от⟩ celebrate; **~ость** *f* [8] idleness; **~ый** [14; -ден, -дна] idle, inactive

**пра́кти|к** *m* [1] practical worker *or* person; **~ка** *f* [5] practice (**на** П in); ***войти́ в ~ку*** become customary; **~кова́ть** [7] practice (-ise); **-ся** (*v/i.*); be in use *or* used; **~́ческий** [16], **~́чный** [14; чен, -чна] practical

**пра́порщик** *m* [1] (*in tsarist army*) ensign; (*in Russian army*) warrant officer

**прах** *m* [1; *no pl.*] *obs. rhet.* dust; ashes *pl.* (*fig.*); ***всё пошло́ ~́ом*** our efforts were in vain

**пра́чечная** *f* [14] laundry

**пребыва́|ние** *n* [12], **~ть** [1] stay

**превзойти́** → ***превосходи́ть***

**превоз|мога́ть** [1], ⟨~мо́чь⟩ [26; г/ж: -огу́, -о́жешь, -о́гут; -о́г, -гла́] overcome, surmount; **~носи́ть** [15], ⟨~нести́⟩ [24 -с-] extol, exalt

**превосх|оди́тельство** *n* [9] *hist.* Excellency; **~оди́ть** [15], ⟨превзойти́⟩ [-йду́, -йдёшь, *etc.*, → ***идти́***; -йдённый] excel (in), surpass (in); **~о́дный** [14; -ден, -дна] superb, outstanding; *качество* superior; superlative *a. gr.*; **~о́дство** *n* [9] superiority

**превра|ти́ть(ся)** → ***~ща́ть(ся)***; **~́тность** *f* [8] vicissitude; *судьбы* reverses; **~́тный** [14; -тен, тна] *неверный* wrong, mis-…; **~ща́ть** [1], ⟨~ти́ть⟩ [15 *e.*; -ащу́, -ати́шь; -ащённый] change, convert, turn, transform (**в** В into) (*v/i.* **-ся**); **~ще́ние** *n* [12] change; transformation

**превы|ша́ть** [1], ⟨~́сить⟩ [15] exceed; **~ше́ние** *n* [12] excess, exceeding

**прегра́|да** *f* [5] barrier; obstacle; **~жда́ть** [1], ⟨~ди́ть⟩ [15 *e.*; -ажу́, -ади́шь; -аждённый] bar, block, obstruct

**пред** → ***пе́ред***

**преда|ва́ть** [5], ⟨~́ть⟩ [-да́м, -да́шь, *etc.*, → ***да́ть***; пре́дал, -а́, -о; -да́й(те)!; пре́данный (-ан, -а́, -о)] betray; ***~́ть гла́сности*** make public; ***~́ть забве́нию*** consign to oblivion; ***~́ть суду́*** bring to trial; **-ся** (Д) indulge (in); devote o.s., give o.s. up (to); *отчаянию* give way to (*despair*); **~́ние** *n* [12] legend; tradition; **´~нный** [14 *sh.*] devoted, faithful, true; → ***и́скренний***; **~́тель** *m* [4] traitor; **~́тельский** [16] treacherous; **~́тельство** *n* [9] *pol.* betrayal, perfidy, treachery; **~́ть(ся)** → ***~ва́ть(ся)***

**предвар|и́тельно** as a preliminary, before(hand); **~и́тельный** [14] preliminary; **~я́ть** [28], ⟨~и́ть⟩ [13] (В) forestall; anticipate; *выступление и т. д.* preface

**предве́|стие** → ***предзнаменова́ние***; **~стник** *m* [1] precursor, herald; **~ща́ть** [1] portend, presage

**предвзя́тый** [14 *sh.*] preconceived

**предви́деть** [11] foresee

**предвку|ша́ть** [1], ⟨~си́ть⟩ [15] look forward (to); **~ше́ние** *n* [12] (pleasurable) anticipation

**предводи́тель** *m* [4] leader; *hist.* marshal of the nobility; ringleader, **~ство** *n* [9] leadership

**предвосх|ища́ть** [1], ⟨~и́тить⟩ [15; -ищу́] anticipate, forestall

**предвы́борный** [14] (pre)election…

**преде́л** *m* [1] limit, bound(ary) (**в** П within); *страны* border; *pl.* precincts; ***положи́ть ~*** put an end (to); **~ьный** [14] maximum…, utmost, extreme

**предзнаменова́|ние** *n* [12] omen, augury, portent; **~ть** [7] *pf.* portend, augur, bode

**предисло́вие** *n* [12] preface

**предл|ага́ть** [1], ⟨~ожи́ть⟩ [16] offer (a p. s.th. Д/В); *идею и т. д.* propose, suggest; (*велеть*) order

**предло́|г** *m* [1] pretext (on, under ***под*** Т), pretense (under); *gr.* preposition; **~же́ние** *n* [12] offer; proposal, proposition, suggestion; *parl.* motion; *comm.* supply; *gr.* sentence, clause; **~жи́ть** → ***предлага́ть***; **~жный** [14] *gr.* prepositional (*case*)

**предме́стье** *n* [10] suburb

**предме́т** *m* [1] object; subject (matter); *comm.* article; **на ~** (Р) with the object of; **~ный** [14]: ***~ный указа́тель*** index

**предназн|ача́ть** [1], ⟨~а́чить⟩ [16] (**-ся** be) intend(ed) for, destine(d) for

**преднаме́ренный** [14 *sh.*] premeditated, deliberate

**пре́док** *m* [1; -дка] ancestor

П

**предопредел|éние** *n* [12] predestination; **~я́ть** [28], ⟨**~и́ть**⟩ [13] predetermine
**предост|авля́ть** [28], ⟨**~а́вить**⟩ [14] (Д) let (a p.) leave (to); give; *кредит, право* grant; *в распоряжение* place (at a p.'s disposal)
**предостер|ега́ть** [1], ⟨**~е́чь**⟩ [26; г/ж] warn (**от** Р of, against); **~еже́ние** *n* [12] warning, caution
**предосторо́жност|ь** *f* [8] precaution(-ary measure ***ме́ра ~и***)
**предосуди́тельный** [14; -лен, льна] reprehensible, blameworthy
**предотвра|ща́ть** [1], ⟨**~ти́ть**⟩ [15 *е.*; -ащу́; -ати́шь; -ащённый] avert, prevent; **~ще́ние** *n* [12] prevention
**предохран|е́ние** *n* [12] protection (**от** Р from, against); **~и́тельный** [14] precautionary; *med.* preventive; *tech.* safety…; **~я́ть** [28], ⟨**~и́ть**⟩ [13] guard, preserve (**от** Р from, against)
**предпис|а́ние** *n* [12] order, injunction; instructions, directions; **~ывать** [1], ⟨**~а́ть**⟩ [3] order, prescribe
**предпол|ага́ть** [1], ⟨**~ожи́ть**⟩ [16] suppose, assume; *impf.* (*намереваться*) intend, plan; (*быть условием*) presuppose; **~ожи́тельный** [14; -лен, -льна] conjectural; hypothetical; *дата* estimated; **~ожи́ть** → ***~ага́ть***
**предпо|сла́ть** → ***~сыла́ть***; **~сле́дний** [15] penultimate, last but one; **~сыла́ть** [1], ⟨**~сла́ть**⟩ [-шлю́, -шлёшь; → ***слать***] preface (with); **~сы́лка** *f* [5; *g/pl.*: -лок] (pre)condition, prerequiste
**предпоч|ита́ть** [1], ⟨**~е́сть**⟩ [25; -т-: -чту́, -чтёшь; -чёл, -чла́; -чтённый] prefer; *pt.* + ***бы*** would rather; **~те́ние** *n* [12] preference; predilection; ***отда́ть ~те́ние*** (Д) show a preference for; give preference to; **~ти́тельный** [14; -лен, -льна] preferable
**предпри|и́мчивость** *f* [8] enterprise; **~и́мчивый** [14 *sh.*] enterprising; **~нима́тель** *m* [4] entrepreneur; employer; **~нима́ть** [1], ⟨**~ня́ть**⟩ [-иму́, -и́мешь; -и́нял, -а́, -о; -и́нятый (-и́нят, -а́, -о)] undertake; **~я́тие** *n* [12] undertaking, enterprise; *завод и т. д.* plant, works, factory (**на** П at); ***риско́ванное ~я́тие*** risky undertaking
**предраспол|ага́ть** [1], ⟨**~ожи́ть**⟩ [16] predispose; **~оже́ние** *n* [12] predisposition (to)
**предрассу́док** *m* [1; -дка] prejudice
**предрешённый** [14; -шён, -шена́] predetermined, already decided
**председа́тель** *m* [4] chairman; president; **~ство** *n* [9] chairmanship; presidency; **~ствовать** [7] preside (**на** П over), be in the chair
**предсказ|а́ние** *n* [12] prediction; *погоды* forecast; (*прорицание*) prophecy; **~ывать** [1], ⟨**~а́ть**⟩ [3] foretell, predict; forecast; prophesy
**предсме́ртный** [14] occurring before death
**представи́тель** *m* [4] representative; → *а.* ***полпре́д***; **~ный** [14; -лен, -льна] representative; *о внешности* stately, imposing; **~ство** *n* [9] representation; → *а.* ***полпре́дство***
**предста́в|ить(ся)** → ***~ля́ть(ся)***; **~ле́ние** *n* [12] *книги и т. д.* presentation; *thea.* performance; *при знакомстве* introduction; idea, notion; **~ля́ть** [28], ⟨**~ить**⟩ [14] present; **-ся** present o.s., occur, offer; (*предъявлять*) produce; introduce (o.s.); (*а.* ***собо́й***) represent, be; act (*а.* = feign **~ля́ться** [Т]); (*esp.* ***~ля́ть себе́***) imagine; (*к званию*) propose (**к** Д for); *refl. а.* appear; seem
**предст|ава́ть** [5], ⟨**~а́ть**⟩ [-а́ну, -а́нешь] appear (before); **~оя́ть** [-ои́т] be in store (Д for), lie ahead; (will) have to; **~оя́щий** [17] (forth)coming
**преду|бежде́ние** *n* [12] prejudice, bias; **~га́дывать**, ⟨**~гада́ть**⟩ [1] guess; foresee; **~мы́шленный** [14] → ***преднаме́ренный***
**предупре|ди́тельный** [14; -лен, -льна] preventive; *человек* obliging; **~жда́ть** [1], ⟨**~ди́ть**⟩ [15 *е.*; -ежу́, -еди́шь; -еждённый] forestall; anticipate (*p.*); (*предотвращать*) prevent (*th.*); *об опасности и т. д* warn (**о** П of); *об уходе* give notice (of); **~жде́ние** *n* [12] warning; notice; notification; prevention

П

**предусм|áтривать** [1], ⟨**~отрéть**⟩ [9; -отрю́, -óтришь] foresee; (*обеспечивать*) provide (for), stipulate; **~отри́тельный** [14; -лен, -льна] prudent, far-sighted

**предчу́вств|ие** *n* [12] presentiment; foreboding; **~овать** [7] have a presentiment (of)

**предшéств|енник** *m* [1] predecessor; **~овать** [7] (Д) precede

**предъяв|и́тель** *m* [4] bearer; **~ля́ть** [28], ⟨**~и́ть**⟩ [14] present, produce, show; *law* ***~ля́ть иск*** bring a suit *or* an action (***прóтив*** Д against); ***~ля́ть прáво на*** (В) raise a claim to

**пре|дыду́щий** [17] preceding, previous; **~éмник** *m* [1] successor

**прéж|де** formerly; (at) first; (Р) before (*a.* ***~де чем***); **~деврéменный** [14; -енен, -енна] premature, early; **~ний** [15] former, previous

**презид|éнт** *m* [1] president; **~иум** *m* [1] presidium

**през|ирáть** [1] despise; ⟨**~рéть**⟩ [9] scorn, disdain; **~рéние** *n* [12] contempt (***к*** Д for); **~рéть** → ***~ирáть***; **~ри́тельный** [14; -лен, -льна] contemptuous, scornful, disdainful

**преиму́ществ|енно** chiefly, principally, mainly; **~о** *n* [9] advantage; preference; privilege; **по ~у** → ***~енно***

**прейскурáнт** *m* [1] price list

**преклон|éние** *n* [12] admiration (***пéред*** Т of); **~и́ться** → ***~я́ться***; **~ный** [14] old; advanced; **~я́ться** [28], ⟨**~и́ться**⟩ [13] revere, worship

**прекослóвить** [14] contradict

**прекрáсный** [14; -сен, -сна] beautiful; fine; splendid, excellent; ***~ пол*** the fair sex; *adv. a.* perfectly well

**прекра|щáть** [1], ⟨**~ти́ть**⟩ [15 *e.*; -ащу́, -ати́шь; -ащённый] stop, cease, end (*v/i.* **-ся**); (*прерывать*) break off; **~щéние** *n* [12] cessation, discontinuance

**прелéст|ный** [14; -тен, -тна] lovely, charming, delightful; **ˊ~ь** *f* [8] charm; *coll.* → ***~ный***

**прелом|лéние** *n* [12] *phys.* refraction; *fig.* interpretation; **~ля́ть** [28], ⟨**~и́ть**⟩ [14; -млённый] (**-ся** be) refract(ed)

**прéлый** [14 *sh.*] rotten; musty

**прель|щáть** [1], ⟨**~сти́ть**⟩ [15 *e.*; -льщу́, -льсти́шь; -льщённый] (**-ся** be) charm(ed), tempt(ed), attract(ed)

**прелю́дия** *f* [7] prelude

**преми́нуть** [19] *pf.* fail (*used only with* ***не*** + *inf.*:) not fail to

**прéмия** *f* [7] prize; bonus; *страховая* premium

**премьéр** *m* [1] premier, (*usu.* **~-мини́стр**) prime minister; **~а** *f* [5] *thea.* première, first night

**пренебр|егáть** [1], ⟨**~éчь**⟩ [26 г/ж]; **~ежéние** *n* [12] (Т) (*невнимание*) neglect, disregard; (*презрение*) disdain, scorn, slight; **~ежи́тельный** [14; -лен, -льна] slighting; scornful, disdainful; **~éчь** → ***~егáть***

**прéния** *n/pl.* [12] debate, discussion

**преобладá|ние** *n* [12] predominance; **~ть** [1] prevail; *численно* predominate

**преобра|жáть** [1], ⟨**~зи́ть**⟩ [15 *e.*; -ажу́, -ази́шь, -ажённый] change, (*vi.* **-ся**); **~жéние** *n* [12] transformation; **Ƨ~жéние** *eccl.* Transfiguration; **~зи́ть(ся)** → ***~жáть(ся)***; **~зовáние** *n* [12] transformation; reorganization; reform; **~зóвывать** [1], ⟨**~зовáть**⟩ [7] reform, reorganize; transform

**преодол|евáть** [1], ⟨**~éть**⟩ [8] overcome, surmount

**препарáт** *m* [1] *chem.*, *pharm.* preparation

**препирáтельство** *n* [9] altercation, wrangling

**преподавá|ние** *n* [12] teaching, instruction; **~тель** *m* [4], **~тельница** *f* [5] teacher; lecturer; instructor; **~ть** [5] teach

**преподн|оси́ть** [15], ⟨**~ести́**⟩ [24 -с-] present with, make a present of; ***~ести́ сюрпри́з*** give s.o. a surprise

**препрово|ждáть** [1], ⟨**~ди́ть**⟩ [15 *e.*; -ожу́, -оди́шь; -ождённый] *документы* forward, send, dispatch

**препя́тств|ие** *n* [12] obstacle, hindrance; ***скáчки с ~иями*** steeplechase; ***бег с ~иями*** hurdles (race); **~овать** [7], ⟨вос-⟩ hinder, prevent (Д/***в*** П a p. from)

**прер|вáть(ся)** → ***~ывáть(ся)***; **~екáние** *n* [12] squabble, argument; **~ывáть** [1], ⟨**~вáть**⟩ [-вý, -вёшь; -áл, -á, -о; прéрванный (-ан, -á, -о)] interrupt; break (off), *v/i.* **-ся**; **~ы́вистый** [14 *sh.*] broken, faltering

**пересе|кáть** [1], ⟨**~́чь**⟩ [26] cut short; *попытки* suppress; ***~́чь в кóрне*** nip in the bud; **-ся** break; stop

**преслéдов|ание** *n* [12] pursuit; (*притеснение*) persecution; *law* prosecution; **~ать** [7] pursue; persecute; *law* prosecute

**пресловýтый** [14] notorious

**пресмыкá|ться** [1] creep, crawl; *fig.* grovel, cringe (***пéред*** Т to); **~ющиеся** *n/pl.* [17] reptiles

**прéсный** [14; -сен, -снá, -о] *вода* fresh, *fig.* insipid, stale

**пресс** *m* [1] the press; **~́а** *f* [5] the press; **~-конферéнция** *f* [7] press conference

**престарéлый** [14] aged, advanced in years

**престóл** *m* [1] throne; *eccl.* altar

**преступ|áть** [1], ⟨**~и́ть**⟩ [14] break, infringe; **~лéние** *n* [12] crime; ***на мéсте ~лéния*** red-handed; **~́ник** *m* [1] criminal, offender; **~́ность** *f* [8] criminality; crime

**пресы|щáться** [1], ⟨**~́титься**⟩ [15], **~щéние** *n* [12] satiety

**претвор|я́ть** [28], ⟨**~и́ть**⟩ [13]: ***~я́ть в жизнь*** put into practice, realize

**претен|дéнт** *m* [1] claimant (to); candidate (for); *на престол* pretender; **~довáть** [7] (***на*** В) (lay) claim (to); **~́зия** *f* [7] claim, pretension (***на*** В, ***к*** Д to); ***быть в ~́зии*** (***на*** В [***за*** В]) have a grudge against s.o.

**претерп|евáть** [1], ⟨**~éть**⟩ [10] suffer, endure; (*подвергнуться*) undergo

**преувел|ичéние** *n* [12] exaggeration; **~и́чивать** [1], ⟨**~и́чить**⟩ [16] exaggerate

**преусп|евáть** [1], ⟨**~éть**⟩ [8] succeed; (*процветать*) thrive, prosper

**при** (П) by, at, near; (*битва*) of; under, in the time of; in a p.'s possession: by, with, on; about (one ***~ себé***), with; in (*погоде и т. д.*); for (all that ***~ всём том***); when, on (-ing); ***~ э́том*** at that; ***быть ни ~ чём*** *coll.* have nothing to do with (it ***тут***), not be a p.'s fault

**прибáв|ить(ся)** → ***~ля́ть(ся)***; **~ка** [5; *g/pl.*: -вок], **~лéние** *n* [12] augmentation, supplement; *семейства* addition; **~ля́ть** [28], ⟨**~ить**⟩ [14] (В *or* Р) add; augment; put on (*weight* ***в*** П); ***~ля́ть шáгу*** quicken one's steps; **-ся** increase; be added; (a)rise; grow longer; **~очный** [14] additional; *стоимость* surplus…

**прибалти́йский** [16] Baltic

**прибе|гáть** [1] **1.** ⟨**~жáть**⟩ [4; -егý, -ежи́шь, -егýт] come running; **2.** ⟨**~́гнуть**⟩ [20] resort, have recourse (***к*** Д to); **~регáть** [1], ⟨**~рéчь**⟩ [26 г/ж] save up, reserve

**приби|вáть** [1], ⟨**~́ть**⟩ [-бью́, -бьёшь, *etc.*, → ***бить***] nail; *пыль и т. д.* lay, flatten; *к берегу* throw *or* wash ashore (*mst. impers.*); **~рáть** [1], ⟨**прибрáть**⟩ [-берý, -рёшь; -брáл -á, -о; при́бранный] tidy *or* clean (up); ***прибрáть к рукáм*** lay one's hands on s.th.; take s.o. in hand; **~́ть** → ***~вáть***

**прибли|жáть** [1], ⟨**~́зить**⟩ [15] approach, draw near (***к*** Д; *v/i.* **-ся**); *событие* hasten; *о величинах* approximate; **~жéние** *n* [12] approach(ing); approximation; **~зи́тельный** [14; -лен, -льна] approximate; **~́зить(ся)** → ***~жáть(-ся)***

**прибóй** *m* [3] surf

**прибóр** *m* [1] apparatus; instrument

**прибрáть** → ***прибирáть***

**прибрéжный** [14] coastal, littoral

**прибы|вáть** [1], ⟨**~́ть**⟩ [-бýду, -дешь; при́был, -á, -о] arrive (***в*** В in, at); *о воде* rise; **´~ль** *f* [8] profit, gains *pl.*; **´~льный** [14; -лен, -льна] profitable; **~́тие** *n* [12] arrival (***в*** В in, at; ***по*** Д upon); **~́ть** → ***~вáть***

**привáл** *m* [1] halt, rest

**привезти́** → ***привози́ть***

**приверéдливый** [14 *sh.*] fastidious; squeamish

**привéржен|ец** *m* [1; -нца] adherent; **~ность** *f* [8] devotion; **~ный** [14 *sh.*] devoted

**привести́** → ***приводи́ть***

**привéт** *m* [1] greeting(s); regards, compliments *pl.*; *coll.* hello!, hi!; **~ливый**

П

[14 *sh.*] affable; **~ственный** [14] salutatory, welcoming; **~ствие** *n* [12] greeting, welcome; **~ствовать** [7; *pt. a. pf.*] greet, salute; (*одобрять*) welcome

**приви|ва́ть** [1], ⟨**∠ть**⟩ [-вью́, -вьёшь, *etc.*, → **вить**] inoculate, vaccinate; *bot.* graft; *привычки и т. д. fig.* cultivate, inculcate; **-ся** take; **∠вка** *f* [5; *g/pl.*: -вок] inoculation, vaccination; grafting; **~де́ние** *n* [12] ghost; **~легиро́ванный** [14] privileged; *акции* preferred; **~ле́гия** *f* [7] privilege; **∠нчивать** [1], ⟨**~нти́ть**⟩ [15 *e.*; -нчу́, -нти́шь] screw on; **∠ть(ся)** → **~ва́ть(ся)**

**при́вкус** *m* [1] aftertaste; smack (of) (*a. fig.*)

**привле|ка́тельный** [14; -лен, -льна] attractive; **~ка́ть** [1], ⟨**∠чь**⟩ [26] draw, attract; *к работе* recruit (**к** Д in); call (*к ответственности* to account); bring (*к суду* to trial)

**при́вод** *m* [1] *tech.* drive, driving gear; **~и́ть** [15], ⟨**привести́**⟩ [25] bring; lead; result (**к** Д in); (*цитировать*) adduce, cite; *math.* reduce; *в порядок* put, set; *в отчаяние* drive; **~но́й** [14] driving (*ремень и т. д. belt, etc.*)

**привоз|и́ть** [15], ⟨**привезти́**⟩ [24] bring (*other than on foot*); import; **~но́й** [14] imported

**приво́лье** *n* [10] open space, vast expanse; freedom

**привы|ка́ть** [1], ⟨**∠кнуть**⟩ [21] get *or* be(come) accustomed *or* used (**к** Д to); **∠чка** *f* [5; *g/pl.*: -чек] habit; custom; **∠чный** [14; -чен, -чна] habitual, usual

**привя́з|анность** *f* [8] attachment (to); **~а́ть(ся)** → **~ывать(ся)**; **~чивый** [14 *sh.*] *coll.* affectionate; (*надоедливый*) obtrusive; **~ывать** [1], ⟨**~а́ть**⟩ [3] (**к** Д) tie, attach (to); **-ся** become attached; *coll.* pester; **′~ь** [8] leash, tether

**пригла|си́тельный** [14] invitation…; **~ша́ть** [1], ⟨**~си́ть**⟩ [15 *e.*; -ашу́, -аси́шь; -ашённый] invite (to *mst* **на** В), ask; *врача* call; **~ше́ние** *n* [12] invitation

**пригна́ть** → **пригоня́ть**

**пригов|а́ривать** [1], ⟨**~ори́ть**⟩ [13] sentence; condemn; *impf. coll.* keep saying; **~о́р** *m* [1] sentence; verdict (*a. fig.*); **~ори́ть** → **~а́ривать**

**приго́дный** [14; -ден, -дна] → **го́дный**

**пригоня́ть** [28], ⟨**пригна́ть**⟩ [-гоню́, -го́нишь; -гна́л, -а́, -о; при́гнанный] fit, adjust

**пригор|а́ть** [1], ⟨**~е́ть**⟩ [9] be burnt; **′~од** *m* [1] suburb; **′~одный** [14] suburban; *поезд и т. д.* local; **′~шня** *f* [6; *g/pl.*: -ней & -шен] hand(ful)

**пригот|а́вливать(ся)** [1] → **~овля́ть(ся)**; **~о́вить(ся)** → **~овля́ть(ся)**; **~овле́ние** *n* [12] preparation (**к** Д for); **~овля́ть** [28], ⟨**~о́вить**⟩ [14] prepare; **-ся** (*v/i.*) prepare o.s. (**к** Д for)

**прида|ва́ть** [5], ⟨**∠ть**⟩ [-да́м, -да́шь, *etc.*, → **дать**; при́да́л, -а́, -о; при́данный (-ан, -а́, -о)] add; give; *значение* attach; **∠ное** *n* [14] dowry; **∠точный** [14] supplementary; *gr.* subordinate (*clause*); **∠ть** → **~ва́ть**; **∠ча** *f* [5]: **в ∠чу** in addition

**придви|га́ть** [1], ⟨**∠нуть**⟩ [20] move up (*v/i.* **-ся**; draw near)

**придво́рный** [14] court (*of a sovereign or similar dignitary*); courtier (*su. m*)

**приде́л|ывать**, ⟨**~ать**⟩ [1] fasten, fix (**к** Д to)

**приде́рж|ивать** [1], ⟨**~а́ть**⟩ [4] hold (back); **-ся** *impf.* (P) hold, adhere (to)

**придир|а́ться** [1], ⟨**придра́ться**⟩ [-деру́сь, -рёшься; -дра́лся, -ала́сь, -а́лось] (**к** Д) find fault (with), carp *or* cavil (at); **∠ка** *f* [5; *g/pl.*: -рок] faultfinding, carping; **∠чивый** [14 *sh.*] captious, faultfinding

**придира́ться** → **придра́ться**

**приду́м|ывать**, ⟨**~ать**⟩ [1] think up, devise, invent

**прие́з|д** *m* [1] arrival (**в** В in); **по ~е** on arrival (in, at); **~жа́ть** [1], ⟨**прие́хать**⟩ [-е́ду, -е́дешь] arrive (*other than on foot* **в** В in, at); **~жий** [17] newly arrived; guest…

**при|ём** *m* [1] reception; *в университет и т. д.* admission; *лекарства* taking; (*способ действия*) way, mode; device, trick; method; **в оди́н ~ём** at one go; **~е́млемый** [14 *sh.*] acceptable; *допустимый* admissible; **~ёмная** *f* [14] *su.* reception room; waiting room;

П

**~ёмник** *m* [1] *tech.* receiver; *для детей* reception center, *Brt.* -tre; → **радиоприёмник**; **~ёмный** *часы* office; *экзамен* entrance; *отец, сын* foster

**при|ехать** → **~езжать**; **~жать(ся)** → **~жимать(ся)**; **~жигать** [1], ⟨**~жечь**⟩ [26 г/ж: -жгу, -жжёшь, → **жечь**] cauterize; **~жимать** [1], ⟨**~жать**⟩ [-жму, -жмёшь; -атый] press, clasp (**к** Д to, on); **-ся** press o.s. (to, against); nestle, cuddle up (to); **~жимистый** [14 *sh.*] tightfisted, stingy; **~з** *m* [1] prize

**призва|ние** *n* [12] vocation, calling; **~ть** → **призывать**

**приземл|яться** [28], ⟨**~иться**⟩ [13] *ae.* land; **~ение** *n* [12] landing, touchdown

**призёр** *m* [1] prizewinner

**призма** *f* [5] prism

**призна|вать** [5], ⟨**~ть**⟩ [1] (Т; *a.* **за** В) recognize, acknowledge (as); (*сознавать*) see, admit, own; (*считать*) find, consider; **-ся** confess (**в** П s.th.), admit; **~ться** *or* **~юсь** tell the truth, frankly speaking; **~к** *m* [1] sign; indication; **~ние** *n* [12] acknowledg(e)ment, recognition; **~ние в преступлении** confession; declaration (**в любви** of love); **~тельность** *f* [8] gratitude; **~тельный** [14; -лен, -льна] grateful, thankful (for **за** В); **~ть(ся)** → **~вать(ся)**

**призра|к** *m* [1] phantom, specter (*Brt.* -tre); **~чный** [14; -чен, -чна] spectral, ghostly; *надежда* illusory

**призыв** *m* [1] appeal, call (**на** В for); *mil.* draft, conscription; **~ать** [1], ⟨призвать⟩ [-зову, -вёшь; -звал, -а, -о; призванный] call, move dawn appeal (**на** В for); *mil.* draft, call up (**на** В for); **~ник** *m* [1 *e.*] draftee, conscript; **~ной** [14]: **~ной возраст** call-up age

**прииск** *m* [1] mine (*for precious metals*); **золотой ~** gold field

**прийти(сь)** → **приходить(ся)**

**приказ** *m* [1] order, command; **~ать** → **~ывать**; **~ывать** [1], ⟨**~ать**⟩ [3] order, command; give orders

**при|калывать** [1], ⟨колоть⟩ [17] pin, fasten; **~касаться** [1], ⟨коснуться⟩ [20] (**к** Д) touch (lightly); **~кидывать**, ⟨**~кинуть**⟩ [20] weigh; estimate (approximately); **~кинуть в уме** *fig.* ponder, weigh up; **-ся** pretend *or* feign to be, act (the Т)

**приклад** *m* [1] *винтовки* butt

**приклад|ной** [14] applied; **~ывать** [1], ⟨приложить⟩ [16] (**к** Д) apply (to), put (on); *к письму и т. д.* enclose (with); *печать* affix a seal

**приклеи|вать** [1], ⟨**~ть**⟩ [13] paste

**приключ|аться** *coll.* [1], ⟨**~иться**⟩ [16 *e.*; 3rd *p. only*] happen, occur; **~ение** *n* [12] (**~енческий** [16] of) adventure(…)

**прико|вывать** [1], ⟨**~вать**⟩ [7 *e.*; -кую, -куёшь] chain; *внимание и т. д.* arrest; **~лачивать** [1], ⟨**~лотить**⟩ [15] nail (on, to **к**), fasten with nails; **~лоть** → **прикалывать**; **~мандировать** [7] *pf.* attach; **~сновение** *n* [12] touch, contact; **~снуться** → **прикасаться**

**прикрас|а** *f* [5] *coll.* embellishment; **без ~** unvarnished

**прикреп|ить(ся)** → **~лять(ся)**; **~лять** [28], ⟨**~ить**⟩ [14 *e.*; -плю, -пишь; -плённый] fasten; attach; **-ся** register (at, with **к** Д)

**прикрик|ивать** [1], ⟨**~нуть**⟩ [20] shout (at **на** В)

**прикры|вать** [1], ⟨**~ть**⟩ [22] cover; (*защищать*) protect; **~тие** *n* [12] cover, escort (*a. mil*); *fig.* cloak

**прилавок** *m* [1; -вка] (*shop*) counter

**прилага|тельное** *n* [14] *gr.* adjective (*a.* **имя ~тельное**); **~ть** [1], ⟨приложить⟩ [16] (**к** Д) enclose; apply (to); *усилия* take, make (*efforts*); **~емый** enclosed

**прила|живать** [1], ⟨**~дить**⟩ [15] fit to, adjust to

**приле|гать** [1] **1.** (**к** Д) (ad)join, border; **2.** ⟨**~чь**⟩ [26 г/ж: -лягу, -ляжешь, -лягут; -лёг, легла, -ляг(те)!] lie down (for a while); **3.** *об одежде* fit (closely); **~жание** *n* [12] diligence; **~жный** [14; -жен, -жна] industrious; **~плять** [28], ⟨**~пить**⟩ [14] stick to; **~тать** [1], ⟨**~теть**⟩ [11] arrive by air, fly in; **~чь** → **~гать** *2*

**прили|в** *m* [1] flood, flow; *fig. крови* rush; **~в энергии** surge of energy; **~вать** [1], ⟨**~ть**⟩ [-лью, -льёшь; → **лить**]

П

flow to; rush to; ~**пать** [1], ⟨~**пнуть**⟩ [21] stick; ~**ть** → ~***вать***

**прили́ч|ие** *n* [12] decency, decorum; ~**ный** [14; -чен, -чна] decent, proper; *coll. сумма и т. д.* decent, fair

**прилож|е́ние** *n* [12] enclosure (*document with a letter etc.*); *журнальное* supplement; *сил и т. д.* application (putting to use); *в книге* appendix, addendum; *gr.* apposition; ~**и́ть** → ***прикла́дывать*** & ***прилага́ть***

**прима́нка** *f* [5; *g/pl.*: -нок] bait, lure; (*fig.*) enticement

**примен|е́ние** *n* [12] application; use; ~**и́мый** [14 *sh.*] applicable; ~**и́тельно** in conformity with; ~**я́ть** [28], ⟨~**и́ть**⟩ [13; -еню́, -е́нишь; -енённый] apply (**к** Д to); use, employ

**приме́р** *m* [1] example; ***привести́ в ~*** cite as an example; **не в ~** *coll.* unlike; ***к ~у*** *coll.* → ***наприме́р***; ~**ивать** [1], ⟨~**ить**⟩ [13] try on; fit; ~**ка** *f* [5; *g/pl.*: -рок] trying on; fitting; ~**ный** [14; -рен, -рна] exemplary; (*приблизительный*) approximate; ~**я́ть** [28] → ~***ивать***

**при́месь** *f* [8] admixture; *fig.* touch

**приме́|та** *f* [5] mark, sign; *дурная* omen; **на ~те** in view; ~**тный** → ***заме́тный***; ~**ча́ние** *n* [12] (foot)note; ~**ча́тельный** [14; -лен, -льна] notable, remarkable

**примир|е́ние** *n* [12] reconciliation; ~**и́тельный** [14; -лен, -льна] conciliatory; ~**я́ть(ся)** [28] → ***мири́ть*(ся)**

**примити́вный** [14; -вен, -вна] primitive, crude

**прим|кну́ть** → ~***ыка́ть***; ~**о́рский** [16] coastal, seaside…; ~**о́чка** *f* [5; *g/pl.*: -чек] lotion; ~**ула** *f* [5] primrose; ~**ус** *m* [1] *trademark* Primus (stove); ~**ча́ться** [4 *e.*; ~мчу́сь, -чи́шься] *pf.* come in a great hurry; ~**ыка́ть** [1], ⟨~**кну́ть**⟩ [20] join (*v/t.* **к** Д); *о здании и т. д. impf.* adjoin

**принадл|ежа́ть** [4 *e.*; -жу́, -жи́шь] belong ([**к**] Д to); ~**е́жность** *f* [8] belonging (**к** Р to); *pl.* accessories

**принести́** → ***приноси́ть***

**принима́ть** [1], ⟨приня́ть⟩ [приму́, -и́мешь; при́нял, -а́, -о; при́нятый (-ят, а́, -о)] take (*a.* over; **за** В for; *measures*); *предложение* accept; *гостей* receive; *в школу и т. д.* admit (**в, на** В [in] to); *закон и т. д.* pass, adopt; *обязанности* assume; ***~ на себя́*** take (up)on o.s., undertake; ***~ на свой счёт*** take as referring to o.s.; **-ся** [-нялся́, -ла́сь] (**за** В) start, begin; set to, get down to; *coll.* take in hand; *bot.*, *med.* take effect (injections)

**приноровиться** [14 *e.*; -влю́сь, -ви́шься] *pf. coll.*adapt o.s. to

**прин|оси́ть** [15], ⟨~**ести́**⟩ [24 -с-: -есу́; -ёс, -есла́] bring (*a.* forth, in), *плоды* yield; make (sacrifice **в** В); ***~оси́ть по́льзу*** be of use *or* of benefit

**прину|ди́тельный** [14; -лен, -льна] forced, compulsory, coercive; ~**жда́ть** [1], ⟨~**ди́ть**⟩ [15] force, compel, constrain; ~**жде́ние** *n* [12] compulsion, coercion, constraint (**по** Д under)

**при́нцип** *m* [1] principle; ***в ~е*** in principle; ***из ~а*** on principle; ~**иа́льный** [14; -лен, -льна] of principle; guided by principle

**приня́|тие** *n* [12] taking, taking up; acceptance; admission (**в, на** В to); *закона и т. д.* passing, adoption; ´~**тый** [14] customary; ~**ть(ся)** → ***принима́ть*(ся)**

**приобре|та́ть** [1], ⟨~**сти́**⟩ [25 -т-] acquire, obtain, get; buy; ~**те́ние** *n* [12] acquisition

**приоб|ща́ть** [1], ⟨~**щи́ть**⟩ [16 *e.*; -щу́, -щи́шь; -щённый] (**к** Д) *документ* file; introduce (to); **-ся** join (in); consort with

**приостан|а́вливать** [1], ⟨~**ови́ть**⟩ [14] call a halt to (*v/i.* **-ся**); *law* suspend

**припа́док** *m* [1; -дка] fit, attack

**припа́сы** *m/pl.* [1] supplies, stores; ***съестны́е ~*** provisions

**припая́ть** [28] *pf.* solder (**к** Д to)

**припе́|в** *m* [1] refrain; ~**ка́ть** [1], ⟨~**чь**⟩ [26] *coll.* (*of the sun*) burn, be hot

**припи́с|ка** *f* [5; *g/pl.*: -сок] postscript; addition; ~**ывать** [1], ⟨~**а́ть**⟩ [3] ascribe, attribute (**к** Д to)

**припла́та** *f* [5] extra payment

**припло́д** *m* [1] increase (*in number of animals*)

П

**приплы|ва́ть** [1], ⟨**∠ть**⟩ [23] swim; sail (**к** Д up to)
**приплю́снутый** [14] flat (*nose*)
**приподн|има́ть** [1], ⟨**~я́ть**⟩ [-ниму́, -ни́мешь; -по́днял, -а́, -о; -по́днятый (-ят, -а́, -о)] lift *or* raise (**-ся** rise) (a little); **∠ятый** [14] *настроение* elated; animated
**приполз|а́ть** [1], ⟨**~ти́**⟩ [24] creep up, in
**припом|ина́ть** [1], ⟨**∠нить**⟩ [13] remember, recollect; ***он тебе́ это ∠нит*** he'll get even with you for this
**припра́в|а** *f* [5] seasoning; dressing; **~ля́ть** [28], ⟨**~ить**⟩ [14] season; dress
**припух|а́ть** [1], ⟨**∠нуть**⟩ [21] swell (a little)
**прира|ба́тывать** [1], ⟨**~бо́тать**⟩ [1] earn in addition
**прира́вн|ивать** [1], ⟨**~я́ть**⟩ [28] equate (with); place on the same footing (as)
**прира|ста́ть** [1], ⟨**~сти́**⟩ [24 -ст-: -стёт; -ро́с, -сла́] take; grow (**к** Д to); increase (**на** В by); **~ще́ние** *n* [12] increment
**приро́|да** *f* [5] nature; ***от ~ды*** by nature, congenitally; ***по ~де*** by nature, naturally; **~дный** [14] natural; *a.* = **~ждённый** [14] (in)born, innate; **~ст** *m* [1] increase, growth
**прируч|а́ть** [1], ⟨**~и́ть**⟩ [16 *e.*; -чу́, -чи́шь; -чённый] tame
**при|са́живаться** [1], ⟨**~се́сть**⟩ [25; -ся́ду; -се́л] sit down (for a while), take a seat
**присв|а́ивать** [1], ⟨**~о́ить**⟩ [13] appropriate; *степень и т. д.* confer ([up] on Д); ***~о́ить зва́ние*** promote to the rank (of); ***~о́ить и́мя*** name; **~ое́ние** *n* [12] appropriation
**присе|да́ть** [1], ⟨**∠сть**⟩ [25; -ся́ду, -се́л] sit down; squat; **∠ст** *m* [1]: ***в один ∠ст*** at one sitting; **∠сть** → ***~да́ть & приса́живаться***
**приско́рб|ие** *n* [12] sorrow; regret; **~ный** [14; -бен, -бна] regrettable, deplorable
**присла́ть** → ***присыла́ть***
**прислон|я́ть** [28], ⟨**~и́ть**⟩ [13] lean (*v/i.* **-ся**; **к** Д against)
**прислу́|га** [5] maid; servant; **~живать** [1] wait (up)on (Д), serve; **~шиваться**, ⟨**~шаться**⟩ [1] listen, pay attention (**к** Д to)
**присм|а́тривать** [1], ⟨**~отре́ть**⟩ [9; -отрю́, -о́тришь; -о́тренный] look after (**за** Т); *coll. новый дом и т. д.* find; **-ся** (**к** Д) peer, look narrowly (at); examine (closely); *к кому-л.* size s.o. up; *к работе и т. д.* familiarize o.s., get acquainted (with); **~о́тр** *m* [1] care, supervision; surveillance; **~отре́ть(ся)** → ***~а́тривать(ся)***
**присоедин|е́ние** *n* [12] addition; *pol.* annexation; **~я́ть** [28], ⟨**~и́ть**⟩ [13] (**к** Д) join (*a.* **-ся**); connect, attach (to); annex, incorporate
**приспосо́б|ить(ся)** → ***~ля́ть(ся)***; **~ле́ние** *n* [12] adaptation; (*устройство*) device; **~ля́ть** [28], ⟨**~ить**⟩ [14] fit, adapt (**-ся** o.s.; **к** Д, **под** В to, for)
**приста|ва́ть** [5], ⟨**∠ть**⟩ [-а́ну, -а́нешь] (**к** Д) stick (to); *к кому-л.* bother, pester; *о лодке* put in; *о судне* tie up; **∠вить** → ***~вля́ть***; **∠вка** *f* [5; *g/pl.*: -вок] *gr.* prefix; **~вля́ть** [28], ⟨**∠вить**⟩ [14] (**к** Д) set, put (to), lean (against); (*приделать*) add on; **´~льный** [14; -лен, -льна] steadfast, intent; **∠нь** *f* [8; *from g/pl. e.*] landing stage; quay, wharf, pier; **∠ть** → ***~ва́ть***
**пристёгивать** [1], ⟨**пристегну́ть**⟩ [20] button (up), fasten
**пристр|а́ивать** [1], ⟨**~о́ить**⟩ [13] (**к** Д) add *or* attach (to); settle; place; provide; **-ся** *coll.* → ***устра́иваться***; join
**пристра́ст|ие** *n* [12] predilection, weakness (**к** Д for); bias; **~ный** [14; -тен, -тна] bias(s)ed, partial (**к** Д to)
**пристре́ли|вать** [1], ⟨**∠ть**⟩ [13; -стрелю́, -е́лишь] shoot (down)
**пристр|о́ить(ся)** → ***~а́ивать(ся)***; **~о́йка** *f* [5; *g/pl.*: -о́ек] annex(e); out-house
**при́ступ** *m* [1] *mil.* assault, onslaught, storm (by Т); *med. fig.* fit, attack; *боли* pang; *болезни* bout; **~а́ть** [1], ⟨**~и́ть**⟩ [14] set about, start, begin
**прису|жда́ть** [1], ⟨**~ди́ть**⟩ [15; -уждённый] (**к** Д) *law* sentence to; condemn to; *приз и т. д.* award; **~жде́ние** *n* [12] awarding; adjudication
**прису́тств|ие** *n* [12] presence (in **в** П; of mind ***ду́ха***); **~овать** [7] be present (**на,**

П

***в, при*** П at); **~ующий** [17] present
**прису́щий** [17 *sh.*] inherent (in Д)
**прис|ыла́ть** [1], ⟨**~ла́ть**⟩ [-шлю́, -шлёшь; при́сланный] send (***за*** T for)
**прися́|га** *f* [5] oath (***под*** T on); **~га́ть** [1], ⟨**~гну́ть**⟩ [20] swear (to); **~жный** [14] juror; ***суд ~жных*** jury; *coll.* born, inveterate
**прита|и́ться** [13] *pf.* hide; keep quiet; **∠скивать** [1], ⟨**~щи́ть**⟩ [16] drag, haul (**-ся** *coll.* o.s.; ***к*** Д [up] to); *coll.* bring (come)
**притвор|и́ть(ся)** → ***~я́ть(ся)***; **∠ный** [14; -рен, -рна] feigned, pretended, sham; **∠ство** *n* [9] pretense, -nce; **~я́ть** [28], ⟨**~и́ть**⟩ [13; -орю́, -о́ришь; -о́ренный] leave ajar; **-ся** [13] feign, pretend (to be T); be ajar
**притесн|е́ние** *n* [12] oppression; **~и́тель** *m* [4] oppressor; **~я́ть** [28], ⟨**~и́ть**⟩ [13] oppress
**притих|а́ть** [1], ⟨**∠нуть**⟩ [21] become silent, grow quiet; *ветер* abate
**прито́к** *m* [1] tributary; influx (*a. fig.*)
**прито́м** (and) besides
**прито́н** *m* [1] den
**при́торный** [14; -рен, -рна] too sweet, cloying (*a. fig.*)
**притр|а́гиваться** [1], ⟨**~о́нуться**⟩ [20] touch (*v/t.* ***к*** Д)
**притуп|ля́ть** [28], ⟨**~и́ть**⟩ [14] (**-ся** become) blunt; *fig.* dull
**при́тча** *f* [5] parable
**притя́|гивать** [1], ⟨**~ну́ть**⟩ [19] drag, pull; *о магните* attract; *coll.* → ***привлека́ть***; **~жа́тельный** [14] *gr.* possessive; **~же́ние** *n* [12] (*phys.*) attraction; **~за́ние** *n* [12] claim, pretension (***на*** В to); **~ну́ть** → ***~гивать***
**приу|ро́чить** [16] *pf.* time, date (for *or* to coincide with ***к*** Д); **~са́дебный** [14]: ***~са́дебный уча́сток*** plot adjoining the (farm)house; **~ча́ть** [1], ⟨**~чи́ть**⟩ [16] accustom; train
**при|хва́рывать** *coll.* [1], ⟨**~хворну́ть**⟩ [20] be(come *pf.*) unwell
**прихо́д** *m* [1] **1.** arrival, coming; **2.** *comm.* receipt(s); **3.** *eccl.* parish; **~и́ть** [15], ⟨**прийти́**⟩ [приду́, -дёшь; пришёл, -шла́, -ше́дший; *g. pt.*: прийдя́] come (to), arrive (***в, на*** В in, at, ***за*** T for); ***~и́ть в упа́док*** fall into decay; ***~и́ть в я́рость*** fly into a rage; ***~и́ть в го́лову, на ум***, *etc.* think of, cross one's mind, take into one's head; ***~и́ть в себя́*** (*or* ***чу́вство***) come to (o.s.); **-ся** *родственником* be; *праздник* fall (***в*** В on, ***на*** В to); ***мне ~ится*** I have to, must; **~ский** [16] parish…
**прихож|а́нин** *m* [1; *pl.* -а́не, -а́н] parishioner; **∠ая** *f* [17] → ***пере́дняя***
**прихот|ли́вый** [14 *sh.*] *узор* fanciful; **´~ь** *f* [8] whim
**прихра́мывать** [1] limp slightly
**прице́л** *m* [1] sight; **~иваться** [1], ⟨**~иться**⟩ [13] (take) aim (at ***в*** В)
**прице́п** *m* [1] trailer; **~ля́ть** [28], ⟨**~и́ть**⟩ [14] hook on (***к*** Д to); couple; **-ся** stick, cling; → *a.* ***приста́(ва́)ть***
**прича́л** *m* [1] mooring; **~ивать** [1], ⟨**~ить**⟩ [13] moor
**прича́|стие** *n* [12] *gr.* participle; *eccl.* Communion; the Eucharist; **~стный** [14; -тен, -тна] participating *or* involved (***к*** Д in); **~ща́ть** [1], ⟨**~сти́ть**⟩ [15 *e.*; -ащу́, -асти́шь; -ащённый] administer (**-ся** receive) Communion; **~ще́ние** *n* [12] receiving Communion
**причём** moreover; in spite of the fact that; while
**причё́с|ка** *f* [5; *g/pl.*: -сок] haircut; hairdo, coiffure; **~ывать** [1], ⟨**причеса́ть**⟩ [3] do, brush, comb (**-ся** one's hair)
**причи́н|а** *f* [5] cause; reason (***по*** Д for); ***по ~е*** because of; ***по той и́ли ино́й ~е*** for some reason or other; **~я́ть** [28], ⟨**~и́ть**⟩ [13] cause, do
**причи|сля́ть** [28], ⟨**∠слить**⟩ [13] rank, number (***к*** Д among); **~та́ние** *n* [12] (ritual) lamentation; **~та́ть** [1] lament; **~та́ться** [1] be due, (p.: ***с*** P) have to pay
**причу́д|а** *f* [5] whim, caprice; *характера* oddity; **~ливый** [14 *sh.*] odd; quaint; *coll.* whimsical, fanciful
**при|ше́лец** *m* [1; -льца] newcomer, stranger; a being from space; **~ши́бленный** *coll.* [14] dejected; **~шива́ть** [1], ⟨**~ши́ть**⟩ [-шью́, -шьёшь, *etc.* → ***шить***] (***к*** Д) sew ([on] to); **~щемля́ть** [28], ⟨**~щеми́ть**⟩ [14 *e.*; -млю́, -ми́шь;

-млённый] pinch, squeeze; ~**щёпка** *f* [5; *g/pl.*: -пок] clothes-peg; ~**щу́ривать** [1], ⟨~щу́рить⟩ [13] → ***жму́рить***

**приют** *m* [1] refuge, shelter; ~**и́ть** [15 *e.*; -ючу́, -юти́шь] *pf.* give shelter (*v/i.* **-ся**)

**прия́|тель** *m* [4], ~**тельница** *f* [5] friend; ~**тельский** [16] friendly; ~**тный** [14; -тен, -тна] pleasant, pleasing, agreeable

**про** *coll.* (В) about, for, of; ~ ***себя́*** to o.s., (*read*) silently

**про́ба** *f* [5] *для анализа* sample; *о золоте* standard; *на изделии* hallmark

**пробе́|г** *m* [1] *sport* run, race; ~**га́ть** [1], ⟨~жа́ть⟩ [4 *e.*; -егу́, -ежи́шь, -гу́т] run (through, over), pass (by); *расстояние* cover; *глазами* skim

**пробе́л** *m* [1] blank, gap (*a. fig.*)

**проби|ва́ть** [1], ⟨~ть⟩ [-бью́, -бьёшь; -бе́й(те)!; проби́л, -а, -о] break through; pierce, punch; **-ся** fight (*or* make) one's way (***сквозь*** В through); *bot* come up; *солнце* shine through; ~**ра́ть** [1], ⟨пробра́ть⟩ [-беру́, -рёшь, → ***брать***] *coll.* scold; *до костей* chill (*to the bone*); **-ся** [-бра́лся, -ла́сь, -ло́сь] force one's way (***сквозь*** В through); steal, slip; ~**рка** *f* [5; *g/pl.*: -рок] test tube; ~**ть(ся)** → ~***ва́ть*****(ся)**

**про́бк|а** *f* [5; *g/pl.*: -бок] cork (*material of bottle*); stopper, plug; *el.* fuse; *fig.* traffic jam; ~**овый** [14] cork…

**пробле́ма** [5] problem; ~**ти́чный** [14; -чен, -чна] problematic(al)

**про́блеск** *m* [1] gleam; flash; ~ ***наде́жды*** ray of hope

**про́б|ный** [14] trial…, test…; ***экземпля́р*** specimen…, sample…; ~***ный ка́мень*** touchstone (a. *fig.*); ~**овать** [7], ⟨по-⟩ try; *на вкус* taste

**пробо́ина** *f* [5] hole; *naut.* leak

**пробо́р** *m* [1] parting (*of the hair*)

**пробра́ться** → ***пробира́ть*****(ся)**

**пробу|жда́ть** [1], ⟨~ди́ть⟩ [15; -уждённый] waken, rouse; **-ся** awake, wake up; ~**жде́ние** *n* [12] awakening

**пробы́ть** [-бу́ду, -бу́дешь; про́был, -а́, -о] *pf.* stay

**прова́л** *m* [1] collapse; *fig.* failure; ~**ивать** [1], ⟨~и́ть⟩ [13; -алю́, -а́лишь; -а́ленный] *на экзамене* fail; ~***ивай*****(те)*!*** *coll.* beat it!; **-ся**; collapse, fall in; fail, flunk; (*исчезнуть*) *coll.* disappear, vanish

**прове́|дать** *coll.* [1] *pf.* visit; (*узнать*) find out; ~**де́ние** *n* [12] carrying out, implementation; ~**зти́** → ***провози́ть***; ~**рить** → ~***ря́ть***; ~**рка** [5; *g/pl.*: -рок] inspection, check(up), examination, control; ~**ря́ть** [28], ⟨~рить⟩ [13] inspect, examine, check (up on), control; ~**сти́** → ***проводи́ть***; ~**тривать** [1], ⟨~трить⟩ [13] air, ventilate

**прови|ни́ться** [13] *pf.* commit an offense (-nce), be guilty (**в** П of), offend (***пе́ред*** Т p.; **в** П with); ~**нциа́льный** [14; -лен, -льна] *mst. fig.* provincial; ~**нция** *f* [7] province(s)

**про́во|д** *m* [1; *pl.*: -да́, *etc. e.*] wire, line; *el.* lead; ~**ди́мость** *f* [8] conductivity; ~**ди́ть** [15] **1.** ⟨провести́⟩ [25] lead, *a. el. impf.* conduct, guide; (*осуществлять*) carry out (*or* through), realize, put (*into practice*); put *or* get through; pass; spend (*время*; **за** Т at); *линию и т. д.* draw; *водопровод и т. д.* lay; *политику* pursue; *собрание* hold; *coll.* trick, cheat; **2.** → ~***жа́ть***; ~**дка** *f* [5; *g/pl.*: -док] installation; *el.* wiring; *tel.* line, wire(s); ~**дни́к** *m* [1 *e.*] guide; *rail.*, *el.* conductor (*Brt. rail.* guard); ~**жа́ть** [1], ⟨~ди́ть⟩ [15] see (off), accompany; *глазами* follow with one's eyes; ~**з** *m* [1] conveyance; transport(ation)

**провозгла|ша́ть** [1] ⟨~си́ть⟩ [15 *e.*; -ашу́, -аси́шь; -ашённый] proclaim; *тост* propose

**провози́ть** [15], ⟨провезти́⟩ [24] convey, transport, bring (with one)

**провока́|тор** *m* [1] agent provocateur; instigator; ~**ция** *f* [7] provocation

**про́вол|ока** *f* [5] wire; ~**о́чка** *coll.* *f* [5; *g/pl.*: -чек] delay (**с** Т in), protraction

**прово́р|ный** [14; -рен, -рна] quick, nimble, deft; ~**ство** *n* [9] quickness, nimbleness, deftness

**провоци́ровать** [7] (*im*)*pf.*, *a.* ⟨с-⟩ provoke (***на*** В to)

**прогада́ть** [1] *pf. coll.* miscalculate (***на*** П by)

П

**прога́лина** *f* [5] glade
**прогл|а́тывать** [1], ⟨~оти́ть⟩ [15] swallow, gulp; *coll.* **~а́тывать язы́к** lose one's tongue; **~я́дывать** [1] **1.** ⟨~ядéть⟩ [11] overlook; (*просматривать*) look over (*or* through); **2.** ⟨~януть⟩ [19] peep out, appear
**прогн|а́ть** → **прогоня́ть**; **~óз** *m* [1] (**пого́ды**) (weather) forecast; *med.* prognosis
**прого|ва́ривать** [1], ⟨~вори́ть⟩ [13] say; talk; **-ся** blab (out) (*v/t.* **о** П); **~лода́ться** [1] *pf.* get *or* feel hungry; **~ня́ть** [28], ⟨прогна́ть⟩ [-гоню́, -го́нишь; -гна́л, -а́, -о; про́гнанный] drive (away); *coll.* *работы* fire; **~ра́ть** [1], ⟨~ре́ть⟩ [9] burn through; *coll.* (*обанкротиться*) go bust
**прого́рклый** [14] rancid
**програ́мм|а** *f* [5] program(me *Brt.*); **~и́ровать** [1] program(me); **~и́ст** *m* [1] (computer) program(m)er
**прогре́сс** *m* [1] progress; **~и́вный** [14; -вен, -вна] progressive; **~и́ровать** [1] (make) progress; *о болезни* get progressively worse
**прогрыз|а́ть** [1], ⟨́~ть⟩ [24; *pt. st.*] gnaw *or* bite through
**прогу́л** *m* [1] truancy; absence from work; **~ивать** [1], ⟨~я́ть⟩ [28] shirk (work); play truant; **-ся** take (*or* go for a) walk; **~ка** *f* [5; *g/pl.*: -лок] walk (**на** В for), stroll, *верхом* ride; **~ьщик** *m* [1] shirker; truant; **~я́ть(ся)** → **~ивать(ся)**
**прода|ва́ть** [5], ⟨́~ть⟩ [-да́м, -да́шь, *etc.*, → **дать**; про́дал, -а́, -о; про́данный (про́дан, -а́, -о)] sell; **-ся** (*v/i.*); *a.* be for *or* on sale; **~ве́ц** *m* [1; -вца́], **~вщи́ца** *f* [5] seller, sales(wo)man, (store) clerk, *Brt.* shop assistant; **́~жа** *f* [5] sale (**в** П on; **в** В for); **́~жный** [14] for sale; *цена* sale; [-жен, -жна] venal, corrupt; **́~ть(ся)** → **~ва́ть(ся)**
**продви|га́ть** [1], ⟨́~нуть⟩ [20] move, push (ahead); **-ся** advance; **~же́ние** *n* [12] advance(ment)
**проде́л|ать** → **~ывать**; **~ка** *f* [5; *g/pl.*: -лок] trick, prank; **~ывать**, ⟨~ать⟩ [1] *отверстие* break through, make; *работу и т. д.* carry through *or* out, do
**проде́ть** [-де́ну, -де́нешь; -де́нь (-те)!; -де́тый] *pf.* pass, run through; *нитку* thread
**продл|ева́ть** [1], ⟨~и́ть⟩ [13] extend, prolong; **~е́ние** *n* [12] extension, prolongation
**продово́льств|енный** [14] food…; grocery…; **~ие** *n* [12] food(stuffs), provisions *pl.*
**продол|гова́тый** [14 *sh.*] oblong; **~жа́тель** *m* [4] continuer; **~жа́ть** [1], ⟨́~жить⟩ [16] continue, go on; lengthen; prolong; **-ся** last; **~же́ние** *n* [12] continuation; *романа* sequel; **~же́ние сле́дует** to be continued; **~жи́тельность** *f* [8] duration; **~жи́тельный** [14; -лен, -льна] long; protracted; **́~жить(ся)** → **~жа́ть(ся)**; **́~ьный** [14] longitudinal
**продро́гнуть** [21] *pf.* be chilled to the marrow
**проду́к|т** *m* [1] product; *pl. a.* foodstuffs; **~ти́вный** [14; -вен, -вна] productive; fruitful; **~то́вый** [14] grocery (*store*); **~ция** *f* [7] production, output
**проду́м|ывать**, ⟨~ать⟩ [1] think over, think out
**про|еда́ть** [1], ⟨~е́сть⟩ [-е́м, -е́шь, *etc.*, → **есть**[1]] eat through, corrode; *coll.* spend on food
**прое́з|д** *m* [1] passage, thoroughfare; **~да нет!** "no thoroughfare!"; **~дом** on the way, en route; **пла́та за ~д** fare; **~дить** → **~жа́ть**; **~дно́й** [14]: **~дно́й биле́т** season ticket; **~жа́ть** [1], ⟨прое́хать⟩ [-е́ду, -е́дешь; -езжа́й(те)!] pass, drive *or* ride through (*or* past, by); travel; **-ся** *coll.* take a drive *or* ride; **~жий** [17] (through) travel(l)er; passerby transient; **~жая доро́га** thoroughfare
**прое́к|т** *m* [1] project, plan, scheme; *документа* draft; **~ти́ровать** [7], ⟨с-⟩ project, plan; design; **~ция** *f* [7] *math.* projection; view
**прое́|сть** → **~да́ть**; **~хать** → **~зжа́ть**
**проже́ктор** *m* [1] searchlight
**прожи|ва́ть** [1], ⟨́~ть⟩ [-иву́, -ивёшь; про́жил, -а́, -о; про́житый (про́жит, -а́, -о)] live; *pf.* spend; **~га́ть** [1], ⟨проже́чь⟩ [26 г/ж: -жгу́, -жжёшь] burn (through);

**~га́ть жизнь** *coll.* live fast; **~́точный** [14]: **~́точный ми́нимум** *m* living *or* subsistence wage; **~́ть** → **~ва́ть**

**прожо́рлив|ость** *f* [8] gluttony, voracity; **~ый** [14 *sh.*] gluttonous

**про́за** *f* [5] prose; **~́ик** *m* [1] prose writer; **~и́ческий** [16] prosaic; prose…

**про́|звище** *n* [11] nickname; **по ~звищу** nicknamed; **~зва́ть** → **~зыва́ть**; **~зева́ть** *coll.* [1] *pf.* miss; let slip; **~зорли́вый** [14 *sh.*] perspicacious; **~зра́чный** [14; -чен, -чна] transparent; *a. fig.* limpid; **~зре́ть** [9] *pf.* recover one's sight; begin to see clearly; perceive; **~зыва́ть** [1], ⟨**~зва́ть**⟩ [-зову́, -вёшь; -зва́л, -а́, -о; про́званный] (T) nickname; **~зяба́ть** [1] vegetate; **~зя́бнуть** [21] *coll.* → **продро́гнуть**

**проигр|ывать** [1], ⟨**~а́ть**⟩ [1] lose (at play); *coll.* play; **-ся** lose all one's money; **~́ыш** *m* [1] loss (**в** П)

**произв|еде́ние** *n* [12] work, product(ion); **~вести́** → **~оди́ть**; **~оди́тель** *m* [4] producer; (*animal*) male parent, sire; **~оди́тельность** *f* [8] productivity; *завода* output; **~оди́тельный** [14; -лен, -льна] productive; **~оди́ть** [15], ⟨**~ести́**⟩ [25] (**-ся** *impf.* be) make (made), carry (-ried) out, execute(d), effect(ed); (*tech. usu. impf.*) produce(d); *на свет* bring forth; *impf.* derive (d; **от** P from); **~о́дный** [14] *слово* derivative (*a. su. f math.*); **~о́дственный** [14] production…; manufacturing; works…; **~о́дство** *n* [9] production, manufacture; *coll.* plant, works, factory (**на** П at)

**произ|во́л** *m* [1] arbitrariness; *судьбы* mercy; tyranny; **~во́льный** [14; -лен, -льна] arbitrary; **~носи́ть** [15], ⟨**~нести́**⟩ [24 -с-] pronounce; *речь* deliver, make; utter; **~ноше́ние** *n* [12] pronunciation; **~ойти́** → **происходи́ть**

**про́ис|ки** *m/pl.* [1] intrigues; **~ходи́ть** [15], ⟨произойти́⟩ [-зойдёт; -зошёл, -шла; *g. pt.*: произойдя́] take place, happen; (*возникать*) arise, result (**от** P from); *о человеке* descend (**от, из** P from); **~хожде́ние** *n* [12] origin (by [= birth] **по** Д), descent; **~ше́ствие** *n* [12] incident, occurrence, event

**про|йти́(сь)** → **~ходи́ть** & **~ха́живаться**

**прок** *coll. m* [1] → **по́льза**

**прока́з|а** *f* [5] **1.** prank, mischief; **2.** *med.* leprosy; **~ник** *m* [1], **~ница** *f* [5] → *coll.* **шалу́н(ья)**; **~ничать** [1] *coll.* → **шали́ть**

**прока́|лывать** [1], ⟨проколо́ть⟩ [17] pierce; perforate; *шину* puncture; **~пывать** [1], ⟨прокопа́ть⟩ [1] dig (through); **~рмливать** [1], ⟨прокорми́ть⟩ [14] support, nourish; feed

**прока́т** *m* [1] hire (**на** B for); *фильма* distribution; **~и́ть(ся)** [15] *pf.* give (take) a drive *or* ride; **~ывать** ⟨**~ать**⟩ [1] mangle; ride; **-ся** → *coll.* **~и́ться**

**прокла́д|ка** *f* [5; *g/pl.*: -док] *трубопровода* laying; *дороги* construction; *tech.* gasket, packing; **~ывать** [1], ⟨проложи́ть⟩ [16] lay (*a.* = build); *fig.* pave; force (one's *way* себе́); *между* interlay

**прокл|ина́ть** [1], ⟨**~я́сть**⟩ [-яну́, -янёшь; про́клял, -а́, -о; про́клятый (про́клят, -а́, -о)] curse, damn; **~я́тие** *n* [12] damnation; **~я́тый** [14] cursed, damned

**проко́|л** *m* [1] perforation; *mot.* puncture; **~ло́ть** → **прока́лывать**; **~па́ть** → **прока́пывать**; **~рми́ть** → **прока́рмливать**

**прокра́|дываться** [1], ⟨**~сться**⟩ [25; *pt. st.*] steal, go stealthily

**прокуро́р** *m* [1] public prosecutor; *на суде* counsel for the prosecution

**про|лага́ть** → **~кла́дывать**; **~ла́мывать**, ⟨**~лома́ть**⟩ [1] & ⟨**~ломи́ть**⟩ [14] break (through; *v/i.* **-ся**); fracture; **~лега́ть** [1] lie; run; **~леза́ть** [1], ⟨**~ле́зть**⟩ [24 *st.*] climb *or* get (in[to], through); **~лёт** *m* [1] flight; *моста* span; *лестницы* well; **~летариа́т** *m* [1] proletariat; **~лета́рий** *m* [3], **~лета́рский** [16] proletarian; **~лета́ть** [1], ⟨**~лете́ть**⟩ [11] fly (covering a certain distance); fly (past, by, over); *fig.* flash, flit

**проли́|в** *m* [1] strait (*e.g.* **~в Паде-Кале́** Strait of Dover [the Pas de Calais]); **~ва́ть** [1], ⟨**~ть**⟩ [-лью́, -льёшь; ле́й(те)!; про́ли́ло; про́ли́тый (про́ли́т, -а́, -о)] spill; (*v/i.* **-ся**); *слёзы*, *свет* shed;

П

**~вно́й** [14]: **~вно́й дождь** pouring rain, pelting rain; **~ть** → **~ва́ть**

**проло́|г** *m* [1] prologue; **~жи́ть** → **про-кла́дывать**; **~м** *m* [1] breach; **~ма́ть**, **~ми́ть** → **прола́мывать**

**про́мах** *m* [1] miss; blunder (make **дать** *or* **сде́лать** *a.* slip, fail); *coll.* **он па́рень не ~** he is no fool; **~ива́ться** [1], ⟨**~ну́ться**⟩ [20] miss

**промедле́ние** *n* [12] delay; procrastination

**промежу́то|к** *m* [1; -тка] interval (**в** П at; **в** В of); period; **~чный** [14] intermediate

**проме|лькну́ть** → **мелькну́ть**; **~нивать** [1], ⟨**~ня́ть**⟩ [28] exchange (**на** В for); **~рза́ть** [1], ⟨**промёрзнуть**⟩ [21] freeze (through); *coll.* → **продро́гнуть**

**промо|ка́ть** [1], ⟨**~кнуть**⟩ [21] get soaked *or* drenched; *impf. only* let water through; not be water proof; **~лча́ть** [4 *e.*; -чу́, -чи́шь] *pf.* keep silent; **~чи́ть** [16] *pf.* get soaked *or* drenched

**промтова́ры** *m/pl.* [1] manufactured goods (*other than food stuffs*)

**промча́ться** [4] *pf.* dart, tear *or* fly (past, by)

**промы|ва́ть** [1], ⟨**~ть**⟩ [22] wash (out, away); *med.* bathe, irrigate

**про́мы|сел** *m* [1; -сла]: **наро́дные ~слы** folk crafts; **~сло́вый** [14]: **~сло́вый сезо́н** fishing (hunting, *etc.*) season; **~ть** → **~ва́ть**

**промы́шлен|ник** *m* [1] manufacturer, industrialist; **~ность** *f* [8] industry; **~ный** [14] industrial

**пронести́(сь)** → **проноси́ть(ся)**

**прон|за́ть** [1], ⟨**~зи́ть**⟩ [15 *e.*; -нжу́, -нзи́шь; -нзённый] pierce, stab; **~зи́тельный** [14; -лен, -льна] shrill, piercing; *взгляд* penetrating; **~и́зывать** [1], ⟨**~иза́ть**⟩ [3] penetrate, pierce

**прони|ка́ть** [1], ⟨**~кнуть**⟩ [21] penetrate; permeate (**че́рез** through); get (in); **-ся** be imbued (T with); **~кнове́ние** *n* [12] penetration; *fig.* fervo(u)r; **~кнове́нный** [14; -е́нен, -е́нна] heartfelt; **~ца́емый** [14 *sh.*] permeable; **~ца́тельный** [14; -лен, -льна] penetrating, searching; *человек* acute, shrewd

**про|носи́ть** [15] **1.** ⟨**~нести́**⟩ [24 -с-: -есу́; -ёс, -есла́] carry (through, by, away); **-ся**, ⟨**-сь**⟩ *о пуле, камне* fly (past, by); pass *or слухи* spread (swiftly); **2.** *pf. coll.* wear out; **~ны́рливый** [14 *sh.*] crafty; pushy; **~ню́хать** [1] *coll.* get wind of

**прообраз** *m* [1] prototype

**пропага́нда** *f* [5] propaganda

**пропа|да́ть** [1], ⟨**~сть**⟩ [25; *pt. st.*] get *or* be lost; *даром* go to waste; be (missing; *a.* **~сть бе́з вести**); *интерес* lose, vanish; **~жа** *f* [5] loss; **~сть**¹ → **~да́ть**; **´~сть**² *f* [8] precipice, abyss; **на краю́ ´~сти** on the verge of disaster; *coll. много* lots *or* a lot (of)

**пропи|ва́ть** [1], ⟨**~ть**⟩ [-пью́, -пьёшь; -пе́й(те)!; про́пи́л, -а́, -о; про́пи́тый (про́пи́т, -а́, -о)] spend on drink

**пропис|а́ть(ся)** → **~ывать(ся)**; **~ска** *f* [5; *g/pl.*: -сок] registration; **~но́й** [14] capital, → **бу́ква**; **~на́я и́стина** truism; **~ывать** [1], ⟨**~а́ть**⟩ [3] *med.* prescribe (Д for); register (*v/i.* **-ся**); **´~ью** (*write*) in full

**пропи́|тывать**, ⟨**~та́ть**⟩ [1] (**-ся** be[-come]) steeped in, saturate(d; T with); **~ть** → **~ва́ть**

**проплы|ва́ть** [1], ⟨**~ть**⟩ [23] swim *or* sail (by); float, drift (by, past); *fig. joc.* sail (by, past)

**пропове́д|ник** *m* [1] preacher; **~овать** [1] preach; *fig.* advocate; **´~ь** ('pro-) *f* [8] *eccl.* sermon

**пропол|за́ть** [1], ⟨**~зти́**⟩ [24] creep, crawl (by, through, under); **~ка** *f* [5] weeding

**пропорциона́льный** [14; -лен, -льна] proportional, proportionate

**про́пус|к** *m* [1] **1.** [*pl.*: -ки] omission, blank; (*отсутствие*) absence; **2.** [*pl.*: -ка́, *etc. e.*] pass, permit; admission; **~ка́ть** [1], ⟨**~ти́ть**⟩ [15] let pass (or through), admit; (*опустить*) omit; *занятие и т. д.* miss; let slip; *impf.* (*течь*) leak

**прора|ба́тывать**, ⟨**~бо́тать**⟩ *coll.* [1] study; **~ста́ть** [1], ⟨**~сти́**⟩ [24 -ст-: -стёт; -ро́с, -росла́] germinate; sprout,

shoot (*of plant*)
**прорва́ть(ся)** → ***прорыва́ть(ся)***
**проре́з|ать** [1], 〈**~а́ть**〉 [3] cut through; **-ся** *о зубах* cut (*teeth*)
**проре́ха** *f* [5] slit, tear
**проро́|к** *m* [1] prophet; **~ни́ть** [13; -оню́, -о́нишь; -о́ненный] *pf.* utter; **~ческий** [16] prophetic; **~чество** *n* [9] prophecy; **~чить** [16] prophesy
**проруб|ать** [1], 〈**~и́ть**〉 [14] cut (through); **´~ь** *f* [8] hole cut in ice
**прор|ы́в** *m* [1] break; breach; **~ыва́ть** [1] **1.** 〈**~ва́ть**〉 [-ву́, -вёшь; -ва́л, -а́, -о; про́рванный (-ан, -а́, -о)] break through; **-ся** (*v/i.*) break through; burst open; force one's way; **2.** 〈**~ы́ть**〉 [22] dig (through)
**про|са́чиваться** [1], 〈**~сочи́ться**〉 [16 *e.*; *3*rd *p. only*] ooze (out), percolate; **~сверли́ть** [13] *pf.* drill, bore (through)
**просве́|т** *m* [1] *в облаках* gap; (*щель*) chink; *fig.* ray of hope; **~ти́ть** → ***~ща́ть & ~чивать* 2.**; **~тле́ть** [8] *pf.* clear up, brighten up; **~чивать** [1] **1.** shine through, be seen; **2.** 〈**~ти́ть**〉 [15] *med.* X-ray; **~ща́ть** [1], 〈**~ти́ть**〉 [15 *e.*; -ещу́, -ети́шь; -ещённый] enlighten, educate, instruct; **~ще́ние** *n* [12] education; **♀ще́ние** Enlightenment
**про́|седь** *f* [8] streaks of gray (*Brt.* grey), grizzly hair; **~се́ивать** [1], 〈**~се́ять**〉 [27] sift; **~сека** *f* [5] cutting, opening (*in a forest*); **~сёлочный** [14]: ***~сёлочная доро́га*** country road, cart track, unmetalled road; **~се́ять** → ***~се́ивать***
**проси́|живать** [1], 〈**~де́ть**〉 [11] sit (up); stay, remain (*for a certain time*); *над чем-л.* spend; **~ть** [15], 〈по-〉 ask (В/***о*** П; ***у*** Р/Р p. for), beg, request; (*пригласить*) invite; intercede (***за*** В for); ***прошу́, про́сят*** *a.* please; ***прошу́!*** please come in!; **-ся** (***в, на*** В) ask (for; leave [to enter, go]); **~я́ть** [28] *pf.* begin to shine; light up with
**проск|ользну́ть** [20] *pf.* slip, creep (***в*** В in); **~очи́ть** [16] *pf.* rush by, tear by; slip through; fall between *or* through
**просл|авля́ть** [28], 〈**~а́вить**〉 [14] glorify, make (**-ся** become) famous; **~еди́ть** [15 *e.*; -ежу́, -еди́шь; -ежённый] *pf.* track down; trace; **~ези́ться** [15 *e.*; -ежу́сь, -ези́шься] *pf.* shed (a few) tears
**просло́йка** *f* [5; *g/pl.*: -оек] layer
**про|слу́шать** [1] *pf.* hear; (through); *med.* auscultate; *coll.* miss, not catch (*what is said e.g.*); **~сма́тривать** [1], 〈**~смотре́ть**〉 [9; -отрю́, -о́тришь; -о́тренный] survey; view; look through *or* over; (*не заметить*) overlook; **~смо́тр** *m* [1] *документов* examination, survey; review (*о фильме тж.* preview); **~сну́ться** → ***~сыпа́ться***; **~со** *n* [9] millet; **~со́вывать** [1], 〈**~су́нуть**〉 [20] pass or push (through); **~со́хнуть** → ***~сыха́ть***; **~сочи́ться** → ***~са́чиваться***; **~спа́ть** → ***~сыпа́ть***
**проспе́кт**[1] *m* [1] avenue
**проспе́кт**[2] *m* [1] prospectus
**просро́ч|ивать** [1], 〈**~ить**〉 [16] let lapse *or* expire; exceed the time limit; **~ка** *f* [5; *g/pl.*: -чек] expiration; (*превышение срока*) exceeding
**прост|а́ивать** [1], 〈**~оя́ть**〉 [-ою́, -ои́шь] stand stay (*for a certain time*); *tech.* stand idle; **~а́к** *m* [1 *e.*] simpleton
**прост|ира́ть** [1], 〈**~ере́ть**〉 [12] stretch (*v/i.* **-ся**), extend
**прости́тельный** [14; -лен, -льна] pardonable, excusable
**проститу́тка** *f* [5; *g/pl.*: -ток] prostitute
**прости́ть(ся)** → ***проща́ть(ся)***
**простоду́ш|ие** *n* [12] naiveté; **~ный** [14; -шен, -шна] ingenuous, artless; simple-minded
**просто́|й**[1] [14; прост, -а́, -о; *comp.*: про́ще] simple, plain; easy; *манеры и т. д.* unaffected, unpretentious; *о людях* ordinary, common; *math.* prime
**просто́й**[2] *m* [3] stoppage, standstill
**простокваша** *f* [5] sour milk, yog(h)urt
**просто́|р** *m* [1] open (space); freedom (***на*** П in); *fig.* scope; **~ре́чие** *n* [12] popular speech; common parlance; **~рный** [14; -рен, -рна] spacious, roomy; **~та́** *f* [5] simplicity; naiveté; **~я́ть** → ***проста́ивать***
**простра́н|ный** [14; -а́нен, -а́нна] vast; *о речи, письме* long-winded, verbose; **~ство** *n* [9] space; expanse
**простра́ция** *f* [7] prostration, complete

physical *or* mental exhaustion
**прострéл** *m* [1] *coll.* lumbago; **~ивать** [1], ⟨**~и́ть**⟩ [13; -елю́, -éлишь; -елённый] shoot (through)
**просту́|да** *f* [5] common cold; **~жáть** [1], ⟨**~ди́ть**⟩ [15] chill; **-ся** catch a cold
**просту́пок** *m* [1; -пка] misdeed; offense (-ce); *law* misdemeano(u)r
**простыня́** *f* [6; *pl*.: прóстыни, -ы́нь, *etc*. *e*.] (bed) sheet
**просу́|нуть** → ***просо́вывать***; **~шивать** [1], ⟨**~ши́ть**⟩ [16] dry thoroughly
**просчитáться** [1] *pf.* miscalculate
**просыпáть** [1], ⟨**~проспáть**⟩ [-плю́, -пи́шь; -спáл, -á, о] oversleep; sleep; *coll.* miss (by sleeping); **~ся**, ⟨**про-сну́ться**⟩ [20] awake, wake up
**прос|ыхáть** [1], ⟨**~óхнуть**⟩ [21] get dry, dry out
**прóсьба** *f* [5] request (***по*** П at; ***о*** П for); please (don't ***не*** + *inf.*) ***у меня́ к вам ~*** I have a favo(u)r to ask you
**про|тáлкивать** [1], *once* ⟨**~толкну́ть**⟩ [20], *coll.* ⟨**~толкáть**⟩ [1] push (through); **-ся** force one's way (through); **~тáптывать** [1], ⟨**~топтáть**⟩ [3] *дорожку* tread; **~тáскивать** [1], ⟨**~тащи́ть**⟩ [16] carry *or* drag (past, by); *coll.* smuggle in
**протéз** ('tes) *m* [1] prosthetic appliance; artificial limb; ***зубнóй ~*** false teeth, dentures
**проте|кáть** [1], ⟨**~́чь**⟩ [26] *impf. only* (*of a river or stream*) flow, run (by); *лодка* leak; *pf. время* pass, elapse; take its course; **~́кция** *f* [7] patronage; **~рéть** → ***протирáть***; **~́ст** *m* [1], **~стовáть** [7], *v/t.* (*im*)*pf.* & ⟨о-⟩ protest; **~́чь** → ***~кáть***
**прóтив** (Р) against; opposite; ***быть*** *or* ***имéть ~*** (have) object(ion; to), mind; **~́иться** [14], ⟨вос-⟩ (Д) oppose, object; **~́ник** *m* [1] opponent, adversary; enemy; **~́ный**[1] [14; -вен, -вна] repugnant, disgusting, offensive, nasty; **~́ный**[2] opposite, contrary; opposing, opposed; ***мне ~́но*** *a*. I hate; ***в ~́ном слу́чае*** otherwise
**противо|вéс** *m* [1] counterbalance; **~возду́шный** [14] antiaircraft…; ***~возду́шная оборóна*** air defense (-ce); **~дéйствие** *n* [12] counteraction; (*сопротивление*) resistance; **~дéйствовать** [7] counteract; resist; **~естéственный** [14 *sh.*] unnatural; **~закóнный** [14; -óнен, -óнна] unlawful, illegal; **~зачáточный** [14] contraceptive; **~показáние** *n* [12] *med.* contra-indication; **~полóжность** *f* [8] contrast, opposition (***в*** В in); antithesis; **~полóжный** [14; -жен, -жна] opposite; contrary, opposed; **~поставля́ть** [28], ⟨-постáвить⟩ [14] oppose; **~поставлéние** *n* [12] opposition; **~ракéтный** [14] antimissile; **~речи́вый** [14 *sh.*] contradictory; **~рéчие** *n* [12] contradiction; **~рéчить** [16] (Д) contradict; **~стоя́ть** [-ою́, -ои́шь] (Д) withstand; stand against; **~я́дие** *n* [12] antidote
**про|тирáть** [1], ⟨**~терéть**⟩ [12] wear (through); *стекло* wipe; **~ткну́ть** → ***~тыкáть***; **~тóкол** *m* [1] (**~токоли́ровать** [7] [*im*]*pf*., *a*., ⟨за-⟩ take down the) minutes *pl*., record; *su. a*. protocol; **~толкáть**, **~толкну́ть** → ***~тáлкивать***; **~топтáть** → ***~тáптывать***; **~торённый** [14] *дорога* beaten well-trodden; **~тоти́п** *m* [1] prototype; **~тóчный** [14] flowing, running; **~трезвля́ться** [28], ⟨**~трезви́ться**⟩ [14 *e*.; -влю́сь, -ви́шься; -влённый] sober up; **~тыкáть** [1], *once* ⟨**~ткну́ть**⟩ [20] pierce, skewer; transfix
**протя́|гивать** [1], ⟨**~ну́ть**⟩ [19] stretch (out), extend, hold out; (*передать*) pass; **~жéние** *n* [12] extent, stretch (***на*** П over, along); (*of time*) space (***на*** П for, during); **~жный** [14; -жен, -жна] *звук* drawn-out; **~ну́ть** → ***~́гивать***
**проучи́ть** *coll.* [16] *pf.* teach a lesson
**професс|ионáльный** [14] professional; trade… (*e.g.* trade union → ***профсою́з***); **~́ия** *f* [7] profession, trade (***по*** Д by); **~́ор** *m* [1; *pl*.; -рá, *etc*. *e*.] professor; **~у́ра** *f* [5] professorship; *collect.* the professors
**прóфиль** *m* [4] **1.** profile; **2. ~ *учи́лища*** type of school or college
**профóрма** *coll.* *f* [5] form, formality
**профсою́з** *m* [1], **~ный** [14] trade union

**про|ха́живаться** [1], ⟨**~йти́сь**⟩ [-йду́сь, -йдёшься; -шёлся, -шла́сь] (go for a) walk, stroll; *coll.* have a go at s.o. (**на чей-либо счёт**); **~хво́ст** *coll. m* [1] scoundrel

**прохла́д|а** *f* [5] coolness; **~и́тельный** [14; -лен, льна]: ***~и́тельные напи́тки*** soft drinks; **~ный** [14; -ден, -дна] cool (*a. fig.*), fresh

**прохо́|д** *m* [1] passage, pass; *anat.* duct (***за́дний ~д*** anus); **~ди́мец** *m* [1; -мца] rogue, scoundrel; **~ди́мость** *f* [8] *дороги* passability; *anat.* permeability; **~ди́ть** [15], ⟨**пройти́**⟩ [пройду́, -дёшь; прошёл; ше́дший; про́йденный; *g. pt.*: пройдя́] pass, go (by, through, over, along); take a … course, be; **~дно́й** [14] *двор* (with a) through passage; **~жде́ние** *n* [12] passage, passing; **~жий** *m* [17] passerby

**процвета́ть** [1] prosper, thrive

**проце|ду́ра** *f* [5] procedure; **~живать** [1], ⟨**~ди́ть**⟩ [15] filter, strain; **~нт** *m* [1] percent(age) (**на** В by); (*usu. pl.*) interest; ***ста́вка ~нта*** rate of interest; **~сс** *m* [1] process; *law* trial (**на** П at); **~ссия** [7] procession

**проче́сть** → ***прочи́тывать***

**про́ч|ий** [17] other; *n & pl. a. su.* the rest; ***и ~ее*** and so on *or* forth, *etc.*; ***ме́жду ~им*** by the way, incidentally; ***поми́мо всего́ ~его*** in addition

**прочи|стить** → ***~ща́ть***; **~тывать**, ⟨**~та́ть**⟩ [1] & ⟨**проче́сть**⟩ [25 -т-: -чту́, -тёшь; -чёл, -чла́; *g. pt.*: -чтя́, -чтённый] read (through); **~ть** [16] intend (for), have s.o. in mind (**в** В as); *успех* destine (for); **~ща́ть** [1], ⟨**~стить**⟩ [15] clean

**про́чн|ость** *f* [8] durability, firmness; **~ый** [14; -чен, -чна; -о] firm, solid, strong; *мир* lasting; *знания* sound

**прочте́ние** *n* [12] reading; perusal; *fig.* interpretation

**прочь** away → ***доло́й***; ***я не ~*** + *inf. coll.* I wouldn't mind …ing

**прош|е́дший** [17] past, last (*a. su. n* ***~е́дшее*** the past); *gr.* past (tense); **~е́ствие** *n* [12] → ***истече́ние***; **~лого́дний** [15] last year's; **~лый** [14] past (*a. su. n* ***~лое***), bygone; **~мыгну́ть** *coll.* [20] *pf.* slip, whisk (by, past)

**прощ|а́й(те)!** farewell!, goodby(e)!, adieu!; **~а́льный** [14] farewell…; *слова* parting; **~а́ние** *n* [12] parting (**при** П, **на** В when, at), leavetaking, farewell; **~а́ть** [1], ⟨**прости́ть**⟩ [15 *e.*; -ощу́, -ости́шь; -ощённый] forgive (р. Д), excuse, pardon; **-ся** (**с** Т) take leave (of), say goodby (to); **~е́ние** *n* [12] forgiveness, pardon

**прояв|и́тель** *m* [4] *phot.* developer; **~и́ть(ся)** → ***~ля́ть(ся)***; **~ле́ние** *n* [12] manifestation, display, demonstration; *phot.* development; **~ля́ть** [28], ⟨**~и́ть**⟩ [14] show, display, manifest; *phot.* develop

**проясн|я́ться** [28], ⟨**~и́ться**⟩ [13] (*of weather*) clear up (*a. fig.*); brighten

**пруд** *m* [1 *e.*; в ~у́] pond

**пружи́на** *f* [5] spring; ***скры́тая ~*** motive

**прут** *m* [1; *a. e.*; *pl.*: -ья, -ьев] twig; *железный* rod

**пры́|гать** [1], *once* ⟨**~гнуть**⟩ [20] jump, spring, leap; **~гу́н** *m* [1 *e.*] (*sport*) jumper; **~жо́к** *m* [1; -жка́] jump, leap, bound; *в воду* dive; **~ткий** [16; -ток, -тка, -о] nimble, quick; **~ть** *coll. f* [8] agility; speed (***во всю*** at full); **~щ** *m* [1 *e.*], **~щик** *m* [1] pimple

**пряди́льный** [14] spinning

**пря|дь** *f* [8] lock, tress, strand; **~жа** *f* [5] yarn; **~жка** *f* [5; *g/pl.*: -жек] buckle

**прям|изна́** *f* [5] straightness; **~о́й** [14; прям, -á, -о] straight (*a.* = bee) line (***~а́я*** *su. f*); direct (*a. gr.*); *rail* through…; *угол* right; *fig.* straight (-forward), downright, outspoken, frank; ***~а́я кишка́*** rectum; **~олине́йный** [14; -е́ен, -е́йна] rectilinear; *fig.*; → ***~о́й*** *fig.*; **~ота́** *f* [5] straightforwardness, frankness; **~оуго́льник** *m* [1] rectangle; **~оуго́льный** [14] rectangular

**пря́н|ик** *m* [1] *имбирный* gingerbread; ***медо́вый ~ик*** honeycake; **~ость** *f* [8] spice; **~ый** [14 *sh.*] spicy, *fig.* piquant

**прясть** [25; -ял, -á, -о], ⟨с-⟩ spin

**пря́т|ать** [3], ⟨с-⟩ hide (*v/i.* **-ся**), conceal; **~ки** *f/pl.* [5; *gen.*: -ток] hide-and-seek

**псал|о́м** *m* [1; -лма́] psalm; **~ты́рь** *f* [8] Psalter

П

**псевдони́м** *m* [1] pseudonym
**псих|иатр** *m* [1] psychiatrist; **ꜜика** *f* [5] state of mind; psyche; mentality; **~и́ческий** [16] mental, psychic(al); ***~и́ческое заболева́ние*** mental illness; **~о́лог** *m* [1] psychologist; **~оло́гия** *f* [7] psychology
**птене́ц** [1; -нца́] nestling, fledgling
**пти́|ца** *f* [5] bird; ***дома́шняя ~ца*** *collect.* poultry; **~цево́дство** *n* [9] poultry farming; **~чий** [18] bird('s); poultry…; ***вид с ~чьего полёта*** bird's-eye view; **~чка** *f* [5; *g/pl.*: -чек] (*галочка*) tick
**пу́бли|ка** *f* [5] audience; public; **~ка́ция** *f* [7] publication; **~кова́ть** [7], ⟨о-⟩ publish; **~ци́ст** *m* [1] publicist; **ꜜчный** [14] public; ***ꜜчный дом*** brothel
**пу́г|ало** *n* [9] scarecrow; **~а́ть** [1], ⟨ис-, на-⟩, *once* ⟨~ну́ть⟩ [20] (**-ся** be) frighten(ed; of Р), scare(d); **~ли́вый** [14 *sh.*] timid, fearful
**пу́говица** *f* [5] button
**пу́дель** *m* [4; *pl. a. etc. e.*] poodle
**пу́др|а** *f* [5] powder; ***са́харная ~а*** powdered (*Brt.* caster) sugar; **~еница** *f* [5] powder compact; **~ить** [13], ⟨на-⟩ powder
**пуз|а́тый** P [14 *sh.*] paunchy; **ꜜо** P *n* [9] paunch, potbelly
**пузыр|ёк** *m* [1; -рька́] vial; *a. dim.* → **ꜜь** *m* [4 *e.*] bubble; *anat.* bladder; *coll. на коже* blister
**пулемёт** *m* [1] machine gun
**пуль|веризáтор** *m* [1] spray(er); **~с** *m* [1] pulse; *coll.* ***щу́пать ~с*** feel the pulse; **~си́ровать** [7] puls(at)e; **~т** *m* [1] conductor's stand; *tech.* control panel *or* desk
**пу́ля** *f* [6] bullet
**пункт** *m* [1] point, station; place, spot; *документа* item, clause, article; ***по ꜜам*** point by point; **~и́р** *m* [1] dotted line; **~уа́льность** *f* [8] punctuality; accuracy; **~уа́льный** [14; -лен, -льна] punctual; accurate; **~уа́ция** *f* [7] punctuation
**пунцо́вый** [1] crimson
**пунш** *m* [1] punch (*drink*)
**пуп|о́к** *m* [1; -пка́], *coll.* **~** *m* [1 *e.*] navel
**пурга́** *f* [5] blizzard, snowstorm

**пу́рпур** *m* [1], **ꜜный**, **ꜜовый** [14] purple
**пуск** *m* [1] (*a.* ***~ в ход***) start(ing), setting in operation; **~а́й** → *coll.* **пусть**; **~а́ть** [1], ⟨пусти́ть⟩ [15] let (go; in[to]), set going, in motion *or* operation [*a.* ***~а́ть в ход***]; start; (*бросить*) throw; *корни* take root; *fig.* begin; *в продажу* offer (*for sale*); ***~а́ть под отко́с*** derail; **-ся** (+ *inf.*) *в путь* start (…ing; *v/ct.* **в** В), set out (**в** В on); begin, undertake; enter upon
**пуст|е́ть** [8], ⟨о-, за-⟩ become empty *or* deserted; **~и́ть** → ***пуска́ть***
**пуст|о́й** [14; пуст, -о́, -о] empty; *надежда, разговор* vain, idle (talk **~о́е**; *n su.* → *a.* **~я́к**); *место* vacant; *взгляд* blank; *geol. порода* barren rock; (*полый*) hollow; **~ота́** *f* [5; *pl. st.*: -о́ты] emptiness; void; *phys.* vacuum
**пусты́|нный** [14; -ы́нен, -ы́нна] uninhabited, deserted; **~ня** *f* [6] desert, wilderness; **~рь** *m* [4 *e.*] waste land; **~шка** *f* [5; *g/pl.*: -шек] *coll.* baby's dummy; *fig.* hollow man
**пусть** let (him, *etc.* + *vb.*; **~ [он] +** *vb.* 3rd *p.*); even (if)
**пустя́|к** *coll. m* [1 *e.*] trifle; *pl* (it's) nothing; ***па́ра ~ко́в*** child's play; **~ко́вый**, **~чный** *coll.* [14] trifling, trivial
**пу́та|ница** *f* [5] confusion, muddle, mess; **~ть** [1], ⟨за-, с-, пере-⟩ (**-ся** get) confuse(d), muddle(d), mix(ed) up, entangled, ***-ся под нога́ми*** get in the way
**путёвка** *f* [5; *g/pl.*: -вок] pass, authorization (*for a place on a tour, in a holiday home, etc.*)
**путе|води́тель** *m* [4] guide(book) (***по*** Д to); **~во́дный** [14] *звезда* lodestar; **~во́й** [14] travel(l)ing; ***~вы́е заме́тки*** travel notes
**путеше́ств|енник** *m* [1] travel(l)er; **~ие** *n* [12] journey, trip; voyage, *морем* cruise; **~овать** [7] travel (**по** Д through)
**пу́т|ник** *m* [1] travel(l)er, wayfarer; **~ный** *coll.* [14] → ***де́льный***
**путч** *m* [1] *pol.* coup, putsch
**пут|ь** *m* [8 *e.*; *instr/sg.*: -тём] way (*a. fig.*: [in] *that* way **~ём**, *a.* by means of Р); road, path; *rail* track, line; (*способ*) means; (*поездка*) trip, journey (**в** В

П

*or* П on); route; ***в*** *or* ***по ~й*** on the way; in passing; ***нам по ~й*** I (we) am (are) going the same way (**с** T as); ***быть на ло́жном ~й*** be on the wrong track

**пух** *m* [1; в -ху́] down, fluff; ***в ~ (и прах)*** (*defeat*) utterly, totally; **~ленький** *coll.* [16], **~лый** [14; пухл, -á, -о] chubby, plump; **~нуть** [21], ⟨рас-⟩ swell; **~о́вый** [14] downy

**пучи́на** *f* [5] gulf, abyss (*a. fig.*)

**пучо́к** *m* [1; -чка] bunch; *coll.* bun (hairdo)

**пу́ш|ечный** [14] gun…, cannon…; **~и́нка** *f* [5; *g/pl.*: -нок] down, fluff; **~и́стый** [14 *sh.*] downy, fluffy; **~ка** *f* [5; *g/pl.*: -шек] gun, cannon; **~ни́на** *f* [5] *collect.* furs, pelts *pl.*; **~но́й** [14] fur…; **~о́к** *coll. m* [1; -шка́] fluff

**пчел|á** *f* [5; *pl. st.*: пчёлы] bee; **~ово́д** *m* [1] beekeeper; **~ово́дство** *n* [9] beekeeping

**пшен|и́ца** *f* [5] wheat; **~и́чный** [14] wheaten; **пшённый** ('pʃo-) [14] millet…; **~о́** *n* [9] millet

**пыл** *m* [1] *fig.* ardo(u)r, zeal; ***в ~у́ сраже́ния*** in the heat of the battle; **~áть** [1], ⟨за-⟩ blaze, flame, *о лице* glow, burn; rage; (T) *гневом*; **~есо́с** *m* [1] vacuum cleaner; **~и́нка** *f* [5; *g/pl.*: -нок] mote, speck of dust; **~и́ть** [13], ⟨за-⟩ get dusty; **-ся** be(come) dusty; **~кий** [16; -лок, -лка́, -о] ardent, passionate

**пыль** *f* [8; в пыли́] dust; **~ный** [14; -лен, -льнá, -о] dusty (*a.* = ***в -ли́***); **~цá** *f* [5] pollen

**пыт|áть** [1] torture; **~áться** [1], ⟨по-⟩ try, attempt; **~ка** *f* [5; *g/pl.*: -ток] torture; **~ли́вый** [14 *sh.*] inquisitive, searching

**пыхте́ть** [11] puff, pant; *coll.* ***~ над че́м-либо*** sweat over something

**пы́шн|ость** *f* [8] splendo(u)r, pomp; **~ый** [14; -шен, -шнá, -о] magnificent, splendid, sumptuous; *волосы, растительность* luxuriant, rich

**пьедестáл** *m* [1] pedestal

**пье́са** *f* [5] *thea.* play; *mus.* piece

**пьян|е́ть** [8], ⟨о-⟩ get drunk (*a. fig.*; from, on **от** P); **~и́ца** *m/f* [5] drunkard; **~ство** *n* [9] drunkenness; **~ствовать** [7] drink heavily; *coll.* booze; **~ый** [14; пьян, -á, -о] drunk(en), *a. fig.* (**от** P with)

**пюре́** (-'re) *n* [*indecl.*] purée; ***карто́фельное ~*** mashed potatoes *pl.*

**пятá** *f* [5; *nom/pl. st.*] heel; ***ходи́ть за ке́м-л. по ~м*** follow on s.o.'s heels

**пят|áк** *coll. m* [1 *e.*], **~ачо́к** *coll. m* [1; -чкá] five-kopeck (*Brt.* -copeck) coin; **~ёрка** *f* [5; *g/pl.*: -рок] five (→ ***дво́йка***); *coll.* → ***отли́чно***; five-ruble (*Brt.* -rouble) note; **~еро** [37] five (→ ***дво́е***)

**пяти|деся́тый** [14] fiftieth; ***~деся́тые го́ды*** *pl.* the fifties; → ***пя́тый***; **~ле́тний** [15] five-year (old), of five; **~со́тый** [14] five hundredth

**пя́титься** [15], ⟨по-⟩ (move) back

**пя́тк|а** *f* [5; *g/pl.*: -ток] heel (take to one's heels ***показáть ~и***)

**пятнáдцат|ый** [14] fifteenth; → ***пя́тый***; **~ь** [35] fifteen; → ***пять***

**пятни́стый** [14 *sh.*] spotted, dappled

**пя́тн|ица** *f* [5] Friday (on: **в** B; *pl.*: **по** Д); **~о́** *n* [9; *pl. st.*; *g/pl.*: -тен] spot, stain (*a. fig.*), blot(ch) (*pl.* **в** B with); ***роди́мое ~о́*** birthmark

**пя́т|ый** [14] fifth; (*page, chapter, etc.*) five; **~ая** *f su. math.* a fifth (*part*); **~ое** *n su.* the fifth (*date*; on P: **~ого**; → ***число́***); ***~ь мину́т ~ого*** five (minutes) past four; **~ь** [35] five; ***без ~и́ (мину́т) час*** (***два***, *etc.*, [часá], five (minutes) to one (two, *etc.* [o'clock]); **~ь**, *etc.* (**часо́в**) five, etc. (o'clock); **~ьдеся́т** [35] fifty; **~ьсо́т** [36] five hundred; **~ью** five times

П

# Р

**раб** *m* [1 *e.*], **~á** *f* [5] slave

**рабо́т|а** *f* [5] work (**за** Т; **на** П at); job; labo(u)r, toil; *качество* workmanship; **~ать** [1] work (**над** Тon; **на** В for; Т as); labo(u)r, toil; *tech.* run, operate; *магазин и т. д.* be open; **~ник** *m* [1], **~ница** *f* [5] worker, working (wo)man; day labo(u)rer, (farm)hand; official; functionary; employee; *научный* scientist; **~ода́тель** *m* [4] employer, *coll.* boss; **~оспосо́бный** [14; -бен, -бна] able-bodied; hard-working; **~я́щий** [17 *sh.*] industrious

**рабо́ч|ий** *m* [17] (*esp. industrial*) worker; *adj.*: working, work (*a. day*); workers', labo(u)r…; **~ая си́ла** manpower; work force; labo(u)r

**ра́б|ский** [16] slave…; slavish, servile; **~ство** *n* [9] slavery, servitude; **~ы́ня** *f* [6] → **~á**

**ра́в|енство** *n* [9] equality; **~ни́на** *f* [5] *geog.* plain; **~но́** alike; as well as; **всё ~но́** it's all the same, it doesn't matter; anyway, in any case; **не всё ли ~но́?** what's the difference?

**равно|ве́сие** *n* [12] balance (*a. fig.*), equilibrium; **~ду́шие** *n* [12] indifference (**к** Д to); **~ду́шный** [14; -шен, -шна] indifferent (**к** Д to); **~ме́рный** [14; -рен, -рна] uniform, even; **~пра́вие** *n* [12] equality (of rights); **~пра́вный** [14; -вен, -вна] (enjoying) equal (rights); **~си́льный** [14; -лен, -льна] of equal strength; tantamount to; equivalent; **~це́нный** [14; -е́нен, -е́нна] equal (in value)

**ра́вн|ый** [14; ра́вен, -вна́] equal (*a. su.*); **~ым о́бразом** → **~о́**; **ему́ нет ~ого** he is unrivalled; **~я́ть** [28], ⟨с-⟩ equalize; *coll.* compare with, treat as equal to; (*v/i.* **-ся**; *a.* be [equal to Д])

**рад** [14; ра́да] (be) glad (Д at, of; *a.* to see *p.*), pleased, delighted; **не ~** (be) sorry; regret

**рада́р** *m* [1] radar

**ра́ди** (Р) for the sake of; for (…'s) sake; for

**радиа́тор** *m* [1] radiator

**радика́л** [1], **~ьный** [14; -лен, -льна] radical

**ра́дио** *n* [*indecl.*] radio (**по** Д on); **~акти́вность** *f* [8] radioactivity; **~акти́вный** [14; -вен, -вна] radioactive; **~акти́вное загрязне́ние** (**оса́дки**) radioactive contamination (fallout); **~веща́ние** *n* [12] broadcasting (system); **~люби́тель** *m* [4] radio amateur; **~переда́ча** *f* [5] (radio) broadcast, transmission; **~приёмник** *m* [1] radio set; receiver; **~слу́шатель** *m* [4] listener; **~ста́нция** *f* [7] radio station; **~телефо́н** *m* [1] radiotelephone

**ради́ст** *m* [1] radio operator

**ра́диус** *m* [1] radius

**ра́до|вать** [7], ⟨об-, по-⟩ (В) gladden, please; **-ся** (Д) rejoice (at), be glad *or* pleased (of, at); **~стный** [14; -тен, -тна] joyful, glad; merry; **~сть** *f* [8] joy, gladness; pleasure

**ра́ду|га** *f* [5] rainbow; **~жный** [14] iridescent, rainbow…; *fig.* rosy; **~жная оболо́чка** *anat.* iris

**раду́ш|ие** *n* [12] cordiality; kindness; (*гостеприимство*) hospitality; **~ный** [14; -шен, -шна] kindly, hearty; hospitable

**раз** *m* [1; *pl. e.*, *gen.* раз] time ([**в**] В this, *etc.*); one; **оди́н ~** once; **два ~а** twice; **ни ~у** not once, never; **не ~** repeatedly; **как ~** just (in time *coll.* **в са́мый** → *a.* **впо́ру**), the very; **вот тебе́ ~** → **на**²

**разба|вля́ть** [28], ⟨~вить⟩ [14] dilute; **~лтывать** *coll.*, ⟨разболта́ть⟩ [1] blab out, give away

**разбе́|г** *m* [1] running start, run (with, at **с** Р); **~га́ться** [1], ⟨**~жа́ться**⟩ [4; -егу́сь, -ежи́шься, -егу́тся] take a run; *в разные стороны* scatter; **у меня́ глаза́ ~жа́лись** I was dazzled

**разби|ва́ть** [1], ⟨~ть⟩ [разобью́, -бьёшь; разбе́й(те)!; -и́тый] break (to pieces), crash, crush; defeat (*a. mil.*); (*разде-*

*лить*) divide up (into **на** В); *парк* lay out; *палатку* pitch; *колено и т. д.* hurt badly; *доводы и т. д.* smash; **-ся** break; get broken; *на группы* break up, divide; hurt o.s. badly; **~ра́тельство** *n* [9] examination, investigation; **~ра́ть** [1], ⟨разобра́ть⟩ [разберу́, -рёшь; разобра́л, -а́, -о; -о́бранный] take to pieces, dismantle; *дом* pull down; *дело* investigate, inquire into; (*различать*) make out, decipher, understand; *вещи* sort out; (*раскупать*) buy up; **-ся** (**в** П) grasp, understand; **~́тый** [14 *sh.*] broken; *coll.* (*усталый*) jaded; **~́ть(ся)** → ***~ва́ть(ся)***

**разбо́й** *m* [3] robbery; **~ник** *m* [1] robber; *joc.* (little) rogue; scamp

**разболта́ть** → ***разба́лтывать***

**разбо́р** *m* [1] analysis; *произведения* review, critique; *дела* investigation, inquiry (into); ***без ~а, ~у*** *coll.* indiscriminately; **~ка** *f* [5] taking to pieces, dismantling; (*сортировка*) sorting (out); **~ный** [14] collapsible; **~чивость** *f* [8] *почерка* legibility; *о человеке* scrupulousness; **~чивый** [14 *sh.*] scrupulous, fastidious; legible

**разбр|а́сывать**, ⟨**~оса́ть**⟩ [1] scatter, throw about, strew; **~еда́ться** [1], ⟨**~ести́сь**⟩ [25] disperse; **~о́д** [1] disorder; **~о́санный** [14] sparse; scattered; **~оса́ть** → ***~а́сывать***

**разбух|а́ть** [1], ⟨**~́нуть**⟩ [21] swell

**разва́л** *m* [1] collapse, breakdown; disintegration; **~ивать** [1], ⟨**~и́ть**⟩ [13; -алю́, -а́лишь] pull (*or* break) down; disorganize; **-ся** fall to pieces, collapse; *coll. в кресле* collapse, sprawl; **~ины** *f pl.* [5] ruins (*coll. a. sg.* = *p.*)

**ра́зве** really; perhaps; only; except that

**развева́ться** [1] fly, flutter, flap

**разве́д|ать** → ***~ывать***; **~е́ние** *n* [12] breeding; *растений* cultivation; **~ённый** [14] divorced; divorcé(e) *su.*; **~ка** *f* [5; *g/pl.*: -док] *mil.* reconnaissance; intelligence service; *geol.* prospecting; **~чик** *m* [1] scout; intelligence officer; reconnaissance aircraft; **~ывательный** [14] reconnaissance…; **~ывать**, ⟨**~ать**⟩ [1] reconnoiter (*Brt.* -tre); *geol.* prospect; *coll.* find out

**разве|зти́** → ***развози́ть***; **~нча́ть** [1] *pf. fig.* debunk

**развёр|нутый** [14] (*широкомасштабный*) large-scale; detailed; **~тывать** [1], ⟨разверну́ть⟩ [20] unfold, unroll, unwrap; *mil.* deploy; *fig.* develop; (**-ся** *v/i.*; *a.* turn)

**разве|сно́й** [14] sold by weight; **~́сить** → ***~́шивать***; **~сти́(сь)** → ***разводи́ть(ся)***; **~твле́ние** *n* [12] ramification, branching; **~твля́ться** [28], ⟨**~тви́ться**⟩ [14 *e.*; 3rd *p. only*] ramify, branch; **~́шивать** [1], ⟨**~́сить**⟩ [15] weigh (out); *бельё* hang (out); **~́ять** [27] *pf.* disperse; *сомнения* dispel

**разви|ва́ть** [1], ⟨**~́ть**⟩ [разовью́, -вьёшь; разве́й(те)!; разви́л, -а́, -о; -ви́тый (ра́звит, -а́, -о)] develop (*v/i.* **-ся**); evolve; **~́нчивать** [1], ⟨**~нти́ть**⟩ [15 *e.*; -нчу́, -нти́шь; -и́нченный] unscrew; **~́тие** *n* [12] development, evolution; **~то́й** [14; ра́звит, -а́, -о] developed; *ребёнок* advanced, well-developed; **~́ть(ся)** → ***~ва́ть(ся)***

**развле|ка́ть** [1], ⟨**~́чь**⟩ [26] entertain, amuse (**-ся** o.s.); (*развлечь отвлекая*) divert; **~че́ние** *n* [12] entertainment, amusement; diversion

**разво́д** *m* [1] divorce; ***быть в ~е*** be divorced; **~и́ть** [15], ⟨развести́⟩ [25] take (along), bring; divorce (**с** T from); (*растворить*) dilute; *животных* rear, breed; *agric.* plant, cultivate; *огонь* light, make; *мост* raise; **-ся**, ⟨**-сь**⟩ get *or* be divorced (**с** T from); *coll.* multiply, grow *or* increase in number

**раз|вози́ть** [15], ⟨**~везти́**⟩ [24] *товары* deliver; *гостей* drive; **~вора́чивать** *coll.* → ***~вёртывать***

**развра́|т** *m* [1] debauchery; depravity; **~ти́ть(ся)** → ***~ща́ть(ся)***; **~тник** *m* [1] profligate; debauchee, rake; **~тный** [14; -тен, -тна] depraved, corrupt; **~ща́ть** [1], ⟨**~ти́ть**⟩ [15 *e.*; -ащу́, -ати́шь; -ащённый] (**-ся** become) deprave(d), debauch(ed), corrupt; **~щённость** *f* [8] depravity

**развяз|а́ть** → ***~́ывать***; **~́ка** *f* [5; *g/pl.*: -зок] *lit.* denouement; outcome; up-

Р

shot; ***де́ло идёт к ҫке*** things are coming to a head; **ҫный** [14; -зен, -зна] forward, (overly) familiar; **ҫывать** [1], ⟨**~а́ть**⟩ [3] untie, undo; *fig. войну* unleash; *coll. язык* loosen; **-ся** come untied; *coll.* (*освободиться*) be through (**с** T with)

**разгад|а́ть** → ***ҫывать***; **ҫка** [5; *g/pl.*: -док] solution; **ҫывать**, ⟨**~а́ть**⟩ [1] guess; *загадку* solve

**разга́р** *m* [1] (**в** П *or* В) ***в ~е*** *спора* in the heat of; ***в ~е*** *лета* at the height of; ***в по́лном ~е*** in full swing

**раз|гиба́ть** [1], ⟨**~огну́ть**⟩ [20] unbend, straighten (**-ся** o.s.)

**разгла́|живать** [1], ⟨**~дить**⟩ [15] smooth out; *швы и т. д.* iron, press; **~ша́ть** [1], ⟨**~си́ть**⟩ [15 *e.*; -ашу́, -аси́шь; -ашённый] divulge, give away, let out

**разгляд|е́ть** [11] *pf.* make out; discern; **ҫывать** [1] examine, scrutinize

**разгне́ванный** [14] angry

**разгов|а́ривать** [1] talk (**с** T to, with; **о** П about, of), converse, speak; **~о́р** *m* [1] talk, conversation; → ***речь***; ***перемени́ть те́му ~о́ра*** change the subject; **~о́рный** [14] colloquial; **~о́рчивый** [14 *sh.*] talkative, loquacious

**разго́н** *m* [1] dispersal; *a.* → ***разбе́г***; **~я́ть** [28], ⟨**разогна́ть**⟩ [разгоню́, -о́нишь; разгна́л, -а́, -о; разо́гнанный] drive away, disperse; *тоску и т. д.* dispel; *coll.* drive at high speed; **-ся** gather speed; gather momentum

**разгор|а́ться** [1], ⟨**~е́ться**⟩ [9] flare up; *щёки* flush

**разгра|бля́ть** [28], ⟨**ҫбить**⟩ [14], **~бле́ние** *n* [12] plunder, pillage, loot; **~ниче́ние** *n* [12] delimitation, differentiation; **~ни́чивать** [1], ⟨**~ни́чить**⟩ [16] demarcate, delimit; *обязанности* divide

**разгро́м** *m* [1] *mil.*, *etc.* crushing defeat, rout; *coll.* (*полный беспорядок*) havoc, devastation, chaos

**разгру|жа́ть** [1], ⟨**~зи́ть**⟩ [15 & 15 *e.*; -ужу́, -у́зи́шь; -у́женный & -ужённый] (**-ся** be) unload(ed); **ҫзка** *f* [5; *g/pl.*: -зок] unloading

**разгу́л** *m* [1] (*кутёж*) revelry, carousal; *шовинизма* outburst of; **~ивать** F [1] stroll, saunter; **-ся**, ⟨**~я́ться**⟩ [28] *о погоде* clear up; **~ьный** *coll.* [14; -лен, -льна]: ***~ьный о́браз жи́зни*** life of dissipation

**разда|ва́ть** [5], ⟨**ҫть**⟩ [-да́м, -да́шь, *etc.* → ***дать***; ро́здал, раздала́, ро́здало; ро́зданный, (-ан, раздана́, ро́здано)] distribute; dispense; give (*cards*: deal) out; **-ся** (re)sound, ring out, be heard; **ҫвливать** [1] → ***дави́ть 2.***; **ҫть(ся)** → ***~ва́ть(ся)***; **ҫча** *f* [5] distribution

**раздва́иваться** → ***двои́ться***

**раздви|га́ть** [1], ⟨**ҫнуть**⟩ [20] part, move apart; *занавески* draw back; **~жно́й** [14] *стол* expanding; *дверь* sliding

**раздвое́ние** *n* [12] division into two, bifurcation; ***~ ли́чности*** *med.* split personality

**раздева́|лка** *coll. f* [5; *g/pl.*: -лок] checkroom, cloakroom; **~ть** [1], ⟨**разде́ть**⟩ [-де́ну, -де́нешь; -де́тый] undress (*v/i.* **-ся**) strip (of)

**разде́л** *m* [1] division; *книги* section; **~аться** *coll.* [1] *pf.* get rid *or* be quit (**с** T o); **~е́ние** *n* [12] division (**на** B into); **~и́тельный** [14] dividing; *gr.* disjunctive; **~и́ть(ся)** → ***~я́ть(ся)*** & ***дели́ть(ся)***; **~ьный** [14] separate; (*отчётливый*) distinct; **~я́ть** [28], ⟨**~и́ть**⟩ [13; -елю́, -е́лишь; -елённый] divide (**на** B into; *a.* [-ed] by); separate; *горе и т. д.* share; **-ся** (be) divide(d)

**разде́ть(ся)** → ***раздева́ть(ся)***

**раз|дира́ть** *coll.* [1], ⟨**~одра́ть**⟩ [раздеру́, -рёшь; разодрал, -а́, -о; -о́дранный] *impf.* rend; *pf. coll.* tear up; **~добы́ть** *coll.* [-бу́ду, -бу́дешь] *pf.* get, procure, come by

**раздо́лье** *n* [10] → ***приво́лье***

**раздо́р** *m* [1] discord, contention; ***я́блоко ~а*** bone of contention

**раздоса́дованный** *coll.* [14] angry

**раздраж|а́ть** [1], ⟨**~и́ть**⟩ [16 *e.*; -жу́, -жи́шь; -жённый] irritate, provoke; vex, annoy; **-ся** become irritated; **~е́ние** *n* [12] irritation; **~и́тельный** [14; -лен, -льна] irritable, short-tempered; **~и́ть(ся)** → ***~а́ть(ся)***

**раздробл|е́ние** *n* [12] breaking, smashing to pieces; **~я́ть** [28] → ***дроби́ть***

Р

**разду|ва́ть** [1], ⟨**:ть**⟩ [18] fan; blow, blow about; (*распухнуть*) swell; (*преувеличивать*) inflate; exaggerate; **-ся** swell

**разду́м|ывать**, ⟨**~ать**⟩ [1] (*передумать*) change one's mind; *impf.* deliberate, consider; ***не ~ывая*** without a moment's thought; **~ье** *n* [10] thought(s), meditation; (*сомнение*) doubt(s)

**разду́ть(ся)** → ***раздува́ть(ся)***

**раз|ева́ть** *coll.* [1], ⟨**~и́нуть**⟩ [20] open wide; ***~ева́ть рот*** gape; **~жа́лобить** [14] *pf.* move to pity; **~жа́ть** → ***~жима́ть***; **~жёвывать** [1], ⟨**~жева́ть**⟩ [7 *e.*; -жую́, -жуёшь] chew; **~жига́ть** [1], ⟨**~же́чь**⟩ [г/ж: -зожгу́, -жжёшь; -жгут; разжёг, -зожгла́; разожжённый] kindle (*a. fig.*); *страсти* rouse; *вражду* stir up; **~жима́ть** [1], ⟨**~жа́ть**⟩ [разожму́, -мёшь; разжа́тый] unclasp, undo; **~и́нуть** → ***~ева́ть***; **~и́ня** *coll. m/f* [6] scatterbrain; **~и́тельный** [14; -лен, -льна] striking; **~и́ть** [13] reek (T of)

**раз|лага́ть** [1], ⟨**~ложи́ть**⟩ [16] break down, decompose; (*v/i.* **-ся**); (become) demoralize(d), corrupt(ed); go to pieces; **~ла́д** *m* [1] discord; **~ла́живаться** [1], ⟨**~ла́диться**⟩ [1] get out of order; *coll.* go wrong; **~ла́мывать** [1], ⟨**~лома́ть**⟩ [1], ⟨**~ломи́ть**⟩ [14] break (in pieces); **~лета́ться** [1], ⟨**~лете́ться**⟩ [11] fly (away, asunder); *coll.* shatter (to pieces); *надежды* come to naught; *о новостях и т. д.* spread quickly

**разли́|в** *m* [1] flood; **~ва́ть** [1], ⟨**~ть**⟩ [разолью́, -льёшь; → ***лить***; -ле́й(те); -и́л, -а́, -о; -и́тый (-и́т, -а́, -о)] spill; pour out; bottle; *суп и т. д.* ladle; **-ся** (*v/i.*) flood, overflow

**различ|а́ть** [1], ⟨**~и́ть**⟩ [16 *e.*; -чу́, -чи́шь; -чённый] (*отличать*) distinguish; (*разглядеть*) discern; **-ся** *impf.* differ (T, **по** Д in); **:ие** *n* [12] distinction, difference; **~и́тельный** [14] distinctive; **~и́ть** → ***~а́ть***; **:ный** [14; -чен, -чна] different, various, diverse

**разлож|е́ние** *n* [12] decomposition, decay; *fig.* corruption; **~и́ть(ся)** → ***разлага́ть*** (**-ся**) & ***раскла́дывать***

**разлом|а́ть**, **~и́ть** → ***разла́мывать***

**разлу́|ка** *f* [5] separation (**с** T from), parting; **~ча́ть** [1], ⟨**~чи́ть**⟩ [16 *e.*; -чу́, -чи́шь; -чённый] separate (*v/i.* **-ся**; **с** T from), part

**разма́|зывать** [1], ⟨**~зать**⟩ [3] smear, spread; **~тывать** [1], ⟨**размота́ть**⟩ unwind, uncoil; **~х** *m* [1] swing; span (*ae.* & *fig.*); sweep; *маятника* amplitude; *fig.* scope; **~хивать** [1], *once* ⟨**~хну́ть**⟩ [20] (T) swing, sway; *саблей и т. д.* brandish; gesticulate; **-ся** lift (one's hand T); *fig.* do things in a big way; **~шистый** *coll.* [14 *sh.*] *шаг, жест* wide; *почерк* bold

**разме|жева́ть** [7] *pf.* delimit, demarcate; **~льча́ть** [1], ⟨**~льчи́ть**⟩ [16 *e.*; -чу́, -чи́шь; -чённый] pulverize

**разме́н** [1], **~ивать** [1], ⟨**~я́ть**⟩ [28] (ex)change (**на** B for); **~ный** [14]: ***~ная моне́та*** small change

**разме́р** *m* [1] size, dimension(s); rate (**в** П at), amount; scale; extent; ***в широ́ких ~ах*** on a large scale; ***доска́ ~ом 0.2 x 2 ме́тра*** board measuring 0.2 x 2 meters, *Brt.* -tres; **~енный** [14 *sh.*] measured; **~я́ть** [28], ⟨**~ить**⟩ [13] measure (off)

**разме|сти́ть** → ***~ща́ть***; **~ча́ть** [1], ⟨**:тить**⟩ [15] mark (out); **:шивать** [1], ⟨**~ша́ть**⟩ [1] stir (up); **~ща́ть** [1], ⟨**~сти́ть**⟩ [15 *e.*; -ещу́, -ести́шь; -ещённый] place; lodge, accommodate (**в** П, **по** Д in, at, with); (*распределить*) distribute; stow; **~ще́ние** *n* [12] distribution; accommodation; arrangement, order; *груза* stowage; *mil.* stationing, quartering; *fin.* placing, investment

**разми|на́ть** [1], ⟨**размя́ть**⟩ [разомну́, -нёшь; размя́тый] knead; *coll. ноги* stretch (*one's legs*); **~ну́ться** *coll. pf.* [20] *о письмах* cross; miss o.a.

**размнож|а́ть** [1], ⟨**:ить**⟩ [16] multiply; duplicate; (*v/i.* **-ся**); reproduce; breed; **~е́ние** *n* [12] multiplication; mimeographing; *biol.* propagation, reproduction; **:ить(ся)** → ***~а́ть(ся)***

**размо|зжи́ть** [16 *e.*; -жу́, -жи́шь; -жённый] *pf.* smash; **~ка́ть** [1], ⟨**:кнуть**⟩ [21] get soaked; **:лвка** *f* [5; *g/pl.*: -вок] tiff, quarrel; **~ло́ть** [17;

-мелю́, -ме́лешь] grind; ~та́ть → ***разма́тывать***; ~чи́ть [16] *pf.* soak; steep

**размы|ва́ть** [1], 〈~ть〉 [22] *geol.* wash away; erode; ~ка́ть [1], 〈разомкну́ть〉 [20] open (*mil.* order, ranks); disconnect, break (*el.* circuit); ~ть → ***~ва́ть***

**размышл|е́ние** *n* [12] reflection (**о** П on), thought; ***по зре́лому ~е́нию*** on second thoughts; **~я́ть** [28] reflect, meditate (**о** П on)

**размягч|а́ть** [1], 〈~и́ть〉 [16 *e.*; -чу́, -чи́шь; -чённый] soften; *fig.* mollify

**раз|мя́ть** → ***~мина́ть***; ~на́шивать, 〈~носи́ть〉 [15] *туфли* wear in; **~нести́** → ***~носи́ть 1.***; ~нима́ть [1], 〈~ня́ть〉 [-ниму́, -ни́мешь; -ня́л & ро́знял, -а́, -о; -ня́тый (-ня́т, -а́, -о)] *дерущихся* separate, part

**ра́зница** *f* [5; *sg. only*; -цей] difference

**разнобо́й** *m* [3] disagreement; *в действиях* lack of coordination

**разно|ви́дность** *f* [8] variety; **~гла́сие** *n* [12] discord, disagreement; difference; (*расхождение*) discrepancy; **~кали́берный** *coll.* [14], **~ма́стный** [14; -тен, -тна] → ***~шёрстный***; **~обра́зие** *n* [12] variety, diversity, multiplicity; **~обра́зный** [14; -зен, -зна] varied, various; **~реч...** → ***противореч...***; **~ро́дный** [14; -ден, -дна] heterogeneous

**разно́с** *m* [1] *почты* delivery; *coll.* ***устро́ить ~*** give s.o. a dressingdown; **~и́ть** [15] **1.** 〈разнести́〉 [25 -с-] deliver (**по** Д to, at), carry; *слухи и т. д.* spread; (*разбить*) smash, destroy; *ветром* scatter; *coll.* (*распухнуть*) swell; **2.** → ***разна́шивать***

**разно|сторо́нний** [15; -о́нен, -о́нна] many-sided; *fig.* versatile; *math.* scalene; ′**~сть** *f* [8] difference; **~́счик** *m* [1] peddler (*Brt.* pedlar); *газет* delivery boy; ***~́счик телегра́мм*** one delivering telegrams; **~цве́тный** [14; -тен, -тна] of different colo(u)rs; multicolo(u)red; **~шёрстный** [14; -тен, -тна] *coll.* *публика* motley, mixed

**разну́зданный** [14 *sh.*] unbridled

**ра́зн|ый** [14] various, different, diverse; **~я́ть** → ***~има́ть***

**разо|блача́ть** [1], 〈~блачи́ть〉 [16 *e.*; -чу́, -чи́шь; -чённый] *eccl.* disrobe, divest; *fig.* expose, unmask; **~блаче́ние** *n* [12] exposure, unmasking; **~бра́ть(ся)** → ***разбира́ть(ся)***; **~гна́ть(ся)** → ***разгоня́ть(ся)***; **~гну́ть(ся)** → ***разгиба́ть(ся)***; **~грева́ть** [1], 〈~гре́ть〉 [8; -е́тый] warm (up); **~де́тый** *coll.* [14 *sh.*] dressed up; **~дра́ть** → ***раздира́ть***; **~йти́сь** → ***расходи́ться***; **~мкну́ть** → ***размыка́ть***; **~рва́ть(ся)** → ***разрыва́ть(ся)***

**разор|е́ние** *n* [12] *fig.* ruin; *в результате войны* devastation; **~и́тельный** [14; -лен, -льна] ruinous; **~и́ть(ся)** → ***~я́ть(ся)***; **~ужа́ть** [1], 〈~ужи́ть〉 [16 *e.*; -жу́, -жи́шь; -жённый] disarm (*v/i.* **-ся**); **~уже́ние** *n* [12] disarmament; **~я́ть** [28], 〈~и́ть〉 [13] ruin; devastate; (**-ся** be ruined, bankrupt)

**разосла́ть** → ***рассыла́ть***

**разостла́ть** → ***расстила́ть***

**разочар|ова́ние** *n* [12] disappointment; **~о́вывать** [1], 〈~ова́ть〉 [7] (**-ся** be) disappoint(ed) (**в** П in)

**разра|ба́тывать**, 〈~бо́тать〉 [1] *agric.* cultivate; work out, develop, elaborate; *mining* exploit; **~бо́тка** *f* [5; *g/pl.*: -ток] *agric.* cultivation; working (out), elaboration; exploitation; **~жа́ться** [1], 〈~зи́ться〉 [15 *e.*; -ажу́сь, -ази́шься] *о шторме, войне* break out; *смехом* burst out laughing; **~ста́ться** [1], 〈~сти́сь〉 [24; 3rd *p. only*: -тётся; -ро́сся, -сла́сь] grow (*a. fig.*); *растения* spread

**разрежённый** [14] *phys.* rarefied; rare

**разре́з** *m* [1] cut; (*сечение*) section; slit; *глаз* shape of the eyes; **~а́ть** [1], 〈~ать〉 [3] cut (up), slit; **~ывать** [1] → ***~а́ть***

**разреш|а́ть** [1], 〈~и́ть〉 [16 *e.*; -шу́, -ши́шь; -шённый] permit, allow; *проблему* (re)solve; (*улаживать*) settle; **-ся** be (re)solved; **~е́ние** *n* [12] permission (**с** Р with); permit; authorization (**на** В for); *проблемы* (re)solution; *конфликтов и т. д.* settlement; **~и́ть(ся)** → ***~а́ть(ся)***

**раз|рисова́ть** [7] *pf.* cover with drawings; ornament; **~ро́зненный** [14] broken up (as, e.g., a set); left over *or* apart (from, e.g., a set); odd; **~руба́ть** [1],

Р

⟨~руби́ть⟩ [14] chop; ***~руби́ть го́рдиев у́зел*** cut the Gordian knot

**разру́|ха** *f* [5] ruin; ***экономи́ческая ~ха*** dislocation; **~ша́ть** [1], ⟨**~ши́ть**⟩ [16] destroy, demolish; *здоровье* ruin; (*расстроить*) frustrate; **-ся** fall to ruin; **~ше́ние** *n* [12] destruction, devastation; **~ши́ть(ся)** → ***~ша́ть*(ся)**

**разры́|в** *m* [1] breach, break, rupture; (*взрыв*) explosion; (*промежуток*) gap; **~ва́ть** [1] **1.** ⟨разорва́ть⟩ [-ву́, -вёшь; -ва́л, -а́, -о; -о́рванный] tear (to *pieces* **на** В); break (off); (**-ся** *v/i*., *a*. explode); **2.** ⟨**~ть**⟩ [22] dig up; **~да́ться** [1] *pf*. break into sobs; **~ть** → ***~ва́ть 2.***; **~хля́ть** [28] → ***рыхли́ть***

**разря́|д** *m* [1] **1.** category, class; *sport* rating; **2.** *el*. discharge; **~ди́ть** → ***~жа́ть***; **~дка** *f* [5; *g/pl*.: -док] **1.** *typ*. letterspacing; **2.** discharging; unloading; *pol*. détente; **~жа́ть** [1], ⟨**~ди́ть**⟩ [15 *e*. & 15; -яжу́, -яди́шь; -яжённый & -я́женный] discharge; *typ*. space out; ***~ди́ть атмосфе́ру*** relieve tension

**разу|бежда́ть** [1], ⟨**~беди́ть**⟩ [15 *e*.; -ежу́, -еди́шь; -еждённый] (**в** П) dissuade (from); **-ся** change one's mind about; **~ва́ться** [1], ⟨**~́ться**⟩ [18] take off one's shoes; **~веря́ться** [28], ⟨**~ве́риться**⟩ [13] (**в** П) lose faith (in); **~знава́ть** *coll*. [5], ⟨**~зна́ть**⟩ [1] find out (**о** П, В about); *impf*. make inquiries about; **~кра́шивать** [1], ⟨**~кра́сить**⟩ decorate, embellish; **~крупня́ть** [28], ⟨**~крупни́ть**⟩ [14] break up into smaller units

**ра́зум** *m* [1] reason; intellect; **~е́ть** [8] understand; know; mean, imply (***под*** Т by); **~е́ться** [8]: ***само́ собо́й ~е́ется*** it goes without saying; ***разуме́ется*** of course; **~́ный** [14; -мен, -мна] rational; reasonable, sensible; wise

**разу́|ться** → ***~ва́ться***; **~чивать** [1], ⟨**~чи́ть**⟩ [16] learn, study, *стихи и т. д*. learn; **-ся** forget

**разъе|да́ть** [1] → ***есть***[1] ***2.***; **~диня́ть** [28], ⟨**~дини́ть**⟩ [13] separate; *el*. disconnect; **~зжа́ть** [1] drive, ride, go about; be on a journey *or* trip; **-ся** ⟨**~́хаться**⟩ [-е́дусь, -е́дешься; -езжа́йтесь!] leave (***по*** Д for); *о супругах* separate; *о машинах* pass o.a. (**с** Т)

**разъярённый** [14] enraged, furious

**разъясн|е́ние** *n* [12] explanation; clarification; **~я́ть** [28], ⟨**~и́ть**⟩ [13] explain, elucidate

**разы́|грывать**, ⟨**~гра́ть**⟩ [1] play; *в лотерее* raffle; (*подшутить*) play a trick (on); **-ся** *о буре* break out; *о страстях* run high; happen; **~скивать** [1], ⟨**~ска́ть**⟩ [3] seek, search (for; *pf*. out = find)

**рай** *m* [3; в раю́] paradise

**рай|о́н** *m* [1] district; region, area; **~о́нный** [14] district…; regional; **~сове́т** *m* [1] (***райо́нный сове́т***) district soviet (*or* council)

**рак** *m* [1] crayfish; *med*. cancer; *astron*. Cancer; ***кра́сный как ~*** red as a lobster

**раке́т|а** *f* [5] rocket; missile; **~ка** *f* [5; *g/pl*.: -ток] *sport* racket; **~ный** [14] rocket-powered; missile…; **~чик** *m* [1] missile specialist

**ра́ковина** *f* [5] shell; *на кухне* sink; ***ушна́я ~*** helix

**ра́м|(к)а** *f* [5; (*g/pl*.: -мок)] frame (-work, *a*. *fig*. = limits; **в** П within); **~па** *f* [5] footlights

**ра́н|а** *f* [5] wound; **~г** *m* [1] rank; **~е́ние** *n* [12] wound(ing); **~еный** [14] wounded (*a. su*.); **~ец** *m* [1; -нца] *школьный* schoolbag, satchel; **~ить** [13] (*im*)*pf*. wound, injure (**в** В in)

**ра́н|ний** [15] early (*adv*. **~о**); ***~о и́ли по́здно*** sooner *or* late; **~ова́то** *coll*. rather early; **~ьше** earlier; formerly; (*сперва*) first; (Р) before; ***как мо́жно ~ьше*** as soon as possible

**рап|и́ра** *f* [5] foil; **~́орт** [1], **~ортова́ть** [7] (*im*)*pf*. report; **~со́дия** *f* [7] *mus*. rhapsody

**ра́са** *f* [5] race

**раска́|иваться** [1], ⟨**~яться**⟩ [27] repent (*v/t*.; **в** П of); **~лённый** [14], **~ли́ть(ся)** → ***~ля́ть*(ся)**; **~́лывать** [1], ⟨раско-ло́ть⟩ [17] split, cleave; crack; (*v/i*. **-ся**); **~ля́ть** [28], ⟨**~ли́ть**⟩ [13] make (**-ся** become) red-hot, white-hot; **~пывать** [1], ⟨раскопа́ть⟩ [1] dig out *or* up; **~т** *m* [1] roll, peal; **~тистый** [14 *sh*.] rolling; **~тывать**, ⟨**~та́ть**⟩ [1] (un)roll; *v/i*.

Р

**-ся**; **~чивать**, ⟨~ча́ть⟩ [1] swing; shake; **-ся** *coll*. bestir o.s.; **~яние** *n* [12] repentance (**в** П of); **~яться** → **~иваться**

**раски́дистый** [14 *sh*.] spreading

**раски́|дывать** [1], ⟨~нуть⟩ [20] spread (out); stretch (out); *шатёр* pitch, set up

**раскла|дно́й** [14] folding, collapsible; **~ду́шка** *coll*. *f* [5; *g/pl*.: -шек] folding *or* folding bed; **∠дывать** [1], ⟨разложи́ть⟩ [16] lay *or* spread out, distribute; *костёр* make, light; (*распределить*) apportion

**раско́|л** *m* [1] *hist*. schism, dissent; *pol*. division, split; **~ло́ть(ся)** → **раска́лывать(ся)**; **~па́ть** → **раска́пывать**; **~пка** *f* [5; *g/pl*.: -пок] excavation

**раскр|а́шивать** [1], → **кра́сить**; **~епоща́ть** [1], ⟨~епости́ть⟩ [15 *e*.; -ощу́, -ости́шь; -ощённый] emancipate, liberate; **~епоще́ние** *n* [12] emancipation, liberation; **~итикова́ть** [7] *pf*. severely criticize; **~ича́ться** [4 *e*.; -чу́сь, -чи́шься] *pf*. shout, bellow (**на** В at); **~ыва́ть** [1], ⟨~ы́ть⟩ [22] open wide (*v/i*. **-ся**); uncover, disclose, reveal; **~ы́ть свои́ ка́рты** show one's cards *or* one's hand

**раску|па́ть** [1], ⟨~пи́ть⟩ [14] buy up; **~по́ривать** [1], ⟨∠порить⟩ [13] uncork; open; **∠сывать** [1], ⟨~си́ть⟩ [15] bite through; *pf. only* get to the heart of; *coll*. *кого-л*. see through; *что-л*. understand; **∠тывать**, ⟨∠тать⟩ [1] unwrap

**ра́совый** [14] racial

**распа́д** *m* [1] disintegration; *радиоактивный* decay

**распа|да́ться** [1], ⟨∠сться⟩ [25; -па́лся, -лась; -па́вшийся] fall to pieces; disintegrate; break up (**на** В into); collapse; *chem*. decompose; **~ко́вывать** [1], ⟨~кова́ть⟩ [7] unpack; **∠рывать** [1] → **поро́ть**; **∠сться** → **~да́ться**; **∠хивать** [1] **1.** ⟨~ха́ть⟩ [3] plow (*Brt*. plough) up; **2.** ⟨~хну́ть⟩ [20] throw *or* fling open (*v/i*. **-ся**); **~шо́нка** *f* [5; *g/pl*.: -нок] baby's undershirt (*Brt*. vest)

**распе|ва́ть** [1] sing for a time; **~ка́ть** *coll*. [1], ⟨∠чь⟩ [26] scold; **~ча́тка** *f* [5; *g/pl*.: -ток] *tech*. hard copy; *comput*. printout; **~ча́тывать**, ⟨~ча́тать⟩ [1] **1.** unseal; open; **2.** print out

**распи́|ливать** [1], ⟨~ли́ть⟩ [13; -илю́, -и́лишь; -и́ленный] saw up; **~на́ть** [1], ⟨распя́ть⟩ [-пну́, -пнёшь; -пя́тый] crucify

**распис|а́ние** *n* [12] timetable (*rail*.) **~а́ние поездо́в**; **~а́ние уро́ков** schedule (**по** Д of, for); **~а́ть(ся)** → **∠ывать(ся)**; **∠ка** *f* [5; *g/pl*.: -сок] receipt (**под** В against); **∠ывать** [1], ⟨~а́ть⟩ [3] write, enter; *art* paint; ornament; **-ся** sign (one's name); (acknowledge) receipt (**в** П); *coll*. register one's marriage

**распл|авля́ть** [28] → **пла́вить**; **~а́каться** [3] *pf*. burst into tears; **~а́та** *f* [5] payment; (*возмездие*) reckoning; **~а́чиваться** [1], ⟨~ати́ться⟩ [15] (**с** Т) pay off, settle accounts (with); pay (**за** В for); **~еска́ть** [3] *pf*. spill

**расплe|та́ть** [1], ⟨~сти́⟩ [25 -т-] (**-ся**, ⟨-сь⟩ come) unbraid(ed); untwist(ed), undo(ne)

**расплы|ва́ться** [1], ⟨∠ться⟩ [23] spread; *чернила и т. д.* run; *на воде* swim about; *очертания* blur; **∠ться в улы́бке** break into a smile; **∠вчатый** [14 *sh*.] blurred, vague

**расплю́щить** [16] *pf*. flatten out, hammer out

**распозн|ава́ть** [5], ⟨~а́ть⟩ [1] recognize, identify; *болезнь* diagnose

**распол|ага́ть** [1], ⟨~ожи́ть⟩ [16] arrange; *войск* dispose; *impf*. (Т) dispose (of), have (at one's disposal); **-ся** settle; encamp; *pf*. be situated; **~ага́ющий** [17] prepossessing; **~за́ться** [1], ⟨~зти́сь⟩ [24] creep *or* crawl away; *слухи* spread; **~оже́ние** *n* [12] arrangement; (dis)position (**к** Д toward[s]); location, situation; (*влечение, доброе отношение*) inclination, propensity; **~оже́ние ду́ха** mood; **~о́женный** [14 *sh*.] *a*. situated; (well-)disposed (**к** Д toward[s]); inclined; **~ожи́ть(ся)** → **~ага́ть(ся)**

**распор|яди́тельность** *f* [8] good management; **~яди́тельный** [14; -лен, -льна] capable; efficient; **~яди́ться** → **~яжа́ться**; **~я́док** [1; -дка] order; *в больнице и т. д.* regulations *pl*.; **~яжа́ться** [1], ⟨~яди́ться⟩ [15 *e*.;

Р

-яжу́сь, -яди́шься] order; (T) dispose (of); see to, take care of; *impf.* (*управлять*) be the boss; manage; **~яже́ние** *n* [12] order(s), instruction(s); disposal (**в** В; **в** П at); ***име́ть в своём ~яже́нии*** have at one's disposal

**распра́в|а** *f* [5] violence; reprisal; *кровавая* massacre; **~ля́ть** [28], ⟨**~ить**⟩ [14] straighten; smooth; *крылья* spread; *ноги* stretch; **-ся** (**с** T) deal with; make short work of

**распредел|е́ние** *n* [12] distribution; **~и́тельный** [14] distributing; *el. щит* switch…; **~я́ть** [28], ⟨**~и́ть**⟩ [13] distribute; *задания и т. д.* allot; (*направить*) assign (**по** Д to)

**распрод|ава́ть** [5], ⟨**~а́ть**⟩ [-да́м, -да́шь; *etc.*, → ***дать***; -про́дал, -а́, -о; -про́данный] sell out (*or* off); **~а́жа** *f* [5] (clearance) sale

**распрост|ира́ть** [1], ⟨**~ере́ть**⟩ [12] stretch out; *влияние* extend (*v/i.* **-ся**); **~ёртый** *a.* open (arms *объятия pl.*); outstretched; prostrate, prone; **~и́ться** [15 *e.*; -ощу́сь, -ости́шься] (**с** T) bid farewell (to); (*отказаться*) give up, abandon

**распростран|е́ние** *n* [12] *слухов и т. д.* spread(ing); *знаний* dissemination, propagation; ***получи́ть широ́кое ~е́ние*** become popular; be widely practiced; **~ённый** [14] widespread; **~я́ть** [28], ⟨**~и́ть**⟩ [13] spread, diffuse (*v/i.* **-ся**); propagate, disseminate; extend; *запах* give off; **~я́ться** *coll.* enlarge upon

**распро|ща́ться** [1] *coll.* → ***~сти́ться***

**ра́спря** *f* [6; *g/pl.*: -рей] strife, conflict; **~га́ть** [1], ⟨**~чь**⟩ [26 г/ж: -ягу́, -яжёшь] unharness

**распу|ска́ть** [1], ⟨**~сти́ть**⟩ [15] dismiss, disband; *parl.* dissolve; *на каникулы* dismiss for; *знамя* unfurl; *вязание* undo; *волосы* loosen; *слухи* spread; *масло* melt; *fig.* spoil; **-ся** *цветок* open; (*раствориться*) dissolve; *coll.* become intractable; let o.s. go; **~тать** → ***~тывать***; **~тица** *f* [5] season of bad roads; **~тывать**, ⟨**~тать**⟩ [1] untangle; **~тье** *n* [10] crossroad(s); **~ха́ть** [1], ⟨**~хнуть**⟩ [21] swell; **~хший** [17] swollen; **~щенный** [14 *sh.*] spoiled, undisciplined; dissolute

**распыл|и́тель** *m* [4] spray(er), atomizer; **~я́ть** [28], ⟨**~и́ть**⟩ [13] spray, atomize; *fig.* dissipate

**распя́|тие** *n* [12] crucifixion; crucifix; **~ть** → ***распина́ть***

**расса́|да** *f* [5] seedlings; **~ди́ть** → ***~живать***; **~дник** *m* [1] seedbed; *a. fig.* hotbed; **~живать** [1], ⟨**~ди́ть**⟩ [15] transplant; *людей* seat; **-ся**, ⟨**рассе́сться**⟩ [рася́дусь, -дешься; -се́лся, -се́лась] sit down, take one's seat; *fig.* sprawl

**рассве́|т** *m* [1] dawn (***на*** П at), daybreak; **~та́ть** [1], ⟨**~сти́**⟩ [25 -т-: -светёт; -свело́] dawn

**рассе|дла́ть** [1] *pf.* unsaddle; **~ивать** [1], ⟨**~ять**⟩ [27] sow; *толпу* scatter, *тучи* disperse (*v/i.* **-ся**); *сомнения* dispel; **~ка́ть** [1], ⟨**~чь**⟩ [26] cut through, cleave; (*of a cane, etc.*) swish; **~ля́ть** [28], ⟨**~ли́ть**⟩ [13] settle in a new location (*v/i.* **-ся**); **~сться** → ***расса́живаться***; **~янность** *f* [8] absent-mindedness; **~янный** [14 *sh.*] absent-minded; scattered; *phys.* diffused; **~ять(ся)** → ***~ивать(ся)***

**расска́з** *m* [1] account, narrative; tale, story; **~а́ть** → ***~ывать***; **~чик** *m* [1] narrator; storyteller; **~ывать** [1], ⟨**~а́ть**⟩ [3] tell; recount, narrate

**расслаб|ля́ть** [28], ⟨**~ить**⟩ [14] weaken, enervate (*v/i.* **~е́ть** [8] *pf.*)

**рассл|е́дование** *n* [12] investigation, inquiry; **~е́довать** [7] (*im*)*pf.* investigate, inquire into; **~ое́ние** *n* [12] stratification; **~ы́шать** [16] *pf.* catch (*what a p. is saying*); ***не ~ы́шать*** not (quite) catch

**рассм|а́тривать** [1], ⟨**~отре́ть**⟩ [-отрю́, -о́тришь; -о́тренный] examine, view; consider; (*различить*) discern, distinguish; **~ея́ться** [27 *e.*; -ею́сь; -еёшься] *pf.* burst out laughing; **~отре́ние** *n* [12] examination (***при*** П at); consideration; **~отре́ть** → ***~а́тривать***

**рассо́л** *m* [1] brine

**расспр|а́шивать** [1], ⟨**~оси́ть**⟩ [15] inquire, ask; **~о́сы** *pl.* [1] inquiries

Р

**рассро́чка** *f* [5] (payment by) instal(l)-ments (**в** B *sg.* by)

**расста|ва́ние** → ***проща́ние***; **~ва́ться** [5], ⟨**~́ться**⟩ [-а́нусь, -а́нешься] part (**с** T with); leave; *с мечтой и т. д.* give up; **~вля́ть** [28], ⟨**~́вить**⟩ [14] place; arrange; set up; (*раздвигать*) move apart; **~но́вка** *f* [5; *g/pl.*: -вок] arrangement; punctuation; *персонал* placing; ***~но́вка полити́ческих сил*** political scene; **~́ться** → ***~ва́ться***

**расст|ёгивать** [1], ⟨**~егну́ть**⟩ [20] unbutton; unfasten (*v/i.* **-ся**); **~ила́ть** [1], ⟨разостла́ть⟩ [расстелю́, -е́лешь; разо́стланный] spread out; lay (*v/i.* **-ся**); **~оя́ние** *n* [12] distance (at a **на** П); ***держа́ться на ~оя́нии*** keep aloof

**расстр|а́ивать** [1], ⟨**~о́ить**⟩ [13] upset; disorganize; disturb, spoil; shatter; *планы* frustrate; *mus.* put out of tune; **-ся** be(come) upset, illhumo(u)red, *etc.*

**расстре́л** *m* [1] execution by shooting; **~ивать** [1], ⟨**~я́ть**⟩ [28] shoot

**расстро́|ить(ся)** → ***расстра́ивать(ся)***; **~йство** *n* [9] disorder, confusion; derangement; frustration; *желудка* stomach disorder; *coll.* diarrh(o)ea

**расступ|а́ться** [1], ⟨**~и́ться**⟩ [14] make way; *о толпе* part

**рассу|ди́тельность** *f* [8] judiciousness; **~ди́тельный** [14; -лен, -льна] judicious, reasonable; **~ди́ть** [15] *pf.* judge; arbitrate; think, consider; decide; **~́док** *m* [1; -дка] reason; common sense; **~́дочный** [14; -чен, -чна] rational; **~жда́ть** [1] argue, reason; discourse (on); argue (about); discuss; **~жде́ние** *n* [12] reasoning, argument, debate, discussion

**рассчи́т|ывать**, ⟨**~а́ть**⟩ [1] calculate, estimate; *с работы* dismiss, sack; *impf.* count *or* reckon (**на** B on); (*ожидать*) expect; (*намереваться*) intend; **-ся** settle accounts, *fig.* get even (**с** T with); (*расплатиться*) pay off

**рассыл|а́ть** [1], ⟨разосла́ть⟩ [-ошлю́, -ошлёшь; -о́сланный] send out (*or* round); **~́ка** *f* [5] distribution; dispatch

**рассып|а́ть** [1], ⟨**~́ать**⟩ [2] scatter, spill; *v/i.* **-ся** crumble, fall to pieces; break up; ***~а́ться в комплиме́нтах*** shower compliments (on Д)

**раста́|лкивать**, ⟨растолка́ть⟩ [1] push asunder, apart; (*будить*) shake; **~пливать** [1], ⟨растопи́ть⟩ [14] light, kindle; *жир* melt; (*v/i.* **-ся**); **~птывать** [1], ⟨растопта́ть⟩ [3] trample, stamp (on); crush; **~скивать** [1], ⟨**~щи́ть**⟩ [16], *coll.* ⟨**~ска́ть**⟩ [1] (*раскрасть*) pilfer; *на части* take away, remove little by little; *дерущихся* separate

**раство́р** *m* [1] *chem.* solution; *цемента* mortar; **~и́мый** [14 *sh.*] soluble; **~я́ть** [28], ⟨**~и́ть**⟩ **1.** [13] dissolve; **2.** [13; -орю́, -о́ришь; -о́ренный] open

**расте́|ние** *n* [12] plant; **~ре́ть** → ***растира́ть***; **~рза́ть** [1] *pf.* tear to pieces; **~рянный** [14 *sh.*] confused, perplexed, bewildered; **~ря́ть** [28] *pf.* lose (little by little); (**-ся** get lost, lose one's head; be[-come] perplexed *or* puzzled)

**расти́** [24 -ст-: -сту́, -стёшь; рос, -сла́; ро́сший] ⟨вы́-⟩ grow; grow up; (*увеличиваться*) increase

**раст|ира́ть** [1], ⟨**~ере́ть**⟩ [12; разотру́, -трёшь] grind, pulverize; rub in; rub, massage

**расти́тельн|ость** *f* [8] vegetation; verdure; *на лице* hair; **~ый** [14] vegetable; ***вести́ ~ый о́браз жи́зни*** vegetate

**расти́ть** [15 *e.*; ращу́, расти́шь] rear; grow, cultivate

**расто|лка́ть** → ***раста́лкивать***; **~лкова́ть** [7] *pf.* expound, explain; **~пи́ть** → ***раста́пливать***; **~пта́ть** → ***раста́птывать***; **~пы́рить** [13] *pf.* spread wide; **~рга́ть** [1], ⟨**~́ргнуть**⟩ [21] *договор* cancel, annul; *брак* dissolve; **~рже́ние** *n* [12] cancellation; annulment; dissolution; **~ро́пный** [14; -пен, -пна] *coll.* smart, deft, quick; **~ча́ть** [1], ⟨**~чи́ть**⟩ [16 *e.*; -чу́, -чи́шь; -чённый] squander, waste, dissipate; *похвалы* lavish (Д on); **~чи́тель** *m* [4], squanderer, spendthrift; **~чи́тельный** [14; -лен, -лен] wasteful, extravagant

**растра|вля́ть** [28], ⟨**~ви́ть**⟩ [14] irritate; *душу* aggravate; ***~ви́ть ра́ну*** *fig.* rub salt in the wound; **~́та** *f* [5] squandering; embezzlement; **~́тчик** *m* [1] embezzler;

Р

**~чивать** [1], ⟨**~тить**⟩ [15] spend, waste; embezzle
**растр|епа́ть** [2] *pf.* (**-ся** be[come]) tousle(d, **~ёпанный** [14]), dishevel([l]ed); ***в ~ёпанных чу́вствах*** confused, mixed up
**растрога́ть** [1] *pf.* move, touch
**растя́|гивать** [1], ⟨**~ну́ть**⟩ [19] stretch (*v/i.* **-ся**; *coll.* fall flat); *med.* sprain, strain; *слова* drawl; *во времени* drag out, prolong; **~же́ние** *n* [12] stretching; strain(ing); **~жи́мый** [14 *sh.*] extensible, elastic; *fig.* vague; **~нутый** [14] long-winded, prolix; **~ну́ться** → ***~гиваться***
**рас|формирова́ть** [8] *pf.* disband; **~ха́живать** [1] walk about, pace up and down; **~хва́ливать** [1], ⟨**~хвали́ть**⟩ [13; -алю́, -а́лишь; -а́ленный] shower praise on; **~хва́тывать**, *coll.* ⟨**~хвата́ть**⟩ [1] snatch away; (*раскупить*) buy up (quickly)
**расхи|ща́ть** [1], ⟨**~тить**⟩ [15] plunder; misappropriate; **~ще́ние** *n* [12] theft; misappropriation
**расхо́|д** *m* [1] expenditure (***на*** В for), expense(s); *топлива и т. д.* consumption; **~ди́ться** [15], ⟨разойти́сь⟩ [-ойду́сь, -ойдёшься; -оше́дшийся; *g. pt.*: -ойдя́сь] go away; disperse; break up; *во мнениях* differ (**с** Т from); *т. ж. о линиях* diverge; (*расстаться*) part, separate; pass (*without meeting*); (*letters*) cross; *товар* be sold out, sell; *деньги* be spent, (***у*** Р) run out of; **~дова́ть** [7], ⟨из-⟩ spend, expend; *pf. a.* use up; **~жде́ние** *n* [12] divergence, difference (***в*** П of)
**расцара́п|ывать**, ⟨**~ать**⟩ [1] scratch (all over)
**расцве́|т** *m* [1] bloom, blossoming; *fig.* flowering; heyday, prime; *искусства и т. д.* flourishing; ***в ~те лет*** in his prime; **~та́ть** [1], ⟨**~сти́**⟩ [25; -т] blo(s-s)om; flourish, thrive; **~тка** *f* [5; *g/pl.*: -ток] colo(u)ring, colo(u)rs
**расце́|нивать** [1], ⟨**~ни́ть**⟩ [13; -еню́, -е́нишь; -енённый] estimate, value, rate; (*считать*) consider, think; **~нка** *f* [5; *g/pl.*: -нок] valuation; *цена* price; *об оплате* rate; **~пля́ть** [28], ⟨**~пи́ть**⟩ [14] uncouple, unhook; disengagc
**рас|чеса́ть** → **~чёсывать**; **~чёска** *f* [5; *g/pl.*: -сок] comb; **~че́сть** → ***рассчита́ть***; **~чёсывать** [1], ⟨**~чеса́ть**⟩ [3] comb (one's hair **-ся** *coll.*)
**расчёт** *m* [1] calculation; estimate; settlement (of accounts); payment; (*увольнение*) dismissal, sack; account, consideration; ***принима́ть в ~*** take into account; ***из ~а*** on the basis (of); ***в ~е*** quits with; ***безнали́чный ~*** payment by written order; by check (*Brt.* cheque); ***~ нали́чными*** cash payment; **~ливый** [14 *sh.*] provident, thrifty; circumspect
**рас|чища́ть** [1], ⟨**~чи́стить**⟩ [15] clear; **~членя́ть** [28], ⟨**~члени́ть**⟩ [13] dismember; divide; **~ша́тывать**, ⟨**~шата́ть**⟩ [1] loosen (*v/i.* **-ся** become lose); *о нервах, здоровье* (be[come]) impair(ed); shatter(ed); **~шевели́ть** *coll.* [13] *pf.* stir (up)
**расши|ба́ть** → ***ушиба́ть***; **~ва́ть** [1], ⟨**~ть**⟩ [разошью́, -шьёшь; → ***шить***] embroider; **~ре́ние** *n* [12] widening, enlargement; expansion; **~ря́ть** [28], ⟨**~рить**⟩ [13] widen, enlarge; extend, expand; *med.* dilate; ***~рить кругозо́р*** broaden one's mind; **~ть** → ***~ва́ть***; **~фро́вывать** [1], ⟨**~фрова́ть**⟩ [7] decipher, decode
**рас|шнуро́вывать** [7] *pf.* unlace; **~ще́лина** *f* [5] crevice, cleft, crack; **~щепле́ние** *n* [12] splitting; *phys.* fission; **~щепля́ть** [28], ⟨**~щепи́ть**⟩ [14 *e.*; -плю́, -пи́шь; -плённый] split
**ратифи|ка́ция** *f* [7] ratification; **~ци́ровать** [7] (*im*)*pf.* ratify
**ра́товать** [7] *за что-л.* fight for, stand up for; *против* inveigh against, declaim against
**рахи́т** *m* [1] rickets
**рацион|ализи́ровать** [7] (*im*)*pf.* rationalize, improve; **~а́льный** [14; -лен, -льна] rational (*a. math.*, *no sh.*); efficient
**рвану́ть** [20] *pf.* jerk; tug (***за*** В at); **-ся** dart

Р

**рвать** [рву, рвёшь; рвал, -á, -o] **1.** ⟨разо-, изо-⟩ [-óрванный] tear (***на, в*** B to *pieces*), *v/i.* **-ся**; **2.** ⟨со-⟩ pluck; **3.** ⟨вы-⟩ pull out; *impers.* (B) vomit, spew; **4.** ⟨пре-⟩ break off; **5.** ⟨взо-⟩ blow up; **~ *и метáть*** *coll.* be in a rage; **-ся** break; (*стремиться*) be spoiling for

**рвéние** *n* [12] zeal; eagerness

**рвóт|а** *f* [5] vomit(ing); **~ный** [14] emetic (*a. n, su.*)

**реа|билитúровать** [7] (*im*)*pf.* rehabilitate; **~гúровать** [7] (***на*** B) react (to); respond (to); **~ктúвный** [14] *chem.* reactive; *tech. ae.* jet-propelled; **~ктор** *m* [1] *tech.* reactor, pile; **~кционéр** *m* [1], **~кциóнный** [14] reactionary; **~кция** *f* [7] reaction

**реал|úзм** *m* [1] realism; **~изовáть** [7] realize; *comm. a.* sell; **~истúческий** [16] realistic; **~ьность** *f* [8] reality; **~ьный** [14; -лен, -льна] real; (*осуществимый*) realizable

**ребёнок** *m* [2; *pl. a.* дéти] child, *coll.* kid; baby; ***груднóй* ~** suckling

**ребрó** *n* [9; *pl.*: рёбра, рёбер, рёбрам] rib; edge (on **~м**); ***постáвить вопрóс* ~м** *fig.* put a question point-blank

**ребя́|та** *pl. of* **ребёнок**; *coll.* children; (*of adults*) boys and lads; **~ческий** [16], **~чий** *coll.* [18] childish; **~чество** *n* [9] *coll.* childishness; **~читься** *coll.* [16] behave childishly

Р

**рёв** *m* [1] roar; bellow; howl

**рев|áнш** *m* [1] revenge; *sport* return match; **~éнь** *m* [4 *e.*] rhubarb; **~éть** [-ý, -вёшь] roar; bellow; howl; *coll.* cry

**ревúз|ия** *f* [7] inspection; *fin.* audit; *наличия товаров и т. д.* revision; **~óр** *m* [1] inspector; auditor

**ревматú|зм** *m* [1] rheumatism; **~ческий** [16] rheumatic

**ревн|úвый** [14 *sh.*] jealous; **~овáть** [7], ⟨при-⟩ be jealous (***к*** Д [В] of [p.'s]); **~ость** *f* [8] jealousy; **~остный** [14; -тен, -тна] zealous, fervent

**револ|ьвéр** *m* [1] revolver; **~юционéр** *m* [1], **~юциóнный** [14] revolutionary; **~юция** *f* [7] revolution

**регúстр** *m* [1], **~úровать** [7], *pf. and impf.*, *pf. also* ⟨за-⟩ register, record; (*v/i.* **~úроваться**); register (o.s.); register one's marriage

**рег|лáмент** *m* [1] order, regulation *pl.*; **~рéсс** *m* [1] regression

**регул|úровать** [7], ⟨у-⟩ regulate; adjust; (*esp. pf.*) settle; **~ирóвщик** *m* [1] traffic controller; **~я́рный** [14; -рен, -рна] regular; **~я́тор** *m* [1] regulator

**редак|тúровать** [7], ⟨от-⟩ edit; **~тор** *m* [1] editor; **~ция** *f* [7] editorial staff; editorial office; wording; ***под* ~цией** edited by

**ред|éть** [8], ⟨по-⟩ thin, thin out; **~úска** *f* [5; *g/pl.*: -сок] (*red*) radish

**рéдк|ий** [16; -док, -дкá, -o; *comp.*: рéже] uncommon; *волосы* thin, sparse; *книга и т. д.* rare; *adv. a.* seldom; **~ость** *f* [8] rarity, curiosity; uncommon (thing); ***на* ~ость** *coll.* exceptionally

**рéдька** *f* [5; *g/pl.*: -дек] radish

**режúм** *m* [1] regime(n); routine; (*условия работы*) conditions

**режисс|ёр** *m* [1] *cine.* director; *thea.* producer

**рéзать** [3] **1.** ⟨раз-⟩ cut (up, open); slice; *мясо* carve; **2.** ⟨за-⟩ slaughter, kill; **3.** ⟨вы-⟩ carve, cut (***по*** В, ***на*** П in *wood*); **4.** ⟨с-⟩ *coll. на экзамене* fail; **5. -ся** *coll.* cut (one's teeth)

**резв|úться** [14 *e.*; -влю́сь, -вúшься] frolic, frisk, gambol; **~ый** [14; -резв, -á, -o] frisky, sportive, frolicsome; quick; *ребёнок* lively

**резéрв** *m* [1] *mil., etc.* reserve(s); **~úст** *m* [1] reservist; **~ный** [14] reserve

**резéц** *m* [1; -зцá] *зуб* incisor; *tech.* cutter; cutting tool

**резúн|а** *f* [5] rubber; **~овый** [14] rubber...; **~ка** *f* [5; *g/pl.*: -нок] eraser; rubber band, (*piece of*) elastic

**рéз|кий** [16; -зок, -зкá, -o; *comp.*: рéзче] sharp, keen; *ветер* biting, piercing; *боль* acute; *звук* harsh; shrill; *свет* glaring; *манера* rough, abrupt; **~кость** *f* [8] sharpness, *etc.*, → **~кий**; harsh word; **~нóй** [14] carved; **~ня́** *f* [6] slaughter; **~олю́ция** *f* [7] resolution; instruction; **~óн** *m* [1] reason; **~онáнс** *m* [1] resonance; (*отклик*) response; **~óнный** *coll.* [14; -óнен, -óнна] reasonable;

**~ультáт** *m* [1] result (as a **в** П); **~ьбá** *f* [5] carving, fretwork
**резюм|é** *n* [*indecl.*] summary; **~úровать** [7] (*im*)*pf.* summarize
**рейд**[1] *m* [1] *naut.* road(stead)
**рейд**[2] *m* [1] *mil.* raid
**рейс** *m* [1] trip; voyage; flight
**рекá** *f* [5; *ac/sg a. st.*; *pl. st.*; *from dat/pl. a. e.*] river
**рéквием** *m* [1] requiem
**реклáм|а** *f* [5] advertising; advertisement; publicity; **~úровать** [7] (*im*)*pf.* advertise; publicize; boost; **~ный** [14] publicity
**реко|мендáтельный** [14] of recommendation; **~мендáция** *f* [7] (*совет*) advice, recommendation; (*документ*) reference; **~мендовáть** [7] (*im*)*pf.*, *a.*, ⟨по-⟩ recommend, advise; **~нструúровать** [7] (*im*)*pf.* reconstruct; **~рд** *m* [1] record; ***установúть ~рд*** set a record; **~рдный** [14] record…; record-breaking; **~рдсмéн** *m* [1], **~рдсмéнка** *f* [5; *g/pl.*: -нок] record-holder
**рéктор** *m* [1] president, (*Brt.* vice-) chancellor of a university
**рели|гиóзный** [14; -зен, -зна] religious; **~гия** *f* [7] religion; **~квия** [7] relic
**рельс** [1], **~овый** [14] rail; track
**ремéнь** *m* [4; -мня́] strap, belt
**ремéсл|енник** *m* [1] craftsman, artisan; *fig.* bungler; **~енный** [14] trade…; handicraft…; **~ó** *n* [9; -мёсла, -мёсел, -мёслам] trade; (handi)craft; occupation
**ремóнт** *m* [1] repair(s); maintenance; *капитальный* overhaul; **~úровать** [7] (*im*)*pf.*, **~ный** [14] repair…
**рентáбельный** [14; -лен, -льна] profitable, cost effective
**рентгéновск|ий** [16]: ***~ий снúмок*** X-ray photograph
**реорганизовáть** [7] (*im*)*pf.* reorganize
**рéп|а** *f* [5] turnip; ***прóще пáреной ~ы*** (as) easy as ABC
**репа|рáция** *f* [7] reparation; **~триúровать** [7] (*im*)*pf.* repatriate
**репéйник** *m* [1] burdock
**репертуáр** *m* [1] repertoire, repertory
**репетú|ровать** [7], ⟨про-⟩ rehearse; **~тор** *m* [1] coach (*teacher*); **~ция** *f* [7] rehearsal
**рéплика** *f* [5] rejoinder, retort; *thea.* cue
**репортáж** *m* [1] report(ing)
**репортёр** *m* [1] reporter
**репресс|úрованный** *m* [14] *su.* one subjected to repression; **~ия** *f* [7] *mst. pl.* repressions *pl.*
**ресníца** *f* [5] eyelash
**респýблик|а** *f* [5] republic; **~áнец** *m* [1; -нца], **~áнский** [16] republican
**рессóра** *f* [5] *tech.* spring
**ресторáн** *m* [1] restaurant (**в** П at)
**ресýрсы** *m/pl.* [5] resources
**реферáт** *m* [1] synopsis; essay
**референдум** *m* [1] referendum
**рефóрм|а** *f* [5], **~úровать** [7] (*im*)*pf.* reform; **~áтор** *m* [1] reformer
**рефрижерáтор** *m* [1] *tech.* refrigerator; *rail.* refrigerator car, *Brt.* van
**реценз|éнт** *m* [1] reviewer; **~úровать** [7], ⟨про-⟩, **~ия** *f* [7] review
**рецéпт** *m* [1] *cul.* recipe; *med.* prescription
**рецидúв** *m* [1] *med.* relapse; recurrence; *law* repeat offence
**рéч|ка** *f* [5; *g/pl.*: -чек] (small) river; **~нóй** [14] river…
**реч|ь** *f* [8; *from g/pl. e.*] speech; (*выступление*) address, speech; ***об э́том не мóжет быть и ~и*** that is out of the question; → ***идтú***
**реш|áть** [1], ⟨**~úть**⟩ [16 *e.*; -шý, -шúшь; -шённый] *проблему* solve; (*принять решение*) decide, resolve (*a.* **-ся** [**на** В on, to], make up one's mind); (*осмелиться*) dare, risk; ***не ~áться*** hesitate; **~áющий** [17] decisive; **~éние** *n* [12] decision; (re)solution; **~ётка** *f* [5; -ток] grating; lattice; trellis; fender; **~етó** *n* [9; *pl. st.*: -шёта] sieve; **~úмость** *f* [8] resoluteness; determination; **~úтельный** [14; -лен, -льна] *человек* resolute, firm; decisive; definite; **~úть(ся)** → **~áть(ся)**
**ржа|вéть** [8], ⟨за-⟩, **~вчина** *f* [5] rust; **~вый** [14] rusty; **~нóй** [14] rye…; **~ть** [ржёт], ⟨за-⟩ neigh
**рúм|ский** [14] Roman; ***~ская цúфра*** Roman numeral

**ри́нуться** [20] *pf.* dash; rush; dart
**рис** *m* [1] rice
**риск** *m* [1] risk; ***на свой*** (***страх и***) **~** at one's own risk; **с ~́ом** at the risk (**для** P of); **~о́ванный** [14 *sh.*] risky; **~ова́ть** [7], 〈**~ну́ть**〉 [20] (*usu.* T) risk, venture
**рисова́|ние** *n* [12] drawing; **~ть** [7], 〈на-〉 draw; *fig.* depict, paint; **-ся** act, pose
**ри́совый** [14] rice…
**рису́нок** *m* [1; -нка] drawing; design; picture, illustration; figure
**ритм** *m* [1] rhythm; **~и́чный** [14; -чен, -чна] rhythmical
**ритуа́л** *m* [1], **~ьный** [14; -лен, -льна] ritual
**риф** *m* [1] reef
**ри́фма** *f* [5] rhyme
**роб|е́ть** [8], 〈о-〉 be timid, quail; ***не ~е́й!*** don't be afraid!; **~́кий** [16; -бок, -бка́, -о; *comp.*: ро́бче] shy, timid; **~́ость** *f* [8] shyness, timidity
**ро́бот** *m* [1] robot
**ров** *m* [1; рва; во рву] ditch
**рове́сник** *m* [1] of the same age
**ро́вн|ый** [14; -вен, -вна́, -о] even, level, flat; straight; equal; *характер* equable; **~о** precisely, exactly; *о времени тж.* sharp; *coll.* absolutely; **~я** *f* [5] equal, match
**рог** *m* [1; *pl. e.*: -га́] horn; antler; **~ *изоби́лия*** horn of plenty; **~а́тый** [14 *sh.*] horned; ***кру́пный ~а́тый скот*** cattle; **~ови́ца** *f* [5] cornea; **~ово́й** [14] horn…
**род** *m* [1; в, на -у́; *pl. e.*] *biol.* genus; *человеческий* human race; (*поколение*) generation; family; (*сорт*) kind; *gr.* gender; (*происхождение*) birth (T by); ***в своём ~́е*** in one's own way; ***~́ом из,* с** P come *or* be from; ***о́т ~у*** (Д) *be* … old; ***с ~́у*** in one's life
**роди́|льный** [14] maternity (hospital ***дом*** *m*); **~мый** [14] → **´~нка**; **´~на** *f* [5] native land, home(land) (***на*** П in); **´~нка** *f* [5; *g/pl.*: -нок] birthmark; mole; **~тели** *m/pl.* [4] parents; **~тельный** [14] *gr.* genitive; **~тельский** [16] parental, parent's
**роди́ть** [15 *e.*; рожу́, роди́шь; -ил, -а (*pf.*: -а́), -о; рождённый] (*im*)*pf.* (*impf. a.* ***рожда́ть***, *coll.* ***рожа́ть*** [1]) bear, give birth to; *fig.* give rise to; **-ся** [*pf.* -и́лся] be born; come into being
**родн|и́к** *m* [1 *e.*] (*source of water*) spring; **~о́й** [14] own (*by blood relationship*); *город и т. д.* native; (my) dear; *pl.* = **~я́** *f* [6] relative(s), relation(s)
**родо|нача́льник** *m* [1] ancestor, (*a. fig.*) father; **~сло́вный** [14] genealogical; ***~сло́вная*** *f* family tree
**ро́дствен|ник** *m* [1], **~ница** *f* [5] relative, relation; **~ный** [14 *sh.*] related, kindred; *языки* cognate; of blood
**родств|о́** *n* [9] relationship; ***в ~е́*** related (**с** T to)
**ро́ды** *pl.* [1] (child)birth
**ро́жа** *f* [5] **1.** *med.* erysipelas; **2.** P mug
**рожд|а́емость** *f* [8] birthrate; **~а́ть(ся)** → ***роди́ть*(ся)**; **~е́ние** *n* [12] birth (**от** P by); ***день ~е́ния*** birthday (***в*** B on); **~е́ственский** [16] Christmas…; **~ество́** *n* [9] (*a.* ***Ⴈество́*** [**христо́во**]) Christmas (***на*** B at); ***поздра́вить с Ⴈество́м христо́вым*** wish a Merry Christmas; ***до*** (***по́сле***) ***Р.хр.*** B.C. (A.D.)
**рож|о́к** *m* [1; -жка́] feeding bottle; *для обуви* shoehorn; **~ь** *f* [8; ржи; *instr./sg.*: ро́жью] rye
**ро́за** *f* [5] rose
**розе́тка** *f* [5; *g/pl.*: -ток] **1.** jam-dish; **2.** *el.* socket, wall plug
**ро́зн|ица** *f* [5]: ***в ~ицу*** retail; **~ичный** [14] retail…
**ро́зовый** [14 *sh.*] pink, rosy
**ро́зыгрыш** *m* [1] (*жеребьёвка*) draw; drawing in a lottery; (*шутка*) (practical) joke; **~ *ку́бка*** play-off
**ро́зыск** *m* [1] search; *law* inquiry; ***уголо́вный ~*** criminal investigation department
**ро|и́ться** [13] swarm (*of bees*); crowd (*of thoughts*); **~й** [3; в рою́; *pl. e.*: рои́, роёв] swarm
**рок** *m* [1] **1.** fate; **2.** *mus.* rock; **~́ер** *m* [1] rocker; **~ово́й** [14] fatal; **~́от** *m* [1], **~ота́ть** [3] roar, rumble
**роль** *f* [8; *from g/pl. e.*] *thea.* part, role; ***э́то не игра́ет ро́ли*** it is of no importance
**ром** *m* [1] rum

**рома́н** *m* [1] novel; *coll.* (love) affair; **~и́ст** *m* [1] novelist; **~с** *m* [1] *mus.* romance; **~ти́зм** *m* [1] romanticism; **~ти́ка** *f* [5] romance; **~ти́ческий** [16], **~ти́чный** [14; -чен, -чна] romantic

**ром|а́шка** *f* [5; *g/pl.*: -шек] *bot.* camomile; **~б** *m* [1] *math.* rhombus

**роня́ть** [28], ⟨урони́ть⟩ [13; -оню́, -о́нишь; -о́ненный] drop; *листья* shed; *fig.* disparage, discredit

**ро́п|от** *m* [1], **~та́ть** [3; -пщу́, ро́пщешь] murmur, grumble, complain (about **на** В)

**роса́** *f* [5; *pl. st.*] dew

**роско́ш|ный** [14; -шен, -шна] luxurious; sumptuous, luxuriant; **ˊ~ь** *f* [8] luxury; luxuriance

**ро́слый** [14] big, tall

**ро́спись** *f* [8] *art* fresco, mural

**ро́спуск** *m* [1] *parl.* dissolution; *на каникулы* breaking up

**рост** *m* [1] growth; *цен и т. д.* increase, rise; *человека* stature, height; ***высо́кого ~а*** tall

**рос|то́к** *m* [1; -тка́] sprout, shoot; **~черк** *m* [1] flourish; ***одни́м ~черком пера́*** with a stroke of the pen

**рот** *m* [1; рта, во рту́] mouth

**ро́та** *f* [5] *mil.* company

**ро́ща** *f* [5] grove

**роя́ль** *m* [4] (grand) piano

**ртуть** *f* [8] mercury, quicksilver

**руба́|нок** *m* [1; -нка] plane; **~шка** *f* [5; *g/pl.*: -шек] shirt; ***ни́жняя ~шка*** undershirt (*Brt.* vest); ***ночна́я ~шка*** nightshirt; *женская* nightgown

**рубе́ж** *m* [1 *e.*] boundary; border(line), frontier; ***за ~о́м*** abroad

**рубero̍ид** *m* [1] ruberoid

**рубе́ц** *m* [1; -бца́] *шов* hem; *на теле* scar

**руби́н** *m* [1] ruby

**руби́ть** [14] **1.** ⟨на-⟩ chop, cut, hew, hack; **2.** ⟨с-⟩ fell

**ру́бка**[1] *f* [5] *леса* felling

**ру́бка**[2] *f* [5] *naut.* wheelhouse

**ру́бленый** [14] minced, chopped

**рубль** *m* [4 *e.*] ruble (*Brt.* rouble)

**ру́брика** *f* [5] heading

**руга́|нь** *f* [8] abuse; **~тельный** [14] abusive; **~тельство** *n* [9] swearword, oath; **~ть** [1], ⟨вы́-⟩ abuse, swear at; attack verbally; **-ся** swear, curse; abuse o.a.

**руд|а́** *f* [5; *pl. st.*] ore; **~ни́к** *m* [1 *e.*] mine, pit; **~око́п** *m* [1] miner

**руж|е́йный** [14] gun…; **~ьё** *n* [10; *pl. st.*; *g/pl.*: -жей] (hand)gun, rifle

**руи́на** *f* [5] ruin (*mst. pl.*)

**рук|а́** *f* [5; *ac/sg.*: ру́ку; *pl.*: ру́ки, рук, -ка́м] hand; arm; ***~а́ об ~у*** hand in hand (arm in arm); ***по́д ~у*** arm in arm; with s.o. on one's arm; ***из ~ вон*** (***пло́хо***) *coll.* wretchedly; ***быть на́ ~у*** (Д) suit (well); ***махну́ть ~о́й*** give up as a bad job; ***на́ ~у нечи́ст*** light-fingered; ***от ~и́*** handwritten; ***пожа́ть ~у*** shake hands (Д with); ***по ~а́м!*** it's a bargain!; ***под ~о́й*** at hand, within reach; ***~о́й пода́ть*** it's no distance (a stone's throw); (***у*** Р) ***~и ко́ротки́*** Р not in one's power; ***из пе́рвых ~*** at first hand; ***приложи́ть ~у*** take part in s.th. bad

**рука́в** *m* [1 *e.*; *pl.*: -ва́, -во́в] sleeve; *реки* branch; *tech.* hose; **~и́ца** *f* [5] mitten; gauntlet

**руковод|и́тель** *m* [4] leader; head, manager; ***нау́чный ~и́тель*** supervisor (of studies); **~и́ть** [15] (Т) lead; direct, manage; **~ство** *n* [9] leadership; guidance; *mst. tech.* instruction(s); handbook, guide, manual; **~ствовать(ся)** [7] manual; follow; be guided (by Т); **~я́щий** [17] leading

**руко|де́лие** *n* [12] needlework; **~мо́йник** *m* [1] washstand; **~па́шный** [14] hand-to-hand; **ˊ~пись** *f* [8] manuscript; **~плеска́ние** *n* [12] (*mst. pl.*) applause; **~пожа́тие** *n* [12] handshake; **~я́тка** *f* [5; *g/pl.*: -ток] handle, grip; hilt

**рул|ево́й** [14] steering; *su. naut.* helmsman; **~о́н** *m* [1] roll; **~ь** *m* [4 *e.*] *судна* rudder, helm; *mot.* steering wheel; *велосипеда* handlebars

**румы́н** *m* [1], **~ка** *f* [5; *g/pl.*: -нок], **~ский** [16] Romanian

**румя́н|ец** *m* [1; -нца] ruddiness; blush; **~ить** [13] **1.** ⟨за-⟩ redden; **2.** ⟨на-⟩ rouge; **~ый** [14 *sh.*] ruddy, rosy; *яблоко* red

**ру́пор** *m* [1] megaphone; *fig.* mouthpiece

Р

**руса́лка** *f* [5; *g/pl.*: -лок] mermaid
**ру́сло** *n* [9] (river)bed, (*a. fig.*) channel
**ру́сский** [16] Russian (*a. su.*); *adv.* **по-ру́сски** (in) Russian
**ру́сый** [14 *sh.*] light brown
**рути́н|а** *f* [5], **~ный** [14] routine
**ру́хлядь** *coll. f* [8] lumber, junk
**ру́хнуть** [20] *pf.* crash down; *fig.* fail
**руча́ться** [1], ⟨поручи́ться⟩ [16] (**за** В) warrant, guarantee, vouch for
**руче́й** *m* [3; -чья́] brook, stream
**ру́чка** *f* [5; -чек] *dim.* → **рука́**; *двери* handle, knob; *кресла* arm; **ша́риковая ~** ballpoint pen
**ручно́й** [14] hand…; *труд* manual; **~ рабо́ты** handmade; small; *животное* tame
**ру́шить** [16] (*im*)*pf.* pull down; **-ся** collapse
**ры́б|а** *f* [5] fish; **~а́к** *m* [1 *e.*] fisherman; **~ий** [18] fish…; *жир* cod-liver oil; **~ный** [14] fish(y); **~ная ло́вля** fishing
**рыболо́в** *m* [1] fisherman; angler; **~ный** [14] fishing; fish…; **~ные принадле́жности** fishing tackle; **~ство** *n* [9] fishery
**рыво́к** *m* [1; -вка́] jerk; *sport* spurt, dash
**рыг|а́ть** [1], ⟨**~ну́ть**⟩ [20] belch
**рыда́|ние** *n* [12] sob(bing); **~ть** [1] sob
**ры́жий** [17; рыж, -á, -o] red (haired), ginger
**ры́ло** *n* [9] snout; P mug
**ры́но|к** *m* [1; -нка] market (**на** П in); **~чный** [14] market…

**рыс|а́к** *m* [1 *e.*] trotter; **~ка́ть** [3] rove, run about; **~ь** *f* [8] **1.** trot (at T); **2.** *zo.* lynx
**ры́твина** *f* [5] rut, groove; hole
**рыть** [22], ⟨вы́-⟩ dig; burrow; **~ся** rummage
**рыхл|и́ть** [13], ⟨вз-, раз-⟩ loosen (*soil*); **~ый** [14; рыхл, -á, -o] friable, loose; *мело* flabby; podgy
**ры́цар|ский** [16] knightly, chivalrous; knight's; **~ь** *m* [4] knight
**рыча́г** *m* [1 *e.*] lever
**рыча́ть** [4; -чу́, -чи́шь] growl, snarl
**рья́ный** [14 *sh.*] zealous
**рюкза́к** *m* [1] rucksack, knapsack
**рю́мка** *f* [5; *g/pl.*: -мок] (wine)glass
**ряби́на** *f* [5] mountain ash
**ряби́ть** [14; -и́т] *воду* ripple; *impers.* flicker (**в глаза́х у** Р before one's eyes)
**ря́б|чик** *m* [1] *zo.* hazelhen; **~ь** *f* ripples *pl.*; *в глазах* dazzle
**ря́вк|ать** *coll.* [1], *once* ⟨**~нуть**⟩ [20] bellow, roar (**на** В at)
**ряд** *m* [1; в -у́; *pl. e.*; *after 2, 3, 4*, ряда́] row; line; series; **в ~е слу́чаев** in a number of cases; *pl.* ranks; *thea.* tier; **~а́ми** in rows; **из ~а вон выходя́щий** remarkable, extraordinary; **~ово́й** [14] ordinary; *su. mil.* private; **~ом** side by side; (**с** Т) beside, next to; next door; close by; **сплошь и ~ом** more often than not
**ря́са** *f* [5] cassock

С

# С

**с**, **со 1.** (Р) from; since; with; for; **2.** (В) about; **3.** (Т) with; of; to; **мы ~ ва́ми** you and I; **ско́лько ~ меня́?** how much do I owe you?
**са́бля** *f* [6; *g/pl.*: -бель] saber (*Brt.* -bre)
**сабот|а́ж** *m* [1], **~и́ровать** [7] (*im*)*pf.* sabotage
**сад** *m* [1; в ~у́; *pl. e.*] garden; **фрукто́вый ~** orchard
**сади́ть** [15], ⟨по-⟩ → **сажа́ть**; **~ся**, ⟨сесть⟩ [25; ся́ду, -дешь; сел, -а; се́вший] (**на, в** В) sit down; *в машину и т. д.* get in(to) *or* on, board *a. rail.*; *naut.* embark; *на лошадь* mount; *о птице* alight; *ae.* land; *солнце* set, sink; *ткань* shrink; set (**за** В to *work*); run (aground **на мель**)
**садо́в|ник** *m* [1] gardener; **~о́дство** *n* [9] gardening, horticulture
**са́ж|а** *f* [5] soot; **в ~е** sooty
**сажа́ть** [1] (*iter. of* **сади́ть**) seat; *в тюрьму* put into; *растения* plant

**са́женец** *m* [1; -нца и т. д.] seedling; sapling
**са́йра** *f* [5] saury
**сала́т** *m* [1] salad; *bot.* lettuce
**са́ло** *n* [9] fat, lard
**сало́н** *m* [1] lounge; showroom; saloon; *ae.* passenger cabin; ***космети́ческий ~*** beauty salon
**салфе́тка** *f* [5; *g/pl.*: -ток] (table) napkin
**са́льдо** *n* [*indecl.*] *comm.* balance
**са́льный** [14; -лен, -льна] greasy; *анекдот* bawdy
**салю́т** *m* [1], **~ова́ть** [7] (*im*)*pf.* salute
**сам** *m*, **~а́** *f*, **~о́** *n*, **~и** *pl.* [30] -self: **я ~(а́)** I … myself; **мы ~и** we … ourselves; ***~о́ собо́й разуме́ется*** it goes without saying; **~е́ц** *m* [1; -мца́] *zo.* male; **~ка** *f* [5; *g/pl.*: -мок] *zo.* female
**само|бы́тный** [14; -тен, -тна] original; **~ва́р** *m* [1] samovar; **~во́льный** [14; -лен, -льна] unauthorrized; **~го́н** *m* [1] home-brew, moonshine; **~де́льный** [14] homemade
**самодержа́вие** *n* [12] autocracy
**само|де́ятельность** *f* [8] independent action *or* activity; *художественная* amateur performances (*theatricals, musicals, etc.*); **~дово́льный** [14; -лен, -льна] self-satisfied, self-complacent; **~защи́та** *f* [5] self-defense (-nce); **~кри́тика** *f* [5] self-criticism
**самолёт** *m* [1] airplane (*Brt.* aeroplane), aircraft; ***пассажи́рский ~*** airliner
**само|люби́вый** [14 *sh.*] proud, touchy; **~лю́бие** *n* [12] pride, self-esteem; **~мне́ние** *n* [12] conceit; **~наде́янный** [14 *sh.*] self-confident, presumptuous; **~облада́ние** *n* [12] self-control; **~обма́н** *m* [1] self-deception; **~оборо́на** *f* [5] self-defense (-nce); **~обслу́живание** *n* [12] self-service; **~определе́ние** *n* [12] self-determination; **~отве́рженный** [14 *sh.*] selfless; **~отво́д** *m* [1] *кандидатуры* withdrawal; **~поже́ртвование** *n* [12] self-sacrifice; **~сва́л** *m* [1] dump truck; **~сохране́ние** *n* [12] self-preservation
**самостоя́тельн|ость** *f* [8] independence; **~ый** [14; -лен, -льна] independent
**само|су́д** *m* [1] lynch *or* mob law; **~уби́йство** *n* [9], **~уби́йца** *m/f* [5] suicide; **~уве́ренный** [14 *sh.*] self-confident; **~управле́ние** *n* [12] self-government; **~у́чка** *m/f* [5; *g/pl.*: -чек] self-taught pers.; **~хо́дный** [14] self-propelled; **~цве́ты** *m/pl.* [1] semiprecious stones; **~це́ль** *f* [8] end in itself; **~чу́вствие** *n* [12] (state of) health
**са́м|ый** [14] the most, …est; the very; the (self)same; just, right; early or late; ***~ое большо́е* (*ма́лое*)** *coll.* at (the) most (least)
**сан** *m* [1] dignity, office
**санато́рий** *m* [3] sanatorium
**санда́лии** *f/pl.* [7] sandals
**са́ни** *f/pl.* [8; *from gen. e.*] sled(ge), sleigh
**санита́р** *m* [1], **~ка** *f* [5; *g/pl.*: -рок] hospital attendant, orderly; **~ный** [14] sanitary
**сан|кциони́ровать** [7] (*im*)*pf.* sanction; **~те́хник** *m* [1] plumber
**сантиме́тр** *m* [1] centimeter (*Brt.* -tre)
**сану́зел** *m* [1] lavatory
**сапёр** *m* [1] engineer
**сапо́г** *m* [1 *e.*; *g/pl.*: сапо́г] boot
**сапо́жник** *m* [1] shoemaker
**сапфи́р** *m* [1] sapphire
**сара́й** *m* [3] shed
**саранча́** *f* [5; *g/pl.*: -че́й] locust
**сарафа́н** *m* [1] sarafan (*Russian peasant women's dress*)
**сард|е́лька** *f* [5; *g/pl.*: -лек] (*sausage*) saveloy, polony.; **~и́на** *f* [5] sardine
**сарка́зм** *m* [1] sarcasm
**сатана́** *m* [5] Satan
**сати́н** *m* [1] sateen, glazed cotton
**сати́р|а** *f* [5] satire; **~ик** *m* [1] satirist; **~и́ческий** [16] satirical
**са́хар** *m* [1; *part.g.*: -у] sugar; **~истый** [14 *sh.*] sugary; **~ница** *f* [5] sugar bowl; **~ный** [14] sugar…; ***~ная боле́знь*** diabetes
**сачо́к** *m* [1; -чка́] butterfly net
**сбав|ля́ть** [28], 〈**~ить**〉 [14] reduce
**сбе|га́ть**[1] [1], 〈**~жа́ть**〉 [4; -егу́, -ежи́шь, -егу́т] run down (from); *pf.* run away, escape, flee; **-ся** come running; **~гать**[2] [1] *pf.* run for, run to fetch (***за*** T)
**сбере|га́тельный** [14] savings

(bank)…; **~гáть** [1], 〈**~́чь**〉 [26 г/ж: -регу́, -режёшь, -регу́т] save; preserve; **~же́ние** *n* [12] economy; savings *pl.*

**сберкáсса** *f* [5] savings bank

**сби|вáть** [1], 〈**~ть**〉 [собью́, -бьёшь; сбей!; сби́тый] knock down (*or* off, *a.* **с ног**); *ae.* shoot down; *сливки* whip; *яйца* beat up; *масло* churn; (*сколотить*) knock together; lead (astray **с пути́**; **-ся** lose one's way); **~ть с то́лку** confuse; *refl. a.* run o.s. off (one's legs **с ноги́**); flock, huddle (together **в ку́чу**); **~́вчивый** [14 *sh.*] confused; inconsistent; **~́ть(ся)** → **~ва́ть(ся)**

**сбли|жáть** [1], 〈**~́зить**〉 [15] bring *or* draw together; **-ся** become friends (**с** T with) *or* lovers; **~же́ние** *n* [12] (*a. pol.*) rapprochement; approach(es)

**сбо́ку** from one side; on one side; (*рядом*) next to

**сбор** *m* [1] collection; gathering; **~ урожа́я** harvest; **~ нало́гов** tax collection; **порто́вый ~** harbo(u)r dues; **тамо́женный ~** customs duty; *pl.* preparations; **в ~́е** assembled; **~́ище** *n* [11] mob, crowd; **~́ка** *f* [5; *g/pl.*: -рок] *sew.* gather; *tech.* assembly, assembling; **~́ник** *m* [1] collection; **~́ный** [14] *sport* combined team; **~́очный** [14] assembly

**сбр|áсывать** [1], 〈**~о́сить**〉 [15] throw down; drop; *одежду и т. д.* shed; **~од** *m* [1] rabble, riff-raff; **~о́сить** → **~а́сывать**; **~у́я** *f* [6] harness

**сбы|вáть** [1], 〈**~ть**〉 [сбу́ду, -дешь; сбыл, -á, -о] sell, market; get rid of (*a.* **с рук**); **-ся** come true; **~т** *m* [1] sale; **~ть(ся)** → **~ва́ть(ся)**

**свáд|ебный** [14], **~ьба** *f* [5; *g/pl.*: -деб] wedding

**свáл|ивать** [1], 〈**~и́ть**〉 [13; -алю́, -áлишь] bring down; *дерево* fell; *в кучу* dump; heap up; *вину* shift (**на** B to); **-ся** fall down; **~ка** *f* [5; *g/pl.*: -лок] dump; (*драка*) brawl

**свáр|ивать** [1], 〈**~и́ть**〉 [13; сварю́, свáришь, свáренный] weld; **~ка** *f* [5], **~очный** [14] welding

**сварли́вый** [14 *sh.*] quarrelsome

**свáя** *f* [6; *g/pl.*: свай] pile

**свéд|ение** *n* [12] information; **приня́ть к ~ению** note; **~ущий** [17 *sh.*] well-informed, knowledgable

**свéж|есть** *f* [8] freshness; coolness; **~éть** [8], 〈по-〉 freshen, become cooler; *pf. a.* look healthy; **~ий** [15; свеж, -á, -ó, свéжи́] fresh; cool; *новости* latest; *хлеб* new

**свезти́** → **свози́ть**

**свёкла** *f* [5; *g/pl.*: -кол] red beet

**свёк|ор** *m* [1; -кра] father-in-law (*husband's father*); **~ро́вь** *f* [8] mother-in-law (*husband' mother*)

**свер|гáть** [1], 〈**~́гнуть**〉 [21] overthrow; dethrone (*с престола*); **~же́ние** *n* [12] overthrow; **~́ить** → **~я́ть**

**сверк|áть** [1], *once* 〈**~ну́ть**〉 [20] sparkle, glitter; *молнии* flash

**сверл|éние** *n* [12], **~и́льный** [14] drilling; **~и́ть** [13], 〈про-〉, **~ó** *n* [9; *pl. st.*: свёрла] drill

**свер|ну́ть(ся)** → **свёртывать(ся)** & **свора́чивать**; **~́стник** → **рове́сник**

**свёрт|ок** *m* [1; -тка] roll; parcel; bundle; **~ывать** [1], 〈сверну́ть〉 [20] roll (up); *за угол* turn; (*сократить*) curtail; *строительство* stop; twist; **-ся** coil up; *молоко* curdle; *кровь* coagulate

**сверх** (P) above, beyond; over; besides; **~ вся́ких ожида́ний** beyond (all) expectations; **~ того́** moreover; **~звукoво́й** [14] supersonic; **~при́быль** *f* [8] excess profit; **~́у** from above; **~уро́чный** [14] overtime; **~ъесте́ственный** [14 *sh.*] supernatural

**сверчо́к** *m* [1; -чкá] *zo.* cricket

**свер|я́ть** [28], 〈**~́ить**〉 [13] compare, collate

**свéсить** → **свéшивать**

**свести́(сь)** → **своди́ть(ся)**

**свет** *m* [1] light; world (**на** П in); **вы́пустить в ~** publish; **чуть ~** at dawn; **~áть** [1] dawn; **~и́ло** *n* [9] *poet.* the sun; luminary (*a. fig.*); **~и́ть(ся)** [15] shine

**светл|éть** [8], 〈по-〉 brighten; grow light(er); **~о…** light…; **~́ый** [14; -тел, -тлá, -о] light, bright; lucid; **~́ая голова́** good head; **~я́к** *m* [1 *e.*; -чкá] glowworm

**свето|во́й** [14] light…; **~фо́р** *m* [1] traffic light

**свéтский** [16] worldly

**светя́щийся** [17] luminous
**свеча́** *f* [5; *pl.*: све́чи, -е́й, -а́м] candle; *el.* spark(ing) plug; candlepower
**све́|шивать** [1], ⟨~сить⟩ [15] let down; dangle; **-ся** hang over; *pf.* lean over
**сви|ва́ть** [1], ⟨~ть⟩ [совью́, -вьёшь; → ***вить***] wind, twist; *гнездо* build
**свида́ни|е** *n* [12] appointment, meeting, date; ***до ~я*** good-by(e)
**свиде́тель** *m* [4], **~ница** *f* [5] witness; **~ство** *n* [9] evidence; testimony; certificate; ***~ство о рожде́нии*** birth certificate; **~ствовать** [7], ⟨за-⟩ testify; attest *тж. подпись*; *impf.* (**о** П) show
**свине́ц** *m* [1; -нца́] *metal* lead
**свин|и́на** *f* [5] pork; **∠ка** *f* [5; *g/pl.*: -нок] *med.* mumps; ***морска́я ∠ка*** guinea pig; **~о́й** [14] pig…, pork…; **∠ство** *n* [9] dirty *or* rotten act
**сви́н|чивать** [1], ⟨~ти́ть⟩ [15 *e.*; -нчу́, -нти́шь; сви́нченный] screw together, fasten with screws; unscrew
**свинь|я́** *f* [6; *pl. st.*, *gen.*: -не́й; *a.* -нья́м] pig, sow; *fig.* swine; ***подложи́ть ~ю́ кому́-л.*** play a mean trick (on)
**свире́п|ствовать** [7] rage; **~ый** [14 *sh.*] fierce, ferocious
**свиста́ть** [1] hang down, droop
**свист** *m* [1] whistle; hiss; **~а́ть** [13] & **~е́ть** [11], *once* ⟨∠нуть⟩ [20] whistle; *pf.* P (*стянуть*) pilfer; **~о́к** *m* [1; -тка́] whistle
**свистопля́ска** *f* [5; *g/pl.*: -сок] turmoil and confusion
**сви́т|а** *f* [5] retinue, suite; **~ер** (-tɛr) *m* [1] sweater; **~ок** *m* [1; -тка] scroll; **~ь** → ***свива́ть***
**свихну́ть** *coll.* [20] *pf.* sprain; **-ся** go mad
**свищ** *m* [1 *e.*] *med.* fistula
**свобо́д|а** *f* [5] freedom, liberty; ***вы́пустить на ~у*** set free; **~ный** [14; -ден, -дна] free (**от** Р from, of); *место и т. д.* vacant; *время и т. д.* spare; *доступ* easy; *одежда* loose; *владение* fluent; exempt (**от** Р from); **~омы́слящий** [17] freethinking; *su.* freethinker, liberal
**свод** *m* [1] *arch.* arch, vault
**своди́ть** [15], ⟨свести́⟩ [25] lead; take down (from, off); bring (together); reduce (**к** Д to); *счёты* square; *ногу* cramp; drive (mad **с ума́**); ***~ на нет*** bring to nought; **-ся**, ⟨-сь⟩ (**к** Д) come *or* amount (to), result (in)
**сво́д|ка** *f* [5; *g/pl.*: -док] report, communiqué; **~ный** [14] *таблица* summary; *брат* step…; **~чатый** [14] vaulted
**свое|во́льный** [14; -лен, -льна] self-willed, wil(l)ful; **~вре́менный** [14; -менен, -менна] timely; **~нра́вный** [14; -вен, -вна] capricious; **~обра́зный** [14; -зен, -зна] original; peculiar, distinctive
**свози́ть** [15], ⟨свезти́⟩ [24] take, convey
**сво|й** *m*, **~я́** *f*, **~ё** *n*, **~и́** *pl.* [24] my, his, her, its, our, your, their (*refl.*); one's own; peculiar; ***в ~ё вре́мя*** at one time; in due course; *su. pl.* one's people, folks, relations; ***не ~й*** frantic (*voice* in T); **∠йственный** [14 *sh.*] peculiar (Д to); (Д p.'s) usual; **∠йство** *n* [9] property, quality, characteristic
**сво́|лочь** *f* [8] scum, swine; **~ра** *f* [5] pack; **~ра́чивать** [1], ⟨сверну́ть⟩ [20] turn (**с** P off); roll (up); **~я́ченица** *f* [5] sister-in-law (*wife's sister*)
**свы|ка́ться** [1], ⟨∠кнуться⟩ [21] get used (**с** T to); **~сока́** haughtily; **∠ше** from above; (P) over, more than
**свя́з|а́ть(ся)** → **∠ывать(ся)**; **~и́ст** *m* [1] signalman; **∠ка** *f* [5; *g/pl.*: -зок] bunch; *anat.* ligament; *anat.* (*vocal*) cord; *gr.* copula; **∠ный** [14; -зен, -зна] coherent; **∠ывать** [1], ⟨~а́ть⟩ [3] tie (together), bind; connect, join; unite; associate; *teleph.* put through, connect; **-ся** get in touch (with), contact; get involved with (**с** T); **~ь** *f* [8; в -зи́] tie, bond; connection; relation; contact; *половая* liaison; communication (radio, telephone, post, *etc.*)
**свят|и́ть** [15 *e.*; -ячу́, -яти́шь], ⟨о-⟩ consecrate, hallow; **∠ки** *f/pl.* [5; *gen.*: -ток] Christmas (**на** П at); **~о́й** [14; свят, -а́, -о] holy; sacred (*a. fig.*); *su.* saint; **∠ость** *f* [8] holiness, sanctity; **~ота́тство** *n* [9] sacrilege; **~ы́ня** *f* [6] *eccl.* sacred place; (*fig.*) sacred object
**свяще́нн|ик** *m* [1] priest; **~ый** [14 *sh.*]

**С**

holy; sacred
**сгиб** *m* [1], **~áть** [1], ⟨согнýть⟩ [20] bend, fold; *v/i.* **-áтся**
**слá|живать** [1], ⟨~дить⟩ [15] smooth out; **-ся** become smooth
**сгнивáть** → ***гнить***
**сгóвор** *m* [1] *usu. pej* agreement; collusion; **~и́ться** [13] *pf.* agree; come to terms; **~чивый** [14 *sh.*] compliant, amenable
**сго|ня́ть** [28], ⟨согнáть⟩ [сгоню́, сгóнишь; сóгнанный] drive (off); **~рáние** *n* [12] combustion; **~рáть** [1], ⟨~рéть⟩ [9] burn down; ***~рáть от стыдá*** burn with shame; **~рячá** in a fit of temper
**сгр|ебáть** [1], ⟨~ести́⟩ [24 -б-: сгребý; сгрёб, сгреблá] rake up; shovel off, from; **~ужáть** [1], ⟨~узи́ть⟩ [15 & 15 *e.*; -ужý, -ýзишь; -ýженный & -ужённый] unload
**сгу|сти́ть** → ***~щáть***; **~сток** *m* [1; -тка] clot; **~щáть** [1], ⟨~сти́ть⟩ [15 *e.*; -ущý, -усти́шь; -ущённый] thicken; condense; ***~щáть крáски*** lay it on thick, exaggerate; **~щёнка** *f* [5; *g/pl.*: -нок] condensed milk
**сда|вáть** [5], ⟨~ть⟩ [сдам, сдашь *etc.* → ***дать***] deliver, hand in (*or* over); *багаж* check, register; *дом и т. д.* rent, let (out); *карты* deal; *экзамен* pass; *mil.* surrender; **-ся** surrender; ***~ётся...*** for rent (*Brt.* to let); **~вливать** [1], ⟨~ви́ть⟩ [14] squeeze; **~ть(ся)** → ***~вáть(ся)***; **~ча** *f* [5] *mil.* surrender; (*передача*) handing over; *деньги* change
**сдвиг** *m* [1] shift; *geol.* fault; *fig.* change (for the better), improvement; **~áть** [1], ⟨сдви́нуть⟩ [20] move, shift (*v/i.* **-ся**); *брови* knit; push together
**сдéл|ка** *f* [5; *g/pl.*: -лок] bargain, transaction, deal; **~ьный** [14] piecework
**сдéрж|анный** [14 *sh.*] reserved, (self-)restrained; **~ивать** [1], ⟨~áть⟩ [4] check, restrain; *гнев и т. д.* suppress; *слово и т. д.* keep; **-ся** control o.s.
**сдирáть** [1], ⟨содрáть⟩ [сдерý, -рёшь; содрáл, -á, -о; сóдранный] tear off (*or* down), strip; *шкуру* flay (*a. fig.*)
**сдóбн|ый** [14] *cul.* rich, short; ***~ая бýл(оч)ка*** bun
**сдружи́ться** → ***подружи́ться***
**сду|вáть** [1], ⟨~ть⟩ [16], *once* ⟨~нуть⟩ [20] blow off (*or* away); **~ру** *coll.* foolishly
**сеáнс** *m* [1] sitting; *cine.* show
**себестóимость** *f* [8] cost; cost price
**себ|я́** [21] myself, yourself, himself, herself, itself, ourselves, yourselves, themselves (*refl.*); oneself; ***к ~é*** home; into one's room; ***мне не по ~é*** I don't feel quite myself, I don't feel too well; ***тáк ~é*** so-so
**сев** *m* [1] sowing
**сéвер** *m* [1] north; → ***востóк***; **~ный** [14] north(ern); northerly; arctic; **~о-востóк** *m* [1] northeast; **~о-востóчный** [14] northeast…; **~о-зáпад** *m* [1] northwest; **~о-зáпадный** [14] northwest…; **~я́нин** *m* [1; *pl.* -я́не, -я́н *и т. д.*] northerner
**севрю́га** *f* [5] stellate sturgeon
**сегóдня** (ṣɪv'ɔ-) today; ***~ ýтром*** this morning; **~шний** [15] today's
**сед|éть** [8], ⟨по-⟩ turn gray (*Brt.* grey); **~инá** *f* [5] gray hair
**седл|áть** [1], **~ó** *n* [9; *pl. st.*: сёдла, сёдел, сёдлам] saddle
**седо|волóсый** [14 *sh.*], **~й** [14; сед, -á, -о] gray-haired (*Brt.* grey)
**седóк** *m* [1 *e.*] horseman, rider; fare (*passenger*)
**седьмóй** [14] seventh; → ***пя́тый***
**сезóн** *m* [1] season; **~ный** [14] seasonal
**сей** *m*, **сия́** *f*, **сиé** *n*, **сии́** *pl. obs.* [29] this; ***по ~ день*** till now; ***на ~ раз*** this time; ***сию́ минýту*** at once; right now; ***сегó гóда*** (***мéсяца***) of this year (month)
**сейф** *m* [1] safe
**сейчáс** now, at present; (*очень скоро*) presently, (*a.* ***~ же***) immediately, at once; (*только что*) just (now)
**секáтор** *m* [1] secateurs, pruning shears
**секрéт** *m* [1] secret (***по*** Д, ***под*** Т in); **~ариáт** *m* [1] secretariat; **~áрь** *m* [4 *e.*] secretary; **~ничать** *coll.* [1] be secretive; **~ный** [14; -тен, -тна] secret; confidential
**сек|суáльный** [14; -лен, -льна] sexual; **~та** *f* [5] sect; **~тор** *m* [1] sector
**секýнд|а** *f* [5] (*of time*) second; **~ный**

[14] second…; **~ная стре́лка** (*of timepiece*) second hand; **~оме́р** *m* [1] stopwatch
**селёдка** *f* [5; *g/pl.*: -док] herring
**селез|ёнка** *f* [5; *g/pl.*: -нок] *anat.* spleen; **ʹ~ень** *m* [4; -зня] drake
**селе́кция** *f* [7] *agric.* selection, breeding
**сели́ть(ся)** [13] → **поселя́ть(ся)**
**сел|о́** *n* [9; *pl. st.*: сёла] village (**в** *or* **на** П in); **ни к ~у́ ни к го́роду** *coll.* for no reason at all; neither here nor there
**сельд|ере́й** *m* [3] celery; **ʹ~ь** *f* [8; *from g/pl. e.*] herring
**се́ль|ский** [16] rural, country…, village…; **~ское хозя́йство** agriculture; **~скохозя́йственный** [14] agricultural; **~сове́т** *m* [1] village soviet
**сёмга** *f* [5] salmon
**семе́й|ный** [14] family…; having a family; **~ство** *n* [9] family
**семена́** → **се́мя**
**семен|и́ть** *coll.* [13] (*when walking*) mince; **~но́й** [14] seed…; *biol.* seminal
**семёрка** [5; *g/pl.*: -рок] seven; → **дво́йка**
**се́меро** [37] seven; → **дво́е**
**семе́стр** *m* [1] term, semester
**се́мечко** *n* [9; *pl.*: -чки, -чек, -чкам] *dim. of* **се́мя**; (*pl.*) sunflower seeds
**семи|деся́тый** [14] seventieth; → **пя́(тидеся́)тый**; **~ле́тний** [15] seventy-year-old; of seventy
**семина́р** *m* [1] seminar; **~ия** *f* [7] seminary; **духо́вная ~ия** theological college
**семисо́тый** [14] seven hundredth
**семна́дцат|ый** [14] seventeenth; → **пя́тый**; **ʹ~ь** [35] seventeen; → **пять**
**семь** [35] seven; → **пять & пя́тый**; **ʹ~десят** [35] seventy; **~со́т** [36] seven hundred; **ʹ~ю** seven times
**семья́** [6; *pl.*: се́мьи, семе́й, се́мьям] family; **~ни́н** *m* [1] family man
**се́мя** *n* [13; *pl.*: -мена́, -мя́н, -мена́м] seed (*a. fig.*); *biol.* semen
**сена́т** *m* [1] senate; **~ор** *m* [1] senator
**се́ни** *f/pl.* [8; *from gen. e.*] entryway (*in a Russian village house*)
**се́но** *n* [9] hay; **~ва́л** *m* [1] hayloft; **~ко́с** *m* [1] haymaking; → **коси́лка**
**сен|сацио́нный** [14; -о́нен, -о́нна] sensational; **~тимента́льный** [14; -лен, -льна] sentimental
**сентя́брь** *m* [4 *e.*] September
**сень** *f* [8; в -ни́] *obs. or poet.* canopy, shade; *fig.* protection
**сепарат|и́ст** *m* [1] separatist; **ʹ~ный** [14] separate
**се́п|сис** *m* [1] *med.* sepsis
**се́ра** *f* [5] sulfur; *coll.* earwax
**серб** *m* [1], **ʹ~(ия́н)ка** *f* [5; *g/pl.*: -б(ия́н)ок] Serb(ian); **ʹ~ский** [16] Serbian
**серви́|з** *m* [1] service, set; **~рова́ть** [7] (*im*)*pf.* serve
**се́рвис** *m* [1] (*consumer*) service
**серде́чный** [14; -чен, -чна] of the heart; *приём* hearty, cordial; *челове́к* warm-hearted; *благода́рность* heartfelt; **~ при́ступ** heart attack
**серди́|тый** [14 *sh.*] angry, mad (**на** В with, at); **~ть** [15], ⟨рас-⟩ annoy, vex, anger; **-ся** be(come) angry, cross (**на** В with)
**се́рдц|е** *n* [11; *pl. e.*: -дца́, -де́ц, -дца́м] heart; **в ~а́х** in a fit of temper; **принима́ть бли́зко к ~у** take to heart; **от всего́ ~а** wholeheartedly; **по́ ~у** (Д) to one's liking; **положа́ ру́ку на́ сердце** *coll.* (quite) frankly; **~ебие́ние** *n* [12] palpitation; **~еви́на** *f* [5] core, pith, heart
**серебр|и́стый** [14 *sh.*] silvery; **~и́ть** [13], ⟨по-, вы́-⟩ silver; **-ся** become silvery; **~о́** *n* [9] silver; **ʹ~яный** [14] silver(y)
**середи́на** *f* [5] middle; midst; mean
**серёжка** *f* [5; *g/pl.*: -жек] earring; *bot.* catkin
**сере́ть** [8], ⟨по-⟩ turn (*impf.* show) gray (*Brt.* grey)
**сержа́нт** *m* [1] sergeant
**сери́|йный** [14] serial; **ʹ~я** *f* [7] series
**се́рна** *f* [5] *zo.* chamois
**се́р|ный** [14] sulfuric; sulfur…; **~ова́тый** [14 *sh.*] grayish, *Brt.* greyish
**серп** *m* [1 *e.*] sickle; *луны* crescent
**серпанти́н** *m* [1] paper streamer; road with sharp, U-shaped curves
**сертифика́т** *m* [1] *ка́чества и т. д.* certificate
**се́рфинг** *m* [1] surfing
**се́рый** [14; сер, -á, -о] gray, *Brt.* grey;

dull, dim
**серьги** *f/pl.* [5; серёг, серьгам; *sg. e.*] earrings
**серьёзн|ый** [14; -зен, -зна] serious, grave; earnest; **~о** *a.* indeed, really
**сессия** *f* [7] session (**на** П in)
**сестра** *f* [5; *pl.*: сёстры, сестёр, сёстрам] sister; (first) cousin; nurse
**сесть** → ***садиться***
**сет|ка** *f* [5; *g/pl.*: -ток] net; *тарифов и т. д.*; **~овать** [1] complain (**на** В about); **~чатка** *f* [5; *g/pl.*: -ток] *anat.* retina; **~ь** *f* [8; в сети; *from g/pl. e.*] net; (*система*) network
**сечение** *n* [12] section; cutting; ***кесарево ~*** cesarean birth
**сечь**[1] [26; *pt. e.*; сек, секла] cut (up); **-ся** split; **~**[2] [26; *pt. st.*; сек, секла], ⟨вы-⟩ whip
**сеялка** *f* [5; *g/pl.*: -лок] drill
**сеять** [27], ⟨по-⟩ sow (*a. fig.*)
**сжалиться** [13] *pf.* (**над** Т) have *or* take pity (on)
**сжат|ие** *n* [12] pressure; compression; **~ый** [14] (*воздух и т. д.*) compressed; *fig.* compact, concise, terse; **~ь(ся)** → ***сжимать(ся)*** & ***жать***[1], ***жать***[2]
**сжигать** [1], ⟨сжечь⟩ → ***жечь***
**сжимать** [1], ⟨сжать⟩ [сожму, -мёшь; сжатый] (com)press, squeeze; (*кулаки*) clench; **-ся** contract; shrink; become clenched
**сзади** (from) behind (*as prp.*: Р)
**сзывать** → ***созывать***
**сибир|ский** [16], **~як** *m* [1 *e.*], **~ячка** *f* [5; *g/pl.*: -чек] Siberian
**сигар(ет)а** *f* [5] cigar(ette)
**сигнал** [1], **~изировать** [7] (*im*)*pf.*, **~ьный** [14] signal, alarm
**сиделка** *f* [5; *g/pl.*: -лок] nurse
**сиде|нье** *n* [10] seat; **~ть** [11; сидя] sit (***за*** Т at, over); *дома* be, stay; *об одежде* fit (**на** П a p.); *на корточках* squat; **-ся**: ***ему не сидится на месте*** he can't sit still
**сидр** *m* [1] cider
**сидячий** [17] *образ жизни* sedentary; sitting
**сизый** [14; сиз, -а, -о] blue-gray, *Brt.* -grey; dove-colo(u)red

**сил|а** *f* [5] strength; force (*тж. привычки*); power, might; vigo(u)r; intensity; energy; *звука* volume; ***своими ~ами*** unaided, by o.s.; ***в ~у*** (Р) by virtue of; ***не в ~ах*** unable; ***не по ~ам, свыше чьих-л. сил*** beyond one's power; ***изо всех сил*** *coll.* with all one's might; **~ач** *m* [1 *e.*] strong man; **~иться** [13] try, endeavo(u)r; **~овой** [14] power…
**силуэт** *m* [1] silhouette
**сильн|ый** [14; силен & силён, -льна, -о, сильны] strong; powerful, mighty; intense; *дождь* heavy; *насморк* bad; **~о** *a.* very much; strongly; badly
**символ** *m* [1] symbol; **~ический** [16], **~ичный** [14; -чен, -чна] symbolic
**симметри|чный** [14; -чен, -чна] symmetrical; **~я** *f* [7] symmetry
**симпат|изировать** [7] sympathize (with Д); **~ичный** [14; -чен, -чна] nice, attractive; ***он мне ~ичен*** I like him; **~ия** *f* [7] liking (***к*** Д for)
**симптом** *m* [1] symptom
**симул|ировать** [7] (*im*)*pf.* feign, sham; simulate; **~янт** *m* [1], **~янтка** *m* [5; *g/pl.*: -ток] simulator; malingerer
**симфони|ческий** [16] symphonic, symphony…; **~я** *f* [7] symphony
**син|ева** *f* [5] blue; **~еватый** [14 *sh.*] bluish; **~еть** [8], ⟨по-⟩ turn (*impf.* show) blue; **~ий** [15; синь, синя, сине] blue; **~ить** [13], ⟨под-⟩ blue; apply blueing to; **~ица** *f* [5] titmouse
**син|од** *m* [1] *eccl.* synod; **~оним** *m* [1] synonym; **~таксис** *m* [1] syntax; **~тез** *m* [1] synthesis; **~тетика** *f* [5] synthetic material; **~тетический** [16] synthetic; **~хронизировать** [7] (*im*)*pf.* synchronize; **~хронный** [14] synchronous; ***~хронный перевод*** interpretation
**синь** *f* [8] blue colo(u)r; **~ка** *f* [5; *g/pl.*: -нек] blue; blueing; blueprint
**синяк** *m* [1 *e.*] bruise
**сиплый** [14; сипл, -а, -о] hoarse
**сирена** *f* [5] siren
**сирен|евый** [14], **~ь** *f* [8] lilac (colo[u]r)
**сироп** *m* [1] syrup
**сирота** *m/f* [5; *pl. st.*: сироты] orphan
**система** *f* [5] system; ***~ управления*** control system; **~тический** [16],

С

**~ти́чный** [14; -чен, -чна] systematic
**си́тец** *m* [1; -тца] chintz, cotton
**си́то** *n* [9] sieve
**ситуа́ция** *f* [7] situation
**сия́|ние** *n* [12] radiance; (*нимб*) halo; ***се́верное ~ние*** northern lights; **~ть** [28] shine; *от радости* beam; *от счастья* radiate
**сказ|а́ние** *n* [12] legend; story; tale; **~а́ть** → ***говори́ть***; **~ка** *f* [5; *g/pl.*: -зок] fairy tale; *coll.* tall tale, fib; **~очный** [14; -чен, -чна] fabulous; fantastic; fairy (tale)…
**сказу́емое** *n* [14] *gr.* predicate
**скак|а́ть** [3] skip, hop, jump; gallop; race; **~ово́й** [14] race…; racing
**скал|а́** [5; *pl. st.*] rock face, crag; cliff; reef; **~и́стый** [14 *sh.*] rocky, craggy; **~ить** [13], 〈о-〉 show, bare; *coll.* ***~ить зу́бы*** *impf.* grin; jeer; **~ка** *f* [5; *g/pl.*: -лок] rolling pin; **~ывать** [1], 〈сколо́ть〉 [17] pin together; (*откалывать*) break (off)
**скам|е́ечка** *f* [5; -чек] footstool; *a. dim. of* **~е́йка** *f* [5; *g/pl.*: -е́ек], **~ья́** *f* [6; *nom/pl. a. st.*] bench; ***~ья́ подсуди́мых*** *law* dock
**сканда́л** *m* [1] scandal; disgrace; *coll.* shame; **~ить** [13], 〈на-〉 row, brawl; **~ьный** [14; -лен, -льна] scandalous
**скандина́вский** [16] Scandinavian
**ска́пливать(ся)** [1] → ***скопля́ть(ся)***
**скар|б** *coll.* [1] belongings; goods and chattels; **~лати́на** *f* [5] scarlet fever
**скат** *m* [1] slope, pitch
**скат|а́ть** → ***ска́тывать*** *2*; **~ерть** *f* [8; *from g/pl. e.*] tablecloth; ***~ертью доро́га*** good riddance!
**ска́т|ывать** [1] **1.** 〈~и́ть〉 [15] roll (*or* slide) down (*v/i.* **-ся**); **2.** 〈~а́ть〉 [1] roll (up)
**ска́ч|ка** *f* [5; *g/pl.*: -чек] galloping; *pl.* horse race(s); **~о́к** → ***прыжо́к***
**ска́шивать** [1], 〈скоси́ть〉 [15] mow
**сква́жина** *f* [5] slit, hole; ***замо́чная ~*** keyhole; ***нефтяна́я ~*** oil well
**сквер** *m* [1] public garden; **~нosло́вить** [14] use foul language; **~ный** [14; -рен, -рна́, -о] *качество* bad, poor; *человек, поступок* nasty, foul

**сквоз|и́ть** [15 *e.*; -и́т] *о свете* shine through; **~и́т** there is a draft, *Brt.* draught; **~но́й** [14] through…; **~ня́к** *m* [1 *e.*] draft, *Brt.* draught; **~ь** (В) *prp.* through
**скворе́|ц** *m* [1; -рца́] starling; **~чница** *f* (-ʃn-) [5] nesting box
**скеле́т** *m* [1] skeleton
**скепти́ческий** [16] skeptical (*Brt.* sceptical)
**ски́|дка** *f* [5; *g/pl.*: -док] discount, rebate; ***де́лать ~дку*** make allowances (***на*** for); **~дывать** [1], 〈~нуть〉 [20] throw off *or* down; *одежду* take *or* throw off; *coll.* *цену* knock off (from); **~петр** *m* [1] scepter, *Brt.* -tre; **~пида́р** *m* [1] turpentine; **~рда́** *f* [5] stack, rick
**скис|а́ть** [1], 〈~нуть〉 [21] turn sour
**скита́ться** [1] wander, rove
**склад** *m* [1] **1.** warehouse, storehouse (***на*** П in); *mil.* depot; **2.** (*нрав*) disposition, turn of mind; **~ка** *f* [5; *g/pl.*: -док] pleat, fold; *на брюках и т. д.* crease; *на лбу* wrinkle; **~но́й** [14] fold(-ing), collapsible; camp…; **~ный** [14; -ден, -дна] *речь* coherent, smooth; P well-made (*or* -built); **~чина** *f* [5]: ***в ~чину*** by clubbing together; **~ывать** [1], 〈сложи́ть〉 [16] lay *or* put (together); pile up; pack (up); fold; *числа* add up; *песню* compose; *оружие, жизнь* lay down; *сложа руки* idle; **-ся** (be) form(ed), develop; *coll.* club together
**скле́и|вать** [1], 〈~ть〉 [13; -е́ю] stick together, glue together (*v/i.* **-ся**)
**склеп** *m* [1] crypt, vault
**скло́ка** *f* [5] squabble
**склон** *m* [1] slope; **~е́ние** *n* [12] *gr.* declension; *astr.* declination; **~и́ть(ся)** → ***~я́ть(ся)***; **~ность** *f* [8] inclination (*fig.*; ***к*** Д to, for), disposition; **~ный** [14; -о́нен, -онна́, -о] inclined (***к*** Д to), disposed; **~я́ть** [28] **1.** 〈~и́ть〉 [13; -оню́, -о́нишь, -онённый] bend, incline (*a. fig.*; *v/i.* **-ся**; о *солнце* sink); (*убедить*) persuade; **2.** 〈просклоня́ть〉 *gr.* (**-ся** be) decline(d)
**скó6|a** *f* [5; *pl.*: ско́бы, скоб, скоба́м] cramp (iron), clamp; **~ка** *f* [5; *g/pl.*: -бок] cramp; *gr.*, *typ.* bracket, parenthe-

sis; **~ли́ть** [13; -облю́, -о́блишь, -о́бленный] scrape; plane
**скова́ть** → ***ско́вывать***
**сковорода́** *f* [5; *pl.*: ско́вороды, -ро́д, -да́м] frying pan
**ско́в|ывать** [1], ⟨**~а́ть**⟩ [7 *e.*; скую́, скуёшь] forge (together); weld; *fig.* fetter; bind; arrest
**сколо́ть** → ***ска́лывать***
**скольз|и́ть** [15 *e.*; -льжу́, -льзи́шь], *once* ⟨**~ну́ть**⟩ [20] slide, glide, slip; **ˊкий** [16; -зок, -зка́, -о] slippery
**ско́лько** [32] how (*or* as) much, many; *coll.* **~ лет, ~ зим** → ***ве́чность*** *coll.*
**сконча́ться** [1] *pf.* die, expire
**скоп|ля́ть** [28], ⟨**~и́ть**⟩ [14] accumulate, gather (*v/i.* **-ся**), amass; save; **~ле́ние** *n* [12] accumulation; *людей* gathering, crowd
**скорб|е́ть** [10 *e.*; -блю́, -би́шь] grieve (**о** П over); **ˊный** [14; -бен, -бна] mournful, sorrowful; **ˊь** *f* [8] grief, sorrow
**скорлупа́** *f* [5; *pl. st.* -лу́пы] shell
**скорня́к** *m* [1 *e.*] furrier
**скоро|гово́рка** *f* [5; *g/pl.*: -рок] tongue twister; *речь* patter; **~пали́тельный** [14 *sh.*] hasty, rash; **~пости́жный** [14; -жен, -жна] sudden; **~спе́лый** [14 *sh.*] early; *fig.* hasty; **~стно́й** [14] (high-) speed…; **ˊ~сть** *f* [8; *from g/pl. e.*] speed; *света и т. д.* velocity; *mot.* gear; **со ˊ~стью** at the rate of; ***груз ма́лой ˊ~стью*** slow freight
**ско́р|ый** [14; скор, -а́, -о] quick, fast, rapid, swift; *помощь* first (*aid*); *будущем* near; **~о** *a.* soon; ***~е́е всего́*** *coll.* most probably; ***на ~ую ру́ку*** *coll.* in haste, anyhow
**скоси́ть** → ***ска́шивать***
**скот** *m* [1 *e.*] cattle, livestock; **~и́на** *f* [5] *coll.* cattle; P beast, brute; **ˊный** [14]: ***ˊный двор*** cattle yard; **~обо́йня** *f* [6; *g/pl.*: -о́ен] slaughterhouse; **~ово́дство** *n* [9] cattle breeding; **ˊский** [16] brutish, bestial
**скра́|шивать** [1], ⟨**~сить**⟩ [15] *fig.* relieve, lighten, smooth over
**скребо́к** *m* [1; -бка́] scraper
**скре́жет** [1], ***~а́ть*** [3] (T) gnash
**скреп|и́ть** → ***~ля́ть***; **ˊка** *f* [5; *g/pl.*: -пок] (paper) clip; **~ле́ние** *n* [12] fastening; **~ля́ть** [28], ⟨**~и́ть**⟩ [14 *e.*; -плю́, -пи́шь; -плённый] fasten together; clamp; make fast; *подписью* countersign; ***~я́ се́рдце*** reluctantly
**скрести́** [24 -б-: скребу́; скрёб] scrape; scratch
**скре́щива|ть** [1], ⟨скрести́ть⟩ [15 *e.*; -ещу́, -ести́шь; -ещённый] cross; clash (*v/i.* **-ся**); **~ние** *n* [12] crossing; intersection
**скрип** *m* [1] creak, squeak; *снега* crunch; **~а́ч** *m* [1 *e.*] violinist; **~е́ть** [10 *e.*; -плю́, -пи́шь], ⟨про-⟩, *once* ⟨**ˊнуть**⟩ [20] creak, squeak; crunch; *зубами* grit, gnash; **ˊка** *f* [5; *g/pl.*: -пок] violin
**скро́мн|ость** *f* [8] modesty; **~ый** [14; -мен, -мна́, -о] modest; *обед* frugal
**скру́|чивать** [1], ⟨**~ти́ть**⟩ [15] twist; roll; bind
**скры|ва́ть** [1], ⟨**ˊть**⟩ [22] hide, conceal (**от** P from); **-ся** disappear; (*прятаться*) hide; **ˊтность** *f* [8] reserve; **ˊтный** [14; -тен, -тна] reserved, reticent; **ˊтый** [14] concealed; latent (*a. phys.*); secret; *смысл* hidden; **ˊть(ся)** → ***~ва́ть(ся)***
**скря́га** *m/f* [5] miser, skinflint
**ску́дный** [14; -ден, -дна] scanty, poor
**ску́ка** *f* [5] boredom, ennui
**скула́** *f* [5; *pl. st.*] cheekbone; **~стый** [14 *sh.*] with high *or* prominent cheek-bones
**скули́ть** [13] whimper
**ску́льпт|ор** *m* [1] sculptor; **~у́ра** *f* [5] sculpture
**ску́мбрия** *f* [7] mackerel
**скуп|а́ть** [1], ⟨**~и́ть**⟩ [14] buy up, corner
**скуп|и́ться** [14], ⟨по-⟩ be stingy (*or* sparing), stint (***на*** B in, of); **~о́й** [14; скуп, -а́, -о] stingy; sparing (***на*** B in); inadequate; taciturn (*на слова*); *su.* miser; **ˊость** *f* [8] stinginess, miserliness
**скуч|а́ть** [1] be bored (**о** П, ***по*** Д) long (for), miss; **ˊный** (-ʃn-) [14; -чен, -чна́, -о] boring, tedious, dull; (Д) **ˊно** feel bored
**слаб|е́ть** [8], ⟨о-⟩ weaken; *о ветре и т. д.* slacken; **~и́тельный** [14] laxative (*n*

С

*a. su.*); **~ово́льный** [14; -лен, -льна] weak-willed; **~ость** *f* [8] weakness, *a. fig.* = foible (**к** Д for); infirmity; **~оу́мный** [14; -мен, -мна] feeble-minded; **~охара́ктерный** [14; -рен, -рна] characterless; of weak character; **~ый** [14; слаб, -á, -о] weak (*a. el.*); feeble; *звук, сходство* faint; *здоровье* delicate; *характер* flabby; *зрение* poor

**сла́в|а** *f* [5] glory; fame, renown; reputation, repute; **~а бо́гу!** thank goodness!; **на ~у** *coll.* first-rate, wonderful, right-on; **~ить** [14], ⟨про-⟩ glorify; praise, extol; **-ся** be famous (T for); **~ный** [14; -вен, -вна, -о] famous, glorious; *coll.* nice; splendid

**славян|и́н** *m* [1; *pl.*: -я́не, -я́н], **~ка** *f* [5; *g/pl.*: -нок] Slav; **~ский** [16] Slavic, Slavonic

**слага́ть** [1], ⟨сложи́ть⟩ [16] *песню* compose; *оружие* lay down; *полномочия* resign (from); *обязанности* relieve o.s. (of); → **скла́дывать(ся)**

**сла́д|кий** [16; -док, -дка́, -о; *comp.*: -сла́ще] sweet; sugary; **~кое** *su.* dessert (**на** В for); **~остный** [14; -тен, -тна] sweet, delightful; **~остра́стие** *n* [12] voluptuousness; **~остра́стный** [14] voluptuous; **~ость** *f* [8] sweetness, delight; → **сла́сти**

**сла́женный** [14 *sh.*] harmonious; *действия* coordinated

**слайд** *m* [1] slide, transparency

**сла́нец** *m* [1; -нца] shale, slate

**сла́сти** *f/pl.* [8; *from gen. e.*] candy *sg.*, *Brt. a.* sweets

**слать** [шлю, шлёшь], ⟨по-⟩ send

**слаща́вый** [14 *sh.*] sugary, sickly sweet

**сле́ва** on, to (*or* from) the left

**слегка́** slightly; somewhat; *прикоснуться* lightly, gently

**след** *m* [1; *g/sg. e.* & -ду; на -ду́; *pl. e.*] trace (*a. fig.*); track; footprint; (*запах*) scent; **~ом** (right) behind; **его́ и ~ просты́л** *coll.* he vanished into thin air; **~и́ть** [15 *e.*; -ежу́, -еди́шь] (**за** T) watch, follow; (*присматривать*) look after; *тайно* shadow; *за событиями* keep up (**за** T with)

**сле́доват|ель** *m* [4] investigator; **~ельно** consequently, therefore; so; **~ь** [7] (**за** T; Д) follow; result (**из** P from); be bound for; (Д) *impers.* should, ought to; **как сле́дует** properly, as it should be; **кому́** *or* **куда́ сле́дует** to the proper person *or* quarter

**сле́дствие** *n* [12] **1.** consequence; **2.** investigation

**сле́дующий** [17] following, next

**сле́жка** *f* [5; *g/pl.*: -жек] shadowing

**слез|а́** *f* [5; *pl.*: слёзы, слёз, слеза́м] tear; **~а́ть** [1], ⟨**~ть**⟩ [24 *st.*] come or get down (from); *с лошади* dismount; *coll. о коже, краске* come off; **~и́ться** [15; -и́тся] water; **~ли́вый** [14 *sh.*] given to crying; tearful, lachrymose; **~оточи́вый** [14] *глаза* running; *газ* tear; **~ть** → **~а́ть**

**слеп|е́нь** *m* [4; -пня́] gadfly; **~е́ц** *m* [1; -пца́] blind man; *fig.* one who fails to notice the obvious; **~и́ть 1.** [14 *e.*; -плю́, -пи́шь], ⟨о-⟩ [ослеплённый] blind; *ярким светом* dazzle; **2.** [14] *pf.*; *impf.*: **~ля́ть** [28] stick together (*v/i.* **-ся**) → *a.* **лепи́ть**; **~нуть** [21], ⟨о-⟩ go (*or* become) blind; **~о́й** [14; слеп, -á, -о] blind (*a. fig.*); *текст* indistinct; *su.* blind man; **~ок** *m* [1; -пка] mo(u)ld, cast; **~ота́** *f* [5] blindness

**сле́сар|ь** *m* [4; *pl.*: -ря́, *etc. e.*, & -ри] metalworker; fitter; locksmith

**слет|а́ть** [1], ⟨**~е́ть**⟩ [11] fly down, (from); *coll.* fall (down, off); **-ся** fly together

**слечь** *coll.* [26 г/ж: сля́гу, сля́жешь; сля́г(те)!] *pf.* fall ill; take to one's bed

**сли́ва** *f* [5] plum

**сли|ва́ть** [1], ⟨**~ть**⟩ [солью́, -льёшь; → **лить**] pour (off, out, together); *о фирмах и т. д.* merge, amalgamate (*v/i.* **-ся**)

**сли́в|ки** *f/pl.* [5; *gen.*: -вок] cream (*a. fig.* = elite); **~очный** [14] creamy; **~очное ма́сло** butter; **~очное моро́женое** ice cream

**сли́з|истый** [14 *sh.*] mucous; slimy; **~истая оболо́чка** mucous membrane; **~ь** *f* [8] slime; mucus, phlegm

**слипа́ться** [1] stick together; *о глазах* close

С

**сли́т|ный** [14] joined; united; **~ное написа́ние слов** omission of hyphen from words; **~но** *a.* together; **~ок** *m* [1; -тка] ingot; **~ь(ся)** → **слива́ться**
**слич|а́ть** [1], ⟨**~и́ть**⟩ [16 *e.*; -чу́, -чи́шь; -чённый] compare, collate
**сли́шком** too; too much; **э́то (уж) ~** *coll.* that beats everything
**слия́ние** *n* [12] *рек* confluence; *фирм* amalgamation, merger
**слова́к** *m* [1] Slovak
**слова́р|ный** [14]: **~ный соста́в** stock of words; **~ь** *m* [4 *e.*] dictionary; vocabulary, glossary; lexicon
**слов|а́цкий** [16], **~а́чка** *f* [5; *g/pl.*: -чек] Slovak; **~е́нец** *m* [1; -нца], **~е́нка** *f* [5; *g/pl.*: -нок], **~е́нский** [16] Slovene
**слове́сн|ость** *f* [8] literature; *obs.* philology; **~ый** [14] verbal, oral
**сло́вно** as if; like; *coll.* as it were
**сло́в|о** *n* [9; *pl. e.*] word; **~ом** in a word; **~о за ~о** word for word; speech; **к ~у сказа́ть** by the way; **по слова́м** according to; **проси́ть (предоста́вить** Д**) ~** ask (give p.) permission to speak; **~оизмене́ние** *n* [12] inflection (*Brt.* -xion); **~оохо́тливый** [14 *sh.*] talkative
**слог** *m* [1; *from g/pl. e.*] syllable; style
**слоёный** [14] *тесто* puff pastry
**слож|е́ние** *n* [12] *math.* addition; *человека* constitution, build; *полномочий* laying down; **~и́ть(ся)** → **скла́дывать(ся), слага́ть(ся)** & **класть 2.**; **~ность** *f* [8] complexity; **в о́бщей ~ности** all in all; **~ный** [14; -жен, -жна́, -о] complicated, complex, intricate; *слово* compound
**сло|и́стый** [14 *sh.*] stratiform; flaky; **~й** *m* [3; *pl. e.*: слои́, слоёв] layer, stratum (in T *pl.*); *краски* coat(ing)
**слом** *m* [1] demolition, pulling down; **~и́ть** [14] *pf.* break, smash; *fig.* overcome; **~я́ го́лову** *coll.* headlong, at breakneck speed
**слон** *m* [1 *e.*] elephant; bishop (*chess*); **~о́вый** [14]: **~о́вая кость** ivory
**слоня́ться** *coll.* [28] loiter about
**слу|га́** *m* [5; *pl. st.*] servant; **~жащий** [17] employee; **~жба** *f* [5] service; work; employment; **~жéбный** [14] office…; official; **~же́ние** *n* [12] service; **~жи́ть** [16], ⟨по-⟩ serve (a p./th. Д); be in use
**слух** *m* [1] hearing; ear (**на** B by; **по** Д); rumo(u)r, hearsay; **~ово́й** [14] of hearing; acoustic; ear…
**слу́ча|й** *m* [3] case; occurrence, event; occasion (**по** Д on; **при** П), opportunity, chance; (*a.* **несча́стный ~й**) accident; **во вся́ком ~е** in any case; **в проти́вном ~е** otherwise; **на вся́кий ~й** to be on the safe side; **по ~ю** on the occasion (of P); **~йность** *f* [8] chance; **~йный** [14; -а́ен, -а́йна] accidental, fortuitous; casual, chance (**~йно** by chance); **~ться** [1], ⟨случи́ться⟩ [16 *e.*; *3rd p. or impers.*] happen (**с** T to); come about; take place; **что бы не случи́лось** come what may
**слу́ша|тель** *m* [4] listener, hearer; student; *pl. collect.* audience; **~ть** [1], ⟨по-⟩ listen (B to); *лекции* attend; **~ю!** (*on telephone*) hello!; **-ся** obey (P p.); *совета* take
**слыть** [23], ⟨про-⟩ (T) have a reputation for
**слы́|шать** [4], ⟨у-⟩ hear (of, about **о** П); **~шаться** [4] be heard; **~шимость** *f* [8] audibility; **~шно** one can hear; **мне ~шно** I can hear; **что ~шно?** what's new?; **~шный** [14; -шен, -шна, -о] audible
**слюда́** *f* [5] mica
**слюн|а́** *f* [5], **~и** *coll. pl.* [8; *from gen. e.*] saliva, spittle; **~ки** *coll. f/pl.*: (**у** P) **от э́того ~ки теку́т** makes one's mouth water
**сля́коть** *f* [8] slush
**сма́з|ать** → **~ывать**; **~ка** *f* [5; *g/pl.*: -зок] greasing, oiling, lubrication; lubricant; **~очный** [14] lubricating; **~ывать** [1], ⟨**~ать**⟩ [3] grease, oil, lubricate; *coll. очертания* slur; blur
**сма́|нивать** [1], ⟨**~ни́ть**⟩ [13; сманю́, -а́нишь; -а́ненный & -анённый] lure, entice; **~тывать**, ⟨смота́ть⟩ [1] wind, reel; **~хивать** [1], ⟨**~хну́ть**⟩ [20] brush off (*or* aside); *impf. coll.* (*походить*) have a likeness (**на** B to); **~чивать** [1], ⟨смочи́ть⟩ [16] moisten
**сме́жный** [14; -жен, -жна́] adjacent

С

**смéл|ость** *f* [8] boldness; courage; **~ый** [14; смел, -á, -о] courageous; bold; **~о** *a. coll.* easily; ***могý ~о сказáть*** I can safely say

**смéн|а** *f* [5] shift (**в** В in); change; changing; replacement; successors *pl.*; ***прийтú на ~у → ~úться***; **~я́ть** [28], ⟨**~úть**⟩ [13; -еню́, -éнишь; -енённый] (**-ся** be) supersede(d; o.a.), relieve(d), replace(d by T), substitut(ed; for); give way to

**смерк|áться** [1], ⟨**~нуться**⟩ [20] grow dusky *or* dark

**смерт|éльный** [14; -лен, -льна] mortal; *исход* fatal; *яд* deadly; **~ность** *f* [8] mortality, death rate; **~ный** [14; -тен, -тна] mortal (*a. su.*); *грех* deadly; *law* death…; *казнь* capital; **~ь** *f* [8; *from g/pl. e.*] death; *coll.* ***надоéсть дó ~и*** bore to death; ***прú ~и*** at death's door

**смерч** *m* [1] waterspout; tornado

**сместú → сметáть**; **~ть → смещáть**

**сме|сь** *f* [8] mixture; blend, compound; **~та** *f* [5] *fin.* estimate

**сметáна** *f* [5] sour cream

**сметáть** [1], ⟨**~стú**⟩ [25 -т-] sweep off *or* away; sweep into; ***~ с лицá землú*** wipe off the face of the earth

**смéтливый** [14 *sh.*] sharp, quick on the uptake

**сметь** [8], ⟨по-⟩ dare, venture

**смех** *m* [1] laughter; ***сó ~у*** with laughter; ***~а рáди*** for a joke, for fun, in jest; ***поднять нá ~*** ridicule; **→ *шýтка***

**смéш|анный** [14] mixed; **~áть(ся) → ~ивать(ся)**; **~ивать**, ⟨**~áть**⟩ [1] mix with, blend with (*v/i.* **-ся**; get *or* be[-come]) confuse(d); *с толпой* mingle with

**смеш|úть** [16 *e.*; -шý, -шúшь], ⟨рас-⟩ [-шённый] make laugh; **~нóй** [14; -шóн, -шнá] laughable, ludicrous; ridiculous; funny; ***мне не ~нó*** I don't see anything funny in it

**сме|щáть** [1], ⟨**~стúть**⟩ [15 *e.*; -ещý, -естúшь; -ещённый] displace, shift, remove; **~щéние** *n* [12] displacement, removal

**смея́ться** [27 *e.*; -ею́сь, -еёшься], ⟨за-⟩ laugh (*impf.* **над** T at); mock (at); deride; *coll. шутить* joke

**смир|éние** *n* [12], **~éнность** *f* [8] humility; meekness; **~úть(ся) → ~я́ть(ся)**; **~ный** [14; -рен (*coll.* -рён), -рнá, -о] meek, gentle; (*покорный*) submissive; **~я́ть** [28], ⟨**~úть**⟩ [13] subdue; restrain, check; **-ся** resign o.s. (**с** T to)

**смóкинг** *m* [1] tuxedo, dinner jacket

**смол|á** *f* [5; *pl. st.*] resin; pitch; tar; **~úстый** [14 *sh.*] resinous; **~úть** [13], ⟨вы-, за-⟩ pitch, tar; **~кáть** [1], ⟨**~кнуть**⟩ [21] grow silent; *звук* cease; **~оду** *coll.* from *or* in one's youth; **~янóй** [14] pitch…, tar…

**сморкáться** [1], ⟨вы́-⟩ blow one's nose

**смоpóдина** *f* [5] currant(s *pl.*)

**смотáть → смáтывать**

**смотр|éть** [9; -отрю́, -óтришь; -óтренный], ⟨по-⟩ look (**на** В at), gaze; view, see, watch; *больного и т. д.* examine, inspect; **~я́** depending (**по** Д on), according (to); ***~éть в óба*** keep one's eyes open, be on guard; ***~ú не опоздáй!*** mind you are not late!; **~úтель** *m* [4] supervisor; *музея* custodian, keeper

**смочúть → смáчивать**

**смрад** *m* [1] stench; **~ный** [14; -ден, -дна] stinking

**смýглый** [14; смугл, -á, -о] swarthy

**смут|úть(ся) → смущáть(ся)**; **~ный** [14; -тен, -тна] vague, dim; *на душе* restless, uneasy

**смущ|áть** [1], ⟨смутúть⟩ [15 *e.*; -ущý, -утúшь; -ущённый] (**-ся** be[come]) embarrass(ed), confuse(d), perplex(ed); **~éние** *n* [12] embarrassment, confusion; **~ённый** [14] embarrassed, confused

**смы|вáть** [1], ⟨**~ть**⟩ [22] wash off (*or* away); **~кáть** [1], ⟨сомкнýть⟩ [20] close (*v/i.* **-ся**); **~сл** *m* [1] sense, meaning; ***в э́том ~сле*** in this respect; *coll.* ***какóй ~сл?*** what's the point?; **~слить** *coll.* [13] understand; **~ть → ~вáть**; **~чкóвый** [14] *mus.* stringed; **~чóк** *m* [1; -чкá] *mus.* bow; **~шлёный** *coll.* [14 *sh.*] clever, bright

**смягч|áть** (-xtʃ-) [1], ⟨**~úть**⟩ [16 *e.*; -чý, -чúшь; -чённый] soften (*v/i.* **-ся**); *наказание, боль* mitigate, alleviate; **-ся** *a.*

relent; **~ающий** *law* extenuating; **~ение** *n* [12] mitigation; **~ить(ся)** → **~ать(ся)**
**смятение** *n* [12] confusion
**снаб|жать** [1], ⟨**~дить**⟩ [15 *e.*; -бжу, -бдишь; -бжённый] supply, furnish, provide (with P); **~жение** *n* [12] supply, provision
**снайпер** *m* [1] sharpshooter, sniper
**снаружи** on the outside; from (the) outside
**снаря|д** projectile, missile, shell; *гимнастический* apparatus; **~жать** [1], ⟨**~дить**⟩ [15 *e.*; -яжу, -ядишь; -яжённый] equip, fit out (T with); **~жение** *n* [12] equipment; outfit; *mil.* munitions *pl.*
**снасть** *f* [8; *from g/pl. e.*] tackle; *usu. pl.* rigging
**сначала** at first; first; (*снова*) all over again
**снег** *m* [1; в -у; *pl. e.*: -а] snow; **~ идёт** it is snowing; **~ирь** *m* [4 *e.*] bullfinch; **~опад** *m* [1] snowfall
**снеж|инка** *f* [5; *g/pl.*: -нок] snowflake; **~ный** [14; -жен, -жна] snow(y); **~ок** *m* [1; -жка] *dim.* → **снег**; light snow; snowball
**сни|жать** [1], ⟨**~зить**⟩ [15] lower; (*уменьшить*) reduce, decrease; (**-ся** *v/i.*; *a.* fall) (*себестоимости*) cut production costs; **~жение** *n* [12] lowering; reduction, decrease; fall; **~зойти** → **~сходить**; **~зу** from below
**сним|ать** [1], ⟨**снять**⟩ [сниму, снимешь; снял, -а, -о; снятый (снят, -а, -о)] take (off *or* down); remove, discard; *с работы* sack, dismiss; *кандидатуру* withdraw; *фильм* shoot; *комнату* rent; (take a) photograph (of); *урожай* reap, gather; *осаду* raise; *копию* make; **~ать сливки** skim; **-ся** weigh (**с якоря** anchor); have a picture of o.s. taken; *с учёта* be struck off; **~ок** *m* [1; -мка] photograph, photo, print (**на** П in)
**снискать** [3] get, win
**снисхо|дительный** [14; -лен, -льна] condescending; indulgent; **~дить** [15], ⟨**снизойти**⟩ [-ойду, -ойдёшь; → **идти**] condescend; **~ждение** *n* [12] indulgence, leniency; condescension
**сниться** [13], ⟨**при-**⟩ *impers.* (Д) dream (of И)
**снова** (over) again, anew
**сно|вать** [7 *e.*] scurry about, dash about; **~видение** *n* [12] dream
**сноп** *m* [1 *e.*] sheaf
**сноровка** *f* [5] knack, skill
**снос|ить** [15], ⟨**снести**⟩ [24 -с-: снесу, снёс] carry (down, away *or* off); take; *здание* pull down, demolish; (*терпеть*) endure, bear, tolerate; → *a.* **нести**; **~ка** *f* [5; *g/pl.*: -сок] footnote; **~ный** [14; -сен, -сна] tolerable
**снотворное** *n* [14] *su.* soporific
**сноха** *f* [5; *pl. st.*] daughter-in-law
**снят|ой** [14]: **~ое молоко** skimmed milk; **~ь(ся)** → **снимать(ся)**
**соба|ка** *f* [5] dog; hound; **~чий** [18] dog('s), canine
**собеседник** *m* [1] interlocutor
**собират|ель** *m* [4] collector; **~ельный** [14] *gr.* collective; **~ь** [1], ⟨**собрать**⟩ [-беру, -рёшь; -ал, -а, -о; собранный (-ан, -а, -о)] gather, collect; *tech.* assemble; prepare; **-ся** gather, assemble; prepare for, make o.s. (*or* be) ready to start (*or* set out *or* go; **в путь** on a journey); (*намереваться*) be going to, intend to; collect (**с мыслями** one's thoughts); (*с силами*) brace up
**соблазн** *m* [1] temptation; **~итель** *m* [4] tempter; seducer; **~ительный** [14; -лен, -льна] tempting, seductive; **~ять** [28], ⟨**~ить**⟩ [13] (**-ся** be) tempt(ed); allured, enticed
**соблю|дать** [1], ⟨**~сти**⟩ [25] observe, obey, adhere (to); *порядок* maintain; **~дение** *n* [12] observance; maintenance; **~сти** → **~дать**
**соболезнова|ние** *n* [12] sympathy, condolences; **~ть** [7] sympathize (Д with)
**собо|ль** *m* [4; *pl. a.* -ля, *etc. e.*] sable; **~р** *m* [1] cathedral
**собра|ние** *n* [12] meeting (**на** В at, in), assembly; collection; **~ть(ся)** → **собирать(ся)**
**собственн|ик** *m* [1] owner, proprietor; **~ость** *f* [8] property; possession, ownership; **~ый** [14] own; *имя* proper; person-

С

al
**собы́тие** *n* [12] event, occurrence
**сова́** *f* [5; *pl. st.*] owl
**сова́ть** [7 *e.*; сую́, суёшь], ⟨**су́нуть**⟩ [20] shove, thrust; *coll.* slip; butt in, poke one's nose into
**соверш|а́ть** [1], ⟨**~и́ть**⟩ [16 *e.*; -шу́, -ши́шь; -шённый] accomplish; *преступление и т. д.* commit; *поездку и т. д.* make; *сделку* strike; **-ся** happen, take place; **~еннолéтие** *n* [12] majority, full age; **~еннолéтний** [15] (***стать*** T come) of age; **~éнный** [14; -éнен, -éнна] perfect(ive *gr.*); *coll.* absolute, complete; *adv. a.* quite; **~éнство** *n* [9] perfection; ***в ~éнстве*** *a.* perfectly; **~éнствовать** [7], ⟨**у-**⟩ perfect (**-ся** o.s.), improve, develop; **~и́ть(ся)** → ***соверша́ть(ся)***
**со́вест|ливый** [14 *sh.*] conscientious; **~но** (р. Д) ashamed; **~ь** *f* [8] conscience; ***по ~и*** honestly, to be honest
**совéт** *m* [1] advice; *law* opinion; board; soviet; **≈ *Безопа́сности*** Security Council; **~ник** *m* [1] adviser; (*as title of office or post*) councillor; **~овать** [7], ⟨**по-**⟩ advise (Д р.); **-ся** ask advice, consult (**о** П on); **~ский** [16] soviet (of local bodies); **~чик** *m* [1] adviser
**совеща́|ние** *n* [12] conference (at ***на*** П), meeting (*a.* in); (*обсуждение*) deliberation; **~тельный** [14] deliberative, consultative; **~ться** [1] confer, consult, deliberate
**совме|сти́мый** [14 *sh.*] compatible; **~сти́ть** → ***~ща́ть***; **~́стный** [14] joint, combined; **~́стно** common; **~ща́ть** [1], ⟨**~сти́ть**⟩ [15 *e.*; -ещу́, -ести́шь; -ещённый] combine; *tech.* match
**совóк** *m* [1; -вка́] shovel; scoop; *для мусора* dustpan
**совоку́пн|ость** *f* [8] total(ity), aggregate, whole; **~ый** [14] joint
**совпа|да́ть** [1], ⟨**~́сть**⟩ [25; *pt. st.*] coincide with; agree with; **~дéние** *n* [12] coincidence, *etc.* → *vb.*
**совремéнн|ик** *m* [1] contemporary; **~ый** [14; -éнен, -éнна] contemporaneous; of the time (of); present-day; up-to-date; → *a.* ***~ик*** contemporary
**совсéм** quite, entirely; at all; ***я его́ ~ не зна́ю*** I don't know him at all
**совхóз** *m* [1] (**совéтское хозя́йство**) state farm; → ***колхóз***
**согла́|сие** *n* [12] consent (***на*** В to; **с** Р with); agreement (***по*** Д by); harmony, concord; **~си́ться** → ***~ша́ться***; **~сно** (Д) according to, in accordance with; **~сный** [14; -сен, -сна] agreeable; harmonious; ***я ~сен*** (*f* ***~сна***) I agree (**с** T with; ***на*** В to); (*a. su.*) consonant; **~сова́ние** *n* [12] coordination; *gr.* agreement; **~сова́ть** → ***~сóвывать***; **~сова́ться** [7] (*im*)*pf.* (**с** T) conform (to); agree (with); **~сóвывать** [1], ⟨**~сова́ть**⟩ [7] coordinate; come to an agreement (**с** T with); (*a. gr.*) make agree; **~ша́ться** [1], ⟨**~си́ться**⟩ [15 *e.*; -ашу́сь, -аси́шься] agree (**с** T with; ***на*** В to), consent (to); *coll.* (*признавать*) admit; **~шéние** *n* [12] agreement, understanding; covenant
**согна́ть** → ***сгоня́ть***
**согну́ть(ся)** → ***сгиба́ть(ся)***
**согре|ва́ть** [1], ⟨**~́ть**⟩ [28] warm, heat
**содéйств|ие** *n* [12] assistance, help; **~овать** [7] (*im*)*pf.*, *a.* ⟨**по-**⟩ (Д) assist, help; *успеху, согласию* contribute (to), further, promote
**содерж|а́ние** *n* [12] content(s); *семьи и т. д.* maintenance, support, upkeep; **~а́тельный** [14; -лен, -льна] pithy, having substance and point; **~а́ть** [4] contain, hold; maintain, support; keep; **-ся** be contained, *etc.*; **~и́мое** [14] contents *pl.*
**содра́ть** → ***сдира́ть***
**содрог|а́ние** *n* [12], **~а́ться** [1], *once* ⟨**~ну́ться**⟩ [20] shudder
**содру́жеств|о** *n* [9] community; concord; ***Брита́нское ~о на́ций*** the British Commonwealth; ***в тéсном ~е*** in close cooperation (**с** T with)
**соедин|éние** *n* [12] joining; conjunction, (at *a.* ***на*** П), connection; combination; *chem.* compound; *tech.* joint; **~и́тельный** [14] connective; *a. gr.* copulative; **~я́ть** [28], ⟨**~и́ть**⟩ [13] unite, join; connect; link (*by telephone, etc.*); (*v/i.* **-ся**); → ***США***

С

**сожал|éние** *n* [12] regret (**о** П for); ***к ~éнию*** unfortunately, to (p.'s) regret; **~éть** [8] (**о** П) regret

**сожжéние** *n* [12] burning; cremation

**сожúтельство** *n* [9] cohabitation

**созв|áть** → ***созывáть***; **~éздие** *n* [12] constellation; **~онúться** *coll.* [13] *pf.* (**с** Т) speak on the phone; arrange s.th. on the phone; phone; **~ýчный** [14; -чен, -чна] in keeping with, consonant with

**созда|вáть** [5], ⟨**~́ть**⟩ [-дáм, -дáшь *etc.*, → ***дать***; сóздал, -á, -о; сóзданный (-ан, -á, -о)] create; produce; found; establish; **-ся** arise, form; ***у меня́ ~лóсь впечатлéние*** I have gained the impression that …; **~́ние** *n* [12] creation; (*существо*) creature; **~́тель** *m* [4] creator; founder; **~́ть(ся)** → ***~вáть(ся)***

**созерцáт|ельный** [14; -лен, -льна] contemplative; **~ь** [1] contemplate

**созидáтельный** [14; -лен, -льна] creative

**созна|вáть** [5], ⟨**~́ть**⟩ [1] realize, be conscious of, see; **-ся** (**в** П) confess; **~́ние** *n* [12] consciousness; ***без ~́ния*** unconscious; **~́тельный** [14; -лен, -льна] conscious; *отношение и т. д.* conscientious; **~́ть(ся)** → ***~вáть(ся)***

**созы́в** *m* [1] convocation; **~́ать** [1], ⟨**созвáть**⟩ [созовý, -вёшь; -звáл, -á, -о; сóзванный] *гостей* invite; *собрание* call, convene; *parl.* convoke

**соизмерúмый** [14 *sh.*] commensurable

**сойтú(сь)** → ***сходúть(ся)***

**сок** *m* [1; в -ý] juice; *берёзовый и т. д.* sap; **~овыжимáлка** *f* [5; -лок] juice extractor

**сóкол** *m* [1] falcon

**сокра|щáть** [1], ⟨**~тúть**⟩ [15 *e.*; -ащý, -атúшь; -ащённый] shorten; abbreviate; abridge; *расходы* reduce, curtail; *p. pt. p. a.* short, brief; **-ся** grow shorter; decrease; *о мышцах и т. д.* contract; **~щéние** *n* [12] shortening, abbreviation, reduction, curtailment; *текста* abridgement; contraction

**сокров|éнный** [14 *sh.*] innermost; secret; concealed; **~́ище** *n* [11] treasure; **~́ищница** *f* [5] treasury

**сокруш|áть** [1], ⟨**~úть**⟩ [16 *e.*; -шý, -шúшь; -шённый] shatter, smash; ***~úть врагá*** rout the enemy; **-ся** *impf.* grieve, be distressed; **~úтельный** [14; -лен, -льна] shattering; **~úть** → ***~áть***

**солдáт** *m* [1; *g/pl.*: солдáт] soldier; **~ский** [16] soldier's

**сол|éние** *n* [12] salting; **~ёный** [14; сóлон, -á, -о] salt(y); corned; pickled; *fig.* spicy; (*short forms only*) hot

**солидáрн|ость** *f* [8] solidarity; **~ый** [14; -рен, -рна] in sympathy with, at one with; *law* jointly liable

**солúдн|ость** *f* [8] solidity; **~ый** [14; -ден, -дна] solid, strong, sound; *фирма* reputable, respectable; *coll.* sizable

**солúст** *m* [1], **~ка** *f* [5; *g/pl.*: -ток] soloist

**солúть** [13; солю́, сóлишь; сóленный] **1.** ⟨по-⟩ salt; **2.** ⟨за-⟩ corn; pickle; ⟨на-⟩ *coll.* spite; cause annoyance; do s.o. a bad turn

**сóлн|ечный** [14; -чен, -чна] sun(ny); solar; **~це** ('son-) *n* [11] sun (**на** П *lie* in); **~цепёк** *m* [1]: ***на ~цепёке*** in the blazing sun

**соловéй** *m* [3; -вья́] nightingale

**сóлод** *m* [1], **~овый** [14] malt

**солóм|а** *f* [5] straw; thatch; **~енный** [14] straw…; thatched; grass (*widow*); **~инка** *f* [5; *g/pl.*: -нок] straw; ***хватáться за ~инку*** clutch at straws

**солóнка** *f* [5; *g/pl.*: -нок] saltcellar

**сол|ь** *f* [8; *from g/pl. e.*] salt (*a. fig.*); *coll.* ***вот в чём вся ~ь*** that's the whole point; **~янóй** [14] salt…; saline

**сом** *m* [1 *e.*] catfish

**сомкнýть(ся)** → ***смыкáть(ся)***

**сомн|евáться** [1], ⟨усомнúться⟩ [13] (**в** П) doubt; **~éние** *n* [12] doubt (**в** П about); question (**под** Т in); **~úтельный** [14; -лен, -льна] doubtful; questionable, dubious

**сон** *m* [1; сна] sleep; dream (in **в** П); **~лúвый** [14 *sh.*] sleepy; **~́ный** [14] sleeping (*a. med.*); sleepy, drowsy; **~́я** *coll. m/f* [6; *g/pl.*: -ней] sleepyhead

**сообра|жáть** [1], ⟨**~зúть**⟩ [15 *e.*; -ажý, -азúшь; -ажённый] consider, weigh, think (over); (*понять*) grasp, understand; **~жéние** *n* [12] consideration;

С

(*причина*) reason; **~зи́тельный** [14; -лен, -льна] sharp, quick-witted; **~зи́ть** → **~жа́ть**; **~зный** [14; -зен, -зна] conformable (**с** T to); *adv. a.* in conformity (with); **~зова́ть** [7] (*im*)*pf.* (make) comform, adapt (to) (**с** T); **-ся** conform, adapt (**с** T to)

**сообща́** together, jointly

**сообщ|а́ть** [1], ⟨**~и́ть**⟩ [16 *e.*; -щу́, -щи́шь; -щённый] communicate (*v/i.* **-ся** *impf.*), report; inform (Д/**о** П p. of); impart; **~е́ние** *n* [12] communication, report; statement; announcement; information; **~ество** *n* [9] association, fellowship; community; **~и́ть** → **~а́ть**; **~ник** *m* [1], **~ница** *f* [5] accomplice

**соору|жа́ть** [1], ⟨**~ди́ть**⟩ [15 *e.*; -ужу́, -уди́шь; -ужённый] build, construct, erect, raise; **~же́ние** *n* [12] construction, building, structure

**соотве́тств|енный** [14 *sh.*] corresponding; *adv. a.* according(ly) (Д to), in accordance (with); **~ие** *n* [12] conformity, accordance; **~овать** [7] (Д) correspond, conform (to), agree; **~ующий** [17] corresponding, appropriate; suitable

**соotéчественни|к** *m* [1], **~ца** *f* [5] compatriot, fellow country (wo)man

**соотноше́ние** *n* [12] correlation

**сопе́рни|к** *m* [1] rival; **~чать** [1] compete, vie (with); rival; be a match (for **с** T); **~чество** *n* [9] rivalry

**соп|е́ть** [10 *e.*; соплю́, сопи́шь] breathe heavily through the nose; wheeze; **~ка** *f* [5; *g/pl.*: -пок] hill; volcano; **~ли** P *pl.* [6; *gen.*: -лей, *etc. e.*] snot

**сопостав|ле́ние** *n* [12] comparison; confrontation; **~ля́ть** [28], ⟨**~вить**⟩ [14] compare

**сопри|каса́ться** [1], ⟨**~косну́ться**⟩ [20] (**с** T) (*примыкать*) adjoin; (*касаться*) touch; *с людьми* deal with; **~косновéние** *n* [12] contact

**сопрово|ди́тельный** [14] covering (*letter*); **~жда́ть** [1] **1.** accompany; escort; **2.** ⟨**~ди́ть**⟩ [15 *e.*; -ожу́, -оди́шь; -ождённый] *примечанием и т. д.* provide (T with); **-ся** *impf.* be accompanied (T by); entail; **~жде́ние** *n* [12] accompaniment; **в ~жде́нии** (P) accompanied (by)

**сопротивл|е́ние** *n* [12] resistance; opposition; **~я́ться** [28] (Д) resist; oppose

**сопряжённый** [14; -жён, -жена́] connected with; entailing

**сопу́тствовать** [14] (Д) accompany

**сор** *m* [1] dust; litter

**соразме́рно** in proportion (Д to)

**сорв|ане́ц** *coll. m* [1; -нца́] madcap; (*of a child*) a terror; **~а́ть(ся)** → **срыва́ть(ся)**; **~иголова́** *coll. m/f* [5; *ac/sg.*: сорвиголову́; *pl.* → **голова́**] daredevil

**соревнова́|ние** *n* [12] competition; contest; ***отбо́рочные ~ния*** heats, qualifying rounds; **~ться** [7] (**с** T) compete (with)

**сор|и́ть** [13], ⟨на-⟩ litter; *fig. деньгами* squander; **~ный** [14]: ***~ная трава́*** = **~ня́к** *m* [1 *e.*] weed

**со́рок** [35] forty; **~а** *f* [5] magpie

**сороко|во́й** [14] fortieth; → ***пят(идеся́т)ый***; **~но́жка** *f* [5; *g/pl.*: -жек] centipede

**соро́чка** *f* [5; -чек] shirt; undershirt; chemise

**сорт** *m* [1; *pl.*: -та́, *etc. e.*] sort, brand; variety, quality; **~ирова́ть** [7], ⟨рас-⟩ sort out; *по размеру* grade; **~иро́вка** *f* [5] sorting

**соса́ть** [-су́, -сёшь; со́санный] suck

**сосе́д** *m* [*sg.*: 1; *pl.*: 4], **~ка** *f* [5; *g/pl.*: -док] neighbo(u)r; **~ний** [15] neighbo(u)ring, adjoining; **~ский** [16] neighbo(u)r's; **~ство** *n* [9] neighbo(u)rhood

**соси́ска** *f* [5; *g/pl.*: -сок] sausage; frankfurter

**со́ска** *f* [5; *g/pl.*: -сок] (*baby's*) dummy, pacifier

**соск|а́кивать** [1], ⟨**~очи́ть**⟩ [16] jump *or* spring (off, down); come off; **~а́льзывать** [1], ⟨**~ользну́ть**⟩ [20] slide (down, off); slip (off); **~у́читься** [16] *pf.* become bored; miss (**по** Д); → **скуча́ть**

**сосл|ага́тельный** [14] *gr.* subjunctive; **~а́ть(ся)** → **ссыла́ться**; **~ужи́вец** *m* [1; -вца] colleague

**сосна́** *f* [5; *pl. st.*: со́сны, со́сен, со́снам] pine tree

**сосо́к** *m* [1; -ска́] nipple, teat

С

**сосредото́ч|ение** *n* [12] concentration; **~ивать** [1], ⟨**~ить**⟩ [16] concentrate (*v/i.* **-ся**); *p. pt. p. a.* intent

**соста́в** *m* [1] composition (*a. chem.*); structure; *студентов и т. д.* body; *thea.* cast; *rail.* train; ***подвижно́й ~*** rolling stock; ***в ~е*** (P) *a.* consisting of; **~и́тель** *m* [4] compiler; author; **~ить** → ***~ля́ть***; **~ле́ние** *n* [12] *словаря и т. д.* compilation; *документа и т. д.* drawing up; **~ля́ть** [28], ⟨**~ить**⟩ [14] compose, make (up); put together; *план и т. д.* draw up, work out; compile; (*образовывать*) form, constitute; (*равняться*) amount (*or* come) to; **~ной** [14]: composite; ***~на́я часть*** constituent part; component

**состоя́|ние** *n* [12] state, condition; position; (*богатство*) fortune; ***быть в ~нии ...*** *a.* be able to ...; ***я не в ~нии*** I am not in a position ...; **~тельный** [14; -лен, -льна] well-to-do, well-off; (*обоснованный*) sound, well-founded; **~ть** [-ою́, -ои́шь] consist (***из*** P of; **в** П in); *членом и т. д.* be (*a.* T); **-ся** *pf.* take place

**сострада́ние** *n* [12] compassion, sympathy

**состяза́|ние** *n* [12] contest, competition; match; **~ться** [1] compete, vie, contend (with)

**сосу́д** *m* [1] vessel

**сосу́лька** *f* [5; *g/pl.*: -лек] icicle

**сосуществова́|ние** *n* [12] coexistence; **~ть** [7] coexist

**сотворе́ние** *n* [12] creation

**со́тня** *f* [6; *g/pl.*: -тен] a hundred

**сотру́дни|к** *m* [1] employee; *pl.* staff; *газеты* contributor; colleague; **~чать** [1] collaborate with; contribute to; **~чество** *n* [9] collaboration, cooperation

**сотрясе́ние** *n* [12] shaking; *мозга* concussion

**со́ты** *m/pl.* [1] honeycomb(s); **~й** [14] hundredth; → ***пя́тый***; ***две це́лых и два́дцать пять ~х*** 2.25

**со́ус** *m* [1] sauce; gravy

**соуча́ст|ие** *n* [12] complicity; **~ник** *m* [1] accomplice

**со́хнуть** [21] **1.** ⟨вы́-⟩ dry; **2.** ⟨за-⟩ *coll.* wither; **3.** *coll. impf.* pine away

**сохран|е́ние** *n* [12] preservation; conservation; **~и́ть(ся)** → **~я́ть(ся)**; **~́ность** *f* [8] safety; undamaged state; ***в ~́ности*** *a.* safe; **~я́ть** [28], ⟨**~и́ть**⟩ [13] keep; preserve; retain; maintain; reserve (for o.s. ***за собо́й***); ***Бо́же сохрани́!*** God forbid!; **-ся** be preserved; *в памяти и т. д.* remain

**социа́л|-демокра́т** *m* [1] social democrat; **~́-демократи́ческий** [16] social democrat(ic); **~и́зм** *m* [1] socialism; **~и́ст** *m* [1] socialist; **~исти́ческий** [16] socialist(ic); **~ьный** [14] social

**соцстра́х** *m* [1] social insurance

**соче́льник** *m* [1] Christmas Eve

**сочета́|ние** *n* [12] combination; **~ть** [1] combine (*v/i.* **-ся**)

**сочин|е́ние** *n* [12] composition; writing, work; *научное* thesis; *gr.* coordination; **~я́ть** [28], ⟨**~и́ть**⟩ [13] compose (*a lit. or mus. work*); write; (*выдумать*) invent, make up

**соч|и́ться** [16 *e.*; 3[rd] *p. only*] exude; ooze (out); *о крови* bleed; **~** [14; -чен, -чна] juicy; *fig.* succulent; rich

**сочу́вств|енный** [14 *sh.*] sympathetic, sympathizing; **~ие** *n* [12] sympathy (**к** Д with, for); **~овать** [7] (Д) sympathize with, feel for; **~ующий** [17] sympathizer

**сою́з** *m* [1] union; alliance; confederation; league; *gr.* conjunction; **~ник** *m* [1] ally; **~ный** [14] allied

**со́я** *f* [6] soya bean

**спа|д** *m* [1] *econ.* recession, slump; **~да́ть** [1], ⟨**~сть**⟩ [25; *pt. st.*] fall; **~́ивать 1.** ⟨**~я́ть**⟩ [28] solder; **2.** *coll.* ⟨спои́ть⟩ [13] accustom to drinking; **~́йка** *f* [5] *fig.* union

**спа́льн|ый** [14] sleeping; bed…; ***~ое ме́сто*** bunk, berth; **~я** *f* [6; *g/pl.*: -лен] bedroom

**спа́ржа** *f* [5] asparagus

**спас|а́тель** *m* [4] one of a rescue team; (*at seaside*) lifeguard; **~а́тельный** [14] rescue…; life-saving; **~а́ть** [1], ⟨**~ти́**⟩ [24 -с-] save, rescue; ***~ти́ положе́ние*** save the situation; **-ся**, ⟨-сь⟩ save o.s.; *a.* escape (*v/i.* **от** P); **~е́ние** *n* [12] rescue;

escape; salvation

**спаси́бо (вам)** thank you (very much **большо́е ~**), thanks (**за** В, **на** П for)

**спаси́тель** *m* [4], ♀ the Savio(u)r; rescuer; **~ный** [14] saving

**спас|ти́** → **~а́ть**; **~ть** → **спада́ть**

**спать** [сплю, спишь; спал, -á, -о] sleep; be asleep; (*a.* **идти́, ложи́ться ~**) go to bed; *coll.* **мне не спи́тся** I can't (get to) sleep

**спая́ть** → **спа́ивать** *1*

**спека́ться** [1] *coll.* → **запека́ться**

**спекта́кль** *m* [4] *thea.* performance; show

**спекул|и́ровать** [7] speculate (Т in); **~я́нт** *m* [1] speculator, profiteer; **~я́ция** *f* [7] speculation (in); profiteering; *philos.* speculation

**спе́лый** [14; спел, -á, -о] ripe

**сперва́** *coll.* (at) first

**спе́реди** in front (of); at the front, from the front (*as prp.*: Р)

**спёртый** *coll.* [14 *sh.*] stuffy, close

**спеть** [8], ⟨по-⟩ ripen; → *a.* **петь**

**спех** *coll. m* [1]: **не к ~у** there is no hurry

**специ|ализи́роваться** [7] (*im*)*pf.* specialize (**в** П, **по** Д in); **~али́ст** *m* [1] specialist, expert (**по** Д in); **~а́льность** *f* [8] speciality, special interest, profession (**по** Д by); **~а́льный** [14; -лен, -льна] special; **~фи́ческий** [16] specific

**спе́ция** *f* [7] *mst.pl.* spice

**спецоде́жда** *f* [5] working clothes; overalls *pl.*

**спеш|и́ть** [16 *e.*; -шу́, -ши́шь] hurry (up), hasten; of *clock* be fast (**на пять мину́т** 5 min.); **~ка** *coll. f* [5] haste, hurry; **~ный** [14; -шен, -шна] urgent, pressing; **в ~ном поря́дке** quickly

**спин|а́** *f* [5; *ac. sg.*: спи́ну; *pl. st.*] back; **~ка** *f* [5; *g/pl.*: -нок] *of piece of clothing or furniture* back; **~но́й** [14] spinal (**мозг** cord); vertebral (**хребе́т** column), back (*bone*)

**спи́ннинг** *m* [1] (*method of fishing*) spinning

**спира́ль** *f* [8], **~ный** [14] spiral

**спирт** *m* [1; *a.* в -у́; *pl. e.*] alcohol, spirit(s *pl.*); **~но́й** [14] alcoholic; *напиток тж.* strong

**спис|а́ть** → **~ывать**; **~ок** *m* [1; -ска] list, register; **~ывать** [1], ⟨**~а́ть**⟩ [3] copy; *долг и т. д.* write (off); plagiarize, crib; *naut.* transfer, post (out of)

**спи́х|ивать** [1], *once* ⟨**~ну́ть**⟩ *coll.* [20] push (down, aside)

**спи́ца** *f* [5] spoke; knitting needle

**спи́чка** *f* [5; *g/pl.*: -чек] match

**сплав** *m* [1] **1.** alloy; **2.** *леса* float(ing); **~ля́ть** [28], ⟨**~ить**⟩ [14] **1.** alloy; **2.** float

**спла́чивать** [1], ⟨сплоти́ть⟩ [15 *e.*; -очу́, -оти́шь; -очённый] rally (*v/i.* **-ся**)

**сплет|а́ть** [1], ⟨сплести́⟩ [25 -т-] plait, braid; (inter)lace; **~е́ние** *n* [12] interlacing; **со́лнечное ~е́ние** solar plexus; **~ник** *m* [1], **~ница** *f* [5] scandalmonger; **~ничать** [1], ⟨на-⟩ gossip; **~ня** *f* [6; *g/pl.*: -тен] gossip

**спло|ти́ть(ся)** → **спла́чивать(ся)**; **~хова́ть** *coll.* [7] *pf.* blunder; **~че́ние** *n* [12] rallying; **~шно́й** [14] *масса и т. д.* solid, compact; (*непрерывный*) continuous; *coll.* sheer, utter; **~шь** throughout, entirely, all over; **~шь и ря́дом** quite often

**сплю́щить** [16] *pf.* flatten, laminate

**спои́ть** → **спа́ивать** *2*

**споко́й|ный** [14; -оен, -о́йна] calm, quiet, tranquil; (*сдержанный*) composed; **~но** *coll.* → **сме́ло** *coll.*; **~ной но́чи!** good night!; **бу́дьте ~ны!** don't worry!; **~ствие** *n* [12] calm(ness), tranquillity; composure; *в обществе и т. д.* peace, order

**сполз|а́ть** [1], ⟨**~ти́**⟩ [24] climb down (from); *fig. coll.* slip (into)

**сполна́...** wholly, in full

**сполосну́ть** [20] *pf.* rinse (out)

**спо́нсор** *m* [1] sponsor

**спор** *m* [1] dispute, controversy, argument; **~у нет** undoubtedly; **~ить** [13], ⟨по-⟩ dispute, argue, debate; *coll. держать пари* bet (on); **~иться** *coll.* [13] *работа* go well; **~ный** [14; -рен, -рна] disputable, questionable

**спорт** *m* [1] sport; **лы́жный ~** skiing; **~и́вный** [14] sporting, athletic; sport(s)...; **~и́вный зал** gymnasium; **~сме́н** *m* [1] sportsman; **~сме́нка** *f* [5; *g/pl.*: -нок] sportswoman

**спо́соб** *m* [1] method, means; way, mode

(T in); *употребления* directions *pl.* (for *use* P); **˷ность** *f* [8] (cap)ability (**к** Д for), talent; *к языкам и т. д.* faculty, capacity; power; ***покупáтельная ˷ность*** purchasing power; **˷ный** [14; -бен, -бна] (**к** Д) able, talented, clever (at); capable (of; *a.* **на** B); **˷ствовать** [7], 〈по-〉 (Д) promote, further, contribute to

**спот|ыкáться** [1], 〈**˷кнýться**〉 [20] stumble (**о** B against, over)

**спохвáт|ываться** [1], 〈**˷иться**〉 [15] suddenly remember

**спрáва** to the right (of)

**справедлúв|ость** *f* [8] justice, fairness; **˷ый** [14 *sh.*] just, fair; (*правильный*) true, right

**спрáв|иться** → ***˷ля́ться***; **˷ка** *f* [5; *g/pl.*: -вок] inquiry (make ***наводúть***); information; certificate; **˷ля́ться** inquiry (**о** П about); consult (*v/t.* **в** П); (**с** T) manage, cope with; **˷очник** *m* [1] reference book; *телефонный* directory; *путеводитель* guide; **˷очный** [14] (of) *бюро* inquiries…; *книга* reference…

**спрáшива|ть** [1], 〈спросúть〉 [15] ask (p. *a.* **у** P; for s.th. *a.* P), inquire; (**с** P) make answer for, call to account; ***˷ется*** one may ask

**спрос** *m* [1] *econ.* demand (**на** B for); ***без ˷а*** *or* ***˷у*** *coll.* without permission; ***˷ и предложéние*** supply and demand

**спросóнок** *coll.* half asleep

**спростá**: *coll.* **не ˷** it's not by chance

С

**спры|гивать** [1], *once* 〈**˷гнуть**〉 [20] jump down (from); **˷скивать** [1], 〈**˷снуть**〉 [20] sprinkle

**спря|гáть** [1], 〈про-〉 *gr.* (**-ся** *impf.* be) conjugate(d); **˷жéние** *n* [12] *gr.* conjugation

**спуг|ивать** [1], 〈**˷нýть**〉 [20; -нý, -нёшь] frighten off

**спус|к** *m* [1] lowering; descent; *склон* slope; *корабля* launch(ing); *воды* drain(ing); ***не давáть ˷ку*** (Д) *coll.* give no quarter; **˷кáть** [1], 〈**˷тúть**〉 [15] lower, let down; launch; drain; *собаку* unchain, set free; *курок* pull; *о шине* go down; **-ся** go (*or* come) down (*stairs по лестнице*), descend; **˷тя́** (B) later, after

**спýтни|к** *m* [1], **˷ца** *f* [5] travelling companion; *жизни* companion; **˷к** *astr.* satellite; *искусственный тж.* sputnik

**спя́чка** *f* [5] hibernation

**сравн|éние** *n* [12] comparison (**по** Д/**с** T in/with); *lit.* simile; **˷ивать** [1] **1.** 〈**˷úть**〉 [13] compare (**с** T; *v/i.* **-ся** to, with); **2.** 〈**˷я́ть**〉 [28] level, equalize; **˷úтельный** [14] comparative; **˷úть(ся)** → ***˷ивать(ся)***; **˷я́ть** → ***˷ивать*** *2*

**сра|жáть** [1], 〈**˷зúть**〉 [15 *e.*; -ажý, -азúшь; -ажённый] smite; overwhelm; **-ся** fight, battle; *coll.* contend, play; **˷жéние** *n* [12] battle; **˷зúть(ся)** → ***˷жáть*(ся)**

**срáзу** at once, straight away

**срам** *m* [1] shame, disgrace; **˷úть** [14 *e.*; -млю́, -мúшь], 〈о-〉 [осрамлённый] disgrace, shame, compromise; **-ся** bring shame upon o.s

**сраст|áться** [1], 〈**˷úсь**〉 [24 -ст-; срóсся, срослáсь] *med.* grow together, knit

**сред|á** *f* **1.** [5; *ac/sg.*: срéду; *nom/pl. st.*] Wednesday (on: **в** B, *pl.*: **по** Д); **2.** [5; *ac/sg.*: *-ду*; *pl. st.*] environment, surroundings *pl.*, milieu; *phys.* medium; midst; ***в нáшей ˷é*** in our midst; **˷ú** (P) among, in the middle (of), amid(st); **˷изéмный** [14], **˷иземномóрский** [16] Mediterranean; **˷невекóвый** [14] medieval; **˷ний** [15] middle; medium…; central; (*посредственный*) middling; average… (**в** П on); *math.* mean; *gr.* neuter; *школа* secondary

**средотóчие** *n* [12] focus, center (*Brt.* -tre)

**срéдство** *n* [9] means ([**не**] **по** Д *pl.* within [beyond] one's); (*лекарство*) remedy; *pl. a.* facilities

**срéз|ать**, **˷ывать** [1], 〈**˷ать**〉 [3] cut off; *coll. на экзамене* fail (*v/i.* **˷аться**)

**сровня́ть** → ***срáвнивать*** *2*

**сро|к** *m* [1] term (T/**на** B for/of), date, deadline; time (**в** B; **к** Д in, on), period; ***продлúть ˷к вúзы*** extend a visa; **˷чный** [14; -чен, -чнá, -о] urgent, pressing; at a fixed date

**сруб|áть** [1], 〈**˷úть**〉 [14] cut down, fell; *дом* build of logs

**сры|в** *m* [1] frustration; derangement; *переговоров* breakdown; **~вáть** [1], ⟨сорвáть⟩ [-ву, -вёшь; сорвáл, -á, -о; сóрванный] tear off; *цветы и т. д.* pluck, pick; *планы и т. д.* disrupt, frustrate; *злость* vent; **-ся** (**с** P) come off; break away (*or* loose); fall down; *coll. с места* dart off; *о планах* fail, miscarry

**ссáди|на** *f* [5] scratch, abrasion; **~ть** [15] *pf.* graze

**ссáживать** [1], ⟨ссади́ть⟩ [15; -жý, -дишь] help down; help alight; make get off (*public transport*)

**ссóр|а** *f* [5] quarrel; **~иться** [13], ⟨по-⟩ quarrel, falling-out

**ссýд|а** *f* [5] loan; **~и́ть** [15] *pf.* lend, loan

**ссыл|áть** [1], ⟨сослáть⟩ [сошлю́, -лёшь; сóсланный] exile, deport, banish; **-ся** (**на** B) refer to, cite; **~ка** *f* [5; *g/pl.*: -лок] **1.** exile; **2.** reference (**на** B to)

**ссыпá|ть** [1], ⟨**~ть**⟩ [2] pour

**стабил|из(и́р)овать** [7] (*im*)*pf.* stabilize; **~ьный** [14; -лен, -льна] stable, firm

**стáвень** *m* [4; -вня] shutter (*for window*)

**стáв|ить** [14], ⟨по-⟩ put, place, set, stand; *часы и т. д.* set; *памятник и т. д.* put (*or* set) up; *на лошадь* stake, (**на** B) back; *thea.* stage; *условия* make; *в известность* inform, bring to the notice of; **~ить в тупи́к** nonplus; **~ка** *f* [5; *g/pl.*: -вок] (*учётная и т. д.*) rate; (*зарплата*) wage, salary; **сдéлать ~ку** gamble (on **на** B); **~ленник** *m* [1] protegé; **~ня** *f* [6; *g/pl.*: -вен] → **~ень**

**стадиóн** *m* [1] stadium (**на** П in)

**стáдия** *f* [7] stage

**стáдо** *n* [9; *pl. e.*] herd, flock

**стаж** *m* [1] length of service

**стажёр** *m* [1] probationer; student in special course not leading to degree

**стакáн** *m* [1] glass

**стáлкивать** [1], ⟨столкнýть⟩ [20] push (off, away); **-ся** (**с** T) come into collision with; *a. fig.* conflict with; *с кем-л.* come across; run into

**сталь** *f* [8] steel; **нержавéющая ~** stainless steel; **~нóй** [14] steel…

**стамéска** *f* [5; *g/pl.*: -сок] chisel

**стандáрт** *m* [1] standard; **~ный** [14; -тен, -тна] standard…

**стани́ца** *f* [5] Cossack village

**станови́ться** [14], ⟨стать⟩ [стáну, -нешь] *impf.* (T) become, grow, get; stand; stop; **~ в óчередь** get in line, *Brt.* queue up; *pf.* begin to; start; *лучше* feel; **во что бы то ни стáло** at all costs, at any cost

**станóк** *m* [1; -нка] machine; *токарный* lathe; *печатный* press; **ткáцкий ~** loom

**стáнция** *f* [7] station (**на** П at); *tel.* exchange

**стáптывать** [1], ⟨стоптáть⟩ [3] trample; (*сносить*) wear out

**старá|ние** *n* [12] pains *pl.*, care; endeavo(u)r; **~тельный** [14; -лен, -льна] assiduous, diligent; painstaking; **~ться** [1], ⟨по-⟩ endeavo(u)r, try (hard)

**стар|éть** [21] **1.** ⟨по-⟩ grow old, age; **2.** ⟨у-⟩ grow obsolete; **~и́к** *m* [1 *e.*] old man; **~инá** *f* [5] olden times, days of yore (**в** B in); *coll.* old man *or* chap; **~и́нный** [14] ancient, antique; old; *обычай* time-hono(u)red; **~ить** [13], ⟨со-⟩ make (**-ся** grow) old

**старо|мóдный** [14; -ден, -дна] old-fashioned, out-of-date; **´~ста** *m класса* prefect, monitor; **´~сть** *f* [8] old age (in one's **на** П **лет**)

**стартовáть** [7] (*im*)*pf. sport* start; *ae.* take off

**стар|ýха** *f* [5] old woman; **~ческий** [16] old man's; senile; **~ший** [17] elder, older, senior; eldest, oldest; *по должности* senior, superior; head, chief; *лейтенант* first; **~шинá** *m* [5] *mil.* first sergeant (*naut.* mate); **~шинствó** *n* [9] seniority

**стáр|ый** [14; стар, -á, -о; *comp.*: стáрше *or* -рée] old; *времена* olden; **~ьё** *n* [10] *coll.* old clothes *pl.*; junk, *Brt.* lumber

**стá|скивать** [1], ⟨**~щи́ть**⟩ [16] drag off, pull off; drag down; take, bring; *coll.* filch

**стати́ст** *m* [1], **~ка** *f* [5; *g/pl.*: -ток] *thea.* supernumerary; *film* extra; **~ика** *f* [5] statistics; **~и́ческий** [16] statistical

**стáт|ный** [14; -тен, -тна, -о] wellbuilt;

С

~уя *f* [6; *g/pl.*: -уй] statue; **~ь**[1] *f* [8]: ***с ка-ко́й ~и?*** *coll.* why (should I, *etc.*)?

**стать**[2] → ***станови́ться***; **∠ся** *coll.* (*impers.*) happen (to **с** T); ***мо́жет ∠ся*** it may be, perhaps

**статья́** *f* [6; *g/pl.*: -те́й] article; *договора и т. д.* clause, item, entry; *coll.* matter (another *особая*)

**стациона́р** *m* [1] permanent establishment; ***лече́бный ~*** hospital; **~ный** [14] permanent, fixed; ***~ный больно́й*** in-patient

**ста́чка** *f* [5; *g/pl.*: -чек] strike

**стащи́ть** → ***ста́скивать***

**ста́я** *f* [6; *g/pl.*: стай] flight, flock; *волков* pack

**ста́ять** [27] *pf.* thaw, melt

**ствол** *m* [1 *e.*] trunk; *ружья* barrel

**сте́бель** *m* [4; -бля; *from g/pl. e.*] stalk, stem

**стёганый** [14] quilted

**сте|ка́ть** [1], ⟨~чь⟩ [26] flow (down); **-ся** flow together; (*собираться*) gather, throng

**стек|ло́** [9; *pl.*: стёкла, стёкол, стёклам] glass; *оконное* pane; ***пере́днее ~ло́*** windshield (*Brt.* windscreen); **~ля́нный** [14] glass…; glassy; **~о́льщик** *m* [1] glazier

**стел|и́ть(ся)** *coll.* → ***стла́ть(ся)***; **~ла́ж** *m* [1 *e.*] shelf; **∠ька** *f* [5; *g/pl.*: -лек] inner sole

**стен|а́** *f* [5; *as/sg.*: сте́ну; *pl.*: сте́ны, стен, стена́м] wall; **~газе́та** *f* [5] (***стенна́я газе́та***) wall newspaper; **~д** *m* [1] stand; **∠ка** *f* [5; *g/pl.*: -нок] wall; ***как об ∠ку горо́х*** like talking to a brick wall; **~но́й** [14] wall…

**стеногра́|мма** *f* [5] shorthand (verbatim) report *or* notes *pl.*; **~фи́стка** *f* [5; *g/pl.*: -ток] stenographer; **~фия** *f* [7] shorthand

**сте́пень** *f* [8; *from g/pl. e.*] degree (to **до** P), extent; *math.* power

**степ|но́й** [14] steppe…; **~ь** *f* [8; в -пи́; *from g/pl. e.*] steppe

**сте́рва** P *f* [5] (*as term of abuse*) bitch

**сте́рео-** *combining* form stereo-; **стереоти́п** *m* [1], **стереоти́пный** [14; -пен, -пна] stereotype

**стере́ть** → ***стира́ть***

**стере́чь** [26 г/ж: -егу́, -ежёшь; -ёг, -егла́] guard, watch (over)

**сте́ржень** *m* [4; -жня] *tech.* rod, pivot

**стерил|изова́ть** [7] (*im*)*pf.* sterilize; **∠ьный** [14; -лен, -льна] sterile, free of germs

**стерпе́ть** [10] *pf.* endure, bear

**стесн|е́ние** *n* [12] constraint; **~и́тельный** [14; -лен, -льна] shy; **~я́ть** [28], ⟨~и́ть⟩ [13] constrain, restrain; (*смущать*) embarrass; (*мешать*) hamper; **~я́ться**, ⟨по-⟩ feel (*or* be) shy, self-conscious *or* embarrassed; (P) be ashamed of; (*колебаться*) hesitate

**стеч|е́ние** *n* [12] confluence; *обстоятельств* coincidence; *народа* concourse; **~ь(ся)** → ***стека́ть(ся)***

**стиль** *m* [4] style; ***но́вый ~*** New Style (*according to the Gregorian calendar*); ***ста́рый ~*** Old Style (*according to the Julian calendar*)

**сти́мул** *m* [1] stimulus, incentive

**стипе́ндия** *f* [7] scholarship, grant

**стир|а́льный** [14] washing; **~а́ть** [1] **1.** ⟨стере́ть⟩ [12; сотру́, -трёшь; стёр(ла); стёрши & стере́в] wipe *or* rub off; erase, efface, blot out; *ногу* rub sore; **2.** ⟨вы-⟩ wash, launder; **∠ка** *f* [5] wash(-ing), laundering; ***отда́ть в ∠ку*** send to the wash

**сти́с|кивать** [1], ⟨~нуть⟩ [20] squeeze, clench; *в объятиях* hug

**стих** (*a.* -и́ *pl.*) *m* [1 *e.*] verse; *pl. a.* poem(s); **~а́ть** [1], ⟨∠нуть⟩ [21] *ве-тер и т. д.* abate; subside; (*успокоиться*) calm down, become quiet; **~и́йный** [14; -и́ен, -и́йна] elemental; *fig.* spontaneous; *бедствие* natural; **~и́я** *f* [7] element(s); **∠нуть** → ***~а́ть***

**стихотворе́ние** *n* [12] poem

**стлать** & *coll.* **стели́ть** [стелю́, сте́лешь], ⟨по-⟩ [по́стланный] spread, lay; *постель* make; **-ся** *impf.* (be) spread; drift; *bot.* creep

**сто** [35] hundred

**стог** *m* [1; в сто́ге & в стогу́; *pl.*: -а́, *etc. e.*] *agric.* stack, rick

**сто́и|мость** *f* [8] cost; value, worth (…

Т/**в** В); **~ть** [13] cost; be worth; (*заслуживать*) deserve; **не ~т** *coll.* → **не́ за что**

**стой!** stop!, halt!

**сто́й|ка** *f* [5; *g/pl.*: сто́ек] stand; *tech.* support; *в банке* counter; *в ресторане* bar; **~кий** [16; сто́ек, стойка́, -o; *comp.*: сто́йче] firm, stable, steady; (*in compounds*) … proof; **~кость** *f* [8] firmness; steadfastness

**сток** *m* [1] flowing (off); drainage, drain

**стол** *m* [1 *e.*] table (**за** Т at); (*питание*) board, fare; diet; **~ нахо́док** lost property office

**столб** *m* [1 *e*] post, pole; *дыма* pillar; **~е́ц** *m* [1; -бца́], **~ик** *m* [1] column (*in newspaper, etc.*); **~ня́к** *m* [1 *e.*] *med.* tetanus

**столе́тие** *n* [12] century; (*годовщина*) centenary

**сто́лик** *m* [1] *dim.* → **стол**; small table

**столи́|ца** *f* [5] capital; **~чный** [14] capital…; metropolitan

**столкн|ове́ние** *n* [12] collision; *fig. mil.* clash; **~у́ть(ся)** → **ста́лкивать(ся)**

**столо́в|ая** *f* [14] dining room; café, restaurant; *на предприятии* canteen; **~ый** [14]: **~ая ло́жка** table spoon; **~ый серви́з** dinner service

**столп** *m* [1 *e.*] *arch.* pillar, column

**столь** so; **~ко** [32] so much, so many; **~ко же** as much *or* many

**столя́р** *m* [1 *e.*] joiner, cabinetmaker; **~ный** [14] joiner's

**стон** *m* [1], **~а́ть** [-ну́, сто́нешь; стона́я], ⟨про-⟩ groan, moan

**стоп|!** stop!; **~ сигна́л** *mot.* stoplight; **~а́** **1.** [5 *e.*] foot; **идти́ по чьи́м-л. стопа́м** follow in s.o.'s footsteps; **~ка** *f* [5; *g/pl.*: -пок] pile, heap; **~орить** [13], ⟨за-⟩ stop; bring to a standstill; **~та́ть** → **ста́птывать**

**сто́рож** *m* [1; *pl.*: -á; *etc. e.*] guard, watchman; **~ево́й** [14] watch…; on duty; *naut.* escort…; patrol…; **~и́ть** [16 *e.*; -жу́, -жи́шь] guard, watch (over)

**сторон|а́** *f* [5; *ac/sg.*: сто́рону; *pl.*: сто́роны, сторо́н, -на́м] side (on *a.* **по** Д; **с** Р); (*направление*) direction; part (**с** Р on); (*местность*) place, region, country; *в суде и т. д.* party; distance (**в** П at; **с** Р from); **в ´~у** aside, apart (*a.* joking **шу́тки**); **в ~е́ от** at some distance (from); **с одно́й ~ы́** on the one hand; **… с ва́шей ~ы́** *a.* … of you; **со свое́й ~ы́** on my part; **~и́ться** [13; -оню́сь, -о́нишься], ⟨по-⟩ make way, step aside; (*избегать*) (Р) avoid, shun; **~ник** *m* [1] adherent, follower, supporter

**сто́чный** [14] waste…; *воды* sewage

**стоя́нка** *f* [5; *g/pl.*: -нок] stop (**на** П at); **автомоби́льная ~** parking place *or* lot; *naut.* anchorage; **~ такси́** taxi stand (*Brt.* rank)

**стоя́|ть** [стою́, стои́шь; сто́я] stand; be; stop; stand up (**за** В for), defend, insist (**на** П on); **сто́йте!** stop!; *coll.* wait!; **~чий** [17] *положение* upright; *вода* stagnant; *воротник* stand-up

**сто́ящий** [17] worthwhile; *человек* worthy, deserving

**страда́|лец** *m* [1; -льца] sufferer; *iro.* martyr; **~ние** *n* [12] suffering; **~тельный** [14] *gr.* passive; **~ть** [1], ⟨по-⟩ suffer (**от** Р, Т from); **он ~ет забы́вчивостью** he has a poor memory

**стра́жа** *f* [5] guard, watch; **~ поря́дка** *mst. pl.* the militia

**стран|а́** *f* [5; *pl. st.*] country; **~и́ца** *f* [5] page (→ **пя́тый**); **~ность** *f* [8] strangeness, oddity; **~ный** [14; -а́нен, -а́нна, -о] strange, odd; **~ствовать** [7] wander, travel

**страст|но́й** [14] *неделя* Holy; *пятница* Good; **~ный** (-sn-) [14; -тен, -тна́, -о] passionate, fervent; **он ~ный люби́тель джа́за** he's mad about jazz; **~ь** *f* [8; *from g/pl. e.*] passion (**к** Д for)

**стратег|и́ческий** [16] strategic; **~ия** *f* [7] strategy

**стра́ус** *m* [1] ostrich

**страх** *m* [1] fear (**от, со** Р for); risk, terror (**на** В at); **~ова́ние** *n* [12] insurance (*fire*… **от** Р); **~ова́ть** [7], ⟨за-⟩ insure (**от** Р against); *fig.* safeguard o.s. (against); **~о́вка** *f* [5; *g/pl.*: -вок] insurance (rate); **~ово́й** [14] insurance…

**страш|и́ть** [16 *e.*; -шу́, -ши́шь], ⟨у-⟩ [-шённый] (**-ся** be) frighten(ed; at Р; fear, dread, be afraid of); **~ный** [14;

С

-шен, -шна́, -о] terrible, frightful, dreadful; *coll.* awful; **2ный суд** the Day of Judg(e)ment; **мне ∠но** I'm afraid, I fear

**стрекоза́** *f* [5; *pl. st.*: -о́зы, -о́з, -о́зам] dragonfly

**стрел|а́** *f* [5; *pl. st.*] arrow; *a. fig.* shaft, dart; **∠ка** *f* [5; *g/pl.*: -лок] (*of a clock or watch*) hand; *компаса и т. д.* needle; *на рисунке* arrow; **~ко́вый** [14] shooting…; (of) rifles *pl.*; **~о́к** *m* [1; -лка́] marksman, shot; **~ьба́** *f* [5; *pl. st.*] shooting, fire; **~я́ть** [28], ⟨вы́стрелить⟩ [13] shoot, fire (**в** В, **по** Д at; *gun* **из** Р)

**стрем|гла́в** headlong; **~и́тельный** [14; -лен, -льна] impetuous, headlong, swift; **~и́ться** [14 *e.*; -млю́сь, -ми́шься] (**к** Д) aspire (to), strive (for); **~ле́ние** *n* [12] aspiration (to), striving (for), urge, desire (to)

**стремя́нка** *f* [5; *g/pl.*: -нок] stepladder

**стресс** *m* [1] *psych.* stress

**стриж** *m* [1 *e.*] sand martin

**стри́|жка** *f* [5] haircut(ting); *овец* shearing; *ногтей* clipping; **~чь** [26; -игу́, -ижёшь; *pl. st.*], ⟨по-, о-(об-)⟩ cut; shear; clip, (*подровнять*) level, trim; **-ся** have one's hair cut

**строга́ть** [1], ⟨вы́-⟩ plane

**стро́г|ий** [16; строг, -а́, -о; *comp.*: стро́же] severe; strict; *стиль и т. д.* austere; *взгляд* stern; **~о говоря́** strictly speaking; **~ость** *f* [8] severity; austerity; strictness



**строе|во́й** [14] building…; **~во́й лес** timber; **∠ние** *n* [12] construction, building; structure

**строи́тель** *m* [4] builder, constructor; **~ный** [14] building…; **~ная площа́дка** building *or* construction site; **~ство** *n* [9] construction

**стро́ить** [13], ⟨по-⟩ build (up), construct; *планы и т. д.* make, scheme; play *fig.* (**из** Р); **-ся** ⟨вы́-, по-⟩ be built; build (*a house, etc.*); *в очередь* form

**строй** *m* **1.** [3; в строю́; *pl. e.*: строй, строёв] order, array; line; **2.** [3] system, order, regime; **ввести́ в ~** put into operation; **∠ка** *f* [5; *g/pl.*: -о́ек] construction; building site; **∠ность** *f* [8] proportion; *mus.* harmony; *о сложении* slenderness; **∠ный** [14; -о́ен, -ойна́, -о] slender, slim; well-shaped; *mus., etc.* harmonious, well-balanced

**строка́** [5; *ac/sg.*: стро́ку́; *pl.* стро́ки, строк, стро́кам] line; **кра́сная ~** *typ.* indent

**стропи́ло** *n* [9] rafter, beam

**строптúвый** [14 *sh.*] obstinate, refractory

**строфа́** *f* [5; *nom/pl. st.*] stanza

**строч|и́ть** [16 & 16 *e.*; -очу́, -о́чи́шь; -о́ченный & -очёный] stitch, sew; *coll.* (*писать*) scribble, dash off; **∠ка** *f* [5; *g/pl.*: -чек] line; *sew.* stitch

**стру́|жка** *f* [5; *g/pl.*: -жек] shavings *pl.*; **~и́ться** [13] stream, flow; **~йка** *f* [5; *g/pl.*: -у́ек] *dim.* → **~я́**

**структу́ра** *f* [5] structure

**струн|а́** *f* [5; *pl. st.*] *mus.*, **∠ный** [14] string

**стрюч|ко́вый** → **бобо́вый**; **~о́к** *m* [1; -чка́] pod

**струя́** *f* [6; *pl. st.*: -у́и] stream (T in); jet; *воздуха* current; **бить струёй** spurt

**стря́|пать** *coll.* [1], ⟨со-⟩ cook; concoct; **~хивать** [1], ⟨**~хну́ть**⟩ [20] shake off

**студе́н|т** *m* [1], **~тка** *f* [5; *g/pl.*: -ток] student, undergraduate; **~ческий** [16] students'…

**сту́день** *m* [4; -дня] aspic

**сту́дия** *f* [7] studio, atelier

**сту́жа** *f* [7] hard frost

**стук** *m* [1] *в дверь* knock; rattle, clatter, noise; **∠нуть** → **стуча́ть**

**стул** *m* [1; *pl.*: сту́лья, -льев] chair; seat; *med.* stool

**ступ|а́ть** [1], ⟨**~и́ть**⟩ [14] step, tread, go; **~е́нь** *f* **1.** [8; *pl.*: ступе́ни, ступе́ней] step (*of stairs*); rung (*of* ladder); **2.** [8; *pl.*: ступе́ни, -не́й, *etc. e.*] stage, grade; *ракеты* rocket stage; **~е́нька** *f* [5; *g/pl.*: -нек] = 2.; **~и́ть** → **~а́ть**; **∠ка** *f* [5; *g/pl.*: -пок] (small) mortar; **~ня́** *f* [6; *g/pl.*: -не́й] foot, sole (*of foot*)

**сту|ча́ть** [4 *e.*; -чу́, -чи́шь], ⟨по-⟩, *once* ⟨**∠кнуть**⟩ [20] knock (*door* **в** В at; *a.* **-ся**); rap, tap; *о сердце и т. д.* throb; (*зубами*) chatter; clatter, rattle; **~ча́т** there's a knock at the door; **∠кнуть** → **испо́л-**

***ниться***

**стыд** *m* [1 *e.*] shame; **~и́ть** [15 *e.*; -ыжу́, -ыди́шь], ⟨при-⟩ [пристыжённый] shame, make ashamed; **-ся**, ⟨по-⟩ be ashamed (P of); **~ли́вый** [14 *sh.*] shy, bashful; ***~но!*** (for) shame!; ***мне ~но*** I am ashamed (***за*** B of p.)

**стык** *m* [1] joint, juncture (***на*** П at); **~о́вка** *f* [5; *g/pl.*: -вок] docking (*of space vehicles*), rendezvous

**сты́(ну)ть** [21], ⟨о-⟩ (become) cool

**сты́чка** *f* [5; *g/pl.*: -чек] skirmish; scuffle

**стюарде́сса** *f* [5] stewardess, air hostess

**стя́|гивать** [1], ⟨**~ну́ть**⟩ [19] tighten; pull together; *mil.* gather, assemble; pull off; *coll.* pilfer

**суб|бо́та** *f* [5] Saturday (on: ***в*** B *pl.*: ***по*** Д); **~си́дия** *f* [7] subsidy

**субтропи́ческий** [16] subtropical

**субъе́кт** *m* [1] subject; *coll.* fellow; **~и́вный** [14; -вен, -вна] subjective

**сувени́р** *m* [1] souvenir

**суверен|ите́т** *m* [1] sovereignty; **~ный** [14; -е́нен, -е́нна] sovereign

**суг|ро́б** *m* [1] snowdrift; **~у́бо** *adv.* especially; ***э́то ~у́бо ча́стный вопро́с*** this is a purely private matter

**суд** *m* [1 *e.*] (*суждение*) judg(e)ment; court (of law); trial (***отда́ть под ~*** put on trial; ***преда́ть ~у́*** bring to trial, prosecute; (*правосудие*) justice

**суда́к** *m* [1 *e.*] pike perch

**суда́р|ыня** *f* [6] *obs.* (*mode of address*) madam; **´~ь** *m* [4] *obs.* (*mode of address*) sir

**суд|е́бный** [14] judicial, legal; forensic; law…; (of the) court; **~и́ть** [15; суждённый] **1.** ⟨по-⟩ judge (***по*** Д by); *fig.* form an opinion (***о*** П of); **2.** (*im*)*pf.* try, judge; ***~я по*** (Д) judging by

**су́д|но** *n* [9; *pl.*: суда́, -о́в] *naut.* ship, vessel; ***~но на возду́шной поду́шке*** hovercraft; ***~но на возду́шных кры́льях*** hydrofoil

**судопроизво́дство** *n* [9] legal proceedings

**су́доро|га** *f* [5] cramp, convulsion, spasm; **~жный** [14; -жен, -жна] convulsive, spasmodic

**судо|строе́ние** *n* [12] shipbuilding; **~строи́тельный** [14] shipbuilding…; ship(yard); **~хо́дный** [14; -ден, -дна] navigable; **~хо́дство** *n* [9] navigation

**судьб|а́** *f* [5; *pl.*: су́дьбы, су́деб, су́дьбам] destiny, fate; ***благодари́ть ~у́*** thank one's lucky stars

**судья́** *m* [6; *pl.*: су́дьи, судей, су́дьям] judge; *sport* referee, umpire

**суеве́р|ие** *n* [12] superstition; **~ный** [14; -рен, -рна] superstitious

**сует|а́** *f* [5], **~и́ться** [15 *e.*; суечу́сь, суети́шься] bustle, fuss; **~ли́вый** [14 *sh.*] bustling, fussy

**суж|де́ние** *n* [12] opinion, judg(e)ment; **~е́ние** *n* [12] narrowing; **~ивать** [1], ⟨су́зить⟩ [15] narrow (*v/i.*: **-ся**; taper); *платье* take in

**сук** *n* [1 *e.*; на ~у́; *pl.*: су́чья, -ьев & -и́, -о́в] bough; *в древесине* knot

**су́к|а** *f* [5] bitch (*also as term of abuse*); **~ин** [19]: ***~ин сын*** son of a bitch

**сукно́** *n* [9; *pl. st.*; су́кна, су́кон, су́кнам] broadcloth; heavy, coarse cloth; ***положи́ть под ~*** *fig.* shelve

**сули́ть** [13], ⟨по-⟩ promise

**султа́н** *m* [1] sultan

**сумасбро́д|ный** [14; -ден, -дна] wild, extravagant; **~ство** *n* [9] madcap *or* extravagant behavio(u)r

**сумасше́|дший** [17] mad, insane; *su.* madman; **~дший дом** *fig.* madhouse; **~ствие** *n* [12] madness, lunacy

**сумато́ха** *f* [5] turmoil, confusion, hurly-burly

**сум|бу́р°** *m* [1] → ***пу́таница***; **~ерки** *f/pl.* [5; *gen.*: -рек] dusk, twilight; **~ка** *f* [5; *g/pl.*: -мок] (hand)bag; *biol.* pouch; **~ма** *f* [5] sum (***на*** B/***в*** B for/of), amount; **~ма́рный** [14; -рен, -рна] total; **~ми́ровать** [7] (*im*)*pf.* sum up

**су́мочка** *f* [5; *g/pl.*: -чек] handbag

**су́мра|к** *m* [1] twilight, dusk; gloom; **~чный** [14; -чен, -чна] gloomy

**сунду́к** *m* [1 *e.*] trunk, chest

**су́нуть(ся)** → ***сова́ть(ся)***

**суп** *m* [1; *pl. e.*], **~ово́й** [14] soup(…)

**супероблóжка** *f* [5; *g/pl.*: -жек] dust jacket

**супру́|г** *m* [1] husband; **~га** *f* [5] wife; **~жеский** [16] matrimonial, conjugal;

С

*жизнь* married; **~жество** *n* [9] matrimony, wedlock
**сургу́ч** *m* [1 *e.*] sealing wax
**суро́в|ость** *f* [8] severity; **~ый** [14 *sh.*] harsh, rough; *климат и т. д.* severe; stern; *дисциплина* rigorous
**суррога́т** *m* [1] substitute
**суста́в** *m* [1] *anat.* joint
**су́тки** *f/pl.* [5; *gen.*: -ток] twentyfour-hour period; ***кру́глые ~*** round the clock
**су́точный** [14] day's, daily; twentyfour-hour, round-the-clock; *pl. su.* daily allowance
**суту́лый** [14 *sh.*] round-shouldered
**сут|ь** *f* [8] essence, crux, heart; ***по ~и де́ла*** as a matter of fact
**суфле́** *n* [*indecl.*] soufflé
**сух|а́рь** *m* [4 *e.*] *сдобный* rusk, zwieback; dried piece of bread; **~ожи́лие** *n* [12] sinew; **~о́й** [14; сух, -á, -o; *comp.*: су́ше] dry; *климат* arid; *дерево* dead; *fig.* cool, cold; *доклад* boring, dull; ***~óе молокó*** dried milk; **~опу́тный** [14] land…; **~ость** *f* [8] dryness, *etc.* → ***~óй***; **~оща́вый** [14 *sh.*] lean; skinny; **~офру́кты** *pl.* [1] dried fruit
**сучо́к** *m* [1; -чкá] *dim.* → **сук**
**су́ш|а** *f* [5] (dry) land; **~ёный** [14] dried; **~и́лка** *m* [5; *g/pl.*: -лок] *coll.* dish drainer; **~ить** [16], 〈вы́-〉 dry; **~ка** *f* [5; *g/pl.*: -шек] drying; dry, ring-shaped cracker
**суще́ств|енный** [14 *sh.*] essential, substantial; **~и́тельное** [14] noun, substantive (*a.* **имя ~и́тельное**); **~о́** *n* [9] creature, being; *суть* essence; ***по ~у́*** at bottom; to the point; **~ова́ние** *n* [12] existence, being; ***сре́дства к ~ова́нию*** livelihood; **~ова́ть** [7] exist, be; live, subsist
**су́щ|ий** [17] *coll. правда* plain; *вздор* absolute, sheer, downright; **~ность** *f* [8] essence, substance; ***в ~ности*** in fact; really and truly
**сфе́ра** *f* [5] sphere; field, realm
**схват|и́ть(ся)** → ***~ывать(ся)***; **~ка** *f* [5; *g/pl.*: -ток] skirmish, fight, combat; scuffle; *a. pl.* contractions, labo(u)r, birth pangs; **~ывать** [1], 〈~и́ть〉 [15] seize (***за*** В by), grasp (*a. fig.*), grab; snatch; (*поймать*) catch (*a cold, etc.*); **-ся** seize; *coll.* grapple (with)
**схе́ма** *f* [5] diagram, chart (in ***на*** П), plan, outline; **~ти́ческий** [16] schematic; *fig.* sketchy
**сход|и́ть** [15], 〈сойти́〉 [сойду́, -дёшь; сошёл, -шлá, *g. pt.*: сойдя́] go (*or* come) down, descend (from **с** Р); *о коже и т. д.* come off; *о снеге* melt; *coll.* pass (***за*** В for); Р do; pass off; ***ей всё ~ит с рук*** she can get away with anything; **~и́ть** *pf.* go (& get *or* fetch ***за*** Т); → ***ум***; **-ся**, 〈-сь〉 meet; gather; become friends; agree (***в*** П upon); (*совпасть*) coincide; *coll.* click; **~ни** *f/pl.* [6; *gen.*: -ней] gangplank, gangway; **~ный** [14; -ден, -днá, -o] similar (**с** Т to), like; *coll. цена* reasonable; **~ство** *n* [9] similarity (**с** Т to), likeness
**сцеди́ть** [15] *pf.* pour off; draw off
**сце́н|а** *f* [5] stage; scene (*a. fig.*); **~а́рий** *m* [3] scenario, script; **~и́ческий** [16] stage…, scenic
**сцеп|и́ть(ся)** → ***~ля́ть(ся)***; **~ка** [5; *g/pl.*: -пок] coupling; **~ле́ние** *n* [12] *phys.* adhesion; cohesion; *tech.* clutch, coupling; **~ля́ть** [28], 〈~и́ть〉 [14] link; couple (*v/i.* **-ся**: *coll.* quarrel, grapple)
**счаст|ли́вец** *m* [1; -вца] lucky man; **~ли́вый** [14; счáстли́в, -a, -o] happy; fortunate; lucky; ***~ли́вого пути́!*** bon voyage!; ***~ли́во*** *coll.* good luck!; ***~ли́во отде́латься*** have a narrow escape; **~ье** *n* [10] happiness; luck; good fortune; ***к ~ью*** fortunately
**сче́сть(ся)** → ***счита́ть(ся)***
**счёт** *m* [1; на ~e & счету́; *pl.*: счетá, *etc.* *e.*] count, calculation; *в банке* account (***в*** В; ***на*** В on); *счёт к оплате* bill; *sport* score; ***в два ~а*** in a jiffy, in a trice; ***в коне́чном ~е*** ultimately; ***за ~*** (Р) at the expense (of); ***на э́тот ~*** on this score, in this respect; ***ска́зано на мой ~*** aimed at me; ***быть на хоро́шем счету́*** (***у*** Р) be in good repute
**счёт|чик** *m* [1] meter; counter; **~ы** *pl.* [1] abacus *sg.*; ***свести́ ~ы*** square accounts, settle a score (with)
**счита́|ть** [1], 〈со-〉 & 〈счесть〉 [25; сочту́, -тёшь; счёл, сочлá; сочтённый; *g. pt.*: сочтя́] count; (*pf.* счесть) (Т, ***за*** В) consider, regard (*a.* as), hold, think;

**~я** *a.* including; **~нные** *pl.* very few; **~ться** (T) be considered (*or* reputed) to be; (**с** T) consider, respect

**сши|ва́ть** [1], ⟨**~ть**⟩ [сошью́, -шьёшь; сше́й(те)!; сши́тый] sew (together)

**съед|а́ть** [1], ⟨съесть⟩ → **есть** *1*; **~о́бный** [14; -бен, -бна] edible

**съез|д** *m* [1] congress (**на** П at); **~ди́ть** [15] *pf.* go; (**за** T) fetch; (**к** Д) visit; **~жа́ть** [1], ⟨съе́хать⟩ [съе́ду, -дешь] go *or* drive (*or* slide) down; **-ся** meet; gather

**съёмка** *m* [5; *g/pl.*: -мок] survey; *фильма* shooting

**съёмный** [14] detachable

**съестно́й** [14] food…

**съе́хать(ся)** → **съезжа́ть(ся)**

**сы́|воротка** *f* [5; *g/pl.*: -ток] whey; *med.* serum; **~гра́ть** → **игра́ть**

**сы́знова** *coll.* anew, (once) again

**сын** *m* [1; *pl.*: сыновья́, -ве́й, -вья́м; *fig. pl.* сыны́] son; *fig. a.* child; **~о́вний** [15] filial; **~о́к** *coll. m* [1; -нка́] (*as mode of address*) sonny

**сы́п|ать** [2], ⟨по-⟩ strew, scatter; pour; **-ся** pour; *удары, град* hail; *дождь, град* pelt; **~но́й** [14]: **~но́й тиф** typhus; spotted fever; **~у́чий** [17 *sh.*] *тело* dry; **~ь** *f* [8] rash

**сыр** *m* [1; *pl. e.*] cheese; **ката́ться как ~ в ма́сле** live off the fat of the land; **~е́ть** [8], ⟨от-⟩ become damp; **~е́ц** *m* [1; -рца́]: **шёлк-~е́ц** raw silk; **~ник** *m* [1] curd fritter; **~ный** [14] cheese…; **~ова́тый** [14 *sh.*] dampish; rare, undercooked; **~о́й** [14; сыр, -á, -o] damp; moist; (*не варёный*) raw; *нефть* crude; *хлеб* sodden; **~ость** *f* [8] dampness; humidity; **~ьё** *n* [10] *collect.* raw material

**сы́т|ный** [14; сы́тен, -тна́, -o] substantial, copious; **~ый** [14; сыт, -á, -o] satisfied, full

**сыч** *m* [1 *e.*] little owl

**сы́щик** *m* [1] detective

**сюда́** here; hither

**сюже́т** *m* [1] subject; plot

**сюи́та** *f* [5] *mus.* suite

**сюрпри́з** *m* [1] surprise

# Т

**та** → **тот**

**таба́|к** *m* [1 *e.*; *part.g.*: -ý] tobacco; **~чный** [14] tobacco…

**та́бе|ль** *m* [1] table; time-keeping *or* attendance record (*in a factory, school, etc.*); **~ле́тка** *f* [5; *g/pl.*: -ток] pill, tablet; **~ли́ца** *f* [5] table; **~ли́ца умноже́ния** multiplication table; **электро́нная ~ли́ца** *comput.* spreadsheet; **~ло́** *n* [*indecl.*] indicator *or* score board; **~ор** *m* [1 *e.*] camp; Gypsy encampment

**табу́н** *m* [1 *e.*] herd, drove

**табуре́тка** *f* [5; *g/pl.*: -ток] stool

**таджи́к** *m* [1], **~ский** [16] Tajik

**таз** *m* [1; в -ý; *pl. e.*] basin; *anat.* pelvis

**таи́нств|енный** [14 *sh.*] mysterious; secret(ive); **´~о** *n* [9] sacrament

**таи́ть** [13] hide, conceal; **-ся** be in hiding; *fig.* lurk

**тайга́** *f* [5] *geog.* taiga

**тай|ко́м** secretly; behind (one's) back (**от** P); **~м** *m* [1] *sport* half, period; **~мер** *m* [1] timer; **~на** *f* [5] secret; mystery; **~ни́к** *m* [1 *e.*] hiding (place); **~ный** [14] secret; stealthy

**так** so, thus; like that; (**~ же** just) as; so much; just so; then; well; yes; one way…; → *a.* **пра́вда**; *coll.* properly; **не ~** wrong(ly); **~ и** (*both*…) and; **~ как** as, since; **и ~** even so; without that; **~же** also, too; **~же не** neither, nor; **а ~же** as well as; **~и** *coll.* all the same; indeed; **~ называ́емый** socalled; alleged; **~ово́й** [14; -ко́в, -ква́] such; (a)like; same; **был(á) ~о́в(á)** disappeared, vanished; **~о́й** [16] such; so; **~о́е** *su.* such things; **~о́й же** the same; as…; **~о́й-то** such-and-such; so-and-so; **что (э́то) ~о́е?** *coll.* what's that?; what did you say?, what's on?; **кто вы ~о́й (~а́я)?**

**= кто вы?**
**та́кса¹** *f* [5] statutory price; tariff
**та́кса²** *f* [5] dachshund
**такси́** *n* [*indecl.*] taxi(cab); **~ст** *m* [1] taxi driver
**такт** *m* [1] *mus.* time, measure, bar; *fig.* tact; **~ика** *f* [5] tactics *pl.* & *sg.*; **~и́ческий** [16] tactical; **~и́чность** *f* [8] tactfulness; **~и́чный** [14; -чен, -чна] tactful
**тала́нт** *m* [1] talent, gift (**к** Д for); man of talent; gifted person; **~ливый** [14 *sh.*] talented, gifted
**та́лия** *f* [7] waist
**тало́н** *m* [1] coupon
**та́лый** [14] thawed; melted
**там** there; when; **~ же** in the same place; ibid; **~ ви́дно бу́дет** we shall see; **~ и сям** here, there, and everywhere; **как бы ~ ни́ было** at any rate
**та́мбур** *m* [1] *rail.* vestibule
**тамо́ж|енный** [14] customs…; **~ня** [6; *g/pl.*: -жен] customs house
**та́мошний** [15] *coll.* of that place
**та́н|ец** *m* [1; -нца] dance (*go* dancing **на** В; *pl.*); **~к** *m* [1] tank; **~кер** *m* [1] tanker; **~ковый** [14] tank…
**танц|ева́льный** [14] dancing…; **~ева́ть** [7], ⟨с-⟩ dance; **~о́вщик** *m* [1], **~о́вщица** *f* [5] (ballet) dancer; **~о́р** *m* [1] dancer
**та́почка** *f* [5; *g/pl.*: -чек] *coll.* slipper; *sport* sneaker, *Brt.* trainer
**та́ра** *f* [5] packing, packaging
**тарака́н** *m* [1] cockroach
**тарахте́ть** *coll.* [11] rumble, rattle
**тара́щить** [16], ⟨вы́-⟩: **~ глаза́** goggle (at **на** В; with *suprise* **от** Р)
**таре́л|ка** *f* [5; *g/pl.*: -лок] plate; *глубо́кая* soup plate; **лета́ющая ~ка** flying saucer; **чу́вствовать себя́ не в свое́й ~ке** feel out of place; feel ill at ease
**тари́ф** *m* [1] tariff; **~ный** [14] tariff…; standard (*wages*)
**таска́ть** [1] carry; drag, pull; *coll.* steal; P wear; **-ся** wander, gad about
**тасова́ть** [7], ⟨с-⟩ shuffle (cards)
**тата́р|ин** *m* [1; *pl.*: -ры, -р, -рам], **~ка** *f* [5; *g/pl.*: -рок], **~ский** [16] Ta(r)tar
**тахта́** *f* [5] ottoman
**та́чка** *f* [5] wheelbarrow
**тащи́ть** [16] **1.** ⟨по-⟩ drag, pull, carry; ⟨при-⟩ bring; **2.** *coll.* ⟨с-⟩ steal, pilfer; **-ся** *coll.* trudge, drag o.s. along
**та́ять** [27], ⟨рас-⟩ thaw, melt; *fig.* fade, wane, languish (**от** Р with)
**тварь** *f* [8] creature; *collect.* creatures; (*a. pej.* miscreant)
**тверде́ть** [8], ⟨за-⟩ harden
**твёрд|ость** *f* [8] firmness, hardness; **~ый** [14; твёрд, тверда, -о] hard; solid; firm; (*a. fig.*) stable, steadfast; *зна́ния* sound, good; *це́ны* fixed, *coll.* sure; **~о** *a.* well, for sure; **~о обеща́ть** make a firm promise
**тво|й** *m*, **~я́** *f*, **~ё** *n*, **~и́** *pl.* [24] your; yours; *pl. su. coll.* your folks; → **ваш**
**твор|е́ние** *n* [12] creation; work; (*существо*) creature; being; **~е́ц** *m* [1; -рца́] creator, author; **~и́тельный** [14] *gr.* instrumental (case); **~и́ть** [13], ⟨со-⟩ create, do; **-ся** *coll.* be (going) on; **~о́г** *m* [1 *e.*] curd(s); **~о́жник** curd pancake
**тво́рче|ский** [16] creative; **~ство** *n* [9] creation; creative work(s)
**теа́тр** *m* [1] theater (*Brt.* -tre; **в** П at); the stage; **~а́льный** [14; -лен, -льна] theatrical; theater…, drama…
**тёзка** *f* [5; *g/pl.*: -зок] namesake
**текст** *m* [1] text; words, libretto
**тексти́ль** *m* [4] *collect.* textiles *pl.*; **~ный** [14] textile; *комбина́т* weaving
**теку́|щий** [17] current; *ме́сяц* the present; *ремо́нт* routine; **~щие собы́тия** current affairs
**телеви́|дение** *n* [12] television, TV; **по ~дению** on TV; **~зио́нный** [14] TV; **~зор** *m* [1] TV set
**теле́га** *f* [5] cart
**телегра́мма** *f* [5] telegram
**телегра́ф** *m* [1] telegraph (office); **~и́ровать** [7] (*im*)*pf.* (Д) telegraph, wire, cable; **~ный** [14] telegraph(ic); telegram…; by wire
**теле́жка** *f* [5; *g/pl.*: -жек] handcart
**те́лекс** *m* [1] telex
**телёнок** *m* [2] calf
**телепереда́ча** *f* [5] telecast
**телеско́п** *m* [1] telescope
**теле́сный** [14] *наказа́ние* corporal; *по-*

Т

*вреждения* physical; fleshcolo(u)red
**телефо́н** *m* [1] telephone (***по*** Д by); ***звони́ть по ~у*** call, phone, ring up; **~-автома́т** *m* [1] telephone booth, *Brt.* telephone box; **~и́ст** *m* [1], **~и́стка** *f* [5; *g/pl.*: -ток] telephone operator; **~ный** [14] tele(phone)…
**Теле́ц** *m* [1] *astr.* Taurus
**те́ло** *n* [9; *pl. e.*] body; ***иноро́дное ~*** foreign body; ***всем ~м*** all over; **~сложе́ние** *n* [12] build; **~храни́тель** *m* [4] bodyguard
**теля́|тина** *f* [5], **~чий** [18] veal
**тем** → ***тот***
**те́м(а́тик)а** *f* [5] subject, topic, theme(s)
**тембр** ('tɛ-) *m* [1] timbre
**темн|е́ть** [8] **1.** ⟨по-⟩ darken; **2.** ⟨с-⟩ grow *or* get dark; **3.** (*a.* **-ся**) appear dark; loom
**тёмно…** (*in compds.*) dark…
**темнота́** *f* [5] darkness; dark
**тёмный** [14; тёмен, темна́] dark; *fig.* obscure; gloomy; (*подозрительный*) shady, dubious; (*силы*) evil; (*невежественный*) ignorant
**темп** ('tɛ-) *m* [1] tempo; rate, pace, speed
**темпера́мент** *m* [1] temperament; spirit; **~ный** [14; -тен, -тна] energetic; vigorous; spirited
**температу́ра** *f* [5] temperature
**те́мя** *n* [13] crown, top of the head
**тенденци|о́зный** (-tɛndɛ-) [-зен, -зна] biased; **´~я** (tɛn'de-) *f* [7] tendency
**те́ндер** *fin.* ('tɛndɛr) *m* [1] *naut. rail.* tender
**тени́стый** [14 *sh.*] shady
**те́ннис** *m* [1] tennis; ***насто́льный ~*** table tennis; **~и́ст** *m* [1] tennis player
**те́нор** *m* [1; *pl.*: -ра́, *etc. e.*] *mus.* tenor
**тень** *f* [8; в тени́; *pl.*: те́ни, тене́й; *etc. e.*] shade; shadow; ***ни те́ни сомне́ния*** not a shadow of doubt
**теор|е́тик** *m* [1] theorist; **~ети́ческий** [16] theoretical; **~́ия** *f* [7] theory
**тепе́р|ешний** [1] *coll.* present; **~ь** now, nowadays, today
**тепл|е́ть** [8; 3[rd] *p. only*], ⟨по-⟩ grow warm; **~и́ться** [13] *mst. fig.* gleam, flicker, glimmer; **~и́ца** *f* [5], **~и́чный** [14] greenhouse, hothouse; **~о́** **1.** *n* [9] warmth; *phys.* heat; warm weather; **2.** *adv.* → ***тёплый***; **~ово́з** *m* [1] diesel locomotive; **~ово́й** [14] (of) heat, thermal; **~ота́** *f* [5] warmth; *phys.* heat; **~охо́д** *m* [1] motor ship
**тёплый** [14; тёпел, тепла́, -о́ & тёпло] warm (*a. fig.*); (***мне***) ***тепло́*** it is (I am) warm
**терапи́я** *f* [7] therapy
**тере|би́ть** [14 *e.*; -блю́, -би́шь] pull (at); pick (at); tousle; *coll.* (*надоедать*) pester; **~́ть** [12] rub; *на тёрке* grate
**терза́|ние** *n* [12] *lit.* torment, agony; **~ть** [1] **1.** ⟨ис-⟩ torment, torture; **2.** ⟨рас-⟩ tear to pieces
**тёрка** *f* [5; *g/pl.*: -рок] grater
**те́рмин** *m* [1] term
**термо́|метр** *m* [1] thermometer; **´~с** ('te-) *m* [1] vacuum flask; **~я́дерный** [14] thermonuclear
**тёрн** *m* [1] *bot.* blackthorn, sloe
**терни́стый** [14 *sh.*] thorny
**терп|ели́вый** [14 *sh.*] patient; **~е́ние** *n* [12] patience; **~е́ть** [10], ⟨по-⟩ suffer, endure; (*мириться*) tolerate, bear, stand; ***вре́мя не ~́ит*** there is no time to be lost; (Д) ***не*** **-ся** *impf.* be impatient *or* eager; **~и́мость** *f* [8] tolerance (***к*** Д toward[s]); **~и́мый** [14 *sh.*] tolerant; *условия и т. д.* tolerable, bearable
**те́рпкий** [16; -пок, -пка́, -о; *comp.*: те́рпче] tart, astringent
**терра́са** *f* [5] terrace
**террит|ориа́льный** [14] territorial; **~о́рия** *f* [7] territory
**терро́р** *m* [1] terror; **~изи́ровать** &; **~изова́ть** [7] *im(pf.)* terrorize
**тёртый** [14] ground, grated
**теря́ть** [28], ⟨по-⟩ lose; *время* waste; *листву* shed; *надежду* give up; ***не ~ из ви́ду*** keep in sight; *fig.* bear in mind; **-ся** get lost; disappear, vanish; (*смущаться*) become flustered, be at a loss
**теса́ть** [3], ⟨об-⟩ hew, cut
**тесн|и́ть** [13], ⟨с-⟩ press, crowd; **-ся** crowd, throng; jostle; **~ота́** *f* [5] crowded state; narrowness; crush; **~́ый** [14; те́сен, тесна́, -о] crowded; cramped; narrow; *fig.* tight; close; *отношения* inti-

Т

mate; ***мир те́сен*** it's a small world
**те́ст|о** *n* [9] dough, pastry; **~ь** *m* [4] father-in-law (*wife's father*)
**тесьма́** *f* [5; *g/pl.*: -сём] tape; ribbon
**те́терев** *m* [1; *pl.*: -а́, *etc. e.*] *zo.* black grouse, blackcock
**тетива́** *f* [5] bowstring
**тётка** *f* [5; *g/pl.*: -ток] aunt; (*as term of address to any older woman*) ma'am, lady
**тетра́д|ь** *f* [8], **~ка** *f* [5; *g/pl.*: -док] exercise book, notebook, copybook
**тётя** *coll. f* [6; *g/pl.*: -тей] aunt
**те́хн|ик** *m* [1] technician; **~ика** *f* [5] engineering; *исполнения и т. д.* technique; equipment; **~икум** *m* [1] technical college; **~и́ческий** [16] technical; engineering…; ***~и́ческое обслу́живание*** maintenance; ***~и́ческие усло́вия*** specifications; **~ологи́ческий** [16] technological; **~оло́гия** *f* [7] technology
**теч|е́ние** *n* [12] current; stream (***вверх*** [***вниз***] ***по*** Д up[down]); course (***в*** В in; **с** Т/Р in/of *time*) *fig.* trend; tendency; **~ь** [26] **1.** flow, run; stream; *время* pass; (*протекать*) leak; **2.** *f* [8] leak (spring ***дать***)
**тёща** *f* [5] mother-in-law (*wife's mother*)
**тибе́тец** *m* [1; -тца] Tibetan
**тигр** *m* [1] tiger; **~и́ца** *f* [5] tigress
**ти́ка|нье** [10], **~ть** [1] *of clock* tick
**ти́на** *f* [5] slime, mud, ooze
**тип** *m* [1] type; *coll.* character; **~и́чный** [14; -чен, -чна] typical; **~огра́фия** *f* [7] printing office
**тир** *m* [1] shooting gallery
**тира́да** *f* [5] tirade
**тира́ж** *m* [1 *e.*] circulation; edition; *лотереи* drawing; ***~о́м в 2000*** edition of 2,000 copies
**тира́н** *m* [1] tyrant; **~ить** [13] tyranize; **~и́я** *f* [7], **~ство** *n* [9] tyranny
**тире́** *n* [*indecl.*] dash
**ти́с|кать** [1], ⟨**~нуть**⟩ [20] squeeze, press; **~ки́** *m/pl.* [1 *e.*] vise, *Brt.* vice; grip; ***в ~ка́х*** in the grip of (P); **~нёный** [14] printed
**титр** *m* [1] *cine.* caption, subtitle, credit
**ти́тул** *m* [1] title; **~ьный лист** [14] title page
**тиф** *m* [1] typhus
**ти́|хий** [16; тих, -а́, -о; *comp.*: ти́ше] quiet, still; calm; soft, gentle; *ход* slow; **~ше!** be quiet!, silence!; **~шина́** *f* [5] silence, stillness, calm; **~шь** [8; в тиши́] quiet, silence
**тка|нь** *f* [8] fabric, cloth; *anat.* tissue; **~ть** [тку, ткёшь; ткал, ткала́, -о], ⟨со-⟩ [со́тканный] weave; **~́цкий** [16] weaver's; weaving; **~ч** *m* [1 *e.*], **~чи́ха** *f* [5] weaver
**ткну́ть(ся)** → ***ты́кать(ся)***
**тле́|ние** *n* [12] decay, putrefaction; *углей* smo(u)ldering; **~ть** [8], ⟨ис-⟩ smo(u)lder; decay, rot, putrefy; *о надежде* glimmer
**то 1.** [28] that; ***~ же*** the same; ***к ~му́ (же)*** in addition (to that), moreover; add to this; ***ни ~ ни сё*** *coll.* neither fish nor flesh; ***ни с ~го́ ни с сего́*** *coll.* all of a sudden, without any visible reason; ***до ~го́*** so; ***она́ до ~го́ разозли́лась*** she was so angry; ***до ~го́ вре́мени*** before (that); **2.** (*cj.*) then; **~ … ~** now … now; ***не ~ … не ~ …*** *or* ***~ ли … ~ ли …*** either … or …, half … half …; ***не ~, что́бы*** not that; ***а не ~*** (or) else; **3.** **~-~** just, exactly; ***в то́м-~ и де́ло*** that's just it
**това́р** *m* [1] commodity, article; *pl.* goods, wares; ***~ы широ́кого потребле́ния*** consumer goods
**това́рищ** *m* [1] comrade, friend; mate, companion (***по*** Д in *arms*); colleague; ***~ по шко́ле*** schoolmate; ***~ по университе́ту*** fellow student; **~еский** [16] friendly; **~ество** *n* [9] comradeship, fellowship; *comm.* association, company
**това́р|ный** [14] goods…; ***~ный склад*** warehouse; *rail.* freight…; **~ообме́н** *m* [1] barter; **~ооборо́т** *m* [1] commodity circulation
**тогда́** then, at that time; ***~ как*** whereas, while; **~шний** [15] of that (*or* the) time, then
**то́ есть** that is (to say), i.e
**тожде́ств|енный** [14 *sh.*] identical; **´~о** *n* [9] identity
**то́же** also, too, as well; → ***та́кже***
**ток** *m* [1] current
**тока́р|ный** [14] turner's; *станок* turn-

ing; ˊ**~ь** *m* [4] turner, lathe operator
**токси́чный** [14; -чен, -чна] toxic
**толк** *m* [1; бе́з ~у] sense; use; understanding; ***знать ~*** (**в** П) know what one is talking about; ***бе́з ~у*** senselessly; ***сбить с ~у*** muddle; **~а́ть** [1], *once* ⟨~ну́ть⟩ [20] push, shove, jog; *fig.* induce, prompt; *coll.* urge on, spur; **-ся** push (o.a.); **~ова́ть** [7] **1.** ⟨ис-⟩ interpret, expound, explain; comment; **2.** ⟨по-⟩ talk (**с** T to); **~о́вый** [14] explanatory; [*sh.*] smart, sensible; **~ом** plainly; ***я ~ом не зна́ю …*** I don't really know …; **~отня́** *coll. f* [6] crush, crowding
**толо|кно́** *n* [9] oat meal; **~чь** [26; -лку́, -лчёшь, -лку́т; -ло́к, -лкла́; -лчённый], ⟨рас-, ис-⟩ pound, crush
**толп|а́** *f* [5; *pl. st.*], **~и́ться** [14 *e.*; *no 1st. & 2nd p. sg.*], ⟨с-⟩ crowd, throng
**толст|е́ть** [8], ⟨по-, рас-⟩ grow fat; grow stout; **~око́жий** [17 *sh.*] thick-skinned; **~ый** [14; толст, -а́, -о; *comp.*: -то́лще] thick; heavy; (*тучный*) stout; fat; **~я́к** *coll. m* [1 *e.*] fat man
**толч|ёный** [14] pounded; **~ея́** *coll. f* [6] crush, crowd; **~о́к** *m* [1; -чка́] push; shove; jolt; *при землетрясении* shock, tremor; *fig.* impulse, spur
**толщин|а́** *f* [5] fatness; corpulence; thickness; ***~о́й в*** (B), ***… в ~у́*** …thick
**толь** *m* [4] roofing felt
**то́лько** only, but; ***как ~*** as soon as; ***лишь*** (*or* ***едва́***) **~** no sooner … than; ***~ бы*** if only; ***~ что*** just now; **~-~** *coll.* barely
**том** *m* [1; *pl.*: -а́; *etc. e.*] volume
**тома́т** *m* [1], **~ный** [14] tomato; ***~ный сок*** tomato juice
**том|и́тельный** [14; -лен, -льна] wearisome; trying; *ожидание* tedious; *жара* oppressive; **~ность** *f* [8] languor; **~ный** [14; -мен, -мна́, -о] languid, languorous
**тон** *m* [1; *pl.*: -а́; *etc. e.*] *mus. and fig.* tone
**то́нк|ий** [16; -нок, -нка́, -о; *comp.*: то́ньше] thin; *талия и т. д.* slim, slender; *шёлк и т. д.* fine; *вопрос и т. д.* delicate, subtle; *слух* keen; *голос* high; *политик* clever, cunning; **~ость** *f* [8] thinness, *etc.* → **~ий**; delicacy, subtlety; *pl.* details (go into ***вдава́ться в*** B; *coll.* split hairs)

**то́нна** *f* [5] ton; **~ж** *m* [1] (*metric*) ton
**тонне́ль** (-'nɛã-) *m* [4] tunnel
**то́нус** *m* [1] *med.* tone
**тону́ть** [19] *v/i.* **1.** ⟨по-, за-⟩ sink; **2.** ⟨у-⟩ drown
**то́п|ать** [1], *once* ⟨~нуть⟩ [20] stamp; **~и́ть** [14] *v/t.* **1.** ⟨за-, по-⟩ sink; *водой* flood; **2.** ⟨за-, ис-, на-⟩ stoke (*a stove, etc.*); heat up; **3.** ⟨рас-⟩ melt; **4.** ⟨у-⟩ drown; **~кий** [16; -пок, -пка́, -о] boggy, marshy; **~лёный** [14] melted; *молоко* baked; **~ливо** *n* [9] fuel; ***жи́дкое ~ливо*** fuel oil; **~нуть** → ***~ать***
**топогра́|фия** *f* [7] topography
**то́поль** *m* [4; *pl.*: -ля́; *etc. e.*] poplar
**топо́р** *m* [1 *e.*] ax(e); **~ный** [14; -рен, -рна] clumsy; coarse, uncouth
**то́пот** *m* [1] stamp(ing), tramp(ing)
**топта́ть** [3], ⟨по-, за-⟩ trample, tread; ⟨вы́-⟩ trample down; ⟨с-⟩ wear out; **-ся** tramp(le); *coll.* hang about; mark time (*на месте*)
**топь** *f* [8] marsh, bog, swamp
**торг** *m* [1; на -у́; *pl.*: -и́; *etc. e.*] trading; bargaining, haggling; *pl.* auction (**с** P by; ***на*** П at); **~а́ш** *m* [1 *e.*] *pej.* (petty) tradesman; mercenaryminded person; **~ова́ть** [8] trade, deal (in T); sell; **-ся**, ⟨с-⟩ (strike a) bargain (**о** П for); **~о́вец** *m* [1; -вца] dealer, trader, merchant; **~о́вка** *f* [5; *g/pl.*: -вок] market woman; **~о́вля** *f* [6] trade, commerce; *наркотиками* traffic; **~о́вый** [14] trade…, trading, commercial, of commerce; *naut.* merchant…; **~пре́д** *m* [1] trade representative; **~пре́дство** *n* [9] trade delegation
**торже́ств|енность** *f* [8] solemnity; **~енный** [14 *sh.*] solemn; festive; **~о** *n* [9] triumph; (*празднество*) festivity, celebration; **~ова́ть** [7], ⟨вос-⟩ triumph (***над*** T over); *impf.* celebrate
**то́рмо|з** *m* **1.** [1; *pl.*: -а́, *etc. e.*] brake; **2.** [1] *fig.* drag; **~зи́ть** [15 *e.*; -ожу́, -ози́шь; -ожённый], ⟨за-⟩ (put the) brake(s on); *fig.* hamper; *psych.* inhibit; **~ши́ть** *coll.* [16; -шу́, -ши́шь] → ***теребить***
**тороп|и́ть** [14], ⟨по-⟩ hasten, hurry up (*v/i.* **-ся**; *a.* be in hurry); **~ли́вый** [14 *sh.*] hasty, hurried

**торпе́д|а** *f* [5], **~и́ровать** [7] (*im*)*pf.* torpedo (*a. fig.*); **~ный** [14] torpedo..
**торт** *m* [1] cake
**торф** *m* [1] peat; **~яно́й** [14] peat…
**торча́ть** [4 *e.*; -чу́, -чи́шь] stick up, stick out; *coll.* hang about
**торше́р** *m* [1] standard lamp
**тоск|а́** *f* [5] melancholy; (*томление*) yearning; (*скука*) boredom, ennui; **~а́ по ро́дине** homesickness; **~ли́вый** [14] melancholy; *погода* dull, dreary; **~ова́ть** [7] grieve, feel sad (*or* lonely); feel bored; yearn *or* long (for **по** П *or* Д); be homesick (*по родине*)
**тост** *m* [1] toast; **предложи́ть ~** propose a toast (**за** В to)
**тот** *m*, **та** *f*, **то** *n*, **те** *pl.* [28] that, *pl.* those; the one; the other; **не ~** wrong; **(н)и тот (н)и друго́й** both (neither); **тот же (са́мый)** the same; **тем бо́лее** the more so; **тем лу́чше** so much the better; **тем са́мым** thereby; → *a.* **то**
**тоталитар|и́зм** *m* [1] totalitarianism; **~ный** [14] totalitarian
**то́тчас (же)** immediately, at once
**точёный** [14] sharpened; *черты лица* chisel(l)ed; *фигура* shapely
**точи́|льный** [14]: **~льный брусо́к** whetstone; **~ть 1.** ⟨на-⟩ whet, grind; sharpen; **2.** ⟨вы́-⟩ turn; **3.** ⟨ис-⟩ eat (*or* gnaw) away
**то́чк|а** *f* [5; *g*/*pl.*: -чек] point; dot; *gr.* period, full stop; **вы́сшая ~а** zenith, climax (**на** П at); **~а с запято́й** *gr.* semicolon; **~а зре́ния** point of view; **попа́сть в са́мую ~у** hit the nail on the head; **дойти́ до ~и** *coll.* come to the end of one's tether
**то́чн|о** *adv.* → **~ый**; *a.* → **сло́вно**; indeed; **~ость** *f* [8] accuracy, exactness, precision; **в ~ости** → **~о**; **~ый** [14; -чен, -чна́, -о] exact, precise, accurate; punctual; *прибор* (of) precision
**точь**: **~ в ~** *coll.* exactly
**тошн|и́ть** [13]: **меня́ ~и́т** I feel sick; I loathe; **~ота́** *f* [5] nausea
**то́щий** [17; тощ, -á, -о] lean, lank, gaunt; *coll.* empty; *растительность* scanty, poor
**трава́** *f* [5; *pl. st.*] grass; *med. pl.* herbs; *сорная* weed
**трав|и́ть** [14 *sh.*] **1.** ⟨за-⟩ *fig.* persecute; **2.** ⟨вы́-⟩ exterminate; **~ля** *f* [6; *g*/*pl.*: -лей] persecution
**травян|и́стый** [14 *sh.*], **~о́й** [14] grass(y)
**траг|е́дия** *f* [7] tragedy; **~ик** *m* [1] tragic actor, tragedian; **~и́ческий** [16], **~и́чный** [14; -чен, -чна] tragic
**традици|о́нный** [14; -о́нен, -о́нна] traditional; **~я** *f* [7] tradition, custom
**тракт** *m* [1]: high road, highway; *anat.* **желу́дочно-кише́чный ~** alimentary canal; **~ова́ть** [7] treat; discuss; interpret; **~о́вка** [5; *g*/*pl.*: -вок] treatment; interpretation; **~ори́ст** *m* [1] tractor driver; **~орный** [14] tractor…
**тра́льщик** *m* [1] trawler; *mil.* mine sweeper
**трамбова́ть** [7], ⟨у-⟩ ram
**трамва́й** *m* [3] streetcar, *Brt.* tram(car) (Т, **на** П by)
**трампли́н** *m* [1] *sport* springboard (*a. fig.*); **лы́жный ~** ski-jump
**транзи́стор** *m* [1] *el.* (*component*) transistor
**транзи́т** *m* [1], **~ный** [14] transit
**транс|криби́ровать** [7] (*im*)*pf.* transcribe; **~ли́ровать** [7] (*im*)*pf.* broadcast, transmit (*by radio*); relay; **~ля́ция** *f* [7] transmission; **~пара́нт** *m* [1] transparency; banner
**тра́нспорт** *m* [1] transport; transport(ation; *a.* system [of]); **~и́ровать** [7] (*im*)*pf.* transport, convey; **~ный** [14] (of) transport(ation)…
**трансформа́тор** *m* [1] *el.* transformer
**транше́я** *f* [6; *g*/*pl.*: -е́й] trench
**трап** *m* [1] *naut.* ladder; *ae.* gangway
**тра́сса** *f* [5] route, line
**тра́т|а** *f* [5] expenditure; waste; **пуста́я ~а вре́мени** a waste of time; **~ить** [15], ⟨ис-, по-⟩ spend, expend; use up; waste
**тра́ур** *m* [1] mourning; **~ный** [14 mourning…; *марш и т. д.* funeral…
**трафаре́т** *m* [1] stencil; stereotype; cliché (*a. fig.*)
**трах** *int.* bang!
**тре́бова|ние** *n* [12] demand (**по** Д on); request, requirement; (*претензия*)

claim; *судьи* order; **~тельный** [14; -лен, -льна] exacting; (*разборчивый*) particular; **~ть** [7], ⟨по-⟩ (P) demand; require; claim; summon, call for; **-ся** be required (*or* wanted); be necessary
**трево́|га** *f* [5] alarm, anxiety; *mil. etc.* warning, alert; **~жить** [16] **1.** ⟨вс-, рас-⟩ alarm, disquiet; **2.** ⟨по-⟩ disturb, trouble; **-ся** be anxious; worry; **~жный** [14; -жен, -жна] worried, anxious, uneasy; *известия и т. д.* alarm(ing), disturbing
**тре́зв|ость** *f* [8] sobriety; **~ый** [14; трезв, -á, -о] sober (*a. fig.*)
**тре́нер** *m* [1] trainer, coach
**тре́ние** *n* [12] friction (*a. fig.*)
**тренир|ова́ть** [12], ⟨на-⟩ train, coach; *v/i.* **-ся**; **~о́вка** *f* [7] training, coaching
**трепа́ть** [2], ⟨по-⟩ *ветром* tousle; dishevel; blow about; ***~ кому́-л. не́рвы*** get on s.o.'s nerves
**тре́пет** *m* [1] trembling, quivering; **~а́ть** [3], ⟨за-⟩ tremble (**от** P with); quiver, shiver; *о пламени* flicker; *от ужаса* palpitate; **~ный** [14; -тен, -тна] quivering; flickering
**треск** *m* [1] crack, crackle
**треска́** *f* [5] cod
**тре́ск|аться** [1], ⟨по-, тре́снуть⟩ [20] crack, split; *о коже и т. д.* chap; **~отня́** *f* [6] *о речи* chatter, prattle; **~у́чий** [17 *sh.*] *мороз* hard, ringing; *fig.* bombastic
**тре́снуть** → ***тре́скаться & треща́ть***
**трест** *m* [1] *econ.* trust
**тре́т|ий** [18] third; **~и́ровать** [7] slight; **~ь** *f* [8; *from g/pl. e.*] (one) third
**треуго́льн|ик** *m* [1] triangle; **~ый** [14] triangular
**тре́фы** *f/pl.* [5] clubs (*cards*)
**трёх|годи́чный** [14] three-year; **~дне́вный** [14] three-day; **~колёсный** [14] three-wheeled; **~ле́тний** [15] three--year; threeyear-old; **~со́тый** [14] three hundredth; **~цве́тный** [14] tricolo(u)r; **~эта́жный** [14] threestoried (*Brt.* -reyed)
**трещ|а́ть** [4 *e.*; -щу́, -щи́шь] **1.** ⟨за-⟩ crack; crackle; *о мебели* creak; *coll.* prattle; ***голова́ ~и́т*** have a splitting headache; **2.** ⟨тре́снуть⟩ [20] burst; **~и́на** *f* [5] split (*a. fig.*), crack, cleft, crevice, fissure; *на коже* chap
**три** [34] three; → ***пять***
**трибу́н|а** *f* [5] platform; rostrum; tribune; (*at sports stadium*) stand; **~а́л** *m* [1] tribunal
**тривиа́льный** [14; -лен, -льна] trivial; trite
**тригономе́трия** *f* [7] trigonometry
**тридца́|тый** [14] thirtieth; → ***пятидеся́тый***; **´~ть** [35 *e.*] thirty
**три́жды** three times
**трикота́ж** *m* [1] knitted fabric; *collect.* knitwear
**трило́гия** *f* [7] trilogy
**трина́дца|тый** [14] thirteenth; → ***пя́тый***; **~ть** [35] thirteen; → ***пять***
**три́ста** [36] three hundred
**триу́мф** *m* [1] triumph; **~а́льный** [14] *арка* triumphal; triumphant
**тро́га|тельный** [14; -лен, -льна] touching, moving; **~ть** [1], *once* ⟨тро́нуть⟩ [20] touch (*a. fig.* = affect, move); *coll.* pester; ***не тронь её!*** leave her alone!; **-ся** start; set out (***в путь*** on a journey)
**тро́е** [37] three (→ ***дво́е***); **~кра́тный** [14; -тен, -тна] thrice-repeated
**Тро́ица** *f* [5] Trinity; Whitsun(day); ♀ *coll.* trio
**тро́й|ка** *f* [5; *g/pl.*: тро́ек] three (→ ***дво́йка***); troika (*team of three horses abreast* [+ *vehicle*]); *coll.* (*of school mark* =) ***посре́дственно***; **~но́й** [14] threefold, triple, treble; **~ня** *f* [6; *g/pl.*: тро́ен] triplets *pl.*
**тролле́йбус** *m* [1] trolley bus
**трон** *m* [1] throne; **≈ный** [14] *речь* King's, Queen's
**тро́нуть(ся)** → ***тро́гать(ся)***
**троп|а́** *f* [5; *pl.*: тро́пы, троп, -па́м] path, track; **~и́нка** [5; *g/pl.*: -нок] (small) path
**тропи́ческий** [16] tropical
**трос** *m* [1] *naut.* line; cable, hawser
**трост|ни́к** *m* [1 *e.*] reed; *сахарный* cane; **~нико́вый** [14] reed…; cane…; **~ь** *f* [8; *from g/pl. e.*] cane, walking stick
**тротуа́р** *m* [1] sidewalk, *Brt.* pavement
**трофе́й** *m* [3] trophy (*a. fig.*); *pl.* spoils of war; booty; **~ный** [14] *mil.* captured
**тро|ю́родный** [14] second (cousin ***брат***

*m*, **сестра́** *f*); **~я́кий** [16 *sh*.] threefold, triple

**труб|а́** *f* [5; *pl. st.*] pipe; *печная* chimney; *naut*. funnel; *mus*. trumpet; **вы́лететь в ~у́** go bust; **~а́ч** *m* [1 *e*.] trumpeter; **~и́ть** [14; -блю́, -би́шь], ⟨про-⟩ blow (the **в** B); **~ка** [5; *g/pl*.: -бок] tube; *для курения* pipe; *teleph*. receiver; **~опрово́д** *m* [1] pipeline; **~очный** [14] *табак* pipe

**труд** *m* [1 *e*.] labo(u)r, work; pains *pl*., trouble; difficulty (**с** T with; *a*. hard[ly]); scholarly work; *pl*. (*in published records of scholarly meetings, etc*.) transactions; *coll*. (*услуга*) service; **взять на себя́ ~** take the trouble (to); **~и́ться** [15], ⟨по-⟩ work; toil; **~ность** *f* [8] difficulty; **~ный** [14; -ден, -дна́, -о] difficult, hard; *coll*. heavy; **де́ло оказа́лось ~ным** it was heavy going; **~ово́й** [14] labo(u)r…; *день* working; *доход* earned; *стаж* service…; **~олюби́вый** [14 *sh*.] industrious; **~оспосо́бный** [14; -бен, -бна] able-bodied, capable of working; **~я́щийся** [17] working; *su. mst. pl*. working people

**тру́женик** *m* [1] toiler, worker

**труп** *m* [1] corpse, dead body

**тру́ппа** *f* [5] company, troupe

**трус** *m* [1] coward

**тру́сики** *no sg*. [1] shorts, swimming trunks, undershorts

**тру́с|ить** [15], be a coward; ⟨с-⟩ be afraid (of P); **~и́ха** *coll./f* [5] *f* → **трус**; **~ли́вый** [14 *sh*.] cowardly; **~ость** *f* [8] cowardice

**трусы́** *no sg*. = **тру́сики**

**трущо́ба** *f* [5] thicket; *fig*. out-of-the-way place; slum

**трюк** *m* [1] feat, stunt; *fig*. gimmick; *pej*. trick

**трюм** *m* [1] *naut*. hold

**трюмо́** *n* [*indecl*.] pier glass

**тря́п|ка** *f* [5; *g/pl*.: -пок] rag; *для пыли* duster; *pl. coll*. finery; *о человеке* milksop; **~ьё** *n* [10] rag(s)

**тря́с|ка** *f* [5] jolting; **~ти́** [24; -с-], *once* ⟨тряхну́ть⟩ [20] shake (a *p.'s* Д *hand, head, etc*. T; *a. fig*.); (*impers*.) jolt; **~ти́сь** shake; shiver (with **от** P)

**тряхну́ть** → **трясти́**

**тсс!** *int*. hush!; ssh!

**туале́т** *m* [1] toilet, lavatory; dress, dressing

**туберкулёз** *m* [1] tuberculosis; **~ный** [14] *больной* tubercular

**туго́|й** [14; туг, -а́, -о *comp*.: ту́же] tight, taut; *замок* stiff; (*туго набитый*) crammed; hard (*a*. of hearing *на ухо*); *adv. a. открываться* hard; with difficulty; **у него́ ~ с деньга́ми** he is short of money

**туда́** there, thither; that way

**туз** *m* [1 *e*.] *cards* ace

**тузе́м|ец** *m* [1; -мца] native; **~ный** [14] native

**ту́ловище** *n* [11] trunk, torso

**тулу́п** *m* [1] sheepskin coat

**тума́н** *m* [1] fog, mist; *дымка* haze (*a. fig*.); **~ный** [14; -а́нен, -а́нна] foggy, misty; *fig*. hazy, vague

**ту́мбочка** *f* [5; *g/pl*.: -чек] bedside table

**ту́ндра** *f* [5] *geog*. tundra

**туне́ц** *m* [1; -нца́ и т. д.] tuna *or* tunny fish

**тунне́ль** → **тонне́ль**

**туп|е́ть** [8], ⟨(п)о-⟩ *fig*. grow blunt; **~и́к** *m* [1 *e*.] blind alley, cul-de-sac; *fig*. deadlock, impasse; **ста́вить в ~и́к** reach a deadlock; **стать в ~и́к** be at a loss, be nonplussed; **~о́й** [14; туп, -а́, -о] blunt; *math*. obtuse; *fig*. dull, stupid; **~ость** *f* [8] bluntness; dullness; **~оу́мный** [14; -мен, -мна] dull, obtuse

**тур** *m* [1] *переговоров* round; tour; turn (*at a dance*); *zo*. aurochs

**турба́за** *f* [5] hostel

**турби́на** *f* [5] turbine

**туре́цкий** [16] Turkish

**тури́|зм** *m* [1] tourism; **~ст** *m* [1] tourist

**туркме́н** *m* [1] Turkmen; **~ский** [16] Turkmen

**турне́** (-'nɛ) *n* [*indecl*.] tour (*esp. of performers or sports competitors*)

**турни́к** *m* [1 *e*.] *sport* horizontal bar

**турнике́т** [1] turnstile; *med*. tourniquet

**турни́р** *m* [1] tournament (**на** П in)

**ту́р|ок** *m* [1; -рка; *g/pl*.: ту́рок], **~ча́нка** [5; *g/pl*.: -нок] Turk

**ту́ск|лый** [14; тускл, -а́, -о] *свет* dim; dull; **~не́ть** [8], ⟨по-⟩ & **~нуть** [20] grow dim *or* dull; lose luster (-tre); pale (**пе́-**

Т

***ред*** T before)

**тут** here; there; then; **~**! present!, here!; **~ *же*** there and then, on the spot; ***~ как ~*** *coll.* there he is; there they are; that's that

**ту́тов|ый** [14]: ***~ое де́рево*** mulberry tree

**ту́фля** *f* [6; *g*/*pl.*: -фель] shoe; *домашняя* slipper

**ту́х|лый** [14; тухл, -á, -о] *яйцо* bad, rotten; **~нуть** [21] **1.** ⟨по-⟩ *о свете* go out; *о костре* go *or* die out; **2.** ⟨про-⟩ go bad

**ту́ч|а** *f* [5] cloud; rain *or* storm cloud *народа* crowd; *мух* swarm; *dim.* **~ка** *f* [5; *g*/*pl.*: -чек], **~ный** [14; -чен, -чнá, -о] corpulent, stout

**туш** *m* [1] *mus.* flourish

**ту́ша** *f* [5] carcass

**туш|ёнка** *f* [5] *coll.* corned beef *or* pork; **~ёный** [14] stewed; **~и́ть** [16], ⟨по-⟩ **1.** switch off, put out, extinguish; *скандал* quell; **2.** *impf.* stew

**тушь** *f* [8] Indian ink; mascara

**тща́тельн|ость** *f* [8] thoroughness; care(fulness); **~ый** [14; -лен, -льна] painstaking; careful

**тще|ду́шный** [14; -шен, -шна] sickly; **~сла́вие** *n* [12] vanity; **~сла́вный** [14; -вен, -вна] vain (-glorious); **~́тный** [14; -тен, -тна] vain, futile; ***~́тно*** in vain

**ты** [21] you; *obs.* thou; ***быть на ~*** (**с** T) be on familiar terms with s.o.

**ты́кать** [3], ⟨ткнуть⟩ [20] poke, jab, thrust; (*v*/*i.* **-ся**) knock (***в*** B against, into)

**ты́ква** *f* [5] pumpkin

**тыл** *m* [1; в -у́; *pl. e.*] rear, back

**ты́сяч|а** *f* [5] thousand; **~еле́тие** *n* [12] millenium; **~ный** [14] thousandth; of thousand(s)

**тьма** *f* [5] dark(ness); *coll.* a host of, a multitude of

**тьфу!** *coll.* fie!, for shame!

**тю́бик** *m* [1] tube (*of toothpaste, etc.*)

**тюк** *m* [1 *e.*] bale, pack

**тюле́нь** *m* [4] *zo.* seal

**тюль** *m* [4] tulle

**тюльпа́н** *m* [1] tulip

**тюр|е́мный** [14] prison…; **~е́мный контролёр** jailer, *Brt.* gaoler, warder; **~ьма́** *f* [5; *pl.*: тю́рьмы, -рем, -рьмам] prison, jail, *Brt.* gaol

**тюфя́к** *m* [1 *e.*] mattress (*filled with straw, etc.*)

**тя́вкать** *coll.* [1] yap, yelp

**тя́г|а** *f* [5] *в печи* draft, *Brt.* draught; *сила* traction; *fig.* bent (**к** Д for); craving (for); **~а́ться** *coll.* [1] (**с** T) be a match (for), vie (with); **~остный** [14; -тен, -тна] (*обременительный*) burdensome; (*неприятный*) painful; **~ость** *f* [8] burden (*be… to* **в** В/Д); **~оте́ние** *n* [12] *земное* gravitation; *a.* → **~а** *fig.*; **~оте́ть** [8] gravitate (toward[s] **к** Д); weigh (upon ***над*** T); **~оти́ть** [15 *e.*; -ощу́, -оти́шь] weigh upon, be a burden to; **-ся** feel a burden (T of); **~у́чий** [17 *sh.*] *жидкость* viscous; *речь* drawling

**тяж|елове́с** *m* [1] *sport* heavyweight; **~елове́сный** [14; -сен, -сна] heavy, ponderous; **~ёлый** [14; -жел, -желá] heavy, difficult, hard; *стиль* laborious; *ранение и т. д.* serious; *удар, положение* severe, grave; *обстоятельства и т. д.* grievous, sad, oppressive, painful; *воздух* close; (Д) ***~ело́*** feel miserable; **~́есть** *f* [8] heaviness; weight; load; burden; gravity; seriousness; **~́кий** [16; тя́жек, тяжкá, -о] heavy (*fig.*), *etc.*, → ***~ёлый***

**тян|у́ть** [19] pull, draw; *naut.* tow; *медлить* protract; *слова* drawl (out); (*влечь*) attract; long; have a mind to; would like; *о запахе* waft; ***~́ет*** there is a draft (*Brt.* draught) (T of); *coll.* *красть* steal; take (**с** P from); **-ся** stretch (*a.* = extend); last; drag; draw on; reach out (**к** Д for)

T

# У

**у** (Р) at, by, near; with; (at) …'s; at …'s place; ***у меня*** (***был, -á …***) I have (had); my; *взять, узнать и т. д.* from, of; *берега и т. д.* off; in; ***у себя́*** in (at) one's home *or* room *or* office

**убав|ля́ть** [28], ⟨**҆ить**⟩ [14] reduce, diminish, decrease; ***҆ить в ве́се*** lose weight; *v/i.* **-ся**

**убе|га́ть** [1], ⟨**~жа́ть**⟩ [4; -егу́, -жи́шь, -гу́т] run away; *тайком* escape

**убе|ди́тельный** [14; -лен, -льна] convincing; *просьба* urgent; **~жда́ть** [1], ⟨**~ди́ть**⟩ [15 *e.*; *no 1*[st] *p. sg.*; -еди́шь, -еждённый] convince (**в** П of); (*уговорить*) persuade (*impf. a.* try to…); **~жде́ние** *n* [12] persuasion; conviction, belief

**убеж|а́ть** → ***убега́ть***; **҆ище** *n* [11] shelter, refuge; *политическое* asylum

**убер|ега́ть** [1], ⟨**~е́чь**⟩ [26 г/ж] keep safe, safeguard

**уби|ва́ть** [1], ⟨**҆ть**⟩ [убью́, -ьёшь; уби́тый] kill, murder; assassinate; *fig.* drive to despair; ***~ва́ть вре́мя*** kill *or* waste time

**убий|ственный** [14 *sh.*] killing; *взгляд* murderous; **~ство** *n* [9] murder; *политическое* assassination; ***покуше́ние на ~ство*** murderous assault; **~ца** *m/f* [5] murderer; assassin

**убира́|ть** [1], ⟨**убра́ть**⟩ [уберу́, -рёшь; убра́л, -á, -о; у́бранный] take (*or* put, clear) away (in); gather, harvest; tidy up; (*украшать*) decorate, adorn, trim; **-ся** *coll.* clear off; ***~йся*** (***вон***)**!** get out of here!, beat it!

**убить** → ***убива́ть***

**убо́|гий** [16 *sh.*] (*бедный*) needy, poor; *жилище* miserable; **~жество** *n* [9] poverty; mediocrity

**убо́й** *m* [3] slaughter (*of livestock*) (for ***на*** В)

**убо́р** *m* [1]: ***головно́й ~*** headgear; **~истый** [14 *sh.*] close; **~ка** *f* [5; *g/pl.*: -рок] harvest, gathering; *комнаты и т. д.* tidying up; **~ная** *f* [14] lavatory, toilet; *thea.* dressing room; **~очный** [14] harvest(ing); **~щица** *f* [5] cleaner (*in offices, etc.*); charwoman

**убра́|нство** *n* [9] furniture, appointments; interior decor; **~ть(ся)** → ***убира́ть(ся)***

**убы|ва́ть** [1], ⟨**҆ть**⟩ [убу́ду, -убу́дешь; у́был, -á, -о] *о воде* subside, fall; (*уменьшаться*) decrease; **́~ль** *f* [8] diminution, fall; **҆ток** *m* [1; -тка] loss, damage; **҆точный** [14; -чен, -чна] unprofitable; **҆ть** → ***~ва́ть***

**уваж|а́емый** [14] respected; dear (*as salutation in letter*); **~а́ть** [1], **~е́ние** *n* [12] respect, esteem (*su.* **к** Д for); **~и́тельный** [14; -лен, -льна] *причина* valid; *отношение* respectful

**уведом|ля́ть** [28], ⟨**́~ить**⟩ [14] inform, notify, advise (**о** П of); **~ле́ние** *n* [12] notification, information

**увезти́** → ***увози́ть***

**увекове́чи|вать** [1], ⟨**~ть**⟩ [16] immortalize, perpetuate

**увелич|е́ние** *n* [12] increase; *phot.* enlargement; **҆ивать** [1], ⟨**҆ить**⟩ [16] increase; enlarge; extend; *v/i.* **-ся**; **~и́тельный** [14] magnifying

**увенча́ться** [1] *pf.* (Т) be crowned

**увер|е́ние** *n* [12] assurance (of **в** П); **҆енность** *f* [8] assurance; certainty; confidence (**в** П in); **҆енный** [14 *sh.*] confident, sure, certain (**в** П of); ***бу́дьте ҆ены*** you may be sure, you may depend on it; **҆ить** → ***~я́ть***

**увёрт|ка** *coll. f* [5; *g/pl.*: -ток] subterfuge, dodge, evasion; **~ливый** [14 *sh.*] evasive, shifty

**увертю́ра** *f* [5] overture

**увер|я́ть** [28], ⟨**҆ить**⟩ [13] assure (**в** П of); *убедить*(*ся*) make believe (sure **-ся**), persuade

**уве́систый** [14 *sh.*] rather heavy; *coll.* weighty

**увести́** → ***уводи́ть***

**уве́ч|ить** [16], ⟨**из-**⟩ maim, mutilate; **~ный** [14] maimed, mutilated, crippled;

**\~ье** *n* [10] mutilation
**увещ(ев)á|ние** *n* [12] admonition; **\~ть** [1] admonish
**уви́л|ивать** [1], ⟨**\~ьну́ть**⟩ [20] shirk
**увлажн|я́ть** [28], ⟨**\~и́ть**⟩ [13] wet, dampen, moisten
**увле|ка́тельный** [14; -лен, -льна] fascinating, absorbing; **\~ка́ть** [1], ⟨**\~́чь**⟩ [26] carry (away; *a. fig.* = transport, captivate); **-ся** (T) be carried away (by), be(-come) enthusiastic (about); (*погрузиться*) be(come) absorbed (in); (*влюбиться*) fall (*or* be) in love (with); **\~че́ние** *n* [12] enthusiasm, passion (for T)
**уво|ди́ть** [15], ⟨**увести́**⟩ [25] take, lead (away, off); *coll.* (*украсть*) steal; **\~зи́ть** [15], ⟨**увезти́**⟩ [24] take, carry, drive (away, off); abduct, kidnap
**уво́л|ить** → **\~ьня́ть**; **\~ьне́ние** *n* [12] dismissal (**с** P from); **\~ьня́ть** [28], ⟨**\~ить**⟩ [13] dismiss (**с** P from)
**увы́!** *int.* alas!
**увя|да́ние** *n* [12] withering; *о человеке* signs of aging; **\~да́ть** [21], ⟨**\~́нуть**⟩ [20] wither, fade; **\~́дший** [17] withered
**увяз|а́ть** [1] **1.** ⟨**\~́нуть**⟩ [21] get stuck (in); *fig.* get bogged down (in); **2.** → **\~́ывать(ся)**; **\~́ка** *f* [5] coordination; **\~́ывать** [1], ⟨**\~а́ть**⟩ [3] tie up; (*согласовывать*) coordinate (*v/i.* **-ся**)
**уга́д|ывать** [1], ⟨**\~а́ть**⟩ [1] guess
**уга́р** *m* [1] charcoal fumes; *fig.* ecstasy, intoxication
**угас|а́ть** [1], ⟨**\~́нуть**⟩ [21] *об огне* die down; *о звуке* die (*or* fade) away; *надежда* die; *силы* fail; *о человеке* fade away
**угле|ки́слый** [14] *chem.* carbonate (of); (**\~ки́слый газ** carbon dioxide); **\~ро́д** *m* [1] carbon
**углово́й** [14] *дом* corner…; angle…; angular
**углуб|и́ть(ся)** → **\~ля́ть(ся)**; **\~ле́ние** *n* [12] deepening; (*впадина*) hollow, cavity, hole; *знаний* extension; **\~лённый** [14 *sh.*] profound; *a. p. pt. p. of* **\~и́ть(ся)**; **\~ля́ть** [28], ⟨**\~и́ть**⟩ [14 *e.*; -блю, -би́шь; -блённый] deepen (*v/i.* **-ся**); make (become) more profound, extend; **-ся** *a.* go deep (**в** B into), be(-come) absorbed (in)
**угна́ть** → **угоня́ть**
**угнет|а́тель** *m* [4] oppressor; **\~а́ть** [1] oppress; (*мучить*) depress; **\~е́ние** *n* [12] oppression; (*a.* **\~ённость** *f* [8]) depression; **\~ённый** [14; -тён, -тена́] oppressed; depressed
**угов|а́ривать** [1], ⟨**\~ори́ть**⟩ [13] (B) (*impf.* try to) persuade; **-ся** arrange, agree; **\~о́р** *m* [1] agreement; *pl.* persuasion; **\~ори́ть(ся)** → **\~а́ривать(ся)**
**уго́д|а** *f* [5]: **в \~у** (Д) for the benefit of, to please; **\~и́ть** → **угожда́ть**; **\~ливый** [14 *sh.*] fawning, ingratiating, toadyish; **\~ник** *m* [1]: **свято́й \~ник** saint; **\~но** please; **как (что) вам \~но** just as (whatever) you like; **(что) вам \~но?** what can I do for you?; **ско́лько (душе́) \~но** → **вдо́воль & вла́сть**
**уго|жда́ть** [1], ⟨**\~ди́ть**⟩ [15 *e.*; -ожу́, -оди́шь] (Д, **на** B) please; *pf. coll. в яму* fall (into); *в беду* get; *в глаз и т. д.* hit
**у́гол** *m* [1; угла́; в, на углу́] corner (**на** П at); *math.* angle
**уголо́вный** [14] criminal; **\~ ко́декс** criminal law
**уголо́к** *m* [1; -лка́] nook, corner
**у́голь** *m* [4; у́гля] coal; **как на \~я́х** *coll.* on tenterhooks; **\~ный** [14] coal…; carbonic
**угомони́ть(ся)** [13] *pf. coll.* calm (down)
**угоня́ть** [28], ⟨**угна́ть**⟩ [угоню́, уго́нишь; угна́л] drive (away, off); *машину* steal; *самолёт* hijack; **-ся** *coll.* catch up (**за** T with)
**угор|а́ть** [1], ⟨**\~е́ть**⟩ [9] be poisoned by carbon monoxide fumes
**у́горь¹** *m* [4 *e.*; угря́] eel
**у́горь²** *m* [4 *e.*; угря́] *med.* blackhead
**уго|ща́ть** [1], ⟨**\~сти́ть**⟩ [15 *e.*; -ощу́, -ости́шь; -ощённый] treat (T), entertain; **\~ще́ние** *n* [12] entertaining; treating (to); refreshments; food, drinks *pl.*
**угро|жа́ть** [1] threaten (p. with Д/T); **\~́за** *f* [5] threat, menace
**угрызе́ни|е** *n* [12]: **\~я** *pl.* **со́вести** pangs of conscience; remorse
**угрю́мый** [14 *sh.*] morose, gloomy

**уда́в** *m* [1] boa, boa constrictor
**уда|ва́ться** [5], ⟨**∠ться**⟩ [уда́стся, -аду́тся; уда́лся, -ала́сь] succeed; ***мне ~ётся*** (***~ло́сь***) (+ *inf.*) I succeed(ed) (in …ing)
**удал|е́ние** *n* [12] removal; *зуба* extraction; sending away (*sport* off); ***на ~е́нии*** at a distance; **~и́ть(ся)** → ***~я́ть(ся)***; **~о́й**, **∠ый** [14; уда́л, -а́, -о] bold, daring; **∠ь** *f* [8], *coll.* **~ьство́** *n* [9] boldness, daring; **~я́ть** [28], ⟨**~и́ть**⟩ [13] remove; *зуб* extract; **-ся** retire, withdraw; move away
**уда́р** *m* [1] blow (*a. fig.*); (*a. med.*) stroke; *el.* shock (*a. fig.*); (*столкновение*) impact; *ножом* slash; *грома* clap; *coll.* form; ***он в ~е*** he's in good form; **~е́ние** *n* [12] stress, accent; **~иться** → ***~я́ться***; **~ный** [14]: ***~ные инструме́нты*** percussion instruments; **~я́ть** [28], ⟨**~ить**⟩ [13] strike (***по*** Д on), hit; knock; beat; sound (*тревогу*); punch (*кулаком*); butt (*головой*); kick (*ногой*); *морозы* set in; **-ся** strike *or* knock (Т/***о*** В with/against); hit (***в*** В); ***~я́ться в кра́йности*** go to extremes
**уда́ться** → ***удава́ться***
**уда́ч|а** *f* [5] success, (good) luck; **~ник** *coll. m* [1] lucky person; **~ный** [14; -чен, -чна] successful; good
**удв|а́ивать** [1], ⟨**~о́ить**⟩ [13] double (*v/i.* **-ся**)
**уде́л** *m* [1] lot, destiny; **~и́ть** → ***~я́ть***; **~ьный** [14] *phys.* specific; **~я́ть** [28], ⟨**~и́ть**⟩ [13] devote, spare; allot
**уде́рж|ивать** [1], ⟨**~а́ть**⟩ [4] withhold, restrain; *в памяти* keep, retain; *деньги* deduct; **-ся** hold (***за*** В on; to; *a.* out); refrain (from ***от*** Р)
**удешев|ля́ть** [28], ⟨**~и́ть**⟩ [14 *e.*; -влю́, -ви́шь, -влённый] reduce the price of
**удив|и́тельный** [14; -лен, -льна] astonishing, surprising; (*необычный*) amazing, strange; (***не***) ***~и́тельно*** it is a (no) wonder; **~и́ть(ся)** → ***~ля́ть(ся)***; **~ле́ние** *n* [12] astonishment, surprise; **~ля́ть** [28], ⟨**~и́ть**⟩ [14 *e.*; -влю́, -ви́шь, -влённый] (**-ся** be) astonish(ed at Д), surprise(d, wonder)
**удила́** *n/pl.* [9; -и́л, -ила́м]: ***закуси́ть ~*** get (*or* take) the bit between one's teeth
**удира́ть** *coll.* [1], ⟨**удра́ть**⟩ [удеру́, -рёшь; удра́л, -а́, -о] make off; run away
**уди́ть** [15] angle (for *v/t.*), fish
**удлин|е́ние** *n* [12] lengthening; **~я́ть** [28], ⟨**~и́ть**⟩ [13] lengthen, prolong
**удо́б|ный** [14; -бен, -бна] (*подходящий*) convenient; *мебель и т. д.* comfortable; ***воспо́льзоваться ~ным слу́чаем*** take an opportunity; **~о...** easily…; **~ре́ние** *n* [12] fertilizer; fertilization; **~ря́ть** [28], ⟨**~рить**⟩ [13] fertilize, manure; **~ство** *n* [9] convenience; comfort
**удовлетвор|е́ние** *n* [12] satisfaction; **~и́тельный** [14; -лен, -льна] satisfactory; *adv. a.* "fair" (*as school mark*); **~я́ть** [28], ⟨**~и́ть**⟩ [13] satisfy; *просьбу* grant; (Д) meet; **-ся** content o.s. (Т with)
**удо|во́льствие** *n* [12] pleasure; **~рожа́ть** [1], ⟨**~рожи́ть**⟩ [16] raise the price of
**удост|а́ивать** [1], ⟨**~о́ить**⟩ [13] (**-ся** be) award(ed); deign (*взгляда, -ом* В to look at p.); **~овере́ние** *n* [12] certificate, certification; ***~овере́ние ли́чности*** identity card; **~оверя́ть** [28], ⟨**~ове́рить**⟩ [13] certify, attest; *личность* prove; *подпись* witness; convince (***в*** П of; **-ся** o.s.; *a.* make sure); **~о́ить(ся)** → ***~а́ивать(ся)***
**удосу́житься** *coll.* [16] find time
**у́дочк|а** *f* [5; *g/pl.*: -чек] fishing rod; ***заки́нуть ~у*** *fig.* cast a line, put a line out; ***попа́сться на ~у*** swallow the bait
**удра́ть** → ***удира́ть***
**удружи́ть** [16 *e.*; -жу́, -жи́шь] *coll.* do a service *or* good turn; *iro.* unwittingly do a disservice
**удруч|а́ть** [1], ⟨**~и́ть**⟩ [16 *e.*; -чу́, -чи́шь; -чённый] deject, depress
**удуш|е́ние** *n* [12] suffocation; **∠ливый** [14 *sh.*] stifling, suffocating; **∠ье** *n* [10] asthma; asphyxia
**уедин|е́ние** *n* [12] solitude; **~ённый** [14 *sh.*] secluded, lonely, solitary; **~я́ться** [28], ⟨**~и́ть(ся)**⟩ [13] withdraw, go off (by o.s.); seclude o.s.
**уе́зд** *m* [1] *hist.*, **~ный** [14] district
**уезжа́ть** [1], ⟨**уе́хать**⟩ [уе́ду, -де́шь] (***в*** В) leave (for), go (away; to)

**уж 1.** *m* [1 *e.*] grass snake; **2.** → ***уже́***; indeed, well; *do, be* (+ *vb.*)

**у́жас** *m* [1] horror; terror, fright; *coll.* → **∠ный, ∠но; ~а́ть** [1], ⟨**~ну́ть**⟩ [20] horrify; **-ся** be horrified *or* terrified (Р, Д at); **~а́ющий** [17] horrifying; **∠ный** [14; -сен, -сна] terrible, horrible, dreadful; awful

**уже́** already; by this time; by now; **~ *не*** not… any more; (***вот***) **~** for; **~ *пора́*** it's time (to + *inf.*)

**уже́ние** *n* [12] angling, fishing

**ужи|ва́ться** [1], ⟨**∠ться**⟩ [14; -иву́сь, -вёшься; -и́лся, -ила́сь] get accustomed (**в** П to); get along (**с** T with); **∠вчивый** [14 *sh.*] easy to get on with

**у́жин** *m* [1] supper (***за*** T at; ***на*** B, ***к*** Д for); **~ать** [1], ⟨по-⟩ have supper

**ужи́ться** → ***ужива́ться***

**узако́н|ивать** [1], ⟨**~ить**⟩ [13] legalize

**узбе́к** *m* [1], **~ский** [16] Uzbek

**узд|а́** *f* [5; *pl. st.*], **~е́чка** *f* [5; *g/pl.*: -чек] bridle

**у́зел** *m* [1; узла́] knot; *rail.* junction; *tech.* assembly; *вещей* bundle; **~о́к** *m* [1; -лка́] knot; small bundle

**у́зк|ий** [16; у́зок, узка́, -о; *comp.*: у́же] narrow (*a. fig.*); (*тесный*) tight; **~ое ме́сто** bottleneck; weak point; **~околе́йный** [14] narrowgauge

**узлов|а́тый** [14 *sh.*] knotty; **~о́й** [14] (*основной*) central, chief

**узна|ва́ть** [5], ⟨**∠ть**⟩ [1] recognize (by ***по*** Д); learn (***от*** P from: p.; ***из*** P th.), find out, (get to) know

**у́зник** *m* [1] prisoner

**узо́р** *m* [1] pattern, design; **с *~ами*** = **~чатый** [14 *sh.*] figured; decorated with a pattern

**у́зость** *f* [8] narrow(-minded)ness

**у́зы** *f/pl.* [5] bonds, ties

**у́йма** *coll. f* [5] lots of, heaps of

**уйти́** → ***уходи́ть***

**ука́з** *m* [1] decree, edict; **~а́ние** *n* [12] instruction (***по*** Д by), direction; indication (P, ***на*** B of); **~а́тель** *m* [4] *в книге* index; indicator (*a. mot.*); **~а́тельный** [14] indicating; (*палец*) index finger; *gr.* demonstrative; **~а́ть** → ***~ывать***; **~ка** *f* [5] pointer; *coll.* orders *pl.*, bidding (*of s.o. else*) (***по*** Д by); **~ывать** [1], ⟨**~а́ть**⟩ [3] point out; point (***на*** B to); *путь и т. д.* show; indicate

**ука́ч|ивать**, ⟨**~а́ть**⟩ [1] rock to sleep, lull; *impers.* make (sea)sick

**укла́д** *m* [1] structure; mode, way (*жизни*); **~ка** *f* [5] packing; *рельсов и т. д.* laying; *волос* set(ting); **~ывать** [1], ⟨уложи́ть⟩ [16] put (to bed); lay; stack, pack (up *coll.* **-ся**); place; cover; **-ся** *a.* go into; fit; *coll.* manage; ***~ываться в голове́*** sink in

**укло́н** *m* [1] slope, incline; slant (*a. fig.* = bias, bent, tendency); *pol.* deviation; **~е́ние** *n* [12] evasion; **~и́ться** → ***~я́ться***; **~чивый** [14 *sh.*] evasive; **~я́ться** [28], ⟨**~и́ться**⟩ [13; -оню́сь, -о́нишься] *от темы и т. д.* digress, deviate; evade (*v/t.* **от** P)

**уклю́чина** *f* [5] oarlock (*Brt.* row-)

**уко́л** *m* [1] prick; jab; *med.* injection

**укомплекто́в|ывать** [1], ⟨**~а́ть**⟩ [7] complete, bring up to (full) strength; supply (fully; with T)

**уко́р** *m* [1] reproach

**укор|а́чивать** [1], ⟨**~оти́ть**⟩ [15 *e.*; -очу́, -оти́шь; -о́ченный] shorten; **~еня́ться** [28], ⟨**~ени́ться**⟩ [13] take root; **~и́зна** *f* [5] → **~**; **~и́зненный** [14] reproachful; **~и́ть** → ***~я́ть***; **~оти́ть** → ***~а́чивать***; **~я́ть** [28], ⟨**~и́ть**⟩ [13] reproach (with), blame (for) (**в** П, ***за*** B)

**укра́дкой** furtively

**украи́н|ец** *m* [1; -нца], **~ка** *f* [5; *g/pl.*: -нок], **~ский** [16] Ukranian

**укра|ша́ть** [1], ⟨**∠сить**⟩ [15] adorn; (**-ся** be) decorat(ed); trim; embellish; **~ше́ние** *n* [12] adornment; decoration; ornament; embellishment

**укреп|и́ть(ся)** → ***~ля́ть(ся)***; **~ле́ние** *n* [12] strengthening; (*положения*) reinforcing; *mil.* fortification; **~ля́ть** [28], ⟨**~и́ть**⟩ [14 *e.*; -плю́, -пи́шь; -плённый] strengthen; make fast; consolidate; *mil.* fortify; **-ся** strengthen, become stronger

**укро́|мный** [14; -мен, -мна] secluded; **~п** *m* [1] dill fennel

**укро|ти́тель** *m* [4], **~ти́тельница** *f* [5] (animal) tamer; **~ща́ть** [1], ⟨**~ти́ть**⟩

У

[15 *e.*; -ощу́, -оти́шь; -ощённый] tame; (*умерить*) subdue, restrain; **~ще́ние** *n* [12] taming

**укрупн|я́ть** [28], ⟨**~и́ть**⟩ [13] enlarge, extend; amalgamate

**укры|ва́ть** [1], ⟨**~́ть**⟩ [22] cover; give shelter; (*прятать*) conceal, harbo(u)r; **-ся** cover o.s.; hide; take shelter *or* cover; **~́тие** *n* [12] cover, shelter

**у́ксус** *m* [1] vinegar

**уку́с** *m* [1] bite; **~и́ть** → ***куса́ть***

**уку́т|ывать**, ⟨**~ать**⟩ [1] wrap up (in)

**ула́|вливать** [1], ⟨**улови́ть**⟩ [14] catch; perceive, detect; *coll.* seize (*an opportunity, etc.*); (*понять*) grasp; **~живать** [1], ⟨**~дить**⟩ [15] settle, arrange, resolve

**у́лей** *m* [3; у́лья] beehive

**улет|а́ть** [1], ⟨**~е́ть**⟩ [11] fly (away)

**улету́чи|ваться** [1], ⟨**~ться**⟩ [16] evaporate, volatilize; *coll.* disappear, vanish

**уле́чься** [26 г/ж: уля́гусь, уля́жешься, уля́гутся; улётся *pf.*] lie down, go (to bed); *о пыли и т. д.* settle; (*утихнуть*) calm down, abate

**ули́ка** *f* [5] evidence

**ули́тка** *f* [5; *g/pl.*: -ток] snail

**у́лиц|а** *f* [5] street (in, on **на** П); ***на ~е*** *a.* outside, outdoors

**улич|а́ть** [1], ⟨**~и́ть**⟩ [16 *e.*: -чу́, -чи́шь, -чённый] (**в** П) catch out in lying; establish the guilt (of); ***~и́ть во лжи*** give s.o. the lie

**у́личн|ый** [14] street…; ***~ое движе́ние*** road traffic

**уло́в** *m* [1] catch; **~и́мый** [14 *sh.*] perceptible; **~и́ть** → ***ула́вливать***; **~ка** *f* [5; *g/pl.*: -вок] trick, ruse

**уложи́ть(ся)** → ***укла́дывать(ся)***

**улуч|а́ть** *coll.* [1], ⟨**~и́ть**⟩ [16 *e.*; -чу́, -чи́шь; -чённый] find, seize, catch

**улучш|а́ть** [1], ⟨**~и́ть**⟩ [16] improve; *v/i.* **-ся**; **~е́ние** *n* [12] improvement; **~́ить(ся)** → ***~а́ть(ся)***

**улыб|а́ться** [1], ⟨**~ну́ться**⟩ [20], **~́ка** *f* [5; *g/pl.*: -бок] smile (at Д)

**ультимат|и́вный** [14; -вен, -вна] categorical, express; **~́ум** *m* [1] ultimatum

**ультра|звуково́й** [14] ultrasonic; **~коро́ткий** [16] ultra-short (frequency)

**ум** *m* [1 *e.*] intellect; mind; sense(s); ***без ~а́*** mad (about **от** Р); ***за́дним ~о́м кре́пок*** wise after the event; ***быть на ~е́ (у*** Р) be on one's mind; ***э́то не его́ ~а́ де́ло*** it's not his business; ***сойти́ с ~а́*** go mad; ***сходи́ть с ~а́*** *coll. a.* be mad (about **по** П); *coll.* ***~ за ра́зум захо́дит*** I'm at my wits end

**умал|е́ние** *n* [12] belittling; **~и́ть** → ***~я́ть***; **~́чивать** [1], ⟨**умолча́ть**⟩ [4 *e.*; -чу́, -чи́шь] (**о** П) pass over in silence; **~я́ть** [28], ⟨**~и́ть**⟩ [13] belittle, derogate, disparage

**уме́|лый** [14] able, capable, skilled; **~ние** *n* [12] skill, ability, know-how

**уменьш|а́ть** [1], ⟨**~́ить**⟩ [16 & 16 *e.*; -е́ньшу́, -е́ньши́шь; -е́ньшенный & -шённый] reduce, diminish, decrease (*v/i.* **-ся**); ***~́ить расхо́ды*** cut down expenditures; **~е́ние** *n* [12] decrease, reduction; **~и́тельный** [14] diminishing; *gr.* diminutive; **~́ить(ся)** → ***~а́ть(ся)***

**уме́ренн|ость** *f* [8] moderation; **~ый** [14 *sh.*] moderate, (*a. geogr.* [*no sh.*]) temperate

**умер|е́ть** → ***умира́ть***; **~́ить** → ***~я́ть***; **~тви́ть** → ***~щвля́ть***; **~́ший** [17] dead; **~щвля́ть** [28], ⟨**~тви́ть**⟩ [14; -рщвлю́, -ртви́шь; -рщвлённый] kill; **~я́ть** [28], ⟨**~́ить**⟩ [13] become moderate

**уме|сти́ть(ся)** → ***~ща́ть(ся)***; **~́стный** (-'mesn) [14; -тен, -тна] appropriate; **~́ть** [8], ⟨с-⟩ be able to; know how to; **~ща́ть** [1], ⟨**~сти́ть**⟩ [15 *e.*; -ещу́, -ести́шь; -ещённый] fit, get (into **в** В); **-ся** find room

**умил|е́ние** *n* [12] emotion, tenderness; **~ённый** [14] touched, moved; **~я́ть** [28], ⟨**~и́ть**⟩ [13] (**-ся** be) move(d), touch(ed)

**умира́ть** [1], ⟨**умере́ть**⟩ [12; *pt.*: у́мер, умерла́, -о; уме́рший] die (of, from **от**); ***~ от ску́ки*** be bored to death

**умиротворённый** [14; -ена, -ён] tranquil; contented

**умн|е́ть** [8], ⟨по-⟩ grow wiser; **~́ик** *coll. m* [1], **~́ица** *m/f* [5] clever person; **~́ичать** *coll.* [1] → ***мудри́ть***

**умнож|а́ть** [1], ⟨**~́ить**⟩ [16] multiply (by **на** В); (*увеличивать*) increase; *v/i.* **-ся**; **~е́ние** *n* [12] multiplication

**у́м|ный** [14; умён, умна́, у́мно́] clever, smart, wise, intelligent; **\~озаключе́ние** *n* [12] conclusion; **\~озри́тельный** [14; -лен, -льна] speculative

**умол|и́ть** → **\~*я́ть***; **´\~к**: ***без ´\~ку*** incessantly; **\~ка́ть** [1], ⟨**´\~кнуть**⟩ [21] *шум* stop; lapse into silence, become silent; **\~ча́ть** → ***ума́лчивать***; **\~я́ть** [28], ⟨**\~и́ть**⟩ [13; -олю́, -о́лишь] implore (*v/t.*), beseech, entreat (for **о** П)

**умопомрачи́тельный** [14; -лен, -льна] *coll.* fantastic

**умо́р|а** *coll.* *f* [5], **\~и́тельный** *coll.* [14; -лен, -льна] side-splitting, hilarious; **\~и́ть** *coll.* [13] *pf.* kill; exhaust, fatigue (*a.* with laughing ***со́ смеху***)

**у́мственный** [14] intellectual, mental; *работа* brainwork

**умудр|я́ть** [28], ⟨**\~и́ть**⟩ [13] teach; make wiser; **-ся** *coll.* contrive, manage

**умыва́|льник** *m* [1] washbowl, *Brt.* wash-basin; **\~ние** *n* [12] washing; wash; **\~ть** [1], ⟨**умы́ть**⟩ [22] **(-ся)** wash (*a.* o.s.)

**у́мы|сел** *m* [1; -сла] design, intent(ion); **с \~слом (без \~сла)** (un-) intentionally; **´\~ть(ся)** → **\~*ва́ть*** **(-*ся*)**; **´\~шленный** [14] deliberate; intentional

**унести́(сь)** → ***уноси́ть(ся)***

**универ|ма́г** *m* [1] (***\~са́льный магази́н***) department store; **\~са́льный** [14; -лен, -льна] universal; **\~са́м** *m* [1] supermarket; **\~сите́т** *m* [1] university (at, in **в** П)

**уни|жа́ть** [1], ⟨**´\~зить**⟩ [15] humiliate; **\~же́ние** *n* [12] humiliation; **\~жённый** [14 *sh.*] humble; **\~зи́тельный** [14; -лен, -льна] humiliating; **´\~зить** → **\~*жа́ть***

**унима́ть** [1], ⟨**уня́ть**⟩ [уйму́, уймёшь; уня́л, -а́, -о; -я́тый (-я́т, -а́, -о)] appease, soothe; *боль* still; **-ся** calm *or* quiet down; *ветер и т. д.* subside

**уничт|ожа́ть** [1], ⟨**\~о́жить**⟩ [16] annihilate, destroy; **\~оже́ние** *n* [12] annihilation; **\~о́жить** → **\~*ожа́ть***

**уноси́ть** [15], ⟨**унести́**⟩ [24 -с-] carry, take (away, off); **-ся** ⟨**сь-**⟩ speed away

**уны|ва́ть** [1] be depressed, be dejected; **´\~лый** [14 *sh.*] depressed; dejected; **´\~ние** *n* [12] despondency; depression; dejection

**уня́ть(ся)** → ***унима́ть(ся)***

**упа́до|к** *m* [1; -дка] decay, decline; ***\~к ду́ха*** depression; ***\~к сил*** breakdown

**упаков|а́ть** → **´\~*ывать***; **´\~ка** *f* [5; *g/pl.*: -вок] packing; wrapping; **´\~щик** *m* [1] packer; **´\~ывать** [1] ⟨**\~а́ть**⟩ [7] pack (up), wrap up

**упа́сть** → ***па́дать***

**упира́ть** [1], ⟨**упере́ть**⟩ [12] rest, prop (against **в** В); **-ся** lean, prop (s.th. T; against **в** В); *в стенку и т. д.* knock *or* run against; (*настаивать*) insist on; be obstinate

**упи́танный** [14 *sh.*] well-fed, fattened

**упла́|та** *f* [5] payment (in **в** В); **\~чивать** [1], ⟨**\~ти́ть**⟩ [15] pay; *по счёту* pay, settle

**уплотн|е́ние** *n* [12] compression; packing; **\~я́ть** [28], ⟨**\~и́ть**⟩ [13] condense, make compact; fill up (with work); *tech.* seal

**уплы|ва́ть** [1], ⟨**´\~ть**⟩ [23] swim or sail (away, off); pass (away), vanish

**упова́ть** [1] (**на** В) trust (in), hope (for)

**упод|обля́ть** [28], ⟨**\~о́бить**⟩ [14] liken, become like (*v/i.* **-ся**)

**упо|е́ние** *n* [12] rapture, ecstasy; **\~ённый** [14; -ён, -ена] enraptured; **\~и́тельный** [14; -лен, -льна] rapturous, intoxicating

**уползти́** [24] *pf.* creep away

**уполномо́ч|енный** [14 *sh.*] authorized; **\~ивать** [1], ⟨**\~ить**⟩ [16] authorize, empower (to **на** В)

**упомина́|ние** *n* [12] mention (of **о** П); **\~ть** [1], ⟨**упомяну́ть**⟩ [19] mention (*v/t.* В, **о** П)

**упо́р** *m* [1] rest; support, prop; stop; ***де́лать \~*** lay stress *or* emphasis (on **на** В); **в \~** point-blank, straightforward; ***смотре́ть в \~ на кого́-л.*** look full in the face of s.o.; **\~ный** [14; -рен, -рна] persistent, persevering; (*упрямый*) stubborn, obstinate; **\~ство** *n* [9] persistence, perseverance; obstinacy; **\~ствовать** [7] be stubborn; persevere, persist (in **в** П)

**употреб|и́тельный** [14; -лен, -льна] common, customary; *слово* in current use; **\~и́ть** → **\~*ля́ть***; **\~ле́ние** *n* [12] use; usage; **\~ля́ть** [28], ⟨**\~и́ть**⟩ [14 *e.*; -блю́,

У

-би́шь; -блённый] (*impf.* **-ся** be) use(d), employ(ed); **~и́ть все сре́дства** make every effort; **~и́ть во зло** abuse

**упра́в|иться** → **~ля́ться**; **~ле́ние** *n* [12] administration (of P; T), management; *tech.* control; *gr.* government; *машиной* driving; **орке́стр под ~ле́нием** orchestra conducted by (P); **~ля́ть** (T) manage, operate; rule; govern (*a. gr.*); drive; *naut.* steer; *tech.* control; *mus.* conduct; **-ся**, ⟨**~иться**⟩ *coll.* [14] (**с** T) manage; finish; **~ля́ющий** [17] manager

**упражн|е́ние** *n* [12] exercise; practice; **~я́ть** [28] exercise (*v/i.*, *v/refl.* **-ся в** П: practice (-ise) s.th.)

**упраздн|е́ние** *n* [12] abolition; liquidation; **~я́ть** [28], ⟨**~и́ть**⟩ [13] abolish; liquidate

**упра́шивать** [1], ⟨упроси́ть⟩ [15] (*impf.*) beg, entreat; (*pf.*) prevail upon

**упрёк** *m* [1] reproach

**упрек|а́ть** [1], ⟨**~ну́ть**⟩ [20] reproach (with **в** П)

**упро|си́ть** → **упра́шивать**; **~сти́ть** → **~ща́ть**; **~че́ние** *n* [12] consolidation; **~чивать** [1], ⟨**~чить**⟩ [16] consolidate (*v/i.* **-ся**), stabilize; **~ща́ть** [1], ⟨**~сти́ть**⟩ [15 *e.*; -ощу́, -ости́шь; -ощённый] simplify; **~ще́ние** *n* [12] simplification

**упру́г|ий** [16 *sh.*] elastic, resilient; **~ость** *f* [8] elasticity

**упря́м|иться** [14] be obstinate; persist in; **~ство** *n* [9] obstinacy, stubbornness; **~ый** [14 *sh.*] obstinate, stubborn

**упря́т|ывать** [1], ⟨**~ать**⟩ [3] hide

**упу|ска́ть** [1], ⟨**~сти́ть**⟩ [15] let go; let slip; let fall; *возможность* miss; **~ще́ние** *n* [12] neglect, ommission

У

**ура́!** *int.* hurrah!

**уравн|е́ние** *n* [12] equalization; *math.* equation; **~ивать** [1] **1.** ⟨уровня́ть⟩ [28] level; **2.** ⟨**~я́ть**⟩ [28] level, equalize *fig.*; **~и́ловка** *f* [5; *g/pl.*: -вок] *pej.* egalitarianism (*esp.* with respect to economic rights and wage level[l]ing); **~ове́шивать** [1], ⟨**~ове́сить**⟩ [15] balance; *p. pt. p. a.* well-balanced, composed, calm; **~я́ть** → **~ивать** *2*

**ураға́н** *m* [1] hurricane

**ура́льский** [16] Ural(s)

**ура́н** *m* [1], **~овый** [14] uranium

**урегули́рование** *n* [12] settlement; regulation; *vb.* → **регули́ровать**

**урез|а́ть** &; **~ывать** *coll.* [1], ⟨**~ать**⟩ [3] cut down, curtail; axe; **~о́нить** *coll.* [13] *pf.* bring to reason

**у́рна** *f* [5] ballot box; refuse bin

**у́ров|ень** *m* [4; -вня] level (at, on **на** П; **в** В); standard; *tech.* gauge; (*показатель*) rate; **жи́зненный ~ень** standard of living; **~ня́ть** → **ура́внивать** *1*

**уро́д** *m* [1] monster; *coll.* ugly creature; **~ливый** [14 *sh.*] deformed; ugly; abnormal; **~овать** [7], ⟨из-⟩ deform, disfigure; (*калечить*) mutilate; maim; **~ство** *n* [9] deformity; ugliness; *fig.* abnormality

**урож|а́й** *m* [3] harvest, (abundant) crop; **~а́йность** *f* [8] yield (heavy высо́кая), productivity; **~а́йный** [14] productive; *год* good year for crops; **~е́нец** *m* [1; -нца], **~е́нка** *f* [5; *g/pl.*: -нок] native (of)

**уро́|к** *m* [1] lesson; **~н** *m* [1] (*ущерб*) loss(es); *репутации* injury; **~ни́ть** → **роня́ть**

**урча́ть** [4 *e.*; -чу́, -чи́шь] *в желудке* rumble; *пёс* growl

**уры́вками** *coll.* by fits and starts; in snatches; at odd moments

**ус** *m* [1; *pl. e.*] (*mst. pl.*) m(o)ustache

**уса|ди́ть** → **~живать**; **~дьба** *f* [5; *g/pl.*: -деб] farmstead, farm center (-tre); *hist.* country estate, country seat; **~живать** [1], ⟨**~ди́ть**⟩ [15] seat; set; *деревьями и т. д.* plant (with T); **-ся**, ⟨усе́сться⟩ [25; уся́дусь, -дешься; уся́дься!; усе́лся, -лась] sit down, take a seat; settle down (to **за** В)

**уса́тый** [14] with a m(o)ustache; (*of animals*) with whiskers

**усв|а́ивать** [1], ⟨**~о́ить**⟩ [13] *привычку* adopt; *знания* acquire, assimilate; *язык и т. д.* master, learn; **~о́ение** *n* [12] adoption; acquirement, assimilation; mastering, learning

**усе́|ивать** [1], ⟨**~ять**⟩ [27] sow, cover litter, strew (with); *звёздами* stud

**усе́рд|ие** *n* [12] zeal; (*прилежание*) diligence, assiduity; **~ный** [14; -ден, -дна] zealous; diligent, assiduous

**усе́сться** → ***уса́живаться***
**усе́ять** → ***усе́ивать***
**усид|е́ть** [11] *pf.* remain sitting; keep one's place; sit still; *coll.* (*выдержать*) hold out, keep a job; **⁓́чивый** [14 *sh.*] assiduous, persevering
**усил|е́ние** *n* [12] strengthening, *звука* intensification; *el.* amplification; **⁓́енный** [14] intensified; *питание* high-caloric; **⁓́ивать** [1], 〈**⁓́ить**〉 [13] strengthen, reinforce; intensify; *звук* amplify; *боль и т. д.* aggravate; **-ся** increase; **⁓́ие** *n* [12] effort, exertion; ***приложи́ть все ⁓́ия*** make every effort; **⁓и́тель** *m* [4] *el.* amplifier; *tech.* booster; **⁓́ить(ся)** → ***⁓́ивать*(ся)**
**ускольз|а́ть** [1], 〈**⁓ну́ть**〉 [20] slip (off, away), escape (from **от** Р)
**ускор|е́ние** *n* [12] acceleration; **⁓я́ть** [28], 〈**⁓́ить**〉 [13] quicken; speed up, accelerate; *v/i.* **-ся**
**усла́|вливаться** [1], 〈**усло́виться**〉 [14] arrange; settle, agree (up on **о** П); **⁓ть** → ***усыла́ть***
**усло́в|ие** *n* [12] condition (on **с** Т, ***при*** П; under ***на*** П), term; stipulation; proviso; *pl.* circumstances; **⁓иться** → ***усла́вливаться***; **⁓ленный** [14 *sh.*] agreed, fixed; **⁓ность** *f* [8] conditionality; convention; **⁓ный** [14; -вен, -вна] *рефлекс* conditional; (*относительный*) relative; ***⁓ный пригово́р*** suspended, sentence; ***⁓ный знак*** conventional sign
**усложн|я́ть** [28], 〈**⁓и́ть**〉 [13] (**-ся** become) complicate(d)
**услу́|га** *f* [5] service (at ***к*** Д *pl.*), favo(u)r; **⁓живать** [1], 〈**⁓жить**〉 [16] do (р. Д) a service or favo(u)r; → *iro.* ***удружи́ть***; **⁓жливый** [14 *sh.*] obliging
**усм|а́тривать** [1], 〈**⁓отре́ть**〉 [9; -отрю́, -о́тришь; -о́тренный] see (in ***в*** П); **⁓еха́ться** [1], 〈**⁓ехну́ться**〉 [20], **⁓е́шка** *f* [5; *g/pl.*: -шек] smile, grin; **⁓ире́ние** *n* [12] suppression; **⁓иря́ть** [28], 〈**⁓ири́ть**〉 [13] pacify; *силой* suppress; **⁓отре́ние** *n* [12] discretion (at ***по*** Д; to ***на*** В), judg(e)ment; **⁓отре́ть** → ***⁓а́тривать***
**усну́ть** [20] *pf.* go to sleep, fall asleep
**усоверше́нствован|ие** *n* [12] improvement, refinement; **⁓ный** [14] improved, perfected
**усомни́ться** → ***сомнева́ться***
**усо́пший** [17] *lit.* deceased
**успе|ва́емость** *f* [8] progress (*in studies*); **⁓ва́ть** [1], 〈**⁓́ть**〉 [8] have (*or* find) time, manage, succeed; arrive, be in time (for ***к*** Д, ***на*** В); catch (*train* ***на по́езд***); *impf.* get on, make progress, learn; ***не ⁓́л(а)*** (+ *inf.*), ***как*** no sooner + *pt.* than; **⁓́ется** *pf. impers.* there is no hurry; **⁓́х** *m* [1] success; *pl. a.* progress; ***с тем же ⁓́хом*** with the same result; **⁓́шный** [14; -шен, -шна] successful; ***⁓́шно*** *a.* with success
**успок|а́ивать** [1], 〈**⁓о́ить**〉 [13] calm, soothe; reassure; **-ся** calm down; *ветер, боль* subside; become quiet; content o.s. (with **на** П); **⁓ое́ние** *n* [12] peace; calm; **⁓о́ительный** [14; -лен, -льна] soothing, reassuring; **⁓о́ить(ся)** → ***⁓а́ивать*(ся)**
**уст|а́** *n/pl.* [9] *obs. or poet.* mouth, lips *pl.*; ***узна́ть из пе́рвых ⁓*** learn at first hand; ***у всех на ⁓а́х*** everybody is talking about it
**уста́в** *m* [1] statute(s); regulations *pl.*; ⁓ *ООН и т. д.* charter
**уста|ва́ть** [5], 〈**⁓́ть**〉 [-а́ну, -а́нешь] get tired; **⁓вля́ть** [28], 〈**⁓́вить**〉 [14] place; cover (with Т), fill; *взгляд* direct, fix (*eyes* on **на** В); **-ся** stare (at **на** *or* **в** В); **⁓́лость** *f* [8] weariness, fatigue; **⁓́лый** [14] tired, weary; **⁓на́вливать** [1], 〈**⁓нови́ть**〉 [14] set *or* put up; *tech.* mount; arrange; fix; *порядок* establish; (*узнать*) find out, ascertain; adjust (to **на** В); **-ся** be established; form; *погода* set in; **⁓но́вка** *f* [5; *g/pl.*: -вок] *tech.* mounting, installation; *силовая* plant; *fig.* orientation (toward[s] **на** В); **⁓новле́ние** *n* [12] establishment; **⁓ре́лый** [14] obsolete, out-of-date; **⁓́ть** → ***⁓ва́ть***
**устила́ть** [1], 〈**устла́ть**〉 [-телю́, -те́лешь; у́стланный] cover, pave (with Т)
**у́стный** [14] oral, verbal
**усто́|и** *m/pl.* [3] foundation; **⁓́йчивость** *f* [8] stability; **⁓́йчивый** [14 *sh.*] stable; **⁓я́ть** [-ою́, -ои́шь] keep one's balance; stand one's ground; resist (*v/t.* ***про́тив***

У

P; ***перед*** T)

**устр|а́ивать** [1], ⟨**~о́ить**⟩ [13] arrange, organize; (*создавать*) set up, establish; *сцену* make; provide (*job* **на** B; *place* in **в** B); *coll. impers.* (*подходить*) suit; **-ся** be settled; settle; get a job (*a.* ***на рабо́ту***); **~ане́ние** *n* [12] removal; elimination; **~аня́ть** [28], ⟨**~ани́ть**⟩ [13] remove; eliminate, clear; **~аша́ть** [1] (**-ся**) → ***страши́ться***; **~емля́ть** [28], ⟨**~еми́ть**⟩ [14 *e.*; -млю́, -ми́шь; -млённый] (**на** B) direct (to, at), fix (on); **-ся** rush; be directed; **~́ица** *f* [5] oyster; **~о́ить(ся)** → ***~а́ивать(ся)***; **~о́йство** *n* [9] arrangement; organization; *общественное* structure, system; device; mechanism

**усту́п** *m* [1] *скалы* ledge; projection; terrace; **~а́ть** [1], ⟨**~и́ть**⟩ [14] cede, let (р. Д) have; *в споре* yield; (*быть хуже*) be inferior to (Д); (*продать*) sell; ***~а́ть доро́гу*** (Д) let pass, give way; ***~а́ть ме́сто*** give up one's place; **~ка** *f* [5; *g/pl.*: -пок] concession; cession; **~чивый** [14 *sh.*] compliant, pliant

**устыди́ть** [15 *e.*; -ыжу́, -ыди́шь; -ыжённый] (**-ся** be) ashame(d; of P)

**у́стье** *n* [10; *g/pl.*: -ьев] (*of a river*) mouth, estuary (at **в** П)

**усугуб|ля́ть** [28], ⟨**~и́ть**⟩ [14 & 14 *e.*; -гу́блю, -гу́бишь; -гу́бленный & -гублённый] increase, intensify; aggravate

**усы́** → ***ус***; **~ла́ть** [1], ⟨усла́ть⟩ [ушлю́, ушлёшь; у́сланный] send (away); **~новля́ть** [28], ⟨**~нови́ть**⟩ [14 *e.*; -влю́, -ви́шь; -влённый] adopt; **~пать** [1], ⟨**~па́ть**⟩ [2] (be)strew (with P); **~пля́ть** [28], ⟨**~пи́ть**⟩ [14 *e.*; -плю́, -пи́шь; -плённый] put to sleep (*by means of narcotics, etc.*) lull to sleep; *животное* put to sleep; *fig.* lull, weaken, neutralize

**ута́|ивать** [1], ⟨**~и́ть**⟩ [13] conceal, keep to o.s.; appropriate; **~йка** *coll.*: ***без ~йки*** frankly; **~птывать** [1], ⟨утопта́ть⟩ [3] tread *or* trample (down); **~скивать** [1], ⟨**~щи́ть**⟩ [16] carry, drag *or* take (off, away); *coll.* walk off with, pilfer

**у́тварь** *f* [8] *collect.* equipment; utensils *pl.*; ***церко́вная ~*** church plate

**утвер|ди́тельный** [14; -лен, -льна] affirmative; ***~ди́тельно*** in the affirmative; **~жда́ть** [1], ⟨**~ди́ть**⟩ [15 *e.*; -ржу́, -рди́шь; -рждённый] confirm; (*укреплять*) consolidate (*v/i.* **-ся**); *impf.* affirm, assert, maintain; **~жде́ние** *n* [12] confirmation; affirmation, assertion; consolidation

**уте|ка́ть** [1], ⟨**~́чь**⟩ [26] flow (away); leak; (*of gas, etc.*) escape; *coll.* run away; **~ре́ть** → ***утира́ть***; **~рпе́ть** [10] *pf.* restrain o.s.; ***не ~рпе́л, что́бы не*** (+ *inf. pf.*) could not help …ing

**утёс** *m* [1] cliff, crag

**уте́|чка** *f* [5] leakage (*a. fig.*); *газа* escape; ***~чка мозго́в*** brain drain; **~чь** → ***~ка́ть***; **~ша́ть** [1], ⟨**~шить**⟩ [16] console, comfort; **-ся** *a.* take comfort in (T); **~ше́ние** *n* [12] comfort, consolation; **~ши́тельный** [14; -лен, -льна] comforting, consoling

**ути́|ль** *m* [4] *collect.* salvage, waste, scrap; **~ра́ть** [1], ⟨утере́ть⟩ [12] wipe; **~ха́ть** [1], ⟨**~хнуть**⟩ [21] subside, abate; *звуки* cease; (*успокоиться*) calm down

**у́тка** *f* [5; *g/pl.*: у́ток] duck; *газетная* canard; false *or esp.* fabricated report

**уткну́ть(ся)** *coll.* [20] *pf. лицом* bury, hide; *в книгу* be(come) engrossed; (*наткнуться*) run up against

**утол|и́ть** → ***~я́ть***; **~ща́ть** [1], ⟨**~сти́ть**⟩ [15 *e.*; -лщу́, -лсти́шь; -лщённый] become thicker; **~ще́ние** *n* [12] thickening; **~я́ть** [28], ⟨**~и́ть**⟩ [13] *жажду* slake, quench; *голод* appease; *желание* satisfy

**утом|и́тельный** [14; -лен, -льна] wearisome, tiring; tedious, tiresome; **~и́ть(ся)** → ***~ля́ть(ся)***; **~ле́ние** *n* [12] fatigue, exhaustion; **~лённый** [14; -лён, -ена́] tired, weary; **~ля́ть** [28], ⟨**~и́ть**⟩ [14 *e.*; -млю́, -ми́шь; -млённый] tire, weary (*v/i.* **-ся**; *a.* get tired)

**утонч|а́ть** [1], ⟨**~и́ть**⟩ [16 *e.*; -чу́, -чи́шь; -чённый] make thinner; *p. pt. p.* thin; *fig.* refine; make refined (*v/i.* **-ся**)

**утоп|а́ть** [1] **1.** ⟨утону́ть⟩ → ***тону́ть 2.***; **2.** drown; **~́ленник** *m* [1] drowned man;

**~ленница** *f* [5] drowned woman; **~тáть** → ***утáптывать***
**уточн|éние** *n* [12] expressing *or* defining more precisely; amplification; elaboration; **~я́ть** [28], ⟨**~и́ть**⟩ [13] amplify; elaborate
**утрá|ивать** [1], ⟨**утрóить**⟩ [13] treble; *v/i.* **-ся**; **~мбовáть** [7] *pf.* ram, tamp; **~та** *f* [5] loss; **~чивать** [1], ⟨**~тить**⟩ [15] lose
**ýтренний** [15] morning
**утри́ровать** [7] exaggerate
**ýтр|о** *n* [9; с, до -á; к -ý] morning (in the **~ом**; **по ~áм**); **...~á** *a*... A.M. → ***день***; **~óба** *f* [5] womb; **~óить(ся)** → ***~áивать(ся)***; **~уждáть** [1], ⟨**~уди́ть**⟩ [15 *e.*; -ужý, -уди́шь; -уждённый] trouble, bother
**утря|сáть** [3; -сти́, -сý, -сёшь], ⟨**~сти́**⟩ [25] *fig.* settle
**утю́|г** *m* [1] (flat)iron; **~жить** [16], ⟨вы-, от-⟩ iron
**ухá** *f* [5] fish soup; **~б** *m* [1] pothole; **~бистый** [14 *sh.*] bumpy
**ухáживать** [1] (***за*** Т) nurse, look after; *за женщиной* court, woo
**ухвáт|ывать** [1], ⟨**~и́ть**⟩ [15] (***за*** В) seize, grasp; **-ся** snatch; cling to; *fig.* seize, jump at
**ухи|тря́ться** [28], ⟨**~три́ться**⟩ [13] contrive, manage; **~щрéние** *n* [12] contrivance; **~щря́ться** [28] contrive
**ухмыл|я́ться** *coll.* [28], ⟨**~ьнýться**⟩ [20] grin, smirk
**ýхо** *n* [9; *pl.*: ýши, ушéй, *etc. e.*] ear (in ***на*** В); ***влюби́ться пó уши*** be head over heels in love; ***пропускáть ми́мо ушéй*** turn a deaf ear (to В); ***держáть ~ востро́*** → ***настóроже***
**ухóд** *m* [1] going away, leaving, departure; (***за*** Т) care, tending, nursing; **~и́ть** [15], ⟨**уйти́**⟩ [уйдý, уйдёшь; ушёл, ушлá; ушéдший; *g. pl.*: уйдя́] leave (*v/t.* ***из, от*** Р) go away; (*миновать*) pass; *от наказания* escape; *от ответа* evade, *в отставку* resign; *на пенсию* retire; *coll.* be worn out, spent (for ***на*** В); ***уйти́ в себя́*** shrink into o.s.
**ухудш|áть** [1], ⟨**~ить**⟩ [16] deteriorate (*v.i.* **-ся**); **~éние** *n* [12] deterioration; worsening
**уцелéть** [8] *pf.* come through alive; survive; escape
**уцепи́ться** [14] *coll.* → ***ухвати́ться***
**учáст|вовать** [7] participate, take part (in ***в*** П); **~вующий** [17] → ***~ник***; **~ие** *n* [12] (***в*** П) participation (in); (*сочувствие*) interest (in), sympathy (with); **~и́ть(ся)** → ***учащáть(ся)***; **~ливый** [14 *sh.*] sympathizing, sympathetic; **~ник** *m* [1], **~ница** *f* [5] participant, participator; competitor (*sports*); *член* member; **~ок** *m* [1; -тка] *земли* plot; (*часть*) part, section; ***избирáтельный ~ок*** electoral district; polling station; **´~ь** [8] fate, lot
**уча|щáть** [1], ⟨**~сти́ть**⟩ [15 *e.*; -ащý, -асти́шь; -ащённый] make (**-ся** become) more frequent
**уч|áщийся** *m* [17] schoolchild, pupil, student; **~ёба** *f* [5] studies *pl.*, study; (*подготовка*) training; **~éбник** *m* [1] textbook; **~éбный** [14] school...; educational; (*пособие*) text (*book*), exercise...; ***~éбный план*** curriculum
**учён|ие** *n* [12] learning; instruction apprenticeship; *mil.* training, practice; teaching, doctrine; **~и́к** *m* [1 *e.*] *and* **~и́ца** *f* [5] pupil; student; *слесаря и т. д.* apprentice; (*последователь*) disciple; **~и́ческий** [16] crude, immature
**учён|ость** *f* [8] learning; erudition; **~ый** [14 *sh.*] learned; ***~ая стéпень*** (university) degree; *su.* scholar, scientist
**уч|éсть** → ***учи́тывать***; **~ёт** *m* [1] calculation; registration; *товаров* stock-taking; ***с ~ётом*** taking into consideration
**учи́лище** *n* [11] school, college (at ***в*** П)
**учиня́ть** [28] → ***чини́ть*** *2*
**учи́тель** *m* [4; *pl.*: -ля, *etc. e.*; *fig. st.*], **~ница** *f* [5] teacher, instructor; **~ский** [16] (of) teachers('); **~ская** *as. su.* teachers' common room
**учи́тывать** [1], ⟨**учéсть**⟩ [25; учтý, -тёшь; учёл, учлá; *g. pt.*: учтя́; учтённый] take into account, consider; register; *вексель* discount
**учи́ть** [16] **1.** ⟨на-, об-, вы́-⟩ teach (p. s.th. В/Д), instruct; train; (*a.* **-ся** Д); **2.** ⟨вы́-⟩ learn, study

**учреди́тель** *m* [4] founder; **~ный** [14] constituent

**учре|жда́ть** [1], 〈**~ди́ть**〉 [15 *e.*; -ежу́, -еди́шь; -еждённый] found, establish, set up; **~жде́ние** *n* [12] founding, setting up, establishment; (*заведение*) institution

**учти́вый** [14 *sh.*] polite, courteous

**уша́нка** *f* [5; *g/pl.*: -нок] cap with earflaps

**уши́б** *m* [1] bruise; injury; **~а́ть** [1], 〈**~и́ть**〉 [-бу́, -бёшь; -и́б(ла); уши́бленный] hurt, bruise (o.s. **-ся**)

**ушко́** *n* [9; *pl.*: -ки́, -ко́в] *tech.* eye, lug; (*of a needle*) eye

**ушно́й** [14] ear…; aural

**уще́лье** *n* [10] gorge, ravine

**ущем|ля́ть** [28], 〈**~и́ть**〉 [14 *e.*; -млю́, -ми́шь; -млённый] *права* infringe

**уще́рб** *m* [1] damage; loss; ***в ~*** to the detriment

**ущипну́ть** → ***щипа́ть***

**ую́т** *m* [1] coziness (*Brt.* cosiness); **~ный** [14; -тен, -тна] snug, cozy (*Brt.* cosy), comfortable

**уязв|и́мый** [14 *sh.*] vulnerable; **~ля́ть** [28], 〈**~и́ть**〉 [14 *e.*; -влю́, -ви́шь; -влённый] *fig.* hurt

**уясн|я́ть** [28], 〈**~и́ть**〉 [13] *себе* understand

# Ф

**фа́бри|ка** *f* [5] factory (in ***на*** П); mill; **~кова́ть** [7], *pf.* 〈с-〉 *fig. coll.* fabricate

**фа́була** *f* [5] plot, story

**фа́за** *f* [5] phase

**фаза́н** *m* [1] pheasant

**файл** *m* [1] *comput.* file

**фа́кел** *m* [1] torch

**факс** *m* [1] fax

**факт** *m* [1] fact; ***~ тот, что*** the fact is that; **~и́ческий** [16] (f)actual, real; *adv. a.* in fact; **~у́ра** *f* [5] *lit.* style, texture

**факульте́т** *m* [1] faculty (in ***на*** П); department

**фаль|сифици́ровать** [7] (*im*)*pf.* falsify; forge; **~ши́вить** [14], 〈с-〉 sing out of tune, play falsely; *coll.* act incincerely, be false; **~ши́вка** *f* [5; *g/pl.*: -вок] forged document; false information; **~ши́вый** [14 *sh.*] false, forged, counterfeit; *монета* base; **~шь** *f* [8] falseness; *лицемерие* hypocrisy, insincerity

**фами́л|ия** *f* [7] surname; ***как ва́ша ~ия?*** what is your name?; **~ья́рный** [14; -рен, -рна] familiar

**фанати́|зм** *m* [1] fanaticism; **~чный** [14; -чен, -чна] fanatical

**фане́ра** *f* [5] plywood; veneer

**фанта|зёр** *m* [1] dreamer, visionary; **~зи́ровать** [7] *impf. only* indulge in fancies, dream; 〈с-〉 invent; **~зия** *f* [7] imagination; fancy; (*выдумка*) invention, fib; *mus.* fantasia; *coll.* (*прихоть*) whim; **~стика** *f* [5] *lit.* fantasy, fiction; ***нау́чная ~стика*** science fiction; *collect.* the fantastic, the unbelievable; **~сти́ческий** [16], **~сти́чный** [14; -чен, -чна] fantastic

**фа́р|а** *f* [5] headlight; **~ва́тер** *m* [1] *naut.* fairway; **~маце́вт** *m* [1] pharmacist; **~тук** *m* [1] apron; **~фо́р** [1], **~фо́ровый** [14] china, porcelain; **~ш** *m* [1] stuffing; minced meat; **~широва́ть** [7] *cul.* stuff

**фаса́д** *m* [1] facade, front

**фасов|а́ть** [7] *impf.*; **~ка** *f* [5; *g/pl.*: -вок] prepackage

**фасо́|ль** *f* [8] string (*Brt.* runner) bean(s); **~н** *m* [1] cut, style

**фата́льный** [14; -лен, -льна] fatal

**фаши́|зм** *m* [1] fascism; **~ст** *m* [1] fascist; **~стский** [16] fascist…

**фая́нс** *m* [1], **~овый** [14] faience

**февра́ль** *m* [4 *e.*] February

**федера́|льный** [14] federal; **~ти́вный** [14] federative, federal; **~ция** *f* [7] federation

**фейерве́рк** *m* [1] firework(s)

**фельд|ма́ршал** *m* [1] *hist.* field marshal; **~шер** *m* [1] doctor's assistant,

Ф

medical attendant
**фельетóн** *m* [1] satirical article
**фен** *m* [1] hairdryer
**фенóмен** *m* [1] phenomenon
**феодáльный** [14] feudal
**ферзь** *m* [4 *e.*] queen (*chess*)
**фéрм|а** *f* [5] farm; **~ер** *m* [1] farmer
**фестивáль** *m* [4] festival
**фетр** *m* [1] felt; **ˆовый** [14] felt…
**фехтовá|льщик** *m* [1] fencer; **~ние** *n* [12] fencing; **~ть** [7] fence
**фиáлка** *f* [5; *g/pl.*: -лок] violet
**фи́г|а** *f* [5], **~овый** [14] fig
**фигу́р|а** *f* [5] figure; chess piece (*excluding pawns*); **~áльный** [14; -лен, -льна] figurative; **~и́ровать** [7] figure, appear; **~ный** [14] figured; ***~ное катáние*** figure skating
**фи́зи|к** *m* [1] physicist; **~ка** *f* [5] physics; **~олóгия** *f* [7] physiology; **~онóмия** [7] physiognomy; **ˆческий** [14] physical; *труд* manual
**физкульту́р|а** *f* [5] physical training; gymnastics; **~ник** *m* [1] sportsman; **~ница** *f* [5] sportswoman
**фик|си́ровать** [7], ⟨за-⟩ record in writing; fix; **~ти́вный** [14; -вен, -вна] fictitious; **ˆция** *f* [7] fiction; invention, untruth
**фила|нтрóп** *m* [1] philantropist; **~рмони́ческий** [16] philharmonic; **~рмóния** *f* [7] philharmonic society, the philharmonic
**филé** *n* [*indecl.*] tenderloin, fil(l)et
**филиáл** *m* [1] branch (*of an institution*)
**фи́лин** *m* [1] eagle owl
**филóл|ог** *m* [1] philologist; **~оги́ческий** [16] philological; **~óгия** *f* [7] philology
**филóс|оф** *m* [1] philosopher; **~óфия** *f* [7] philosophy; **~óфский** [16] philosophical; **~óфствовать** [7] philosophize
**фильм** *m* [1] film (*vb.* ***снимáть ~***); ***документáльный ~*** documentary (film); ***мультипликациóнный ~*** cartoon; ***худóжественный ~*** feature film
**фильтр** *m* [1], **~овáть** [7] filter
**финáл** *m* [1] final; *mus.* finale
**финанс|и́ровать** [7] (*im*)*pf.* finance; **ˆовый** [14] financial; **ˆы** *m/pl.* [1] finance(s)
**фи́ник** *m* [1] date (*fruit*)
**фини́фть** *f* [8] *art* enamel
**фи́ниш** *m* [1] *sport* finish; **~ный** [14]: ***~ная прямáя*** last lap
**финн** *m* [1], **ˆка** *f* [5; *g/pl.*: -ок], **ˆский** [16] Finnish
**фиолéтовый** [14] violet
**фи́рма** *f* [5] firm
**фискáльный** [14] fiscal
**фити́ль** *m* [4 *e.*] wick; (*igniting device*) fuse; (*detonating device*) *usu.* fuze
**флаг** *m* [1] flag, colo(u)rs *pl.*
**фланг** *m* [1], **ˆовый** [14] *mil.* flank
**фланéл|евый** [14], **~ь** *f* [8] flannel
**флегмати́чный** [14; -чен, -чна] phlegmatic
**флéйта** *f* [5] flute
**фли́|гель** *arch.* *m* [4; *pl.*: -ля, *etc. e.*] wing; outbuilding; **~рт** *m* [1] flirtation; **~ртовáть** [7] flirt
**фломáстер** *m* [1] felt-tip pen
**флот** *m* [1] fleet; ***воéнно-морскóй ~*** navy; ***воéнно-возду́шный ~*** (air) force; **ˆский** [16] naval
**флю́|гер** *m* [1] weather vane; weathercock; **~с** *m* [1] gumboil
**фля́|га** *f* [5], **~жка** *f* [5; *g/pl.*: -жек] flask; *mil.* canteen
**фойé** *n* [*indecl.*] lobby, foyer
**фóкус** *m* [1] (juggler's *or* conjurer's) trick, sleight of hand; *coll.* caprice; whim; **~ник** *m* [1] juggler, conjurer; **~ничать** *coll.* [1] play tricks; *о ребёнке* play up; behave capriciously
**фольгá** *f* [5] foil
**фольклóр** *m* [1], **~ный** [14] folklore
**фон** *m* [1] background (against ***на*** П)
**фонáр|ик** *m* [1] flashlight, *Brt.* torch; **~ь** *m* [4 *e.*] lantern; (street) lamp; *coll.* black eye
**фонд** *m* [1] fund; *pl.* reserves, stock(s); **ˆовый** [14] stock…
**фонéт|ика** *f* [5] phonetics; **~и́ческий** [16] phonetic(al)
**фонтáн** *m* [1] fountain
**форéль** *f* [8] trout
**фóрм|а** *f* [5] form, shape; *tech.* mo(u)ld; cast; *mil.* uniform; dress (*sports*); **~áльность** *f* [8] formality; **~áльный** [14;

Ф

-лен, -льна] formal; **~áт** *m* [1] size, format (*a. tech.*); **~енный** [14] uniform; *coll.* proper; regular; ***~енная одéжда*** uniform; **~ировáть** [7], ⟨с-⟩ (**-ся** be) form(ed); **~ули́ровать** [7] (*im*)*pf.* & ⟨с-⟩ formulate; **~улирóвка** [5; *g*/*pl.*: -вок] formulation

**форпóст** *m* [1] *mil.* advanced post; outpost (*a. fig.*)

**форси́ровать** [7] (*im*)*pf.* force

**фó|рточка** *f* [5; *g*/*pl.*: -чек] window leaf; **~рум** *m* [1] forum; **~сфор** *m* [1] phosphorus

**фото|аппарáт** *m* [1] camera; **~граф** *m* [1] photographer; **~графи́ровать** [7], ⟨с-⟩ photograph; **~графи́ческий** [16] photographic; → ***~аппарáт***; **~грáфия** *f* [7] photograph; photography; photographer's studio

**фрагментáрный** [14; -рен, -рна] fragmentary

**фрáза** *f* [5] phrase

**фрак** *m* [1] tailcoat, full-dress coat

**фрáкция** *f* [7] *pol.* faction; (*chem.*) fraction

**франт** *m* [1] dandy, fop

**франц|ýженка** *f* [5; *g*/*pl.*: -нок] Frenchwoman; **~ýз** *m* [1] Frenchman; **~ýзский** [16] French

**фрахт** *m* [1], **~овáть** [7] freight

**фрéска** *f* [5] fresco

**фронт** *m* [1] *mil.* front; **~овóй** [14] front…; front-line

**фрукт** *m* [1] (*mst. pl.*) fruit; **~óвый** [14] fruit…; ***~óвый сад*** orchad

**фу!** *int.* (*expressing revulsion*) ugh!; (*expressing surprise*) oh!; ooh!

**фундáмент** *m* [1] foundation; *основа* basis; **~áльный** [14; -лен, -льна] fundamental

**функциони́ровать** [7] function

**фунт** *m* [1] pound

**фур|áж** *m* [1 *e.*] fodder; **~áжка** *f* [5; *g*/*pl.*: -жек] *mil.* service cap; **~гóн** *m* [1] van; **~óр** *m* [1] furor(e); **~ýнкул** *m* [1] furuncle, boil

**футбóл** *m* [1] football, soccer (*Brt. a.* association football); **~и́ст** *m* [1] soccer player; **~ьный** [14] soccer…, football…

**футля́р** *m* [1] case, container

**фы́рк|ать** [1], ⟨**~нуть**⟩ [20] snort; *coll.* grouse

# Х

**хáки** [*indecl.*] khaki

**халáт** *m* [1] dressing gown, bathrobe; *врача* smock; **~ный** *coll.* [14; -тен, -тна] careless, negligent

**халтýра** *coll.* *f* [5] potboiler; hackwork; extra work (*usu.* inferior) chiefly for profit

**хам** *m* [1] cad, boor, lout

**хандр|á** *f* [5] depression, blues *pl.*; **~и́ть** [13] be depressed *or* in the dumps

**ханж|á** *coll.* *m*/*f* [5; *g*/*pl.*: -жéй] hypocrite; **~ествó** *n* [9] hypocrisy

Х

**хаó|с** *m* [1] chaos; **~ти́ческий** [16], **~ти́чный** [14; -чен, -чна] chaotic

**харáктер** *m* [1] character, nature; *человека* temper, disposition; **~изовáть** [7] (*im*)*pf.* & ⟨о-⟩ characterize; (*описывать*) describe; **~и́стика** *f* [5] character(istic); characterization; (*документ*) reference; **~ный** [14; -рен, -рна] characteristic (**для** Р of)

**хáриус** *m* [1] *zo.* grayling

**хáря** *coll.* *f* [6] mug (= *face*)

**хáта** *f* [5] peasant house

**хвал|á** *f* [5] praise; **~éбный** [14; -бен, -бна] laudatory; **~ёный** [14] *iro.* much-vaunted; **~и́ть** [13; хвалю́, хвáлишь] praise; **-ся** boast (Т of)

**хвáст|аться** & *coll.* **~ать** [1], ⟨по-⟩ boast, brag (Т of); **~ли́вый** [14 *sh.*] boastful; **~овствó** *n* [9] boasting; **~ýн** *m* [1 *e.*] *coll.* boaster, braggart

**хват|áть** [1] **1.** ⟨(с)хвати́ть⟩ [15] (**за** В) snatch (at); grasp, seize (by); *a., coll.,* (**-ся *за*** В; lay hold of); **2.** ⟨**~и́ть**⟩ (*impers.*) (Р) suffice, be sufficient; (р. Д,

**у** P) have enough; last (*v/t.* **на** B); (**э́того мне**) **~и́т** (that's) enough (for me)
**хво́йный** [14] coniferous
**хвора́ть** *coll.* [1] be sick *or* ill
**хво́рост** *m* [1] brushwood
**хвост** *m* [1 *e.*] tail; *coll.* (*очередь*) line, *Brt.* queue; **в ~е́** get behind, lag behind; **поджа́ть ~** *coll.* become more cautious
**хво́я** *f* [6] (pine) needle(s *or* branches *pl.*)
**хе́рес** *m* [1] sherry
**хи́жина** *f* [5] hut, cabin
**хи́лый** [14; хил, -á, -o] weak, sickly, puny
**хи́ми|к** *m* [1] chemist; **~́ческий** [16] chemical; **~я** *f* [7] chemistry
**химчи́стка** *f* [5; *g/pl.*: -ток] dry cleaning; dry cleaner's
**хини́н** *m* [1] quinine
**хире́ть** [8] weaken, grow sickly; *растение* wither; *fig.* decay
**хиру́рг** *m* [1] surgeon; **~и́ческий** [16] surgical; **~и́я** *f* [7] surgery
**хитр|е́ц** *m* [1 *e.*] cunning person; **~и́ть** [13], ⟨с-⟩ use guile; → **мудри́ть**; **~́ость** *f* [8] craft(iness), cunning; (*приём*) artifice, ruse, trick; stratagem; **~́ый** [14; -тёр, -трá, хи́тро] cunning, crafty, sly, wily; *coll.* artful; (*изобретательный*) ingenious
**хихи́кать** [1] giggle, titter
**хище́ние** *n* [12] theft; embezzlement
**хи́щн|ик** *m* [1] beast (*or* bird) of prey; **~́ический** [14] predatory; *fig.* injurious (*to nature*); **~ый** [16; -щен, -щна] rapacious, predatory; of prey
**хладнокро́в|ие** *n* [12] composure; **~ный** [14; -вен, -вна] cool(headed), calm
**хлам** *m* [1] trash, rubbish
**хлеб** *m* [1] **1.** bread; **2.** [1; *pl.*: -бá, *etc. e.*] grain, *Brt.* corn; (*пропитание*) livelihood; *pl.* cereals; **~́ный** [14] grain…, corn…, cereal…; bread…; **~опека́рня** *f* [6; *g/pl.*: -рен] bakery; **~осо́льный** [14; -лен, -льна] hospitable
**хлев** *m* [1; в -е & -ý; *pl.*: -á, *etc. e.*] cattle shed; *fig.* pigsty
**хлест|а́ть** [3] *once*, ⟨**~ну́ть**⟩ [20] lash, whip, beat; *о воде* gush, spurt; *о дожде* pour
**хлоп|!** *int.* bang! crack!, plop!; → *a.* **~́ать** [1], ⟨по-⟩, *once* ⟨**~́нуть**⟩ [20] *по спине* slap; *в ладоши* clap; *дверью и т. д.* bang, slam (*v/t.* T)
**хло́пок** *m* [1; -пка] cotton
**хлопо́к** *m* [1; -кá *и т. д.*] clap; bang
**хлопот|а́ть** [3], ⟨по-⟩ (**о** П) busy *or* exert o.s. (**о** П, **за** B on behalf of); *impf. по хозяйству* toil, bustle (about); **~ли́вый** [14 *sh.*] *о человеке* busy, fussy; **~́ный** [14] troublesome; exacting; **´~ы** *f/pl.* [5; *g/pl.*: -по́т] trouble(s), efforts (on behalf of, for); cares
**хлопчатобума́жный** [14] cotton…
**хло́пья** *n/pl.* [10; *gen.*: -ьев] flakes; **кукуру́зные ~** corn flakes
**хлор** *m* [1] chlorine; **~́истый** [14] chlorine…; chloride…
**хлы́нуть** [20] *pf.* gush (forth); rush; *дождь* (begin to) pour in torrents
**хлыст** *m* [1 *e.*] whip; switch
**хлю́пать** *coll.* [1] squelch
**хмель¹** *m* [4] hop(s)
**хмель²** *m* [4] intoxication
**хму́р|ить** [13], ⟨на-⟩ frown, knit one's brows; **-ся** frown, scowl; *погода* be(-come) overcast; **~ый** [14; хмур, -á, -o] gloomy, sullen; *день* cloudy
**хны́кать** *coll.* [3] whimper, snivel; *fig.* whine
**хо́бби** *n* [*indecl.*] hobby
**хо́бот** *m* [1] *zo.* trunk
**ход** *m* [1; в (на) -ý & -е; *pl.*: хóды́] motion; (*скорость*) speed (**на** П at), pace; *истории и т. д.* course; *подземный* passage; *поршня* stroke; *чёрный* entrance; lead (*cards*); move (*chess, etc.*); **на ~ý** in transit; *a.* while walking, *etc.*; **пусти́ть в ~** start; motion; *оружие* use; **знать все ~ы и вы́ходы** know all the ins and outs; **по́лным ~́ом** in full swing; **~ мы́слей** train of thought
**хода́тай|ство** *n* [9] intercession; petition; **~ствовать** [7], ⟨по-⟩ intercede (**у** P, **за** B with/for); petition (**о** П for)
**ход|и́ть** [15] go (**в, на** B to); walk; *под парусом* sail; *поезд и т. д.* run, ply; *в шашках и т. д.* move; visit, attend (*v/t.* **в, на** B; *p.* **к** Д); *о слухах* circulate; (*носить*) (**в** П) wear; **~́кий** [16; хóдок, -дкá, -o; *comp.*: хóдче] *coll.* fast; *товар*

Х

marketable, saleable; in great demand; **~ýльный** [14; -лен, -льна] stilted; **~ьбá** *f* [5] walking; walk; **~я́чий** [17] popular; current; *coll. больной* ambulant

**хождéние** *n* [12] going, walking; (*распространение*) circulation

**хозя́|ин** *m* [1; *pl*.: хозя́ева, хозя́ев] owner; boss, master; *домовладелец* landlord; *принимающий гостей* host; **~ева** → **~ин & ~йка**; **~йка** *f* [5; *g/pl*.: -я́ек] mistress; landlady; hostess; housewife; **~йничать** [1] keep house; manage (at will); make o.s. at home; **~йственный** [14 *sh*.] economic(al), thrifty; **~йственные товáры** household goods; **~йство** *n* [9] economy; household; farm

**хоккéй** *m* [3] hockey; **~ с шáйбой** ice hockey

**холéра** *f* [5] cholera

**хóлить** [13] tend, care for

**холл** *m* [1] vestibule, foyer

**хол|м** *m* [1 *e*.] hill; **~ми́стый** [14 *sh*.] hilly

**хóлод** *m* [1] cold (**на** П in); chill (*a. fig*.); *pl*. [-á, *etc. e*.] cold (weather) (**в** В in); **~éть** [8], ⟨по-⟩ grow cold, chill; **~и́льник** *m* [1] refrigerator; **~ность** *f* [8] coldness; **~ный** [14; хóлоден, -днá, -о] cold (*a. fig*.); *geogr. & fig*. frigid; (**мне**) **~но** it is (I am) cold

**холост|óй** [14; хóлост] single, unmarried; bachelor('s); *патрон* blank; *tech. ход* idle; **~я́к** *m* [1 *e*.] bachelor

**холст** *m* [1 *e*.] canvas

**хомя́к** *m* [1 *e*.] hamster

**хор** *m* [1] choir; **~ом** all together

**хорвáт** *m* [1], **~ка** *f* [5; *g/pl*.: -ток] Croat; **~ский** [16] Croatian

**хорёк** *m* [1; -рькá] polecat, ferret

**хореогрáфия** *f* [7] choreography

**хоровóд** *m* [1] round dance

**хорони́ть** [13; -оню́, -óнишь], ⟨по-⟩ bury

**хорóш|енький** [16] pretty; **~éнько** *coll*. properly, throughly; **~éть** [8], ⟨по-⟩ grow prettier; **~ий** [17; хорóш, -á; *comp*.: лу́чше] good; fine, nice; (*a*. **собóй**) pretty, goodlooking, handsome; **~ó** well; *отметка* good, B (→ **четвёрка**); all right!, OK!, good!; **~ó, что вы** it's a good thing you…; **~ó вам** (+ *inf*.) it is all very well for you to…

**хотé|ть** [хочу́, хóчешь, хóчет, хоти́м, хоти́те, хотя́т], ⟨за-⟩ (P) want, desire; **я ~л(а) бы** I would (*Brt*. should) like; **я хочу́, чтóбы вы** + *pt*. I want you to…; **хóчешь не хóчешь** willy-nilly; **-ся** (*impers*.): **мне хóчется** I'd like; *a*. → **~ть**

**хоть** (*a*. **~ бы**) at least; even; even (if *or* though); if only; **~ … ~** whether … whether, (either) or; *coll*. **~ бы и так** even if it be so; **~ убéй** for the life of me; *a*. **хотя́**

**хотя́** although, though (*a*. **~ и**); **~ бы** even though; if; → *a*. **хоть**

**хóхот** *m* [1] guffaw; loud laugh; **~áть** [3], ⟨за-⟩ roar (with laughter)

**храбр|éц** *m* [1 *e*.] brave person; **~ость** *f* [8] valo(u)r, bravery; **~ый** [14; храбр, -а, -о] brave, valiant

**храм** *m* [1] *eccl*. temple, church

**хран|éние** *n* [12] keeping; *товаров* storage; **кáмера ~éния** *rail., ae., etc*.; cloakroom, *Brt*. left-luggage office; *автоматическая* left-luggage locker; **~и́лище** *n* [11] storehouse; depository; **~и́тель** *m* [4] keeper, custodian; *музея* curator; **~и́ть** [13], ⟨со-⟩ keep; maintain; store *tech. a. of computer*; *памяти* preserve; (*соблюдать*) observe

**храп** *m* [1], **~éть** [10 *e*.; -плю́, -пи́шь] snore; snorting

**хребéт** *m* [1; -бтá] *anat*. spine; spinal column; (mountain) range

**хрен** *m* [1] horseradish

**хрип** *m* [1], **~éние** *n* [12] wheeze; wheezing; **~éть** [10; -плю́, -пи́шь] wheeze; be hoarse; *coll*. speak hoarsely; **~лый** [14; хрипл, -á, -о] hoarse, husky; **~нуть** [21], ⟨о-⟩ become hoarse; **~отá** [5] hoarseness; husky voice

**христ|иани́н** *m* [1; *pl*.: -áне, -áн], **~иáнка** *f* [5; *g/pl*.: -нок], **~иáнский** [16] Christian; **~иáнство** *n* [9] Christianity; **2óс** *m* [Христá] Christ

**хром** *m* [1] chromium; chrome

**хром|áть** [1] limp; be lame; **~óй** [14; хром, -á, -о] lame

**хрóн|ика** *f* [5] chronicle; current events; newsreel; **~и́ческий** [16] chronic(al);

Х

**~ологи́ческий** [16] chronological; **~оло́гия** *f* [7] chronology

**хру́|пкий** [16; -пок, -пка́, -о; *comp*.: хру́пче] brittle, fragile, frail, infirm; **~ста́ль** *m* [4 *e*.] crystal; **~сте́ть** [11] crunch; **~щ** *m* [1 *e*.] cockchafer

**худо́ж|ественный** [14 *sh*.] artistic; art(s)…; of art; belles(*-lettres*); applied (*arts*); **~ество** *n* [9] (applied) art; **~ник** *m* [1] artist; painter

**худ|о́й** [14; худ, -á, -о; *comp*.: худе́е] thin, lean, scrawny; [*comp*.: ху́же] bad, evil; **~́ший** [16] worse, worst; → ***лу́чший***

**ху́же** worse; → ***лу́чше & тот***

**хулига́н** *m* [1] rowdy, hooligan

# Ц

**ца́п|ать** *coll*. [1], *once* ⟨~нуть⟩ [20] snatch, grab; scratch

**ца́пля** *f* [6; *g/pl*.: -пель] heron

**цара́п|ать** [1], ⟨(п)о-⟩, *once* ⟨~нуть⟩ [20], **~ина** *f* [5] scratch

**цар|е́вич** *m* [1] czarevitch; prince; **~е́вна** *f* [5; *g/pl*.: -вен] princess; **~и́ть** [13] *fig*. reign; **~и́ца** *f* [5] czarina, (Russian) empress; *fig*. queen; **~́ский** [16] of the czar(s), czarist; royal; **~́ство** *n* [9] realm; kingdom (*a*. *fig*.); rule; *a*. → **~́ствование** *n* [12] reign (**в** В in); **~́ствовать** [7] reign, rule; **~ь** *m* [4 *e*.] czar, (Russian) emperor; *fig*. king; ***без ~я́ в голове́*** stupid

**цвести́** [25 -т-] bloom, blossom

**цвет** *m* [1] **1.** [*pl*.: -á, *etc*. *e*.] colo(u)r; *fig*. cream, pick; *лица* complexion; ***защи́тного ~́а*** khaki; **2.** [*only pl*.: -ы́, *etc*. *e*.] flowers; **3.** [*no pl*.: **в -у́** in bloom] blossom, bloom; **~е́ние** *n* [12] flowering; **~и́стый** [14 *sh*.] multicolo(u)red, florid; **~ни́к** [1 *e*.] flower bed, garden; **~но́й** [14] colo(u)red; colo(u)r; *металлы* nonferrous; ***~на́я капу́ста*** cauliflower; **~о́к** *m* [1; -тка́; *pl*. *usu*. = 2] flower; **~о́чный** [14] flower…; ***~о́чный магази́н*** florist's; **~у́щий** [17 *sh*.] flowering; *fig*. flourishing; *возраст* prime (of life)

**целе́|бный** [14; -бен, -бна] curative, medicinal; **~во́й** [14] special, having a special purpose; **~сообра́зный** [14; -зен, -зна] expedient; **~устремлённый** [14 *sh*.] purposeful

**цели|ко́м** entirely, wholly; **~на́** *f* [5] virgin lands; virgin soil; **~́тельный** [14; -лен, -льна] salutary, curative; **~́ть(ся)** [13], ⟨при-⟩ aim (**в** В at)

**целлюло́за** *f* [5] cellulose

**целова́ть(ся)** [7], ⟨по-⟩ kiss

**це́л|ое** [14] whole (**в** П on the); **~ому́дренный** [14 *sh*.] chaste; **~ому́дрие** *n* [12] chastity; **~остность** *f* [8] integrity; **~ость** *f* [8]: safety; ***в ~ости*** intact; **~ый** [14; цел, -á, -о] whole, entire, intact; ***~ый и невреди́мый*** safe and sound; ***~ое число́*** whole number, integer; → ***деся́тый*** & ***со́тый***

**цель** *f* [8] aim, end, goal, object; (*мишень*) target; purpose (**с** Т, **в** П *pl*. for); ***име́ть ~́ю*** aim at; **~́ность** *f* [8] integrity; **~́ный** [14; це́лен, -льна́, -о] of one piece; entire, whole; *человек* self-contained; *молоко* [*no sh*.] unskimmed

**цеме́нт** *m* [1] cement; **~и́ровать** [7] *tech*. cement, case-harden

**цен|а́** *f* [5; *ac/sg*.: це́ну; *pl*. *st*.] price (P of; **по** Д/**в** В at/of), cost; value (Д of *or* one's); ***знать себе́ ~́у*** know one's worth; ***~ы́ нет*** (Д) be invaluable; ***любо́й ~о́й*** at any price; **~зу́ра** *f* [5] censorship

**цен|и́тель** *m* [4] judge, connoisseur; **~и́ть** [13; ценю́, це́нишь], ⟨о-⟩ estimate; value, appreciate; **~́ность** *f* [8] value; *pl*. valuables; **~́ный** [14; -е́нен, -е́нна] valuable; *fig*. precious, important; ***~́ные бума́ги*** *pl*. securities

**це́нтнер** *m* [1] centner

**центр** *m* [1] center, *Brt*. centre; **~ализо-**

Ц

**ва́ть** [7] (*im*)*pf.* centralize; **~а́льный** [14] central; ***~а́льная газе́та*** national newspaper; **~обе́жный** [14] centrifugal
**цеп|ене́ть** [8], ⟨о-⟩ become rigid, freeze; be rooted to the spot; *fig.* be transfixed; **ˆкий** [16; -пок, -пка́, -о] tenacious (*a. fig.*); **~ля́ться** [28] cling (to ***за*** В); **~но́й** [14] chain(ed); **~о́чка** *f* [5; *g/pl.*: -чек] chain; **~ь** *f* [8; в, на -и́; *from g/pl. e.*] chain (*a. fig.*); *mil.* line; *el.* circuit
**церемо́н|иться** [13], ⟨по-⟩ stand on ceremony; **~ия** *f* [7] ceremony; **~ный** [14] ceremonious
**церко́в|ный** [14] church…; ecclesiastical; **ˊ~ь** *f* [8; -кви; *instr./sg.*: -ковью; *pl.*: -кви, -ве́й, -ва́м] church (*building and organization*)
**цех** *m* [1] shop (*section of factory*)
**цивилиз|а́ция** *f* [7] civilization; **~о́ванный** [14] civilized
**цикл** *m* [1] cycle; *лекций* course; **~о́н** *m* [1] cyclone
**цико́рий** *m* [3] chicory
**цили́ндр** *m* [1] cylinder; **~и́ческий** [16] cylindrical
**цинга́** *f* [5] *med.* scurvy
**цини́|зм** *m* [1] cynicism; **ˊ~к** *m* [1] cynic; **~чный** [14; -чен, -чна] cynical
**цинк** *m* [1] zinc; **ˆовый** [14] zinc…
**цино́вка** *f* [5; *g/pl.*: -вок] mat
**цирк** *m* [1], **~ово́й** [14] circus
**циркул|и́ровать** [7] circulate; **ˊ~ь** *m* [4] (a pair of) compasses *pl.*; **~я́р** *m* [1] (official) instruction
**цисте́рна** *f* [5] cistern, tank
**цитаде́ль** (-ˈdɛ-) *f* [8] citadel; *fig.* bulwark; stronghold
**цита́та** *f* [5] quotation
**цити́ровать** [7], ⟨про-⟩ quote
**ци́трусовые** [14] citrus (trees)
**циф|ербла́т** *m* [1] dial; *часов* face; **ˆра** *f* [5] figure; number
**цо́коль** *m* [4] *arch.* socle; *el.* screw base (*of light bulb*)
**цыга́н** *m* [1; *nom./pl.*: -е & -ы; *gen.*: цыга́н], **~ка** *f* [5; *g/pl.*: -нок], **~ский** [16] Gypsy, *Brt.* Gipsy
**цыплёнок** *m* [2] chicken
**цы́почк|и**: ***на ~ах*** (***~и***) on tiptoe

# Ч

**чад** *m* [1; в -у́] fume(s); *fig.* daze; intoxication; **~и́ть** [15 *e.*; чажу́, чади́шь], ⟨на-⟩ smoke
**ча́до** *n* [9] *obs. or joc.* child
**чаевы́е** *pl.* [14] tip, gratuity
**чай** *m* [3; *part. g.*: -ю; в -е & -ю́; *pl. e.*: чаи́, чаёв] tea; ***дать на ~*** tip
**ча́йка** [5; *g/pl.*: ча́ек] (sea) gull
**ча́й|ник** *m* [1] *для заварки* teapot; teakettle; **~ный** [14] *ложка и т. д.* tea
**чалма́** *f* [5] turban
**чан** *m* [1; *pl. e.*] tub, vat
**ча́р|ка** *f* [5; *g/pl.*: -рок] *old use* cup, goblet; **~ова́ть** [20] charm; **~оде́й** *m* [3] magician, wizard (*a. fig.*)
**час** *m* [1; в -е & -у́; *after* 2, 3, 4: -а́; *pl. e.*] hour (for *pl.* ***~а́ми***); (one) o'clock (at ***в*** В); time, moment (at ***в*** В); an hour's…; ***второ́й ~*** (it is) past one; ***в пя́том ~у́*** between four and five; (→ ***пять & пя́тый***); ***кото́рый ~?*** what's the time?; ***с ˆу на ~*** soon; ***~ от ˆу не ле́гче*** things are getting worse and worse; **~о́вня** *f* [6; *g/pl.*: -вен] chapel; **~ово́й** [14] hour's; watch…, clock…; *su.* sentry, guard; ***~ово́й по́яс*** time zone; ***~ово́й ма́стер*** = **~овщи́к** *m* [1 *e.*] watchmaker
**част|и́ца** *f* [5] particle; **~и́чный** [14; -чен, -чна] partial; **ˆник** *coll.* private trader; owner of a small business; **ˆное** *n* [14] *math.* quotient; **ˆность** *f* [8] detail; **ˆный** [14] private; particular, individual; ***ˆная со́бственность*** private property; **~ота́** *f* [5; *pl. st.*: -о́ты] frequency; **~у́шка** *f* [5; *g/pl.*: -шек] humorous *or* topical two- or four-lined verse; **ˆый** [14; част, -а́, -о; *comp.*: ча́ще] frequent (*adv. a.* often); *густой* thick, dense;

*стежки и т. д.* close; *пульс и т. д.* quick, rapid; **~ь** *f* [8; *from g/pl. e.*] part (in T; *pl. a.* **по** Д); (*доля*) share; piece; section; *mil.* unit; ***бо́льшей ~ью, по бо́льшей ~и*** for the most part, mostly; ***разобра́ть на ~и*** take to pieces

**час|ы́** *no sg.* [1] *ручные* watch; clock; ***по моим ~а́м*** by my watch

**ча́х|лый** [14 *sh.*] sickly; *растительность* stunted; **~нуть** [21], ⟨за-⟩ wither away; *о человеке* become weak, waste away

**ча́ш|а** *f* [5] cup, bowl; *eccl.* chalice; **~ечка** *f* [5] *dim.* → ***ча́шка: коле́нная ~ечка*** kneecap; **~ка** *f* [5; *g/pl.*: -шек] cup; *весов* pan

**ча́ща** *f* [5] thicket

**ча́ще** more (***~ всего́*** most) often

**ча́яние** *n* [12] expectation, aspiration

**чей** *m*, **чья** *f*, **чьё** *n*, **чьи** *pl.* [26] whose; ***~ э́то дом?*** whose house is this?

**чек** *m* [1] check, *Brt.* cheque; *для оплаты* chit, bill; *оплаченный* receipt; **~а́нить** [13], ⟨вы́-⟩ mint, coin; *узор* chase; **~а́нка** *f* [5; *g/pl.*: -нок] minting, coinage; chasing; **~и́ст** *m* [1] (state) security officer; *hist.* member of the cheka; **~о́вый** [14] check…

**челно́|к** *m* [1 *e.*], **~чный** [14] shuttle

**чело́** *n* [9; *pl. st.*] *obs.* brow

**челове́|к** *m* [1; *pl.*: лю́ди; 5, 6, *etc.* -е́к] man, human being; person, individual; ***ру́сский ~к*** Russian; **~колю́бие** *n* [12] philanthropy; **~ческий** [16] human(e); **~чество** *n* [9] mankind, humanity; **~чный** [14; -чен; -чна] humane

**че́люсть** *f* [8] jaw; (full) denture

**чем** than; rather than, instead of; ***~ …, тем …*** the more … the more …; ***~ скоре́е, тем лу́чше*** the sooner, the better; **~ода́н** *m* [1] suitcase

**чемпио́н** *m* [1] champion; **~а́т** *m* [1] championship

**чепуха́** *f* [5] *coll.* nonsense; (*мелочь*) trifle

**че́пчик** *m* [1] baby's bonnet

**че́рв|и** *f/pl.* [4; *from gen. e.*] **& ~ы** *f/pl.* [5] hearts (*cards*)

**черви́вый** [14 *sh.*] worm-eaten

**черво́нец** *m* [1; -нца] *hist.* (*gold coin*) chervonets; (*ten-r(o)uble bank note in circulation 1922-47*)

**черв|ь** [4; *e.*; *nom/pl. st.*: че́рви, черве́й], **~я́к** *m* [1 *e.*] worm

**черда́к** *m* [1 *e.*] garret, attic, loft

**черёд** *coll. m* [1 *e.*] (*очередь*) turn; (*порядок*) course

**чередова́|ние** *n* [12] alternation; **~ть(ся)** [7] alternate (with)

**че́рез** (В) through; *улицу* across, over; *время* in, after; *ехать* via; ***~ день*** *a.* every other day

**черёмуха** *f* [5] bird cherry

**че́реп** *m* [1; *pl.*: -á, *etc. e.*] skull

**черепа́|ха** *f* [5] tortoise; *морская* turtle; **~ховый** [14] tortoise(shell)…; **~ший** [18] tortoise's, snail's

**череп|и́ца** *f* [5] tile (*of roof*); **~и́чный** [14] tiled; **~о́к** [1; -пка́] fragment, piece

**чере|счу́р** too, too much; **~шня** *f* [6; *g/pl.*: -шен] (sweet) cherry, cherry tree

**черкну́ть** *coll.* [20] *pf.*: scribble; dash off; ***~ па́ру*** (*or* ***не́сколько***) ***слов*** drop a line

**черн|е́ть** [8], ⟨по-⟩ blacken, grow black; *impf.* show up black; **~и́ка** *f* [5] bilberry, -ries *pl.*; **~и́ла** *n/pl.* [9] ink; **~и́ть** [13], ⟨о-⟩ *fig.* blacken, denigrate, slander

**черно|ви́к** *m* [1 *e.*] rough copy; draft; **~во́й** [14] draft…; rough; **~воло́сый** [14 *sh.*] black-haired; **~гла́зый** [14 *sh.*] black-eyed; **~зём** *m* [1] chernozem, black earth; **~ко́жий** [17 *sh.*] black; *as su.* [-его́] *m* black (man), negro; **~мо́рский** [16] Black Sea…; **~сли́в** *m* [1] prune(s); **~та́** *f* [5] blackness

**чёрн|ый** [14; чёрен, черна́] black (*a. fig.*); *хлеб* brown; *металл* ferrous; *работа* rough; *ход* back; ***на ~ый день*** for a rainy day; ***~ым по бе́лому*** in black and white

**чернь** *f* [8] *art* niello

**че́рп|ать** [1], ⟨**~ну́ть**⟩ [20] scoop, ladle; *знания, силы* derive, draw (from **из** Р, **в** П)

**черстве́ть** [8], ⟨за-, по-⟩ grow stale; *fig.* harden

**чёрствый** [14; чёрств, -á, -о] stale, hard; *fig.* callous

**чёрт** *m* [1; *pl.* 4: че́рти, -те́й, *etc. e.*] devil;

*coll.* **~побери́** the devil take it; **на кой ~** *coll.* what the deuce; **ни черта́** *coll.* nothing at all; **~а с два!** like hell!

**черт|а́** *f* [5] line; trait, feature (*a.* **~ы́ лица́**); **в ~е́ го́рода** within the city boundary

**чертёж** *m* [1 *e.*] drawing, draft (*Brt.* draught), design; **~ник** *m* [1] draftsman, *Brt.* draughtsman; **~ный** [14] *доска и т. д.* drawing (*board*, *etc.*)

**черт|и́ть** [15], ⟨на-⟩ draw, design; **~о́вский** [16] *coll.* devilish

**чёрточка** *f* [5; *g/pl.*: -чек] hyphen

**черче́ние** *n* [12] drawing

**чеса́ть** [3] **1.** ⟨по-⟩ scratch; **2.** ⟨при-⟩ *coll.* comb; **-ся** itch

**чесно́к** *m* [1 *e.*] garlic

**чесо́тка** *f* [5] scab, rash, mange

**че́ст|вование** *n* [12] celebration; **~вовать** [7] celebrate, hono(u)r; **~ность** *f* [8] honesty; **~ный** [14; че́стен, -тна́, -о] honest, upright; (*справедливый*) fair; **~олюби́вый** [14 *sh.*] ambitious; **~олю́бие** *n* [12] ambition; **~ь** *f* [8] hono(u)r (in **в** B); credit; **э́то де́лает вам ~ь** it does you credit; *coll.* **~ь ~ью** properly, well

**чета́** *f* [5] couple, pair; match; **она́ ему́ не ~** she is no match for him

**четве́р|г** *m* [1 *e.*] Thursday (on **в** B, *pl.*: **по** Д); **~е́ньки** *coll. f/pl.* [5] all fours (on **на** B, П); **четвёрка** *f* [5; *g/pl.*: -рок] four (→ **тро́йка**); *coll.* (*mark*) → **хорошо́**; **´~о** [37] four (→ **дво́е**); **четвёртый** (-'vɔr-) [14] fourth → **пя́тый**; **´~ть** *f* [8; *from g/pl. e.*] (one) fourth; *школьная* (school-)term; quarter (to **без** P; past one **второ́го**)

**чёткий** [16; чёток, четка́, -о] precise; clear; *почерк* legible; (*точный*) exact, accurate

**чётный** [14] even (*of numbers*)

**четы́ре** [34] four; → **пять**; **~жды** four times; **~ста** [36] four hundred

**четырёх|ле́тний** [15] of four years; four-year; **~ме́стный** [14] fourseater; **~со́тый** [14] four hundredth; **~уго́льник** *m* [1] quadrangle; **~уго́льный** [14] quadrangular

**четы́рнадца|тый** [14] fourteenth; → **пя́тый**; **~ть** [35] fourteen; → **пять**

**чех** *m* [1] Czech

**чехарда́** *f* [5] leapfrog; **министе́рская ~** frequent changes in personnel (*esp. in government appointments*)

**чехо́л** *m* [1; -хла́] case, cover

**чечеви́ца** *f* [5] lentil(s)

**че́ш|ка** *f* [5; *g/pl.*: -шек] Czech (woman); **~ский** [16] Czech

**чешуя́** *f* [6] *zo.* scales *pl.*

**чи́бис** *m* [1] *zo.* lapwing

**чиж** *m* [1 *e.*], *coll.* **´~ик** *m* [1] *zo.* siskin

**чин** *m* [1; *pl. e.*] *mil.* rank

**чин|и́ть** [13; чиню́, чи́нишь] a) ⟨по-⟩ mend, repair; b) ⟨о-⟩ *карандаш* sharpen, point; **~и́ть препя́тствие** (Д) obstruct, impede; **´~ный** [14; чи́нен, чинна́, чи́нно] proper; sedate; **~о́вник** *m* [1] official, functionary

**чири́к|ать** [1], ⟨~нуть⟩ [20] chirp

**чи́рк|ать** [1], ⟨~нуть⟩ [20] strike

**числ|енность** *f* [8] number; **~енный** [14] numerical; **~и́тель** *m* [4] *math.* numerator; **~и́тельное** *n* [14] *gr.* numeral (*a.* **и́мя ~и́тельное**); **~иться** [13] be *or* be reckoned (**в** П *or* **по** Д/P); **~о́** *n* [9; *pl. st.*: чи́сла, чи́сел, чи́слам] number; date, day; **како́е сего́дня ~о́?** what is the date today? (→ **пя́тый**); **в ~е́** (P) among, **в том ~е́** including

**чи́ст|ить** [15] **1.** ⟨по-, вы-⟩ clean(se); brush; *обувь* polish; **2.** ⟨о-⟩ peel; **~ка** [5; *g/pl.*: -ток] clean(s)ing; *pol.* purge; **~окро́вный** [14; -вен, -вна] thoroughbred; **~оплo´тный** [14; -тен, -тна] cleanly; *fig.* clean, decent; **~осерде́чный** [14; -чен, -чна] openhearted, frank, sincere; **~ота́** *f* [5] clean(li)ness; purity; **~ый** [14; чист, -á, -о; *comp.*: чи́ще] clean; *золото и т. д.* pure; *спирт* neat; *небо* clear; *вес* net; *лист* blank; *работа* fine, faultless; *правда* plain; *случайность* mere

**чита́|льный** [14]: **~льный зал** reading room; **~тель** *m* [4] reader; **~ть** [1], ⟨про-⟩ & *coll.* ⟨проче́сть⟩ [25; -чту́, -чтёшь; чёл, -чла́; -чтённый] read, recite; give (*lecture* on **о** П), deliver; **~ть мора́ль** lecture

**чи́тка** *f* [5; *g/pl.*: -ток] reading (*usu. by a*

Ч

*group*)

**чих|а́ть** [1], *once* ⟨**~ну́ть**⟩ [20] sneeze

**член** *m* [1] member; (*конечность*) limb; part; **~ораздéльный** [14; -лен, -льна] articulate; **~ский** [16] member(-ship)…; **~ство** *n* [9] membership

**чмóк|ать** *coll.* [1], *once* ⟨**~нуть**⟩ [20] smack; (*поцеловать*) give s.o. a smacking kiss

**чóк|аться** [1], *once* ⟨**~нуться**⟩ [20] clink (glasses T) (with **с** T)

**чó|порный** [14; -рен, -рна] prim, stiff; **~рт** → ***чёрт***

**чрев|áтый** [14 *sh.*] fraught (with T); **~о** [9] womb

**чрез** → ***чéрез***

**чрез|вычáйный** [14; -áен, -áйна] extraordinary; extreme; special; ***~вычáйное положéние*** state of emergency; **~мéрный** [14; -рен, -рна] excessive

**чтé|ние** *n* [12] reading; *художественное* recital; **~ц** *m* [1 *e.*] reader

**чтить** → ***почитáть***[1]

**что** [23] **1.** *pron.* what (*a.* ***~ за***); that, which; how; (*a.* ***а ~?***) why (so?); (*a.* ***а ~***) what about; what's the matter; *coll.* ***а ~?*** well?; ***вот ~*** the following; listen; that's it; ***~ до меня́*** as for me; ***~ вы (ты)!*** you don't say!, what next!; ***нé за ~*** (you are) welcome, *Brt.* don't mention it; ***ни за ~*** not for the world; ***ну и ~?*** what of that; ***(уж) на ~*** *coll.* however; ***с чегó бы э́то?*** *coll.* why? why …?; ***~ и говори́ть*** *coll.* sure; → ***ни***; *coll.* → **~-нибудь**, **~-то**; **2.** *cj.* that; like, as if; ***~ (ни) …, то …*** every … (a) …

**чтóб(ы)** (in order) that *or* to (*a.* ***с тем, ~***); ***~ не*** lest, for fear that; ***вмéсто тогó ~*** + *inf.* instead of …ing; ***скажи́ ему́, ~ он*** + *pt.* tell him to *inf.*

**чтó|-либо**, **~-нибудь**, **~-то** [23] something; anything; ***~-то*** *a. coll.* somewhat; somehow, for some reason or other

**чу́вств|енный** [14 *sh.*] sensuous; (*плотский*) sensual; **~и́тельность** *f* [8] sensibility; **~и́тельный** [14; -лен, -льна] sensitive; sentimental; sensible (*a.* = considerable, great, strong); **~о** *n* [9] sense; feeling; sensation; *coll.* love; ***óрганы ~*** organs of sense; **~овать** [7], ⟨по-⟩ feel (*a.* ***себя́*** [T *s.th.*]); **-ся** be felt

**чугу́н** *m* [1 *e.*] cast iron; **~ный** [14] cast-iron…

**чуд|áк** *m* [1 *e.*] crank, eccentric; **~áчество** *n* [9] eccentricity; **~éсный** [14; -сен, -сна] wonderful, marvel(l)ous; *спасение* miraculous; **~и́ть** [15 *e.*] *coll.* → ***дури́ть***; **~иться** [15] *coll.* → ***мерéщиться***; **~ный** [14; -ден, -дна] wonderful, marvel(l)ous; **~о** *n* [9; *pl.*: чудеса́, -éс, -еса́м] miracle, marvel; wonder; *a.* → ***~но***; **~óвище** *n* [11] monster; **~óвищный** [14; -щен, -щна] monstrous; *потери и т. д.* enormous

**чуж|би́на** *f* [5] foreign country (in ***на*** П; *a.* abroad); **~да́ться** [1] (P) shun, avoid; **~дый** [14; чужд, -á, -o] foreign; alien; free (from P); **~óй** [14] someone else's, others'; alien; strange, foreign; *su. a.* stranger, outsider

**чул|áн** *m* [1] storeroom, larder; **~óк** *m* [1; -лкá; *g/pl.*: -лóк] stocking

**чумá** *f* [5] plague

**чурбáн** *m* [1] block; *fig.* blockhead

**чу́тк|ий** [16; -ток, -ткá, -o; *comp.*: чу́тче] sensitive (to ***на*** B), keen; *сон* light; *слух* quick (of hearing); *человек* sympathetic; **~ость** *f* [8] keenness; delicacy (of feeling)

**чу́точку** *coll.* a wee bit

**чуть** hardly, scarcely; a little; ***~ не*** nearly, almost; ***~ ли не*** *coll.* almost, all but; ***~ что*** *coll.* on the slightest pretext; **чуть-чуть** → ***чуть***

**чутьё** *n* [10] instinct (for ***на*** B); flair

**чу́чело** *n* [9] stuffed animal; ***~ горóховое*** scarecrow; *coll.* dolt

**чушь** *coll. f* [8] bosh, twaddle

**чу́ять** [27], ⟨по-⟩ scent, *fig.* feel

Ч

# Ш

**шаба́шник** *m* [1] *coll. pej.* moonlighter
**шабло́н** *m* [1] stencil, pattern, cliché; **~ный** [14] trite, hackneyed
**шаг** *m* [1; *after* 2, 3, 4: -á; в -ý; *pl. e.*] step (by step **~ за** Т) (*a. fig.*); *большой* stride; *звук* footsteps; *tech.* pitch; **приба́вить ~у** quicken one's pace; **ни ~у** (**да́льше**) not a step futher; **на ка́ждом ~ý** everywhere, at every turn, continually; **~а́ть** [1], *once* ⟨**~ну́ть**⟩ [20] step, stride; walk; pace; (*через*) cross; *pf.* take a step; **далеко́ ~ну́ть** *fig.* make great progress; **~а́ть взад и вперёд** pace back and forth
**ша́йба** *f* [5] *tech.* washer; *sport* puck
**ша́йка** *f* [5; *g/pl.*: ша́ек] gang
**шака́л** *m* [1] jackal
**шала́ш** *m* [1] hut
**шал|и́ть** [13] be naughty, frolic, romp; fool (about), play (pranks); **~и́шь!** *coll.* (*rebuke*) don't try that on me!; none of your tricks!; **~овли́вый** [14 *sh.*] mischievous, playful; **~опа́й** *coll. m* [3] loafer; **~ость** *f* [8] prank; **~ýн** *m* [1 *e.*] naughty boy; **~ýнья** *f* [6; *g/pl.*: -ний] naughty girl
**шалфе́й** *m* [3] *bot.* sage
**шаль** *f* [8] shawl
**шальн|о́й** [14] mad, crazy; *пуля* stray…; **~ы́е де́ньги** easy money
**ша́мкать** [1] mumble
**шампа́нское** *n* [16] champagne
**шампиньо́н** *m* [1] field mushroom
**шампу́нь** *m* [4] shampoo
**шанс** *m* [1] chance, prospect (of **на** В)
**шанта́ж** *m* [1], **~и́ровать** [7] blackmail
**ша́пка** *f* [5; *g/pl.*: -пок] cap; *typ.* banner headlines
**шар** *m* [1; *after* 2, 3, 4: -á; *pl. e.*] sphere; ball; **возду́шный ~** balloon; **земно́й ~** globe
**шара́х|аться** *coll.* [1], ⟨**~нуться**⟩ [20] dash, jump (aside), recoil; *о лошади* shy
**шарж** *m* [1] cartoon, caricature; **дру́жеский ~** harmless, wellmeant caricature

**ша́рик** *m* [1] *dim.* → **шар**; **~овый** [14] → **ру́чка**; **~оподши́пник** *m* [1] ball bearing
**ша́рить** [13], ⟨по-⟩ *в чём-л.* rummage; grope about, feel
**ша́р|кать** [1], *once* ⟨**~кнуть**⟩ [20] shuffle
**шарни́р** *m* [1] *tech.* hinge, joint
**шаро|ва́ры** *f/pl.* [5] baggy trousers; **~ви́дный** [14; -ден, -дна] **~обра́зный** [14; -зен, -зна] spherical, globe-shaped
**шарф** *m* [1] scarf, neckerchief
**шасси́** *n* [*indecl.*] chassis; *ae.* undercarriage
**шат|а́ть** [1], *once* ⟨(по)шатну́ть⟩ [20] shake; rock; **-ся** *о зубе и т. д.* be loose; *о человеке* stagger, reel, totter; *coll. без дела* lounge *or* loaf, gad about
**шатёр** *m* [1; -тра́] tent, marquee
**ша́т|кий** [16; -ток, -тка] shaky, unsteady (*a. fig.*); *мебель* rickety; *fig. friend, etc.* unreliable; fickle; **~ну́ть(ся)** → **~а́ть(ся)**
**шах** *m* [1] shah; check (*chess*)
**шахмат|и́ст** *m* [1] chess player; **~ный** [14] chess…; **´~ы** *f/pl.* [5] chess; **игра́ть в ´~ы** play chess; chessmen
**ша́хт|а** *f* [5] mine, pit; *tech.* shaft; **~ёр** *m* [1] miner; **~ёрский** [16] miner's
**ша́шка**[1] *f* [5; *g/pl.*: -шек] saber, *Brt.* sabre
**ша́шка**[2] *f* [5; *g/pl.*: -шек] checker, draughtsman; *pl.* checkers, *Brt.* draughts
**шашлы́к** *m* [1] shashlik, kebab
**швартова́ться** [7], ⟨при-⟩ *naut.* moor, make fast
**швед** *m* [1], **~ка** *f* [5; *g/pl.*: -док] Swede; **~ский** [16] Swedish
**шве́йн|ый** [14] sewing; **~ая маши́на** sewing machine
**швейца́р** *m* [1] doorman, doorkeeper, porter
**швейца́р|ец** *m* [1; -рца], **~ка** *f* [5; *g/pl.*: -рок] Swiss; **Ƨия** [7] Switzerland; **~ский** [16] Swiss
**швыр|я́ть** [28], *once* ⟨**~ну́ть**⟩ [20] hurl, fling (*a.* Т)

**шеве|ли́ть** [13; -елю́, -е́ли́шь], ⟨по-⟩, *once* ⟨(по)~льну́ть⟩ [20] stir, move (*v/i.* **-ся**); **~ли́ть мозга́ми** *coll.* use one's wits
**шевелю́ра** *f* [5] (head of) hair
**шеде́вр** (-'dɛvr) *m* [1] masterpiece, chef d'œuvre
**ше́йка** *f* [5; *g/pl.*: ше́ек] neck
**ше́лест** *m* [1], **~е́ть** [11] rustle
**шёлк** *m* [1; *g/sg. a.* -у; в шелку́; *pl.*: шелка́, *etc. e.*] silk
**шелкови́|стый** [14 *sh.*] silky; **~ца** *f* [5] mulberry (tree)
**шёлковый** [14] silk(en); ***как* ~** meek as a lamb
**шел|охну́ться** [20] *pf.* stir; **~уха́** *f* [5], **~уши́ть** [16 *e.*; -шу́, -ши́шь] peel, husk; **~уши́ться** *о коже* peel
**шельмова́ть** [7], ⟨о-⟩ *hist.* punish publicly; *coll.* defame, charge falsely
**шепеля́в|ить** [14] lisp; **~ый** [14 *sh.*] lisping
**шёпот** *m* [1] whisper (in a T)
**шеп|та́ть** [3], ⟨про-⟩, *once* ⟨~ну́ть⟩ [20] whisper (*v/i. a.* **-ся**)
**шере́нга** *f* [5] file, rank
**шероховáтый** [14 *sh.*] rough, *fig.* uneven, rugged
**шерст|ь** *f* [8; *from g/pl. e.*] wool; *животного* coat; *овцы* fleece; **~яно́й** [14] wool([l]en)
**шершáвый** [14 *sh.*] rough
**шест** *m* [1 *e.*] pole
**ше́ств|ие** *n* [12] procession; **~овать** [7] stride, walk (*as in a procession*)
**шест|ёрка** *f* [5; *g/pl.*: -рок] six (→ ***тро́йка***); six-oar boat; **~ерня́** *f* [6; *g/pl.*: -рён] *tech.* pinion; cogwheel; **´~еро** [37] six (→ ***дво́е***); **~идеся́тый** [14] sixtieth; → ***пя́т(идеся́т)ый***; **~име́сячный** [14] of six months; six-month; **~исо́тый** [14] six hundredth; **~иуго́льник** *m* [1] hexagon; **~на́дцатый** [14] sixteenth; → ***пя́тый***; **~на́дцать** [35] sixteen; → ***пять***; **~о́й** [14] sixth; → ***пя́тый***; **~ь** [35 *e.*] six; → ***пять***; **~ьдеся́т** [35] sixty; **~ьсо́т** [36] six hundred; **´~ью** six times
**шеф** *m* [1] chief, head; *coll.* boss
**ше́я** *f* [6; *g/pl.*: -шей] neck
**ши́ворот**: ***взять за* ~** seize by the collar
**шик|а́рный** [14; -рен, -рна] chic, smart; **´~ать** *coll.* [1], *once* ⟨´~нуть⟩ [20] shush, hush, urge to be quiet
**ши́ло** *n* [1; *pl.*: -лья, -льев] awl
**ши́на** *f* [5] tire, *Brt.* tyre; *med.* splint
**шине́ль** *f* [8] greatcoat
**шинкова́ть** [7] chop, shred
**шип** *m* [1 *e.*] thorn; *на обуви* spike
**шипе́|ние** *n* [12] hiss(ing); **~ть** [10], ⟨про-⟩ hiss; *о кошке* spit; *на сковороде* sizzle
**шипо́вник** *m* [1] *bot.* dogrose
**шип|у́чий** [17 *sh.*] sparkling, fizzy; **~у́чка** *f* [5; *g/pl.*: -чек] *coll.* fizzy drink; **~я́щий** [17] sibilant
**шири|на́** *f* [5] width, breadth; ***~но́й в*** (В) *or* **… *в ~ну́* …** wide; **´~ть** [13] **(-ся)** widen, expand
**ши́ри́нка** *f* [5; *g/pl.*: -нок] fly (of trousers)
**ши́рма** *f* [5] (*mst. pl.*) screen
**широ́к|ий** [16; широ́к, -ока́, -óко́; *comp.*: ши́ре] broad; wide; vast; great; mass…; *наступление и т. д.* large-scale; ***на ~ую но́гу*** in grand style; **~омасшта́бный** [14; -бен, -бна] large-scale; **~опле́чий** [17 *sh.*] broad-shouldered
**шир|ота́** *f* [5; *pl. st.*: -о́ты] breadth; *geogr.* latitude; **~потре́б** *coll. m* [1] consumer goods; **~ь** *f* [8] expanse width; extent
**шить** [шью, шьёшь; ше́й(те)!; ши́тый], ⟨с-⟩ [сошью, -ьёшь, сши́тый] sew (*pf. a.* together); (*вышить*) embroider; себе́ have made; **~ё** *n* [10] sewing; needlework; embroidery
**ши́фер** *m* [1] (roofing) slate
**шифр** *m* [1] cipher, code; *библиотечный* pressmark (*chiefly Brt.*); **~ова́ть** [7], ⟨за-⟩ encipher, encode
**шиш** *coll. m* [1 *e.*]: ***ни ~а́*** damn all
**ши́шка** *f* [5; *g/pl.*: -шек] *на голове* bump, lump; *bot.* cone; *coll.* bigwig
**шка|ла́** *f* [5; *pl. st.*] scale; **~ту́лка** *f* [5; *g/pl.*: -лок] casket; **~ф** *m* [1; в -у́; *pl. e.*] cupboard; *платяной* wardrobe; ***кни́жный ~ф*** bookcase
**шквал** *m* [1] squall, gust
**шкив** *m* [1] *tech.* pulley
**шко́л|а** *f* [5] school (*go* to ***в*** В; *be* at, in ***в*** П); ***вы́сшая ~а*** higher education establishment(s); ***~а-интерна́т*** boarding

school; **~ьник** *m* [1] schoolboy; **~ьница** *f* [5] schoolgirl; **~ьный** [14] school…
**шку́р|а** *f* [5] skin (*a*. **~ка** *f* [5; *g/pl*.: -рок]), hide
**шлагба́ум** *m* [1] barrier (*at road or rail crossing*)
**шлак** *m* [1] slag
**шланг** *m* [1] hose
**шлем** *m* [1] helmet
**шлёпать** [1], *once* 〈**~нуть**〉 [20] slap, spank (*v/i. coll*. **-ся** fall with a plop); plump down
**шлифова́ть** [7], 〈от-〉 grind; (*полировать*) polish
**шлю|з** *m* [1] sluice, lock; **~́пка** *f* [5; *g/pl*.: -пок] launch, boat; *спасательная* lifeboat
**шля́п|а** *f* [5] hat; **~ка** *f* [5; *g/pl*.: -пок] *dim*. → **~а** hat; *гвоздя* head
**шля́ться** *coll*. [1] → ***шата́ться***
**шмель** *m* [4 *e*.] bumblebee
**шмы́г|ать** *coll*. [1], *once* 〈**~ну́ть**〉 [20] whisk, scurry, dart; *носом* sniff
**шни́цель** *m* [4] cutlet, schnitzel
**шнур** *m* [1 *e*.] cord; **~ова́ть** [7], 〈за-〉 lace up; **~о́к** *m* [1; -рка́] shoestring, (shoe) lace
**шныря́ть** *coll*. [28] dart about
**шов** *m* [1; шва] seam; *tech*. joint; *в вышивке* stitch (*a. med*.)
**шок** *m* [1], **~и́ровать** [7] shock
**шокола́д** *m* [1] chocolate
**шо́рох** *m* [1] rustle
**шо́рты** *no sg*. [1] shorts
**шоссе́** *n* [*indecl*.] highway
**шотла́нд|ец** *m* [1; -дца] Scotsman, *pl*. the Scots; **~ка** *f* [5; *g/pl*.: -док] Scotswoman; **~ский** [16] Scottish
**шофёр** *m* [1] driver, chauffeur
**шпа́га** *f* [5] *sport* épée; sword
**шпага́т** *m* [1] cord, string; *gymnastics* split(s)
**шпа́л|а** *rail*. *f* [5] cross tie, *Brt*. sleeper; **~е́ра** *f* [5] *для винограда и т. д*. trellis
**шпарга́лка** *coll*. *f* [5; *g/pl*.: -лок] pony, *Brt*. crib (*in school*)
**шпигова́ть** [7], 〈на-〉 lard
**шпик** *m* [1] lard; fatback; *coll*. secret agent
**шпиль** *m* [4] spire, steeple
**шпи́|лька** *f* [5; *g/pl*.: -лек] hairpin; hat pin; tack; *fig*. taunt, caustic remark, (*v/b*.: **подпусти́ть** В); **~на́т** *m* [1] spinach
**шпио́н** *m* [1], **~ка** *f* [5; *g/pl*.: -нок] spy; **~а́ж** *m* [1] espionage; **~ить** [13] spy
**шприц** *m* [1] syringe
**шпро́ты** *m* [1] sprats
**шпу́лька** *f* [5; *g/pl*.: -лек] spool, bobbin
**шрам** *m* [1] scar
**шрифт** *m* [1] type, typeface; script
**штаб** *m* [1] *mil*. staff; headquarters
**шта́бель** *m* [4; *pl*.: -ля́, *etc. e*.] pile
**штамп** *m* [1], **~ова́ть** [7], 〈от-〉 stamp, impress
**шта́нга** *f* [5] *sport*: weight; (*перекладина*) crossbar
**штаны́** *coll*. *m/pl*. [1 *e*.] trousers
**штат**¹ *m* [1] state (*administrative unit*)
**штат**² *m* [1] staff; **~́ный** [14] (on the) staff; **~́ский** [16] civilian; *одежда* plain
**штемпел|ева́ть** ('ʃtɛ-) [6], **~ь** *m* [4; *pl*.: -ля́, *etc. e*.] stamp; postmark
**ште́псель** ('ʃtɛ-) *m* [4; *pl*.: -ля́, *etc. e*.] plug; **~ный** [14]: ***~ная розе́тка*** socket
**штиль** *m* [4] *naut*. calm
**штифт** *m* [1 *e*.] *tech*. joining pin, dowel
**што́п|ать** [1], 〈за-〉 darn, mend; **~ка** *f* [5] darning, mending
**што́пор** *m* [1] corkscrew; *ae*. spin
**што́ра** *f* [5] blind; curtain
**шторм** *m* [1] *naut*. gale; storm
**штраф** *m* [1] fine; ***наложи́ть ~*** impose a fine; **~но́й** [14] *sport* penalty…; **~ова́ть** [7], 〈о-〉 fine
**штрейкбре́хер** *m* [1] strikebreaker
**штрих** *m* [1 *e*.] stroke (*in drawing*), hachure; *fig*. trait; ***доба́вить не́сколько ~́ов*** add a few touches; **~ова́ть** [7], 〈за-〉 shade, hatch
**штуди́ровать** [7], 〈про-〉 study
**шту́ка** *f* [5] item; piece; *coll*. thing; (*выходка*) trick
**штукату́р|ить** [13], 〈о-〉, **~ка** *f* [5] plaster
**штурва́л** *m* [1] *naut*. steering wheel
**штурм** *m* [1] storm, onslaught
**шту́рм|ан** *m* [1] navigator; **~ова́ть** [7] storm, assail; **~ови́к** *m* [1 *e*.] combat aircraft
**шту́чный** [14] (by the) piece (*not by*

*weight*)
**штык** *m* [1 *e*.] bayonet
**шу́ба** *f* [5] fur (coat)
**шум** *m* [1] noise; din; *воды* rush; *листьев* rustle; *машины, в ушах* buzz; *coll.* hubbub, row, ado; **~ и гам** hullabaloo; **наде́лать ~у** cause a sensation; **~е́ть** [10 *e*.; шумлю́, шуми́шь] make a noise; rustle; rush; roar; buzz; **~и́ха** *coll. f* [5] sensation, clamo(u)r; **~ный** [14; -мен, -мна́, -о] noisy, loud; sensational; **~о́вка** *f* [5; *g/pl*.: -вок] skimmer; **~о́к** [1; -мка́]: **под ~о́к** *coll.* on the sly
**шу́р|ин** *m* [1] brother-in-law (*wife's brother*); **~ша́ть** [4 *e*.; -шу́, -ши́шь], ⟨за-⟩ rustle
**шу́стрый** *coll.* [14; -тёр, -тра́, -о] nimble
**шут** *m* [1 *e*.] fool, jester; *гороховый* clown, buffoon; *coll.* **~ его́ зна́ет** deuce knews; **~и́ть** [15], ⟨по-⟩ joke, jest; make fun (of **над** T); **~ка** *f* [5; *g/pl*.: -ток] joke, jest (in **в** B); fun (for **ра́ди** P); *coll.* trifle (it's no **~ка ли**); **кро́ме ~ок** joking apart; are you in earnest?; **не на ~ку** serious(ly); (Д) **не до ~ок** be in no laughing mood; **~ли́вый** *coll.* [14 *sh.*] jocose, playful; **~ни́к** *m* [1 *e*.] joker, wag; **~очный** [14] joking, sportive, comic; *дело* laughing; **~я́** jokingly (**не** in earnest)
**шушу́кать(ся)** *coll.* [1] whisper
**шху́на** *f* [5] schooner
**ш-ш** shush!

# Щ

**щаве́ль** *m* [4 *e*.] *bot.* sorrel
**щади́ть** [15 *e*.; щажу́, щади́шь], ⟨по-⟩ [щажённый] spare; have mercy (on)
**щё́бень** *m* [4; -бня] broken stone or cinders; road metal
**щебета́ть** [3] chirp, twitter
**щего́л** *m* [1; -гла́] goldfinch
**щегол|ева́тый** [14 *sh.*] foppish, dandified; **~ь** *m* [4] dandy, fop; **~я́ть** [28] overdress; give exaggerated attention to fashion; *coll.* flaunt, parade, show off
**ще́др|ость** *f* [8] generosity; **~ый** [14; щедр, -а́, -о] liberal, generous
**щека́** [5; *ac/sg*.: щёку; *pl*.: щёки, щёк, щека́м, *etc. e*.] cheek
**щеко́лда** *f* [5] latch
**щекот|а́ть** [3], ⟨по-⟩, **~ка** *f* [5] tickle; **~ли́вый** [14 *sh.*] ticklish, delicate
**щёлк|ать** [1], *once* ⟨~нуть⟩ [20] **1.** *языком и т. д. v/i.* click (T), *пальцами* snap; *кнутом* crack; *зубами* chatter; *птица* warble, sing; **2.** *v/t.* flick, fillip (on **по́ лбу**); *орехи* crack
**щёло|чь** *f* [8; *from g/pl. e*.] alkali; **~чно́й** [14] alkaline
**щелчо́к** *m* [1; -чка́] flick, fillip; crack
**щель** *f* [8; *from g/pl. e*.] chink, crack, crevice; slit
**щеми́ть** [14 *e*.; *3rd p. only, a. impers.*] *о сердце* ache
**щено́к** *m* [1; -нка́; *pl*.: -нки́ & (2) -ня́та] puppy; *дикого животного* whelp
**щеп|ети́льный** [14; -лен, -льна] scrupulous, punctilious; fussy, finicky; **~ка** *f* [5; *g/pl*.: -пок] chip; **худо́й как ~ка** thin as a rake
**щепо́тка** *f* [5; *g/pl*.: -ток] pinch (*of salt, ect.*)
**щети́н|а** *f* [5] bristle(s); *coll.* stubble; **~иться** [13], ⟨о-⟩ bristle
**щётка** *f* [5; *g/pl*.: -ток] brush
**щи** *f/pl.* [5; *gen*.: -щей] shchi (cabbage soup)
**щи́колотка** *f* [5; *g/pl*.: -ток] ankle
**щип|а́ть** [2], *once* ⟨(у)~ну́ть⟩ [20], pinch, tweak (*v/t.* **за** B), (*тж. от мороза*) nip, bite; ⟨об-⟩ pluck; *траву* browse; **~цы́** *m/pl.* [1 *e*.] tongs, pliers, pincers, nippers; *med.* forceps; (nut)crackers; **~чики** *m/pl.* [1] tweezers
**щит** *m* [1 *e*.] shield; **распредели́тельный ~** switchboard
**щитови́дный** [14] *железа* thyroid
**щу́ка** *f* [5] *zo.* pike (fish)
**щу́п|альце** *n* [11; *g/pl*.: -лец] feeler, ten-

tacle; **~ать** [1], ⟨по-⟩ feel; probe; touch; ⟨про-⟩ *fig.* sound; **~лый** *coll.* [14; щупл, -á, -o] puny, frail
**щýрить** [13] screw up (one's eyes **-ся**)

# Э

**эваку|áция** *f* [7] evacuation; **~úровать** [7] (*im*)*pf.* evacuate
**эволюциóнный** [14] evolutionary
**эгúд|а** *f* [5]: ***под ~ой*** under the aegis (of P)
**эгоú|зм** [1] ego(t)ism, selfishness; **~ст** *m* [1], **~стка** *f* [5; *g*/*pl*.: -ток] egoist; **~стúческий** [16], **~стúчный** [14; -чен, -чна] selfish
**эй!** *int.* hi!, hey!
**эквивалéнт** [1], **~ный** [14; -тен, -тна] equivalent
**экзáм|ен** *m* [1] examination (in ***по*** Д); **~енáтор** *m* [1] examiner; **~еновáть** [7], ⟨про-⟩ examine; **-ся** be examined (by **у** P), have one's examination (with); *p. pr. p.* examine
**экземпля́р** *m* [1] copy; (*образец*) specimen
**экзотúческий** [16] exotic
**экип|áж** *m* [1] *naut.*, *ae.* crew; **~ировáть** [7] (*im*)*pf.* fit out, equip; **~ирóвка** *f* [5; *g*/*pl*.: -вок] equipping; equipment
**эколóги|я** *f* [7] ecology; **~ческий** [16] ecologic(al)
**эконóм|ика** *f* [5] economy; *наука* economics; **~ить** [14], ⟨с-⟩ save; economize; **~úческий** [16] economic; **~ия** *f* [7] economy; saving (of P, **в** П); **~ный** [14; -мен, -мна] economical, thrifty
**экрáн** *m* [1] *cine.* screen; *fig.* film industry; shield, shade
**экскавáтор** *m* [1] excavator
**экскурс|áнт** *m* [1] tourist, excursionist; **~ия** *f* [7] excursion, outing, trip; **~овóд** *m* [1] guide
**экспедú|тор** *m* [1] forwarding agent; **~ция** *f* [7] dispatch, forwarding; expedition
**экспер|иментáльный** [14] experimental; **~т** *m* [1] expert (in ***по*** Д); **~тúза** *f* [5] examination; (expert) opinion
**эксплуа|тáтор** *m* [1] exploiter; **~тáция** *f* [7] exploitation; *tech.* operation; ***сдать в ~тáцию*** comission, put into operation; **~тúровать** [7] exploit; *tech.* operate, run
**экспон|áт** *m* [1] exhibit; **~úровать** [7] (*im*)*pf.* exhibit; *phot.* expose
**э́кспорт** *m* [1], **~úровать** [7] (*im*)*pf.* export; **~ный** [14] export…
**экс|прóмт** *m* [1] impromptu, improvisation; ***~прóмтом*** *a.* extempore; **~тáз** *m* [1] ecstasy; **~трáкт** *m* [1] extract; **~тренный** [14 *sh.*] *выпуск* special; urgent; ***в ~тренных слýчаях*** in case of emergency; **~центрúчный** [14; -чен, -чна] eccentric
**эластúчн|ость** *f* [8] elasticity; **~ый** [14; -чен, -чна] elastic
**элегáнтн|ость** *f* [8] elegance; **~ый** [14; -тен, -тна] elegant, stylish
**элéктр|ик** *m* [1] electrician; **~úческий** [16] electric(al); **~úчество** *n* [9] electricity; **~úчка** *f* [5; *g*/*pl*.: -чек] *coll.* suburban electric train; **~овóз** *m* [1] electric locomotive; **~омонтёр** → ***~ик***; **~óн** *m* [1] electron; **~óника** *f* [5] electronics; **~опроводка** *f* [5; *g*/*pl*.: -док] electric wiring; **~остáнция** *f* [7] electric power station; **~отéхник** *m* [1] → ***элéктрик***; **~отéхника** *f* [5] electrical engineering
**элемéнт** *m* [1] element; *comput.* pixel; *el.* cell, battery; *coll.* type, character; **~áрный** [14; -рен, -рна] elementary
**эмáл|евый** [14], **~ировáть** [7], **~ь** *f* [8] enamel
**эмбáрго** *n* [*indecl.*] embargo; ***наложúть ~*** place an embargo (on ***на*** B)
**эмблéма** *f* [5] emblem; *mil.* insignia
**эмигр|áнт** *m* [1], **~áнтка** *f* [5; *g*/*pl*.: -ток], **~áнтский** [16] emigrant; émigré; **~úровать** [7] (*im*)*pf.* emigrate
**эмúссия** *f* [7] *денег* emission

**эмоциона́льный** [14; -лен, -льна] emotional
**энерге́тика** *f* [5] power engineering
**энерг|и́чный** [14; -чен, -чна] energetic; forceful, drastic; **∠ия** *f* [7] energy; *fig. a.* vigo(u)r; **~оёмкий** [16; -мок, -мка] power-consuming
**энтузиа́зм** *m* [1] enthusiasm
**энциклопе́д|ия** *f* [7] (*a.* **~и́ческий слова́рь** *m*) encyclop(a)edia
**эпи|гра́мма** *f* [5] epigram; **~деми́ческий** [16], **~де́мия** *f* [7] epidemic; **~зо́д** *m* [1] episode; **~ле́псия** *f* [7] epilepsy; **~ло́г** *m* [1] epilogue; **∠тет** *m* [1] epithet; **~це́нтр** *m* [1] epicenter, *Brt.* -tre
**э́по|с** *m* [1] epic (literature), epos; **∠ха** *f* [5] epoch, era, period (in **в** B)
**эроти́ческий** [16] erotic
**эруди́ция** *f* [5] erudition
**эска́др|а** *f* [5] *naut.* squadron; **~и́лья** *f* [6; *g/pl.*: -лий] *ae.* squadron
**эс|кала́тор** *m* [1] escalator; **~ки́з** *m* [1] sketch; **~кимо́с** *m* [1] Eskimo, Inuit; **~корти́ровать** [7] escort; **~ми́нец** *m* [1; -нца] *naut.* destroyer; **~се́нция** *f* [7] essence; **~тафе́та** *f* [5] relay race; **~тети́ческий** [16] aesthetic
**эсто́н|ец** *m* [1; -нца], **~ка** *f* [5; *g/pl.*: -нок], **~ский** [16] Estonian
**эстра́да** *f* [5] stage, platform; → ***варьете́***
**эта́ж** *m* [1 *e.*] floor, stor(e)y; **дом в три ~а́** three-storied (*Brt.* -reyed) house
**э́так(ий)** *coll.* → **так(о́й)**
**эта́п** *m* [1] stage, phase; *sport* lap
**э́тика** *f* [5] ethics (*a. pl.*)
**этике́тка** *f* [5; *g/pl.*: -ток] label
**этимоло́гия** *f* [7] etymology
**этногра́фия** *f* [7] ethnography
**э́т|от** *m*, **~а** *f*, **~о** *n*, **~и** *pl.* [27] this, *pl.* these; *su.* this one; the latter; that; it; there
**этю́д** *m* [1] *mus.* étude, exercise; *art lit.* study, sketch; *chess* problem
**эф|е́с** *m* [1] (*sword*) hilt; **~и́р** *m* [1] ether; *fig.* air; ***переда́ть в ~и́р*** broadcast; **~и́рный** [14; -рен, -рна] ethereal
**эффект|и́вность** *f* [8] effectiveness, efficacy; **~и́вный** [14; -вен, -вна] efficacious; **∠ный** [14; -тен, -тна] effective, striking
**эх!** *int.* eh!; oh!; ah!
**эшело́н** *m* [1] echelon; train

# Ю

**юбил|е́й** *m* [3] jubilee, anniversary; **~е́йный** [14] jubilee…; **~я́р** *m* [1] pers. (*or* institution) whose anniversary is being marked
**ю́бка** *f* [5; *g/pl.*: ю́бок] culotte, split skirt
**ювели́р** *m* [1] jewel(l)er; **~ный** [14]) jewel(l)er's
**юг** *m* [1] south; ***е́хать на ~*** travel south; → ***восто́к***; **∠о-восто́к** *m* [1] southeast; **∠о-восто́чный** [14] southeast…; **∠о-за́пад** *m* [1] southwest; **∠о-за́падный** [14] southwest
**ю́жный** [14] south(ern); southerly
**ю́зом** *adv.* skidding
**ю́мор** *m* [1] humo(u)r; **~исти́ческий** [16] humorous; comic
**ю́нга** *m* [5] sea cadet
**ю́ность** *f* [8] youth (*age*)
**ю́нош|а** *m* [5; *g/pl.*: -шей] youth (*person*); **~ество** *n* [9] youth
**ю́ный** [14; юн, -á, -о] young, youthful
**юри|ди́ческий** [16] juridical, legal; of the law; ***~ди́ческая консульта́ция*** legal advice office; **~ско́нсульт** *m* [1] legal adviser
**юри́ст** *m* [1] lawyer; legal expert
**ю́рк|ий** [16; ю́рок, юрка́, -о] nimble, quick; **~нуть** [20] *pf.* scamper, dart (away)
**ю́рта** *f* [5] yurt, nomad's tent
**юсти́ция** *f* [7] justice
**юти́ться** [15 *e.*; ючу́сь, юти́шься] huddle together; take shelter

# Я

**я** [20] I; ***это я*** it's me
**ябед|а** *coll.* *f* [5] tell-tale; **~ничать** [1] tell tales; inform on
**ябло|ко** *m* [9; *pl.*: -ки, -к] apple; *глазное* eyeball; **~ня** *f* [6] apple tree
**яв|и́ть(ся)** → ***~ля́ть(ся)***; **~ка** *f* [5] appearance; attendance; rendezvous; *место* place of (secret) meeting; **~ле́ние** *n* [12] phenomenon; occurrence, event; *thea.* scene; **~ля́ть** [28], ⟨**~и́ть**⟩ [14] present; display, show; **-ся** appear, turn up; come; (Т) be; **~ный** [14; я́вен, я́вна] obvious, evident; *вздор* sheer; **~ствовать** [7] follow (*logically*); be clear
**ягнёнок** *m* [2] lamb
**я́год|а** *f* [5], **~ный** [14] berry
**я́годица** *f* [5] buttock
**яд** *m* [1] poison; *fig. a.* venom
**я́дерный** [14] nuclear
**ядови́тый** [14 *sh.*] poisonous; *fig.* venomous
**ядр|ёный** *coll.* [14 *sh.*] *здоровый* strong, stalwart, *мороз* severe; **~о́** *n* [9; *pl. st.*; *g*/*pl.*: я́дер] kernel; *phys.*, nucleus; *fig.* core, pith
**я́зв|а** *f* [5] ulcer, sore; *fig.* plague; **~и́тельный** [14; -лен, -льна] sarcastic, caustic
**язы́к** *m* [1 *e.*] tongue; language (in ***на*** П); speech; ***на ру́сском ~е́*** (*speak, write, etc.*) in Russian; ***держа́ть ~ за зуба́ми*** hold one's tongue; **~ово́й** [14] language…; linguistic; **~озна́ние** *n* [12] linguistics
**язы́ч|еский** [16] pagan; **~ество** *n* [9] paganism; **~ник** *m* [1] pagan
**язычо́к** *m* [1; -чка́] *anat.* uvula
**яи́чн|ица** *f* [5] (*a.* **~ица-глазу́нья**) fried eggs *pl.*; **~ый** [14] egg…
**яйцо́** *n* [9; *pl.*: я́йца, яиц, я́йцам] egg; ***~ вкрутую*** (***всмя́тку***) hard-boiled (soft-boiled) egg
**я́кобы** allegedly; as it were
**я́кор|ь** *m* [4; *pl.*: -ря́, *etc. e.*] anchor (at ***на*** П); ***стоя́ть на ~е*** ride at anchor
**я́м|а** *f* [5] hole, pit; **~(оч)ка** [5; *g*/*pl.*: я́мо(че)к] dimple
**ямщи́к** *m* [1 *e.*] *hist.* coachman
**янва́рь** *m* [4 *e.*] January
**янта́рь** *m* [4 *e.*] amber
**япо́н|ец** *m* [1; -нца], **~ка** *f* [5; *g*/*pl.*: -нок], **~ский** [16] Japanese
**я́ркий** [16; я́рок, ярка́, -о; *comp.*: я́рче] *свет* bright; *цвет* vivid, rich; *пламя* blazing; *fig.* striking, outstanding
**яр|лы́к** *m* [1 *e.*] label; **~марка** *f* [5; *g*/*pl.*: -рок] fair (at ***на*** П)
**яров|о́й** [14] *agric.* spring; *as su.* ***~о́е*** spring crop
**я́рост|ный** [14; -тен, -тна] furious, fierce; **~ь** *f* [8] fury, rage
**я́рус** *m* [1] *thea.* circle; *geol.* layer
**я́рый** [14 *sh.*] ardent; vehement
**я́сень** *m* [4] ash tree
**я́сли** *m*/*pl.* [4; *gen.*: я́слей] day nursery, *Brt.* crèche
**ясн|ови́дец** *m* [1; -дца] clairvoyant; **~ость** *f* [8] clarity; **~ый** [14; я́сен, ясна́, -о] clear; bright; *погода* fine; (*отчётливый*) distinct; (*очевидный*) evident; *ответ* plain
**я́стреб** *m* [1; *pl.*: -ба́ & -бы] hawk
**я́хта** *f* [5] yacht
**яче́|йка** *f* [5; *g*/*pl.*: -е́ек] *biol. pol.* cell; ***~йка па́мяти*** *computer* storage cell; **~я́** *f* [6; *g*/*pl.*: ячей] mesh
**ячме́нь** *m* [4 *e.*] barley; *med.* sty
**я́щерица** *f* [5] lizard
**я́щик** *m* [1] box, case, chest; *выдвигающийся* drawer; ***почто́вый ~*** mailbox (*Brt.* letter-box); ***откла́дывать в до́лгий ~*** shelve, put off
**я́щур** *m* [1] foot-and-mouth disease

# Activity Section

The following section contains two parts to help you in learning:

**Games and puzzles** to help you learn how to use this dictionary and practice your Russian language skills. You'll learn about the different features of this dictionary and how to look something up effectively.

**Basic words and expressions** to reinforce your learning and help you master the basics.

Also, you will be provided with some important **grammatical information** where necessary.

# Using Your Dictionary

Using a bilingual dictionary is important if you want to speak, read or write in a foreign language. Unfortunately, if you don't understand the symbols in your dictionary or the structure of the entries, you will make mistakes.

What kind of mistakes? Think of some of the words you know in English that look or sound alike. For example, think about the word *mark*. How many meanings can you think of for the word *mark*? Try to list at least three:

**a.** ____________________

**b.** ____________________

**c.** ____________________

Now look up *mark* in the English side of the dictionary. There are more than ten Russian words that correspond to the single English word *mark*. Some of these Russian words are listed below in scrambled form.

Unscramble the jumbled Russian words, then draw a line connecting each Russian word or expression with the appropriate English meaning.

| ***Russian jumble*** | ***English meaning*** |
|---|---|
| **1.** ОМТАТКЕ | **a.** a trace |
| **2.** ЯТПНО | **b.** a target |
| **3.** МТИТОЕЬТ | **c.** a grade in school |
| **4.** ИШМЬНЕ | **d.** a stain |
| **5.** СДЕЛ | **e.** to make a mark |

With so many Russian meanings to choose from, each meaning something different, you must be careful to choose the right one to fit the context of your translation. Using the wrong word can make it hard for people to understand you. Imagine the confusing sentences you would make if you never looked beyond the first translation.

***For example:***

The hunter was following the stains left by a moose.

A good sniper can hit a very small stain from very far away.

She always gets good stains in school.

Another potential pitfall in finding a correct translation from English to Russian lies with irregular verbs. When some irregular verbs are used in the past tense, they look and sound identical to other words (nouns, adverbs, etc.) that have completely different meanings.

Let's take the verb *to feel* as an example. Look at the following sentence, where this verb is used in the past tense: *I **felt** alone*. Let's see what happens if, instead of converting the past form of the verb to its infinitive *to feel*, you look up the word *felt*. The dictionary does not give you a direct translation of verbs in their past tense form, but it does direct you to the infinitive form. So, the first entry under *felt* states that it is a past form of the verb *to feel*. But because the word *felt* is also a noun, the second entry provides a translation for the noun, which is a type of fabric. So, if in searching for the translation of your verb you skip to the very first entry that has a Russian word in it, you risk ending up with the following: *I **a type of fabric** alone*. Doesn't make much sense, does it?

Below you'll find several phrases that contain irregular verbs in the past tense. Find Russian translations of those verbs by looking up their infinitive forms. Write out the Russian infinitives.

**1.** He **left** school early.

**2.** I **thought** today was Monday.

**3.** She **bent** her knees.

**4.** He **spoke** very softly.

Now find the direct translations for the words in bold (i.e., without going to the infinitive form).

1. ______________________

2. ______________________

3. ______________________

4. ______________________

And, finally, translate the four Russian words you just found back into English.

1. ______________________

2. ______________________

3. ______________________

4. ______________________

Are those words similar in meaning to the words you started out with? Imagine putting these new words back into the sentences above. Would those sentences make sense?

If you choose the wrong meaning, you simply won't be understood. Mistakes like these are easy to avoid once you know what to look for when using your dictionary. The following pages will review the structure of your dictionary and show you how to pick the right word when you use it. Read the tips and guidelines, then complete the puzzles and exercises to practice what you have learned.

# Running Heads

Running heads are words printed at the top of each page. The running head on the left tells you the first headword on the left-hand page. The running head on the right tells you the last headword on the right-hand page. All the words that fall in alphabetical order between the two running heads appear on those two dictionary pages.

Look up the running head on the page where each headword appears and write it in the space provided. Then unscramble the jumbled running heads and match them with what you wrote.

| *Headword* | *Running head* | *Jumbled running head* |
|---|---|---|
| **1.** свита | СВОЕВОЛЬНЫЙ | КИШП |
| **2.** покаяние | ______ | ЬИНУОРТ |
| **3.** льстец | ______ | АСЯТРЬАЫЛКСАВ |
| **4.** голод | ______ | СВЕ |
| **5.** балкон | ______ | ЦАРБОТИНА |
| **6.** аэробус | ______ | ЦИЬНЕМЛА |
| **7.** вето | ______ | ОСЛГВЬТОАО |
| **8.** мелочность | ______ | АЛБАД |
| **9.** распад | ______ | УЛАЖ |
| **10.** ураган | ______ | ВОЗПОНКО |
| **11.** шинель | ______ | ВОВОЙСЬЛЫНЕ |
| **12.** пыль | ______ | АРИБАНЛЕ |

# Pronunciation

Correct pronunciation is important if you want others to understand what you are saying. This is especially true in a language like Russian, where the alphabet is so diametrically different from English. Pages 13-19 of your dictionary show you some of the basic pronunciation rules of the Russian language. Let's first take a look at the vowels on pages 13 through 15. Russian has 10 vowels: **а**, **о**, **у**, **ы**, **э**, **я**, **ё**, **ю**, **и**, and **е**. And, as your dictionary points out, most of those vowels change in pronunciation depending on whether they fall in a stressed or an unstressed syllable. Take, for example, the word **молокó** – milk. As you can see, the stress here falls on the very last syllable – **ко**. Your dictionary tells you that letter **о**, when stressed, is pronounced similar to the English *o* in the word *obey*. When it is unstressed, however, its pronunciation is closer to the letter a in *father* in the syllable closest to the stressed one (i.e., first pretonic) and as a slightly different *a* in the word *ago* in the syllables that are further away from the stressed one (i.e., post-tonic). Thus a word can have three identical vowels that are all pronounced differently.

Below you will see a list of words that have stressed and unstressed syllables. Find the words in your dictionary and mark the stressed syllable by circling it.

| | |
|---|---|
| **1.** иногда ________________ | **5.** наделать ________________ |
| **2.** математик ________________ | **6.** ветеринар ________________ |
| **3.** течение ________________ | **7.** платье ________________ |
| **4.** оборванец ________________ | **8.** омоним ________________ |

Now look up the pronunciation of all vowels for each of the words above in the pronunciation table on pages 13-15 and write out the transcription symbols for those vowels in the spaces provided.

The pronunciation of consonants in Russian is also subject to change, depending on their surroundings. Russian consonants **б**, **в**, **г**, **д**, **з**, **к**, **л**, **м**, **н**, **п**, **р**, **с**, **т**, **ф**, and **х** can change from hard to soft sounding, when followed by the soft sign **ь** or any of the following vowels: **я**, **ё**, **ю**, **и**, **е**. (Consonants **ж**, **ш**, and **ц** are always hard-sounding, and consonants **ч** and **щ** are always soft-sounding, regardless of what vowel follows them.)

Take a look at the eight words from the previous activity. Can you find the consonants that become softened by the vowels that follow them? List your findings below by writing the word where you think the soft consonant is and circle the consonant(s) in question.

________________ ________________ ________________

________________ ________________ ________________

Your dictionary also mentions the so-called voiced versus voiceless consonants. The voiced consonants **б**, **в**, **г**, **д**, **ж**, and **з** have their voiceless counterparts **п**, **ф**, **к**, **т**, **ш**, and **с**. When any of the voiced consonants is followed by any of the voiceless ones, the voiced will be pronounced as its voiceless counterpart. Thus, for example, in the word **всегда** *(always)* letter **в** is pronounced as its counterpart **ф**. Similarly, when a voiceless consonant is followed by any of the voiced ones, it will be pronounced as its voiced counterpart. For instance, in the word **сбор** *(collection)* letter **с** is pronounced as its counterpart **з**.

Below you'll find a list of words that contain voiced and voiceless consonant pairs. Identify the consonant pairs by drawing a circle around them and indicate which consonant in the pair is going to be pronounced differently and how.

***Example***: вторник __в → ф__

**1.** отговаривать __________ **4.** предшественник __________

**2.** вплавь __________ **5.** обкладывать __________

**3.** отдавать __________ **6.** из-под __________

# Identifying Headwords

If you are looking for a single word in the dictionary, you simply look for that word's location in alphabetical order. However, if you are looking for a phrase, or an object that is described by several words, you will have to decide which word to look up.

Two-word terms are listed by their first word. If you are looking for the Russian equivalent of *shooting* star, you will find it under *shooting*.

So-called phrasal verbs in English are found in a block under the main verb. The phrasal verbs *get ahead, get away,* and *get up* are all found in a block after *get*.

Idiomatic expressions are found under the key word in the expression. The phrase *at the same time* is found in the entry for *time*.

On the Russian-English side of your dictionary, feminine headwords that are variants of a masculine headword and share a meaning with that word are listed in alphabetical order with their masculine counterpart. Such feminine headwords are easily identified by their endings – **-а** or **-я**. Thus in Russian, a male teacher is called **учитель** and a female teacher is **учительница**. Both words are found in alphabetical order under the masculine form, **учитель**. (Note: Further, more detailed explanation of gender is presented further in a separate section.)

Find the following words and phrases in your dictionary. Identify the headword that each is found under and write it next to each word or expression.

**1.** call someone's attention to

**2.** it appears to me

**3.** have a shot

**4.** try one's luck

**5.** watch out

**6.** come to a halt

**7.** get the feel of

**8.** come what may

**9.** dot the i's

**10.** look into

11. показатель

12. карманный вор

13. на мой взгляд

14. быть под каблуком

15. сахарница

Now try to find all of the headwords in the word-search puzzle that follows.

| | | | | | | | | | | | | | | | | | |
|---|---|---|---|---|---|---|---|---|---|---|---|---|---|---|---|---|---|
| О | Ш | A | D | Q | Q | V | Y | N | D | O | T | B | T | L | E | S | S |
| Е | К | V | F | G | N | M | C | Y | R | V | C | F | E | U | H | G | T |
| У | Ц | А | Г | Ш | Щ | Л | А | D | A | L | Z | E | R | T | Y | U | B |
| Д | Л | П | Б | К | Ы | Е | L | B | N | O | E | A | S | Q | Q | C | X |
| П | В | О | Ж | Л | Ъ | И | L | H | W | O | Y | T | R | O | K | J | G |
| О | Е | F | L | Г | У | Е | R | X | Y | K | O | S | H | O | T | L | D |
| К | Ы | А | П | Щ | Г | К | Y | R | C | E | Z | V | N | K | I | T | E |
| А | Х | F | A | P | P | E | A | R | S | I | З | Н | У | Е | Ё | W | Y |
| З | И | В | Е | Х | С | Т | В | З | Г | Л | Я | Д | Н | У | Т | Ь | Ж |
| Н | Б | J | Y | R | H | N | U | Ш | C | M | Ь | Й | Х | Ъ | З | Л | M |
| О | Т | T | Y | W | E | O | B | Ы | J | O | P | L | G | F | R | E | W |
| К | Л | Н | A | I | T | I | Y | Ф | F | Z | M | M | N | I | T | U | A |
| Ж | А | Н | A | L | T | E | R | З | E | V | X | E | E | D | G | S | T |
| Д | V | P | N | M | R | E | W | Й | E | L | M | Y | A | J | O | I | C |
| О | К | А | Р | М | А | Н | А | З | L | O | C | S | C | P | H | J | H |
| Щ | Л | Ь | Ю | Ф | Ы | А | Р | Р | Т | Y | H | B | E | A | S | X | V |
| О | Р | Ф | А | Ы | У | Б | Ь | Т | Y | J | J | E | Y | G | K | E | S |
| Р | А | Х | А | С | Д | И | Т | Q | S | E | E | I | M | E | Y | R | T |

# Alphabetization

The entries in a bilingual dictionary are in alphabetical order. If words begin with the same letter or letters, they are alphabetized from **А** to **Я** (or from *A* to *Z* on the English side) using the first unique letter in each word.

Practice alphabetizing the following words. Rewrite the words in alphabetical order, using the space provided below. Then insert the words in alphabetical order in the grid below and use the bold squares to reveal a mystery message.

| | | |
|---|---|---|
| балаган | дебют | туризм |
| мужчина | вклад | доступ |
| осока | калина | осмотр |
| помидор | блюдечко | нотариус |
| армия | район | уныние |
| зачинщик | школа | рояль |
| карта | верблюд | ладонь |
| март | | |

| | | |
|---|---|---|
| ______________ | ______________ | ______________ |
| ______________ | ______________ | ______________ |
| ______________ | ______________ | ______________ |
| ______________ | ______________ | ______________ |
| ______________ | ______________ | ______________ |
| ______________ | ______________ | ______________ |
| ______________ | ______________ | ______________ |
| ______________ | | |

What message is written in the blue squares?

______________________________________________

# Parts of Speech

In English and Russian, words are categorized into different ***parts of speech***. These labels tell us what function a word performs in a sentence.

***Nouns*** are things. (Hint: On the Russian side of your dictionary, all nouns are followed by the letters *m, f,* or *n,* which indicate their gender. Thus if you see any of those letters following an entry in the vocabulary, you can assume that it is a noun.) *Flower, people, book, doctor,* and *tiger* are all nouns.

***Verbs*** describe actions. *Eat, go, observe,* and *build* are all verbs.

***Adjectives*** describe nouns in sentences. For example, the adjective *pretty* tells us about the noun *girl* in the phrase *a pretty girl.*

***Adverbs*** also describe, but they modify verbs, adjectives, and other adverbs. The adverb *quickly* tells you more about how the action is carried out in the phrase *ran quickly.*

***Prepositions*** specify relationships in time and space. They are words such as *in, on, before,* or *with.*

***Articles*** are words that accompany nouns. Words like *the* and *a* or *an* modify the noun, marking it as specific or general, and known or unknown. (Note: Russian nouns do not take articles.)

***Conjunctions*** are words like *and, but,* and *if* that join phrases and sentences together.

***Pronouns*** take the place of nouns in a sentence, such as *it, me,* and *they.*

On the next page is a list of nouns, adjectives and verbs that have been jumbled up together. Look up each word to find out what part of speech it represents and then classify them according to their part of speech into one of the three columns provided below.

| | | | | |
|---|---|---|---|---|
| маленький | большой | мальчик | лужайка | спать |
| полк | ловить | ползать | знамя | зыбкий |
| иголка | бежевый | бедненький | кавалер | испуг |
| предлог | презирать | разминать | разлив | трасса |
| торт | узкий | широкий | волокнистый | вожак |
| бамбук | бегать | агитировать | бессменный | душа |
| макет | любить | лысый | лук | годный |

| *Adjectives* | *Nouns* | *Verbs* |
|---|---|---|
| | | |

# Gender

Russian nouns belong to one of three groups: masculine, feminine and neuter. A noun's gender is indicated in an entry after the headword with *m* for masculine, *f* for feminine, and *n* for neuter.

In its nominative case (i.e., the way the word is given to you in the dictionary), each noun has a gender-specific ending. Thus all masculine nouns end either in a consonant, the semivowel **й**, or the soft sign **ь**. All feminine nouns end either in the vowel **а** or **я** or the soft sign **ь**. All neuter nouns end either in the vowel **о**, **е**, **ё** or **я**. (Note: **я** endings of neuter nouns are preceded by the consonant **м**. E.g.: **пламя**, **бремя**, **время**.)

Below you will find a set of words with a dot next to each one of them. Look up these words in your dictionary. First, underline all feminine words. Then draw lines to connect all the dots that belong to feminine words (make sure to draw your lines moving from word to word in a clockwise direction, starting from the top).

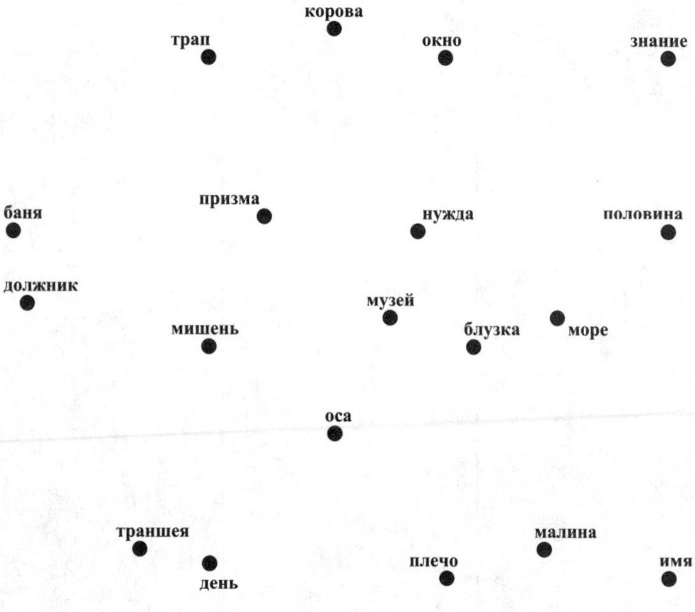

What figure do you see?

Now do the same for all the masculine nouns you find. And now for all the neuter ones. You should end up with three distinct figures that look like this:

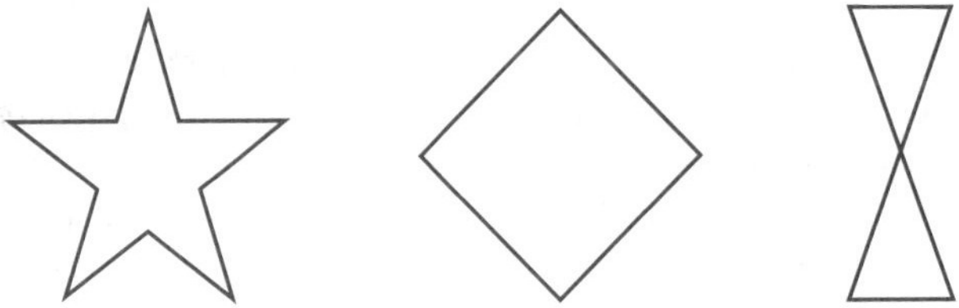

# Declensions

In Russian, nouns change endings to reflect their position in a sentence (or what is known as a *case*). Your dictionary gives you a declension table for the nouns on pages 667-668. That table shows you the changes that a noun goes through from the nominative to the prepositional case. (Note that endings are different for each gender.)

In the English language nouns do not change explicitly to reflect different cases. Thus in the phrases *George sees a bird* and *A bird sees George* neither *George* nor *a bird* look any different despite the change in their position in the phrase. That is not the case in Russian, where the first phrase would look like this: **Джордж видит птицу**. And the second phrase will look like this: **Птица видит Джорджа**.

In the following set of sentences the word *girl* (**девочка**) is placed in different positions to showcase the different cases. The Russian word for *girl* is written next to each sentence, but it is missing the ending. For each sentence look up the ending for a feminine noun for the case that is written in parentheses and write the appropriate ending to the Russian word in the space provided next to each sentence.

Note: Letters **к**, **г**, **х**, **ж**, **ч**, **ш** and **щ** cannot be followed by the letter **ы**. Therefore, feminine nouns that have either of those letters immediately before the ending will be declined with a letter **и** <u>not</u> **ы** in the genitive singular and nominative and accusative plural cases. E.g. the word **книга** will become **книги** in the genitive singular <u>not</u> **книгы**. The same applies to the word **девочка**.

1. The **girl** is a student. (Nominative) — девочк _______
2. I was at the **girl's** house. (Genitive) — (у) девочк ____
3. I gave flowers <u>to</u> the **girl**. (Dative) — девочк _______
4. I see the **girl**. (Accusative) — девочк _______
5. I am going out <u>with</u> the **girl**. (Instrumental) — (с) девочк ____
6. I am thinking <u>about</u> the **girl**. (Prepositional) — (о) девочк ____

Now let's try a few sentences with nouns of different genders and numbers and in different cases. As before, the noun will be given to you without the ending. You will need to look up the correct ending and write it in.

1. Jim met his future **wife** at a dinner reception. (Acc., feminine, singular) жен ____________
2. I love swimming in the **sea**. (Prep., neuter, singular) (в) мор _________
3. The dog was barking outside the **window**. (Inst., neuter, singular) (за) окн _________
4. I don't have a **pencil**. (Gen., masculine, singular) карандаш _______
5. The teacher gave a lecture to his **students**. (Dat., masculine, plural) студент _________

# Adjectives

Adjectives in Russian change endings to agree in gender and number with the noun they modify. Masculine adjectives can have endings **-ый, -ий,** and **-ой**. Feminine adjectives can have endings **-ая** and **-яя**. Neuter adjectives can have endings **-ое** and **-ее**. And plural adjectives have endings **-ые** and **-ие**. You may notice that those endings match the endings for the nouns of the corresponding genders and number – i.e., **-й** for masculine nouns, **-я** for feminine nouns, **-е** for neuter nouns, and **-ы** and **-и** for plural nouns.

Use the dictionary to determine whether the nouns in the following phrases are feminine, masculine, or neuter. Look up the Russian translations of the English adjectives and write them next to the English phrases. Then write in the correct forms of the adjectives to complete the phrase.

1. a **sad** smile = ____________ ____________ улыбка
2. a **small** boy = ____________ ____________ мальчик
3. a **cool** day = ____________ ____________ день
4. a **hot** summer = ____________ ____________ лето
5. an **important** message = ____________ ____________ сообщение
6. a **blue** sea = ____________ ____________ море
7. a **heavy** bag = ____________ ____________ сумка
8. a **strange** question = ____________ ____________ вопрос
9. an **interesting** idea = ____________ ____________ идея
10. a **dark** night = ____________ ____________ ночь
11. a **late** hour = ____________ ____________ час

Check your answers against the word search. The correct forms are found in the puzzle.

| | | | | | | | | | | | | | | | | | |
|---|---|---|---|---|---|---|---|---|---|---|---|---|---|---|---|---|---|
| Ф | Т | Я | Ж | Ё | Л | А | Я | У | Й | Э | Ю | Р | Л | Х | П | О | Н |
| С | В | Н | Ш | Й | А | М | И | К | Ф | Х | Е | Л | Л | Ё | А | Д | У |
| С | С | И | Н | Т | Е | Р | Е | С | Н | А | Я | О | Д | Х | В | Л | О |
| И | В | Г | Щ | С | П | Е | Ч | А | Л | Ь | Н | А | Я | Ш | П | Р | А |
| Т | К | Н | Г | И | У | И | Ь | Г | В | Ё | Ё | Р | Ж | Н | Р | П | Ы |
| П | В | А | Ж | Н | О | Е | Б | Щ | П | Й | А | К | Э | Г | О | А | Ф |
| Н | О | Ш | Н | Т | Е | Т | Ю | Ш | И | А | В | Ц | О | Е | Х | В | Я |
| О | Ы | Я | О | Л | Н | Т | Р | К | О | Е | Ы | У | П | К | Л | Ы | Э |
| Й | Я | Щ | Ю | Ж | Щ | Ш | Ь | А | В | В | А | К | У | Д | А | Ж | Т |
| М | В | Т | Б | Е | Г | Н | В | Г | И | Е | М | К | В | У | Д | Ф | Ё |
| Л | Ы | А | Р | Л | Е | Р | Ы | Н | Д | Р | Т | А | П | Ы | Н | М | М |
| Д | Ф | Е | О | Л | Ы | Й | И | Н | Д | З | О | П | И | В | Ы | С | Н |
| Ж | Ы | У | А | Д | Ц | О | Ф | К | С | О | И | П | Ь | С | Й | Ч | А |
| З | П | М | В | Ж | У | П | Ы | А | П | В | М | Т | С | М | В | Т | Я |
| Х | А | Р | А | Э | В | Р | С | А | Р | К | С | Ь | И | И | У | И | Щ |
| Ъ | А | П | П | Ж | А | О | Е | О | К | Р | А | Ж | Н | Ь | А | Г | Ш |
| Ю | Л | В | Р | Л | О | Л | М | Т | О | М | Ч | Т | Е | И | Ы | Щ | Р |
| Е | С | Т | Р | А | Н | Н | Ы | Й | Л | Д | С | М | Е | Ч | Ф | Д | Р |

# Verbs

Verbs in the dictionary are presented in their infinitive form. All the verb entries on the Russian side of the dictionary are followed by numbers in square brackets. Those numbers correspond to model conjugations provided to you on pages 662-666 of your dictionary. Thus a verb like **говорить** (*to speak*) is followed by number 13. If we look up that number in the table, we find it next to the verb **мирить** on page 664. This tells us that the verb **говорить** will be conjugated in exactly the same way as the verb **мирить**, which is presented to you in the table.

To conjugate the verb, you must use the form that agrees with that verb's subject. The majority of Russian verbs fall into one of two groups (see page 661 of your dictionary). Verbs of the 1st group generally have endings of **-ать**, **-ять**, **-еть**, **-уть**, **ыть**, and **-ти** (for example: **читать**, **терять**, **петь**, **гнуть**, **рыть**, **идти**); while the 2nd group verbs generally end with **-ить** (for example: **говорить**). Your dictionary shows you the conjugated endings of the 1st and 2nd group verbs in the conjugation table on page 661. Note that the entries in that conjugation table from left to right correspond to 1st, 2nd, and 3rd person singular (i.e., **я** *[I]*, **ты** *[you singular]*, **он/она/оно** *[he/she/it]**) and 1st, 2nd, and 3rd person plural (i.e., **мы** *[we]*, **вы** *[you plural or formal]*, **они** *[they]*) respectively. Thus, for instance, if you wanted to use the verb **читать** (*to read*) in a phrase *A boy* (**мальчик**) is reading, you would select the ending for the 3rd person singular (i.e., *a boy*) from the 1st group verbs: **Мальчик читает**.
(Note: There are also some verbs with 1st group endings that are conjugated as 2nd group verbs and some verbs with 2nd group endings that are conjugated as 1st group verbs. Those verbs are exceptions and, if possible, should be memorized.)

| |
|---|
| * Note: In Russian, pronouns **он** and **она** can be used to replace both animate and inanimate objects. |

### *Reflexive verbs*

Some of the verbs in the Russian language are what is called reflexive verbs. A reflexive verb is one whose subjcct is the same as its direct object – in other words, the verb's action is reflected back onto its subject. A good example is a phrase **Я умываюсь**, which literally means *I am washing myself*. Here the object of the verb *to wash* is the same as its subject – *I*.

In English, such reflection is accomplished by reflexive pronouns, such as *myself, herself, yourself*, etc. In Russian, the endings of reflexive verbs are followed by **-ся** in the infinitive form. **-ся** changes to **-сь** in the 1st person singular and 2nd person plural. You can see the complete endings on page 661 of your dictionary.

For the following exercise, conjugate the given verbs in the present tense. Use the context and/or the subject pronouns to determine the person and the number of verb form you will need. Finally, use the correct answers to fill in the crossword that follows.

Hint: Follow the numbers in square brackets in the dictionary entry to determine which model conjugation to follow.

*Across*

| | |
|---|---|
| **1.** Я вас ______________ на свой день рождения. | **приглашать** |
| **3.** Я постепенно ______________ к новой обстановке. | **привыкать** |
| **5.** Я не ____________________, зачем вам это нужно. | **понимать** |
| **7.** Куда вы ______________? | **бежать** |
| **9.** Ваш сын очень много _______________. | **шалить** |
| **11.** Машина ___________________ по шоссе. | **мчаться** |
| **13.** Что вы здесь ________________? | **делать** |
| **15.** От этой музыки у меня ______________ голова. | **трещать** |
| **17.** Вадим ________________ вместе со своей женой. | **завтракать** |
| **19.** Ваза с цветами ____________ в комнате на столе. | **стоять** |
| **21.** Собака _____________ за окном. | **лаять** |
| **23.** Маша ____________________ от холода. | **ёжиться** |

*Down*

| | | |
|---|---|---|
| **2.** | Неправда, ты всё ______________. | **придумывать** |
| **4.** | Самолет ______________ в Нью-Йорк через пол-часа. | **прибывать** |
| **6.** | Мы ______________ свежим воздухом. | **дышать** |
| **8.** | Вы ни о чём не ______________ ? | **жалеть** |
| **10.** | Ну зачем вы ______________ ? | **упрямиться** |
| **12.** | Он часто ______________ свою бабушку. | **навещать** |
| **14.** | Телефон ______________ в соседней комнате. | **звонить** |
| **16.** | Дождь ______________ по стеклу. | **стучать** |
| **18.** | Они ______________ ходить в кино. | **любить** |

When you are reading Russian, you face a different challenge. You see a conjugated verb in context and you need to determine what is its infinitive in order to understand its meaning.

For the next puzzle, you will see conjugated verbs in the sentences. Figure out which verbs represent the conjugated forms and write the infinitive (the headword form) for each one in the crossword puzzle.

*Across*

1. Корабль **швартуется** в гавани.
3. Что ты всё время **ворочаешься**?
5. Где вы сегодня **обедали**?
7. **Благодарю** вас за помощь.
9. Этот поступок **вдохновил** его на подвиг.
11. Стрела чуть-чуть не **долетела** до цели.
13. Вы не **желаете** присесть?
15. Он **лязгал** зубами от холода и от страха.
17. Паровоз **гудел**, подъезжая к станции.
19. Вы меня случайно не **избегаете**?
21. После разговора с ней, Вадим **воспрянул** духом.

*Down*

2. У Светы простуда – она очень сильно **кашляет**.
4. Что он **намеревается** делать по этому поводу?
6. Сегодня так холодно, что я просто **замерзаю**.
8. Он очень **заботится** о своей семье.
10. Я **исполнил** вашу просьбу.
12. Кому вы **адресовали** это письмо?
14. Они **возлагали** большие надежды на эту встречу.
16. Мы с вами так не **договаривались**.
18. Эта женщина его совсем **зачаровала**.

## *Perfective vs. imperfective verbs*

You will notice that some verb entries in your dictionary are followed by letters *impf.* or *pf.* Those stand for imperfective and perfective verb aspects.

**Imperfective verbs** describe actions that are continuous in nature (such as *a bird is singing, a boy is reading,* etc.).

**Perfective verbs** describe actions that are completed (for example: *a boy read [finished reading] a book; a bird sang [i.e., finished singing] a song,* etc.) or that will be completed (for example: *a boy will finish reading a book; a bird will finish singing a song*).

Almost every imperfective verb can be given a perfective aspect and vice versa. Your dictionary provides perfective aspects in the entries for imperfective verbs and imperfective aspects for perfective verbs when applicable. Those are presented in angle brackets following the main verb entry.

Notice that not all of the verb forms listed in your dictionary have prefixes written next to them. That is because those verb forms are continuous and, as such, cannot express completed actions (which is what a perfective form is).

The conjugation tables in the back of your dictionary provide some examples of how imperfective verbs can become perfective by adding a prefix in front of the verb. Thus the verb **читать** (*to read*), which is an imperfective verb, becomes perfective when given a prefix **про-**. So a sentence **Я читаю книгу**, meaning *I am reading a book*, becomes *I will read* (or *will finish reading*) *a book* in the following case: **Я прочитаю книгу**.

Below there are several sentences that contain imperfective verbs that you will find in your conjugation tables. Put those sentences in the future by adding the prefixes listed next to those verbs.

1. Собака гложет кость. ______________________________
2. Я рисую стол. ______________________________
3. Дует ветер. ______________________________
4. Снег тает. ______________________________

Now provide the English translations of the new sentences that you have created.

1. ______________________________
2. ______________________________
3. ______________________________
4. ______________________________

# Entries in Context

In this dictionary, in addition to the literal translation of each headword, entries sometimes include phrases using that word. When the headword is repeated within an English-Russian entry, a symbol called a tilde (~) takes the place of the entire headword. For example, the phrase *beyond reach*, which is listed under the headword *reach*, in your dictionary looks like this: ***beyond ~***.

On the Russian-English side, some headwords are split by a vertical bar, which serves as a mark of repetition. The tilde replaces only the part of the headword that precedes the vertical bar. For example, when the headword **понимá|ние** (*comprehension, understanding*) is used in a phrase **в моём понимáнии** (*as I see it*), in your dictionary it looks like this: ***в моём ~нии***.

Fill in the sentences below, using the correct word in context. Then find those words in the puzzle that follows.

Hint: Each clue contains key words that will help you find the answer. Look up the bold words in each clue. You will find the answers in expressions within each entry.

1. Soldiers are marching to the beat of the drum.

   **барабанный** ______________

2. There is so much information that my thoughts are in a whirl.

   **голова** ___________________________

3. Mind your own business!

   ___ **мешайтесь** _________________!

4. He seems so downcast lately.

   _________ **воду** ___________________

5. That's what you call hitting the nail on the head!

   __________________ **бровь,** ___________

6. Would you stop beating around the bush?

   ______________ **вокруг** __________________

7. to shake hands

**здороваться** ______________

8. Sometimes trying to get through to you is like hitting one's head against a brick wall.

**биться** ______________________________

9. to gain the upper hand

__________________ **верх**

10. He shouted at the top of his voice.

________________ **голос**

11. What is the time? It's a quarter to one.

**без** ________________________________

12. time and again

_____________ **дело**

13. The die is cast.

**жребий** ______________

14. to take something into consideration

____________________________ **внимание**

15. There's nothing to do but be bored to death.

**изнывать** ______________________

16. She is nothing but skin and bone.

**кожа** ____________________

17. It all happened in the twinkling of an eye.

_____ **мгновение** ________

**18.** I don't really care. It's all the same to me.

________________________ **безразлично**

**19.** It serves him right!

________________ **надо**!

**20.** an optical illusion

**обман**________________

| | | | | | | | | | | | | | | | | | | | |
|---|---|---|---|---|---|---|---|---|---|---|---|---|---|---|---|---|---|---|---|
| О | Д | В | Р | Т | Щ | У | С | О | П | Ж | Л | В | Ш | А | И | В | О | К | А |
| С | П | Ф | В | Ч | Е | Т | В | Е | Р | Т | И | Ч | А | С | И | С | К | У | И |
| Ъ | Р | Х | О | Д | И | Т | Ь | Д | А | О | К | О | Л | О | З | Г | А | Ф | К |
| С | И | И | С | Й | К | Ц | Я | Ч | В | Ж | Ю | Б | Т | Ь | Л | О | К | Ш | Р |
| О | Н | Ж | Ш | Б | О | Л | Б | Ю | О | З | Т | О | И | Г | М | Л | В | Н | У |
| О | Я | О | Ш | А | О | С | Е | Н | В | У | Щ | Ш | И | Ь | Н | О | О | Т | Г |
| Ц | Т | Н | Г | Ж | Э | Й | Л | А | Е | Ш | З | Н | Ш | Г | Е | В | П | Т | О |
| Щ | Ь | К | А | Ю | Ж | М | Б | К | С | Л | А | В | И | Е | Э | О | У | С | М |
| Ш | В | Т | А | К | Е | М | У | И | Ь | Ь | Р | П | А | В | Т | Й | Щ | Ю | И |
| Г | О | Ц | Ы | Б | Ъ | Н | Ш | Ц | Й | Т | У | Р | В | А | О | О | Е | У | Д |
| Н | Г | К | М | Ь | Е | Д | Г | З | У | Ь | К | О | У | И | Э | Б | Н | Ы | Ё |
| Е | Ш | Е | И | Ш | В | Г | К | М | Р | М | У | Л | Ч | Ь | Ф | С | Н | Й | Т |
| К | Л | Г | О | И | И | О | Ы | О | К | Е | Д | Д | С | Б | Ы | Т | Ы | Ц | Щ |
| У | П | Р | Т | М | Т | Т | В | Л | Е | Н | Н | Д | И | Ю | Й | Е | Й | И | И |
| К | Б | Г | Ь | С | Ь | С | А | Т | Г | К | Д | И | Т | Э | Ц | Н | З | Т | С |
| Ш | Р | Р | Б | Ч | Л | К | Е | Г | Ш | Ы | Л | П | Я | Х | В | У | Э | С | Я |
| Г | Л | А | Ю | С | П | У | Н | Е | В | А | В | Г | Л | А | З | Щ | Х | О | С |
| А | Д | Ч | С | Я | В | К | К | Н | В | В | Ж | О | Ь | З | Р | Г | Ъ | К | Ч |
| В | З | Я | Т | Ь | К | И | П | О | А | Ё | П | Л | Б | К | Р | О | З | А | И |
| Ж | Н | Е | Н | Е | В | С | В | О | Ё | Д | Е | Л | О | В | Т | Р | Ё | Д | Т |

# Riddles

Solve the following riddles in English. Then write the Russian translation of the answer on the lines. You will need the numbers below the lines for the activity "Cryptogram."

**1.** This cold season is followed by spring.

___ ___ ___ ___

5 10 2 15

**2.** The direction opposite of North.

___ ___

27 12

**3.** This thing protects you from the rain, but it's bad luck to open it indoors.

___ ___ ___ ___ ___ ___

5 13 25 9 10 22

**4.** The sound a dog makes.

___ ___ ___

18 15 34

**5.** The couple you call Mom and Dad.

___ ___ ___ ___ ___ ___ ___ ___

7 13 30 10 9 16 18 10

**6.** If you are injured or very ill, you should go to this place.

___ ___ ___ ___ ___ ___ ___ ___

29 13 18 41 25 10 38 15

**7.** This mode of transportation has only two wheels. It is also good exercise!

___ ___ ___ ___ ___ ___ ___ ___ ___

23 16 18 13 11 10 20 16 30

**8.** This animal is a horse's baby.

_____ _____ _____ _____ _____ _____ _____ _____ _____

33 16 7 16 29 31 25 13 22

**9.** A weapon that shoots out cannonballs.

_____ _____ _____ _____ _____

20 40 35 22 15

**10.** A tool used by fishermen.

_____ _____ _____ _____ _____ _____

40 30 13 37 22 15

**11.** This celestial object replaces the sun at night.

_____ _____ _____ _____

18 40 25 15

**12.** Snow White bit into this red fruit and fell into a long slumber.

_____ _____ _____ _____ _____ _____

8 29 18 13 22 13

**13.** This professional brings letters and packages to your door.

_____ _____ _____ _____ _____ _____ _____ _____ _____

20 13 37 9 15 18 41 13 25

**14.** An Australian mammal that carries her babies in a small pouch on her belly.

_____ _____ _____ _____ _____ _____ _____

22 16 25 12 40 7 40

**15.** A very young dog is referred to as this.

_____ _____ _____ _____ _____

6 16 25 13 22

# Cryptogram

Write the letter that corresponds to each number (refer to the previous activity "Riddles") in the spaces. When you are done, you will discover a message in Russian. What does it say? Try your best to translate this message into English.

| | | | | | | | | | | | | | | | | | | | | |
|---|---|---|---|---|---|---|---|---|---|---|---|---|---|---|---|---|---|---|---|---|
| 40 | 2 | 13 | 2 | | 7 | 13 | 11 | 11 | 10 | 27 | | 25 | 16 | | 20 | 13 | 25 | 8 | 9 | 41 |
| 15 | 7 | 35 | 10 | 25 | 13 | 2 | | 13 | 29 | 6 | 10 | 2 | | | | | | | | |
| 25 | 16 | | 10 | 5 | 2 | 16 | 7 | 10 | 9 | 41 | | | | | | | | | | |
| 40 | | 25 | 16 | 34 | | 13 | 11 | 13 | 29 | 16 | 25 | 25 | 15 | 8 | | 11 | 9 | 15 | 9 | 41 |
| 23 | | 7 | 13 | 11 | 11 | 10 | 27 | | 2 | 13 | 33 | 25 | 13 | | | | | | | |
| 9 | 13 | 18 | 41 | 22 | 13 | | 23 | 16 | 7 | 10 | 9 | 41 | | | | | | | | |

# Answer Key

## Using Your Dictionary

**a-c** *Answers will vary*

***Russian word jumble***

**1.** отметка, **c**

**2.** пятно, **d**

**3.** отметить, **e**

**4.** мишень, **b**

**5.** след, **a**

***Russian verb infinitives***

**1.** уходить

**2.** думать

**3.** согнуть

**4.** говорить

***Direct translations of words in bold***

**1.** левый

**2.** мысль

**3.** склонность

**4.** спица

***Translation back into English***

**1.** *left, left-hand*

**2.** *thought, idea*

**3.** *inclination*

**4.** *spoke, knitting needle*

## Running Heads

| *Headword* | *Running head* | *Jumbled running head* |
|---|---|---|
| 1. свита | СВОЕВОЛЬНЫЙ | КИШП |
| 2. покаяние | ПОЗВОНОК | ЬИНУОРТ |
| 3. льстец | ЛУЖА | АСЯТРЬАЫЛКСАВ |
| 4. голод | ГОЛОСОВАТЬ | СВЕ |
| 5. балкон | БАЛЕРИНА | ЦАРБОТИНА |
| 6. аэробус | БАЛДА | ЦИЬНЕМЛА |
| 7. вето | ВЕС | ОСЛГВЬТОАО |
| 8. мелочность | МЕЛЬНИЦА | АЛБАД |
| 9. распад | РАСКАЛЫВАТЬСЯ | УЛАЖ |
| 10. ураган | УРОНИТЬ | ВОЗПОНКО |
| 11. шинель | ШПИК | ВОВОЙСЬЛЫНЕ |
| 12. пыль | РАБОТНИЦА | АРИБАНЛЕ |

## Pronunciation

1. иногда ɪ ə a
2. математик ə ɪ a ɪ
3. течение ɪ ɛ ɪ jɪ
4. оборванец ə a a ɪ
5. наделать a ɛ ə
6. ветеринар ɪ ɪ i a
7. платье ~~a jɪ~~
8. омоним a ɔ ɪ

### *Softened consonants*

математик наделать омоним

течение ветеринар

оборванец платье

### *Voiced vs. voiceless consonants*

1. сговаривать т → д
2. вплавь в → ф
3. отдавать т → д
4. предшественник д → т
5. сбкладывать б → п
6. из-под з → с

## Identifying Headwords

1. *call*
2. *appear*
3. *shot*
4. *try*
5. *watch*
6. *halt*
7. *feel*
8. *come*
9. *dot*
10. *look*
11. показ
12. карман
13. взгляд
14. каблук
15. сахар

| | | | | | | | | | | | | | | | | | |
|---|---|---|---|---|---|---|---|---|---|---|---|---|---|---|---|---|---|
| О | Ш | Λ | D | Q | Q | V | Y | N | D | O | T | B | T | L | E | S | S |
| Е | К | V | F | G | N | M | C | Y | R | V | C | F | E | U | H | G | T |
| У | Ц | А | Г | Ш | Щ | Л | A | D | A | L | Z | E | R | T | Y | U | B |
| Д | Л | П | Б | К | Ы | Е | L | B | N | O | E | A | S | Q | Q | C | X |
| П | В | О | Ж | Л | Ь | И | L | H | W | O | Y | T | R | O | K | J | G |
| О | E | F | L | I | У | E | R | X | Y | K | O | S | H | O | T | L | D |
| К | Ы | А | П | Щ | Г | К | Y | R | C | E | Z | V | N | K | I | T | E |
| А | X | F | A | P | P | E | A | R | S | I | З | H | У | E | Ё | W | Y |
| З | И | В | Е | Х | С | Т | В | З | Г | Л | Я | Д | Н | У | Т | Ь | Ж |
| Н | Б | J | Y | R | H | N | U | Ш | С | М | Ь | Й | Х | Ъ | З | Л | M |
| О | Т | Т | Y | W | E | O | B | Ы | J | O | P | L | G | F | R | E | W |
| К | Л | Н | A | I | T | I | Y | Ф | F | Z | M | M | N | I | T | U | A |
| Ж | А | H | A | L | T | E | R | З | E | V | X | E | E | D | G | S | T |
| Д | V | P | N | M | R | E | W | Й | E | L | M | Y | A | J | O | I | C |
| О | К | А | Р | М | А | Н | А | З | L | O | C | S | C | P | H | J | H |
| Щ | Л | Ь | Ю | Ф | Ы | А | Р | Р | T | Y | H | B | E | A | S | X | V |
| О | Р | Ф | А | Ы | У | Б | Ь | Т | Y | J | J | E | Y | G | K | E | S |
| Р | А | Х | А | С | Д | И | Т | Q | S | E | E | I | M | E | Y | R | T |

## Alphabetization

армия

балаган

блюдечко

верблюд

вклад

дебют

доступ

зачинщик

калина

карта

ладонь

март

мужчина

нотариус

осока

осмотр

помидор

район

рояль

туризм

уныние

школа

| | | | | | | | | | | | | |
|---|---|---|---|---|---|---|---|---|---|---|---|---|
| | | | А | Р | М | И | Я | | | | | |
| | | | | | Б | А | Л | А | Г | А | Н | |
| | | | | | Б | Л | Ю | Д | Е | Ч | К | О |
| | | | | В | Е | Р | Б | Л | Ю | Д | | |
| | | | | | В | К | Л | А | Д | | | |
| | | | | Д | Е | Б | Ю | Т | | | | |
| | | | Д | О | С | Т | У | П | | | | |
| | | | | | З | А | Ч | И | Н | Щ | И | К |
| | | | | К | А | Л | И | Н | А | | | |
| | | | | К | А | Р | Т | А | | | | |
| | | Л | А | Д | О | Н | Ь | | | | | |
| | | | | | М | А | Р | Т | | | | |
| | | | | | | М | У | Ж | Ч | И | Н | А |
| Н | О | Т | А | Р | И | У | С | | | | | |
| | | | | | | О | С | М | О | Т | Р | |
| | | | | О | С | О | К | А | | | | |
| | | | | П | О | М | И | Д | О | Р | | |
| | | | | | Р | А | Й | О | Н | | | |
| | | | | | Р | О | Я | Л | Ь | | | |
| | | | Т | У | Р | И | З | М | | | | |
| | | | | | У | Н | Ы | Н | И | Е | | |
| | | | | | | Ш | К | О | Л | А | | |

**Я люблю учить русский язык.**

*(I love to study Russian language.)*

## Parts of Speech

| *Adjectives* | *Nouns* | *Verbs* |
|---|---|---|
| маленький | мальчик | спать |
| большой | лужайка | ловить |
| бежевый | полк | ползать |
| бедненький | знамя | презирать |
| узкий | иголка | разминать |
| зыбкий | кавалер | бегать |
| широкий | испуг | агитировать |
| волокнистый | предлог | любить |
| бессменный | разлив | |
| лысый | трасса | |
| годный | торт | |
| | вожак | |
| | бамбук | |
| | душа | |
| | макет | |
| | лук | |

## Gender

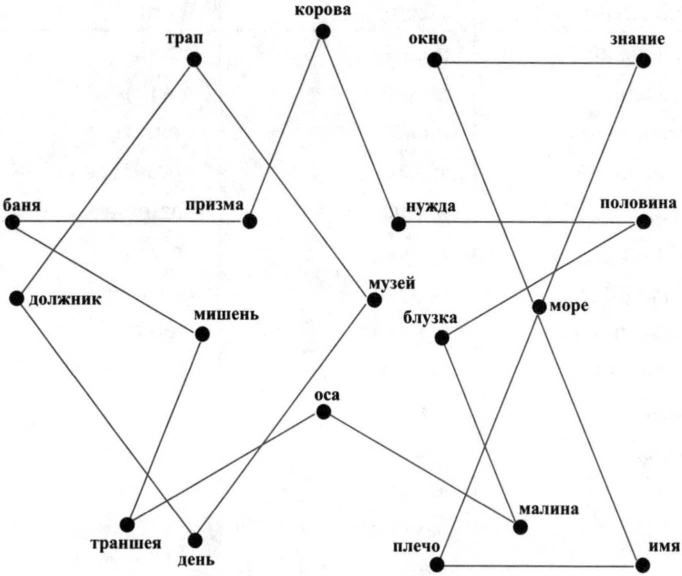


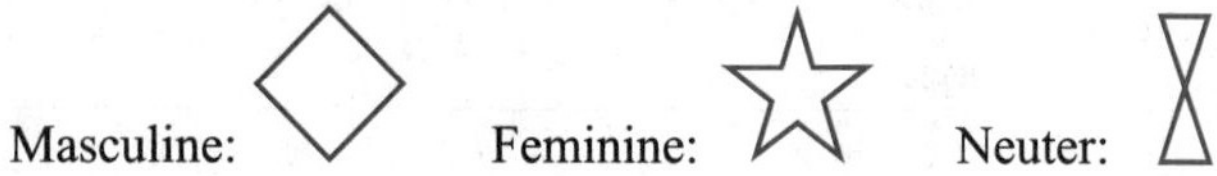


## Declensions

| | |
|---|---|
| 1. (Nominative) | девочка |
| 2. (Genitive) | (у) девочки |
| 3. (Dative) | девочке |
| 4. (Accusative) | девочку |
| 5. (Instrumental) | (с) девочкой |
| 6. (Prepositional) | (о) девочке |

### *Nouns of different gender and number*

1. (Acc., feminine, singular) жену
2. (Prep., neuter, singular) (в) море
3. (Inst., neuter, singular) (за) окном
4. (Gen., masculine, singular) карандаша
5. (Dat., masculine, plural) студентам

## Adjectives

1. печальная улыбка
2. маленький мальчик
3. прохладный день
4. жаркое лето
5. важное сообщение
6. синее море
7. тяжёлая сумка
8. странный вопрос
9. интересная идея
10. тёмная ночь
11. поздний час

| | | | | | | | | | | | | | | | | | |
|---|---|---|---|---|---|---|---|---|---|---|---|---|---|---|---|---|---|
| Ф | Т | Я | Ж | Ё | Л | А | Я | У | Й | Э | Ю | Р | Л | Х | П | О | Н |
| С | В | Н | Ш | Й | А | М | И | К | Ф | Х | Е | Л | Л | Ё | А | Д | У |
| С | С | И | Н | Т | Е | Р | Е | С | Н | А | Я | О | Д | Х | В | Л | О |
| И | В | Г | Щ | С | П | Е | Ч | А | Л | Ь | Н | А | Я | Ш | П | Р | А |
| Т | К | Н | Г | И | У | И | Ь | Г | В | Ё | Ё | Р | Ж | Н | Р | П | Ы |
| П | В | А | Ж | Н | О | Е | Б | Щ | П | Й | А | К | Э | Г | О | А | Ф |
| Н | О | Ш | Н | Т | Е | Т | Ю | Ш | И | А | В | Ц | О | Е | Х | В | Я |
| О | Ы | Я | О | Л | Н | Т | Р | К | О | Е | Ы | У | П | К | Л | Ы | Э |
| Й | Я | Щ | Ю | Ж | Щ | Ш | Ь | А | В | В | А | К | У | Д | А | Ж | Т |
| М | В | Т | Б | Е | Г | Н | В | Г | И | Е | М | К | В | У | Д | Ф | Ё |
| Л | Ы | А | Р | Л | Е | Р | Ы | Н | Д | Р | Т | А | П | Ы | Н | М | М |
| Д | Ф | Е | О | Л | Ы | Й | И | Н | Д | З | О | П | И | В | Ы | С | Н |
| Ж | Ы | У | А | Д | Ц | О | Ф | К | С | О | И | П | Ь | С | Й | Ч | А |
| З | П | М | В | Ж | У | П | Ы | А | П | В | М | Т | С | М | В | Т | Я |
| Х | А | Р | А | Э | В | Р | С | А | Р | К | С | Ь | И | И | У | И | Щ |
| Ъ | А | П | П | Ж | А | О | Е | О | К | Р | А | Ж | Н | Ь | А | Г | Ш |
| Ю | Л | В | Р | Л | О | Л | М | Т | О | М | Ч | Т | Е | И | Ы | Щ | Р |
| Е | С | Т | Р | А | Н | Н | Ы | Й | Л | Д | С | М | Е | Ч | Ф | Д | Р |

## Verbs

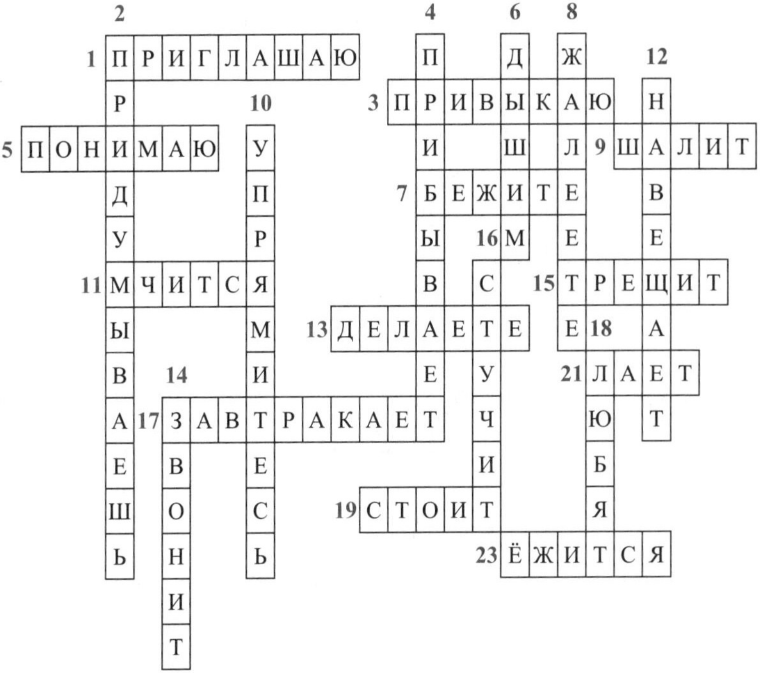
1 ПРИГЛАШАЮ
2 ПРИДУМЫВАЕШЬ
3 ПРИВЫКАЮ
4 ПРИБЫВАЕТ
5 ПОНИМАЮ
6 ДЫШИМ
7 БЕЖИТЕ
8 ЖАЛЕЕТЕ
9 ШАЛИТ
10 УПРЯМИТЕСЬ
11 МЧИТСЯ
12 НАВЕЩАЕТ
13 ДЕЛАЕТЕ
14 ЗВОНИТ
15 ТРЕЩИТ
16 СТУЧИТ
17 ЗАВТРАКАЕТ
18 ЛЮБЯТ
19 СТОИТ
21 ЛАЕТ
23 ЁЖИТСЯ

1 швартоваться
3 ворочаться
5 обедать
7 благодарить
11 долететь
13 желать
14 вдохновить
15 лязгать
19 избегать
21 воспрянуть
гудеть
кашлять
4 намереваться
6 замерзать
8 заботиться
исполнить
адресовать
возлагать
16 договариваться
18 зачаровать

### *Perfective vs. imperfective verbs*

| | |
|---|---|
| **1.** Собака обгложет кость. | *A dog will finish gnawing at a bone.* |
| **2.** Я нарисую стол. | *I will draw a table.* |
| **3.** Подует ветер. | *The wind will blow.* |
| **4.** Снег растает. | *The snow will melt.* |

## Entries in Context

**1.** барабанный бой

**2.** голова кругом идёт

**3.** Не мешайтесь не в своё дело!

**4.** Он как в воду опущенный.

**5.** Не в бровь, а в глаз.

**6.** ходить вокруг да около

**7.** здороваться за руку

**8.** биться головой об стену

**9.** взять верх

**10.** во весь голос

**11.** без четверти час

**12.** то и дело

**13.** жребий брошен

**14.** принять во внимание

**15.** изнывать от скуки

**16.** кожа да кости

**17.** в мгновение ока

**18.** мне это безразлично

**19.** Так ему и надо!

**20.** обман зрения

| | | | | | | | | | | | | | | | | | | | |
|---|---|---|---|---|---|---|---|---|---|---|---|---|---|---|---|---|---|---|---|
| О | Д | В | Р | Т | Щ | У | С | О | П | Ж | Л | В | Ш | А | И | В | О | К | А |
| С | П | Ф | В | Ч | Е | Т | В | Е | Р | Т | И | Ч | А | С | И | С | К | У | И |
| Ъ | Р | Х | О | Д | И | Т | Ь | Д | А | О | К | О | Л | О | З | Г | А | Ф | К |
| С | И | И | С | Й | К | Ц | Я | Ч | В | Ж | Ю | Б | Т | Ь | Л | О | К | Ш | Р |
| О | Н | Ж | Ш | Б | О | Л | Б | Ю | О | З | Т | О | И | Г | М | Л | В | Н | У |
| О | Я | О | Ш | А | О | С | Е | Н | В | У | Щ | Ш | И | Ь | Н | О | О | Т | Г |
| Ц | Т | Н | Г | Ж | Э | Й | Л | А | Е | Ш | З | Н | Ш | Г | Е | В | П | Т | О |
| Щ | Ь | К | А | Ю | Ж | М | Б | К | С | Л | А | В | И | Е | Э | О | У | С | М |
| Ш | В | Т | А | К | Е | М | У | И | Ь | Ь | Р | П | А | В | Т | Й | Щ | Ю | И |
| Г | О | Ц | Ы | Б | Ъ | Н | Ш | Ц | Й | Т | У | Р | В | А | О | О | Е | У | Д |
| Н | Г | К | М | Ь | Е | Д | Г | З | У | Ь | К | О | У | И | Э | Б | Н | Ы | Ё |
| Е | Ш | Е | И | Ш | В | Г | К | М | Р | М | У | Л | Ч | Ь | Ф | С | Н | Й | Т |
| К | Л | Г | О | И | И | О | Ы | О | К | Е | Д | Д | С | Б | Ы | Т | Ы | Ц | Щ |
| У | П | Р | Г | М | Т | Т | В | Л | Е | Н | Н | Д | И | Ю | Й | Е | Й | И | И |
| К | Б | Г | Ь | С | Ь | С | А | Т | Г | К | Д | И | Т | Э | Ц | Н | З | Т | С |
| Ш | Р | Р | Б | Ч | Л | К | Е | Г | Ш | Ы | Л | П | Я | Х | В | У | Э | С | Я |
| Г | Л | А | Ю | С | П | У | Н | Е | В | А | В | Г | Л | А | З | Щ | Х | О | С |
| А | Д | Ч | С | Я | В | К | К | Н | В | В | Ж | О | Ь | З | Р | Г | Ъ | К | Ч |
| В | З | Я | Т | Ь | К | И | П | О | А | Ё | П | Л | Б | К | Р | О | З | А | И |
| Ж | Н | Е | Н | Е | В | С | В | О | Ё | Д | Е | Л | О | В | Т | Р | Ё | Д | Т |

## Riddles

1. зима
2. юг
3. зонтик
4. лай
5. родители
6. больница
7. велосипед
9. пушка
10. удочка
11. луна
12. яблоко
13. почтальон
14. кенгуру
15. щенок

## Cryptogram

| | | | | | | | | | | | | | | | | | | | | |
|---|---|---|---|---|---|---|---|---|---|---|---|---|---|---|---|---|---|---|---|---|
| 40 | 2 | 13 | 2 | | 7 | 13 | 11 | 11 | 10 | 27 | | 25 | 16 | | 20 | 13 | 25 | 8 | 9 | 41 |
| у | м | о | м | | р | о | с | с | и | ю | | н | е | | п | о | н | я | т | ь |
| 15 | 7 | 35 | 10 | 25 | 13 | 2 | | 13 | 29 | 6 | 10 | 2 | | | | | | | | |
| а | р | ш | и | н | о | м | | о | б | щ | и | м | | | | | | | | |
| 25 | 16 | | 10 | 5 | 2 | 16 | 7 | 10 | 9 | 41 | | | | | | | | | | |
| н | е | | и | з | м | е | р | и | т | ь | | | | | | | | | | |
| 40 | | 25 | 16 | 34 | | 13 | 11 | 13 | 29 | 16 | 25 | 25 | 15 | 8 | | 11 | 9 | 15 | 9 | 41 |
| у | | н | е | й | | о | с | о | б | е | н | н | а | я | | с | т | а | т | ь |
| 23 | | 7 | 13 | 11 | 11 | 10 | 27 | | 2 | 13 | 33 | 25 | 13 | | | | | | | |
| в | | р | о | с | с | и | ю | | м | о | ж | н | о | | | | | | | |
| 9 | 13 | 18 | 41 | 22 | 13 | | 23 | 16 | 7 | 10 | 9 | 41 | | | | | | | | |
| т | о | л | ь | к | о | | в | е | р | и | т | ь | | | | | | | | |

*Russia cannot be understood by mind alone,*
*Cannot be measured by a common yardstick,*
*She has a stature of its own.*
*Believe in Russia is all that one can do.*
(F. Tyutchev)

# Basic Russian Phrases

## Pronunciation

This section uses a simplified phonetic transcription. Simply read the pronunciation as if it were English.

Stress in Russian is irregular and has been marked in the following phrases. The stressed syllable is underlined, and any pronunciation changes are reflected in the phonetic transcription.

## Essential

| | | |
|---|---|---|
| Yes./No. | **Да./Нет.** | *da/nyet* |
| Okay. | **Хорошо/О кей.** | *kharasho/o ke* |
| Please. | **Пожалуйста.** | *pazhalsta* |
| Thank you (very much). | **Спасибо (большое).** | *spaseeba (bal'shoye)* |
| Hello./Hi! | **Здравствуй(те)!/ Привет!** | *zdrastvooy(tye)/ preevyet* |
| Good morning. | **Доброе утро.** | *dobraye ootra* |
| Good afternoon/ evening. | **Добрый день/ вечер.** | *dobriy dyen'/ vyechyeer* |
| Good night. | **Спокойной ночи.** | *spakoyniy nochyee* |
| Good-bye. | **До свидания.** | *da sveedaneeya* |
| Excuse me. *[getting attention]* | **Извините./ Простите.** | *eezveeneetye/ prasteetye* |
| Excuse me. *[May I get past?]* | **Разрешите. (Разрешите пройти).** | *razreeshitye (razreeshitye praytee)* |
| Excuse me!/ Sorry! | **Извините!/ Простите!** | *eezveeneetye/ prasteetye* |
| Don't mention it. | **Не за что.** | *nye za shta* |
| Never mind. | **Ничего.** | *neechyeevo* |

## Communication Difficulties

| | | |
|---|---|---|
| Do you speak English? | **Вы говорите по-английски?** | *vi gavareetye pa-angleeyskee* |
| Does anyone here speak English? | **Здесь кто-нибудь говорит по-английски?** | *zdyes' ktoneebood' gavareet pa-angleeyskee* |
| I don't speak (much) Russian. | **Я плохо говорю по-русски.** | *ya plokha gavaryoo pa-rooskee* |
| Could you speak more slowly? | **Говорите медленнее, пожалуйста.** | *gavareetye myedleennee pazhalsta* |
| Could you repeat that? | **Повторите, пожалуйста.** | *paftareetye pazhalsta* |
| Excuse me? *[Pardon?]* | **Извините.** | *eezveeneetye* |
| What was that? | **Что такое?** | *shto takoye* |
| Could you spell it? | **Назовите по буквам, пожалуйста.** | *nazaveetye pa bookvam pazhalsta* |
| Please write it down. | **Напишите, пожалуйста.** | *napeeshitye pazhalsta* |
| Can you translate this for me? | **Переведите мне это, пожалуйста.** | *peereeveedeetye mnye eta pazhalsta* |
| What does this/ that mean? | **Что это/ то значит?** | *shto eta/to znachyeet* |
| Please point to the phrase in the book. | **Пожалуйста, покажите эту фразу в книге.** | *pazhalsta pakazhitye etoo frazoo f kneegye* |
| I understand. | **Я понимаю.** | *ya paneemayoo* |
| I don't understand. | **Я не понимаю.** | *ya nee paneemayoo* |
| Do you understand? | **Вы понимаете?** | *vi paneemayetye* |

You can form a simple question in Russian by repeating the same words of the positive statement, without altering the word order, but adding interrogatory intonation (letting the voice rise at the end of the sentence).

| | | |
|---|---|---|
| There is a fax machine here. | **Здесь есть факс.** | *zdyes' yest' faks* |
| Is there a fax machine here? | **Здесь есть факс?** | *zdyes' yest' faks* |

## Emergency

| | | |
|---|---|---|
| Help! | **Помогите!** | *pamageetye* |
| Go away! | **Идите отсюда!** | *eedeetye atsyooda* |
| Leave me alone! | **Оставьте меня в покое!** | *astaf'tye meenya f pakoye* |
| Call the police! | **Вызовите милицию!** | *vizaveetye meeleetsiyoo* |
| Stop thief! | **Держите вора!** | *deerzhitye vora* |
| Get a doctor! | **Вызовите врача!** | *vizaveetye vrachya* |
| Fire! | **Пожар!** | *pazhar* |
| I'm ill. | **Я заболел(а).** | *ya zabalyel(a)* |
| I'm lost. | **Я заблудился(-лась).** | *ya zabloodeelsa (las')* |
| Can you help me? | **Помогите мне, пожалуйста.** | *pamageetye mnye pazhalsta.* |

# English – Russian

# English – Russian

## A

**a** [eɪ, ə] *неопределённый артикль; как правило, не переводится*; **~ table** стол; **ten r(o)ubles a dozen** десять рублей дюжина
**A** [eɪ] *su.*: **from ~ to Z** от "А" до "Я"
**aback** [əˈbæk] *adv.*: **taken ~** поражён, озада́чен
**abandon** [əˈbændən] **1.** (*give up*) отка́зываться [-за́ться] от (Р); (*desert*) оставля́ть [-а́вить], покида́ть [-и́нуть]; **~ o.s.** преда́(ва́)ться (**to** Д); **2.** непринуждённость *f*; **~ed** поки́нутый
**abase** [əˈbeɪs] унижа́ть [уни́зить]; **~ment** [-mənt] униже́ние
**abash** [əˈbæʃ] смуща́ть [смути́ть]
**abate** [əbˈeɪt] *v/t.* уменьша́ть [-е́ньшить]; *of wind, etc. v/i.* утиха́ть [ути́хнуть]
**abb|ess** [ˈæbɪs] настоя́тельница монастыря́; **~ey** [ˈæbɪ] монасты́рь *m*; **~ot** [ˈæbət] абба́т, настоя́тель *m*
**abbreviat|e** [əˈbriːvɪeɪt] сокраща́ть [-рати́ть]; **~ion** [əbriːvɪˈeɪʃn] сокраще́ние
**ABC** [eiːbiːˈsiː] а́збука, алфави́т; (**as**) **easy as ~** ле́гче лёгкого
**abdicat|e** [ˈæbdɪkeɪt] отрека́ться от престо́ла; *of rights, office* отка́зываться [-за́ться] от (Р); **~ion** [æbdɪˈkeɪʃn] отрече́ние от престо́ла
**abdomen** [ˈæbdəmən] брюшна́я по́лость *f*, *coll.* живо́т
**aberration** [æbəˈreɪʃn] *judg(e)ment or conduct* заблужде́ние; *mental* помраче́ние ума́; *deviation* отклоне́ние от но́рмы; *astr.* аберра́ция
**abeyance** [əˈbeɪəns] состоя́ние неизве́стности; **in ~** *law* вре́менно отменённый
**abhor** [əbˈhɔː] ненави́деть; (*feel disgust*) пита́ть отвраще́ние (к Д); **~rence** [əbˈhɔrəns] отвраще́ние; **~rent** [-ənt] □ отврати́тельный
**abide** [əˈbaɪd] [*irr.*]: **~ by** приде́рживаться (Р); *v/t.* **not ~** не терпе́ть
**ability** [əˈbɪlətɪ] спосо́бность *f*
**abject** [ˈæbdʒekt] □ жа́лкий; **~ poverty** кра́йняя нищета́
**ablaze** [əˈbleɪz]: **be ~** пыла́ть; **~ with anger** *of eyes, cheeks* пыла́ть гне́вом; **~ with light** я́рко освещён(ный)
**able** [ˈeɪbl] □ спосо́бный; **be ~** мочь, быть в состоя́нии; **~-bodied** [-bɔdɪd] здоро́вый; го́дный
**abnormal** [æbˈnɔːməl] ненорма́льный; анома́льный; *med.* **~ psychology** психопатоло́гия
**aboard** [əˈbɔːd] *naut.* на су́дне, на борту́; **go ~** сади́ться на су́дно (в самолёт; в авто́бус, на по́езд)
**abolish** [əˈbɒlɪʃ] отменя́ть [-ни́ть]; *of custom, etc.* упраздня́ть [-ни́ть]
**A-bomb** [ˈeɪbɒm] а́томная бо́мба
**abomina|ble** [əˈbɒmɪnəbl] □ отврати́тельный; **~ snowman** сне́жный челове́к; **~tion** [əbɒmɪˈneɪʃn] отвраще́ние; *coll.* како́й-то *or* про́сто у́жас
**aboriginal** [æbəˈrɪdʒənl] = **aborigine** [-ˈrɪdʒɪnɪ] *as su.* коренно́й жи́тель, тузе́мец *m*, -мка *f*, абориге́н; *as adj.* коренно́й, тузе́мный
**abortion** [əˈbɔːʃn] або́рт
**abound** [əˈbaʊnd] быть в изоби́лии; изоби́ловать (**in** Т)
**about** [əˈbaʊt] **1.** *prp.* вокру́г (Р); о́коло (Р); о (П), об (П), обо (П) насчёт (Р); у (Р); про (В); **2.** *adv.* вокру́г, везде́; приблизи́тельно; **be ~ to** собира́ться
**above** [əˈbʌv] **1.** *prp.* над (Т); вы́ше (Р); свы́ше (Р); **~ all** пре́жде всего́; **2.** *adv.* наверху́, наве́рх; вы́ше; **3.** *adj.* вышеска́занный; **~-board**

[~'bɔːd] *adv. & adj.* чéстный, откры́тый; **~-mentioned** [~'menʃənd] вышеупомя́нутый
**abrasion** [ə'breɪʒn] *of skin* ссáдина
**abreast** [ə'brest] в ряд; ***keep ~ of*** *fig.* быть в кýрсе; ***keep ~ of the times*** идти́ в нóгу со врéменем
**abridg|e** [ə'brɪdʒ] сокращáть [-ратить]; **~(e)ment** [~mənt] сокращéние
**abroad** [ə'brɔːd] за грани́цей, за грани́цу; ***there is a rumo(u)r ~*** хóдит слух
**abrogate** [ə'brəgeɪt] *v/t.* отменя́ть [-ни́ть]; аннули́ровать *(im)pf.*
**abrupt** [ə'brʌpt] (*steep*) крутóй; (*sudden*) внезáпный; (*blunt*) рéзкий
**abscess** ['æbsɪs] нары́в, абсцéсс
**abscond** [əb'skɒnd] *v/i.* скры(вá)ться, укры́(вá)ться
**absence** ['æbsəns] отсýтствие; ***~ of mind*** рассéянность *f*
**absent 1.** ['æbsənt] □ отсýтствующий (*a. fig.*); **2.** [æb'sent] ***~ o.s.*** отлучáться [-чи́ться]; **~-minded** рассéянный
**absolute** ['æbsəluːt] □ абсолю́тный; *coll.* пóлный, совершéнный
**absorb** [æb'sɔːb] впи́тывать [впитáть], поглощáть [-лоти́ть] (*a. fig.*); *of gas, etc.* абсорби́ровать *(im)pf.*; **~ing** [~ɪŋ] *fig.* увлекáтельный
**abstain** [əb'steɪn] воздéрживаться [-жáться] (***from*** от Р)
**abstention** [æb'stenʃən] воздержáние
**abstinence** ['æbstɪnəns] умéренность *f*; *from drink* трéзвость *f*
**abstract 1.** ['æbstrækt] отвлечённый, абстрáктный (*a. gr.*); **2.** резюмé, крáткий обзóр; ***in the ~*** теорети́чески; **3.** [æb'strækt] (*take out*) извлекáть [-лéчь]; (*purloin*) похищáть [-хи́тить]; резюми́ровать *(im)pf.*; **~ed** [~ɪd] *of person* погружённый в свои́ мы́сли; **~ion** [~kʃn] абстрáкция
**abstruse** [æb'struːs] □ *fig.* непоня́тный, тёмный, мудрёный
**abundan|ce** [ə'bʌndəns] изоби́лие; **~t** [~dənt] □ оби́льный, богáтый
**abus|e** [ə'bjuːs] **1.** (*misuse*) злоупотреблéние; (*insult*) оскорблéние; (*curse*) брань *f*; **2.** [ə'bjuːz] злоупотребля́ть [-би́ть] (T); [вы́]ругать; **~ive** [ə'bjuːsɪv] □ оскорби́тельный
**abyss** [ə'bɪs] бéздна
**acacia** [ə'keɪʃə] акáция
**academic|(al** □) [ækə'demɪk(əl)] академи́ческий; **~ian** [əkædə'mɪʃn] акадéмик
**accede** [æk'siːd]: ***~ to*** (*assent*) соглашáться [-аси́ться] (с T); *of office* вступáть [-пи́ть] в (B)
**accelerat|e** [ək'seləreɪt] ускоря́ть [-óрить]; **~or** [ək'seləreɪtə] *mot.* педáль гáза
**accent** ['æksənt] (*stress*) ударéние; (*mode of utterance*) произношéние, акцéнт; **~uate** [æk'sentjʊeɪt] дéлать и́ли стáвить ударéние на (П); *fig.* подчёркивать [-черкнýть]
**accept** [ək'sept] принимáть [-ня́ть]; соглашáться [-гласи́тсься] с (T); **~able** [ək'septəbl] □ приéмлемый; *of a gift* прия́тный; **~ance** [ək'septəns] приня́тие; (*approval*) одобрéние; *comm.* акцéпт
**access** ['ækses] дóступ; (*way*) прохóд, проéзд; ***easy of ~*** достýпный; ***access code*** *comput.* код дóступа; **~ory** [æk'sesərɪ] соучáстник (-ица); **~ible** [æk'sesəbl] □ достýпный, достижи́мый; **~ion** [æk'seʃn]: ***~ to the throne*** вступлéние на престóл
**accessory** [æk'sesərɪ] □ **1.** дополни́тельный, второстепéнный; **2.** *pl.* принадлéжности *f/pl.*; *gloves, etc.* аксессуáры
**accident** ['æksɪdənt] (*chance*) случáйность *f*; (*mishap*) несчáстный слýчай; *mot.*, *tech.* авáрия; *rail.* крушéние; **~al** [æksɪ'dentl] случáйный
**acclaim** [ə'kleɪm] **1.** аплоди́ровать; привéтствовать; **2.** привéтствие; овáция
**acclimatize** [ə'klaɪmətaɪz] акклиматизи́ровать(ся) *(im)pf.*
**accommodat|e** [ə'kɒmədeɪt] (*adapt*) приспособля́ть [-пособить]; предостáвить жильё (Д); (*hold*) вмещáть [вмести́ть]; *comm.* вы́да(вá)ть ссýду; **~ion** [əkɒmə'deɪʃn] жильё, помещéние

**accompan|iment** [əˈkʌmpənɪmənt] сопровождéние; аккомпанемéнт; **~y** [~pənɪ] *v/t.* (*escort*) сопровождáть [-води́ть]; *mus.* аккомпани́ровать (Д)
**accomplice** [əˈkʌmplɪs] соучáстник (-ица) (*in crime*)
**accomplish** [əˈkʌmplɪʃ] (*fulfill*) выполня́ть [вы́полнить]; (*achieve*) достигáть [-и́гнуть] (Р); (*complete*) завершáть [-и́ть]; **~ment** [~mənt] выполнéние; достижéние
**accord** [əˈkɔːd] **1.** (*agreement*) солáсие; соглашéние; ***of one's own ~*** по сóбственному желáнию; ***with one ~*** единодýшно; **2.** *v/i.* согласóвываться [-сováться] (с Т), гармони́ровать (с Т); *v/t.* предоставля́ть [-стáвить]; **~ance** [-əns] соглáсие; ***in ~ with*** в соотвéтствии с (Т);**~ing** [~ɪŋ]: ***~ to*** соглáсно (Д); **~ingly** [~ɪŋlɪ] *adv.* соотвéтственно; таки́м óбразом
**accost** [əˈkɒst] заговáривать [-вори́ть] с (Т)
**account** [əˈkaʊnt] **1.** *comm.* счёт; (*report*) отчёт; (*description*) сообщéние, описáние; ***by all ~s*** сýдя по всемý; ***on no ~*** ни в кóем слýчае; ***on ~ of*** из-за (Р); ***take into ~, take ~ of*** принимáть во внимáние; ***turn to*** (***good***) ***~*** испóльзовать (*im*)*pf.* (с вы́годой); ***call to ~*** призывáть к отвéту; ***~ number*** нóмер счёта; **2.** *v/i.* ***~ for*** отвечáть [-éтить] за (В); (*explain*) объясня́ть [-ни́ть]; *v/t.* (*consider*) считáть [счесть] (В/Т); **~able** [əˈkauntəbl] □ (*responsible*) отвéтственный (***to*** пéред Т, ***for*** за В); **~ant** [-ənt] квалифици́рованный бухгáлтер
**accredit** [əˈkredɪt] *of ambassador, etc.* аккредитовáть (*im*)*pf.*; (*attribute*) припи́сывать [-сáть]; *credit* выдавáть [-дать] креди́т
**accrue** [əˈkruː]: ***~d interest*** нарóсшие процéнты
**accumulat|e** [əˈkjuːmjʊleɪt] накáпливать(ся) [-копи́ть(ся)]; скопля́ть(ся) [-пи́ть(ся)];**~ion** [əkjuːmjuːˈleɪʃn] накоплéние; скоплéние
**accura|cy** [ˈækjʊrəsɪ] тóчность *f*; *in shooting* мéткость *f*; **~te** [~rɪt] тóчный; *of aim or shot* мéткий
**accurs|ed** [əˈkɜːsɪd], **~t** [-st] проклятый
**accus|ation** [ækjuːˈzeɪʃn] обвинéние; **~e** [əˈkjuːz] *v/t.* обвиня́ть [-ни́ть]; **~er** [~ə] обвини́тель *m*, -ни́ца *f*
**accustom** [əˈkʌstəm] приучáть [-чи́ть] (***to*** к Д); ***get ~ed*** привыкáть [-вы́кнуть] (***to*** к Д); **~ed** [~d] привы́чный; (*inured*) приýченный; (*usual*) обы́чный
**ace** [eɪs] туз; *fig.* первоклáссный лётчик, ас; ***be within an ~ of*** быть на волосóк от (Р)
**acerbity** [əˈsɜːbətɪ] тéрпкость *f*
**acet|ic** [əˈsiːtɪk] ýксусный
**ache** [eik] **1.** боль *f*; **2.** *v/i.* болéть
**achieve** [əˈtʃiːv] достигáть [-и́гнуть] (Р); **~ment** [~mənt] достижéние
**acid** [ˈæsid] **1.** кислотá; **2.** ки́слый; *fig.* éдкий; ***~ rain*** кислóтный дождь
**acknowledg|e** [əkˈnɒlɪdʒ] *v/t.* подтверждáть [-ерди́ть]; *confess* признá(вá)ть; **~(e)ment** [~mənt] признáние; подтверждéние
**acorn** [ˈeɪkɔːn] *bot.* жёлудь *m*
**acoustics** [əˈkaustɪks] акýстика
**acquaint** [əˈkweɪnt] *v/t.* [по]знакóмить; ***~ o.s. with*** ознакóмиться с (Т); ***be ~ed with*** быть знакóмым с (Т); **~ance** [~əns] знакóмство; *pers.* знакóмый; ***make s.o.'s ~*** познакóмиться с кéм-л.
**acquire** [əˈkwaɪə] *v/t.* приобретáть [-ести́]
**acquisition** [ækwɪˈzɪʃn] приобретéние
**acquit** [əˈkwɪt] *law v/t.* опрáвдывать [-дáть]; ***~ o.s. well*** хорошó прояви́ть себя́; **~tal** [~l] оправдáние
**acrid** [ˈækrɪd] óстрый, едкий (*a. fig.*)
**across** [əˈkrɒs] **1.** *adv.* поперёк; на ту стóрону; ***two miles ~*** ширинóй в две ми́ли; **2.** *prp.* чéрез (В)
**act** [ækt] **1.** *v/i.* дéйствовать; поступáть [-пи́ть]; *v/t. thea.* игрáть [сыгрáть]; **2.** постýпок; постановлéние, закон; *thea.* дéйствие, акт; **~ing** [~ɪŋ] **1.** исполня́ющий обя́занности; **2.** *thea.* игрá

**action** ['ækʃn] (*conduct*) посту́пок; (*acting*) де́йствие; (*activity*) де́ятельность *f*; *mil.* бой; *law* иск; ***take ~*** принима́ть ме́ры

**activ|e** ['æktɪv] □ акти́вный; энерги́чный; де́ятельный; **~ity** [æk'tɪvətɪ] де́ятельность *f*, рабо́та; акти́вность *f*; эне́ргия

**act|or** ['æktə] актёр; **~ress** [-trɪs] актри́са

**actual** ['æktʃuəl] □ действи́тельный; факти́ческий; **~ly** факти́чески, на са́мом де́ле

**acute** [ə'kjuːt] □ си́льный, о́стрый; (*penetrating*) проница́тельный

**adamant** ['ædəmənt] *fig.* непреклонный

**adapt** [ə'dæpt] приспособля́ть [-посо́бить] (***to, for*** к Д); *text* адапти́ровать; ***~ o.s.*** адапти́роваться; **~ation** [ædæp'teɪʃn] приспособле́ние; *of text* обрабо́тка; *of organism* адапта́ция

**add** [æd] *v/t.* прибавля́ть [-а́вить]; *math.* скла́дывать [сложи́ть]; *v/i.* увели́чи(ва)ть (***to*** В)

**addict** ['ædɪkt]: ***drug ~*** наркома́н; **~ed** [ə'dɪktɪd] скло́нный (***to*** к Д)

**addition** [ə'dɪʃn] *math.* сложе́ние; прибавле́ние; ***in ~*** кро́ме того́, к тому́ же; ***in ~ to*** вдоба́вок к (Д); **~al** [-əl] доба́вочный, дополни́тельный

**address** [ə'dres] *v/t.* **1.** *a letter* адресова́ть *(im)pf.*; (*speak to*) обраща́ться [обрати́ться] к (Д); **2.** а́дрес; обраще́ние; речь *f*; **~ee** [ædre'siː] адреса́т

**adept** ['ædept] иску́сный; уме́лый

**adequa|cy** ['ædɪkwəsɪ] соотве́тствие; доста́точность *f*; адеква́тность; **~te** [-kwɪt] (*sufficient*) доста́точный; (*suitable*) соотве́тствующий, адеква́тный

**adhere** [əd'hɪə] прилипа́ть [-ли́пнуть] (***to*** к Д); *fig.* приде́рживаться (***to*** Р); **~nce** [-rəns] приве́рженность *f*; **~nt** [-rənt] приве́рженец (-нка)

**adhesive** [əd'hiːsɪv] □ ли́пкий, клейкий; ***~ plaster*** лейкопла́стырь *m*; ***~ tape*** ли́пкая ле́нта

**adjacent** [ə'dʒeɪsənt] □ сме́жный (***to*** с Т), сосе́дний

**adjoin** [ə'dʒɔɪn] примыка́ть [-мкну́ть] к (Д); прилега́ть *pf.* к (Д)

**adjourn** [ə'dʒɜːn] *v/t.* (*suspend proceedings*) закрыва́ть [-ы́ть]; (*carry over*) переноси́ть [-нести́]; (*postpone*) отсро́чи(ва)ть; *parl.* де́лать переры́в; **~ment** [-mənt] отсро́чка; переры́в

**administ|er** [əd'mɪnɪstə] руководи́ть, управля́ть (Т); ***~ justice*** отправля́ть правосу́дие; **~ration** [ədmɪnɪ'streɪʃn] администра́ция; **~rative** [əd'mɪnɪstrətɪv] администрати́вный; исполни́тельный; **~rator** [əd'mɪnɪstreɪtə] администра́тор

**admir|able** ['ædmərəbl] превосхо́дный; замеча́тельный; **~ation** [ædmɪ'reɪʃən] восхище́ние; **~e** [əd'maiə] восхища́ться [-и́ться] (Т); [по]любова́ться (Т *or* на В)

**admiss|ible** [əd'mɪsəbl] □ допусти́мый, прие́млемый; **~ion** [əd'mɪʃən] (*access*) вход; (*confession*) призна́ние; ***~ fee*** пла́та за вход

**admit** [əd'mɪt] *v/t.* (*let in*) впуска́ть [-сти́ть]; (*allow*) допуска́ть [-сти́ть]; (*confess*) призна́(ва́)ть(ся); **~tance** [-əns] до́ступ, вход

**admixture** [əd'mɪkstʃə] при́месь *f*

**admon|ish** [əd'mɒnɪʃ] (*exhort*) увещ(ев)а́ть *impf.*; (*warn*) предостерега́ть [-ре́чь] (***of*** от Р); **~ition** [ædmə'nɪʃn] увеща́ние; предостереже́ние

**ado** [ə'duː] сует́а; хло́поты *f/pl.*; ***without much ~*** без вся́ких церемо́ний

**adolescen|ce** [ædə'lesəns] отро́чество; **~t** [-snt] **1.** подростко́вый; **2.** *person* подро́сток

**adopt** [ə'dɒpt] *v/t.* усыновля́ть [-ви́ть]; *girl* удочеря́ть [-ри́ть]; *resolution, etc.* принима́ть [-ня́ть]; **~ion** [ə'dɒpʃn] усыновле́ние; удочере́ние; приня́тие

**ador|able** [ə'dɔːrəbl] обожа́емый, преле́стный; **~ation** [ædə'reɪʃn] обожа́ние; **~e** [ə'dɔː] *v/t.* обожа́ть

**adorn** [ə'dɔːn] украша́ть [укра́сить]; **~ment** [-mənt] украше́ние

**adroit** [ə'drɔɪt] □ ло́вкий, иску́сный

**adult** ['ædʌlt] взрóслый, совершеннолéтний

**adulter|ate** [ə'dʌltəreɪt] (*debase*) [ис]пóртить; (*dilute*) разбавля́ть [-áвить]; фальсифици́ровать (*im*)*pf*.; **~y** [-rɪ] нарушéние супрýжеской вéрности, адюльтéр

**advance** [əd'vɑːns] **1.** *v/i. mil.* наступáть; (*move forward*) продвигáться [продви́нуться]; (*a. fig.*) дéлать успéхи; *v/t.* продвигáть [-и́нуть]; *idea, etc.* выдвигáть [вы́двинуть]; плати́ть авáнсом; **2.** *mil.* наступлéние; *in studies* успéх; прогрéсс; *of salary* авáнс; **~d** [əd'vaːnst] передовóй; *in years* престарéлый, пожилóй; **~ment** [~mənt] успéх; продвижéние

**advantage** [əd'vɑːntɪdʒ] преимýщество; (*benefit*) вы́года; ***take ~ of*** [вос]пóльзоваться (Т); **~ous** [ædvən'teɪdʒəs, ædvæn~] вы́годный, полéзный, благоприя́тный

**adventur|e** [əd'ventʃə] приключéние; **~er** [-rə] искáтель приключéний; авантюри́ст; **~ous** [-rəs] предприи́мчивый; авантю́рный

**advers|ary** ['ædvəsərɪ] (*antagonist*) проти́вник (-ица); (*opponent*) сопéрник (-ица); **~e** ['ædvɜːs] неблагоприя́тный; **~ity** [əd'vɜːsɪti] несчáстье, бедá

**advertis|e** ['ædvətaɪz] реклами́ровать (*im*)*pf*.; *in newspaper* помещáть [-ести́ть] объявлéние; **~ement** [əd'vɜːtɪsmənt] объявлéние; реклáма; **~ing** ['ædvətaɪzɪŋ] реклáмный

**advice** [əd'vaɪs] совéт

**advis|able** [əd'vaɪzəbl] □ желáтельный, целесообрáзный; **~e** [əd'vaɪz] *v/t.* [по]совéтовать (Д), [по]рекомендовáть; (*inform*) сообщáть [-щи́ть]; **~er** [~ə] *official* совéтник, *professional* консультáнт

**advocate** **1.** ['ædvəkət] сторóнник (-ица); *law* адвокáт, защи́тник; **2.** [~keɪt] поддéрживать, *speak in favo*(*u*)*r of* выступáть [вы́ступить] (за В)

**aerial** ['eərɪəl] антéнна; ***outdoor ~*** нарýжная антéнна

**aero...** [eərə] áэро...; **~bics** [~bɪks] аэрóбика; **~drome** ['eərədrəʊm] аэродрóм; **~naut** [~nɔːt] аэронáвт; **~nautics** [~nɔːtɪks] аэронáвтика; **~plane** [~pleɪn] самолёт; **~sol** [~sɔl] аэрозóль *m*; **~stat** [~stæt] аэростáт

**aesthetic** [iːs'θetɪk] эстети́ческий; **~s** [~s] эстéтика

**afar** [ə'fɑː] *adv*.: вдалекé; ***from ~*** издалекá

**affable** ['æfəbl] привéтливый

**affair** [ə'feə] *business* дéло; *love* любóвная связь *f*, ромáн

**affect** [ə'fekt] *v/t.* [по]влия́ть на (В); задé(вá)ть; *med.* поражáть [-рази́ть]; (*pretend*) притворя́ться [-ри́ться]; **~ation** [æfek'teɪʃən] жемáнство; **~ed** [ə'fektɪd] □ притвóрный; манéрный; **~ion** [ə'fekʃn] привя́занность *f*, любóвь *f*; **~ionate** [ə'fekʃnət] □ нéжный, лáсковый, лю́бящий

**affiliate** [ə'fɪlɪeɪt] **1.** *v/t. join, attach* присоединя́ть [-ни́ть] (как филиáл); **2.** дочéрняя компáния; компáния-филиáл

**affinity** [ə'fɪnətɪ] *closeness* бли́зость *f*, *relationship* родствó; *attraction* влечéние

**affirm** [ə'fɜːm] утверждáть [-рди́ть]; **~ation** [æfə'meɪʃn] утверждéние; **~ative** [ə'fɜːmətɪv] □ утверди́тельный

**affix** [ə'fɪks] прикрепля́ть [-пи́ть] (***to*** к Д)

**afflict** [ə'flɪkt]: ***be ~ed*** страдáть (***with*** Т, от Р); постигáть [-и́чь *or* -и́гнуть]; **~ion** [ə'flɪkʃn] гóре; недýг

**affluen|ce** ['æfluəns] изоби́лие, богáтство; **~t** [~ənt] □ оби́льный, богáтый

**afford** [ə'fɔːd] позволя́ть [-вóлить] себé; ***I can ~ it*** я могý себé э́то позвóлить; *yield, give* (пре-)доставля́ть [-áвить]

**affront** [ə'frʌnt] **1.** оскорбля́ть [-би́ть]; **2.** оскорблéние

**afield** [ə'fiːld] *adv.* вдалекé; ***far ~*** далекó

**afloat** [ə'fləʊt] на водé, на плавý (*a. fig.*)

**afraid** [ə'freɪd] испу́ганный; ***be ~ of*** боя́ться (Р)
**afresh** [ə'freʃ] *adv.* сно́ва, сы́знова
**African** ['æfrɪkən] **1.** африка́нец (-нка); **2.** африка́нский
**after** ['ɑːftə] **1.** *adv.* пото́м, по́сле, зате́м; позади́; ***shortly ~*** вско́ре; **2.** *prp.* за (Т), позади́ (Р); че́рез (В); по́сле (Р); ***time ~ time*** ско́лько раз; ***~ all*** в конце́ концо́в; всё же; **3.** *cj.* с тех пор, как; по́сле того́, как; **4.** *adj.* после́дующий; **~math** ['ɑːftəmæθ] ота́ва; *fig.* после́дствия *n/pl.*; **~noon** [~'nuːn] вре́мя по́сле полу́дня; **~taste** (остаю́щийся) при́вкус; **~thought** мысль, прише́дшая по́здно; **~wards** [~wədz] *adv.* впосле́дствии, пото́м
**again** [ə'gen] *adv.* сно́ва, опя́ть; ***~ and ~, time and ~*** неоднокра́тно; сно́ва и сно́ва; ***as much ~*** ещё сто́лько же
**against** [ə'genst] *prp.* про́тив (Р); о, об (В); на (В); ***as ~*** по сравне́нию с (Т); ***~ the wall*** у стены́, к стене́
**age** [eɪdʒ] **1.** век, во́зраст; года́ *m/pl.*; век, эпо́ха; ***of ~*** совершенноле́тний; ***under ~*** несовершенноле́тний; **2.** *v/t.* [со]ста́рить; *v/i.* [по]ста́рить; **~d** ['eɪdʒɪd] престаре́лый
**agency** ['eɪdʒənsɪ] аге́нтство
**agenda** [ə'dʒendə] пове́стка дня
**agent** ['eɪdʒənt] аге́нт; дове́ренное лицо́; *chem.* сре́дство
**aggravate** ['ægrəveɪt] (*make worse*) усугубля́ть [-би́ть]; ухудша́ть [уху́дшить]; (*irritate*) раздража́ть [-жи́ть]
**aggregate** ['ægrɪgət] совоку́пность; о́бщее число́; ***in the ~*** в це́лом
**aggress|ion** [ə'greʃn] агре́ссия; **~or** [ə'gresə] агре́ссор
**aghast** [ə'gɑːst] ошеломлённый, поражённый у́жасом
**agil|e** ['ædʒaɪl] □ прово́рный, подви́жный, живо́й; ***~ mind*** живо́й ум; **~ity** [ə'dʒɪlɪtɪ] прово́рство; жи́вость *f*
**agitat|e** ['ædʒɪteɪt] *v/t.* [вз]волнова́ть, возбужда́ть [-уди́ть]; *v/i.* агити́ровать (***for*** за В); **~ion** [ædʒɪ'teɪʃn] волне́ние; агита́ция
**agnail** ['ægneɪl] заусе́ница
**ago** [ə'gəu]: ***a year ~*** год тому́ наза́д; ***long ~*** давно́; ***not long ~*** неда́вно
**agonizing** ['ægənaɪzɪŋ] мучи́тельный
**agony** ['ægənɪ] аго́ния; муче́ние
**agree** [ə'griː] *v/i.* (*consent, accept*) соглаша́ться [-ласи́ться] (***to*** с Т, на В); ***~ [up]on*** (*settle, arrange*) усла́вливаться [усло́виться] о (П); (*reach a common decision*) догова́риваться [-вори́ться]; **~able** [~əbl] (*pleasing*) прия́тный; (*consenting*) согла́сный (***to*** с Т, на В); **~ment** [~mənt] согла́сие; (*contract, etc.*) соглаше́ние, догово́р
**agricultur|al** [ægrɪ'kʌltʃərəl] сельскохозя́йственный; **~e** ['ægrɪkʌltʃə] се́льское хозя́йство; земледе́лие; **~ist** [ægrɪ'kʌltʃərɪst] агроно́м
**ahead** [ə'hed] вперёд, впереди́; ***straight ~*** пря́мо, вперёд
**aid** [eɪd] **1.** по́мощь *f*; помо́щник (-ица); *pl.* (*financial, etc.*) посо́бия; **2.** помога́ть [помо́чь] (Д)
**AIDS** [eɪdz] *med.* СПИД (синдро́м приобретённого иммунодефици́та); **~-infected** инфици́рованный СПИДом
**ail|ing** ['eɪlɪŋ] больно́й, нездоро́вый; **~ment** ['eɪlmənt] недомога́ние, боле́знь *f*
**aim** [eɪm] **1.** *v/i.* прице́ли(ва)ться (***at*** в В); *fig.* ***~ at*** име́ть в виду́; *v/t.* направля́ть [-ра́вить] (***at*** на В); **2.** цель *f*, наме́рение; **~less** [eɪmlɪs] □ бесце́льный
**air**[1] [eə] **1.** во́здух; ***by ~*** самолётом; авиапо́чтой; ***go on the ~*** *of person* выступа́ть [вы́ступить] по ра́дио; ***in the ~*** (*uncertain*) висе́ть в во́здухе; *of rumour, etc.* носи́ться в во́здухе; ***clear the ~*** разряжа́ть [-яди́ть] атмосфе́ру; **2.** (*ventilate*) прове́три(ва)ть(ся) (*a. fig.*)
**air**[2] [~] вид; ***give o.s. ~s*** ва́жничать
**air**[3] [~] *mus.* мело́дия; пе́сня
**air|bag** поду́шка безопа́сности; **~base** авиаба́за; **~-conditioned** с кондициони́рованным во́здухом; **~craft** самолёт; **~field** аэродро́м; **~force** вое́нно-возду́шные си́лы; **~ hostess** стюарде́сса; **~lift** возду́шная перево́зка; **~line** авиали́ния; **~liner** (авиа)ла́й-

нер; **~mail** авиапо́чта; **~man** лётчик, авиа́тор; **~plane** *Am.* самолёт; **~port** аэропо́рт; **~ rald** возду́шный налёт; **~shelter** бомбоубе́жище; **~strip** взлётнопоса́дочная полоса́; **~tight** гермети́ческий

**airy** ['eəri] □ по́лный во́здуха; *of plans, etc.* беспе́чный, легкомы́сленный

**aisle** [ɑil] *thea.* прохо́д (ме́жду ряда́ми)

**ajar** [ə'dʒɑː] приоткры́тый

**akin** [ə'kɪn] ро́дственный, сро́дный (***to*** Д)

**alacrity** [ə'lækrɪtɪ] гото́вность *f*; рве́ние

**alarm** [ə'lɑːm] **1.** трево́га; (*fear*) страх; *tech.* трево́жно-предупреди́тельная сигнализа́ция; **2.** [вс]трево́жить, [вз]волнова́ть; **~ clock** буди́льник; **~ing** [-ɪŋ] *adj.*: **~ *news*** трево́жные изве́стия *n/pl.*

**album** ['ælbəm] альбо́м

**alcohol** ['ælkəhɒl] алкого́ль *m*; спирт; **~ic** [ælkə'hɒlɪk] **1.** алкого́льный; **2.** алкого́лик; **~ism** ['ælkəhɒlɪzəm] алкоголи́зм

**alcove** ['ælkəʊv] альков, ни́ша

**alder** ['ɔːldə] ольха́

**ale** [eɪl] пи́во, эль *m*

**alert** [ə'lɜːt] **1.** □ (*lively*) живо́й, прово́рный; (*watchful*) бди́тельный; насторо́женный; **2.** сигна́л трево́ги; ***on the ~*** настороже́

**algorithm** ['ælgərɪðəm] алгори́тм

**alien** ['eɪlɪən] **1.** иностра́нный; чу́ждый; **2.** иностра́нец *m*, -ка *f*; **~ate** [-eɪt] *law* отчужда́ть; (*estrange*) отдаля́ть [-ли́ть]; (*turn away*) отта́лкивать [-толкну́ть]

**alight**[1] [ə'laɪt] сходи́ть [сойти́] (с Р)

**alight**[2] [-] *pred. adj.* (*on fire*) зажжённый; в огне́; (*lit up*) освещённый

**align** [ə'laɪn] выра́внивать(ся) [вы́ровнять(ся)]; **~ment** [-mənt] выра́внивание; (*arrangement*) расстано́вка

**alike** [ə'laɪk] **1.** *pred. adj.* (*similar*) подо́бный, похо́жий; (*as one*) одина́ковый; **2.** *adv.* то́чно так же; подо́бно

**alimentary** [ælɪ'mentərɪ]: **~ *canal*** пищевари́тельный тракт

**alimony** ['ælɪmənɪ] алиме́нты *m/pl.*

**alive** [ə'laɪv] (*living*) живо́й; (*alert, keen*) чу́ткий (***to*** к Д); (*infested*) кища́щий (***with*** Т); ***be ~ to*** я́сно понима́ть

**all** [ɔːl] **1.** *adj.* весь *m*, вся *f*, всё *n*, все *pl*; вся́кий; всевозмо́жный; ***for ~ that*** несмотря́ на то; **2.** всё, все; ***at ~*** вообще́; ***not at ~*** во́все не; ***not at ~!*** не́ за что!; ***for ~ (that) I care*** мне безразли́чно; ***for ~ I know*** наско́лько я зна́ю; **3.** *adv.* вполне́, всеце́ло, соверше́нно; ***~ at once*** сра́зу; ***~ the better*** тем лу́чше; ***~ but*** почти́; ***~ right*** хорошо́, ла́дно

**allay** [ə'leɪ] успока́ивать [-ко́ить]

**allegation** [ælɪ'geɪʃn] голосло́вное утвержде́ние

**allege** [ə'ledʒ] утвержда́ть (без основа́ния)

**allegiance** [ə'liːdʒəns] ве́рность *f*, пре́данность *f*

**allerg|ic** [ə'lɜːdʒɪk] аллерги́ческий; **~y** ['ælədʒɪ] аллерги́я

**alleviate** [ə'liːvɪeɪt] облегча́ть [-чи́ть]

**alley** ['ælɪ] переу́лок; ***blind ~*** тупи́к

**alliance** [ə'laɪəns] сою́з

**allocat|e** ['æləkeɪt] *money* ассигнова́ть; *land, money* выделя́ть [вы́делить] (*distribute*); распределя́ть [-ли́ть]; **~ion** [ælə'keɪʃn] распределе́ние

**allot** [ə'lɒt] *v/t.* распределя́ть [-ли́ть]; разда́(ва́)ть; **~ment** [-mənt] распределе́ние; до́ля, часть *f*; *Brt.* (*plot of land*) земе́льный уча́сток

**allow** [ə'laʊ] позволя́ть [-о́лить]; допуска́ть [-сти́ть]; *Am.* утвержда́ть; **~able** [-əbl] □ позволи́тельный; **~ance** [-əns] посо́бие, пе́нсия; *fin.* ски́дка; ***make ~ for*** принима́ть во внима́ние

**alloy** ['ælɔɪ] сплав

**all-purpose** многоцелево́й, универса́льный

**all-round** всесторо́нний

**allude** [ə'luːd] ссыла́ться [сосла́ться] (***to*** на В); (*hint at*) намека́ть [-кну́ть] (***to*** на В)

**allur|e** [ə'ljʊə] (*charm*) привлека́ть

[-лéчь]; (*lure*) завлекáть [-лéчь]; **~ing** привлекáтельный, замáнчивый
**allusion** [ə'lu:ʒn] намёк, ссы́лка
**ally** [ə'laɪ] **1.** соединя́ть [-ни́ть] (***to, with*** с Т); **2.** сою́зник
**almighty** [ɔ:l'maɪtɪ] всемогу́щий
**almond** [ɑ:mənd] миндáль *m*
**almost** ['ɔ:lməʊst] почти́, едвá не
**alone** [ə'ləun] оди́н *m*, однá *f*, однó *n*, одни́ *pl.*; одинóкий (-кая); ***let*** (*или* ***leave***) **~** остáвить *pf.* в покóе; ***let ~ ...*** не говоря́ ужé о … (П)
**along** [ə'lɒŋ] **1.** *adv.* вперёд; ***all ~*** всё врéмя; ***~ with*** вмéсте с (Т); *coll.* ***get ~ with you!*** убирáйтесь; **2.** *prp.* вдоль (Р), по (Д); **~side** [~saɪd] бок ó бок, ря́дом
**aloof** [ə'lu:f]: ***stand ~*** держáться в сторонé *or* особнякóм
**aloud** [ə'laʊd] грóмко, вслух
**alpha|bet** ['ælfəbet] алфави́т; **~betic** [ˌ~'etɪk] áзбучный, алфави́тный; **~numeric** *comput.* алфави́тно- *or* бу́квенно-цифровóй
**already** [ɔ:l'redɪ] ужé
**also** ['ɔ:lsəʊ] тáкже, тóже
**altar** ['ɔ:ltə] алтáрь *m*
**alter** ['ɔ:ltə] *v/t.* & *v/i.* меня́т(ся) (*impf.*); изменя́ть(ся) [-ни́ть(ся)]; **~ation** [ɔ:ltə'reɪʃn] изменéние, передéлка (***to*** Р)
**alternat|e** **1.** ['ɔ:ltəneɪt] чередовáть(ся); **2.** [ɔ:l'tɜ:nɪt] □ перемéнный; ***alternating current*** перемéнный ток; **~ion** [ɔ:ltə'neɪʃn] чередовáние; **~ive** [ɔ:l'tɜ:nətɪv] **1.** альтернати́вный; перемéнно дéйствующий; **2.** альтернати́ва; вы́бор
**although** [ɔ:l'ðəʊ] хотя́
**altitude** ['æltɪtju:d] высотá
**altogether** [ɔ:ltə'geðə] (*entirely*) вполнé, совершéнно; (*in general*; *as a whole*) в цéлом, в óбщем
**alumin(i)um** [æljʊ'mɪnɪəm, *Am*: ə'lu:mɪnəm] алюми́ний
**always** ['ɔ:lweɪz] всегдá
**Alzheimer's disease** ['æltshɑɪməz] болéзнь Альцгéймера
**am** [æm; *в предложении*: əm] [*irr.*] *1st pers. sg. pr. om* **be**

**A.M.** (*abbr. of* ***ante meridiem***) утрá, у́тром
**amalgamate** [ə'mælgəmeɪt] *v/t.* объединя́ть [-ни́ть]; *v/i.* объединя́ться [-ни́ться] (***with*** с Т)
**amass** [ə'mæs] соб(и)рáть; (*accumulate*) накопля́ть [-пи́ть]
**amateur** ['æmətə] люби́тель *m*, -ница *f*; дилетáнт *m*, -ка *f*, *attr.* люби́тельский
**amaz|e** [ə'meɪz] изумля́ть [-ми́ть], поражáть [порази́ть]; **~ement** [~mənt] изумлéние; **~ing** [ə'meɪzɪŋ] удиви́тельный, порази́тельный
**ambassador** [æm'bæsədə] посóл
**amber** ['æmbə] янтáрь *m*
**ambigu|ity** [æmbɪ'gju:ətɪ] двусмы́сленность *f*; **~ous** [æm'bɪgjʊəs] □ двусмы́сленный
**ambitio|n** [æm'bɪʃn] честолю́бие; (*aim*) мечтá, стремлéние; **~us** [~ʃəs] честолюби́вый
**amble** ['æmbl] идти́ лёгкой похóдкой, прогу́ливаться
**ambulance** ['æmbjʊləns] маши́на скóрой пóмощи
**ambush** ['æmbʊʃ] засáда
**amenable** [ə'mi:nəbl] (*tractable*) □ подáтливый; (*obedient*) послу́шный; (*complaisant*) сговóрчивый
**amend** [ə'mend] исправля́ть(ся) [-áвить(ся)]; вноси́ть [внести́] попрáвки в (В); **~ment** [~mənt] исправлéние; попрáвка; **~s** [ə'mendz]: ***make ~ for*** компенси́ровать (В)
**amenity** [ə'mi:nətɪ] *mst. pl.* удóбства; *in town* местá óтдыха и развлечéний; *of family life* прéлести
**American** [ə'merɪkən] **1.** америкáнец *m*, -нка *f*; **2.** америкáнский
**amiable** ['eɪmjəbl] □ доброду́шный; (*sweet*) ми́лый
**amicable** ['æmɪkəbl] □ дружелю́бный, дру́жественный
**amid(st)** [ə'mɪd(st)] среди́ (Р), посреди́ (Р), мéжду (Т)
**amiss** [ə'mɪs] *adv.* непрáвильно; ***take ~*** обижáться [оби́деться]
**amity** ['æmɪtɪ] дру́жба
**ammonia** [ə'məʊnɪə] аммиáк; ***liquid ~***

нашаты́рный спирт
**ammunition** [æmjʊ'nɪʃn] боеприпа́сы *m/pl.*
**amnesty** ['æmnəstɪ] **1.** амни́стия; **2.** амнисти́ровать *(im)pf.*
**among(st)** [ə'mʌŋ(st)] среди́ (P), ме́жду (T *sometimes* P)
**amoral** [eɪ'morəl] □ амора́льный
**amorous** ['æmərəs] □ (*in love*) влюблённый (***of*** в B); (*inclined to love*) влю́бчивый
**amount** [ə'maʊnt] **1.** ~ ***to*** равня́ться (Д); *fig.* быть равноси́льным; ***it ~s to this*** де́ло сво́дится к сле́дующему; **2.** су́мма, коли́чество
**ample** ['æmpl] (*sufficient*) доста́точный, (*abundant*) оби́льный; (*spacious*) просто́рный
**ampli|fier** ['æmplɪfaɪə] *el.* усили́тель *m*; **~fy** [~faɪ] уси́ли(ва)ть; (*expand*) расширя́ть [-и́рить]; **~tude** [~tjuːd] широта́, разма́х; амплиту́да
**ampoule** ['æmpuːl] а́мпула
**amputate** ['æmpjʊteɪt] ампути́ровать *(im)pf.*
**amuse** [ə'mjuːz] забавля́ть, позаба́вить *pf.*, развлека́ть [-е́чь]; **~ment** [~mənt] развлече́ние, заба́ва; ~ ***park*** площа́дка с аттракцио́нами
**an** [æn, ən] *неопределённый артикль*
**an(a)emi|a** [ə'niːmɪə] анеми́я; **~c** [~mɪk] анеми́чный
**an(a)esthetic** [ænɪs'θetɪk] обезбо́ливающее сре́дство; ***general ~*** о́бщий нарко́з; ***local ~*** ме́стный нарко́з
**analog|ous** [ə'næləgəs] □ аналоги́чный, схо́дный; **~y** [ə'nælədʒɪ] анало́гия, схо́дство
**analysis** [ə'næləsɪs] ана́лиз
**analyze**, *Brit.* **-yse** ['ænəlaɪz] анализи́ровать *(im)pf.*, *pf. a.* [про-]
**anarchy** ['ænəkɪ] ана́рхия
**anatomy** [ə'nætəmɪ] (*science*) анато́мия; (*dissection*) анатоми́рование; (*analysis*) разбо́р; (*human body*) те́ло
**ancest|or** ['ænsɪstə] пре́док; **~ral** [æn'sestrəl] родово́й; **~ry** ['ænsestrɪ] (*lineage*) происхожде́ние; (*ancestors*) пре́дки *m/pl.*
**anchor** ['æŋkə] **1.** я́корь *m*; ***at ~*** на я́коре; **2.** ***come to ~*** станови́ться [стать] на я́корь
**anchovy** ['æntʃəvɪ] анчо́ус
**ancient** [eɪnʃənt] дре́вний; анти́чный
**and** [ənd, ən, ænd] и; а
**anew** [ə'njuː] (*again*) сно́ва; (*in a different way*) по-но́вому, за́ново
**angel** ['əɪndʒəl] а́нгел; **~ic(al** □) [æn'dʒelɪk(l)] а́нгельский
**anger** ['æŋgə] **1.** гнев; **2.** [рас]серди́ть
**angle**[1] ['æŋgl] у́гол; (*viewpoint*) то́чка зре́ния
**angle**[2] [~] уди́ть ры́бу; *fig.* напра́шиваться (***for*** на B); **~r** [~ə] рыболо́в
**Anglican** ['æŋglɪkən] **1.** член англика́нской це́ркви; **2.** англика́нский
**angry** ['æŋgrɪ] серди́тый (***with*** на B)
**anguish** ['æŋgwɪʃ] страда́ние, му́ка
**angular** ['æŋgjʊlə] *mst. fig.* углова́тый; (*awkward*) нело́вкий
**animal** ['ænɪml] **1.** живо́тное; ***pack ~*** вью́чное живо́тное; **2.** живо́тный; ~ ***kingdom*** живо́тное ца́рство
**animat|e** ['ænɪmeɪt] оживля́ть [-ви́ть]; **~ion** [ænɪ'meɪʃn] жи́вость *f*; оживле́ние
**animosity** [ænɪ'mɒsətɪ] вражде́бность *f*
**ankle** ['æŋkl] лоды́жка
**annals** ['ænlz] *pl.* ле́топись *f*
**annex** [ə'neks] аннекси́ровать *(im)pf.*; присоединя́ть [-ни́ть]; **~ation** [ænek'seɪʃn] анне́ксия
**annex(e)** ['ænəks] (*to a building*) пристро́йка; крыло́; (*to document*, *etc.*) приложе́ние
**annihilate** [ə'naɪəleɪt] уничтожа́ть [-о́жить], истребля́ть [-би́ть]
**anniversary** [ænɪ'vɜːsərɪ] годовщи́на
**annotat|e** ['ænəteɪt] анноти́ровать *(im)pf.*; снабжа́ть примеча́ниями; **~ion** [ænə'teɪʃn] аннота́ция; примеча́ние
**announce** [ə'naʊns] объявля́ть [-ви́ть]; заявля́ть [-ви́ть]; **~ment** [~mənt] объявле́ние, заявле́ние; *on the radio*, *etc.* сообще́ние; **~r** [~ə] *radio* ди́ктор
**annoy** [ə'nɔɪ] надоеда́ть [-е́сть] (Д); досажда́ть [досади́ть] (Д); раздра-

жать; **~ance** [-əns] доса́да; раздраже́ние; неприя́тность *f*
**annual** ['ænjuəl] **1.** *publication* □ ежего́дный; годово́й; **2.** *plant* ежего́дник; однолетнее расте́ние
**annul** [ə'nʌl] аннули́ровать (*im*)*pf*.; отменя́ть [-ни́ть]; *contract* растор-га́ть [-о́ргнуть]; **~ment** [-mənt] отме́на, аннули́рование
**anodyne** ['ænədaɪn] болеутоля́ющее сре́дство; успока́ивающее сре́дство
**anomalous** [ə'nɒmələs] □ *adj*. анома́льный
**anonymous** [ə'nɒnɪməs] □ анони́мный
**another** [ə'nʌðə] друго́й, ещё; ***one after ~*** оди́н за други́м; ***quite ~ thing*** совсе́м друго́е де́ло
**answer** ['ɑːnsə] **1.** *v/t*. отвеча́ть [-е́тить] (Д); (*fulfil*) удовлетворя́ть [-ри́ть]; ***~ back*** дерзи́ть; ***~ the bell*** *or* ***door*** открыва́ть дверь на звоно́к; ***~ the telephone*** взять *or* сня́ть тру́бку; *v/i*. отвеча́ть [-е́тить] (***to a p.*** Д, ***to a question*** на вопро́с); ***~ for*** отвеча́ть [-е́тить] за (В); **2.** отве́т (***to*** на В); реше́ние *a. math*.; **~able** ['ɑːnsərəbl] □ отве́тственный; **~ing machine** автоотве́тчик
**ant** [ænt] мураве́й
**antagonism** [æn'tægənɪzəm] антагони́зм, вражда́
**antagonize** [æn'tægənaɪz] настра́ивать [-ро́ить] (***against*** про́тив Р)
**antenatal** [æntɪ'neɪtl]: ***~ clinic*** *approx*. же́нская консульта́ция
**antenna** [æn'tenə] *Am*. → ***aerial***
**anterior** [æn'tɪərɪə] *of time* предше́ствующий (***to*** Д); *of place* пере́дний
**anthem** ['ænθəm] хора́л, гимн; ***national ~*** госуда́рственный гимн
**anti…** [æntɪ…] противо…, анти…
**antiaircraft** [æntɪ'ɛəkrɑːft] противовозду́шный; ***~ defence*** противовозду́шная оборо́на (ПВО)
**antibiotic** [-baɪ'ɒtɪk] антибио́тик
**anticipat|e** [æn'tɪsɪpeɪt] (*foresee*) предви́деть, предчу́вствовать; (*expect*) ожида́ть; предвкуша́ть [-уси́ть]; (*forestall*) предупрежда́ть [-реди́ть]; **~ion** [æntɪsɪ'peɪʃn] ожида́ние; предчу́вствие; ***in ~*** в ожида́нии, в предви́дении
**antics** ['æntɪks] ша́лости *f/pl*., прока́зы *f/pl*., проде́лки *f/pl*.
**antidote** ['æntɪdəʊt] противоя́дие
**antipathy** [æn'tɪpəθɪ] антипа́тия
**antiqua|ry** ['æntɪkwərɪ] антиква́р; **~ted** [-kweɪtɪd] устаре́лый; (*old-fashioned*) старомо́дный
**antiqu|e** [æn'tiːk] **1.** анти́чный; стари́нный; **2.** ***the ~*** (*art*) анти́чное иску́сство; **~ity** [æn'tɪkwətɪ] дре́вность *f*; старина́; анти́чность *f*
**antiseptic** [æntɪ'septɪk] антисепти́ческое сре́дство
**antlers** ['æntləz] *pl*. оле́ньи рога́ *m/pl*.
**anvil** ['ænvɪl] накова́льня
**anxiety** [æŋ'zaɪətɪ] (*worry*) беспоко́йство, (*alarm*) трево́га; (*keen desire*) стра́стное жела́ние; (*apprehension*) опасе́ние
**anxious** ['æŋkʃəs] озабо́ченный; беспоко́ящийся (***about, for*** о П); *of news, warning signals, etc*. трево́жный
**any** ['enɪ] **1.** *pron. & adj*. како́йнибудь; вся́кий, любо́й; ***at ~ rate*** во вся́ком слу́чае; ***not ~*** никако́й; **2.** *adv*. ско́лько-нибудь, ниско́лько; **~body**, **~one** кто́-нибудь; вся́кий; **~how** ка́к-нибудь; так и́ли ина́че, всё же; **~thing** что́-нибудь; ***~ but*** то́лько не…; **~where** где́-нибудь, куда́-нибудь
**apart** [ə'pɑːt] отде́льно; по́рознь; ***~ from*** кро́ме (Р); **~ment** [-mənt] → ***flat*** *Brt*.; *mst. pl*. апартаме́нты *m/pl*.; *Am*. кварти́ра; ***~ house*** многокварти́рный дом
**ape** [eɪp] **1.** обезья́на; **2.** подража́ть (Д), [с]обезъя́нничать
**aperient** [ə'pɪərɪənt] слаби́тельное
**aperitif** [ə'perɪtɪf] аперити́в
**aperture** ['æpətʃə] отве́рстие; *phot*. диафра́гма
**apex** ['eɪpeks] верши́на
**apiece** [ə'piːs] за шту́ку; за ка́ждого, с челове́ка
**apolog|etic** [əpɒlə'dʒetɪk] (***~ally***): ***be ~*** извиня́ться [-ни́ться] (***about, for*** за В); ***~ air*** винова́тый вид; **~ize**

[ə'pɒlədʒaɪz] извиня́ться [-ни́ться] (**for** за В; **to** пе́ред Т); **~y** [-dʒɪ] извине́ние

**apoplectic** [æpə'plektɪk]: **~ stroke** уда́р, инсу́льт

**apostle** [ə'pɒsl] апо́стол

**apostrophe** [ə'pɒstrəfɪ] *gr.* апостро́ф

**appall** *or Brt.* **appal** [ə'pɔːl] ужаса́ть [-сну́ть]

**apparatus** [æpə'reɪtəs] прибо́р; аппарату́ра, аппара́т; *sport* снаря́ды *m/pl.*

**appar|ent** [ə'pærənt] (*obvious*) очеви́дный; (*visible, evident*) ви́димый; **for no ~ reason** без ви́димой причи́ны; **~ently** по-ви́димому; **~ition** [æpə'rɪʃən] при́зрак

**appeal** [ə'piːl] **1.** апелли́ровать (*im*)*pf.*; обраща́ться [обрати́ться] (**to** к Д); (*attract*) привлека́ть [-е́чь] (**to** В); *law* обжа́ловать; **2.** воззва́ние, призы́в; привлека́тельность *f*; обжа́лование; **~ing** [-ɪŋ] (*moving*) тро́гательный; (*attractive*) привлека́тельный

**appear** [ə'pɪə] появля́ться [-ви́ться]; (*seem*) пока́зываться [-за́ться]; *on stage etc.* выступа́ть [вы́ступить]; **it ~s to me** мне ка́жется; **~ance** [ə'pɪərəns] появле́ние; вне́шний вид; *person's* вне́шность *f*; **~ances** *pl.* прили́чия *n/pl.*; **keep up ~** соблюда́ть прили́чия

**appease** [ə'piːz] умиротворя́ть [-ри́ть]; успока́ивать [-ко́ить]

**append** [ə'pend] прилага́ть [-ложи́ть] (к Д); **~icitis** [əpendɪ'saɪtɪs] аппендици́т; **~ix** [ə'pendɪks] *of a book, etc.* приложе́ние; *anat.* аппе́ндикс

**appetite** ['æpɪtaɪt] аппети́т (**for** на В); *fig.* влече́ние, скло́нность *f* (**for** к Д)

**appetizing** ['æpɪtaɪzɪŋ] аппети́тный

**applaud** [ə'plɔːd] *v/t.* аплоди́ровать (Д); (*approve*) одобря́ть [одо́брить]

**applause** [ə'plɔːz] аплодисме́нты *m/pl*; *fig.* (*approval*) одобре́ние

**apple** [æpl] я́блоко; **~ of discord** я́блоко раздо́ра; **~ tree** я́блоня

**appliance** [ə'plaɪəns] устро́йство, приспособле́ние, прибо́р

**applica|ble** ['æplɪkəbl] примени́мый, (*appropriate*) подходя́щий (**to** к Д); **delete where ~** зачеркни́те, где необходи́мо; **~nt** [-kənt] кандида́т (**for** на В); **not ~** не отно́сится (**to** к Д); **~tion** [æplɪ'keɪʃn] примене́ние; заявле́ние; про́сьба (**for** о П); **send in an ~** пода́ть заявле́ние, зая́вку

**apply** [ə'plaɪ] *v/t.* (*bring into action*) прилага́ть [-ложи́ть] (**to** к Д); (*lay or spread on*) прикла́дывать [приложи́ть]; (*use*) применя́ть [-ни́ть] (**to** к Д); **~ o.s. to** занима́ться [заня́ться] (Т); *v/i.* (*approach, request*) обраща́ться [обрати́ться] (**for** за Т; **to** к Д); (*concern, relate to*) относи́ться

**appoint** [ə'pɔɪnt] назнача́ть [-на́чить]; **~ment** [-mənt] назначе́ние; (*meeting*) встре́ча; (*agreement*) договорённость *f*; **by ~** по предвари́тельной договорённости, по за́писи

**apportion** [ə'pɔːʃn] разделя́ть [-ли́ть]

**apprais|al** [ə'preɪzl] оце́нка; **~e** [ə'preɪz] оце́нивать [-ни́ть], расце́нивать [-ни́ть]

**apprecia|ble** [ə'priːʃəbl] □ заме́тный, ощути́мый; **~te** [-ɪeɪt] *v/t.* оце́нивать [-ни́ть]; [о]цени́ть; (*understand*) понима́ть [-ня́ть]; *v/i.* повыша́ться [-вы́ситься] в цене́; **~tion** [əpriːʃɪ'eɪʃn] (*gratitude*) призна́тельность *f*; оце́нка, понима́ние

**apprehen|d** [æprɪ'hend] (*foresee*) предчу́вствовать; (*fear*) опаса́ться; (*seize, arrest*) заде́рживать [-жа́ть], аресто́вывать [-ова́ть]; **~sion** [-'henʃn] опасе́ние, предчу́вствие; аре́ст; **~sive** [-'hensɪv] □ озабо́ченный, по́лный трево́ги

**apprentice** [ə'prentɪs] учени́к; **~ship** [-ʃɪp] уче́ние, учени́чество

**approach** [ə'prəʊtʃ] **1.** приближа́ться [-бли́зиться] к (Д); (*speak to*) обраща́ться [обрати́ться] к (Д); **2.** приближе́ние; по́дступ; *fig.* подхо́д; **~ing** [-ɪŋ] приближа́ющийся; **~ traffic** встре́чное движе́ние

**approbation** [æprə'beɪʃn] одобре́ние; са́нкция, согла́сие

**appropriate** **1.** [ə'prəʊprɪeɪt] (*take possession of*) присва́ивать [-сво́ить]; **2.** [-ət] (*suitable*) подходя́щий, соот-

вéтствующий
**approv|al** [ə'pruːvl] одобрéние; утверждéние; **~e** [ə'pruːv] одобря́ть [одóбрить]; утверждáть [-дить]; санкциони́ровать *(im)pf.*
**approximate** **1.** [ə'prɒksɪmeɪt] приближáть(ся) [-бли́зить(ся)] к (Д); **2.** [~mət] приблизи́тельный
**apricot** ['eɪprɪkɒt] абрикóс
**April** ['eɪprəl] апрéль *m*
**apron** ['eɪprən] перéдник, фáртук
**apt** [æpt] □ (*suitable*) подходя́щий, (*pertinent*) умéстный; (*gifted*) спосóбный; **~ *to*** склóнный к (Д); **~itude** ['æptɪtjuːd], **~ness** [~nɪs] спосóбность *f*; склóнность *f* (***for, to*** к Д); умéстность *f*
**aqualung** ['ækwəlʌŋ] акваля́нг
**aquarium** [ə'kweərɪəm] аквáриум
**Aquarius** [ə'kweərɪəs] Водолéй
**aquatic** [ə'kwætɪk] **1.** водянóй, вóдный; **2.** **~s** *pl.* вóдный спорт
**aqueduct** ['ækwɪdʌkt] акведу́к
**Arab** ['ærəb] арáб *m*, -ка *f*; **~ic** ['ærəbɪk] **1.** арáбский язы́к; **2.** арáбский
**arable** ['ærəbl] пáхотный
**arbit|er** ['ɑːbɪtə] (*judge*) арби́тр; (*third party*) третéйский судья́; **~rariness** ['ɑːbɪtrərɪnɪs] произвóл; **~rary** [ɪ~trərɪ] произвóльный; **~rate** ['ɑːbɪtreɪt] выступáть в кáчестве арби́тра; **~ration** [ɑːbɪ'treɪʃn] арбитрáж; **~rator** ['ɑːbɪtreɪtə] третéйский судья́, арби́тр
**arbo(u)r** ['ɑːbə] бесéдка
**arc** [ɑːk] дугá; **~ade** [ɑː'keɪd] (*covered passageway*) аркáда; *with shops* пассáж
**arch**[1] [ɑːtʃ] **1.** áрка; свод; дугá; **2.** придавáть фóрму áрки; выгибáться
**arch**[2] [~] **1.** хи́трый, лукáвый; **2.** *pref.* архи...; глáвный
**archaic** [ɑː'keɪɪk] (***~ally***) устарéлый, устарéвший; дрéвний
**archbishop** [ɑːtʃ'bɪʃəp] архиепи́скоп
**archery** ['ɑːtʃərɪ] стрельбá из лу́ка
**architect** ['ɑːkɪtekt] архитéктор; **~ural** [ɑːkɪ'tektʃərəl] архитекту́рный; **~ure** ['ɑːkɪtektʃə] архитекту́ра
**archway** ['ɑːtʃweɪ] сводчáтый прохóд
**arctic** ['ɑːktɪk] аркти́ческий; ***the Arctic*** Áрктика
**ardent** ['ɑːdənt] □ *mst. fig.* горя́чий, пы́лкий; я́рый
**ardo(u)r** ['ɑːdə] рвéние, пыл
**arduous** ['ɑːdjʊəs] □ тру́дный
**are** [ɑː; *в предложении*: ə] → ***be***
**area** ['eərɪə] (*measurement*) плóщадь *f*; ***~ of a triangle*** плóщадь треугóльника; (*region*) райóн, край, зóна; (*sphere*) óбласть
**Argentine** ['ɑːdʒəntaɪn] **1.** аргенти́нский; **2.** аргенти́нец *m*, -нка *f*
**argue** ['ɑːgjuː] *v/t.* обсуждáть [-уди́ть]; докáзывать [-зáть]; ***~ a p. into*** убеждáть [убеди́ть] в (П); *v/i.* [по-] спóрить (с Т); ***~ against*** приводи́ть дóводы прóтив (Р)
**argument** ['ɑːgjʊmənt] дóвод, аргумéнт; (*discussion, debate*) спор; **~ation** [ɑːgjʊmen'teɪʃn] аргументáция
**arid** ['ærɪd] сухóй (*a. fig.*); засу́шливый
**Aries** ['eəriːz] Овен
**arise** [ə'raɪz] (*get up, stand up*) вставáть [встать]; (*fig., come into being*) возникáть [-ни́кнуть] (***from*** из Р); явля́ться [яви́ться] результáтом (***from*** из Р); **~n** [ə'rɪzn] *p. pt. om* ***arise***
**aristocra|cy** [ærɪ'stɒkrəsɪ] аристокрáтия; **~t** ['ærɪstəkræt] аристокрáт; **~tic** [ærɪstə'krætɪk] аристократи́ческий
**arithmetic** [ə'rɪθmətɪk] арифмéтика
**ark** [ɑːk]: ***Noah's ~*** Нóев ковчéг
**arm**[1] [ɑːm] рукá; (*sleeve*) рукáв
**arm**[2] [~] вооружáть(ся) [-жи́ть(ся)]; ***~ed forces*** вооружённые си́лы
**armament** ['ɑːməmənt] вооружéние
**armchair** крéсло
**armful** ['ɑːmfʊl] охáпка
**armistice** ['ɑːmɪstɪs] переми́рие
**armo(u)r** ['ɑːmə] *hist.* доспéхи *m/pl.*; броня́; **~y** [~rɪ] арсенáл; оружéйная палáта
**armpit** ['ɑːmpɪt] подмы́шка
**arms** [ɑːmz] ору́жие
**army** ['ɑːmɪ] áрмия; *fig.* мнóжество
**arose** [ə'rəʊz] *pt. om* ***arise***
**around** [ə'raʊnd] **1.** *adv.* всю́ду, кругóм; **2.** *prp.* вокру́г (Р)
**arouse** [ə'raʊz] [раз]буди́ть (*a. fig.*);

*fig*. возбуждáть [-удúть]; *interest, envy etc*. вызывáть [вы́звать]
**arrange** [əˈreɪndʒ] приводúть в порядок; *a party etc*. устрáивать [-рóить]; (*agree in advance*) услáвливаться [услóвиться]; *mus*. аранжи́ровать (*im*)*pf*.; **~ment** [~mənt] устрóйство; расположéние; соглашéние, мероприя́тие; *mus*. аранжирóвка
**array** [əˈreɪ] *fig. assemblage* мнóжество, *display* коллéкция; цéлый ряд
**arrear(s)** [əˈrɪə] *mst. pl*. отставáние; задóлженность *f*
**arrest** [əˈrest] **1.** арéст, задержáние; **2.** арестóвывать [-овáть], задéрживать [-жáть]
**arriv|al** [əˈraɪvl] прибы́тие, приéзд; **~als** *pl*. прибы́вшие *pl*.; **~e** [əˈraɪv] прибы́(вá)ть; приезжáть [-éхать] (***at*** в, на В)
**arroga|nce** [ˈærəgəns] надмéнность *f*, высокомéрие; **~nt** [~nt] надмéнный, высокомéрный
**arrow** [ˈærəʊ] стрелá; *as symbol on road sign, etc*. стрéлка
**arsenal** [ˈɑːsənl] арсенáл
**arsenic** [ˈɑːsnɪk] мышья́к
**arson** [ˈɑːsn] *law* поджóг
**art** [ɑːt] искýсство; ***fine ~s*** изя́щные *or* изобразúтельные искýсства
**arter|ial** [ɑˈtɪərɪəl]: **~ *road*** магистрáль *f*; **~y** [ˈɑːtərɪ] *anat*. артéрия
**artful** [ˈɑːtfəl] лóвкий; хúтрый
**article** [ˈɑːtɪkl] (*object*) предмéт, вещь *f*; (*piece of writing*) статья́; (*clause*) пункт, парáграф; артúкль *m*
**articulat|e** [ɑːˈtɪkjʊleɪt] **1.** отчётливо, я́сно произносúть; **2.** [~lət] отчётливый; членораздéльный; **~ion** [ɑːtɪkjʊˈleɪʃn] артикуля́ция
**artificial** [ɑːtɪˈfɪʃl] искýсственный
**artillery** [ɑːˈtɪlərɪ] артиллéрия; **~man** [~mən] артиллерúст
**artisan** [ɑːtɪˈzæn] ремéсленник
**artist** [ˈɑːtɪst] худóжник (-ица); (*actor*) актёр, актрúса; **~e** [ɑːˈtiːst] артúст(-ка); **~ic(al** □) [ɑːˈtɪstɪk(l)] артистúческий, худóжественный
**artless** [ˈɑːtlɪs] естéственный; (*ingenuous*) простодýшный; (*unskilled*) неискýсный
**as** [əz, æz] *cj. a. adv*. когдá; в то врéмя как; тáк как; хотя́; ***~ far ~ I know*** наскóлько мне извéстно; ***~ it were*** так сказáть; кáк бы; ***~ well*** тáкже; в такóй же мéре; ***such ~*** такóй как; как напримéр; ***~ well ~*** и … и …; *prp*. ***~ for, ~ to*** что касáется (Р); ***~ from*** с (Р)
**ascend** [əˈsend] поднимáться [-ня́ться]; восходúть [взойтú]
**ascension** [əˈsenʃn]: ♀ (***Day***) Вознесéние
**ascent** [əˈsent] восхождéние; (*upward slope*) подъём
**ascertain** [æsəˈteɪn] удостоверя́ться [-вéриться] в (П); устанáвливать [-новúть]
**ascribe** [əˈskraɪb] припúсывать [-сáть] (Д/В)
**aseptic** [eɪˈseptɪk] *med*. асептúческий, стерúльный
**ash**[1] [æʃ] *bot*. я́сень *m*; ***mountain ~*** рябúна
**ash**[2] [~] *mst. pl*. **~es** [ˈæʃɪz] золá, пéпел
**ashamed** [əˈʃeɪmd] пристыжённый; ***I'm ~ of you*** мне сты́дно за тебя́; ***feel ~ of o.s.*** стыдúться
**ash can** *Am*. ведрó для мýсора
**ashen** [ˈæʃən] пéпельного цвéта; (*pale*) блéдный
**ashore** [əˈʃɔː] на бéрег, на берегý
**ashtray** пéпельница
**ashy** [ˈæʃɪ] *of or relating to ashes* пéпельный
**Asian** [ˈeɪʃn] **1.** азиáтский; **2.** азиáт *m*, -ка *f*
**aside** [əˈsaɪd] в стóрону, в сторонé
**ask** [ɑːsk] *v/t*. (*request*) [по]просúть (***a th. of, from a p.*** чтó-нибудь у когó-нибудь); ***~ that*** просúть, чтóбы …; (*inquire*) спрáшивать [спросúть]; ***~ (a p.) a question*** задавáть вопрóс (Д); *v/i*. ***~ for*** [по]просúть (В *or* Р *or* о П)
**askance** [əˈskæns]: ***look ~*** кóсо посмотрéть (***at*** на В)
**askew** [əˈskjuː] крúво
**asleep** [əˈsliːp] спя́щий; ***be ~*** спать
**asparagus** [əˈspærəgəs] спáржа
**aspect** [ˈæspekt] вид (*a. gr*.); аспéкт, сторонá

**aspen** ['æspən] оси́на
**asperity** [æ'sperətɪ] (*sharpness*) ре́зкость *f*; ***with ~*** ре́зко; (*severity*) суро́вость *f*
**asphalt** ['æsfælt] **1.** асфа́льт; **2.** покрыва́ть асфа́льтом
**aspir|ation** [æspə'reɪʃn] стремле́ние; **~e** [ə'spaɪə] стреми́ться (***to, after, at*** к Д)
**aspirin** ['æsprɪn] аспири́н
**ass** [æs] осёл (*a. fig.*); ***make an ~ of o.s.*** поста́вить себя́ в глу́пое положе́ние; *coll.* валя́ть дурака́
**assail** [ə'seɪl] (*attack*) напада́ть [-па́сть] на (В); *fig.* энерги́чно бра́ться за; *with questions* засыпа́ть [засы́пать] вопро́сами; **~ant** [-ənt] напада́ющий
**assassin** [ə'sæsɪn] уби́йца *m/f*; **~ate** [-ɪneɪt] уби́(ва́)ть; **~ation** [əsæsɪ'neɪʃn] уби́йство
**assault** [ə'sɔːlt] **1.** нападе́ние; *mil.* ата́ка, штурм; **2.** напада́ть [напа́сть], набра́сываться [-ро́ситься] на (В)
**assembl|e** [ə'sembl] (*gather*) собира́ть(ся) [-бра́ть(ся)]; *tech.* [с]монти́ровать, собира́ть [-бра́ть]; **~y** [-i] собра́ние; ассамбле́я; *tech.* сбо́рка
**assent** [ə'sent] **1.** согла́сие; **2.** соглаша́ться [-ласи́ться] (***to*** на В; с Т)
**assert** [ə'sɜːt] утвержда́ть [-рди́ть]; **~ion** [ə'sɜːʃn] утвержде́ние
**assess** [ə'ses] оце́нивать [-ни́ть] (*a. fig.*); *taxes etc.* определя́ть [-ли́ть], устана́вливать [-нови́ть]; **~ment** [-mənt] *for taxation* обложе́ние; *valuation* оце́нка
**asset** ['æset] це́нное ка́чество; *fin.* статья́ дохо́да; **~s** *pl. fin.* акти́в(ы); ***~ and liabilities*** акти́в и пасси́в
**assiduous** [ə'sɪdjʊəs] приле́жный
**assign** [ə'saɪn] (*appoint*) назнача́ть [-на́чить]; (*allot*) ассигно́вывать, ассигнова́ть (*im*)*pf.*; (*charge*) поруча́ть [-чи́ть]; *room, etc.* отводи́ть [-вести́]; **~ment** [-mənt] назначе́ние; зада́ние, поруче́ние
**assimilat|e** [ə'sɪmɪleɪt] ассимили́ровать(ся) (*im*)*pf.*; (*absorb*) усва́ивать [-во́ить]; **~ion** [əsɪmɪ'leɪʃn] ассимиля́ция; усвое́ние
**assist** [ə'sɪst] помога́ть [-мо́чь] (Д), [по]соде́йствовать (*im*)*pf.* (Д); **~ance** [~əns] по́мощь *f*; **~ant** [~ənt] ассисте́нт(ка); помо́щник (-ица); ***~ professor*** *univ. Am.* ассисте́нт; ***shop ~*** *Brt.* продаве́ц
**associa|te** [ə'səʊʃɪeɪt] **1.** обща́ться (***with*** с Т); (*connect*) ассоции́ровать(ся) (*im*)*pf.*; **2.** [~ʃɪət] колле́га *m*; соуча́стник; *comm.* компаньо́н; **~tion** [əsəʊsɪ'eɪʃn] ассоциа́ция; объедине́ние, о́бщество
**assort|ed** [ə'sɔːtɪd] разнообра́зный; ***~ chocolates*** шокола́д ассорти́ *indecl.*; **~ment** [~mənt] ассортиме́нт
**assum|e** [ə'sjuːm] (*suppose*) предполага́ть [-ложи́ть]; (*take up*) вступа́ть [-пи́ть]; **~ption** [ə'sʌmpʃn] предположе́ние; *eccl.* **Ձption** Успе́ние
**assur|ance** [ə'ʃʊərəns] (*promise*) увере́ние; (*confidence*) уве́ренность *f*; (*insurance*) страхо́вка; **~e** [ə'ʃʊə] уверя́ть [уве́рить]; **~edly** [~rɪdlɪ] *adv.* коне́чно, несомне́нно
**aster** ['æstə] *bot.* а́стра
**astir** [əs'tɜː] в движе́нии; на нога́х
**astonish** [ə'stɒnɪʃ] удивля́ть [-ви́ть], изумля́ть [-ми́ть]; ***be ~ed*** удивля́ться [-ви́ться] (***at*** Д); **~ing** [~ɪʃɪŋ] удиви́тельный, порази́тельный; **~ment** [~mənt] удивле́ние, изумле́ние
**astound** [ə'staʊnd] поража́ть [порази́ть]
**astrakhan** [æstrə'kæn] (*lambskin*) кара́куль *m*
**astray** [ə'streɪ]: ***go ~*** заблуди́ться, сби́ться с пути́ (*a. fig.*); ***lead s.o. ~*** сбить с пути́ (и́стинного)
**astride** [ə'straɪd] верхо́м (***of*** на П)
**astringent** [ə'strɪndʒənt] *med.* вя́жущее сре́дство
**astro|logy** [ə'strɒlədʒɪ] астроло́гия; **~nomer** [ə'strɒnəmə] астроно́м; **~nomy** [ə'strɒnəmɪ] астроно́мия
**astute** [ə'stjuːt] □ (*cunning*) хи́трый; (*shrewd*) проница́тельный; **~ness** [~nɪs] хи́трость *f*; проница́тельность *f*
**asylum** [ə'saɪləm] (*place of refuge*) убе́жище; (*shelter*) прию́т; (*mental in-*

*stitution*) сумасше́дший дом

**at** [æt, ət] *prp*. в (П, В); у (Р); при (П); на (П, В); о́коло (Р); за (Т); **~ *school*** в шко́ле; **~ *the age of*** в во́зрасте (Р); **~ *first*** снача́ла; **~ *first sight*** с пе́рвого взгля́да; на пе́рвый взгляд; **~ *last*** наконе́ц

**ate** [et, eit] *pt. om* **eat**

**atheism** ['eɪθɪɪzəm] атеи́зм

**athlet|e** ['æθliːt] спортсме́н, атле́т; **~ic(al □)** [æθ'letɪk(əl)] атлети́ческий; **~ics** [æθ'letɪks] *pl*. (лёгкая) атле́тика

**atmospher|e** ['ætməsfɪə] атмосфе́ра (*a. fig*.); **~ic(al □)** [ætməs'ferɪk(əl)] атмосфе́рный

**atom** ['ætəm] а́том; ***not an ~ of truth*** нет и до́ли и́стины; **~ic** [ə'tɒmɪk] а́томный; **~ *pile*** а́томный реа́ктор; **~ *power plant*** а́томная электроста́нция; **~ *waste*** отхо́ды а́томной промы́шленности

**atone** [ə'təʊn]: **~ *for*** загла́живать [-ла́дить], искупа́ть [-пи́ть]

**atroci|ous** [ə'trəʊʃəs] □ зве́рский, *coll*. ужа́сный; **~ty** [ə'trɒsətɪ] зве́рство

**attach** [ə'tætʃ] *v/t. com*. прикрепля́ть [-пи́ть]; *document* прилага́ть [-ложи́ть]; *importance, etc*. прид(ав)а́ть; *law* налага́ть аре́ст на (В); **~ *o.s. to*** привя́зываться [-за́ться] к (Д); **~ment** [-mənt] (*affection*) привя́занность *f*, (*devotion*) пре́данность *f*

**attack** [ə'tæk] **1.** *mil*. ата́ка; нападе́ние (*a. mil*.); *in press, etc*. ре́зкая кри́тика; *med*. при́ступ; **2.** *v/t*. атакова́ть (*im*)*pf*.; напада́ть [напа́сть] на (В), набра́сываться [-ро́ситься] на (В); подверга́ть [-ве́ргнуть] ре́зкой кри́тике

**attain** [ə'teɪn] *v/t*. достига́ть [-и́гнуть] (Р), доби́(ва́)ться; (Р); **~ment** [-mənt] достиже́ние

**attempt** [ə'tempt] **1.** попы́тка; *on s.o.'s life* покуше́ние; **2.** [по]пыта́ться, [по]-про́бовать

**attend** [ə'tend] (*wait, serve*) обслу́живать [-жи́ть]; (*go to*) посеща́ть [-ети́ть]; *med*. уха́живать за (Т); *be present* прису́тствовать (***at*** на П); (*accompany*) сопровожда́ть *mst. impf*.; (*give care*) быть внима́тельным; **~ance** [ə'tendəns] прису́тствие (***at*** на П); наплы́в пу́блики; посеща́емость *f*; *med*. ухо́д (за Т); **~ant** [-ənt] **1.**: **~ *nurse*** дежу́рная медсестра́; **2.** *in elevator* (*Brt. lift*) лифтёр

**attent|ion** [ə'tenʃn] внима́ние; **~ive** [-tɪv] внима́тельный

**attest** [ə'test] (*certify*) удостоверя́ть [-ве́рить]; (*bear witness to*) [за]свиде́тельствовать

**attic** ['ætɪk] черда́к; манса́рда

**attire** [ə'taɪə] наря́д

**attitude** ['ætɪtjuːd] отноше́ние, пози́ция; (*pose*) по́за

**attorney** [ə'tɜːnɪ] уполномо́ченный, дове́ренный; *at law* пове́ренный в суде́, адвока́т; ***power of ~*** дове́ренность *f*; ***attorney general*** *Am*. мини́стр юсти́ции

**attract** [ə'trækt] *v/t*. привлека́ть [-вле́чь] (*a. fig*.); *magnet* притя́гивать [-яну́ть]; *fig*. прельща́ть [-льсти́ть]; **~ion** [ə'trækʃn] притяже́ние; *fig*. привлека́тельность *f*; ***the town has many ~s*** в го́роде мно́го достопримеча́тельностей; **~ive** [-tɪv] привлека́тельный, зама́нчивый; **~ivness** [-tɪvnɪs] привлека́тельность *f*

**attribute 1.** [ə'trɪbjuːt] припи́сывать [-са́ть] (Д/В); (*explain*) объясня́ть [-сни́ть]; **2.** ['ætrɪbjuːt] сво́йство, при́знак; *gr*. определе́ние

**aubergine** ['əʊbəʒiːn] баклажа́н

**auction** ['ɔːkʃn] **1.** аукцио́н, торги́ *m/pl*.; ***sell by ~, put up for ~*** продава́ть с аукцио́на; **2.** продава́ть с аукцио́на (*mst*. **~ *off***); **~eer** [ɔːkʃə'niə] аукционе́р

**audaci|ous** [ɔː'deɪʃəs] (*daring*) отва́жный, де́рзкий; (*impudent*) на́глый; **~ty** [ɔː'dæsətɪ] отва́га; де́рзость *f*; на́глость *f*

**audible** ['ɔːdəbl] вня́тный, слы́шный

**audience** ['ɔːdɪəns] слу́шатели *m/pl*., зри́тели *m/pl*., пу́блика; (*interview*) аудие́нция (***of, with*** у Р)

**audiovisual** [ɔːdɪəʊ'vɪʃʊəl] аудиовизуа́льный

**audit** ['ɔːdɪt] **1.** прове́рка фина́нсовой

отчётности, аудит; **2.** проверять [-ерить] отчётность *f*; **~or** ['ɔːdɪtə] бухгалтер-ревизор, контролёр
**auditorium** [ɔːdɪ'tɔːrɪəm] аудитория; зрительный зал
**augment** [ɔːg'ment] увеличи(ва)ть
**August** ['ɔːgəst] август
**aunt** [ɑːnt] тётя, тётка
**auspices** ['ɔːspɪsɪz] *pl.*: ***under the ~*** под эгидой
**auster|e** [ɒ'stɪə] □ строгий, суровый; **~ity** [ɒ'sterətɪ] строгость *f*, суровость *f*
**Australian** [ɒ'streɪlɪən] **1.** австралиец *m*, -ийка *f*; **2.** австралийский
**Austrian** ['ɒstrɪən] **1.** австриец *m*, -ийка *f*; **2.** австрийский
**authentic** [ɔː'θentɪk] (***~ally***) подлинный, достоверный
**author** ['ɔːθə] автор; **~itative** [ɔː'θɒrɪtətɪv] □ авторитетный; **~ity** [ɔː'θɒrɪtɪ] авторитет; (*right*) полномочие; власть *f* (***over*** над Т); ***on the ~ of*** на основании (Р); по утверждению (Р); **~ize** ['ɔːθəraiz] уполномочи(ва)ть; (*sanction*) санкционировать (*im*)*pf*.; **~ship** [-ʃɪp] авторство
**autobiography** [ɔːtəbaɪ'ɒgrəfɪ] автобиография
**autogenic** [ɔːtə'dʒenɪk]: ***~ training*** аутогенная тренировка
**autograph** ['ɔːtəgrɑːf] автограф
**automatic** [ɔːtə'mætɪk] (***~ally***) автоматический; *fig.* машинальный; ***~ machine*** автомат
**automobile** ['ɔːtəməbiːl] автомашина, автомобиль *m*.; *attr.* автомобильный
**autonomy** [ɔː'tɒnəmɪ] автономия
**autumn** ['ɔːtəm] осень *f*; **~al** [ɔː'tʌmnəl] осенний
**auxiliary** [ɔːg'zɪlɪərɪ] вспомогательный; (*additional*) дополнительный
**avail** [ə'veɪl] **1.** помогать [помочь] (Д); ***~ o.s. of*** [вос]пользоваться (Т); **2.** польза, выгода; ***of no ~*** бесполезный; ***to no ~*** напрасно; **~able** [ə'veɪləbl] (*accessible*) доступный; (*on hand*) имеющийся (в наличии)
**avalanche** ['ævəlɑːnʃ] лавина
**avaric|e** ['ævərɪs] скупость *f*; (*greed*) жадность *f*; **~ious** [ævə'rɪʃəs] скупой; жадный
**aveng|e** [ə'vendʒ] [ото]мстить (Д за В); **~er** [~ə] мститель *m*, -ница *f*
**avenue** ['ævənjuː] аллея; *Am.* широкая улица, проспект; *fig.* (*approach, way*) путь *m*
**aver** [ə'vɜː] утверждать [-дить]
**average** ['ævərɪdʒ] **1.**: ***on an*** (***the***) ***~*** в среднем; **2.** средний; **3.** (в среднем) составлять [-авить]
**avers|e** [ə'vɜːs] □ нерасположенный (***to, from*** к Д); ***I'm not ~ to*** я не прочь, я люблю; **~ion** [ə'vɜːʃn] отвращение, антипатия
**avert** [ə'vɜːt] отвращать [-ратить]; *eyes* отводить [-вести] (*a. fig.*); *head* отворачивать [-вернуть]
**aviation** [eɪvɪ'eɪʃn] авиация
**avocado** [ævə'kɑːdəʊ], ***~ pear*** авокадо *indecl.*
**avoid** [ə'vɔɪd] избегать [-ежать]
**await** [ə'weɪt] ожидать (Р)
**awake** [ə'weɪk] **1.** бодрствующий; ***be ~ to*** ясно понимать; **2.** [*irr.*]. *v/t*. (*mst.* ***~n*** [ə'weɪkən]) [раз]будить; *interest, etc.* пробуждать [-удить] (к Д); *v/i*. просыпаться [проснуться]; ***~ to a th.*** осозн(а-в)ать (В)
**award** [ə'wɔːd] **1.** награда; *univ.* стипендия; **2.** присуждать [-удить]
**aware** [ə'weə]: ***be ~ of*** знать (В *or* о П), сознавать (В); ***become ~ of*** почувствовать
**away** [ə'weɪ] прочь; далеко
**awe** [ɔː] благоговение, трепет (***of*** перед Т)
**awful** [ɔːfʊl] □ страшный, ужасный (*a. coll.*)
**awhile** [ə'waɪl] на некоторое время; ***wait ~*** подожди немного
**awkward** ['ɔːkwəd] (*clumsy*) неуклюжий, неловкий (*a. fig.*); (*inconvenient, uncomfortable*) неудобный
**awl** [ɔːl] шило
**awning** ['ɔːnɪŋ] навес, тент
**awoke** [ə'wəʊk] *pt.* и *pt. p. om* ***awake***
**awry** [ə'raɪ] косо, набок; ***everything went ~*** всё пошло скверно

**ax**(**e**) [æks] топóр, колýн
**axis** ['æksɪs], *pl.* **axes** [~siːz] ось *f*
**axle** ['æksl] *tech.* ось *f*

**ay**(**e**) [aɪ] *affirmative vote* гóлос "за"
**azure** ['æʒə] **1.** лазýрь *f*; **2.** лазýрный

# B

**babble** ['bæbl] **1.** лéпет; болтовня́; **2.** [по]болтáтъ; [за]лепетáть
**baboon** [bə'buːn] *zo.* бабуи́н
**baby** ['beɪbɪ] **1.** младéнец, ребёнок, дитя́ *n*; **2.** небольшóй; мáлый; ***~ carriage*** дéтская коля́ска; ***~ grand*** кабинéтный роя́ль; **~hood** ['beɪbɪhud] младéнчество
**bachelor** ['bætʃələ] холостя́к; *univ.* бакалáвр
**back** [bæk] **1.** спинá; *of chair, dress, etc.* спи́нка; *of cloth* изнáнка; *sport* **full~** защи́тник; *of head* заты́лок; *of coin, etc.* обрáтная сторонá; **2.** *adj.* зáдный; обрáтный; отдалённый; **3.** *adv.* назáд, обрáтно; томý назáд; **4.** *v/t.* поддéрживать [-жáть]; подкрепля́ть [-пи́ть]; *fin.* субсиди́ровать, финанси́роватъ; гаранти́ровать; *v/i.* отступáть [-пи́ть]; [по]пя́титься; **~bone** позвонóчник, спиннóй хребéт; *fig.* опóра; **~er** ['bækə] *fin.* субсиди́рующий; гарáнт; **~ground** зáдний план, фон; **~ing** поддéржка; **~side** (*coll. buttocks*) зад; зáдница; **~stairs** тáйный, закули́сный; **~stroke** плáвание на спинé; **~ talk** *Am.* дéрзкий отвéт; **~up** **1.** поддéржка, *comput.* резéрвная кóпия; **2.** создавáть [создáть] резéрвную кóпию; **~ward** ['bækwəd] **1.** *adj.* обрáтный; отстáлый; **2.** *adv.* (*a.* **~ward**[**s**] [-z]) назáд; зáдом; наоборóт; обрáтно
**bacon** ['beɪkən] бекóн
**bacteri|ologist** [bæktɪərɪ'ɒlədʒɪst] бактериóлог; **~um** [bæk'tɪərɪəm], *pl.* **~a** [~rɪə] бактéрия
**bad** [bæd] □ плохóй, дурнóй, сквéрный; (*harmful*) врéдный; ***~ cold*** си́льный нáсморк; ***~ mistake*** серьёзная (грýбая оши́бка); ***he is ~ly off*** он в невы́годном положéнии; ***~ly wounded*** тяжелорáненый; *coll.* ***want ~ly*** óчень хотéть
**bade** [beɪd, bæd] *pt. om* ***bid***
**badge** [bædʒ] значóк
**badger** ['bædʒə] **1.** *zo.* барсýк; **2.** изводи́ть [извести́]
**baffle** ['bæfl] (*confuse*) сбивáть с тóлку
**bag** [bæg] **1.** *large* мешóк; сýмка, *small, hand~* сýмочка; **2.** клáсть [положи́ть] в мешóк
**baggage** ['bægɪdʒ] багáж; ***~ check*** *Am.* багáжная квитáнция
**bagpipe** ['bægpaɪp] волы́нка
**bail** [beɪl] **1.** залóг; (*guarantee*) поручи́тельство; **2.** поручáться [-чи́ться]
**bait** [beɪt] **1.** нажи́вка, примáнка (*a. fig.*); *fig.* искушéние; **2.** примáнивать [-ни́ть]; *fig.* преслéдовать, изводи́ть [-вести́]
**bak|e** [beɪk] [ис]пéчь(ся); **~er** ['beɪkə] пéкарь *m*; **~'s** (***shop***) бýлочная; **~ery** [~rɪ] пекáрня; **~ing soda** сóда (питьевáя)
**balance** ['bæləns] **1.** (*scales*) весы́ *m/pl.*; (*equilibrium*) равновéсие; *fin.* балáнс; сáльдо *n indecl.*; *coll.* (*remainder*) остáток; ***~ of power*** полити́ческое равновéсие; ***~ of trade*** торгóвый балáнс; **2.** [с]баланси́ровать (В); сохраня́ть равновéсие; *fin.* подводи́ть балáнс; *mentally* взвéшивать [-éсить]; быть в равновéсии
**balcony** ['bælkənɪ] балкóн
**bald** [bɔːld] лы́сый, плеши́вый; *fig.* (*unadorned*) неприкрáшенный; **~ly**: ***to put it ~*** говоря́ пря́мо
**bale** [beɪl] ки́па, тюк
**balk** [bɔːk] *v/t.* (*hinder*) [вос]препя́тствовать (Д), [по]мешáть (Д)

**ball**[1] [bɔːl] мяч; шар; *of wool* клубóк; ***keep the ~ rolling*** *of a conversation* поддéрживать разговóр
**ball**[2] [~] бал, танцевáльный вéчер
**ballad** ['bæləd] баллáда
**ballast** ['bæləst] баллáст
**ballbearing(s** *pl.*) шарикоподшúпник
**ballet** ['bæleɪ] балéт
**balloon** [bə'luːn] воздýшный шар, аэростáт
**ballot** ['bælət] **1.** голосовáние; **2.** [про]голосовáть; ~ **box** избирáтельная ýрна; ~ **paper** избирáтельный бюллетéнь *m*
**ballpoint** → ***pen***
**ballroom** танцевáльный зал
**ballyhoo** [bælɪ'huː] шумúха
**balm** [bɑːm] бальзáм; *fig.* утешéние
**balmy** ['bɑːmɪ] □ аромáтный; успокóительный; *air* благоухáнный
**baloney** [bə'ləʊnɪ] *Am. sl.* вздор
**balsam** ['bɔːlsəm] бальзáм; *bot.* бальзамúн
**balustrade** [bælə'streɪd] балюстрáда
**bamboo** [bæm'buː] бамбýк
**bamboozle** *coll.* [bæm'buːzl] надý(вá)ть, обмáнывать [-нýть]
**ban** [bæn] **1.** запрéт; ***be under a ~*** быть под запрéтом; ***raise the ~*** снять запрéт; **2.** налагáть запрéт на (В)
**banana** [bə'nɑːnə] банáн
**band** [bænd] **1.** лéнта; *of robbers, etc.* шáйка, бáнда; грýппа, отря́д; *mus.* оркéстр; **2.**: ~ ***together*** объединя́ться [-нúться] (***against*** прóтив Р)
**bandage** ['bændɪdʒ] **1.** бинт, повя́зка; **2.** [за]бинтовáть, перевя́зывать [-зáть]
**bandit** ['bændɪt] бандúт
**bandmaster** ['bændmɑːstə] капельмéйстер
**bandy** ['bændɪ] обмéниваться [-ня́ться] (*словами, мячом и т.п.*) *coll.* перебрáниваться
**bane** [beɪn] *fig.* погúбель, бедá; прокля́тие
**bang** [bæŋ] **1.** удáр, стук; **2.** (*hit*) ударя́ть(ся) [удáрить(ся)]; стучáть; *once* [стýкнуть(ся)]; *door* хлóпать, *once* [-пнуть]
**banish** ['bænɪʃ] *from country* высылáть [вы́слать]; *from one's mind* гнать
**banisters** ['bænɪstəz] *pl.* перúла *n/pl.*
**bank**[1] [bæŋk] бéрег
**bank**[2] [~] **1.** банк; ~ ***of issue*** эмиссиóнный банк; **2.** *fin.* класть (дéньги) в банк; *v/i.* ~ ***on*** полагáться [-ложúться] на (В); ~ ***account*** счёт в бáнке; **~er** ['bæŋkə] банкúр; **~ing** ['bæŋ-kɪŋ] бáнковое дéло; ~ ***rate*** учётная стáвка; **~rupt** ['bæŋkrʌpt] **1.** банкрóт; **2.** обанкрóтившийся; неплатёжеспосóбный; **3.** дéлать банкрóтом; **~ruptcy** ['bæŋkrʌptsɪ] банкрóтство
**banner** ['bænə] знáмя *n*, *poet.* стяг, флаг
**banquet** ['bæŋkwɪt] пир; *formal* банкéт
**banter** ['bæntə] подшýчивать [-утúть], поддрáзнивать [-нúть]
**baptism** ['bæptɪzəm] крещéние
**Baptist** ['bæptɪst] баптúст
**baptize** [bæp'taɪz] [о]крестúть
**bar** [bɑː] **1.** брусóк, *of chocolate* плúтка; *across door* засóв; (*bank*) óтмель *f*; *in pub* бар; *mus.* такт; *fig.* преграда, препя́тствие; *law* адвокатýра; **2.** запирáть на засóв; (*obstruct*) преграждáть [-радúть]; (*exclude*) исключáть [-чúть]
**barbed** [bɑːbd]: ~ ***wire*** колю́чая прóволока
**barbar|ian** [bɑː'beərɪən] **1.** вáрвар; **2.** вáрварский; **~ous** ['bɑːbərəs] □ дúкий; (*cruel*) жестóкий
**barbecue** ['bɑːbɪkjuː] гриль для жáрки мя́са на откры́том вóздухе
**barber** ['bɑːbə] (мужскóй) парикмáхер; **~shop** парикмáхерская
**bare** [beə] **1.** гóлый, обнажённый; (*empty*) пустóй; ***the ~ thought*** дáже мысль (о П); **2.** обнажáть [-жúть], откры́(вá)ть; **~faced** ['beəfeɪst] бесстыдный; **~foot** босикóм; **~footed** босóй; **~headed** с непокры́той головóй; **~ly** ['beəlɪ] едвá, éле-éле
**bargain** ['bɑːgɪn] **1.** сдéлка; (*sth. bought*) вы́годная покýпка; ***into the ~*** в придáчу; **2.** [по]торговáться (о

П, с Т)

**barge** [bɑːdʒ] **1.** ба́ржа; **2.**: (**~ *into***) *coll.* ната́лкиваться [-толкну́ться]; влеза́ть [влезть]; **~ *in*** вва́ливаться [-и́ться]

**bark**[1] [bɑːk] **1.** кора́; **2.** *strip* сдира́ть кору́ с (Р)

**bark**[2] [~] **1.** *of dog* лай; **2.** [за]ла́ять

**barley** ['bɑːlɪ] ячме́нь *m*

**bar|maid** ['bɑːmeɪd] официа́нтка в ба́ре; **~man** [~mən] ба́рмен

**barn** [bɑːn] амба́р, сара́й

**baron** ['bærən] баро́н; **~ess** [~ɪs] баро́несса

**baroque** [bə'rɒk, bə'rəʊk] **1.** баро́чный; **2.** баро́кко *n indecl.*

**barrack(s** *pl.*) ['bærək(s)] бара́к; каза́рма

**barrel** ['bærəl] (*cask*) бо́чка, (*keg*) бочо́нок; *of gun* ствол

**barren** ['bærən] □ неплодоро́дный, беспло́дный

**barricade** [bærɪ'keɪd] **1.** баррика́да; **2.** [за]баррикади́ровать

**barrier** ['bærɪə] барье́р; *rail.* шлагба́ум; *fig.* препя́тствие, поме́ха

**barring** ['bɑːrɪŋ] *prp.* кро́ме; за исключе́нием

**barrister** ['bærɪstə] адвока́т

**barrow** ['bærəʊ] та́чка; ручна́я теле́жка

**barter** ['bɑːtə] **1.** ба́ртер, обме́н; ба́ртерная сде́лка; **2.** [по]меня́ть, обме́нивать [-ня́ть] (***for*** на В)

**base**[1] [beɪs] □ по́длый, ни́зкий

**base**[2] [~] **1.** осно́ва, ба́зис, фунда́мент; **2.** осно́вывать [-ова́ть] (В на П), бази́ровать

**base|ball** ['beɪsbɔːl] бейсбо́л; **~less** [~lɪs] необосно́ванный; **~ment** [~mənt] подва́л, подва́льный эта́ж

**bashful** ['bæʃfəl] □ засте́нчивый, ро́бкий

**basic** ['beɪsɪk] основно́й; ***~ally*** в основно́м

**basin** [beɪsn] таз, ми́ска; (*sink*) ра́ковина; *geogr.* бассе́йн

**bas|is** ['beɪsɪs], *pl.* **~es** [~iːz] основа́ние, осно́ва

**bask** [bɑːsk]: **~ *in the sun*** гре́ться на со́лнце

**basket** ['bɑːskɪt] корзи́на; **~ball** баскетбо́л

**bass** [beɪs] *mus.* **1.** бас; **2.** басо́вый

**bassoon** [bə'suːn] фаго́т

**bastard** ['bæstəd] внебра́чный ребёнок

**baste** [beɪst] *sew.* смётывать [смета́ть]

**bat**[1] [bæt] *zo.* лету́чая мышь

**bat**[2] [~] **1.** *at games* бита́ (в крике́те); **2.** бить, ударя́ть в мяч

**bat**[3] [~]: ***without ~ting an eyelid*** и гла́зом не моргну́в

**batch** [bætʃ] па́ртия; *of letters, etc.* па́чка

**bath** [bɑːθ] **1.** ва́нна; **2.** [вы́-, по]мы́ть, [вы́]купа́ть

**bathe** [beɪð] [вы́]купа́ться

**bathing** ['beɪðɪŋ] купа́ние

**bath|robe** ['bɑːθrəʊb] (купа́льный) хала́т; **~room** ва́нная (ко́мната); **~ towel** купа́льное полоте́нце

**batiste** [bæ'tiːst] бати́ст

**baton** ['bætən] *mus.* дирижёрская па́лочка

**battalion** [bə'tæljən] батальо́н

**batter** ['bætə] **1.** взби́тое те́сто; **2.** си́льно бить, [по]колоти́ть, изби́ть *pf.*; **~ *down*** взла́мывать [взлома́ть]; **~y** [~rɪ] батаре́я; *mot.* аккумуля́тор; *for clock, etc.* батаре́йка

**battle** ['bætl] **1.** би́тва, сраже́ние (***of*** под Т); **2.** сража́ться [срази́ться]; боро́ться

**battle|field** поле сраже́ния; **~ship** лине́йный кора́бль, линко́р

**bawdy** ['bɔːdɪ] непристо́йный

**bawl** [bɔːl] крича́ть [кри́кнуть], [за]ора́ть; **~ *out*** выкри́кивать [вы́крикнуть]

**bay**[1] [beɪ] зали́в, бу́хта

**bay**[2] [~] лавро́вое де́рево

**bay**[3] [~] **1.** (*bark*) лай; **2.** [за]ла́ять; ***bring to ~*** *fig.* припере́ть *pf.* к стене́; ***keep at ~*** не подпуска́ть [-сти́ть]

**bayonet** ['beɪənɪt] *mil.* штык

**bay window** [beɪ'wɪndəʊ] *arch.* э́ркер

**bazaar** [bə'zɑː] база́р

**be** [biː, bɪ] [*irr.*]: **a**) быть, быва́ть; (*be*

*situated*) находи́ться; *of position* лежа́ть, стоя́ть; ***there is, are*** есть; **~ *about to*** соб(и)ра́ться (+ *inf*.); **~ *away*** отсу́тствовать; **~ *at s.th.*** де́лать, быть за́нятым (Т); **~ *off*** уходи́ть [уйти́], отправля́ться [-а́виться]; **~ *on*** идти́ *of a film, etc*.; **~ *going on*** происходи́ть; ***how are you?*** как вы пожива́ете?, как вы себя́ чу́вствуете? **b**) *v/aux*. (*для образования длительной формы*) **~ *reading*** чита́ть; **c**) *v/aux*. (*для образования пассива*): **~ *read*** чита́ться, быть чи́танным (чита́емым)

**beach** [biːtʃ] **1.** пляж, взмо́рье; **2.** (*pull ashore*) вы́тащить *pf*. на бе́рег

**beacon** [ˈbiːkən] сигна́льный ого́нь; мая́к; ба́кен

**bead** [biːd] бу́сина, би́серина; *of sweat* ка́пля

**beads** [biːdz] *pl*. бу́сы *f/pl*.

**beak** [biːk] клюв

**beam** [biːm] **1.** ба́лка, брус; (*ray*) луч; **2.** сия́ть; излуча́ть [-чи́ть]

**bean** [biːn] боб; ***full of ~s*** экспанси́вный, живо́й; ***spill the ~s*** проболта́ться *pf*.

**bear**[1] [beə] медве́дь *m* (-ве́дица *f*)

**bear**[2] [~] [*irr*.] *v/t*. носи́ть, нести́; (*endure*) [вы́]терпе́ть, выде́рживать [вы́держать]; (*give birth*) рожда́ть [роди́ть]; **~ *down*** преодоле́(ва́)ть; **~ *out*** подтвержда́ть [-рди́ть]; **~ *o.s.*** держа́ться, вести́ себя́; **~ *up*** подде́рживать [-жа́ть]; **~ (*up*)*on*** каса́ться [косну́ться] (Р); име́ть отноше́ние (к Д); ***bring to ~*** употребля́ть [-би́ть]

**beard** [bɪəd] борода́; **~ed** [~ɪd] борода́тый

**bearer** [ˈbeərə] челове́к, несу́щий груз; *in expedition, etc*. носи́льщик; *of letter* предъяви́тель(ница *f*) *m*

**bearing** [ˈbeərɪŋ] (*way of behaving*) мане́ра держа́ть себя́; (*relation*) отноше́ние; ***beyond*** (***all***) **~** невыноси́мо; ***find one's ~s*** [с]ориенти́роваться (*a*. *fig*.); ***lose one's ~s*** заблуди́ться, *fig*. растеря́ться

**beast** [biːst] зверь *m*; скоти́на; **~ly** [~lɪ] *coll*. ужа́сный

**beat** [biːt] **1.** [*irr*.] *v/t*. [по]би́ть; (*one blow*) ударя́ть [уда́рить]; **~ *a retreat*** отступа́ть [-пи́ть]; **~ *up*** изби́(ва́)ть; *eggs, etc*. взби(ва́)ть; **~ *about the bush*** ходи́ть вокру́г да о́коло; *v/i*. *drums* бить; *heart* би́ться; *on door* колоти́ть; **2.** уда́р; бой; бие́ние; ритм; **~en** [ˈbiːtn] **1.** *p. pt*. от ***beat***; **2.** би́тый, побеждённый; *track* проторённый

**beautician** [bjuːˈtɪʃn] космето́лог

**beautiful** [ˈbjuːtɪfl] □ краси́вый, прекра́сный, *day, etc*. чу́дный

**beautify** [ˈbjuːtɪfaɪ] украша́ть [укра́сить]

**beauty** [ˈbjuːtɪ] красота́, краса́вица; **~ *parlo*(*u*)*r***, *Brt*. **~ *salon*** космети́ческий кабине́т

**beaver** [ˈbiːvə] бобр

**became** [bɪˈkeɪm] *pt*. от ***become***

**because** [bɪˈkɒz] потому́ что, так как; **~ *of*** из-за (Р)

**beckon** [ˈbekən] [по]мани́ть

**becom|e** [bɪˈkʌm] [*irr*. (***come***)] *v/i*. [с]де́латься; станови́ться [стать]; *of clothes v/t*. быть к лицу́, идти́ (Д); подоба́ть (Д); **~ing** [~ɪŋ] □ подоба́ющий; *of dress, etc*. (иду́щий) к лицу́

**bed** [bed] **1.** посте́ль *f*; крова́ть *f*; *agric*. гря́дка, клу́мба; *of river* ру́сло; **2.** (*plant*) выса́живать [вы́садить]

**bedclothes** *pl*. посте́льное бельё

**bedding** [ˈbedɪŋ] посте́льные принадле́жности *f/pl*.

**bed|ridden** [ˈbedrɪdn] прико́ванный к посте́ли; **~room** спа́льня; **~spread** покрыва́ло; **~time** вре́мя ложи́ться спать

**bee** [biː] пчела́; ***have a ~ in one's bonnet*** *coll*. быть поме́шанным на чём-л.

**beech** [biːtʃ] бук, бу́ковое де́рево

**beef** [biːf] говя́дина; **~steak** бифште́кс; **~ tea** кре́пкий бульо́н; **~y** [biːfɪ] му́скулистый

**bee|hive** у́лей; **~keeping** пчелово́дство; **~line**: ***make a ~*** пойти́ напрями́к, стрело́й помча́ться

**been** [biːn, bɪn] *pt. p*. от ***be***

**beer** [bɪə] пи́во; ***small ~*** сла́бое пи́во, *fig*. ме́лкая со́шка

**beet** [biːt] свёкла (*chiefly Brt.*: *beetroot*)
**beetle** [biːtl] жук
**before** [bɪ'fɔː] **1.** *adv.* впереди́, вперёд; ра́ньше; **~ long** вско́ре; **long ~** задо́лго; **2.** *cj.* пре́жде чем; пока не; перед тем как; скоре́е чем; **3.** *prp.* пе́ред (Т); впереди́ (Р); до (Р); **~hand** зара́нее, заблаговре́менно
**befriend** [bɪ'frend] относи́ться подру́жески к (Д)
**beg** [beg] *v.t.* [по]проси́ть (Р); умоля́ть [-ли́ть] (**for** о П); выпра́шивать [вы́просить] (*of* у Р); *v/i.* ни́щенствовать
**began** [bɪ'gæn] *pt. om* **begin**
**beggar** ['begə] **1.** ни́щий, ни́щенка; **lucky ~** счастли́вчик; **poor ~** бедня́га; **2.** разоря́ть [-ри́ть], доводи́ть [-вести́] до нищеты́; **it ~s all description** не поддаётся описа́нию
**begin** [bɪ'gɪn] [*irr.*] нач(ин)а́ть (**with** с Р); **to ~ with** во-пе́рвых; снача́ла, для нача́ла; **~ner** [~ə] начина́ющий, новичо́к; **~ning** [~ɪŋ] нача́ло; **in** *or* **at the ~** внача́ле
**begrudge** [bɪ'grʌdʒ] (*envy*) [по]зави́довать (Д в П); жале́ть, скупи́ться
**begun** [bɪ'gʌn] *p. pt. om* **begin**
**behalf** [bɪ'hɑːf]: **on** *or* **in ~ of** для (Р), ра́ди (Р); от и́мени (Р)
**behav|e** [bɪ'heɪv] вести́ себя́; держа́ться; поступа́ть [-пи́ть]; **~iour** [~jə] поведе́ние
**behind** [bɪ'haɪnd] **1.** *adv.* позади́, сза́ди; **look ~** огляну́ться *pf.*; **be ~ s.o.** отстава́ть [-ста́ть] от кого́-л. (**in** в П); **2.** *prp.* за (Т); позади́ (Р), сза́ди (Р); по́сле (Р)
**beige** [beɪʒ] бе́жевый
**being** ['biːɪŋ] бытие́, существова́ние; (*creature*) живо́е существо́; **for the time ~** в настоя́щее вре́мя; на не́которое вре́мя, пока́
**belated** [bɪ'leɪtɪd] запозда́лый
**belch** [beltʃ] **1.** отры́жка; **2.** рыга́ть [рыгну́ть]
**belfry** ['belfrɪ] колоко́льня
**Belgian** ['beldʒən] **1.** бельги́ец *m*, -и́йка *f*; **2.** бельги́йский
**belief** [bɪ'liːf] ве́ра (**in** в В); убежде́ние; **beyond ~** (про́сто) невероя́тно; **to the best of my ~** по моему́ убежде́нию; наско́лько мне изве́стно
**believe** [bɪ'liːv] [по]ве́рить (**in** в В); **~r** [~ə] ве́рующий
**belittle** [bɪ'lɪtl] *fig.* умаля́ть [-ли́ть]; принижа́ть [-ни́зить]
**bell** [bel] ко́локол; звоно́к
**belles-lettres** [bel'letrə] *pl.* худо́жественная литерату́ра, беллетри́стика
**bellicose** ['belɪkəʊs] □ во́инственный, агресси́вный
**belligerent** [bɪ'lɪdʒərənt] **1.** вою́ющая сторона́; **2.** вою́ющий
**bellow** ['beləʊ] **1.** *of animal* мыча́ние; *of wind, storm* рёв; **2.** реве́ть; ора́ть
**belly** ['belɪ] **1.** живо́т, *coll.* брю́хо; **2.** наду́(ва́)ть(ся); **~ful** [~fʊl]: **have had a ~** *coll., fig.* быть сы́тым по го́рло (**of** Т)
**belong** [bɪ'lɒŋ] принадлежа́ть (Д); относи́ться (к Д); **~ings** [~ɪŋz] *pl.* ве́щи *f/pl.*, пожи́тки
**beloved** [bɪ'lʌvɪd, *pred.* bɪ'lʌvd] возлю́бленный, люби́мый
**below** [bɪ'ləʊ] **1.** *adv.* внизу́; ни́же; **2.** *prp.* ни́же (Р); под (В, Т)
**belt** [belt] **1.** по́яс, *of leather* реме́нь; зо́на; *tech.* приводно́й реме́нь; *mil.* портупе́я; **safety ~** *mot.* реме́нь безопа́сности; *ae.* привязно́й реме́нь; **2.** подпоя́с(ыв)ать; (*thrash*) поро́ть ремнём
**bemoan** [bɪ'məʊn] опла́к(ив)ать
**bench** [bentʃ] скамья́; (*work~*) верста́к
**bend** [bend] **1.** сгиб, изги́б; *of road* поворо́т, изги́б; *of river* излу́чина; **2.** [*irr.*] *v/t.* [по-, со]гну́ть; *head, etc.* наклоня́ть [-ни́ть]; *v/i.* наклоня́ться [-ни́ться]; сгиба́ться [согну́ться]
**beneath** [bɪ'niːθ] → **below**
**benediction** [benɪ'dɪkʃn] благослове́ние
**benefactor** ['benɪfæktə] благоде́тель; (*donor*) благотвори́тель
**beneficial** [benɪ'fɪʃl] □ благотво́рный, поле́зный
**benefit** ['benɪfɪt] **1.** вы́года, по́льза; (*allowance*) посо́бие; *thea.* бенефи́с; **2.** приноси́ть по́льзу; извлека́ть по́льзу

**benevolen|ce** [bɪ'nevələns] благожела́тельность *f*; **~t** [~ənt] □ благожела́тельный
**benign** [bɪ'naɪn] □ добросерде́чный; *climate* благотво́рный; *med.* доброка́чественный
**bent** [bent] **1.** *pt. и p. pt. от* ***bend***; ***~ on*** поме́шанный на (П); **2.** скло́нность *f*, спосо́бность *f*; ***follow one's ~*** сле́довать свои́м накло́нностям
**bequeath** [bɪ'kwi:ð] завеща́ть *(im)pf.*
**bequest** [bɪ'kwest] насле́дство
**bereave** [bɪ'ri:v] [*irr.*] лиша́ть [-ши́ть] (Р); отнима́ть [-ня́ть]
**beret** ['bereɪ] бере́т
**berry** ['beri] я́года
**berth** [bɜ:θ] *naut.* я́корная стоя́нка; (*cabin*) каю́та; (*sleeping place*) ко́йка; *rail.* спа́льное ме́сто, по́лка; *fig.* (вы́годная) до́лжность
**beseech** [bɪ'si:tʃ] [*irr.*] умоля́ть [-ли́ть], упра́шивать [упроси́ть] (+ *inf.*)
**beset** [bɪ'set] [*irr.* (***set***)] окружа́ть [-жи́ть]; *with questions, etc.* осажда́ть [осади́ть]; ***I was ~ by doubts*** меня́ одолева́ли сомне́ния
**beside** [bɪ'saɪd] *prp.* ря́дом с (Т), о́коло (Р), близ (Р); ми́мо ***~ o.s.*** вне себя́ (***with*** от Р); ***~ the point*** не по существу́; не отно́сится к де́лу; **~s** [~z] **1.** *adv.* кро́ме того́, сверх того́; **2.** *prp.* кро́ме (Р)
**besiege** [bɪ'si:dʒ] осажда́ть [осади́ть]
**besought** [bɪ'sɔ:t] *pt. от* ***beseech***
**bespatter** [bɪ'spætə] забры́зг(ив)ать
**best** [best] **1.** *adj.* лу́чший; ***~ man*** *at a wedding* ша́фер; ***the ~ part*** бо́льшая часть; **2.** *adv.* лу́чше всего́, всех; **3.** са́мое лу́чшее; ***to the ~ of …*** наско́лько …; ***make the ~ of*** испо́льзовать наилу́чшим о́бразом; ***at ~*** в лу́чшем слу́чае; ***all the ~!*** всего́ са́мого лу́чшего!
**bestial** ['bestɪəl, 'bestʃəl] □ (*behaviour*) ско́тский; *cruelty, etc.* зве́рский
**bestow** [bɪ'stəʊ] ода́ривать [-ри́ть]; награжда́ть [-ради́ть] (В/Т); *title* присва́ивать [-во́ить]
**bet** [bet] **1.** пари́ *n indecl.*; **2.** [*irr.*] держа́ть пари́; би́ться об закла́д; ***~ on horses*** игра́ть на ска́чках
**betray** [bɪ'treɪ] преда́(ва́)ть; (*show*) вы́да(ва́)ть; **~al** [~əl] преда́тельство; **~er** [~ə] преда́тель *m*, -ница *f*
**betrothal** [bɪ'trəʊðl] помо́лвка
**better** ['betə] **1.** *adj.* лу́чший; ***he is ~*** ему́ лу́чше; **2.**: ***change for the ~*** переме́на к лу́чшему; ***get the ~ of*** взять верх над (Т); [пре]одоле́ть; **3.** *adv.* лу́чше; бо́льше; ***so much the ~*** тем лу́чше; ***you had ~ go*** вам бы лу́чше уйти́; ***think ~ of it*** переду́мать *pf.*; **4.** *v/t.* улучша́ть [улу́чшить]
**between** [bɪ'twi:n] **1.** *adv.* ме́жду; **2.** *prp.* ме́жду (Т); ***~ you and me*** ме́жду на́ми (говоря́)
**beverage** ['bevərɪdʒ] напи́ток
**beware** [bɪ'weə] бере́чься, остерега́ться (Р) *impf.*; ***~ of the dog!*** осторо́жно, зла́я соба́ка!
**bewilder** [bɪ'wɪldə] смуща́ть [смути́ть]; ста́вить в тупи́к; (*confuse*) сбива́ть с то́лку; **~ment** [~mənt] смуще́ние, замеша́тельство; пу́таница
**bewitch** [bɪ'wɪtʃ] околдо́вывать [-дова́ть], очаро́вывать [-рова́ть]
**beyond** [bɪ'jɒnd] **1.** *adv.* вдали́, на расстоя́нии; ***this is ~ me*** э́то вы́ше моего́ понима́ния; **2.** *prp.* за (В, Т); вне (Р); сверх (Р); по ту сто́рону (Р)
**bias** ['baɪəs] **1.** (*prejudice*) предубежде́ние (про́тив Р); (*tendency of mind*) скло́нность *f*; **2.** склоня́ть [-ни́ть]; ***~ed opinion*** предвзя́тое мне́ние
**bib** [bɪb] де́тский нагру́дник
**Bible** [baɪbl] Би́блия
**biblical** ['bɪblɪkəl] □ библе́йский
**bicarbonate** [baɪ'kɑ:bənət]: ***~ of soda*** питьева́я со́да
**bicker** ['bɪkə] препира́ться (с Т)
**bicycle** ['baɪsɪkl] **1.** велосипе́д; **2.** е́здить на велосипе́де
**bid** [bɪd] **1.** [*irr.*] *price* предлага́ть [-ложи́ть]; **2.** предложе́ние, (*at sale*) зая́вка; ***final ~*** оконча́тельная цена́; **~den** [bɪdn] *p. pt. от* ***bid***
**biennial** [baɪ'enɪəl] двухле́тний
**bifocal** [baɪ'fəʊkl] бифока́льный
**big** [bɪg] большо́й, кру́пный; (*tall*) вы-

со́кий; *of clothes* вели́к; *coll. fig.* ва́жный; *coll. fig.* **~ shot** ши́шка; **talk ~** [по]хва́статься
**bigamy** ['bigəmɪ] двоебра́чие
**bigot** ['bɪgət] слепо́й приве́рженец, фана́тик
**bigwig** ['bɪgwɪg] *coll.* ши́шка
**bike** [baɪk] *coll.* велосипе́д
**bilateral** [baɪ'lætərəl] двусторо́нний
**bilberry** ['bɪlbəri] черни́ка
**bile** [baɪl] жёлчь *f*; *fig.* жёлчность *f*
**bilious** ['bɪlɪəs]: **~ attack** при́ступ тошноты́; рво́та
**bill**[1] [bɪl] *of a bird* клюв
**bill**[2] [~] законопрое́кт, билль *m*; счёт; (*poster*) афи́ша; *fin.* ве́ксель *m*; **~ of credit** аккредити́в; **~ of fare** меню́; **that will fill the ~** э́то подойдёт; **foot the ~** оплати́ть счёт *pf.*
**billiards** ['bɪljədz] *pl.* билья́рд
**billion** ['bɪljən] биллио́н; *Am.* миллиа́рд
**billow** ['bɪləʊ] **1.** вал, больша́я волна́; **2.** *of sea* вздыма́ться; *sails* надува́ть [-ду́ть]
**bin** [bɪn]: **rubbish ~** му́сорное ведро́
**bind** [baɪnd] *v/t.* [с]вяза́ть; свя́зывать [-за́ть]; (*oblige*) обя́зывать [-за́ть]; *book* переплета́ть [-плести́]; **~er** ['baɪndə] переплётчик; **~ing** [~ɪŋ] (*book cover*) переплёт
**binoculars** [bɪ'nɒkjʊləz] бино́кль *m*
**biography** [baɪ'ɒgrəfɪ] биогра́фия
**biology** [baɪ'ɒlədʒɪ] биоло́гия
**biosphere** ['bɑɪəsfɪə] биосфе́ра
**birch** [bɜːtʃ] (**~ tree**) берёза
**bird** [bɜːd] пти́ца; **early ~** ра́нняя пта́шка (*о челове́ке*); **~'s-eye** ['bɜːdzaɪ]: **~ view** вид с пти́чьего полёта
**Biro** ['baɪərəʊ] *Brt. trademark* ша́риковая ру́чка
**birth** [bɜːθ] рожде́ние; (*origin*) происхожде́ние; **give ~** рожда́ть [роди́ть]; **~day** день рожде́ния; **~place** ме́сто рожде́ния; **~rate** рожда́емость *f*
**biscuit** ['bɪskɪt] пече́нье
**bishop** ['bɪʃəp] *eccl.* епи́скоп; *chess* слон; **~ric** [~rɪk] епа́рхия
**bison** ['baɪsn] *zo.* бизо́н, зубр
**bit**[1] [bɪt] кусо́чек, части́ца; немно́го
**bit**[2] [~] *comput.* бит, двои́чная ци́фра
**bit**[3] [~] *pt. от* **~e**
**bitch** [bɪtʃ] су́ка
**bit|e** [baɪt] **1.** уку́с; *of fish* клёв; кусо́к; **have a ~** перекуси́ть *pf.*; **2.** [*irr.*] куса́ть [укуси́ть]; клева́ть [клю́нуть]; *of pepper, etc.* жечь; *of frost* щипа́ть; **~ing** *wind* прони́зывающий; *remark, etc.* язви́тельный
**bitten** ['bɪtn] *p. pt. от* **bite**
**bitter** ['bɪtə] □ го́рький, ре́зкий; *fig.* го́рький, мучи́тельный; *struggle, person* ожесточённый
**blab** [blæb] *coll.* разба́лтывать [-болта́ть]
**black** [blæk] **1.** чёрный; тёмный, мра́чный; **~ eye** синя́к под гла́зом; **in ~ and white** чёрным по бе́лому; **give s.o. a ~ look** мра́чно посмотре́ть на (B); **2.** *fig.* очерни́ть; **~ out** потеря́ть созна́ние; **3.** чёрный цвет; (*Negro*) чернoко́жий; **~berry** ежеви́ка; **~bird** чёрный дрозд; **~board** кла́ссная доска́; **~en** ['blækn] *v/t.* [за]черни́ть; *fig.* [о]черни́ть; *v/i.* [по]черне́ть; **~guard** ['blægɑːd] негодя́й, подле́ц; **~head** *med.* угри́ *m/pl.*; **~-letter day** несчастли́вый день; **~mail 1.** вымога́тельство, шанта́ж; **2.** вымога́ть (*pf.*) де́ньги у (P); **~out** затемне́ние; *med.* поте́ря созна́ния; **~smith** кузне́ц
**bladder** ['blædə] *anat.* пузы́рь *m*
**blade** [bleɪd] ло́пасть *f*; *of knife* ле́звие; **~ of grass** трави́нка
**blame** [bleɪm] **1.** вина́; **2.** вини́ть, обвиня́ть [-ни́ть]; **he has only himself to ~** он сам во всем винова́т; **~less** ['bleɪmləs] безупре́чный
**blanch** [blɑːntʃ] (*grow pale*) побледне́ть *pf.*; *cul.* бланши́ровать
**blank** [blæŋk] **1.** □ (*empty*) пусто́й; (*expressionless*) невырази́тельный; *of form, etc.* незапо́лненный; **~ cartridge** холосто́й патро́н; **2.** (*empty space*) пробе́л; **my mind was a ~** у меня́ в голове́ не́ было ни одно́й мы́сли
**blanket** [blæŋkɪt] шерстяно́е одея́ло; *fig.* покро́в
**blare** [bleə] *radio* труби́ть, реве́ть

**blasphemy** ['blæsfəmɪ] богохýльство

**blast** [blɑːst] **1.** сúльный порыв вéтра; *of explosion* взрыв; ***at full ~*** на пóлную мóщность; **2.** взрывáть [взорвáть]; *mus.* трубúть; **~ed** [-ɪd] *coll.* проклятый; **~ furnace** дóменная печь *f*

**blatant** ['bleɪtənt] нáглый, вопиющий

**blaze** [bleɪz] **1.** плáмя *n*; *of flame, passion* вспышка; **2.** *v/i.* горéть; пылáть (*a. fig.*); сверкáть [-кнýть]; **~r** ['bleɪzə] спортúвная кýртка

**bleach** [bliːtʃ] белúть

**bleak** [bliːk] унылый, безрáдостный; *prospects etc.* мрáчный

**bleary** ['blɪərɪ] затумáненный, неясный; **~-eyed** ['blɪərɪaɪd] с мýтными глазáми

**bleat** [bliːt] **1.** блéяние; **2.** [за]блéять

**bled** [bled] *pt. и pt. p. от* ***bleed***

**bleed** [bliːd] [*irr.*] *v/i.* кровотóчить; истекáть [-тéчь] крóвью; **~ing** ['bliːdɪŋ] кровотечéние

**blemish** ['blemɪʃ] недостáток; пятнó (*a. fig.*)

**blend** [blend] **1.** смéшивать(ся) [-шáть(ся)]; (*harmonize*) сочетáть(ся) (*im*)*pf.*; **2.** смесь *f*

**bless** [bles] благословлять [-вúть]; одарять [-рúть]; **~ed** ['blesɪd] *adj.* счастлúвый, блажéнный; **~ing** ['blesɪŋ] *eccl.* благословéние; блáго, счáстье

**blew** [bluː] *pt. от* ***blow***

**blight** [blaɪt] **1.** *disease* головня; ржáвчина; мучнúстая росá *и т.д.*; то, что разрушáет (*планы*), отравляет (*жизнь и т.д.*); **2.** *hopes, etc.* разбú(вá)ть

**blind** [blaɪnd] **1.** □ слепóй (*fig.* ***~ to*** к Д); *handwriting* нечёткий, неясный; ***~ alley*** тупúк; ***turn a ~ eye*** закрывáть [закрыть] глазá (***to*** на В); **~ly** *fig.* наугáд, наобýм; **2.** штóра; жалюзú *n indecl.*; **3.** ослеплять [-пúть]; **~fold** ['blaɪndfəʊld] завязывать глазá (Д); **~ness** слепотá

**blink** [blɪŋk] **1.** (*of eye*) моргáние, *of light* мерцáние; **2.** *v/i.* моргáть [-гнýть]; мигáть [мигнýть]

**bliss** [blɪs] блажéнство

**blister** ['blɪstə] **1.** волдырь *m*; **2.** покрывáться волдырями

**blizzard** ['blɪzəd] бурáн, сúльная метéль *f*

**bloat** [bləʊt] распухáть [-пýхнуть]; раздý(вá)ться

**block** [blɒk] **1.** *of wood* колóда, чурбáн; *of stone, etc.* глыба; *between streets* квартáл; ***~ of apartments*** (*Brt.* ***flats***) многоэтáжный дом; **2.** (*obstruct*) преграждáть [-адúть]; ***~ in*** набрáсывать вчернé; (*mst.* ***~ up***) блокúровать (*im*)*pf*; *of pipe* засоряться [-рúться]

**blockade** [blɒ'keɪd] **1.** блокáда; **2.** блокúровать (*im*)*pf.*

**blockhead** ['blɒkhed] болвáн

**blond(e)** [blɒnd] блондúн *m*, -ка *f*; белокýрый

**blood** [blʌd] кровь *f*; ***in cold ~*** хладнокрóвно; **~shed** кровопролúтие; **~thirsty** кровожáдный; **~ vessel** кровенóсный сосýд; **~y** ['blʌdɪ] окровáвленный, кровáвый

**bloom** [bluːm] **1.** цветóк, цветéние; *fig.* расцвéт; ***in ~*** в цветý; **2.** цвестú, быть в цветý

**blossom** ['blɒsəm] **1.** цветóк (фруктóвого дéрева); **2.** цвестú, расцветáть [-естú]

**blot** [blɒt, blɑːt] **1.** пятнó (*a. fig.*); **2.** *fig.* запятнáть *pf.*

**blotch** [blɒtʃ] клякса, пятнó

**blouse** [blaʊz] блýза, блýзка

**blow**[1] [bləʊ] удáр (*a. fig.*)

**blow**[2] [~] [*irr.*] **1.** [по]дýть; ***~ up*** взрывáть(ся) [взорвáть(ся)]; ***~ one's nose*** [вы]сморкáться; **2.** дуновéние; **~n** [~n] *pt. p. от* ***blow***

**blue** [bluː] **1.** голубóй; лазýрный; (*dark ~*) сúний; *coll.* (*be sad, depressed*) унылый, подáвленный; **2.** голубóй цвет; сúний цвет; **3.** окрáшивать в сúний, голубóй цвет; *of washing* [под]сúнúть; **~bell** колокóльчик

**blues** [bluːz] *pl.* меланхóлия, хандрá

**bluff**[1] [blʌf] (*abrupt*) рéзкий; (*rough*) грубовáтый; *of headlands, etc.* обрывистый

**bluff**[2] [~] **1.** обма́н, блеф; **2.** *v/t.* обма́нывать[-ну́ть]; *v/i.* блефова́ть

**blunder** ['blʌndə] **1.** гру́бая оши́бка; **2.** де́лать гру́бую оши́бку

**blunt** [blʌnt] **1.** □ тупо́й; *remark, etc.* ре́зкий; **2.** [за]тупи́ть; *fig.* притупля́ть [-пи́ть]

**blur** [blɜː] **1.** (*indistinct outline*) нея́сное очерта́ние; пятно́; **2.** *v/t.* сде́лать нея́сным *pf.*; сма́зывать [-зать]; *tears, etc.* затума́нить *pf.*

**blush** [blʌʃ] **1.** кра́ска от смуще́ния *или* стыда́; **2.** [по]красне́ть

**boar** [bɔː] бо́ров, *hunt.* каба́н

**board** [bɔːd] **1.** доска́; (*food*) стол; *of ship* борт; *thea.* сце́на, подмо́стки *m/pl.*; *council* правле́ние; ***~ of directors*** правле́ние директоро́в; **2.** *v/t.* наст(и)ла́ть; *v/i.* столова́ться; *train, plane, etc.* сади́ться [сесть] на, в (В); **~er** ['bɔːdər] жиле́ц, опла́чивающий ко́мнату и пита́ние; **~ing house** пансио́н; **~ing school** шко́ла-интерна́т

**boast** [bəʊst] **1.** хвастовство́; **2.** горди́ться (Т); (*of, about*) [по]хва́статься (Т); **~ful** ['bəʊstfəl] хвастли́вый

**boat** [bəʊt] *small* ло́дка, *vessel* су́дно; **~ing** ['bəʊtɪŋ] ката́ние на ло́дке подпры́гивать [-гнуть]

**bobbin** ['bɒbɪn] кату́шка; шпу́лька

**bode** [bəʊd]: (*portend*) ***~ well*** быть хоро́шим знако́м

**bodice** ['bɒdɪs] лиф

**bodily** ['bɒdɪlɪ] теле́сный, физи́ческий

**body** ['bɒdɪ, 'bɑːdɪ] те́ло; (*corpse*) труп; *mot.* ку́зов; **~ building** бо́дибилдинг, культури́зм

**bog** [bɒg] **1.** боло́то, тряси́на; **2.** ***get ~ged down*** увяза́ть [увя́знуть]

**boggle** ['bɒgl] отша́тываться [-тну́ться] отпря́нуть (*out of surprise, fear, or doubt*); ***the mind ~s*** уму́ непостижи́мо

**bogus** ['bəʊgəs] подде́льный

**boil**[1] [bɔɪl] *med.* фуру́нкул

**boil**[2] [~] **1.** кипе́ние; **2.** [с]вари́ть(ся); [вс]кипяти́ть(ся); кипе́ть; **~er** ['bɔɪlə] *tech.* котёл

**boisterous** ['bɔɪstərəs] □ бу́рный, шу́мный; *child* ре́звый

**bold** [bəʊld] □ (*daring*) сме́лый; *b.s.* на́глый; *typ.* жи́рный; **~ness** ['bəʊldnɪs] сме́лость *f*; на́глость *f*

**bolster** ['bəʊlstə] **1.** ва́лик; опо́ра; **2.** (*prop*) подде́рживать [-жа́ть]; подпира́ть [-пере́ть]

**bolt** [bəʊlt] **1.** болт; *on door* засо́в, задви́жка; (*thunder~*) уда́р гро́ма; ***a ~ from the blue*** гром среди́ я́сного не́ба; **2.** *v/t.* запира́ть на засо́в; *v/i.* нести́сь стрело́й; (*run away*) убега́ть [убежа́ть]

**bomb** [bɒm] **1.** бо́мба; **2.** бомби́ть

**bombard** [bɒm'bɑːd]: ***~ with questions*** бомбардирова́ть, забра́сывать [-роса́ть] вопро́сами

**bombastic** [bɒm'bæstɪk] напы́щенный

**bond** [bɒnd] *pl. fig.*: **~s** у́зы *f/pl.*; *fin.* облига́ции *f/pl.*

**bone** [bəʊn] **1.** кость *f*; ***~ of contention*** я́блоко раздо́ра; ***make no ~s about*** *coll.* не [по]стесня́ться; не церемо́ниться с (Т); **2.** вынима́ть, выреза́ть ко́сти

**bonfire** ['bɒnfaɪə] костёр

**bonnet** ['bɒnɪt] *baby's* че́пчик; *mot.* капо́т

**bonus** ['bəʊnəs] *fin.* пре́мия, вознагражде́ние

**bony** ['bəʊnɪ] костля́вый

**book** [bʊk] **1.** кни́га; **2.** (*tickets*) зака́зывать, заброни́ровать (*a. room in a hotel*); **~case** кни́жный шкаф; **~ing clerk** ['bʊkɪŋklɑːk] *rail.* касси́р; **~ing office** биле́тная ка́сса; **~keeping** бухгалте́рия; **~let** брошю́ра, букле́т; **~seller** продаве́ц книг; ***second-hand ~*** букини́ст

**boom**[1] [buːm] **1.** *econ.* бум; **2.** *of business* процвета́ть *impf.*

**boom**[2] [~] **1.** *of gun, thunder, etc.* гул; ро́кот; **2.** бу́хать, рокота́ть

**boon** [buːn] бла́го

**boor** [bʊə] гру́бый, невоспи́танный челове́к; **~ish** ['bʊərɪʃ] гру́бый, невоспи́танный

**boost** [buːst] *trade* стимули́ровать (разви́тие); *tech.* уси́ливать [-лить];

***it ~ed his morale*** э́то его́ подбодри́ло; (*advertise*) реклами́ровать

**boot**[1] [buːt]: ***to ~*** в прида́чу, вдоба́вок *adv.*

**boot**[2] [~] сапо́г, боти́нок; *mot.* бага́жник; **~lace** ['~leɪs] шнуро́к для боти́нок

**booth** [buːð] кио́ск; ***telephone ~*** телефо́нная бу́дка; ***polling ~*** каби́на для голосова́ния

**booty** ['buːtɪ] добы́ча

**border** ['bɔːdə] **1.** грани́ца; (*edge*) край; *on tablecloth, etc.* кайма́; **2.** грани́чить (***upon*** с Т)

**bore**[1] [bɔː] **1.** расто́ченное отве́рстие; *of gun* кали́бр; *fig.* зану́да; **2.** [про]сверли́ть; *fig.* надоеда́ть [-е́сть] (Д); наводи́ть ску́ку на (В)

**bore**[2] [~] *pt. от* ***bear***[2]

**boredom** ['bɔːdəm] ску́ка

**born** [bɔːn] рождённый; *fig.* прирождённый; **~e** [~] *pt. p. от* ***bear***[2]

**borough** ['bʌrə] (*town*) го́род; (*section of a town*) райо́н

**borrow** ['bɒrəʊ] *money* брать [взять] взаймы́; занима́ть [-ня́ть] (***from*** у Р); *book* взять почита́ть

**Bosnian** ['bɒznɪən] **1.** босни́ец *m*, -и́йка *f*; **2.** босни́йский

**bosom** ['bʊzəm] грудь *f*; *fig.* ло́но; ***~ friend*** закады́чный друг

**boss** [bɒs] *coll.* **1.** шеф, босс, нача́льник; **2.** кома́ндовать (Т); **~y** ['bɒsɪ] лю́бящий кома́ндовать

**botany** ['bɒtənɪ] бота́ника

**botch** [bɒtʃ] по́ртить; сде́лать *pf.* пло́хо и́ли ко́е-как

**both** [bəʊθ] о́ба, о́бе; и тот и друго́й; ***~ … and …*** как … так и …; и … и …

**bother** ['bɒðə] *coll.* **1.** беспоко́йство; ***oh ~!*** кака́я доса́да!; **2.** вози́ться; надоеда́ть [-е́сть] (Д); [по]беспоко́ить

**bottle** ['bɒtl] **1.** бу́тылка; *for scent* флако́н; ***baby's ~*** рожо́к; ***hotwater ~*** гре́лка; **2.** разлива́ть по бу́тылкам; **~opener** ключ, открыва́лка

**bottom** ['bɒtəm] **1.** дно; *of boat* дни́ще; ни́жняя часть *f*; *of hill* подно́жье; *coll.* зад; *fig.* осно́ва, суть *f*; ***at the ~*** внизу́; ***be at the ~ of sth.*** быть причи́ной и́ли зачи́нщиком (Р); ***get to the ~ of sth.*** добра́ться до су́ти (Р); **2.** са́мый ни́жний

**bough** [baʊ] сук; ве́тка, ветвь *f*

**bought** [bɔːt] *pt.* и *pt. p. от* ***buy***

**boulder** ['bəʊldə] валу́н

**bounce** [baʊns] **1.** прыжо́к, скачо́к; ***full of ~*** по́лный эне́ргии; **2.** подпры́гивать [-гнуть]; *of ball* отска́кивать [отскочи́ть]

**bound**[1] [baʊnd] **1.** грани́ца; преде́л (*a. fig.*); ограниче́ние; **2.** (*limit*) ограни́чивать; (*be the boundary of*) грани́чить (с Т)

**bound**[2] [~]: ***be ~*** направля́ться (***for*** в В)

**bound**[3] [~] **1.** прыжо́к, скачо́к; **2.** пры́гать [-гнуть], [по]скака́ть; (*run*) бежа́ть скачка́ми

**bound**[4] [~] **1.** *pt. и pt. p. от* ***bind***; **2.** свя́занный; (*obliged*) обя́занный; *of book* переплетённый

**boundary** ['baʊndərɪ] грани́ца; *between fields* межа́; *fig.* преде́л

**boundless** ['baʊndlɪs] безграни́чный

**bouquet** [bʊ'keɪ] буке́т (*a. of wine*)

**bout** [baʊt] *of illness* при́ступ; *in sports* встре́ча

**bow**[1] [baʊ] **1.** покло́н; **2.** *v/i.* [со]гну́ться; кла́няться [поклони́ться]; (*submit*) подчиня́ться [-ни́ться] (Д); *v/t.* [со]гну́ть

**bow**[2] [bəʊ] лук; (*curve*) дуга́; (*knot*) бант; *mus.* смычо́к

**bow**[3] [baʊ] *naut.* нос

**bowels** ['baʊəlz] *pl.* кишки́ *f/pl.*; *of the earth* не́дра *n/pl.*

**bowl**[1] [bəʊl] ми́ска; ва́за

**bowl**[2] [~] **1.** шар; *pl.* игра́ в шары́; **2.** *v/t.* [по]кати́ть; *v/i.* игра́ть в шары́; ***be ~ed over*** быть покорённым *или* ошеломлённым (***by*** Т)

**box**[1] [bɒks] **1.** коро́бка; я́щик; *thea.* ло́жа; **2.** укла́дывать в я́щик

**box**[2] [~] *sport* **1.** бокси́ровать; **2.** ***~ on the ear*** пощёчина; **~er** ['~ə] *sportsman, dog* боксёр; **~ing** ['~ɪŋ] *sport* бокс

**box office** театра́льная ка́сса

**boy** [bɔɪ] ма́льчик; ю́ноша; **~friend** ['~frend] друг (*девушки*); **~hood** ['~hʊd] о́трочество; **~ish** ['bɔɪɪʃ] □

мальчи́шеский
**brace** [breɪs] **1.** *tech.* коловоро́т, скоба́; **~ *and bit*** дрель; **2.** (*support*) подпира́ть [-пере́ть]; **~ *up*** подбодря́ть [-бодри́ть]; **~ *o.s.*** собра́ться с ду́хом
**bracelet** ['breɪslɪt] брасле́т
**braces** [breɪsɪz] *pl. suspenders* подтя́жки *f/pl.*
**bracket** ['brækɪt] **1.** *tech.* кроншт́ейн; (*income* **~**) катего́рия, гру́ппа; *typ.* ско́бка; **2.** заключа́ть [-чи́ть] в ско́бки; *fig.* ста́вить на одну́ до́ску с (Т)
**brag** [bræg] [по]хва́статься
**braggart** ['brægət] хвасту́н
**braid** [breɪd] **1.** *of hair* коса́; (*band*) тесьма́; *on uniform* галу́н; **2.** заплета́ть [-ести́]; обшива́ть тесьмо́й
**brain** [breɪn] мозг; (*fig. mst.* **~s**) рассу́док, ум; у́мственные спосо́бности *f/pl.* ***rack one's ~s*** лома́ть себе́ го́лову (над Т); ***use your ~s!*** шевели́ мозга́ми!; **~wave** блестя́щая иде́я; **~y** ['~ɪ] *coll.* башкови́тый
**brake** [breɪk] **1.** *mot.* то́рмоз; **2.** [за]тормози́ть
**branch** [brɑːntʃ] **1.** ветвь *f*, ве́тка (*a. rail*), сук (*pl.*: су́чья); *of science* о́трасль; *of bank*, *etc.* отделе́ние, филиа́л; **2.** разветвля́ть(ся) [-етви́ть(ся)]; расширя́ться [-ши́риться]
**brand** [brænd] **1.** клеймо́; сорт; торго́вая ма́рка; **2.** *fig.* (*stigmatize*) [за]клейми́ть, [о]позо́рить
**brandish** ['brændɪʃ] разма́хивать [-хну́ть] (Т)
**brand-new** [brænd'njuː] *coll.* соверше́нно но́вый, с иго́лочки
**brandy** ['brændɪ] конья́к
**brass** [brɑːs] лату́нь; *coll.* (*impudence*) на́глость *f*, наха́льство; **~ *band*** духово́й орке́стр
**brassière** ['bræsɪə] ли́фчик, бюстга́льтер
**brave** [breɪv] **1.** хра́брый, сме́лый; **2.** хра́бро встреча́ть; **~ry** ['breɪvərɪ] хра́брость *f*, сме́лость *f*
**brawl** [brɔːl] **1.** шу́мная ссо́ра, потасо́вка; **2.** [по]сканда́лить, [по]дра́ться
**brawny** ['brɔːnɪ] си́льный; му́скулистый
**brazen** ['breɪzn] ме́дный, бронзо́вый; бессты́дный, на́глый (*a.* **~faced**)
**Brazilian** [brə'zɪlɪən] **1.** брази́льский; **2.** брази́лец *m*, бразилья́нка *f*
**breach** [briːtʃ] **1.** проло́м; *fig.* (*breaking*) разры́в; *of rule*, *etc.* наруше́ние; (*gap*) брешь *f*; **2.** пробива́ть брешь в (П)
**bread** [bred] хлеб
**breadth** [bredθ] ширина́; *fig.* широта́ (кругозо́ра); широ́кий разма́х
**break** [breɪk] **1.** (*interval*) переры́в; па́уза; (*crack*) тре́щина; разры́в; *coll.* шанс; ***a bad ~*** неуда́ча; **2.** [*irr.*] *v/t.* [с]лома́ть; разби́(ва́)ть; разруша́ть [-ру́шить]; (*interrupt*) прер(ы)ва́ть; (*a lock*, *etc.*) взла́мывать [взлома́ть]; **~ *up*** разла́мывать [-лома́ть]; разби́(-ва́)ть; *v/i.* пор(ы)ва́ть (с Т); [по]лома́ться, разби́(ва́)ться; **~ *away*** отделя́ться [-ли́ться] (от Р); **~ *down*** *tech.* потерпе́ть *pf.* ава́рию, вы́йти *pf.* из стро́я; **~ *out*** вспы́хивать [-хнуть]; **~able** ['breɪkəbl] ло́мкий, хру́пкий; **~age** ['breɪkɪdʒ] поло́мка; **~down** *of talks*, *etc.* прекраще́ние; *tech.* поло́мка; ***nervous ~*** не́рвное расстро́йство
**breakfast** ['brekfəst] **1.** за́втрак; **2.** [по]за́втракать
**breakup** распа́д, разва́л
**breast** [brest] грудь *f*; ***make a clean ~ of sth.*** чистосерде́чно сознава́ться в чём-л.; **~stroke** *sport* брасс
**breath** [breθ] дыха́ние; вздох; ***take a ~*** перевести́ *pf.* дух; ***with bated ~*** затаи́в дыха́ние; **~e** [briːð] *v/i.* дыша́ть [дохну́ть]; **~er** [briːðə] *pause* переды́шка; **~less** ['breθlɪs] запыха́вшийся; *of a day* безве́тренный
**bred** [bred] *pt. и pt. p. от* ***breed***
**breeches** ['brɪtʃɪz] *pl.* бри́джи *pl.*
**breed** [briːd] **1.** поро́да; **2.** [*irr.*] *v/t.* выводи́ть [вы́вести]; разводи́ть *v/i.* [-вести́], размножа́ться [-о́житься]; [рас]плоди́ться; **~er** ['briːdə] *of animal* производи́тель *m*; скотово́д; **~ing** [-dɪŋ] разведе́ние (живо́тных); *of person* воспита́ние; ***good ~*** воспи́танность *f*

**breez|e** [bri:z] лёгкий ветеро́к, бриз; **~y** ['bri:zɪ] ве́тренный; *person* живо́й, весёлый

**brevity** ['brevətɪ] кра́ткость *f*

**brew** [bru:] *v/t. beer* [с]вари́ть; *tea* зава́ривать [-ри́ть]; *fig.* затева́ть [затéять]; **~ery** ['bru:ərɪ] пивова́ренный заво́д

**brib|e** [braɪb] **1.** взя́тка; по́дкуп; **2.** подкупа́ть [-пи́ть]; дава́ть взя́тку (Д); **~ery** ['braɪbərɪ] взя́точничество

**brick** [brɪk] кирпи́ч; *fig.* молодчи́на; сла́вный па́рень *m*; ***drop a ~*** сморо́зить *pf.* глу́пость; (*say*) ля́пнуть *pf.*; **~layer** ка́менщик

**bridal** ['braɪdl] □ сва́дебный

**bride** [braɪd] неве́ста; *just married* новобра́чная; **~groom** жени́х; *just married* новобра́чный; **~smaid** подру́жка неве́сты

**bridge** [brɪdʒ] **1.** мост; ***~ of the nose*** перено́сица; **2.** соединя́ть мо́стом; стро́ить мост че́рез (В); (*overcome*) *fig.* преодоле́(ва́)ть

**bridle** ['braɪdl] **1.** узда́; **2.** *v/t.* взну́здывать [-да́ть]

**brief** [bri:f] **1.** коро́ткий, кра́ткий, сжа́тый; **2.** [про]инструкти́ровать; **~case** портфе́ль *m*

**brigade** [brɪ'geɪd] *mil.* брига́да

**bright** [braɪt] □ я́ркий; све́тлый, я́сный; (*intelligent*) смышлёный; **~en** ['braɪtn] *v/t.* оживля́ть [-ви́ть]; *v/i. weather* проясня́ться [-ни́ться]; *person:* оживля́ться [-ви́ться]; **~ness** ['~nɪs] я́ркость *f*; блеск

**brillian|ce, ~cy** ['brɪljəns, -sɪ] я́ркость *f*; блеск; (*splendo[u]r*) великоле́пие; (*intelligence*) блестя́щий ум; **~t** [-jənt] **1.** □ блестя́щий (*a. fig.*); сверка́ющий; **2.** бриллиа́нт

**brim** [brɪm] **1.** край; *of hat* поля́ *n/pl.*; **2.** наполня́ть(ся) до краёв; ***~ over*** *fig.* перелива́ться [-ли́ться] че́рез край

**brine** [braɪn] *cul.* рассо́л

**bring** [brɪŋ] [*irr.*] приноси́ть [-нести́]; доставля́ть [-а́вить]; *in car, etc.* привози́ть [-везти́]; (*lead*) приводи́ть [-вести́]; ***~ about*** осуществля́ть [-ви́ть]; ***~ down*** *prices* снижа́ть [сни́зить]; ***~ down the house*** вы́звать *pf.* бу́рю аплодисме́нтов; ***~ home to*** довести́ что́-нибудь до чего́-нибудь созна́ния; ***~ round*** приводи́ть [-вести́] в созна́ние; ***~ up*** воспи́тывать [-та́ть]

**brink** [brɪŋk] (*edge*) край (*a. fig.*); (круто́й) бе́рег; ***on the ~ of war*** на гра́ни войны́

**brisk** [brɪsk] ско́рый, оживлённый

**bristl|e** ['brɪsl] **1.** щети́на; **2.** [о]щети́ниться; ***~ with anger*** [рас]серди́ться; ***~ with*** изоби́ловать (Т); **~y** [~ɪ] щети́нистый, колю́чий

**British** ['brɪtɪʃ] брита́нский; ***the ~*** брита́нцы *m/pl.*

**brittle** ['brɪtl] хру́пкий, ло́мкий

**broach** [brəʊtʃ] *question* поднима́ть [-ня́ть]; (*begin*) нач(ин)а́ть

**broad** [brɔ:d] □ широ́кий, обши́рный; *of humour* грубова́тый; ***in ~ daylight*** средь бе́ла дня; **~cast** [*irr.* (***cast***)] **1.** *rumour, etc.* распространя́ть [-ни́ть]; передава́ть по ра́дио, трансли́ровать; **2.** радиопереда́ча, трансля́ция; радиовеща́ние

**brocade** [brə'keɪd] парча́

**broil** [brɔɪl] жа́рить(ся) на огне́; *coll.* жа́риться на со́лнце

**broke** [brəʊk] *pt. от* ***break***; ***be ~*** быть без гроша́; ***go ~*** обанкро́титься *pf.*

**broken** ['brəʊkən] **1.** *pt. p. от* ***break***; **2.** разби́тый, раско́лотый; ***~ health*** надло́мленное здоро́вье

**broker** ['brəʊkə] бро́кер, ма́клер

**bronchitis** [brɒŋ'kaɪtɪs] бронхи́т

**bronze** [brɒnz] **1.** бро́нза; **2.** бро́нзовый; **3.** загора́ть [-ре́ть]

**brooch** [brəʊtʃ] брошь, бро́шка

**brood** [bru:d] **1.** вы́водок; *fig.* ора́ва; **2.** *fig.* гру́стно размышля́ть

**brook** [brʊk] руче́й

**broom** [bru:m] метла́, ве́ник

**broth** [brɒθ] бульо́н

**brothel** ['brɒθl] публи́чный дом

**brother** ['brʌðə] брат; собра́т; **~hood** [~hʊd] бра́тство; **~-in-law** [~rɪnlɔ:] (*wife's brother*) шу́рин; (*sister's husband*) зять *m*; (*husband's brother*) де́верь *m*; **~ly** [~lɪ] бра́тский

**brought** [brɔ:t] *pt. и pt. p. от* ***bring***

**brow** [braʊ] лоб; (*eye~*) бровь *f*; *of hill* вершина; **~beat** ['braʊbi:t] [*irr.* (**beat**)] запугивать [-гать]

**brown** [braʊn] **1.** коричневый цвет; **2.** коричневый; смуглый; загорелый; **3.** загорать [-реть]

**browse** [braʊz] пастись; *fig.* читать беспорядочно, просматривать

**bruise** [bru:z] **1.** синяк, кровоподтёк; **2.** ушибать [-бить]; поставить *pf.* (себе) синяки

**brunt** [brʌnt]: ***bear the ~ of sth.*** *fig.* выносить всю тяжесть чего-л.

**brush** [brʌʃ] **1.** *for sweeping, brushing, etc.* щётка; *for painting* кисть *f*; **2.** *v/t.* чистить щёткой; причёсывать щёткой; ***~ aside*** отмахиваться [-хнуться] (от Р); ***~ up*** приводить в порядок; *fig.* освежать в памяти; *v/i.* ***~ by*** прошмыгивать [-гнуть]; ***~ against s.o.*** слегка задеть кого-либо; **~wood** ['brʌʃwʊd] хворост, валежник

**brusque** [brʊsk] □ грубый; (*abrupt*) резкий

**brussels sprouts** [brʌsəls'spraʊts] брюссельская капуста

**brut|al** ['bru:tl] □ грубый; (*cruel*) жестокий; **~ality** [bru:'tælətɪ] грубость *f*; жестокость *f*; **~e** [bru:t] **1.** жестокий; ***by ~ force*** грубой силой; **2.** *animal* животное; *pers.* скотина

**bubble** ['bʌbl] **1.** пузырь *m*, *dim.* пузырёк; **2.** пузыриться; (*boil*) кипеть; *of spring* бить ключом (*a. fig.*)

**buck** [bʌk] **1.** *zo.* самец (*оленя, зайца и др.*); **2.** становиться на дыбы; ***~ up*** *coll.* встряхнуться *pf.*; оживляться [-виться]

**bucket** ['bʌkɪt] ведро; *of dredging machine* ковш

**buckle** ['bʌkl] **1.** пряжка; **2.** *v/t.* застёгивать [-тегнуть]; *v/i. of metal, etc.* [по]коробиться; ***~ down to*** приниматься за дело

**buckwheat** ['bʌkwi:t] гречиха; *cul.* гречневая крупа

**bud** [bʌd] **1.** почка, бутон; *fig.* зародыш; ***nip in the ~*** подавить *pf.* в зародыше; **2.** *v/i. bot.* давать почки; *fig.* разви(ва)ться

**budge** ['bʌdʒ] *mst. v/i.* сдвигаться [-инуться]; шевелить(ся) [-льнуть(ся)]; *fig.* уступать [-пить]

**budget** ['bʌdʒɪt] **1.** бюджет; финансовая смета; **2.**: ***~ for*** ассигновать определённую сумму на что-то; предусматривать [-смотреть]

**buff** [bʌf] тёмно-жёлтый

**buffalo** ['bʌfələʊ] *zo.* буйвол

**buffer** ['bʌfə] *rail.* буфер

**buffet**[1] ['bʌfɪt] ударять [-арить]; ***~ about*** бросать из стороны в сторону

**buffet**[2] **1.** [~] буфет; **2.** ['bʊfeɪ] буфетная стойка; ***~ supper*** ужин "аля-фуршет"

**buffoon** [bə'fu:n] шут

**bug** [bʌg] клоп; *Am.* насекомое; *hidden microphone* подслушивающее устройство

**build** [bɪld] **1.** [*irr.*] [по]строить; сооружать [-рудить]; *nest* [с]вить; ***~ on*** полагаться [положиться], возлагать надежды на (В); **2.** (тело)сложение; **~er** ['bɪldə] строитель *m*; **~ing** ['~ɪŋ] здание; строительство

**built** [bɪlt] *pt. и pt. p. от* ***build***

**bulb** [bʌlb] *bot.* луковица; *el.* лампочка

**bulge** [bʌldʒ] **1.** выпуклость *f*; **2.** выпячиваться [выпятиться], выдаваться [выдаться]

**bulk** [bʌlk] объём; основная часть *f*; ***in ~*** навалом; **~y** ['bʌlkɪ] громоздкий; *person* тучный

**bull** [bʊl] бык; ***take the ~ by the horns*** взять *pf.* быка за рога; ***~ in a china shop*** слон в посудной лавке

**bulldog** ['bʊldɒg] бульдог

**bulldozer** ['bʊldəʊʒə] бульдозер

**bullet** ['bʊlɪt] пуля

**bulletin** ['bʊlətɪn] бюллетень *m*

**bull's-eye** ['bʊlzaɪ] яблочко мишени; ***hit the ~*** попасть *pf.* в цель (*a. fig.*)

**bully** ['bʊlɪ] **1.** задира *m*; **2.** задирать, запугивать [-гать]

**bum** [bʌm] *coll.* зад(ница); *Am. sl.* лодырь *m*; бродяга *m*

**bumblebee** ['bʌmblbi:] шмель *m*

**bump** [bʌmp] **1.** глухой удар; (*swelling*) шишка; **2.** ударять(ся) [уда-

рить(ся)]; ~ ***into*** натáлкиваться [-толкнýться] (*a. fig.*); *of cars*, *etc.* стáлкиваться [столкнýться]; ~ ***against*** стýкаться [-кнуться]
**bumper** ['bʌmpə] *mot.* бýфер
**bumpy** ['bʌmpɪ] ухáбистый, нерóвный
**bun** [bʌn] бýлочка
**bunch** [bʌntʃ] *of grapes* гроздь, кисть; *of keys* свя́зка; *of flowers* букéт; *of people* грýппа
**bundle** ['bʌndl] **1.** ýзел; **2.** *v/t.* (*put together*) собирáть вмéсте, свя́зывать в ýзел (*a.* ~ ***up***)
**bungalow** ['bʌŋgələʊ] одноэтáжный коттéдж
**bungle** ['bʌŋgl] неумéло, небрéжно рабóтать; [на] пóртить; *coll.* завалúть
**bunk**[1] [bʌŋk] вздор
**bunk**[2] [~] кóйка (*a. naut.*); *rail.* спáльное мéсто, пóлка
**buoy** [bɔɪ] *naut.* бáкен, буй; ~**ant** ['bɔɪənt] □ плавýчий; (*cheerful*) жизнерáдостный; бóдрый
**burden** ['bɜːdn] **1.** нóша; *fig.* брéмя *n*, груз; **2.** нагружáть [-рузúть]; обременя́ть [-нúть]; ~**some** [~səm] обременúтельный
**bureau** ['bjʊərəʊ] контóра; бюрó *n indecl.*; ***information*** ~ спрáвочное бюрó; ~**cracy** [bjʊə'rɒkrəsɪ] бюрокрáтия
**burglar** ['bɜːglər] взлóмщик; ~**y** [~rɪ] крáжа со взлóмом
**burial** ['berɪəl] пóхороны *f/pl.*; ~ ***service*** заупокóйная слýжба
**burly** ['bɜːlɪ] здоровéнный, дю́жий
**burn** [bɜːn] **1.** ожóг; **2.** [*irr.*] *v/i.* горéть; *of food* подгорáть [-рéть]; *sting* жечь; *v/t.* [с]жечь; сжигáть [сжечь]; ~**er** ['bɜːnə] горéлка
**burnt** [bɜːnt] *pt. u pt. p. om* **burn**
**burrow** ['bʌrəʊ] **1.** норá; **2.** [вы́]рыть нóру
**burst** [bɜːst] **1.** (*explosion*) взрыв *a. fig.*; *of anger*, *etc.* вспы́шка; **2.** [*irr.*] *v/i.* взрывáться [взорвáться]; *dam* прор(ы)вáться; *pipe*, *etc.* лóпаться [лóпнуть]; ~ ***into the room*** врывáться [ворвáться] в кóмнату; ~ ***into tears*** разрыдáться; *v/t.* взрывáть [взорвáть]
**bury** ['berɪ] [по]хоронúть; *a bone*, *etc. in earth* зары́(вá)ть
**bus** [bʌs] автóбус
**bush** [bʊʃ] куст, кустáрник; ***beat about*** *or* ***around the*** ~ ходúть вокрýг да óколо
**business** ['bɪznɪs] дéло; бúзнес; торгóвое предприя́тие; ***have no*** ~ ***to*** *inf.* не имéть прáва (+ *inf.*); ~**like** [~laɪk] деловóй; практúчный; ~**man** бизнесмéн, предпринимáтель; ~ **trip** деловáя поéздка
**bus|station** автовокзáл; ~ **stop** автóбусная остановка
**bust** [bʌst] бюст; жéнская грудь *f*
**bustle** ['bʌsl] **1.** суматóха; суетá; **2.** *v/i.* [по]торопúться, [за]суетúться; *v/t.* [по]торопúть
**busy** ['bɪzɪ] **1.** □ занятóй (***at*** Т); зáнятый (*a. tel.*); **2.** (*mst.* ~ ***o.s.***) занимáться [заня́ться] (***with*** Т)
**but** [bʌt, bət] **1.** *cj.* но, а; однáко; тем не мéнее; éсли бы не; **2.** *prp.* крóме (Р), за исключéнием (Р); ***the last*** ~ ***one*** предпоследний; ~ ***for*** без (Р); **3.** *adv.* тóлько, лишь; ~ ***now*** тóлько что; ***all*** ~ едвá не ...; ***nothing*** ~ ничегó крóме, тóлько; ***I cannot help*** ~ *inf.* не могý не (+ *inf.*)
**butcher** ['bʊtʃə] **1.** мяснúк; *fig.* убúйца *m*; **2.** *cattle* забивáть; *people* убú(вá)ть; ~**y** [~rɪ] бóйня, резня́
**butler** ['bʌtlə] дворéцкий
**butt** [bʌt] **1.** (*blow*) удáр; *of rifle* приклáд; (*of cigarette*) окýрок; *fig. of person* мишéнь для насмéшек; **2.** ударя́ть головóй; (*run into*) натыкáться [наткнýться]; ~ ***in*** перебивáть [-бúть]
**butter** ['bʌtə] **1.** (слúвочное) мáсло; **2.** намáзывать мáслом; ~**cup** *bot.* лю́тик; ~**fly** бáбочка
**buttocks** ['bʌtəks] *pl.* я́годицы *f/pl.*
**button** ['bʌtn] **1.** пýговица; *of bell*, *etc.* (*knob*) кнóпка; **2.** застёгивать [-тегнýть]; ~**hole** петля́
**buxom** ['bʌksəm] пы́шная, полногрýдая
**buy** [baɪ] [*irr.*] *v/t.* покупáть [купúть]

(**from** у Р); **~er** ['baɪə] покупа́тель *m*, -ница *f*

**buzz** [bʌz] **1.** жужжа́ние; *of crowd* гул; **2.** *v/i.* [за]жужжа́ть

**by** [baɪ] **1.** *prp.* у (Р), при (П), о́коло (Р); к (Д); вдоль (Р); **~ *the dozen*** дю́жинами; **~ *o.s.*** оди́н *m*, одна́ *f*; **~ *land*** назе́мным тра́нспортом; **~ *rail*** по желе́зной доро́ге; ***day ~ day*** день за днём; **2.** *adv.* бли́зко, ря́дом; ми́мо; **~ *and ~*** вско́ре; **~ *the way*** ме́жду про́чим; **~ *and large*** в це́лом; **~-election** ['baɪɪlekʃn] дополни́тельные вы́боры *m/pl.*; **~gone** про́шлый; **~pass** объе́зд, объездна́я доро́га; **~-product** побо́чный проду́кт; **~stander** ['~stændə] очеви́дец (-дица); **~street** у́лочка

**byte** [baɪt] *comput.* байт

**by|way** глуха́я доро́га; **~word** при́тча во язы́цех

# C

**cab** [kæb] такси́ *n indecl.*; *mot.*, *rail.* каби́на

**cabbage** ['kæbɪdʒ] капу́ста

**cabin** ['kæbɪn] (*hut*) хи́жина; *ae.* каби́на; *naut.* каю́та

**cabinet** ['kæbɪnɪt] *pol.* кабине́т; *of TV, radio, etc.* ко́рпус

**cable** ['keɪbl] **1.** ка́бель *m*; (*rope*) кана́т; телегра́мма; **~ *television*** ка́бельное телеви́дение; **2.** *tel.* телеграфи́ровать (*im*)*pf.*

**cackle** ['kækl] **1.** куда́хтанье; гогота́нье; **2.** [за]куда́хтать; *of geese and man* [за]гогота́ть

**cad** [kæd] негодя́й

**cadaverous** [kə'dævərəs] исхуда́вший как скеле́т

**caddish** ['kædɪʃ] по́длый

**cadet** [kə'det] каде́т, курса́нт

**cadge** [kædʒ] *v/t.* кля́нчить; *v/i.* попроша́йничать; **~r** ['kædʒə] попроша́йка

**café** ['kæfeɪ] кафе́ *n indecl.*

**cafeteria** [kæfɪ'tɪərɪə] кафете́рий; *at factory, univ.* столо́вая

**cage** [keɪdʒ] *for animals* кле́тка; (*of elevator*) каби́на ли́фта

**cajole** [kə'dʒəʊl] угова́ривать [-вори́ть]; *coll.* обха́живать; доби́ться *pf.* чего-л. ле́стью и́ли обма́ном

**cake** [keɪk] кекс, торт; *fancy* пиро́жное; *of soap* кусо́к

**calamity** [kə'læmətɪ] бе́дствие

**calcium** ['kælsɪəm] ка́льций

**calculat|e** ['kælkjʊleɪt] *v/t.* вычисля́ть [вы́числить]; *cost, etc.* подсчи́тывать [-ита́ть]; *v/i.* рассчи́тывать (***on*** на В); **~ion** [kælkjʊ'leɪʃn] вычисле́ние; расчёт; **~or** ['kælkjʊleɪtə] калькуля́тор

**calendar** ['kælɪndə] календа́рь

**calf**[1] [kɑːf], *pl.* **calves** [kɑːvz] телёнок (*pl.*: теля́та); (*a.* **~skin**) теля́чья ко́жа, опо́ек

**calf**[2] [~], *pl.* **calves** *of the leg*(*s*) [~] икра́

**caliber** *or* **calibre** ['kælɪbə] кали́бр (*a. fig.*)

**calico** ['kælɪkəʊ] си́тец

**call** [kɔːl] **1.** крик, зов, о́клик; *tel.* звоно́к; (*summon*) вы́зов; (*appeal*) призы́в; визи́т, посеще́ние; ***on ~*** *of nurse, doctor* дежу́рство на дому́; **2.** *v/t.* [по]зва́ть; оклика́ть [-и́кнуть]; (*summon*) соз(ы)ва́ть; вызыва́ть [вы́звать]; [раз]буди́ть; призыва́ть; **~ *off*** отменя́ть [-ни́ть] (Р); **~ *up*** призыва́ть на вое́нную слу́жбу; **~ *s.o.'s attention to*** привле́чь *pf.* чьё-л. внима́ние (к Д); *v/i.* крича́ть [кри́кнуть]; *tel.* [по]звони́ть; (*visit*) заходи́ть [зайти́] (***at*** в В; ***on a p.*** к Д); **~ *for*** [по]тре́бовать; **~ *for a p.*** заходи́ть [зайти́] за (Т); **~ *in*** *coll.* забега́ть [-ежа́ть] (к Д); **~ *on*** навеща́ть [-ести́ть] (В); приз(ы)ва́ть (***to do*** *etc.* сде́лать *и т.д.*); **~box** ['kɔːlbɒks] *Am.* телефо́н-автома́т, телефо́нная бу́дка; **~er** ['kɔːlə] го́сть(я

C

*f*) *m*
**calling** ['kɔːlɪŋ] (*vocation*) призва́ние; профе́ссия
**call|ous** ['kæləs] □ огрубе́лый; мозо́листый; *fig.* бессерде́чный; **~us** ['kæləs] мозо́ль
**calm** [kɑːm] **1.** □ споко́йный; безве́тренный; **2.** тишина́; *of sea* штиль *m.*; споко́йствие; **3.** **~ down** успока́ивать(ся) [-ко́ить(ся)]; *of wind, etc.* стиха́ть [-и́хнуть]
**calorie** ['kælərɪ] *phys.* кало́рия
**calve** [kɑːv] [о]тели́ться; **~s** *pl. от* **calf**
**cambric** ['keɪmbrɪk] бати́ст
**came** [keɪm] *pt. от* **come**
**camera** ['kæmərə] фотоаппара́т; *cine.* киноаппара́т; **in ~** при закры́тых дверя́х
**camomile** ['kæməmaɪl] рома́шка
**camouflage** ['kæməflɑːʒ] **1.** камуфля́ж, маскиро́вка (*a. mil.*); **2.** [за] маскирова́ть(ся)
**camp** [kæmp] **1.** ла́герь *m*; **~ bed** похо́дная крова́ть; **2.** стать ла́герем; **~ out** расположи́ться *pf.* и́ли ночева́ть на откры́том во́здухе
**campaign** [kæm'peɪn] **1.** *pol., etc.* камп́ания; **2.** проводи́ть камп́анию; агити́ровать (**for** за В, **against** про́тив Р)
**camphor** ['kæmfə] камфара́
**camping** ['kæmpɪŋ] ке́мпинг (= *a.* **~ site**)
**campus** ['kæmpəs] *Am. university grounds and buildings* университе́тский городо́к
**can**[1] [kæn] *v/aux.* [с]мочь, быть в состоя́нии; [с]уме́ть
**can**[2] [~] **1.** *for milk* бидо́н; (*tin*) ба́нка; *for petrol* кани́стра; **2.** консерви́ровать (*im*)*pf.*, *pf. a.* [за-]; **~ opener** консе́рвный нож
**canal** [kə'næl] кана́л
**canary** [kə'neərɪ] канаре́йка
**cancel** ['kænsl] (*call off*) отменя́ть [-ни́ть]; (*cross out*) вычёркивать [вы́черкнуть]; *agreement, etc.* аннули́ровать (*im*)*pf.*; *stamp* погаша́ть [погаси́ть]; *math.* (*a.* **~ out**) сокраща́ть [-рати́ть]
**cancer** ['kænsə] *astr.* созве́здие Ра́ка; *med.* рак; **~ous** [~rəs] ра́ковый
**candid** ['kændɪd] □ и́скренний, прямо́й; **~ camera** скры́тая ка́мера
**candidate** ['kændɪdət] кандида́т (**for** на В)
**candied** ['kændɪd] заса́харенный
**candle** ['kændl] свеча́; **the game is (not) worth the ~** игра́ (не) сто́ит свеч; **~stick** [~stɪk] подсве́чник
**cando(u)r** ['kændə] открове́нность *f*; и́скренность *f*
**candy** ['kændɪ] ледене́ц; *Am.* конфе́ты *f/pl.*, сла́сти *f/pl.*
**cane** [keɪn] *bot.* тростни́к; *for walking* трость *f*
**canned** [kænd] консерви́рованный
**cannon** ['kænən] пу́шка; ору́дие
**cannot** ['kænɒt] не в состоя́нии, → **can**[1]
**canoe** [kə'nuː] като́э
**canon** ['kænən] *eccl.* кано́н; пра́вило
**cant** [kænt] пусты́е слова́; ханжество́
**can't** [kɑːnt] = **cannot**
**canteen** [kæn'tiːn] *eating place* буфе́т; столо́вая
**canvas** ['kænvəs] *cloth* холст; *for embroidery* канва́; *fig.* карти́на; паруси́на
**canvass** [~] *v/t.*: **~ opinions** иссле́довать обще́ственное мне́ние; собира́ть голоса́ перед вы́борами
**caoutchouc** ['kaʊtʃʊk] каучу́к
**cap** [kæp] **1.** *with peak* ке́пка, *mil.* фура́жка; *without peak* ша́пка; *tech.* колпачо́к; *of mushroom* шля́пка; **~ in hand** в ро́ли проси́теля; **2.** накрыва́ть [-ры́ть] кры́шкой; *coll.* перещеголя́ть *pf.*; **to ~ it all** в доверше́ние всего́
**capab|ility** [keɪpə'bɪlətɪ] спосо́бность *f*; **~le** ['keɪpəbl] □ спосо́бный (**of** на В); (*gifted*) одарённый
**capaci|ous** [kə'peɪʃəs] □ вмести́тельный; **~ty** [kə'pæsətɪ] объём, вмести́мость *f*; (*ability*) спосо́бность *f*; *tech.* производи́тельность *f*; *of engine* мо́щность *f*; *el.* ёмкость *f*; **in the ~ of** в ка́честве (Р)
**cape**[1] [keɪp] плащ
**cape**[2] [~] *geogr.* мыс

**caper** ['keɪpə] прыжо́к, ша́лость; ***cut ~s*** выде́лывать антраша́; дура́читься

**capital** ['kæpɪtl] **1.** □ (*crime*) кара́емый сме́ртью; (*sentence, punishment*) сме́ртный; **2.** столи́ца; (*wealth*) капита́л; (*a.* ***~ letter***) загла́вная бу́ква; **~ism** ['kæpɪtəlɪzəm] капитали́зм; **~ize** ['kæpɪtəlaɪz]: ***~ on*** обраща́ть в свою́ по́льзу

**capitulate** [kə'pɪtʃʊleɪt] капитули́ровать, сд(ав)а́ться (***to*** Д) (*a. fig.*)

**capric|e** [kə'priːs] капри́з, прич́уда; **~ious** [kə'prɪʃəs] □ капри́зный

**capsize** [kæp'saɪz] *v/i. naut.* опроки́дываться [-ки́нуться]; *v/t.* опроки́дывать [-ки́нуть]

**capsule** ['kæpsjuːl] *med.* ка́псула

**captain** ['kæptɪn] *mil., naut., sport* капита́н

**caption** ['kæpʃn] *title, words accompanying picture* по́дпись к карти́нке; заголо́вок; *cine.* ти́тры *m/pl.*

**captiv|ate** ['kæptɪveɪt] пленя́ть [-ни́ть], очаро́вывать [-ова́ть]; **~e** ['kæptɪv] пле́нный; *fig.* пле́нник; **~ity** [kæp'tɪvətɪ] плен; нево́ля

**capture** ['kæptʃə] **1.** пойма́ть; захва́тывать [-ти́ть]; брать в плен; **2.** по́имка; захва́т

**car** [kɑː] *rail vehicle* ваго́н; *motor vehicle* автомоби́ль, маши́на; ***by ~*** маши́ной

**caramel** ['kærəmel] караме́ль *f*

**caravan** ['kærəvæn] карава́н; дома́втоприце́п

**caraway** ['kærəweɪ] тмин

**carbohydrate** [ˌkɑːbəʊ'haɪdreɪt] углево́д

**carbon** ['kɑːbən] углеро́д; ***~ paper*** копи́рка

**carburet(t)or** [kɑːbjʊ'retə] *mot.* карбюра́тор

**carcase** ['kɑːkəs] ту́ша

**card** [kɑːd] ка́рта, ка́рточка; **~board** ['kɑːdbɔːd] карто́н

**cardigan** ['kɑːdɪgən] кардига́н

**cardinal** ['kɑːdənəl] **1.** □ (*chief*) гла́вный, основно́й; (*most important*) кардина́льный; ***~ number*** коли́чественное числи́тельное; **2.** *eccl.* кардина́л

**card|index** ['kɑːdɪndeks] картоте́ка; **~ phone** ка́рточный телефо́н

**care** [keə] **1.** забо́та; (*charge*) попече́ние; (*attention*) внима́ние; (*tending*) присмо́тр (за Т); (*nursing*) ухо́д (за Т); ***~ of*** (*abbr.* ***c/o***) по а́дресу (Р); ***take ~ of*** [с]бере́чь (В); присмотре́ть за (Т); ***handle with ~!*** осторо́жно!; **2.** име́ть жела́ние, [за]хоте́ть (***to***: + *inf.*); ***~ for***: **a**) [по]забо́титься о (П); **b**) люби́ть (В); *coll.* ***I don't ~!*** мне всё равно́!; ***well ~d for*** ухо́женный

**career** [kə'rɪə] **1.** *fig.* карье́ра; **2.** нести́сь, мча́ться

**carefree** ['keəfriː] беззабо́тный

**careful** ['keəfl] □ (*cautious*) осторо́жный; (*done with care*) аккура́тный, тща́тельный; внима́тельный (к Д); ***be ~*** (***of, about, with***) забо́титься (о П); стара́ться (+ *inf.*); **~ness** [-nɪs] осторо́жность *f*; тща́тельность *f*

**careless** ['keəlɪs] □ *work, etc.* небре́жный; *driving, etc.* неосторо́жный; **~ness** [-nɪs] небре́жность *f*

**caress** [kə'res] **1.** ла́ска; **2.** ласка́ть

**caretaker** ['keəteɪkə] сто́рож

**carfare** ['kɑːfeə] *Am.* пла́та за прое́зд

**cargo** ['kɑːgəʊ] *naut., ae.* груз

**caricature** ['kærɪkətʃʊə] **1.** карикату́ра; **2.** изобража́ть в карикату́рном ви́де

**car jack** ['kɑːdʒæk] *lifting device* домкра́т

**carnal** ['kɑːnl] □ *sensual* чу́вственный, пло́тский; *sexual* полово́й

**carnation** [kɑː'neɪʃn] гвозди́ка

**carnival** ['kɑːnɪvl] карнава́л

**carol** ['kærəl] рожде́ственский гимн

**carp**[1] [kaːp] *zo.* карп

**carp**[2] [~] придира́ться

**carpent|er** ['kɑːpəntə] пло́тник; **~ry** [~trɪ] пло́тничество

**carpet** ['kɑːpɪt] **1.** ковёр; **2.** устила́ть ковро́м

**carriage** ['kærɪdʒ] *rail.* ваго́н; перево́зка, транспортиро́вка; *of body* оса́нка; ***~ free, ~ paid*** опла́ченная до-

ста́вка
**carrier** ['kærɪə] (*porter*) носи́льщик; *med.* носи́тель инфе́кции; **~s** тра́нспортное аге́нтство; **~ bag** су́мка
**carrot** ['kærət] морко́вка; *collect.* морко́вь *f*
**carry** ['kærɪ] **1.** *v/t.* носи́ть, [по]нести́; *in train, etc.* вози́ть, [по]везти́; ***~ o.s.*** держа́ться, вести́ себя́; *of law, etc.* ***be carried*** быть при́нятым; ***~ s.th. too far*** заходи́ть сли́шком далеко́; ***~ on*** продолжа́ть [-до́лжить]; ***~ out*** *или* ***through*** доводи́ть до конца́; выполня́ть [вы́полнить]; *v/i. of sound* доноси́ться [донести́сь]
**cart** [kɑːt] теле́га, пово́зка
**cartilage** ['kɑːtɪlɪdʒ] хрящ
**carton** ['kɑːtn] *container* карто́нка; *for milk, etc.* паке́т
**cartoon** [kɑː'tuːn] карикату́ра, шарж; *animated* мультфи́льм, *coll.* му́льтик
**cartridge** ['kɑːtrɪdʒ] патро́н
**carve** [kɑːv] *on wood* ре́зать; *meat* наре́за́ть [наре́зать]
**carving** ['kɑːvɪŋ] *object* резьба́
**case**[1] [keɪs] я́щик; *for spectacles, etc.* футля́р; (*suit~*) чемода́н; (*attaché ~*) (портфе́ль-)диплома́т
**case**[2] [~] слу́чай; (*state of affairs*) положе́ние; (*circumstances*) обстоя́тельство; *law* суде́бное де́ло; ***in any ~*** в любо́м слу́чае; ***in ~ of need*** в слу́чае необходи́мости; ***in no ~*** ни в ко́ем слу́чае
**cash** [kæʃ] **1.** де́ньги, нали́чные де́ньги *f/pl.*; ***on a ~ basis*** за нали́чный расчёт; ***~ on delivery*** нало́женным платежо́м; **2.** получа́ть де́ньги по (Д); ***~ in on*** воспо́льзоваться; **~ier** [kæ'ʃɪə] касси́р(ша)
**cask** [kɑːsk] бо́чка, бочо́нок
**casket** ['kɑːskɪt] шкату́лка; *Am. a.* = *coffin* гроб
**casserole** ['kæsərəʊl] гли́няная кастрю́ля; запека́нка
**cassette** [kə'set] кассе́та
**cassock** ['kæsək] ря́са, сута́на
**cast** [kɑːst] **1.** (*act of throwing*) бросо́к, мета́ние; *thea.* (*actors*) соста́в исполни́телей; **2.** [*irr.*] *v/t.* броса́ть [бро́сить] (*a. fig.*); *shadow* отбра́сывать; *tech. metals* отли́(ва́)ть; *thea. roles* распределя́ть [-ли́ть]; ***~ light on*** пролива́ть [-ли́ть] свет на (В); ***~ lots*** броса́ть жре́бий; ***be ~ down*** быть в уны́нии; *v/i.* ***~ about for*** разы́скивать
**caste** [kɑːst] ка́ста
**castigate** ['kæstɪgeɪt] нака́зывать [-за́ть]; *fig.* жесто́ко критикова́ть
**cast iron** чугу́н; *attr.* чугу́нный
**castle** ['kɑːsl] за́мок; *chess* ладья́
**castor** ['kɑːstə]: ***~ oil*** касто́ровое ма́сло
**castrate** [kæ'streɪt] кастри́ровать (*im*)*pf.*
**casual** ['kæʒʊl] □ (*chance*) случа́йный; (*careless*) небре́жный; **~ty** [~tɪ] несча́стный слу́чай; *person* пострада́вший, же́ртва; *pl. mil.* поте́ри
**cat** [kæt] ко́шка; (*male*) кот
**catalog**(**ue**) ['kætəlɒg] **1.** катало́г; **2.** составля́ть [-вить] катало́г, вноси́ть в катало́г
**cataract** ['kætərækt] (*waterfall*) водопа́д; *med.* катара́кта
**catarrh** [kə'tɑː] ката́р
**catastrophe** [kə'tæstrəfɪ] катастро́фа; *natural* стихи́йное бе́дствие
**catch** [kætʃ] **1.** *of fish* уло́в; (*trick*) подво́х; *on door* задви́жка; **2.** [*irr.*] *v/t.* лови́ть [пойма́ть]; (*take hold of*) схва́тывать [схвати́ть]; *disease* заража́ться [зарази́ться] (Т); *train, etc.* поспе́(-ва́)ть к (Д); ***~ cold*** просту́живаться [-уди́ться]; ***~ s.o.'s eye*** пойма́ть взгляд (Р); ***~ up*** догоня́ть [догна́ть]; **3.** *v/i.* зацепля́ться [-пи́ться]; *coll.* ***~ on*** станови́ться мо́дным; ***~ up with*** догоня́ть [догна́ть] (В); **~ing** ['kætʃɪŋ] *fig.* зарази́тельный; *med.* зара́зный; **~word** (*popular phrase*) мо́дное слове́чко
**categor|ical** [kætɪ'gɒrɪkl] □ категори́ческий; **~y** ['kætɪgərɪ] катего́рия, разря́д
**cater** ['keɪtə]: ***~ for*** обслу́живать (В)
**caterpillar** *zo.* ['kætəpɪlə] гу́сеница
**catgut** ['kætgʌt] струна́; *med.* ке́тгут
**cathedral** [kə'θiːdrəl] собо́р
**Catholic** ['kæθəlɪk] **1.** като́лик; **2.** ка-

толи́ческий

**catkin** ['kætkɪn] *bot.* серёжка

**cattle** ['kætl] кру́пный рога́тый скот; **~ breeding** скотово́дство

**caught** [kɔːt] *pt.* и *pt. p. от* ***catch***

**cauliflower** ['kɒlɪflaʊə] цветна́я капу́ста

**cause** ['kɔːz] **1.** причи́на, основа́ние; (*motive*) по́вод; **2.** причиня́ть [-ни́ть]; (*make happen*) вызыва́ть [вы́звать]; **~less** ['kɔːzlɪs] □ беспричи́нный, необосно́ванный

**caution** ['kɔːʃn] **1.** (*prudence*) осторо́жность *f*; (*warning*) предостереже́ние; **2.** предостерега́ть [-ре́чь] (***against*** от Р)

**cautious** ['kɔːʃəs] □ осторо́жный, осмотри́тельный; **~ness** [-nɪs] осторо́жность *f*, осмотри́тельность *f*

**cavalry** ['kævlrɪ] кавале́рия

**cave** [keɪv] **1.** пеще́ра; **2. ~ *in***: *v/i.* оседа́ть [осе́сть]; *fig., coll.* сда́ться *pf.*

**caviar(e)** ['kævɪɑː] икра́

**cavil** ['kævəl] **1.** приди́рка; **2.** прид(и)ра́ться (***at, about*** к Д, за В)

**cavity** ['kævɪtɪ] впа́дина; по́лость *f*; *in tooth, tree* дупло́

**cease** [siːs] *v/i.* перест(ав)а́ть; *v/t.* прекраща́ть [-крати́ть]; остана́вливать [-нови́ть]; **~-fire** прекраще́ние огня́; переми́рие; **~less** ['siːsləs] □ непреры́вный, непреста́нный

**cedar** ['siːdə] кедр

**cede** [siːd] уступа́ть [-пи́ть] (В)

**ceiling** ['siːlɪŋ] потоло́к; *attr.* максима́льный; ***price ~*** преде́льная цена́

**celebrat|e** ['selɪbreɪt] [от]пра́здновать; **~ed** [-ɪd] знамени́тый; **~ion** [selɪ'breɪʃn] торжества́ *n/pl.*; пра́зднование

**celebrity** [sɪ'lebrɪtɪ] *pers. and state of being* знамени́тость *f*

**celery** ['selərɪ] сельдере́й

**celestial** [sɪ'lestɪəl] □ небе́сный

**cell** [sel] *pol.* яче́йка; *in prison* ка́мера; *eccl.* ке́лья; *biol.* кле́тка; *el.* элеме́нт

**cellar** ['selə] подва́л; ***wine ~*** ви́нный по́греб

**cello** ['tʃeləʊ] виолонче́ль

**Cellophane®** ['seləfeɪn] целлофа́н

**cement** [sɪ'ment] **1.** цеме́нт; **2.** цементи́ровать (*im*)*pf.*; *fig.* **~ *relations*** укрепля́ть [-пи́ть] свя́зи

**cemetery** ['semɪtrɪ] кла́дбище

**censor** ['sensə] **1.** це́нзор; **2.** подверга́ть цензу́ре; **~ship** ['sensəʃɪp] цензу́ра

**censure** ['senʃə] **1.** осужде́ние, порица́ние; **2.** осужда́ть [осуди́ть], порица́ть

**census** ['sensəs] пе́репись *f*

**cent** [sent] *Am. coin* цент

**centenary** [sen'tiːnərɪ] столе́тняя годовщи́на, столе́тие

**center** (*Brt.* **-tre**) ['sentə] **1.** центр; (*focus*) средото́чие; ***in the ~*** в середи́не; **2.** [с]концентри́ровать(ся); сосредото́чи(ва)ть(ся)

**centi|grade** ['sentɪgreɪd]: ***... degrees ~*** ... гра́дусов по Це́льсию; **~meter** (*Brt. -tre*) [-miːtə] сантиме́тр; **~pede** [-piːd] *zo.* сороконо́жка

**central** ['sentrəl] □ центра́льный; гла́вный; **~ *office*** управле́ние; **~ize** [-laɪz] централизова́ть (*im*)*pf.*

**centre** → ***center***

**century** ['sentʃərɪ] столе́тие, век

**ceramics** [sɪ'ræmɪks] кера́мика

**cereal** ['sɪərɪəl] хле́бный злак

**cerebral** ['serɪbrəl] мозгово́й, церебра́льный

**ceremon|ial** [serɪ'məʊnɪəl] □ торже́ственный; **~ious** [-nɪəs] церемо́нный; **~y** ['serɪmənɪ] церемо́ния

**certain** ['sɜːtn] □ (*definite*) определённый; (*confident*) уве́ренный; (*undoubted*) несомне́нный; не́кий; не́который; ***a ~ Mr. Jones*** не́кий г-н Джо́унз; ***to a ~ extent*** до не́которой сте́пени; **~ty** [-tɪ] уве́ренность *f*; определённость *f*

**certi|ficate** **1.** [sə'tɪfɪkət] свиде́тельство; спра́вка; ***birth ~*** свиде́тельство о рожде́нии; **2.** [-keɪt] вы́дать удостовере́ние (Д); **~fy** ['sɜːtɪfaɪ] удостоверя́ть [-е́рить]; **~tude** [-tjuːd] уве́ренность *f*

**cessation** [se'seɪʃn] прекраще́ние

**CFC *chlorofluorocarbon*** фрео́н

**chafe** [tʃeɪf] *v/t. make sore* натира́ть

[натере́ть]; *v/i.* раздража́ться [-жи́ться]
**chaff** [tʃɑːf] подшу́чивать [-шути́ть] над (Т), подтру́нивать [-ни́ть]
**chagrin** ['ʃægrɪn] **1.** доса́да, огорче́ние; **2.** досажда́ть [досади́ть] (Д); огорча́ть [-чи́ть]
**chain** [tʃeɪn] **1.** цепь *f* (*a. fig.*); *dim.* цепо́чка; **~s** *pl. fig.* око́вы *f/pl.*; у́зы *f/pl.*; **~ reaction** цепна́я реа́кция; **2.** *dog.* держа́ть на цепи́
**chair** [tʃeə] стул; **be in the ~** председа́тельствовать; **~man** ['tʃeəmən] председа́тель *m*; **~woman** [~wʊmən] (же́нщина-)председа́тель, председа́тельница
**chalk** [tʃɔːk] **1.** мел; **2.** писа́ть, рисова́ть ме́лом; **~ up** (*register*) отмеча́ть [е́тить]
**challenge** ['tʃælɪndʒ] **1.** вы́зов; **2.** вызыва́ть [вы́звать]; *s.o.'s right, etc.* оспа́ривать [оспо́рить]
**chamber** ['tʃeɪmbə] (*room*) ко́мната; (*official body*) **~ of commerce** торго́вая пала́та; **~maid** го́рничная; **~ music** ка́мерная му́зыка
**chamois** ['ʃæmwaː] за́мша
**champagne** [ʃæm'peɪn] шампа́нское
**champion** ['tʃæmpɪən] **1.** чемпио́н *m*, -ка *f*; защи́тник *m*, -ница *f*; **2.** защища́ть [-ити́ть]; боро́ться за (В); **~ship** пе́рвенство, чемпиона́т
**chance** [tʃɑːns] **1.** случа́йность *f*; риск; (*opportunity*) удо́бный слу́чай; шанс (**of** на В); **by ~** случа́йно; **take a ~** рискова́ть [-кну́ть]; **2.** случа́йный; **3.** *v/i.* случа́ться [-чи́ться]
**chancellor** ['tʃɑːnsələ] ка́нцлер
**chancy** ['tʃɑːnsɪ] *coll.* риско́ванный
**chandelier** [ʃændə'lɪə] лю́стра
**change** [tʃeɪndʒ] **1.** переме́на, измене́ние; *of linen* сме́на; **small ~** *money* сда́ча; **for a ~** для разнообра́зия; **2.** *v/t.* [по]меня́ть; изменя́ть [-ни́ть]; *money* разме́нивать [-ня́ть]; *v/i.* [по]меня́ться; изменя́ться [-ни́ться]; *into different clothes* переоде́(ва́)ться; обме́ниваться [-ня́ть]; *rail.* переса́живаться [-се́сть]; **~able** ['tʃeɪndʒəbl] □ непостоя́нный, изме́нчивый
**channel** ['tʃænl] *river* ру́сло; (*naut. fairway*) фарва́тер; *geogr.* проли́в; *fig.* (*source*) исто́чник; **through official ~s** по официа́льным кана́лам
**chaos** ['keɪɒs] ха́ос, беспоря́док
**chap¹** [tʃæp] **1.** (*split, crack of skin*) тре́щина; **2.** [по]тре́скаться
**chap²** [~] *coll.* па́рень *m*
**chapel** ['tʃæpl] часо́вня
**chapter** ['tʃæptə] глава́
**char** [tʃɑː] (*burn*) обу́гли(ва)ть(ся)
**character** ['kærəktə] хара́ктер; (*individual*) ли́чность *f*; *thea.* де́йствующее лицо́; *lit.* геро́й, персона́ж; (*letter*) бу́ква; **~istic** [kærəktə'rɪstɪk] **1.** (**~ally**) характе́рный; типи́чный (**of** для Р); **2.** характе́рная черта́; сво́йство; **~ize** ['kærəktəraɪz] характеризова́ть (*im*)*pf*.
**charcoal** ['tʃɑːkəʊl] древе́сный у́голь *m*
**charge** [tʃɑːdʒ] **1.** пла́та; *el.* заря́д; (*order*) поруче́ние; *law* обвине́ние; *mil.* ата́ка; *fig.* попече́ние, забо́та; **~s** *pl. comm.* расхо́ды *m/pl.*; изде́ржки *f/pl.*; **be in ~ of** руководи́ть (Т); быть отве́тственным (за В); **2.** *v/t. battery* заряжа́ть [-яди́ть]; поруча́ть [-чи́ть] (Д); обвиня́ть [-ни́ть] (**with** в П); *price* проси́ть (**for** за В); (*rush*) броса́ться ['-ситься]
**charisma** [kə'rɪzmə] ли́чное обая́ние
**charitable** ['tʃærətəbl] □ благотвори́тельный; (*kind*) милосе́рдный
**charity** ['tʃærətɪ] милосе́рдие; благотвори́тельность *f*
**charm** [tʃɑːm] **1.** (*trinket*) амуле́т; *fig.* ча́ры *f/pl.*; обая́ние, очарова́ние; **2.** заколдо́вывать [-дова́ть]; *fig.* очаро́вывать [-ова́ть]; **~ing** ['tʃɑːmɪŋ] □ очарова́тельный, обая́тельный
**chart** [tʃɑːt] *naut.* морска́я ка́рта; диагра́мма; *pl.* спи́сок шля́геров, бестсе́ллеров
**charter** ['tʃɑːtə] **1.** *hist.* ха́ртия; **~ of the UN** Уста́в ООН; **2.** *naut.* [за]фрахтова́ть (*су́дно*)
**charwoman** ['tʃɑːwʊmən] убо́рщица, приходя́щая домрабо́тница
**chase** [tʃeɪs] **1.** пого́ня *f*; *hunt.* охо́та; **2.**

охо́титься за (Т); пресле́довать; **~ *away*** прогоня́ть [-гна́ть]
**chasm** [kæzəm] бе́здна, про́пасть *f*
**chaste** [tʃeɪst] □ целому́дренный
**chastity** ['tʃæstətɪ] целому́дрие; де́вственность *f*
**chat** [tʃæt] **1.** бесе́да; **2.** [по]болта́ть, [по]бесе́довать
**chattels** ['tʃætlz] *pl.* (*mst.* ***goods and ~***) иму́щество, ве́щи *f/pl.*
**chatter** ['tʃætə] **1.** болтовня́ *f*; щебета́ние; **2.** [по]болта́ть; **~box**, **~er** [-rə] болту́н *m*, -нья *f*
**chatty** ['tʃætɪ] разгово́рчивый
**chauffeur** ['ʃəʊfə] води́тель *m*; шофёр
**cheap** [tʃiːp] □ дешёвый; *fig.* плохо́й; **~en** ['tʃiːpən] [по]дешеве́ть; *fig.* унижа́ть [уни́зить]
**cheat** [tʃiːt] **1.** *pers.* обма́нщик, плут; (*fraud*) обма́н; **2.** обма́нывать [-ну́ть]
**check** [tʃek] **1.** *chess* шах; (*restraint*) препя́тствие; остано́вка; (*verification, examination*) контро́ль *m* (***on*** над Т), прове́рка (***on*** P); *luggage/baggage ticket* бага́жная квита́нция; *bank draft* (*Brt.* ***cheque***), *receipt or bill in restaurant, etc.* чек; **2.** проверя́ть [-ве́рить]; [про]контроли́ровать; приостана́вливать [-нови́ть]; препя́тствовать; **~book** че́ковая кни́жка; **~er** ['tʃekə] контролёр; **~ers** ['tʃekəz] *pl. Am.* ша́шки *f/pl.*; **~mate 1.** шах и мат; **2.** де́лать мат; **~-up** прове́рка; *med.* осмо́тр
**cheek** [tʃiːk] щека́ (*pl.*: щёки); *coll.* на́глость *f*, де́рзость *f*
**cheer** [tʃɪə] **1.** весе́лье; одобри́тельные во́згласы *m/pl.*; **2.** *v/t.* подба́дривать [-бodри́ть]; приве́тствовать во́згласами; *v/i.* **~ *up*** приободри́ться; **~ful** ['tʃɪəfl] □ бо́дрый, весёлый; **~less** [-ləs] □ уны́лый, мра́чный; **~y** [-rɪ] □ живо́й, весёлый, ра́достный
**cheese** [tʃiːz] сыр
**chemical** ['kemɪkl] **1.** □ хими́ческий; **2. ~s** [-s] *pl.* хими́ческие препара́ты *m/pl.*, химика́лии *f/pl.*
**chemist** ['kemɪst] *scientist* хи́мик; *pharmacist* апте́карь *m*; **~ry** ['kemɪstrɪ] хи́мия; **~'s** *Brt.* апте́ка
**cherish** ['tʃerɪʃ] *hope* леле́ять; *in memory* храни́ть; (*love*) не́жно люби́ть
**cherry** ['tʃerɪ] ви́шня
**chess** [tʃes] ша́хматы *f/pl.*; **~board** ша́хматная доска́; **~man** ша́хматная фигу́ра
**chest** [tʃest] я́щик, сунду́к; *anat.* грудна́я кле́тка; **~ *of drawers*** комо́д; ***get s.th. off one's ~*** облегчи́ть ду́шу
**chestnut** ['tʃesnʌt] **1.** кашта́н; **2.** кашта́новый
**chew** [tʃuː] жева́ть; **~ *over*** (*think about*) размышля́ть; **~ing gum** ['tʃuːɪŋgʌm] жева́тельная рези́нка, *coll.* жва́чка
**chic** [ʃiːk] элега́нтный
**chick** [tʃɪk] цыплёнок; **~en** ['tʃɪkɪn] ку́рица; *cul.* куря́тина; **~enpox** ветряна́я о́спа
**chief** [tʃiːf] **1.** □ гла́вный; **2.** глава́, руководи́тель, нача́льник, *coll.* шеф; **~ly** гла́вным о́бразом
**child** [tʃaɪld] ребёнок, дитя́ *n* (*pl.*: де́ти); **~ *prodigy*** ['prɒdɪdʒɪ] вундерки́нд; **~birth** ро́ды *m/pl.*; **~hood** ['-hʊd] де́тство; ***from ~*** с де́тства; **~ish** ['tʃaɪldɪʃ] □ ребя́ческий; **~like** [-laɪk] как ребёнок; **~ren** ['tʃɪldrən] *pl. om* ***child***
**chill** [tʃɪl] **1.** хо́лод; *fig.* хо́лодность *f*; *med.* просту́да; **2.** холо́дный; *fig.* расхола́живающий; **3.** *v/t.* охлажда́ть [-лади́ть]; [о]студи́ть; *v/i.* охлажда́ться [-лади́ться]; **~y** ['tʃɪlɪ] холо́дный, прохла́дный (*both a. fig.*)
**chime** [tʃaɪm] **1.** звон колоколо́в; бой часо́в; **2.** [за]звони́ть; *of clock* проби́ть *pf.*; **~ *in*** вме́шиваться [-ша́ться]; *fig.* **~ (*in*) *with*** гармонизи́ровать; соотве́тствовать
**chimney** ['tʃɪmnɪ] дымова́я труба́
**chin** [tʃɪn] подборо́док
**china** ['tʃaɪnə] фарфо́р
**Chinese** [tʃaɪ'niːz] **1.** кита́ец *m*, -а́янка *f*; **2.** кита́йский
**chink** [tʃɪŋk] *crevice* щель *f*, тре́щина
**chip** [tʃɪp] **1.** *of wood* ще́пка; *of glass* оско́лок; *on plate, etc.* щерби́нка; **~s** *Brt.* карто́фель-чи́псы; **2.** *v/t.* отби́ть

*pf.* край; *v/i.* отла́мываться [отлома́ться]

**chirp** [tʃɜːp] **1.** чири́канье; щебета́ние; **2.** чири́кать [-кнуть]; [за]щебета́ть

**chisel** ['tʃɪzl] **1.** долото́, стаме́ска; *sculptor's* резе́ц; **2.** рабо́тать долото́м, резцо́м; **~led features** точёные черты́ лица́

**chitchat** ['tʃɪt tʃæt] болтовня́

**chivalrous** ['ʃɪvəlrəs] □ *mst. fig.* ры́царский

**chlor|inate** ['klɔːrɪneɪt] хлори́ровать; **~oform** ['klɒrəfɔːm] хлорофо́рм

**chocolate** ['tʃɒklɪt] шокола́д; *pl.* шокола́дные конфе́ты *f/pl.*

**choice** ['tʃɔɪs] **1.** вы́бор; альтернати́ва; **2.** □ отбо́рный

**choir** ['kwaɪə] хор

**choke** [tʃəʊk] *v/t.* [за]души́ть; (*mst.* **~ down**) глота́ть с трудо́м; *laughter* дави́ться (**with** от P); *v/i.* (*suffocate*) задыха́ться [-дохну́ться]; [по]дави́ться (**on** T)

**choose** [tʃuːz] [*irr.*] выбира́ть [вы́брать]; (*decide*) предпочита́ть [-че́сть]; **~ to** *inf.* хоте́ть (+ *inf.*)

**chop** [tʃɒp] **1.** отбивна́я (котле́та); **2.** *v/t. wood, etc.* [на]руби́ть; *parsley, etc.* [на]кроши́ть; **~ down** сруба́ть [-би́ть]; **~ and change** бесконе́чно меня́ть свои́ взгля́ды, пла́ны *и т.д.*; **~per** ['tʃɒpə] *tool* топо́р; *sl. helicopter* вертолёт; **~py** ['tʃɒpɪ] *sea* неспоко́йный

**choral** ['kɔːrəl] □ хорово́й; **~(e)** [kɒ'rɑːl] хора́л

**chord** [kɔːd] струна́; *mus.* акко́рд

**chore** [tʃɔː] ну́дная рабо́та; повседнёвные дела́

**chorus** ['kɔːrəs] хор; му́зыка для хо́ра; *of song* припе́в, рефре́н; **in ~** хо́ром

**chose** [tʃəʊz] *pt. от* **choose**; **~n** [-n] **1.** *pt. p. от* **choose**; **2.** и́збранный

**Christ** [kraɪst] Христо́с

**christen** ['krɪsn] [о]крести́ть; **~ing** [-ɪŋ] крести́ны *f/pl.*; креще́ние

**Christian** ['krɪstʃən] **1.** христиа́нский; **~ name** и́мя (*в отличие от фамилии*); **2.** христиа́нин *m*, -а́нка *f*; **~ity** [krɪstɪ'ænətɪ] христиа́нство

**Christmas** ['krɪsməs] Рождество́

**chromium** ['krəʊmɪəm] хром; **~-plated** хроми́рованный

**chronic** ['krɒnɪk] (**~ally**) хрони́ческий (*a. med.*); **~le** [-l] хро́ника, ле́топись *f*

**chronolog|ical** [ˌkrɒnə'lɒdʒɪkl] □ хронологи́ческий; **~y** [krə'nɒlədʒɪ] хроноло́гия

**chubby** ['tʃʌbɪ] *coll.* по́лный; *child* пу́хленький

**chuck** [tʃʌk] броса́ть [бро́сить]; *coll.* швыря́ть [-рну́ть]; **~ out** выбра́сывать [вы́бросить]; *from work* вышвы́ривать [вы́швырнуть]

**chuckle** ['tʃʌkl] посме́иваться

**chum** [tʃʌm] *coll.* **1.** прия́тель; **2.** быть в дру́жбе

**chump** [tʃʌmp] коло́да, чурба́н; *sl.* (*fool*) болва́н

**chunk** [tʃʌnk] *coll. of bread* ло́моть *m*; *of meat, etc.* то́лстый кусо́к

**church** [tʃɜːtʃ] це́рковь *f*; **~ service** богослуже́ние; **~yard** пого́ст, кла́дбище

**churlish** ['tʃɜːlɪʃ] □ (*ill-bred*) гру́бый; (*bad-tempered*) раздражи́тельный

**churn** [tʃɜːn]: маслобо́йка; бидо́н

**chute** [ʃuːt] *slide, slope* спуск; (*rubbish* **~**) мусоропрово́д; *for children* го́рка

**cider** ['saɪdə] сидр

**cigar** [sɪ'gɑː] сига́ра

**cigarette** [sɪgə'ret] сигаре́та; (*of Russian type*) папиро́са; **~ holder** мундшту́к

**cinch** [sɪntʃ] *coll.* не́что надёжное, ве́рное

**cinder** ['sɪndə]: **~s** *pl.* у́гли; **~track** *sport* га́ревая доро́жка

**cinema** ['sɪnɪmə] кинематогра́фия, кино́ *n indecl.*

**cinnamon** ['sɪnəmən] кори́ца

**cipher** ['saɪfə] **1.** шифр; (*zero*) нуль *m or* ноль *m*; **2.** зашифро́вывать [-ова́ть]

**circle** ['sɜːkl] **1.** круг (*a. fig.*); (*ring*) кольцо́; *thea.* я́рус; **business ~s** делово́е круги́; **2.** враща́ться вокру́г (P); соверша́ть круги́, кружи́ть(ся)

**circuit** ['sɜːkɪt] (*route*) маршру́т; объе́зд; *el.* цепь *f*, схе́ма

**circular** ['sɜːkjʊlə] **1.** □ кру́глый; *road*

круговóй; **~ *letter*** циркуля́рное письмó; **2.** циркуля́р; (*advertisement*) проспéкт

**circulat|e** ['sɜːkjʊleɪt] *v/i. rumo(u)r* распространя́ться [-ни́ться]; циркули́ровать (*a. fig.*); **~ing** [-ɪŋ]: **~ library** библиотéка с вы́дачей книг нá дом; **~ion** [sɜːkjʊ'leɪʃn] кровообращéние; циркуля́ция; *of newspapers etc.* тирáж; *fig.* распространéние

**circum…** ['sɜːkəm] *pref.* (*в сложных словах*) вокрýг, кругóм

**circum|ference** [sə'kʌmfərəns] окрýжность *f*; перифери́я; **~spect** ['sɜːkəmspekt] □ осмотри́тельный, осторóжный; **~stance** ['sɜːkəmstəns] обстоя́тельство; **~stantial** [sɜːkəm'stænʃl] □ обстоя́тельный, подрóбный; **~vent** [~'vent] (*law, etc.*) обходи́ть [обойти́]

**circus** ['sɜːkəs] цирк; *attr.* цирковóй

**cistern** ['sɪstən] бак; *in toilet* бачóк

**cit|ation** [saɪ'teɪʃn] цитáта, ссы́лка, цити́рование; **~e** [saɪt] ссылáться [сослáться] на (В)

**citizen** ['sɪtɪzn] граждани́н *m*, -дáнка *f*; **~ship** [~ʃɪp] граждáнство

**citrus** ['sɪtrəs]: **~ fruit** ци́трусовые

**city** ['sɪtɪ] гóрод; *attr.* городскóй; ***the*** **♀** Си́ти (*деловой центр в Лондоне*)

**civic** ['sɪvɪk] граждáнский; *of town* городскóй

**civil** ['sɪvl] □ *of a community* граждáнский (*a. law*); штáтский; (*polite*) вéжливый; **~ *servant*** госудáрственный слýжащий, *contp.* чинóвник; **~ *service*** госудáрственная слýжба; **~ian** [sɪ'vɪljən] штáтский; **~ity** [sɪ'vɪlətɪ] вéжливость *f*; **~ization** [sɪvəlaɪ'zeɪʃn] цивилизáция

**clad** [klæd] *pt. и pt. p. от* ***clothe***

**claim** [kleɪm] **1.** претендовáть, (*demand*) на (В); [по]трéбовать; (*assert*) утверждáть [-рди́ть]; предъявля́ть правá на (В); **2.** трéбование; претéнзия; *law* иск; **~ *for damages*** иск за причинённый ущéрб; **~ *to be*** выдавáть себя́ за (В); **~ant** ['kleɪmənt] претендéнт; *law* истéц

**clairvoyant** [kleə'vɔɪənt] ясновидец

**clamber** ['klæmbə] [вс]карáбкаться

**clammy** ['klæmɪ] □ (*sticky*) ли́пкий; *hands* холóдный и влáжный; *weather* сырóй и холóдный

**clamo(u)r** ['klæmə] **1.** шум, кри́ки *m/pl.*; шýмные протéсты *m/pl.*; **2.** шýмно трéбовать (Р)

**clamp** [klæmp] **1.** *tech.* скобá; зажи́м; **2.** скрепля́ть [-пи́ть]; заж(им)áть

**clandestine** [klæn'destɪn] □ тáйный

**clang** [klæŋ] **1.** лязг; *of bell* звон; **2.** ля́згать [-гнуть]

**clank** [klæŋk] **1.** звон, лязг, бря́цание; **2.** бря́цать, [за]гремéть

**clap** [klæp] **1.** хлопóк; хлóпанье; *of thunder* удáр; **2.** хлóпать, аплоди́ровать; **~trap** пустáя болтовня́; (*nonsense*) чепухá

**clarify** ['klærɪfaɪ] *v/t. liquid, etc.* очищáть [очи́стить]; (*make transparent*) дéлать прозрáчным; *fig.* выясня́ть [вы́яснить]; *v/i.* дéлаться прозрáчным, я́сным

**clarity** ['klærətɪ] я́сность *f*

**clash** [klæʃ] **1.** столкновéние; (*contradiction*) противорéчие; конфли́кт; **2.** стáлкиваться [столкнýться]; *of opinions, etc.* расходи́ться [разойти́сь]

**clasp** [klɑːsp] **1.** пря́жка, застёжка; *fig.* (*embrace*) объя́тия *n/pl.*; **2.** *v/t.* (*fasten*) застёгивать [застегнýть]; (*hold tightly*) сж(им)áть; *fig.* заключáть в объя́тия; *hand* пож(им)áть

**class** [klɑːs] **1.** *school* класс; *social* общéственный класс; **(*evening*) ~es** (вечéрние) кýрсы; **2.** классифици́ровать (*im*)*pf.*

**classic** ['klæsɪk] **1.** клáссик; **2. ~(al** □) [~(əl)] класси́ческий

**classi|fication** [klæsɪfɪ'keɪʃn] классификáция; **~fy** ['klæsɪfaɪ] классифици́ровать (*im*)*pf.*

**clatter** ['klætə] **1.** *of dishes* звон; *of metal* грóхот (маши́н); (*talk*) болтовня́; *of hoofs, etc.* тóпот; **2.** [за]гремéть; [за]тóпать; *fig.* [по]болтáть

**clause** [klɔːz] *of agreement, etc.* пункт, статья́; *gr.* ***principal/subordinate ~*** глáвное/придáточное предложéние

**claw** [klɔː] **1.** *of animal* кóготь *m*; *of*

*crustacean* клешня́; **2.** разрыва́ть, терза́ть когтя́ми
**clay** [kleɪ] гли́на
**clean** [kliːn] **1.** *adj.* □ чи́стый; (*tidy*) опря́тный; **2.** *adv.* на́чисто; соверше́нно, по́лностью; **3.** [по]чи́стить; **~ up** уб(и)ра́ть; приводи́ть в поря́док; **~er** ['kliːnə] убо́рщик *m*, -ица *f*; **~er's** химчи́стка; **~ing** ['kliːnɪŋ] чи́стка; *of room* убо́рка; **~liness** ['klenlɪnɪs] чистопло́тность *f*; **~ly 1.** *adv.* ['kliːnlɪ] чи́сто; **2.** *adj.* ['klenlɪ] чистопло́тный; **~se** [klenz] очища́ть [очи́стить]
**clear** [klɪər] **1.** □ све́тлый, я́сный (*a. fig.*); (*transparent*) прозра́чный; *fig.* свобо́дный (**from, of** от Р); *profit, etc.* чи́стый; (*distinct*) отчётливый; (*plain*) я́сный, поня́тный; **2.** *v/t.* убира́ть [-бра́ть]; очища́ть [очи́стить] (**from, of** от Р); расчища́ть [-и́стить]; (*free from blame*) опра́вдывать [-да́ть]; **~ the air** разряди́ть атмосфе́ру; *v/i.* (*a.* **~ up**) *of mist* рассе́иваться [-е́яться]; *of sky* проясня́ться [-ни́ться]; **~ance** ['klɪərəns] *comm.* разреше́ние (на прово́з, на вы́воз, *naut.* на вы́ход); **~ing** ['klɪərɪŋ] *tech.* зазо́р; *mot.* кли́ренс; *in forest* про́сека, поля́на; *fin.* кли́ринг; **~ly** я́сно; (*obviously*) очеви́дно
**cleave** [kliːv] [*irr.*] *split* раска́лывать(ся) [-коло́ть(ся)]; рассека́ть [-е́чь]; *adhere* прилипа́ть [-ли́пнуть]
**clef** [klef] *mus.* ключ
**cleft** [kleft] рассе́лина
**clemen|cy** ['klemənsɪ] милосе́рдие; снисхожде́ние; **~t** ['klemənt] милосе́рдный; *weather* мя́гкий
**clench** [klentʃ] заж(им)а́ть; *fists* сж(им)а́ть; *teeth* сти́скивать [сти́снуть]; → ***clinch***
**clergy** ['klɜːdʒɪ] духове́нство; **~man** [-mən] свяще́нник
**clerical** ['klerɪkl] □ *eccl.* духо́вный; *of clerks* канцеля́рский
**clerk** [klɑːk] клерк, конто́рский слу́жащий; *Am.* ***sales*** **~** продаве́ц
**clever** ['klevə] □ у́мный; (*skilled*) уме́лый; *mst. b.s.* ло́вкий
**click** [klɪk] **1.** щёлканье; **2.** *lock* щёлкать [-кнуть]; *tongue* прищёлкивать [-кнуть]; *fig.* идти́ гла́дко; **~ *on*** *comput.* щёлкнуть мы́шью
**client** ['klaɪənt] клие́нт; покупа́тель *m*; **~èle** [kliːən'tel] клиенту́ра
**cliff** [klɪf] утёс, скала́
**climate** ['klaɪmɪt] кли́мат
**climax** ['klaɪmæks] **1.** кульмина́ция; **2.** достига́ть [-и́гнуть] кульмина́ции
**climb** [klaɪm] [*irr.*] влез(а́)ть на (В); *mountain* поднима́ться [-ня́ться] (на В); **~er** ['klaɪmə] альпини́ст; *fig.* карьери́ст; *bot.* вью́щееся расте́ние
**clinch** [klɪntʃ] *fig.* оконча́тельно договори́ться *pf.*, реши́ть *pf.*; ***that ~ed the matter*** э́тим вопро́с был оконча́тельно решён
**cling** [klɪŋ] [*irr.*] (***to***) [при]льну́ть к (Д); **~ *together*** держа́ться вме́сте
**clinic** ['klɪnɪk] кли́ника; поликли́ника; **~al** [-ɪkəl] клини́ческий
**clink** [klɪŋk] **1.** звон; **2.** [за]звене́ть; **~ *glasses*** чо́каться [-кнуться]
**clip**[1] [klɪp] **1.** *newspaper* вы́резка; *TV* клип; **2.** выреза́ть [вы́резать]; (*cut*) [о-, под]стри́чь
**clip**[2] [~] **1.** скре́пка; **2.**: **~ *together*** скрепля́ть [-пи́ть]
**clipp|er** ['klɪpə]: (*a pair of*) (*nail-*) **~ers** *pl.* маникю́рные но́жницы *f/pl.*; *hort.* сека́тор; **~ings** [~ɪŋz] *pl.* газе́тные вы́резки *f/pl.*; обре́зки *m/pl.*
**cloak** [kləʊk] **1.** плащ; *of darkness* покро́в; *fig.* (*pretext*) предло́г; **2.** покры́(ва́)ть; *fig.* прикры́(ва́)ть; **~room** гардеро́б, *coll.* раздева́лка; *euph.*, *mst. Brt.* туале́т; **~room attendant** гардеро́бщик *m*, -щица *f*
**clock** [klɒk] часы́ *m/pl.* (*стенные и т.д.*); **~wise** по часово́й стре́лке
**clod** [klɒd] ком; (*fool*) ду́рень *m*, о́лух
**clog** [klɒg] засоря́ть(ся) [-ри́ть(ся)], забива́ться [-би́ться]
**cloister** ['klɔɪstə] монасты́рь *m*; *arch.* кры́тая арка́да
**close 1.** [kləʊs] □ (*restricted*) закры́тый; (*near*) бли́зкий; (*tight*) те́сный; *air* ду́шный, спёртый; (*stingy*) скупо́й; *study, etc.* внима́тельный, тща́тельный; **~ *by*** *adv.* ря́дом, побли́зости; **~**

***to*** около (Р); **2.** [kləʊz] конéц; (*conclusion*) завершéние; ***come to a ~*** закóнчиться, завершиться; **3.** [kləʊz] *v/t.* закры́(вá)ть; закáнчивать [-кóнчить]; кончáть [кóнчить]; заключáть [-чи́ть] (речь); *v/i.* закры́(вá)ться; кончáться [кóнчиться]; ***~ in*** приближáться [-ли́зиться]; наступáть [-пи́ть]; **~ness** ['kləʊsnɪs] бли́зость *f*; скýпость *f*

**closet** ['klɒzɪt] *Am.* чулáн; стеннóй шкаф

**close-up**: ***take a ~*** снимáть [снять] крýпным плáном

**closure** ['kləʊʒə] закры́тие

**clot** [klɒt] **1.** *of blood* сгýсток; комóк; **2.** *mst. of blood* свёртываться [свернýться]

**cloth** [klɒθ], *pl.* **~s** [klɒθs] ткань *f*, материáл; ***length of ~*** отрéз

**clothe** [kləʊð] [*a. irr.*] одé(вá)ть; *fig.* облекáть [облéчь]

**clothes** [kləʊðz] *pl.* одéжда; ***change one's ~*** переодéться; **~line** верёвка для сýшки бельá; **~ peg** прищéпка

**clothing** ['kləʊðɪŋ] одéжда; ***ready-made ~*** готóвая одéжда

**cloud** [klaʊd] **1.** óблако, тýча; ***have one's head in the ~s*** витáть в облакáх; **2.** покрывáть(ся) тýчами, облакáми; *fig.* омрачáть(ся) [-чи́ть(ся)]; **~burst** ли́вень *m*; **~less** ['klaʊdləs] □ безóблачный; **~y** [-ɪ] □ óблачный; *liquid* мýтный; *ideas* тумáнный

**clove**[1] [kləʊv] гвозди́ка (прáность)

**clove**[2] [~] *pt. от* ***cleave***

**clover** ['kləʊvə] клéвер; ***in ~*** жить припевáючи

**clown** [klaʊn] клóун

**club** [klʌb] **1.** *society* клуб; (*heavy stick*) дуби́на; *Am.* дуби́нка (полицéйского); **~s** *pl. at cards* трéфы *f/pl.*; **2.** *v/t.* [по]би́ть; *v/i.* собирáться вмéсте; ***~ together*** сложи́ться [склáдываться]; (*share expense*) устрáивать склáдчину

**clue** [klu:] ключ к разгáдке; ***I haven't a ~*** понáтия не имéю

**clump** [klʌmp] **1.** *of bushes* кустáрник; *of trees* кýпа, грýппа; **2.** *tread heavily* тяжелó ступáть

**clumsy** ['klʌmzɪ] □ неуклю́жий; нелóвкий (*a. fig.*); (*tactless*) бестáктный

**clung** [klʌŋ] *pt. и pt. p. от* ***cling***

**cluster** ['klʌstə] **1.** кисть *f*; гроздь *f*; **2.** расти́ грóздьями; ***~ round*** окружáть [-жи́ть]

**clutch** [klʌtʃ] **1.** *of car* сцеплéние; ***fall into s.o.'s ~es*** попáсть *pf.* в чьи́-л. лáпы; **2.** (*seize*) схвáтывать [-ти́ть]; ухвати́ться *pf.* (***at*** за В)

**clutter** ['klʌtə] **1.** беспорáдок; **2.** завали́ть, загромозди́ть

**coach** [kəʊtʃ] **1.** *Brt.* междугорóдный автóбус; (*trainer*) трéнер; (*tutor*) репети́тор; *rail.* пассажи́рский вагóн; **2.** [на]тренировáть; натáскивать к экзáмену

**coagulate** [kəʊ'ægjʊleɪt] свёртываться, коагули́роваться

**coal** [kəʊl] (кáменный) ýголь *m*

**coalition** [kəʊə'lɪʃn] коали́ция

**coal|mine**, **~ pit** ýгольная шáхта

**coarse** [kɔ:s] □ *material* грýбый; *sugar, etc.* крýпный; *fig.* неотёсанный; *joke* непристóйный

**coast** [kəʊst] морскóй бéрег, побережье; **~al**: ***~ waters*** прибрéжные вóды; **~er** ['kəʊstə] *naut.* сýдно каботáжного плáвания

**coat** [kəʊt] **1.** (*man's jacket*) пиджáк; (*over~*) пальтó *n indecl.*; (*fur*) мех, шерсть *f*; (*layer of paint, etc.*) слой; ***~ of arms*** герб; **2.** (*cover*) покры́(вá)ть; **~ hanger** вéшалка; **~ing** ['kəʊtɪŋ] слой

**coax** [kəʊks] уговáривать [уговори́ть]

**cob** [kɒb] *of maize* початóк

**cobbler** ['kɒblə] сапóжник

**cobblestone** ['kɒblstəʊn] булы́жник; *attr.* булы́жный

**cobweb** ['kɒbweb] паути́на

**cock** [kɒk] **1.** (*rooster*) петýх; (*tap*) кран; *in gun* курóк; **2.** *ears* насторáживать [-рожи́ть]

**cockatoo** [kɒkə'tu:] какадý *m indecl.*

**cockchafer** ['kɒktʃeɪfər] мáйский жук

**cock-eyed** ['kɒkaɪd] *sl.* косоглáзый; косóй; *Am.* пья́ный

**cockpit** ['kɒkpɪt] *ae.* каби́на

**cockroach** ['kɒkrəʊtʃ] *zo.* таракáн

C

**cock|sure** [kɒk'ʃʊə] *coll.* самоуве́ренный; **~tail** ['~teɪl] кокте́йль *m*; **~y** ['kɒkɪ] □ *coll.* наха́льный, де́рзкий
**cocoa** ['kəʊkəʊ] *powder or drink* кака́о *n indecl.*
**coconut** ['kəʊkənʌt] коко́с, коко́совый оре́х
**cocoon** [kə'kuːn] ко́кон
**cod** [kɒd] треска́
**coddle** ['kɒdl] [из]ба́ловать, [из]не́жить
**code** [kəʊd] **1.** *of conduct, laws* ко́декс; *of symbols, ciphers* код; **2.** коди́ровать *(im)pf.*
**cod-liver**: **~ *oil*** ры́бий жир
**coerc|e** [kəʊ'ɜːs] принужда́ть [-ну́дить]; **~ion** [~ʃn] принужде́ние
**coexist** [kəʊɪg'zɪst] сосуществова́ть (с Т)
**coffee** ['kɒfɪ] ко́фе *m indecl.*; ***instant* ~** раствори́мый ко́фе; **~ *grinder*** кофемо́лка; **~ *set*** кофе́йный серви́з; **~pot** кофе́йник
**coffin** ['kɒfɪn] гроб
**cog** [kɒg] зубе́ц
**cogent** ['kəʊdʒənt] □ (*convincing*) убеди́тельный
**cognac** ['kɒnjæk] конья́к
**cohabit** [kəʊ'hæbɪt] сожи́тельствовать, жить вме́сте
**coheren|ce** [kəʊ'hɪərəns] связь *f*; свя́зность *f*; согласо́ванность *f*; **~t** [~rənt] □ *story, etc.* свя́зный; поня́тный; согласо́ванный
**cohesion** [kəʊ'hiːʒn] сцепле́ние; сплочённость *f*
**coiffure** [kwɑː'fjʊə] причёска
**coil** [kɔɪl] **1.** кольцо́; *el.* кату́шка; **2.** (*a.* **~ *up***) свёртываться кольцо́м (спира́лью)
**coin** [kɔɪn] **1.** моне́та; ***pay s.o. back in his own* ~** отплати́ть *pf.* кому́-л. той же моне́той; **2.** (*mint*) чека́нить; **~age** ['kɔɪnɪdʒ] чека́нка
**coincide** [kəʊɪn'saɪd] совпада́ть [-па́сть]; **~nce** [kəʊ'ɪnsɪdəns] совпаде́ние; *fig.* случа́йное стече́ние обстоя́тельств; ***by sheer* ~** по чи́стой случа́йности
**coke**[1] [kəʊk] кокс
**coke**[2] [~] *coll.* ко́ка-ко́ла
**colander** ['kʌləndə] дуршла́г
**cold** [kəʊld] **1.** □ холо́дный; *fig.* неприве́тливый; **2.** хо́лод; просту́да; ***catch* (*a*) ~** простуди́ться; **~ness** ['kəʊldnɪs] *of temperature* хо́лод; *of character, etc.* хо́лодность *f*
**colic** ['kɒlɪk] *med.* ко́лики *f/pl.*
**collaborat|e** [kə'læbəreɪt] сотру́дничать; **~ion** [kəlæbə'reɪʃn] сотру́дничество; ***in* ~ *with*** в сотру́дничестве (с Т)
**collapse** [kə'læps] **1.** (*caving in*) обва́л; разруше́ние; *of plans, etc.* круше́ние; *med.* по́лный упа́док сил, колла́пс; **2.** *of a structure* обру́ши(ва)ться, ру́хнуть; *of person* упа́сть без созна́ния
**collar** ['kɒlər] **1.** воротни́к; *dog's* оше́йник; **2.** схвати́ть *pf.* за ши́ворот; *sl. a criminal* схвати́ть *pf.*; **~bone** *anat.* ключи́ца
**collateral** [kə'lætərəl] побо́чный; *evidence* ко́свенный
**colleague** ['kɒliːg] колле́га *f/m*, сослужи́вец *m*, -вица *f*
**collect** [kə'lekt] *v/t.* (*get together*) соб(ир)а́ть; *stamps etc.* коллекциони́ровать; (*call for*) заходи́ть [зайти́] за (Т); *o.s.* (*control o.s.*) овладева́ть собо́й; *v/i.* (*gather*) соб(и)ра́ться (*a. fig.*); **~ *on delivery*** *Am.* нало́женным платежо́м; **~ed** [kə'lektɪd] □ *fig.* споко́йный; **~ *works*** собра́ние сочине́ний; **~ion** [kə'lekʃn] колле́кция, собра́ние; **~ive** [~tɪv] □ коллекти́вный; совоку́пный; **~or** [~tə] коллекционе́р; *of tickets, etc.* контролёр
**college** ['kɒlɪdʒ] колле́дж; институ́т, университе́т
**collide** [kə'laɪd] ста́лкиваться [столкну́ться]
**collie** ['kɒlɪ] ко́лли *m/f indecl.*
**collier** ['kɒlɪər] углеко́п, шахтёр; **~y** ['kɒljərɪ] каменноуго́льня ша́хта
**collision** ['kəlɪʒn] столкнове́ние
**colloquial** [kə'ləʊkwɪəl] □ разгово́рный
**colon** ['kəʊlən] *typ.* двоето́чие
**colonel** ['kɜːnl] полко́вник
**colonial** [kə'ləʊnɪəl] колониа́льный

**colony** ['kɒlənɪ] коло́ния

**colo(u)r** ['kʌlə] **1.** цвет; (*paint*) кра́ска; *on face* румя́нец; *fig.* колори́т; **~s** *pl.* госуда́рственный флаг; ***be off ~*** нева́жно себя́ чу́вствовать; **2.** *v/t.* [по]кра́сить; окра́шивать [окра́сить]; *fig.* приукра́шивать [-кра́сить]; *v/i.* [по]красне́ть; **~-blind:** ***be ~*** быть дальто́ником; **~ed** [~d] окра́шенный; цветно́й; **~ful** [~fʊl] я́ркий; **~ing** [~rɪŋ] окра́ска, раскра́ска; *fig.* приукра́шивание; **~less** [~ləs] □ бесцве́тный (*a. fig.*)

**colt** [kəʊlt] жеребёнок (*pl.:* жеребя́та); *fig.* птене́ц

**column** ['kɒləm] *arch.*, *mil.* коло́нна; *of smoke, etc.* столб; *of figures* столбе́ц

**comb** [kəʊm] **1.** гре́бень *m*, гребёнка; **2.** *v/t.* расчёсывать [-чеса́ть], причёсывать [-чеса́ть]

**combat** ['kɒmbæt] **1.** бой, сраже́ние; **2.** сража́ться [срази́ться]; боро́ться (*a. fig.*); **~ant** ['kɒmbətənt] бое́ц

**combin|ation** [kɒmbɪ'neɪʃn] сочета́ние; **~e** [kəm'baɪn] объединя́ть(ся) [объедини́ть(ся)]; сочета́ть(ся) (*im*)*pf.*; ***~ business with pleasure*** сочета́ть прия́тное с поле́зным

**combusti|ble** [kəm'bʌstəbl] горю́чий, воспламеня́емый; **~on** [~tʃən] горе́ние, сгора́ние; ***internal ~ engine*** дви́гатель вну́треннего сгора́ния

**come** [kʌm] [*irr.*] приходи́ть [прийти́]; *by car, etc.* приезжа́ть [прие́хать]; ***to ~*** бу́дущий; ***~ about*** случа́ться [-чи́ться], происходи́ть [произойти́]; ***~ across*** встреча́ться [-ре́титься] с (Т), ната́лкиваться [наткну́ться] на (В); ***~ back*** возвраща́ться [-ти́ться]; ***~ by*** дост(ав)а́ть (случа́йно); ***~ from*** быть ро́дом из (Р); ***~ off***, (*be successful*) уда́сться *pf.*; *of skin, etc.* сходи́ть [сойти́]; ***~ round*** приходи́ть в себя́; *coll.* заходи́ть [зайти́] к (Д); *fig.* идти на усту́пки; ***~ to*** доходи́ть [дойти́] до (Р); (*equal*) равня́ться (Д), сто́ить (В *or* Р); ***~ up to*** соотве́тствовать (Д); ***~ to know s.o.*** (***sth.***) познако́миться *pf.* (с Т) (узнава́ть [-на́ть] В); ***~ what may*** что бы ни случи́лось

**comedian** [kə'miːdɪən] ко́мик

**comedy** ['kɒmədɪ] коме́дия

**comeliness** ['kʌmlɪnɪs] милови́дность *f*

**comfort** ['kʌmfət] **1.** комфо́рт, удо́бство; *fig.* (*consolation*) утеше́ние; (*support*) подде́ржка; **2.** утеша́ть [уте́шить]; успока́ивать [-ко́ить]; **~able** [~əbl] удо́бный, комфорта́бельный; *income, life* вполне́ прили́чный; **~less** [~lɪs] □ неую́тный

**comic** ['kɒmɪk] **1.** коми́ческий, смешно́й; юмористи́ческий; **2.** ко́мик; ***the ~s*** ко́миксы

**coming** ['kʌmɪŋ] **1.** прие́зд, прибы́тие; **2.** бу́дущий; наступа́ющий

**comma** ['kɒmə] запята́я

**command** [kə'mɑːnd] **1.** кома́нда, прика́з; (*authority*) кома́ндование; ***have at one's ~*** име́ть в своём распоряже́нии; **2.** прика́зывать [-за́ть] (Д); владе́ть (Т); *mil.* кома́ндовать; **~er** [kə'mɑːndə] *mil.* команди́р; *navy* капита́н; **Ωer-in-chief** [~rɪn'tʃiːf] главнокома́ндующий; **~ment** [~mənt] *eccl.* за́поведь *f*

**commemora|te** [kə'meməreɪt] *anniversary* ознаменова́ть; *event* отмеча́ть [отме́тить]; **~tion** [kəmemə'reɪʃn] ознаменова́ние

**commence** [kə'mens] нач(ин)а́ть(-ся); **~ment** [~mənt] нача́ло, торже́ственное вруче́ние дипло́мов

**commend** [kə'mend] отмеча́ть [-е́тить], [по]хвали́ть (***for*** за В); рекомендова́ть (*im*)*pf.*

**comment** ['kɒment] **1.** (*remark*) замеча́ние; *on text, etc.* коммента́рий; ***no ~!*** коммента́рии изли́шни!; **2.** (***on***) комменти́ровать (*im*)*pf.*; отзыва́ться [отозва́ться]; [с]де́лать замеча́ние; **~ary** ['kɒməntrɪ] коммента́рий; **~ator** ['kɒmənteɪtə] коммента́тор

**commerc|e** ['kɒmɜːs] торго́вля, комме́рция; **~ial** [kə'mɜːʃl] □ торго́вый, комме́рческий; *su. radio, TV* рекла́ма

**commiseration** [kəmɪzə'reɪʃn] сочу́вствие, соболе́знование

**commission** [kə'mɪʃn] **1.** (*body of per-*

*sons*) коми́ссия; (*authority*) полномо́чие; (*errand*) поруче́ние; (*order*) зака́з; *comm.* комиссио́нные; **2.** зака́зывать [-за́ть]; поруча́ть [-чи́ть]; **~er** [-ʃənə] уполномо́ченный; член коми́ссии

**commit** [kə'mɪt] (*entrust*) поруча́ть [-чи́ть]; вверя́ть [вве́рить]; *for trial, etc.* преда́(ва́)ть; *crime* соверша́ть [-ши́ть]; **~** (**o.s.**) обя́зывать(ся) [-за́ть(ся)]; **~** (**to prison**) заключа́ть [-чи́ть] (в тюрму́); **~ment** [-mənt] (*promise*) обяза́тельство; **~tee** [-ɪ] коми́ссия; комите́т; ***be on a ~*** быть чле́ном коми́ссии

**commodity** [kə'mɒdətɪ] това́р, предме́т потребле́ния

**common** ['kɒmən] □ о́бщий; (*ordinary*) просто́й, обыкнове́нный; (*mediocre*) зауря́дный; (*widespread*) распространённый; ***it is ~ knowledge that …*** общеизве́стно, что …; ***out of the ~*** незауря́дный; **~ *sense*** здра́вый смысл; ***we have nothing in ~*** у нас нет ничего́ о́бщего; **~place 1.** бана́льность *f*; **2.** бана́льный, *coll.* изби́тый; **~s** [-z] *pl.* простонаро́дье; (*mst. **House of***) ♀ Пала́та общи́н; **~wealth** [-welθ] госуда́рство, содру́жество; ***the British ♀ of Nations*** Брита́нское Содру́жество На́ций

**commotion** [kə'məʊʃn] волне́ние, смяте́ние, возня́

**communal** ['kɒmjʊnl] (*pertaining to community*) обще́ственный, коммуна́льный; **~ *apartment** or **flat*** коммуна́льная кварти́ра

**communicat|e** [kə'mjuːnɪkeɪt] *v.t.* сообща́ть [-щи́ть]; перед(ав)а́ть; *v/i.* сообща́ться; **~ion** [kəmjuːnɪ'keɪʃn] сообще́ние; коммуника́ция; связь *f*; **~ *satellite*** спу́тник свя́зи; **~ive** [kə'mjuːnɪkətɪv] □ общи́тельный, разгово́рчивый

**communion** [kə'mjuːnjən] обще́ние; *sacrament* прича́стие

**communiqué** [kə'mjuːnɪkeɪ] коммюнике́ *n indecl.*

**communis|m** ['kɒmjʊnɪzəm] коммуни́зм; **~t 1.** коммуни́ст *m*, -ка *f*; **2.** коммунисти́ческий

**community** [kə'mjuːnətɪ] о́бщество; ***local ~*** ме́стные жи́тели

**commute** [kə'mjuːt] *law* смягчи́ть наказа́ние; *travel back and forth regularly* е́здить на рабо́ту (*напр. из при́города в город*)

**compact** [kəm'pækt] *adj.* компа́ктный; (*closely packed*) пло́тный; *style* сжа́тый; *v/t.* сж(им)а́ть; уплотня́ть [-ни́ть]; **~ *disc*** компа́ктдиск

**companion** [kəm'pænjən] това́рищ, подру́га; (*travel*[*l*]*ing* **~**) спу́тник; **~ship** [-ʃɪp] компа́ния; дру́жеские отноше́ния *n/pl.*

**company** ['kʌmpənɪ] о́бщество; *comm.* компа́ния; акционе́рное о́бщество, фи́рма; (*guests*) го́сти *pl.*; *thea.* тру́ппа; ***have ~*** принима́ть госте́й

**compar|able** ['kɒmpərəbl] □ сравни́мый; **~ative** [kəm'pærətɪv] □ сравни́тельный; **~e** [kəm'peər] **1. *beyond ~*** вне вся́кого сравне́ния; **2.** *v/t.* сра́внивать [-ни́ть], слича́ть [-чи́ть], (***to*** с Т); *v/i.* сра́вниваться [-ни́ться]; **~ *favo*(*u*)*rably with*** вы́годно отлича́ться от Р; **~ison** [kəm'pærɪsn] сравне́ние; ***by ~*** по сравне́нию (с Т)

**compartment** [kəm'pɑːtmənt] отделе́ние; *rail.* купе́ *n indecl.*

**compass** ['kʌmpəs] ко́мпас; (*extent*) преде́л; (***a pair of***) **~es** *pl.* ци́ркуль *m*

**compassion** [kəm'pæʃn] сострада́ние, жа́лость *f*; **~ate** [-ʃənət] □ сострада́телный, сочу́вствующий

**compatible** [kəm'pætəbl] □ совмести́мый (*a. comput.*)

**compatriot** [kəm'pætrɪət] сооте́чественник *m*, -ница *f*

**compel** [kəm'pel] заставля́ть [-а́вить]; принужда́ть [-нуди́ть]

**compensat|e** ['kɒmpənseɪt] *v/t.* компенси́ровать; *losses* возмеща́ть [-ести́ть]; **~ion** [kɒmpən'seɪʃn] возмеще́ние, компенса́ция

**compete** [kəm'piːt] соревнова́ться, состяза́ться; конкури́ровать (***with*** с Т, ***for*** за В)

**competen|ce**, **~cy** ['kɒmpɪtəns, -ɪ]

спосо́бность *f*; компете́нтность *f*; **~t** [-tənt] □ компете́нтный

**competit|ion** [kɒmpəˈtɪʃn] состяза́ние, соревнова́ние; *comm.* конкуре́нция; *of pianists, etc.* ко́нкурс; **~ive** [kəmˈpetətɪv] конкурентоспосо́бный; **~or** [kəmˈpetɪtə] конкуре́нт *m*, -ка *f*; (*rival*) сопе́рник *m*, -ица *f*; уча́стник ко́нкурса

**compile** [kəmˈpaɪl] составля́ть [-а́вить]

**complacen|ce, ~cy** [kəmˈpleɪsəns, ~ɪ] самодово́льство

**complain** [kəmˈpleɪn] [по]жа́ловаться (***of*** на В); *law* обжа́ловать *pf*.; **~t** [-t] жа́лоба; *med.* боле́знь *f*; *comm.* реклама́ция

**complement** [ˈkɒmplɪmənt] **1.** дополне́ние; компле́кт; **2.** дополня́ть [допо́лнить]; [у]комплектова́ть

**complet|e** [kəmˈpliːt] **1.** □ (*whole*) по́лный; (*finished*) зако́нченный; *coll. fool* кру́глый; **~ *stranger*** соверше́нно незнако́мый челове́к; **2.** зака́нчивать [зако́нчить]; **~ion** [~ˈpliʃn] оконча́ние

**complex** [ˈkɒmpleks] **1.** □ (*intricate*) сло́жный; (*composed of parts*) ко́мплексный, составно́й; *fig.* сло́жный, запу́танный; **2.** ко́мплекс; **~ion** [kəmˈplekʃn] цвет лица́; **~ity** [~sɪtɪ] сло́жность *f*

**compliance** [kəmˈplaɪəns] усту́пчивость *f*; согла́сие; ***in ~ with*** в соотве́тствии с (Т)

**complicat|e** [ˈkɒmplɪkeɪt] усложня́ть(ся) [-ни́ть(ся)]; **~ion** [~ˈkeɪʃn] сло́жность *f*, тру́дность *f*; *pl.* осложне́ния *n/pl., a. med.*

**compliment 1.** [ˈkɒmplɪmənt] комплиме́нт; (*greeting*) приве́т; **2.** [~ment] *v/t.* говори́ть комплиме́нты (Д); поздравля́ть [-а́вить] (***on*** с Т)

**comply** [kəmˈplaɪ] уступа́ть [-и́ть], соглаша́ться [-ласи́ться] (***with*** с Т); (*yield*) подчиня́ться [-ни́ться] (***with*** Д)

**component** [kəmˈpəʊnənt] **1.** компоне́нт; составна́я часть *f*; **2.** составно́й

**compos|e** [kəmˈpəʊz] (*put together*) составля́ть [-а́вить]; (*create*) сочиня́ть [-ни́ть]; *compose o.s.* успока́иваться [-ко́иться]; **~ed** [~d] □ споко́йный, сде́ржанный; **~er** [~ə] компози́тор; **~ition** [kɒmpəˈzɪʃn] *art* компози́ция; (*structure*) соста́в; *lit., mus.* сочине́ние; **~ure** [kəmˈpəʊʒə] самооблада́ние, споко́йствие

**compound 1.** [ˈkɒmpaʊnd] *chem.* соста́в, соедине́ние; *gr.* сло́жное сло́во; **2.** сло́жный; **~ *interest*** сло́жные проце́нты *m/pl.*

**comprehend** [kɒmprɪˈhend] постига́ть [пости́гнуть], понима́ть [-ня́ть]; (*include*) охва́тывать [охвати́ть]

**comprehen|sible** [kɒmprɪˈhensəbl] поня́тный, постижи́мый; **~sion** [~ʃn] понима́ние; поня́тливость *f*; **~sive** [~sɪv] □ (*inclusive*) (все)объе́млющий; исче́рпывающий; *study* всесторо́нний

**compress** [kəmˈpres] сж(им)а́ть; ***~ed air*** сжа́тый во́здух

**comprise** [kəmˈpraɪz] состоя́ть; заключа́ть в себе́

**compromise** [ˈkɒmprəmaɪz] **1.** компроми́сс; **2.** *v/t.* [с]компромети́ровать; *v/i.* пойти́ *pf.* на компроми́сс

**compuls|ion** [kəmˈpʌlʃn] принужде́ние; **~ory** [~ˈpʌlsərɪ] *education, etc.* обяза́тельный; принуди́тельный

**comput|e** [kəmˈpjuːt] вычисля́ть [вы́числить]; **~er** [~ə] компью́тер

**comrade** [ˈkɒmreɪd] това́рищ

**con** [kɒn] = ***contra*** про́тив; ***the pros and ~s*** (голоса́) за и про́тив

**conceal** [kənˈsiːl] скры́(ва́)ть; ута́ивать [-и́ть], ума́лчивать [умолча́ть]

**concede** [kənˈsiːd] уступа́ть [-пи́ть]; (*allow*) допуска́ть [-сти́ть]

**conceit** [kənˈsiːt] самонаде́янность, самомне́ние; **~ed** [~ɪd] самонаде́янный

**conceiv|able** [kənˈsiːvəbl] мы́слимый; постижи́мый; ***it's hardly ~*** вряд ли; **~e** [kənˈsiːv] *v/i.* представля́ть себе́; *v/t.* заду́м(ыв)ать

**concentrate** [ˈkɒnsəntreɪt] сосредото́чи(ва)ть(ся)

**conception** [kənˈsepʃn] конце́пция; за́мысел; *biol.* зача́тие

**concern** [kənˈsɜːn] **1.** де́ло; (*anxiety*)

C

беспоко́йство; интере́с; *comm.* предприя́тие; ***what ~ is it of yours?*** како́е вам до э́того де́ло?; **2.** каса́ться [косну́ться] (Р); име́ть отноше́ние к (Д); **~ *o.s. about, with*** [за]интересова́ться, занима́ться [заня́ться] (Т); **~ed** [-d] □ заинтересо́ванный; име́ющий отноше́ние; озабо́ченный; **~ing** [-ɪŋ] *prp.* относи́тельно (Р)

**concert** ['kɒnsət] конце́рт; ***act in ~*** де́йствовать согласо́ванно

**concerto** [kən'tʃeətəʊ] конце́рт

**concession** [kən'seʃn] усту́пка; *econ.* конце́ссия; *in price* ски́дка

**conciliat|e** [kən'sɪlɪeɪt] примиря́ть [-ри́ть]; **~or** [-ə] посре́дник

**concise** [kən'saɪs] □ сжа́тый, кра́ткий; **~ness** [-nɪs] сжа́тость *f*, кра́ткость *f*

**conclude** [kən'kluːd] *agreement, etc.* заключа́ть [-чи́ть]; (*finish*) зака́нчивать [зако́нчить]; ***to be ~d*** оконча́ние сле́дует

**conclusi|on** [kən'kluːʒn] оконча́ние; (*inference*) заключе́ние; вы́вод; ***draw a ~*** сде́лать *pf.* вы́вод; **~ve** [-sɪv] □ (*final*) заключи́тельный; (*convincing*) убеди́тельный

**concoct** [kən'kɒkt] [со]стря́пать (*a. fig.*); *fig.* приду́м(ыв)ать

**concord** ['kɒŋkɔːd] (*agreement*) согла́сие

**concrete** ['kɒŋkriːt] **1.** конкре́тный; **2.** бето́н; **3.** [за]бетони́ровать

**concur** [kən'kɜː] (*agree*) соглаша́ться [-ласи́ться]; (*coincide*) совпада́ть [-па́сть]

**concussion** [kən'kʌʃn]: сотрясе́ние мо́зга

**condemn** [kən'dem] осужда́ть [осуди́ть]; (*blame*) порица́ть; пригова́ривать [-вори́ть] (к Д); [за]бракова́ть; **~ation** [kɒndəm'neɪʃn] осужде́ние

**condens|ation** [kɒnden'seɪʃn] конденса́ция, сгуще́ние; **~e** [kən'dens] сгуща́ть(ся); *fig.* сокраща́ть [-рати́ть]

**condescen|d** [kɒndɪ'send] снисходи́ть [снизойти́]; **~sion** [-'senʃn] снисхожде́ние; снисходи́тельность *f*

**condiment** ['kɒndɪmənt] припра́ва

**condition** [kən'dɪʃn] **1.** усло́вие; (*state*) состоя́ние; **~s** *pl.* (*circumstances*) обстоя́тельства *n/pl.*; усло́вия *n/pl.*; ***on ~ that*** при усло́вии, что; **2.** ста́вить усло́вия; обусло́вливать [-о́вить]; **~al** [~əl] □ усло́вный

**condol|e** [kən'dəʊl] соболе́зновать (***with*** Д); **~ence** [~əns] соболе́знование

**condom** ['kɒndəm] презервати́в, кондо́м

**condone** [kən'dəʊn] проща́ть; (*overlook*) смотре́ть сквозь па́льцы

**conduct** **1.** ['kɒndʌkt] поведе́ние; **2.** [kən'dʌkt] вести́ себя́; *affairs* руководи́ть; *mus.* дирижи́ровать; **~or** [kən'dʌktə] *mus.* дирижёр; *el.* проводни́к

**cone** [kəʊn] ко́нус; *bot.* ши́шка

**confectionery** [kən'fekʃənərɪ] конди́терские изде́лия *n/pl.*

**confedera|te** **1.** [kən'fedərət] федерати́вный; **2.** [~] член конфедера́ции; сою́зник; (*accomplice*) соуча́стник, соо́бщник; **3.** [~reɪt] объединя́ться в сою́з; **~tion** [kənfedə'reɪʃn] конфедера́ция

**confer** [kənfɜː] *v/t.* (*award*) присужда́ть [-уди́ть]; *v/i.* (*consult*) совеща́ться; **~ence** ['kɒnfərəns] конфере́нция; совеща́ние

**confess** [kən'fes] призн(ав)а́ться, созн(ав)а́ться в (П); **~ion** [~'feʃn] призна́ние; *to a priest* и́споведь *f*; *creed, denomination* вероиспове́дание

**confide** [kən'faɪd] доверя́ть (***in*** Д); (*entrust*) вверя́ть [вве́рить]; (*trust*) полага́ться [положи́ться] (***in*** на В); **~nce** [kɒnfɪdəns] дове́рие; (*firm belief*) уве́ренность *f*; **~nt** ['kɒnfɪdənt] □ уве́ренный; **~ntial** [kɒnfɪ'denʃəl] конфиденциа́льный; секре́тный

**configure** [kən'fɪgə] *comput.* конфигури́ровать

**confine** [kən'faɪn] ограни́чи(ва)ть; *to prison* заключа́ть [-чи́ть]; ***be ~d*** *of pregnant woman* рожа́ть [роди́ть]; **~ment** [~mənt] ограниче́ние; заключе́ние; ро́ды *m/pl.*

**confirm** [kən'fɜːm] подтвержда́ть

[-рди́ть]; **~ed bachelor** убеждённый холостя́к; **~ation** [kɒnfə'meɪʃn] подтвержде́ние
**confiscat|e** ['kɒnfɪskeɪt] конфискова́ть (*im*)*pf.*; **~ion** [ˌkɒnfɪ'skeɪʃn] конфиска́ция
**conflagration** [kɒnflə'greɪʃn] бушу́ющий пожа́р
**conflict 1.** ['kɒnflɪkt] конфли́кт, столкнове́ние; **2.** [kən'flɪkt] быть в конфли́кте; *v/i.* противоре́чить
**confluence** ['kɒnfluəns] *of rivers* слия́ние
**conform** [kən'fɔːm] согласо́вывать [-сова́ть] (***to*** с Т); (*obey*) подчиня́ться [-ни́ться] (***to*** Д); *to standards etc.* удовлетворя́ть [-ри́ть], соотве́тствовать; **~ity** [~ɪtɪ] соотве́тствие; подчине́ние; ***in ~ with*** в соотве́тствии с (Т)
**confound** [kən'faʊnd] (*amaze*) поража́ть [порази́ть]; (*stump*) [по]ста́вить в тупи́к; (*confuse*) [с]пу́тать; ***~ it!*** чёрт побери́!
**confront** [kən'frʌnt] стоя́ть лицо́м к лицу́ с (Т)
**confus|e** [kən'fjuːz] [с]пу́тать; (*embarrass*) смуща́ть [-ути́ть]; **~ion** [kən'fjuːʒən] смуще́ние; (*disorder*) беспоря́док; ***throw into ~*** привести́ в замеша́тельство
**congeal** [kən'dʒiːl] засты́(ва́)ть
**congenial** [kən'dʒiːnɪəl] □ бли́зкий по ду́ху, прия́тный; *climate* благоприя́тный
**congenital** [kən'dʒenɪtl] врождённый
**congestion** [kən'dʒestʃən] *traffic* перегру́женность *f*; перенаселённость *f*
**conglomeration** [kənglɒmə'reɪʃn] скопле́ние, конгломера́т
**congratulat|e** [kən'grætʃʊleɪt] поздравля́ть [-а́вить] (***on*** с Т); **~ion** [kəngrætʃʊ'leɪʃn] поздравле́ние
**congregat|e** ['kɒŋgrɪgeɪt] соб(и)ра́ть(ся); **~ion** [kɒŋgrɪ'geɪʃn] *in Bitte church* собра́ние прихожа́н
**congress** ['kɒŋgres] конгре́сс; съезд; **~man** *Am.* конгрессме́н
**congruous** ['kɒŋgrʊəs] □ (*fitting*) соотве́тствующий; гармони́рующий (***to*** с Т)
**conifer** ['kɒnɪfə] де́рево хво́йной поро́ды
**conjecture** [kən'dʒektʃə] **1.** дога́дка, предположе́ние; **2.** предполага́ть [-ложи́ть]
**conjugal** ['kɒndʒʊgl] супру́жеский
**conjunction** [kən'dʒʌŋkʃn] соедине́ние; *gr.* сою́з; связь *f*; ***in ~ with*** совме́стно (с Т)
**conjunctivitis** [kəndʒʌŋktɪ'vaɪtɪs] конъюнктиви́т
**conjur|e** ['kʌndʒə] ***~ up*** *fig.* вызыва́ть в воображе́нии; *v/i.* пока́зывать фо́кусы; **~er, ~or** [~rə] фо́кусник
**connect** [kə'nekt] соединя́ть(ся) [-ни́ть(ся)]; (*link*) свя́зывать(ся) [-за́ть(ся)]; *tel.* соединя́ть [-ни́ть]; **~ed** [~ɪd] □ свя́занный; ***be ~ with*** име́ть свя́зи (с Т); **~ion** [kə'nekʃn] связь *f*; соедине́ние; **~s** свя́зи; (*family*) ро́дственники
**connive** [kə'naɪv]: ***~ at*** потво́рствовать (Д), попусти́тельствовать
**connoisseur** [kɒnə'sɜː] знато́к
**conquer** ['kɒŋkə] *country* завоёвывать [-оева́ть]; (*defeat*) побежда́ть [победи́ть]; **~or** [~rə] победи́тель(-ница *f*) *m*; завоева́тель *m*, -ница *f*
**conquest** ['kɒŋkwest] завоева́ние; побе́да
**conscience** ['kɒnʃəns] со́весть *f*; ***have a guilty ~*** чу́вствовать угрызе́ния со́вести
**conscientious** [kɒnʃɪ'enʃəs] □ добросо́вестный
**conscious** ['kɒnʃəs] □ *effort, etc.* созна́тельный; (*aware*) сознаю́щий; **~ness** [~nɪs] созна́ние
**conscript** [kən'skrɪpt] призывни́к; **~ion** [kən'skrɪpʃn] во́инская пови́нность *f*
**consecrate** ['kɒnsɪkreɪt] *a church, etc.* освяща́ть [-яти́ть]
**consecutive** [kən'sekjʊtɪv] □ после́довательный
**consent** [kən'sent] **1.** согла́сие; **2.** соглаша́ться [-ласи́ться]
**consequen|ce** ['kɒnsɪkwens] (по)сле́дствие; (*importance*) ва́жность *f*;

C

~t [~kwənt] обусло́вленный; (*subsequent*) после́дующий; ~tly [~kwəntlı] сле́довательно; поэ́тому

**conserv|ation** [kɒnsə'veıʃn] сохране́ние; ***nature*** ~ охра́на приро́ды; ~**ative** [kən'sɜːvətıv] **1.** □ консервати́вный; **2.** *pol.* консерва́тор; ~**atory** [~trı] оранжере́я; *mus.* консервато́рия; ~**e** [kən'sɜːv] сохраня́ть [-ни́ть]

**consider** [kən'sıdə] *v/t.* обсужда́ть [-уди́ть]; (*think over*) обду́м(ыв)ать; (*regard*) полага́ть, счита́ть; (*take into account*) счита́ться с (Т); ~**able** [~rəbl] □ значи́тельный; большо́й; ~**ate** [~rət] внима́тельный (к Д); ~**ation** [kənsıdə'reıʃn] обсужде́ние; факт; соображе́ние; внима́ние; ***take into*** ~ принима́ть во внима́ние, учи́тывать; ~**ing** [kən'sıdərıŋ] *prp.* учи́тывая (В), принима́я во внима́ние (В)

**consign** [kən'saın] перед(ав)а́ть; поруча́ть [-чи́ть]; *comm.* пос(ы)ла́ть (груз) по а́дресу; ~**ee** [kɒnsaı'niː] грузополуча́тель, адреса́т гру́за; ~**ment** [~mənt] груз, па́ртия това́ров

**consist** [kən'sıst] состоя́ть (***of*** из Р); заключа́ться (***in*** в П); ~**ence**, ~**ency** [~əns, ~ənsı] логи́чность *f*; консисте́нция *f*; ~**ent** [~ənt] □ после́довательный; согласу́ющийся (***with*** с Т)

**consol|ation** [kɒnsə'leıʃn] утеше́ние; ~**e** [kən'səʊl] утеша́ть [уте́шить]

**consolidate** [kən'sɒlıdeıt] *position*, *etc.* укрепля́ть [-пи́ть]; (*unite*) объединя́ть(ся) [-ни́ть(ся)]; *comm.* слива́ться [-и́ться]

**consonant** ['kɒnsənənt] □ (*in accord*) согла́сный, созву́чный

**conspicuous** [kən'spıkjʊəs] □ заме́тный, броса́ющийся в глаза́

**conspir|acy** [kən'spırəsı] за́говор; ~**ator** [~tə] загово́рщик *m*, -ица *f*; ~**e** [kən'spaıə] устра́ивать за́говор; сгова́риваться [сговори́ться]

**constable** ['kʌnstəbl] *hist.* консте́бль *m*; (*policeman*) полице́йский

**constan|cy** ['kɒnstənsı] постоя́нство; (*faithfulness*) ве́рность *f*; ~**t** [~stənt] □ постоя́нный; ве́рный

**consternation** [kɒnstə'neıʃn] смяте́ние; замеша́тельство (*от стра́ха*)

**constipation** [kɒnstı'peıʃn] запо́р

**constituen|cy** [kən'stıtjʊənsı] избира́тельный о́круг; (*voters*) избира́тели *m/pl.*; ~**t** [~ənt] **1.** (*part*) составно́й; *pol.* учреди́тельный; **2.** избира́тель *m*; составна́я часть *f*

**constitut|e** ['kɒnstıtjuːt] (*make up*) составля́ть [-а́вить]; (*establish*) осно́вывать [-нова́ть]; ~**ion** [kɒnstı'tjuːʃn] (*makeup*) строе́ние; конститу́ция; учрежде́ние; физи́ческое *or* душе́вное здоро́вье; ~**ional** [~ʃənl] □ конституцио́нный; *of body* органи́ческий

**constrain** [kən'streın] принужда́ть [-нуди́ть]; вынужда́ть [вы́нудить]; (*limit*) сде́рживать [-жа́ть]; ~**t** [~t] принужде́ние; вы́нужденность *f*; *of feelings* ско́ванность *f*

**constrict** [kən'strıkt] стя́гивать [стяну́ть]; сж(им)а́ть; ~**ion** [~kʃn] сжа́тие; стя́гивание

**construct** [kən'strʌkt] [по]стро́ить; сооружа́ть [-уди́ть]; *fig.* созд(ав)а́ть; ~**ion** [~kʃn] строи́тельство, стро́йка; (*building*, *etc.*) строе́ние; ~ ***site*** стро́йка; ~**ive** [~tıv] конструкти́вный

**construe** [kən'struː] истолко́вывать [-кова́ть]

**consul** ['kɒnsl] ко́нсул; ~ ***general*** генера́льный ко́нсул; ~**ate** ['kɒnsjʊlət] ко́нсульство

**consult** [kən'sʌlt] *v/t.* спра́шивать сове́та у (Р); *v/i.* [про]консульти́роваться, совеща́ться; ~ ***a doctor*** пойти́ на консульта́цию к врачу́; ~**ant** [~ənt] консульта́нт; ~**ation** [kɒnsl'teıʃn] *specialist advice and advice bureau* консульта́ция, конси́лиум (враче́й)

**consum|e** [kən'sjuːm] *v/t.* съеда́ть [съесть]; (*use*) потребля́ть [-би́ть]; [из]расхо́довать; ~**er** [~ə] потреби́тель *m*; ~ ***goods*** потреби́тельские това́ры

**consummate** [kən'sʌmıt] □ соверше́нный, зако́нченный

**consumption** [kən'sʌmpʃn] потребле́ние, расхо́д; *med.* туберкулёз лёгких

**contact** ['kɒntækt] конта́кт (*a. fig.*);

***business ~s*** деловы́е свя́зи
**contagious** [kən'teɪdʒəs] □ зара́зный, инфекцио́нный
**contain** [kən'teɪn] содержа́ть (в себе́), вмеща́ть [-ести́ть]; ***~ o.s.*** сде́рживаться [-жа́ться]; **~er** [~ə] конте́йнер
**contaminat|e** [kən'tæmɪneɪt] *water, etc.* загрязня́ть [-ни́ть]; заража́ть [зарази́ть]; *fig.* ока́зывать [-за́ть] па́губное влия́ние; **~ion** [kəntæmɪ'neɪʃn]: ***radioactive ~*** радиоакти́вное загрязне́ние
**contemplat|e** ['kɒntəmpleɪt] обду́м(ыв)ать; **~ion** [kɒntem'pleɪʃn] созерца́ние; размышле́ние
**contempora|neous** [kəntempə'reɪnɪəs] □ совпада́ющий по вре́мени, одновреме́нный; **~ry** [kən'tempərərɪ] **1.** совреме́нный; **2.** совреме́нник *m*, -ица *f*
**contempt** [kən'tempt] презре́ние (***for*** к Д); **~ible** [~əbl] □ презре́нный; **~uous** [~ʃʊəs] □ презри́тельный
**contend** [kən'tend] *v/i.* боро́ться; сопе́рничать; *v/t.* утвержда́ть
**content** [kən'tent] **1.** дово́льный; **2.** удовлетворя́ть [-ри́ть]; **3.** удовлетворе́ние; ***to one's heart's ~*** вво́лю; **4.** ['kɒntent] содержа́ние; ***table of ~s*** оглавле́ние; **~ed** [kən'tentɪd] □ дово́льный, удовлетворённый
**contention** [kən'tenʃn] *dissension* спор, ссо́ра; *assertion* утвержде́ние
**contentment** [kən'tentmənt] удовлетворённость *f*
**contest 1.** ['kɒntest] ко́нкурс; *sport* соревнова́ние; **2.** [kən'test] оспа́ривать [оспо́рить]; *one's rights, etc.* отста́ивать [отстоя́ть]; (*struggle*) боро́ться (за В); **~ant** уча́стник (-ица) состяза́ния
**context** ['kɒntekst] конте́кст
**continent** ['kɒntɪnənt] матери́к, контине́нт; ***the ≈*** *Brt.* (материко́вая) Евро́па
**contingen|cy** [kən'tɪndʒənsɪ] случа́йность *f*; непредви́денное обстоя́тельство; ***be prepared for every ~*** быть гото́вым ко вся́ким случа́йностям; **~t** [~dʒənt] □ **1.** случа́йный, непредви́денный; **2.** гру́ппа; *mil.* континге́нт
**continu|al** [kən'tɪnjʊəl] □ непреры́вный, беспреста́нный; **~ation** [kəntɪnjʊ'eɪʃn] продолже́ние; **~e** [kən'tɪnjuː] *v/t.* продолжа́ть [-до́лжить]; ***to be ~d*** продолже́ние сле́дует; *v/i.* продолжа́ться [-до́лжиться]; *of forest, road, etc.* простира́ться, тяну́ться; **~ity** [kɒntɪ'njuːətɪ] непреры́вность *f*; **~ous** [kən'tɪnjʊəs] □ непреры́вный; (*unbroken*) сплошно́й
**contort** [kən'tɔːt] *of face* искажа́ть [искази́ть]
**contour** ['kɒntʊə] ко́нтур, очерта́ние
**contraband** ['kɒntrəbænd] контраба́нда
**contraceptive** [kɒntrə'septɪv] противозача́точное сре́дство
**contract 1.** [kən'trækt] *v/t. muscle* сокраща́ть [-рати́ть]; *alliance* заключа́ть [-чи́ть]; *v/i.* сокраща́ться [-рати́ться]; *of metal* сж(им)а́ть(ся); **2.** ['kɒntrækt] контра́кт, догово́р; **~ion** [~ʃən] сжа́тие; сокраще́ние; **~or** [~tə] подря́дчик
**contradict** [kɒntrə'dɪkt] противоре́чить (Д); **~ion** [~kʃn] противоре́чие; **~ory** [~tərɪ] □ противоречи́вый
**contrary** ['kɒntrərɪ] **1.** противополо́жный; *person* упря́мый; ***~ to*** *prp.* вопреки́ (Д); **2.** обра́тное; ***on the ~*** наоборо́т
**contrast 1.** ['kɒntrɑːst] противополо́жность *f*; контра́ст; **2.** [kən'trɑːst] *v/t.* сопоставля́ть [-а́вить], сра́внивать [-ни́ть]; *v/i.* отлича́ться от (Р); контрасти́ровать с (Т)
**contribut|e** [kən'trɪbjuːt] (*donate*) [по]же́ртвовать; *to a newspaper, etc.* сотру́дничать (***to*** в П); **~ion** [kɒntrɪ'bjuːʃn] вклад; взнос; **~or** [kən'trɪbjʊtə] а́втор; же́ртвователь
**contriv|ance** [kən'traɪvəns] вы́думка; *mechanism, etc.* приспособле́ние; **~e** [kən'traɪv] *v/t.* (*invent*) приду́м(ыв)ать; (*scheme*) затева́ть [-е́ять]; *v/i.* ухитря́ться [-ри́ться]; умудря́ться [-ри́ться]

C

**control** [kən'trəʊl] **1.** управле́ние (*a. tech.*), регули́рование; контро́ль *m*; **~ desk** пульт управле́ния; **lose ~ of o.s.** потеря́ть самооблада́ние; **under ~** в поря́дке; **2.** управля́ть (Т); [про]контроли́ровать (*im*)*pf*.; *feelings*, *etc*. сде́рживать [-жа́ть]; **~ler** [~ə] контролёр, инспе́ктор; *ae*., *rail*. диспе́тчер

**controver|sial** [kɒntrə'vɜːʃl] □ спо́рный; **~sy** ['kɒntrəvɜːsɪ] спор, поле́мика

**convalesce** [kɒnvə'les] выздора́вливать *impf*.; **~nce** [~ns] выздоровле́ние; **~nt** [~nt] □ выздора́вливающий

**convene** [kən'viːn] *meeting*, *etc*. со-з(ы)ва́ть; (*come together*) соб(и)ра́ть(ся)

**convenien|ce** [kən'viːnɪəns] удо́бство; **at your earliest ~** как то́лько вы смо́жете; **public ~** *euph*. убо́рная; **~t** [~ɪənt] □ удо́бный

**convent** ['kɒnvənt] монасты́рь *m*; **~ion** [kən'venʃn] съезд; (*agreement*) конве́нция, соглаше́ние; (*custom*) обы́чай, усло́вность *f*

**converge** [kən'vɜːdʒ] сходи́ться [сойти́сь] (в одну́ то́чку)

**convers|ation** [kɒnvə'seɪʃn] разгово́р, бесе́да; **~ational** [~ʃənl] разгово́рный; **~e** [kən'vɜːs] разгова́ривать, бесе́довать; **~ion** [kən'vɜːʃn] превраще́ние; *eccl*., *etc*. обраще́ние; *el*. преобразова́ние; *stocks*, *etc*. конве́рсия

**convert** [kən'vɜːt] превраща́ть [-ати́ть]; *el*. преобразо́вывать [-ва́ть]; *fin*. конверти́ровать; *eccl*., *etc*. обраща́ть [-рати́ть] (в другу́ю ве́ру); **~ible** [~əbl]: **~ currency** конверти́руемая валю́та

**convey** [kən'veɪ] *goods* перевози́ть [-везти́], переправля́ть [-пра́вить]; *greetings*, *electricity*, *etc*. перед(ав)а́ть; **~ance** [~əns] перево́зка; доста́вка; тра́нспортное сре́дство; **~or** [~ə] (**~ belt**) конве́йер

**convict 1.** ['kɒnvɪkt] осуждённый; **2.** [kən'vɪkt] признава́ть вино́вным; **~ion** [kən'vɪkʃn] *law* осужде́ние; (*firm belief*) убежде́ние

**convinc|e** [kən'vɪns] убежда́ть [убеди́ть] (**of** в П); **~ing** [~ɪŋ] убеди́тельный

**convoy** ['kɒnvɔɪ] *naut*. конво́й; сопровожде́ние

**convuls|e** [kən'vʌls] содрога́ться [-гну́ться]; **be ~d with laughter** смея́ться до упа́ду; **her face was ~d with pain** её лицо́ искази́лось от бо́ли; **~ion** [~ʃn] *of ground* колеба́ние; *of muscles* су́дорога; **~ive** [~sɪv] су́дорожный

**coo** [kuː] ворkова́ть

**cook** [kʊk] **1.** по́вар; **2.** [при]гото́вить еду́; **~ery** ['kʊkərɪ] кулина́рия; пригото́вле́ние еды́; **~ie**, **~y** ['kʊkɪ] *Am*. пече́нье

**cool** [kuːl] **1.** прохла́дный; *fig*. хладнокро́вный; (*imperturbable*) невозмути́мый; *pej*. де́рзкий, наха́льный; **keep ~!** не горячи́сь!; **2.** прохла́да; **3.** охлажда́ть(ся) [охлади́ть(ся)]; осты́(ва́)ть; **~headed** [kuːl'hedɪd] □ хладнокро́вный

**coolness** ['kuːlnɪs] холодо́к; прохла́да; хладнокро́вие

**coop** [kuːp] **~ up** *или* **in** держа́ть взаперти́

**cooperat|e** [kəʊ'ɒpəreɪt] сотру́дничать; **~ion** [kəʊɒpə'reɪʃn] сотру́дничество; **~ive** [kəʊ'ɒpərətɪv] кооперати́вный; **~ society** кооперати́в

**coordinat|e** [kəʊ'ɔːdɪneɪt] координи́ровать (*im*)*pf*.; согласо́вывать [-ова́ть]; **~ion** [kəʊɔːdɪ'neɪʃn] координа́ция

**cope** [kəʊp]: **~ with** справля́ться [-а́виться] с (Т)

**copier** ['kɒpɪə] копирова́льный аппара́т

**copious** ['kəʊpɪəs] □ оби́льный

**copper** ['kɒpə] **1.** медь *f*; (*coin*) ме́дная моне́та; **2.** ме́дный

**copy** ['kɒpɪ] **1.** ко́пия; (*single example*) экземпля́р; **2.** перепи́сывать [-са́ть]; снима́ть [снять] ко́пию с (Р); **~book** тетра́дь *f*; **~right** а́вторское пра́во

**coral** ['kɒrəl] кора́лл

**cord** [kɔːd] **1.** верёвка, шнур; **vocal ~s** голосовы́е свя́зки; **2.** свя́зывать

[-за́ть] верёвкой
**cordial** ['kɔːdɪəl] **1.** □ серде́чный, и́скренний; **2.** стимули́рующий напи́ток; **~ity** [kɔːdɪ'ælətɪ] серде́чность *f*; раду́шие
**cordon** ['kɔːdn] **1.** кордо́н; **2.** **~ *off*** отгора́живать [-роди́ть]
**corduroy** ['kɔːdərɔɪ] вельве́т в ру́бчик; **~s** *pl.* вельве́товые брю́ки *m/pl.*
**core** [kɔː] сердцеви́на; *fig.* суть *f*; ***to the ~*** *fig.* до мо́зга косте́й
**cork** [kɔːk] **1.** про́бка; **2.** затыка́ть про́бкой; '**~screw** што́пор
**corn**[1] [kɔːn] зерно́; хлеба́ *m/pl.*; *Am.*, *maize* кукуру́за
**corn**[2] [~] *on a toe* мозо́ль
**corner** ['kɔːnə] **1.** у́гол; **2.** *fig.* загна́ть *pf.* в у́гол; припере́ть *pf.* к стене́
**cornflakes** корнфле́кс; кукуру́зные хло́пья
**cornice** ['kɔːnɪs] *arch.* карни́з
**coronary** ['kɒrənərɪ] корона́рный; *su. coll.* инфа́ркт
**coronation** [kɒrə'neɪʃn] корона́ция
**corpor|al** ['kɔːpərəl] **1.** □ теле́сный; **2.** *mil. approx.* ефре́йтор; **~ation** [kɔːpə'reɪʃn] корпора́ция
**corps** [kɔː]: ***diplomatic ~*** дипломати́ческий ко́рпус
**corpse** [kɔːps] труп
**corpulen|ce** ['kɔːpjʊləns] ту́чность *f*; **~t** [~lənt] ту́чный
**correct** [kə'rekt] **1.** □ пра́вильный, ве́рный, то́чный; (*proper*) корре́ктный; **2.** *v/t.* исправля́ть [-а́вить], корректи́ровать; *manuscript* пра́вить; **~ion** [kə'rekʃn] (*act of correcting*) исправле́ние; (*the correction made*) попра́вка
**correlat|e** ['kɒrəleɪt] устана́вливать соотноше́ние; **~ion** [kɒrə'leɪʃn] соотноше́ние, взаимосвя́зь *f*
**correspond** [kɒrɪ'spɒnd] соотве́тствовать (***with, to*** Д); *by letter* перепи́сываться (с Т); **~ence** [~əns] соотве́тствие, перепи́ска; **~ent** [~ənt] **1.** соотве́тствующий; **2.** корреспонде́нт *m*, -ка *f*; **~ing** [~ɪŋ] □ соотве́тствующий (Д)
**corridor** ['kɒrɪdɔː] коридо́р
**corroborate** [kə'rɒbəreɪt] подтвержда́ть [-рди́ть]
**corro|de** [kə'rəʊd] разъеда́ть [-е́сть]; [за]ржаве́ть; **~sion** [kə'rəʊʒn] корро́зия, ржа́вчина; **~sive** [~sɪv] **1.** коррозио́нный; **2.** разъеда́ющее вещество́
**corrugated** ['kɒrəgeɪtɪd]: **~ *iron*** рифлёное желе́зо
**corrupt** [kə'rʌpt] **1.** □ коррумпи́рованный, прода́жный; (*containing mistakes*) искажённый; (*depraved*) развращённый; **2.** *v/t.* искажа́ть [-зи́ть]; развраща́ть [-рати́ть]; подкупа́ть [-пи́ть]; *v/i.* [ис]по́ртиться; искажа́ться [-зи́ться]; **~ion** [~pʃn] искаже́ние; корру́пция, прода́жность *f*; развращённость *f*
**corset** ['kɔːsɪt] корсе́т
**cosmetic** [kɒz'metɪk] **1.** космети́ческий; **2.** *pl.* косме́тика
**cosmic** ['kɒzmɪk] косми́ческий
**cosmonaut** ['kɒzmənɔːt] космона́вт
**cosmos** ['kɒzmɒs] ко́смос
**cost** [kɒst] **1.** цена́, сто́имость *f*; *pl.* расхо́ды, изде́ржки; **~ *effectiveness*** рента́бельность *f*; **2.** [*irr.*] сто́ить
**costly** ['kɒstlɪ] дорого́й, це́нный
**costume** ['kɒstjuːm] костю́м; **~ *jewel(-le)ry*** бижуте́рия
**cosy** ['kəʊzɪ] □ ую́тный
**cot** [kɒt] де́тская крова́ть
**cottage** ['kɒtɪdʒ] котте́дж, небольшо́й дом (*обычно в деревне*); *Am.* ле́тняя да́ча; **~ *cheese*** тво́рог
**cotton** ['kɒtn] **1.** хло́пок; хлопчатобума́жная ткань; (*thread*) ни́тки; **2.** хлопчатобума́жный; **~ *wool*** ва́та; **3.**: **~ *on*** *coll.* понима́ть [-ня́ть]
**couch** [kaʊtʃ] дива́н, *Brt.* куше́тка
**cough** [kɒf] **1.** ка́шель *m*; ***a bad ~*** си́льный ка́шель; **2.** ка́шлять [ка́шлянуть]
**could** [kəd; *strong* kʊd] *pt. om* **can**
**council** ['kaʊnsl] сове́т; ***Security ♀*** Сове́т Безопа́сности; ***town ~*** городско́й сове́т, муниципалите́т; **~(l)or** [~sələ] член сове́та
**counsel** ['kaʊnsl] **1.** сове́т, совеща́ние; *law* адвока́т; ***~ for the prosecution*** об-

винитель *m*; **2.** давать совет (Д); **~(l)or** [~ələ] *dipl., pol.* советник

**count**[1] [kaʊnt] **1.** счёт; (*counting up*) подсчёт; **2.** *v/t.* [со]считать; подсчитывать [-итать]; (*include*) включать [-чить]; *v/i.* считаться; (*be of account*) иметь значение

**count**[2] [~] граф

**countenance** ['kaʊntənəns] **1.** лицо; выражение лица; (*support*) поддержка; ***lose ~*** потерять самообладание; **2.** поддерживать [-жать], поощрять [-рить]

**counter**[1] ['kaʊntə] прилавок; *in bar, bank* стойка; *tech.* счётчик

**counter**[2] [~] **1.** противоположный (***to*** Д); встречный; **2.** *adv.* обратно; напротив; **3.** [вос]противиться (Д); *a blow* наносить встречный удар

**counteract** [kaʊntər'ækt] противодействовать (Д); нейтрализовать (*im*)*pf.*

**counterbalance** **1.** ['kaʊntəbæləns] *mst. fig.* противовес; **2.** [kaʊntə'bæləns] уравновешивать [-весить]; служить противовесом (Д)

**counterespionage** [kaʊntər'espɪənɑːʒ] контрразведка

**counterfeit** ['kaʊntəfɪt] **1.** поддельный; **2.** подделка; **3.** поддел(ыв)ать

**counterfoil** ['kaʊntəfɔɪl] корешок (билета, квитанции)

**countermand** [kaʊntə'mɑːnd] *order* отменять [-нить]

**countermove** ['kaʊntəmuːv] *fig.* ответная мера, контрудар

**counterpane** ['kaʊntəpeɪn] покрывало

**counterpart** ['kaʊntəpɑːt] представитель другой стороны (*занимающий тот же пост, должность и т.д*); ***the English MPs met their Russian ~s*** английские парламентарии встретились со своими русскими коллегами

**countersign** ['kaʊntəsaɪn] *v/t.* [по]ставить вторую подпись (на П)

**countess** ['kaʊntɪs] графиня

**countless** ['kaʊntlɪs] бесчисленный, несчётный

**country** ['kʌntrɪ] **1.** страна; местность *f*; ***go to the ~*** поехать за город; ***live in the ~*** жить в сельской местности; **2.** деревенский; **~man** [~mən] сельский житель; земляк, соотечественник; **~side** [~saɪd] сельская местность *f*

**county** ['kaʊntɪ] графство; *Am.* округ

**coup** [kuː] удачный ход (*удар и т.п.*)

**couple** ['kʌpl] **1.** пара; **2.** соединять [-нить]; *zo.* спариваться

**coupling** ['kʌplɪŋ] *tech.* муфта сцепления

**coupon** ['kuːpɒn] купон, талон

**courage** ['kʌrɪdʒ] мужество, смелость *f*, храбрость *f*, отвага; ***pluck up one's ~*** набраться *pf.* храбрости; **~ous** [kə'reɪdʒəs] □ мужественный, смелый, храбрый

**courier** ['kʊrɪə] курьер, нарочный

**course** [kɔːs] (*direction*) направление, курс; *of events* ход; *of river* течение; (*food*) блюдо; ***of ~*** конечно; ***in the ~ of*** в течение

**court** [kɔːt] **1.** двор (*a. fig.*); (*law ~*) суд; *sport* площадка; ***tennis ~*** теннисный корт; **2.** (*woo*) ухаживать за (Т); (*seek favo[u]r of*) искать расположения (Р); **~eous** ['kɜːtɪəs] □ вежливый, учтивый; **~esy** ['kɜːtəsɪ] учтивость *f*, вежливость *f*; **~ martial** *mil.* **1.** военный трибунал; **2.** судить военным трибуналом; **~ship** ['~ʃɪp] ухаживание; **~yard** двор

**cousin** ['kʌzn] *male* кузен, двоюродный брат; *female* кузина, двоюродная сестра

**cove** [kəʊv] (маленькая) бухта

**cover** ['kʌvə] **1.** (*lid, top*) крышка; *for bed, etc.* покрывало; *of book* обложка; (*shelter*) укрытие; *fig.* покров; ***send under separate ~*** послать в отдельном письме, пакете; **2.** покры(-ва)ть (*a. comm.*); прикры(ва)ть; (*a. ~ up*) скры(ва)ть; **~ing** [~rɪŋ]: ***~ letter*** сопроводительное письмо

**coverage** ['kʌvərɪdʒ] репортаж; охват

**covert** ['kʌvət] □ скрытый, тайный

**covet** ['kʌvɪt] жаждать (Р); **~ous** [~əs] □ жадный, алчный; скупой

**cow**¹ [kaʊ] коро́ва
**cow**² [~] запу́гивать [-га́ть]; терроризова́ть *(im)pf.*
**coward** ['kaʊəd] трус *m*, -и́ха *f*; **~ice** [~ɪs] тру́сость *f*; малоду́шие; **~ly** [~lɪ] трусли́вый
**cowboy** ['kaʊbɔɪ] *Am.* ковбо́й
**cower** ['kaʊə] съёжи(ва)ться
**cowl** [kaʊl] капюшо́н
**coy** [kɔɪ] □ засте́нчивый
**cozy** ['kəʊzɪ] ую́тный
**crab**¹ [kræb] *zo.* краб
**crab**² [~] *bot.* ди́кая я́блоня; *coll.* ворчу́н
**crack** [kræk] **1.** *(noise)* треск; тре́щина; щель *f*; рассе́лина; *coll.* *(blow)* уда́р; *Am.* саркасти́ческое замеча́ние; ***at the ~ of dawn*** на заре́; **2.** *coll.* первокла́ссный; **3.** *v/t.* раска́лывать [-коло́ть], коло́ть; ***~ a joke*** отпусти́ть шу́тку; *v/i.* производи́ть треск, шум; [по]тре́скаться; раска́лываться [-коло́ться]; *of voice* лома́ться; **~ed** [~t] тре́снувший; *coll.* вы́живший из ума́; **~er** ['~ə] хлопу́шка; *Am.* кре́кер; **~le** ['~l] потре́скивание, треск
**cradle** ['kreɪdl] **1.** колыбе́ль *f*; *fig.* нача́ло; младе́нчество; **2.** бе́режно держа́ть в рука́х (как ребёнка)
**craft** [krɑːft] *(skill)* ло́вкость *f*, сноро́вка; *(trade)* ремесло́; *(boat)* су́дно *(pl.* суда́); **~sman** ['~smən] ма́стер; **~y** ['~ɪ] ло́вкий, хи́трый
**crag** [kræg] скала́, утёс; **~gy** ['~ɪ] скали́стый
**cram** [kræm] набива́ть [-би́ть]; впи́хивать [-хну́ть]; [на]пи́чкать; *coll.* [за]зубри́ть
**cramp** [kræmp] **1.** су́дорога; **2.** *(hamper)* стесня́ть [-ни́ть]; *(limit)* сужи́вать [су́зить]
**cranberry** ['krænbərɪ] клю́ква
**crane** [kreɪn] **1.** *bird* жура́вль *m*; *tech.* подъёмный кран; **2.** поднима́ть кра́ном; *neck* вытя́гивать [вы́тянуть] ше́ю
**crank** [kræŋk] **1.** *mot.* заводна́я ру́чка; *coll. person* челове́к с причу́дами; **2.** заводи́ть [-вести́] ру́чкой (автомаши́ну); **~shaft** *tech.* коле́нчатый вал; **~y** ['~ɪ] капри́зный; эксцентри́чный
**cranny** ['krænɪ] щель *f*; тре́щина
**crape** [kreɪp] креп
**crash** [kræʃ] **1.** гро́хот, гром; *ae.* ава́рия; *rail.* круше́ние; *fin.* крах; **2.** па́дать, ру́шиться с тре́ском; разби́(ва́)ться *(a. ae.)*; *ae.* потерпе́ть *pf.* ава́рию; **~ helmet** защи́тный шлем; **~ landing** авари́йная поса́дка
**crater** ['kreɪtə] кра́тер; *mil.* воро́нка
**crave** [kreɪv] стра́стно жела́ть, жа́ждать (***for*** P)
**crawl** [krɔːl] **1.** по́лзание; *swimming* кроль; **2.** по́лзать, [по]ползти́; *fig.* пресмыка́ться
**crayfish** ['kreɪfɪʃ] рак
**crayon** ['kreɪən] цветно́й каранда́ш; пасте́ль *f*, рису́нок пасте́лью *или* цветны́м карандашо́м
**craz|e** [kreɪz] **1.** *coll.* ма́ния, пова́льное увлече́ние; ***be the ~*** быть в мо́де; **2.** своди́ть с ума́; **~y** ['kreɪzɪ] □ поме́шанный; *plan, etc.* безу́мный; ***be ~ about*** быть поме́шанным (на П)
**creak** [kriːk] **1.** скрип; **2.** [за]скрипе́ть
**cream** [kriːm] **1.** сли́вки *f/pl.*; крем; *(the best part)* са́мое лу́чшее; ***shoe ~*** крем для о́буви; ***sour ~*** смета́на; ***whipped ~*** взби́тые сли́вки; **2.** снима́ть сли́вки с (Р); **~y** ['kriːmɪ] □ *(containing cream)* сли́вочный
**crease** [kriːs] **1.** скла́дка; *(on paper)* сгиб; **2.** [по]мя́ть(ся); загиба́ть [загну́ть]; **~-proof** немну́щийся
**creat|e** [kriː'eɪt] [со]твори́ть; созд(а-в)а́ть; **~ion** [~'eɪʃn] созда́ние; (со)творе́ние; **~ive** [~ɪv] тво́рческий; **~or** [~ə] созда́тель *m*, творе́ц; **~ure** ['kriːtʃə] созда́ние, существо́
**creden|ce** ['kriːdns] ве́ра, дове́рие; **~tials** [krɪ'denʃlz] *pl.* *dipl.* вери́тельные гра́моты *f/pl.*; удостовере́ние
**credible** ['kredəbl] □ заслу́живающий дове́рия; *story* правдоподо́бный; ***it's hardly ~ that*** маловероя́тно, что
**credit** ['kredɪt] **1.** дове́рие; хоро́шая репута́ция; *fin.* креди́т; **2.** ве́рить, доверя́ть (Д); *fin.* кредитова́ть *(im)pf.*; ***~ s.o. with s.th.*** счита́ть, что; **~able**

C

['~əbl] □ похва́льный; **~ card** креди́тная ка́рточка; **~or** [~ə] кредито́р; **~worthy** кредитоспосо́бный

**credulous** ['kredjʊləs] □ легкове́рный, дове́рчивый

**creek** [kri:k] бу́хта, небольшо́й зали́в; *Am.* руче́й

**creep** [kri:p] [*irr.*] по́лзать, [по]ползти́; *of plants* стла́ться, ви́ться; (*stealthily*) кра́сться; *fig.* **~ in** вкра́дываться [вкра́сться]; **~er** ['~ə] вью́щееся расте́ние

**cremate** [krə'meɪt] креми́ровать

**crept** [krept] *pt.* и *pt. p. от* ***creep***

**crescent** ['kresnt] полуме́сяц

**crest** [krest] *of wave, hill* гре́бень *m*; **~fallen** ['krestfɔ:lən] упа́вший ду́хом; уны́лый

**crevasse** [krɪ'væs] рассе́лина

**crevice** ['krevɪs] щель *f*, расще́лина, тре́щина

**crew**[1] [kru:] *of train* брига́да; *naut., ae.* экипа́ж, *mil.* кома́нда

**crew**[2] [~] *chiefly Brt. pt. от* ***crow***

**crib** [krɪb] *Am.* де́тская крова́тка; *educ.* шпарга́лка

**cricket**[1] ['krɪkɪt] *zo.* сверчо́к

**cricket**[2] [~] *game* крике́т; *coll.* ***not ~*** не по пра́вилам, нече́стно

**crime** [kraɪm] преступле́ние

**criminal** ['krɪmɪnl] **1.** престу́пник; **2.** престу́пный; кримина́льный, уголо́вный; ***~ code*** уголо́вный ко́декс

**crimson** ['krɪmzn] **1.** багро́вый, мали́новый; **2.** [по]красне́ть

**cringe** [krɪndʒ] пресмыка́ться

**crinkle** ['krɪŋkl] **1.** скла́дка; морщи́на; **2.** [с]мо́рщиться; [по]мя́ться

**cripple** ['krɪpl] **1.** кале́ка *m/f*, инвали́д; **2.** [ис]кале́чить, [из]уро́довать; *fig.* парализова́ть (*im*)*pf.*

**crisis** ['kraɪsɪs] кри́зис

**crisp** [krɪsp] **1.** *having curls* кудря́вый; *snow, etc.* хрустя́щий; *air* бодря́щий; **2.** ***potato ~s*** хрустя́щий карто́фель

**crisscross** ['krɪskrɒs] **1.** *adv.* крестна́крест, вкось; **2.** перечёркивать крест-на́крест; ***~ed with roads*** покры́тый се́тью доро́г

**criteri|on** [kraɪ'tɪərɪən], *pl.* **~a** [~rɪə] крите́рий, мери́ло

**criti|c** ['krɪtɪk] кри́тик; **~cal** ['krɪtɪkl] крити́ческий; **~cism** [~sɪzəm], **~que** ['krɪti:k] кри́тика; реце́нзия; **~cize** ['krɪtɪsaɪz] [рас]критикова́ть; (*judge severely*) осужда́ть [осуди́ть]

**croak** [krəʊk] [за]ка́ркать; [за]ква́кать

**Croat** ['krəʊæt] хорва́т, хорва́тка; **~ian** [krəʊ'eɪʃən] хорва́тский

**crochet** ['krəʊʃeɪ] **1.** вяза́ние (крючко́м); **2.** вяза́ть

**crock** [krɒk] гли́няный горшо́к; **~ery** ['krɒkərɪ] гли́няная/фая́нсовая посу́да

**crony** ['krəʊnɪ] *coll.* закады́чный друг

**crook** [krʊk] **1.** (*bend*) поворо́т; изги́б; *sl.* моше́нник; **2.** сгиба́ть(ся) [согну́ть(ся)]; **~ed** ['krʊkɪd] изо́гнутый; криво́й; *coll.* нече́стный

**croon** [kru:n] напева́ть вполго́лоса

**crop** [krɒp] **1.** урожа́й; посе́вы *m/pl.*; ***~ failure*** неурожа́й; **2.** (*bear a crop*) уроди́ться; *hair* подстрига́ть [-ри́чь]; ***~ up*** возника́ть [-и́кнуть]; обнару́житься

**cross** [krɒs] **1.** крест; **2.** □ (*transverse*) попере́чный; *fig.* серди́тый; **3.** *v/t.* *arms, etc.* скре́щивать [-ести́ть]; (*go across*) переходи́ть [перейти́], переезжа́ть [перее́хать]; *fig.* противоде́йствовать (Д); пере́чить; ***~ o.s.*** [пере]крести́ться; *v/i. of mail* размину́ться *pf.*; **~-bar** попере́чина; **~breed** по́месь *f*; (*plant*) гибри́д; **~-eyed** косогла́зый; **~ing** ['krɒsɪŋ] перекрёсток; перепра́ва; перехо́д; **~roads** *pl. или sg.* перекрёсток; **~ section** попере́чное сече́ние; **~wise** попере́к; крестна́крест; **~word puzzle** кроссво́рд

**crotchet** ['krɒtʃɪt] *mus.* четвертна́я но́та; *caprice* фанта́зия

**crouch** [kraʊtʃ] нагиба́ться [нагну́ться]

**crow** [krəʊ] **1.** воро́на; пе́ние петуха́; **2.** кукаре́кать; **~bar** лом

**crowd** [kraʊd] **1.** толпа́; (*large number*) мно́жество, ма́сса; *coll.* толкотня́, да́вка; *coll.* компа́ния; **2.** собира́ться толпо́й, толпи́ться; набива́ться битко́м

**crown** [kraʊn] **1.** коро́на; *fig.* вене́ц; *of tree* кро́на; *of head* маку́шка; **2.** коронова́ть *(im)pf.*; *fig.* увенча́ть(ся); ***to ~ it all*** в доверше́ние всего́
**cruci|al** ['kruːʃl] □ крити́ческий; реша́ющий; **~fixion** [kruːsɪ'fɪkʃn] распя́тие; **~fy** ['kruːsɪfaɪ] распина́ть [-пя́ть]
**crude** [kruːd] □ *(raw)* сыро́й; *(unrefined)* неочи́щенный; *statistics* гру́бый
**cruel** ['krʊəl] □ жесто́кий; *fig.* мучи́тельный; **~ty** [-tɪ] жесто́кость *f*
**cruise** [kruːz] **1.** *naut.* круи́з; **2.** крейси́ровать; соверша́ть ре́йсы; **~r** ['kruːzə] *naut.* кре́йсер
**crumb** [krʌm] кро́шка; **~le** ['krʌmbl] [рас-, ис]кроши́ть(ся)
**crumple** ['krʌmpl] [из-, по-, с]мя́ть(ся); [с]ко́мкать(ся)
**crunch** [krʌntʃ] жева́ть с хру́стом; хрусте́ть [хру́стнуть]
**crusade** [kruː'seɪd] кресто́вый похо́д; кампа́ния; **~r** [-ə] крестоно́сец; *fig.* боре́ц
**crush** [krʌʃ] **1.** да́вка; толкотня́; **2.** *v/t.* [раз]дави́ть; (**~** *out*) выжима́ть [вы́жать]; *enemy* разбива́ть [-би́ть]
**crust** [krʌst] **1.** *of bread* ко́рка; *of earth* кора́; покрыва́ть(ся) ко́ркой; **~y** ['krʌstɪ] □ покры́тый ко́ркой
**crutch** [krʌtʃ] косты́ль *m*
**crux** [krʌks]: ***the ~ of the matter*** суть де́ла
**cry** [kraɪ] **1.** крик; вопль; плач; **2.** [за]пла́кать; *(exclaim)* восклица́ть [-и́кнуть]; *(shout)* крича́ть [кри́кнуть]; **~** ***for*** [по]тре́бовать (P)
**cryptic** ['krɪptɪk] *(mysterious)* таинственный; *(secret)* сокрове́нный
**crystal** ['krɪstl] *cut glass or rock* хруста́ль *m*; *tech.* криста́лл; *attr.* хруста́льный; **~lize** [-təlaɪz] кристаллизова́ть(ся) *(im)pf.*
**cub** [kʌb] детёныш
**cub|e** [kjuːb] *math.* **1.** куб; **~** ***root*** куби́ческий ко́рень *m*; **2.** возводи́ть в куб; **~ic(al)** ['kjuːbɪk(l)] куби́ческий
**cubicle** ['kjuːbɪkl] каби́нка
**cuckoo** ['kʊkuː] куку́шка
**cucumber** ['kjuːkʌmbə] огуре́ц
**cuddle** ['kʌdl] *v/t.* прижима́ть к себе́; *v/i.* приж(им)а́ться (друг к дру́гу)
**cue** [kjuː] (билья́рдный) кий; *(hint)* намёк; *thea.* ре́плика
**cuff** [kʌf] **1.** манже́та, обшла́г; **2.** *(blow)* шлепо́к; дать затре́щину; **~links** за́понки
**culminat|e** ['kʌlmɪneɪt] достига́ть [-ти́гнуть] вы́сшей то́чки *(или* сте́пени); **~ion** [kʌlmɪ'neɪʃn] кульмина́ция
**culprit** ['kʌlprɪt] *(offender)* престу́пник; вино́вник
**cultivat|e** ['kʌltɪveɪt] обраба́тывать [-бо́тать], возде́л(ыв)ать; *plants* культиви́ровать; *friendship* стреми́ться завяза́ть дру́жеские отноше́ния; **~ion** [kʌltɪ'veɪʃn] *of soil* обрабо́тка, возде́лывание; *of plants* разведе́ние
**cultural** ['kʌltʃərəl] □ культу́рный
**cultur|e** ['kʌltʃə] культу́ра (*a. agric.*); **~ed** [-d] культу́рный; интеллиге́нтный
**cumbersome** ['kʌmbəsəm] громо́здкий; *fig.* обремени́тельный
**cumulative** ['kjuːmjʊlətɪv] □ совоку́пный; накопи́вшийся
**cunning** ['kʌnɪŋ] **1.** ло́вкий; хи́трый; кова́рный; *Am. a.* привлека́тельный; **2.** ло́вкость *f*; хи́трость *f*; кова́рство
**cup** [kʌp] ча́шка; ча́ша; *as prize* ку́бок; **~board** ['kʌbəd] шка́ф(чик); **~** ***final*** фина́л ро́зыгрыша ку́бка
**cupola** ['kjuːpələ] ку́пол
**curable** ['kjʊərəbl] излечи́мый
**curb** [kɜːb] **1.** узда́ (*a. fig.*); подгу́бный ремéнь; **2.** обу́здывать [-да́ть] (*a. fig.*)
**curd** [kɜːd] простоква́ша; *pl.* творо́г; **~le** ['kɜːdl] свёртываться [сверну́ться]
**cure** [kjʊə] **1.** лече́ние; сре́дство; **2.** [вы́]лечи́ть, излéчивать [-чи́ть]; *meat* [за]копти́ть
**curfew** ['kɜːfjuː] коменда́нтский час
**curio** ['kjʊərɪəʊ] ре́дкая антиква́рная вещь *f*; **~sity** [kjʊərɪ'ɒsətɪ] любопы́тство; ре́дкая вещь; *f*; **~us** ['kjʊərɪəs] любопы́тный; пытли́вый;

C

стра́нный; **~ly enough** как э́то ни стра́нно
**curl** [kɜːl] **1.** ло́кон, завито́к; *pl.* ку́дри *f/pl.*; **2.** ви́ться; *of smoke* клуби́ться; **~y** ['kɜːlɪ] кудря́вый, вью́щийся
**currant** ['kʌrənt] сморо́дина; кори́нка
**curren|cy** ['kʌrənsɪ] *fin.* де́ньги *f/pl.*, валю́та; ***hard* (*soft*) ~** конверти́руемая (неконверти́руемая) валю́та; **~t** [-ənt] **1.** □ теку́щий; *opinion, etc.* ходя́чий; **2.** пото́к; *in sea* тече́ние; *el.* ток
**curriculum** [kəˈrɪkjələm] учебный план
**curry¹** ['kʌrɪ] ка́рри *n*
**curry²** [~]: **~ *favo(u)r with*** заискивать пе́ред (T)
**curse** [kɜːs] **1.** прокля́тие; руга́тельство; *fig.* бич, бе́дствие; **2.** проклина́ть [-кля́сть]; руга́ться; **~d** ['kɜːsɪd] □ прокля́тый
**cursory** ['kɜːsərɪ] бе́глый, бы́стрый; ***give a ~ glance*** пробежа́ть глаза́ми
**curt** [kɜːt] *answer* ре́зкий
**curtail** [kɜːˈteɪl] укора́чивать [-роти́ть]; уре́з(ыв)ать; *fig.* сокраща́ть [сократи́ть]
**curtain** ['kɜːtn] **1.** занаве́ска; *thea.* за́навес; **2.** занаве́шивать [-ве́сить]
**curv|ature** ['kɜːvətʃə] кривизна́; **~e** [kɜːv] **1.** *math.* крива́я; *of road, etc.* изги́б; **2.** повора́чивать [-верну́ть]; изгиба́ть(ся) [изогну́ть(ся)]; *of path, etc.* ви́ться
**cushion** ['kʊʃn] **1.** поду́шка; **2.** *on falling* смягча́ть [-чи́ть] уда́р
**custody** ['kʌstədɪ] опе́ка, попече́ние; ***take into ~*** задержа́ть, арестова́ть
**custom** ['kʌstəm] обы́чай; (*habit*) привы́чка; клиенту́ра; **~s** *pl.* тамо́жня; (*duties*) тамо́женные по́шлины *f/pl.*; **~ary** [~ərɪ] □ обы́чный; **~er** [~ə] покупа́тель *m*, -ница *f*, клие́нт *m*, -ка *f*; **~s examination** тамо́женный досмо́тр; **~s house** тамо́жня
**cut** [kʌt] **1.** разре́з, поре́з; *of clothes* покро́й; ***short ~*** коро́ткий путь *m*; **2.** [*irr.*] *v/t.* [от]ре́зать; разре́зать [-реза́ть]; *hair* [по]стри́чь; *precious stone* [от]шлифова́ть; *grass* [с]коси́ть; *teeth* проре́з(ыв)а́ться; **~ *short*** оборва́ть [обрыва́ть]; **~ *down*** сокраща́ть [-рати́ть]; **~ *out*** выреза́ть [вы́резать]; *dress* [с]крои́ть; *fig.* вытесня́ть [вы́теснить]; ***be ~ out for*** быть сло́вно со́зданным для (Р); *v/i.* ре́зать; **~ *in*** вме́шиваться [-ша́ться]; ***it ~s both ways*** па́лка о двух конца́х
**cute** [kjuːt] □ *coll.* хи́трый; *Am.* ми́лый, привлека́тельный
**cutlery** ['kʌtlərɪ] нож, ножевы́е изде́лия; столо́вые прибо́ры
**cutlet** ['kʌtlɪt] отбивна́я (котле́та)
**cut|out** *el.* автомати́ческий выключа́тель *m*, предохрани́тель *m*; **~ter** ['kʌtər] *cutting tool* резе́ц; *chopping knife* реза́к; *naut.* ка́тер; **~ting** ['kʌtɪŋ] **1.** □ о́стрый, ре́зкий; язви́тельный; **2.** ре́зание; *of clothes* кро́йка; *bot.* черено́к
**cyber|netics** [saɪbəˈnetɪks] киберне́тика; **~space** ['saɪbəspeɪs] виртуа́льная реа́льность
**cycl|e** ['saɪkl] **1.** цикл (*a. tech.*); круг; (*bicycle*) велосипе́д; **2.** е́здить на велосипе́де; **~ist** [~ɪst] велосипеди́ст *m*, -ка *f*
**cyclone** ['saɪkləʊn] цикло́н
**cylinder** ['sɪlɪndə] *geometry* цили́ндр
**cymbal** ['sɪmbl] *mus.* таре́лки *f/pl.*
**cynic** ['sɪnɪk] ци́ник; **~al** [~l] цини́чный
**cypress** ['saɪprəs] *bot.* кипари́с
**czar** [zɑː] царь
**Czech** [tʃək] **1.** чех *m*, че́шка *f*; **2.** че́шский

# D



**dab** [dæb] **1.** *with brush* мазóк; *of colour* пятнó; **2.** слегкá прикасáться, приклáдывать (В); дéлать лёгкие мазки́ на (П)
**dabble** ['dæbl] плескáть(ся); *hands, feet etc.* болтáть ногáми *и т.* в водé; занимáться чем-л. повéрхностно
**dad** [dæd], **~dy** ['dædı] *coll.* пáпа
**daffodil** ['dæfədıl] жёлтый нарци́сс
**dagger** ['dægə] кинжáл; ***be at ~s drawn*** быть на ножáх (с Т)
**dahlia** ['deılıə] георги́н
**daily** ['deılı] **1.** *adv.* ежеднéвно; **2.** ежеднéвный; *cares etc.* повседнéвный; **3.** ежеднéвная газéта
**dainty** ['deıntı] **1.** □ лáкомый; изя́щный; изы́сканный; **2.** лáкомство, деликатéс
**dairy** ['deərı] *shop* магази́н молóчных продýктов
**daisy** ['deızı] маргари́тка
**dale** [deıl] доли́на, дол
**dally** ['dælı] зря терять врéмя
**dam** [dæm] **1.** дáмба, плоти́на; **2.** запрýживать [-уди́ть]
**damage** ['dæmıdʒ] **1.** вред; повреждéние; (*loss*) ущéрб; **~s** *pl. law* ущéрб; компенсáция (за причинённый ущéрб); **2.** повреждáть [-еди́ть], [ис]пóртить
**damn** [dæm] проклинáть [-ля́сть]; (*censure*) осуждáть [осуди́ть]; (*swear at*) ругáться
**damnation** [dæm'neıʃn] *int.* проклятие; осуждéние
**damp** [dæmp] **1.** сы́рость *f*, влáжность *f*; **2.** влáжный, сырóй; **~en** ['dæmpən] [на]мочи́ть; *fig.* обескурáжи(ва)ть
**danc|e** [dɑːns] **1.** тáнец; тáнцы *m/pl.*; **2.** танцевáть; **~er** [~ə] танцóр, танцóвщик *m*, -и́ца *f*; **~ing** [~ıŋ] тáнцы *m/pl.*; пля́ска; *attr.* танцевáльный; ***~ partner*** партнёр, дáма
**dandelion** ['dændılaıən] одувáнчик
**dandle** ['dændl] [по]качáть (на рукáх)
**dandruff** ['dændrʌf] пéрхоть *f*
**dandy** ['dændı] **1.** щёголь *m*; **2.** *Am. sl.* первоклáссный
**Dane** [deın] датчáнин *m*, -чáнка *f*
**danger** ['deındʒə] опáсность *f*; **~ous** ['deındʒrəs] □ опáсный
**dangle** ['dæŋgl] висéть, свисáть [сви́снуть]; *legs* болтáть (Т)
**Danish** ['deınıʃ] дáтский
**dar|e** [deər] *v/i.* [по]смéть; отвáжи(ва)ться; *v/t.* пытáться подби́ть; **~edevil** смельчáк, сорвиголовá *m*; **~ing** ['deərıŋ] **1.** □ смéлый, отвáжный; **2.** смéлость *f*, отвáга
**dark** [dɑːk] **1.** тёмный; *skin* смýглый; (*hidden*) тáйный; *look etc.* мрáчный; ***~ horse*** тёмная лошáдка; **2.** темнотá, тьма; невéдение; ***keep s.o. in the ~*** держáть когó-л. в невéдении; ***keep s.th. ~*** держáть в тáйне; **~en** ['dɑːkən] [с]темнéть; [по]мрачнéть; **~ness** ['dɑːknıs] темнотá, тьма
**darling** ['dɑːlıŋ] **1.** люби́мец (-мица); **2.** ми́лый, люби́мый
**darn** [dɑːn] [за]штóпать
**dart** [dɑːt] **1.** *in game* стрелá; (*sudden movement*) прыжóк, рывóк; **2.** *v/i. fig.* мчáться стрелóй
**dash** [dæʃ] **1.** *of wave etc.* удáр; (*rush*) стреми́тельное движéние; (*dart*) рывóк; *fig.* при́месь *f*, чýточка; *typ.* тирé *n indecl.*; **2.** *v/t.* бросáть [брóсить]; разби́(вá)ть; *v/i.* бросáться [брóситься]; ***I'll have to ~*** мне нýжно бежáть; **~board** *mot.* прибóрная доскá; **~ing** ['dæʃıŋ] □ лихóй
**data** ['deıtə] *pl., Am. a. sg.* дáнные *n/pl.*; фáкты *m/pl.*; ***~ bank*** банк дáнных; ***~ processing*** обрабóтка дáнных
**date**[1] [deıt] **1.** дáта, числó; *coll.* свидáние; ***out of ~*** устарéлый; ***up to ~*** новéйший; совремéнный; **2.** дати́ровать (*im*)*pf.*; *Am. coll.* услáвливаться [-óвиться] с (Т) (о встрéче); имéть свидáние
**date**[2] [~] *bot.* фи́ник
**daub** [dɔːb] **1.** [вы́-, из-, на]мáзать;

D

[на]малева́ть; **2.** мазня́
**daughter** ['dɔːtə] дочь *f*; **~-in-law** [~rɪn-lɔː] неве́стка, сноха́
**daunt** [dɔːnt] устраша́ть [-ши́ть], запу́гивать [-га́ть]; **~less** ['dɔːntlɪs] неустраши́мый, бесстра́шный
**dawdle** ['dɔːdl] *coll.* безде́льничать
**dawn** [dɔːn] **1.** рассве́т, у́тренняя заря́; *fig.* заря́; **2.** света́ть
**day** [deɪ] день *m*; (*mst.* **~s** *pl.*) жизнь *f*; **~ *off*** выходно́й день *m*; ***every other ~*** че́рез день; ***the ~ after tomorrow*** послеза́втра; ***the other ~*** на днях; неда́вно; **~break** рассве́т; **~dream** мечта́ть, гре́зить наяву́
**daze** [deɪz] ошеломля́ть [-ми́ть]
**dazzle** ['dæzl] ослепля́ть [-пи́ть]
**dead** [ded] **1.** мёртвый; *flowers* увя́дший; (*numbed*) онеме́вший; *silence etc.* по́лный; ***come to a ~ stop*** ре́зко останови́ться; ***~ end*** тупи́к; **2.** *adv.* по́лно, соверше́нно; ***~ against*** реши́тельно про́тив; **3.** ***the ~*** мёртвые *m/pl.*; ***in the ~ of night*** глубо́кой но́чью; **~en** ['dedn] лиша́ть(ся) си́лы; *sound* заглуша́ть [-ши́ть]; **~lock** *fig.* тупи́к; **~ly** [~lɪ] смерте́льный; *weapon* смертоно́сный
**deaf** [def] □ глухо́й; **~en** [defn] оглуша́ть [-ши́ть]
**deal** [diːl] **1.** (*agreement*) соглаше́ние; (*business agreement*) сде́лка; ***a good ~*** мно́го; ***a great ~*** о́чень мно́го; **2.** [*irr.*] *v/t.* (*distribute*) разд(ав)а́ть; распределя́ть [-ли́ть]; *at cards* сдава́ть [сдать]; *v/i.* торгова́ть; ***~ with*** обходи́ться [обойти́сь] *or* поступа́ть [-пи́ть] с (Т); име́ть де́ло с (Т); **~er** ['diːlə] ди́лер, торго́вец; **~ing** ['diːlɪŋ] (*mst.* **~s** *pl.*): ***have ~s with*** вести́ дела́ (с Т); **~t** [delt] *pt. u pt. p. от* **~**
**dean** [diːn] настоя́тель собо́ра; *univ.* дека́н
**dear** [dɪə] **1.** дорого́й (*a. = costly*), ми́лый; (*in business letter*) (глубоко)уважа́емый; **2.** прекра́сный челове́к; **3.** *coll.* ***oh ~!, ~ me!*** Го́споди!
**death** [deθ] смерть *f*; **~ duty** нало́г на насле́дство; **~ly** [~lɪ]: ***~ pale*** бле́дный как смерть; **~ rate** сме́ртность *f*; **~ trap** опа́сное ме́сто
**debar** [dɪ'bɑː] [вос]препя́тствовать; не допуска́ть [-сти́ть]; (*exclude*) исключа́ть [-чи́ть]; *from voting etc.* лиша́ть пра́ва
**debase** [dɪ'beɪs] унижа́ть [-и́зить]; снижа́ть ка́чество (Р), курс (валю́ты)
**debat|able** [dɪ'beɪtəbl] □ спо́рный; дискуссио́нный; **~e** [dɪ'beɪt] **1.** диску́ссия; пре́ния *n/pl.*, деба́ты *m/pl.*; **2.** обсужда́ть [-уди́ть]; [по]спо́рить; (*ponder*) обду́м(ыв)ать
**debauch** [dɪ'bɔːtʃ] **1.** развра́т; (*carouse*) попо́йка; **2.** развраща́ть [-рати́ть]
**debilitate** [dɪ'bɪlɪteɪt] (*weaken*) ослабля́ть [-а́бить]
**debit** ['debɪt] *fin.* **1.** де́бет; **2.** дебетова́ть (*im*)*pf.*, вноси́ть в де́бет
**debris** ['deɪbriː] разва́лины *f/pl.*, обло́мки *m/pl.*
**debt** [det] долг; **~or** ['detə] должни́к *m*, -и́ца *f*
**decade** ['dekeɪd] десятиле́тие; *of one's age* деся́ток
**decadence** ['dekədəns] упа́док; *in art* декаде́нтство
**decant** [dɪ'kænt] сце́живать [сцеди́ть]; **~er** [~ə] графи́н
**decay** [dɪ'keɪ] **1.** гние́ние; разложе́ние; *of teeth* разруше́ние; ка́риес; ***fall into ~*** *of building* [об] ветша́ть; *fig.* приходи́ть [прийти́] в упа́док; **2.** [с]гнить; разлага́ться [-ложи́ться]
**decease** [dɪ'siːs] *part. law* смерть *f*, конч́ина; **~d** [~t] поко́йный
**deceit** [dɪ'siːt] обма́н; **~ful** [~fʊl] лжи́вый; (*deceptive*) обма́нчивый
**deceiv|e** [dɪ'siːv] обма́нывать [-ну́ть]; **~er** [~ə] обма́нщик (-ица)
**December** [dɪ'sembə] дека́брь *m*
**decen|cy** ['diːsnsɪ] прили́чие; **~t** [~nt] □ прили́чный; *kind, well-behaved coll.* поря́дочный; *coll.* сла́вный; ***it's very ~ of you*** о́чень любе́зно с ва́шей стороны́
**deception** [dɪ'sepʃn] обма́н; ложь *f*
**decide** [dɪ'saɪd] реша́ть(ся) [реши́ть(ся)]; принима́ть реше́ние;

D

**~d** [-ɪd] (*clear-cut*) □ определённый; (*unmistakable*) бесспо́рный
**decimal** ['desɪml] **1.** десяти́чный; **2.** десяти́чная дробь *f*
**decipher** [dɪ'saɪfə] расшифро́вывать [-ова́ть]; *poor handwriting* разбира́ть [разобра́ть]
**decisi|on** [dɪ'sɪʒn] реше́ние (*a. law*); **~ve** [dɪ'saɪsɪv] *conclusive* реша́ющий; *resolute* реши́тельный; **~veness** реши́тельность *f*
**deck** [dek] *naut.* па́луба; *Am. cards* коло́да; **~chair** шезло́нг
**declar|able** [dɪ'kleərəbl] подлежа́щий деклара́ции; **~ation** [deklə'reɪʃn] заявле́ние; деклара́ция (*a. fin.*); ***customs ~*** тамо́женная деклара́ция; **~e** [dɪ'kleər] объявля́ть [-ви́ть]; заявля́ть [-ви́ть]; выска́зываться [вы́сказаться] (***for*** за В, ***against*** про́тив Р); *to customs officials* предъявля́ть [-ви́ть]
**decline** [dɪ'klaɪn] **1.** (*fall*) паде́ние; *of strength* упа́док; *in prices* сниже́ние; *of health* ухудше́ние; *of life* зака́т; **2.** *v/t. an offer* отклоня́ть [-ни́ть]; *gr.* [про]склоня́ть; *v/i.* приходи́ть в упа́док; *of health etc.* ухудша́ться [уху́дшиться]
**decode** [diː'kəʊd] расшифро́вывать [-рова́ть]
**decompose** [diːkəm'pəʊz] разлага́ть(ся) [-ложи́ть(ся)]; [с]гнить
**decorat|e** ['dekəreɪt] украша́ть [укра́сить]; (*confer medal, etc. on*) награжда́ть [-ди́ть]; **~ion** [dekə'reɪʃn] украше́ние; о́рден, знак отли́чия; **~ive** ['dekərətɪv] декорати́вный
**decor|ous** ['dekərəs] □ присто́йный; **~um** [dɪ'kɔːrəm] этике́т
**decoy** [dɪ'kɔɪ] прима́нка (*a. fig.*)
**decrease** **1.** ['diːkriːs] уменьше́ние, пониже́ние; **2.** [dɪ'kriːs] уменьша́ть(ся) [уме́ньшить(ся)], снижа́ть [-и́зить]
**decree** [dɪ'kriː] **1.** *pol.* ука́з, декре́т, постановле́ние; *law* реше́ние; **2.** постановля́ть [-ви́ть]
**decrepit** [dɪ'krepɪt] дря́хлый
**dedicat|e** ['dedɪkeɪt] посвяща́ть [-яти́ть]; **~ion** [dedɪ'keɪʃn] (*devotion*) пре́данность *f*; (*inscription*) посвяще́ние; ***work with ~*** по́лностью отдава́ть себя́ рабо́те
**deduce** [dɪ'djuːs] [с]де́лать вы́вод; заключа́ть [-чи́ть]
**deduct** [dɪ'dʌkt] вычита́ть [вы́честь]; **~ion** [dɪ'dʌkʃn] вы́чет; (*conclusion*) вы́вод, заключе́ние; *comm.* ски́дка
**deed** [diːd] **1.** де́йствие; посту́пок; *law* акт; ***~ of purchase*** догово́р ку́пли/прода́жи; **2.** *Am.* передава́ть по а́кту
**deem** [diːm] *v/t.* счита́ть [счесть]; *v/i.* полага́ть
**deep** [diːp] **1.** глубо́кий; *colo(u)r* густо́й; **2.** *poet.* мо́ре, океа́н; **~en** ['diːpən] углубля́ть(ся) [-би́ть(ся)]; уси́ливать(ся) [уси́лить(ся)]; **~-freeze** → ***freezer***, **~ness** [-nɪs] глубина́; **~-rooted** глубоко́ укорени́вшийся
**deer** [dɪə] оле́нь *m*
**deface** [dɪ'feɪs] обезобра́живать [-а́зить]
**defam|ation** [defə'meɪʃn] клевета́; **~e** [dɪ'feɪm] [о]клевета́ть
**default** [dɪ'fɔːlt] **1.** невыполне́ние обяза́тельств; не́явка; *comput.* автомати́ческий вы́бор; **2.** не выполня́ть обяза́тельства
**defeat** [dɪ'fiːt] **1.** пораже́ние; *of plans* расстро́йство; **2.** *mil.*, *sport etc.* побежда́ть [-еди́ть]; расстра́ивать [-ро́ить]
**defect** [dɪ'fekt] недоста́ток; (*fault*) неиспра́вность *f*; дефе́кт, изъя́н; **~ive** [-tɪv] несоверше́нный, □ повреждённый; ***~ goods*** брако́ванные това́ры; ***mentally ~*** у́мственно отста́лый
**defence** → ***defense***
**defend** [dɪ'fend] обороня́ть(ся), [-ни́ть(ся)], защища́ть на суде́; **~ant** [-ənt] *law* подсуди́мый; *civil* отве́тчик; **~er** [-ə] защи́тник
**defense** [dɪ'fens] оборо́на, защи́та; **~less** [-lɪs] беззащи́тный
**defensive** [dɪ'fensɪv] **1.** оборо́на; **2.** оборо́нный, оборони́тельный
**defer** [dɪ'fɜː] откла́дывать [отложи́ть]; отсро́чи(ва)ть

D

**defian|ce** [dɪ'faɪəns] (*challenge*) вы́зов; (*disobedience*) неповинове́ние; (*scorn*) пренебреже́ние; **~t** [-ənt] □ вызыва́ющий

**deficien|cy** [dɪ'fɪʃənsɪ] недоста́ток, нехва́тка; **~t** [-ənt] недоста́точный; несоверше́нный

**deficit** ['defɪsɪt] недочёт; недоста́ча; дефици́т

**defile** [dɪ'faɪl] загрязня́ть [-ни́ть]

**defin|e** [dɪ'faɪn] определя́ть [-ли́ть]; дава́ть характери́стику; (*show limits of*) оче́рчивать [-рти́ть], обознача́ть; **~ite** ['defɪnɪt] □ определённый; (*exact*) то́чный; **~ition** [defɪ'nɪʃn] определе́ние; **~itive** [dɪ'fɪnɪtɪv] □ (*final*) оконча́тельный

**deflect** [dɪ'flekt] отклоня́ть(ся) [-ни́ть(ся)]

**deform|ed** [dɪ'fɔːmd] изуро́дованный; искажённый; **~ity** [dɪ'fɔːmətɪ] уро́дство

**defraud** [dɪ'frɔːd] обма́нывать [-ну́ть]; выма́нивать (***of*** В)

**defray** [dɪ'freɪ] опла́чивать [оплати́ть]

**defrost** [diːfrɒst] отта́ивать [-а́ять]; размора́живать [-ро́зить]

**deft** [deft] □ ло́вкий, иску́сный

**defy** [dɪ'faɪ] вызыва́ть [вы́звать]; броса́ть [бро́сить] вы́зов; вести́ себя́ вызыва́юще; (*flout*) пренебрега́ть [-бре́чь] (Т)

**degenerate** [dɪ'dʒenəreɪt] вырожда́ться [вы́родиться]

**degrad|ation** [degrə'deɪʃn] деграда́ция; **~e** [dɪ'greɪd] *v/t.* (*lower in rank*) понижа́ть [пони́зить]; (*abase*) унижа́ть [уни́зить]

**degree** [dɪ'griː] (*unit of measurement*) гра́дус; (*step or stage in a process*) у́ровень *m*; сте́пень *f*; (*a. univ.*) зва́ние; ***honorary ~*** почётное зва́ние; ***by ~s*** постепе́нно; ***in no ~*** ничу́ть, ниско́лько; ***to some ~*** в изве́стной сте́пени

**deign** [deɪn] снисходи́ть [снизойти́]; соизволя́ть [-о́лить]; *usu. iron.* удоста́ивать [-сто́ить]

**deity** ['diːɪtɪ] божество́

**deject|ed** [dɪ'dʒektɪd] □ удручённый; угнетённый; **~ion** [dɪ'dʒekʃn] уны́ние

**delay** [dɪ'leɪ] **1.** заде́ржка; отсро́чка; **2.** *v/t.* заде́рживать [-жа́ть]; откла́дывать [отложи́ть]; ме́длить с (Т); *v/i.* ме́длить, ме́шкать

**delega|te 1.** ['delɪgət] делега́т, представи́тель(ница *f*) *m*; **2.** [~geɪt] делеги́ровать (*im*)*pf.*, поруча́ть [-чи́ть]; **~tion** [delɪ'geɪʃn] делега́ция

**deliberat|e 1.** [dɪ'lɪbəreɪt] *v/t.* обду́м(ыв)ать; взве́шивать [-е́сить]; обсужда́ть [обсуди́ть]; *v/i.* совеща́ться; **2.** [~rət] □ преднаме́ренный, умы́шленный; **~ion** [dɪlɪbə'reɪʃn] размышле́ние; обсужде́ние; осмотри́тельность *f*; ***act with ~*** де́йствовать с осмотри́тельностью

**delica|cy** ['delɪkəsɪ] делика́тность *f*; *food* ла́комство; утончённость *f*; не́жность *f*; **~te** [~kɪt] □ делика́тный; (*fragile*) хру́пкий; изя́щный; *work* иску́сный; чувстви́тельный; щепети́льный; **~tessen** [delɪkə'tesn] магази́н делика́те́сов, гастроно́м

**delicious** [dɪ'lɪʃəs] восхити́тельный; о́чень вку́сный

**delight** [dɪ'laɪt] **1.** удово́льствие; восто́рг; наслажде́ние; **2.** восхища́ть [-ити́ть]; наслажда́ться [-ди́ться]; доставля́ть удово́льствие (***in*** Т): ***be ~ed with*** быть в восто́рге (от Р); ***be ~ed to*** *inf.* име́ть удово́льствие (+ *inf.*); **~ful** [~ful] □ *girl etc.* очарова́тельный; восхити́тельный

**delinquent** [dɪ'lɪŋkwənt]: ***juvenile ~*** несовершенноле́тний престу́пник

**deliri|ous** [dɪ'lɪrɪəs] находя́щийся в бреду́, вне себя́, в исступле́нии; ***~ with joy*** вне себя́ от ра́дости; **~um** [~əm] бред

**deliver** [dɪ'lɪvə] *newspapers etc.* доставля́ть [-а́вить]; *a speech* произноси́ть [-нести́]; *order* сда́(ва́)ть; *a blow* наноси́ть [нанести́] (*уда́р*); ***be ~ed*** *med.* роди́ть; **~ance** [~rəns] освобожде́ние; (*rescue*) спасе́ние

**delude** [dɪ'luːd] вводи́ть в заблужде́ние; (*deceive*) обма́нывать [-ну́ть]

**deluge** ['deljuːdʒ] **1.** наводне́ние;

(*rain*) ли́вень; *fig.* пото́к; **2.** затопля́ть [-пи́ть]; наводня́ть [-ни́ть] *a. fig.*

**delus|ion** [dɪ'lu:ʒn] заблужде́ние; иллю́зия; **~ive** [~sɪv] □ обма́нчивый; иллюзо́рный

**demand** [dɪ'mɑ:nd] **1.** тре́бование; потре́бность *f*; *comm.* спрос; ***be in great ~*** по́льзоваться больши́м спро́сом; **2.** [по]тре́бовать (Р)

**demilitarize** [di:'mɪlɪtəraɪz] демилитаризова́ть *(im)pf.*

**demobilize** [di:'məʊbɪlaɪz] демобилизова́ть *(im)pf.*

**democra|cy** [dɪ'mɒkrəsɪ] демокра́тия; **~tic(al** □) [demə'krætɪk(əl)] демократи́ческий

**demolish** [dɪ'mɒlɪʃ] разруша́ть [-ру́шить]; (*pull down*) сноси́ть [снести́]

**demon** ['di:mən] де́мон, дья́вол

**demonstrat|e** ['demənstreɪt] [про]демонстри́ровать; (*prove*) дока́зывать [-за́ть]; **~ion** [demən'streɪʃn] демонстра́ция; доказа́тельство; **~ive** [dɪ'mɒnstrətɪv] □ *person, behaviour* экспанси́вный; *gr.* указа́тельный

**demoralize** [dɪ'mɒrəlaɪz] деморализова́ть

**demure** [dɪ'mjʊə] □ скро́мный; *smile* засте́нчивый

**den** [den] ло́говище; берло́га; прито́н

**denial** [dɪ'naɪəl] отрица́ние; *official* опроверже́ние; (*refusal*) отка́з

**denomination** [dɪnɒmɪ'neɪʃn] *eccl.* вероиспове́дание; се́кта

**denote** [dɪ'nəʊt] означа́ть *impf.*, обознача́ть [-на́чить]

**denounce** [dɪ'naʊns] (*expose*) разоблача́ть [-чи́ть]; *to police* доноси́ть; *termination of a treaty, etc.* денонси́ровать *(im)pf.*

**dens|e** [dens] □ густо́й; пло́тный (*a. phys.*); *fig.* глу́пый, тупо́й; **~ity** ['densətɪ] густота́; пло́тность *f*

**dent** [dent] **1.** вмя́тина; **2.** вда́вливать [вдави́ть]; *v/i.* [по]гну́ться

**dentist** ['dentɪst] зубно́й врач

**denture** ['dentʃə] *mst. pl.* зубно́й проте́з

**denunciation** [dɪnʌnsɪ'eɪʃn] доно́с; обличе́ние, обвине́ние

**deny** [dɪ'naɪ] отрица́ть; отка́зываться [-за́ться] от (Р); (*refuse to give, allow*) отка́зывать [-за́ть] в (П); ***there is no ~ing*** сле́дует призна́ть

**deodorant** [di:'əʊdərənt] дезодора́нт

**depart** [dɪ'pɑ:t] *v/i.* уходи́ть [уйти́], уезжа́ть [уе́хать], отбы́(ва́)ть, отправля́ться [-а́виться]; отступа́ть [-пи́ть] (***from*** от Р); **~ment** [~mənt] *univ.* отделе́ние, факульте́т; *of science* о́бласть *f*, о́трасль; *in shop* отде́л; *Am.* министе́рство; ***State*** ♀ министе́рство иностра́нных дел; ***~ store*** универма́г; **~ure** [dɪ'pɑ:tʃə] отъе́зд; ухо́д; *rail.* отправле́ние; (*deviation*) отклоне́ние

**depend** [dɪ'pend]: ***~ (up)on*** зави́сеть от (Р); *coll.* ***it ~s*** смотря́ по обстоя́тельствам; ***you can ~ on him*** на него́ мо́жно положи́ться; **~able** [~əbl] надёжный; **~ant** [~ənt] иждиве́нец *m*, -нка *f*; **~ence** [~əns] зави́симость *f*; (*trust*) дове́рие; **~ent** [~ənt] □ (***on***) зави́сящий (от Р)

**depict** [dɪ'pɪkt] изобража́ть [-рази́ть]; *fig.* опи́сывать [-са́ть]

**deplete** [dɪ'pli:t] истоща́ть [-щи́ть]

**deplor|able** [dɪ'plɔ:rəbl] □ приско́рбный, заслу́живающий сожале́ния; *state* плаче́вный; **~e** [dɪ'plɔ:] (*disapprove of*) порица́ть; сожале́ть о (П)

**deport** [dɪ'pɔ:t] депорти́ровать

**depose** [dɪ'pəʊz] *from office* смеща́ть [смести́ть]; (*dethrone*) сверга́ть [све́ргнуть]

**deposit** [dɪ'pɒzɪt] **1.** *geol.* отложе́ние; за́лежь *f*; *fin.* вклад; депози́т; зада́ток; ***~ account*** депози́тный счёт; **2.** класть [положи́ть]; депони́ровать *(im)pf.*; дава́ть [дать] зада́ток; **~or** [dɪ'pɒzɪtə] вкла́дчик *m*, -ица *f*, депози́тор

**depot** **1.** ['depəʊ] *rail.* депо́ *n indecl.*; *storage place* склад; **2.** ['di:pəʊ] *Am. rail.* железнодоро́жная ста́нция

**deprave** [dɪ'preɪv] развраща́ть [-рати́ть]

**depreciat|e** [dɪ'pri:ʃɪeɪt] обесце́ни(-ва)ть; **~ion** [dɪpri:ʃɪ'eɪʃn] сниже́ние сто́имости; обесце́нение; амортиза́-

D

ция
**depress** [dɪˈpres] угнета́ть *impf.*; подавля́ть [-ви́ть]; **~ed** [-t] *fig.* уны́лый; **~ion** [dɪˈpreʃn] угнетённое состоя́ние; *geogr.* впа́дина; *econ.* депре́ссия
**deprive** [dɪˈpraɪv] лиша́ть [лиши́ть] (**of** P)
**depth** [depθ] глубина́; ***be out of one's ~*** быть не под си́лу, быть недосту́пным понима́нию
**deput|ation** [depjʊˈteɪʃn] делега́ция; **~y** [ˈdepjʊtɪ] делега́т; депута́т; замести́тель(ница *f*) *m*
**derange** [dɪˈreɪndʒ] *plans etc.* расстра́ивать [-ро́ить]; (*put out of order*) приводи́ть в беспоря́док
**derelict** [ˈderəlɪkt] *ship* поки́нутый; *house* (за)бро́шенный
**deri|de** [dɪˈraɪd] осме́ивать [-ея́ть], высме́ивать [вы́смеять]; **~sion** [dɪˈrɪʒn] высме́ивание; **~sive** [dɪˈraɪsɪv] □ издева́тельский; *scornful* насме́шливый
**derive** [dɪˈraɪv] (*originate*) происходи́ть [-изойти́]; *benefit* извлека́ть [-вле́чь] (***from*** от P)
**derogatory** [dɪˈrɒgətrɪ] пренебрежи́тельный
**descend** [dɪˈsend] спуска́ться [спусти́ться]; сходи́ть [сойти́]; *ae.* снижа́ться [сни́зиться]; *from a person* происходи́ть [-изойти́] (***from*** из P); **~** (***up***)***on*** обру́ши(ва)ться на (В); **~ant** [-ənt] пото́мок
**descent** [dɪˈsent] спуск; сниже́ние; (*slope*) склон; происхожде́ние
**describe** [dɪˈskraɪb] опи́сывать [-са́ть]
**description** [dɪˈskrɪpʃn] описа́ние; ***of every ~*** са́мые ра́зные
**desert**[1] [dɪˈzɜːt]: ***get one's ~s*** получи́ть по заслу́гам
**desert**[2] **1.** [ˈdezət] пусты́ня; **2.** [dɪˈzɜːt] *v/t.* (*leave*) броса́ть [бро́сить]; (*go away*) покида́ть [поки́нуть]; *v/i.* дезерти́ровать (*im*)*pf.*; **~ed** [-ɪd] *street* пусты́нный; (*neglected*) забро́шенный; (*abandoned*) поки́нутый; **~er** [-ə] дезерти́р; **~ion** [-ʃn] дезерти́рство; *spouse's* ухо́д
**deserv|e** [dɪˈzɜːv] заслу́живать [-жи́ть]; **~edly** [-ɪdlɪ] заслу́женно; **~ing** [-ɪŋ] заслу́живающий; досто́йный (***of*** P)
**design** [dɪˈzaɪn] **1.** (*intention*) за́мысел, наме́рение, план; *arch.* прое́кт; *tech.* диза́йн; (*pattern*) узо́р; **2.** предназнача́ть [-зна́чить]; заду́м(ыв)ать; [с]проекти́ровать; *machinery* [с]конструи́ровать
**designat|e** [ˈdezɪgneɪt] определя́ть [-ли́ть]; (*mark out*) обознача́ть [-зна́чить]; (*appoint*) назнача́ть [-зна́чить]
**designer** [dɪˈzaɪnə] (*engineer*) констру́ктор; диза́йнер; ***dress ~*** моделье́р
**desir|able** [dɪˈzaɪərəbl] □ жела́тельный; **~e** [dɪˈzaɪə] **1.** жела́ние; тре́бование; **2.** [по]жела́ть (P); [по]тре́бовать (P); ***leave much to be ~d*** оставля́ть жела́ть лу́чшего; **~ous** [-rəs] жела́ющий (***of*** P); ***be ~ of knowing*** стреми́ться/жела́ть узна́ть
**desk** [desk] пи́сьменный стол; ***~ diary*** насто́льный календа́рь; **~top publishing** насто́льное изда́тельство
**desolat|e 1.** [ˈdesəleɪt] опустоша́ть [-ши́ть]; разоря́ть [-ри́ть]; **2.** [-lət] □ опустошённый; несча́стный; одино́кий; **~ion** [desəˈleɪʃn] опустоше́ние; одино́чество
**despair** [dɪˈspeə] **1.** отча́яние; ***drive s.o. to ~*** доводи́ть [-вести́] кого́-л. до отча́яния; **2.** отча́иваться [-ча́яться]; теря́ть наде́жду (***of*** на В); **~ing** [-rɪŋ] □ отча́ивающийся
**despatch** → ***dispatch***
**desperat|e** [ˈdespərət] □ *effort etc.* отча́янный; *state* безнадёжный; *adv.* отча́янно, стра́шно; **~ion** [despəˈreɪʃn] отча́яние
**despise** [dɪˈspaɪz] презира́ть
**despite** [dɪˈspaɪt] *prp.* несмотря́ на (В)
**despondent** [dɪˈspɒndənt] □ пода́вленный, удручённый
**dessert** [dɪˈzɜːt] десе́рт; *attr.* десе́ртный
**destin|ation** [destɪˈneɪʃn] (*purpose, end*) назначе́ние; ме́сто назначе́ния;

**~e** ['destɪn] предназнача́ть [-зна́чить]; ***be ~d*** (*be fated*) предопределя́ть [-ли́ть]; **~y** [-tɪnɪ] судьба́

**destitute** ['destɪtju:t] нужда́ющийся; лишённый (***of*** Р)

**destroy** [dɪ'strɔɪ] уничтожа́ть [-о́жить]; истребля́ть [-би́ть]; *buildings, etc.* разруша́ть [-ру́шить]; **~er** [-ə] *warship* эсми́нец

**destruct|ion** [dɪ'strʌkʃn] разруше́ние; уничтоже́ние; **~ive** [-tɪv] □ разруши́тельный; па́губный; вре́дный

**detach** [dɪ'tætʃ] отделя́ть [-ли́ть]; разъединя́ть [-ни́ть]; (*tear off*) отрыва́ть [оторва́ть]; **~ed** [-t] отде́льный; *fig.* беспристра́стный; **~ment** [-mənt] *mil.* отря́д; *fig.* беспристра́стность *f*

**detail** ['di:teɪl] подро́бность *f*, дета́ль *f*; ***in ~*** дета́льно, подро́бно; ***go into ~s*** вника́ть (вдава́ться) в подро́бности

**detain** [dɪ'teɪn] заде́рживать [-жа́ть] (*a. by the police*); ***he was ~ed at work*** он задержа́лся на рабо́те

**detect** [dɪ'tekt] обнару́жи(ва)ть; (*notice*) замеча́ть [-е́тить]; **~ion** [dɪ'tekʃn] обнаруже́ние; *of crime* рассле́дование; **~ive** [-tɪv] **1.** детекти́в, операти́вник; **2.** детекти́вный

**detention** [dɪ'tənʃn] (*holding*) задержа́ние; (*custody*) содержа́ние под аре́стом; (*confinement*) заключе́ние

**deter** [dɪ'tɜ:] уде́рживать [-жа́ть] (***from*** от Р)

**deteriorat|e** [dɪ'tɪərɪəreɪt] ухудша́ть(ся) [уху́дшить(ся)]; [ис]по́ртить(ся); **~ion** [dɪtɪərɪə'reɪʃn] ухудше́ние

**determin|ation** [dɪtɜ:mɪ'neɪʃn] определе́ние; (*firmness*) реши́тельность *f*; **~e** [dɪ'tɜ:mɪn] *v/t.* определя́ть [-ли́ть]; реша́ть [реши́ть]; *v/i.* реша́ться [реши́ться]; **~ed** [-d] реши́тельный

**detest** [dɪ'test] ненави́деть; пита́ть отвраще́ние к (Д); **~able** [-əbl] отврати́тельный

**detonate** ['detəneɪt] детони́ровать; взрыва́ть(ся) [взорва́ть(ся)]

**detour** ['di:'tʊə] око́льный путь *m*; объе́зд; ***make a ~*** сде́лать *pf.* крюк

**detract** [dɪ'trækt] умаля́ть [-ли́ть], уменьша́ть [уме́ньшить]

**detriment** ['detrɪmənt] уще́рб, вред

**devalue** [di:'vælju:] обесце́ни(ва)ть

**devastat|e** ['devəsteɪt] опустоша́ть [-ши́ть]; разоря́ть [-ри́ть]; **~ion** [devə'steɪʃn] опустоше́ние

**develop** [dɪ'veləp] разви́(ва́)ть(ся); *mineral resources* разраба́тывать [-бо́тать]; *phot.* проявля́ть [-ви́ть]; **~ment** [-mənt] разви́тие; разрабо́тка; (*event*) собы́тие

**deviat|e** ['di:vɪeɪt] отклоня́ться [-ни́ться]; **~ion** [di:vɪ'eɪʃn] отклоне́ние

**device** [dɪ'vaɪs] *tech.* приспособле́ние, устро́йство; (*way, method, trick*) приём; ***leave a p. to his own ~s*** предоставля́ть челове́ка самому́ себе́

**devil** ['devl] дья́вол, чёрт, бес; **~ish** [-əlɪʃ] □ дья́вольский, *coll.* черто́вский; **~ry** [-vlrɪ] чертовщи́на

**devious** ['di:vɪəs]: □ ***by ~ means*** нече́стным путём

**devise** [dɪ'vaɪz] приду́м(ыв)ать; изобрета́ть [-рести́]

**devoid** [dɪ'vɔɪd] (***of***) лишённый (Р)

**devot|e** [dɪ'vəʊt] посвяща́ть [-яти́ть] (В/Д); **~ed** [-ɪd] □ пре́данный, лю́бящий; **~ion** [dɪ'vəʊʃn] пре́данность *f*, привя́занность *f*

**devour** [dɪ'vaʊə] пож(и)ра́ть; ***be ~ed with curiosity*** сгора́ть от любопы́тства

**devout** [dɪ'vaʊt] □ *supporter, etc.* пре́данный; *relig.* благочести́вый

**dew** [dju:] роса́; **~y** [-ɪ] роси́стый, покры́тый росо́й

**dexter|ity** [dek'sterətɪ] ло́вкость *f*; **~ous** ['dekstrəs] ло́вкий

**diabolic(al** □) [daɪə'bɒlɪk(əl)] дья́вольский; *fig.* жесто́кий, злой

**diagnosis** [daɪəg'nəʊsɪs] диа́гноз

**diagram** ['daɪəgræm] диагра́мма; схе́ма

**dial** ['daɪəl] **1.** *of clock, etc.* цифербла́т; *tech.* шкала́ (цифербла́тного ти́па); *tel.* диск; **2.** *tel.* набира́ть [-бра́ть] номер; позвони́ть *pf.*

**dialect** ['daɪəlekt] диале́кт, наре́чие

**dialogue** ['daɪəlɒg] диало́г; разгово́р

**diameter** [daɪ'æmɪtə] диа́метр

**diamond** ['daɪəmənd] алма́з; *precious stone* бриллиа́нт; ромб; **~s** [~s] *pl. cards*: бу́бны *f/pl.*

**diaper** ['daɪəpər] (*Brt.*: *nappy*) пелёнка

**diaphragm** ['daɪəfræm] *anat.* диафра́гма *a. optics*

**diarrh(o)ea** [daɪə'rɪə] поно́с

**diary** ['daɪərɪ] дневни́к

**dice** [daɪs] (*pl. om* ***die***[2]) игра́льные ко́сти *f/pl.*

**dictat|e 1.** ['dɪkteɪt] (*order*) предписа́ние; *of conscience* веле́ние; *pol.* дикта́т; **2.** [dɪk'teɪt] [про]диктова́ть (*a. fig.*); предпи́сывать [-са́ть]; **~ion** [dɪk'teɪʃn] *educ.* дикто́вка, дикта́нт; предписа́ние; **~orship** [dɪk'teɪtəʃɪp] диктату́ра

**diction** ['dɪkʃn] ди́кция; **~ary** [~rɪ] слова́рь *m*

**did** [dɪd] *pt. om* ***do***

**die**[1] [daɪ] умира́ть [умере́ть], сконча́ться *pf.*; *coll.* стра́стно жела́ть; ***~ away, ~ down*** *of sound* замира́ть [-мере́ть]; *of wind* затиха́ть [-и́хнуть]; *of flowers* увяда́ть [-я́нуть]; *of fire* угаса́ть [уга́снуть]

**die**[2] [~] (*pl.* **dice**) игра́льная кость *f*; ***the ~ is cast*** жре́бий бро́шен

**diet** ['daɪət] **1.** *customary* пи́ща; *med.* дие́та; **2.** *v/t.* держа́ть на дие́те; *v/i.* быть на дие́те

**differ** ['dɪfə] различа́ться, отлича́ться; (*disagree*) не соглаша́ться [-ласи́ться], расходи́ться [разойти́сь] (***from*** с Т, ***in*** в П); ***tastes ~*** о вку́сах не спо́рят; **~ence** ['dɪfrəns] ра́зница; разли́чие; разногла́сие; *math.* ра́зность *f*; ***it makes no ~ to me*** мне всё равно́; **~ent** [~nt] □ ра́зный; друго́й, не тако́й (***from*** как), ино́й; **~entiate** [dɪfə'renʃɪeɪt] различа́ть(ся) [-чи́ть(-ся)], отлича́ться [-чи́ть(ся)]

**difficult** ['dɪfɪkəlt] □ тру́дный; **~y** [~ɪ] тру́дность *f*; затрудне́ние

**diffiden|ce** ['dɪfɪdəns] (*lack of confidence*) неуве́ренность *f*; (*shyness*) засте́нчивость *f*; **~t** [~dənt] неуве́ренный; засте́нчивый

**diffus|e 1.** [dɪ'fjuːz] *fig.* распространя́ть [-ни́ть]; **2.** [dɪ'fjuːs] распространённый; *light* рассе́янный; **~ion** [dɪ'fjuːʒn] распростране́ние; рассе́ивание; *of gas, liquids* диффу́зия

**dig** [dɪg] **1.** [*irr.*] копа́ться; [вы́]копать; ры́ться; [вы́]рыть; **2.** *coll.* (*a. cutting remark*) толчо́к

**digest 1.** [dɪ'dʒest] *food* перева́ривать [-ри́ть]; *information, etc.* усва́ивать [усво́ить] (*a. fig.*); *v/i.* перева́риваться [-ри́ться]; усва́иваться [усво́иться]; **2.** ['daɪdʒest] (*literary*) дайдже́ст; **~ible** [dɪ'dʒestəbl] *fig.* удобовари́мый; легко́ усва́иваемый (*a. fig.*); **~ion** [~tʃən] *of food* пищеваре́ние; *of knowledge* усвое́ние

**digital** ['dɪdʒɪtl] цифрово́й

**dignif|ied** ['dɪgnɪfaɪd] преиспо́лненный досто́инства; **~y** [~faɪ] *fig.* облагора́живать [-ро́дить]

**dignit|ary** ['dɪgnɪtərɪ] сано́вник; лицо́, занима́ющее высо́кий по́ст; *eccl.* иера́рх; **~y** [~tɪ] досто́инство

**digress** [daɪ'gres] отклоня́ться [-ни́ться]

**dike** [daɪk] да́мба; плоти́на; (*ditch*) кана́ва

**dilapidated** [dɪ'læpɪdeɪtɪd] ве́тхий, ста́рый

**dilate** [daɪ'leɪt] расширя́ть(ся) [-ши́рить(ся)]

**diligen|ce** ['dɪlɪdʒəns] прилежа́ние, усе́рдие; **~t** □ приле́жный, усе́рдный

**dill** [dɪl] укро́п

**dilute** [daɪ'ljuːt] разбавля́ть [-ба́вить]; разводи́ть [-вести́]

**dim** [dɪm] **1.** □ *light* ту́склый; *outlines, details* нея́сный; *eyesight* сла́бый; *recollections* сму́тный; *coll.* (*stupid*) тупо́й; **2.** [по]тускне́ть; [за]тума́нить(ся); ***~ one's headlights*** включи́ть бли́жний свет

**dime** [daɪm] *Am.* моне́та в де́сять це́нтов

**dimension** [dɪ'menʃn] разме́р; объём; измере́ние

**dimin|ish** [dɪ'mɪnɪʃ] уменьша́ть(ся) [уме́ньшить(ся)]; убы́(ва)ть; **~utive** [dɪ'mɪnjʊtɪv] □ миниатю́рный
**dimple** ['dɪmpl] я́мочка (на щеке́)
**din** [dɪn] шум; гро́хот
**dine** [daɪn] [по]обе́дать; [по]у́жинать; **~r** ['daɪnə] обе́дающий; *rail.* (*part. Am.*) ваго́н-рестора́н
**dinghy** ['dɪŋgɪ] ма́ленькая ло́дка
**dingy** ['dɪndʒɪ] □ гря́зный
**dining|car** *rail.* ваго́н-рестора́н; **~ room** столо́вая
**dinner** ['dɪnər] обе́д; ***at ~*** за обе́дом; ***formal ~*** официа́льный обе́д
**dint** [dɪnt]: ***by ~ of*** посре́дством (Р)
**dip** [dɪp] **1.** *v/t.* погружа́ть [-узи́ть], окуна́ть [-ну́ть]; *brush* обма́кивать [-кну́ть]; *into pocket* су́нуть; *v/i.* погружа́ться [-узи́ться], окуна́ться [-ну́ться]; *of flag* приспуска́ть [-сти́ть]; *of road* спуска́ться [-сти́ться]; **2.** (*slope*) укло́н; купа́ние; ***have a ~*** искупа́ться
**diploma** [dɪ'pləʊmə] дипло́м; **~cy** [~sɪ] диплма́тия; **~t** ['dɪpləmæt] диплома́т; **~tic(al** □) [dɪplə'mætɪk(əl)] дипломати́ческий
**dire** ['daɪə] ужа́сный
**direct** [dɪ'rekt, daɪ-] **1.** □ прямо́й; (*immediate*) непосре́дственный; (*straightforward*) я́сный; откры́тый; ***~ current*** *el.* постоя́нный ток; ***~ train*** прямо́й по́езд; **2.** *adv.* = **~ly**; **3.** руководи́ть (Т); управля́ть (Т); направля́ть [-а́вить]; ука́зывать доро́гу (Д); **~ion** [dɪ'rekʃən, daɪ-] направле́ние; руково́дство; указа́ние; инстру́кция; **~ive** [dɪ'rektɪv] директи́ва; **~ly** [~lɪ] **1.** *adv.* пря́мо, непосре́дственно; неме́дленно; **2.** *cj.* как то́лько
**director** [dɪ'rektər, daɪ-] дире́ктор; *cine.* режиссёр; ***board of ~s*** сове́т директоро́в; **~ate** [~rɪt] дире́кция; правле́ние; **~y** [~rɪ] (телефо́нный) спра́вочник
**dirt** [dɜːt] грязь *f*; **~ cheap** *coll.* о́чень дешёвый; *adv.* по дешёвке; **~y** ['dɜːtɪ] **1.** □ гря́зный; *joke* неприли́чный; *weather* нена́стный; ***~ trick*** по́длый посту́пок; **2.** [за]па́чкать
**disability** [dɪsə'bɪlətɪ] нетрудоспосо́бность *f*; бесси́лие; физи́ческий недоста́ток; ***~ pension*** пе́нсия по нетрудоспосо́бности
**disabled** [dɪs'eɪbld] искале́ченный; (*unable to work*) нетрудоспосо́бный; ***~ veteran*** инвали́д войны́
**disadvantage** [dɪsəd'vɑːntɪdʒ] недоста́ток; невы́годное положе́ние; уще́рб; неудо́бство
**disagree** [dɪsə'griː] расходи́ться во взгля́дах; противоре́чить друг дру́гу; (*quarrel*) [по]спо́рить; быть вре́дным (***with*** для Р); **~able** [~əbl] □ неприя́тный; **~ment** [~mənt] разногла́сие; несогла́сие
**disappear** [dɪsə'pɪə] исчеза́ть [-е́знуть]; пропада́ть [-па́сть]; *from sight* скры́(ва́)ться; **~ance** [~rəns] исчезнове́ние
**disappoint** [dɪsə'pɔɪnt] разочаро́вывать [-рова́ть]; *hopes etc.* обма́нывать [-ну́ть]; **~ment** [~mənt] разочарова́ние
**disapprov|al** [dɪsə'pruːvl] неодобре́ние; **~e** [dɪsə'pruːv] не одобря́ть [одо́брить] (Р); неодобри́тельно относи́ться (***of*** к Д)
**disarm** [dɪs'ɑːm] *v/t. mst. fig.* обезору́жи(ва)ть; разоружа́ть [-жи́ть]; *v/i.* разоружа́ться [-жи́ться]; **~ament** [dɪs'ɑːməmənt] разоруже́ние
**disarrange** [dɪsə'reɪndʒ] (*upset*) расстра́ивать [-ро́ить]; (*put into disorder*) приводи́ть в беспоря́док
**disast|er** [dɪ'zɑːstə] бе́дствие; катастро́фа; **~rous** [~trəs] □ бе́дственный; катастрофи́ческий
**disband** [dɪs'bænd] распуска́ть [-усти́ть]
**disbelieve** [dɪsbɪ'liːv] не [по]ве́рить; не доверя́ть (Д)
**disc** [dɪsk] диск
**discard** [dɪs'kɑːd] (*throw away*) выбра́сывать [-росить]; *hypothesis* отверга́ть [-е́ргнуть]
**discern** [dɪ'sɜːn] различа́ть [-чи́ть]; распозн(ав)а́ть *pf.*; отлича́ть [-чи́ть]; **~ing** [~ɪŋ] □ *person* проница́тельный
**discharge** [dɪs'tʃɑːdʒ] **1.** *v/t.* (*unload*)

разгружа́ть [-узи́ть]; *prisoner* освобожда́ть [-боди́ть]; *from work* увольня́ть [уво́лить]; *duties* выполня́ть [вы́полнить]; *gun, etc.* разряжа́ть [-яди́ть]; *from hospital* выпи́сывать [вы́писать]; *v/i. of wound* гнои́ться; **2.** разгру́зка; (*shot*) вы́стрел; освобожде́ние; увольне́ние; *el.* разря́д; выполне́ние

**disciple** [dɪ'saɪpl] после́дователь (-ница *f*) *m*; *Bibl.* апо́стол

**discipline** ['dɪsɪplɪn] **1.** дисципли́на, поря́док; **2.** дисциплини́ровать (*im*)*pf.*

**disclose** [dɪs'kləʊz] обнару́жи(ва)ть; раскры́(ва́)ть

**disco** ['dɪskəʊ] *coll.* дискоте́ка

**discolo(u)r** [dɪs'kʌlə] обесцве́чивать(ся) [-е́тить(ся)]

**discomfort** [dɪs'kʌmfət] **1.** неудо́бство; дискомфо́рт; (*uneasiness of mind*) беспоко́йство; **2.** причиня́ть [-ни́ть] неудо́бство (Д)

**disconsert** [dɪskən'sɜːt] [вз]волнова́ть; смуща́ть [смути́ть]; приводи́ть в замеша́тельство

**disconnect** [dɪskə'nekt] разъединя́ть [-ни́ть] (*a. el.*); разобща́ть [-щи́ть]; (*uncouple*) расцепля́ть [-пи́ть]; **~ed** [-ɪd] □ *thoughts, etc.* бессвя́зный

**disconsolate** [dɪs'kɒnsələt] □ неуте́шный

**discontent** [dɪskən'tent] недово́льство; неудовлетворённость *f*; **~ed** [-ɪd] □ недово́льный; неудовлетворённый

**discontinue** [dɪskən'tɪnjuː] прер(ы)ва́ть; прекраща́ть [-рати́ть]

**discord** ['dɪskɔːd] разногла́сие; разла́д

**discotheque** ['dɪskətek] → ***disco***

**discount 1.** ['dɪskaʊnt] *comm.* ди́сконт, учёт векселе́й; ски́дка; ***at a ~*** со ски́дкой; **2.** [dɪs'kaʊnt] дисконти́ровать (*im*)*pf.*, учи́тывать [учёсть] (векселя́); де́лать ски́дку

**discourage** [dɪs'kʌrɪdʒ] обескура́жи(ва)ть; отбива́ть охо́ту (Д; ***from*** к Д)

**discourse 1.** [dɪs'kɔːs] рассужде́ние; речь *f*; бесе́да; **2.** ['dɪskɔːs] вести́ бесе́ду

**discourte|ous** [dɪs'kɜːtɪəs] □ неве́жливый, неучти́вый; **~sy** [-tɪsɪ] неве́жливость *f*, неучти́вость *f*

**discover** [dɪs'kʌvə] де́лать откры́тие (P); обнару́жи(ва́)ть; **~y** [-rɪ] откры́тие

**discredit** [dɪs'kredɪt] **1.** дискредита́ция; **2.** дискредити́ровать (*im*)*pf.*; [о]позо́рить

**discreet** [dɪ'skriːt] □ (*careful*) осторо́жный, осмотри́тельный; такти́чный

**discrepancy** [dɪs'krepənsɪ] (*lack of correspondence*) расхожде́ние; противоречи́вость *f*; (*difference*) несхо́дство

**discretion** [dɪ'skreʃn] благоразу́мие; осторо́жность *f*; усмотре́ние; ***at your ~*** на ва́ше усмотре́ние

**discriminat|e** [dɪs'krɪmɪneɪt] относи́ться по-ра́зному; **~ *between*** отлича́ть, различа́ть; **~ *against*** дискримини́ровать; относи́ться предвзя́то (к Д); **~ing** [-ɪŋ] □ дискриминацио́нный; *taste, etc.* разбо́рчивый; **~ion** [-'neɪʃn] (*judgment, etc.*) проница́тельность *f*; (*bias*) дискримина́ция

**discuss** [dɪ'skʌs] обсужда́ть [-уди́ть], дискути́ровать; **~ion** [-ʌʃən] обсужде́ние, диску́ссия; *public* пре́ния *n/pl.*

**disdain** [dɪs'deɪn] **1.** (*scorn*) презира́ть [-зре́ть]; (*think unworthy*) счита́ть ни́же своего́ досто́инства; **2.** презре́ние; пренебреже́ние

**disease** [dɪ'ziːz] боле́знь *f*; **~d** [-d] больно́й

**disembark** [dɪsɪm'bɑːk] выса́живать(ся) [вы́садить(ся)]; сходи́ть на бе́рег; *goods* выгружа́ть [вы́грузить]

**disengage** [dɪsɪn'geɪdʒ] (*make free*) высвобожда́ть(ся) [вы́свободить(ся)]; *tech.* (*detach*) разъединя́ть [-ни́ть]

**disentangle** [dɪsɪn'tæŋgl] распу́т(ыв)ать(ся); *fig.* выпу́тываться [вы́путать(ся)]

**disfavo(u)r** [dɪs'feɪvə] **1.** неми́лость *f*; ***regard with ~*** относи́ться отрица́-

тельно; **2.** не одобря́ть [одо́брить]
**disfigure** [dɪsˈfɪgə] обезобра́живать [-ра́зить], [из]уро́довать
**disgrace** [dɪsˈgreɪs] **1.** (*loss of respect*) бесче́стье; (*disfavour*) неми́лость *f*; (*cause of shame*) позо́р; **2.** [о]позо́рить; **~ful** [-fʊl] □ посты́дный, позо́рный
**disguise** [dɪsˈgaɪz] **1.** маскиро́вка; переодева́ние; обма́нчивая вне́шность *f*; ма́ска; ***in*** **~** переоде́тый; **2.** [за]маскирова́ть(ся); переоде́(ва́)ть(ся); (*hide*) скры(ва́)ть
**disgust** [dɪsˈgʌst] **1.** отвраще́ние; **2.** внуша́ть [-ши́ть] отвраще́ние (Д); (*make indignant*) возмуща́ть [-ути́ть]; **~ing** [-ɪŋ] □ отврати́тельный
**dish** [dɪʃ] **1.** блю́до, таре́лка, ми́ска; ***the ~es*** *pl.* посу́да; (*food*) блю́до; **2.**: **~ *out*** раскла́дывать на таре́лки
**dishearten** [dɪsˈhɑːtn] приводи́ть [-вести́] в уны́ние
**dishevel(l)ed** [dɪˈʃevld] растрёпанный, взъеро́шенный
**dishonest** [dɪsˈɒnɪst] □ нече́стный; недобросо́вестный; **~y** [-ɪ] нече́стность *f*; недобросо́вестность *f*; обма́н
**dishono(u)r** [dɪsˈɒnə] **1.** бесче́стье, позо́р; **2.** [о]позо́рить; *young girl* [о]бесче́стить; **~able** [-rəbl] □ бесче́стный, ни́зкий
**disillusion** [dɪsɪˈluːʒn] **1.** разочарова́ние; **2.** разруша́ть [-у́шить] иллю́зии (Р); **~ed** [-d] разочаро́ванный
**disinclined** [dɪsɪnˈklaɪnd] нерасполо́женный
**disinfect** [dɪsɪnˈfekt] дезинфици́ровать (*im*)*pf*.; **~ant** [-ənt] дезинфици́рующее сре́дство
**disintegrate** [dɪsˈɪntɪgreɪt] распада́ться [-па́сться]; разруша́ться [-у́шиться]
**disinterested** [dɪsˈɪntrəstɪd] □ (*without self-interest*) бескоры́стный; (*without prejudice*) беспристра́стный
**disk** [dɪsk] диск; **~ drive** дисково́д
**diskette** [dɪˈsket] *comput.* диске́та
**dislike** [dɪsˈlaɪk] **1.** не люби́ть; **2.** нелюбо́вь *f* (***of*** к Д); антипа́тия; ***take a ~ to*** невзлюби́ть (В)
**dislocate** [ˈdɪsləkeɪt] *med.* выви́хивать [вы́вихнуть]; (*put out of order*) наруша́ть [нару́шить]
**dislodge** [dɪsˈlɒdʒ] (*move*) смеща́ть [смести́ть]; *mil.* выбива́ть [вы́бить]
**disloyal** [dɪsˈlɔɪəl] □ *to state*, *etc.* нелоя́льный; *friend* неве́рный
**dismal** [ˈdɪzməl] □ (*gloomy*) мра́чный; уны́лый; гнету́щий
**dismantl|e** [dɪsˈmæntl] *tech.* разбира́ть [разобра́ть]; демонти́ровать (*im.*)*pf*.; **~ing** [-ɪŋ] демонта́ж
**dismay** [dɪsˈmeɪ] **1.** смяте́ние, потрясе́ние; **2.** *v/t.* приводи́ть [-вести́] в смяте́ние
**dismiss** [dɪsˈmɪs] *v/t.* (*allow to go*) отпуска́ть [-сти́ть]; *from work*, *service*, *etc.* увольня́ть [уво́лить]; **~ *all thoughts of*** отбро́сить да́же мы́сль (о П); **~al** [-l] увольне́ние; отстране́ние
**dismount** [dɪsˈmaʊnt] *v/i.* слеза́ть с ло́шади, с велосипе́да
**disobedien|ce** [dɪsəˈbiːdɪəns] непослуша́ние, неповинове́ние; **~t** [-t] □ непослу́шный
**disobey** [dɪsəˈbeɪ] не [по]слу́шаться (Р); *order* не подчиня́ться [-ни́ться] (Д)
**disorder** [dɪsˈɔːdə] беспоря́док; *med.* расстро́йство; **~s** *pl.* (*riots*) беспоря́дки *m/pl.*; ***throw into ~*** переверну́ть всё вверх дном; **~ly** [-lɪ] беспоря́дочный; неорганизо́ванный, бу́йный
**disorganize** [dɪsˈɔːgənaɪz] дезорганизова́ть (*im*)*pf*., расстра́ивать [-ро́ить]
**disown** [dɪsˈəʊn] не призн(ав)а́ть; отка́зываться [-за́ться] от (Р)
**dispassionate** [dɪˈspæʃənət] □ (*impartial*) беспристра́стный; (*cool*) бесстра́стный
**dispatch** [dɪˈspætʃ] **1.** отпра́вка; отправле́ние; (*message*) сообще́ние; **2.** пос(ы)ла́ть; отправля́ть [-а́вить]
**dispel** [dɪˈspel] рассе́ивать [-се́ять]; *crowd etc.* разгоня́ть [разогна́ть]
**dispensary** [dɪˈspensərɪ] больни́чная

D

аптéка; *in drugstore* рецептýрный отдéл
**dispense** [dɪ'spens] *v/t. prescription* приготовлять; (*deal out*) раздавáть [-дáть]; **~ justice** отправлять [-áвить] правосýдие; **~ with** обходиться [обойтись], откáзываться [-зáться]
**disperse** [dɪ'spɜːs] разгонять [разогнáть]; рассéивать(ся) [-éять(ся)]; (*spread*) распространять [-нить]
**dispirit** [dɪ'spɪrɪt] удручáть [-чить]; приводить в уныние
**displace** [dɪs'pleɪs] (*take the place of*) занять мéсто, замещáть [заместить]
**display** [dɪ'spleɪ] **1.** (*exhibit*) выставлять [выставить]; *courage, etc.* проявлять [-явить]; **2.** выставка; проявлéние; *comput.* дисплéй
**displeas|e** [dɪs'pliːz] вызывáть [вызвать] недовóльство, не [по]нрáвиться (Д); быть не по вкýсу (Д); **~ed** [~d] недовóльный; **~ure** [dɪs'pleʒə] недовóльство
**dispos|al** [dɪ'spəʊzl] *of troops, etc.* расположéние; (*removal*) удалéние; ***put at s.o.'s ~*** предостáвить в чьё-л. распоряжéние; **~e** [dɪ'spəʊz] *v/t.* располагáть [-ложить] (В); *v/i.* **~ *of*** распоряжáться [-ядиться] (Т); **~ed** [~d] расположенный; настрóенный; (*be inclined to*) быть склóнным; **~ition** [dɪspə'zɪʃn] расположéние; харáктер; предрасположéние (к Д), склóнность (к Д)
**disproportionate** [dɪsprə'pɔːʃənət] □ непропорционáльный, несоразмéрный
**disprove** [dɪs'pruːv] опровергáть [-вéргнуть]
**dispute** [dɪs'pjuːt] **1.** (*discuss*) обсуждáть [-удить]; (*call into question*) оспáривать [оспóрить]; (*argue*) [по]спóрить; **2.** диспут; дебáты *m/pl.*; полéмика; дискýссия
**disqualify** [dɪs'kwɒlɪfaɪ] дисквалифицировать (*im*)*pf.*; лишáть прáва
**disquiet** [dɪs'kwaɪət] [о]беспокóить
**disregard** [dɪsrɪ'gɑːd] **1.** пренебрежéние; игнорирование; **2.** игнорировать (*im*)*pf.*; пренебрегáть [-брéчь] (Т)
**disreput|able** [dɪs'repjʊtəbl] □ *behavio(u)r* дискредитирующий; пóльзующийся дурнóй репутáцией; **~e** [dɪsrɪ'pjuːt] дурнáя слáва
**disrespect** [dɪsrɪ'spekt] неуважéние; **~ful** [~fl] □ непочтительный
**dissatis|faction** [dɪsætɪs'fækʃn] недовóльство; неудовлетворённость *f*; **~factory** [~tərɪ] неудовлетворительный; **~fy** [dɪs'sætɪsfaɪ] не удовлетворять [-рить]
**dissect** [dɪ'sekt] *anat.* вскры(вá)ть; *fig.* анализировать
**dissent** [dɪ'sent] **1.** несоглáсие; **2.** расходиться во взглядах, мнéниях
**disservice** [dɪs'sɜːvɪs]: ***he did her a ~*** он оказáл ей плохýю услýгу
**dissimilar** [dɪ'sɪmɪlə] □ непохóжий, несхóдный, разнорóдный
**dissipat|e** ['dɪsɪpeɪt] (*disperse*) рассéивать [-éять]; (*spend, waste*) растрáчивать [-трáтить]; **~ion** [dɪsɪ'peɪʃn]: ***life of ~*** беспýтный óбраз жизни
**dissociate** [dɪ'səʊʃɪeɪt] разобщáть [-щить] отмежёвываться [-евáться] (от Р)
**dissolut|e** ['dɪsəluːt] □ распýщенный; беспýтный; **~ion** [dɪsə'luːʃn] *of marriage, agreement* расторжéние; *parl.* рóспуск; *of firm, etc.* ликвидáция, расформировáние
**dissolve** [dɪ'zɒlv] *v/t. parl. etc.* распускáть [-устить]; *salt, etc.* растворять [-рить]; *marriage, agreement* расторгáть [-óргнуть]; аннулировать (*im*)*pf.*; *v/i.* растворяться [-риться]
**dissonant** ['dɪsənənt] нестрóйный, диссонирующий
**dissuade** [dɪ'sweɪd] отговáривать [-ворить] (***from*** от Р)
**distan|ce** ['dɪstəns] расстояние; *sport* дистáнция; даль *f*; *of time* промежýток, период; ***in the ~*** вдали; вдалекé; ***keep s.o. at a ~*** держáть когó-л. на расстоянии; **~t** [~t] □ дáльний, далёкий; отдалённый; *fig.* (*reserved*) сдéржанный, холóдный
**distaste** [dɪs'teɪst] отвращéние; **~ful**

[-fl] □ неприя́тный (на В, ***to*** Д)
**distend** [dɪ'stend] разу́(ва́)ть(ся), наду́(ва́)ть(ся)
**distil** [dɪ'stɪl] *chem.* перегоня́ть [-гна́ть], дистиллирова́ть (*im*)*pf*.; ***~led water*** дистилли́рованная вода́; **~lery** [-ərɪ] перего́нный заво́д
**distinct** [dɪ'stɪŋkt] □ (*different*) разли́чный, осо́бый, индивидуа́льный; (*clear*) отчётливый; (*definite*) определённый; **~ion** [dɪs'tɪŋkʃn] разли́чие; (*hono(u)r*) честь; ***draw a ~ between*** де́лать разли́чие ме́жду (Т); ***writer of ~*** изве́стный писа́тель; **~ive** [-tɪv] □ отличи́тельный, характе́рный
**distinguish** [dɪ'stɪŋgwɪʃ] различа́ть [-чи́ть]; отлича́ть [-чи́ть]; ***~ o.s.*** отличи́ться; **~ed** [-t] выдаю́щийся, изве́стный; *guest* почётный
**distort** [dɪ'stɔːt] искажа́ть [искази́ть] (*a. fig.*)
**distract** [dɪ'strækt] отвлека́ть [отвле́чь]; **~ion** [dɪ'strækʃn] отвлече́ние; (*amusement*) развлече́ние
**distress** [dɪ'stres] **1.** огорче́ние, го́ре; *naut*. бе́дствие; (*suffering*) страда́ние; (*poverty*) нужда́, нищета́; ***~ signal*** сигна́л бе́дствия; **2.** (*upset*) огорча́ть [-чи́ть]; расстра́ивать [-ро́ить]
**distribut|e** [dɪ'strɪbjuːt] распределя́ть [-ли́ть]; (*hand out*) разд(ав)а́ть; *printed matter* распространя́ть [-ни́ть]; **~ion** [dɪstrɪ'bjuːʃn] распределе́ние; разда́ча; распростране́ние
**district** ['dɪstrɪkt] райо́н; о́круг; ***election ~*** избира́тельный о́круг
**distrust** [dɪs'trʌst] **1.** недове́рие; (*suspicion*) подозре́ние; **2.** не доверя́ть (Д); **~ful** [-fl] □ недове́рчивый; подозри́тельный; ***~ of o.s.*** неуве́ренный в себе́
**disturb** [dɪ'stɜːb] [по]беспоко́ить; (*worry*) взволнова́ть; *peace*, *etc*. наруша́ть [-у́шить]; **~ance** [-əns] шум, трево́га, волне́ние; *pl*. волне́ния *n/pl*.
**disuse** [dɪs'juːz] неупотребле́ние; ***fall into ~*** вы́йти из употребле́ния; *of law*, *etc*. не применя́ться, не испо́льзоваться
**ditch** [dɪtʃ] кана́ва, ров
**dive** [daɪv] **1.** ныря́ть [нырну́ть]; погружа́ться [-узи́ться]; пры́гать [-гнуть] в во́ду; *ae*. пики́ровать (*im*)*pf*.; **2.** прыжо́к в во́ду; погруже́ние; пики́рование; (*disreputable bar*, *etc.*) прито́н, погребо́к; ***make a ~ for*** броса́ться [бро́ситься]; **~r** ['daɪvə] водола́з; ныря́льщик *m*, -ица *f*; *sport* спортсме́н по прыжка́м в во́ду
**diverge** [daɪ'vɜːdʒ] расходи́ться [разойти́сь] (*a. fig.*); (*turn away*) отклоня́ться [-ни́ться]; **~nce** [-əns] расхожде́ние; отклоне́ние; **~nt** [-ənt] □ расходя́щийся; ***~ opinions*** ра́зные мне́ния
**divers|e** [daɪ'vɜːs] □ разли́чный, разнообра́зный; (*different*) ино́й; **~ion** [daɪ'vɜːʃən] (*amusement*) развлече́ние; (*turning away*) отклоне́ние; **~ity** [-sɪtɪ] разнообра́зие; разли́чие
**divert** [daɪ'vɜːt] *attention* отвлека́ть [-е́чь]; (*amuse*) развлека́ть [-е́чь]
**divid|e** [dɪ'vaɪd] *v/t. math.* [раз]дели́ть; (*share out*) разделя́ть [-ли́ть]; *v/i.* [раз]дели́ться; разделя́ться [-ли́ться]; *math.* дели́ться без оста́тка; **~end** ['dɪvɪdend] *fin*. дивиде́нд; *math*. дели́мое
**divine** [dɪ'vaɪn] **1.** □ боже́ственный; ***~ service*** богослуже́ние; **2.** (*guess*) уга́дывать [-да́ть]
**diving** ['daɪvɪŋ] ныря́ние; *sport* прыжки́ в во́ду; **~ board** трампли́н
**divinity** [dɪ'vɪnɪtɪ] (*theology*) богосло́вие; (*a divine being*) божество́
**divis|ible** [dɪ'vɪzəbl] (раз)дели́мый; **~ion** [dɪ'vɪʒn] деле́ние; разделе́ние; (*department*) отде́л; *mil*. диви́зия; *math*. деле́ние
**divorce** [dɪ'vɔːs] **1.** разво́д; **2.** (*dissolve a marriage*) расторга́ть брак (Р); разводи́ться [-вести́сь] с (Т); ***be ~d*** быть в разво́де
**divulge** [daɪ'vʌldʒ] разглаша́ть [-ласи́ть]
**dizz|iness** ['dɪzɪnɪs] головокруже́ние; **~y** ['dɪzɪ] □ головокружи́тельный; ***I feel ~*** у меня́ кру́жится голова́
**do** [duː] [*irr.*] **1.** *v/t.* [с]де́лать; *duty*, *etc.* выполня́ть [вы́полнить]; (*arrange*)

D

D

устра́ивать [-ро́ить]; *homework etc.* приготовля́ть [-то́вить]; **~ *London*** осма́тривать Ло́ндон; ***have done reading*** ко́нчить чита́ть; *coll.* **~ *in*** (*exhaust*), *a. sl.* (*kill*) уби́(ва́)ть; **~ *out*** убира́ть [убра́ть]; **~ *out of*** выма́нивать [вы́манить] (обма́ном); **~ *over*** переде́л(ыв)ать; *with paint* покры́(ва́т)ь; **~ *up*** завора́чивать [заверну́ть]; [с]де́лать ремо́нт; *coat* застёгивать [-егну́ть]; (*tie*) завя́зывать [-за́ть]; **2.** *v/i.* [с]де́лать; поступа́ть [-пи́ть], де́йствовать; **~ *so as to …*** устра́ивать так, что́бы …; ***that will ~*** доста́точно, дово́льно; сойдёт; ***how ~ you ~?*** здра́вствуй(те)!; как вы пожива́ете?; **~ *well*** успева́ть; хорошо́ вести́ де́ло; **~ *away with*** уничтожа́ть [-о́жить]; ***I could ~ with …*** мне мог бы пригоди́ться (И); ***I could ~ with a shave*** мне не помеша́ло бы побри́ться, **~ *without*** обходи́ться [обойти́сь] без (Р); **~ *be quick!*** поспеши́те!, скоре́й!; **~ *you like London? – I ~*** вам нра́вится Ло́ндон? – Да

**docil|e** ['dəʊsaɪl] послу́шный; (*easily trained*) поня́тливый; **~ity** [dəʊ'sɪlɪtɪ] послуша́ние; поня́тливость *f*

**dock** [dɑk] **1.** *naut.* док; *law* скамья́ подсуди́мых; **2.** *naut.* ста́вить су́дно в док; *of space vehicles* [со]стыкова́ться

**dockyard** ['dɒkjɑːd] верфь *f*

**doctor** ['dɒktə] *acad.* до́ктор; *med.* врач; **~ate** [~rət] сте́пень до́ктора

**doctrine** ['dɒktrɪn] уче́ние, доктри́на

**document 1.** ['dɒkjʊmənt] докуме́нт; **2.** [~ment] документи́ровать, подтвержда́ть докуме́нтами

**dodge** [dɒdʒ] **1.** увёртка, уло́вка, хи́трость *f*; **2.** увиливать [-льну́ть]; [с]хитри́ть; избега́ть [-ежа́ть] (Р)

**doe** [dəʊ] *mst.* са́мка оле́ня

**dog** [dɒg] **1.** соба́ка, пёс; **2.** ходи́ть по пята́м (Р); *fig.* пресле́довать; **~ *collar*** оше́йник

**dogged** ['dɒgɪd] □ упря́мый, упо́рный, насто́йчивый

**dogma** ['dɒgmə] до́гма; *specific* до́гмат; **~tic** [dɒg'mætɪk] *person* догмати́чный; **~tism** ['dɒgmətɪzəm] догмати́зм

**dog-tired** [dɒg'taɪəd] уста́лый как соба́ка

**doings** ['duːɪŋz] дела́ *n/pl.*, посту́пки *m/pl.*

**do-it-yourself**: **~ *kit*** набо́р инструме́нтов "сде́лай сам"

**doleful** ['dəʊlfʊl] □ ско́рбный, печа́льный

**doll** [dɒl] ку́кла

**dollar** ['dɒlə] до́ллар

**domain** [də'meɪn] (*estate*) владе́ние; (*realm*) сфе́ра; *fig.* о́бласть *f*

**dome** [dəʊm] ку́пол; (*vault*) свод

**domestic** [də'mestɪk] **1.** дома́шний; семе́йный; **2.** дома́шняя рабо́тница; слуга́ *m*; **~ate** [~tɪkeɪt] *animal* приуча́ть [-чи́ть]

**domicile** ['dɒmɪsaɪl] местожи́тельство

**domin|ant** ['dɒmɪnənt] госпо́дствующий, преоблада́ющий; **~ate** [~neɪt] госпо́дствовать, преоблада́ть; **~ation** [dɒmɪ'neɪʃn] госпо́дство, преоблада́ние; **~eer** [dɒmɪ'nɪə] вести́ себя́ деспоти́чески; **~eering** [~rɪŋ] □ деспоти́чный, вла́стный

**don** [dɒn] *univ.* преподава́тель

**donat|e** [dəʊ'neɪt] [по]же́ртвовать; **~ion** [~ʃn] поже́ртвование

**done** [dʌn] **1.** *pt. p. om* **do**; **2.** *adj.* гото́вый; **~ *in*** уста́лый; ***well ~(!)*** хорошо́ прожа́ренный; молоде́ц!

**donkey** ['dɒŋkɪ] осёл

**donor** ['dəʊnə] дари́тель(ница *f*) *m*; *of blood, etc.* до́нор

**doom** [duːm] **1.** рок, судьба́; (*ruin*) ги́бель; **2.** обрека́ть [-е́чь] (***to*** на В)

**door** [dɔː] дверь *f*; ***next ~*** ря́дом, в сосе́днем до́ме; ***out of ~s*** на откры́том во́здухе; **~ *handle*** дверна́я ру́чка; **~keeper** швейца́р; **~way** вход, дверно́й проём

**dope** [dəʊp] нарко́тик; *sport* до́пинг; *coll.* (*blockhead*) о́лух

**dormant** ['dɔːmənt] *mst. fig.* безде́йствующий, спя́щий; **~ *capital*** мёртвый капита́л

**dormitory** ['dɔːmɪtrɪ] большо́е спальное помеще́ние (*в школах, интернатах и т.д.*); *Am.* общежи́тие

**dose** [dəʊs] **1.** до́за; **2.** дози́ровать (*im*)*pf.*; дава́ть до́зами

**dot** [dɒt] **1.** то́чка; ***come on the ~*** прийти́ то́чно; **2.**: ***~ the i's*** ста́вить то́чки над i; **~ted line** пункти́р

**dot|e** [dəʊt]: **~ (*up*)*on*** души́ не ча́ять; **~ing** ['dəʊtɪŋ] о́чень лю́бящий

**double** ['dʌbl] **1.** двойно́й; *fig.* двоя́кий; **2.** *person* двойни́к; двойно́е коли́чество; па́рная игра́; *thea.* (*understudy*) дублёр; **3.** *v/t.* удва́ивать [удво́ить]; скла́дывать вдво́е; ***~d up*** скрю́чившийся; *v/i.* удва́иваться [удво́иться]; **~-breasted** двубо́ртный; **~-dealing** двуру́шничество; **~-edged** обоюдоо́стрый

**doubt** [daʊt] **1.** *v/t.* сомнева́ться [усомни́ться] в (П); не доверя́ть (Д); *v/i.* име́ть сомне́ния; **2.** сомне́ние; ***no ~*** без сомне́ния; **~ful** ['daʊtfʊl] □ сомни́тельный; ***~ blessing*** па́лка о двух конца́х; **~less** ['daʊtlɪs] несомне́нно; вероя́тно

**dough** [dəʊ] те́сто; **~nut** ['dəʊnʌt] по́нчик

**dove** [dʌv] го́лубь *m*

**down**[1] [daʊn] пух; *dim.* пушо́к

**down**[2] [~] **1.** *adv.* вниз, внизу́; ***~ to*** вплоть до (Р); ***it suits me ~ to the ground*** меня́ э́то вполне́ устра́ивает; **2.** *prp.* вниз по (Д); вдоль по (Д); ***~ the river*** вниз по реке́; **3.** *adj.* напра́вленный вниз; ***prices are ~*** це́ны сни́зились; **4.** *v/t.* опуска́ть [опусти́ть]; *enemies* одоле́(ва́)ть; **~cast** удручённый; **~fall** паде́ние; **~hearted** [daʊn'hɑːtɪd] па́вшийду́хом; **~hill** [daʊn'hɪl] вниз; под го́ру; **~pour** ли́вень *m*; **~right 1.** *adv.* соверше́нно; пря́мо; **2.** *adj.* прямо́й; (*frank*) открове́нный; (*honest*) че́стный; **~stairs** [daʊn'steəz] вниз, внизу́; **~stream** [daʊn'striːm] вниз по тече́нию; **~town** [daʊn'taʊn] *part. Am.* в це́нтре го́рода; **~ward(s)** [~wəd(z)] вниз, кни́зу

**downy** ['daʊnɪ] пуши́стый, мя́гкий как пух

**dowry** ['daʊərɪ] прида́ное

**doze** [dəʊz] **1.** дремо́та; ***have a ~*** вздремну́ть; **2.** дрема́ть

**dozen** ['dʌzn] дю́жина

**drab** [dræb] ту́склый, однообра́зный

**draft** [drɑːft] **1.** = ***draught***; набро́сок; чернови́к; *fin.* чек; су́мма, полу́ченная по че́ку; *mil.* призы́в, набо́р; *arch.* эски́з; **2.** набра́сывать [-роса́ть]; призыва́ть [призва́ть]

**drag** [dræg] **1.** обу́за, бре́мя *n*; **2.** *v/t.* [по]тяну́ть, [по]волочи́ть; ***I could hardly ~ my feet*** я е́ле волочи́л но́ги; *v/i.* [по]волочи́ться; ***~ on*** тяну́ться

**dragon** ['drægən] драко́н; **~fly** стрекоза́

**drain** [dreɪn] **1.** дрена́ж; *pl.* канализа́ция; *from roof* водосто́к; **2.** *v/t.* осуша́ть [-ши́ть]; *fig.* истоща́ть [-щи́ть]; **~age** ['dreɪnɪdʒ] дрена́ж; сток; канализа́ция

**drake** [dreɪk] се́лезень *m*

**drama|tic** [drə'mætɪk] (***~ally***) драмати́ческий; театра́льный; драмати́чный; **~tist** ['dræmətɪst] драмату́рг; **~tize** [~taɪz] драматизи́ровать (*im*)*pf.*

**drank** [dræŋk] *pt. om* ***drink***

**drape** [dreɪp] [за]драпирова́ть; располага́ть скла́дками; **~ry** ['dreɪpərɪ] драпиро́вка; (*cloth*) тка́ни *f/pl.*

**drastic** ['dræstɪk] (***~ally***) реши́тельный, круто́й; сильноде́йствующий

**draught** [drɑːft] *chiefly Brt.* тя́га; *in room* сквозня́к; (*drink*) глото́к; (*rough copy*) чернови́к, набро́сок; **~s** *pl.* ша́шки *f/pl.*; → ***draft***; ***~ beer*** бочково́е пи́во; **~sman** [~smən] чертёжник; (*artist*) рисова́льщик *m*, -щица *f*

**draw** [drɔː] **1.** [*irr.*] [на]рисова́ть; [по]тяну́ть; [по]тащи́ть; *tooth* вырыва́ть [вы́рвать]; *water* черпа́ть; *attention* привлека́ть [-е́чь]; *conclusion* приходи́ть [-йти́] (к Д); *sport* зака́нчивать [-ко́нчить] (игру́) вничью́; ***~ near*** приближа́ться [-ли́зиться]; ***~ out*** вытя́гивать [вы́тянуть]; ***~ up** paper* составля́ть [-а́вить]; (*stop*) остана́вливаться [-нови́ться]; **2.** (*lottery*) жеребьёвка; *sport* ничья́; **~back** ['drɔːbæk] недоста́ток; **~er** [drɔː] вы-

движно́й я́щик; **~ers**: *a.* ***pair of ~*** *pl.* кальсо́ны *f/pl.*, *short* трусы́
**drawing** ['drɔːɪŋ] рису́нок; рисова́ние; чертёж; **~ board** чертёжная доска́; **~ room** гости́ная
**drawn** [drɔːn] *pt. p. om* ***draw***
**dread** [dred] **1.** боя́ться, страши́ться (P); **2.** страх, боя́знь *f*; **~ful** ['dredfl] □ ужа́сный, стра́шный
**dream** [driːm] **1.** сон, сновиде́ние; (*reverie*) мечта́; **2.** [*a. irr.*] ви́деть во сне; мечта́ть; ***~ up*** приду́мывать [-мать]; вообража́ть [-рази́ть]; **~er** [~ə] мечта́тель(ница *f*) *m*, фантазёр(ка); **~y** [~ɪ] □ мечта́тельный
**dreary** ['drɪərɪ] □ тосбли́вый; *weather* нена́стный; *work*, *etc.* ску́чный
**dredge** [dredʒ] землечерпа́лка
**dregs** [dregz] *pl.* оса́док; *of society* отбро́сы *m/pl.*; ***drink to the ~*** [вы́]пить до дна
**drench** [drentʃ] промока́ть [-мо́кнуть]; ***get ~ed*** промо́кнуть до ни́тки
**dress** [dres] **1.** пла́тье; *collect.* оде́жда; *thea.* ***~ rehearsal*** генера́льная репети́ция; **2.** оде́(ва́)ть(ся); (*adorn*) украша́ть(ся) [укра́сить(ся)]; *hair* де́лать причёску; *med.* перевя́зывать [-за́ть]; **~ circle** *thea.* бельэта́ж; **~er** [~ə] ку́хонный шкаф; *Am. a.* комо́д, туале́тный сто́лик
**dressing** ['dresɪŋ] перевя́зочный материа́л; перевя́зка; *cul.* припра́ва; ***~ down*** головомо́йка; **~ gown** хала́т; **~ table** туале́тный сто́лик
**dressmaker** портни́ха
**drew** ['druː] *pt. om* ***draw***
**dribble** ['drɪbl] ка́пать; пуска́ть слю́ни
**dried** [draɪd] сухо́й; вы́сохший
**drift** [drɪft] **1.** *naut.* дрейф; (*snow~*) сугро́б; *of sand* нано́с; *fig.* тенде́нция; ***did you get the ~ of what he said?*** ты улови́л смысл его́ слов?; **2.** *v/t.* сноси́ть [снести́]; наноси́ть [нанести́]; *leaves*, *snow* мести́; *v/i.* дрейфова́ть (*im*)*pf.*; намести́; *fig. of person* плыть по тече́нию
**drill** [drɪl] **1.** дрель; бу́рав; *tech.* бур; (*exercise*) упражне́ние; *sport* трениро́вка; **2.** [на]тренирова́ть
**drink** [drɪŋk] **1.** питьё; напи́ток; **2.** [*irr.*] [вы́]пить; пья́нствовать
**drip** [drɪp] ка́пать, па́дать ка́плями
**drive** [draɪv] **1.** езда́; пое́здка; подъе́зд (к до́му); *tech.* при́вод; *fig.* эне́ргия; си́ла; ***go for a ~*** пое́хать ката́ться на маши́не; **2.** [*irr.*] *v/t.* (*force along*) [по]гна́ть; *nail*, *etc.* вби(ва́)ть; (*convey*) вози́ть, [по]везти́; *v/i.* е́здить, [по]е́хать; ката́ться; [по]нести́сь; ***~ at*** намека́ть на (В)
**drivel** ['drɪvl] бессмы́слица, чепуха́
**driven** ['drɪvn] *pt. p. om* ***drive***
**driver** ['draɪvə] *mot.* води́тель *m*, шофёр; *rail.* машини́ст; ***racing ~*** го́нщик
**drizzle** ['drɪzl] **1.** и́зморось *f*; ме́лкий дождь *m*; **2.** мороси́ть
**drone** [drəʊn] **1.** *zo.* тру́тень *m*; **2.** жужжа́ть; *plane* гуде́ть
**droop** [druːp] *v/t. head* опуска́ть [-сти́ть]; пове́сить; *v/i.* поника́ть [-и́кнуть]; *of flowers* увяда́ть [увя́нуть]
**drop** [drɒp] **1.** ка́пля; (*fruit ~*) ледене́ц; *in prices*, *etc.* паде́ние, сниже́ние; *thea.* за́навес; **2.** *v/t.* роня́ть [урони́ть]; *smoking*, *etc.* броса́ть [бро́сить]; ***~ a p. a line*** черкну́ть кому́-л. слове́чко; *v/i.* ка́пать [ка́пнуть]; спада́ть [спасть]; па́дать [упа́сть]; понижа́ться [-и́зиться]; *of wind* стиха́ть [сти́хнуть]; ***~ in*** заходи́ть [зайти́], загля́дывать [загляну́ть]
**drought** [draʊt] за́суха
**drove** [drəʊv] **1.** (*herd*) ста́до; **2.** *pt. om* ***drive***
**drown** [draʊn] *v/t.* [у]топи́ть; *fig. sound* заглуша́ть [-ши́ть]; *v/i.* [у]тону́ть = ***be ~ed***; **~ o.s.** [у]топи́ться
**drows|e** [draʊz] [за]дрема́ть; **~y** ['draʊsɪ] со́нный
**drudge** [drʌdʒ] исполня́ть ску́чную, тяжёлую рабо́ту, тяну́ть ля́мку
**drug** [drʌg] лека́рство; *pl.* медикаме́нты *m/pl.*; нарко́тик; ***take ~s*** употребля́ть нарко́тики; **~ addict** наркома́н; **~gist** ['drʌgɪst] апте́карь *m*; **~store** *Am.* апте́ка
**drum** [drʌm] **1.** бараба́н; **2.** бить в бараба́н, бараба́нить

**drunk** [drʌŋk] **1.** *pt. p. от* ***drink***; **2.** пья́ный; ***get ~*** напива́ться пья́ным; **~ard** ['drʌŋkəd] пья́ница *m/f*; **~en** ['drʌŋkən] пья́ный
**dry** [draɪ] **1.** □ сухо́й, вы́сохший; ***~ as dust*** ску́чный; **2.** [вы́]суши́ть; [вы́]со́хнуть; ***~ up*** высу́шивать [вы́сушить]; *of river etc.* высыха́ть [вы́сохнуть], пересыха́ть [-со́хнуть]; **~ cleaner's** химчи́стка
**dual** ['dju:əl] □ двойно́й
**dubious** ['dju:bɪəs] □ сомни́тельный подозри́тельный
**duchess** ['dʌtʃɪs] герцоги́ня
**duck**¹ [dʌk] у́тка; *fig.* ***a lame ~*** неуда́чник
**duck**² [~] ныря́ть [нырну́ть]; окуна́ться [-ну́ться]; (*move quickly*) увёртываться [уверну́ться]
**duckling** ['dʌklɪŋ] утёнок
**due** [dju:] **1.** до́лжный, надлежа́щий; ***~ to*** благодаря́; ***the train is ~ ...*** по́езд до́лжен прибы́ть ...; ***in ~ course*** в своё вре́мя; **2.** *adv. naut. east, etc.* то́чно, пря́мо; **3.** до́лжное; то, что причита́ется; ***give s.o. his ~*** отдава́ть до́лжное кому́-л.; *mst.* **~s** *pl.* сбо́ры *m/pl.*, нало́ги *m/pl.*; по́шлины *f/pl.*; чле́нский взнос
**duel** ['dju:əl] **1.** дуэ́ль *f*; **2.** дра́ться на дуэ́ли
**duet** [dju:'et] дуэ́т
**dug** [dʌg] *pt. и pt. p. от* ***dig***
**duke** [dju:k] ге́рцог
**dull** [dʌl] **1.** (**~y**) (*not sharp*) тупо́й (*a. fig.*); (*boring*) ску́чный; *comm.* вя́лый; *day* па́смурный; **2.** притупля́ть(ся) [-пи́ть(ся)]; *fig.* де́лать(-ся) ску́чным; **~ness** ['dʌlnɪs] ску́ка; вя́лость *f*; ту́пость *f*
**duly** ['dju:lɪ] до́лжным о́бразом
**dumb** [dʌm] □ немо́й; *Am.* глу́пый; **~found** [dʌm'faʊnd] ошеломля́ть [-ми́ть]
**dummy** ['dʌmɪ] *tailor's* манеке́н; *mil.* маке́т; *Brt.* ***baby's ~*** (*Am. pacifier*) со́ска, пусты́шка
**dump** [dʌmp] **1.** сва́лка; **2.** сбра́сывать [сбро́сить]; сва́ливать [-ли́ть]; **~ing** *comm.* де́мпинг; **~s** *pl.*: ***be down in the ~*** плохо́е настрое́ние
**dunce** [dʌns] тупи́ца *m/f*
**dune** [dju:n] дю́на
**dung** [dʌŋ] наво́з
**duplic|ate 1.** ['dju:plɪkɪt] **a)** двойно́й; запасно́й; **b)** дублика́т; ко́пия; ***in ~*** в двух экземпля́рах; **2.** [~keɪt] снима́ть, де́лать ко́пию с (Р); удва́ивать [удво́ить]; **~ity** [dju:'plɪsɪtɪ] двули́чность *f*
**dura|ble** ['djʊərəbl] □ про́чный; дли́тельный; **~tion** [djʊə'reɪʃn] продолжи́тельность *f*
**during** ['djʊərɪŋ] *prp.* в тече́ние (Р), во вре́мя (Р)
**dusk** [dʌsk] су́мерки; **~y** ['kʌskɪ] □ су́меречный; *skin* сму́глый
**dust** [dʌst] **1.** пыль *f*; **2.** (*wipe*) вытира́ть пыль; **~bin** *Brt.* (*Am. trash can*) му́сорное ведро́; **~er** ['dʌstə] тря́пка для вытира́ния пы́ли; **~y** ['dʌstɪ] □ пы́льный
**Dutch** [dʌtʃ] **1.** голла́ндец *m*, -дка *f*; **2.** голла́ндский; ***the ~*** голла́ндцы *pl.*
**duty** ['dju:tɪ] долг, обя́занность *f*; дежу́рство; *fin.* по́шлина; ***off ~*** свобо́дный от дежу́рства; **~-free** *adv.* беспо́шлинно
**dwarf** [dwɔ:f] **1.** ка́рлик; **2.** [по]меша́ть ро́сту; каза́ться ма́леньким (по сравне́нию с Т)
**dwell** [dwel] [*irr.*] жить; ***~ (up)on*** остана́вливаться [-нови́ться] на (П); **~ing** ['dwelɪŋ] жили́ще, дом
**dwelt** [dwelt] *pt. и pt. p. от* ***dwell***
**dwindle** ['dwɪndl] уменьша́ться [уме́ньшиться], сокраща́ться [-рати́ться]
**dye** [daɪ] **1.** кра́ска; краси́тель; *fig.* ***of the deepest ~*** отъя́вленный; **2.** [по-, вы́]кра́сить, окра́шивать [окра́сить]
**dying** ['daɪɪŋ] (*s.* ***die***¹) **1.** умира́ющий; *words* предсме́ртный; **2.** умира́ние; смерть
**dynam|ic** [daɪ'næmɪk] динами́ческий; *fig.* динами́чный; акти́вный; энерги́чный; **~ics** [~ɪks] *mst. sg.* дина́мика; **~ite** ['daɪnəmaɪt] динами́т

# E

**each** [iːtʃ] ка́ждый; **~ *other*** друг дру́га
**eager** [ˈiːgə] □ стремя́щийся; (*diligent*) усе́рдный; энерги́чный; **~ness** [~nɪs] пыл, рве́ние
**eagle** [ˈiːgl] орёл, орли́ца
**ear** [ɪə] у́хо (*pl.*: у́ши); *mus.* слух; **~drum** бараба́нная перепо́нка
**earl** [ɜːl] граф (англи́йский)
**early** [ˈɜːlɪ] **1.** ра́нний; (*premature*) преждевре́менный; ***at the earliest*** в лу́чшем слу́чае; ***it is too ~ to draw conclusions*** де́лать вы́воды преждевре́менно; **2.** *adv.* ра́но; (*timely*) заблаговре́менно; ***as ~ as*** уже́, ещё; как мо́жно ра́ньше
**earmark** [ˈɪəmɑːk] (*set aside*) предназнача́ть [-зна́чить]
**earn** [ɜːn] зараба́тывать [-бо́тать]; *fig.* заслу́живать [-жи́ть]
**earnest** [ˈəːnɪst] **1.** □ серьёзный; убеждённый; и́скренний; **2.** серьёзность *f*; ***in ~*** серьёзно, всерьёз
**earnings** [ˈɜːnɪŋz] за́работок
**ear|phones** [ˈɪəfəʊnz] нау́шники *m./pl.*; **~ring** серьга́, серёжка; **~shot** преде́лы слы́шимости
**earth** [ɜːθ] **1.** земля́, земно́й шар; (*soil*) земля́, по́чва; **2.** *v/t.* (*~ up*) зары́(ва́)ть; зака́пывать [закопа́ть]; *el.* заземля́ть [-ли́ть]; **~en** [~n] земляно́й; **~enware** [~nweə] гли́няная посу́да; **~ly** [~lɪ] земно́й; **~quake** [~kweɪk] землетрясе́ние; **~worm** земляно́й червь *m.*, *coll.* червя́к
**ease** [iːz] **1.** лёгкость *f*; непринуждённость *f*; ***at ~*** свобо́дно, удо́бно; ***feel ill at ~*** чу́вствовать себя́ нело́вко; **2.** облегча́ть [-чи́ть]; успока́ивать [-ко́ить]
**easel** [ˈiːzl] мольбе́рт
**easiness** [ˈiːzɪnɪs] → ***ease*** *1*
**east** [iːst] **1.** восто́к; **2.** восто́чный; **3.** *adv.* на восто́к; к восто́ку (***of*** от Р)
**Easter** [ˈiːstə] Па́сха
**easter|ly** [ˈiːstəlɪ] с восто́ка; **~n** [ˈiːstən] восто́чный
**eastward(s)** [ˈiːstwəd(z)] на восто́к
**easy** [ˈiːzɪ] лёгкий; споко́йный; непринуждённый; ***take it ~!*** не торопи́(те)сь; споко́йнее!; **~ chair** кре́сло; **~going** *fig.* благоду́шный; беззабо́тный
**eat** [iːt] **1.** [*irr.*] [съ]есть; (*damage*) разъеда́ть [-е́сть] (*mst.* ***away, into***); **2.** [et] *pt. от* ***eat 1***; **~able** [ˈiːtəbl] съедо́бный; **~en** [ˈiːtn] *pt. p. от* ***eat 1***
**eaves** [iːvz] *pl.* карни́з; **~drop** подслу́ш(ив)ать
**ebb** [eb] **1.** (*a.* **~-tide**) отли́в; *fig.* переме́на к ху́дшему; **2.** *of tide* убы́(ва́)ть; *fig.* ослабе́(ва́)ть
**ebony** [ˈebənɪ] чёрное де́рево
**eccentric** [ɪkˈsentrɪk] **1.** *fig.* эксцентри́чный; **2.** чуда́к
**ecclesiastical** [ɪkliːzɪˈæstɪkl] □ духо́вный, церко́вный
**echo** [ˈekəʊ] **1.** э́хо; *fig.* отголо́сок; **2.** отдава́ться э́хом
**eclair** [ɪˈkleə] экле́р
**eclipse** [ɪˈklɪps] **1.** затме́ние; **2.** затмева́ть [-ми́ть] (*a. fig.*); заслоня́ть [-ни́ть]
**ecology** [ɪˈkɒlədʒɪ] эколо́гия
**econom|ic** [iːkəˈnɒmɪk] экономи́ческий; **~ical** [~l] эконо́мный, бережли́вый; **~ics** [~ɪks] *pl.* эконо́мика
**econom|ist** [ɪˈkɒnəmɪst] экономи́ст; **~ize** [~maɪz] [с]эконо́мить; **~y** [~mɪ] эконо́мия; бережли́вость *f*; ***national ~*** эконо́мика страны́
**ecsta|sy** [ˈekstəsɪ] экста́з, восто́рг; **~tic** [ɪkˈstætɪk] (***~ally***) восто́рженный
**eddy** [ˈedɪ] водоворо́т
**edge** [edʒ] **1.** край; *of knife* ле́звие, остриё; *of forest* опу́шка; *of cloth* кро́мка; *of road* обо́чина; ***be on ~*** быть в не́рвном состоя́нии; **2.** (*border*) окаймля́ть [-ми́ть]; ***~ one's way ...*** пробира́ться [-бра́ться]; **~ways** [~weɪz], **~wise** [~waɪz] кра́ем, бо́ком
**edging** [ˈedʒɪŋ] край, кайма́, бордю́р; *of photo, etc.* оканто́вка
**edible** [ˈedɪbl] съедо́бный

**edit** ['edɪt] [от]редакти́ровать; *film* [с]монти́ровать; **~ion** [ɪ'dɪʃn] изда́ние; **~or** ['edɪtə] реда́ктор; **~orial** [edɪ'tɔːrɪəl] **1.** реда́кторский; редакцио́нный; **~ *office*** реда́кция; **2.** передова́я статья́; **~orship** ['edɪtəʃɪp]: ***under the ~*** под реда́кцией

**educat|e** ['edjʊkeɪt] дава́ть образова́ние (Д); (*bring up*) воспи́тывать [-та́ть]; **~ion** [edjʊ'keɪʃn] образова́ние, воспита́ние; **~ional** [edjʊ'keɪʃnl] образова́тельный; педагоги́ческий; учёбный

**eel** [iːl] у́горь *m*

**effect** [ɪ'fekt] **1.** (*result*) сле́дствие; результа́т; *phys.* эффе́кт; (*action*) де́йствие; (*impression*) эффе́кт, впечатле́ние; (*influence*) влия́ние; ***~s*** *pl.* иму́щество; ***come into ~*** вступа́ть в си́лу; ***in ~*** в су́щности; ***to no ~*** напра́сный; ***to the ~*** сле́дующего содержа́ния; **2.** производи́ть [-вести́]; выполня́ть [вы́полнить]; соверша́ть [-ши́ть]; **~ive** [~ɪv] эффекти́вный, действи́тельный; *tech.* поле́зный; **~ual** [~ʃʊəl] *remedy, etc.* де́йственный, эффекти́вный

**effeminate** [ɪ'femɪnət] □ женоподо́бный

**effervescent** [efə'vesnt] **1.** шипу́чий; **2.** *fig.* бры́зжущий весе́льем

**efficacy** ['efɪkəsɪ] де́йственность *f*

**efficien|cy** [ɪ'fɪʃnsɪ] делови́тость *f*; эффекти́вность *f*; **~t** [~nt] □ делови́тый; уме́лый, продукти́вный; эффекти́вный

**effort** ['efət] уси́лие; попы́тка

**effrontery** [ɪ'frʌntərɪ] на́глость *f*

**effusive** [ɪ'fjuːsɪv] □ экспанси́вный; несде́ржанный

**egg**[1] [eg] яйцо́; ***scrambled ~s*** *pl.* яи́чница-болту́нья; ***fried ~s*** *pl.* яи́чница-глазу́нья; ***hard-boiled*** (***soft-boiled***) **~** яйцо́ вкруту́ю (всмя́тку); **~shell** яи́чная скорлупа́

**egg**[2] [~] подстрека́ть [-кну́ть] (*mst.* ***~ on***)

**egotism** ['egəʊtɪzəm] эгои́зм, самомне́ние

**Egyptian** [ɪ'dʒɪpʃn] **1.** египтя́нин *m*, -я́нка *f*; **2.** еги́петский

**eight** [eɪt] **1.** во́семь; **2.** восьмёрка; **~een** [eɪ'tiːn] восемна́дцать; **~eenth** [eɪ'tiːnθ] восемна́дцатый; **~h** [eɪtθ] **1.** восьмо́й; **2.** восьма́я часть *f*; **~ieth** ['eɪtɪəθ] восьмидеся́тый; **~y** ['eɪtɪ] во́семьдесят

**either** ['aɪðə] **1.** *pron.* оди́н из двух; любо́й, ка́ждый; тот и́ли друго́й; и тот и друго́й, о́ба; **2.** *cj.* ***~ ... or ...*** и́ли ... и́ли ...; ли́бо ... ли́бо ...; ***not (...) ~*** та́кже не

**ejaculate** [ɪ'dʒækjʊleɪt] (*cry out*) восклица́ть [-ли́кнуть]; изверга́ть се́мя

**eject** [ɪ'dʒekt] (*throw out*) выгоня́ть [вы́гнать]; *from house* выселя́ть [вы́селить]; *lava* изверга́ть [-е́ргнуть]; *smoke* выпуска́ть [вы́пустить]

**eke** [iːk]: ***~ out*** восполня́ть [-по́лнить]; ***~ out a livelihood*** перебива́ться кое-ка́к

**elaborat|e** **1.** [ɪ'læbərət] □ сло́жный; тща́тельно разрабо́танный; **2.** [~reɪt] разраба́тывать [-бо́тать]; разви́(-ва́)ть; **~ion** [ɪˌlæbə'reɪʃn] разрабо́тка; разви́тие; уточне́ние

**elapse** [ɪ'læps] проходи́ть [пройти́], протека́ть [проте́чь]

**elastic** [ɪ'læstɪk] **1.** (***~ally***) эласти́чный; упру́гий; **2.** рези́нка; **~ity** [elæ'stɪsətɪ] эласти́чность *f*, упру́гость *f*

**elated** [ɪ'leɪtɪd] □ в припо́днятом настрое́нии

**elbow** ['elbəʊ] **1.** ло́коть *m*; *of pipe, etc.* коле́но; ***at one's ~*** под руко́й, ря́дом; **2.** прота́лкиваться [-толкну́ться]; ***~ out*** выта́лкивать [вы́толкнуть]; **~room** ме́сто, простра́нство; *fig.* свобо́да де́йствий

**elder**[1] ['eldə] *bot.* бузина́

**elder**[2] [~] **1.** ста́рец, ста́рший; **~ly** ['eldəlɪ] пожило́й

**eldest** ['eldɪst] са́мый ста́рший

**elect** [ɪ'lekt] **1.** *by vote* изб(и)ра́ть; (*choose, decide*) выбира́ть [вы́брать]; реша́ть [-ши́ть]; **2.** и́збранный; **~ion** [~kʃn] вы́боры *m/pl.*; **~or** [~tə] избира́тель *m*; **~oral** [~tərəl] избира́тельный; **~orate** [~tərət] избира́тели *m/pl.*

E

**electri|c** [ɪ'lektrɪk] электри́ческий; *~ **circuit*** электри́ческая цепь *f*; **~cal** [~trɪkl] □ электри́ческий; ***~ engineering*** электроте́хника; **~cian** [ɪlek'trɪʃn] электромонтёр

**electri|city** [ɪˌlek'trɪsətɪ] электри́чество; **~fy** [ɪ'lektrɪfaɪ] электрифици́ровать (*im*)*pf*.; [на]электризова́ть (*a. fig.*)

**electron** [ɪ'lektrɒn] электро́н; **~ic** [ɪlek'trɒnɪk] электро́нный; ***~ data processing*** электро́нная обрабо́тка да́нных; **~ics** электро́ника

**elegan|ce** ['elɪɡəns] элега́нтность *f*; изя́щество; **~t** ['elɪɡənt] □ элега́нтный, изя́щный

**element** ['elɪmənt] элеме́нт (*a. tech., chem.*); черта́; до́ля; ***the ~s*** стихи́я; ***~s*** *pl.* осно́вы *f/pl.*; ***in one's ~*** в свое́й стихи́и; ***there is an ~ of truth in this*** в э́том есть до́ля пра́вды; **~al** [elɪ'mentl] стихи́йный; **~ary** [~trɪ] □ элемента́рный; ***elementaries*** *pl.* осно́вы *f/pl.*

**elephant** ['elɪfənt] слон

**elevat|e** ['elɪveɪt] поднима́ть [-ня́ть]; повыша́ть [-вы́сить]; *fig.* возвыша́ть [-вы́сить]; **~ion** [elɪ'veɪʃn] возвыше́ние; (*elevated place*) возвы́шенность *f*; (*height*) высота́; **~or** ['elɪveɪtə] *for grain* элева́тор, *for lifting loads* грузоподъёмник; *Am.* лифт

**eleven** [ɪ'levn] оди́ннадцать; **~th** [~θ] **1.** оди́ннадцатый; **2.** оди́ннадцатая часть *f*

**elf** [elf] эльф; прока́зник

**elicit** [ɪ'lɪsɪt]: ***~ the truth*** добива́ться [-би́ться] и́стины

**eligible** ['elɪdʒəbl] □ име́ющий пра́во быть и́збранным; (*suitable*) подходя́щий

**eliminat|e** [ɪ'lɪmɪneɪt] устраня́ть [-ни́ть]; уничтожа́ть [-то́жить]; (*exclude*) исключа́ть [-чи́ть]; **~ion** [ɪlɪmɪ'neɪʃn] устране́ние; уничтоже́ние; ***by a process of ~*** ме́тодом исключе́ния

**elk** [elk] *zo.* лось *m*

**elm** [elm] *bot.* вяз

**eloquen|ce** ['eləkwəns] красноре́чие; **~t** [~t] □ красноречи́вый

**else** [els] ещё; кро́ме; ина́че; ино́й, друго́й; ***or ~*** а то; и́ли же; **~where** [els'weə] где́-нибудь в друго́м ме́сте

**elucidate** [ɪ'lu:sɪdeɪt] разъясня́ть [-ни́ть]

**elude** [ɪ'lu:d] избега́ть [-ежа́ть] (Р), уклоня́ться [-ни́ться] от (Р); *of meaning* ускольза́ть [-зну́ть]

**elusive** [ɪ'lu:sɪv] неулови́мый

**emaciated** [ɪ'meɪʃɪeɪtɪd] истощённый, худо́й

**email**, **E-mail** ['i:meɪl] электро́нная по́чта

**emanate** ['eməneɪt] идти́ из (Р); *rumours* исходи́ть (***from*** из, от Р)

**emancipat|e** [ɪ'mænsɪpeɪt] освобожда́ть [освободи́ть]; **~ion** [ɪmænsɪ'peɪʃn] освобожде́ние, эмансипа́ция

**embankment** [ɪm'bæŋkmənt] на́сыпь *f*; *by river or sea* на́бережная

**embargo** [em'bɑ:ɡəʊ] эмба́рго *n indecl.*; запре́т; ***be under ~*** быть под запре́том

**embark** [ɪm'bɑ:k] *of goods* [по]грузи́ть(ся); *of passengers* сади́ться [сесть]; *fig.* ***~ (up)on*** бра́ться [взя́ться] (за В); предпринима́ть [-ня́ть]

**embarrass** [ɪm'bærəs] смуща́ть [смути́ть]; приводи́ть [-вести́] в замеша́тельство; стесня́ть [-ни́ть]; ***~ed by lack of money*** в стеснённом положе́нии; **~ing** [~ɪŋ] □ затрудни́тельный; неудо́бный; стеснённый; **~ment** [~mənt] (*difficulties*) затрудне́ние; смуще́ние; (*confusion*) замеша́тельство

**embassy** ['embəsɪ] посо́льство

**embellish** [ɪm'belɪʃ] украша́ть [укра́сить]

**embers** ['embəz] *pl.* тле́ющие у́гли *m/pl.*

**embezzle** [ɪm'bezl] растра́чивать [-а́тить]; **~ment** [~mənt] растра́та

**embitter** [ɪm'bɪtə] озлобля́ть [озло́бить], ожесточа́ть [-чи́ть]

**emblem** ['embləm] эмбле́ма; си́мвол; ***national ~*** госуда́рственный герб

**embody** [ɪm'bɒdɪ] воплоща́ть [-лоти́ть]; (*personify*) олицетворя́ть [-ри́ть]; (*include*) включа́ть [-чи́ть]

**embrace** [ɪm'breɪs] **1.** объя́тие; **2.** об-

нима́ть(ся) [-ня́ть(ся)]; (*accept*) принима́ть [-ня́ть]; (*include*) охва́тывать [охвати́ть]
**embroider** [ɪm'brɔɪdə] вы́ши(ва́)ть; **~y** [~rɪ] вышива́ние; вы́шивка
**embroil** [ɪm'brɔɪl] запу́т(ыв)ать(ся); ввя́зываться [-за́ться]
**emerald** ['emərəld] изумру́д
**emerge** [ɪ'mɜːdʒ] появля́ться [-ви́ться]; (*surface*) всплы(ва́)ть (*a. fig.*); **~ncy** [~ənsɪ] чрезвыча́йная (авари́йная) ситуа́ция; ***in an ~*** в слу́чае кра́йней необходи́мости; *attr.* запасно́й, вспомога́тельный; ***~ landing*** вы́нужденная поса́дка
**emigra|nt** ['emɪgrənt] эмигра́нт; **~te** [~greɪt] эмигри́ровать (*im*)*pf.*; **~tion** [emɪ'greɪʃn] эмигра́ция
**eminen|ce** ['emɪnəns] *geogr.* возвы́шенность *f*; *fig.* знамени́тость *f*; ***win ~ as a scientist*** стать *pf.* знамени́тым учёным; **~t** [~ənt] □ *fig.* выдаю́щийся; *adv.* чрезвыча́йно
**emit** [ɪ'mɪt] *sound, smell* изд(ав)а́ть, испуска́ть [-усти́ть]; *light* излуча́ть; *heat* выделя́ть [вы́делить]
**emoti|on** [ɪ'məʊʃn] чу́вство; возбужде́ние; волне́ние; эмо́ция *mst. pl.*; **~onal** [~ʃənl] □ эмоциона́льный; *voice* взволно́ванный; *music, etc.* волну́ющий
**emperor** ['empərə] импера́тор
**empha|sis** ['emfəsɪs] вырази́тельность *f*; ударе́ние, акце́нт; ***place ~ on s.th.*** подчёркивать [-еркну́ть] ва́жность чего́-л.; **~size** [~saɪz] подчёркивать [-черкну́ть]; **~tic** [ɪm'fætɪk] (***~ally***) *gesture etc.* вырази́тельный; *request* насто́йчивый
**empire** ['empaɪə] импе́рия
**employ** [ɪm'plɔɪ] употребля́ть [-би́ть], применя́ть [-ни́ть], испо́льзовать (*im*)*pf.*; предоставля́ть, нанима́ть на рабо́ту (Д); **~ee** [emplɔɪ'iː] слу́жащий [-щая], рабо́тник (-ица); **~er** [ɪm'plɔɪə] нанима́тель *m*, работода́тель *m*; **~ment** [~mənt] (*use*) примене́ние; рабо́та, заня́тие; ***~ agency*** бюро́ по трудоустро́йству; ***full ~*** по́лная за́нятость
**empower** [ɪm'paʊə] уполномо́чи(ва)ть
**empress** ['emprɪs] императри́ца
**empt|iness** ['emptɪnɪs] пустота́; **~y** [~tɪ] **1.** □ пусто́й, поро́жний; *coll.* голо́дный; ***I feel ~*** я го́лоден; **2.** опорожня́ть(ся) [-ни́ть(ся)]; [о]пусте́ть; *liquid* вылива́ть [вы́лить]; *sand, etc.* высыпа́ть [вы́сыпать]
**enable** [ɪ'neɪbl] дава́ть возмо́жность *f*; [с]де́лать возмо́жным (Д)
**enact** [ɪ'nækt] *law* постановля́ть [-ви́ть]; *thea.* игра́ть роль; ста́вить на сце́не
**enamel** [ɪ'næml] **1.** эма́ль *f*; *art* эма́ль, *obs.* фи́нифть; **2.** эмалирова́ть (*im*)*pf.*; покрыва́ть эма́лью
**enamo(u)red** [ɪ'næməd]: ***~ of*** влюблённый в (В)
**enchant** [ɪn'tʃɑːnt] очаро́вывать [-ова́ть]; **~ment** [~mənt] очарова́ние; **~ress** [~rɪs] *fig.* обворожи́тельная же́нщина, волше́бница
**encircle** [ɪn'sɜːkl] окружа́ть [-жи́ть]
**enclos|e** [ɪn'kləʊz] (*fence in*) огора́живать [-роди́ть]; *in letter, etc.* прилага́ть [-ложи́ть]; **~ure** [~ʒə] огоро́женное ме́сто; вложе́ние, приложе́ние
**encompass** [ɪn'kʌmpəs] окружа́ть [-жи́ть]
**encore** ['ɒŋkɔː] *thea.* **1.** бис!; **2.** крича́ть "бис"; вызыва́ть [вы́звать] на бис; (*give an encore*) биси́ровать
**encounter** [ɪn'kaʊntə] **1.** встре́ча; столкнове́ние; (*contest, competition*) состяза́ние; **2.** встреча́ть(ся) [-е́тить(ся)]; *difficulties etc.* ста́лкиваться [столкну́ться] (с Т); ната́лкиваться [натолкну́ться] (на В)
**encourage** [ɪn'kʌrɪdʒ] ободря́ть [-ри́ть]; поощря́ть [-ри́ть]; **~ment** [~mənt] ободре́ние; поощре́ние
**encroach** [ɪn'krəʊtʃ]: ***~ (up)on*** вторга́ться [вто́ргнуться] в (В); *rights* посяга́ть (на В); *time* отнима́ть [-ня́ть]; **~ment** [~mənt] вторже́ние
**encumb|er** [ɪn'kʌmbər] обременя́ть [-ни́ть]; (*cram*) загроможда́ть [-мозди́ть]; (*hamper*) затрудня́ть [-ни́ть]; [вос]препя́тствовать (Д); **~rance**

[-brəns] бре́мя *n*; обу́за; *fig.* препя́тствие
**encyclop(a)edia** [ɪnsaɪklə'piːdɪə] энциклопе́дия
**end** [end] **1.** коне́ц, оконча́ние; цель *f*; ***no ~ of*** о́чень мно́го (Р); ***in the ~*** в конце́ концо́в; ***on ~*** стоймя́; *hair* ды́бом; беспреры́вно, подря́д; ***to that ~*** с э́той це́лью; **2.** конча́ть(ся) [ко́нчить(ся)]
**endanger** [ɪn'deɪndʒə] подверга́ть опа́сности
**endear** [ɪn'dɪə] внуша́ть любо́вь, заставля́ть полюби́ть; **~ment** [-mənt] ла́ска; ***words of ~*** ла́сковые слова́
**endeavo(u)r** [ɪn'devə] **1.** [по]пыта́ться, прилага́ть уси́лия, [по]стара́ться; **2.** попы́тка, стара́ние; ***make every ~*** сде́лать всё возмо́жное
**end|ing** ['endɪŋ] оконча́ние; **~less** ['endlɪs] □ бесконе́чный
**endorse** [ɪn'dɔːs] *fin.* индосси́ровать (*im*)*pf*.; (*approve*) одобря́ть [одо́брить]; **~ment** [ɪn'dɔːsmənt] индоссаме́нт, одобре́ние
**endow** [ɪn'daʊ] одаря́ть [-ри́ть]; (*give*) [по]же́ртвовать; **~ment** [-mənt] поже́ртвование, дар
**endur|ance** [ɪn'djʊərəns] *physical* про́чность *f*; *mental* выно́сливость *f*; **~e** [ɪn'djʊə] выноси́ть [вы́нести], терпе́ть
**enema** ['enɪmə] кли́зма
**enemy** ['enəmɪ] враг; неприя́тель *m*; проти́вник
**energ|etic** [enə'dʒetɪk] (***~ally***) энерги́чный; **~y** ['enədʒɪ] эне́ргия
**enfold** [ɪn'fəʊld] (*embrace*) обнима́ть [обня́ть]; (*wrap up*) заку́тывать [-тать]
**enforce** [ɪn'fɔːs] заставля́ть [-а́вить], принужда́ть [-ди́ть]; *a law* вводи́ть [ввести́]; *strengthen* уси́ли(ва)ть
**engage** [ɪn'geɪdʒ] *v/t.* (*employ*) нанима́ть [наня́ть]; *rooms* заброни́ровать; *in activity* занима́ть [заня́ть]; (*attract*) привлека́ть [-е́чь]; завладе́(-ва́)ть; *in conversation* вовлека́ть [-е́чь]; ***be ~d*** быть за́нятым; быть помо́лвленным; *v/i.* (*pledge*) обя́зываться [-за́ться]; занима́ться [заня́ться] (***in*** Т); **~ment** [-mənt] обяза́тельство; встре́ча, свида́ние; помо́лвка
**engaging** [ɪn'geɪdʒɪŋ] □ очарова́тельный
**engender** [ɪn'dʒendə] *fig.* порожда́ть [породи́ть]
**engine** ['endʒɪn] *mot.* дви́гатель; мото́р; *rail.* парово́з; **~ driver** машини́ст
**engineer** [endʒɪ'nɪə] **1.** инжене́р; *naut.* меха́ник; *Am.* машини́ст; **2.** *fig.* подстра́ивать [-ро́ить]; **~ing** [-rɪŋ] машинострое́ние
**English** ['ɪŋglɪʃ] **1.** англи́йский; **2.** англи́йский язы́к; ***the ~*** англича́не *pl.*; **~man** [-mən] англича́нин; **~woman** [-ˌwʊmən] англича́нка
**engrav|e** [ɪn'greɪv] [вы́]гравирова́ть; *fig. in mind* запечатле́(ва́)ть; **~ing** [-ɪŋ] гравирова́ние; гравю́ра, эста́мп
**engross** [ɪn'grəʊs] поглоща́ть [-лоти́ть]; ***~ing book*** захва́тывающая кни́га
**enhance** [ɪn'hɑːns] *value, etc.* повыша́ть [повы́сить]; (*intensify*) уси́ли(ва)ть
**enigma** [ɪ'nɪgmə] зага́дка; **~tic** [enɪg'mætɪk] □ зага́дочный
**enjoy** [ɪn'dʒɔɪ] наслажда́ться [наслади́ться] (Т); получа́ть [-чи́ть] удово́льствие; ***~ o.s.*** развлека́ться [-ле́чься]; ***~ good health*** облада́ть хоро́шим здоро́вьем; **~able** [-əbl] прия́тный; **~ment** [-mənt] наслажде́ние, удово́льствие
**enlarge** [ɪn'lɑːdʒ] увели́чи(ва)ть(-ся); распространя́ться (***on*** о П); ***~ one's mind*** расширя́ть [-ши́рить] кругозо́р; **~ment** [-mənt] расшире́ние; *of photo, etc.* увеличе́ние
**enlighten** [ɪn'laɪtn] просвеща́ть [-ети́ть]; разъясня́ть [-ни́ть]; **~ment** просвеще́ние; *of a person* просвещённость *f*
**enlist** [ɪn'lɪst] *v/i. mil.* поступа́ть [-пи́ть] на вое́нную слу́жбу; ***~ help*** привле́чь на по́мощь
**enliven** [ɪn'laɪvn] оживля́ть [-ви́ть]
**enmity** ['enmɪtɪ] вражда́, неприя́знь *f*
**ennoble** [ɪ'nəʊbl] облагора́живать

[-ро́дить]
**enorm|ity** [ɪ'nɔːmətɪ] необъя́тность *f*; *pej.* чудо́вищность *f*; преступле́ние; **~ous** [~əs] □ огро́мный, грома́дный; чудо́вищный
**enough** [ɪ'nʌf] доста́точно, дово́льно
**enquire** [ɪn'kwaɪə] → ***inquire***
**enrage** [ɪn'reɪdʒ] [вз]беси́ть, приводи́ть в я́рость
**enrapture** [ɪn'ræptʃə] восхища́ть [-ити́ть], очаро́вывать
**enrich** [ɪn'rɪtʃ] обогаща́ть [-гати́ть]
**enrol(l)** [ɪn'rəʊl] *v/t.* запи́сывать [-са́ть]; [за]регистри́ровать; *v/i.* запи́сываться [-са́ться]; **~ment** [~mənt] регистра́ция; за́пись *f*
**en route** [ˌɒn'ruːt] по доро́ге
**ensign** ['ensaɪn] флаг; *Am. naut.* мла́дший лейтена́нт
**ensue** [ɪn'sjuː] (*follow*) [по]сле́довать; получа́ться в результа́те
**ensure** [ɪn'ʃʊə] обеспе́чивать [-чить]; (*guarantee*) руча́ться [поручи́ться] (за В)
**entail** [ɪn'teɪl] влечь за собо́й, вызыва́ть [вы́звать]
**entangle** [ɪn'tæŋgl] запу́тывать(ся), (*a. fig.*)
**enter** ['entə] *v/t. room, etc.* входи́ть [войти́] в (В); *university* поступа́ть [-пи́ть] в (В); *in book* вноси́ть [внести́]; (*penetrate*) проника́ть [-ни́кнуть] в (В); *v/i.* входи́ть [войти́], вступа́ть [-пи́ть]
**enterpris|e** ['entəpraɪz] предприя́тие; (*quality*) предприи́мчивость *f*; **~ing** [~ɪŋ] □ предприи́мчивый
**entertain** [entə'teɪn] *guests* принима́ть [-ня́ть]; (*give food to*) угоща́ть [угости́ть]; (*amuse*) развлека́ть [-ле́чь], занима́ть [заня́ть]; **~ment** [~mənt] развлече́ние; приём
**enthusias|m** [ɪn'θjuːzɪæzm] восто́рг; энтузиа́зм; **~t** [~æst] энтузиа́ст(ка); **~tic** [ɪnθjuːzɪ'æstɪk] (***~ally***) восто́рженный; по́лный энтузиа́зма
**entice** [ɪn'taɪs] зама́нивать [-ни́ть]; (*tempt*) соблазня́ть [-ни́ть]; **~ment** [~mənt] собла́зн, прима́нка
**entire** [ɪn'taɪə] □ це́лый, весь; сплошно́й; **~ly** [~lɪ] всеце́ло; соверше́нно
**entitle** [ɪn'taɪtl] (*give a title to*) озагла́вливать [-ла́вить]; дава́ть пра́во (Д)
**entity** ['entɪtɪ] бытие́; су́щность *f*
**entrails** ['entreɪlz] *pl.* вну́тренности *f/pl.*
**entrance** ['entrəns] вход, въезд; *actor's* вы́ход; (*right to enter*) до́ступ; ~ ***examinations*** вступи́тельные экза́мены
**entreat** [ɪn'triːt] умоля́ть; **~y** [~ɪ] мольба́, про́сьба
**entrench** [ɪn'trentʃ] *fig.* укореня́ться [-ни́ться]
**entrust** [ɪn'trʌst] поруча́ть [-чи́ть]; доверя́ть [-ве́рить]
**entry** ['entrɪ] вход, въезд; *of an actor on stage* вход/вы́ход; *in book* за́пись; ***No*** ~ вход (въезд) запрещён
**enumerate** [ɪ'njuːməreɪt] перечисля́ть [-и́слить]
**envelop** [ɪn'veləp] (*wrap*) заку́т(ыв)ать; *of mist, etc.* оку́т(ыв)ать; **~e** ['envələʊp] конве́рт
**envi|able** ['envɪəbl] □ зави́дный; **~ous** [~əs] □ зави́стливый
**environ|ment** [ɪn'vaɪərənmənt] окружа́ющая среда́; **~mental** окружа́ющий; ~ ***protection*** охра́на окружа́ющей среды́; **~s** [ɪn'vaɪərənz] *pl.* окре́стности *f/pl.*
**envisage** [ɪn'vɪzɪdʒ] представля́ть себе́; (*anticipate*) предви́деть; (*consider*) рассма́тривать [-смотре́ть]
**envoy** ['envɔɪ] (*messenger*) посла́нец; (*diplomat*) посла́нник; полномо́чный представи́тель *m*
**envy** ['envɪ] **1.** за́висть *f*; **2.** [по]зави́довать (Д)
**epic** ['epɪk] **1.** эпи́ческая поэ́ма; **2.** эпи́ческий
**epicenter** (**-tre**) ['epɪsentə] эпице́нтр
**epidemic** [epɪ'demɪk] эпиде́мия
**epilogue** ['epɪlɒg] эпило́г
**episode** ['epɪsəʊd] слу́чай, эпизо́д, происше́ствие
**epitome** [ɪ'pɪtəmɪ] (*embodiment*) воплоще́ние
**epoch** ['iːpɒk] эпо́ха

E

**equable** ['ekwəbl] □ ро́вный; *fig.* уравнове́шенный
**equal** ['iːkwəl] **1.** □ ра́вный; одина́ковый; **~ *to*** *fig.* спосо́бный на (В); **2.** равня́ться (Д); **~ity** [ɪ'kwɒlətɪ] ра́венство; **~ization** [iːkwəlaɪ'zeɪʃn] ура́внивание; **~ize** [~aɪz] ура́внивать [-ня́ть]
**equanimity** [ekwə'nɪmətɪ] споко́йствие, душе́вное равнове́сие
**equat|ion** [ɪ'kweɪʒn] *math.* уравне́ние; **~or** [~tə] эква́тор
**equilibrium** [iːkwɪ'lɪbrɪəm] равнове́сие
**equip** [ɪ'kwɪp] *office, etc.* обору́довать; *expedition, etc.* снаряжа́ть [-яди́ть]; (*provide*) снабжа́ть [-бди́ть]; **~ment** [~mənt] обору́дование; снаряже́ние
**equity** ['ekwɪtɪ] справедли́вость *f*; беспристра́стность *f*; *fin. pl.* обыкнове́нные а́кции *f/pl.*
**equivalent** [ɪ'kwɪvələnt] **1.** эквивале́нт (***to*** Д); **2.** равноце́нный; равноси́льный
**equivocal** [ɪ'kwɪvəkəl] □ двусмы́сленный; (*questionable*) сомни́тельный
**era** ['ɪərə] э́ра; эпо́ха
**eradicate** [ɪ'rædɪkeɪt] искореня́ть [-ни́ть]
**eras|e** [ɪ'reɪz] стира́ть [стере́ть]; подчища́ть [-и́стить]; **~er** [~ə] *Am.* рези́нка
**erect** [ɪ'rekt] **1.** □ прямо́й; (*raised*) по́днятый; **2.** [по]стро́ить, воздвига́ть [-и́гнуть]; **~ion** [ɪ'rekʃn] постро́йка, сооруже́ние, строе́ние
**ermine** ['ɜːmɪn] *zo.* горноста́й
**erosion** [ɪ'rəʊʒn] эро́зия
**erotic** [ɪ'rɒtɪk] эроти́ческий
**err** [ɜː] ошиба́ться [-би́ться], заблужда́ться
**errand** ['erənd] поруче́ние
**errat|ic** [ɪ'rætɪk] (**~*ally***) неусто́йчивый; *player, behavio(u)r* неро́вный; **~um** [e'rɑːtəm], *pl.* **~a** [~tə] опеча́тка, опи́ска
**erroneous** [ɪ'rəʊnɪəs] □ оши́бочный
**error** ['erə] оши́бка, заблужде́ние; погре́шность *f* (*a. astr.*)
**eruption** [ɪ'rʌpʃn] изверже́ние; *on face, etc.* высыпа́ние (сы́пи); *of teeth* проре́зывание
**escalator** ['eskəleɪtə] эскала́тор
**escapade** ['eskəpeɪd] проде́лка; шальна́я вы́ходка
**escape** [ɪ'skeɪp] **1.** *v/i. from prison* бежа́ть; *from death* спаса́ться [спасти́сь]; *v/t. danger, etc.* избега́ть [-ежа́ть]; ускольза́ть [-зну́ть] (от Р); ***his name ~s me*** не могу́ припо́мнить его́ и́мени; **2.** побе́г, спасе́ние; (*leak*) уте́чка
**escort** **1.** ['eskɔːt] сопровожде́ние, эско́рт; *mil.* конво́й; **2.** [ɪs'kɔːt, ~ɔːrt] сопровожда́ть, конвои́ровать
**esoteric** [esəʊ'terɪk] эзотери́ческий
**especial** [ɪ'speʃl] осо́бый; специа́льный; **~ly** [~ɪ] осо́бенно
**espionage** ['espɪənɑːʒ] шпиона́ж
**essay** ['eseɪ] о́черк, эссе́; (*attempt*) попы́тка; *educ.* сочине́ние
**essen|ce** ['esns] су́щность *f*, существо́; суть *f*; (*substance*) эссе́нция; **~tial** [ɪ'senʃl] **1.** □ суще́ственный (***to*** для Р), ва́жный; **2.** *pl.* всё необходи́мое
**establish** [ɪ'stæblɪʃ] *the truth, etc.* устана́вливать [-нови́ть]; (*set up*) учрежда́ть [-реди́ть], осно́вывать [-ова́ть]; **~ *o.s.*** поселя́ться [-ли́ться], устра́иваться [-ро́иться] (в П); **~ *order*** наводи́ть [-вести́] поря́док; **~ment** [~mənt] установле́ние; учрежде́ние; ***the*** **♀** исте́блишмент
**estate** [ɪ'steɪt] (*property*) иму́щество; (*land with a large house*) име́ние; ***real* ~** недви́жимость *f*
**esteem** [ɪ'stiːm] **1.** уваже́ние; **2.** уважа́ть
**estimable** ['estɪməbl] досто́йный уваже́ния
**estimat|e** **1.** ['estɪmeɪt] оце́нивать [-ни́ть]; **2.** [~mɪt] сме́та, калькуля́ция; оце́нка; ***at a rough ~*** в гру́бом приближе́нии; **~ion** [estɪ'meɪʃn] оце́нка; (*opinion*) мне́ние
**estrange** [ɪ'streɪndʒ] отта́лкивать [-толкну́ть], сде́лать чужи́м
**etching** ['etʃɪŋ] *craft* гравиро́вка;

*product* гравю́ра; травле́ние
**etern|al** [ɪ'tɜːnl] ве́чный; неизме́нный; **~ity** [~nɪtɪ] ве́чность *f*
**ether** ['iːθə] эфи́р
**ethic|al** ['eθɪkl] □ эти́чный, эти́ческий; **~s** ['eθɪks] э́тика
**etiquette** ['etɪket] этике́т
**euro** ['jʊrəʊ] е́вро
**European** [jʊərə'piːən] **1.** европе́ец *m*, -пе́йка *f*; **2.** европе́йский
**Eurovision** ['jʊərəvɪʒn] Еврови́дение
**evacuate** [ɪ'vækjʊeɪt] эвакуи́ровать (*im*)*pf*.
**evade** [ɪ'veɪd] (*avoid*) избега́ть [-ежа́ть] (P); уклоня́ться [-ни́ться] от (P); *law, etc*. обходи́ть [обойти́]
**evaluat|e** [ɪ'væljʊeɪt] оце́нивать [-ни́ть]; **~ion** [ɪvæljʊ'eɪʃn] оце́нка
**evaporat|e** [ɪ'væpəreɪt] испаря́ть(-ся) [-ри́ть(ся)]; *fig*. разве́иваться [-е́яться]; **~ion** [ɪvæpə'reɪʃn] испаре́ние
**evasi|on** [ɪ'veɪʒn] уклоне́ние, увёртка; **~ve** [~sɪv] □ укло́нчивый
**eve** [iːv] кану́н; ***on the ~ of*** накану́не (P)
**even** ['iːvn] **1.** *adj*. □ (*level, smooth*) ро́вный, гла́дкий; (*equal*) ра́вный, одина́ковый; *number* чётный; **2.** *adv*. ро́вно; как раз; ***not ~*** да́же не; ***~ though, ~ if*** да́же е́сли; **3.** выра́внивать [вы́ровнять]; сгла́живать [сгла́дить]; **~ly** [~lɪ] ро́вно, по́ровну
**evening** ['iːvnɪŋ] ве́чер; вечери́нка; ***~ dress*** вече́рнее пла́тье; *man's* фрак
**event** [ɪ'vent] собы́тие, слу́чай; *sport* соревнова́ние; ***at all ~s*** во вся́ком слу́чае; ***be wise after the ~*** за́дним умо́м кре́пок; ***in the ~ of*** в слу́чае (P); **~ful** [~fʊl] по́лный собы́тий
**eventual** [ɪ'ventʃʊəl] возмо́жный; коне́чный; **~ly** [~ɪ] в конце́ концо́в; со вре́менем
**ever** ['evə] всегда́; когда́-нибудь, когда́-либо; ***~ so*** о́чень; ***as soon as ~ I can*** как то́лько я смогу́; ***for ~*** навсегда́; ***hardly ~*** почти́ не; **~green** вечнозелёный; **~lasting** [evə'lɑːstɪŋ] □ ве́чный; **~present** постоя́нный
**every** ['evrɪ] ка́ждый; ***~ now and then*** вре́мя от вре́мени; ***~ other day*** че́рез день; ***have ~ reason*** име́ть все основа́ния; **~body** все *pl*.; ка́ждый, вся́кий; **~day** ежедне́вный; **~one** ка́ждый, вся́кий; все *pl*.; **~thing** всё; **~where** везде́, всю́ду
**evict** [ɪ'vɪkt] выселя́ть [вы́селить]
**eviden|ce** ['evɪdəns] доказа́тельство; (*sign*) при́знак; (*data*) да́нные, фа́кты; *law* ули́ка; свиде́тельское показа́ние; ***in ~*** в доказа́тельство; **~t** [~nt] □ очеви́дный, я́вный
**evil** ['iːvl] **1.** □ злой; *influence* па́губный; дурно́й, плохо́й; **2.** зло
**evince** [ɪ'vɪns] проявля́ть [-ви́ть]
**evoke** [ɪ'vəʊk] вызыва́ть [вы́звать]
**evolution** [iːvə'luːʃn] эволю́ция; разви́тие
**evolve** [ɪ'vɒlv] разви́(ва́)ться
**ewe** [juː] овца́
**exact** [ɪg'zækt] **1.** □ то́чный, аккура́тный; **2.** (*demand*) [по]тре́бовать (P); взы́скивать [-ка́ть]; ***~ taxes*** взима́ть нало́ги; **~ing** [~ɪŋ] тре́бовательный, взыска́тельный
**exaggerate** [ɪg'zædʒəreɪt] преувели́чи(ва)ть
**exalt** [ɪg'zɔːlt] (*make higher*) повыша́ть [повы́сить]; (*praise*) превозноси́ть [-нести́]; **~ation** [egzɔːl'teɪʃn] восто́рг
**examin|ation** [ɪgzæmɪ'neɪʃn] (*inspection*) осмо́тр; (*study*) иссле́дование; *by experts* эксперти́за; *in school, etc*. экза́мен; **~e** [ɪg'zæmɪn] *patient, etc*. осма́тривать [-мотре́ть]; иссле́довать (*im*)*pf*.; [про]экзаменова́ть
**example** [ɪg'zɑːmpl] приме́р; (*sample*) образе́ц; ***for ~*** наприме́р
**exasperate** [ɪg'zɑːspəreɪt] изводи́ть [извести́]; раздража́ть [-жи́ть]; доводи́ть до бе́лого кале́ния
**excavate** ['ekskəveɪt] выка́пывать [вы́копать]; *archaeology* вести́ раско́пки
**excavator** ['ekskəveɪtə] экскава́тор
**exceed** [ɪk'siːd] *speed, etc*. превыша́ть [-вы́сить]; (*be greater than*) превосходи́ть [-взойти́]; ***this ~s all limits!*** э́то перехо́дит все грани́цы!; **~ing** [~ɪŋ]

□ превыша́ющий

**excel** [ɪk'sel] *v/t.* преуспева́ть [-пе́ть] (***in, at*** Т); *v/i.* выделя́ться [вы́делиться]; **~lence** ['eksələns] высо́кое ка́чество; соверше́нство; **~lent** ['eksələnt] □ превосхо́дный

E

**except** [ɪk'sept] **1.** исключа́ть [-чи́ть]; **2.** *prp.* исключа́я (В); кро́ме (Р); ***~ for*** за исключе́нием (Р); **~ing** [~ɪŋ] *prp.* за исключе́нием (Р); **~ion** [ɪk'sepʃn] исключе́ние; ***take ~ to*** возража́ть [-рази́ть] (про́тив Р); **~ional** [~l] исключи́тельный; *person* незауря́дный

**excess** [ɪk'ses] избы́ток, изли́шек; эксце́сс; ***~ fare*** допла́та; ***~ luggage*** изли́шек багажа́; бага́ж сверх но́рмы; ***~ profits*** сверхпри́быль; **~ive** [~ɪv] □ чрезме́рный

**exchange** [ɪks'tʃeɪndʒ] **1.** обме́ниваться [-ня́ться] (Т); обме́нивать [-ня́ть] (***for*** на В), [по]меня́ться (Т); **2.** обме́н; (*a.* ♀) би́ржа; ***foreign ~*** иностра́нная валю́та

**exchequer** [ɪks'tʃekə]: ***Chancellor of the*** ♀ мини́стр фина́нсов Великобрита́нии

**excise** [ek'saɪz] *fin.* акци́з, акци́зный сбор

**excit|able** [ɪk'saɪtəbl] возбуди́мый; **~e** [ɪk'saɪt] возбужда́ть [-уди́ть], [вз]волнова́ть; **~ement** [~mənt] возбужде́ние, волне́ние

**exclaim** [ɪk'skleɪm] восклица́ть [-и́кнуть]

**exclamation** [ekslə'meɪʃn] восклица́ние

**exclude** [ɪk'skluːd] исключа́ть [-чи́ть]

**exclusi|on** [ɪk'skluːʒn] исключе́ние; **~ve** [~sɪv] □ исключи́тельный; (*sole*) еди́нственный; ***~ of*** без; не счита́я; за исключе́нием (Р)

**excrement** ['ekskrɪmənt] экскреме́нты *m/pl.*, испражне́ния *n/pl.*

**excruciating** [ɪk'skruːʃɪeɪtɪŋ] мучи́тельный

**excursion** [ɪk'skɜːʒn] экску́рсия; ***go on an ~*** отпра́виться (пое́хать) на экску́рсию

**excus|able** [ɪk'skjuːzəbl] □ прости́тельный; **~e** **1.** [ɪk'skjuːz] извиня́ть [-ни́ть], проща́ть [прости́ть]; **2.** [ɪk'skjuːs] извине́ние; (*reason*) оправда́ние; (*pretext*) отгово́рка

**execut|e** ['eksɪkjuːt] (*carry out*) исполня́ть [-о́лнить]; (*fulfil*) выполня́ть [вы́]полнить); (*put to death*) казни́ть (*im*)*pf.*; **~ion** [eksɪ'kjuːʃn] исполне́ние; выполне́ние; (*capital punishment*) казнь *f*; **~ive** [ɪg'zekjʊtɪv] **1.** исполни́тельный; администрати́вный; **2.** исполни́тельная власть *f*; (*person*) администра́тор

**exemplary** [ɪg'zemplərɪ] образцо́вый, приме́рный

**exemplify** [ɪg'zemplɪfaɪ] (*illustrate by example*) поясня́ть приме́ром; (*serve as example*) служи́ть приме́ром (Р)

**exempt** [ɪg'zempt] **1.** освобожда́ть [-боди́ть] (от Р); **2.** освобождённый, свобо́дный (***of*** от Р)

**exercise** ['eksəsaɪz] **1.** упражне́ние; (*drill*) трениро́вка; (*walk*) прогу́лка; **2.** [на]тренирова́ть(ся); *patience, etc.* проявля́ть [-ви́ть]; (*use*) [вос]по́льзоваться

**exert** [ɪg'zɜːt] *strength, etc.* напряга́ть [-ря́чь]; *influence, etc.* ока́зывать [-за́ть]; ***~ o.s.*** прилага́ть [-ложи́ть] уси́лия; **~ion** [ɪg'zɜːʃn] напряже́ние, уси́лие

**exhale** [eks'heɪl] выдыха́ть [вы́дохнуть]

**exhaust** [ɪg'zɔːst] **1.** изнуря́ть [-ри́ть], истоща́ть [-щи́ть]; **2.** *pipe* выхлопна́я труба́; вы́хлоп; **~ion** [~ʃn] истоще́ние, изнуре́ние; **~ive** [~ɪv] □ (*very tiring*) изнуря́ющий; *study, etc.* всесторо́нний; *answer* исче́рпывающий

**exhibit** [ɪg'zɪbɪt] **1.** *interest etc.* проявля́ть [-ви́ть]; *at exhibition* выставля́ть [вы́ставить]; **2.** экспона́т; **~ion** [eksɪ'bɪʃn] проявле́ние; вы́ставка; **~or** [ɪg'zɪbɪtə] экспоне́нт

**exhilarat|e** [ɪg'zɪləreɪt] оживля́ть [-ви́ть]; [вз]бодри́ть; **~ing** [~ɪŋ] *weather, etc.* бодря́щий

**exhort** [ɪg'zɔːt] призыва́ть [-зва́ть]; увещева́ть; побужда́ть [-уди́ть] (к Д)

**exigency** ['eksɪdʒənsɪ] о́страя необ-

ходи́мость *f*
**exile** ['eksaɪl] **1.** *lit., hist.* изгна́ние, ссы́лка; изгна́нник, ссы́льный; **2.** ссыла́ть [сосла́ть]; *from a country* высыла́ть [вы́слать]
**exist** [ɪg'zɪst] существова́ть, жить; **~ence** [-əns] существова́ние, жизнь *f*; ***in ~*** = **~ent** [-ənt] существу́ющий
**exit**['eksɪt] вы́ход; ***emergency ~*** запасно́й вы́ход
**exodus** ['eksədəs] ма́ссовый отъе́зд; *Bibl.* Исхо́д
**exonerate** [ɪg'zɒnəreɪt] опра́вдывать [-да́ть]; (*free from blame*) снима́ть [снять] обвине́ние; *from responsibility* снима́ть [снять] отве́тственность
**exorbitant** [ɪg'zɔːbɪtənt] □ непоме́рный, чрезме́рный
**exotic** [ɪg'zɒtɪk] экзоти́ческий
**expan|d** [ɪk'spænd] расширя́ть(ся) [-и́рить(ся)], увели́чи(ва)ть(ся); (*develop*) разви́(ва́)ть(ся); **~se** [ɪk'spæns] простра́нство; протяже́ние; **~sion** [~nʃn] расшире́ние; (*spread*) распростране́ние; разви́тие; **~sive**[~sɪv] □ обши́рный; *fig.* экспанси́вный
**expect** [ɪks'pekt] ожида́ть (P); (*count on*) рассчи́тывать, наде́яться; (*think*) полага́ть, ду́мать; **~ant**[~ənt]: ***~ mother*** бере́менная же́нщина; **~ation** [ekspek'teɪʃn] ожида́ние; (*hope*) *mst. pl.* наде́жда
**expedi|ent** [ɪk'spiːdɪənt] **1.** подходя́щий, целесообра́зный, соотве́тствующий; **2.** сре́дство достиже́ния це́ли; приём; **~tion**[ekspɪ'dɪʃn] экспеди́ция; (*speed*) быстрота́
**expel** [ɪk'spel] *from school, etc.* исключа́ть [-чи́ть] (из P)
**expen|d** [ɪk'spend] [ис]тра́тить; [из]расхо́довать; **~diture** [~ɪtʃə] расхо́д, тра́та; **~se** [ɪk'spens] расхо́д, тра́та; ***at his ~*** за его́ счёт; ***travel ~s*** командиро́вочные; **~sive**[~sɪv] □ дорого́й, дорогосто́ящий
**experience** [ɪk'spɪərɪəns] **1.** (жи́зненный) о́пыт; (*event*) слу́чай, приключе́ние; **2.** испы́тывать [испыта́ть]; (*suffer*) пережи́(ва́)ть; **~d** [~t] о́пытный; квалифици́рованный
**experiment** **1.** [ɪk'sperɪmənt] о́пыт, экспериме́нт; **2.** [~ment] производи́ть о́пыты; **~al** [ɪksperɪ'mentl] □ эксперимента́льный, о́пытный, про́бный
**expert** ['ekspɜːt] **1.** о́пытный, иску́сный; **2.** экспе́рт, знато́к, специали́ст; *attr.* высококвалифици́рованный
**expir|ation**[ekspɪ'reɪʃn] (*end*) оконча́ние, истече́ние; **~e**[ɪk'spaɪə] (*breathe out*) выдыха́ть [вы́дохнуть]; (*die*) умира́ть [умере́ть]; *fin.* истека́ть [-е́чь]
**explain** [ɪk'spleɪn] объясня́ть [-ни́ть]; (*justify*) опра́вдывать [-да́ть]
**explanat|ion** [eksplə'neɪʃn] объясне́ние; (*justification*) оправда́ние; (*reason*) причи́на; **~ory** [ɪk'splænətrɪ] □ объясни́тельный
**explicable** [ɪk'splɪkəbl] объясни́мый
**explicit** [ɪk'splɪsɪt] □ я́сный, недвусмы́сленный, то́чный
**explode** [ɪk'spləʊd] (*blow up*) взрыва́ть(ся) [взорва́ть(ся)] (*a. fig.*); *of applause etc.* разража́ться [-рази́ться] (***with*** T)
**exploit** **1.** ['eksplɔɪt] по́двиг; **2.** [ɪk'splɔɪt] эксплуати́ровать; *mining* разраба́тывать [-бо́тать]; **~ation** [eksplɔɪ'teɪʃn] эксплуата́ция; разрабо́тка
**explor|ation**[eksplə'reɪʃn] иссле́дование; **~e**[ɪk'splɔː] иссле́довать (*im*)*pf.*; *geol.* разве́д(ыв)ать; *problem, etc.* изуча́ть [-чи́ть]; **~er** [~rə] иссле́дователь(ница *f*) *m*
**explosi|on** [ɪk'spləʊʒn] взрыв; *of anger* вспы́шка; **~ve** [~sɪv] **1.** □ взры́вчатый; *fig.* вспы́льчивый; **2.** взры́вчатое вещество́
**exponent** [ɪk'spəʊnənt] (*advocate*) сторо́нник, представи́тель *m*; *math.* показа́тель *m* сте́пени; (*interpreter*) толкова́тель *m*
**export** **1.** ['ekspɔːt] э́кспорт, вы́воз; **2.** [ɪk'spɔːt] экспорти́ровать (*im*)*pf.*, вывози́ть [вы́везти]; **~er** [~ə] экспортёр
**expos|e** [ɪk'spəʊz] *to danger, etc.* подверга́ть [-е́ргнуть]; (*display*) вы-

E

ставля́ть [вы́ставить]; (*unmask*) разоблача́ть [-чи́ть]; *phot.* экспони́ровать (*im*)*pf*.; **~ition** [ekspə'zɪʃn] вы́ставка; изложе́ние

**exposure** [ɪk'spəʊʒə] (*unmasking*) разоблаче́ние; *phot.* экспози́ция, вы́держка; возде́йствие вне́шней среды́; ***die of ~*** умере́ть от *переохлажде́ния и т.д.*

**expound** [ɪk'spaʊnd] излага́ть [изложи́ть]; (*explain*) разъясня́ть [-ни́ть]

**express** [ɪk'spres] **1.** □ (*clearly stated*) определённый, то́чно вы́раженный; (*urgent*) сро́чный; **2. ~** (***train***) экспре́сс; **3.** *adv.* спе́шно; **4.** выража́ть [вы́разить]; **~ion** [ɪk'spreʃn] выраже́ние; (*quality*) вырази́тельность *f*; **~ive** [~ɪv] □ (*full of feeling*) вырази́тельный; (*~ of joy, etc.*) выража́ющий

**expulsion** [ɪk'spʌlʃn] изгна́ние; *form school, etc.* исключе́ние; *from country* вы́сылка

**exquisite** [ɪk'skwɪzɪt] □ изы́сканный, утончённый; *sensibility* обострённый; *torture* изощрённый

**extant** [ek'stænt] сохрани́вшийся

**extempor|aneous** [ekstempə'reɪnɪəs] □, **~ary** [ɪk'stempərərɪ] импровизи́рованный; **~e** [~pərɪ] *adv.* экспро́мтом

**extend** [ɪk'stend] *v/t.* протя́гивать [-тяну́ть]; (*spread*) распространя́ть [-ни́ть]; (*prolong*) продлева́ть [-ли́ть]; (*enlarge*) расширя́ть [-ши́рить]; *v/i.* простира́ться [простере́ться]

**extensi|on** [ɪk'stenʃn] (*enlargement*) расшире́ние; *of knowledge etc.* распростране́ние; (*continuance*) продле́ние; *arch.* пристро́йка; **~ve** [~sɪv] □ обши́рный, простра́нный

**extent** [ɪk'stent] (*area, length*) протяже́ние; (*degree*) разме́р, сте́пень *f*, ме́ра; ***to the ~ of*** в разме́ре (Р); ***to some ~*** до изве́стной сте́пени

**extenuate** [ɪk'stenjʊeɪt] (*lessen*) уменьша́ть [уме́ньшить]; (*find excuse for*) стара́ться найти́ оправда́ние; (*soften*) ослабля́ть [-а́бить]

**exterior** [ek'stɪərɪə] **1.** вне́шний, нару́жный; **2.** вне́шняя сторона́

**exterminate** [ek'stɜːmɪneɪt] (*destroy*) истребля́ть [-би́ть]; *fig.* искореня́ть [-ни́ть]

**external** [ek'stɜːnl] □ нару́жный, вне́шний

**extinct** [ɪk'stɪŋkt] уга́сший; *species, etc.* вы́мерший; *volcano etc.* потýхший

**extinguish** [ɪk'stɪŋgwɪʃ] [по]гаси́ть; [по]туши́ть; *debt* погаша́ть [погаси́ть]

**extol** [ɪk'stəʊl] превозноси́ть [-нести́]

**extort** [ɪk'stɔːt] *money* вымога́ть; *secret* выпы́тывать [вы́пытать]; **~ion** [ɪk'stɔːʃn] вымога́тельство

**extra** ['ekstrə] **1.** доба́вочный, дополни́тельный; ***~ charges*** дополни́тельная (о)пла́та; **2.** *adv.* осо́бо; осо́бенно; дополни́тельно; **3.** припла́та; **~s** *pl.* дополни́тельные расхо́ды; побо́чные дохо́ды

**extract** **1.** ['ekstrækt] экстра́кт; *from text* вы́держка, отры́вок; **2.** [ɪk'strækt] *tooth* удаля́ть [-ли́ть]; *bullet etc.* извлека́ть [-е́чь]; *chem.* экстраги́ровать; **~ion** [~kʃn] экстраги́рование; (*ancestry, origin*) происхожде́ние

**extraordinary** [ɪk'strɔːdnrɪ] чрезвыча́йный, необы́чный, экстраордина́рный, выдаю́щийся

**extrasensory** [ekstrə'sensərɪ] внечу́вственный, экстрасенсо́рный

**extravagan|ce** [ɪk'strævəgəns] экстрава́гантность *f*; (*wastefulness*) расточи́тельность *f*; (*excess*) изли́шество; **~t** [~gənt] □ расточи́тельный; сумасбро́дный, экстрава́гантный

**extrem|e** [ɪk'striːm] **1.** □ кра́йний; преде́льный; чрезвыча́йный; **2.** кра́йность *f*; ***go to ~*** пойти́ на кра́йние ме́ры; **~ity** [ɪk'stremətɪ] (*end*) оконе́чность *f*, край; кра́йность *f*; кра́йняя нужда́; кра́йняя ме́ра; **~ities** [~z] *pl.* коне́чности *f/pl.*

**extricate** ['ekstrɪkeɪt] высвобожда́ть [вы́свободить], вы́зволить *mst. pl.*; ***~ o.s.*** выпу́тываться [вы́путаться]

**exuberan|ce** [ɪg'zjuːbərəns] изоби́лие, избы́ток; **~t** [~t] *vegetation* бу́й-

ный; *speech* обильный, несдержанный; (*full of life*) полный жизни, экспансивный
**exult** [ɪɡ'zʌlt] ликовать; торжествовать
**eye** [aɪ] **1.** глаз; *of needle* ушко; ***with an ~ to*** с целью (+ *inf.*); ***catch s.o.'s ~*** поймать чей-л. взгляд; обратить на себя внимание; **2.** смотреть на (В), пристально разглядывать; **~ball** глазное яблоко; **~brow** бровь *f*; **…~d** [aɪd] …глазый; **~lash** ресница; **~lid** веко; **~sight** зрение; **~ shadow** тени для век; **~witness** свидетель, очевидец



# F

**fable** ['feɪbl] басня; *fig.* выдумка
**fabric** ['fæbrɪk] (*structure*) структура; (*cloth*) ткань *f*; **~ate** ['fæbrɪkeɪt] (*mst. fig.*) выдумывать [выдумать]; (*falsify*) [с]фабриковать
**fabulous** ['fæbjʊləs] □ баснословный; (*excellent*) великолепный
**face** [feɪs] **1.** лицо, *joc. or pej.* физиономия; *of cloth* лицевая сторона; *of watch* циферблат; ***on the ~ of it*** с первого взгляда; **2.** *v/t.* встречать смело; смотреть в лицо (Д); стоять лицом к (Д); *of window, etc.* выходить на (В); *tech.* облицовывать [-цевать]
**facetious** [fə'siːʃəs] □ шутливый
**face value** номинальная стоимость; ***take s.th. at (its) ~*** принимать [-нять] за чистую монету
**facil|itate** [fə'sɪlɪteɪt] облегчать [-чить]; **~ity** [fə'sɪlətɪ] лёгкость *f*; способность *f*; *of speech* плавность *f*
**facing** ['feɪsɪŋ] *of wall, etc.* облицовка
**fact** [fækt] факт; ***as a matter of ~*** собственно говоря; ***I know for a ~ that*** я точно знаю, что
**faction** ['fækʃn] фракция
**factor** ['fæktə] *math.* множитель; (*contributing cause*) фактор; **~y** [-rɪ] фабрика, завод
**faculty** ['fækəltɪ] способность *f*; *fig.* дар; *univ.* факультет
**fad** [fæd] (*craze*) увлечение; (*fancy*) прихоть *f*, причуда; (*fashion*) преходящая мода
**fade** [feɪd] увядать [увянуть]; постепенно уменьшать [уменьшить]; *of colo(u)r* [по]линять
**fag** [fæɡ] усталость, утомление
**fail** [feɪl] **1.** *v/i.* (*grow weak*) ослабе(-ва)ть; (*be wanting in*) недост(ав)ать; потерпеть *pf.* неудачу; *at examination* проваливаться [-литься]; ***he ~ed to do*** ему не удалось сделать (В); забы(-ва)ть; *v/t. of courage, etc.* покидать [-инуть]; **2.** *su.*: ***without ~*** наверняка; непременно; **~ing** ['feɪlɪŋ] недостаток; слабость *f*; **~ure** ['feɪljə] неудача, неуспех; провал; банкротство; неудачник *m*, -ница *f*; *tech.* повреждение, отказ
**faint** [feɪnt] **1.** □ слабый; *light* тусклый; **2.** [о]слабеть; потерять сознание (***with*** от Р); **3.** обморок, потеря сознания; **~-hearted** [feɪnt'hɑːtɪd] трусливый, малодушный
**fair**[1] [feə] **1.** *adj.* прекрасный, красивый; (*favo[u]rable*) благоприятный; *hair* белокурый; *weather* ясный; (*just*) справедливый; **2.** *adv.* честно; прямо, ясно; ***~ copy*** чистовик; ***~ play*** честная игра
**fair**[2] [~] ярмарка
**fair|ly** ['feəlɪ] справедливо; (*quite*) довольно; **~ness** ['feənɪs] справедливость *f*; красота (→ ***fair***[1]); ***in all ~*** со всей справедливостью
**fairy** ['feərɪ] фея; **~land** сказочная страна; **~ tale** сказка
**faith** [feɪθ] доверие, вера, *a. relig.*; **~ful** ['feɪθfl] верный, преданный; (*accurate*) точный, правдивый; ***yours ~ly*** преданный Вам; **~less** ['feɪθlɪs] □ вероломный
**fake** [feɪk] *sl.* **1.** подделка, фальшивка;

**2.** поддéл(ыв)ать

**falcon** ['fɔːlkən] сóкол

**fall** [fɔːl] **1.** падéние; (*decline*) упáдок; (*declivity*, *slope*) обры́в, склон; *Am.* óсень *f*; (*mst.* **~s** *pl.*) водопáд; **2.** [*irr.*] пáдать [упáсть]; спадáть [спасть]; *of water* убы́(вá)ть; **~ back** отступáть [-пи́ть]; **~ ill** *или* **sick** заболé(вá)ть; **~ out** [по]ссóриться; **~ short of** не оправдáть (ожидáний); не достигáть [-и́чь] *a.* [-и́гнуть] (цéли); **~ short** уступáть в чём-л., не хватáть [-ти́ть]; **~ to** принимáться [-ня́ться] за (В)

**fallacious** [fə'leɪʃəs] □ оши́бочный, лóжный

**fallacy** ['fæləsɪ] заблуждéние, оши́бочный вы́вод

**fallen** ['fɔːlən] *pt. p. om* **fall**

**falling** ['fɔːlɪŋ] падéние; понижéние

**fallout** ['fɔːləʊt]: **radioactive ~** радиоакти́вные осáдки

**fallow** ['fæləʊ] *adj.* вспáханный под пар

**false** [fɔːls] □ лóжный, оши́бочный; *coin* фальши́вый; *friend* верoлóмный; *teeth* искýсственный; **~hood** ['fɔːlshʊd] ложь *f*; (*falseness*) лжи́вость *f*

**falsi|fication** [fɔːlsɪfɪ'keɪʃn] поддéлка; *of theories, etc.* фальсификáция; **~fy** ['fɔːlsɪfaɪ] поддéл(ыв)ать; фальсифици́ровать

**falter** ['fɔːltə] *in walking* двигаться неувéренно; *in speech* запинáться [запнýться]; *fig.* колебáться

**fame** [feɪm] слáва; извéстность *f*; **~d** [feɪmd] извéстный, знамени́тый; **be ~ for** слáвиться (T)

**familiar** [fə'mɪlɪə] □ бли́зкий, хорошó знакóмый; (*usual*) привы́чный; **~ity** [fəmɪlɪ'ærətɪ] (*of manner*) *a. pej.* фамилья́рность *f*; (*knowledge*) осведомлённость *f*; **~ize** [fə'mɪlɪəraɪz] ознакомля́ть [-кóмить]

**family** ['fæməlɪ] семья́, семéйство; **~ tree** родословное дéрево

**fami|ne** ['fæmɪn] гóлод; **~sh**: **I feel ~ed** я умирáю от гóлода

**famous** ['feɪməs] □ знамени́тый

**fan**[1] [fæn] **1.** вéер; *tech.* вентиля́тор; **2.**: **~ o.s.** обмáхивать(ся) [-хнýть(ся)] вéером

**fan**[2] [~] *sport* болéльщик *m*, -щица *f*, фанáт; (*admirer*) поклóнник *m*, -ница *f*

**fanatic** [fə'nætɪk] **1.** (*a.* **~al** [~ɪkəl] □) фанати́чный; **2.** фанáтик *m*, -ти́чка *f*

**fanciful** ['fænsɪfl] □ прихотли́вый, причýдливый

**fancy** ['fænsɪ] **1.** фантáзия, воображéние; (*whim*) при́хоть *f*; (*love*) пристрáстие; (*inclination*) склóнность *f*; **2.** *prices* фантасти́ческий; **~ goods** *pl.* мóдные товáры *m/pl.*; **3.** воображáть [-рази́ть]; представля́ть [-áвить] себе; [по]люби́ть; [за]хотéть; **just ~!** предстáвьте себé!

**fang** [fæŋ] клык

**fantas|tic** [fæn'tæstɪk] (**~ally**) причýдливый, фантасти́чный; *coll.* невероя́тный; потрясáющий, **~y** ['fæntəsɪ] фантáзия, воображéние

**far** [fɑː] *adj.* дáльний, далёкий, отдалённый; *adv.* далекó; горáздо; **as ~ as** до (Р); **as ~ as I know** наскóлько мне извéстно; **inso~** (*Brt.* **in so ~**) **as** поскóльку; **~ away** далекó

**fare** [feə] плáта за проéзд; **~well** [fɛə'wel, feər~] **1.** прощáй(те)!; **2.** прощáние

**farfetched** [fɑː'fetʃt] *fig.* притя́нутый зá уши

**farm** [fɑːm] **1.** фéрма; **2.** обрабáтывать зéмлю; **~er** ['fɑːmə] фéрмер; **~house** жилóй дом на фéрме; **~ing** заня́тие сéльским хозя́йством, фéрмерство; **~stead** ['fɑːmsted] усáдьба

**far-off** ['fɑːrɔf] далёкий

**farthe|r** ['fɑːðə] **1.** *adv.* дáльше; **2.** *adj.* бóлее отдалённый; **~st** [~ðɪst] **1.** *adj.* сáмый далёкий, сáмый дáльний; **2.** *adv.* дáльше всегó

**fascinat|e** ['fæsɪneɪt] **очаровывать [-овать], пленять [-нить]**; **~ion** [fæsɪ'neɪʃn] очаровáние

**fashion** ['fæʃn] **1.** (*prevailing style*) мóда; стиль *m*; (*manner*) óбраз, манéра; **in** (**out of**) **~** (не)мóдный; **2.** придавáть фóрму, вид (Д **into** Р); **~able** ['fæʃnəbl] мóдный

**fast**[1] [fɑːst] (*fixed*, *firm*) про́чный, кре́пкий, твёрдый; (*quick*) бы́стрый; ***my watch is ~*** мои́ часы́ спеша́т

**fast**[2] [~] **1.** (*going without food*) пост; **2.** пости́ться

**fasten** ['fɑːsn] *v/t.* (*fix*) прикрепля́ть [-пи́ть]; (*tie*) привя́зывать [-за́ть]; *coat, etc.* застёгивать [-тегну́ть]; *door* запира́ть [-пере́ть]; *v/i.* застёгмра́ться [запере́ться]; застёгивать(ся) [-тегну́ть(ся)]; ***~ upon*** *fig.* ухвати́ться за (В); **~er** [~ə] застёжка

**fast food** фаст-фу́д

**fastidious** [fæ'stɪdɪəs] □ разбо́рчивый; *about food* привере́дливый

**fat** [fæt] **1.** жи́рный; *person* ту́чный; **2.** жир; са́ло

**fatal** ['feɪtl] рокова́й, фата́льный; (*causing death*) смерте́льный; **~ity** [fə'tælətɪ] (*doom*) обречённость *f*; (*destiny*) фата́льность *f*; (*caused by accident*) же́ртва; смерть *f*

**fate** [feɪt] рок, судьба́

**father** ['fɑːðə] оте́ц; **~hood** [~hʊd] отцо́вство; **~-in-law** ['fɑːðərɪnlɔː] *husband's* свёкор; *wife's* тесть *m*; **~less** [~lɪs] оста́вшийся без отца́; **~ly** [~lɪ] оте́ческий

**fathom** ['fæðəm] *fig.* вника́ть [вни́кнуть] в (В), понима́ть [поня́ть]

**fatigue** [fə'tiːg] **1.** утомле́ние, уста́лость *f*; **2.** утомля́ть [-ми́ть]

**fat|ness** ['fætnɪs] жи́рность *f*; **~ten** ['fætn] *animal* отка́рмливать [откорми́ть]; [рас]толсте́ть

**fatuous** ['fætʃʊəs] □ бессмы́сленный, глу́пый

**faucet** ['fɔːsɪt] *esp. Am.* водопрово́дный кран

**fault** [fɔːlt] (*shortcoming*) недоста́ток; *tech.* неиспра́вность *f*, дефе́кт; (*blame*) вина́; ***find ~ with*** прид(и)ра́ться к (Д); ***be at ~*** быть вино́вным; **~finder** приди́ра *m/f*; **~less** ['fɔːltlɪs] □ безупре́чный; **~y** ['fɔːltɪ] □ *thing* с бра́ком, десфе́ктом; *method* поро́чный

**favo(u)r** ['feɪvə] **1.** благосклóнность *f*, расположе́ние; одолже́ние, любе́зность *f*; ***do s.o. a ~*** оказа́ть *pf.* кому́-л. любе́зность; **2.** (*approve*) одобря́ть [-рить]; (*regard with goodwill*) хорошо́ относи́ться к (Д); **~able** [~rəbl] □ благоприя́тный; *opportunity* удо́бный; **~ite** ['feɪvərɪt] **1.** люби́мец *m*, -мица *f*, фавори́т; **2.** люби́мый

**fawn** [fɔːn] све́тло-кори́чневый цвет

**fax** [fæks] **1.** факс; **2.** передава́ть [-да́ть] по фа́ксу

**fear** [fɪə] **1.** страх, боя́знь *f*; (*apprehension*) опасе́ние; **2.** боя́ться (Р) ***for ~ of*** из-за боя́зни; **~ful** ['fɪəfl] □ стра́шный, ужа́сный; **~less** ['fɪəlɪs] бесстра́шный

**feasible** ['fiːzəbl] (*capable of being done*) выполни́мый, осуществи́мый; возмо́жный

**feast** [fiːst] банке́т; пир, пи́ршество; *eccl.* церко́вный *или* престо́льный пра́здник

**feat** [fiːt] по́двиг

**feather** ['feðə] перо́, ***show the white ~*** *coll.* прояви́ть тру́сость *f*; **~brained** пустоголо́вый

**feature** ['fiːtʃə] **1.** черта́; осо́бенность *f*, сво́бство; *Am.* выдаю́щаяся газе́тная статья́; **~s** *pl.* черты́лица́; **2.** *in story* фигури́ровать; *of a film* пока́зывать [-за́ть]; ***the film ~s a new actor as …*** фильм с уча́стием но́вого актёра в ро́ли …

**February** ['febrʊərɪ] февра́ль *m*

**fed** [fed] *pt. и pt. p. от* ***feed***; ***I am ~ up with …*** мне надое́л (-ла, -ло)

**federa|l** ['fedərəl] федера́льный; *in names of states* федерати́вный; **~tion** [fedə'reɪʃn] федера́ция

**fee** [fiː] *doctor's, etc.* гонора́р; *member's* взнос; *for tuition* пла́та

**feeble** ['fiːbl] □ сла́бый, хи́лый

**feed** [fiːd] **1.** *agric.* корм, фура́ж; *baby's* еда́, кормле́ние; *of a machine* пита́ние; **2.** [*irr.*] *v/t.* [по]корми́ть; пита́ть, подава́ть; *v/i.* пита́ться, корми́ться; (*graze*) пасти́сь; **~back** *tech.* обра́тная связь; **~ing bottle** де́тский рожо́к

**feel** [fiːl] **1.** [*irr.*] [по]чу́вствовать

(себя́); (*experience*) испы́тывать [-та́ть]; *by contact* ощуща́ть [ощути́ть]; (*touch*) [по]тро́гать; (*grope*) нащу́п(ыв)ать; ~ ***like doing*** быть скло́нным сде́лать; **2.**: ***get the ~ of*** привыка́ть [-ы́кнуть]; **~ing** ['fiːlɪŋ] чу́вство, ощуще́ние
**feet** [fiːt] *pl. om* ***foot 1***
**feign** [feɪn] притворя́ться [-ри́ться], симули́ровать (*im*)*pf.*
**feint** [feɪnt] (*sham offensive*) финт, диве́рсия
**fell** [fel] **1.** *pt. om* ***fall***; **2.** *tree*, *etc.* [с]руби́ть
**fellow** ['feləʊ] па́рень; (*companion*) това́рищ; *professional* колле́га, сотру́дник; *of a college* член сове́та; **~-countryman** соотéчественник; **~ship** [~ʃɪp] това́рищество
**felt**¹ [felt] *pt. и pt. p. om* ***feel***
**felt**² [~] во́йлок, фетр
**female** ['fiːmeɪl] **1.** же́нский; **2.** же́нщина; *zo.* са́мка
**feminine** ['femɪnɪn] □ же́нский; же́нственный
**fen** [fen] боло́то, топь *f*
**fence** [fens] **1.** забо́р, и́згородь *f*, огра́да; ***sit on the ~*** занима́ть нейтра́льную пози́цию; **2.** *v/t.* отгора́живать [-роди́ть]; *v/i. sport* фехтова́ть
**fencing** ['fensɪŋ] **1.** и́згородь *f*, забо́р, огра́да; *sport* фехтова́ние; **2.** *attr.* фехтова́льный
**fender** ['fendə] (*fire screen*) ками́нная решётка; *of car*, *Am.* крыло́
**ferment** **1.** ['fəːment] заква́ска, ферме́нт; *chem..* броже́ние (*a. fig.*); **2.** [fə'ment] вызыва́ть броже́ние; броди́ть; **~ation** [fɜːmen'teɪʃn] броже́ние
**fern** [fɜːn] па́поротник
**feroci|ous** [fə'rəʊʃəs] □ свире́пый; *dog* злой; **~ty** [fə'rɒsətɪ] свире́пость *f*
**ferret** ['ferɪt] **1.** *zo.* хорёк; **2.** [по]ры́ться, [по]ша́рить; ~ ***out*** вы́искивать [вы́искать]; *secret* разню́хивать [-хать]; вы́ведать *pf.*
**ferry** ['ferɪ] **1.** (*place for crossing river, etc.*) перево́з, перепра́ва; (*boat*) паро́м; **2.** перевози́ть [-везти́]; **~man** перево́зчик
**fertil|e** ['fɜːtaɪl] □ *soil* плодоро́дный; *humans, animals* плодови́тый (*a. fig.*); ~ ***imagination*** бога́тое воображе́ние; **~ity** [fə'tɪlətɪ] плодоро́дие; плодови́тость *f*; **~ize** ['fɜːtɪlaɪz] удобря́ть [удо́брить]; оплодотворя́ть [-ри́ть]; **~izer** ['fɜːtɪlaɪzə] удобре́ние
**fervent** ['fɜːvənt] горя́чий, пы́лкий
**fervor(u)r** ['fɜːvə] жар, пыл, страсть *f*
**fester** ['festə] гнои́ться
**festiv|al** ['festəvl] пра́здник; фестива́ль *m*; **~e** ['festɪv] □ пра́здничный; **~ity** [fe'stɪvətɪ] пра́зднество; торжество́
**fetch** [fetʃ] сходи́ть, съе́здить за (Т); приноси́ть [-нести́]; **~ing** [~ɪŋ] □ привлека́тельный
**fetter** ['fetə] **1.** *mst.* **~s** *pl.* пу́ты *f/pl.*; *fig.* око́вы *f/pl.*, у́зы *f/pl.*; **2.** *fig.* свя́зывать [-за́ть] по рука́м и нога́м
**feud** [fjuːd] *family* вражда́ *f*
**feudal** ['fjuːdl] □ феода́льный
**fever** ['fiːvə] лихора́дка, жар; **~ish** [~rɪʃ] □ лихора́дочный
**few** [fjuː] немно́гие; немно́го, ма́ло (Р); ***a ~*** не́сколвко (Р); ***a good ~*** дово́льно мно́го
**fiancé(e)** [fɪ'ɒnseɪ] жени́х (неве́ста)
**fiasco** [fɪ'æskəʊ] прова́л, по́лная неуда́ча, фиа́ско
**fib** [fɪb] **1.** вы́думка, нелра́вда; **2.** прив(и)ра́ть
**fiber**, *Brt.* **fibre** ['faɪbə] волокно́, нить *f*
**fickle** ['fɪkl] непостоя́нный
**fiction** ['fɪkʃn] вы́мысел, вы́думка; худо́жественная литерату́ра, беллетри́стика; ***science ~*** нау́чная фанта́стика; **~al** [~l] □ вы́мышленный
**fictitious** [fɪk'tɪʃəs] □ подло́жный, фикти́вный; вы́мышленный
**fiddle** ['fɪdl] *coll.* **1.** скри́пка; *fig. a cheat* жу́льничество; **2.** игра́ть на скри́пке; *fig.* обма́нывать
**fidelity** [fɪ'delətɪ] ве́рность *f*, пре́данность *f*; (*accuracy*) то́чность *f*
**fidget** ['fɪdʒɪt] *coll.* **1.** непосе́да; **2.** ёрзать, верте́ться; **~y** [~ɪ] суетли́вый, беспоко́йный, не́рвный; *child* непосе́дливый
**field** [fiːld] по́ле; (*meadow*) луг; *fig.* об-

ласть; ~ **events** лёгкая атлéтика; ~ **glasses** полевóй бинóкль *m*; ~ **of vision** пóле зрéния; ~**work** *geol., etc.* рабóта в пóле
**fiend** [fiːnd] дья́вол; *person* злодéй; ~**ish** ['fiːndɪʃ] □ дья́волвский, жестóкий, злой
**fierce** [fɪəs] □ свирéпый; *frost, etc.* лю́тый; *wind, etc.* си́льный; ~**ness** ['fɪəsnɪs] свирéпость *f*, лю́тость *f*
**fif|teen** [fɪf'tiːn] пятнáдцать; ~**teenth** [~θ] пятнáдцатый; ~**th** [fɪfθ] **1.** пя́тый; **2.** пя́тая часть *f*; ~**tieth** ['fɪftɪɪθ] пятидеся́тый; ~**ty** ['fɪftɪ] пятьдеся́т
**fig** [fɪg] инжи́р
**fight** [faɪt] **1.** *mil.* сражéние, бой; *between persons* дрáка; (*struggle*) борьбá; ***show*** ~ быть готóвым к борьбé; **2.** [*irr.*] *v/t.* борóться прóтив (Р); дрáться (с Т); *v/i.* сражáться [срази́ться]; (*wage war*) воевáть; борóться; ~**er** ['faɪtər] боéц; *fig.* борéц; ~**er plane** истреби́тель *m*; ~**ing** ['faɪtɪŋ] сражéние, бой; дрáка; *attr.* боевóй
**figment** ['fɪgmənt]: ~ ***of imagination*** плод воображéния
**figurative** ['fɪgjʊrətɪv] □ перенóсный, метафори́ческий
**figure** ['fɪgə] **1.** фигу́ра; *math.* числó; ци́фра; (*diagram etc.*) рису́нок; *coll* (*price*) ценá; **2.** *v/t.* представля́ть себé; рассчи́тывать [-итáть]; *Am.* считáть, полагáть; *v/i.* фигури́ровать
**filch** [fɪltʃ] [у]крáсть; *coll.* [у-, с]тащи́ть (***from*** у Р)
**file**[1] [faɪl] **1.** *tool* напи́льник; (*nail* ~) пи́лочка (для ногтéй); **2.** (*a.* ~ ***down***) подпи́ливать [-ли́ть]
**file**[2] [~] **1.** (*folder*) пáпка; *of papers* подши́вка; *for reference* картотéка; *computer* файл; **2.** регистри́ровать (*im*)*pf.*; подшивáть к дéлу
**filial** ['fɪlɪəl] □ сынóвний, дочéрний
**fill** [fɪl] **1.** наполня́ть(ся) [-óлнить(ся)]; *tooth* [за]пломби́ровать; (*satisfy*) удовлетворя́ть [-ри́ть]; *Am. an order* выполня́ть [вы́полнить]; ~ ***in*** заполня́ть [-óлнить]; **2.** достáточное коли́чество; ***eat one's*** ~ наéсться дóсыта
**fillet** ['fɪlɪt] *cul.* филé(й) *n indecl.*
**filling** ['fɪlɪŋ] наполнéние; (зубнáя) плóмба; *cul.* фарш, начи́нка; *mot.* ~ **station** бензозапрáвочная стáнция
**film** [fɪlm] **1.** (фото) плёнка; *cine.* фильм; (*thin layer*) плёнка; **2.** производи́ть киносъёмку (Р); снимáть [снять]; экранизи́ровать (*im*)*pf.*
**filter** ['fɪltə] **1.** фильтр; **2.** [про-] фильтровáть; ~**-tipped** с фи́льтром
**filth** [fɪlθ] грязь *f*; ~**y** ['fɪlθɪ] □ гря́зный (*a. fig.*); ~ ***weather*** гну́сная погóда
**fin** [fɪn] *zo.* плавни́к
**final** ['faɪnl] **1.** □ заключи́тельный; окончáтельный; **2.** *sport* финáл; ~**s** *univ.* выпускны́е экзáмены; ~**ly** [~nəlɪ] в концé концóв; (*in conclusion*) в заключéние
**financ|e** ['faɪnæns] **1.** ~**es** *pl.* финáнсы *m/pl.*; дéньги; **2.** *v/t.* финанси́ровать (*im*)*pf.*; ~**ial** [faɪ'nænʃl] финáнсовый; ~**ier** [~sɪə] финанси́ст
**finch** [fɪntʃ] *zo.* зя́блик
**find** [faɪnd] [*irr.*] **1.** находи́ть [найти́]; *by searching* оты́скивать [-кáть]; (*discover*) обнару́живать [-ить]; (*consider*) считáть [счесть]; *rhet.* обретáть [обрести́]; заст(ав)áть; **2.** нахóдка; ~**ing** ['faɪndɪŋ] *law* решéние; *pl.* вы́воды
**fine**[1] [faɪn] □ тóнкий, изя́щный; прекрáсный; ***not to put too*** ~ ***a point on it*** говоря́ напрями́к
**fine**[2] [~] **1.** штраф; пéня; **2.** [о]штрафовáть
**finesse** [fɪ'nes] деликáтность *f*, утончённость *f*; *at cards, etc.* иску́сный манёвр
**finger** ['fɪŋgə] **1.** пáлец; ***not to lift a*** ~ пáлец о пáлец не удáрить; **2.** трóгать; *an instrument* перебирáть пáльцами; ~**print** отпечáток пáльцев
**finish** ['fɪnɪʃ] **1.** *v/t.* кончáть [кóнчить]; (*complete*) завершáть [-ши́ть]; (*make complete*) отдéл(ыв)ать; *v/i.* кончáться [кóнчить(ся)]; *sport* финиши́ровать; **2.** конéц; (*polish*) отдéлка; *sport* фи́ниш
**Finn** [fɪn] финн, фи́нка, ~**ish 1.** фи́нский; **2.** фи́нский язы́к
**fir** [fɜː] ель *f*, пи́хта; ~ **cone** ['fəːkəʊn]

еловая шишка

**fire** [faɪə] **1.** огонь *m*; ***be on ~*** гореть; **2.** *v/t.* (*set fire to*) зажигать [зажечь], поджигать [-жечь]; *stove* [за]топить; *fig.* воспламенять [-нить]; (*dismiss*) увольнять [уволить]; *v/i.* (*shoot*) стрелять [выстрелить]; **~ alarm** ['faɪərəlɑːm] пожарная тревога; **~ brigade**, *Am.* **~ department** пожарная команда; **~ engine** ['faɪərendʒɪn] пожарная машина; **~ escape** ['faɪərɪskeɪp] пожарная лестница; **~ extinguisher** ['faɪərɪkstɪŋgwɪʃə] огнетушитель *m*; **~ fighter** пожарный; **~place** камин; **~plug** пожарный кран, гидрант; **~proof** огнеупорный; **~side** место около камина; **~ station** пожарное депо; **~wood** дрова *n/pl.*; **~works** *pl.* фейерверк

**firing** ['faɪərɪŋ] (*shooting*) стрельба

**firm**[1] [fɜːm] фирма

**firm**[2] [~] □ крепкий, плотный, твёрдый; (*resolute*) устойчивый; **~ness** ['fɜːmnɪs] твёрдость *f*

**first** [fɜːst] **1.** *adj.* первый; ***at ~ sight*** с первого взгляда; ***in the ~ place*** во-первых; **2.** *adv.* сперва, сначала; впервые; скорее, ***at ~*** сначало; ***~ of all*** прежде всего; **3.** начало; ***the ~*** первое число; ***from the ~*** с самого начала; **~-born** первенец; **~-class** *quality* первоклассный; *travel* первым классом; **~ly** ['fɜːstlɪ] во-первых; **~-rate** превосходный; *int.* прекрасно!

**fiscal** ['fɪskl] фискальный, финансовый

**fish** [fɪʃ] **1.** рыба; *coll.* ***odd*** (*или* ***queer***) **~** чудак; **2.** ловить рыбу; ***~ for compliments*** напрашиваться на комплименты; ***~ out*** выудить; **~bone** рыбная кость *f*

**fisherman** ['fɪʃəmən] рыбак, рыболов

**fishing** ['fɪʃɪŋ] рыбная ловля; **~ line** леса; **~ rod** удочка; (*without line*) удилище; **~ tackle** рыболовные принадлежности *f/pl.*

**fiss|ion** ['fɪʃn] *phys.* расщепление; **~ure** ['fɪʃə] трещина, расселина

**fist** [fɪst] кулак

**fit**[1] [fɪt] **1.** годный, подходящий; (*healthy*) здоровый; (*deserving*) достойный; **2.** *v/t.* подгонять [-догнать] (***to*** к Д); (*be suitable for*) подходить [подойти] к (Д); приспособлять [-пособить] (***for, to*** к Д); ***~ out*** (*equip*) снаряжать [-ядить]; (*supply*) снабжать [-бдить]; *v/i.* (*suit*) годиться; *of dress* сидеть; приспособляться [приспособиться]

**fit**[2] [~] *med.* припадок, приступ; *of generosity, etc.* порыв; ***by ~s and starts*** урывками; ***give s.o. a ~*** потрясти *pf.*

**fit|ful** ['fɪtfl] □ судорожный, порывистый; **~ter** [~ə] механик, монтёр; **~ting** [~ɪŋ] **1.** □ подходящий, годный; **2.** установка; монтаж; *of clothes* примерка; **~tings** *pl.* арматура

**five** [faɪv] **1.** пять; **2.** *in cards, bus number, etc.*; *school mark* пятёрка

**fix** [fɪks] **1.** устанавливать [-новить]; (*make fast*) укреплять [-пить]; *attention, etc.* сосредоточивать [-точить], останавливать [-новить] (на П); (*repair*) починять [-нить]; *Am.* (*prepare*) приготавливать [-товить]; *Am. hair etc.* приводить в порядок; ***~ up*** организовать (*im*)*pf.*; улаживать [уладить]; (*arrange*) устраивать [-роить]; *v/i.* затверде(ва)ть; останавливаться [-новиться] (***on*** на П); **2.** *coll.* дилемма, затруднительное положение; **~ed** [fɪkst] (*adv.* **~edly** ['fɪksɪdlɪ]) неподвижный; **~ture** ['fɪkstʃə] приспособление; арматура; (*equipment*) оборудование; ***lighting ~*** осветительное устройство

**fizzle** ['fɪzl] шипеть

**flabby** ['flæbɪ] □ вялый; *fig.* слабохарактерный

**flag**[1] [flæg] флаг, знамя *n*; ***~ of convenience*** *naut.* удобный флаг

**flag**[2] [~] **1.** (***~stone***) плита; **2.** мостить плитами

**flagrant** ['fleɪgrənt] □ вопиющий

**flagstaff** флагшток

**flair** [fleə] чутьё, нюх; (*ability*) способности *f/pl.*

**flake** [fleɪk] **1.** **~s** *of snow* снежинки

*f/pl.*; *pl.* хло́пья *m/pl.*; **2. ~ *off*** [об]лупи́ться, шелуши́ться
**flame** [fleɪm] **1.** пла́мя *n*; ого́нь *m*; *fig.* страсть *f*; **2.** горе́ть, пламене́ть; пыла́ть
**flan** [flæn] откры́тый пиро́г; ола́дья
**flank** [flæŋk] **1.** бок, сторона́; *mil.* фланг; **2.** быть располо́женным сбо́ку, на фла́нге (Р); грани́чить (с Т), примыка́ть (к Д)
**flannel** ['flænl] шерстяна́я флане́ль *f*; **~s** [-z] *pl.* флане́левые брю́ки *f/pl.*
**flap** [flæp] **1.** *of wings* взмах; (*sound*) хло́панье; *of hat* у́хо; ***get into a ~*** засуети́ться *pf.*, паникова́ть; взма́хивать [-хну́ть]; **2.** *v/t.* (*give a light blow to*) шлёпать [-пнуть]; легко́ ударя́ть; *v/i.* свиса́ть; *of flag* развева́ться [-ве́яться]
**flare** [fleə] **1.** горе́ть я́рким пла́менем; ***~ up*** вспы́хивать [-хнуть]; *fig.* вспыли́ть *pf.*; **2.** вспы́шка пла́мени; сигна́льная раке́та
**flash** [flæʃ] **1.** → ***flashy***; **2.** вспы́шка; *fig.* про́блеск; ***in a ~*** мгнове́нно; **3.** сверка́ть [-кну́ть]; вспы́хивать [-хнуть]; пронести́сь *pf.* (*a.* ***~ by***); **~light** *phot.* вспы́шка; *Am.* карма́нный фона́рик *m*; **~y** показно́й; безвку́сный
**flask** [flɑːsk] фля́жка
**flat** [flæt] **1.** □ (*level*) пло́ский; (*smooth*) ро́вный; (*dull*) ску́чный; *voice* глухой; ***fall ~*** не вызыва́ть [вы́звать] интере́са; не име́ть успе́ха; ***~ tire*** (*Brt.* ***tyre***) спу́щенная ши́на; **2.** (*apartment*) кварти́ра; пло́скость *f*; *land* равни́на, низи́на; *mus.* бемо́ль *m*; **~iron** утю́г; **~ten** ['flætn] де́лать(ся) пло́ским, ро́вным
**flatter** ['flætə] [по]льсти́ть (Д); ***I am ~ed*** я польщена́; **~er** [-rər] льстец *m*, льсти́ца *f*; **~ing** [-rɪŋ] ле́стный; **~y** [-rɪ] лесть *f*
**flaunt** [flɔːnt] выставля́ть [вы́ставить] на пока́з, афиши́ровать
**flavo(u)r** ['fleɪvə] **1.** (*taste*) вкус; *fig.* при́вкус; **2.** приправля́ть [-ра́вить]; придава́ть запах, при́вкус (Д); **~ing** [-rɪŋ] припра́ва; **~less** [-lɪs] безвку́сный
**flaw** [flɔː] (*crack*) тре́щина, щель *f*; *in character, etc.* недоста́ток; (*defect*) дефе́кт, изъя́н; **~less** ['flɔːlɪs] безупре́чный
**flax** [flæks] лён
**flea** [fliː] блоха́
**fled** [fled] *pt. и pt. p. от* ***flee***
**flee** [fliː] [*irr.*] бежа́ть, спаса́ться бе́гством
**fleece** [fliːs] **1.** ове́чья шерсть *f*; **2.** [о]стри́чь; *fig.* обдира́ть [ободра́ть]
**fleet**[1] [fliːt] □ бы́стрый
**fleet**[2] [~] флот
**flesh** [fleʃ] *soft or edible parts of animal bodies* мя́со; *body as opposed to mind or soul* плоть *f*; *of fruit or plant* мя́коть *f*; **~y** [~ɪ] мяси́стый; то́лстый
**flew** [fluː] *pt. от* ***fly***
**flexib|ility** [fleksə'bɪlətɪ] ги́бкость *f*; **~le** ['fleksəbl] □ ги́бкий; *fig.* пода́тливый, усту́пчивый
**flicker** ['flɪkə] **1.** *of light* мерца́ние; *of movement* трепета́ние; **2.** мерца́ть; трепета́ть *of smile* мелька́ть [-кну́ть]
**flight**[1] [flaɪt] полёт, перелёт; *of birds* стая́; ***~ number*** но́мер ре́йса
**flight**[2] [~] бе́гство; ***put to ~*** обраща́ть в бе́гство
**flighty** ['flaɪtɪ] □ ве́треный
**flimsy** ['flɪmzɪ] (*not strong*) непро́чный; (*thin*) то́нкий; ***~ argument*** малоубеди́тельный до́вод
**flinch** [flɪntʃ] вздра́гивать [вздро́гнуть]; отпря́дывать [отпря́нуть]
**fling** [flɪŋ] **1.** бросо́к; весе́лье; ***have a ~*** кутну́ть, пожи́ть в своё удово́льствие; **2.** [*irr.*] *v/i.* кида́ться [ки́нуться], броса́ться [бро́ситься]; *v/t.* (*throw*) кида́ть [ки́нуть], броса́ть [бро́сить]; ***~ open*** распа́хивать [-хну́ть]
**flint** [flɪnt] кре́мень *m*
**flippan|cy** ['flɪpənsɪ] легкомы́слие; **~t** □ легкомы́сленный
**flirt** [flɜːt] **1.** коке́тка; **2.** флиртова́ть, коке́тничать; **~ation** [flɜː'teɪʃn] флирт
**flit** [flɪt] порха́ть [-хну́ть] (*a. fig.*); *of smile, etc.* пробежа́ть

**float** [fləʊt] **1.** *on fishing line* поплаво́к; **2.** *v/t. timber* сплавля́ть [-а́вить]; *fin.* вводи́ть [ввести́] пла́вающий курс; *v/i. of object* пла́вать, [по]плы́ть; держа́ться на воде́; *fig.* плыть по тече́нию

**flock** ['flɒk] **1.** *of sheep* ста́до; *of birds* ста́я; **2.** стека́ться [сте́чься]; держа́ться вме́сте

F

**flog** [flɒg] [вы́]поро́ть; ~ ***a dead horse*** стара́ться возроди́ть безнадёжно устаре́лое де́ло

**flood** [flʌd] **1.** (*a.* ~ ***tide***) прили́в, подъём воды́; (*inundation*) наводне́ние, полово́дье, разли́в; *Bibl.* ***the*** ♀ всеми́рный пото́п; **2.** поднима́тся [-ня́ться], выступа́ть из берего́в; (*inundate*) затопля́ть [-пи́ть]; *the market* наводня́ть [-ни́ть]; **~gate** шлюз

**floor** [flɔː] **1.** пол; (*stor(e)y*) эта́ж; ***take the*** ~ *parl.* взять *pf.* сло́во; **2.** настила́ть пол; *coll.* (*knock down*) сбива́ть [сбить] с ног; *fig.* (*nonplus*) [по]ста́вить в тупи́к; **~ing** ['flɔːrɪŋ] насти́лка поло́в; пол

**flop** [flɒp] **1.** шлёпаться [-пнуться]; плю́хать(ся) [-хнуть(-ся)]; *Am.* потерпе́ть *pf.* фиа́ско; **2.** *sl.* прова́л; **~py** [-ɪ]: ~ ***disk*** *comput.* ги́бкий диск

**florid** ['flɒrɪd] □ цвети́стый (*a. fig.*)

**florist** ['flɒrɪst] продаве́ц цвето́в

**flounce** [flaʊns] *out of room* броса́ться [бро́ситься]

**flounder**[1] *zo.* ['flaʊndə] ка́мбала

**flounder**[2] [~] *esp. in water* бара́хтаться; *fig.* [за]пу́таться

**flour** [flaʊə] мука́

**flourish** ['flʌrɪʃ] *v/i.* пы́шно расти́; (*prosper*) процвета́ть, преуспева́ть; *v/t.* (*wave*) разма́хивать (Т)

**flout** [flaʊt] попира́ть [попра́ть]; пренебрега́ть [-ре́чь] (Т)

**flow** [fləʊ] **1.** тече́ние; пото́к; (*a. of speech*) струя́; *of sea* прпли́в; **2.** течь; струи́ться; ли́ться

**flower** ['flaʊə] **1.** цвето́к; *fig.* цвет; ***in*** ~ в цвету́; **2.** цвести́; **~y** [-rɪ] *fig.* цвети́стый

**flown** [fləʊn] *pt. p. om* ***fly***

**flu** [fluː] = ***influenza*** *coll.* грипп

**fluctuat|e** ['flʌktʃʊeɪt] колеба́ться; **~ion** [flʌktʃʊ'eɪʃn] колеба́ние

**flue** [fluː] дымохо́д

**fluen|cy** ['fluːənsɪ] *fig.* пла́вность *f*, бе́глость *f*; **~t** [-t] □ пла́вный, бе́глый; ***she speaks*** ~ ***German*** она́ бе́гло говори́т по-неме́цки

**fluff** [flʌf] пух, пушо́к, **~y** ['flʌfɪ] пуши́стый

**fluid** ['fluːɪd] **1.** жи́дкость *f*; **2.** жи́дкий; *fig.* неопределённый

**flung** [flʌŋ] *pt. и pt. p. om* ***fling***

**flurry** ['flʌrɪ] волне́ние, сумато́ха

**flush** [flʌʃ] **1.** румя́нец; *of shame* кра́ска; *of feeling* прили́в; **2.** *v/t. toilet* спуска́ть [-сти́ть] во́ду (в убо́рной); (*rinse or wash clean*) промыва́ть [-мы́ть]; *v/i.* [по]карсне́ть

**fluster** ['flʌstə] **1.** сует́а, волне́ние; **2.** [вз]волнова́ть(ся)

**flute** [fluːt] *mus.* фле́йта

**flutter** ['flʌtə] **1.** порха́ние; *of leaves*, *a. fig.* тре́пет; *fig.* волне́ние; **2.** *v/i.* маха́ть [-хну́ть]; *in the wind* развева́ться; порха́ть [-хну́ть]

**flux** [flʌks] *fig.* тече́ние; пото́к; ***in a state of*** ~ в состоя́нии непреры́вного измене́ния

**fly** [flaɪ] **1.** му́ха; ***a*** ~ ***in the ointment*** ло́жка дёгтя в бо́чке мёда; **2.** [*irr.*] лета́ть, [по]лете́ть; пролета́ть [-ете́ть]; (*hurry*) [по]спеши́ть; *of flag* поднима́ть [-ня́ть]; *ae.* пилоти́ровать; ~ ***at*** набра́сываться [-ро́ситься] (с бра́нью) на (В); ~ ***into a passion*** вспылть *pf.*

**flying** ['flaɪɪŋ] лета́тельный; лётный; ~ ***saucer*** лета́ющая таре́лка; ~ ***visit*** мимолётный визи́т

**fly|over** путепро́вод; эстака́да; **~weight** *boxer* наилегча́йший вес; **~wheel** махови́к

**foal** [fəʊl] жеребёнок

**foam** [fəʊm] **1.** пе́на; ~ ***rubber*** пенорези́на; **2.** [вс]пе́ниться; *of horse* взмы́ли(ва)ться; **~y** ['fəʊmɪ] пе́нящийся; взмы́ленный

**focus** ['fəʊkəs] **1.** *phot.*, *phys.* фо́кус; **2.** быть в фо́кусе; сосредото́чи(ва)ть (*a. fig.*)

**fodder** ['fɒdə] фура́ж, корм
**foe** [fəʊ] враг
**fog** [fɒg] **1.** тума́н; (*bewilderment*) замеша́тельство; **2.** [за]тума́нить; *fig.* напуска́ть [-сти́ть] тума́ну; озада́чи(ва)ть; **~gy** ['fɒgɪ] □ тума́нный
**foible** ['fɔɪbl] *fig.* сла́бость *f*
**foil**[1] [fɔɪl] (*thin metal*) фольга́; (*contrast*) противопоставле́ние
**foil**[2] [~] **1.** расстра́ивать пла́ны (Р); **2.** рапи́ра
**fold** [fəʊld] **1.** скла́дка, сгиб; **2.** *v/t.* скла́дывать [сложи́ть]; сгиба́ть [согну́ть]; *one's arms* скре́щивать [-ести́ть]; **~er** ['fəʊldə] *for papers* па́пка; брошю́ра
**folding** ['fəʊldɪŋ] складно́й; ***~ doors*** двуство́рчатые две́ри; **~ chair** складно́й стул; **~ umbrella** складно́й зо́нтик
**foliage** ['fəʊlɪɪdʒ] листва́
**folk** [fəʊk] наро́д, лю́ди *m/pl.*; **~lore** ['fəʊklɔː] фолькло́р; **~song** наро́дная пе́сня
**follow** ['fɒləʊ] сле́довать (за Т *or* Д); (*watch*) следи́ть (за Т); (*pursue*) пресле́довать (В); (*engage in*) занима́ться [-ня́ться] (Т); (*understand*) понима́ть [-ня́ть]; ***~ suit*** сле́довать приме́ру; **~er** ['fɒləʊə] после́дователь(ница *f*) *m*; (*admirer*) покло́нник; **~ing** ['fɒləʊɪŋ] сле́дующий
**folly** ['fɒlɪ] безрассу́дство, глу́пость *f*, безу́мие
**fond** [fɒnd] □ не́жный, лю́бящий, ***be ~ of*** люби́ть (В)
**fond|le** ['fɒndl] [при]ласка́ть; **~ness** [~nɪs] не́жность *f*, любо́вь *f*
**food** [fuːd] пи́ща, еда́; **~stuffs** *pl.* (пищевы́е) проду́кты *m/pl.*
**fool** [fuːl] **1.** дура́к, глупе́ц; ***make a ~ of s.o.*** [о]дура́чить кого́-л.; **2.** *v/t.* обма́нывать [-ну́ть]; *v/i.* [по]дура́читься; ***~ about*** валя́ть дурака́
**fool|ery** ['fuːlərɪ] дура́чество; **~hardy** ['fuːlhɑːdɪ] □ безрассу́дно хра́брый; **~ish** ['fuːlɪʃ] глу́пый, неразу́мный; **~ishness** [~nɪs] глу́пость *f*; **~proof** безопа́сный; безотка́зный
**foot** [fʊt] **1.** (*pl.* **feet**) нога́, ступня́; (*base*) основа́ние; *of furniture* но́жка; ***on ~*** пешко́м; **2.** *v/t.* (*mst.* ***~ up***) подсчи́тывать [-ита́ть]; ***~ the bill*** заплати́ть по счёту; ***~ it*** идти́ пешко́м; **~ball** футбо́л; **~fall** шаг; звук шаго́в; **~gear** *coll.* о́бувь *f*; **~hold** опо́ра (*a. fig.*)
**footing** ['fʊtɪŋ] опо́ра; ***on a friendly ~*** быть на дру́жеской ноге́; ***lose one's ~*** оступа́ться [-пи́ться]
**foot|lights** *pl. thea.* ра́мпа; **~path** тропи́нка; тропа́; **~print** след; **~sore** со стёртыми нога́ми; **~step** по́ступь *f*; шаг; ***follow in s.o.'s ~s*** идти́ по чьи́м-л. стопа́м; **~wear** о́бувь *f*
**for** [fə; *strong* fɔː] *prp. mst.* для (Р); ра́ди (Р); за (В); в направле́нии (Р), к (Д); из-за (Р), по причи́не (Р), всле́дствие; в тече́ние (Р); в продолже́ние (Р); ***~ three days*** в тече́ние трёх дней; уже́ три дня; вме́сто (Р); в обме́н на (В); ***~ all that*** несмотря́ на всё э́то; ***~ my part*** с мое́й стороны́; **2.** *cj.* так как, потому́ что, и́бо
**forbad**(**e**) [fə'bæd] *pt. om* ***forbid***
**forbear** [fɔː'beə] [*irr.*] (*be patient*) быть терпели́вый; (*refrain from*) возде́рживаться [-жа́ться] (***from*** от Р)
**forbid** [fə'bɪd] [*irr.*] запреща́ть [-ети́ть]; **~den** [~n] *pt. p. om* ***forbid***; **~ing** [~ɪŋ] □ (*threatening*) угрожа́ющий
**forbor|e** [fɔː'bɔː] *pt. om* ***forbear***, **~ne** [~n] *pt. p. om* ***forbear***
**force** [fɔːs] **1.** си́ла; (*violence*) наси́лие; (*constraint*) принужде́ние; (*meaning*) смысл, значе́ние; ***armed ~s*** *pl.* вооружённые си́лы *f/pl.*; ***come into ~*** вступа́ть в си́лу; **2.** заставля́ть [-а́вить], принужда́ть [-уди́ть]; (*get by force*) брать си́лой; ***join ~s*** объединя́ть [-ни́ть] уси́лия; ***~ open*** взла́мывать [взлома́ть]; **~d** [~t]: ***~ landing*** вы́нужденная поса́дка; **~ful** [~fl] □ си́льный, де́йственный; *argument* убеди́тельный
**forcible** ['fɔːsəbl] □ (*using force*) наси́льственный; (*convincing*) убеди́тельный
**ford** [fɔːd] **1.** брод; **2.** переходи́ть вброд
**fore** [fɔː] **1.** *adv.* впереди́; **2.** *adj.* пере́-

F

дний; **~bode** [fɔː'bəʊd] предвеща́ть; (*have a feeling*) предчу́вствовать; **~boding** предчу́вствие; **~cast 1.** ['fɔː-kɑːst] предсказа́ние; ***weather ~*** прогно́з пого́ды; **2.** [fɔː'kɑːst] [*irr.* (***cast***)] [с]де́лать (дава́ть [дать]) прогно́з; предска́зывать [-каза́ть] **~father** пре́док; **~finger** указа́тельный па́лец; **~gone** [fɔː'gɒn]: ***it's a ~ conclusion*** э́то предрешённый исхо́д; **~ground** пере́дний план; **~head** ['fɔːrɪd] лоб

F

**foreign** ['fɒrɪn] иностра́нный; *Brt.* ***the ♀ Office*** Министе́рство иностра́нных дел; ***~ policy*** вне́шняя поли́тика; **~er** [~ə] иностра́нец *m*, -нка *f*

**fore|lock** ['fɔːlɒk] прядь воло́с на лбу; **~man** бригади́р; ма́стер; **~most** пере́дний, передово́й; **~runner** предве́стник *m*, -ица *f*; **~see** [fɔː'siː] [*irr.* (***see***)] предви́деть; **~sight** ['fɔːsaɪt] предви́дение; (*provident care*) преду-смотри́тельность *f*

**forest** ['fɒrɪst] лес

**forestall** [fɔː'stɔːl] (*avert*) предупрежда́ть [-упреди́ть]; (*do s.th. first*) опережа́ть [-ди́ть]

**forest|er** ['fɒrɪstə] лесни́к, лесни́чий; **~ry** [~trɪ] лесни́чество, лесово́дство

**fore|taste** ['fɔːteɪst] **1.** предвкуше́ние; **2.** предвкуша́ть [-уси́ть]; **~tell** [fɔː'tel] [*irr.* (***tell***)] предска́зывать [-за́ть]

**forever** [fə'revə] навсегда́

**forfeit** ['fɔːfɪt] **1.** штраф; *in game* фант; **2.** [по]плати́ться (Т); *right* утра́чивать [-а́тить]

**forgave** [fə'geɪv] *pt. от* ***forgive***

**forge**[1] [fɔːdʒ] (*mst.* ***~ ahead***) насто́йчиво продвига́ться вперёд

**forge**[2] [~] **1.** ку́зница; **2.** кова́ть; *signature, etc.* подде́л(ыв)ать; **~ry** ['fɔːdʒərɪ] подде́лка; *of document* подло́г

**forget** [fə'get] [*irr.*] забы́(ва́)ть; **~ful** [~fl] □ забы́вчивый; **~-me-not** [~mɪnɒt] незабу́дка

**forgiv|e** [fə'gɪv] [*irr.*] проща́ть [прости́ть]; **~en** [fə'gɪvən] *pt. p. от* **~**; **~eness** [~nɪs] проще́ние; **~ing** [~ɪŋ] всепроща́ющий; □ великоду́шный, снисходи́тельный

**forgo** [fɔː'gəʊ] [*irr.* (***go***)] возде́рживаться [-жа́ться] от (Р), отка́зываться [-за́ться] от (Р)

**forgot**, **~ten** [fə'gɒt(n)] *pt. a. pt. p. от* ***forget***

**fork** [fɔːk] ви́лка; *agric.* ви́лы *f/pl.*; *mus.* камерто́н; *of road* разветвле́ние

**forlorn** [fə'lɔːn] забро́шенный, несча́стный

**form** [fɔːm] **1.** фо́рма; фигу́ра; (*document*) бланк; *Brt. educ.* класс; ***matter of ~*** чи́стая форма́льность; **2.** обра-зо́вывать(ся) [-ова́ть(ся)]; составля́ть [-а́вить]; (*create*) создава́ть [-а́ть]; (*organize*) организо́вывать [-ва́ть]; [с]формирова́ть

**formal** ['fɔːml] □ форма́льный; официа́льный; **~ity** [fɔː'mælətɪ] форма́льность *f*

**formation** [fɔː'meɪʃn] образова́ние; формирова́ние; *mil.* строй; (*structure*) строе́ние

**former** ['fɔːmə] пре́жний, бы́вший; предше́ствующий; ***the ~*** пе́рвый; **~ly** [~lɪ] пре́жде

**formidable** ['fɔːmɪdəbl] □ гро́зный; *size* грома́дный; (*difficult*) тру́дный

**formula** ['fɔːmjʊlə] фо́рмула; **~te** [~leɪt] формули́ровать (*im*)*pf.*, *pf. a.* [с-]

**forsake** [fə'seɪk] [*irr.*] оставля́ть [-а́вить], покида́ть [-и́нуть]

**forswear** [fɔː'sweə] [*irr.* (***swear***)] (*give up*) отка́зываться [-за́ться] от (Р)

**fort** [fɔːt] *mil.* форт

**forth** [fɔːθ] *adv.* вперёд; да́льше; впредь; ***and so ~*** и так да́лее; **~coming** предстоя́щий

**fortieth** ['fɔːtɪɪθ] сороково́й; сорокова́я часть *f*

**forti|fication** [fɔːtɪfɪ'keɪʃn] укрепле́ние; **~fy** ['fɔːtɪfaɪ] *mil.* укрепля́ть [-пи́ть]; *fig.* подкрепля́ть [-пи́ть]; ***~ o.s.*** подкрепля́ться [-пи́ться] (***with*** Т); **~tude** [~tjuːd] си́ла ду́ха, сто́йкость *f*

**fortnight** ['fɔːtnaɪt] две неде́ли *f/pl.*

**fortress** ['fɔːtrɪs] кре́пость *f*

**fortuitous** [fɔː'tjuːɪtəs] □ случа́йный

**fortunate** ['fɔːtʃənət] счастли́вый, уда́чный; ***I was ~ enough*** мне посчастли́вилось; **~ly** *adv.* к сча́стью

**fortune** ['fɔːtʃən] судьба́; (*prosperity*) бога́тство, состоя́ние; ***good*** (***bad***) **~** (не)уда́ча; **~ teller** гада́лка

**forty** ['fɔːtɪ] со́рок

**forward** ['fɔːwəd] **1.** *adj.* пере́дний; (*familiar*) развя́зный, де́рзкий; *spring* ра́нний; **2.** *adv.* вперёд, да́льше; впредь; **3.** *sport* напада́ющий, фо́вард; **4.** перес(ы-) ла́ть, направля́ть [-а́вить] (по но́вому а́дресу)

**forwent** [fɔː'went] *pt. om* ***forgo***

**foster** ['fɒstər] воспи́тывать [-ита́ть]; (*look after*) присма́тривать [-мотре́ть] (за Т); *fig. hope etc.* пита́ть; (*cherish*) леле́ять; (*encourage*) поощря́ть [-ри́ть]; благоприя́тствовать (Д)

**fought** [fɔːt] *pt. u pt. p. om* ***fight***

**foul** [faʊl] **1.** □ (*dirty*) гря́зный; (*loathsome*) отврати́тельный (*a. weather*); нече́стный; **2.** *sport* наруше́ние пра́вил; **~ play** гру́бая игра́, **3.** [за]па́чкать(ся); (*pollute*) загрязня́ть [-ни́ть], допусти́ть *pf.* наруше́ние

**found** [faʊnd] **1.** *pt. u pt. p. om* ***find***; **2.** (*lay the foundation of*) закла́дывать [заложи́ть]; (*establish*) осно́вывать (основа́ть); учрежда́ть [-еди́ть]

**foundation** [faʊn'deɪʃn] фунда́мент, осно́ва; *for research, etc.* фонд

**founder** ['faʊndə] основа́тель(ница *f*) *m*; *of society* учреди́тель(ница *f*) *m*

**foundry** ['faʊndrɪ] *tech.* лите́йный цех

**fountain** ['faʊntɪn] фонта́н; **~ pen** автору́чка

**four** [fɔː] **1.** четы́ре; **2.** четвёрка (→ ***five 2.***); **~teen** [ˌfɔː'tiːn] четы́рнадцать; **~teenth** [-θ] четы́рнадцатый; **~th** [fɔːθ] **1.** четвёртый; **2.** че́тверть *f*

**fowl** [faʊl] дома́шняя пти́ца

**fox** [fɒks] **1.** лиси́ца, лиса́; **2.** [с]хитри́ть; обма́нывать [-ну́ть]; ***the question ~ed me*** вопро́с поста́вил меня́ в тупи́к; **~y** ['fɒksɪ] хи́трый

**foyer** ['fɔɪeɪ] фойе́ *n indecl.*

**fraction** ['frækʃn] *math.* дробь *f*; (*small part or amount*) части́ца

**fracture**['fræktʃə] **1.** тре́щина, изло́м; *med.* перело́м; **2.** [с]лома́ть (*a. med.*)

**fragile** ['frædʒaɪl] хру́пкий (*a. fig.*), ло́мкий

**fragment** ['frægmənt] обло́мок, оско́лок; *of text* отры́вок; **~ary** [-ərɪ] фрагмента́рный; (*not complete*) отры́вочный

**fragran|ce** ['freɪgrəns] арома́т; **~t** [-t] □ арома́тный

**frail** [freɪl] *in health* хру́пкий; хи́лый, боле́зненный; *morally* сла́бый

**frame** [freɪm] **1.** *anat.* скеле́т, о́стов; телосложе́ние; *of picture, etc.* ра́мка, ра́ма; *of spectacles* опра́ва; ***~ of mind*** настрое́ние; **2.** (*construct*) [по]стро́ить, выраба́тывать [вы́работать]; вставля́ть в ра́му; **~work** *tech.* ра́ма; карка́с; *fig.* структу́ра; ра́мки *f/pl.*

**franchise** ['fræntʃaɪz] пра́во уча́ствовать в вы́борах; *comm.* привиле́гия; лице́нзия

**frank** [fræŋk] □ и́скренний, открове́нный

**frankfurter** ['fræŋkfɜːtə] соси́ска

**frankness** ['fræŋknɪs] открове́нность *f*

**frantic** ['fræntɪk] (***~ally***) безу́мный; *efforts, etc.* отча́янный

**fratern|al** [frə'tɜːnl] □ бра́тский; *adv.* по-бра́тски; **~ity** [-nətɪ] бра́тство; *Am. univ.* студе́нческая организа́ция

**fraud** [frɔːd] обма́н, моше́нничество; **~ulent** ['frɔːdjʊlənt] □ обма́нный, моше́ннический

**fray**[1] [freɪ] дра́ка; (*quarrel*) ссо́ра

**fray**[2] [~] обтрепа́ться

**freak** [friːk] *of nature* капри́з, причу́да; *person, animal* уро́д; (*enthusiast*) фана́т; ***film ~*** киноман́

**freckle** ['frekl] весну́шка; **~d** [~d] весну́шчатый

**free** [friː] **1.** □ *com.* свобо́дный, во́льный; (*not occupied*) неза́нятый; (***~*** *of charge*) беспла́тный; ***give s.o. a ~ hand*** предоста́вить по́лную свобо́ду де́йствий; ***he is ~ to*** он во́лен (+ *inf.*); ***make ~ to*** *inf.* позволя́ть себе́; ***set ~*** выпуска́ть на свобо́ду; **2.** освобожда́ть [-боди́ть]; **~dom** ['friːdəm] свобо́да;

~holder свобо́дный со́бственник; ♀mason масо́н; ~style *sport* во́льный стиль; ~ trade area свобо́дная экономи́ческая зо́на

**freez|e** [fri:z] [*irr.*] *v/i.* замерза́ть [замёрзнуть]; (*congeal*) засты́(ва́)ть; мёрзнуть; *v/t.* замора́живать [-ро́зить]; ~er ['fri:zə] *domestic appliance* морози́льник; ~ing **1.** □ леденя́щий; **2.** замора́живание; замерза́ние; ~ ***point*** то́чка замерза́ния

**freight** [freɪt] **1.** фрахт, груз; (*cost*) сто́имость перево́зки; **2.** [по]грузи́ть; [за]фрахтова́ть; ~ car *Am. rail.* това́рный ваго́н; ~ train *Am.* това́рный по́езд/соста́в

**French** [frentʃ] **1.** францу́зский; ***take ~ leave*** уйти́, не проща́ясь (*или* по-англи́йски); **2.** францу́зский язы́к; ***the ~*** францу́зы *pl.*; ~man ['frentʃmən] францу́з; ~woman ['frentʃwʊmən] францу́женка

**frenz|ied** ['frenzɪd] безу́мный, неисто́вый; ~y [~zɪ] безу́мие, неи́стовство

**frequen|cy** ['fri:kwənsɪ] частота́ (*a. phys.*); ча́стое повторе́ние; ~t **1.** [~t] □ ча́стый; **2.** [fri:'kwənt] регуля́рно посеща́ть

**fresh** [freʃ] □ све́жий; но́вый; чи́стый; *Am.* развя́зный, дёрзкий; ***~ water*** пре́сная вода́; ***make a ~ start*** нача́ть *pf.* всё снача́ла; ~en ['freʃn] освежа́ть [-жи́ть]; *of the wind* [по]свеже́ть; ~man [~mən] (*firstyear student*) первоку́рсник; ~ness [~nɪs] све́жесть *f*

**fret** [fret] **1.** волне́ние, раздраже́ние; **2.** беспоко́ить(ся), [вз]волнова́ть(ся); (*wear away*) подта́чивать [-точи́ть]

**fretful** ['fretfl] □ раздражи́тельный, капри́зный

**friction** ['frɪkʃn] тре́ние (*a. fig.*)

**Friday** ['fraɪdɪ] пя́тница

**fridge** [frɪdʒ] *coll.* холоди́льник

**friend** [frend] прия́тель(ница *f*) *m*, друг, подру́га; ***make ~s*** подружи́ться; ~ly [~lɪ] дру́жеский; ~ship [~ʃɪp] дру́жба

**frigate** ['frɪgət] фрега́т

**fright** [fraɪt] испу́г; *fig.* (*scarecrow*) пу́гало, страши́лище; ~en ['fraɪtn] [ис]пуга́ть; (~*en away*) вспу́гивать [-гну́ть]; ***~ed at*** *или* ***of*** испу́ганный (Т); ~ful [~fl] □ стра́шный, ужа́сный

**frigid** ['frɪdʒɪd] □ холо́дный

**frill** [frɪl] обо́рка

**fringe** [frɪndʒ] **1.** бахрома́; *of hair* чёлка; *of forest* опу́шка; ***~ benefits*** дополни́тельные льго́ты; **2.** отде́лывать бахромо́й; *with trees, etc.* окаймля́ть [-ми́ть]

**frisk** [frɪsk] резви́ться; ~y ['frɪskɪ] □ ре́звый, игри́вый

**fritter** ['frɪtə]: ***~ away*** транжи́рить; растра́чиваться

**frivol|ity** [frɪ'vɒlətɪ] легкомы́слие; фриво́льность *f*; ~ous ['frɪvələs] □ легкомы́сленный; несерьёзный

**frizzle** ['frɪzl] *of hair* завива́ть(ся) [-ви́ть(ся)]; *with a sizzle* жа́рить(ся) с шипе́нием

**fro** [frəʊ]: ***to and ~*** взад и вперёд

**frock** [frɒk] да́мское или де́тское пла́тье; *monk's habit* ря́са

**frog** [frɒg] лягу́шка

**frolic** ['frɒlɪk] **1.** ша́лость *f*; весе́лье; **2.** резви́ться; ~some [~səm] □ игри́вый, ре́звый

**from** [frəm; *strong* frɒm] *prp.* от (Р); из (Р); с (Р); по (Д); ***defend ~*** защища́ть от (Р); ***~ day to day*** со дня на́ день

**front** [frʌnt] **1.** фаса́д; пере́дняя сторона́; *mil.* фронт; ***in ~ of*** пе́ред (Т); впереди́ (Р); **2.** пере́дний; **3.** (*face*) выходи́ть на (В) (*a.* ***~ on***); ~al ['frʌntl] лобово́й; *anat.* ло́бный; *attack, etc.* фронта́льный; ~ier ['frʌntɪə] **1.** грани́ца; **2.** пограни́чный

**frost** [frɒst] **1.** моро́з; **2.** *plants* поби́ть моро́зом; ~bite обмороже́ние; ~y ['frɒstɪ] □ моро́зный; *fig.* (*unfriendly*) ледяно́й

**froth** [frɒθ] **1.** пе́на; **2.** [вс-, за]пе́нить(ся); ~y ['frɒθɪ] пе́нистый

**frown** [fraʊn] **1.** хму́рый взгляд; **2.** *v/i.* [на]хму́риться; ***~ on*** относи́ться [-нести́сь] неодобри́тельно

**froze** [frəʊz] *pt. от* ***freeze***; ~n [~n] **1.** *pt. p. от* ***freeze***; **2.** замёрзший; *meat, etc.* заморо́женный

**frugal** ['fru:gl] □ *person* бережли́вый;

*meal* скро́мный; *with money etc.* эконо́мный
**fruit** [fru:t] **1.** плод (*a. fig.*); фрукт *mst. pl.*; ***dried ~*** сухофру́кты; **2. *bear ~*** плодоноси́ть, дава́ть плоды́; **~ful** ['fru:tfl] *fig.* плодотво́рный; **~less** [-lɪs] □ беспло́дный
**frustrat|e** [frʌ'streɪt] *plans* расстра́ивать [-ро́ить]; *efforts* де́лать тще́тным; **~ed** [-ɪd] обескура́женный, неудовлетворённый; **~ion** [frʌ'streɪʃn] расстро́йство, *of hopes* круше́ние
**fry** [fraɪ] [за-, под]жа́рить(ся); **~ing pan** ['fraɪɪŋpæn] сковорода́
**fudge** [fʌdʒ] (*sweet*) пома́дка
**fuel** [fju:əl] **1.** то́пливо; **2.** *mot.* горю́чее; ***add ~ to the fire*** подлива́ть ма́сла в ого́нь
**fugitive** ['fju:dʒətɪv] (*runaway*) бегле́ц; *from danger, persecution, etc.* бе́женец *m*, -нка *f*
**fulfil(l)** [fʊl'fɪl] выполня́ть [вы́полнить], осуществля́ть [-ви́ть]; **~ment** [-mənt] осуществле́ние, выполне́ние
**full** [fʊl] **1.** □ по́лный; *hour* це́лый; **2.** *adv.* вполне́; как раз; о́чень; **3. *in ~*** по́лностью; ***to the ~*** в по́лной ме́ре; **~ dress** пара́дная фо́рма; **~-fledged** вполне́ опери́вшийся; *fig.* зако́нченный; полнопра́вный; **~scale** [fʊl'skeɪl] в по́лном объёме
**fumble** ['fʌmbl] (*feel about*) ша́рить; (*rummage*) ры́ться; ***~ for words*** поды́скивать слова́
**fume** [fju:m] **1.** дым; (*vapour*) испаре́ние; **2.** дыми́ть(ся); *fig.* возмуща́ться
**fumigate** ['fju:mɪgeɪt] оку́ривать
**fun** [fʌn] весе́лье; заба́ва; ***have ~*** хорошо́ провести́ вре́мя; ***make ~ of*** высме́ивать [вы́смеять] (В)
**function** ['fʌŋkʃn] **1.** фу́нкция, назначе́ние; **2.** функциони́ровать, де́йствовать
**fund** [fʌnd] запа́с; *fin.* капита́л, фонд; **~s** *pl.* (*resources*) фо́нды *m/pl.*; ***public ~*** госуда́рственные сре́дства
**fundament|al** [fʌndə'mentl] □ основно́й, коренно́й, суще́ственный; **~als** *pl.* осно́вы *f/pl.*
**funeral** ['fju:nərəl] по́хороны *f/pl.*; *attr.* похоро́нный
**funnel** ['fʌnl] воро́нка; *naut.* дымова́я труба́
**funny** ['fʌnɪ] □ заба́вный, смешно́й; (*strange*) стра́нный
**fur** [fɜ:] мех; (*skin with ~*) шку́р(к)а; ***~ coat*** шу́ба; **~s** *pl.* меха́ *m/pl.*, мехов́ые това́ры *m/pl.*, пушни́на
**furious** ['fjʊərɪəs] □ (*violent*) бу́йный; (*enraged*) взбешённый
**furl** [fɜ:l] *sails* свёртывать [сверну́ть]; *umbrella* скла́дывать [сложи́ть]
**fur-lined** ['fɜ:laɪnd] подби́тый ме́хом
**furnace** ['fɜ:nɪs] горн; печь *f*
**furnish** ['fɜ:nɪʃ] (*provide*) снабжа́ть [снабди́ть] (***with*** T); *room, etc.* обставля́ть [-а́вить], меблирова́ть (*im*)*pf.*; **~ings** обстано́вка; дома́шние принадле́жности
**furniture** ['fɜ:nɪtʃər] ме́бель *f*, обстано́вка
**furrier** ['fʌrɪə] скорня́к
**furrow** ['fʌrəʊ] *agric.* борозда́; (*groove*) коле́я
**further** ['fɜ:ðə] **1.** да́льше, да́лее; зате́м; кро́ме того́; **2.** соде́йствовать, спосо́бствовать (Д); **~ance** [-rəns] продвиже́ние (***of*** P), соде́йствие (***of*** Д); **~more** [fɜ:ðə'mɔ:] *adv.* к тому́ же, кро́ме того́
**furthest** ['fɜ:ðɪst] са́мый да́льний
**furtive** ['fɜ:tɪv] □ скры́тый, та́йный; ***~ glance*** взгляд укра́дкой
**fury** ['fjʊərɪ] нейстовство, я́рость *f*; ***fly into a ~*** прийти́ в я́рость
**fuse**[1] [fju:z] *el.* пла́вкий предохрани́тель *m*, *coll.* про́бка
**fuse**[2] [~]: ***the lights have ~d*** про́бки перегоре́ли
**fuss** [fʌs] *coll.* **1.** суета́; (*row*) шум, сканда́л; ***make a ~*** подня́ть *pf.* шум; ***make a ~ of s.o.*** носи́ться с ке́м-л.; **2.** [за]суети́ться; [вз]волнова́ться (***about*** из-за P)
**futile** ['fju:taɪl] бесполе́зный, тще́тный
**future** ['fju:tʃə] **1.** бу́дущий; **2.** бу́дущее, бу́дущность *f*; ***in the near ~***

в ближа́йшее вре́мя; ***there is no ~ in it*** э́то бесперспекти́вно

**fuzzy** ['fʌzɪ] (*blurred*) сму́тный; (*fluffy*) пуши́стый

# G



**gab** [gæb]: ***the gift of the ~*** хорошо́ подве́шенный язы́к

**gabardine** ['gæbədiːn] габарди́н

**gabble** ['gæbl] тарато́рить

**gable** ['geɪbl] *arch.* фронто́н

**gad** [gæd]: ***~ about*** шля́ться, шата́ться

**gadfly** ['gædflaɪ] *zo.* сле́пень *m*

**gadget** ['gædʒɪt] приспособле́ние; *coll.* техни́ческая нови́нка

**gag** [gæg] **1.** *for stopping mouth* кляп; (*joke*) шу́тка, остро́та; **2.** затыка́ть рот (Д); заста́вить *pf.* замолча́ть

**gaiety** ['geɪətɪ] весёлость *f*

**gaily** ['geɪlɪ] *adv. om* ***gay*** ве́село; (*brightly*) я́рко

**gain** [geɪn] **1.** (*profit*) при́быль *f*; (*winnings*) вы́игрыш; (*increase*) приро́ст; **2.** выи́грывать [вы́играть]; приобрета́ть [-ести́]; ***~ weight*** [по]полне́ть

**gait** [geɪt] похо́дка

**galaxy** ['gæləksɪ] гала́ктика; *fig.* плея́да

**gale** [geɪl] шторм, си́льный ве́тер

**gall** [gɔːl] **1.** *med.* жёлчь *f*; *bitterness* жёлчность *f*; (*bad temper*) зло́ба; **2.** раздража́ть [-жи́ть]

**gallant** ['gælənt] **1.** гала́нтный; **2.** *adj.* ['gælənt] □ хра́брый, до́блестный

**gall bladder** жёлчный пузы́рь

**gallery** ['gælərɪ] галере́я; *thea.* балко́н; *coll.* галёрка

**galley** ['gælɪ] *naut.* ка́мбуз

**gallon** ['gælən] галло́н

**gallop** ['gæləp] **1.** гало́п; **2.** скака́ть гало́пом

**gallows** ['gæləʊz] *sg.* ви́селица

**gamble** ['gæmbl] **1.** аза́ртная игра́; риско́ванное предприя́тие; **2.** игра́ть в аза́ртные и́гры; *on stock exchange* игра́ть; **~r** [~ə] картёжник, игро́к

**gambol** ['gæmbl] **1.** прыжо́к; **2.** пры́гать, скака́ть

**game** [geɪm] **1.** игра́; *of chess, etc.* па́ртия; *of tennis* гейм; (*wild animals*) дичь *f*; ***~s*** *pl.* состяза́ния *n/pl.*, и́гры *f/pl.*; ***beat s.o. at his own ~*** бить кого́-л. его́ со́бственным ору́жием; **2.** *coll.* охо́тно гото́вый (сде́лать что́-л.); **3.** игра́ть на де́ньги; **~ster** [~stə] игро́к, картёжник

**gander** ['gændə] гуса́к

**gang** [gæŋ] **1.** *of workers* брига́да; *of criminals* ба́нда; **2.** ***~ up*** объедини́ться *pf.*

**gangster** ['gæŋstə] га́нгстер

**gangway** [gæŋweɪ] *naut.* схо́дни; *ae.* трап; (*passage*) прохо́д

**gaol** [dʒeɪl] тюрьма́; → ***jail***

**gap** [gæp] *in text, knowledge* пробе́л; (*cleft*) брешь *f*, щель *f*; *fig. between ideas, etc.* расхожде́ние

**gape** [geɪp] разева́ть рот; [по]глазе́ть; зия́ть

**garage** ['gærɑːʒ] гара́ж

**garbage** ['gɑːbɪdʒ] отбро́сы *m/pl.*; му́сор; ***~ chute*** мусоропро́вод

**garden** ['gɑːdn] **1.** сад; ***kitchen ~*** огоро́д; **2.** занима́ться садово́дством; **~er** [~ə] садо́вник, садово́д; **~ing** [~ɪŋ] садово́дство

**gargle** ['gɑːgl] **1.** полоска́ть го́рло; **2.** полоска́ние для го́рла

**garish** ['geərɪʃ] бро́ский, крича́щий; я́ркий

**garland** ['gɑːlənd] гирля́нда, вено́к

**garlic** ['gɑːlɪk] чесно́к

**garment** ['gɑːmənt] предме́т оде́жды

**garnish** ['gɑːnɪʃ] **1.** (*decoration*) украше́ние, *mst. cul.*; **2.** украша́ть [укра́сить]; гарни́ровать

**garret** ['gærɪt] манса́рда

**garrison** ['gærɪsn] гарнизо́н

**garrulous** ['gærʊləs] □ болтли́вый

**gas** [gæs] **1.** газ; *Am.* бензи́н, горю́чее;

**~bag** *coll.* болту́н; пустоме́ля; **2.** отравля́ть га́зом
**gash** [gæʃ] **1.** глубо́кая ра́на, разре́з; **2.** наноси́ть глубо́кую ра́ну (Д)
**gas lighter** га́зовая зажига́лка
**gasoline**, **gasolene** ['gæsəliːn] *mot. Am.* бензи́н
**gasp** [gɑːsp] задыха́ться [задохну́ться]; лови́ть во́здух
**gas station** *Am.* автозапра́вочная ста́нция; **~ stove** га́зовая плита́
**gastri|c** ['gæstrɪk] желу́дочный; ***~ ulcer*** я́зва желу́дка; **~tis** [gæ'straɪtɪs] гастри́т
**gate** [geɪt] воро́та *n/pl.*; *in fence* кали́тка; **~way** воро́та *n/pl.*; вход; подворо́тня
**gather** ['gæðə] *v/t.* соб(и)ра́ть; *harvest* снима́ть [снять]; *flowers* [на-, со]рва́ть; *fig.* де́лать вы́вод; ***~ speed*** набира́ть ско́рость; *v/i.* соб(и)ра́ться; **~ing** [~rɪŋ] собра́ние; *social* встре́ча; *med.* нары́в
**gaudy** ['gɔːdɪ] □ я́ркий, крича́щий, безвку́сный
**gauge** [geɪdʒ] **1.** *tech.* кали́бр; измери́тельный прибо́р; ***fuel ~*** *mot.* бензоме́р; **2.** измеря́ть [-е́рить]; градуи́ровать *(im)pf.*; *fig. person* оце́нивать [-ни́ть]
**gaunt** [gɔːnt] □ исхуда́лый, измождённый; *place* забро́шенный, мра́чный
**gauze** [gɔːz] ма́рля
**gave** [geɪv] *pt. om* ***give***
**gawky** ['gɔːkɪ] неуклю́жий
**gay** [geɪ] □ весёлый; *colo(u)r* я́ркий, пёстрый; гомосексуа́льный
**gaze** [geɪz] **1.** при́стальный взгляд; **2.** при́стально смотре́ть
**gazette** [gə'zet] *official* бюллете́нь *m*, ве́стник
**gear** [gɪə] **1.** механи́зм; приспособле́ния *n/pl.*; *tech.* шестерня́; зубча́тая переда́ча; *mot.* переда́ча; ско́рость *f*; *(equipment)* принадле́жности *f/pl.*; *(belongings)* ве́щи *f/pl.*; ***change ~*** переключи́ть переда́чу; ***in ~*** включённый, де́йствующий; **2.** приводи́ть в движе́ние; включа́ть [-чи́ть]
**geese** [giːs] *pl. om* ***goose***
**gem** [dʒem] драгоце́нный ка́мень *m*; *fig.* сокро́вище
**gender** ['dʒendə] *gr.* род
**gene** [dʒiːn] *biol.* ген
**general** ['dʒenərəl] **1.** □ о́бщий; обы́чный; *(in all parts)* повсеме́стный; *(chief)* гла́вный, генера́льный; ***~ election*** всео́бщие вы́боры *m/pl.*; **2.** *mil.* генера́л; **~ization** [dʒenrəlaɪ'zeɪʃn] обобще́ние; **~ize** ['dʒenrəlaɪz] обобща́ть [-щи́ть]; **~ly** [~lɪ] вообще́; обы́чно
**generat|e** ['dʒenəreɪt] порожда́ть [-роди́ть]; производи́ть [-вести́]; *el.* вырaба́тывать [вы́работать]; **~ion** [dʒenə'reɪʃn] поколе́ние; **~or** ['dʒenəreɪtə] генера́тор
**gener|osity** [dʒenə'rɒsətɪ] великоду́шие; *with money, etc.* ще́дрость *f*; **~ous** ['dʒenərəs] □ великоду́шный, ще́дрый
**genetics** [dʒɪ'netɪks] гене́тика
**genial** ['dʒiːnɪəl] □ *climate* тёплый, мя́гкий; до́брый, серде́чный
**genius** ['dʒiːnɪəs] ге́ний; тала́нт, гениа́льность *f*
**genocide** ['dʒenəsaɪd] геноци́д
**genre** ['ʒɑːnrə] жанр
**gentle** ['dʒentl] □ мя́гкий; кро́ткий; ти́хий; не́жный; *animals* сми́рный; *breeze* лёгкий; **~man** джентельме́н; господи́н; **~manlike**, **~manly** [~lɪ] воспи́танный; **~ness** [~nɪs] мя́гкость *f*; доброта́
**genuine** ['dʒenjʊɪn] □ *(real)* по́длинный; *(sincere)* и́скренний, непodде́льный
**geography** [dʒɪ'ɒgrəfɪ] геогра́фия
**geology** [dʒɪ'ɒlədʒɪ] геоло́гия
**geometry** [dʒɪ'ɒmətrɪ] геоме́трия
**germ** [dʒɜːm] микро́б; *(embryo)* заро́дыш *(a. fig.)*
**German** ['dʒɜːmən] **1.** герма́нский, неме́цкий; ***~ silver*** мельхио́р; **2.** не́мец, не́мка; неме́цкий язы́к
**germinate** ['dʒɜːmɪneɪt] дава́ть ростки́, прораста́ть [-расти́]
**gesticulat|e** [dʒe'stɪkjʊleɪt] жестикули́ровать; **~ion** [~stɪkjʊ'leɪʃn] жести-

G

куля́ция
**gesture** ['dʒestʃə] жест (*a. fig.*)
**get** [get] [*irr.*] **1.** *v/t.* (*obtain*) дост(а-в)а́ть; (*receive*) получа́ть [-чи́ть]; (*earn*) зараба́тывать [-бо́тать]; (*buy*) покупа́ть, купи́ть; (*fetch*) приноси́ть [-нести́]; (*induce*) заставля́ть [-ста́вить]; ***I have got to …*** мне ну́жно, я до́лжен; ***~ one's hair cut*** [по]стри́чься; **2.** *v/i.* (*become, be*) [с]де́латься, станови́ться [стать]; ***~ ready*** [при]гото́виться; ***~ about*** (*travel*) разъезжа́ть; *after illness* начина́ть ходи́ть; ***~ abroad*** *of rumo(u)rs* распространя́ться [-ни́ться]; ***~ across*** *fig.* заставля́ть [-а́вить] поня́ть; ***~ ahead*** продвига́ться вперёд; ***~ at*** доб(и)ра́ться до (Р); ***~ away*** уд(и)ра́ть, уходи́ть [уйти́]; ***~ down*** *from shelf* снима́ть [снять]; *from train* сходи́ть [сойти́]; ***~ in*** входи́ть [войти́]; ***~ on well with a p.*** хорошо́ ла́дить с ке́м-л.; ***~ out*** вынима́ть [вы́нуть]; ***~ to hear*** (***know, learn***) узн(ав)а́ть; ***~ up*** вст(ав)а́ть; **~up** ['getʌp] (*dress*) наря́д
**geyser** ['gi:zə] **1.** ге́йзер; **2.** *Brt.* га́зовая коло́нка
**ghastly** ['gɑ:stlɪ] ужа́сный
**gherkin** ['gɜ:kɪn] огу́рчик; ***pickled ~s*** корнишо́ны
**ghost** [gəʊst] при́зрак, привиде́ние; дух (*a. eccl.*); *fig.* тень *f*, лёгкий след; **~like** ['gəʊstlaɪk], **~ly** [~lɪ] похо́жий на привиде́ние, при́зрачный
**giant** ['dʒaɪənt] **1.** велика́н, гига́нт; **2.** гига́нтский
**gibber** ['dʒɪbə] говори́ть невня́тно; **~ish** [~rɪʃ] тараба́рщина
**gibe** [dʒaɪb] *v/i.* насмеха́ться (***at*** над Т)
**gidd|iness** ['gɪdɪnɪs] *med.* головокруже́ние; легкомы́слие; **~y** ['gɪdɪ] □ испы́тывающий головокруже́ние; (*not serious*) легкомы́сленный; ***I feel ~*** у меня́ кру́жится голова́; ***~ height*** головокружи́тельная высота́
**gift** [gɪft] дар, пода́рок; спосо́бность *f*, тала́нт (***of*** к Д); **~ed** ['gɪftɪd] одарённый, спосо́бный
**gigantic** [dʒaɪ'gæntɪk] (***~ally***) гига́нтский, грома́дный
**giggle** ['gɪgl] **1.** хихи́канье; **2.** хихи́кать [-кнуть]
**gild** [gɪld] [*irr.*] [по]золоти́ть
**gill** [gɪl] *zo.* жа́бра
**gilt** [gɪlt] **1.** позоло́та; **2.** позоло́ченный
**gin** [dʒɪn] (*machine or alcoholic beverage*) джин
**ginger** ['dʒɪndʒə] **1.** имби́рь *m*; **2. ~ up** *coll.* подстёгивать [-стегну́ть], оживля́ть [-ви́ть]; **~bread** имби́рный пря́ник; **~ly** [~lɪ] осторо́жный, ро́бкий
**gipsy** ['dʒɪpsɪ] цыга́н(ка)
**giraffe** [dʒɪ'rɑ:f] жира́ф
**girder** ['gɜ:də] (*beam*) ба́лка
**girdle** ['gɜ:dl] (*belt*) по́яс, куша́к; (*corset*) корсе́т
**girl** [gɜ:l] де́вочка, де́вушка; **~friend** подру́га; **~hood** ['gɜ:lhʊd] деви́чество; **~ish** □ деви́чий
**giro** ['dʒaɪrəʊ] *banking* безнали́чная опера́ция
**girth** [gɜ:θ] обхва́т, разме́р; *for saddle* подпру́га
**gist** [dʒɪst] суть *f*
**give** [gɪv] [*irr.*] **1.** *v/t.* да(ва́)ть; *as gift* [по]дари́ть; (*hand over*) передава́ть [-да́ть]; (*pay*) [за]плати́ть; *pleasure* доставля́ть [-а́вить]; ***~ birth to*** роди́ть; ***~ away*** отд(ав)а́ть; *coll.* вы́да(ва́)ть, пред(ав)а́ть; ***~ in*** *application* под(ав)а́ть; ***~ off*** *smell* изд(ав)а́ть; ***~ up*** отка́зываться [-за́ться] от (Р); ***2.*** *v/i.* ***~*** (***in***) уступа́ть [-пи́ть]; ***~ into*** выходи́ть на (В); ***~ out*** конча́ться [ко́нчиться]; обесси́леть *pf.*; **~n** ['gɪvn] **1.** *pt. p. от* ***give***; **2.** *fig.* да́нный; (*disposed*) скло́нный (***to*** к Д)
**glaci|al** ['gleɪsɪəl] □ леднико́вый; **~er** ['glæsɪə] ледни́к
**glad** [glæd] □ дово́льный; ра́достный, весёлый; ***I am ~*** я ра́д(а); **~ly** охо́тно; **~den** ['glædn] [об]ра́довать
**glade** [gleɪd] поля́на
**gladness** ['glædnɪs] ра́дость *f*
**glamo|rous** ['glæmərəs] обая́тельный, очарова́тельный; **~(u)r** ['glæmə] очарова́ние
**glance** [glɑ:ns] **1.** бы́стрый взгляд; **2.** (*slip*) скользи́ть [-зну́ть] (*mst.* **~**

***off***); **~ *at*** взглянýть на (В); **~ *back*** оглядываться [-нýться]; **~ *through*** просмáтривать [-смо-трéть]
**gland** [glænd] жéлеза
**glare** [gleə] **1.** ослепи́тельно сверкáть; (*stare*) серди́то смотрéть; **2.** серди́тый *or* свирéпый взгляд; ослепи́тельный блеск
**glass** [glɑːs] **1.** стеклó; стакáн; *for wine* рю́мка; (*looking* **~**) зéркало; (***a pair of***) **~*es*** *pl.* очки́ *n/pl.*; **2.** *attr.* стекля́нный; **~*house*** *Brt.* (*greenhouse*) тепли́ца; *Am.* (*place where glass is made*) стекóльный завóд; **~y** ['glɑːsɪ] □ зеркáльный; *eyes* тýсклый
**glaz|e** [gleɪz] **1.** глазýрь *f*; **2.** глази́ровать (*im*)*pf*.; *windows* застекля́ть [-ли́ть]; **~ier** ['gleɪzɪə] стекóльщик
**gleam** [gliːm] **1.** мя́гкий, слáбый свет; прóблеск, луч; **2.** поблёскивать
**glean** [gliːn] *v/t. fig. information, etc.* тщáтельно собирáть
**glee** [gliː] ликовáние
**glib** [glɪb] □ *tongue* бóйкий; **~ *excuse*** благови́дный предлóг
**glid|e** [glaɪd] **1.** скользи́ть, плáвно дви́гаться; **2.** плáвное движéние; **~er** ['glaɪdə] *ae.* планёр
**glimmer** ['glɪmə] **1.** мерцáние, тýсклый свет; **2.** мерцáть, тýскло свети́ть
**glimpse** [glɪmps] **1.**: ***at a*** **~** с пéрвого взгля́да; ***catch a*** **~** = *v.* ***glimpse***; **2.** [у]ви́деть мéльком
**glint** [glɪnt] **1.** блеск; **2.** блестéть
**glisten** ['glɪsn], **glitter** ['glɪtə] блестéть, сверкáть, сия́ть
**gloat** [gləʊt] злорáдствовать
**global** ['gləʊbl] глобáльный, всеми́рный
**globe** [gləʊb] шар; земнóй шар; глóбус; **~trotter** [~trɒtə] заядлый путешéственник
**gloom** [gluːm] мрак; ***throw a*** **~** ***over ...*** повергáть [-вéргнуть] в уны́ние; **~y** ['gluːmɪ] □ мрáчный; угрю́мый
**glori|fy** ['glɔːrɪfaɪ] прославля́ть [-áвить]; **~ous** ['glɔːrɪəs] □ великолéпный, чудéсный
**glory** ['glɔːrɪ] **1.** слáва; **2.** торжествовáть; (*take pride*) горди́ться (***in*** Т)
**gloss** [glɒs] **1.** внéшний блеск; глянец; (*explanatory comment*) пояснéние, толковáние; **2.** наводи́ть глянец на (В); **~ *over*** приукрáшивать [-крáсить]; обойти́ молчáнием
**glossary** ['glɒsərɪ] глоссáрий; *at end of book* словáрь *m*
**glossy** ['glɒsɪ] □ *hair* блестя́щий; *photo, etc.* глянцевый
**glove** [glʌv] перчáтка; **~ *compartment*** *mot. coll.* бардачóк
**glow** [gləʊ] **1.** (*burn*) горéть; *of coals* тлеть; *with happiness* сия́ть; **2.** зáрево; *on face* румя́нец; **~worm** светлячóк
**glucose** ['gluːkəʊs] глюкóза
**glue** [gluː] **1.** клей; **2.** [с]клéить; ***be ~d to*** быть прикóванным (к Д)
**glum** [glʌm] мрáчный, хмýрый
**glut** [glʌt] избы́ток; затовáривание
**glutton** ['glʌtn] обжóра *m/f*; **~y** [~ɪ] обжóрство
**gnash** [næʃ] [за]скрежетáть
**gnat** [næt] комáр; (*midge*) мóшка
**gnaw** [nɔː] глодáть; грызть (*a. fig.*)
**gnome** [nəʊm] гном, кáрлик
**go** [gəʊ] **1.** [*irr.*] ходи́ть, идти́; (*pass*) проходи́ть [пройти́]; (*leave*) уходи́ть [уйти́]; *by car, etc.* éздить, [по]éхать; (*become*) [с]дéлаться; (*function*) рабóтать; ***let*** **~** отпускáть [отпусти́ть]; выпускáть из рук; **~ *to see*** заходи́ть [зайти́] к (Д), навещáть [-ести́ть]; **~ *at*** набрáсываться [-рóситься] на (В); **~ *by*** проходи́ть [пройти́] ми́мо; (*be guided by*) руковóдствоваться (Т); **~ *for*** идти́ [пойти́] за (Т); **~ *for a walk*** пойти́ на прогýлку; **~ *in for*** занимáться [-ня́ться]; **~ *on*** продолжáть [-дóлжить]; идти́ дáльше; **~ *through with*** доводи́ть до концá (В); **~ *without*** обходи́ться (обойти́сь) без (Р); **2.** ходьбá, движéние; *coll.* энéргия; ***on the*** **~** на ходý; на ногáх; ***no*** **~** *coll.* не вы́йдет; не пойдёт; ***in one*** **~** с пéрвой попы́тки; в одно́м захóде; ***have a*** **~** ***at*** [по]прóбовать (В)
**goad** [gəʊd] побуждáть [побуди́ть]; подстрекáть [-кнýть]
**goal** [gəʊl] цель *f*; *sport* ворóта *n/pl.*;

G

гол; **~keeper** вратáрь *m*
**goat** [gəʊt] козёл, козá
**gobble** ['gɒbl] есть жáдно, бы́стро
**go-between** ['gəʊbɪtwiːn] посрéдник
**goblin** ['gɒblɪn] домовóй
**god** [gɒd] (*deity*) бог; (*supreme being*) (***God***) Бог; божествó; *fig.* кумúр; ***thank God!*** слáва Бóгу!; **~child** крéстник *m*, -ница *f*; **~dess** ['gɒdɪs] богúня; **~father** крёстный отéц; **~forsaken** ['~fəseɪkən] бóгом забы́тый; забрóшенный; **~less** ['~lɪs] безбóжный; **~mother** крёстная мать *f*
**goggle** ['gɒgl] **1.** тарáщить глазá; **2.** (***a pair of***) **~*s*** *pl.* защúтные очкú *n/pl.*
**going** ['gəʊɪŋ] **1.** дéйствующий; ***be ~ to*** *inf.* намéреваться, собирáться (+ *inf.*); ***~ concern*** процветáющее предприя́тие; **2.** (*leave*) ухóд; отъéзд; **~s-on** [gəʊɪŋz'ɒn]: ***what ~!*** ну и делá!
**gold** [gəʊld] **1.** зóлото; **2.** золотóй; **~en** ['gəʊldən] золотóй; **~finch** *zo.* щегóл
**golf** [gɒlf] гольф
**gondola** ['gɒndələ] гондóла
**gone** [gɒn] *pt. p. от* ***go***
**good** [gʊd] **1.** хорóший; (*kind*) дóбрый; (*suitable*) гóдный, (*beneficial*) полéзный; ***~ for colds*** помогáет при простýде; ***Good Friday*** *relig.* Страстнáя пя́тница; ***be ~ at*** быть спосóбным к (Д); **2.** добрó, блáго; пóльза; **~*s*** *pl.* товáр; ***that's no ~*** это бесполéзно; ***for ~*** навсегдá; **~by**(**e**) [gʊd'baɪ] **1.** до свидáния!, прощáйте!; **2.** прощáние; **~-natured** добродýшный; **~ness** ['~nɪs] добротá; *int.* Гóсподи!; **~will** доброжелáтельность *f*
**goody** ['gʊdɪ] *coll.* конфéта, лáкомство
**goose** [guːs], *pl.* **geese** [giːs] гусь *m*
**gooseberry** ['gʊzbərɪ] крыжóвник (*no pl.*)
**goose|flesh**, *a.* **~pimples** *pl. fig.* гусúная кóжа, мурáшки
**gorge** [gɔːdʒ] (*ravine*) ýзкое ущéлье
**gorgeous** ['gɔːdʒəs] великолéпный
**gorilla** [gə'rɪlə] горúлла
**gory** ['gɔːrɪ] □ окровáвленный, кровáвый
**gospel** ['gɒspəl] Евáнгелие
**gossip** ['gɒsɪp] **1.** сплéтня; сплéтник *m*, -ница *f*; **2.** [на]сплéтничать
**got** [gɒt] *pt. и pt. p. от* ***get***
**Gothic** ['gɒθɪk] готúческий
**gourmet** ['gʊəmeɪ] гурмáн
**gout** [gaʊt] *med.* подáгра
**govern** ['gʌvn] *v/t.* (*rule*) прáвить, (*administer*) управля́ть (Т); **~ess** [~ənɪs] гувернáнтка; **~ment** [~ənmənt] правúтельство; управлéние; *attr.* правúтельственный; **~or** [~ənə] губернáтор; *coll.* (*boss*) хозя́ин; шеф
**gown** [gaʊn] плáтье; *univ.* мáнтия
**grab** [græb] *coll.* схвáтывать [-атúть]
**grace** [greɪs] **1.** грáция, изя́щество; **2.** *fig.* украшáть [укрáсить]; удостáивать [-стóить]; **~ful** ['greɪsfl] □ грациóзный, изя́щный; **~fulness** [~nɪs] грациóзность *f*, изя́щество
**gracious** ['greɪʃəs] □ любéзный; благосклóнный; (*merciful*) мúлостивый; ***goodness ~!*** Гóсподи!
**gradation** [grə'deɪʃn] градáция, постепéнный перехóд
**grade** [greɪd] **1.** стéпень *f*, (*rank*) ранг; (*quality*) кáчество; *Am. educ.* класс; (*slope*) уклóн; **2.** [рас]сортировáть
**gradient** ['greɪdɪənt] уклóн; ***steep ~*** крутóй спуск *or* подъём
**gradua|l** ['grædʒʊəl] □ постепéнный; **~te 1.** [~eɪt] градуúровать (*im*)*pf.*, наносúть делéния; кончáть университéт; *Am.* кончáть (любóе) учéбное заведéние; **2.** [~ɪt] *univ.* выпускнúк университéта; **~tion** [grædʒʊ'eɪʃn] градуирóвка; *Am.* окончáние (вы́сшего) учéбного заведéния
**graft** [grɑːft] **1.** *hort.* (*scion*) черенóк; привúвка; **2.** привú(вá)ть; *med.* пересáживать ткань *f*
**grain** [greɪn] зернó; (*cereals*) хлéбные злáки *m/pl.*; (*particle*) крупúнка; *fig.* ***against the ~*** не по нутрý
**gramma|r** ['græmə] граммáтика; **~tical** [grə'mætɪkəl] □ грамматúческий
**gram(me)** [græm] грамм
**granary** ['grænərɪ] амбáр; жúтница *a. fig.*
**grand** [grænd] **1.** □ *view*, *etc.* велúчественный; *plans*, *etc.* грандиóз-

ный; ***we had a ~ time*** мы прекрасно провели время; **2.** *mus.* (*a.* ***~ piano***) рояль *m*; **~child** ['græntʃaɪld] внук, внучка; **~eur** ['grændʒə] грандиозность *f*; величие

**grandiose** ['grændɪəʊs] □ грандиозный

**grandparents** *pl.* дедушка и бабушка

**grant** [grɑːnt] **1.** предоставлять [-авить]; (*admit as true*) допускать [-стить]; **2.** дар; субсидия; *student's* стипендия; ***take for ~ed*** принимать [принять] как само собой разумеющееся

**granul|ated** ['grænjʊleɪtɪd] гранулированный; **~e** ['grænjuːl] зёрнышко

**grape** [greɪp] *collect.* виноград; ***a bunch of ~s*** гроздь винограда; ***a ~*** виноградина; **~fruit** грейпфрут

**graph** [grɑːf] график; **~ic** ['græfɪk] графический; наглядный; *description* яркий; ***~ arts*** *pl.* графика; **~ite** ['græfaɪt] графит

**grapple** ['græpl]: ***~ with*** бороться с (Т); *fig. difficulties* пытаться преодолеть

**grasp** [grɑːsp] **1.** хватать [схватить] (***by*** за В); *in one's hand* заж(им)ать; хвататься [схватиться] (***at*** за В); **2.** понимать [понять]; ***it's beyond my ~*** это выше моего понимания; ***she kept the child's hand in her ~*** она крепко держала ребёнка за руку

**grass** [grɑːs] трава; (*pasture*) пастбище; **~hopper** ['~hɒpə] кузнечик; **~ widow** [~'wɪdəʊ] соломенная вдова; **~y** ['~ɪ] травяной

**grate** [greɪt] **1.** (*fireplace*) решётка; **2.** *cheese, etc.* [на]тереть; *teeth* [за]скрежетать; ***~ on*** *fig.* раздражать [-жить] (В)

**grateful** ['greɪtfl] □ благодарный

**grater** ['greɪtə] тёрка

**grati|fication** [grætɪfɪ'keɪʃn] удовлетворение; **~fy** ['grætɪfaɪ] удовлетворять [-рить]; (*indulge*) потакать (Д)

**grating**[1] ['greɪtɪŋ] □ скрипучий, резкий

**grating**[2] [~] решётка

**gratitude** ['grætɪtjuːd] благодарность *f*

**gratuit|ous** [grə'tjuːɪtəs] □ бесплатный, безвозмездный; **~y** [~ətɪ] пособие

**grave**[1] [greɪv] □ серьёзный, веский; *illness, etc.* тяжёлый

**grave**[2] [~] могила

**gravel** ['grævl] гравий

**graveyard** кладбище

**gravitation** [grævɪ'teɪʃn] притяжение; тяготение (*a. fig.*)

**gravity** ['grævətɪ] серьёзность *f*; *of situation* тяжесть *f*, опасность *f*

**gravy** ['greɪvɪ] (мясная) подливка

**gray** [greɪ] серый; → *Brt.* ***grey***

**graze**[1] [greɪz] пасти(сь)

**graze**[2] [~] заде(ва)ть; (*scrape*) [по]царапать

**grease** [griːs] **1.** жир; *tech.* консистентная смазка; **2.** [griːz] смаз(ыв)ать

**greasy** ['griːsɪ] □ жирный; *road* скользкий

**great** [greɪt] □ великий; большой; (*huge*) огромный; *coll.* великолепный; **~coat** *mil.* шинель *f*; **~-grandchild** [greɪt'græntʃaɪld] правнук *m*, -учка *f*; **~ly** [~lɪ] очень, сильно; **~ness** [~nɪs] величие

**greed** [griːd] жадность *f*; **~y** ['griːdɪ] □ жадный (***of, for*** к Д)

**Greek** [griːk] **1.** грек *m*, гречанка *f*; **2.** греческий

**green** [griːn] **1.** зелёный; (*unripe*) незрелый; *fig.* неопытный; **2.** зелёный цвет, зелёная краска; (*grassy plot*) лужайка; **~s** *pl.* зелень *f*, овощи *m/pl.*; **~grocery** овощной магазин; **~house** теплица, оранжерея; **~ish** ['griːnɪʃ] зеленоватый

**greet** [griːt] *guests, etc.* приветствовать; [по]здороваться; **~ing** ['griːtɪŋ] приветствие; привет

**grenade** [grɪ'neɪd] *mil.* граната

**grew** [gruː] *pt. от* ***grow***

**grey** [greɪ] **1.** серый; *hair* седой; **2.** серый цвет, серая краска; **3.** посереть; ***turn ~*** [по]седеть; **~hound** борзая

**grid** [grɪd] решётка

G

**grief** [gri:f] róре; ***come to ~*** потерпéть *pf.* неудáчу, попáсть *pf.* в бедý
**griev|ance** ['gri:vns] обúда; (*complaint*) жáлоба; ***nurse a ~*** затаúть обúду (***against*** на В); **~e** [gri:v] горевáть; (*cause grief to*) огорчáть [-чúть]; **~ous** ['gri:vəs] □ гóрестный, печáльный
**grill** [grɪl] **1.** (электро)грúль; (*on cooker*) решётка; жáреное на решётке (в грúле) мя́со; **2.** жáрить на решётке (в грúле); **~room** гриль-бáр
**grim** [grɪm] □ жестóкий; *smile, etc.* мрáчный
**grimace** [grɪ'meɪs] **1.** гримáса, ужúмка; **2.** гримáсничать
**grim|e** [graɪm] грязь *f*; **~y** ['graɪmɪ] □ запáчканный, гря́зный
**grin** [grɪn] **1.** усмéшка; **2.** усмехáться [-хнýться]
**grind** [graɪnd] [*irr.*] **1.** [с]молóть; размáлывать [-молóть]; *to powder* растирáть [растерéть]; (*sharpen*) [на]точúть; *fig.* зубрúть; **2.** размáлывание; тяжёлая, скýчная рабóта; **~stone** точúльный кáмень *m*; ***keep one's nose to the ~*** трудúться без óтдыха
**grip** [grɪp] **1.** (*handle*) рýчка, рукоя́тка; (*understanding*) понимáние; *fig.* тискú *m/pl.*; **2.** (*take hold of*) схвáтывать [схватúть]; *fig.* овладевáть внимáнием (Р)
**gripe** [graɪp] ворчáние; (*colic pains*) кóлики *f/pl.*
**gripping** ['grɪpɪŋ] захвáтывающий
**grisly** ['grɪzlɪ] ужáсный
**gristle** ['grɪsl] хрящ
**grit** [grɪt] **1.** песóк, грáвий; *coll.* твёрдость харáктера; **~s** *pl.* овся́ная крупá; **2.** [за]скрежетáть (Т)
**grizzly** ['grɪzlɪ] **1.** сéрый; *hair* с прóседью; **2.** североамерикáнский медвéдь *m*, грúзли *m indecl.*
**groan** [grəʊn] **1.** óхать [óхнуть]; *with pain, etc.* [за]стонáть; **2.** стон
**grocer|ies** ['grəʊsərɪz] *pl.* бакалéя; **~y** [-rɪ] бакалéйный отдéл
**groggy** ['grɒgɪ] нетвёрдый на ногáх; *after illness* слáбый
**groin** [grɔɪn] *anat.* пах
**groom** [gru:m] **1.** кóнюх; (*bride~*) женúх; **2.** ухáживать за (лóшадью); хóлить; ***well ~ed*** хоро-шó и тщáтельно одéтый, опря́тный ухóженный
**groove** [gru:v] желобóк; *tech.* паз; *fig.* рутúна, привы́чка, колея́
**grope** [grəʊp] идтú óщупью; нащýп(ыв)ать (*a. fig.*)
**gross** [grəʊs] **1.** □ (*flagrant*) вопиющий; (*fat*) тýчный; (*coarse*) грýбый; *fin.* валовóй, брýтто; **2.** мáсса, гросс
**grotesque** [grəʊ'tesk] гротéскный
**grotto** ['grɒtəʊ] грот
**grouch** [graʊtʃ] *Am. coll.* **1.** дурнóе настроéние; **2.** быть не в дýхе; **~y** [-ɪ] ворчлúвый
**ground**¹ [graʊnd] *pt. и pt. p. от* ***grind***; ***~ glass*** мáтовое стеклó
**ground**² [~] **1.** *mst.* земля́, пóчва; (*area of land*) учáсток землú; площáдка; (*reason*) основáние; **~s** *pl. adjoining house* сад, парк; ***on the ~(s)*** на основáнии (Р); ***stand one's ~*** удéрживать свой позúции, проявúть твёрдость; **2.** обоснóвывать [-новáть]; *el.* заземля́ть [-лúть]; (*teach*) обучáть оснóвам предмéта; **~ floor** [graʊnd'flɔ:] *Brt.* пéрвый этáж; **~less** [-lɪs] □ беспричúнный, необоснóванный; **~nut** арáхис; **~work** фундáмент, оснóва
**group** [gru:p] **1.** грýппа; **2.** соб(и)рáться; [с]группировáть(ся)
**grove** [grəʊv] рóща, лесóк
**grovel** ['grɒvl] *fig.* пресмыкáться; заúскивать
**grow** [grəʊ] [*irr.*] *v/i.* растú; вырастáть [вы́расти]; (*become*) [с]дéлаться, становúться [стать]; *v/t. bot.* выращивать [вы́растить]; культивúровать (*im*)*pf.*
**growl** [graʊl] [за]рычáть
**grow|n** [grəʊn] *pt. p. от* ***grow***; **~nup** ['grəʊnʌp] взрóслый; **~th** [grəʊθ] рост; *med.* óпухоль *f*
**grub** [grʌb] **1.** личúнка; **2.** (*dig in dirt*) ры́ться (в П); **~by** ['grʌbɪ] гря́зный
**grudge** [grʌdʒ] **1.** неохóта, недовóльство; (*envy*) зáвисть *f*; **2.** [по]завúдовать (Д, в П); неохóтно давáть; [по]жалéть

**gruff** [grʌf] □ ре́зкий; гру́бый; *voice* хри́плый
**grumble** ['grʌmbl] [за]ворча́ть; (*complain*) [по]жа́ловаться; *of thunder etc.* [за]грохота́ть; **~r** [~ə] *fig.* ворчу́н(ья *f*/*m*)
**grunt** [grʌnt] хрю́кать [-кнуть]; *of person* [про]бурча́ть
**guarant|ee** [gærən'tiː] **1.** гара́нтия; поручи́тельство; **2.** гаранти́ровать (*im*)*pf.*; руча́ться за (B); **~or** [gærən'tɔː] *law* поручи́тель (-ница *f*) *m*; **~y** ['gærəntɪ] гара́нтия
**guard** [gɑːd] **1.** охра́на; *mil.* карау́л; *rail.* проводни́к; **~s** *pl.* гва́рдия; ***be on one's ~*** быть начеку́; **2.** *v/t.* охраня́ть [-ни́ть]; сторожи́ть; (*protect*) защища́ть [защити́ть] (***from*** от P); *v/i.* [по]бере́чься, остерега́ться [-ре́чься] (***against*** P); **~ian** ['gɑːdɪən] *law* опеку́н; **~ianship** [~ʃɪp] *law* опеку́нство
**guess** [ges] **1.** дога́дка, предположе́ние; **2.** отга́дывать [-да́ть], уга́дывать [-да́ть]; *Am.* счита́ть, полага́ть
**guest** [gest] го́сть(я *f*) *m*; **~house** пансио́н
**guffaw** [gə'fɔː] хо́хот
**guidance** ['gaɪdns] руково́дство
**guide** [gaɪd] **1.** *for tourists* экскурсово́д, гид; **2.** направля́ть [-ра́вить]; руководи́ть (T); **~book** путеводи́тель *m*
**guile** [gaɪl] хи́трость *f*, кова́рство; **~ful** ['gaɪlfl] □ кова́рный; **~less** [~lɪs] □ простоду́шный
**guilt** [gɪlt] вина́, вино́вность *f*; **~less** ['gɪltlɪs] невино́вный; **~y** ['gɪltɪ] □ вино́вный, винова́тый
**guise** [gaɪz]: ***under the ~ of*** под ви́дом (P)
**guitar** [gɪ'tɑː] гита́ра
**gulf** [gʌlf] зали́в; *fig.* про́пасть *f*
**gull**[1] [gʌl] ча́йка
**gull**[2] [~] обма́нывать [-ну́ть]; [о]дура́чить
**gullet** ['gʌlɪt] пищево́д; (*throat*) гло́тка
**gullible** ['gʌlɪbl] легкове́рный
**gulp** [gʌlp] **1.** жа́дно глота́ть; **2.** глото́к; ***at one ~*** за́лпом
**gum**[1] [gʌm] десна́
**gum**[2] [~] **1.** клей; ***chewing ~*** жева́тельная рези́нка; **2.** скле́и(ва)ть
**gun** [gʌn] ору́дие, пу́шка; (*rifle*) ружьё; (*pistol*) пистоле́т; **~boat** каноне́рка; **~man** банди́т; **~ner** *mil.*, *naut.* ['gʌnə] артиллери́ст, канони́р, пулемётчик; **~powder** по́рох
**gurgle** ['gɜːgl] *of water* [за]бу́лькать
**gush** [gʌʃ] **1.** си́льный пото́к; ***~ of enthusiasm*** взрыв энтузиа́зма; **2.** хлы́нуть *pf.*; ли́ться пото́ком; *fig.* бу́рно излива́ть чу́вства
**gust** [gʌst] *of wind* поры́в
**gusto** ['gʌstəʊ] смак; ***with ~*** с больши́м энтузиа́змом
**gut** [gʌt] кишка́; **~s** *pl.* вну́тренности *f*/*pl.*; *coll.* ***he has plenty of ~s*** он му́жественный (*or* волево́й) челове́к
**gutter** ['gʌtə] сто́чная кана́ва; *on roof* жёлоб; ***~ press*** бульва́рная пре́сса
**guy** [gaɪ] *chiefly Brt.* (*person of grotesque appearance*) чу́чело; *Am. coll.* (*fellow, person*) ма́лый; па́рень *m*
**guzzle** ['gʌzl] жа́дно пить; (*eat*) есть с жа́дностью
**gymnas|ium** [dʒɪm'neɪzɪəm] спорти́вный зал; **~tics** [dʒɪm'næstɪks] *pl.* гимна́стика
**gypsy** ['dʒɪpsɪ] *esp. Am.* цыга́н(ка)
**gyrate** [dʒaɪ'reɪt] дви́гаться по кру́гу, враща́ться

# H

**haberdashery** ['hæbədæʃərɪ] (*goods*) галантерéя; (*shop*) галантерéйный магазúн
**habit** ['hæbɪt] привы́чка; **~able** ['hæbɪtəbl] гóдный для жилья́; **~ation** [hæbɪ'teɪʃn] жильё
**habitual** [hə'bɪtʃʊəl] обы́чный; (*done by habit*) привы́чный
**hack**[1] [hæk] [на-, с]рубúть
**hack**[2] [~] (*horse*) наёмная лóшадь *f*, кля́ча; (*writer*) халтýрщик; *coll.* писáка
**hackneyed** ['hæknɪd] *fig.* избúтый
**had** [d, əd, həd; *strong* hæd] *pt. u pt. p. om* ***have***
**haddock** ['hædək] пúкша
**h(a)emoglobin** [hiːmə'gləʊbɪn] гемоглобúн
**h(a)emorrhage** ['hemərɪdʒ] кровоизлия́ние
**haggard** ['hægəd] □ измождённый, осýнувшийся
**haggle** ['hægl] (*bargain*) торговáться
**hail**[1] [heɪl]: ***~ a taxi*** подозвáть таксú
**hail**[2] [~] **1.** град; **2.** ***it ~ed today*** сегодня́ был град; **~stone** грáдина
**hair** [heə] вóлос; ***keep your ~ on!*** спокóйно!; **~cut** стрúжка; **~do** причёска; **~dresser** парикмáхер; **~dryer** фен; **~pin** шпúлька; **~-raising** стрáшный; **~'s breadth** минимáльное расстоя́ние; **~splitting** крохобóрство; **~y** [~rɪ] волосáтый
**hale** [heɪl] здорóвый, крéпкий
**half** [hɑːf, hæf] **1.** половúна; ***~ past two*** половúна трéтьего; ***one and a ~*** полторá *n/m*, полторы́ *f*; ***go halves*** делúть пополáм; ***not ~!*** *Brt. coll.* ещё бы!; а кáк же!; **2.** полу…; половúнный; **3.** почтú; наполовúну; **~-caste** метúс; **~-hearted** □ равнодýшный, вя́лый; **~-length** (*a.* ***~ portrait***) пояснóй портрéт; **~penny** ['heɪpnɪ] полпéнни *n indecl.*; **~-time** *sport* конéц тáйма; **~way** на полпутú; **~-witted** полоýмный
**halibut** ['hælɪbət] пáлтус
**hall** [hɔːl] зал; холл, вестибю́ль *m*; (*entrance ~*) прихóжая; *college* (*residence*) общежúтие для студéнтов
**hallow** ['hæləʊ] освящáть [-ятúть]
**halo** ['heɪləʊ] *astr.* ореóл (*a. fig.*); *of saint* нимб
**halt** [hɔːlt] **1.** (*temporary stop*) привáл; остановка; ***come to a ~*** остановúться *pf.*; **2.** останáвливать(ся) [-новúть(ся)]; дéлать привáл; *mst. fig.* (*hesitate*) колебáться; запинáться [запнýться]
**halve** [hɑːv] **1.** делúть пополáм; **2.** **~s** [hɑːvz, hævz] *pl. om* ***half***
**ham** [hæm] (*pig thigh*) óкорок, (*meat of pig thigh*) ветчинá
**hamburger** ['hæmbɜːgə] бýлочка с котлéтой, гáмбургер
**hamlet** ['hæmlɪt] деревýшка
**hammer** ['hæmə] **1.** молотóк; ***sledge ~*** мóлот; **2.** ковáть мóлотом; бить молоткóм; (*knock*) [по-]стучáть; (*form by ~ing*) выкóвывать [вы́ковать]; ***~ into s.o.'s head*** вбивáть [вбить] комý-л. в гóлову
**hammock** ['hæmək] гамáк
**hamper**[1] ['hæmpə] корзúна с кры́шкой
**hamper**[2] [~] [вос]препя́тствовать; [по]мешáть (Д)
**hand** [hænd] **1.** рукá; (*writing*) пóчерк; *of watch* стрéлка; (*worker*) рабóчий; ***at ~*** под рукóй; ***a good*** (***poor***) ***~ at*** (не-) искýсный в (П); ***change ~s*** переходúть [-ейтú] из рук в рýки; ***~ and glove*** в тéсной свя́зи; ***lend a ~*** помогáть [-мóчь]; ***off ~*** экспрóмтом; ***on ~*** *comm.* имéющийся в продáже; в распоряжéнии; ***on the one ~*** с однóй стороны́; ***on the other ~*** с другóй стороны́; ***~-to-~*** рукопáшный; ***come to ~*** попадáться [-пáсться] пóд руку; **2.** ***~ down*** оставля́ть потóмству; ***~ in*** вручáть [-чúть]; ***~ over*** перед(ав)áть; **~bag** дáмская сýмочка; **~brake** *mot.* ручнóй тóрмоз;

~**cuff** нару́чник; ~**ful** ['hændfl] горсть *f*; *coll*. “наказа́ние”; ***she's a real*** ~ она́ су́щее наказа́ние
**handicap** ['hændıkæp] **1.** поме́ха; *sport* гандика́п; **2.** ста́вить в невы́годное положе́ние; ~**ped**: ***physically*** ~ с физи́ческим недоста́тком; ***mentally*** ~ у́мственно отста́лый
**handi|craft** ['hændıkrɑːft] ручна́я рабо́та; ремесло́; ~**work** ручна́я рабо́та; ***is this your*** ~ ***?*** *fig*. э́то твои́х рук де́ло?
**handkerchief** ['hæŋkətʃıf] носово́й плато́к
**handle** ['hændl] **1.** ру́чка; *of tool, etc*. рукоя́тка; **2.** держа́ть в рука́х, тро́гать или брать рука́ми; (*deal with*) обходи́ться [обойти́сь] с (Т); обраща́ться с (Т)
**hand|made** [hænd'meıd] ручно́й рабо́ты; ~**shake** рукопожа́тие; ~**some** ['hænsəm] краси́вый; (*generous*) ще́дрый; (*large*) поря́дочный; ~**writing** по́черк; ~**y** ['hændı] удо́бный; (*nearby*) бли́зкий
**hang** [hæŋ] **1.** [*irr*.] *v/t*. ве́шать [пове́сить]; *lamp, etc*. подве́шивать [-ве́сить]; (*pt. u pt. p.* ~**ed**) ве́шать [пове́сить]; *v/i*. висе́ть; ~ ***about***, ~ ***around*** слоня́ться, окола́чиваться; ~ ***on*** держа́ть(ся) (за В); *fig*. упо́рствовать; ~ ***on!*** подожди́те мину́тку!; **2.**: ***get the*** ~ ***of*** понима́ть [-ня́ть]; разобра́ться [разбира́ться]
**hangar** ['hæŋə] анга́р
**hanger** ['hæŋə] *for clothes* ве́шалка
**hangings** ['hæŋıŋz] *pl*. драпиро́вки *f/pl*., занаве́ски *f/pl*.
**hangover** ['hæŋəʊvə] *from drinking* похме́лье; *survival* пережи́ток
**haphazard** [hæp'hæzəd] **1.** науда́чу, наобу́м; **2.** □ случа́йный
**happen** ['hæpən] случа́ться [-чи́ться], происходи́ть [произойти́]; отка́зываться [-за́ться]; ***he*** ~***ed to be at home*** он оказа́лся до́ма; ***it so*** ~***ed that …*** случи́лось так, что …; ~ (***up***)***on*** случа́йно встре́тить; ~**ing** ['hæpənıŋ] слу́чай, собы́тие
**happi|ly** ['hæpılı] счастли́во, к сча́стью; ~**ness** [~nıs] сча́стье
**happy** ['hæpı] □ *com*. счастли́вый; (*fortunate*) уда́чный; ~**-go-lucky** беспе́чный
**harangue** [hə'ræŋ] разглаго́льствовать
**harass** ['hærəs] [за]трави́ть; (*pester*) изводи́ть [-вести́]; [из]му́чить
**harbo(u)r** ['hɑːbər] **1.** га́вань *f*, порт; ~ ***duties*** порто́вые сбо́ры; **2.** (*give shelter to*) дать убе́жище (Д), приюти́ть; *fig*. зата́ивать [-и́ть]
**hard** [hɑːd] **1.** *adj*. *com*. твёрдый, жёсткий; (*strong*) кре́пкий; (*difficult*) тру́дный; тяжёлый; ~ ***cash*** нали́чные *pl*. (де́ньги); ~ ***currency*** твёрдая валю́та; ~ ***of hearing*** туго́й на у́хо; **2.** *adv*. твёрдо; кре́пко; си́льно; упо́рно; с трудо́м; ~ ***by*** бли́зко, ря́дом; ~ ***up*** в затрудни́тельном фина́нсовом положе́нии; ~**-boiled** [hɑːd'bɔıld] → ***egg***; *fig*. бесчу́вственный, чёрствый; *Am*. хладнокро́вный; ~ **disk** жёсткий диск; ~**en** ['hɑːdn] затвердева́ть, [за]тверде́ть; *fig*. закаля́ть(ся) [-ли́ть(ся)]; ~**-headed** [hɑːd'hedıd] □ практи́чный, тре́звый; ~**-hearted** [hɑːd'hɑːtıd] бесчу́вственный; ~**ly** ['hɑːdlı] с тру-до́м, едва́, едва́ ли; ~**ship** [~ʃıp] невзго́ды; тру́дности; (*lack of money*) нужда́; ~**ware** *comput*. аппа-ра́тное обеспе́чение; ~**y** ['hɑːdı] □ сме́лый, отва́жный; (*able to bear hard work, etc*.) выно́сливый
**hare** [heə] за́яц; ~**brained** опроме́тчивый; (*foolish*) глу́пый
**harm** [hɑːm] **1.** вред, зло; (*damage*) уще́рб; **2.** [по]вреди́ть (Д); ~**ful** ['hɑːmfl] □ вре́дный, па́губный; ~**less** [~lıs] □ безвре́дный, безоби́дный
**harmon|ious** [hɑː'məʊnıəs] □ гармони́чный, стро́йный; ~**ize** ['hɑːmənaız] *v/t*. гармонизи́ровать (*im*)*pf*.; приводи́ть в гармо́нию; *v/i*. гармони́ровать; ~**y** [~nı] гармо́ния, созву́чие; (*agreement*) согла́сие
**harness** ['hɑːnıs] **1.** у́пряжь *f*, сбру́я; **2.** запряга́ть [запря́чь]
**harp** [hɑːp] **1.** а́рфа; **2.** игра́ть на а́рфе; ~ (***up***)***on*** тверди́ть, завести́ *pf*. волы́нку о (П)

H

**harpoon** [hɑːˈpuːn] гарпу́н, острога́
**harrow** [ˈhærəʊ] *agric.* **1.** борона́; **2.** [вз]борони́ть; *fig.* [из]му́чить; **~ing** [-ɪŋ] *fig.* мучи́тельный
**harsh** [hɑːʃ] □ ре́зкий; жёсткий; (*stern*) стро́гий, суро́вый; *to taste* те́рпкий
**harvest** [ˈhɑːvɪst] **1.** *of wheat, etc.* жа́тва, убо́рка; *of apples, etc.* сбор; урожа́й; ***bumper ~*** небыва́лый урожа́й; **2.** собира́ть урожа́й
**has** [z, əz, həz;, *strong* hæz] *3rd p. sg. pres. от* **have**
**H**
**hash** [hæʃ] ру́бленое мя́со; *fig.* пу́таница
**hast|e** [heɪst] спе́шка, поспе́шность *f*, торопли́вость *f*; ***make ~*** [по]спеши́ть; **~en** [ˈheɪsn] спеши́ть, [по-] торопи́ться; (*speed up*) ускоря́ть [-о́рить]; **~y** [ˈheɪstɪ] □ поспе́шный; необду́манный
**hat** [hæt] шля́па; *without brim* ша́пка; ***talk through one's ~*** нести́ чушь *f*
**hatch** [hætʃ] *naut., ae.* люк
**hatchet** [ˈhætʃɪt] топо́рик
**hat|e** [heɪt] **1.** не́нависть *f*; **2.** ненави́деть; **~eful** [ˈheɪtfl] ненави́стный; **~red** [ˈheɪtrɪd] не́нависть *f*
**haught|iness** [ˈhɔːtɪnɪs] надме́нность *f*, высокоме́рие; **~y** [-tɪ] □ надме́нный, высокоме́рный
**haul** [hɔːl] **1.** перево́зка; (*catch*) уло́в; **2.** тяну́ть; перевози́ть [-везти́]; **~age** [-ɪdʒ] транспортиро́вка, доста́вка
**haunch** [hɔːntʃ] бедро́
**haunt** [hɔːnt] **1.** *of ghost* появля́ться [-ви́ться] в (П); (*frequent*) ча́сто посеща́ть; **2.** люби́мое ме́сто; *of criminals, etc.* прито́н; ***~ed look*** затра́вленный вид
**have** [v, əv, həv;, *strong* hæv] **1.** [*irr.*] *v/t.* име́ть; ***I ~ to do*** я до́лжен сде́лать; ***~ one's hair cut*** [по-] стри́чься; ***he will ~ it that ...*** он наста́ивает на том, что́бы (+ *inf.*); ***I had better go*** мне лу́чше уйти́; ***I had rather go*** я предпочёл бы уйти́; ***~ about one*** име́ть при себе́; ***~ it your own way*** поступа́й как зна́ешь; *opinion* ду́май, что хо́чешь; **2.** *v/aux. вспомогательный глагол для образования перфектной формы*: ***I ~ come*** я пришёл
**havoc** [ˈhævək] опустоше́ние; (*destruction*) разруше́ние; ***play ~ with*** вноси́ть [внести́] беспоря́док/хао́с в (В); разру́шить *pf.*
**hawk** [hɔːk] (*a. pol.*) я́стреб
**hawker** [ˈhɔːkə] у́личный торго́вец
**hawthorn** [ˈhɔːθɔːn] боя́рышник
**hay** [heɪ] се́но; ***~ fever*** се́нная лихора́дка; **~loft** сенова́л; **~stack** стог се́на
**hazard** [ˈhæzəd] **1.** риск; (*danger*) опа́сность *f*; **2.** рискова́ть [-кну́ть]; **~ous** [ˈhæzədəs] □ риско́ванный
**haze** [heɪz] ды́мка, тума́н
**hazel** [ˈheɪzl] **1.** (*tree*) оре́шник; **2.** (*colo[u]r*) ка́рий; **~nut** лесно́й оре́х
**hazy** [ˈheɪzɪ] □ тума́нный; *fig.* сму́тный
**H-bomb** водоро́дная бо́мба
**he** [ɪ, hɪ;, *strong* hiː] **1.** *pron. pers.* он; ***~ who ...*** тот, кто ...; **2. ~-...** *перед названием животного обозначает самца*
**head** [hed] **1.** *com.* голова́; *of government, etc.* глава́; *of department, etc.* руководи́тель *m*, нача́льник; *of bed* изголо́вье; *of coin* лицева́я сторона́, орёл; ***come to a ~*** *fig.* дости́гнуть *pf.* крити́ческой ста́дии; ***get it into one's ~ that ...*** вбить себе́ в го́лову, что ...; **2.** гла́вный; **3.** *v/t.* возглавля́ть; ***~ off*** (*prevent*) предотвраща́ть [-ати́ть]; ***~ for*** *v/i.* направля́ться [-а́виться]; держа́ть курс на (В); **~ache** [ˈhedeɪk] головна́я боль *f*; **~dress** головно́й убо́р; **~ing** [ˈ-ɪŋ] загла́вие; **~land** мыс; **~light** *mot.* фа́ра; **~line** (газе́тный) заголо́вок; **~long** *adj.* опроме́тчивый; *adv.* опроме́тчиво; очертя́ го́лову; **~master** дире́ктор шко́лы; **~phone** нау́шник; **~quarters** *pl.* штаб; *of department, etc.* гла́вное управле́ние; **~strong** своево́льный, упря́мый; **~way**: ***make ~*** де́лать успе́хи, продвига́ться; **~y** [ˈhedɪ] □ опьяня́ющий; *with success* опьянённый
**heal** [hiːl] зале́чивать [-чи́ть], исцеля́ть [-ли́ть]; (*a. ~ up*) зажи́(ва́)ть
**health** [helθ] здоро́вье; **~ful** [-fl] □ целе́бный; **~-resort** куро́рт; **~y** [ˈhelθɪ] □

здоро́вый; (*good for health*) поле́зный

**heap** [hi:p] **1.** ку́ча, гру́да; *fig.* ма́сса, у́йма; **2.** нагроможда́ть [-мозди́ть]; *of food, etc.* накла́дывать [-ложи́ть]

**hear** [hɪə] [*irr.*] [у]слы́шать; [по-] слу́шать; **~ s.o. out** вы́слушать *pf.*; **~d** [hɜ:d] *pt. и pt. p. от* **hear**, **~er** ['hɪərə] слу́шатель(ница *f*) *m*; **~ing** [-ɪŋ] слух; *law* слу́шание де́ла; **within ~** в преде́лах слы́шимости; **~say** ['hɪəseɪ] слу́хи, то́лки

**heart** [hɑ:t] се́рдце; му́жество; (*essence*) суть *f*; (*innermost part*) сердцеви́на; *of forest* глубина́; **~s** *pl.* че́рви *f/pl.*; *fig.* се́рдце, душа́; **by ~** наизу́сть; **lose ~** па́дать ду́хом; **take ~** воспря́нуть ду́хом; **take to ~** принима́ть бли́зко к се́рдцу; **~ attack** серде́чный при́ступ; **~broken** уби́тый го́рем; **~burn** изжо́га; **~en** ['hɑ:tn] ободря́ть [-ри́ть]; **~felt** душе́вный, и́скренний

**hearth** [hɑ:θ] оча́г (*a. fig.*)

**heart|less** ['hɑ:tlɪs] □ бессерде́чный; **~rending** [-rendɪŋ] душераздира́ющий; **~-to-~** дру́жеский; **~y** ['hɑ:tɪ] □ дру́жеский, серде́чный; (*healthy*) здоро́вый

**heat** [hi:t] **1.** *com.* жара́, жар; *fig.* пыл; *sport* забе́г, заплы́в, заéзд; **2.** нагре́(-ва́)ть(ся); *fig.* [раз]горячи́ть; **~er** ['hi:tə] обогрева́тель

**heath** [hi:θ] ме́стность *f*, поро́сшая ве́реском; (*waste land*) пу́стошь *f*; *bot.* ве́реск

**heathen** ['hi:ðn] **1.** язы́чник; **2.** язы́ческий

**heating** ['hi:tɪŋ] обогрева́ние; отопле́ние

**heave** [hi:v] **1.** подъём; **2.** [*irr.*] *v/t.* (*haul*) поднима́ть [-ня́ть]; *v/i. of waves* вздыма́ться; (*strain*) напряга́ться [-я́чься]

**heaven** ['hevn] небеса́ *n/pl.*, не́бо; **move ~ and earth** [с]де́лать всё возмо́жное; **~ly** [-lɪ] небе́сный; *fig.* велико́лепный

**heavy** ['hevɪ] □ *com.* тяжёлый; *crop* оби́льный; *sea* бу́рный; *sky* мра́чный; неуклю́жий; **~weight** *sport* тяжелове́с

**heckle** ['hekl] прерыва́ть замеча́ниями; задава́ть ка́верзные вопро́сы

**hectic** ['hektɪk] *activity* лихора́дочный; **~ day** напряжённый день *m*

**hedge** [hedʒ] **1.** жива́я и́згородь *f*; **2.** *v/t.* огора́живать и́згородью; *v/i.* (*evade*) уклоня́ться от прямо́го отве́та; уви́ливать [увильну́ть]; **~hog** *zo.* ёж

**heed** [hi:d] **1.** внима́ние, осторо́жность *f*; **take no ~ of** не обраща́ть внима́ния на (В); **2.** обраща́ть внима́ние на (В); **~less** [-lɪs] □ небре́жный; необду́манный; **~ of danger** не ду́мая об опа́сности

**heel** [hi:l] **1.** *of foot* пя́тка; *of shoe* каблу́к; **head over ~s** вверх торма́шками; **down at ~** *fig.* неря́шливый; **2.** поста́вить *pf.* набо́йку (на В)

**hefty** ['heftɪ] *fellow* здорове́нный; *blow* си́льный

**height** [haɪt] высота́; *person's* рост; (*high place*) возвы́шенность *f*; *fig.* верх; **~en** ['haɪtn] *interest* повыша́ть [повы́сить]; (*make more intense*) уси́ли(ва)ть

**heir** [eə] насле́дник; **~ess** ['eərɪs, 'eərəs] насле́дница

**held** [held] *pt. и pt. p. от* **hold**

**helicopter** ['helɪkɒptə] вертолёт

**hell** [hel] ад; *attr.* а́дский; **raise ~** подня́ть ужа́сный крик; **~ish** [-ɪʃ] а́дский

**hello** [hə'ləʊ] *coll.* приве́т; *tel.* алло́!

**helm** [helm] *naut.* штурва́л; *fig.* корми́ло

**helmet** ['helmɪt] шлем

**helmsman** ['helmzmən] *naut.* рулево́й

**help** [help] **1.** *com.* по́мощь *f*; **there is no ~ for it !** ничего́ не поде́лаешь!; **2.** *v/t.* помога́ть [помо́чь] (Д); **~ yourself to fruit** бери́те фру́кты; **I could not ~ laughing** я не мог не рассмея́ться; *v/i.* помога́ть [-мо́чь]; **~er** ['helpə] помо́щник (-ица); **~ful** ['helpfl] поле́зный; **~ing** ['helpɪŋ] *of food* по́рция; **have another ~** взять *pf.* ещё (**of** Р); **~less** ['helplɪs] □ беспо́мощный; **~lessness** ['helplɪsnɪs] бес-

H

по́мощность *f*
**hem** [hem] **1.** рубе́ц; *of skirt* подо́л; **2.** подруба́ть [-би́ть]; **~ *in*** окружа́ть [-жи́ть]
**hemisphere** ['hemɪsfɪə] полуша́рие
**hemlock** ['hemlɒk] *bot.* болиголо́в
**hemp** [hemp] конопля́; (*fibre*) пенька́
**hen** [hen] ку́рица
**hence** [hens] отсю́да; сле́довательно; ***a year ~*** че́рез год; **~forth** [hens'fɔːθ], **~forward** [hens'fɔːwəd] с э́того вре́мени, впредь
**henpecked** ['henpekt] находя́щийся под башмако́м у жены́
**her** [ə, hə;, *strong* hɜː] *pers. pron.* (*косвенный падеж от* ***she***) её; ей
**herb** [hɜːb] (целе́бная) трава́; (пря́ное) расте́ние
**herd** [hɜːd] **1.** ста́до; *fig.* толпа́; **2.** *v/t.* пасти́ (скот); *v/i.*: **~ *together*** [с]толпи́ться; **~sman** ['hɜːdzmən] пасту́х
**here** [hɪə] здесь, тут; сюда́; вот; ***~'s to you !*** за ва́ше здоро́вье!
**here|after** [hɪər'ɑːftə] в бу́дущем; **~by** э́тим, настоя́щим; таки́м о́бразом
**heredit|ary** [hɪ'redɪtrɪ] насле́дственный; **~y** [~tɪ] насле́дственность *f*
**here|upon** [hɪərə'pɒn] вслед за э́тим; **~with** при сём
**heritage** ['herɪtɪdʒ] насле́дство; насле́дие (*mst. fig.*)
**hermetic** [hɜː'metɪk] (***~ally***) гермети́ческий
**hermit** ['hɜːmɪt] отше́льник
**hero** ['hɪərəʊ] геро́й; **~ic** [~'rəʊɪk] (***~ally***) герои́ческий, геро́йский; **~ine** ['herəʊɪn] герои́ня; **~ism** [~ɪzəm] герои́зм
**heron** ['herən] *zo.* ца́пля
**herring** ['herɪŋ] сельдь *f*; *cul.* селёдка
**hers** [hɜːz] *pron. poss.* её
**herself** [hɜː'self] сама́; себя́, -ся, -сь
**hesitat|e** ['hezɪteɪt] [по]колеба́ться; *in speech* запина́ться [запну́ться]; **~ion** [hezɪ'teɪʃn] колеба́ние; запи́нка
**hew** [hjuː] [*irr.*] руби́ть; разруба́ть [-би́ть]; (*shape*) высека́ть [вы́сечь]
**hey** [heɪ] эй!
**heyday** ['heɪdeɪ] *fig.* зени́т, расцве́т
**hicc|up, ~ough** ['hɪkʌp] **1.** ико́та; **2.** ика́ть [икну́ть]
**hid** [hɪd], **hidden** ['hɪdn] *pt. и pt. p. от* ***hide***
**hide** [haɪd] [*irr.*] [с]пря́тать(ся); (*conceal*) скры(ва́)ть; **~-and-seek** [haɪdn'siːk] пря́тки
**hideous** ['hɪdɪəs] □ отврати́тельный, уро́дливый
**hiding-place** потаённое ме́сто, укры́тие
**hi-fi** ['haɪfaɪ] высо́кая то́чность воспроизведе́ния зву́ка
**high** [haɪ] **1.** □ *adj. com.* высо́кий; (*lofty*) возвы́шенный; *wind* си́льный; *authority* вы́сший, верхо́вный; *meat* с душко́м; ***it's ~ time*** давно́ пора́; **~ *spirits*** *pl.* припо́днятое настрое́ние; **2.** *adv.* высоко́; си́льно; ***aim ~*** высоко́ ме́тить; **~brow** интеллектуа́л; **~-class** первокла́ссный; **~-grade** высо́кого ка́чества; **~-handed** своево́льный; вла́стный; **~lands** *pl.* гори́стая ме́стность *f*
**high|light** выдаю́щийся моме́нт; **~ly** ['haɪlɪ] о́чень, весьма́; ***speak ~ of*** высоко́ отзыва́ться о (П); **~-minded** возвы́шенный, благоро́дный; **~-rise building** высо́тное зда́ние; **~-strung** о́чень чувстви́тельный; напряжённый; **~way** гла́вная доро́га, шоссе́; *fig.* прямо́й путь *m*; **~ *code*** пра́вила доро́жного движе́ния
**hijack** ['haɪdʒæk] *plane* угоня́ть [-на́ть]; *train, etc.* соверша́ть [-ши́ть] налёт; **~er** [~ə] уго́нщик
**hike** [haɪk] *coll.* **1.** прогу́лка; похо́д; **2.** путеше́ствовать пешко́м; **~r** ['haɪkə] пе́ший тури́ст
**hilarious** [hɪ'leərɪəs] □ весёлый, смешно́й; *coll.* умори́тельный
**hill** [hɪl] холм; **~billy** *Am.* ['hɪlbɪlɪ] челове́к из глуби́нки; **~ock** ['hɪlək] хо́лмик; **~side** склон холма́; **~y** [~ɪ] холми́стый
**hilt** [hɪlt] рукоя́тка (*сабли и т.д.*)
**him** [ɪm;, *strong* hɪm] *pers. pron.* (*косвенный падеж от* ***he***) его́, ему́; **~self** [hɪm'self] сам; себя́, -ся, -сь
**hind** [haɪnd] за́дний; **~ *leg*** за́дняя нога́
**hinder** ['hɪndə] **1.** препя́тствовать (Д);

**2.** *v/t.* [по]меша́ть
**hindrance** ['hɪndrəns] поме́ха, препя́тствие
**hinge** [hɪndʒ] **1.** *of door* пе́тля; шарни́р; *fig.* сте́ржень *m*, суть *f*; **2. ~ upon** *fig.* зави́сеть от (Р)
**hint** [hɪnt] **1.** намёк; **2.** намека́ть [-кну́ть] (**at** на В)
**hip**[1] [hɪp] бе́дро; **~ pocket** за́дний карма́н
**hip**[2] [~] я́года шипо́вника
**hippopotamus** [hɪpə'pɒtəməs] гиппопота́м, бегемо́т
**hire** ['haɪə] **1.** *worker* наём; *car, TV, etc.* прока́т; **2.** нанима́ть [наня́ть]; *room, etc.* снима́ть [снять]; брать [взять] напрока́т; **~ out** сдава́ть в прока́т; **~ purchase** поку́пка в рассро́чку
**his** [ɪz;, *strong* hɪz] *poss. pron.* его́, свой
**hiss** [hɪs] *v/i.* [за-, про]шипе́ть; *v/t.* осви́стывать [-ста́ть]
**histor|ian** [hɪ'stɔːrɪən] исто́рик; **~ic(al** □) [hɪs'tɒrɪk(l)] истори́ческий; **~y** ['hɪstərɪ] исто́рия
**hit** [hɪt] **1.** уда́р; попада́ние; *thea., mus.* успе́х; **direct ~** прямо́е попада́ние; **2.** [*irr.*] ударя́ть [уда́рить]; поража́ть [порази́ть]; *target* попада́ть [попа́сть] в (В); **~ town, the beach, etc.** *Am. coll.* (*arrive*) прибы́(ва́)ть в, на (В); *coll.* **~ it off with** [по]ла́дить с (Т); **~ (up)on** находи́ть [найти́] (В); **~ in the eye** *fig.* броса́ться [бро́ситься] в глаза́
**hitch** [hɪtʃ] **1.** толчо́к, рыво́к; *fig.* препя́тствие; **2.** зацепля́ть(ся) [-пи́ть(ся)], прицепля́ть(ся) [-пи́ть(ся)]; **~hike** *mot.* е́здить автосто́пом
**hither** ['hɪðər] *lit.* сюда́; **~to** [~'tuː] *lit.* до сих пор
**hive** [haɪv] **1.** у́лей; (*of bees*) рой пчёл; *fig.* людско́й мураве́йник; **2.** жить вме́сте
**hoard** [hɔːd] **1.** (скры́тый) запа́с, склад; **2.** накопля́ть [-пи́ть]; запаса́ть [-сти́] (В); *secretly* припря́т(ыв)ать
**hoarfrost** ['hɔːfrɒst] и́ней
**hoarse** [hɔːs] □ хри́плый, си́плый
**hoax** [həʊks] **1.** обма́н, ро́зыгрыш; **2.** подшу́чивать [-ути́ть] над (Т), разыгрывать [-ра́ть]
**hobble** ['hɒbl] *v/i.* прихра́мывать
**hobby** ['hɒbɪ] *fig.* хо́бби *n indecl.*, люби́мое заня́тие
**hock** [hɒk] (*wine*) рейнве́йн
**hockey** ['hɒkɪ] хокке́й
**hoe** [həʊ] *agric.* **1.** ца́пка; **2.** ца́пать
**hog** [hɒg] свинья́ (*a. fig.*); бо́ров
**hoist** [hɔɪst] **1.** *for goods* подъёмник; **2.** поднима́ть [-ня́ть]
**hold** [həʊld] **1.** *naut.* трюм; **catch** (*or* **get, lay, take**) **~ of** схва́тывать [схвати́ть] (В); **keep ~ of** уде́рживать [-жа́ть] (В); **2.** [*irr.*] *v/t.* держа́ть; (*sustain*) выде́рживать [вы́держать]; (*restrain*) остана́вливать [-нови́ть]; *meeting, etc.* проводи́ть [-вести́]; *attention* завладе́(ва́)ть; занима́ть [-ня́ть]; (*contain*) вмеща́ть [вмести́ть]; (*think*) счита́ть; **~ one's own** отста́ивать свою́ пози́цию; **~ talks** вести́ переговоры; **~ the line!** *tel.* не ве́шайте тру́бку; **~ over** откла́дывать [отложи́ть]; **~ up** (*support*) подде́рживать [-жа́ть]; (*delay*) заде́рживать [-жа́ть]; останови́ть с це́лью грабежа́; **3.** *v/i.* остана́вливаться [-нови́ться]; *of weather* держа́ться; **~ forth** разглаго́льствовать; **~ good** (*or* **true**) име́ть си́лу; **~ off** держа́ться по́одаль; **~ on** де́ржиться за (В); **~ to** приде́рживаться (Р); **~er** [~ə] аренда́тор; владе́лец; **~ing** [~ɪŋ] уча́сток зе́мли; владе́ние; **~-up** *Am.* налёт, ограбле́ние
**hole** [həʊl] дыра́, отве́рстие; *in ground* я́ма; *of animals* нора́; *coll. fig.* затрудни́тельное положе́ние; **pick ~s in** находи́ть недоста́тки в (П); придира́ться [придра́ться]
**holiday** ['hɒlədɪ] пра́здник, официа́льный день о́тдыха; о́тпуск; **~s** *pl. educ.* кани́кулы *f/pl.*
**hollow** ['hɒləʊ] **1.** □ пусто́й, по́лый; *cheeks* ввали́вшийся; *eyes* впа́лый; **2.** по́лость *f*; *in tree* дупло́; (*small valley*) лощи́на; **3.** выда́лбливать [вы́долбить]
**holly** ['hɒlɪ] остроли́ст, па́дуб
**holster** ['həʊlstə] кобура́
**holy** ['həʊlɪ] свято́й, свяще́нный; ♀

***Week*** Страстна́я неде́ля

**homage** ['hɒmɪdʒ] уваже́ние; ***do*** (*or* ***pay, render***) **~** отдава́ть дань уваже́ния (***to*** Д)

**home** [həʊm] **1.** дом, жили́ще; ро́дина; ***at* ~** до́ма; ***maternity* ~** роди́льный дом; **2.** *adj.* дома́шний; вну́тренний; оте́чественный; **~ *industry*** оте́чественная промы́шленность *f*; **≗ *Office*** министе́рство вну́тренних дел; **≗ *Secretary*** мини́стр вну́тренних дел; **3.** *adv.* домо́й; ***hit*** (*or* ***strike***) **~** попа́сть *pf.* в цель *f*; **~less** [-lɪs] бездо́мный; **~like** ую́тный; непринуждённый; **~ly** [-lɪ] *fig.* просто́й, обы́денный; дома́шний; *Am.* (*plain-looking*) некраси́вый; **~made** дома́шнего изготовле́ния; **~sickness** тоска́ по ро́дине; **~ward(s)** [-wəd(z)] домо́й

**homicide** ['hɒmɪsaɪd] уби́йство; уби́йца *m/f*

**homogeneous** [hɒmə'dʒiːnɪəs] □ одноро́дный, гомоге́нный

**honest** ['ɒnɪst] □ че́стный; **~y** [-ɪ] че́стность *f*

**honey** ['hʌnɪ] мёд; (*mode of address*) дорога́я; **~comb** ['hʌnɪkəʊm] со́ты; **~moon 1.** медо́вый ме́сяц; **2.** проводи́ть медо́вый ме́сяц

**honorary** ['ɒnərərɪ] почётный

**hono(u)r** ['ɒnə] **1.** честь *f*; (*respect*) почёт; *f*; *mil., etc.* по́честь; **2.** чтить, почита́ть; *fin. check/Brt. cheque* опла́чивать [-лати́ть]; **~able** ['ɒnərəbl] □ почётный, благоро́дный; (*upright*) че́стный

**hood** [hʊd] (*covering for head*) капюшо́н; *Am.* (*for car engine*) капо́т

**hoodwink** ['hʊdwɪŋk] обма́нывать [-ну́ть]

**hoof** [huːf] копы́то

**hook** [huːk] **1.** крюк, крючо́к; ***by ~ or by crook*** пра́вдами и непра́вдами, так и́ли ина́че; **2.** зацепля́ть [-пи́ть]; *dress. etc.* застёгивать(ся) [-стегну́ть(ся)]

**hoop** [huːp] о́бруч; ***make s.o. jump through ~s*** подверга́ть кого́-л. тяжёлому испыта́нию

**hoot** [huːt] **1.** шика́нье; *mot.* сигна́л; **2.** *v/i.* оши́кивать [-кать]; дава́ть сигна́л, сигна́лить; *v/t.* (*a.* **~ *down***) освисты́вать [-иста́ть]

**hop**¹ [hɒp] *bot.* хмель *m*

**hop**² [~] **1.** прыжо́к; ***keep s.o. on the ~*** не дава́ть кому́-л. поко́я; **2.** на одно́й ноге́

**hope** [həʊp] **1.** наде́жда; ***past* ~** безнадёжный; ***raise* ~** обнадё-жи(ва)ть; **2.** наде́яться (***for*** на В); **~ful** [-fl] (*promising*) подаю́щий наде́жды; (*having hope*) наде́ющийся; **~less** [-lɪs] безнадёжный

**horde** [hɔːd] орда́; по́лчища; *pl.* то́лпы *f/pl.*

**horizon** [hə'raɪzn] горизо́нт; *fig.* кругозо́р

**hormone** ['hɔːməʊn] гормо́н

**horn** [hɔːn] *animal's* рог; звуково́й сигна́л; *mus* рожо́к; **~ *of plenty*** рог изоби́лия

**hornet** ['hɔːnɪt] *zo.* ше́ршень *m*

**horny** ['hɔːnɪ] *hands* мозо́листый

**horoscope** ['hɒrəskəʊp] гороско́п; ***cast a* ~** составля́ть [-а́вить] гороско́п

**horr|ible** ['hɒrəbl] □ стра́шный, ужа́сный; **~id** ['hɒrɪd] ужа́сный; (*repelling*) проти́вный; **~ify** ['hɒrɪfaɪ] ужаса́ть [-сну́ть]; шоки́ровать; **~or** ['hɒrə] у́жас

**hors d'œuvres** [ɔː'dɜːv] *pl.* заку́ски *f/pl.*

**horse** [hɔːs] ло́шадь *f*, конь *m*; ***get on a* ~** сесть *pf.* на ло́шадь; ***dark* ~** тёмная лоша́дка; **~back**: ***on* ~** верхо́м; **~ laugh** *coll.* гру́бый, гро́мкий хо́хот; **~man** вса́дник; **~power** лошади́ная си́ла; **~ race** ска́чки; **~radish** хрен; **~shoe** подко́ва

**horticulture** ['hɔːtɪkʌltʃə] садово́дство

**hose** [həʊz] (*pipe*) шланг

**hosiery** ['həʊzɪərɪ] чуло́чные изде́лия *n/pl.*

**hospice** ['hɒspɪs] *med.* хо́спис

**hospitable** [hɒs'pɪtəbl] □ гостеприи́мный

**hospital** ['hɒspɪtl] больни́ца; *mil.* го́спиталь *m*; **~ity** [hɒspɪ'tælətɪ] госте-

приимство; **~ize** ['hɒspɪtəlaɪz] госпитализи́ровать
**host**[1] [həʊst] хозя́ин; ***act as ~*** быть за хозя́ина
**host**[2] [~] мно́жество, *coll.* ма́сса, тьма́
**hostage** ['hɒstɪdʒ] зало́жник *m*, -ница *f*
**hostel** ['hɒstl] общежи́тие; (*youth* ~) турба́за
**hostess** ['həʊstɪs] хозя́йка (→ ***host***)
**hostil|e** ['hɒstaɪl] вражде́бный; **~ity** [hɒ'stɪlətɪ] вражде́бность *f*; вражде́бный акт; *pl. mil.* вое́нные де́йствия
**hot** [hɒt] горя́чий; *summer* жа́ркий; *fig.* пы́лкий; **~bed** парни́к; **~ dog** *fig.* бу́лочка с горя́чей соси́ской
**hotchpotch** ['hɒtʃpɒtʃ] *fig.* вся́кая вся́чина, смесь *f*
**hotel** [həʊ'tel] оте́ль *m*, гости́ница
**hot|headed** опроме́тчивый; **~house** оранжере́я, тепли́ца; **~ spot** *pol.* горя́чая то́чка; **~-water bottle** гре́лка
**hound** [haʊnd] **1.** го́нчая; **2.** *fig.* [за]трави́ть
**hour** [aʊə] час; вре́мя; ***24 ~s*** су́тки; ***rush ~*** часы́ пик; **~ly** [~lɪ] ежеча́сный
**house** [haʊs] **1.** *com.* дом; зда́ние; *parl.* пала́та; ***apartment ~*** многокварти́рный дом; **2.** [haʊz] *v/t.* поселя́ть [-ли́ть]; помеща́ть [-ести́ть]; (*give shelter to*) приюти́ть *pf.*; *v/i.* помеща́ться [-ести́ться]; **~hold** дома́шний круг; семья́; **~holder** домовладе́лец; **~keeper** эконо́мка; дома́шняя хозя́йка; **~keeping**: ***do the ~*** вести́ дома́шнее хозя́йство; **~warming** новосе́лье; **~wife** домохозя́йка
**housing** ['haʊzɪŋ] обеспе́чение жильём; ***~ conditions*** жили́щные усло́вия
**hove** [həʊv] *pt. и pt. p. от* ***heave***
**hovel** ['hɒvl] лачу́га, хиба́рка
**hover** ['hɒvə] *of bird* пари́ть; *ae.* кружи́ть(ся); **~craft** су́дно на возду́шной поду́шке
**how** [haʊ] как?, каки́м о́бразом?; ***~ about ...?*** как насчёт (P) ...?; **~ever** [haʊ'evə] **1.** *adv.* как бы ни; **2.** *cj.* одна́ко, и всё же
**howl** [haʊl] **1.** вой, завыва́ние; **2.** [за]вы́ть; **~er** ['haʊlə] *sl.* гру́бая оши́бка; ля́псус
**hub** [hʌb] *of wheel* ступи́ца; *fig. of activity* центр; *of the universe* пуп земли́
**hubbub** ['hʌbʌb] шум; *coll.* го́мон, гам
**huddle** ['hʌdl] **1.** *of things* [с]вали́ть в ку́чу; ***~ together*** *of people* сби́ться *pf.* в ку́чу; **2.** ку́ча; *of people* су́толока, сумато́ха
**hue**[1] [hjuː] оттéнок
**hue**[2] [~]: ***~ and cry*** крик, шум
**huff** [hʌf] раздраже́ние; ***get into a ~*** оби́деться
**hug** [hʌg] **1.** объя́тие; **2.** обнима́ть [-ня́ть]; *fig.* быть приве́рженным; **~ o.s.** поздравля́ть [-а́вить] себя́
**huge** [hjuːdʒ] □ огро́мный, грома́дный
**hulk** [hʌlk] *fig.* у́вален
**hull** [hʌl] *bot.* шелуха́, скорлупа́; *naut.* ко́рпус
**hum** [hʌm] [за]жужжа́ть; (*sing*) напева́ть; *coll.* ***make things ~*** вноси́ть оживле́ние в рабо́ту
**human** ['hjuːmən] **1.** челове́ческий; **2.** *coll.* челове́к; **~e** [hjuː'meɪn] гума́нный, челове́чный; **~eness** гума́нность *f*; **~itarian** [hjuːmænɪ'teərɪən] гумани́ст; гума́нный; **~ity** [hjuː'mænətɪ] челове́чество; **~kind** [hjuː-mən-'kaɪnd] род челове́ческий; **~ly** по-челове́чески
**humble** ['hʌmbl] **1.** □ (*not self-important*) смире́нный, скро́мный; (*lowly*) просто́й; **2.** унижа́ть [уни́зить]; смиря́ть [-ри́ть]
**humbug** ['hʌmbʌg] (*deceit*) надува́тельство; (*nonsense*) чепуха́
**humdrum** ['hʌmdrʌm] однообра́зный, ску́чный
**humid** ['hjuːmɪd] сыро́й, вла́жный; **~ity** [hjuː'mɪdətɪ] вла́жность *f*
**humiliat|e** [hjuː'mɪlɪeɪt] унижа́ть [уни́зить]; **~ion** [hjuːmɪlɪ'eɪʃn] униже́ние
**humility** [hjuː'mɪlətɪ] смире́ние
**humorous** ['hjuːmərəs] □ юмористи́ческий

H

**humo(u)r** ['hjuːmə] **1.** юмор, шутли́вость *f*; (*mood*) настрое́ние; ***out of ~*** не в ду́хе; **2.** (*indulge*) потака́ть (Д); ублажа́ть [-жи́ть]

**hump** [hʌmp] **1.** горб; **2.** [с]го́рбить(ся)

**hunch** [hʌntʃ] **1.** горб; (*intuitive feeling*) чутьё, интуи́ция; ***have a ~ that*** у меня́ тако́е чу́вство, что …; **2.** [с]го́рбить(ся) (*a.* ***up***); **~back** горбу́н(ья)

**hundred** ['hʌndrəd] **1.** сто; **2.** со́тня; **~th** [~θ] со́тый; со́тая часть *f*; **~weight** це́нтнер

H

**hung** [hʌŋ] *pt. и pt. p. от* **hang**

**Hungarian** [hʌŋ'geərɪən] **1.** венгр *m*, -ге́рка *f*; **2.** венге́рский

**hunger** ['hʌŋgə] **1.** го́лод; *fig.* жа́жда; **2.** *v/i.* голода́ть; быть голо́дным; *fig. desire* жа́ждать (***for*** Р)

**hungry** ['hʌŋgrɪ] □ голо́дный; ***get ~*** проголода́ться

**hunk** [hʌŋk] ломо́ть *m*; *of meat* большо́й кусо́к

**hunt** [hʌnt] **1.** охо́та; (*search*) по́иски *m/pl.* (***for*** Р); **2.** охо́титься на (В) *or* за (Т); **~ *out*** *or* ***up*** оты́скивать [-ка́ть]; **~ *for*** *fig.* охо́титься за (Т), иска́ть (Р *or* В); **~er** ['hʌntə] охо́тник; **~ing grounds** охо́тничьи уго́дья

**hurdle** ['hɜːdl] барье́р; **~*s*** ска́чки с препя́тствиями; бег с препя́тствиями

**hurl** [hɜːl] **1.** си́льный бросо́к; **2.** швыря́ть [-рну́ть], мета́ть [метну́ть]

**hurricane** ['hʌrɪkən] урага́н

**hurried** ['hʌrɪd] торопли́вый

**hurry** ['hʌrɪ] **1.** торопли́вость *f*, поспе́шность *f*; ***be in no ~*** не спеши́ть; ***what's the ~?*** заче́м спеши́ть?; **2.** *v/t.* [по]торопи́ть; *v/i.* [по]спеши́ть (*a.* **~ *up***)

**hurt** [hɜːt] [*irr.*] (*injure*) ушиба́ть [-би́ть] (*a. fig.*); причиня́ть боль *f*; боле́ть

**husband** ['hʌzbənd] муж; (*spouse*) супру́г

**hush** [hʌʃ] **1.** тишина́, молча́ние; **2.** ти́ше!; **3.** установи́ть *pf.* тишину́; ***~ up*** *facts* скры(ва́)ть; ***the affair was ~ed up*** де́ло замя́ли

**husk** [hʌsk] **1.** *bot.* шелуха́; **2.** очища́ть от шелухи́, [об]лущи́ть; **~y** ['hʌskɪ] □ (*hoarse*) си́плый; охри́плый; (*burly*) ро́слый

**hustle** ['hʌsl] **1.** *v/t.* (*push*) толка́ть [-кну́ть]; пиха́ть [пихну́ть]; (*hurry*) [по]торопи́ть; *v/i.* толка́ться; [по]торопи́ться; **2.** толкотня́; ***~ and bustle*** шум и толкотня́

**hut** [hʌt] хи́жина

**hutch** [hʌtʃ] *for rabbits, etc.* кле́тка

**hyacinth** ['haɪəsɪnθ] гиаци́нт

**hybrid** ['haɪbrɪd] гибри́д; *animal* по́месь *f*

**hydro** ['haɪdrə] водо…; **~electric power station** гидро(электро-) ста́нция; **~foil** су́дно на подво́дных кры́льях; **~gen** ['haɪdrədʒən] водоро́д; **~phobia** ['haɪdrə'fəʊbɪə] бе́шенство; **~plane** ['haɪdrəpleɪn] гидропла́н

**hygiene** ['haɪdʒiːɪn] гигие́на

**hymn** [hɪm] (церко́вный) гимн

**hyphen** ['haɪfn] дефи́с; **~ate** [~fəneɪt] писа́ть через чёрточку

**hypnotize** ['hɪpnətaɪz] [за]гипнотизи́ровать

**hypo|chondriac** [haɪpə'kɒndrɪæk] ипохо́ндрик; **~crisy** [hɪ'pɒkrəsɪ] лицеме́рие; **~crite** ['hɪpəkrɪt] лицеме́р; **~critical** [hɪpə'krɪtɪkl] лицеме́рный; нейскренний; **~thesis** [haɪ'pɒθəsɪs] гипо́теза, предположе́ние

**hyster|ical** [hɪ'sterɪkl] истери́чный; **~ics** [hɪ'sterɪks] *pl.* исте́рика

# I

**I** [aɪ] *pers. pron.* я; **~ *feel cold*** мне хо́лодно; ***you and* ~** мы с ва́ми

**ice** [aɪs] **1.** лёд; **2.** замора́живать [-ро́зить]; *cul.* глазирова́ть (*im*)*pf.*; **~ *over*** покрыва́ть(ся) льдом; **~ age** леднико́вый пери́од; **~box** *Am.* холоди́льник; **~breaker** ледоко́л; **~ cream** моро́женое; **~d** охлаждённый; *cake* глазиро́ванный; **~ hockey** хокке́й; **~ rink** като́к

**icicle** ['aɪsɪkl] сосу́лька

**icing** ['aɪsɪŋ] *cul.* са́харная глазу́рь *f*

**icon** ['aɪkɔn] ико́на

**icy** ['aɪsɪ] □ ледяно́й (*a. fig.*)

**idea** [aɪ'dɪə] (*concept*) иде́я; (*notion*) поня́тие, представле́ние; (*thought*) мысль *f*; **~l** [~l] **1.** □ идеа́льный; **2.** идеа́л

**identi|cal** [aɪ'dentɪkl] □ тот (же) са́мый; тожде́ственный; иденти́чный, одина́ковый; **~fication** [aɪˌdentɪfɪ'keiʃn] определе́ние; опозна́(ва́)ние; установле́ние ли́чности; **~fy** [~faɪ] определя́ть [-ли́ть]; опозн(ав)а́ть; устана́вливать ли́чность *f* (P); **~ty** [~tɪ]: ***prove s.o.'s* ~** установи́ть *pf.* ли́чность *f*; **~ty card** удостовере́ние ли́чности

**idiom** ['ɪdɪəm] идио́ма; (*language*) наре́чие, го́вор, язы́к

**idiot** ['ɪdɪət] идио́т *m*, -ка *f*; **~ic** [ɪdɪ'ɒtɪk] (**-ally**) идио́тский

**idle** ['aɪdl] **1.** неза́нятый; безрабо́тный; лени́вый; *question* пра́здный; (*futile*) тще́тный; *tech.* безде́йствующий, холосто́й; **2.** *v/t.* проводи́ть (вре́-мя) без де́ла (*mst.* **~ *away***); *v/i.* лени́ться, безде́льничать; **~ness** [~nɪs] пра́здность *f*; безде́лье; **~r** [~ə] безде́льник *m*, -ица *f*, лентя́й *m*, -ка *f*

**idol** ['aɪdl] и́дол; *fig.* куми́р; **~ize** ['aɪdəlaɪz] боготвори́ть

**idyl(l)** ['ɪdɪl] иди́ллия

**if** [ɪf] *cj.* е́сли; е́сли бы; (= ***whether***) ли: ***I don't know* ~ *he knows*** не зна́ю, зна́ет ли он ...; **~ *I were you* ...** на ва́шем ме́сте

**ignit|e** [ɪg'naɪt] зажига́ть [-же́чь]; загора́ться [-ре́ться], воспламеня́ться [-ни́ться]; **~ion** [ɪg'nɪʃn] *mot.* зажига́ние

**ignoble** [ɪg'nəʊbl] □ ни́зкий, неблагоро́дный

**ignor|ance** ['ɪgnərəns] неве́жество; *of intent, etc.* неве́дение; **~ant** [~rənt] неве́жественный; несве́дущий; **~e** [ɪg'nɔː] игнори́ровать

**ill** [ɪl] **1.** *adj.* больно́й; дурно́й; **~ *omen*** дурно́е предзнаменова́ние; **2.** *adv.* едва́ ли; пло́хо; **3.** зло, вред

**ill|-advised** неблагоразу́мный; **~-bred** невоспи́танный

**illegal** [ɪ'liːgl] □ незако́нный

**illegible** [ɪ'ledʒəbl] □ неразбо́рчивый

**illegitimate** [ɪlɪ'dʒɪtɪmət] □ незако́нный; *child* незаконнорождённый

**ill|-fated** злосча́стный, злополу́чный; **~-founded** необосно́ванный; **~-humo(u)red** раздражи́тельный

**illiterate** [ɪ'lɪtərət] □ негра́мотный

**ill|-mannered** невоспи́танный, гру́бый; **~-natured** □ зло́бный, недоброжела́тельный

**illness** ['ɪlnɪs] боле́знь *f*

**ill|-timed** несвоевре́менный, неподходя́щий; **~-treat** пло́хо обраща́ться с (T)

**illumin|ate** [ɪ'luːmɪneɪt] освеща́ть [-ети́ть], озаря́ть [-ри́ть]; (*enlighten*) просвеща́ть [-ети́ть]; (*cast light on*) пролива́ть свет на (B); **~ating** [~neɪtɪŋ] поучи́тельный, освети́тельный; **~ation** [ɪluːmɪ'neɪʃn] освеще́ние; (*display*) иллюмина́ция

**illus|ion** [ɪ'luːʒn] иллю́зия, обма́н чувств; **~ive** [~sɪv], **~ory** [~sərɪ] □ при́зрачный, иллюзо́рный

**illustrat|e** ['ɪləstreɪt] иллюстри́ровать (*im*)*pf.*; (*explain*) поясня́ть [-ни́ть]; **~ion** [ɪlə'streɪʃn] иллюстра́ция; **~ive** ['ɪləstrətɪv] иллюстрати́вный

**illustrious** [ɪ'lʌstrɪəs] □ просла́вленный, знамени́тый

**ill-will** недоброжела́тельность *f*
**image** ['ımıdʒ] о́браз; изображе́ние; (*reflection*) отраже́ние; (*likeness*) подо́бие, ко́пия
**imagin|able** [ı'mædʒınəbl] □ вообрази́мый; **~ary** [~nərı] воображаемый; мни́мый; **~ation** [ımædʒı'neıʃn] воображе́ние, фанта́зия; **~ative** [ı'mædʒınətıv] □ одарённый воображе́нием; **~e** [ı'mædʒın] вообража́ть [-рази́ть], представля́ть [-а́вить] себе́
**imbecile** ['ımbəsi:l] **1.** слабоу́мный; **2.** *coll.* глупе́ц
**imbibe** [ım'baıb] (*absorb*) впи́тывать [впита́ть] (*a. fig.*); *fig. ideas, etc.* усва́ивать [усво́ить]
**imita|te** ['ımıteıt] подража́ть (Д); (*copy, mimic*) передра́знивать [-ни́ть]; подде́л(ыв)ать; **~tion** [ımı'teıʃn] подража́ние; имита́ция, подде́лка; *attr.* иску́сственный
**immaculate** [ı'mækjʊlət] безукори́зненный, безупре́чный
**immaterial** [ımə'tıərıəl] (*unimportant*) несуще́ственный, нева́жный; (*incorporeal*) невеще́ственный, нематериа́льный
**immature** [ımə'tjʊə] незре́лый
**immediate** [ı'mi:djət] □ непосре́дственный; ближа́йший; (*urgent*) безотлага́тельный; **~ly** [~lı] *adv. of time, place* непосре́дственно; неме́дленно
**immemorial** [ımə'mɔ:rıəl]: ***from time ~*** испоко́н веко́в
**immense** [ı'mens] □ огро́мный
**immerse** [ı'mɜ:s] погружа́ть [-узи́ть], окуна́ть [-ну́ть]; *fig.* **~ o.s. in** погружа́ться [-узи́ться]
**immigra|nt** ['ımıgrənt] иммигра́нт *m*, -ка *f*; **~te** [~greıt] иммигри́ровать (*im*)*pf.*; **~tion** [ımı'greıʃn] иммигра́ция
**imminent** ['ımınənt] грозя́щий, нави́сший; ***a storm is ~*** надвига́ется бу́ря
**immobile** [ı'məʊbaıl] неподви́жный
**immoderate** [ı'mɒdərət] непоме́рный, чрезме́рный
**immodest** [ı'mɒdıst] □ нескро́мный
**immoral** [ı'mɒrəl] □ безнра́вственный
**immortal** [ı'mɔ:tl] бессме́ртный
**immun|e** [ı'mju:n] невосприи́мчивый (***from*** к Д); **~ity** [~ıtı] *med.* иммуните́т, невосприи́мчивость *f* (***from*** к Д); *dipl.* иммуните́т
**imp** [ımp] дьяволёнок, бесёнок; шалуни́шка *m/f*
**impact** ['ımpækt] уда́р; (*collision*) столкнове́ние; *fig.* влия́ние, возде́йствие
**impair** [ım'peə] (*weaken*) ослабля́ть [-а́бить]; *health* подрыва́ть [-дорва́ть], (*damage*) поврежда́ть [-ди́ть]
**impart** [ım'pɑ:t] (*give*) прид(ав)а́ть; (*make known*) сообща́ть [-щи́ть]
**impartial** [ım'pɑ:ʃl] □ беспристра́стный, непредвзя́тый
**impassable** [ım'pɑ:səbl] □ непроходи́мый; *for vehicles* непрое́зжий
**impassive** [ım'pæsıv] □ споко́йный, бесстра́стный
**impatien|ce** [ım'peıʃns] нетерпе́ние; **~t** [~nt] □ нетерпели́вый
**impeccable** [ım'pekəbl] (*flawless*) безупре́чный
**impede** [ım'pi:d] [вос]препя́тствовать (Д)
**impediment** [ım'pedımənt] поме́ха
**impel** [ım'pel] (*force*) вынужда́ть [вы́нудить]; (*urge*) побужда́ть [-уди́ть]
**impending** [ım'pendıŋ] предстоя́щий, надвига́ющийся
**impenetrable** [ım'penıtrəbl] □ непроходи́мый; непроница́емый (*a. fig.*); *fig.* непостижи́мый
**imperative** [ım'perətıv] □ *manner, voice* повели́тельный, вла́стный; (*essential*) кра́йне необходи́мый
**imperceptible** [ımpə'septəbl] неощути́мый; незаме́тный
**imperfect** [ım'pɜ:fıkt] □ несоверше́нный; (*faulty*) дефе́ктный
**imperial** [ım'pıərıəl] □ импе́рский; (*majestic*) вели́чественный
**imperil** [ım'perəl] подверга́ть [-ве́ргнуть] опа́сности
**imperious** [ım'pıərıəs] □ (*commanding*) вла́стный; (*haughty*) высокоме́рный
**impermeable** [ım'pɜ:mıəbl] непроница́емый

**impersonal** [ɪm'pɜːsənl] *gr.* безличный; безликий; объективный
**impersonate** [ɪm'pɜːsəneɪt] исполнять роль *f* (P), выдавать себя за; изображать [-азить]
**impertinen|ce** [ɪm'pɜːtɪnəns] дерзость *f.*; **~t** [~nənt] □ дерзкий
**imperturbable** [ɪmpə'ɜːbəbl] □ невозмутимый
**impervious** [ɪm'pɜːvɪəs] → ***impermeable***; *fig.* глухой (***to*** к Д)
**impetu|ous** [ɪm'petjʊəs] □ стремительный; (*done hastily*) необдуманный; **~s** ['ɪmpɪtəs] импульс, толчок
**impinge** [ɪm'pɪndʒ]: **~ (*up*)*on*** [по]влиять, отражаться [-зиться]
**implacable** [ɪm'plækəbl] □ (*relentless*) неумолимый; (*unappeasable*) непримиримый
**implant** [ɪm'plɑːnt] *ideas, etc.* насаждать [насадить]; внушать [-шить]
**implausible** [ɪm'plɔːzəbl] неправдоподобный, невероятный
**implement** ['ɪmplɪmənt] **1.** (*small tool*) инструмент; *agric.* орудие; **2.** выполнять [выполнить]
**implicat|e** ['ɪmplɪkeɪt] вовлекать [-ечь], впут(ыв)ать; **~ion** [ɪmplɪ'keɪʃn] вовлечение; скрытый смысл, намёк
**implicit** [ɪm'plɪsɪt] □ (*unquestioning*) безоговорочный; (*suggested*) подразумеваемый; (*implied*) недосказанный
**implore** [ɪm'plɔː] умолять [-лить]
**imply** [ɪm'plaɪ] подразумевать; (*insinuate*) намекать [-кнуть] на (B); значить
**impolite** [ɪmpə'laɪt] □ невежливый
**impolitic** [ɪm'pɒlətɪk] □ нецелесообразный; неблагоразумный
**import 1.** ['ɪmpɔːt] ввоз, импорт; **~s** *pl.* ввозимые товары *m/pl.*; **2.** [ɪm'pɔːt] ввозить [ввезти], импортировать (*im*)*pf.*; **~ance** [ɪm'pɔːtns] значение, важность *f*; **~ant** [~tnt] важный, значительный
**importunate** [ɪm'pɔːtʃʊnət] □ назойливый
**impos|e** [ɪm'pəʊz] *v/t.* навязывать [-зать]; *a tax* облагать [обложить]; ***~ a fine*** наложить штраф; *v/i.* ***~ upon*** злоупотреблять [-бить] (T); **~ing** [~ɪŋ] внушительный, впечатляющий
**impossib|ility** [ɪmpɒsə'bɪlətɪ] невозможность *f*; **~le** [ɪm'pɒsəbl] □ невозможный; (*unbearable*) *coll.* несносный
**impostor** [ɪm'pɒstə] шарлатан; самозванец
**impoten|ce** ['ɪmpətəns] бессилие, слабость *f*; *med.* импотенция; **~t** [~tənt] бессильный, слабый; импотентный
**impoverish** [ɪm'pɒvərɪʃ] доводить до нищеты; *fig.* обеднять [-нить]
**impracticable** [ɪm'præktɪkəbl] □ неисполнимый, неосуществимый
**impractical** [ɪm'præktɪkl] □ непрактичный
**impregnate** ['ɪmpregneɪt] (*saturate*) пропитывать [-питать]; (*fertilize*) оплодотворять [-творить]
**impress** [ɪm'pres] отпечат(ыв)ать; (*fix*) запечатле(ва)ть; (*bring home*) внушать [-шить] (***on*** Д); производить впечатление на (B); **~ion** [ɪm'preʃn] впечатление; *typ.* оттиск; ***I am under the ~ that*** у меня такое впечатление, что ...; **~ionable** [ɪm'preʃənəbl] впечатлительный; **~ive** [ɪm'presɪv] □ внушительный, впечатляющий
**imprint** [ɪm'prɪnt] **1.** *in memory, etc.* запечатле(ва)ть; **2.** отпечаток
**imprison** [ɪm'prɪzn] сажать [посадить]/заключать [-чить] в тюрьму; **~ment** [~mənt] тюремное заключение
**improbable** [ɪm'prɒbəbl] □ невероятный, неправдоподобный
**improper** [ɪm'prɒpə] неуместный; (*indecent*) непристойный; (*incorrect*) неправильный
**improve** [ɪm'pruːv] *v/t.* улучшать [улучшить]; [у]совершенствовать; *v/i.* улучшаться [улучшиться]; [у]совершенствоваться; ***~ upon*** улучшать [улучшить] (B); **~ment** [~mənt] улучшение; усовершенствование
**improvise** ['ɪmprəvaɪz] импровизировать (*im*)*pf.*

**imprudent** [ɪm'pruːdnt] □ неблагоразу́мный; неосторо́жный

**impuden|ce** ['ɪmpjʊdəns] на́глость *f*; де́рзость *f*; **~t** [-dənt] на́глый; де́рзкий

**impulse** ['ɪmpʌls] и́мпульс, толчо́к; (*sudden inclination*) поры́в

**impunity** [ɪm'pjuːnətɪ] безнака́занность *f*; ***with ~*** безнака́занно

**impure** [ɪm'pjʊə] нечи́стый; гря́зный (*a. fig.*); (*indecent*) непристо́йный; *air* загрязнённый; (*mixed with s.th.*) с при́месью

**impute** [ɪm'pjuːt] припи́сывать [-са́ть] (Д/В)

**in** [ɪn] **1.** *prp.* в, во (П *or* В); ***~ number*** в коли́честве (Р), число́м в (В); ***~ itself*** само́ по себе́; ***~ 1949*** в 1949-ом (в ты́сяча девятьсо́т со́рок девя́том) году́; ***cry out ~ alarm*** закрича́ть в испу́ге (*or* от стра́ха); ***~ the street*** на у́лице; ***~ my opinion*** по моему́ мне́нию, помо́ему; ***~ English*** по-англи́йски; ***a novel ~ English*** рома́н на англи́йском языке́; ***~ thousands*** ты́сячами; ***~ the circumstances*** в э́тих усло́виях; ***~ this manner*** таки́м о́бразом; ***~ a word*** одни́м сло́вом; ***be ~ power*** быть у вла́сти; ***be engaged ~ reading*** занима́ться чте́нием; **2.** *adv.* внутри́; внутрь; ***she's ~ for an unpleasant surprise*** её ожида́ет неприя́тный сюрпри́з; *coll.*; ***be ~ with*** быть в хоро́ших отноше́ниях с (Т)

**inability** [ɪnə'bɪlətɪ] неспосо́бность *f*

**inaccessible** [ɪnæk'sesəbl] □ недосту́пный; непристу́пный

**inaccurate** [ɪn'ækjərət] □ нето́чный

**inactiv|e** [ɪn'æktɪv] □ безде́ятельный; безде́йствующий; **~ity** [ɪnæk'tɪvətɪ] безде́ятельность *f*; ине́ртность *f*

**inadequate** [ɪn'ædɪkwɪt] □ (*insufficient*) недоста́точный; (*not capable*) неспосо́бный; *excuse* неубеди́тельный

**inadmissible** [ɪnəd'mɪsəbl] недопусти́мый, неприе́млемый

**inadvertent** [ɪnəd'vɜːtənt] □ невнима́тельный; неумы́шленный; (*unintentional*) ненаме́ренный

**inalienable** [ɪn'eɪlɪənəbl] □ неотъе́млемый

**inane** [ɪ'neɪn] □ (*senseless*) бессмы́сленный; (*empty*) пусто́й

**inanimate** [ɪn'ænɪmət] □ неодушевлённый; (*lifeless*) безжи́зненный

**inappropriate** [ɪnə'prəʊprɪət] неуме́стный, несоотве́тствующий

**inapt** [ɪn'æpt] □ неспосо́бный; (*not suitable*) неподходя́щий

**inarticulate** [ɪnɑː'tɪkjʊlət] □ нечленоразде́льный, невня́тный

**inasmuch** [ɪnəz'mʌtʃ]: ***~ as*** *adv.* так как; в виду́ того́, что; поско́льку

**inattentive** [ɪnə'tentɪv] невнима́тельный

**inaugura|te** [ɪ'nɔːgjʊreɪt] *launch* откры́(ва́)ть; (*install as president*) вводи́ть в до́лжность; **~tion** [ɪnɔːgjʊ'reɪʃn] вступле́ние в до́лжность, инаугура́ция; (торже́ственное) откры́тие

**inborn** [ɪn'bɔːn] врождённый, прирождённый

**incalculable** [ɪn'kælkjʊləbl] □ неисчисли́мый, бессчётный; *person* капри́зный, ненадёжный

**incapa|ble** [ɪn'keɪpəbl] □ неспосо́бный (***of*** к Д *or* на В); **~citate** [ɪnkə'pæsɪteɪt] де́лать неспосо́бным, непригодным

**incarnate** [ɪn'kɑːnɪt] воплощённый, олицетворённый

**incautious** [ɪn'kɔːʃəs] □ неосторо́жный, опроме́тчивый

**incendiary** [ɪn'sendɪərɪ] *mil.*, *fig.* зажига́тельный

**incense**[1] ['ɪnsens] ла́дан

**incense**[2] [ɪn'sens] приводи́ть в я́рость

**incentive** [ɪn'sentɪv] сти́мул

**incessant** [ɪn'sesnt] □ непреры́вный

**inch** [ɪntʃ] дюйм; *fig.* пядь *f*; ***by ~es*** ма́ло-пома́лу

**inciden|ce** ['ɪnsɪdəns]: ***high ~ of*** большо́е коли́чество слу́чаев; **~t** [-t] слу́чай; происше́ствие; *mil.*, *dipl.* инциде́нт; **~tal** [ɪnsɪ'dentl] □ случа́йный; побо́чный; прису́щий (Д); *pl.* непредви́денные расхо́ды *m/pl.*; **~tally**

случа́йно; ме́жду про́чим; попу́тно
**incinerate** [ɪn'sɪnəreɪt] испепеля́ть [-ли́ть]; сжига́ть [сжечь]
**incis|ion** [ɪn'sɪʒn] разре́з, надре́з; **~ive** [ɪn'saɪsɪv] □ о́стрый; *criticism, etc.* ре́зкий
**incite** [ɪn'saɪt] (*instigate*) подстрека́ть [-кну́ть]; (*move to action*) побужда́ть [-уди́ть]
**inclement** [ɪn'klemənt] суро́вый, холо́дный
**inclin|ation** [ɪnklɪ'neɪʃn] (*slope*) накло́н, укло́н; (*mental leaning*) скло́нность *f*; **~e** [ɪn'klaɪn] **1.** *v/i.* склоня́ться [-ни́ться]; **~ *to*** *fig.* быть скло́нным к (Д); *v/t.* наклоня́ть [-ни́ть]; склоня́ть [-ни́ть] (*a. fig.*); **2.** накло́н
**inclose** [ɪn'kləʊz] → ***enclose***
**inclu|de** [ɪn'klu:d] включа́ть [-чи́ть]; содержа́ть; **~sive** [~sɪv] □ включа́ющий в себя́, содержа́щий; ***from Monday to Friday ~*** с понеде́льника до пя́тницы включи́тельно
**incoheren|ce** [ɪnkəʊ'hɪərəns] несвя́зность *f*; непосле́довательность *f*; **~t** [~t] □ несвя́зный; (*not consistent*) непосле́довательный
**income** ['ɪŋkʌm] дохо́д
**incomparable** [ɪn'kɒmprəbl] □ (*not comparable*) несравни́мый; *matchless* несравне́нный
**incompatible** [ɪŋkəm'pætəbl] несовмести́мый
**incompetent** [ɪn'kɒmpɪtənt] □ несве́дущий, неуме́лый; *specialist* некомпете́нтный; *law* недееспосо́бный
**incomplete** [ɪŋkəm'pli:t] □ непо́лный; (*unfinished*) незако́нченный
**incomprehensible** [ɪŋkɔmprɪ'hensəbl] □ непоня́тный, непостижи́мый
**inconceivable** [ɪŋkən'si:vəbl] □ невообрази́мый
**incongruous** [ɪn'kɒŋgruəs] □ (*out of place*) неуме́стный; (*absurd*) неле́пый; (*incompatible*) несовмести́мый
**inconseqential** [ɪn'kɒnsɪkwəntʃl] □ несуще́ственный
**inconsidera|ble** [ɪŋkən'sɪdərəbl] □ незначи́тельный, нева́жный; **~te** [-rɪt] □ невнима́тельный (***to*** к Д); (*rash*) необду́манный
**inconsisten|cy** [ɪnkən'sɪstənsɪ] непосле́довательность *f*, противоре́чие; **~t** [~tənt] □ непосле́довательный, противоречи́вый
**inconsolable** [ɪnkən'səʊləbl] □ безуте́шный
**inconvenien|ce** [ɪŋkən'vi:nɪəns] **1.** неудо́бство; **2.** причиня́ть [-ни́ть] неудо́бство; [по]беспоко́ить; **~t** [~nɪənt] □ неудо́бный, затрудни́тельный
**incorporat|e** [ɪn'kɔ:pəreɪt] объединя́ть(ся) [-ни́ть(ся)]; включа́ть [-чи́ть] (***into*** в В); **~ed** [~reɪtɪd] зарегистри́рованный в ка́честве юриди́ческого лица́
**incorrect** [ɪŋkə'rekt] □ непра́вильный
**incorrigible** [ɪn'kɒrɪdʒəbl] □ неисправи́мый
**increase** [ɪn'kri:s] **1.** увели́чи(ва)ть(ся); [вы́]расти́; *of wind, etc.* уси́ли(ва)ть(ся); **2.** ['ɪnkri:s] рост; увеличе́ние; приро́ст
**incredible** [ɪn'kredəbl] □ невероя́тный; неимове́рный
**incredul|ity** [ɪnkrɪ'dju:lətɪ] недове́рчивость *f*; **~ous** [ɪn'kredjʊləs] □ недове́рчивый
**increment** ['ɪŋkrəmənt] приро́ст
**incriminate** [ɪn'krɪmɪneɪt] инкримини́ровать (*im*)*pf*.; *law* обвиня́ть в преступле́нии
**incrustation** [ɪnkrʌ'steɪʃn] инкруста́ция
**incubator** ['ɪŋkʊbeɪtə] инкуба́тор
**incur** [ɪn'kɜ:] навлека́ть [-вле́чь] на себя́; **~ *losses*** понести́ *pf.* убы́тки
**incurable** [ɪn'kjʊərəbl] неизлечи́мый; *fig.* неисправи́мый
**indebted** [ɪn'detɪd] *for money* в долгу́ (*a. fig.*); *fig.* обя́занный
**indecen|cy** [ɪn'di:snsɪ] непристо́йность *f*; неприли́чие; **~t** [~snt] неприли́чный
**indecisi|on** [ɪndɪ'sɪʒn] нереши́тельность *f*; (*hesitation*) колеба́ние; **~ve** [~'saɪsɪv] нереши́тельный; не реша́ющий; **~ *evidence*** недоста́точно убеди́тельные доказа́тельства
**indecorous** [ɪn'dekərəs] □ непри-

I

ли́чный; некорре́ктный

**indeed** [ɪn'diːd] в са́мом де́ле, действи́тельно; неужéли!

**indefensible** [ɪndɪ'fensəbl] □ *mil.* незащити́мая пози́ция; (*unjustified*) не име́ющий оправда́ния; *fig.* несостоя́тельный

**indefinite** [ɪn'defɪnət] □ неопределённый (*a. gr.*); неограни́ченный

**indelible** [ɪn'deləbl] □ неизглади́мый

**indelicate** [ɪn'delɪkət] □ неделика́тный; нескро́мный; *remark* беста́ктный

**indemnity** [ɪn'demnətɪ] гара́нтия возмеще́ния убы́тков; компенса́ция

**indent** [ɪn'dent] *v/t. typ.* нач(ин)а́ть с кра́сной строки́; *v/i. comm.* [с]де́лать зака́з на (В)

**independen|ce** [ɪndɪ'pendəns] незави́симость *f*, самостоя́тельность *f*; **~t** [-t] □ незави́симый, самостоя́тельный

**indescribable** [ɪndɪs'kraɪbəbl] □ неопису́емый

**indestructible** [ɪndɪ'strʌktəbl] □ неразруши́мый

**indeterminate** [ɪndɪ'tɜːmɪnət] □ неопределённый; (*vague, not clearly seen*) нея́сный

**index** ['ɪndeks] и́ндекс, указа́тель *m*; показа́тель *m*; **~ finger** указа́тельный па́лец

**India** ['ɪndɪə]: **~ rubber** каучу́к; рези́на; **~n** [-n] **1.** *of India* инди́йский; *of North America* инде́йский; ***~ corn*** кукуру́за; ***~ summer*** ба́бье ле́то; **2.** инди́ец, инди́анка; *of North America* инде́ец, инди́анка

**indicat|e** ['ɪndɪkeɪt] ука́зывать [-за́ть]; (*show*) пока́зывать [-за́ть]; (*make clear*) д(ав)а́ть поня́ть; означа́ть *impf.*; **~ion** [ɪndɪ'keɪʃn] (*sign*) знак, при́знак; **~or** ['ɪndɪkeɪtə] стре́лка; *mot.* сигна́л поворо́та, *coll.* мига́лка

**indifferen|ce** [ɪn'dɪfrəns] равноду́шие, безразли́чие; **~t** [-t] равноду́шный, безразли́чный; ***~ actor*** посре́дственный актёр

**indigenous** [ɪn'dɪdʒɪnəs] тузе́мный; ме́стный

**indigest|ible** [ɪndɪ'dʒestəbl] □ *fig.* неудобовари́мый; **~ion** [-tʃən] расстро́йство желу́дка

**indign|ant** [ɪn'dɪgnənt] □ негоду́ющий; **~ation** [ɪndɪg'neɪʃn] негодова́ние; **~ity** [ɪn'dɪgnɪtɪ] униже́ние, оскорбле́ние

**indirect** ['ɪndɪrekt] □ непрямо́й; *route* око́льный; *answer* укло́нчивый; ***~ taxes*** ко́свенные нало́ги

**indiscre|et** [ɪndɪ'skriːt] □ нескро́мный; (*tactless*) беста́ктный; **~tion** [~'skreʃn] нескро́мность *f*, беста́ктность *f*

**indiscriminate** [ɪndɪ'skrɪmɪnət] □ неразбо́рчивый

**indispensable** [ɪndɪ'spensəbl] □ необходи́мый, обяза́тельный

**indispos|ed** [ɪndɪ'spəʊzd] (*disinclined*) нерасполо́женный; нездоро́вый; **~ition** ['ɪndɪspə'zɪʃn] нежела́ние; недомога́ние

**indisputable** [ɪndɪ'spjuːtəbl] неоспори́мый, бесспо́рный

**indistinct** [ɪndɪ'stɪŋkt] □ нея́сный, неотчётливый; *speech* невня́тный

**individual** [ɪndɪ'vɪdjʊəl] **1.** □ индивидуа́льный; характе́рный; (*separate*) отде́льный; **2.** индиви́дуум, ли́чность *f*; **~ity** [~vɪdjʊ'ælətɪ] индивидуа́льность *f*

**indivisible** [ɪndɪ'vɪzəbl] недели́мый

**indolen|ce** ['ɪndələns] лень *f*; **~t** [-t] лени́вый

**indomitable** [ɪn'dɒmɪtəbl] □ неукроти́мый

**indoor** ['ɪndɔː] вну́тренний; **~s** [ɪn'dɔːz] в до́ме

**indorse** → ***endorse***

**indubitable** [ɪn'djuːbɪtəbl] □ несомне́нный

**induce** [ɪn'djuːs] заставля́ть [-а́вить]; (*bring about*) вызыва́ть [вы́звать]; **~ment** [~mənt] сти́мул, побужде́ние

**indulge** [ɪn'dʌldʒ] *v/t.* доставля́ть удово́льствие (Д ***with*** Т); (*spoil*) балова́ть; потво́рствовать (Д); *v/i.* ***~ in*** увлека́ться [-е́чься] (Т); пред(ав)а́ться (Д); **~nce** [~əns] потво́рство; **~nt** [~ənt] □ снисходи́тельный; нетре́бо-

вательный; потво́рствующий
**industri|al** [ɪn'dʌstrɪəl] □ промы́шленный; произво́дственный; **~alist** [-ɪst] промы́шленник; **~ous** [ɪn'dʌstrɪəs] трудолюби́вый
**industry** ['ɪndəstrɪ] промы́шленность *f*, индустри́я; трудолю́бие
**inedible** [ɪn'edɪbl] несъедо́бный
**ineffect|ive** [ɪnɪ'fektɪv], **~ual** [-tʃʊəl] □ безрезульта́тный; неэффекти́вный
**inefficient** [ɪnɪ'fɪʃnt] □ *person* неспосо́бный, неуме́лый; *method*, *etc*. неэффекти́вный
**inelegant** [ɪn'elɪgənt] □ неэлега́нтный
**ineligible** [ɪn'elɪdʒəbl]: ***be ~ for*** не име́ть пра́ва (на В)
**inept** [ɪ'nept] □ неуме́стный, неподходя́щий; неуме́лый
**inequality** [ɪnɪ'kwɒlətɪ] нера́венство
**inert** [ɪ'nɜːt] □ ине́ртный; (*sluggish*) вя́лый; **~ia** [ɪ'nɜːʃə], **~ness** [ɪ'nɜːtnɪs] ине́рция; вя́лость *f*
**inescapable** [ɪnɪ'skeɪpəbl] □ неизбе́жный
**inessential** [ɪn'əsenʃl] □ несуще́ственный
**inestimable** [ɪn'estɪməbl] □ неоцени́мый
**inevitable** [ɪn'evɪtəbl] □ неизбе́жный, немину́емый
**inexact** [ɪnɪg'zækt] □ нето́чный
**inexhaustible** [ɪnɪg'zɔːstəbl] □ неистощи́мый, неисчерпа́емый
**inexorable** [ɪn'eksərəbl] □ неумоли́мый, непрекло́нный
**inexpedient** [ɪnɪk'spiːdɪənt] □ нецелесообра́зный
**inexpensive** [ɪnɪk'spensɪv] □ недорого́й, дешёвый
**inexperience** [ɪnɪk'spɪərɪəns] нео́пытность *f*; **~d** [-t] нео́пытный
**inexplicable** [ɪnɪk'splɪkəbl] □ необъясни́мый, непоня́тный
**inexpressible** [ɪnɪk'spresəbl] □ невырази́мый, неопису́емый
**inextinguishable** [ɪnɪk'stɪŋgwɪʃəbl] □ неугаси́мый
**inextricable** [ɪnɪk'strɪkəbl] □ запу́танный
**infallible** [ɪn'fæləbl] □ безоши́бочный, непогреши́мый; *method* надёжный
**infam|ous** ['ɪnfəməs] □ посты́дный, позо́рный, бесче́стный; **~y** [-mɪ] бесче́стье, позо́р; (*infamous act*) ни́зость *f*; по́длость *f*
**infan|cy** ['ɪnfənsɪ] младе́нчество; **~t** [-t] младе́нец
**infantile** ['ɪnfəntaɪl] младе́нческий; *behaviour* инфанти́льный
**infantry** ['ɪnfəntrɪ] пехо́та
**infatuated** [ɪn'fætjʊeɪtɪd]: ***be ~ with*** быть без ума́ от (Р)
**infect** [ɪn'fekt] заража́ть [-рази́ть]; **~ion** [ɪn'fekʃn] инфе́кция; **~ious** [-ʃəs] □, **~ive** [-tɪv] инфекцио́нный, зара́зный; *fig*. зарази́тельный
**infer** [ɪn'fɜː] де́лать вы́вод; (*imply*) подразумева́ть; **~ence** ['ɪnfərəns] вы́вод, заключе́ние
**inferior** [ɪn'fɪərɪə] **1.** (*subordinate*) подчинённый; (*worse*) ху́дший, неполноце́нный; *goods* ни́зкого ка́чества; **2.** подчинённый; **~ity** [ɪnfɪərɪ'ɒrətɪ] ни́зкое ка́чество (положе́ние); неполноце́нность *f*; ***~ complex*** ко́мплекс неполноце́нности
**infernal** [ɪn'fɜːnl] □ *mst. fig*. а́дский
**infertile** [ɪn'fəːtaɪl] беспло́дный (*a. fig*.); неплодоро́дный
**infest** [ɪn'fest]: ***be ~ed*** кише́ть (Т)
**infidelity** [ɪnfɪ'delətɪ] неве́рность *f* (***to*** Д)
**infiltrate** ['ɪnfɪltreɪt] (*enter secretly*) проника́ть [-и́кнуть]; проса́чиваться [-сочи́ться]
**infinit|e** ['ɪnfɪnət] □ бесконе́чный, безграни́чный; **~y** [ɪn'fɪnətɪ] бесконе́чность *f*; безграни́чность *f*
**infirm** [ɪn'fɜːm] □ не́мощный, дря́хлый; **~ary** [-ərɪ] больни́ца; **~ity** [-ətɪ] не́мощь *f*
**inflam|e** [ɪn'fleɪm] воспламеня́ть(-ся) [-и́ть(ся)]; *med*. воспаля́ть(ся) [-ли́ть(ся)]; **~ed** [-d] воспалённый
**inflamma|ble** [ɪn'flæməbl] □ воспламеня́ющийся; **~tion** [ɪnflə'meɪʃn] *med*. воспале́ние; **~tory** [ɪn'flæmətrɪ] *speech* подстрека́тельский; *med*. вос-

I

палительный
**inflat|e** [ɪn'fleɪt] наду́(ва́)ть; *tyre* нака́чивать [-ча́ть]; *prices* взви́нчивать [-нти́ть]; **~ion** [ɪn'fleɪʃn] *of balloon, etc.* надува́ние; *econ.* инфля́ция
**inflexible** [ɪn'fleksəbl] □ неги́бкий; *fig.* непрекло́нный, непоколеби́мый
**inflict** [ɪn'flɪkt] *a blow, etc.* наноси́ть [-нести́]; *pain* причиня́ть [-ни́ть]; *views, etc.* навя́зывать(ся)
**influen|ce** ['ɪnflʊəns] **1.** влия́ние, возде́йствие; **2.** [по]влия́ть на (В); возде́йствовать на (В) (*im*)*pf.*; **~tial** [ɪnflʊ'enʃl] влия́тельный
**influenza** [ɪnflʊ'enzə] грипп
**influx** ['ɪnflʌks] прито́к; *of visitors* наплы́в
**inform** [ɪn'fɔːm] *v/t.* информи́ровать (*im*)*pf.*, уведомля́ть [уве́домить] (**of** о П); *v/i.* доноси́ть [-нести́] (***against*** на В); ***keep s.o. ~ed*** держа́ть в ку́рсе де́л
**inform|al** [ɪn'fɔːml] □ неофициа́льный; *conversation* непринуждённый; **~ality** [ɪnfɔː'mælətɪ] несоблюде́ние форма́льностей; непринуждённость *f*
**inform|ation** [ɪnfə'meɪʃn] информа́ция, све́дения *n*/*pl.*; спра́вка; **~ative** [ɪn'fɔːmətɪv] информи́рующий; содержа́тельный; (*educational*) поучи́тельный
**infrequent** [ɪn'friːkwənt] □ ре́дкий
**infringe** [ɪn'frɪndʒ] наруша́ть [-ру́шить] (*a.* **~ *upon***)
**infuriate** [ɪn'fjʊərɪeɪt] [вз]беси́ть
**ingen|ious** [ɪn'dʒiːnɪəs] □ изобрета́тельный; **~uity** [ɪndʒɪ'njuːətɪ] изобрета́тельность *f*; **~uous** [ɪn'dʒenjʊəs] □ (*frank*) чистосерде́чный; (*lacking craft or subtlety*) простоду́шный; просто́й, бесхи́тростный
**ingratitude** [ɪn'grætɪtjuːd] неблаго-да́рность *f*
**ingredient** [ɪn'griːdɪənt] составна́я часть *f*, ингредие́нт (*a. cul.*)
**inhabit** [ɪn'hæbɪt] населя́ть; обита́ть, жить в (П); **~ant** [-ɪtənt] жи́тель(ница *f*) *m*, обита́тель(ница *f*) *m*
**inhal|ation** [ɪnhə'leɪʃn] *med.* ингаля́ция; **~e** [ɪn'heɪl] вдыха́ть [вдохну́ть]
**inherent** [ɪn'hɪərənt] □ прису́щий
**inherit** [ɪn'herɪt] насле́довать (*im*)*pf.*; *fig.* унасле́довать *pf.*; **~ance** [-ɪtəns] насле́дство (*a. fig.*)
**inhibit** [ɪn'hɪbɪt] сде́рживать [сдержа́ть], [вос]препя́тствовать (Д); **~ion** [ɪnhɪ'bɪʃn] *med.* торможе́ние
**inhospitable** [ɪn'hɒspɪtəbl] □ негостеприи́мный
**inhuman** [ɪn'hjuːmən] □ бесчелове́чный; античелове́ческий
**inimitable** [ɪ'nɪmɪtəbl] □ неподража́емый; (*peerless*) несравне́нный
**initia|l** [ɪ'nɪʃl] **1.** □ нача́льный, первонача́льный; **2.** нача́льная бу́ква; ***~s*** *pl.* инициа́лы *m*/*pl.*; **~te** [-ɪeɪt] вводи́ть [ввести́]; *into a secret* посвяща́ть [-вяти́ть]; (*start*) положи́ть *pf.* нача́ло (Д); **~tive** [ɪ'nɪʃətɪv] инициати́ва; **~tor** [-ʃɪəɪtə] инициа́тор
**inject** [ɪn'dʒekt] *med.* [с]де́лать инъе́кцию; **~ion** [-ʃn] инъе́кция, впры́скивание, уко́л
**injur|e** ['ɪndʒə] [по]вреди́ть, поврежда́ть [-еди́ть]; *in war, etc.* ра́нить (*im*)*pf.*; (*wrong*) обижа́ть [-и́деть]; **~ious** [ɪn'dʒʊərɪəs] □ вре́дный; **~y** ['ɪndʒərɪ] оскорбле́ние; поврежде́ние, ра́на; *sport* тра́вма
**injustice** [ɪn'dʒʌstɪs] несправедли́вость *f*
**ink** [ɪŋk] черни́ла *n*/*pl.*
**inkling** ['ɪŋklɪŋ] намёк (на В); (*suspicion*) подозре́ние
**inland** ['ɪnlənd] **1.** вну́тренняя террито́рия страны́; **2.** вну́тренний; **3.** [ɪn'lænd] внутрь, внутри́ (страны́)
**inlay** [ɪn'leɪ] инкруста́ция
**inlet** ['ɪnlet] у́зкий зали́в, бу́хта; впускно́е отве́рстие
**inmate** ['ɪnmeɪt] *of hospital* больно́й, пацие́нт, обита́тель; *of prison* заключённый
**inmost** ['ɪnməʊst] глубоча́йший, *thoughts* сокрове́ннейший
**inn** [ɪn] гости́ница, тракти́р
**innate** [ɪ'neɪt] □ врождённый, приро́дный
**inner** ['ɪnə] вну́тренний; **~most**

[-məʊst] → ***inmost***

**innocen|ce** ['ɪnəsns] *law* невинóвность *f*; невúнность *f*; простотá; **~t** [-snt] □ невúнный; *law* невинóвный

**innocuous** [ɪ'nɒkjʊəs] □ безврéдный; *remark* безобúдный

**innovation** [ɪnə'veɪʃn] нововведéние, нóвшество

**innuendo** [ɪnjuː'endəʊ] кóсвенный намёк, инсинуáция

**innumerable** [ɪ'njuːmərəbl] □ бессчётный, бесчúсленный

**inoculate** [ɪ'nɒkjʊleɪt] [с]дéлать привúвку (Д от Р)

**inoffensive** [ɪnə'fensɪv] безобúдный, безврéдный

**inopportune** [ɪn'ɒpətjuːn] □ несвоеврéменный, неподходя́щий

**inordinate** [ɪ'nɔːdɪnət] непомéрный, чрезмéрный

**in-patient** ['ɪnpeɪʃnt] стационáрный больнóй

**inquest** ['ɪnkwest] *law* расслéдование, выяснéние причúн смéрти

**inquir|e** [ɪn'kwaɪə] *v/t.* спрáшивать [-росúть]; *v/i.* узн(ав)áть; наводúть [-вестú] спрáвки (***about, after, for*** о П; ***of*** у Р); **~ *into*** выясня́ть, расслéдовать (*im*)*pf*; **~ing** [-rɪŋ] □ *mind* пытлúвый; **~y** [-rɪ] расслéдование, слéдствие; (*question*) вопрóс; ***make inquiries*** наводúть спрáвки

**inquisitive** [ɪn'kwɪzɪtɪv] □ любознáтельный; любопы́тный

**insan|e** [ɪn'seɪn] □ психúчески больнóй; *fig.* безу́мный; **~ity** [ɪn'sænətɪ] психúческое заболевáние; безу́мие

**insatiable** [ɪn'seɪʃəbl] □ ненасы́тный; (*greedy*) жáдный

**inscribe** [ɪn'skraɪb] (*write*) надпúсывать [-сáть] (***in, on*** В/Т *or* В на П)

**inscription** [ɪn'skrɪpʃn] нáдпись *f*

**inscrutable** [ɪn'skruːtəbl] □ непостижúмый, загáдочный

**insect** ['ɪnsekt] насекóмое; **~icide** [ɪn'sektɪsaɪd] инсектицúд

**insecure** [ɪnsɪ'kjʊə] □ ненадёжный; (*not safe*) небезопáсный

**insens|ible** [ɪn'sensəbl] □ *to touch, etc.* нечувствúтельный; потеря́вший сознáние; (*unsympathetic*) бесчу́вственный; **~itive** [-ɪtɪv] нечувствúтельный; невосприúмчивый

**inseparable** [ɪn'seprəbl] □ неразлу́чный; неотделúмый (***from*** от Р)

**insert** [ɪn'sɜːt] вставля́ть [-áвить]; *advertisement* помещáть [-естúть]; **~ion** [ɪn'sɜːʃn] *of lace, etc.* встáвка; (*announcement*) объявлéние

**inside** [ɪn'saɪd] **1.** вну́тренняя сторонá; вну́тренность *f*; *of clothing* изнáнка; ***turn ~ out*** вы́вернуть *pf.* на изнáнку; ***he knows his subject ~ out*** он знáет свой предмéт назубóк; **2.** *adj.* вну́тренний; **3.** *adv.* внутрь, внутрú; **4.** *prp.* внутрú (Р)

**insidious** [ɪn'sɪdɪəs] □ предáтельский, ковáрный

**insight** ['ɪnsaɪt] проницáтельность *f*; интуúция

**insignificant** [ɪnsɪg'nɪfɪkənt] незначúтельный, маловáжный

**insincere** [ɪnsɪn'sɪə] неúскренний

**insinuat|e** [ɪn'sɪnjʊeɪt] намекáть [-ну́ть] на (В); **~ *o.s.*** *fig.* вкрáдываться [вкрáсться]; **~ion** [ɪnsɪnjʊ'eɪʃn] инсинуáция

**insipid** [ɪn'sɪpɪd] безвку́сный, прéсный

**insist** [ɪn'sɪst]: **~ (*up*)*on*** настáивать [-стоя́ть] на (П); **~ence** [-əns] настóйчивость *f*; **~ent** [-ənt] настóйчивый

**insolent** ['ɪnsələnt] □ высокомéрный; нáглый

**insoluble** [ɪn'sɒljʊbl] нерастворúмый; *fig.* неразрешúмый

**insolvent** [ɪn'sɒlvənt] неплатёжеспособный

**insomnia** [ɪn'sɒmnɪə] бессóнница

**inspect** [ɪn'spekt] осмáтривать [осмотрéть]; производúть [-вестú] инспéкцию; **~ion** [ɪn'spekʃn] осмóтр; инспéкция

**inspir|ation** [ɪnspə'reɪʃn] вдохновéние; воодушевлéние; **~e** [ɪn'spaɪə] *fig.* вдохновля́ть [-вúть]; *hope* вселя́ть [-лúть]; *fear* внушáть [-шúть]

**install** [ɪn'stɔːl] устанáвливать [-новúть]; *tech.* [с]монтúровать; **~ation**

I

[ɪnstəˈleɪʃn] установка
**instalment** [ɪnˈstɔːlmənt] очерҿдной взнос (при покупке в рассрочку); часть романа *и т.д.*, публикуемого в нескольких номерах
**instance** [ˈɪnstəns] случай; пример; ***for ~*** например
**instant** [ˈɪnstənt] **1.** □ немедленный, безотлагательный; **2.** мгновение; момент; **~aneous** [ɪnstənˈteɪnɪəs] мгновенный; **~ly** [ˈɪnstəntlɪ] немедленно, тотчас
**instead** [ɪnˈsted] взамен, вместо; ***~ of*** вместо (Р)
**instep** [ˈɪnstep] подъём (ноги)
**instigat|e** [ˈɪnstɪgeɪt] (*urge on*) побуждать (-удить); (*incite*) подстрекать [-кнуть]; **~or** [~ə] подстрекатель(-ница *f*) *m*
**instil(l)** [ɪnˈstɪl] *fig.* внушать [-шить] (***into*** Д)
**instinct** [ˈɪnstɪŋkt] инстинкт; **~ive** [ɪnˈstɪŋktɪv] □ инстинктивный
**institut|e** [ˈɪnstɪtjuːt] научное учреждение, институт; **2.** (*set up*) учреждать [-едить]; (*found*) основывать [-вать]; **~ion** [ɪnstɪˈtjuːʃn] учреждение; ***educational ~*** учебное заведение
**instruct** [ɪnˈstrʌkt] обучать [-чить], [на]учить; [про]инструктировать (*im*)*pf*.; **~ion** [ɪnˈstrʌkʃn] обучение; инструкция; **~ive** [~tɪv] □ поучительный; **~or** [~tə] руководитель *m*, инструктор; (*teacher*) преподаватель *m*
**instrument** [ˈɪnstrʊmənt] инструмент; *fig.* орудие; прибор, аппарат; **~al** [ɪnstrʊˈmentl] □ служащий средством; *gr.* творительный
**insubordinate** [ɪnsəˈbɔːdɪnət] (*not submissive*) непокорный
**insufferable** [ɪnˈsʌfrəbl] □ невыносимый, нестерпимый
**insufficient** [ɪnsəˈfɪʃnt] недостаточный
**insula|r** [ˈɪnsjʊlə] □ островной; *fig.* замкнутый; **~te** [~leɪt] *el.* изолировать (*im*)*pf*.; **~tion** [ɪnsjʊˈleɪʃn] *el.* изоляция; ***~ tape*** изоляционная лента
**insulin** [ˈɪnsjʊlɪn] инсулин
**insult 1.** [ˈɪnsʌlt] оскорбление; **2.** [ɪnˈsʌlt] оскорблять [-бить]
**insur|ance** [ɪnˈʃʊərəns] страхование; (*sum insured*) сумма страхования, *coll.* страховка; ***~ company*** страховая компания; **~e** [ɪnˈʃʊə] [за]страховать(ся)
**insurgent** [ɪnˈsɜːdʒənt] повстанец; мятежник
**insurmountable** [ɪnsəˈmaʊntəbl] непреодолимый
**insurrection** [ɪnsəˈrekʃn] восстание
**intact** [ɪnˈtækt] целый, невредимый
**intangible** [ɪnˈtændʒəbl] □ неосязаемый; *fig.* неуловимый
**integ|ral** [ˈɪntɪgrəl] □ неотъемлемый; (*whole*) целый, целостный; ***~ part*** неотъемлемая часть; **~rate** [~greɪt] объединять [-нить]; *math.* интегрировать (*im*)*pf*.; **~rity** [ɪnˈtegrɪtɪ] честность *f*; (*entireness*) целостность *f*
**intellect** [ˈɪntəlekt] ум, интеллект; **~ual** [ɪntɪˈlektjʊəl] **1.** □ интеллектуальный, умственный; ***~ property*** интеллектуальная собственность; **2.** интеллигент *m*, -ка *f*; **~s** *pl.* интеллигенция
**intelligence** [ɪnˈtelɪdʒəns] ум, рассудок, интеллект; *mil.* ***~ service*** разведывательная служба, разведка
**intellig|ent** [ɪnˈtelɪdʒənt] умный; *coll.* смышлёный; **~ible** [~dʒəbl] □ понятный
**intend** [ɪnˈtend] намереваться, собираться; (*mean*) иметь в виду; ***~ for*** (*destine for*) предназначать [-значить] для (Р)
**intense** [ɪnˈtens] □ сильный; интенсивный, напряжённый
**intensify** [ɪnˈtensɪfaɪ] усили(ва)ть(ся); интенсифицировать (*im*)*pf.*
**intensity** [ɪnˈtensətɪ] интенсивность *f*, сила; *of colo(u)r* яркость *f*
**intent** [ɪnˈtent] **1.** □ погружённый (***on*** в В); поглощённый (***on*** Т); *look* внимательный, пристальный; **2.** намерение, цель *f*; ***to all ~s and purposes*** в сущности, на самом деле; **~ion** [ɪnˈtenʃn] намерение; **~ional** [~ʃənl] □

(пред)наме́ренный, умы́шленный

**inter…** ['ıntə] *pref.* меж…, между…; пере…; взаимо…

**interact** [ıntər'ækt] взаимоде́йствовать

**intercede** [ıntə'si:d] [по]хода́тайствовать; *in order to save* заступа́ться [-пи́ться]

**intercept** [ıntə'sept] *letter, etc.* перехва́тывать [-хвати́ть]; (*listen in on*) подслу́шивать [-шать]

**intercession** [ıntə'seʃn] хода́тайство

**interchange** [ıntə'tʃeındʒ] **1.** *v/t.* обме́ниваться [-ня́ться] (T); **2.** обме́н

**intercom** ['ıntəkɒm] вну́тренняя телефо́нная связь, селе́ктор

**intercourse** ['ıntəkɔ:s] *social* обще́ние; *sexual* половы́е сноше́ния *n/pl.*

**interest** ['ıntrəst] **1.** интере́с; заинтересо́ванность *f* (***in*** в П); (*advantage, profit*) по́льза, вы́года; *fin.* проце́нты *m/pl.* ***~ rate*** ста́вка проце́нта; **2.** интересова́ть; заинтересо́вывать [-сова́ть]; **~ing** [-ıŋ] □ интере́сный

**interface** [ıntə'feıs] стык; *comput.* интерфе́йс; *fig.* взаимосвя́зь *f*

**interfere** [ıntə'fıə] вме́шиваться [-ша́ться] (***in*** в В); (*hinder*) [по]меша́ть (***with*** Д); **~nce** [-rəns] вмеша́тельство; поме́ха

**interim** ['ıntərım] **1.** промежу́ток вре́мени; ***in the ~*** тем вре́менем; **2.** вре́менный, промежу́точный

**interior** [ın'tıərıə] **1.** вну́тренний; ***~ decorator*** оформи́тель интерье́ра; **2.** вну́тренняя часть *f*; *of house* интерье́р; вну́тренние о́бласти страны́; *pol.* вну́тренние дела́ *n/pl.*

**interjection** [ıntə'dʒekʃn] восклица́ние; *gr.* междоме́тие

**interlace** [ıntə'leıs] переплета́ть(ся) [-плести́(сь)]

**interlock** [ıntə'lɒk] сцепля́ть(ся) [-пи́ть(ся)]; соединя́ть(ся) [-ни́ть(ся)]

**interlocutor** [ıntə'lɒkjʊtə] собесе́дник

**interlude** ['ıntəlu:d] *thea.* антра́кт; *mus., fig.* интерлю́дия

**intermedia|ry** [ıntə'mi:dıərı] **1.** посре́днический; **2.** посре́дник; **~te** [~'mi:dıət] □ промежу́точный

**interminable** [ın'tɜ:mınəbl] □ бесконе́чный

**intermingle** [ıntə'mıŋgl] сме́шивать(ся) [-ша́ть(ся)]; обща́ться

**intermission** [ıntə'mıʃn] переры́в, па́уза

**intermittent** [ıntə'mıtənt] □ преры́вистый

**intern** [ın'tɜ:n] интерни́ровать (*im*)*pf.*

**internal** [ın'tɜ:nl] □ вну́тренний

**international** [ıntə'næʃnl] □ междунаро́дный, интернациона́льный; ***~ law*** междунаро́дное пра́во; ***♀ Monetary Fund*** Междунаро́дный валю́тный фонд

**Internet** ['ıntənet] *comput.* Интерне́т

**interplanetary** [ıntə'plænətrı] межплане́тный

**interpose** [ıntə'pəʊz] *v/t.* *remark* вставля́ть [-а́вить], вкли́ни(ва)ться (ме́жду T); *v/i.* станови́ться [стать] (***between*** ме́жду T); (*interfere*) вме́шиваться [-ша́ться] (в B)

**interpret** [ın'tɜ:prıt] объясня́ть [-ни́ть], истолко́вывать [-кова́ть]; переводи́ть [-вести́] (у́стно); **~ation** [ıntɜ:prı'teıʃn] толкова́ние, интерпрета́ция, объясне́ние; **~er** [ın'tɜ:prıtə] перево́дчик (-ица *f*) *m*

**interrogat|e** [ın'terəgeıt] допра́шивать [-роси́ть]; **~ion** [ınterə'geıʃn] допро́с; **~ive** [ıntə'rɒgətıv] □ вопроси́тельный (*a. gr.*)

**interrupt** [ıntə'rʌpt] прер(ы)ва́ть; **~ion** [~'rʌpʃn] переры́в

**intersect** [ıntə'sekt] пересека́ть(ся) [-се́чь(ся)]; **~ion** [~kʃn] пересече́ние

**intersperse** [ıntə'spɜ:s] разбра́сывать [-броса́ть], рассыпа́ть; ***~ with jokes*** пересыпа́ть шу́тками

**intertwine** [ıntə'twaın] сплета́ть(ся) [-ести́(сь)]

**interval** ['ıntəvl] *of time* интерва́л, промежу́ток; *of space* расстояние; *thea.* антра́кт; *in school* переме́на

**interven|e** [ıntə'vi:n] вме́шиваться [-ша́ться]; вступа́ться [-пи́ться]; **~tion** [~'venʃn] интерве́нция; вмеша́-

тельство

**interview** ['ɪntəvjuː] **1.** интервью́ *n indecl.*; *for a job* собесе́дование; **2.** брать [взять] интервью́; проводи́ть [-вести́] собесе́дование

**intestine** [ɪn'testɪn] кишка́; **~s** *pl.* кишки́ *f/pl.*, кише́чник

**intima|cy** ['ɪntɪməsɪ] инти́мность *f*, бли́зость *f*; **~te 1.** [-meɪt] сообща́ть [-щи́ть]; (*hint*) намека́ть [-кну́ть] на (В); **2.** [~mɪt] □ инти́мный, ли́чный; бли́зкий; **~tion** [ɪntɪ'meɪʃn] сообще́ние; намёк

**intimidate** [ɪn'tɪmɪdeɪt] [ис]пуга́ть; *by threats* запу́гивать [-га́ть]

**into** ['ɪntʊ, ɪntə] *prp.* в, во (В); ***translate ~ English*** переводи́ть [-вести́] на англи́йский язы́к

**intolera|ble** [ɪn'tɒlərəbl] □ (*unbearable*) невыноси́мый, нестерпи́мый; **~nt** [~rənt] □ (*lacking forbearance, bigoted*) нетерпи́мый

**intonation** [ɪntə'neɪʃn] интона́ция

**intoxica|te** [ɪn'tɒksɪkeɪt] опьяня́ть [-ни́ть] (*a. fig.*); **~tion** [ɪntɒksɪ'keɪʃn] опьяне́ние

**intractable** [ɪn'træktəbl] □ упря́мый; неподáтливый

**intravenous** [ɪntrə'viːnəs] □ внутриве́нный

**intrepid** [ɪn'trepɪd] бесстра́шный, отва́жный

**intricate** ['ɪntrɪkɪt] □ сло́жный, запу́танный

**intrigu|e** [ɪn'triːg] **1.** интри́га; (*love affair*) любо́вная связь *f*; **2.** интригова́ть; [за]интригова́ть, [за]интересова́ть; **~ing** [~ɪŋ] интригу́ющий; *coll.* интере́сный

**intrinsic** [ɪn'trɪnsɪk] (***~ally***) вну́тренний; (*inherent*) сво́йственный, прису́щий

**introduc|e** [ɪntrə'djuːs] вводи́ть [ввести́]; (*acquaint*) представля́ть [-а́вить]; **~tion** [~'dʌkʃn] (*preface*) введе́ние, предисло́вие; представле́ние; *mus.* интроду́кция; **~tory** [~'dʌktərɪ] вступи́тельный, вво́дный

**intru|de** [ɪn'truːd] *into s.o.'s private life* вторга́ться [вто́ргнуться]; появля́ться [-ви́ться] некста́ти; **~der** [~ə] челове́к, прише́дший некста́ти, навя́зчивый челове́к; **~sion** [~uːʒn] вторже́ние; появле́ние без приглаше́ния; ***sorry for the ~*** прости́те за беспоко́йство

**intrust** [ɪn'trʌst] → ***entrust***

**intuition** [ɪntjuː'ɪʃn] интуи́ция

**inundate** ['ɪnʌndeɪt] затопля́ть [-пи́ть], наводня́ть [-ни́ть]

**invade** [ɪn'veɪd] *mil.* вторга́ться [вто́ргнуться]; *of tourists, etc.* наводня́ть [-ни́ть]; ***~ s.o.'s privacy*** нару́шить чьё-л. уедине́ние; **~r** [~ə] захва́тчик

**invalid 1.** [ɪn'vælɪd] недействи́тельный, не име́ющий зако́нной си́лы; *argument* несостоя́тельный; **2.** ['ɪnvəlɪd] инвали́д; **~ate** [ɪn'vælɪdeɪt] сде́лать недействи́тельным

**invaluable** [ɪn'væljʊəbl] □ неоцени́мый

**invariable** [ɪn'veərɪəbl] □ неизме́нный

**invasion** [ɪn'veɪʒn] вторже́ние

**invent** [ɪn'vent] (*create*) изобрета́ть [-брести́]; *story* выду́мывать [вы́думать]; **~ion** [ɪn'venʃn] изобрете́ние; вы́думка; (*faculty*) изобрета́тельность *f*; **~ive** [~tɪv] □ изобрета́тельный; **~or** [~tə] изобрета́тель *m*; **~ory** ['ɪnvəntrɪ] инвента́рная о́пись *f*

**inverse** [ɪn'vɜs] обра́тный; ***in ~ order*** в обра́тном поря́дке

**invert** [ɪn'vɜːt] перевора́чивать [-верну́ть]; (*put in the opposite position*) переставля́ть [-а́вить]; ***~ed commas*** кавы́чки

**invest** [ɪn'vest] *money* вкла́дывать [вложи́ть]; *fig. with authority, etc.* облека́ть [обле́чь] (***with*** Т); инвести́ровать

**investigat|e** [ɪn'vestɪgeɪt] рассле́довать (*im*)*pf.*; (*study*) иссле́довать (*im*)*pf.*; **~ion** [ɪnvestɪ'geɪʃn] (*inquiry*) рассле́дование; *law* сле́дствие; иссле́дование

**invest|ment** [ɪn'vestmənt] вложе́ние де́нег, инвести́рование; (*sum*) инвести́ция, вклад; **~or** [ɪn'vestə]

вкла́дчик, инве́стор
**inveterate** [ɪn'vetərət] (*deep-rooted*) закорене́лый; *coll. smoker*, *etc.* зая́длый; **~ *prejudices*** глубоко́ укорени́вшиеся предрассу́дки
**invidious** [ɪn'vɪdɪəs] □ вызыва́ющий оби́ду, за́висть; *remark* оби́дный
**invigorate** [ɪn'vɪgəreɪt] дава́ть си́лы (Д); бодри́ть
**invincible** [ɪn'vɪnsəbl] непобеди́мый
**inviolable** [ɪn'vaɪələbl] □ наруши́мый; неприкоснове́нный; **~ *right*** неруши́мое пра́во
**invisible** [ɪn'vɪzəbl] неви́димый
**invit|ation** [ɪnvɪ'teɪʃn] приглаше́ние; **~e** [ɪn'vaɪt] приглаша́ть [-ласи́ть]
**invoice** ['ɪnvɔɪs] *comm.* накладна́я, счёт-факту́ра
**invoke** [ɪn'vəʊk] взыва́ть [воззва́ть] о (П)
**involuntary** [ɪn'vɒləntrɪ] □ (*forced*) вы́нужденный; (*contrary to choice*) нево́льный; (*done unconsciously*) непроизво́льный
**involve** [ɪn'vɒlv] вовлека́ть [-е́чь]; впу́т(ыв)ать
**invulnerable** [ɪn'vʌlnərəbl] □ неуязви́мый
**inward** ['ɪnwəd] **1.** вну́тренний; **2.** *adv.* (*mst.* **~s** [~z]) внутрь; вну́тренне
**iodine** ['aɪədiːn] йод
**irascible** [ɪ'ræsəbl] □ раздражи́тельный
**irate** [aɪ'reɪt] гне́вный
**iridescent** [ɪrɪ'desnt] ра́дужный
**iris** ['aɪərɪs] *anat.* ра́дужная оболо́чка; *bot.* и́рис
**Irish** ['aɪərɪʃ] **1.** ирла́ндский; **2.** ***the* ~** ирла́ндцы *m/pl.*
**irksome** ['ɜːksəm] надое́дливый; раздража́ющий
**iron** ['aɪən] **1.** желе́зо; утю́г; ***have many ~s in the fire*** бра́ться сра́зу за мно́го дел; **2.** желе́зный; **3.** [вы́]утю́жить, [вы́]гла́дить
**ironic(al** □) [aɪ'rɒnɪk(l)] ирони́ческий
**iron|ing** ['aɪənɪŋ] **1.** гла́женье; ве́щи для гла́женья; **2.** глади́льный; **~board** глади́льная доска́; **~mongery** ['aɪənmʌŋgərɪ] металлоизде́лия; **~works** *mst. sg.* металлурги́ческий заво́д
**irony** ['aɪərənɪ] ирó́ния
**irrational** [ɪ'ræʃənl] неразу́мный; иррациона́льный (*a. math.*)
**irreconcilable** [ɪ'rekənsaɪləbl] □ непримири́мый; *ideas*, *etc.* несовмести́мый
**irrecoverable** [ɪrɪ'kʌvərəbl] □: **~ *losses*** невосполни́мые поте́ри
**irrefutable** [ɪrɪ'fjuːtəbl] □ неопровержи́мый
**irregular** [ɪ'regjʊlə] □ непра́вильный (*a. gr.*); (*disorderly*) беспоря́дочный; (*not regular*) нерегуля́рный; **~ *features*** непра́вильные черты́ лица́
**irrelevant** [ɪ'reləvənt] □ не относя́щийся к де́лу; не име́ющий значе́ния
**irreparable** [ɪ'repərəbl] □ непоправи́мый
**irreplaceable** [ɪrɪ'pleɪsəbl] незамени́мый
**irreproachable** [ɪrɪ'prəʊtʃəbl] □ безукори́зненный, безупре́чный
**irresistible** [ɪrɪ'zɪstəbl] □ неотрази́мый; *desire*, *etc.* непреодоли́мый
**irresolute** [ɪ'rezəluːt] □ нереши́тельный
**irrespective** [ɪrɪ'spektɪv] безотноси́тельный (***of*** к Д); незави́симый (***of*** от Р)
**irresponsible** [ɪrɪ'spɒnsəbl] □ безотве́тственный
**irreverent** [ɪ'revərənt] □ непочти́тельный
**irrevocable** [ɪ'revəkəbl] □ безвозвра́тный, бесповоро́тный
**irrigate** ['ɪrɪgeɪt] ороша́ть [ороси́ть]
**irrita|ble** ['ɪrɪtəbl] □ раздражи́тельный; **~te** [~teɪt] раздража́ть [-жи́ть]; **~tion** [ɪrɪ'teɪʃn] раздраже́ние
**Islam** [ɪz'lɑːm] исла́м; **~ic** [ɪz'læmɪk] исла́мский
**is** [ɪz] *3rd p. sg. pres. от* ***be***
**island** ['aɪlənd] о́стров; **~er** [~ə] островитя́нин *m*, -тя́нка *f*
**isle** [aɪl] о́стров; **~t** [aɪ'lɪt] острово́к
**isolat|e** ['aɪsəleɪt] изоли́ровать (*im*)*pf.*; (*separate*) отделя́ть [-ли́ть]; **~ed**: ***in* ~ *cases*** в отде́льных слу́чаях;

I

**~ion** [aɪsəˈleɪʃn] изоля́ция; уедине́ние

**issue** [ˈɪʃuː] **1.** (*a. flowing out*) вытека́ние; *law* (*offspring*) пото́мство; (*publication*) вы́пуск, изда́ние; (*outcome*) исхо́д, результа́т; *of money* эми́ссия; ***be at ~*** быть предме́том спо́ра; ***point at ~*** предме́т обсужде́ния; **2.** *v/i. of blood* [по]те́чь (***from*** из P); вытека́ть [вы́течь] (***from*** из P); *of sound* изд(ав)а́ть; *v/t. book, etc.* выпуска́ть [вы́пустить], изд(ав)а́ть

**isthmus** [ˈɪsməs] перешеек

**it** [ɪt] *pres. pron.* он, она́, оно́; э́то; ***~ is cold*** хо́лодно; ***~ is difficult to say …*** тру́дно сказа́ть

**Italian** [ɪˈtælɪən] **1.** италья́нский; **2.** италья́нец *m*, -нка *f*; **3.** италья́нский язы́к

**italics** [ɪˈtælɪks] *typ.* курси́в

**itch** [ɪtʃ] **1.** чесо́тка; зуд (*a. fig.*); **2.** чеса́ться; ***be ~ing to*** *inf.* горе́ть жела́нием (+ *inf.*)

**item** [ˈaɪtem] **1.** (*single article*) пункт, пара́граф; *on agenda* вопро́с; *on programme* но́мер; (*object*) предме́т

**itinerary** [aɪˈtɪnərərɪ] маршру́т

**its** [ɪts] *poss. pron. om* ***it*** его́, её, свой

**itself** [ɪtˈself] (сам *m*, сама́ *f*) само́; себя́, -с, -сь; себе́; ***in ~*** само по себе́; само́ собо́й; (*separately*) отде́льно

**ivory** [ˈaɪvərɪ] слоно́вая кость *f*

**ivy** [ˈaɪvɪ] плющ

J

# J

**jab** [dʒæb] *coll.* **1.** толка́ть [-кну́ть]; ты́кать [ткнуть]; (*stab*) пыря́ть [-рну́ть]; **2.** тычо́к, пино́к; (*prick*) уко́л (*a. coll. injection*)

**jabber** [ˈdʒæbə] болта́ть,тарато́рить

**jack** [dʒæk] **1.** *cards* вале́т; *mot.* домкра́т; ***Union ~*** госуда́рственный флаг Соединённого короле́вства; **2.** ***~ up*** поднима́ть домкра́том; **~ass** осёл; дурак

**jackdaw** [ˈdʒækdɔː] га́лка

**jacket** [ˈdʒækɪt] *lady's* жаке́т; *man's* пиджак; *casual* ку́ртка

**jack|knife** складно́й нож; *fig.* (*dive*) прыжо́к в во́ду согну́вшись; **~-of--all-trades** ма́стер на все ру́ки

**jade** [dʒeɪd] *min.* нефри́т

**jagged** [ˈdʒægɪd] зу́бчатый; ***~ rocks*** о́стрые ска́лы

**jail** [dʒeɪl] **1.** тюрьма́; тюре́мное заключе́ние; **2.** *v/t.* заключа́ть [-чи́ть] в тюрьму́; **~er** [ˈdʒeɪlə] тюре́мный надзира́тель

**jam**[1] [dzæm] варе́нье, джем, пови́дло

**jam**[2] [~] **1.** да́вка, сжа́тие; ***traffic ~*** зато́р, про́бка; ***be in a ~*** быть в затрудни́тельном положе́нии; **2.** заж(им)а́ть; (*pinch*) защемля́ть [-ми́ть]; (*push into confined space*) набива́ть битко́м; (*block*) загроможда́ть [-мозди́ть]; *v/i.* закли́ни(ва)ть

**jangle** [ˈdʒæŋgl] издава́ть [-да́ть] ре́зкий звук

**janitor** [ˈdʒænɪtə] дво́рник

**January** [ˈdʒænjʊərɪ] янва́рь *m*

**Japanese** [dʒæpəˈniːz] **1.** япо́нский; **2.** япо́нец *m*, -нка *f*; ***the ~*** *pl.* япо́нцы *pl.*

**jar**[1] [dʒɑː] (*vessel, usu. of glass*) ба́нка

**jar**[2] [~] **1.** *v/t.* толка́ть [-кну́ть]; *v/i.* ре́зать слух; **2.** толчо́к; (*shock*) потрясе́ние

**jaundice** [ˈdʒɔːndɪs] *med.* желту́ха; *fig.* жёлчность *f*; **~d** [~t] желту́шный; *fig.* зави́стливый

**jaunt** [dʒɔːnt] пое́здка, прогу́лка; ***let's go for a ~ to London*** дава́й-ка съе́здим в Ло́ндон; **~y** [ˈdʒɔːntɪ] □ беспе́чный; бо́йкий

**javelin** [ˈdʒævlɪn] *sport* копьё

**jaw** [dʒɔː] че́люсть *f*; **~s** *pl.* рот; *animal's* пасть *f*; **~bone** че́люстная кость *f*

**jazz** [dʒæz] джаз

**jealous** [ˈdʒeləs] □ ревни́вый; зави́стливый; **~y** [~ɪ] ре́вность *f*; за́висть *f*

**jeans** [dʒiːnz] *pl.* джи́нсы *pl.*

**jeep**® [dʒiːp] *mil.* джип, вездеход
**jeer** [dʒɪə] **1.** насмешка, издёвка; **2.** насмехаться, глумиться (***at*** над T)
**jelly** ['dʒelɪ] **1.** желе *n indecl.*; (*aspic*) студень *m*; **2.** засты(ва)ть; **~fish** медуза
**jeopardize** ['dʒepədaɪz] подвергать опасности, [по]ставить под угрозу
**jerk** [dʒɜːk] **1.** рывок; толчок; ***the car stopped with a ~*** машина резко остановилась; **2.** резко толкать или дёргать; двигаться толчками; **~y** ['dʒɜːkɪ] □ отрывистый; *movement* судорожный; (*bumpy*) тряский; **~ily** *adv.* рывками
**jersey** ['dʒɜːzɪ] *fabric, garment* джерси *indecl.*
**jest** [dʒest] **1.** шутка; ***in ~*** в шутку; **2.** [по]шутить
**jet** [dʒet] **1.** *of water, gas, etc.* струя; **2.** бить струёй; **3.** *ae.* реактивный самолёт; *attr.* реактивный;
**jetty** ['dʒetɪ] *naut.* пристань *f*
**Jew** [dʒuː] еврей(-ка *f*) *m*
**jewel** ['dʒuːəl] драгоценный камень *m.*; **~(l)er** [~ə] ювелир; **~(le)ry** [~rɪ] драгоценности *f/pl.*
**Jew|ess** ['dʒuːɪs] еврейка; **~ish** [~ɪʃ] еврейский
**jiffy** ['dʒɪfɪ] *coll.* миг, мгновение
**jigsaw** ['dʒɪgsɔː]: **~ (*puzzle*)** составная картинка-загадка
**jilt** [dʒɪlt] бросить *pf.*
**jingle** ['dʒɪŋgl] **1.** звон, звяканье; **2.** [за]звенеть, звякать [-кнуть]
**jitters** ['dʒɪtəz] нервное возбуждение; ***she's got the ~*** она трясётся от страха
**job** [dʒɒb] работа, труд; дело; ***by the ~*** сдельно; ***it's a good ~ ...*** хорошо, что ...; ***it's just the ~*** это то, что нужно; ***know one's ~*** знать своё дело; **~ber** ['dʒɑbə] занимающийся случайной работой; брокер, маклер
**jockey** ['dʒɒkɪ] жокей
**jocose** [dʒəʊ'kəʊs] шутливый; *mood* игривый
**jocular** ['dʒɒkjʊlə] шутливый
**jog** [dʒɔg] **1.** толчок (*a. fig.*); тряская езда; **2.** *v/t.* толкать [-кнуть]; *v/i.* (*mst.* **~ *along***,) бегать (бежать) трусцой; трястись; *fig.* понемногу продвигаться; **~ger** любитель *m* оздоровительного бега
**join** [dʒɔɪn] **1.** *v/t.* (*connect*) соединять [-нить], присоединять [-нить]; *a company* присоединяться [-ниться] к (Д); вступить в члены (Р); **~ *hands*** объединяться [-ниться]; браться за руки; *v/i.* соединяться [-ниться]; (*unite*) объединяться [-ниться]; **~ *in with*** присоединяться [-ниться] к (Д); **~ *up*** поступать [-ить] на военную службу; **2.** соединение; *tech.* шов
**joiner** ['dʒɔɪnə] столяр
**joint** [dʒɔɪnt] **1.** *tech.* соединение; стык; *anat.* сустав; *of meat* кусок мяса для жарения; ***put out of ~*** вывихнуть *pf.*; **2.** □ объединённый; общий; **~ *owners*** совладельцы; **~ *venture*** совместное предприятие; **~ stock** акционерный капитал; **~ *company*** акционерное общество
**jok|e** [dʒəʊk] **1.** шутка, острота; **2.** *v/i.* [по]шутить; *v/t.* поддразнивать [-нить]; ***~ing apart ...*** если говорить серьёзно; шутки в сторону; **~er** ['dʒəʊkə] шутник *m*, -ница *f*
**jolly** ['dʒɒlɪ] **1.** весёлый, радостный; **2.** *adv.* очень; ***it's ~ hard ...*** чертовски трудно ...
**jolt** [dʒəʊlt] **1.** трясти [тряхнуть], встряхивать [-хнуть]; **2.** толчок; *fig.* встряска
**jostle** ['dʒɒsl] **1.** толкать(ся); теснить(ся); **2.** толчок; *in crowd* толкотня, давка
**jot** [dʒɒt] **1.** ничтожное количество, йота; ***not a ~ of truth*** ни капли правды; **2. ~ *down*** бегло набросать *pf.*, кратко записать *pf.*
**journal** ['dʒɜːnl] журнал; дневник; **~ism** ['dʒɜːnəlɪzəm] журналистика; **~ist** [~ɪst] журналист
**journey** ['dʒɜːnɪ] **1.** поездка, путешествие; ***go on a ~*** отправиться *pf.* в путешествие; **2.** путешествовать
**jovial** ['dʒəʊvɪəl] весёлый, общительный

J

**joy** [dʒɔɪ] ра́дость *f*, удово́льствие; **~ful** ['dʒɔɪfl] □ ра́достный, весёлый; **~less** [~lɪs] □ безра́достный; **~ous** [~əs] □ ра́достный, весёлый

**jubil|ant** ['dʒuːbɪlənt] лику́ющий; **~ee** ['dʒuːbɪliː] юбиле́й

**judge** [dʒʌdʒ] **1.** судья́ *m* (*a. sport*); *art* знато́к, цени́тель *m*; *in competition* член жюри́, *pl.* жюри́ *pl. indecl.*; **2.** *v/i.* суди́ть; быть арби́тром в спо́ре; ***~ for yourself …*** посуди́ сам …; *v/t.* суди́ть о (П); (*decide the merit of*) оце́нивать [-ни́ть]; (*condemn*) осужда́ть [осуди́ть], порица́ть

**judg(e)ment** ['dʒʌdʒmənt] *law* пригово́р, реше́ние суда́; сужде́ние; (*good sense*) рассуди́тельность *f*; (*opinion*) мне́ние, взгляд

**judicial** [dʒuː'dɪʃl] □ суде́бный

**judicious** [dʒuː'dɪʃəs] □ здравомы́слящий, рассуди́тельный; **~ness** [~nɪs] рассуди́тельность *f*

**judo** ['dʒuːdəʊ] дзюдо́ *n indecl.*

**jug** [dʒʌg] (*vessel*) кувши́н; *sl.* (*prison*) тюрьма́

**juggle** ['dʒʌgl] **1.** фо́кус, трюк; **2.** жонгли́ровать (*a. fig.*); **~r** [~ə] жонглёр

**juic|e** [dʒuːs] сок; **~y** ['dʒuːsɪ] □ со́чный; *gossip, etc.* сма́чный, пика́нтный

**July** [dʒu'laɪ] ию́ль *m*

**jumble** ['dʒʌmbl] **1.** пу́таница, беспоря́док; **2.** толка́ться; переме́шивать(ся); дви́гаться беспоря́дочным о́бразом; *chiefly Brt.* **~sale** благотвори́тельная распрода́жа

**jump** [dʒʌmp] **1.** прыжо́к; скачо́к (*a. fig.*); **2.** *v/i.* пры́гать [-гнуть]; скака́ть; ***~ at*** *an offer, etc.* охо́тно приня́ть *pf.*, ухва́тываться [ухвати́ться] за (В); ***~ to conclusions*** де́лать поспе́шные вы́воды; ***~ to one's feet*** вскочи́ть *pf.* (на́ ноги); ***the strange noise made me ~*** э́тот стра́нный звук заста́вил меня́ вздро́гнуть; *v/t.* перепры́гивать [-гнуть]

**jumper¹** ['dʒʌmpə] (*horse, athlete*) прыгу́н

**jumper²** [~] (*garment*) дже́мпер

**jumpy** ['dʒʌmpɪ] не́рвный

**junct|ion** ['dʒʌŋkʃn] соедине́ние (*a. el.*); *rail.* железнодоро́жный у́зел; (*crossroads*) перекрёсток; **~ure** [~ktʃə]: ***at this ~*** в э́тот моме́нт

**June** [dʒuːn] ию́нь *m*

**jungle** ['dʒʌŋgl] джу́нгли *f/pl.*; густы́е за́росли *f/pl.*

**junior** ['dʒuːnɪə] **1.** *in age, rank* мла́дший; моло́же (***to*** Р *or* чем И); **2.** (*person*) мла́дший

**junk** [dʒʌŋk] ру́хлядь *f*, хлам, отбро́сы *m/pl.*

**junta** ['dʒʌntə] ху́нта

**juris|diction** [dʒʊərɪs'dɪkʃn] отправле́ние правосу́дия; юрисди́кция; **~prudence** [dʒʊərɪs'pruːdəns] юриспруде́нция

**juror** ['dʒʊərə] *law* прися́жный

**jury** ['dʒʊrɪ] *law* прися́жные *m/pl.*; *in competiton* жюри́ *n indecl.*; **~man** прися́жный; член жюри́

**just** [dʒʌst] **1.** □ *adj.* справедли́вый; (*exact*) ве́рный, то́чный; **2.** *adv.* то́чно, как раз, и́менно; то́лько что; пря́мо; ***~ now*** сейча́с, сию́ мину́ту; то́лько что

**justice** ['dʒʌstɪs] справедли́вость *f*; *law* правосу́дие; судья́ *m*

**justifiable** ['dʒʌstɪ'faɪəbl] опра́вданный

**justification** [dʒʌstɪfɪ'keɪʃn] оправда́ние; (*ground*) основа́ние

**justify** ['dʒʌstɪfaɪ] опра́вдывать [-да́ть]

**justly** ['dʒʌstlɪ] справедли́во

**justness** ['dʒʌstnɪs] справедли́вость *f*

**jut** [dʒʌt] (*a. **~ out***) выступа́ть, вы́да(-ва́)ться

**juvenile** ['dʒuːvənaɪl] ю́ный, ю́ношеский; *delinquent* несовершенноле́тний

# K

**kaleidoscope** [kəˈlaɪdəskəʊp] калейдоско́п (*a. fig.*)
**kangaroo** [kæŋgəˈruː] кенгуру́ *m/f indecl.*
**karate** [kəˈrɑːtɪ] карате́
**keel** [kiːl] **1.** киль *m*; **2.** ***~ over*** опроки́дывать(ся) [-и́нуть(ся)]
**keen** [kiːn] □ (*sharp*) о́стрый (*a. fig.*); (*acute*) проница́тельный; (*intense*) си́льный; (*enthusiastic*) стра́стный; ***be ~ on*** о́чень люби́ть (В), стра́стно увлека́ться (Т)
**keep** [kiːp] **1.** содержа́ние; (*food*) пропита́ние; ***for ~s*** *coll.* навсегда́; **2.** [*irr.*] *v/t.* *com* держа́ть; сохраня́ть [-ни́ть]; храни́ть; (*manage*) содержа́ть; *diary* вести́; *word* [с]держа́ть; ***~ company with*** подде́рживать знако́мство с (Т); уха́живать за (Т); ***~ waiting*** заставля́ть ждать; ***~ away*** не подпуска́ть (***from*** к Д); ***~ in*** не выпуска́ть; *hat, etc.* ***~ on*** не снима́ть; ***~ up*** подде́рживать [-жа́ть]; **3.** *v/i.* держа́ться; уде́рживаться (-жа́ться) (***from*** от Р); (*remain*) ост(ав)а́ться; *of food* не по́ртиться; ***~ doing*** продолжа́ть де́лать; ***~ away*** держа́ться в отдале́нии; ***~ from*** возде́рживаться [-жа́ться] от (Р); ***~ off*** держа́ться в стороне́ от (Р); ***~ on*** (*talk*) продолжа́ть говори́ть; ***~ to*** приде́рживаться (Р); ***~ up*** держа́ться бо́дро; ***~ up with*** держа́ться наравне́ с (Т), идти́ в но́гу с (Т)
**keep|er** [ˈkiːpə] (*custodian*) храни́тель *m*; **~ing** [ˈkiːpiŋ] хране́ние; содержа́ние; ***be in*** (***out of***) ***~ with …*** (не) соотве́тствовать (Д); **~sake** [ˈkiːpseɪk] суве́нир, пода́рок на па́мять
**keg** [keg] бочо́нок
**kennel** [ˈkenl] конура́
**kept** [kept] *pt. и pt. p. от* ***keep***
**kerb(stone)** [ˈkɜːb(stəʊn)] поре́брик
**kerchief** [ˈkɜːtʃɪf] (головно́й) плато́к; косы́нка
**kernel** [ˈkɜːnl] зерно́, зёрнышко; *of nut* ядро́; *fig.* суть *f*
**kettle** [ˈketl] ча́йник; ***that's a different ~ of fish*** э́то совсе́м друго́е де́ло; **~drum** лита́вра
**key** [kiː] **1.** ключ (*a. fig.*); код; *mus., tech.* кла́виш(а); *mus.* ключ, тона́льность *f*; *fig.* тон; **2.** *mus.* настра́ивать [-ро́ить]; ***~ up*** *fig.* придава́ть реши́мость (Д); ***be ~ed up*** быть в взви́нченном состоя́нии; **~board** клавиату́ра; **~hole** замо́чная сква́жина; **~note** основна́я но́та ключа́; *fig.* основна́я мысль *f*; **~stone** *fig.* краеуго́льный ка́мень *m*
**kick** [kɪk] **1.** *with foot* уда́р; пино́к; *coll.* (*stimulus, pleasure*) удово́льствие; **2.** *v/t.* ударя́ть [уда́рить]; *horse* брыка́ть [-кну́ть]; ***~ out*** (*eject, dismiss*) выгоня́ть [вы́гнать]; вышвы́ривать [вы́швырнуть]; *v/i.* брыка́ться [-кну́ться], ляга́ться [ля́гнуться]; (*complain, resist*) [вос]проти́виться
**kid** [kɪd] **1.** козлёнок; (*leather*) ла́йка; *coll.* ребёнок; **2.** *coll.* (*pretend*) притворя́ться [-ри́ться]; (*deceive as a joke*) шутли́во обма́нывать [-ну́ть]
**kidnap** [ˈkɪdnæp] похища́ть [-хи́тить]; **~(p)er** [~ə] похити́тель *m*; (*extortionist*) вымога́тель *m*
**kidney** [ˈkɪdnɪ] *anat.* по́чка; **~ bean** фасо́ль *f*; **~ machine** *аппарат*: иску́сственная по́чка
**kill** [kɪl] уби́(ва́)ть; (*slaughter*) заби́(ва́)ть; *fig.* [по]губи́ть; ***~ time*** убива́ть вре́мя; **~er** [ˈkɪlə] уби́йца *m/f.*; **~ing** [~ɪŋ] (*exhausting*) уби́йственный; (*amusing*) умори́тельный; ***the work is really ~*** рабо́та про́сто на изно́с
**kin** [kɪn] родня́; ***next of ~*** ближа́йшие ро́дственники
**kind** [kaɪnd] **1.** □ до́брый, серде́чный; **2.** сорт, разнови́дность *f*; род; ***nothing of the ~*** ничего́ подо́бного; ***pay in ~*** плати́ть нату́рой; *fig.* отблагодари́ть; *for bad deed* [от]плати́ть той же моне́той; **~-hearted** добросерде́чный
**kindle** [ˈkɪndl] разжига́ть [-же́чь]; во-

спламеня́ть [-ни́ть]; *interest* возбужда́ть [-ди́ть]
**kindling** ['kɪndlɪŋ] расто́пка
**kind|ly** ['kaɪndlɪ] до́брый; **~ness** [-nɪs] доброта́; до́брый посту́пок; ***do s.o. a ~*** ока́з(ыв)ать кому́-л. любе́зность *f*
**kindred** ['kɪndrɪd] **1.** ро́дственный; **2.** родня́; ро́дственники
**king** [kɪŋ] коро́ль *m*; **~dom** ['kɪŋdəm] короле́вство; *bot. zo.* (расти́тельное, живо́тное) ца́рство; **~ly** [-lɪ] короле́вский, ца́рственный
**kink** [kɪŋk] *in metal* изги́б; *fig., in character* стра́нность *f*; причу́да
**kin|ship** ['kɪnʃɪp] родство́; **~sman** ['kɪnzmən] ро́дственник
**kiosk** ['ki:ɒsk] кио́ск; *Brt.* ***telephone ~*** телефо́нная бу́дка
**kip** [kɪp] *chiefly Brt. coll.* (*bed*) ко́йка; (*sleep*) сон; ***~ down*** [по]кема́рить; устро́иться; вздремну́ть *pf.*
**kiss** [kɪs] **1.** поцелу́й; **2.** [по]целова́ть(ся)
**kit** [kɪt] *mil.* ли́чное снаряже́ние; ***first-aid ~*** апте́чка; ***tool ~*** набо́р инструме́нтов; компле́кт принадле́жностей
**kitchen** ['kɪtʃɪn] ку́хня
**kite** [kaɪt] (бума́жный) змей
**kitten** ['kɪtn] котёнок
**knack** [næk] уме́ние, сноро́вка; ***get the ~*** научи́ться *pf.* (***of*** Д), приобрести́ *pf.* на́вык
**knapsack** ['næpsæk] ра́нец, рюкза́к
**knave** [neɪv] *cards* вале́т
**knead** [ni:d] [с]меси́ть
**knee** [ni:] коле́но; **~cap** *anat.* коле́нная ча́шка; **~l** [ni:l] [*irr.*] станови́ться на коле́ни; стоя́ть на коле́нях (***to*** пе́ред Т)
**knelt** [nelt] *pt. и pt. p. от* ***kneel***
**knew** [nju:] *pt. от* ***know***
**knickknack** ['nɪknæk] безделу́шка
**knife** [naɪf] **1.** (*pl.* **knives**) нож; **2.** зака́лывать [заколо́ть] ножо́м
**knight** [naɪt] **1.** ры́царь *m*; *chess* конь *m*; **2.** *modern use* жа́ловать ти́тул; **~ly** [-lɪ] ры́царский (*a. fig.*)
**knit** [nɪt] [*irr.*] [с]вяза́ть; (*~ together*) *med.* сраста́ться [срасти́сь]; ***~ one's brows*** хму́рить бро́ви; **~ting** ['nɪtɪŋ] **1.** вяза́ние; **2.** вяза́льный
**knives** [naɪvz] *pl. от* ***knife***
**knob** [nɒb] (*swelling*) ши́шка; (*door ~*) ру́чка; *on radio, etc.* кно́пка
**knock** [nɒk] **1.** стук; *on the head, etc.* уда́р; **2.** ударя́ть(ся) [уда́рить(ся)]; [по]стуча́ть(ся); *coll.* ***~ about*** разъезжа́ть по све́ту; ***~ down*** сбива́ть с ног; *mot.* сбить *pf.* маши́ной; ***be ~ed down*** быть сби́тым маши́ной; ***~ off work*** прекраща́ть рабо́ту; ***~ off*** стря́хивать [-хну́ть], сма́хивать [-хну́ть]; ***~ out*** вы́би(ва́)ть, выкола́чивать [вы́колотить]; *sport.* нокаути́ровать (*im*)*pf.*; ***~ over*** сбива́ть [сбить] с ног; *object* опроки́дывать [-ки́нуть]; **~out** нока́ут (*a.* ***~ blow***)
**knoll** [nəʊl] холм, буго́р
**knot** [nɒt] **1.** у́зел; *in wood* сук, сучо́к; ***get tied up in ~s*** запу́тываться [-таться]; **2.** завя́зывать у́зел (*or* узло́м); спу́т(ыв)ать; **~ty** ['nɒtɪ] узлова́тый; сучкова́тый; *fig.* тру́дный
**know** [nəʊ] [*irr.*] знать; быть знако́мым с (Т); (*recognize*) узн(ав)а́ть; ***~ French*** говори́ть пофранцу́зски; ***be in the ~*** быть в ку́рсе де́ла; ***come to ~*** узн(ав)а́ть; **know-how** уме́ние; *tech.* но́у-ха́у; **~ing** ['nəʊɪŋ] □ ло́вкий, хи́трый; *look* многозначи́тельный; **~ledge** ['nɒlɪdʒ] зна́ние; ***to my ~*** по мои́м све́дениям; **~n** [nəʊn] *pt. p. от* ***know***; ***come to be ~*** сде́латься *pf.* изве́стным; ***make ~*** объявля́ть [-ви́ть]
**knuckle** ['nʌkl] **1.** суста́в па́льца руки́; **2.** ***~ down, ~ under*** уступа́ть [-пи́ть]; подчиня́ться [-ни́ться]
**Koran** [kə'rɑ:n] Кора́н

# L

**label** ['leɪbl] **1.** ярлы́к (*a. fig.*); этике́тка; *tie-on* би́рка; *stick-on* накле́йка; **2.** накле́ивать/привя́зывать ярлы́к на (В)/к (Д) (*a. fig.*)

**laboratory** [lə'bɒrətrɪ] лаборато́рия; **~ assistant** лабора́нт *m*, -ка *f*

**laborious** [lə'bɔːrɪəs] □ тру́дный

**labo(u)r** ['leɪbə] **1.** труд; рабо́та; (*childbirth*) ро́ды *pl.*; ***forced* ~** принуди́тельные рабо́ты *f/pl.*; **~ *exchange*** би́ржа труда́; **2.** рабо́чий; **3.** *v/i.* труди́ться, рабо́тать; прилага́ть уси́лия; **~ed** [-d] вы́мученный; тру́дный; **~er** [-rə] рабо́чий; **~-intensive** трудоёмкий

**lace** [leɪs] **1.** кру́жево; (*shoe~*) шнуро́к; **2.** [за]шнурова́ть]

**lacerate** ['læsəreɪt] раздира́ть [разодра́ть]; (*cut*) разреза́ть [-ре́зать]

**lack** [læk] **1.** недоста́ток, нехва́тка; отсу́тствие (Р); **2.** испы́тывать недоста́ток, нужду́ в (П); не хвата́ть [-ти́ть], недостава́ть; ***he* ~*s courage*** у него́ не хвата́ет му́жества

**lacquer** ['lækə] **1.** лак; **2.** [от]лакирова́ть, покрыва́ть [-ы́ть] ла́ком

**lad** [læd] (*boy*) ма́льчик; (*fellow*) па́рень *m*; (*youth*) ю́ноша *m*

**ladder** ['lædə] приставна́я ле́стница, стремя́нка; *in stocking* спусти́вшаяся петля́

**laden** ['leɪdn] нагружённый; *fig.* обременённый

**ladies**, **ladies (room)**, **the ladies'** ['leɪdɪz] же́нский туале́т; *coll.* (*lavatory*) же́нская убо́рная

**ladle** ['leɪdl] **1.** *tech.* ковш; черпа́к; *for soup* поло́вник; **2.** отче́рпывать [отчерпну́ть]; *soup* разли́(ва́)ть (*a.* **~ *out***)

**lady** ['leɪdɪ] да́ма; *title* ле́ди *f indecl.*; **~bird** бо́жья коро́вка

**lag** [læg] (*trail*) тащи́ться (сза́ди); отст(ав)а́ть (*a.* **~ *behind***)

**laggard** ['lægəd] медли́тельный, вя́лый челове́к; отстаю́щий

**lagoon** [lə'guːn] лагу́на

**laid** [leɪd] *pt.* и *pt. p. om* ***lay***

**lain** [leɪn] *pt. p. om* ***lie***²

**lair** [leə] ло́говище, берло́га

**lake** [leɪk] о́зеро

**lamb** [læm] **1.** ягнёнок; (*food*) бара́нина; **2.** [о]ягни́ться; **~skin** овчи́на, ове́чья шку́ра

**lame** [leɪm] **1.** □ хромо́й; *fig. excuse* сла́бый, неубеди́тельный; **2.** [из-]уве́чить, [ис]кале́чить

**lament** [lə'ment] **1.** сетова́ние, жа́лоба; **2.** [по]се́товать, опла́к(ив)ать; **~able** ['læməntəbl] жа́лкий; печа́льный; **~ation** [læmən'teɪʃn] жа́лоба, плач

**lamp** [læmp] ла́мпа; *in street* фона́рь *m*

**lampoon** [læm'puːn] па́сквиль *m*

**lamppost** фона́рный столб

**lampshade** абажу́р

**land** [lænd] **1.** земля́; (*not sea*) су́ша; (*soil*) земля́, по́чва; (*country*) страна́; **~ *register*** земе́льный рее́стр; ***travel by* ~** е́хать (е́здить) су́шей/назе́мным тра́нспортом; **2.** *of ship passengers* выса́живать(ся) [вы́садить(ся)]; *of aircraft* приземля́ться [-ли́ться]

**landing** ['lændɪŋ] вы́садка; *ae.* приземле́ние, поса́дка; при́стань *f*

**land|lady** хозя́йка; **~lord** хозя́ин; **~mark** ориенти́р; *fig.* (*turning point*) ве́ха; **~owner** землевладе́лец; **~scape** ['lændskeɪp] ландша́фт, пейза́ж; **~slide** о́ползень *m*

**lane** [leɪn] тропи́нка; *in town* переу́лок; *of traffic* ряд

**language** ['læŋgwɪdʒ] язы́к (речь); ***strong* ~** си́льные выраже́ния *n/pl.*, брань *f*

**languid** ['læŋgwɪd] □ то́мный

**languish** ['læŋgwɪʃ] (*lose strength*) [за]ча́хнуть; (*pine*) тоскова́ть, томи́ться

**languor** ['læŋgə] апати́чность *f*; томле́ние; то́мность *f*

**lank** ['læŋk] □ высо́кий и худо́й; *hair* прямо́й; **~y** ['læŋkɪ] □ долговя́зый

**lantern** ['læntən] фона́рь *m*
**lap**[1] [læp] **1.** по́ла; *anat.* коле́ни *n/pl*; *fig.* ло́но; *sport.* круг; **2.** перекры́(-ва́)ть
**lap**[2] [~] *v/t.* (*drink*) [вы́]лака́ть; жа́дно пить; *v/i.* плеска́ться
**lapel** [lə'pel] ла́цкан
**lapse** [læps] **1.** *of time* ход; (*slip*) оши́бка, про́мах, *moral* паде́ние; **2.** [в]пасть; приня́ться *pf.* за ста́рое; (*expire*) истека́ть [-е́чь]; **~ *into silence*** умолка́ть [умо́лкнуть]
**larceny** ['lɑːsənɪ] кра́жа, воровство́
**lard** [lɑːd] топлёное свино́е са́ло
**larder** ['lɑːdə] кладова́я
**large** [lɑːdʒ] ☐ большо́й; (*substantial*) кру́пный; (*too big*) вели́к; ***at*~** на свобо́де; **~ly** ['lɑːdʒlɪ] в значи́тельной сте́пени; в основно́м, гла́вным о́бразом; **~-scale** кру́пный, крупномасшта́бный
**lark** [lɑːk] жа́воронок; *fig.* шу́тка, прока́за, заба́ва
**larva** ['lɑːvə] *zo.* личи́нка
**laryngitis** [lærɪn'dʒaɪtɪs] ларинги́т
**larynx** ['lærɪŋks] горта́нь *f*
**lascivious** [lə'sɪvɪəs] ☐ похотли́вый
**laser** ['leɪzə] ла́зер
**lash** [læʃ] **1.** плеть *f*; (*whip*) кнут; (*blow*) уда́р; (*eye*~) ресни́ца; **2.** хлеста́ть [-ну́ть]; (*fasten*) привя́зывать [-за́ть]; *fig.* бичева́ть
**lass**, **lassie** [læs, 'læsɪ] де́вушка, де́вочка
**lassitude** ['læsɪtjuːd] уста́лость *f*
**last**[1] [lɑːst] **1.** *adj.* после́дний; про́шлый; кра́йний; **~ *but one*** предпосле́дний; **~ *night*** вчера́ ве́чером; **2.** коне́ц; ***at*~** наконе́ц; ***at long*~** в конце́ концо́в; **3.** *adv.* в после́дний раз; по́сле всех; в конце́
**last**[2] [~] продолжа́ться [-до́лжиться]; [про]дли́ться; (*suffice*) хвата́ть [-ти́ть]; (*hold out*) сохраня́ться [-ни́ться]
**lasting** ['lɑːstɪŋ] ☐ дли́тельный; *peace* про́чный
**lastly** ['lɑːstlɪ] наконе́ц
**latch** [lætʃ] **1.** щеко́лда, задви́жка; замо́к с защёлкой; **2.** запира́ть [запере́ть]
**late** [leɪt] по́здний; (*delayed*) запозда́лый; (*former*) неда́вний; (*deceased*) поко́йный; *adv.* по́здно; ***at*** (***the***) **~*st*** не поздне́е; ***of*** **~** после́днее вре́мя; ***be*~** опа́здывать [опозда́ть]; **~ly** ['leɪtlɪ] неда́вно; в после́днее вре́мя
**latent** ['leɪtnt] скры́тый
**lateral** ['lætərəl] ☐ боково́й
**lathe** [leɪð] тока́рный стано́к
**lather** ['lɑːðə] **1.** мы́льная пе́на; **2.** *v/t.* намы́ли(ва)ть; *v/i.* мы́литься, намы́ли(ва)ться
**Latin** ['lætɪn] **1.** лати́нский язы́к; **2.** лати́нский; **~American** латиноамерика́нец, -нский
**latitude** ['lætɪtjuːd] *geogr.*, *astr.* широта́; *fig.* свобо́да де́йствий
**latter** ['lætə] после́дний; второ́й; **~ly** [~lɪ] в после́днее вре́мя
**lattice** ['lætɪs] решётка (*a.* **~*work***)
**laudable** ['lɔːdəbl] ☐ похва́льный
**laugh** [lɑːf] **1.** смех; **2.** смея́ться; **~ *at a p.*** высме́ивать [вы́смеять] (В), смея́ться над (Т); **~able** ['lɑːfəbl] ☐ смешно́й; **~ter** ['lɑːftə] смех
**launch** [lɔːntʃ] **1.** ка́тер; мото́рная ло́дка; **2.** *rocket* запуска́ть [-сти́ть]; *boat* спуска́ть [-сти́ть]; *fig.* пуска́ть в ход; **~ing** [~ɪŋ] → ***launch*** *2*; **~ing pad** пускова́я устано́вка; **~ing site** пускова́я площа́дка
**laundry** ['lɔːndrɪ] пра́чечная; бельё для сти́рки *or* из сти́рки
**laurel** ['lɒrəl] лавр
**lavatory** ['lævətrɪ] убо́рная
**lavender** ['lævəndə] лава́нда
**lavish** ['lævɪʃ] **1.** ☐ ще́дрый, расточи́тельный; **2.** расточа́ть [-чи́ть]
**law** [lɔː] зако́н; пра́вило; *law* пра́во; юриспруде́нция; ***lay down the*** **~** кома́ндовать; **~-abiding** законопослу́шный, соблюда́ющий зако́н; **~ court** суд; **~ful** ['lɔːfl] ☐ зако́нный; **~less** ['lɔːlɪs] ☐ *person* непоко́рный; *state* анархи́чный
**lawn**[1] [lɔːn] (*linen*) бати́ст
**lawn**[2] [~] (*grassy area*) лужа́йка, газо́н; **~chair** *Am.* шезло́нг; **~mower** газонокоси́лка

**law|suit** ['lɔːsuːt] судéбный процéсс; **~yer** ['lɔːjə] юрúст; адвокáт
**lax** [læks] □ вя́лый; ры́хлый; (*careless*) небрéжный; (*not strict*) нестрóгий; **~ative** ['læksətɪv] слабúтельное
**lay**[1] [leɪ] **1.** *pt. om* ***lie***[2]; **2.** (*secular*) свéтский
**lay**[2] [~] **1.** положéние, направлéние; **2.** [*irr.*] *v/t.* класть [положúть]; *blame* возлагáть [-ложúть]; *table* накры́(-вá)ть; ***~ in stocks*** запасáться [запастúсь] (***of*** Т); ***~ low*** (*knock down*) повалúть *pf.*; ***I was laid low by a fever*** меня свалúла лихорáдка; ***~ off*** увольня́ть [-лить]; ***~ out*** выкла́дывать [вы́ложить]; *park, etc.* разбú(-вá)ть; ***~ up*** (*collect and store*) [на]копúть; прикóвывать к постéли; *v/i. of hen* [с]нестúсь; держáть парú (*a.* ***~ a wager***)
**layer** ['leɪə] слой, пласт, наслоéние
**layman** ['leɪmən] миря́нин; (*amateur*) неспециалúст, любúтель *m*
**lay|-off** сокращéние кáдров; **~out** планирóвка
**lazy** ['leɪzɪ] ленúвый
**lead**[1] [led] свинéц
**lead**[2] [liːd] **1.** руководствó; инициатúва; *sport.* лúдерство; (*first place*) пéрвое мéсто; *thea.* глáвная роль *f*; *el.* прóвод; **2.** [*irr.*] *v/t.* водúть, [по]вестú; приводúть [-вестú] (***to*** к Д); (*direct*) руководúть (Т); *cards* ходúть [пойтú] с (Р *pl.*); ***~ on*** соблазня́ть [-нúть]; *v/t.* вестú; быть пéрвым; ***~ off*** отводúть; *v/i.* нач(ин)áть
**leaden** ['ledn] свинцóвый (*a. fig.*)
**leader** ['liːdə] руководúтель(ница *f*) *m*; лúдер; *in newspaper* передовáя статья́
**leading** ['liːdɪŋ] **1.** руководя́щий; ведýщий; (*outstanding*) выдаю́щийся; ***~ question*** наводя́щий вопрóс; **2.** руковóдство; ведéние
**leaf** [liːf] (*pl.*: **leaves**) лист (*bot. pl.*: лúстья); (*leafage*) листвá; ***turn over a new ~*** начáть нóвую жизнь; **~let** ['liːflɪt] листóвка
**league** [liːg] лúга; ***in ~ with*** в сою́зе с (Т)
**leak** [liːk] **1.** течь *f*; *of gas, etc.* утéчка (*a. fig.*); **2.** давáть течь, пропускáть вóду; ***~ out*** просáчиваться [-сочúться] (*a. fig.*); **~age** ['liːkɪdʒ] просáчивание; **~y** ['liːkɪ] протекáющий, с тéчью
**lean**[1] [liːn] [*irr.*] прислоня́ть(ся) [-нúть(ся)] (***against*** к Д); опирáться [оперéться] (***on*** на В) (*a. fig.*); наклоня́ть(ся) [-нúть(ся)] (*a.* ***~ forward***)
**lean**[2] [~] тóщий, худóй; *meat* нежúрный
**leant** [lent] *chiefly Brt. pt. p. om* ***lean***
**leap** [liːp] **1.** прыжóк, скачóк; **2.** [*a. irr.*] пры́гать [-гнуть], скакáть *once* [скакнýть]; **~t** [lept] *pt. p. om* ***leap***; ***~ year*** високóсный год
**learn** [lɜːn] [*a. irr.*] изучáть [-чúть], [на]учúться (Д); ***~ from*** узн(ав)áть от (Р); **~ed** ['lɜːnɪd] □ учёный; **~ing** [~ɪŋ] учéние; учёность *f*, эрудúция; **~t** [lɜːnt] *chiefly Brt. pt. p. om* ***learn***
**lease** [liːs] **1.** арéнда; (*period*) срок арéнды; ***long-term ~*** долгосрóчная арéнда, лúзинг; **2.** сдавáть в арéнду; брать в арéнду
**leash** [liːʃ] поводóк, прúвязь *f*
**least** [liːst] *adj.* малéйший; наимéньший; *adv.* мéнее всегó, в наимéньшей стéпени; ***at (the) ~*** по крáйней мéре; ***not in the ~*** ничýть, нискóлько; ***to say the ~*** мя́гко говоря́
**leather** ['leðə] **1.** кóжа; **2.** кóжаный
**leave** [liːv] **1.** разрешéние, позволéние; (*absence, holiday*) óтпуск; **2.** [*irr.*] *v/t.* оставля́ть [-áвить]; (*abandon*) покидáть [покúнуть]; предоставля́ть [-áвить]; (*bequeath, etc.*) оставля́ть; завещáть *im*(*pf*); ***~ it to me*** предостáвь(те) э́то мне; ***~ off*** бросáть [брóсить]; *v/i.* уезжáть [уéхать]; уходúть [уйтú]
**leaves** [liːvz] *pl. om* ***leaf***
**leavings** ['liːvɪŋz] остáтки *m/pl.*
**lecture** ['lektʃə] **1.** лéкция; (*reproof*) нотáция; **2.** *v/i.* читáть лéкции; *v/t.* читáть нотáцию; отчúтывать [-итáть]; **~r** [~rə] (*speaker*) доклáдчик; *professional* лéктор; *univ.* преподавáтель *m*
**led** [led] *pt. и pt. p. om* ***lead***

L

**ledge** [ledʒ] вы́ступ, усту́п
**ledger** ['ledʒə] *fin.* гроссбу́х, бухга́лтерская кни́га
**leech** [liːtʃ] *zo.* пия́вка
**leer** [lɪə] смотре́ть и́скоса (***at*** на В); де́лать гла́зки кому́-нибу́дь; кри́во улыба́ться [улыбну́ться]
**leeway** ['liːweɪ] *naut.* дрейф; *fig.* ***make up ~*** навёрстывать упу́щенное
**left**¹ [left] *pt. и pt. p. от* ***leave***; ***be ~*** ост(ав)а́ться
**left**² [~] **1.** ле́вый; **2.** ле́вая сторона́; **~-hander** левша́ *m/f*
**left-luggage|locker** *rail. Brt.* автомати́ческая ка́мера хране́ния; **~ office** ка́мера хране́ния
**leg** [leg] нога́; *of table, etc.* но́жка; *of trousers* штани́на
**legacy** ['legəsɪ] (*bequest*) насле́дство; *fig.* (*heritage*) насле́дие
**legal** ['liːgl] □ зако́нный, лега́льный; правово́й; **~ize** [~gəlaɪz] узако́ни(ва)ть, легализова́ть (*im*)*pf.*
**legend** ['ledʒənd] леге́нда; **~ary** [~drɪ] легенда́рный
**legible** ['ledʒəbl] □ разбо́рчивый
**legislat|ion** [ledʒɪs'leɪʃn] законода́тельство; **~ive** ['ledʒɪslətɪv] законода́тельный; **~or** [~leɪtə] законода́тель *m*
**legitima|cy** [lɪ'dʒɪtɪməsɪ] зако́нность *f*; **~te** **1.** [~meɪt] узако́ни(ва)ть; **2.** [~mɪt] зако́нный
**leisure** ['leʒə] досу́г; ***at your ~*** когда́ вам удо́бно; **~ly** *adv.* не спеша́, споко́йно; *adj.* неторопли́вый
**lemon** ['lemən] лимо́н; **~ade** [lemə'neɪd] лимона́д
**lend** [lend] [*irr.*] ода́лживать [одолжи́ть]; *money* дава́ть взаймы́; *fig.* д(ав)а́ть, прид(ав)а́ть; ***~ a hand*** помога́ть [-мо́чь]
**length** [leŋð] длина́; расстоя́ние; *of time* продолжи́тельность *f*; *of cloth* отре́з; ***at ~*** наконе́ц; *speak* подро́бно; ***go to any ~s*** быть гото́вым на всё; **~en** ['leŋθən] удлиня́ть(ся) [-ни́ть(ся)]; **~wise** [~waɪz] в длину́; вдоль; **~y** [~ɪ] дли́нный; *time* дли́тельный; *speech* растя́нутый; многосло́вный
**lenient** ['liːnɪənt] □ мя́гкий; снисходи́тельный
**lens** [lenz] ли́нза; *phot.* объекти́в; *anat.* хруста́лик; ***contact ~*** конта́ктная ли́нза
**lent** [lent] *pt. и pt. p. от* ***lend***
**Lent** [lent] вели́кий пост
**lentil** ['lentɪl] чечеви́ца
**leopard** ['lepəd] леопа́рд
**less** [les] **1.** (*comp. от* ***little***) ме́ньший; **2.** *adv.* ме́ньше, ме́нее; **3.** *prp.* ми́нус (Р); ***none the ~*** тем не ме́нее
**lessen** ['lesn] *v/t.* уменьша́ть [уме́ньшить]; *v/i.* уменьша́ться [уме́ньшиться]
**lesser** ['lesə] ме́ньший
**lesson** ['lesn] уро́к; *fig.* ***teach s.o. a ~*** проучи́ть (В) *pf.*; ***let this be a ~ to you*** пусть э́то послу́жит тебе́ уро́ком
**lest** [lest] что́бы не, как бы не
**let** [let] [*irr.*] оставля́ть [-а́вить]; сдава́ть внаём; позволя́ть [-во́лить] (Д), пуска́ть [пусти́ть]; ***~ be*** оста́вить *pf.* в поко́е; ***~ alone*** *adv.* не говоря́ уже́ о … (П); ***~ down*** опуска́ть [-сти́ть]; *fig.* подводи́ть [-вести́]; ***~ go*** выпуска́ть из рук; ***~ o.s. go*** дать *pf.* во́лю чу́вствам; увлека́ться [увле́чься]; ***~ into*** *a secret, etc.* посвяща́ть [-яти́ть] в; ***~ off*** *gun* стреля́ть [вы́стрелить] из (Р); *steam mst. fig.* выпуска́ть [вы́пустить] пар; ***~ out*** выпуска́ть [вы́пустить]; ***~ up*** *Am.* ослабе́(ва́)ть
**lethal** ['liːθl] смерте́льный, лета́льный
**lethargy** ['leθədʒɪ] летарги́я; вя́лость *f*
**letter** ['letə] бу́ква; письмо́; ***capital*** (***small***) ***~*** загла́вная, прописна́я (стро́чная) бу́ква; ***to the ~*** буква́льно; ***man of ~s*** литера́тор; ***registered ~*** заказно́е письмо́; **~ box** почто́вый я́щик; **~ing** [~rɪŋ] *f on gravestone, etc.* на́дпись *f*; *in book* разме́р и фо́рма букв
**lettuce** ['letɪs] сала́т
**level** ['levl] **1.** горизонта́льный; (*even*) ро́вный; (*equal*) одина́ковый, ра́вный, равноме́рный; ***draw ~ with*** поравня́ться *pf.* с (Т); ***keep a ~ head*** сохраня́ть [-ни́ть] хладнокро́вие; **2.** у́ро-

вень *m*; *fig.* масшта́б; **~ of the sea** у́ровень мо́ря; **on the ~** че́стно, правди́во; **3.** *v/t.* выра́внивать [вы́ровнять]; ура́внивать [-вня́ть]; **~ to the ground** сровня́ть *pf.* с землёй; **~ up** повыша́ть ура́внивая; *v/i.* **~ at** прице́ли(ва)ться в (В); **~ crossing** переéзд; **~-headed** рассуди́тельный

**lever** ['liːvə] рыча́г

**levy** ['levɪ]: **~ taxes** взима́ть нало́ги

**lewd** [ljuːd] □ похотли́вый

**liability** [laɪə'bɪlətɪ] отве́тственность *f* (*a. law*); (*obligation*) обяза́тельство; (*debt*) задо́лженность *f*; *fig.* приве́рженность *f*, скло́нность *f*; **liabilities** *pl.* обяза́тельства *n/pl.*; *fin.* долги́ *m/pl.*

**liable** ['laɪəbl] □ отве́тственный (за В); обя́занный; (*subject to*) подве́рженный; **be ~ to** быть предрасполо́женным к (Д)

**liar** ['laɪə] лгу́н *m*, -ья *f*

**libel** ['laɪbəl] **1.** клевета́; **2.** [на]клевета́ть на (В), оклевета́ть (В) *pf.*

**liberal** ['lɪbərəl] **1.** □ (*generous*) ще́дрый; (*ample*) оби́льный; *mst. pol.* либера́льный; **2.** либера́л(ка)

**liberat|e** ['lɪbəreɪt] освобожда́ть [-боди́ть]; **~ion** [lɪbə'reɪʃn] освобожде́ние; **~or** ['lɪbəreɪtə] освободи́тель *m*

**liberty** ['lɪbətɪ] свобо́да; (*familiar or presumptuous behavio(u)r*) бесцеремо́нность *f*; **be at ~** быть свобо́дным; **take the ~ of** брать [взять] на себя́ сме́лость; **take liberties with s.o.** позволя́ть себе́ во́льности с кем-л.

**librar|ian** [laɪ'breəriən] библиоте́карь *m*; **~y** ['laɪbrərɪ] библиоте́ка

**lice** [laɪs] *pl. om* **louse**

**licen|ce**, *Am. also* **~se** ['laɪsəns] **1.** разреше́ние; *comm.* лице́нзия; (*freedom*) во́льность *f*; **driving ~** води́тельские права́ *n/pl.*; **2.** разреша́ть [-ши́ть]; дава́ть пра́во (В)

**licentious** [laɪ'senʃəs] □ распу́щенный

**lick** [lɪk] **1.** обли́зывание; **2.** лиза́ть [лизну́ть]; обли́зывать [-за́ть]; *coll.* (*thrash*) [по]би́ть, [по]колоти́ть; **~ into shape** привести́ *pf.* в поря́док

**lid** [lɪd] кры́шка; (*eye~*) ве́ко

**lie¹** [laɪ] **1.** ложь *f*; **give the ~ to** облича́ть во лжи; **2.** [со]лга́ть

**lie²** [~] **1.** положе́ние; направле́ние; **explore the ~ of the land** *fig.* зонди́ровать по́чву; **2.** [*irr.*] лежа́ть; быть располо́женным, находи́ться; (*consist*) заключа́ться; **~ ahead** предстоя́ть (Д); **~ down** ложи́ться [лечь]; **~ in wait for** поджида́ть (В) (спря́тавшись)

**lieu** [ljuː]: **in ~ of** вме́сто (Р)

**lieutenant** [lef'tenənt] лейтена́нт

**life** [laɪf] жизнь *f*; (*way of ~*) о́браз жи́зни; биогра́фия; (*vitality*) жи́вость *f*; **for ~** пожи́зненный; на всю жизнь; **~ sentence** пригово́р к пожи́зненному заключе́нию; **~boat** спаса́тельная шлю́пка; **~guard** спаса́тель *m*; **~ insurance** страхова́ние жи́зни; **~ jacket** спаса́тельный жиле́т; **~less** □ бездыха́нный, безжи́зненный; **~like** реалисти́чный; сло́вно живо́й; **~long** всю жизнь; **~time** вся жизнь *f*, це́лая жизнь *f*

**lift** [lɪft] **1.** лифт; *for goods, etc.* подъёмник; *fig.* (*high spirits*) воодушевле́ние; **give s.o. a ~** подвози́ть [-везти́] кого́-л.; **2.** *v/t.* поднима́ть [-ня́ть]; возвыша́ть [-вы́сить]; *sl.* [у]кра́сть; *v/i.* возвыша́ться [вы́ситься]; *of mist, etc.* поднима́ться [-ня́ться]

**ligament** ['lɪgəmənt] *anat.* свя́зка

**light¹** [laɪt] **1.** свет; (*lighting*) освеще́ние; ого́нь *m*; *fig.* (*luminary*) свети́ло; **come to ~** стать изве́стным; обнару́живаться [-жится]; **will you give me a ~?** да́йте мне прикури́ть; **put a ~ to** зажига́ть [заже́чь]; **2.** све́тлый, я́сный; **3.** [*a. irr.*] *v/t.* зажига́ть [заже́чь]; освеща́ть [-ети́ть]; *v/i.* (*mst.* **~ up**) загора́ться [-ре́ться]; освеща́ться [-ети́ться]

**light²** [~] **1.** □ *adj.* лёгкий (*a. fig.*); **make ~ of** относи́ться несерьёзно к (Д); **travel ~** путеше́ствовать налегке́; **2. ~ on** неожи́данно натолкну́ться *pf.* на (В)

**lighten** ['laɪtn] освеща́ть [-ети́ть]; (*become brighter*) [по]светле́ть

**lighter** ['laɪtə] *for cigarettes, etc.* зажи-

га́лка
**light|-headed** легкомы́сленный; **~-hearted** □ беззабо́тный; весёлый; **~house** мая́к
**lighting** ['laɪtɪŋ] освеще́ние
**lightness** лёгкость *f*
**lightning** [laɪtnɪŋ] мо́лния; ***with ~ speed*** молниено́сно; **~ conductor**, **~ rod** громоотво́д
**lightweight** *sport* боксёр лёгкого ве́са; легкове́сный (*a. fig.*)
**like** [laɪk] **1.** похо́жий, подо́бный; ра́вный; ***as ~ as two peas*** похо́жи как две ка́пли воды́; ***such~*** подо́бный тому́, тако́й; *coll.* ***feel ~*** хоте́ть (+ *inf.*); ***what is he ~?*** что он за челове́к?; **2.** не́что подо́бное; ***~s*** *pl.* скло́нности *f/pl.*, влече́ния *n/pl.*; ***his ~*** ему́ подо́бные; **3.** люби́ть; [за]хоте́ть; ***how do you ~ London?*** как вам нра́вится Ло́ндон?; ***I should ~ to know*** я хоте́л бы знать
**likeable** ['laɪkəbl] симпати́чный
**like|lihood** ['laɪklɪhʊd] вероя́тность *f*; **~ly** ['laɪklɪ] вероя́тный; (*suitable*) подходя́щий; ***he is ~ to die*** он вероя́тно умрёт; ***as ~ as not*** вполне́ возмо́жно
**like|n** ['laɪkən] уподобля́ть [-о́бить]; (*compare*) сра́внивать [-ни́ть]; **~ness** ['laɪknɪs] схо́дство; **~wise** [-waɪz] то́же, та́кже; подо́бно
**liking** ['laɪkɪŋ] расположе́ние (***for*** к Д); ***take a ~ to*** полюби́ть *pf.* (В)
**lilac** ['laɪlək] **1.** сире́нь *f*; **2.** сире́невый, лило́вый
**lily** ['lɪlɪ] ли́лия; ***~ of the valley*** ла́ндыш
**limb** [lɪm] коне́чность *f*; *of tree* ве́тка
**lime**[1] [laɪm] *tree* ли́па
**lime**[2] [~] и́звесть *f*; **~light** свет ра́мпы; *fig.* центр внима́ния
**limit** ['lɪmɪt] преде́л, грани́ца; ***be ~ed to*** ограни́чивать(ся) (Т); ***speed ~*** преде́льная ско́рость *f*; ***time ~*** ограниче́ние во вре́мени; преде́льный срок; **~ation** [lɪmɪ'teɪʃn] ограниче́ние; **~ed** ['lɪmɪtɪd]: **~ (*liability*) *company*** компа́ния с ограни́ченной отве́тственностью; **~less** ['lɪmɪtlɪs] □ безграни́чный
**limp**[1] [lɪmp] **1.** [за]хрома́ть; **2.** прихра́мывание, хромота́
**limp**[2] [~] вя́лый; сла́бый; ***her body went ~*** те́ло её обмя́кло
**limpid** ['lɪmpɪd] прозра́чный
**line** [laɪn] **1.** ли́ния (*a. rail.*, *tel.*, *ae*); *typ.* строка́; *in drawing* черта́, штрих; (*fishing ~*) леса́; специа́льность *f*, заня́тие; ***~s*** *pl.* стро́ки; ***~ of conduct*** ли́ния поведе́ния; ***hard ~s*** *pl.* неуда́ча; ***in ~ with*** в согла́сии с (Т); ***stand in ~*** *Am.* стоя́ть в о́череди; ***that's not in my ~*** э́то не по мое́й ча́сти; **2.** *v/t.* разлино́вывать [-нова́ть]; *sew.* класть на подкла́дку; *of trees*, *etc.* тяну́ться вдоль (Р); *v/i.* **~ *up*** выстра́иваться [вы́строиться] (в ряд)
**linear** ['lɪnɪə] лине́йный
**linen** ['lɪnɪn] **1.** полотно́; бельё; **2.** льняно́й
**liner** ['laɪnə] *naut.* ла́йнер; *ae.* возду́шний ла́йнер
**linger** ['lɪŋgə] [по]ме́длить; **~ *over*** заде́рживаться [-жа́ться] на (П)
**lingerie** ['læːnʒərɪː] да́мское бельё
**lining** ['laɪnɪŋ] *of garment* подкла́дка; *tech.* оби́вка, облицо́вка
**link** [lɪŋk] **1.** звено́; связь *f* (*a. fig.*); соедине́ние; **2.** соединя́ть [-ни́ть]
**linoleum** [lɪ'nəʊlɪəm] лино́леум
**linseed** ['lɪnsiːd]: **~ *oil*** льняно́е ма́сло
**lion** ['laɪən] лев; **~ess** [~es] льви́ца
**lip** [lɪp] губа́; (*edge*) край; *coll.* (*impudence*) де́рзость *f*; **~stick** губна́я пома́да
**liquid** ['lɪkwɪd] **1.** жи́дкий; **2.** жи́дкость *f*
**liquidat|e** ['lɪkwɪdeɪt] ликвиди́ровать *im*(*pf.*); *debt* выпла́чивать [вы́платить]; **~ion** [lɪkwɪ'deɪʃn] ликвида́ция; вы́плата до́лга
**liquor** ['lɪkə] спиртно́й напи́ток
**lisp** [lɪsp] **1.** шепеля́вость *f*; **2.** шепеля́вить
**list**[1] [lɪst] **1.** спи́сок, пе́речень *m*; **2.** вноси́ть в спи́сок; составля́ть спи́сок (Р)
**list**[2] [~] **1.** *naut.* крен; **2.** [на]крени́ться
**listen** ['lɪsn] [по]слу́шать; (*heed*) прислу́ш(ив)аться (***to*** к Д); **~ *in*** (*eavesdrop*) подслу́ш(ив)ать (***to*** В); слу́шать ра́дио; **~er** [~ə] слу́шатель(-

ница *f*) *m*
**listless** ['lɪstlɪs] апати́чный, вя́лый
**lit** [lɪt] *pt. и pt. p. от* ***light***[1]
**literacy** ['lɪtərəsɪ] гра́мотность *f*
**literal** ['lɪtərəl] □ буква́льный, досло́вный
**litera|ry** ['lɪtərərɪ] литерату́рный; **~te** [~rət] гра́мотный; **~ture** ['lɪtrətʃə] литерату́ра
**lithe** [laɪð] ги́бкий
**lithography** [lɪ'θɒgrəfɪ] литогра́фия
**litre**, *Am.* **liter** ['li:tə] литр
**litter**[1] ['lɪtə] **1.** помёт (припло́д); **2.** [о]щени́ться, [о]пороси́ться *и т. д.*
**litter**[2] [~] **1.** му́сор; **2.** [на]му́сорить, [на]сори́ть
**little** ['lɪtl] **1.** *adj.* ма́ленький, небольшо́й; *time* коро́ткий; ***a ~ one*** малы́ш; **2.** *adv.* немно́го, ма́ло; **3.** пустя́к; ме́лочь *f*; ***a ~*** немно́го; ***~ by ~*** ма́ло-пома́лу, постепе́нно; ***not a ~*** нема́ло
**liturgy** ['lɪtədʒɪ] *eccl.* литурги́я
**live** [lɪv] **1.** *com.* жить; существова́ть; ***~ to see*** дожи́(ва́)ть до (Р); ***~ down: I'll never ~ it down*** мне э́того никогда́ не забу́дут; ***~ out*** пережи́(ва́)ть; ***~ up to expectations*** опра́вдывать [-да́ть] (В); **2.** [laɪv] живо́й; *coals*, *etc.* горя́щий; *el.* под напряже́нием; **~lihood** ['laɪvlɪhʊd] сре́дства к существова́нию; **~liness** [~nɪs] жи́вость *f*; оживле́ние; **~ly** ['laɪvlɪ] живо́й; оживлённый
**liver** ['lɪvə] *anat.* пе́чень *f*; *cul.* печёнка
**live|s** [laɪvz] *pl. от* ***life***; **~stock** ['laɪvstɒk] дома́шний скот
**livid** ['lɪvɪd] ме́ртвенно-бле́дный; ***~ with rage*** взбешённый
**living** ['lɪvɪŋ] **1.** живо́й; живу́щий, существу́ющий; **2.** сре́дства существова́ния; жизнь *f*, о́браз жи́зни; **~ room** гости́ная
**lizard** ['lɪzəd] я́щерица
**load** [ləʊd] **1.** груз; но́ша; (*weight of cares*, *etc.*) бре́мя *n*; *tech.* нагру́зка; **2.** [на]грузи́ть; *gun* заряжа́ть [-яди́ть]; *fig.* обременя́ть [-ни́ть]; **~ing** [ləʊdɪŋ] погру́зка; груз
**loaf**[1] [ləʊf] (*pl.* **loaves**) (*white*) бато́н; (*mst. brown*) буха́нка
**loaf**[2] [~] безде́льничать; шата́ться, слоня́ться без де́ла
**loafer** ['ləʊfə] безде́льник
**loan** [ləʊn] **1.** заём; *from bank* ссу́да; ***the book is on ~*** кни́га на рука́х; **2.** дава́ть взаймы́; дава́ть [дать] ссу́ду
**loath** [ləʊθ] (*reluctant*) несклóнный; **~e** [ləʊð] пита́ть отвраще́ние к (Д); **~some** ['ləʊðsəm] □ отврати́тельный
**loaves** [ləʊvz] *pl. от* ***loaf***
**lobby** ['lɒbɪ] **1.** *in hotel* вестибю́ль *m*; *parl.* кулуа́ры *m/pl.*; (*group*) ло́бби; *thea.* фойе́ *n indecl.*; **2.** *parl.* пыта́ться возде́йствовать на чле́нов конгре́сса
**lobe** [ləʊb] *of ear* мо́чка
**lobster** ['lɒbstə] ома́р
**local** ['ləʊkəl] **1.** □ ме́стный; ***~ government*** ме́стные о́рганы вла́сти; **2.** ме́стный жи́тель *m*; (*a.* ***~ train***) при́городный по́езд; **~ity** [ləʊ'kælətɪ] ме́стность *f*, райо́н; (*neighbo(u)rhood*) окре́стность *f*; **~ize** ['ləʊkəlaɪz] локализова́ть (*im*)*pf.*
**locat|e** [ləʊ'keɪt] *v/t.* определя́ть ме́сто (Р); располага́ть в определённом ме́сте; назнача́ть ме́сто для (Р); ***be ~d*** быть располо́женным; **~ion** [~ʃn] ме́сто; *Am.* местонахожде́ние
**lock**[1] [lɒk] *of hair* ло́кон
**lock**[2] [~] **1.** замо́к; *on canal* шлюз; **2.** *v/t.* запира́ть [запере́ть]; ***~ in*** запира́ть [запере́ть]; *v/t.* запира́ться [запере́ться]
**lock|er** ['lɒkə] запира́ющийся шка́фчик; **~et** ['lɒkɪt] медальо́н; **~out** лока́ут; **~smith** сле́сарь *m*
**locomotive** ['ləʊkəməʊtɪv] (*или* ***~ engine***) локомоти́в, парово́з, теплово́з, электрово́з
**locust** ['ləʊkəst] саранча́
**lodg|e** [lɒdʒ] **1.** сторо́жка; (*mst.* ***hunting ~***) охо́тничий до́мик; **2.** *v/t.* да(-ва́)ть помеще́ние (Д); *v/i.* снима́ть ко́мнату; *of bullet*, *etc.* застрева́ть [-ря́ть]; **~er** ['lɒdʒə] квартира́нт *m*, -ка *f*; **~ing** ['lɒdʒɪŋ]: ***live in ~s*** снима́ть ко́мнату
**loft** [lɒft] черда́к; ***hay ~*** сенова́л; **~y** ['lɒftɪ] □ (*haughty*) высокоме́рный;

*building* величественный; *style* возвышенный

**log** [lɒg] колода; бревно; **~ cabin** бревенчатая хижина

**loggerhead** ['lɒgəhed]: ***be at ~s*** быть в ссоре, ссориться (***with*** с Т)

**logic** ['lɒdʒɪk] логика; **~al** [ˌlɒdʒɪkl] □ логический

**loin** [lɔɪn] филейная часть *f*; **~s** *pl.* поясница

**loiter** ['lɔɪtə] слоняться без дела; (*linger*) мешкать

**loll** [lɒl] сидеть/стоять развалясь

**lone|liness** ['ləʊnlɪnɪs] одиночество; **~ly** [-lɪ], **~some** [-səm] одинокий

**long**[1] [lɒŋ] **1.** долгий срок, долгое время *n*; ***before ~*** вскоре; ***for ~*** надолго; **2.** *adj.* длинный; долгий; медленный; ***in the ~ run*** в конце концов; ***be ~*** долго длиться; **3.** *adv.* долго; ***as ~ ago as ..*** ещё …; ***~ ago*** давно; ***so ~!*** пока (до свидания)!; **~er** дольше; больше

L

**long**[2] [~] страстно желать, жаждать (***for*** Р), тосковать (по Д)

**long-distance** *attr.* дальний; *sport* на длинные дистанции; *tel.* междугородний

**longing** ['lɒŋɪŋ] **1.** □ тоскующий; **2.** сильное желание, стремление (к Д), тоска (по Д)

**longitude** ['lɒndʒɪtjuːd] *geogr.* долгота

**long|-sighted** дальнозоркий; **~-suffering** многострадальный; **~-term** долгосрочный; **~-winded** □ многословный

**look** [lʊk] **1.** взгляд; *in face, eyes* выражение; (*appearance*) вид, наружность *f* (*a.* **~s** *pl.*); ***have a ~ at a th.*** посмотреть *pf.* на (В); ознакомляться [-комиться] с (Т); **2.** *v/i.* [по]смотреть (***at*** на В); выглядеть; ***~ for*** искать (В *or* Р); ***~ forward to*** предвкушать [-усить] (В); с радостью ожидать (Р); ***~ into*** рассматривать [-мотреть], разбираться [-зобраться]; ***~ out!*** берегись!; ***~ (up)on*** *fig.* смотреть как на (В); считать (за В); ***~ with disdain*** смотреть с презрением; ***~ over*** не замечать [-етить]; ***~ through*** просматривать [-мотреть]; ***~ up*** *in dictionary, etc.* [по]искать; (*visit*) навещать [-естить]

**looker-on** [lʊkər'ɒn] зритель *m*; (невольный) свидетель *m*

**looking glass** зеркало

**lookout** ['lʊkaʊt] (*view*) вид; (*prospects*) виды *m/pl.*, шансы *m/pl.*; ***that is my ~*** это моё дело

**loom**[1] [luːm] ткацкий станок

**loom**[2] [~] маячить, неясно вырисовываться

**loop** [luːp] **1.** петля; **2.** делать петлю; закреплять петлёй; **~hole** *mst. fig.* лазейка

**loose** [luːs] □ *com.* свободный; (*vague*) неопределённый; (*not close-fitting*) просторный; (*not tight*) болтающийся, шатающийся; (*licentious*) распущенный; *earth* рыхлый; **~n** ['luːsn] (*make loose*) ослаблять(ся) [-абить(ся)]; (*untie*) развязывать [-язать]; разрыхлять [-лить]; расшатывать [-шатать]

**loot** [luːt] **1.** [о]грабить; **2.** добыча, награбленное добро

**lopsided** [lɒp'saɪdɪd] кривобокий; кособокий

**loquacious** [lə'kweɪʃəs] болтливый

**lord** [lɔːd] лорд; (*ruler, master*) повелитель *m*; ***the* ♀** Господь *m*; ***my* ♀** [mɪ'lɔːd] милорд; ***the ♀'s Prayer*** Отче наш; ***the ♀'s Supper*** Тайная вечеря; **~ly** ['lɔːdlɪ] высокомерный

**lorry** ['lɒrɪ] *mot.* грузовик

**lose** [luːz] [*irr.*] *v/t.* [по]терять; *a chance, etc.* упускать [-стить]; *game, etc.* проигрывать [-рать]; ***~ o.s.*** заблудиться *pf.*; *v/i.* [по]терять; *sport* проигрывать [-рать]; *of watch* отст(а-в)ать

**loss** [lɒs] потеря, утрата; *comm.* ущерб, убыток; ***at a ~*** в растерянности; ***with no ~ of time*** не теряя времени

**lost** [lɒst] *pt. u pt. p. om* ***lose***; ***be ~*** пропадать [-пасть]; (*perish*) погибать [-гибнуть]; *fig.* растеряться *pf.*; ***~ property office*** стол находок

**lot** [lɒt] (*destiny*) жребий; участь *f*,

до́ля; *comm.* (*consignment*) па́ртия това́ров; уча́сток земли́; *coll.* ма́сса, у́йма; ***draw ~s*** броса́ть жре́бий; ***fall to a p.'s ~*** вы́пасть *pf.* на чью-л. до́лю
**lotion** ['ləʊʃn] лосьо́н
**lottery** ['lɒtərɪ] лотере́я
**loud** [laʊd] □ гро́мкий, зву́чный; (*noisy*) шу́мный; *colo(u)r* крикли́вый, крича́щий
**lounge** [laʊndʒ] **1.** (*loll*) сиде́ть развали́сь; (*walk idly*) слоня́ться; **2.** пра́здное времяпрепровожде́ние; *thea.* фойе́ *n indecl.*; *at airport* зал ожида́ния; *in house* гости́ная
**lous|e** [laʊs] (*pl.*: **lice**) вошь *f* (*pl.*: вши); **~y** ['laʊzɪ] вши́вый (*a. coll. fig.*); *sl.* парши́вый
**lout** [laʊt] ха́мский, неотёсанный челове́к
**lovable** ['lʌvəbl] □ привлека́тельный, ми́лый
**love** [lʌv] **1.** любо́вь *f*; влюблённость *f*; предме́т любви́; ***give*** (*or* ***send***) ***one's ~ to a p.*** передава́ть, посыла́ть приве́т (Д); ***in ~ with*** влюблённый в (В); ***make ~ to*** быть бли́зкими; занима́ться любо́вью; ***not for ~ or money*** ни за что (на све́те); **2.** люби́ть; ***~ to do*** де́лать с удово́льствием; ***~ affair*** любо́вная свя́зь; *coll.* рома́н; **~ly** ['lʌvlɪ] прекра́сный, чу́дный; **~r** ['lʌvə] (*a paramour*) любо́вник *m*, -ница *f*; возлю́бленный; (*one fond of s.th.*) люби́тель(ница *f*) *m*
**loving** ['lʌvɪŋ] □ лю́бящий
**low¹** [ləʊ] ни́зкий, невысо́кий; *fig.* сла́бый; *voice, sound, etc.* ти́хий; *behavio(u)r* ни́зкий, непристо́йный; ***feel ~*** быть в плохо́м настрое́нии; пло́хо себя́ чу́вствовать
**low²** [~] **1.** мыча́ние; **2.** [за]мыча́ть
**lower¹** ['ləʊə] **1.** *comp. от* **low¹**; ни́зший; ни́жний; **2.** *v/t. sails, etc.* спуска́ть [-сти́ть]; *eyes* опуска́ть [-сти́ть]; *prices, voice, etc.* снижа́ть [-и́зить]; *v/i.* снижа́ться [-и́зиться]
**lower²** ['laʊə] смотре́ть угрю́мо; (*scowl*) [на]хму́риться
**low|-grade** ни́зкого со́рта, плохо́го ка́чества; **~land** ни́зменность *f*; **~-necked** с глубо́ким вы́резом; **~-paid** низкоопла́чиваемый; **~-spirited** пода́вленный, уны́лый
**loyal** ['lɔɪəl] □ ве́рный, пре́данный, лоя́льный; **~ty** [~tɪ] ве́рность *f*, пре́данность *f*, лоя́льность *f*
**lubric|ant** ['lu:brɪkənt] сма́зочное вещество́, сма́зка; **~ate** [~keɪt] сма́з(ыв)ать; **~ation** [lu:brɪ'keɪʃn] сма́зывание
**lucid** ['lu:sɪd] □ я́сный; (*transparent*) прозра́чный
**luck** [lʌk] уда́ча, сча́стье; ***good ~*** счастли́вый слу́чай, уда́ча; ***bad ~, hard ~, ill ~*** неуда́ча; **~ily** ['lʌkɪlɪ] к/по сча́стью; **~y** ['lʌkɪ] □ счастли́вый, уда́чный; принося́щий уда́чу
**lucrative** ['lu:krətɪv] □ при́быльный, вы́годный
**ludicrous** ['lu:dɪkrəs] □ неле́пый, смешно́й
**lug** [lʌg] [по]тащи́ть; *coll.* [по]волочи́ть
**luggage** ['lʌgɪdʒ] бага́ж
**lukewarm** ['lu:kwɔ:m] чуть тёплый; *fig.* прохла́дный
**lull** [lʌl] **1.** (*~ to sleep*) убаю́к(ив)ать; *fig.* успока́ивать [-ко́ить]; усыпля́ть [-пи́ть]; **2.** *in fighting, storm, etc.* вре́менное зати́шье
**lullaby** ['lʌləbaɪ] колыбе́льная (пе́сня)
**lumber** ['lʌmbə] *esp. Brt.* (*junk*) хлам; *esp. Am.* пиломатериа́лы *m/pl.*
**lumin|ary** ['lu:mɪnərɪ] *mst. fig.* свети́ло; **~ous** [~nəs] □ светя́щийся, све́тлый
**lump** [lʌmp] **1.** глы́ба, ком; *person* чурба́н; *of sugar, etc.* кусо́к; (*swelling*) ши́шка; ***~ sum*** о́бщая су́мма; ***a ~ in the throat*** комо́к в го́рле; **2.** *v/t.*: ***~ together*** [с]вали́ть в ку́чу; *v/i.* сбива́ться в ко́мья
**lunatic** ['lu:nətɪk] *mst. fig.* сумасше́дший
**lunch** ['lʌntʃ] обе́д в по́лдень, ленч; ***have ~*** [по]обе́дать
**lung** [lʌŋ] лёгкое; **~s** *pl.* лёгкие *n/pl.*
**lunge** [lʌndʒ] **1.** *mst. in fencing* вы́пад,

L

удáр; **2.** *v/i.* наносúть удáр (***at*** Д)
**lurch**[1] [lɜːtʃ] *naut.* [на]кренúться; идтú шатáясь
**lurch**[2] [~]: ***leave a. p. in the ~*** брóсить *pf.* когó-л. в бедé
**lure** [ljʊə] **1.** (*bait*) примáнка; *fig.* соблáзн; **2.** примáнивать [-нúть]; *fig.* соблазнáть [-нúть]
**lurid** ['lʊərɪd] (*glaring*) кричáщий; óчень я́ркий; (*shocking*) жýткий, ужáсный; (*gaudy*) аляповáтый
**lurk** [lɜːk] ждать притаúвшись; скрывáться в засáде; тaúться
**luscious** ['lʌʃəs] □ сóчный
**lust** [lʌst] (*sexual desire*) пóхоть *f*; (*craving*) жáжда
**lust|er**, *Brt.* **lustre** ['lʌstə] блеск; (*pendant*) лю́стра; **~rous** ['lʌstrəs] □ блестя́щий
**lute** [luːt] *mus.* лю́тня
**Lutheran** ['luːθərən] лютерáнин *m*, -анка *f*; лютерáнский
**luxur|iant** [lʌg'ʒʊərɪənt] бýйный, пы́шный; **~ious** [~rɪəs] роскóшный, пы́шный; **~y** ['lʌkʃərɪ] рóскошь *f*; предмéт рóскоши
**lying** ['laɪɪŋ] **1.** *pr. p. от* ***lie***[1] *и* ***lie***[2]; **2.** *adj.* от ***lie*** (*telling lies*) лжúвый
**lymph** [lɪmf] лúмфа
**lynch** [lɪntʃ] линчевáть
**lynx** [lɪnks] *zo.* рысь *f*
**lyric** ['lɪrɪk], **~al** [~ɪkəl] □ лирúческий; **~s** *pl.* лúрика

# M

**macabre** [mə'kɑːbrə] мрáчный; ***~ humour*** чёрный ю́мор
**macaroni** [mækə'rəʊnɪ] макарóны *f/pl.*
**macaroon** [mækə'ruːn] миндáльное печéнье
**machination** [mækɪ'neɪʃn] (*usu. pl.*) махинáции, кóзни *f/pl.*; интрúга
**machine** [mə'ʃiːn] станóк; машúна; механúзм; *attr.* машúнный; ***~ translation*** машúнный перевóд; ***~-made*** машúнного произвóдства; **~ry** [~ərɪ] машúнное оборýдование, машúны
**mackerel** ['mækrəl] макрéль, скýмбрия
**mad** [mæd] □ сумасшéдший, помéшанный; *animals* бéшеный; ***be ~ about*** быть без умá от (Д); ***be ~ with s.o.*** сердúться на (В); ***go ~*** сходúть с умá; ***drive ~*** сводúть с умá
**madam** ['mædəm] мадáм *f indecl.*; сударыня
**mad|cap** сорвиголовá *m/f*; **~den** ['mædn] [вз]бесúть; сводúть с умá; раздражáть [-жúть]
**made** [meɪd] *pt. и pt. p. от* ***make***
**mad|house** *fig.* сумасшéдший дом; **~man** сумасшéдший; *fig.* безýмец **~ness** ['mædnɪs] сумасшéствие; безýмие
**magazine** [mægə'ziːn] (*journal*) журнáл
**maggot** ['mægət] личúнка
**magic** ['mædʒɪk] **1.** (*a.* **~al** ['mædʒɪkəl] □) волшéбный; **2.** волшебствó; **~ian** [mə'dʒɪʃn] волшéбник
**magistrate** ['mædʒɪstreɪt] судья́
**magnanimous** [mæg'nænɪməs] □ великодýшный
**magnet** ['mægnɪt] магнúт; **~ic** [mæg'netɪk] (***~ally***) магнúтный; *fig.* притягáтельный
**magni|ficence** [mæg'nɪfɪsns] великолéпие; **~ficent** [~snt] великолéпный; **~fy** ['mægnɪfaɪ] увелúчи(ва)ть; **~fying glass** лýпа; **~tude** ['mægnɪtjuːd] величинá; вáжность *f*; ***~ of the problem*** масштáбность проблéмы
**mahogany** [mə'hɒgənɪ] крáсное дéрево
**maid** [meɪd] *in hotel* гóрничная; (*house~*) домрабóтница; ***old ~*** стáрая дéва
**maiden** ['meɪdn] **1.** дéвушка; **2.** неза-

му́жняя; *fig. voyage, etc.* пе́рвый; **~ *name*** де́вичья фами́лия; **~ly** [-lɪ] де́вичий

**mail** [meɪl] **1.** по́чта; *attr.* почто́вый; **2.** отправля́ть [-а́вить] по по́чте; посыла́ть по́чтой; **~box** *Am.* почто́вый я́щик; **~man** *Am.* почтальо́н; **~-order** зака́з по по́чте

**maim** [meɪm] [ис]кале́чить

**main** [meɪn] **1.** гла́вная часть *f*; **~s** *pl. el., etc.* магистра́ль *f*; ***in the* ~** в основно́м; **2.** гла́вный, основно́й; **~land** ['meɪnlənd] матери́к; **~ly** ['meɪnlɪ] гла́вным о́бразом; бо́льшей ча́стью; **~ road** шоссе́ *n indecl.*, магистра́ль *f*; **~spring** *fig.* дви́жущая си́ла; **~stay** *fig.* гла́вная опо́ра

**maintain** [meɪn'teɪn] подде́рживать [-жа́ть]; (*support*) содержа́ть *impf.*; утвержда́ть [-рди́ть]; (*preserve*) сохраня́ть [-ни́ть]; **~ *that*** утвержда́ть, что …; **~ *the status quo*** сохраня́ть ста́тус-кво́

**maintenance** ['meɪntənəns] (*up-keep*) поддержа́ние; (*preservation*) сохране́ние; *tech.* техни́ческое обслу́живание; (*child support, etc.*) содержа́ние

**maize** [meɪz] кукуру́за

**majest|ic** [mə'dʒestɪk] (**~*ally***) вели́чественный; **~y** ['mædʒəstɪ] вели́чественность *f*; ***His*** (***Her***) **~** его (её) вели́чество

**major** ['meɪdʒə] **1.** бо́льший; кру́пный; *mus.* мажо́рный; **~ *key*** мажо́рная тона́льность; **2.** майо́р; *Am. univ.* о́бласть/предме́т специализа́ция; **~ general** генера́лмайо́р; **~ity** [mə'dʒɒrətɪ] совершенноле́тие; большинство́; ***in the* ~ *of cases*** в большинстве́ слу́чаев

**make** [meɪk] **1.** [*irr.*] *v/t. com.* [с]де́лать; (*manufacture*) производи́ть [-вести́]; (*prepare*) [при]гото́вить; (*constitute*) составля́ть [-а́вить]; *peace, etc.* заключа́ть [-чи́ть]; (*compel, cause to*) заставля́ть [-ста́вить]; **~ *good*** выполня́ть [вы́полнить]; *loss* возмеща́ть [-мести́ть]; **~ *sure of*** удостоверя́ться [-ве́риться] в (П); **~ *way*** уступа́ть доро́гу (***for*** Д); **~ *into*** превраща́ть [-рати́ть], переде́л(ыв)ать в (В); **~ *out*** разбира́ть [разобра́ть]; *cheque* выпи́сывать [вы́писать]; **~ *over*** перед(ав)а́ть; **~ *up*** составля́ть [-а́вить]; *a quarrel* ула́живать [ула́дить]; сде́лать макия́ж; *time* навёрстывать [наверста́ть]; = **~ *up for*** (*v/i.*); **~ *up one's mind*** реша́ться [-ши́ться]; **2.** *v/i.* направля́ться [-а́виться] (***for*** к Д); **~ *off*** сбежа́ть *pf.* (***with*** с Т); **~ *for*** направля́ться [-а́виться]; **~ *up for*** возмеща́ть [-мести́ть]; *grief caused, etc.* сгла́живать [-дить], искупа́ть [-пи́ть]; **3.** моде́ль *f*; (*firm's*) ма́рка; ***of British* ~** произво́дства Великобрита́нии; **~-believe** фанта́зия; **~shift** заме́на; подру́чное/вре́менное сре́дство; *attr.* вре́менный; **~-up** соста́в; *thea.* грим; косме́тика

**maladjusted** [mælə'dʒʌstɪd] пло́хо приспосо́бленный; **~ *child*** тру́дновоспиту́емый ребёнок

**malady** ['mælədɪ] боле́знь *f* (*a. fig.*)

**male** [meɪl] **1.** мужско́й; **2.** *person* мужчи́на; *animal* саме́ц

**malevolen|ce** [mə'levələns] (*rejoicing in s.o.'s misfortune*) злора́дство; (*wishing evil*) недоброжела́тельность *f*; **~t** [-lənt] □ злора́дный; недоброжела́тельный

**malice** ['mælɪs] *of person* злой; *of act, thought, etc.* зло́ба; ***bear s.o.* ~** затаи́ть *pf.* зло́бу на (В)

**malicious** [mə'lɪʃəs] □ зло́бный

**malign** [mə'laɪn] **1.** □ па́губный, вре́дный; **2.** [на]клевета́ть на (В), оклевета́ть (В); **~ant** [mə'lɪgnənt] □ зло́бный; *med.* злока́чественный

**malinger** [mə'lɪŋgə] притворя́ться, симули́ровать; **~er** [-rə] симуля́нт *m*, -ка *f*

**mallet** ['mælɪt] деревя́нный молото́к

**malnutrition** ['mælnjuː'trɪʃn] недоеда́ние; непра́вильное пита́ние

**malt** [mɔːlt] со́лод

**maltreat** [mæl'triːt] пло́хо обраща́ться с (Т)

**mammal** ['mæml] млекопита́ющее

**mammoth** ['mæməθ] ма́монт

**man** [mæn] (*pl.* **men**) челове́к; мужчи́-

M

на *m*; (~*kind*) челове́чество; *chess* фигу́ра; ***the ~ in the street*** обы́чный челове́к
**manage** ['mænɪdʒ] *v/i.* руководи́ть; управля́ть (Т), заве́довать (Т); *problem, etc.* справля́ться [-а́виться] с (Т); обходи́ться [обойти́сь] (***without*** без Р); ***~ to*** (+ *inf.*) [с]уме́ть ...; **~able** [-əbl] □ *person* послу́шный; сгово́рчивый; *task etc.* выполни́мый; **~ment** [-mənt] (*control*) управле́ние; (*governing body*) правле́ние; (*managerial staff*) администра́ция; (*senior staff*) дире́кция; **~r** [-ə] ме́неджер; дире́ктор
**managing** ['mænɪdʒɪŋ] руководя́щий; ***~ director*** замести́тель дире́ктора
**mandat|e** ['mændeɪt] (*authority*) полномо́чие; *for governing a territory* манда́т; *given by voters* нака́з; *law* прика́з суда́; **~ory** ['mændətərɪ] обяза́тельный
**mane** [meɪn] гри́ва; *man's* копна́ воло́с
**manful** ['mænfl] □ му́жественный
**mangle** ['mæŋgl] [ис]кале́чить; [из]уро́довать; *text, etc.* искажа́ть [искази́ть]
**man|handle** ['mænhændl] гру́бо обраща́ться, избива́ть [-би́ть]; **~hood** ['mænhʊd] возмужа́лость *f*, зре́лый во́зраст
**mania** ['meɪnɪə] ма́ния; **~c** ['meɪnæk] манья́к *m*, -я́чка *f*
**manicure** ['mænɪkjʊə] **1.** маникю́р; **2.** де́лать маникю́р (Д)
**manifest** ['mænɪfest] **1.** □ очеви́дный, я́вный; **2.** *v/t.* обнару́жи(ва)ть; проявля́ть [-ви́ть]; **~ation** ['mænɪfe'steɪʃn] проявле́ние
**manifold** ['mænɪfəʊld] □ (*various*) разнообра́зный, разноро́дный; (*many*) многочи́сленный
**manipulat|e** [mə'nɪpjʊleɪt] манипули́ровать; **~ion** [mənɪpjʊ'leɪʃn] манипуля́ция; *of facts* подтасо́вка
**man|kind** [mæn'kaɪnd] челове́чество; **~ly** [-lɪ] му́жественный; **~-made** иску́сственный
**mannequin** ['mænɪkɪn] (*person*) манеке́нщица; (*dummy*) манеке́н
**manner** ['mænə] спо́соб, ме́тод; мане́ра; о́браз де́йствий; **~s** *pl.* уме́ние держа́ть себя́; мане́ры *f/pl.*; обы́чаи *m/pl.*; ***all ~ of*** вся́кого ро́да; са́мые ра́зные; ***in a ~*** в не́которой сте́пени; ***in this ~*** таки́м о́бразом; ***in such a ~ that*** таки́м о́бразом, что ...; **~ed** [-d] (*displaying a particular manner*) мане́рный; (*precious*) вы́чурный; **~ly** [-lɪ] ве́жливый
**maneuver**; *Brt.* **manœuvre** [mə'nuːvə] **1.** манёвр; махина́ция; интри́га; **2.** маневри́ровать
**manor** ['mænə] поме́стье
**manpower** ['mænpaʊə] рабо́чая си́ла
**mansion** ['mænʃn] большо́й дом; *in town* особня́к
**manslaughter** ['mænslɔːtə] непредумы́шленное уби́йство
**mantelpiece** ['mæntlpiːs] по́лка ками́на
**manual** ['mænjʊəl] **1.** ручно́й; ***~ labo(u)r*** физи́ческий труд; **2.** (*handbook*) руково́дство; (*textbook*) уче́бник; (*reference book*) спра́вочник; *tech.* инстру́кция (по эксплуата́ции)
**manufactur|e** [mænjʊ'fæktʃə] **1.** изготовле́ние; *on large scale* произво́дство; **2.** производи́ть [-вести́]; **~er** [-rə] производи́тель *m*, изготови́тель *m*; **~ing** [-rɪŋ] произво́дство; *attr.* промы́шленный
**manure** [mə'njʊə] **1.** (*dung*) наво́з; **2.** унаво́живать
**many** ['menɪ] **1.** мно́гие, многочи́сленные; мно́го; ***~ a time*** мно́го раз; **2.** мно́жество; ***a good ~*** большо́е коли́чество; ***a great ~*** грома́дное коли́чество; **~-sided** многосторо́нний
**map** [mæp] **1.** ка́рта; **2.** наноси́ть на ка́рту; ***~ out*** [с]плани́ровать
**maple** ['meɪpl] клён
**mar** [mɑː] [ис]по́ртить
**marathon** ['mærəθən] марафо́н (*a. fig.*)
**marble** ['mɑːbl] мра́мор
**March**[1] [mɑːtʃ] март
**march**[2] [~] **1.** *mil.* марш; похо́д; *fig. of*

M

*events* разви́тие; **2.** марширова́ть; *fig.* идти́ вперёд (*a.* **~ on**)
**mare** [meə] кобы́ла; ***~'s nest*** иллю́зия
**margarine** [mɑːdʒə'riːn] маргари́н
**margin** ['mɑːdʒɪn] край; *of page* поля́ *n/pl.*; *of forest* опу́шка; ***~ of profit*** чи́стая при́быль *f*; **~al** [-l] □ находя́щийся на краю́; ***~ notes*** заме́тки на поля́х страни́цы
**marigold** ['mærɪgəʊld] ноготки́ *m/pl.*
**marine** [mə'riːn] **1.** морско́й; **2.** солда́т морско́й пехо́ты; **~r** ['mærɪnə] морепла́ватель *m*; моря́к, матро́с
**marital** ['mærɪtl] □ *of marriage* бра́чный; *of married persons* супру́жеский
**maritime** ['mærɪtaɪm] морско́й
**mark¹** [mɑːk] *currency* ма́рка
**mark²** [~] **1.** ме́тка, знак; (*school~*) балл, отме́тка; (*trade~*) фабри́чная ма́рка; (*target*) мише́нь *f*; (*stain*) пятно́; (*trace*) след; ***a man of ~*** выдаю́щийся челове́к; ***hit the ~*** *fig.* попа́сть *pf.* в цель; ***up to the ~*** *fig.* на до́лжной высоте́; **2.** *v/t.* отмеча́ть [-е́тить] (*a. fig.*); ста́вить отме́тку в (П); ***~ off*** отделя́ть [-ли́ть]; ***~ time*** топта́ться на ме́сте; **~ed** [mɑːkt] □ отме́ченный; (*readily seen*) заме́тный
**market** ['mɑːkə] *comput.* ма́ркер
**market** ['mɑːkɪt] **1.** ры́нок; *comm.* сбыт; ***on the ~*** в прода́же; ***~ economy*** ры́ночная эконо́мика; **2.** прода́(-ва)ть; **~able** [~əbl] хо́дкий; **~ing** [~ɪŋ] (*trade*) торго́вля; (*sale*) сбыт; ма́ркетинг
**marksman** ['mɑːksmən] ме́ткий стрело́к
**marmalade** ['mɑːməleɪd] (апельси́новое) варе́нье
**marquee** [mɑː'kiː] большо́й шатёр
**marriage** ['mærɪdʒ] брак; (*wedding*) сва́дьба; бракосочета́ние; ***civil ~*** гражда́нский брак; **~able** [~əbl] бра́чного во́зраста; ***~ certificate*** свиде́тельство о бра́ке
**married** ['mærɪd] *man* жена́тый; *woman* заму́жняя; ***~ couple*** супру́ги *pl.*
**marrow¹** ['mærəʊ] ко́стный мозг; ***be chilled to the ~*** продро́гнуть *pf.* до мо́зга косте́й
**marrow²** [~] *bot.* кабачо́к
**marry** ['mærɪ] *v/t. of parent* (*give son in marriage*) жени́ть; (*give daughter in marriage*) вы́дать *pf.* за́муж; *relig.* [об]венча́ть; *civil* сочета́ть бра́-ком; *of man* жени́ться на (П); *v/i.* жени́ться; *of woman* выходи́ть [вы́йти] за́муж
**marsh** [mɑːʃ] боло́то
**marshal** ['mɑːʃl] **1.** ма́ршал; *Am. also* суде́бное/полице́йское должностно́е лицо́; **2.**: ***~ one's thoughts*** привести́ *pf.* свои́ мы́сли в систе́му
**marshy** ['mɑːʃɪ] боло́тистый, то́пкий
**marten** ['mɑːtɪn] *zo.* куни́ца
**martial** ['mɑːʃl] □ вое́нный; вои́нственный; ***~ law*** вое́нное положе́ние
**martyr** ['mɑːtə] му́ченик *m*, -ница *f*; *mst. fig.* страда́лец *m*, -лица *f*
**marvel** ['mɑːvl] **1.** чу́до; **2.** удивля́ться [-ви́ться]; **~(l)ous** ['mɑːvələs] □ изуми́тельный
**mascot** ['mæskət] талисма́н
**masculine** ['mɑːskjʊlɪn] мужско́й; (*manly*) му́жественный
**mash** [mæʃ] **1.** *cul.* пюре́ *n indecl.*; **2.** размина́ть [-мя́ть]; ***~ed potatoes*** *pl.* карто́фельное пюре́ *n indecl.*
**mask** [mɑːsk] **1.** ма́ска; **2.** [за]маскирова́ть; (*conceal*) скры́(ва́)ть; **~ed** [~t]: ***~ ball*** маскара́д
**mason** ['meɪsn] ка́менщик; масо́н; **~ry** [~rɪ] ка́менная (*or* кирпи́чная) кла́дка
**masquerade** [mæskə'reɪd] маскара́д
**mass¹** [mæs] *relig.* ме́сса
**mass²** [~] **1.** ма́сса; **2.** соб(и)ра́ться
**massacre** ['mæsəkə] **1.** резня́; **2.** зве́рски убива́ть [уби́ть]
**massage** ['mæsɑːʒ] **1.** масса́ж; **2.** масси́ровать
**massive** ['mæsɪv] масси́вный; кру́пный
**mass media** *pl.* сре́дства ма́ссовой информа́ции
**mast** [mɑːst] *naut.* ма́чта
**master** ['mɑːstə] **1.** хозя́ин; (*teacher*) учи́тель *m*; (*expert*) ма́стер; ***♀ of Arts*** маги́стр иску́сств; **2.** (*overcome*) одоле́(ва́)ть; (*gain control of*)

справля́ться [-а́виться]; (*acquire knowledge of*) овладе́(ва́)ть (Т); **~ful** ['mɑːstəfl] вла́стный, ма́стерский; **~ key** отмы́чка; универса́льный ключ; **~ly** [-lɪ] мастерско́й; **~piece** шеде́вр; **~y** ['mɑːstərɪ] госпо́дство, власть *f*; (*skill*) мастерство́

**masticate** ['mæstɪkeɪt] жева́ть

**mastiff** ['mæstɪf] масти́ф

**mat** [mæt] **1.** цино́вка; *of fabric* ко́врик; *sport.* мат; **2.** *hair* слипа́ться [сли́пнуться]

**match**[1] [mætʃ] спи́чка

**match**[2] [~] **1.** ро́вня *m/f*; *sport.* матч, состяза́ние; (*marriage*) брак, па́ртия; ***be a ~ for*** быть ро́вней (Д); **2.** *v/t.* [с]равня́ться с (Т); *colo(u)rs, etc.* подбира́ть; ***well ~ed couple*** хоро́шая па́ра; *v/i.* соотве́тствовать; сочета́ться; ***to ~*** *in colour, etc.* подходя́щий; **~less** ['mætʃlɪs] несравне́нный, бесподо́бный

**mate** [meɪt] **1.** това́рищ; *coll. address* друг; *of animal* саме́ц (са́мка); *naut.* помо́щник капита́на; **2.** *of animals* спа́ривать(ся)

**material** [mə'tɪərɪəl] **1.** □ материа́льный; *evidence* веще́ственный; **2.** материа́л (*a. fig.*); (*cloth*) мате́рия

**matern|al** [mə'tɜːnl] □ матери́нский; **~ity** [-nɪtɪ] матери́нство; ***~ hospital*** роди́льный дом

**mathematic|ian** [mæθəmə'tɪʃn] матема́тик; **~s** [~'mætɪks] (*mst. sg.*) матема́тика

**matinee** ['mætɪneɪ] *thea., cine.* дневно́е представле́ние

**matriculate** [mə'trɪkjʊleɪt] быть при́нятым в университе́т

**matrimon|ial** [mætrɪ'məʊnɪəl] □ бра́чный; супру́жеский; **~y** ['mætrɪmənɪ] супру́жество, брак

**matrix** ['meɪtrɪks] ма́трица

**matron** ['meɪtrən] матро́на; *in hospital approx.* сестра́-хозя́йка

**matter** ['mætə] **1.** (*substance*) вещество́, материа́л; (*content*) содержа́ние; (*concern*) вопро́с, де́ло; ***what's the ~?*** что случи́лось?, в чём де́ло?; ***no ~ who …*** всё равно́, кто …; ***~ of course*** само́ собо́й разуме́ющееся де́ло; ***for that ~*** что каса́ется э́того; ***~ of fact*** факт; ***as a ~ of fact*** вообще́-то; **2.** име́ть значе́ние; ***it does not ~*** ничего́; **~-of-fact** практи́чный, делово́й

**mattress** ['mætrɪs] матра́с

**matur|e** [mə'tjʊə] **1.** □ зре́лый; *wine* вы́держанный; **2.** созре́(ва́)ть; достига́ть [-ти́чь] зре́лости; **~ity** [~rɪtɪ] зре́лость *f*

**maudlin** ['mɔːdlɪn] □ плакси́вый

**maul** [mɔːl] [рас]терза́ть; *fig.* жесто́ко критикова́ть

**mauve** [məʊv] розова́то-лило́вый

**mawkish** ['mɔːkɪʃ] □ сентимента́льный

**maxim** ['mæksɪm] афори́зм; при́нцип

**maximum** ['mæksɪməm] **1.** ма́ксимум; **2.** максима́льный

**May**[1] [meɪ] май

**may**[2] [~] [*irr.*] (*модальный глагол без инфинитива*) [с]мочь; ***~ I come in?*** мо́жно войти́? ***you ~ want to …*** возмо́жно вы [за]хоти́те …

**maybe** ['meɪbɪː] мо́жет быть

**May Day** ['meɪdeɪ] Первома́йский пра́здник

**mayonnaise** [meɪə'neɪz] майоне́з

**mayor** [meə] мэр

**maze** [meɪz] лабири́нт; *fig.* пу́таница; ***be in a ~*** быть в замеша́тельстве, в растéрянности

**me** [miː, mɪ] *косвенный падеж от I*; мне, меня́; *coll.* я

**meadow** ['medəʊ] луг

**meager**; *Brt.* **meagre** ['miːgə] худо́й, то́щий; *meal, etc.* ску́дный

**meal** [miːl] еда́ (за́втрак, обе́д, у́жин)

**mean**[1] [miːn] □ по́длый, ни́зкий; (*stingy*) скупо́й; (*shabby*) убо́гий, жа́лкий

**mean**[2] [~] **1.** сре́дний; → ***meantime***; **2.** середи́на; **~s** *pl.* состоя́ние, бога́тство; (*a. sg.*) (*way to an end*) сре́дство; спо́соб; ***by all ~s*** обяза́тельно; коне́чно; ***by no ~s*** ниско́лько; отню́дь не …; ***by ~s of*** с по́мощью (Р); посре́дством

**mean**[3] [~] [*irr.*] (*intend*) намерева́ться; име́ть в виду́; хоте́ть сказа́ть, подразумева́ть; (*destine*) предназнача́ть [-зна́чить]; зна́чить; ***~ well*** име́ть до́-

брые намéрения
**meaning** [miːnıŋ] значéние; смысл; **~less** [-lıs] бессмы́сленный
**meant** [ment] *pt. и pt. p. от* **mean**
**mean|time**, **~while** тем врéменем; мéжду тем
**measles** ['miːzlz] *pl.* корь *f*
**measure** ['meʒə] **1.** мéра; ***beyond ~*** сверх мéры; ***in great ~*** в большóй стéпени; ***made to ~*** сдéланный на закáз; ***~ for ~*** *approx.* óко за óко; ***take ~s*** принимáть [-нять] мéры; **2.** мéрить, измерять [-éрить]; [с]мéрить; *sew.* снимáть мéрку с (Р); ***~ one's words*** взвéшивать словá; **~ment** [-mənt] размéр; измерéние
**meat** [miːt] мя́со; *fig.* суть *f*; **~ball** фрикадéлька; **~s** (*pl.*) тéфтели (*pl.*)
**mechanic** [mı'kænık] механик; **~al** [-nıkəl] □ механи́ческий; *fig.* машинáльный; **~al engineering** машинострое́ние; **~s** (*mst. sg.*) механика
**medal** [medl] медáль *f*
**meddle** [medl] (***with, in***) вмéшиваться [-шáться] (в В); **~some** [-səm] □ надоéдливый
**mediat|e** ['miːdıeıt] посрéдничать; **~ion** [miːdı'eıʃn] посрéдничество; **~or** ['miːdıeıtə] посрéдник
**medical** ['medıkəl] □ медици́нский; врачéбный; ***~ certificate*** больни́чный листóк; медици́нское свидéтельство; ***~ examination*** медици́нский осмóтр
**medicin|al** [me'dısınl] □ лекáрственный; целéбный; **~e** ['medsın] медици́на; лекáрство
**medieval** [medı'iːvəl] □ средневекóвый
**mediocre** [miːdı'əʊkə] посрéдственный
**meditat|e** ['medıteıt] *v/i.* размышля́ть; *v/t.* обду́м(ыв)ать (В); **~ion** [medı'teıʃn] размышлéние, медитáция
**medium** ['miːdıəm] **1.** (*middle position or condition*) середи́на; (*means of effecting or transmitting*) срéдство; (*phys., surrounding substance*) средá; **2.** срéдний
**medley** ['medlı] смесь *f*
**meek** [miːk] □ крóткий, мя́гкий; **~ness** ['miːknıs] крóтость *f*
**meet** [miːt] [*irr.*] *v/t.* встречáть [-éтить]; (*become aquainted with*) [по]знакóмиться с (Т); (*satisfy*) удовлетворя́ть [-ри́ть]; *debt* оплáчивать [-лати́ть]; ***go to ~ a p.*** встречáть [-éтить] (В); ***there is more to it than ~s the eye*** это дéло не так прóсто; *v/i.* [по]знакóмиться; (*get together*) со-б(и)рáться; **~ *with*** испы́тывать [-пытáть] (В), подвергáться [-вéргнуться]; **~ing** ['miːtıŋ] заседáние; встрéча; ми́тинг, собрáние
**melancholy** ['meləŋkɒlı] **1.** уны́ние; грусть *f*; **2.** *of person* уны́лый; *of something causing sadness* грýстный, печáльный
**mellow** ['meləʊ] *person* смягчáть(-ся) [-чи́ть(ся)]; *fruit* созрé(вá)ть
**melo|dious** [mı'ləʊdıəs] □ мелоди́чный; **~dy** ['melədı] мелóдия
**melon** ['melən] ды́ня
**melt** [melt] [рас]тáять; *metal* [рас-]плáвить(ся); *fat* растáпливать [-топи́ть]; *fig.* смягчáть(ся) [-чи́ть(ся)]
**member** ['membə] член (*a. parl.*); **~ship** [-ʃıp] члéнство
**memoirs** ['memwɑːz] *pl.* мемуáры *m/pl.*
**memorable** ['memərəbl] □ (досто)пáмятный
**memorandum** [memə'rændəm] запи́ска; *dipl.* меморáндум
**memorial** [mı'mɔːrıəl] **1.** (*commemorative object, monument, etc.*) пáмятник; (*written record, athletic tournament, etc.*) мемориáл; **2.** мемориáльный
**memorize** ['meməraız] запоминáть [запóмнить]; (*learn by heart*) заучивать наизу́сть
**memory** ['memərı] пáмять *f* (*a. of computer*); воспоминáние
**men** [men] (*pl. от* **man**) мужчи́ны *m/pl.*
**menace** ['menəs] **1.** угрожáть, грози́ть (Д; ***by, with*** Т); **2.** угрóза; опáсность *f*; (*annoying person*) занýда
**mend** [mend] **1.** *v/t.* [по]чини́ть; ***~ one's ways*** исправля́ться [-áвиться]; *v/i.*

M

(*improve*) улучша́ться [улу́чшиться]; *of health* поправля́ться [-а́виться]; **2.** почи́нка; ***on the ~*** на попра́вку

**mendacious** [men'deɪʃəs] □ лжи́вый

**meningitis** [menɪn'dʒaɪtɪs] менинги́т

**menstruation** [menstrʊ'eɪʃn] менструа́ция

**mental** ['mentl] □ *of the mind* у́мственный; *illness* психи́ческий; ***make a ~ note of*** отме́тить *pf.* в уме́ (В): ***~ hospital*** психиатри́ческая больни́ца; **~ity** [men'tælətɪ] склад ума́; у́мственная спосо́бность; пси́хика

**mention** ['menʃn] **1.** упомина́ние; **2.** упомина́ть [-мяну́ть] (В *or* о П); ***don't ~ it!*** не́ за что!; ***not to ~*** не говоря́ уж (о П)

**menu** ['menjuː] меню́ *n indecl.*

**meow**, *Brt.* **miaow** [mɪ'aʊ] [за]мяу́кать

**mercenary** ['mɜːsɪnərɪ] □ коры́стный

**merchandise** ['mɜːtʃəndaɪz] това́ры *m/pl.*

**merchant** ['mɜːtʃənt] торго́вец; *chiefly Brt.* **~ bank** комме́рческий банк

**merci|ful** ['mɜːsɪfʊl] □ милосе́рдный; **~less** [-lɪs] □ беспоща́дный

**mercury** ['mɜːkjʊrɪ] ртуть *f*

**mercy** ['mɜːsɪ] милосе́рдие; поща́да; ***be at the ~ of*** быть во вла́сти (Р); по́лностью зави́сеть от (Р)

**mere** [mɪə] просто́й; ***a ~ child*** всего́ лишь ребёнок; **~*ly*** то́лько, про́сто

**merge** [mɜːdʒ] сли́(ва́)ть(ся) (***in*** с Т); объединя́ться [-ни́ться]; **~r** ['mɜːdʒə] *comm.* слия́ние, объедине́ние

**meridian** [mə'rɪdɪən] *geogr.* меридиа́н

**meringue** [mə'ræŋ] *cul.* мере́нга

**merit** ['merɪt] **1.** заслу́га; (*worth*) досто́инство; ***judge s.o. on his ~s*** оце́нивать кого́-л. по заслу́гам; **2.** заслу́живать [-ужи́ть]

**mermaid** ['mɜːmeɪd] руса́лка

**merriment** ['merɪmənt] весе́лье

**merry** ['merɪ] □ весёлый, ра́достный; ***make ~*** весели́ться; **~-go-round** карусе́ль *f*; **~-making** весе́лье; пра́зднество

**mesh** [meʃ] (*one of the spaces in net, etc.*) ячёйка; ***~es*** *pl.* се́ти *f/pl.*

**mess**[1] [mes] **1.** беспоря́док; (*confusion*) пу́таница; (*trouble*) неприя́тность *f*; ***make a ~ of a th.*** прова́ливать де́ло; **2.** *v/t.* приводи́ть в беспоря́док; *v/i. coll.* **~ *about*** рабо́тать ко́е-как; (*tinker*) копа́ться, вози́ться

**mess**[2] [~] *mil.* столо́вая

**message** ['mesɪdʒ] сообще́ние; *dipl., a. coll.* посла́ние; ***did you get the ~?*** поня́тно? усекли́?

**messenger** ['mesɪndʒə] курье́р

**messy** ['mesɪ] неу́бранный; гря́зный; в беспоря́дке

**met** [met] *pt. и pt. p. от* ***meet***

**metal** ['metl] мета́лл; (*road ~*) щёбень *m*; *attr.* металли́ческий; **~lic** [mɪ'tælɪk] металли́ческий; **~lurgy** [mɪ'tælədʒɪ] металлу́ргия

**metaphor** ['metəfə] мета́фора

**meteor** ['miːtɪə] метео́р; **~ology** [miːtɪə'rɒlədʒɪ] метеороло́гия

**meter** ['miːtə] счётчик; **~ *reading*** показа́ние счётчика

**meter**, *Brt.* **metre** ['miːtə] метр

**method** ['meθəd] ме́тод, спо́соб; систе́ма, поря́док; **~ical** [mɪ'θɒdɪkl] системати́ческий, методи́ческий; (*orderly*) методи́чный

**meticulous** [mɪ'tɪkjʊləs] □ тща́тельный

**metric** ['metrɪk] (***~ally***): **~ *system*** метри́ческая систе́ма

**metropoli|s** [mə'trɒpəlɪs] столи́ца; метропо́лия; **~tan** [metrə'pɒlɪtən] **1.** *eccl.* митрополи́т; **2.** *adj.* (*of a capital*) столи́чный

**mettle** ['metl] си́ла хара́ктера; хра́брость *f*; бо́дрость *f*; (*endurance*) выно́сливость *f*

**Mexican** ['meksɪkən] **1.** мексика́нский; **2.** мексика́нец *m*, -нка *f*

**mice** [maɪs] *pl.* мы́ши *f/pl.*

**micro…** ['maɪkrəʊ] ми́кро…

**microbe** ['maɪkrəub] микро́б

**micro|phone** ['maɪkrəfəʊn] микрофо́н; **~scope** ['maɪkrəskəʊp] микроско́п; **~wave oven** микроволно́вая печь *f*

**mid** [mɪd] сре́дний; среди́нный; **~air**: ***in ~*** высоко́ в во́здухе; **~day** **1.** по́лдень *m*; **2.** полу́денный

M

**middle** ['mɪdl] **1.** середи́на; **2.** сре́дний; ♀ ***Ages*** *pl.* средневеко́вье; **~-aged** [~'eɪdʒd] сре́дних лет; **~-class** буржуа́зный; **~man** посре́дник; **~weight** боксёр сре́днего ве́са

**middling** ['mɪdlɪŋ] (*mediocre*) посре́дственный; (*medium*) сре́дний

**midge** [mɪdʒ] мо́шка; **~t** ['mɪdʒɪt] ка́рлик; *attr.* ка́рликовый

**mid|land** ['mɪdlənd] центра́льная часть страны́; **~night** по́лночь *f*; **~riff** ['mɪdrɪf] *anat.* диафра́гма; **~st** [mɪdst]: ***in the ~ of*** среди́ (Р); ***in our ~*** в на́шей среде́; **~summer** [~'sʌmə] середи́на ле́та; **~way** [~'weɪ] на полпути́; **~wife** акуше́рка; **~winter** [~'wɪntə] середи́на зимы́

**might**[1] [maɪt] *pt. от* ***may***

**might**[2] [~] мощь *f*; могу́щество; ***with ~ and main*** и́зо всех сил; **~y** ['maɪtɪ] могу́щественный; *blow* мо́щный; *adv. coll. Am.*: ***that's ~ good of you*** о́чень ми́ло с ва́шей стороны́

**migrat|e** [maɪ'greɪt] мигри́ровать; **~ion** [~ʃn] мигра́ция; *of birds* перелёт

**mike** [maɪk] *coll.* микрофо́н

**mild** [maɪld] □ мя́гкий; *drink*, *tobacco* сла́бый; (*slight*) лёгкий

**mildew** ['mɪldjuː] *bot.* ми́лдью *n indecl.*; *on bread* пле́сень *f*

**mile** [maɪl] ми́ля

**mil(e)age** ['maɪlɪdʒ] расстоя́ние в ми́лях

**milieu** ['miːljɜː] среда́, окруже́ние

**milit|ary** ['mɪlɪtrɪ] **1.** □ вое́нный; во́инский; **~ *service*** вое́нная слу́жба; **2.** вое́нные; вое́нные вла́сти *f/pl.*; **~ia** [mɪ'lɪʃə] мили́ция

**milk** [mɪlk] **1.** молоко́; ***condensed ~*** сгущённое молоко́; ***powdered ~*** сухо́е молоко́; ***whole ~*** це́льное молоко́; **2.** [по]дои́ть; **~maid** доя́рка; **~y** ['mɪlkɪ] моло́чный; ♀ ***Way*** Мле́чный путь *m*

**mill** [mɪl] **1.** ме́льница; (*factory*) фа́брика, заво́д; **2.** [с]моло́ть

**millennium** [mɪ'lenɪəm] тысячеле́тие

**millepede** ['mɪlɪpiːd] *zo.* многоно́жка

**miller** ['mɪlə] ме́льник

**millet** ['mɪlɪt] про́со

**millinery** ['mɪlɪnərɪ] ателье́ да́мских шляп

**million** ['mɪljən] миллио́н; **~aire** [mɪljə'neə] миллионе́р; **~th** ['mɪljənθ] **1.** миллио́нный; **2.** миллио́нная часть *f*

**millstone** жёрнов; ***be a ~ round s.o.'s neck*** ка́мень на ше́е; тяжёлая отве́тственность *f*

**milt** [mɪlt] моло́ки *f/pl.*

**mimic** ['mɪmɪk] **1.** имита́тор; **2.** пароди́ровать (*im*)*pf.*; подража́ть (Д); **~ry** [~rɪ] подража́ние; *zo.* мимикри́я

**mince** [mɪns] **1.** *v/t. meat* пропуска́ть [-сти́ть] через мясору́бку; ***he does not ~ matters*** он говори́т без обиняко́в; *v/i.* говори́ть жема́нно; **2.** мясно́й фарш (*mst.* ***~d meat***); **~meat** фарш из изю́ма, я́блок *и т. п.*; **~ pie** пирожо́к (→ ***mincemeat***)

**mincing machine** мясору́бка

**mind** [maɪnd] **1.** ум, ра́зум; (*opinion*) мне́ние; (*intention*) наме́рение; жела́ние; па́мять *f*; ***to my ~*** на мой взгляд; ***be out of one's ~*** быть без ума́; ***change one's ~*** переду́м(ыв)ать; ***bear in ~*** име́ть в виду́; ***have a ~ to*** хоте́ть (+*inf.*); ***have s.th. on one's ~*** беспоко́иться о чём-л.; ***be in two ~s*** колеба́ться, быть в нереши́тельности; ***make up one's ~*** реша́ться [-ши́ться]; ***set one's ~ to …*** твёрдо реши́ть; **2.** (*look after*) присма́тривать [-смотре́ть] за (Т); (*heed*) остерега́ться [-ре́чься] (Р); ***never ~!*** ничего́!; ***I don't ~ (it)*** я ничего́ не име́ю про́тив; ***would you ~ taking off your hat?*** бу́дьте добры́, сними́те шля́пу; **~ful** ['maɪndfʊl] (***of***) внима́тельный к (Д); забо́тливый

**mine**[1] [maɪn] *pron.* мой *m*, моя́ *f*, моё *n*, мои́ *pl.*

**mine**[2] [~] **1.** рудни́к; (*coal ~*) ша́хта; *fig.* исто́чник; *mil.* ми́на; **2.** добы́(ва́)ть; **~r** ['maɪnə] шахтёр, *coll.* горня́к

**mineral** ['mɪnərəl] **1.** минера́л; **2.** минера́льный; **~ *resources*** поле́зные ископа́емые

**mingle** ['mɪŋgl] сме́шивать(ся) [-ша́ть(ся)]

**miniature** ['mɪnətʃə] **1.** миниатю́ра; **2.** миниатю́рный

M

**minibus** микроавтóбус
**minim|ize** ['mɪnɪmaɪz] доводи́ть [довести́] до ми́нимума; *fig.* преуменьша́ть [-éньшить]; **~um** [~ɪməm] **1.** ми́нимум; **2.** минима́льный
**mining** ['maɪnɪŋ] горнодобыва́ющая промы́шленность *f*
**minister** ['mɪnɪstə] *pol.* мини́стр; *eccl.* свящéнник
**ministry** ['mɪnɪstrɪ] *pol.*, *eccl.* министéрство
**mink** [mɪŋk] *zo.* нóрка
**minor** ['maɪnə] **1.** (*inessential*) несущéственный; (*inferior in importance*) второстепéнный; *mus.* минóрный; **2.** несовершеннолéтний; **~ity** [maɪ'nɒrətɪ] меньшинствó
**mint¹** [mɪnt] **1.** (*place*) монéтный двор; ***a ~ of money*** большáя сýмма; **2.** [от]чекáнить
**mint²** [~] *bot.* мя́та
**minuet** [mɪnjʊ'et] менуэ́т
**minus** ['maɪnəs] **1.** *prp.* без (P), ми́нус; ***it's ~ 10° now*** сейчáс (на ýлице) ми́нус дéсять грáдусов; **2.** *adj.* отрицáтельный
**minute** **1.** [maɪ'nju:t] □ мéлкий; (*slight*) незначи́тельный; (*detailed*) подрóбный, детáльный; **2.** ['mɪnɪt] минýта; момéнт; ***~s*** *pl.* протокóл
**mirac|le** ['mɪrəkl] чýдо; ***work ~s*** твори́ть чудесá; **~ulous** [mɪ'rækjʊləs] □ чудéсный
**mirage** ['mɪrɑ:ʒ] ми́ра́ж
**mire** ['maɪə] тряси́на; (*mud*) грязь *f*
**mirror** ['mɪrə] **1.** зéркало; **2.** отражáть [отрази́ть]
**mirth** [mɜ:θ] весéлье, рáдость *f*; **~ful** [~fl] □ весёлый, рáдостный; **~less** [~lɪs] □ безрáдостный
**miry** ['maɪərɪ] тóпкий
**misadventure** ['mɪsəd'ventʃə] несчáстье; несчáстный слýчай
**misapply** ['mɪsə'plaɪ] неправи́льно испóльзовать
**misapprehend** [mɪsæprɪ'hend] понимáть [-ня́ть] превря́тно
**misbehave** [mɪsbɪ'heɪv] плóхо вести́ себя́
**miscalculate** [mɪs'kælkjʊleɪt] ошибáться в расчёте, подсчёте
**miscarr|iage** [mɪs'kærɪdʒ] (*failure*) неудáча; *med.* вы́кидыш; ***~ of justice*** судéбная оши́бка; **~y** [~rɪ] терпéть неудáчу; имéть вы́кидыш
**miscellaneous** [mɪsə'leɪnɪəs] □ рáзный, смéшанный
**mischief** ['mɪstʃɪf] озорствó; прокáзы *f/pl.*; (*harm*) вред; зло; ***do s.o. a ~*** причиня́ть [-ни́ть] комý-л. зло
**mischievous** ['mɪstʃɪvəs] □ (*injurious*) врéдный; *mst. child* озор нóй; шаловли́вый
**misconceive** [mɪskən'si:v] неправи́льно поня́ть *pf.*
**misconduct** **1.** [mɪs'kɒndʌkt] плохóе поведéние; **2.** [~kən'dʌkt]: ***~ o.s.*** дýрно вести́ себя́
**misconstrue** [mɪskən'stru:] неправи́льно истолкóвывать
**misdeed** [mɪs'di:d] простýпок
**misdirect** [mɪsdɪ'rekt] невéрно напрáвить; *mail* неправи́льно адресовáть
**miser** ['maɪzə] скупéц, скря́га *m/f*
**miserable** ['mɪzrəbl] □ (*wretched*) жáлкий; (*unhappy*) несчáстный; (*squalid*) убóгий; *meal* скýдный
**miserly** ['maɪzəlɪ] скупóй
**misery** ['mɪzərɪ] невзгóда, несчáстье, страдáние; (*poverty*) нищетá
**misfortune** [mɪs'fɔ:tʃən] неудáча, несчáстье, бедá
**misgiving** [mɪs'gɪvɪŋ] опасéние, предчýвствие дурнóго
**misguide** [mɪs'gaɪd] вводи́ть в заблуждéние; давáть [дать] неправи́льный совéт
**mishap** ['mɪshæp] неприя́тное происшéствие, неудáча
**misinform** [mɪsɪn'fɔ:m] неправи́льно информи́ровать, дезинформи́ровать
**misinterpret** [mɪsɪn'tɜ:prɪt] невéрно поня́ть *pf.*, истолкóвывать
**mislay** [mɪs'leɪ] [*irr.* (***lay***)] положи́ть не на мéсто; *lose* затеря́ть; ***I've mislaid my pipe somewhere*** я кудá-то дел своЮ трýбку
**mislead** [mɪs'li:d] [*irr.* (***lead***)] вести́ по неправи́льному пути́; вводи́ть в за-

блужде́ние
**mismanage** [mɪsˈmænɪdʒ] пло́хо вести́ дела́
**misplace** [mɪsˈpleɪs] положи́ть не на ме́сто; *p. pt.* **~d** *fig.* неуме́стный
**misprint** [mɪsˈprɪnt] опеча́тка
**misread** [mɪsˈriːd] [*irr.* (***read***)] непра́вильно проче́сть *pf.*; непра́вильно истолко́вывать
**misrepresent** [mɪsreprɪˈzent] представля́ть в ло́жном све́те; искажа́ть [-кази́ть]
**miss**[1] [mɪs] де́вушка; (*as title*) мисс
**miss**[2] [~] **1.** про́мах; ***give s.th. a ~*** пропусти́ть *pf.*, не сде́лать *pf.* чего́-л.; **2.** *v/t. chance* упуска́ть [-сти́ть]; *train* опа́здывать [-да́ть] на (В); (*fail to notice*) не заме́тить *pf.*; (*not find*) не заста́ть *pf.* до́ма; (*long for*) тоскова́ть по (Т, Д); *v/i.* (*fail to hit*) прома́хиваться [-хну́ться]
**missile** [ˈmɪsaɪl] раке́та; ***guided ~*** управля́емая раке́та
**missing** [ˈmɪsɪŋ] отсу́тствующий, недостаю́щий; *mil.* пропа́вший бе́з вести; ***be ~*** отсу́тствовать
**mission** [ˈmɪʃn] ми́ссия, делега́ция; (*task*) зада́ча; (*calling*) призва́ние
**misspell** [mɪsˈspel] [*a. irr.* (***spell***)] [с]де́лать орфографи́ческую оши́бку; непра́вильно написа́ть
**mist** [mɪst] тума́н; ды́мка
**mistake** [mɪˈsteɪk] **1.** [*irr.* (***take***)] ошиба́ться [-би́ться]; (*understand wrongly*) непра́вильно понима́ть [-ня́ть]; непра́вильно принима́ть [-ня́ть] (***for*** за (В); ***be ~n*** ошиба́ться [-би́ться]; **2.** оши́бка; заблужде́ние; ***by ~*** по оши́бке; **~n** [~ən] оши́бочный, непра́вильно по́нятый; (*ill-judged*) неосмотри́тельный; неуме́стный
**mister** [ˈmɪstə] ми́стер, господи́н
**mistletoe** [ˈmɪsltəʊ] оме́ла
**mistress** [ˈmɪstrɪs] *of household, etc.* хозя́йка до́ма; (*school ~*) учи́тельница; (*a paramour*) любо́вница
**mistrust** [mɪsˈtrʌst] **1.** не доверя́ть (Д); **2.** недове́рие; **~ful** [~fʊl] □ недове́рчивый
**misty** [ˈmɪstɪ] □ тума́нный; (*obscure*) сму́тный
**misunderstand** [mɪsʌndəˈstænd] [*irr.* (***stand***)] непра́вильно понима́ть; **~ing** [~ɪŋ] недоразуме́ние; (*disagreement*) размо́лвка
**misuse** **1.** [mɪsˈjuːz] злоупотребля́ть [-би́ть] (Т); (*treat badly*) ду́рно обраща́ться с (Т); **2.** [~ˈjuːs] злоупотребле́ние
**mite** [maɪt] (*small child*) малю́тка *m/f*
**mitigate** [ˈmɪtɪgeɪt] смягча́ть [-чи́ть]; (*lessen*) уменьша́ть [уме́ньшить]
**mitten** [ˈmɪtn] рукави́ца
**mix** [mɪks] [с]меша́ть(ся); переме́шивать [-ша́ть]; (*mingle with*) обща́ться; **~ed** переме́шанный, сме́шанный; (*of different kind*) разноро́дный; ***~ up*** перепу́т(ыв)ать; ***be ~ up in*** быть заме́шанным в (П); **~ture** [ˈmɪkstʃə] смесь *f*
**moan** [məʊn] **1.** стон; **2.** [за]стона́ть
**mob** [mɒb] **1.** толпа́; **2.** (*throng*) [с]толпи́ться; (*besiege*) осажда́ть [-ди́ть]
**mobil|e** [ˈməʊbaɪl] *person, face, mind* живо́й, подви́жный; *mil.* моби́льный; ***~ phone*** моби́льный телефо́н; **~ization** [məʊbɪlaɪˈzeɪʃn] *mil., etc.* мобилиза́ция; **~ize** [ˈməʊbɪlaɪz] (*a. fig.*) мобилизова́ть (*im*)*pf.*
**moccasin** [ˈmɒkəsɪn] мокаси́н
**mock** [mɒk] **1.** насме́шка; **2.** подде́льный; *v/t.* осме́ивать [-ея́ть]; *v/i.*; ***~ at*** насмеха́ться [-ея́ться] над (Т); **~ery** [~ərɪ] издева́тельство, осмея́ние
**mode** [məʊd] ме́тод, спо́соб; *tech.* режи́м; ***~ of life*** о́браз жи́зни
**model** [ˈmɒdl] **1.** моде́ль *f*; *fashion* манеке́нщица; *art* нату́рщик *m*, -ица *f*; *fig.* приме́р; образе́ц; *attr.* образцо́вый; **2.** *sculpture* вы́лепить; (***~ after, [up]on***) брать приме́р
**modem** [ˈməʊdem] мо́дем
**moderat|e** **1.** [ˈmɒdərət] □ уме́ренный; **2.** [ˈmɒdəreɪt] умеря́ть [уме́рить]; смягча́ть(ся) [-чи́ть(ся)]; *wind* стиха́ть [сти́хнуть]; **~ion** [mɒdəˈreɪʃn] уме́ренность *f*
**modern** [ˈmɒdən] совреме́нный; **~ize** [~aɪz] модернизи́ровать (*im*)*pf.*

M

**modest** ['mɒdɪst] □ скромный; **~y** [~ɪ] скромность *f*
**modi|fication** [mɒdɪfɪ'keɪʃn] видоизменение; *mst. tech.* модификация; **~fy** ['mɒdɪfaɪ] видоизменять [-нить]; (*make less severe*) смягчать [-чить]; модифицировать
**modul|ate** ['mɒdjʊleɪt] модулировать; **~e** ['mɒdjuːl] *math.* модуль *m*; (*separate unit*) блок, секция; (*spacecraft*) модульный отсек; ***lunar ~*** лунная капсула
**moist** [mɔɪst] влажный; **~en** ['mɔɪsn] увлажнять(ся) [-нить(ся)]; **~ure** ['mɔɪstʃə] влага
**molar** ['məʊlə] коренной зуб
**mold**[1] [məʊld] (*Brt.* **mould**) (*fungus*) плесень *f*
**mold**[2] [~] (*Brt.* **mould**) **1.** (литейная) форма; **2.** *tech.* отливать [-лить]; *fig.* [с]формировать
**moldy** ['məʊldɪ] (*Brt.* **mouldy**) заплесневелый
**mole**[1] [məʊl] *zo.* крот; (*secret agent*) «крот»
**mole**[2] [~] (*breakwater*) мол
**mole**[3] [~] *on skin* родинка
**molecule** ['mɒlɪkjuːl] молекула
**molest** [mə'lest] приста(ва)ть к (Д)
**mollify** ['mɒlɪfaɪ] успокаивать [-коить], смягчать [-чить]
**molt** [məʊlt] (*Brt.* **moult**) *zo.* [по]линять
**moment** ['məʊmənt] момент, миг, мгновение; ***at the ~*** в данное время; ***a great ~*** важное событие; **~ary** [~trɪ] (*instantaneous*) мгновенный; (*not lasting*) кратковременный; **~ous** [mə'mentəs] □ важный; **~um** [~təm] *phys.* инерция; движущая сила; ***gather ~*** набирать скорость *f*; разрастаться [-тись]
**monarch** ['mɒnək] монарх; **~y** [~ɪ] монархия
**monastery** ['mɒnəstrɪ] монастырь *m*
**Monday** ['mʌndɪ] понедельник
**monetary** ['mʌnɪtrɪ] валютный; *reform, etc.* денежный
**money** ['mʌnɪ] деньги *f/pl.*; ***ready ~*** наличные деньги *f/pl.*; ***be out of ~*** не иметь денег; **~box** копилка; **~order** денежный перевод
**mongrel** ['mʌŋgrəl] *dog* дворняжка
**monitor** ['mɒnɪtə] *in class* староста; *tech.* монитор
**monk** [mʌŋk] монах
**monkey** ['mʌŋkɪ] **1.** обезьяна; **2.** *coll.* дурачиться; ***~ with*** возиться с (T); **~ wrench** *tech.* разводной гаечный ключ
**mono|logue** ['mɒnəlɒg] монолог; **~polist** [mə'nɒpəlɪst] монополист; **~polize** [~laɪz] монополизировать (*im*)*pf.*; **~poly** [~lɪ] монополия (P); **~tonous** [mə'nɒtənəs] □ монотонный; **~tony** [~tənɪ] монотонность *f*
**monsoon** [mɒn'suːn] муссон
**monster** ['mɒnstə] чудовище; *fig.* монстр; *attr.* (*huge*) гигантский
**monstro|sity** [mɒn'strɒsətɪ] чудовищность *f*; **~us** ['mɒnstrəs] □ чудовищный; безобразный
**month** [mʌnθ] месяц; **~ly** ['mʌnθlɪ] **1.** (еже)месячный; ***~ season ticket*** месячный проездной билет; **2.** ежемесячный журнал
**monument** ['mɒnjʊmənt] памятник; монумент; **~al** [mɒnjʊ'mentl] □ монументальный
**mood** [muːd] настроение
**moody** ['muːdɪ] (*gloomy*) угрюмый; (*in low spirits*) не в духе; переменчивого настроения; капризный
**moon** [muːn] луна, месяц; ***reach for the ~*** желать невозможного; **~light** лунный свет; **~lit** залитый лунным светом
**moor**[1] [mʊə] торфянистая местность *f*, поросшая вереском
**moor**[2] [~] *naut.* [при]швартоваться
**moot** [muːt]: ***~ point*** спорный вопрос
**mop** [mɒp] **1.** швабра; ***~ of hair*** копна волос; **2.** мыть, протирать шваброй
**mope** [məʊp] хандрить
**moped** ['məʊped] мопед
**moral** ['mɒrəl] **1.** □ моральный, нравственный; **2.** мораль *f*; ***~s*** *pl.* нравы *m/pl.*; **~e** [mə'rɑːl] *part. mil.* моральное состояние; **~ity** [mə'rælətɪ] мораль *f*, этика; **~ize** ['mɒrəlaɪz] мо-

рализи́ровать
**morato|rium** [mɒrəˈtɔːrɪəm] *pl.*, **~ria** [-rɪə] *comm.*, *pol.*, *mil.* морато́рий
**morbid** [ˈmɔːbɪd] боле́зненный
**more** [mɔː] бо́льше; бо́лее; ещё; ***~ or less*** бо́лее и́ли ме́нее; ***once ~*** ещё раз; ***no ~*** бо́льше не …; ***the ~ so as …*** тем бо́лее, что …; **~over** [mɔːrˈəʊvə] кро́ме того́, бо́лее того́
**morning** [ˈmɔːnɪŋ] у́тро; ***in the ~*** у́тром; ***tomorrow ~*** за́втра у́тром
**morose** [məˈrəʊs] □ мра́чный
**morphia** [ˈmɔːfɪə], **morphine** [ˈmɔːfiːn] мо́рфий
**morsel** [ˈmɔːsl] кусо́чек
**mortal** [ˈmɔːtl] **1.** □ сме́ртный; *wound* смерте́льный; **2.** сме́ртный; ***ordinary ~*** просто́й сме́ртный; **~ity** [mɔːˈtælətɪ] (*being mortal*; *a. ~ rate*) сме́ртность *f*
**mortar** [ˈmɔːtə] известко́вый раство́р
**mortgage** [ˈmɔːgɪdʒ] **1.** ссу́да (под недви́жимость); закладна́я; **2.** закла́дывать [заложи́ть]
**morti|fication** [mɔːtɪfɪˈkeɪʃn] чу́вство стыда́; ***to my ~*** к моему́ стыду́; **~fy** [ˈmɔːtɪfaɪ] (*shame*, *humiliate*) обижа́ть [оби́деть]; унижа́ть [уни́зить]; (*cause grief*) оскорбля́ть [-би́ть]
**mortuary** [ˈmɔːtʃərɪ] морг
**mosaic** [məʊˈzeɪɪk] моза́ика
**Moslem** [ˈmɒzləm] = **Muslim**
**mosque** [mɒsk] мече́ть *f*
**mosquito** [məsˈkiːtəʊ] кома́р; *in tropics* моски́т
**moss** [mɒs] мох; **~y** [ˈ~ɪ] мши́стый
**most** [məʊst] **1.** *adj.* □ наибо́льший; **2.** *adv.* бо́льше всего́; ***~ beautiful*** са́мый краси́вый; **3.** наибо́льшее коли́чество; бо́льшая часть *f*; ***at*** (***the***) ***~*** са́мое бо́льшее, не бо́льше чем; ***make the ~ of …*** наилу́чшим о́бразом испо́льзовать; ***the ~ I can do*** всё, что я могу́ сде́лать; **~ly** [ˈməʊstlɪ] по бо́льшей ча́сти; гла́вным о́бразом; ча́ще всего́
**motel** [məʊˈtel] моте́ль *m*
**moth** [mɒθ] моль *f*; мотылёк; **~-eaten** изъе́денный мо́лью
**mother** [ˈmʌðə] **1.** мать *f*; **2.** относи́ться по-матери́нски к (Д); **~hood** [ˈmʌðəhʊd] матери́нство; **~-in-law** [-rɪnlɔː] (*wife's mother*) тёща; (*husband's mother*) свекро́вь *f*; **~ly** [-lɪ] матери́нский; **~-of-pearl** [-rəvˈpɜːl] перламу́тровый; **~ tongue** родно́й язы́к
**motif** [məʊˈtiːf] моти́в
**motion** [ˈməʊʃn] **1.** движе́ние; *of mechanism* ход; (*proposal*) предложе́ние; **2.** *v/t.* пока́зывать же́стом; *v/i.* кива́ть [кивну́ть] (***to*** на В); **~less** [-lɪs] неподви́жный; **~ picture** *Am.* (кино)фи́льм
**motiv|ate** [ˈməʊtɪveɪt] мотиви́ровать; **~e** [ˈməʊtɪv] **1.** *of power* дви́жущий; **2.** (*inducement*) по́вод, моти́в
**motley** [ˈmɒtlɪ] пёстрый
**motor** [ˈməʊtə] **1.** дви́гатель *m*, мото́р; **2.** мото́рный; **~ mechanic**, **~ fitter** автомеха́ник; **3.** е́хать (везти́) на автомаши́не; **~boat** мото́рная ло́дка; **~car** автомаши́на, *coll.* маши́на; **~cycle** мотоци́кл; **~ing** [ˈməʊtərɪŋ] автомоби́льный спорт; автоту́ризм; **~ist** [-rɪst] автомобили́ст *m*, -ка *f*; **~ scooter** моторо́ллер; **~way** автостра́да
**mottled** [ˈmɒtld] кра́пчатый
**mound** [maʊnd] (*hillock*) холм; (*heap*) ку́ча
**mount**[1] [maʊnt] возвы́шенность *f*; гора́; **♀ *Everest*** гора́ Эвере́ст
**mount**[2] [~] *v/i.* поднима́ться [-ня́ться]; сади́ться на ло́шадь *f*; *v/t. radio*, *etc.* устана́вливать [-нови́ть], [с]монти́ровать; (*frame*) вставля́ть в ра́му (в опра́ву)
**mountain** [ˈmaʊntɪn] **1.** гора́; **2.** го́рный, наго́рный; **~eer** [maʊntɪˈnɪə] альпини́ст(ка); **~ous** [ˈmaʊntɪnəs] гори́стый
**mourn** [mɔːn] горева́ть; *s.b.'s death* опла́к(ив)ать; **~er** [ˈmɔːnə] скорбя́щий; **~ful** [ˈmɔːnfl] □ печа́льный, ско́рбный; **~ing** [ˈmɔːnɪŋ] тра́ур
**mouse** [maʊs] (*pl.* ***mice***) мышь *f*
**moustache** [məˈstɑːʃ] = ***mustache***
**mouth** [maʊθ], *pl.* **~s** [~z] рот; *of river* у́стье; *of cave*, *etc.* вход; **~ organ** губна́я гармо́ника; **~piece** *of pipe*, *etc.* мундшту́к; *fig.* ру́пор
**move** [muːv] **1.** *v/t. com.* дви́гать [дви́нуть]; передвига́ть [-и́нуть]; (*touch*)

M

тро́гать [тро́нуть]; (*propose*) вноси́ть [внести́]; *v/i.* дви́гаться [дви́нуться]; (*change residence*) переезжа́ть [перее́хать]; *of events* разви́(ва́)ться; *of affairs* идти́ [пойти́]; *fig. in artistic circles, etc.* враща́ться; **~ in** въезжа́ть [въе́хать]; **~ on** дви́гаться вперёд; **2.** движе́ние; перее́зд; *in game pf.* ход; *fig.* шаг; ***on the ~*** на ходу́; ***make a ~*** сде́лать ход; **~ment** ['mu:vmənt] движе́ние; *of symphony, etc.* часть *f*

**movies** ['mu:vɪz] *pl.* кино́ *n indecl.*

**moving** ['mu:vɪŋ] □ дви́жущийся; (*touching*) тро́гательный; ***~ staircase*** эскала́тор

**mow** [məʊ] [*irr.*] [с]коси́ть; **~n** *pt. p. om* ***mow***

**Mr.** ['mɪstə] → ***mister***

**Mrs.** ['mɪsɪz] ми́ссис, госпожа́

**much** [mʌtʃ] *adj.* мно́го; *adv.* о́чень; ***I thought as ~*** я так и ду́мал; ***make ~ of*** придава́ть [прида́ть] большо́е значе́ние; окружи́ть внима́нием; ба́ловать (В); ***I am not ~ of a dancer*** я нева́жно танцу́ю

M

**muck** [mʌk] наво́з; *fig.* дрянь *f*

**mucus** ['mju:kəs] слизь *f*

**mud** [mʌd] грязь *f*

**muddle** ['mʌdl] **1.** *v/t.* перепу́т(ыв)ать; [с]пу́тать (*a.* ***~ up***); **2.** *coll.* пу́таница, неразбери́ха; (*disorder*) беспоря́док

**mud|dy** ['mʌdɪ] гря́зный; **~guard** крыло́

**muffin** ['mʌfɪn] сдо́бная бу́лочка

**muffle** ['mʌfl] *of voice, etc.* глуши́ть, заглуша́ть [-ши́ть]; (*envelop*) заку́т(ыв)ать; **~r** [~ə] (*device for deadening sound; Am. esp. mot.*) глуши́тель *m*

**mug** [mʌg] кру́жка

**muggy** ['mʌgɪ] ду́шный, вла́жный

**mulberry** ['mʌtlbərɪ] (*tree*) ту́товое де́рево, шелкови́ца; (*fruit*) ту́товая я́года

**mule** [mju:l] мул; ***stubborn as a ~*** упря́мый как осёл

**mull** [mʌl]: ***~ over*** обду́м(ыв)ать; размышля́ть [-мы́слить]

**mulled** [mʌld]: ***~ wine*** глинтве́йн

**multi|ple** ['mʌltɪpl] **1.** *math.* кра́тный; **2.** *math.* кра́тное число́; (*repeated*) многокра́тный; *interests. etc.* разнообра́зный; **~plication** [mʌltɪplɪ'keɪʃn] умноже́ние; увеличе́ние; ***~ table*** табли́ца умноже́ния; **~plicity** [~'plɪsətɪ] многочи́сленность *f*; (*variety*) разнообра́зие; **~ply** ['mʌltɪplaɪ] увели́чи(ва)ть(ся); *math.* умножа́ть [-о́жить]; **~purpose** многоцелево́й; **~tude** [~tju:d] мно́жество, ма́сса; толпа́

**mum** [mʌm]: ***keep ~*** пома́лкивать

**mumble** ['mʌmbl] [про]бормота́ть

**mummy** ['mʌmɪ] му́мия

**mumps** [mʌmps] *sg.* сви́нка

**mundane** ['mʌndeɪn] земно́й, мирско́й; □ бана́льный; *life* прозаи́чный

**municipal** [mju:'nɪsɪpl] □ муниципа́льный; **~ity** [~nɪsɪ'pælətɪ] муниципалите́т

**mural** ['mjʊərəl] фре́ска; стенна́я ро́спись *f*

**murder** ['mɜ:də] **1.** уби́йство; **2.** уби́(ва́)ть; **~er** [~rə] уби́йца *m/f*; **~ous** [~rəs] □ уби́йственный

**murky** ['mɜ:kɪ] □ тёмный; *day* па́смурный

**murmur** ['mɜ:mə] **1.** *of brook* журча́ние; *of voices* ти́хие зву́ки голосо́в; шёпот; **2.** [за]журча́ть; шепта́ть; (*grumble*) ворча́ть

**musc|le** ['mʌsl] му́скул, мы́шца; **~ular** ['mʌskjʊlə] (*brawny*) мускули́стый; му́скульный

**muse**¹ [mju:z] му́за

**muse**² [~] заду́м(ыв)аться (***about, on*** над Т)

**museum** [mju:'zɪəm] музе́й

**mushroom** ['mʌʃrʊm] **1.** гриб; ***pick ~s*** собира́ть грибы́; **2.** (*grow rapidly*) расти́ как грибы́

**music** ['mju:zɪk] му́зыка; музыка́льное произведе́ние; (*notes*) но́ты *f/pl.*; ***face the ~*** расхлёбывать ка́шу; ***set to ~*** положи́ть *pf.* на му́зыку; **~al** ['mju:zɪkl] □ музыка́льный; мелоди́чный; **~ hall** мю́зикхолл; эстра́дный теа́тр; **~ian** [mju:'zɪʃn] музыка́нт

**Muslim** ['mʊzlɪm] мусульма́нский

**muslin** ['mʌzlɪn] мусли́н

**musquash** ['mʌskwɒʃ] онда́тра; мех

рнда́тры
**mussel** ['mʌsl] ми́дия
**must** [mʌst]: ***I ~*** я до́лжен (+ *inf.*); ***I ~ not*** мне нельзя́; ***he ~ still be there*** он должно́ быть всё ещё там
**mustache** [mə'stɑːʃ] усы́ *m/pl.*
**mustard** ['mʌstəd] горчи́ца
**muster** ['mʌstə] (*gather*) собира́ться [-бра́ться]; **~ (*up*) *one's courage*** набра́ться *pf.* хра́брости, собра́ться *pf.* с ду́хом
**musty** ['mʌstɪ] за́тхлый
**mutation** [mjuː'teɪʃn] *biol.* мута́ция
**mut|e** [mjuːt] **1.** □ немо́й; **2.** немо́й; **~ed** ['~ɪd] приглушённый
**mutilat|e** ['mjuːtɪleɪt] [из]уве́чить; **~ion** [~'eɪʃn] уве́чье
**mutin|ous** ['mjuːtɪnəs] □ мятéжный (*a. fig.*); **~y** [~nɪ] бунт, мятéж
**mutter** ['mʌtə] **1.** бормота́нье; (*grumble*) ворча́ние; **2.** [про]бормота́ть; [про]ворча́ть
**mutton** ['mʌtn] бара́нина; ***leg of ~*** бара́нья нога́; **~ *chop*** бара́нья отбивна́я
**mutual** ['mjuːtʃʊəl] □ обою́дный, взаи́мный; о́бщий; **~ *friend*** о́бщий друг
**muzzle** ['mʌzl] **1.** мо́рда, ры́ло; *of gun* ду́ло; (*for dog*) намо́рдник; **2.** надева́ть намо́рдник (Д); *fig.* заста́вить *pf.* молча́ть
**my** [maɪ] *poss. pron.* мой *m*, моя́ *f*, моё *n*; мои́ *pl.*
**myrtle** ['mɜːtl] мирт
**myself** [maɪ'self] *refl. pron.* **1.** себя́, меня́ самого́; -ся, -сь; **2.** *pron. emphatic* сам; ***I dit it ~*** я сам э́то сде́лал
**myster|ious** [mɪ'stɪərɪəs] □ зага́дочный, таи́нственный; **~y** ['mɪstərɪ] та́йна; ***it's a ~ to me ...*** остаётся для меня́ зага́дкой
**mysti|c** ['mɪstɪk] (*a.* **~cal** [~kl] □) мисти́ческий; **~fy** [~tɪfaɪ] мистифици́ровать (*im*)*pf.*; (*bewilder*) озада́чи(ва)ть
**myth** [mɪθ] миф

# N

**nab** [næb] *coll.* (*arrest*) накрыва́ть [-ы́ть]; (*take unawares*) застига́ть [-и́гнуть]
**nag** [næg] *coll.* пили́ть
**nail** [neɪl] **1.** *anat.* но́готь *m*; гвоздь *m*; **~ *file*** пи́лка для ногте́й; **2.** заби́(ва́)ть гвоздя́ми; прибива́(ва́)ть; **~ *s.b. down*** заста́вить *pf.* раскры́ть свои́ ка́рты; прижа́ть *pf* к стене́
**naïve** [naɪ'iːv] *or* **naive** □ наи́вный; безыску́сный
**naked** ['neɪkɪd] □ наго́й, го́лый; (*evident*) я́вный; ***with the ~ eye*** невооружённым гла́зом; **~ness** [~nɪs] нагота́
**name** [neɪm] **1.** и́мя *n*; (*surname*) фами́лия; *of things* назва́ние; ***of*** (*coll.* ***by***) ***the ~ of*** по и́мени (И); ***in the ~ of*** во и́мя (Р); от и́мени (Р); ***call a p. ~s*** [об]руга́ть (В); **2.** наз(ы)ва́ть; дава́ть и́мя (Д); **~less** ['neɪmlɪs] □ безымя́нный; **~ly** ['~lɪ] и́менно; **~-plate** табли́чка с фами́лией; **~-sake** тёзка *m/f*
**nap**[1] [næp] **1.** коро́ткий/лёгкий сон; **2.** дрема́ть [вздремну́ть]; ***catch s.b. ~ping*** заст(ав)а́ть кого́-л. враспло́х
**nap**[2] [~] *on cloth* ворс
**nape** [neɪp] заты́лок
**napkin** ['næpkɪn] салфе́тка; *baby's* пелёнка
**narcotic** [nɑː'kɒtɪk] **1.** (**~*ally***) наркоти́ческий; **2.** нарко́тик
**narrat|e** [nə'reɪt] расска́зывать [-за́ть]; **~ion** [~ʃn] расска́з; **~ive** ['nærətɪv] повествова́ние
**narrow** ['nærəʊ] **1.** □ у́зкий; (*confinsed*) те́сный; *person, mind* ограни́ченный, недалёкий; **2. ~s** *pl.* проли́в; **3.** су́живать(ся) [су́зить(-ся)]; уменьша́ть(ся) [уме́ньшить(-ся)]; *of chances, etc.* ограни́чи(ва)ть; **~-minded** у́зкий; с предрассу́дками

N

**nasal** ['neɪzl] □ носово́й; *voice* гнуса́вый
**nasty** ['nɑːstɪ] □ (*offensive*) проти́вный; непри́ятный; гря́зный; (*spiteful*) зло́бный
**nation** ['neɪʃn] на́ция
**national** ['næʃnl] **1.** □ национа́льный, наро́дный; госуда́рственный; **2.** (*citizen*) по́дданный; **~ity** [næʃə'nælətɪ] национальность *f*; гражда́нство, по́дданство; **~ize** ['næʃnəlaɪz] национализи́ровать (*im*)*pf*.
**native** ['neɪtɪv] **1.** □ родно́й; (*indigenous*) тузе́мный, ме́стный, коренно́й; **~ language** родно́й язы́к; **2.** уроже́нец *m*, -нка *f*; ме́стный жи́тель
**natural** ['nætʃrəl] □ есте́ственный; *leather*, *etc*. натура́льный; **~ sciences** есте́ственные нау́ки *f*/*pl*.; **~ize** [~aɪz] предоставля́ть [-а́вить] гражда́нство
**nature** ['neɪtʃə] приро́да; хара́ктер
**naught** [nɔːt] ничто́; ноль *m*; ***set at ~*** ни во что не ста́вить; пренебрега́ть [-бре́чь] (Т)
**naughty** ['nɔːtɪ] □ непослу́шный, капри́зный
**nause|a** ['nɔːzɪə] тошнота́; (*disgust*) отвраще́ние; **~ate** ['nɔːzɪeɪt] *v*/*t*. тошни́ть; ***it ~s me*** меня́ тошни́т от э́того; вызыва́ть [вы́звать] отвраще́ние; ***be ~d*** испы́тывать отвраще́ние
**nautical** ['nɔːtɪkl] морско́й
**naval** ['neɪvl] (вое́нно-)морско́й
**nave** [neɪv] *arch*. неф
**navel** ['neɪvl] пуп, пупо́к
**naviga|ble** ['nævɪgəbl] □ судохо́дный; **~te** [~geɪt] *v*/*i*. *naut*., *ae*. управля́ть; *v*/*t*. *ship*, *plane* вести́; **~tion** [nævɪ'geɪʃn] навига́ция; ***inland ~*** речно́е судохо́дство; **~tor** ['nævɪgeɪtə] шту́рман
**navy** ['neɪvɪ] вое́нно-морски́е си́лы; вое́нно-морско́й флот; **~(blue)** тёмно-си́ний
**near** [nɪə] **1.** *adj*. бли́зкий; бли́жний; (*stingy*) скупо́й; ***in the ~ future*** в ближа́йшее вре́мя; ***~ at hand*** под руко́й; **2.** *adv*. ря́дом; бли́зко, недалеко́; почти́; ско́ро; **3.** *prp*. о́коло (Р), у (Р); **4.** приближа́ться [-ли́зиться] к (Д); **~by** [nɪə'baɪ] близлежа́щий; ря́дом; **~ly** ['nɪəlɪ] почти́; **~-sighted** [nɪə'saɪtɪd] близору́кий
**neat** [niːt] □ чи́стый, опря́тный; *figure* изя́щный; стро́йный; *workmanship* иску́сный; (*undiluted*) неразба́вленный; **~ness** ['niːtnɪs] опря́тность *f*
**necess|ary** ['nesəsərɪ] **1.** □ необходи́мый, ну́жный; **2.** необходи́мое; **~itate** [nɪ'sesɪteɪt] [по]тре́бовать; вынужда́ть [вы́нудить]; **~ity** [~tɪ] необходи́мость *f*, нужда́
**neck** [nek] ше́я; *of bottle*, *etc*. го́рлышко; ***~ of land*** перешéек; ***risk one's ~*** рискова́ть голово́й; ***stick one's ~ out*** рискова́ть; [по]ле́зть в пе́тлю; **~band** во́рот; **~lace** [~lɪs] ожере́лье; **~tie** га́лстук
**neée** [neɪ] урождённая
**need** [niːd] **1.** на́добность *f*; потре́бность *f*; необходи́мость *f*; (*poverty*) нужда́; ***be in ~ of*** нужда́ться в (П); **2.** нужда́ться в (П); ***I ~ it*** мне э́то ну́жно; ***if ~ be*** в слу́чае необходи́мости; **~ful** [~fl] □ ну́жный
**needle** ['niːdl] игла́, иго́лка; (*knitting ~*) спи́ца
**needless** ['niːdlɪs] □ нену́жный; ***~ to say*** разуме́ется
**needlework** вы́шивка
**needy** ['niːdɪ] □ нужда́ющийся
**negat|ion** [nɪ'geɪʃn] отрица́ние; **~ive** ['negətɪv] **1.** □ отрица́тельный; негати́вный; **2.** *phot*. негати́в; ***answer in the ~*** дава́ть [дать] отрицатеʌный отве́т
**neglect** [nɪ'glekt] **1.** пренебреже́ние; (*carelessness*) небре́жность *f*; **2.** пренебрега́ть [-бре́чь] (Т); **~ed** [~ɪd] забро́шенный; **~ful** [~fʊl] небре́жный
**negligen|ce** ['neglɪdʒəns] небре́жность *f*; (*attitude*) хала́тность *f*; **~t** [~t] □ небре́жный; хала́тный
**negligible** ['neglɪdʒəbl] ничто́жный, незначи́тельный
**negotia|te** [nɪ'gəʊʃɪeɪt] вести́ перегово́ры; догова́риваться [-вори́ться] о (П); *obstacles*, *etc*. преодоле́(ва́)ть; **~tion** [nɪgəʊʃɪ'eɪʃn] перегово́ры *m*/*pl*.; **~tor** [nɪ'gəʊʃɪeɪtə] лицо́, веду́щее перегово́ры

N

**Negr|ess** ['ni:grɪs] *contemptuous* афроамерика́нка, негритя́нка; **~o** ['ni:grəʊ], *pl.* **~oes** [-z] афроамерика́нец, негр
**neigh** [neɪ] **1.** ржа́ние; **2.** [за]ржа́ть
**neighbo(u)r** ['neɪbə] сосе́д(ка); **~hood** [-hʊd] окру́га, райо́н; **~ing** [-rɪŋ] сосе́дний
**neither** ['naɪðə] **1.** ни тот, ни друго́й; **2.** *adv.* та́кже не; **~ ... nor ...** ни … ни …
**nephew** ['nevju:] племя́нник
**nerve** [nɜ:v] **1.** нерв; (*courage*) му́жество, хладнокро́вие; на́глость *f*; ***get on s.b.'s ~s*** де́йствовать на не́рвы; ***have the ~ to ...*** име́ть на́глость *f*; **2.** придава́ть си́лы (хра́брости) (Д)
**nervous** ['nɜ:vəs] □ не́рвный; (*highly strung, irritable*) нерво́зный; **~ness** [-nɪs] не́рвность *f*, нерво́зность *f*
**nest** [nest] **1.** гнездо́ (*a. fig.*); **2.** вить гнездо́; **~le** ['nesl] *v/i.* удо́бно устро́иться *pf.*; приж(им)а́ться (***to, on, against*** к Д); *v/t. one's head* приж(има́ть (го́лову)
**net**[1] [net] **1.** сеть *f*; **2.** расставля́ть се́ти; пойма́ть *pf.* се́тью
**net**[2] [-] **1.** не́тто *adj. indecl.*, *weight, profit* чи́стый; **2.** приноси́ть (получа́ть) чи́стый дохо́д
**nettle** ['netl] **1.** *bot.* крапи́ва; **2.** обжига́ть крапи́вой; *fig.* раздража́ть, [рас]серди́ть
**network** ['netwɜ:k] *tech.*, *rail*, *etc.* сеть *f*
**neuralgia** [njʊə'rældʒə] невралги́я
**neurosis** [njʊə'rəʊsɪs] невро́з
**neuter** ['nju:tə] *gr.* сре́дний род
**neutral** ['nju:trəl] **1.** □ нейтра́льный; **2.** нейтра́льное госуда́рство; **~ity** [nju:'trælətɪ] нейтралите́т; **~ize** ['nju:trəlaɪz] нейтрализова́ть (*im*)*pf.*
**never** ['nevə] никогда́; совсе́м не; **~-ending** бесконе́чный, несконча́емый; **~more** никогда́ бо́льше; **~theless** [nevəðə'les] тем не ме́нее; несмотря́ на э́то
**new** [nju:] но́вый; *vegetables, moon* молодо́й; *bread, etc.* све́жий; **~born** новоро́жденный; **~comer** вновь прибы́вший; новичо́к; **~fangled** ['-fæŋgld] новомо́дный; **~ly** ['nju:lɪ] за́ново, вновь; неда́вно
**news** [nju:z] но́вости *f/pl.*, изве́стия *n/pl.*; ***what's the ~?*** что но́вого?; **~agent** продаве́ц газе́т; **~paper** газе́та; **~print** газе́тная бума́га; **~reel** киножурна́л; **~stall**, **~stand** газе́тный кио́ск
**New Testament** Но́вый заве́т
**New Year** Но́вый год; ***~'s Eve*** кану́н Но́вого го́да; ***Happy ~!*** С Но́вым Го́дом!
**next** [nekst] **1.** *adj.* сле́дующий; ближа́йший; ***~ door to*** в сле́дующем до́ме; *fig.* чуть (ли) не, почти́; ***~ to*** во́зле (Р); вслед за (Т); **2.** *adv.* пото́м, по́сле, зате́м; в сле́дующий раз; **~ of kin** ближа́йший (-шая) ро́дственник (-ица)
**nibble** ['nɪbl] *v/t.* обгры́з(а́)ть
**nice** [naɪs] □ прия́тный, ми́лый, сла́вный; (*fine, delicate*) то́нкий; **~ty** ['naɪsətɪ] (*delicate point, detail*) то́нкости *f/pl.*, дета́ли *f/pl.*
**niche** [nɪtʃ] ни́ша
**nick** [nɪk] **1.** (*notch*) зару́бка; ***in the ~ of time*** как раз во́время; **2.** сде́лать *pf.* зару́бку в (П); *Am.* (*cheat*) обма́нывать [-ну́ть]; *Brt. coll.* (*steal*) стащи́ть *pf.*
**nickel** ['nɪkl] **1.** *min.* ни́кель *m*; *Am.* моне́та в 5 це́нтов; **2.** [от]никели́ровать
**nickname** ['nɪkneɪm] **1.** про́звище; **2.** прозыва́ть [-зва́ть]; да(ва́)ть про́звище (Д)
**nicotine** ['nɪkəti:n] никоти́н
**niece** [ni:s] племя́нница
**niggard** ['nɪgəd] скупе́ц; **~ly** [-lɪ] скупо́й; *sum, etc.* жа́лкий
**night** [naɪt] ночь *f*, ве́чер; ***by ~, at ~*** но́чью; ***stay the ~*** переночева́ть; **~club** ночно́й клуб; **~fall** су́мерки *f/pl.*; **~dress, ~gown** ночна́я руба́шка; **~ingale** ['naɪtɪŋgeɪl] солове́й; **~ly** ['naɪtlɪ] ночно́й; *adv.* но́чью; ка́ждую ночь; **~mare** кошма́р
**nil** [nɪl] *sport* ноль *m or* нуль *m*; ничего́
**nimble** ['nɪmbl] □ прово́рный, ло́вкий; *mind* живо́й
**nimbus** ['nɪmbəs] *eccl. art* нимб

N

**nine** [naɪn] де́вять; девя́тка; → ***five***; **~pins** *pl.* ке́гли *f/pl.*; **~teen** [naɪn'tiːn] девятна́дцать; **~ty** ['naɪntɪ] девяно́сто
**ninny** ['nɪnɪ] *coll.* простофи́ля *m/f*
**ninth** [naɪnθ] **1.** девя́тый; **2.** девя́тая часть *f*
**nip** [nɪp] **1.** щипо́к; (*bite*) уку́с; (*frost*) моро́з; ***there is a ~ in the air*** во́здух моро́зный; **2.** щипа́ть [щипну́ть]; *finger* прищемля́ть [-ми́ть]; *flowers* поби́ть *pf.* моро́зом; ***~ in the bud*** пресека́ть в заро́дыше
**nipper** ['nɪpə] (***a pair of***) ***~s*** *pl.* клёщи *pl.*; *coll.* малы́ш
**nipple** ['nɪpl] сосо́к
**nitrate** ['naɪtreɪt] нитра́т
**nitrogen** ['naɪtrədʒən] азо́т
**no** [nəʊ] **1.** *adj.* никако́й; ***in ~ time*** в мгнове́ние о́ка; ***~ one*** никто́; **2.** *adv.* нет; **3.** отрица́ние
**Nobel prize** [nəʊ'bel] Но́белевская пре́мия
**nobility** [nəʊ'bɪlətɪ] дворя́нство; благоро́дство
**noble** ['nəʊbl] **1.** □ благоро́дный; (*highborn*) зна́тный; ***~ metal*** благоро́дный мета́лл; **2.** = **~man** титуло́ванное лицо́, дворяни́н
**nobody** ['nəʊbədɪ] *pron.* никто́; *su.* ничто́жный челове́к
**nocturnal** [nɒk'tɜːnl] ночно́й
**nod** [nɒd] **1.** кива́ть голово́й; (*doze*) дрема́ть; *coll.* (*drowse*) клева́ть но́сом; **2.** криво́к голово́й
**noise** [nɔɪz] шум; (*din*) гро́хот; ***make a ~*** *fig.* поднима́ть [-ня́ть] шум; **~less** ['nɔɪzlɪs] □ бесшу́мный
**noisy** ['nɔɪzɪ] □ шу́мный; *child* шумли́вый
**nomin|al** ['nɒmɪnl] □ номина́льный; *gr.* именно́й; ***~ value*** номина́льная цена́; **~ate** ['nɒmɪmeɪt] (*appoint*) назнача́ть [-зна́чить]; *candidate* выдвига́ть ['-инуть]; **~ation** [nɒmɪ'neɪʃn] выдвиже́ние; назначе́ние
**non** [nɒn] *prf.* не…, бес.., без…
**nonalcoholic** безалкого́льный
**nonchalance** ['nɒnʃələns] беззабо́тность *f*
**noncommittal** [nɒnkə'mɪtl] укло́нчивый
**nondescript** ['nɒndɪskrɪpt] (*dull*) невзра́чный; *colo(u)r* неопределённый
**none** [nʌn] **1.** ничто́, никто́; ни оди́н; никако́й; **2.** нисколько, совсе́м не …; ***~theless*** тем не ме́нее
**nonentity** [nɒ'nentətɪ] *person* ничто́жество
**nonexistent** несуществу́ющий
**nonpayment** *mst. fin.* неплатёж, неупла́та
**nonplus** [nɒn'plʌs] приводи́ть в замеша́тельство, озада́чи(ва)ть
**nonpolluting** [nɒnpə'luːtɪŋ] не загрязня́ющий среду́
**nonprofit** некомме́рческий
**nonresident** не прожива́ющий в да́нном ме́сте
**nonsens|e** ['nɒnsəns] вздор, бессмы́слица; **~ical** [nɒn'sensɪkl] бессмы́сленный
**nonsmoker** *person* некуря́щий; *Brt. rail* ваго́н для некуря́щих
**nonstop** безостано́вочный; *ae.* беспоса́дочный
**noodle** ['nuːdl]: ***~s*** *pl.* лапша́
**nook** [nʊk] укро́мный уголо́к; закоу́лок; ***search every ~ and cranny*** обша́рить *pf.* все углы́ и закоу́лки
**noon** [nuːn] по́лдень *m*
**noose** [nuːs] петля́; (*lasso*) арка́н
**nor** [nɔː] и не; та́кже не; ни
**norm** [nɔːm] но́рма; **~al** ['nɔːml] □ норма́льный; **~alize** [~əlaɪz] приводи́ть [-вести́] в но́рму; нормализова́ть (*im*)*pf.*
**north** [nɔːθ] **1.** се́вер; **2.** се́верный; **3.** *adv.*: ***~ of*** к се́веру от (Р); **~-east 1.** се́веро-восто́к; **2.** се́веро-восто́чный (*a.* **~-eastern**; **~erly** ['nɔːðəlɪ], **~ern** ['nɔːðən] се́верный; **~ward(s)** ['nɔːθwəd(z)] *adv.* на се́вер; к се́веру; **~-west 1.** се́веро-за́пад; *naut.* норд-ве́ст; **2.** се́веро-за́падный (*a.* **~-western**)
**nose** [nəʊz] **1.** нос; (*sense of smell*, *a. fig.*) чутьё; *of boat*, *etc.* нос; **2.** *v/t.* [по]ню́хать; *information* разню́х(ив)ать; **~gay** буке́т цвето́в

**nostril** ['nɒstrəl] ноздря́
**nosy** ['nəʊzɪ] *coll.* любопы́тный
**not** [nɒt] не
**notable** ['nəʊtəbl] □ примеча́тельный, знамена́тельный; *person* выдаю́щийся
**notary** ['nəʊtərɪ] нота́риус (*a.* ***public*** **~**)
**notation** [nəʊ'teɪʃn] *mus.* нота́ция; за́пись *f*
**notch** [nɒtʃ] **1.** зару́бка; (*mark*) ме́тка; **2.** [с]де́лать зару́бку
**note** [nəʊt] **1.** заме́тка; за́пись *f*; (*comment*) примеча́ние; (*bank note*) банкно́т; (*denomination*) де́нежная купю́ра; *dipl.* но́та; *mus.* но́та; ***man of*** **~** знамени́тость *f*; ***worthy of*** **~** досто́йный внима́ния; **2.** замеча́ть [-е́тить]; (*mention*) упомина́ть [-мяну́ть]; (*a.* **~** ***down***) де́лать заме́тки, запи́сывать [-са́ть]; (*make a mental note*) отмеча́ть [-е́тить]; **~book** записна́я кни́жка; **~d** [-ɪd] хорошо́ изве́стный; **~worthy** примеча́тельный
**nothing** ['nʌθɪŋ] ничто́, ничего́; ***for*** **~** зря, да́ром; ***come to*** **~** ни к чему́ не привести́ *pf*; ***to say*** **~** ***of*** не говоря́ уже́ о (П); ***there is*** **~** ***like …*** нет ничего́ лу́чшего, чем …
**notice** ['nəʊtɪs] **1.** внима́ние; извеще́ние, уведомле́ние; (*warning*) предупрежде́ние; (*announcement*) объявле́ние; ***at short*** **~** без предупрежде́ния; ***give*** **~** предупрежда́ть об увольне́нии (*or* об ухо́де); извеща́ть [-ести́ть]; **2.** замеча́ть [-е́тить]; обраща́ть внима́ние на (В); **~able** [-əbl] □ досто́йный внима́ния; заме́тный; **~board** доска́ объявле́ний
**notification** [nəʊtɪfɪ'keɪʃn] извеще́ние, сообще́ние
**notify** ['nəʊtɪfaɪ] извеща́ть [-ести́ть], уведомля́ть [уве́домить]
**notion** ['nəʊʃn] поня́тие, представле́ние
**notorious** [nəʊ'tɔːrɪəs] □ общеизве́стный; *pej.* пресловýтый
**notwithstanding** [nɒtwɪθ'stændɪŋ] несмотря́ на (В), вопреки́ (Д)
**nought** [nɔːt] ничто́; *math.* ноль *m or* нуль *m*; ***bring to*** **~** своди́ть [свести́] на нет
**nourish** ['nʌrɪʃ] пита́ть (*a. fig.*); [на-, по]корми́ть; *fig. hope, etc.* леле́ять; **~ing** [-ɪŋ] пита́тельный; **~ment** [-mənt] пита́ние; пи́ща (*a. fig.*)
**novel** ['nɒvl] **1.** но́вый; (*unusual*) необы́чный; **2.** рома́н; **~ist** [-ɪst] писа́тель *m*, -ница *f*; романи́ст; **~ty** [-tɪ] нови́нка; новизна́; (*method*) но́вшество
**November** [nəʊ'vembə] ноя́брь *m*
**novice** ['nɒvɪs] новичо́к; *eccl.* послу́шник *m*, -ница *f*
**now** [naʊ] **1.** тепе́рь, сейча́с; то́тчас; ***just*** **~** то́лько что; **~** ***and again*** (*или* ***then***) вре́мя от вре́мени; **2.** *cj.* когда́, раз
**nowadays** ['naʊədeɪz] ны́нче; в на́ши дни; в на́ше вре́мя
**nowhere** ['nəʊweə] нигде́, никуда́
**noxious** ['nɒkʃəs] □ вре́дный
**nozzle** ['nɒzl] *of hose* наконе́чник; *tech.* со́пло
**nucle|ar** ['njuːklɪə] я́дерный; **~** ***pile*** я́дерный реа́ктор; **~** ***power plant*** а́томная электроста́нция; **~us** [-s] ядро́
**nude** [njuːd] го́лый, наго́й; *art.* **~** ***figure*** обнажённая фигу́ра
**nudge** [nʌdʒ] *coll.* **1.** подта́лкивать [-толкну́ть]; **2.** лёгкий толчо́к ло́ктем
**nuisance** ['njuːsns] неприя́тность *f*; доса́да; *fig.* надое́дливый челове́к
**null** [nʌl] недействи́тельный; ***become*** **~** ***and void*** утра́чивать [утра́тить] зако́нную си́лу; **~ify** ['nʌlɪfaɪ] аннули́ровать (*im*)*pf*.; расторга́ть [-то́ргнуть]
**numb** [nʌm] *with terror* онеме́вший, оцепене́вший; *with cold* окочене́вший
**number** ['nʌmbə] **1.** число́; но́мер; (*figure*) ци́фра; **2.** нумерова́ть; (*be in number*) насчи́тывать; **~less** [-lɪs] бесчи́сленный; **~plate** *mot.* номерно́й знак
**numeral** ['njuːmərəl] **1.** *gr.* и́мя числи́тельное; (*figure*) ци́фра; **2.** цифрово́й
**numerical** [njuː'merɪkəl] □ числово́й; чи́сленный

N

**numerous** ['nju:mərəs] □ многочи́сленный; ***in ~ cases*** во мно́гих слу́чаях
**nun** [nʌn] мона́хиня
**nunnery** ['nʌnərɪ] же́нский монасты́рь *m*
**nurse** [nɜ:s] **1.** ня́ня (*a.* ***~maid***); медици́нская сестра́, медсестра́; **2.** (*breast-feed*) [на]корми́ть гру́дью; (*take nourishment from the breast*) соса́ть грудь *f*; (*rear*) вска́рмливать; (*look after*) уха́живать за (T); **~ry** ['nɜ:sərɪ] де́тская (ко́мната); *agric.* пито́мник; ***~ school*** де́тский сад
**nursing** ['nɜ:sɪŋ]: ***~ home*** ча́стная лече́бница; ***~ staff*** медсёстры
**nurture** ['nɜ:tʃə] (*bring up*) воспи́тывать [-та́ть]
**nut** [nʌt] оре́х; *tech.* га́йка; ***a hard ~ to crack*** кре́пкий оре́шек; **~cracker** щипцы́ для оре́хов; **~meg** ['nʌtmeg] муска́тный оре́х
**nutri|tion** [nju:'trɪʃn] пита́ние; **~tious** [~ʃəs], **~tive** ['nju:trətɪv] □ пита́тельный
**nut|shell** оре́ховая скорлупа́; ***in a ~*** кра́тко, в двух слова́х; **~ty** ['nʌtɪ] *taste* име́ющий вкус оре́ха; *coll. idea*, *etc.* бредово́й; *person* безу́мный, психо́ванный
**nylon** ['naɪlɒn] нейло́н
**nymph** [nɪmf] ни́мфа

# O

**oaf** [əʊf] дура́к; у́вален *m*
**oak** [əʊk] дуб; *attr.* дубо́вый
**oar** [ɔ:] **1.** весло́; **2.** *poet.* грести́; **~sman** ['ɔ:zmən] гребе́ц
**oasis** [əʊ'eɪsɪs] оа́зис
**oat** [əʊt] овёс (*mst.* ***~s*** *pl.*)
**oath** [əʊθ] кля́тва; *mil.*, *law* прися́га; (*curse*) руга́тельство
**oatmeal** ['əʊtmi:l] овся́нка
**obdurate** ['ɒbdjuərət] □ (*stubborn*) упря́мый; (*unrepentant*) нераска́янный
**obedien|ce** [ə'bi:dɪəns] повинове́ние; **~t** [~t] □ послу́шный
**obelisk** ['ɒbəlɪsk] обели́ск
**obese** [əʊ'bi:s] ту́чный
**obesity** [əʊ'bi:sətɪ] ту́чность *f*
**obey** [ə'beɪ] повинова́ться (*im*)*pf.* (Д); [по]слу́шаться (P)
**obituary** [ə'bɪtʃʊərɪ] некро́лог
**object 1.** ['ɒbdʒɪkt] предме́т, вещь *f*; объе́кт; *fig.* цель *f*; наме́рение; **2.** [əb'dʒekt] (*disapprove*) не одобря́ть (P), протестова́ть; возража́ть [-рази́ть] (***to*** про́тив P); ***if you don't ~*** е́сли вы не возража́ете
**objection** [əb'dʒekʃn] возраже́ние; проте́ст; **~able** [~əbl] □ нежела́тельный; (*distasteful*) неприя́тный
**objective** [əb'dʒektɪv] **1.** □ объекти́вный; **2.** объе́кт, цель *f*
**obligat|ion** [ɒblɪ'geɪʃn] (*promise*) обяза́тельство; (*duty*) обя́занность *f*; **~ory** [ə'blɪgətrɪ] □ обяза́тельный
**oblig|e** [ə'blaɪdʒ] (*require*) обя́зывать [-за́ть]; (*compel*) вынужда́ть [-ну́дить]; ***I was ~d to …*** я был вы́нужден …; ***~ a p.*** де́лать одолже́ние кому́-либо; ***much ~d*** о́чень благода́рен (-рна); **~ing** [~ɪŋ] □ услу́жливый, любе́зный
**oblique** [ə'bli:k] □ косо́й; *gr.* ко́свенный
**obliterate** [ə'blɪtəreɪt] (*efface*) изгла́живать(ся) [-ла́дить(ся)]; (*destroy*) уничтожа́ть [-о́жить]; (*expunge*) вычёркивать [вы́черкнуть]
**oblivi|on** [ə'blɪvɪən] забве́ние; **~ous** [~əs] □ забы́вчивый
**obnoxious** [əb'nɒkʃəs] проти́вный, несно́сный
**obscene** [əb'si:n] □ непристо́йный
**obscur|e** [əb'skjʊə] **1.** □ тёмный; (*not distinct*) нея́сный; *author*, *etc.* малоизве́стный; *meaning*, *etc.* непоня́тный; **2.** *sun. etc.* заслоня́ть [-ни́ть]; **~ity** [~rətɪ] неизве́стность *f*; *in text* нея́сное

O

ме́сто

**obsequious** [əb'siːkwɪəs] □ подобостра́стный

**observ|able** [əb'zɜːvəbl] □ заме́тный; **~ance** [-vəns] *of law, etc.* соблюде́ние; *of anniversary, etc.* пра́зднование; **~ant** [-vənt] □ наблюда́тельный; **~ation** [ɒbzə'veɪʃn] наблюде́ние; наблюда́тельность *f*; (*comment*) замеча́ние; **~atory** [əb'zɜːvətrɪ] обсервато́рия; **~e** [əb'zɜːv] *v/t.* наблюда́ть; *fig.* соблюда́ть [-юсти́]; (*notice*) замеча́ть [-е́тить] (В); *v/i.* замеча́ть [-е́тить]; **~er** [~ə] наблюда́тель *m*

**obsess** [əb'ses]: ***~ed by**, a.* ***with*** одержи́мый (Т); **~ion** [əb'seʃn] навя́зчивая иде́я; одержи́мость *f*

**obsolete** ['ɒbsəliːt] устаре́лый; *words, etc.* устаре́вший

**obstacle** ['ɒbstəkl] препя́тствие

**obstinate** ['ɒbstənət] упря́мый; насто́йчивый

**obstruct** [əb'strʌkt] [по]меша́ть (Д), затрудня́ть [-ни́ть]; (*block*) загражда́ть [-ади́ть] загора́живать [-роди́ть]; **~ion** [əb'strʌkʃn] препя́тствие, поме́ха; загражде́ние; *law* обстру́кция; **~ive** [~tɪv] препя́тствующий; обструкцио́нный

**obtain** [əb'teɪn] *v/t.* (*receive*) получа́ть [-чи́ть]; (*procure*) добы́(ва́)ть; (*acquire*) обрета́ть [-ести́]; **~able** [~əbl] досту́пный; *result, etc.* достижи́мый

**obtru|de** [əb'truːd] навя́зывать(ся) [-за́ть(ся)] (***on*** Д); **~sive** [~sɪv] навя́зчивый

**obvious** ['ɒbvɪəs] □ очеви́дный, я́сный, я́вный

**occasion** [ə'keɪʒn] **1.** слу́чай; возмо́жность *f*; (*reason*) по́вод, причи́на; (*special event*) собы́тие; ***on that ~*** в тот раз; ***on the ~ of*** по слу́чаю (Р); ***rise to the ~*** оказа́ться *pf.* на высоте́ положе́ния; **2.** причиня́ть [-ни́ть]; дава́ть по́вод к (Д); **~al** [~ʒnl] □ случа́йный; ре́дкий

**occult** [ɒ'kʌlt] □ окку́льтный

**occup|ant** ['ɒkjʊpənt] (*inhabitant*) жи́тель *m*, -ница *f*; (*tenant*) жиле́ц; ***the ~s of the car*** е́хавшие (*or* сидя́щие) в маши́не; **~ation** [ɑkjʊ'peɪʃn] *mil.* оккупа́ция; (*work, profession*) заня́тие, профе́ссия; **~y** ['ɒkjʊpɑɪ] *seat, etc.* занима́ть [заня́ть]; (*take possession of*) завладе́(ва́)ть (Т); оккупи́ровать (*im*)*pf.*

**occur** [ə'kɜː] (*take place*) случа́ться [-чи́ться]; (*be met with*) встреча́ться [-е́титься]; ***~ to a p.*** приходи́ть в го́лову; **~rence** [ə'kʌrəns] происше́ствие, слу́чай

**ocean** ['əʊʃn] океа́н

**o'clock** [ə'klɒk]: ***five ~*** пять часо́в

**ocul|ar** ['ɒkjʊlə] глазно́й; **~ist** ['ɒkjʊlɪst] окули́ст, глазно́й врач

**odd** [ɒd] □ нечётный; *sock, etc.* непа́рный; (*extra*) ли́шний; *of incomplete set* разро́зненный; (*strange*) стра́нный; **~ity** ['ɒdɪtɪ] чудакова́тость *f*; **~s** [ɒdz] ша́нсы *m/pl.*; ***be at ~ with*** не ла́дить с (Т); ***~ and ends*** оста́тки *m/pl.*; вся́кая вся́чина

**odious** ['əʊdɪəs] ненави́стный; (*repulsive*) отврати́тельный

**odo(u)r** ['əʊdə] за́пах; арома́т

**of** [ɒv; *mst.* əv, v] *prp.* о, об (П); из (Р); от (Р); *denoting cause, affiliation, agent, quality, source; often corresponds to the genitive case in Russian*; ***think ~ s.th.*** ду́мать о (П); ***out ~ charity*** из милосе́рдия; ***die ~*** умере́ть *pf.* от (Р); ***cheat ~*** обсчи́тывать на (В); ***the battle ~ Quebec*** би́тва под Квебе́ком; ***proud ~*** го́рдый (Т); ***the roof ~ the house*** кры́ша до́ма

**off** [ɔːf, ɒf] **1.** *adv.* прочь; ***far ~*** далеко́; *translated into Russian mst. by verbal prefixes*; ***go ~*** (*leave*) уходи́ть [уйти́]; ***switch ~*** выключа́ть [вы́ключить]; ***take ~*** (*remove*) снима́ть [снять]; ***on and ~, ~ and on*** вре́мя от вре́мени; ***be well ~*** быть обеспе́ченным; **2.** *prp.* с (Р), со (Р) *indicates removal from a surface*; от (Р) *indicates distance*; **3.** *adj.*; ***day ~*** выходно́й день; ***~side*** *Brt.* пра́вая сторона́; *Am.* ле́вая сторона́; ***the ~ season*** мёртвый сезо́н

**offal** ['ɒfl] потроха́ *m/pl.*

**offend** [ə'fend] *v/t.* обижа́ть [оби́деть]; *feelings* оскорбля́ть [-би́ть]; *v/i.* наруша́ть [-у́шить] (***against*** В);

O

**~er** [~ə] оби́дчик; *law* правонаруши́тель(ница *f*) *m*; ***first ~*** челове́к, суди́мый (соверши́вший преступле́ние) впервы́е

**offen|se**, *Brt.* **~ce** [ə'fens] (*transgression*) просту́пок; оби́да, оскорбле́ние; *mil.* наступле́ние

**offensive** [ə'fensɪv] **1.** □ (*insulting*) оскорби́тельный; оби́дный; (*disagreeable*) проти́вный; **2.** *mil.* наступле́ние

**offer** ['ɒfə] **1.** предложе́ние; **2.** *v/t.* предлага́ть [-ложи́ть]; ***~ an explanation*** дава́ть [дать] объясне́ние; ***~ resistance*** оказа́ть [-а́зывать] сопротивле́ние

**offhand** [ɒf'hænd] *manner* бесцеремо́нный; развя́зный; *adv.* без подгото́вки; ***he couldn't tell me ~ ...*** он не смог мне сра́зу отве́тить …

**office** ['ɒfɪs] (*position*) до́лжность *f*; слу́жба; (*premises*) конто́ра; канцеля́рия; *of doctor, dentist, etc.* кабине́т; ~ министе́рство; ***~ hours*** часы́ рабо́ты, приёмные часы́

**officer** ['ɒfɪsə] *mil.* офице́р

**official** [ə'fɪʃl'] **1.** □ официа́льный; служе́бный; ***through ~ channels*** по официа́льным кана́лам; **2.** должностно́е лицо́, слу́жащий; *hist.*, *a. pej.* чино́вник

**officious** [ə'fɪʃəs] □ назо́йливый, навя́зчивый

**off|set** возмеща́ть [-ести́ть]; **~shoot** побе́г; ответвле́ние; **~spring** о́тпрыск, пото́мок; **~-the-record** конфиденциа́льный

**often** ['ɒfn] ча́сто, мно́го раз; ***more ~ than not*** бо́льшей ча́стью; в большинстве́ слу́чаев

**ogle** ['əʊgl] стро́ить гла́зки (Д)

**oil** [ɔɪl] **1.** (*vegetable ~*) ма́сло; (*petroleum*) нефть *f*; ***diesel ~*** соля́рка; ***fuel ~*** жи́дкое то́пливо; **2.** сма́з(ыв)ать; **~cloth** клеёнка; **~field** нефтяно́е месторожде́ние; **~ well** нефтяна́я сква́жина; **~y** ['ɔɪlɪ] масляни́стый, ма́сляный; *fig.* еле́йный

**ointment** ['ɔɪntmənt] мазь *f*

**OK**, **okay** [əʊ'keɪ] *coll.* **1.** *pred.* в поря́дке, хорошо́; **2.** *int.* хорошо́!, ла́дно!, идёт!; слу́шаюсь!

**old** [əʊld] *com.* ста́рый; (***in times***) ***of ~*** в старину́; ***~ age*** ста́рость *f*; **~-fashioned** [~'fæʃnd] старомо́дный

**olfactory** [ɒl'fæktərɪ] обоня́тельный

**olive** ['ɒlɪv] *fruit* масли́на; *colo(u)r* оли́вковый цвет

**Olympic** [ə'lɪmpɪk]: ***the ~ Games*** Олимпи́йские и́гры

**omelet(te)** ['ɒmlɪt] омле́т

**ominous** ['ɒmɪnəs] □ злове́щий

**omission** [ə'mɪʃn] (*oversight*) упуще́ние; (*leaving out*) про́пуск

**omit** [ə'mɪt] пропуска́ть [-сти́ть]; (*on purpose*) опуска́ть [-сти́ть]

**on** [ɒn] **1.** *prp. mst.* на (П *or* В); ***~ the wall*** на стене́; ***~ good authority*** из достове́рного исто́чника; ***~ the 1st of April*** пе́рвого апре́ля; ***~ his arrival*** по его́ прибы́тии; ***talk ~ a subject*** говори́ть на те́му; ***~ hearing it*** услы́шав э́то; **2.** *adv.* да́льше; вперёд; да́лее; ***keep one's hat ~*** остава́ться в шля́пе; ***have a coat ~*** быть в пальто́; ***and so ~*** и так да́лее (и т.д.); ***be ~*** быть запу́щенным в ход, включённым (*и т. п.*)

**once** [wʌns] **1.** *adv.* раз; не́когда; когда́-то; ***at ~*** сейча́с же ***~ and for all*** раз (и) навсегда́; ***~ in a while*** и́зредка; ***this ~*** на э́тот раз; **2.** *cj.* как то́лько

**one** [wʌn] **1.** оди́н; еди́ный; еди́нственный; како́й-то; ***~ day*** одна́жды; ***~ never knows*** никогда́ не зна́ешь; **2.** (число́) оди́н; едини́ца; ***the little ~s*** малыши́ *m/pl.*; ***~ another*** друг дру́га; ***at ~*** заодно́; ***~ by ~*** оди́н за други́м; ***I for ~*** я со свое́й стороны́

**onerous** ['ɒnərəs] □ обремени́тельный

**one|self** [wʌn'self] *pron. refl.* -ся, -сь, (самого́) себя́; **~-sided** □ односторо́нний; **~-way**: ***~ street*** у́лица с односторо́нним движе́нием

**onion** ['ʌnjən] лук, лу́ковица

**onlooker** ['ɒnlʊkə] → ***looker-on***

**only** ['əʊnlɪ] **1.** *adj.* еди́нственный; **2.** *adv.* еди́нственно; то́лько, лишь; исключи́тельно; ***~ yesterday*** то́лько вчера́; **3.** *cj.* но; ***~ that ...*** е́сли бы не то, что …

O

**onset** ['ɒnset] нача́ло
**onslaught** ['ɒnslɔːt] ата́ка, нападе́ние
**onward** ['ɒnwəd] **1.** *adj.* продвига́ющий; **~ *movement*** движе́ние вперёд; **2.** *adv.* вперёд; впереди́
**ooze** [uːz] [про]сочи́ться
**opaque** [əʊ'peɪk] □ непрозра́чный
**open** ['əʊpən] **1.** □ *com.* откры́тый; (*frank*) открове́нный; **~ *to*** досту́пный (Д); ***in the* ~ *air*** на откры́том во́здухе; **2. *bring into the* ~** сде́лать *pf.* достоя́нием обще́ственности; **3.** *v/t.* откры́(ва́)ть; нач(ин)а́ть; *v/i.* откры́(ва́)ться; нач(ин)а́ться; **~ *into*** *of door* откры́(ва́)ться в (В); **~ *on to*** выходи́ть на *or* в (В); **~-handed** ще́дрый; **~ing** [~ɪŋ] отве́рстие; нача́ло; *of exhibition* откры́тие; **~-minded** *fig.* непредубеждённый
**opera** ['ɒpərə] о́пера; **~ glasses** *pl.* театра́льный бино́кль *m*
**operat|e** ['ɒpəreɪt] *v/t.* управля́ть (Т); *part. Am.* приводи́ть в де́йствие; *v/i. med.* опери́ровать *(im)pf.*; рабо́тать; де́йствовать; **~ion** [ɒpə'reɪʃn] де́йствие; *med., mil., comm.* опера́ция; проце́сс; ***be in* ~** быть в де́йствии; **~ive** ['ɒpərətɪv] □ *having force* действи́тельный; *effective* де́йственный; *working* де́йствующий; **~or** ['ɒpəreɪtə] *of a machine* управля́ющий; *tel.* опера́тор; телеграфи́ст(ка *f*) *m*
**opinion** [ə'pɪnjən] мне́ние; взгляд; ***in my* ~** по-мо́ему
**opponent** [ə'pəʊnənt] оппоне́нт, проти́вник
**opportun|e** ['ɒpətjuːn] □ благоприя́тный, подходя́щий; *timely* своевре́менный; **~ity** [ɒpə'tjuːnətɪ] удо́бный слу́чай, возмо́жность *f*
**oppos|e** [ə'pəʊz] противопоставля́ть [-ста́вить]; (*be against*) [вос]проти́виться (Д); **~ed** [~d] противопоста́вленный; ***as* ~ *to*** в отли́чие от (Р); ***be* ~** быть про́тив (Р); **~ite** ['ɒpəzɪt] **1.** □ противополо́жный; **2.** *prp., adv.* напро́тив, про́тив (Р); **3.** противополо́жность *f*; **~ition** [ɒpə'zɪʃn] противопоставле́ние; сопротивле́ние; оппози́ция
**oppress** [ə'pres] притесня́ть [-ни́ть], угнета́ть; **~ion** [~ʃn] притесне́ние, угнете́ние; **~ive** [~sɪv] □ гнету́щий; *weather* ду́шный
**optic** ['ɒptɪk] глазно́й, зри́тельный; **~al** [~l] □ опти́ческий; **~ian** [ɒp'tɪʃn] о́птик
**optimism** ['ɒptɪmɪzəm] оптими́зм
**optimistic** [ɒptɪ'mɪstɪk] *person* оптимисти́чный; *prognosis, etc.* оптимисти́ческий
**option** ['ɒpʃn] вы́бор, пра́во вы́бора; **~al** ['ʃənl] □ необяза́тельный, факультати́вный
**opulence** ['ɒpjʊləns] бога́тство
**or** [ɔː] или; **~ *else*** ина́че; и́ли же
**oracle** ['ɒrəkl] ора́кул
**oral** ['ɔːrəl] □ у́стный; слове́сный
**orange** ['ɒrɪndʒ] **1.** апельси́н; ора́нжевый цвет; **2.** ора́нжевый
**orator** ['ɒrətə] ора́тор
**orbit** ['ɔːbɪt] орби́та; ***put into* ~** выводи́ть [-вести] на орби́ту
**orchard** ['ɔːtʃəd] фрукто́вый сад
**orchestra** ['ɔːkɪstrə] орке́стр
**ordain** [ɔː'deɪn] посвяща́ть в духо́вный сан
**ordeal** [ɔː'diːl] *fig.* испыта́ние
**order** ['ɔːdə] **1.** поря́док; (*command*) прика́з; *comm.* зака́з; ***take* (*holy*) ~s** принима́ть духо́вный сан; ***in* ~ *to*** что́бы; ***in* ~ *that*** с тем, что́бы; ***make to* ~** де́лать на зака́з; ***out of* ~** неиспра́вный; **2.** прика́зывать [-за́ть]; *comm.* зака́зывать [за́ть]; **~ly** [~lɪ] (*well arranged, tidy*) аккура́тный, дисциплини́рованный
**ordinary** ['ɔːdənrɪ] обыкнове́нный; зауря́дный; ***out of the* ~** необы́чный
**ore** ['ɔː] руда́
**organ** ['ɔːgən] о́рган; *mus.* орга́н; **~ic** [ɔː'gænɪk] (***~ally***) органи́ческий; *fig.* органи́чный
**organ|ization** [ɔːgənaɪ'zeɪʃn] организа́ция; **~ize** ['ɔːgənaɪz] организова́ть *(im)pf.*; **~izer** [~ə] организа́тор
**orgy** ['ɔːdʒɪ] о́ргия
**orient** ['ɔːrɪənt] **1.**: ***the* ~** Восто́к, восто́чные стра́ны *f/pl.*; **2.** ориенти́ровать *(im)pf.*; **~al** [ɔːrɪ'entl] □ во-

сто́чный, азиа́тский; **~ate** ['ɔːrɪənteɪt] ориенти́ровать (*im*)*pf.*
**orifice** ['ɒrɪfɪs] (*opening*) отве́рстие
**origin** ['ɒrɪdʒɪn] (*source*) исто́чник; (*derivation*) происхожде́ние; (*beginning*) нача́ло
**original** [ə'rɪdʒənl] **1.** □ (*first*) первонача́льный; *ideas, etc.* оригина́льный; (*not a copy*) по́длинный; **2.** оригина́л, по́длинник; (*eccentric*) чуда́к; ***in the ~*** в оригина́ле; **~ity** [ərɪdʒə'nælətɪ] оригина́льность *f*
**originat|e** [ə'rɪdʒɪneɪt] *v/t.* дава́ть нача́ло (Д), порожда́ть [породить]; *v/i.* происходи́ть [-изойти́] (***from*** от Р); **~or** [~ə] инициа́тор
**ornament** **1.** ['ɔːnəmənt] украше́ние (*a. fig.*), орна́мент; **2.** [~ment] украша́ть [укра́сить]; **~al** [ɔːnə'mentl] □ декорати́вный
**ornate** [ɔː'neɪt] □ бога́то укра́шенный; *style* витиева́тый
**orphan** ['ɔːfn] **1.** сирота́ *m/f.*; **2.** осироте́вший (*a.* ***~ed***); **~age** ['ɔːfənɪdʒ] сиро́тский дом; прию́т для сиро́т
**orthodox** ['ɔːθədɒks] □ ортодокса́льный; *eccl.* правосла́вный
**oscillate** ['ɒsɪleɪt] *swing* кача́ться; (*fluctuate*), *a. fig.* колеба́ться
**ostensible** [ɒ'stensəbl] □ слу́жащий предло́гом; мни́мый; очеви́дный
**ostentatious** [ɒsten'teɪʃəs] □ показно́й
**ostrich** ['ɒstrɪtʃ] *zo.* стра́ус
**other** ['ʌðə] друго́й; ино́й; ***the ~ day*** на днях; ***the ~ morning*** неда́вно у́тром; ***every ~ day*** че́рез день; ***in ~ words*** други́ми слова́ми; **~wise** [~waɪz] ина́че; и́ли же
**otter** ['ɒtə] *zo.* вы́дра
**ought** [ɔːt]: ***I ~ to*** мне сле́довало бы; ***you ~ to have done it*** вам сле́довало э́то сде́лать
**ounce** [aʊns] у́нция
**our** ['aʊə] *poss. adj.*; **~s** ['auəz] *pron. & pred. adj.* наш, на́ша, на́ше; на́ши *pl.*; **~selves** [aʊə'selvz] *pron.* **1.** *refl.* себя́, -ся, -сь; **2.** *for emphasis* (мы) са́ми
**oust** [aʊst] выгоня́ть [вы́гнать], вытесня́ть [вы́теснить]
**out** [aʊt] *adv.* нару́жу; вон; в, на; *often translated by the prefix* вы-; ***take ~*** вынима́ть [вы́нуть]; ***have it ~ with s.o.*** объясни́ться *pf.* с ке́м-л.; ***~ and ~*** соверше́нно; ***a/the way ~*** вы́ход; ***~ size*** разме́р бо́льше норма́льного; *prp.* ***~ of*** из (Р); вне (Р); из-за (Р)
**out|...** [aʊt] пере...; вы...; рас...; про...; воз..., вз...; из...; **~balance** [~'bæləns] переве́шивать [-ве́сить]; **~break** ['aʊtbreɪk] *of anger, etc.* вспы́шка; *of war, etc.* (внеза́пное) нача́ло; **~building** ['aʊtbɪldɪŋ] надво́рное строе́ние; **~burst** [~bɜːst] взрыв, вспы́шка; **~cast** [~kɑːst] отве́рженный; **~come** [~kʌm] результа́т; **~cry** [~kraɪ] кри́ки, шум; проте́ст; **~do** [aʊt'duː] [*irr.* (***do***)] превосходи́ть [-взойти́]; **~door** ['aʊtdɔː] *adj.* (находя́щийся) на откры́том во́здухе; *clothes* ве́рхний; **~doors** [~'dɔːz] *adv.* на откры́том во́здухе; ***it's cold ~*** на у́лице хо́лодно
**outer** ['aʊtə] вне́шний, нару́жный; **~most** [~məʊst] кра́йний; са́мый да́льний от це́нтра
**out|fit** ['aʊtfɪt] (*equipment*) снаряже́ние; (*clothes*) костю́м; **~going** [~gəʊɪŋ] уходя́щий; *letters, etc.* исходя́щий; *person* общи́тельный; ужи́вчивый; **~grow** [aut'grəʊ] [*irr.* (***grow***)] *clothes* выраста́ть [вы́расти] из (Р); **~house** [~haʊs] надво́рное строе́ние; *Am.* убо́рная во дворе́
**outing** ['aʊtɪŋ] (за́городная) прогу́лка, экску́рсия
**out|last** [aʊt'lɑːst] *mst. of person* пережи́(ва́)ть; *of things* служи́ть (носи́ться) до́льше, чем...; **~law** ['aʊtlɔː] **1.** челове́к вне зако́на; **2.** объявля́ть вне зако́на; **~lay** [~leɪ] расхо́ды *m/pl.*; **~let** [~let] выпускно́е отве́рстие; вы́ход; **~line** [~laɪn] **1.** (*a. pl.*) очерта́ние, ко́нтур; **2.** де́лать набро́сок (Р); **~live** [aʊt'lɪv] пережи́(ва́)ть; **~look** ['aʊtlʊk] вид, перспекти́ва; то́чка зре́ния, взгляд; **~lying** [~laɪŋ] отдалённый; **~number** [aʊt'nʌmbə] превосходи́ть чи́сленностью; **~patient** амбулато́рный больно́й; **♀patient De-**

**partment** поликли́ника при больни́це; **~pouring** ['~pɔːrɪŋ] *mst. pl.* излия́ние (чувств); **~put** [~pʊt] (*production*) вы́пуск; проду́кция; (*productivity*) производи́тельность *f*

**outrage** ['aʊtreɪdʒ] **1.** наруше́ние прили́чий; безобра́зие; возмути́тельное явле́ние; **2.** оскорбля́ть [-би́ть] возмуща́ть [-ути́ть]; изнаси́ловать; **~ous** [aʊt'reɪdʒəs] □ возмути́тельный; безобра́зный; сканда́льный

**out|right** ['aʊtraɪt] откры́то, пря́мо, реши́тельно; **~run** [aʊt'rʌn] [*irr.* (***run***)] перегоня́ть [-гна́ть], опережа́ть [-реди́ть]; **~set** ['aʊtset] нача́ло; ***from the ~*** с са́мого нача́ла; **~shine** [aʊt'ʃaɪn] [*irr.* (***shine***)] затмева́ть [-ми́ть]; **~side** ['aʊtsaɪd] нару́жная сторона́; (*surface*) пове́рхность *f*; вне́шний вид; ***at the ~*** са́мое бо́льшее; **2.** ['aʊtsaɪd] нару́жный, вне́шний; кра́йний; **3.** *adv.* нару́жу; снару́жи; на (откры́том) во́здухе; **4.** *prp.* вне (Р); **~sider** [aʊt'saɪdə] посторо́нний (челове́к); **~skirts** ['aʊtskɜːts] *pl.* окра́ина; **~spoken** [aʊt'spəʊkən] □ откровéнный; **~standing** [aʊt'stændɪŋ] *fig.* выдаю́щийся; *bill* неопла́ченный; **~stretch** [aʊt'stretʃ] протя́гивать [-тяну́ть]; **~strip** [~'strɪp] опережа́ть [-реди́ть]; (*surpass*) превосходи́ть [-взойти́]

**outward** ['aʊtwəd] **1.** вне́шний, нару́жный; ***during the ~ journey*** (***to***) **…** во вре́мя пое́здки туда́ (в В); **2.** *adv.* (*mst.* **~s** [~z]) нару́жу; за преде́лы

**outweigh** [aʊt'weɪ] превосходи́ть ве́сом; переве́шивать [переве́сить]

**oven** ['ʌvn] *in bakery, industry, etc.* печь *f*; *in stove* духо́вка

**over** ['əʊvə] **1.** *adv. usually translated by verbal prefixes*; пере…; вы…; про…; сно́ва; вдоба́вок; сли́шком; ***~ and above*** в добавле́ние, к тому́же; (***all***) ***~ again*** сно́ва, ещё раз; ***~ and ~*** (***again***) сно́ва и сно́ва; ***read ~*** перечи́тывать [-чита́ть] ***it's all ~*** всё ко́нчено; **2.** *prp.* над (Т); по (Д); за (В); свы́ше (Р); сверх (Р) че́рез (В); о(б) (П); ***all ~ the town*** по всему́ го́роду

**over|…** ['əʊvə] *pref.* сверх…; над…; пере…; чрезме́рно; **~act** [əʊvə'ækt] переи́грывать [-гра́ть]; **~all** ['əʊvərɔːl] *working clothes* хала́т; **~s** комбинезо́н, *coll.* спецо́вка; **~awe** [əʊvər'ɔː] внуша́ть [-ши́ть] благогове́йный стра́х; **~balance** [əʊvə'bæləns] теря́ть равнове́сие; *fig.* переве́шивать [-ве́сить]; **~bearing** [əʊvə'beərɪŋ] □ вла́стный; **~board** ['əʊvəbɔːd] *naut.* за́ борт, за бо́ртом; **~cast** ['əʊvəkaːst] покры́тый облака́ми; па́смурный; **~charge** [əʊvə'tʃaːdʒ] брать [взять] сли́шком мно́го (***for*** за В); **~coat** ['əʊvəkəʊt] пальто́ *n indecl.*; **~come** [əʊvə'kʌm] [*irr.*(***come***)] (*surmount*) преодоле́(-ва́)ть, (*defeat*) побежда́ть [-еди́ть]; **~crowd** [əʊvə'kraʊd] переполня́ть [-по́лнить]; **~do** [əʊvə'duː] [*irr.* (***do***)] *meat, etc.* пережа́ри(ва)ть; (*go too far*) переусе́рдствовать (*im*)*pf.*; **~draw** [əʊvə'drɔː] [*irr.* (***draw***)]: ***~ one's account*** превы́сить *pf.* креди́т в ба́нке; **~dress** [əʊvə'dres] оде́(ва́)ться; сли́шком наря́дно; **~due** [əʊvə'djuː] *payment* просро́ченный; ***the bus is 5 minutes ~*** авто́бус опа́здывает на пять мину́т; **~eat** [əʊvər'iːt] перееда́ть [-е́сть]; **~flow 1.** [əʊvə'fləʊ] [*irr.* (***flow***)] *v/t.* затопля́ть [-пи́ть]; *v/i.* перели́(-ва́)ться; **2.** ['əʊvəfləʊ] наводне́ние; разли́в; **~grow** [əʊvə'grəʊ] [*irr.* (***grow***)] *with weeds* зараста́ть [-ти́]; **~hang** [əʊvə'hæŋ] [*irr.* (***hang***)] *v/i.* нависа́ть [-и́снуть]; **~haul** [əʊvə'hɔːl] (*repair*) (капита́льно) [от]ремонти́ровать; **~head 1.** [əʊvə'hed] *adv.* над голово́й, наверху́; **2.** ['əʊvəhed] *adj.* ве́рхний; **3. ~s** ['əʊvəhedz] *pl. comm* накладны́е расхо́ды *m/pl.*; **~hear** [əʊvə'hɪə] [*irr.* (***hear***)] подслу́ш(ив)ать; нечá янно услы́шать; **~lap** [əʊvə'læp] *v/i.* заходи́ть оди́н за друго́й; *fig.* совпада́ть; **~lay** [əʊvə'leɪ] [*irr.* (***lay***)] *tech.* покры́(-ва́)ть; **~load** [əʊvə'ləʊd] перегружа́ть [-узи́ть]; **~look** [əʊvə'lʊk] *of windows, etc.* выходи́ть на (В); (*not notice*) пропуска́ть [-сти́ть]; упуска́ть [-сти́ть]; **~pay** [əʊvə'peɪ] [*irr.* (***pay***)] перепла́чивать [-лати́ть]; **~power** [əʊvə'paʊə]

O

переси́ли(ва)ть; **~rate** ['əʊvə-'reɪt] переоце́нивать [-ни́ть]; **~reach** [əʊvə-'riːtʃ] перехитри́ть *pf.*; **~ o.s.** брать сли́шком мно́го на себя́; **~ride** [əʊvə-'raɪd] [*irr.* (**ride**)] *fig.* отверга́ть [-е́ргнуть]; **~run** [əʊvə'rʌn] [*irr.* (**run**)] перелива́ться че́рез край; **~seas** [əʊvə-'siːz] **1.** иностра́нный, заграни́чный; **2.** за рубежо́м, за грани́цей; **~seer** ['əʊvəsɪə] надсмо́трщик; **~shadow** [əʊvə'ʃædəʊ] *fig.* затмева́ть [-ми́ть]; **~sight** [~saɪt] недосмо́тр; **~sleep** [əʊvə'sliːp] [*irr.* (**sleep**)] прос(ы)па́ть; **~state** [əʊvə'steɪt] преувели́чи(ва)ть; **~statement** преувеличе́ние; **~strain** [əʊvə'streɪn] **1.** переутомле́ние; **2.** переутомля́ть [-ми́ть]; **~take** [əʊvə'teɪk] [*irr.* (**take**)] обгоня́ть [обогна́ть]; *of events* засти́гнуть *pf.* врасплóх; **~tax** [əʊvə'tæks] облага́ть чрезме́рным нало́гом; *fig. strength, etc.* перенапряга́ть [-ря́чь]; **don't ~ my patience** не испы́тывай моё терпе́ние; **~throw** [əʊvə'θrəʊ] [*irr.* (**throw**)] сверга́ть [све́ргнуть]; **~time** ['əʊvətaɪm] **1.** сверхуро́чная рабо́та; **2.** *adv.* сверхуро́чно

**overture** ['əʊvətjʊə] *mus.* увертю́ра

**over|turn** [əʊvə'tɜːn] опроки́дывать [-и́нуть]; **~whelm** [əʊvə'welm] (*crush*) подавля́ть [-ви́ть]; переси́ли(ва)ть; **~ed with grief** уби́тый го́рем; **~work** ['əʊvəwəːk] **1.** переутомле́ние; **2.** [əʊvə'wɜːk] переутомля́ть(ся) [-ми́ть(ся)]; **~wrought** [əʊvə'rɔːt] в состоя́нии кра́йнего возбужде́ния; *nerves* перенапряжённый

**owe** [əʊ] быть до́лжным (Д/В); быть обя́занным (Д/Т)

**owing** ['əʊɪŋ] до́лжный; неупла́ченный; **~ to** *prp.* благодаря́ (Д)

**owl** [aʊl] сова́

**own** [əʊn] **1.** свой, со́бственный; родно́й; **2. my ~** моя́ со́бственность *f*; **a house of one's ~** со́бственный дом; **hold one's ~** не сдава́ть свои́ пози́ции; **3.** владе́ть (Т); (*admit, confess*) призна(ва́)ть (В); **~ to** призна́(ва́)ться в (П)

**owner** ['əʊnə] владе́лец *m*, -лица *f*; хозя́ин; **~ship** [~ʃɪp] со́бственность *f*

**ox** [ɒks], *pl.* **oxen** ['ɒksn] вол, бык

**oxid|e** ['ɒksaɪd] о́кись *f*; **~ize** ['ɒksɪdaɪz] окисля́ть(ся) [-ли́ть(ся)]

**oxygen** ['ɒksɪdʒən] кислоро́д

**oyster** ['ɔɪstə] у́стрица

P

# P

**pace** [peɪs] **1.** (*step*) шаг; (*speed*) темп, ско́рость *f*; **2.** *v/t.* ме́рить шага́ми; *v/i.* [за]шага́ть; *room* ходи́ть взад и вперёд; **set the ~** задава́ть темп

**pacify** ['pæsɪfaɪ] (*calm*) умиротворя́ть [-ри́ть]; *rebellion* усмиря́ть [-ри́ть]

**pack** [pæk] **1.** *of cigarettes, etc.*, па́чка; *of papers* ки́па; *cards* коло́да; *of dogs* сво́ра; *of wolves* ста́я; **2.** *v/t.* (*often* **~ up**) упако́вывать [-кова́ть]; укла́дываться [уложи́ться]; (*fill*) заполня́ть [запо́лнить]; наби́(ва́)ть; (*a.* **~ off**) выпрова́живать [вы́проводить]; отгружа́ть [отгрузи́ть]; **~age** ['pækɪdʒ] (*parcel*) паке́т, свёрток, упако́вка; **~ tour** туристи́ческая пое́здка, ко́мплексное турне́; **~er** ['pækə] упако́вщик *m*, -ица *f*; **~et** ['pækɪt] паке́т; па́чка; **small ~** *mail* бандеро́ль *f*

**pact** [pækt] пакт, догово́р

**pad** [pæd] **1.** мя́гкая прокла́дка; (*writing ~*) блокно́т; **2.** подби́(ва́)ть, наби́(ва́)ть (ва́той *и т. д.*); *fig.* **~ out** перегружа́ть [-узи́ть]

**paddle** ['pædl] **1.** гребо́к; байда́рочное весло́; **2.** грести́; плыть на байда́рке

**paddling pool** ['pædlɪŋ] *coll.* лягуша́тник

**paddock** ['pædək] вы́гон

**padlock** ['pædlɒk] вися́чий замо́к

**pagan** ['peɪgən] **1.** язы́чник; **2.** язы́ческий

**page** [peɪdʒ] страни́ца
**pageant** ['pædʒənt] карнава́льное (пра́здничное) ше́ствие; пы́шное зре́лище
**paid** [peɪd] *pt. и pt. p. om* ***pay***
**pail** [peɪl] ведро́
**pain** [peɪn] **1.** боль *f*; ***~s*** *pl.* (*often sg.*) страда́ния *n/pl.*; ***on ~ of*** под стра́хом (P); ***be in ~*** испы́тывать боль; ***spare no ~s*** приложи́ть все уси́лия; ***take ~s*** [по]стара́ться; **2.** причиня́ть боль (Д); **~ful** ['peɪnfl] □ боле́зненный; мучи́тельный; **~less** ['~lɪs] □ безболе́зненный; **~staking** ['peɪnzteɪkɪŋ] усе́рдный, стара́тельный
**paint** [peɪnt] **1.** кра́ска; "***Wet*** ~" Осторо́жно, окра́шено; **2.** [по]кра́сить; **~brush** кисть *f*; **~er** ['peɪntə] *art* худо́жник; (*decorator*) маля́р; **~ing** ['peɪntɪŋ] (*art or occupation*) жи́вопись *f*; (*work of art*) карти́на
**pair** [peə] **1.** па́ра; ***a ~ of scissors*** но́жницы *f/pl.*; **2.** (*~ off*) соединя́ть(ся) по двое́; раздели́ть *pf.* на па́ры; *biol.* спа́ривать(ся)
**pal** [pæl] прия́тель(ница *f*) *m*; *coll.* ко́реш
**palace** ['pælɪs] дворе́ц
**palate** ['pælət] *anat.* нёбо; *fig.* вкус
**pale** [peɪl] **1.** □ бле́дный; ***~ ale*** све́тлое пи́во; **2.** [по]бледне́ть
**paleness** ['peɪlnɪs] бле́дность *f*
**palette** ['pælət] пали́тра
**pall** [pɔːl] *v/i.* приеда́ться [-е́сться]
**palliate** ['pælɪeɪt] *pain* облегча́ть [-чи́ть]
**pall|id** ['pælɪd] □ бле́дный; **~or** [~lə] бле́дность *f*
**palm**[1] [pɑːm] **1.** *of hand* ладо́нь *f*; **2.** ***~ off on s.b.*** *coll.* подсо́вывать [подсу́нуть]; *fig. pej.* всу́чивать [-чи́ть] (Д)
**palm**[2] [~], **~tree** па́льма; ~ **Sunday** Ве́рбное воскресе́нье
**palpable** ['pælpəbl] □ осяза́емый; ощути́мый; *fig.* очеви́дный, я́вный
**palpitat|e** ['pælpɪteɪt] *with fear, etc.* трепета́ть; *of heart* си́льно би́ться; **~ion** [pælpɪ'teɪʃn] сердцебие́ние
**paltry** ['pɔːltrɪ] □ пустяко́вый, ничто́жный
**pamper** ['pæmpə] [из]ба́ловать
**pamphlet** ['pæmflɪt] памфле́т
**pan** [pæn] (*saucepan*) кастрю́ля; (*frying ~*) сковорода́, (-ро́дка)
**pan...** [~] *pref.* пан...; обще...
**panacea** [pænə'sɪə] панаце́я
**pancake** ['pænkeɪk] блин; *without yeast* бли́нчик; *small and thick* ола́дья
**pandemonium** [pændɪ'məʊnɪəm] смяте́ние; *fig.* столпотворе́ние
**pander** ['pændə] потво́рствовать (***to*** Д)
**pane** [peɪn] (око́нное) стекло́
**panel** ['pænl] **1.** *arch.* пане́ль *f*; *mot.* прибо́рная доска́; **2.** обшива́ть пане́лями
**pang** [pæŋ] внеза́пная о́страя боль *f*; ***~s of conscience*** угрызе́ния со́вести
**panic** ['pænɪk] **1.** пани́ческий; **2.** па́ника; **~-stricken** [~strɪkən] охва́ченный па́никой
**pansy** ['pænzɪ] *bot.* аню́тины гла́зки *m/pl.*
**pant** [pænt] задыха́ться; тяжело́ дыша́ть; вздыха́ть; стра́стно жела́ть (***for, after*** P)
**panties** ['pæntɪz] (***a pair of ~***) *women's* тру́сики; *children's* штани́шки
**pantry** ['pæntrɪ] кладова́я
**pants** [pænts] *pl.* (***a pair of ~***) трусы́; *Am.* брю́ки *m/pl.*
**papal** ['peɪpəl] □ па́пский
**paper** ['peɪpə] **1.** бума́га; (*news~*) газе́та; (*wall~*) обо́и *m/pl.*; нау́чный докла́д; докуме́нт; **2.** окле́ивать [окле́ить] обо́ями; **~back** кни́га в мя́гком переплёте; **~ bag** кулёк; **~clip** скре́пка; **~work** канцеля́рская рабо́та
**paprika** ['pæprɪkə] кра́сный пе́рец
**par** [pɑː] ра́венство; (*recognized or face value*) номина́льная сто́имость *f*; ***at~*** по номина́лу; ***be on a ~ with*** быть наравне́, на одно́м у́ровне с (Т)
**parable** ['pærəbl] при́тча
**parachut|e** ['pærəʃuːt] парашю́т; **~ist** [~ɪst] парашюти́ст
**parade** [pə'reɪd] **1.** *mil.* пара́д; ***make a ~ of*** выставля́ть напока́з; **2.** щеголя́ть
**paradise** ['pærədaɪs] рай
**paradox** ['pærədɒks] парадо́кс; **~ical**

P

[~ɪkl] парадокса́льный
**paraffin** ['pærəfɪn] *chiefly Brt.* кероси́н; (~ *wax*) парафи́н
**paragon** ['pærəgən] образе́ц; ***~ of virtue*** образе́ц доброде́тели
**paragraph** ['pærəgrɑːf] абза́ц; газе́тная заме́тка
**parallel** ['pærəlel] **1.** паралле́льный; **2.** паралле́ль *f* (*a. fig.*); *geogr.* паралле́ль *f*; ***without ~*** несравни́мый; **3.** быть паралле́льным с (Т), (*compare*) проводи́ть [-вести́] паралле́ль ме́жду; сра́внивать [-ни́ть]
**paraly|se** *Am.* **~ze** ['pærəlaɪz] парализова́ть (*im*)*pf.* (*a. fig.*); **~sis** [pə'ræləsɪs] *med.* парали́ч
**paramount** ['pærəmaʊnt]: ***of ~ importance*** первостепе́нной ва́жности
**parapet** ['pærəpɪt] парапе́т
**paraphernalia** [pærəfə'neɪlɪə] *pl.* ли́чные ве́щи *f/pl.*, принадле́жности
**parasite** ['pærəsaɪt] парази́т (*a. fig.*)
**paratroops** ['pærətruːps] *pl.* парашю́тно-деса́нтные войска́ *n/pl.*
**parcel** ['pɑːsl] **1.** паке́т; *mail* посы́лка; **2.** (*mst.* ***~ out***) *land* дели́ть на уча́стки; (*mst.* ***~ up***) упако́вывать [-ова́ть]
**parch** [pɑːtʃ] иссуша́ть [-ши́ть]; *of sun* опаля́ть [-ли́ть]; ***my throat is ~ed*** у меня́ пересо́хло в го́рле
**parchment** [pɑːtʃmənt] перга́мент
**pardon** ['pɑːdn] **1.** проще́ние; *law* поми́лование; **2.** проща́ть [прости́ть]; поми́ловать *pf.*; **~able** [~əbl] □ прости́тельный
**pare** [peə] (*peel*) [по]чи́стить; (*cut*) обреза́ть [-ре́зать]; *fig.* [о-, по-] стри́чь; *fig. expenses* уре́з(ыв)ать
**parent** ['peərənt] *mst. pl.* роди́тели *m/pl.*; **~age** [~ɪdʒ] происхожде́ние; **~al** [pə'rentl] □ роди́тельский
**parenthe|sis** [pə'renθəsɪs], *pl.* **~ses** [~siːz] вво́дное сло́во *or* предложе́ние; *pl. typ.* (кру́глые) ско́бки *f/pl.*
**paring** ['peərɪŋ] кожура́, ко́рка, шелуха́; ***~s*** *pl.* обре́зки *m/pl.*; *of vegetables, fruit* очи́стки *f/pl.*
**parish** ['pærɪʃ] **1.** церко́вный прихо́д; **2.** прихо́дский; **~ioners** [pə'rɪʃənəz] прихожа́не *pl.*
**parity** ['pærətɪ] ра́венство; равноце́нность *f*; *fin.* парите́т
**park** [pɑːk] **1.** (*public garden*) парк; *for vehicles* стоя́нка; **2.** *mot.* паркова́ть, ста́вить на стоя́нку; **~ing** ['pɑːkɪŋ] автостоя́нка; ***No ~*** стоя́нка запрещена́
**parlance** ['pɑːləns]: ***in common ~*** в обихо́дной ре́чи
**parliament** ['pɑːləmənt] парла́мент; **~ary** [pɑːlə'mentərɪ] парла́ментский
**parlo(u)r** ['pɑːlə] *in house* гости́ная; *Am., for services* ателье́ *n indecl.*; ***~ games*** ко́мнатные и́гры
**parody** ['pærədɪ] паро́дия
**parole** [pə'rəʊl] че́стное сло́во; усло́вно-досро́чное освобожде́ние
**parquet** ['pɑːkeɪ] парке́т
**parrot** ['pærət] **1.** попуга́й; **2.** повторя́ть как попуга́й
**parry** ['pærɪ] (*ward off*) отража́ть [-рази́ть], пари́ровать (*a. fig.*)
**parsimonious** [pɑːsɪ'məʊnɪəs] □ скупо́й
**parsley** ['pɑːslɪ] петру́шка
**parsnip** ['pɑːsnɪp] пастерна́к
**parson** ['pɑːsn] приходско́й свяще́нник, па́стор
**part** [pɑːt] **1.** часть *f*, до́ля; уча́стие; *thea. a. fig.* роль *f*; ме́стность *f*, край; *mus.* па́ртия; ***in these ~s*** в э́тих края́х; ***take in good ~*** не оби́деться *pf.*, приня́ть *pf.* споко́йно; ***take ~*** принима́ть [-ня́ть] уча́стие; ***for my*** (***own***) ***~*** с мое́й стороны́; ***in ~*** части́чно; ***on the ~ of*** со стороны́ (Р); **2.** *adv.* ча́стью, отча́сти; **3.** *v/t.* разделя́ть [-ли́ть]; ***~ the hair*** де́лать пробо́р; *v/i.* разлуча́ться [-чи́ться], расст(ав)а́ться (***with, from*** с Т)
**partial** ['pɑːʃl] □ части́чный; (*not indifferent*) пристра́стный; неравноду́шный (***to*** к Д); ***I'm ~ to peaches*** я люблю́ пе́рсики
**particip|ant** [pɑː'tɪsɪpənt] уча́стник *m*, -ица *f*; **~ate** [~peɪt] уча́ствовать (***in*** в П); **~ation** [~'peɪʃn] уча́стие
**particle** ['pɑːtɪkl] части́ца
**particular** [pə'tɪkjʊlə] **1.** □ осо́бенный; осо́бый; (*hard to satisfy*) разбо́рчивый; ***in this ~ case*** в да́нном

P

слу́чае; ***for no ~ reason*** без осо́бой причи́ны; **2.** подро́бность *f*, дета́ль *f*; ***in ~*** в осо́бенности; **~ly** [pə'tıkjʊləlı] осо́бенно

**parting** ['pɑːtıŋ] **1.** (*separation*) разлу́ка; (*farewell*) проща́ние; *in hair* пробо́р; **2.** проща́льный

**partisan** [pɑːtı'zæn] **1.** (*adherent*) сторо́нник *m*, -ица *f*; *mil.* партиза́н; **2.** партиза́нский

**partition** [pɑː'tıʃn] **1.** (*division*) разде́л; (*separating structure*) перегоро́дка; **2.**: **~ *off*** отгора́живать [-ради́ть]

**partly** ['pɑːtlı] ча́стью, отча́сти

**partner** ['pɑːtnə] **1.** *in crime* соуча́стник *m*, -ица *f*; *comm.* компаньо́н, партнёр; *sport*, *etc.* партнёр; **2.** быть партнёром; **~ship** [~ʃıp] парнёрство; (*marriage*) сою́з, това́рищество, компа́ния

**part-owner** совладе́лец

**partridge** ['pɑːtrıdʒ] куропа́тка

**part-time** непо́лный рабо́чий день; *attr.* не по́лностью за́нятый; ***~ worker*** рабо́чий, за́нятый непо́лный рабо́чий день

**party** ['pɑːtı] *pol.* па́ртия; (*team*) отря́д; (*group*) гру́ппа, компа́ния, *law* сторона́; уча́стник (***to*** в П); (*social gathering*) вечери́нка

**pass** ['pɑːs] **1.** прохо́д; *mountain* переве́л; (*permit*) про́пуск; беспла́тный биле́т; *univ.* посре́дственная сда́ча экза́мена; *cards*, *sport* пас; **2.** *v/i.* проходи́ть [пройти́]; (*drive by*) проезжа́ть [-е́хать]; переходи́ть (***from … to …*** из (Р) … в (В) …); *cards* пасова́ть; ***~ as, for*** счита́ться (Т), слыть (Т); ***~ away*** умира́ть [умере́ть]; ***~ by*** проходи́ть ми́мо; ***~ into*** переходи́ть [перейти́] в (В); ***~ off*** *of pain*, *etc.* проходи́ть [пройти́]; ***~ on*** идти́ да́льше; ***~ out*** (*faint*) [по]теря́ть созна́ние; **3.** *v/t.* проходи́ть [пройти́]; проезжа́ть [-е́хать]; минова́ть (*im*)*pf.*; *exam* сдать *pf.*; обгоня́ть [обогна́ть], опережа́ть [-реди́ть]; переправля́ть(ся) [-а́вить(ся)] че́рез (В); (*a.* ***~ on***) перед(ав)а́ть; *sentence* выноси́ть [вы́нести]; *time* проводи́ть [-вести́]; *law* принима́ть [-ня́ть]; **~able** ['pɑːsəbl] *road*, *etc.* проходи́мый; (*tolerable*) сно́сный

**passage** ['pæsıdʒ] прохо́д; *of time* тече́ние; переéзд, перепра́ва; *ae.* перелёт; *crossing by ship* пла́вание, рейс; (*corridor*) коридо́р; *from book* отры́вок

**passenger** ['pæsındʒə] пассажи́р; **~ train** пассажи́рский по́езд

**passer-by** [pɑːsə'baı] прохо́жий

**passion** ['pæʃn] *strong emotion*, *desire* страсть *f*; (*anger*) гнев; ***♀ Week*** Страстна́я неде́ля; **~ate** [~ıt] □ стра́стный, пы́лкий

**passive** ['pæsıv] □ пасси́вный; *gr.* ***the ~ voice*** страда́тельный зало́г

**passport** ['pɑːspɔːt] па́спорт

**password** ['pɑːswɜːd] паро́ль *m*

**past** [pɑːst] **1.** *adj.* про́шлый; мину́вший; ***for some time ~*** за после́днее вре́мя; **2.** *adv.* ми́мо; **3.** *prp.* за (Т); по́сле (Р); ми́мо (Р); свы́ше (Р); ***half ~ two*** полови́на тре́тьего; ***~ endurance*** нестерпи́мый; ***~ hope*** безнадёжный; **4.** про́шлое

**paste** [peıst] **1.** (*glue*) клей; **2.** кле́ить, прикле́и(ва)ть

**pastel** ['pæstl] (*crayon*) пасте́ль *f*

**pasteurize** ['pæstəraız] пастеризова́ть (*im*)*pf.*

**pastime** ['pɑːstaım] времяпрепровожде́ние

**pastor** ['pɑːstə] па́стор *m*; **~al** [~rəl] *of shepherds or country life* пастора́льный; *of clergy* па́сторский

**pastry** ['peıstrı] (*dough*) те́сто; (*tart*) пиро́жное; **~ cook** конди́тер

**pasture** ['pɑːstʃə] **1.** па́стбище; вы́гон; **2.** пасти́(сь)

**pat** [pæt] **1.** похло́пывание; **2.** *on back* похло́п(ыв)ать; [по]гла́дить; **3.** кста́ти; как раз подходя́щий; ***a ~ answer*** гото́вый отве́т (*a. fig.* шабло́нный)

**patch** [pætʃ] **1.** *on clothes* запла́та; *of colo(u)r* пятно́; клочо́к земли́; **2.** [за]лата́ть; [по]чини́ть; ***~ up a quarrel*** ула́живать [-а́дить] ссо́ру

**patent** ['peıtnt] **1.** (*obvious*) я́вный; запатенто́ванный; ***~ leather*** лакиро́ванная ко́жа; **2.** (*a.* **letters ~** *pl.*) пате́нт; **3.**

P

[за]патентова́ть; **~ee** [peɪtn'tiː] владе́лец пате́нта
**patern|al** [pə'tɜːnl] □ отцо́вский; (*fatherly*) оте́ческий; **~ity** [~nətɪ] отцо́вство
**path** [pɑːθ], *pl.* **~s** [pɑːðz] тропи́нка, доро́жка
**pathetic** [pə'θetɪk] жа́лкий; печа́льный; тро́гательный
**patien|ce** ['peɪʃns] терпе́ние; **~t** [~nt] **1.** □ терпели́вый; **2.** больно́й *m*, -на́я *f*, пацие́нт *m*, -тка *f*
**patriot** ['pætrɪət] патрио́т; **~ism** ['~ɪzəm] патриоти́зм
**patrol** [pə'trəʊl] *mil.* **1.** патру́ль *m*; **2.** патрули́ровать
**patron** ['peɪtrən] (*supporter, sponsor*) покрови́тель *m*; (*customer*) клие́нт, покупа́тель *m*; **~age** ['pætrənɪdʒ] *support* покрови́тельство; **~ize** [~naɪz] покрови́тельствовать; (*be condescending*) снисходи́тельно относи́ться к (Д)
**patter** ['pætə] говори́ть скороговóркой; [про]бормота́ть; *of rain* бараба́нить; *of feet* топота́ть
**pattern** ['pætn] **1.** образе́ц; (*way*) о́браз; (*design*) узо́р; **2.** де́лать по образцу́ (***on*** P)
**paunch** [pɔːntʃ] брюшко́
**pauper** ['pɔːpə] ни́щий *m*, -щая *f*
**pause** [pɔːz] **1.** па́уза, переры́в; **2.** [с]де́лать па́узу
**pave** [peɪv] [вы́]мости́ть; ***~ the way for*** *fig.* прокла́дывать [проложи́ть] путь; **~ment** ['peɪvmənt] тротуа́р
**pavilion** [pə'vɪlɪən] павильо́н
**paw** [pɔː] **1.** ла́па (*coll a.* = ***hand***); **2.** тро́гать ла́пой
**pawn**[1] [pɔːn] *chess* пе́шка
**pawn**[2] [~] **1.** зало́г, закла́д; ***in ~*** в закла́де; **2.** закла́дывать [заложи́ть]; **~broker** владе́лец ломба́рда; ростовщи́к; **~shop** ломба́рд
**pay** [peɪ] **1.** (о)пла́та, упла́та; *wages* зарпла́та; **2.** [*irr.*] *v/t.* [за]плати́ть; *bill, etc.* опла́чивать [оплати́ть]; ***~ a visit*** посеща́ть [-ети́ть], (*official*) наноси́ть [-нести́] визи́т; ***~ attention to*** обраща́ть внима́ние на (В); ***~ down*** плати́ть нали́чными; *v/i.* (*be profitable*) окупа́ться [-пи́ться] (*a. fig.*); ***~ for*** [у-, за]плати́ть за (В), опла́чивать; *fig.* [по]плати́ться за (В); **~able** ['peɪəbl] опла́чиваемый подлежа́щий упла́те; **~day** день зарпла́ты; *coll.* получка; **~ing** ['peɪɪŋ] вы́годный; **~ment** ['~mənt] упла́та, опла́та, платёж
**pea** [piː] *bot.* горо́х; горо́шина; **~s** *pl.* горо́х; *attr.* горо́ховый
**peace** [piːs] мир; споко́йствие; **~able** ['piːsəbl] □ миролюби́вый, ми́рный; **~ful** ['~fl] □ ми́рный, споко́йный; **~maker** миротво́рец
**peach** [piːtʃ] пе́рсик
**peacock** ['piːkɒk] павли́н
**peak** [piːk] *of mountain* верши́на (*a. fig.*); *of cap* козырёк; ***~ of summer*** разга́р ле́та; *attr.* максима́льный; вы́сший
**peal** [piːl] **1.** звон колоколо́в; *of thunder* раска́т; ***~ of laughter*** взрыв сме́ха; **2.** звони́ть
**peanut** ['piːnʌt] ара́хис
**pear** [peə] гру́ша
**pearl** [pɜːl] *collect.* же́мчуг; жемчу́жина *a. fig.*; *attr.* жемчу́жный; **~ barley** перло́вая крупа́, *coll.* перло́вка
**peasant** ['peznt] **1.** крестья́нин *m*, -янка *f*; **2.** крестья́нский; **~ry** [~ri] крестья́нство
**peat** [piːt] торф
**pebble** ['pebl] га́лька
**peck** [pek] клева́ть [клю́нуть]
**peckish** ['pekɪʃ] *coll.* голо́дный; ***feel ~*** хоте́ть есть
**peculiar** [pɪ'kjuːlɪə] □ (*distinctive*) своеобра́зный; осо́бенный; (*strange*) стра́нный; (*characteristic*) сво́йственный (Д); **~ity** [pɪkjuːlɪ'ærətɪ] осо́бенность *f*; стра́нность *f* сво́йство
**peddler** *or Brt.* **pedlar** ['pedlə] разно́счик; у́личный торго́вец
**pedal** ['pedl] **1.** педа́ль *f*; **2.** е́хать на велосипе́де
**pedest|al** ['pedɪstl] пьедеста́л (*a. fig.*); **~rian** [pɪ'destrɪən] **1.** пешехо́д; **2.** пешехо́дный; **~rian crossing** перехо́д
**pedigree** ['pedɪgriː] родосло́вная; происхожде́ние

P

**peek** [piːk] → ***peep***

**peel** [piːl] **1.** ко́рка, ко́жица, шелуха́; **2.** (*a.* **~ *off***) *v/t.* снима́ть ко́жицу, ко́рку, шелуху́ с (Р); *fruit*, *vegetables* [по]чи́стить; *v/i.* [об]лупи́ться; *of skin* сходи́ть [сойти́]

**peep¹** [piːp] [про]пища́ть

**peep²** [~] **1.** взгляд укра́дкой; ***have a ~*** взгляну́ть *pf.*; **2.** взгляну́ть *pf.* укра́дкой; **~ *in*** загля́дывать [-яну́ть]; **~hole** *in door* глазо́к

**peer¹** [pɪə]: **~ *at*** всма́триваться [всмотре́ться]

**peer²** [~] ро́вня *m/pf.*; пэр; **~less** ['pɪəlɪs] несравне́нный

**peevish** ['piːvɪʃ] □ брюзгли́вый

**peg** [peg] **1.** ко́лышек; *for coats*, *etc.* ве́шалка; (*clothes* **~**) прище́пка; *fig.* ***take a p. down a ~*** сбива́ть спесь с кого́-л.; **2.** прикрепля́ть ко́лышком; отмеча́ть ко́лышками; **~ *away*** *impf. only*, *coll.* вка́лывать; упо́рно рабо́тать

**pellet** ['pelɪt] ша́рик; (*pill*) пилю́ля; *collect.* дробь *f*

**pell-mell** [pel'mel] вперемéшку

**pelt¹** [pelt] ко́жа, шку́ра

**pelt²** [~] (*throw at*) забра́сывать [-роса́ть]; *v/i. of rain*, *etc.* бараба́нить

**pelvis** ['pelvɪs] *anat.* таз

**pen** [pen] **1.** ру́чка; ***ballpoint ~*** ша́риковая ру́чка; ***fountain ~*** авторучка; **2.** [на]писа́ть

**penal** ['piːnl] уголо́вный; **~ *offence***, *Am.* ***-se*** уголо́вное преступле́ние; **~ize** ['piːnəlaɪz] нака́зывать [-за́ть]; **~ty** ['penəltɪ] наказа́ние; *sport.* пена́льти; *attr.* штрафно́й

**pence** [pens] *pl. om* ***penny***

**pencil** ['pensl] **1.** каранда́ш; ***in ~*** карандашо́м; **2.** (*draw*) [на]рисова́ть; писа́ть карандашо́м

**pendant** ['pendənt] куло́н; брело́к

**pending** ['pendɪŋ] **1.** *law* ожида́ющий реше́ния; **2.** *prp.* (вплоть) до (Р)

**pendulum** ['pendjʊləm] ма́ятник

**penetra|ble** ['penɪtrəbl] □ проница́емый; **~te** [~treɪt] проника́ть [-ни́кнуть] в (В); (*pervade*) прони́зывать [-за́ть]; *fig.* вника́ть [вни́кнуть] в (В); **~ting** ['~treɪtɪŋ] (*acute*) проница́тельный; *sound*, *etc.* пронзи́тельный; **~tion** [penɪ'treɪʃn] проникнове́ние; проница́тельность *f*

**peninsula** [pə'nɪnsjʊlə] полуо́стров

**peniten|ce** ['penɪtəns] раска́яние; покая́ние; **~t** [~nt] □ ка́ющийся; **~tiary** [penɪ'tenʃərɪ] исправи́тельный дом; тюрьма́

**penknife** ['pennaɪf] перочи́нный нож

**pen name** псевдони́м

**pennant** ['penənt] вы́мпел

**penniless** ['penɪlɪs] без копе́йки

**penny** ['penɪ] пе́нни *n indecl.*, пенс; ***cost a pretty ~*** влете́ть *pf.* в копе́ечку

**pen pal** друг по перепи́ске

**pension 1.** ['penʃn] пе́нсия; (*disability* **~**) пе́нсия по инвали́дности; **2.** *v/t.* назна́чить *pf.* пе́нсию; (**~** *off*) увольня́ть на пе́нсию; **~er** ['penʃənə] пенсионе́р(ка)

**pensive** ['pensɪv] □ заду́мчивый

**pent** [pent] заключённый; **~-up** *anger*, *etc.* накопи́вшийся; пода́вленный

**penthouse** ['penthaʊs] кварти́ра; вы́строенная на кры́ше до́ма

**people** ['piːpl] **1.** (*race*, *nation*) наро́д; (*persons generally*) лю́ди *m/pl.*; (*inhabitants*) населе́ние; **2.** заселя́ть [-ли́ть]; *country* населя́ть [-ли́ть]

**pepper** ['pepə] **1.** пе́рец; **2.** [по-, на]перчи́ть; **~mint** *bot.* пе́речная мя́та; **~y** [~rɪ] напе́рченный; *fig.* вспы́льчивый, раздражи́тельный

**per** [pɜː] по (Д), че́рез (В), посре́дством (Р); за (В); **~ *annum*** в год, ежего́дно; **~cent** проце́нт

**perambulator** [pə'ræmbjʊleɪtə] де́тская коля́ска

**perceive** [pə'siːv] (*visually*) замеча́ть [-е́тить]; (*discern*) различа́ть [-чи́ть]; *mentally* понима́ть [-ня́ть]; осозн(а-в)а́ть; *through senses* [по-] чу́вствовать; ощуща́ть [-ути́ть]

**percentage** [pə'sentɪdʒ] проце́нт

**percepti|ble** [pə'septəbl] □ ощути́мый, различи́мый; **~on** [~ʃn] восприя́тие

**perch¹** [pɜːtʃ] *zo.* о́кунь *m*

**perch²** [~] сади́ться [сесть]; уса́живаться [усе́сться]

P

**percolator** ['pɜːkəleɪtə] кофева́рка
**percussion** [pə'kʌʃn] уда́р; *mus. collect.* уда́рные инструме́нты
**peremptory** [pə'remptərɪ] безапелляцио́нный, категори́чный, (*manner*) вла́стный
**perennial** [pə'renɪəl] □ *fig.* ве́чный, неувяда́емый; *bot.* многоле́тний
**perfect** ['pɜːfɪkt] **1.** □ соверше́нный; (*exact*) то́чный; **2.** [pə'fekt] [у]соверше́нствовать; **~ion** [~ʃn] соверше́нство
**perfidious** [pə'fɪdɪəs] □ *lit.* вероло́мный
**perforate** ['pɜːfəreɪt] перфори́ровать (*im*)*pf.*
**perform** [pə'fɔːm] исполня́ть [-о́лнить] (*a. thea.*); *thea.*, *mus.* игра́ть [сыгра́ть]; **~ance** [~əns] исполне́ние (*a. thea.*); *thea.* спекта́кль *m*; *sport.* достиже́ние; **~er** [~ə] исполни́тель(ница *f*) *m*
**perfume** ['pɜːfjuːm] *liquid* духи́ *m/pl.*; (*smell*, *bouquet*) арома́т, (*fragrance*) благоуха́ние
**perfunctory** [pə'fʌŋktərɪ] □ (*automatic*) машина́льный; *fig.* (*careless*) небре́жный; (*superficial*) пове́рхностный
**perhaps** [pə'hæps] мо́жет быть
**peril** ['perəl] опа́сность *f*; **~ous** [~əs] □ опа́сный
**period** ['pɪərɪəd] пери́од; эпо́ха; (*full stop*) то́чка, коне́ц; **~ic** [pɪərɪ'ɒdɪk] периоди́ческий; **~ical** [~dɪkl] **1.** → ***periodic***; **2.** периоди́ческое изда́ние
**periphery** [pə'rɪferɪ] окру́жность *f*; *fig.* перифери́я
**perish** ['perɪʃ] погиба́ть [-и́бнуть]; **~able** ['perɪʃəbl] □ *food* скоропо́ртящийся; **~ing** [~ɪŋ]: ***it's ~ here*** здесь жу́тко хо́лодно
**perjur|e** ['pɜːdʒə]: **~ *o.s.*** лжесвиде́тельствовать; **~y** [~rɪ] лжесвиде́тельство
**perk** [pɜːk] *coll.*: *mst.* **~ *up*** *v/i.* оживля́ться [-ви́ться]; **~y** ['pɜːkɪ] □ живо́й; (*self-assured*) самоуве́ренный
**permanen|ce** ['pɜːmənəns] постоя́нство; **~t** [~nt] постоя́нный, неизме́нный; **~ *address*** постоя́нный а́дрес; **~ *wave*** зави́вка «перманент»
**permea|ble** ['pɜːmɪəbl] проница́емый; **~te** [~mɪeɪt] проника́ть [-и́кнуть]; пропи́тывать [-ита́ть]
**permissi|ble** [pə'mɪsəbl] □ допусти́мый; **~on** [~ʃn] разреше́ние
**permit 1.** [pə'mɪt] разреша́ть [-ши́ть], позволя́ть [-во́лить]; допуска́ть [-усти́ть]; ***weather ~ting*** е́сли пого́да позво́лит; **2.** ['pɜːmɪt] разреше́ние; (*document*) про́пуск
**pernicious** [pə'nɪʃəs] □ па́губный, вре́дный
**perpendicular** [pɜːpən'dɪkjʊlə] □ перпендикуля́рный
**perpetrate** ['pɜːpɪtreɪt] соверша́ть [-ши́ть]
**perpetu|al** [pə'petʃuəl] □ постоя́нный, ве́чный; **~ate** [~ʃʊeɪt] увекове́чи(ва)ть
**perplex** [pə'pleks] озада́чи(ва)ть, сбива́ть с то́лку; **~ity** [~ətɪ] озада́ченность *f*; недоуме́ние
**perquisite** ['pɜːkwɪzɪt] побо́чное преиму́щество; льго́та
**persecut|e** ['pɜːsɪkjuːt] пресле́довать; **~ion** [pɜːsɪ'kjuːʃn] пресле́дование
**persever|ance** [pɜːsɪ'vɪərəns] насто́йчивость *f*, упо́рство; **~e** [~'vɪə] *v/i.* упо́рно продолжа́ть (***in*** В)
**persist** [pə'sɪst] упо́рствовать (***in*** в П); **~ence** [~əns] насто́йчивость *f*; **~ent** [~ənt] □ насто́йчивый; (*unceasing*) беспреста́нный
**person** ['pɜːsn] лицо́, ли́чность *f*; персо́на, осо́ба; ***pleasant ~*** прия́тный челове́к; **~age** [~ɪdʒ] ва́жная персо́на; *lit.* персона́ж; **~al** [~l] □ ли́чный, персона́льный; **~ality** [pɜːsə'nælətɪ] ли́чность *f*; **~ify** [pə'sɒnɪfaɪ] (*give human qualities*) олицетворя́ть [-ри́ть]; (*embody*, *exemplify*) воплоща́ть [-лоти́ть]; **~nel** [pɜːsə'nel] персона́л, штат; **~ *department*** отде́л ка́дров
**perspective** [pə'spektɪv] перспекти́ва; (*view*) вид
**perspir|ation** [pɜːspə'reɪʃn] поте́ние; пот; **~e** [pə'spaɪə] [вс]поте́ть
**persua|de** [pə'sweɪd] убежда́ть [убе-

ди́ть]; **~sion** [-ʒn] убежде́ние; убеди́тельность *f*; **~sive** [-sɪv] □ убеди́тельный
**pert** [pɜːt] □ де́рзкий
**pertain** [pə'teɪn] (*relate*) име́ть отноше́ние (к Д); (*belong*) принадлежа́ть
**pertinacious** [pɜːtɪ'neɪʃəs] □ упря́мый; (*determined*) насто́йчивый
**pertinent** ['pɜːtɪnənt] уме́стный; относя́щийся к де́лу
**perturb** [pə'tɜːb] [вз]волнова́ть, [о]беспоко́ить
**perusal** [pə'ruːzl] внима́тельное прочте́ние; рассмотре́ние
**pervade** [pə'veɪd] *of smell*, *etc*. распространя́ться [-ни́ться] по (Д)
**pervers|e** [pə'vɜːs] □ превра́тный, отклоня́ющийся от но́рмы; извращённый; **~ion** [ʃn] *med*. извраще́ние
**pervert** **1.** [pə'vɜːt] извраща́ть [-рати́ть]; совраща́ть [-рати́ть]; **2.** ['pɜːvɜːt] извраще́нец
**pest** [pest] *fig*. я́зва, бич; *zo*. вреди́тель *m*; **~er** ['~ə] докуча́ть (Д); надоеда́ть [-е́сть] (Д); **~icide** ['~tɪsaɪd] пестици́д
**pet** [pet] **1.** дома́шнее живо́тное; (*favourite*) люби́мец, ба́ловень *m*; **2.** люби́мый; *~ name* ласка́тельное и́мя; **3.** ба́ловать; ласка́ть
**petal** ['petl] *bot*. лепесто́к
**petition** [pə'tɪʃn] **1.** проше́ние, хода́тайство; **2.** обраща́ться [-ати́ться] с проше́нием; хода́тайствовать
**petrol** ['petrəl] *chiefly Brt*. бензи́н
**petticoat** ['petɪkəʊt] ни́жняя ю́бка; комбина́ция
**petty** ['petɪ] □ ме́лкий; (*small-minded*) ме́лочный
**petulant** ['petjʊlənt] раздражи́тельный, капри́зный
**pew** [pjuː] церко́вная скамья́
**phantom** ['fæntəm] фанто́м, при́зрак; иллю́зия
**pharmacy** ['fɑːməsɪ] фармаци́я; (*drugstore*) апте́ка
**phase** [feɪz] фа́за; пери́од, эта́п
**phenomen|on** [fə'nɒmɪnən], *pl*. **~a** [-nə] явле́ние; фено́мен
**phial** ['faɪəl] пузырёк
**philologist** [fɪ'lɒlədʒɪst] фило́лог
**philosoph|er** [fɪ'lɒsəfə] филóсоф; **~ize** [-faɪz] филосо́фствовать; **~y** [-fɪ] филосо́фия
**phlegm** [flem] мокро́та; (*sluggishness*) флегмати́чность *f*
**phone** [fəʊn] → ***telephone***
**phonetics** [fə'netɪks] *pl*. фоне́тика
**phon(e)y** ['fəʊnɪ] *coll*. (*false*) фальши́вый, неесте́ственный
**phosphorus** ['fɔsfərəs] фо́сфор
**photograph** ['fəʊtəgrɑːf] **1.** фотогра́фия, сни́мок; **2.** [с]фотографи́ровать; **~er** [fə'tɒgrəfə] фото́граф; **~y** [-fɪ] фотогра́фия
**phrase** [freɪz] **1.** фра́за, выраже́ние; **2.** выража́ть [вы́разить]; [с]формули́ровать
**physic|al** ['fɪzɪkəl] □ физи́ческий; материа́льный; **~ian** [fɪ'zɪʃn] врач; **~ist** ['~sɪst] фи́зик; **~s** ['fɪzɪks] *sg*. фи́зика
**physique** [fɪ'ziːk] телосложе́ние
**pianist** ['pɪənɪst] piани́ст
**piano** [pɪ'ænəʊ] *upright* пиани́но; ***grand ~*** роя́ль *m*; ***~ concerto*** конце́рт для роя́ля с орке́стром
**pick** [pɪk] **1.** вы́бор; (*tool*) кирка́; **2.** выбира́ть [вы́брать]; *nose* ковыря́ть в (П); *flowers*, *fruit* соб(и-)ра́ть; (*pluck*) срыва́ть [сорва́ть]; ***~ out*** выбира́ть [вы́брать]; ***~ up*** подбира́ть [подобра́ть]; поднима́ть [-ня́ть]; (*collect s.o.*) заезжа́ть [зае́хать] за (Т); **~aback** ['pɪkəbæk], = ***piggyback*** ['pɪgɪbæk], на спине́; на заќорках; ***give me a ~*** посади́ меня́ на пле́чи; **~axe** кирка́
**picket** ['pɪkɪt] **1.** (*stake*) кол; *mil*. заста́ва; пост; *of strikers*, *etc*. пике́т; **2.** пикети́ровать
**picking** ['pɪkɪŋ] *of fruit* сбор; **~s** *pl*. оста́тки *m/pl*., объе́дки *m/pl*.
**pickle** ['pɪkl] **1.** марина́д; *pl*. пи́кули *f/pl*.; *coll*. беда́; неприя́тности *f/pl*.; ***be in a ~*** вли́пнуть *pf*.; **2.** [за-] маринова́ть; ***~d herring*** марино́ванная селёдка
**pickup** (*van*) пика́п
**pictorial** [pɪk'tɔːrɪəl] иллюстри́рованный; *art* изобрази́тельный

P

**picture** ['pɪktʃə] **1.** карти́на; **~s** *pl.* (*generally*) жи́вопись *f*; *chiefly Brt.* кино́ *indecl.*; ***put in the ~*** вводи́ть [ввести́] в курс де́ла; **~ *gallery*** карти́нная галере́я; **~ (*post*)*card*** откры́тка с ви́дом; **2.** (*depict*) изобража́ть [-рази́ть]; (*describe*) опи́сывать [-са́ть]; (*imagine*) вообража́ть [-рази́ть]; **~ *to o.s.*** представля́ть [-а́вить] себе́; **~sque** [pɪktʃə'resk] живопи́сный

**pie** [paɪ] пиро́г; *small* пирожо́к

**piece** [pi:s] **1.** кусо́к, часть *f*; (*fragment*) обры́вок, обло́мок; (*single article*) вещь *f*; предме́т; шту́ка; **~ *of advice*** сове́т; **~ *of news*** но́вость *f*; ***by the ~*** пошту́чно; ***give a ~ of one's mind*** выска́зывать своё мне́ние; ***take to ~s*** разбира́ть на ча́сти; **2.**: **~ *together*** соединя́ть в одно́ це́лое, собира́ть из кусо́чков; **~meal** по частя́м, уры́вками; **~work** сде́льная рабо́та

**pier** [pɪə] *naut.* пирс; мол; *of bridge* усто́й, бык; (*breakwater*) волноло́м; (*wharf*) при́стань *f*

**pierce** [pɪəs] пронза́ть [-зи́ть]; прока́лывать [-коло́ть]; *of cold* прони́зывать [-за́ть]

**piety** ['paɪətɪ] благоче́стие; набо́жность *f*

**pig** [pɪg] свинья́

**pigeon** ['pɪdʒɪn] го́лубь *m*; **~hole 1.** отделе́ние (пи́сьменного стола́ *и т. п.*); **2.** раскла́дывать по я́щикам; *fig.* откла́дывать в до́лгий я́щик

**pig|headed** [pɪg'hedɪd] упря́мый; **~skin** свина́я ко́жа; **~sty** свина́рник; **~tail** коси́чка, коса́

**pike** [paɪk] (*fish*) щу́ка

**pile** [paɪl] **1.** ку́ча, гру́да; (*stack*) шта́бель *m*; **2.** скла́дывать [сложи́ть]; сва́ливать в ку́чу

**piles** *pl. med.* геморро́й

**pilfer** ['pɪlfə] ворова́ть; стяну́ть *pf.*

**pilgrim** ['pɪlgrɪm] пало́мник; **~age** ['pɪlgrɪmɪdʒ] пало́мничество

**pill** [pɪl] табле́тка; ***bitter ~*** *fig.* го́рькая пилю́ля

**pillage** ['pɪlɪdʒ] мародёрство

**pillar** ['pɪlə] столб, коло́нна; *Brt.* **~box** почто́вый я́щик

**pillion** ['pɪljən] *on motorcycle* за́днее сиде́нье

**pillow** ['pɪləʊ] поду́шка; **~case**, **~slip** на́волочка

**pilot** ['paɪlət] **1.** *ae.* пило́т; *naut.* ло́цман; **2.** *naut.* проводи́ть [-вести́]; *ae.* пилоти́ровать

**pimple** ['pɪmpl] пры́щик

**pin** [pɪn] **1.** була́вка; ***hair ~*** шпи́лька; *Brt.* ***drawing ~*** (*Am. thumbtack*) кно́пка; **2.** прика́лывать [-коло́ть]; **~ *down*** припере́ть *pf.* к сте́нке; **~ *one's hopes on*** возлага́ть [-ложи́ть] наде́жды на (В)

**pinafore** ['pɪnəfɔ:] пере́дник

**pincers** ['pɪnsəz] *pl.* кле́щи *f/pl.*; (*tweezers*) пинце́т

**pinch** [pɪntʃ] **1.** щипо́к; *of salt, etc.* щепо́тка; *fig.* стеснённое положе́ние; ***at a ~*** в кра́йнем слу́чае; **2.** *v/t.* щипа́ть [щипну́ть]; (*squeeze*) прищемля́ть [-ми́ть]; *v/i.* [по]скупи́ться; *of shoes* жать

**pine**[1] [paɪn]: **~ *away*** [за]ча́хнуть; **~ *for*** тоскова́ть по (П)

**pine**[2] [~] *bot.* сосна́; **~apple** анана́с; **~ cone** сосно́вая ши́шка

**pinion** ['pɪnjən] *tech.* (*cogwheel*) шестерня́

**pink** [pɪŋk] **1.** *bot.* гвозди́ка; ро́зовый цвет; **2.** ро́зовый

**pinnacle** ['pɪnəkl] *arch.* остроконе́чная ба́шенка; *of mountain* верши́на; *fig.* верх

**pint** [paɪnt] пи́нта

**pioneer** [paɪə'nɪə] **1.** пионе́р; первопрохо́дец *m*; **2.** прокла́дывать путь *m* (***for*** Д)

**pious** ['paɪəs] □ на́божный

**pip** [pɪp] *of fruit* ко́сточка, зёрнышко

**pipe** [paɪp] труба́; *smoker's* тру́бка; *mus.* ду́дка; **2.**: **~ *down*** замолча́ть *pf.*; **~ dream** несбы́точная мечта́; **~line** трубопрово́д; нефтепрово́д; **~r** ['paɪpə] *mst.* волы́нщик

**piping** ['paɪpɪŋ]: **~ *hot*** о́чень горя́чий

**piquant** ['pi:kənt] пика́нтный (*a. fig.*)

**pique** [pi:k] **1.** доса́да; **2.** (*nettle*) раздража́ть; вызыва́ть доса́ду; (*wound*) уязвля́ть [-ви́ть] заде́(ва́)ть

P

**pira|cy** ['paɪərəsɪ] пира́тство (*a. in publishing*); **~te** [-rət] **1.** пира́т

**pistol** ['pɪstl] пистоле́т

**piston** ['pɪstən] *tech.* по́ршень *m*; **~ stroke** ход по́ршня

**pit** [pɪt] я́ма; *mining* ша́хта; *thea.* оркестро́вая я́ма

**pitch**[1] [pɪtʃ] смола́; (*tar*) дёготь *m*; ***as black as ~*** чёрный как смоль

**pitch**[2] [~] (*degree*) сте́пень *f*; *mus.* высота́ то́на; *naut.* ки́левая ка́чка; *tech.* (*slope*) накло́н; *tech.* (*thread*) шаг резьбы́; *sport* по́ле, площа́дка; **2.** *v/t.* (*set up camp, tent, etc.*) разби́(ва́)ть; (*throw*) броса́ть [бро́сить]; *naut.* кача́ть; *fig.* ***~ into*** набра́сываться [-ро́ситься] на (В)

**pitcher** ['pɪtʃə] (*jug*) кувши́н; (*sport*) подаю́щий

**pitchfork** ['pɪtʃfɔːk] ви́лы *f/pl.*

**pitfall** ['pɪtfɔːl] *fig.* лову́шка

**pith** [pɪθ] *bot.* сердцеви́на; *fig.* су́щность *f*, суть *f*; **~y** ['pɪθɪ] *fig.* сжа́тый; содержа́тельный

**pitiable** ['pɪtɪəbl] □ (*arousing pity*) несча́стный; (*arousing contempt*) жа́лкий

**pitiful** ['pɪtɪfl] □ (*arousing compassion*) жа́лостливый; (*arousing contempt*) жа́лкий

**pitiless** ['pɪtɪlɪs] □ безжа́лостный

**pittance** ['pɪtəns] гроши́

**pity** ['pɪtɪ] **1.** жа́лость *f* (***for*** к Д), ***it is a ~*** жаль; **2.** [по]жале́ть

**pivot** ['pɪvət] **1.** ось *f* враще́ния; *fig.* сте́ржень *m*; **2.** враща́ться (**[*up*]*on*** вокру́г Р)

**pizza** ['piːtsə] пи́цца

**placard** ['plækɑːd] плака́т

**placate** [plə'keɪt] умиротворя́ть [-ри́ть]

**place** [pleɪs] **1.** ме́сто; го́род, селе́ние; дом; (*station*) до́лжность *f*; ***give ~ to*** уступа́ть ме́сто (Д); ***in ~ of*** вме́сто (Р); ***in ~s*** места́ми; ***out of ~*** неуме́стный; **2.** [по]ста́вить, класть [положи́ть]; *orders, etc.* размеща́ть [-ести́ть]; *article, etc.* помеща́ть [-ести́ть]; ***I can't ~ her*** не могу́ вспо́мнить, отку́да я её зна́ю

**placid** ['plæsɪd] □ споко́йный

**plagiar|ism** ['pleɪdʒərɪzəm] плагиа́т; **~ize** [~raɪz] занима́ться плагиа́том

**plague** [pleɪg] **1.** (*pestilence*) чума́ *fig.* (*calamity*) бе́дствие; (*scourge*) бич; **2.** [из]му́чить; *coll.* надоеда́ть [-е́сть] (Д)

**plaice** [pleɪs] ка́мбала

**plaid** [plæd] шотла́ндка; плед

**plain** [pleɪn] **1.** □ просто́й; поня́тный, я́сный; (*obvious*) очеви́дный; обыкнове́нный; (*smooth, level*) гла́дкий, ро́вный; **2.** *adv.* я́сно; открове́нно; **3.** *geogr.* равни́на; ***~spoken*** прямо́й

**plaint|iff** ['pleɪntɪf] исте́ц *m*, исти́ца *f*; **~ive** ['pleɪntɪv] □ жа́лобный, зауны́вный

**plait** [plæt] **1.** коса́; **2.** заплета́ть [-ести́]

**plan** [plæn] **1.** план, прое́кт; **2.** [за]плани́ровать; составля́ть план; *fig.* намеча́ть [-е́тить]; (*intend*) намерева́ться

**plane**[1] [pleɪn] **1.** пло́ский; **2.** пло́скость *f*; *math.* прое́кция; *ae.* самолёт; *fig.* у́ровень *m*

**plane**[2] [~] **1.** (*tool*) руба́нок; **2.** [вы́]строга́ть

**planet** ['plænɪt] плане́та

**plank** [plæŋk] **1.** доска́; **2.** настила́ть *or* обшива́ть до́сками

**plant** [plɑːnt] **1.** расте́ние; *tech.* заво́д, фа́брика; **2.** *tree* сажа́ть [посади́ть]; [по]ста́вить; **~ation** [plæn'teɪʃən] планта́ция; насажде́ние

**plaque** [plɑːk] (*wall ornament*) таре́лка; *on door, etc.* доще́чка, табли́чка; ***memorial ~*** мемориа́льная доска́

**plasma** ['plæzmə] пла́зма

**plaster** ['plɑːstə] **1.** *for walls* штукату́рка; *med.* пла́стырь *m*; (*mst.* ***~ of Paris***) гипс; ***sticking ~*** *med.* лейкопла́стырь; **2.** [о]штукату́рить; накла́дывать пла́стырь на (В)

**plastic** ['plæstɪk] (***~ally***) **1.** пласти́ческий; **2.** пластма́сса, пла́стик; ***~ surgery*** пласти́ческая хирурги́я

**plate** [pleɪt] **1.** (*dish*) таре́лка; (*metal tableware*) посу́да; (*sheet of glass, metal, etc.*) лист; *on door* доще́чка; ***silver ~*** столо́вое серебро́; **2.** покрыва́ть ме-

P

та́ллом

**plateau** ['plætəʊ] плато́ *n indecl.*

**platform** ['plætfɔːm] *rail.* перро́н, платфо́рма; *for speakers* трибу́на; *on bus, etc.* площа́дка; *pol.* полити́ческая програ́мма

**platinum** ['plætɪnəm] пла́тина; *attr.* пла́тиновый

**platitude** ['plætɪtjuːd] бана́льность *f*; истасканное выраже́ние

**platoon** [plə'tuːn] *mil.* взвод

**platter** ['plætə] блю́до

**plausible** ['plɔːzəbl] □ правдоподо́бный; *of excuse, argument, etc.* благови́дный

**play** [pleɪ] **1.** игра́; пье́са; ***fair ~*** че́стная игра́; **2.** игра́ть [сыгра́ть] (в В, *mus.* на П); (*direct*) направля́ть [-вить]; ***~ off*** *fig.* разы́грывать [-ра́ть]; стра́вливать [страви́ть] (***against*** с Т); ***~ed out*** вы́дохшийся; **~bill** театра́льная афи́ша; **~er** ['pleɪə] игро́к; актёр; **~mate** това́рищ по и́грам, друг де́тства; **~ful** ['pleɪfl] □ игри́вый; **~goer** ['~gəʊə] театра́л; **~ground** де́тская площа́дка; **~house** теа́тр; **~pen** де́тский мане́ж; **~thing** игру́шка; **~wright** ['~raɪt] драмату́рг

**plea** [pliː] про́сьба, мольба́; *law* заявление в суде́; ***on the ~*** (***of*** *или* ***that*** ***…***) под предло́гом (Р *or* что …)

**plead** [pliːd] *v/i.*: ***~ for*** вступа́ться [-пи́ться] за (В); говори́ть за (В); ***~ guilty*** признава́ть себя́ вино́вным; *v/t. in court* защища́ть [-ити́ть]; приводи́ть в оправда́ние

**pleasant** ['pleznt] □ прия́тный

**please** [pliːz] [по]нра́виться (Д); угожда́ть [угоди́ть] (Д); ***if you ~*** с ва́шего позволе́ния; изво́льте!; ***~ come in!*** войди́те, пожа́луйста!; доставля́ть удово́льствие (Д); ***be ~d to do*** де́лать с удово́льствием; ***be ~d with*** быть дово́льным (Т); **~d** [pliːzd] дово́льный

**pleasing** ['pliːzɪŋ] □ прия́тный

**pleasure** ['pleʒə] удово́льствие, наслажде́ние; *attr.* развлека́тельный, увесели́тельный; ***at your ~*** по ва́шему жела́нию

**pleat** [pliːt] **1.** скла́дка; **2.** де́лать скла́дки на (П)

**pledge** [pledʒ] **1.** зало́г, закла́д; (*promise*) обеща́ние; **2.** закла́дывать [заложи́ть]; обеща́ть; (*vow*) [по]кля́сться; обя́зываться [-за́ться]; ***he ~d himself*** он связа́л себя́ обеща́нием

**plenary** ['pliːnərɪ] плена́рный

**plenipotentiary** [plenɪpə'tenʃərɪ] полномо́чный представи́тель *m*

**plentiful** ['plentɪfl] □ оби́льный

**plenty** ['plentɪ] **1.** изоби́лие; ***~ of*** мно́го (Р); **2.** *coll.* вполне́; дово́льно

**pleurisy** ['plʊərəsɪ] плеври́т

**pliable** ['plaɪəbl] □ ги́бкий; *fig.* пода́тливый, мя́гкий

**pliancy** ['plaɪənsɪ] ги́бкость *f*

**pliers** ['plaɪəz] *pl.* плоскогу́бцы *m/pl.*

**plight** [plaɪt] плохо́е положе́ние, состоя́ние

**plod** [plɒd] (*a.* ***~ along, on***) [по]тащи́ться; корпе́ть (***at*** над Т)

**plot** [plɒt] **1.** уча́сток земли́, деля́нка; (*conspiracy*) за́говор; *lit.* фа́була, сюже́т; **2.** *v/i.* гото́вить за́говор; *v/t. on map* наноси́ть [нанести́]; замышля́ть [-ы́слить]; интригова́ть

**plow**, *Brt.* **plough** [plaʊ] **1.** плуг; **2.** [вс]паха́ть; *fig.* [из]борозди́ть; **~land** пахо́тная земля́; па́шня

**pluck** [plʌk] **1.** *coll.* сме́лость *f*, му́жество; **2.** *flowers* срыва́ть [сорва́ть]; *fowl* ощи́пывать [-па́ть]; ***~ at*** дёргать [дёрнуть] (В); хвата́ть(ся) [схвати́ть(ся)] за (В); ***~ up courage*** собра́ться *pf.* с ду́хом; **~y** ['plʌkɪ] сме́лый, отва́жный

**plug** [plʌg] **1.** зату́чка; *in bath, etc.* про́бка; *el.* ште́псель *m*; ***~ socket*** ште́псельная розе́тка; **2.** *v/t. stop up* затыка́ть [заткну́ть]; ***~ in*** включа́ть [-чи́ть]

**plum** [plʌm] сли́ва; *attr.* сли́вовый

**plumage** ['pluːmɪdʒ] опере́ние

**plumb** [plʌm] *adv.* (*exactly*) то́чно; пря́мо, как раз

**plumb|er** ['plʌmə] санте́хник, *coll.* водопрово́дчик; **~ing** [~ɪŋ] *in house* водопрово́д и канализа́ция

**plummet** ['plʌmɪt] свинцо́вый отве́с;

P

*on fishing line* грузи́ло

**plump**[1] [plʌmp] (*chubby*) пу́хлый; (*somewhat fat*) по́лный; *poultry* жи́рный

**plump**[2] [~] **1.** □ *coll.* реши́тельный; **2.** бу́хаться [-хнуться]; **3.** *adv. coll.* пря́мо, без обиняко́в

**plunder** ['plʌndə] [о]гра́бить

**plunge** [plʌndʒ] **1.** (*dive*) ныря́ть [нырну́ть]; *hand, etc.* окуна́ть [-ну́ть]; **2.** ныря́ние; погруже́ние; ***take the ~*** [с]де́лать реши́тельный шаг

**plural** ['pluərəl] *gr.* мно́жественное число́; (*multiple*) многочи́сленный

**plush** [plʌʃ] плюш

**ply**[1] [plaɪ] *v/t. with questions* засыпа́ть [засы́пать], забра́сывать [-роса́ть]; *v/i.* курси́ровать

**ply**[2] [~] слой; **~wood** фане́ра

**pneumatic** [nju:'mætɪk] (***~ally***) пневмати́ческий

**pneumonia** [nju:'məunɪə] воспале́ние лёгких, пневмони́я

**poach**[1] [pəutʃ] браконье́рствовать

**poach**[2] [~]: ***~ed egg*** яйцо́-пашо́т

**poacher** ['pəutʃə] браконье́р

**PO Box** (= *Post Office Box*) почто́вый я́щик (п/я)

**pocket** ['pɒkɪt] **1.** карма́н; (*air~*) возду́шная я́ма; **2.** класть в карма́н; *fig. appropriate* прикарма́ни(ва)ть; *pride* подавля́ть [-ви́ть]; *insult* прогла́тывать [-лоти́ть]; **3.** карма́нный

**pod** [pɒd] **1.** *of seed* стручо́к; **2.** *shell v/t.* лу́щить

**poem** ['pəuɪm] поэ́ма; стихотворе́ние

**poet** ['pəuɪt] поэ́т; **~ess** [~əs] поэте́сса; **~ic(al** □) [pəu'etɪk(əl)] поэти́ческий; поэти́чный; **~ry** ['pəuɪtrɪ] поэ́зия

**poignan|cy** ['pɔɪnjənsɪ] острота́; **~t** [~nt] о́стрый; тро́гательный; *fig.* мучи́тельный

**point** [pɔɪnt] **1.** (*dot*) то́чка; (*item*) пункт; *on thermometer* гра́дус, деле́ние; (*essence*) смысл; суть де́ла; *sport* очко́; (*sharp end*) остриё, о́стрый коне́ц; *rail* стре́лка; ***~ of view*** то́чка зре́ния; ***the ~ is that …*** де́ло в том, что …; ***make a ~ of*** + *ger.* поста́вить себе́ зада́чей (+ *inf.*); ***in ~ of*** в отноше́нии (Р); ***off the ~*** не (относя́щийся) к де́лу; ***be on the ~ of*** + *ger.* соб(и)ра́ться (+ *inf.*); ***win on ~s*** выи́грывать по очка́м; ***to the ~*** к де́лу (относя́щийся); ***a sore ~*** больно́й вопро́с; ***that's beside the ~*** э́то ни при чём; **2.** *v/t.*: ***~ one's finger*** пока́зывать па́льцем (***at*** на В); заостря́ть [-ри́ть]; (*often ~* ***out***) ука́зывать [-за́ть]; ***~ a weapon at*** направля́ть [-ра́вить] ору́жие на (В); *v/i.*; ***~ at*** ука́зывать [-за́ть] на (В); ***~ to*** быть напра́вленным на (В); **~-blank**: ***ask ~*** спра́шивать в упо́р; ***refuse ~*** категори́чески отказа́ть(ся) *pf.*; **~ed** ['pɔɪntɪd] □ остроконе́чный; о́стрый; *fig.* ко́лкий; **~er** ['pɔɪntə] стре́лка *m*; *teacher's* ука́зка; *dog* по́йнтер; **~less** ['~lɪs] бессмы́сленный

**poise** [pɔɪz] **1.** равнове́сие; *carriage* оса́нка; **2.** *v/i.* баланси́ровать

**poison** ['pɔɪzn] **1.** яд, отра́ва; **2.** отравля́ть [-ви́ть]; **~ous** [~əs] (*fig. a.*) ядови́тый

**poke** [pəuk] **1.** толчо́к, тычо́к; **2.** *v/t.* (*prod*) ты́кать [ткнуть]; толка́ть [-кну́ть]; сова́ть [су́нуть]; *fire* меша́ть кочерго́й; ***~ fun at*** подшу́чивать [-шути́ть] над (Т); *v/i.* сова́ть нос (***into*** в В); (*grope for*) иска́ть о́щупью (***for*** В *or* Р)

**poker** ['pəukə] кочерга́

**poky** ['pəukɪ] те́сный; убо́гий

**polar** ['pəulə] поля́рный; ***~ bear*** бе́лый медве́дь *m*; **~ity** [pəu'lærətɪ] поля́рность *f*

**pole**[1] [pəul] (*of planet*; *a. elec.*) по́люс

**pole**[2] [~] (*post*; *a. in sport*) шест

**Pole**[3] [~] поля́к *m*, по́лька *f*

**polemic** [pə'lemɪk] (*a.* **~al** [~mɪkl] □) полеми́чный, полеми́ческий; **~s** [~s] поле́мика

**police** [pə'li:s] **1.** поли́ция; **2.** содержа́ть поря́док в (П); **~man** полице́йский; **~ station** полице́йский уча́сток

**policy**[1] ['pɒləsɪ] поли́тика; ли́ния поведе́ния

**policy**[2] [~]: ***insurance ~*** страхово́й по́лис

**Polish**[1] ['pəulɪʃ] по́льский

**polish**[2] ['pɒlɪʃ] **1.** полиро́вка; *fig.* лоск; **2.** [от]полирова́ть; *floor* натира́ть

P

[-ерéть]; *shoes* почи́стить; *fig.* наводи́ть [-вести́] лоск
**polite** [pəˈlaɪt] □ вéжливый; **~ness** [-nɪs] вéжливость *f*
**politic|al** [pəˈlɪtɪkl] □ полити́ческий; **~ian** [pɒlɪˈtɪʃən] поли́тик, полити́ческий дéятель; **~s** [ˈpɒlətɪks] *pl.* поли́тика
**poll** [pəʊl] **1.** голосовáние; (*elections*) вы́боры; ***opinion ~*** опрóс общéственного мнéния; **2.** *v/t. receive votes* получáть [-чи́ть]; *v/i.* [про]голосовáть
**pollen** [ˈpɒlən] пыльцá
**polling** [ˈpəʊlɪŋ] **1.** → ***poll***; **2.**: ***~ station*** избирáтельный учáсток
**pollute** [pəˈluːt] загрязня́ть [-ни́ть]; осквернять [-ни́ть]
**pollution** [pəˈluːʃn] загрязнéние
**polyethylene** [pɒlɪˈeθɪliːn] *or Brt.*
**polythene** [ˈpɒlɪθiːn] полиэтилéн
**polyp** [ˈpɒlɪp] *zo.*, **~us** [-əs] *med.* поли́п
**pomegranate** [ˈpɒmɪgrænɪt] гранáт
**pommel** [ˈpɒml] *of sword* голóвка; *of saddle* лукá; *v/t.* = ***pummel***
**pomp** [pɒmp] пóмпа; великолéпие
**pompous** [ˈpɒmpəs] □ напы́щенный, помпéзный
**pond** [pɒnd] пруд
**ponder** [ˈpɒndə] *v/t.* обдýм(ыв)ать; *v/i.* задýм(ыв)аться; **~ous** [-rəs] □ *fig.* тяжеловéсный
**pontoon** [pɒnˈtuːn] понтóн; **~ bridge** понтóнный мост
**pony** [ˈpəʊnɪ] *horse* пóни *m indecl.*
**poodle** [ˈpuːdl] пýдель *m*
**pool** [puːl] **1.** (*puddle*) лýжа; (*pond*) пруд; (*swimming* **~**) плáвательный бассéйн; **2.** *cards* банк; *billards* пул; *comm.* фонд; *v/t.* объединя́ть в óбщий фонд; склáдываться [сложи́ться] (***with*** с Т)
**poor** [pʊə] □ бéдный; неимýщий; (*unfortunate*) несчáстный; (*scanty*) скýдный; (*bad*) плохóй; **~ly** [ˈpʊəlɪ] *adj.* нездорóвый
**pop** [pɒp] **1.** (*explosive sound*) хлопóк; *coll.* (*fizzy drink*) шипýчка; **2.** *v/t.* (*put*) совáть [сýнуть]; *of cork v/i.* хлóпать [-пнуть]; ***~ across*** *to a shop, etc.* сбегáть; ***~ in*** заскочи́ть, забежáть
**popcorn** [ˈpɒpkɔːn] попкóрн; воздýшная кукурýза
**pope** [pəʊp] (ри́мский) пáпа *m*
**poplar** [ˈpɒplə] тóполь *m*
**poppy** [ˈpɒpɪ] мак
**popula|ce** [ˈpɒpjʊləs] (*the masses*) мáссы; (*the common people*) простóй нарóд; населéние; **~r** [-lə] (*of the people*) нарóдный; (*generally liked*) популя́рный; **~rity** [-ˈlærətɪ] популя́рность *f*
**populat|e** [ˈpɒpjʊleɪt] населя́ть [-ли́ть]; **~ion** [pɒpjʊˈleɪʃn] населéние
**populous** [ˈpɒpjʊləs] □ многолю́дный
**porcelain** [ˈpɔːsəlɪn] фарфóр
**porch** [pɔːtʃ] крыльцó; пóртик; *Am.* верáнда
**pore**[1] [pɔː] пóра
**pore**[2] [~] *problem* размышля́ть, *book* корпéть (***over*** над Т)
**pork** [pɔːk] свини́на
**pornography** [pɔːˈnɒgrəfɪ] порногрáфия
**porous** [ˈpɔːrəs] □ пóристый
**porridge** [ˈpɒrɪdʒ] овся́ная кáша
**port**[1] [pɔːt] гáвань *f*, порт; *naut.* (*left side*) лéвый борт
**port**[2] [~] портвéйн
**portable** [ˈpɔːtəbl] портати́вный
**portal** [pɔːtl] *arch.* портáл
**portend** [pɔːˈtend] предвещáть
**portent** [ˈpɔːtent] предвéстник, предзнаменовáние
**porter** [ˈpɔːtə] вахтёр; *in hotel* швейцáр; *rail, etc.* носи́льщик; *Am. on train* проводни́к
**portion** [ˈpɔːʃn] **1.** часть *f*; *of food, etc.* пóрция; **2.** (*share out*) [раз-] дели́ть
**portly** [ˈpɔːtlɪ] дорóдный
**portrait** [ˈpɔːtrɪt] портрéт; **~ist** [-ɪst] портрети́ст
**portray** [pɔːˈtreɪ] рисовáть (писáть) портрéт с (Р); изображáть [-рази́ть]; (*describe*) опи́сывать [-сáть]; **~al** [-əl] изображéние; описáние
**pose** [pəʊz] **1.** пóза; **2.** *for an artist* пози́ровать; *question* (по)стáвить; ***~ as*** выдавáть себя́ за (В)

P

**position** [pəˈzɪʃn] ме́сто; положе́ние; пози́ция; состоя́ние; то́чка зре́ния
**positive** [ˈpɒzətɪv] **1.** □ положи́тельный, позити́вный; (*sure*) уве́ренный; (*definite*) определённый; **2.** *phot.* позити́в
**possess** [pəˈzes] *quality* облада́ть (Т); *things* владе́ть (Т); *fig.* овладе́(ва́)ть (Т); ***be ~ed*** быть одержи́мым; **~ion** [~zeʃn] владе́ние; ***take ~ of*** завладе́(ва́)ть (Т); облада́ние; *fig.* одержи́мость *f*; **~or** [~zesə] владе́лец; облада́тель *m*
**possib|ility** [pɒsəˈbɪlətɪ] возмо́жность *f*; **~le** [ˈpɒsəbl] возмо́жный; **~ly** [~ɪ] возмо́жно; ***if I ~ can*** е́сли у меня́ бу́дет возмо́жность *f*
**post**[1] [pəʊst] столб
**post**[2] [~] **1.** (*mail*) по́чта; *mil.* (*duty station*) пост; (*appointment*, *job*) до́лжность *f*; **2.** *v/t.* отправля́ть по по́чте
**postage** [ˈpəʊstɪdʒ] почто́вая опла́та; **~ stamp** почто́вая ма́рка
**postal** [ˈpəʊstl] □ почто́вый; ***~ order*** де́нежный почто́вый перево́д
**post|card** откры́тка; **~code** почто́вый и́ндекс
**poster** [ˈpəʊstə] афи́ша, плака́т
**poste restante** [pəʊstˈrɪstænt] *chiefly Brt.* до востре́бования
**posterior** [pɒˈstɪərɪə] (*subsequent*) после́дующий; (*behind*) за́дний; (*buttocks*) зад
**posterity** [pəˈsterətɪ] пото́мство
**post-free** *chiefly Brt.* → **postpaid**
**postgraduate** [pəʊstˈgrædʒʊət] аспира́нт(ка); (*not working for degree*) стажёр; ***~ study*** аспиранту́ра
**posthumous** [ˈpɒstjʊməs] посме́ртный; *child* рождённый по́сле сме́рти отца́
**post|man** почтальо́н; **~mark** **1.** почто́вый ште́мпель *m*; **2.** [за]штемпелева́ть; **~master** нача́льник почто́вого отделе́ния
**postmortem** [pəʊstˈmɔːtəm] вскры́тие, аутопси́я
**post|office** отделе́ние свя́зи, *coll.* по́чта; **~box** абонеме́нтный почто́вый я́щик; ***general ~ office*** (гла́вный) почта́мт; **~paid** опла́ченный отправи́телем
**postpone** [pəʊsˈpəʊn] отсро́чи(ва)ть; откла́дывать [отложи́ть]; **~ment** [~mənt] отсро́чка
**postscript** [ˈpəʊsskrɪpt] постскри́птум
**postulate** **1.** [ˈpɒstjʊlət] постула́т; **2.** [~leɪt] постули́ровать (*im*)*pf.*
**posture** [ˈpɒstʃə] (*attitude*) по́за; (*carriage*) оса́нка
**postwar** [pəʊstˈwɔː] послевое́нный
**posy** [ˈpəʊzɪ] буке́т цвето́в
**pot** [pɒt] **1.** горшо́к; котело́к; ***~s of money*** ку́ча де́нег; **2.** *plants* сажа́ть в горшо́к; *jam*, *etc.* заготовля́ть впрок, [за]консерви́ровать
**potato** [pəˈteɪtəʊ] (*single*) карто́фелина; **~es** [~z] *pl.* карто́фель *m*; *coll.* карто́шка; ***~ crisps*** хрустя́щий карто́фель
**pot-belly** брю́хо, пу́зо
**poten|cy** [ˈpəʊtnsɪ] эффекти́вность *f*; (*sexual*) поте́нция; *of drink* кре́пость *f*; **~t** [~tnt] □ эффекти́вный; кре́пкий; **~tial** [pəˈtenʃl] **1.** потенциа́льный, возмо́жный; **2.** потенциа́л
**pothole** [ˈpɒthəʊl] вы́боина, ры́твина
**potion** [ˈpəʊʃn] зе́лье; ***love ~*** любо́вный напи́ток
**pottery** [ˈpɒtərɪ] керами́ческие (*or* гонча́рные) изде́лия *n/pl.*
**pouch** [paʊtʃ] су́мка (*a. biol.*); мешо́чек
**poultry** [ˈpəʊltrɪ] дома́шняя пти́ца
**pounce** [paʊns] **1.** прыжо́к; **2.** набра́сываться [-ро́ситься] ([***up***]***on*** на В)
**pound** [paʊnd] (*weight*) фунт; (*money*) **~** (***sterling***) фунт сте́рлингов (*abbr.* £)
**pound**[2] [~] [ис-, рас]толо́чь; (*strike*) колоти́ть; ***~ to pieces*** разби́ть *pf.*
**pour** [pɔː] *v/t.* лить; ***~ out*** нали́(ва́)ть; *dry substance* сы́пать, насыпа́ть [насы́пать]; *v/i.* ли́ться; [по]сы́паться **~ing** [~rɪŋ]: ***~ rain*** проливно́й дождь *m*
**pout** [paʊt] *v/i.* [на]ду́ться; ***~ one's lips*** наду́(ва́)ть гу́бы
**poverty** [ˈpɒvətɪ] бе́дность *f*
**powder** [ˈpaʊdə] **1.** порошо́к; (*face ~*) пу́дра; (*gun~*) по́рох; **2.** [ис]толо́чь;

[на]пу́дрить(ся); посыпа́ть [посы́пать]; ~ **compact** пу́дреница
**power** ['paʊə] си́ла; мощь *f*; *tech.* мо́щность *f*; *atomic*, *etc.* эне́ргия; *pol.* держа́ва; власть *f*; *law* полномо́чие; *math* сте́пень *f*; ***mental ~s*** у́мственные спосо́бности; **~ful** [-fl] мо́щный, могу́щественный; си́льный; **~less** [-lɪs] бесси́льный; ~ **plant**, ~ **station** электроста́нция
**powwow** ['paʊwaʊ] совеща́ние, собра́ние
**practica|ble** ['præktɪkəbl] □ реа́льный, осуществи́мый; **~l** [-kl] практи́ческий; *mind*, *person*, *etc.* практи́чный; факти́ческий; ~ ***joke*** ро́зыгрыш
**practice** ['præktɪs] пра́ктика; (*training*) упражне́ние, трениро́вка; (*habit*) привы́чка; (*custom*) обы́чай; ***in ~*** факти́чески; ***put into ~*** осуществля́ть [-ви́ть]
**practice**, *Brt.* **practise** [~] *v/t.* применя́ть [-ни́ть]; *medicine*, *etc.* занима́ться [-ня́ться] (Т); упражня́ться в (П); практикова́ть; *v/i.* упражня́ться; **~d** [-t] о́пытный
**practitioner** [præk'tɪʃənə]: ***general ~*** врач-терапе́вт
**praise** [preɪz] **1.** похвала́; **2.** [по]хвали́ть
**praiseworthy** ['preɪzwɜːðɪ] досто́йный похвалы́
**prance** [prɑːns] *of child* пры́гать; *of horse* гарцева́ть
**prank** [præŋk] вы́ходка, прока́за
**prattle** ['prætl] болта́ть; *of baby* лепета́ть
**prawn** [prɔːn] *zo.* креве́тка
**pray** [preɪ] [по]моли́ться; [по]проси́ть
**prayer** [preə] моли́тва; ***Lord's ♀*** О́тче наш; ~ **book** моли́твенник
**pre…** [priː, pri] до…; пред…
**preach** [priːtʃ] пропове́довать; **~er** ['priːtʃə] пропове́дник
**precarious** [prɪ'keərɪəs] (*uncertain*) ненадёжный; (*dangerous*) опа́сный
**precaution** [prɪ'kɔːʃn] предосторо́жность *f*; ***take ~s*** принима́ть [-ня́ть] ме́ры предосторо́жности
**precede** [prɪ'siːd] предше́ствовать (Д); **~nce** ['presɪdəns] первоочерёдность, приорите́т; **~nt** ['presɪdənt] righteous прецеде́нт
**precept** ['priːsept] наставле́ние
**precinct** ['priːsɪŋkt] преде́л; *Am.* (*electoral ~*) избира́тельный о́круг; ***~s*** *pl.* окре́стности *f/pl.*
**precious** ['preʃəs] **1.** □ драгоце́нный; ~ ***metals*** благоро́дные мета́ллы; **2.** *coll. adv.* о́чень
**precipi|ce** ['presɪpɪs] про́пасть *f*; **~tate** **1.** [prɪ'sɪpɪteɪt] вверга́ть [-е́ргнуть]; (*hasten*) ускоря́ть [-о́рить]; **2.** [-tɪt] **a**) □ (*rash*) опроме́тчивый; (*violently hurried*) стреми́тельный; **b**) *chem.* оса́док; **~tous** [prɪ'sɪpɪtəs] □ (*steep*) круто́й; обры́вистый
**precis|e** [prɪ'saɪs] □ то́чный; *tech.* прецизио́нный; **~ion** [~'sɪʒn] то́чность *f*
**preclude** [pri'kluːd] исключа́ть зара́нее; (*prevent*) предотвраща́ть [-ратить] (В); (*hinder*) [по]меша́ть (Д)
**precocious** [prɪ'kəʊʃəs] □ не по года́м разви́то́й
**preconceive** ['priːkən'siːv] представля́ть себе́ зара́нее; **~d** [~d] предвзя́тый
**preconception** [priːkən'sepʃn] предвзя́тое мне́ние
**precondition** [priːkən'dʃn] предвари́тельное усло́вие
**predatory** ['predətrɪ] хи́щный
**predecessor** ['priːdɪsesə] предше́ственник [-ица]
**predestine** [priː'destɪn] предопределя́ть [-ли́ть]; ***~d*** предопределённый
**predetermine** [priːdɪ'tɜːmɪn] предопределя́ть [-ли́ть]
**predicament** [prɪ'dɪkəmənt] нело́вкое положе́ние; серьёзное затрудне́ние
**predicate** ['predɪkət] *gr.* сказу́емое; утвержда́ть [-ди́ть]
**predict** [prɪ'dɪkt] предска́зывать [-за́ть]; **~ion** [~kʃn] предсказа́ние
**predilection** [priːdɪ'lekʃn] скло́нность *f*, пристра́стие (***for*** к Д)
**predispose** [priːdɪs'pəʊz] предраспо-

лага́ть [-ложи́ть]
**predomina|nce** [prɪˈdɒmɪnəns] госпо́дство, преоблада́ние; **~nt** [~nənt] □ преоблада́ющий, домини́рующий; **~te** [~neɪt] госпо́дствовать, преоблада́ть (***over*** над T)
**preeminent** [priːˈemɪnənt] превосходя́щий; выдаю́щийся
**prefabricated** [priːˈfæbrɪkeɪtɪd]: **~ *house*** сбо́рный до́м
**preface** [ˈprefɪs] **1.** предисло́вие; **2.** начина́ть [-ча́ть] (В ***with***, с Р); снабжа́ть предисло́вием
**prefect** [ˈpriːfekt] префе́кт
**prefer** [prɪˈfɜː] предпочита́ть [-почу́есть]; (*put forward*) выдвига́ть [вы́двинуть]; **~able** [ˈprefrəbl] □ предпочти́тельный; **~ence** [~rəns] предпочте́ние; **~ential** [prefəˈrenʃl] □ предпочти́тельный; *econ.* льго́тный
**prefix** [ˈpriːfɪks] пре́фикс, приста́вка
**pregnan|cy** [ˈpregnənsɪ] бере́менность *f*; **~t** [~nənt] □ бере́менная; *fig.* чрева́тый; **~ *pause*** многозначи́тельная па́уза
**prejudice** [ˈpredʒʊdɪs] **1.** предрассу́док; предубежде́ние; **2.** предубежда́ть [-ди́ть]; (*harm*) [по]вреди́ть, наноси́ть уще́рб (Д)
**preliminary** [prɪˈlɪmɪnərɪ] **1.** □ предвари́тельный; **2.** подготови́тельное мероприя́тие
**prelude** [ˈpreljuːd] *mus.* прелю́дия (*a. fig.*)
**prematur|e** [ˈprematjʊə] преждевре́менный; **~ *baby*** недоно́шенный ребёнок
**premeditation** [priːmedɪˈteɪʃn] преднаме́ренность *f*
**premier** [ˈpremɪə] пе́рвый, гла́вный; премье́р-мини́стр
**première** [ˈpremɪeə] премье́ра
**premises** [ˈpremɪsɪz] *pl.* помеще́ние
**premium** [ˈpriːmɪəm] (*reward*) награ́да; *payment* пре́мия; ***at a ~*** вы́ше номина́льной сто́имости; в большо́м спро́се
**premonition** [preːməˈnɪʃn] предчу́вствие
**preoccup|ied** [priːˈɒkjʊpaɪd] озабо́ченный; **~y** [~paɪ] поглоща́ть внима́ние (Р); занима́ться [-ня́ться] (***with*** T)
**prepaid** [priːˈpeɪd] заранее опла́ченный; ***carriage ~*** доста́вка опла́чена
**preparat|ion** [prepəˈreɪʃn] приготовле́ние; подгото́вка; *med.* препара́т; **~ory** [prɪˈpærətrɪ] предвари́тельный; подготови́тельный; **~ *to leaving*** пе́ред тем как уйти́
**prepare** [prɪˈpeə] *v/t. of surprise, etc.* пригота́вливать [-то́вить]; *of dinner, etc.* [при]гото́вить; (*for an exam, etc.*) подгота́вливать [-то́вить]; *v/i.* [при]гото́виться; подгота́вливаться [-то́виться] (***for*** к Д); **~d** [~d] □ гото́вый; подгото́вленный
**prepondera|nce** [prɪˈpɒndərəns] переве́с; **~nt** [~rənt] име́ющий переве́с; **~ntly** [~lɪ] преиму́щественно
**prepossessing** [priːpəˈzesɪŋ] □ располага́ющий; привлека́тельный
**preposterous** [prɪˈpɒstərəs] неле́пый, абсу́рдный
**prerequisite** [priːˈrekwɪzɪt] предпосы́лка, непреме́нное усло́вие
**presage** [ˈpresɪdʒ] предвеща́ть; предчу́вствовать
**preschool** [priːˈskuːl] дошко́льный
**prescribe** [prɪˈskraɪb] предпи́сывать [-писа́ть]; *med.* прописывать [-писа́ть]
**prescription** [prɪˈskrɪpʃn] предпи́сывание; распоряже́ние; *med.* реце́пт
**presence** [ˈprezns] прису́тствие; ***~ of mind*** прису́тствие ду́ха
**present**[1] [ˈpreznt] **1.** □ прису́тствующий; (*existing now*) тепе́решний, настоя́щий; (*given*) да́нный; **2.** настоя́щее вре́мя; ***at ~*** сейча́с; в да́нное вре́мя; ***for the ~*** пока́; на э́тот раз
**present**[2] [prɪˈzent] (*introduce, etc.*) представля́ть [-а́вить]; *gift* преподноси́ть[-нести́]; *petition* под(ав)а́ть (проше́ние); *a play* [по]ста́вить; *ticket* предъявля́ть [-ви́ть]
**present**[3] [ˈpreznt] пода́рок
**presentation** [preznˈteɪʃn] представле́ние, презента́ция; (*exposition*) из-

ложéние
**presentiment** [prɪ'zentɪmənt] предчýвствие
**presently** ['prezntlɪ] вскóре; сейчáс
**preservati|on** [prezə'veɪʃn] охрáна, сохранéние; сохрáнность *f*; **~ve** [prɪ'zɜːvətɪv] консервáнт
**preserve** [prɪ'zɜːv] **1.** сохранять [-нить]; предохранять [-нить]; *vegetables, etc.* консервировать; **2.** (*mst. pl.*) консéрвы *m/pl.*; варéнье; (***game*** **~**) заповéдник
**preside** [prɪ'zaɪd] председáтельствовать (***over*** на П)
**presiden|cy** ['prezɪdənsɪ] президéнтство; **~t** [-dənt] президéнт
**press** [pres] **1.** печáть *f*, прéсса; (*crowd*) толпá; *coll.* дáвка; *tech.* пресс; **2.** *v/t.* жать; давить; *button* наж(им)áть; (*force*) навязывать [-зáть] (***on*** Д); ***I am ~ed for time*** меня поджимáют срóки; у меня мáло врéмени; **~ *for*** настáивать [настоять] на (П); **~ *on*** двигаться дáльше; **~ card** журналистское удостоверéние; **~ing** ['presɪŋ] срóчный, неотлóжный; (*insistent*) настоятельный; **~ure** ['preʃə] давлéние (*a. fig.*); сжáтие
**prestig|e** [pre'stiːʒ] престиж; **~ious** [pre'stɪdʒəs] (*having prestige*) влиятельный; *hono(u)red* уважаемый
**presum|able** [prɪ'zjuːməbl] предположительный; **~e** [prɪ'zjuːm] *v/t.* предполагáть [-ложить]; *v/i.* полагáть; (*dare*) осмéли(ва)ться; **~ (*up*)*on*** злоупотреблять [-бить] (Т); ***he ~s too much*** он слишком мнóго себé позволяет
**presumpt|ion** [prɪ'zʌmpʃn] предположéние; *law* презýмпция; **~uous** [-tʃʊəs] самонадéянный, переступáющий границы чегó-то
**presuppos|e** [priːsə'pəʊz] предполагáть [-ложить]; **~ition** [priːsʌpə'zɪʃn] предположéние
**pretend** [prɪ'tend] притворяться [-риться]; [с]дéлать вид
**pretense**, *Brt.* **pretence** [prɪ'tens] (*false show*) притвóрство; (*pretext*) предлóг
**preten|sion** [prɪ'tenʃn] претéнзия, притязáние (***to*** на В); **~tious** [-ʃəs] претенциóзный
**pretext** ['priːtekst] предлóг
**pretty** ['prɪtɪ] **1.** □ красивый; приятный; хорóшенький; **2.** *adv.* довóльно, весьмá; ***be sitting ~*** хорошó устрóился
**prevail** [prɪ'veɪl] одолевáть [-лéть] (***over*** В); преобладáть; превалировать; (***over*** над Т *or* среди Р); **~ (*up*)*on s.b. to do s.th.*** убедить *pf.* когó-л. чтó-л. сдéлать; **~ing** [-ɪŋ] госпóдствующий, преобладáющий
**prevalent** ['prevələnt] □ распространённый
**prevaricate** [prɪ'værɪkeɪt] уклоняться от прямóго отвéта, увиливать [-льнýть]
**prevent** [prɪ'vent] предотвращáть [-атить]; (*hinder*) [по]мешáть (Д); *crime* предупреждáть [-упредить]; **~ion** [prɪ'venʃn] предупреждéние; предотвращéние; **~ive** [-tɪv] **1.** □ предупредительный; профилактический; **2.** *med.* профилактическое срéдство
**pre|view** ['priːvjuː] *of film, etc* предварительный просмóтр
**previous** ['priːvɪəs] □ предыдýщий; (*premature*) преждеврéменный; **~ *to*** до (Р); **~ly** [-lɪ] прéжде (Р); пéред (Т)
**prewar** [priː'wɔː] довоéнный
**prey** [preɪ] **1.** добыча; (*fig., victim*) жéртва; ***beast*** (***bird***) ***of ~*** хищный зверь *m.* (хищная птица); **2.: ~ (*up*)*on*** охóтиться (на В); *fig.* терзáть
**price** [praɪs] **1.** ценá; **2.** (*value*) оцéнивать [-нить]; назначáть цéну (Д); **~less** ['-lɪs] бесцéнный
**prick** [prɪk] **1.** укóл; шип; *of conscience* угрызéния *n/pl.*; **2.** *v/t.* колóть [кольнýть]; **~ *up one's ears*** навострить ýши; *v/i.* колóться; **~le** ['prɪkl] шип, колючка; **~ly** ['-lɪ] (*having prickles or thorns*) колючий; (*causing stinging sensation*) кóлкий; (*touchy*) обидчивый
**pride** [praɪd] **1.** гóрдость *f*; ***take ~ in*** гордиться (Т); **2.: ~ *o.s.*** гордиться ([***up***]***on*** Т)

P

**priest** [priːst] свяще́нник
**prim** [prɪm] □ чо́порный
**prima|cy** ['praɪməsɪ] пе́рвенство; **~ry** [-rɪ] первонача́льный; *colours, etc.* основно́й; нача́льный; *geol.* перви́чный; ***of ~ importance*** первостепе́нной ва́жности
**prime** [praɪm] **1.** □ (*main*) гла́вный, основно́й; (*original*) первонача́льный; перви́чный; (*excellent*) превосхо́дный; ***~ minister*** премье́рмини́стр; **2.** *fig.* расцве́т; ***in one's ~*** в расцве́те сил; **3.** *v/t.* снабжа́ть информа́цией; ната́скивать
**primer** ['prɪmə] (*schoolbook*) буква́рь *m*; (*paint*) грунто́вка
**primeval** [praɪ'miːvl] □ первобы́тный
**primitive** ['prɪmɪtɪv] первобы́тный; примити́вный
**primrose** ['prɪmrəʊz] при́мула
**prince** [prɪns] (*son of royalty*) принц; князь *m*; **~ss** [prɪn'ses] (*daughter of sovereign*) принце́сса; (*wife of nonroyal prince*) княги́ня; (*daughter of nonroyal prince and princess*) княжна́
**principal** ['prɪnsəpl] **1.** □ гла́вный, основно́й; **2.** *univ.* ре́ктор; *of school* дире́ктор шко́лы; *fin.* основно́й капита́л; *thea.* веду́щий актёр
**principle** ['prɪnsəpl] при́нцип; пра́вило; ***on ~*** из при́нципа; ***a matter of ~*** де́ло при́нципа
**print** [prɪnt] **1.** *typ.* печа́ть *f*; о́ттиск; (*type*) шрифт; (*imprint*) след, отпеча́ток (*a. photo*); *art* гравю́ра; ***out of ~*** тира́ж распро́дан; **2.** [на]печа́тать; *phot.* отпеча́т(ыв)ать; *fig.* запечатле́(ва́)ть (***on*** на П); **~er** ['prɪntə] печа́тник; *comput.* при́нтер
**printing** ['prɪntɪŋ] печа́тание; печа́тное де́ло; ***~ of 50,000 copies*** тира́ж в 50 000 экземпля́ров; *attr.* печа́тный; **~ office** типогра́фия
**prior** ['praɪə] **1.** предше́ствующий (***to*** Д); **2.** *adv.*: ***~ to*** до (Р); **~ity** [praɪ'ɒrətɪ] приорите́т; очерёдность *f*; ***of top ~*** первостепе́нной ва́жности
**prism** ['prɪzəm] при́зма
**prison** ['prɪzn] тюрьма́; **~er** [-ə] заключённый; (*~ of war*) военнопле́нный
**privacy** ['praɪvəsɪ] (*seclusion*) уедине́ние; ли́чная/ча́стная жизнь
**private** ['praɪvɪt] **1.** □ ча́стный; (*personal*) ли́чный; (*secluded*) уединённый; *conversation* с гла́зу на глаз; **2.** *mil.* рядово́й; ***in ~*** конфиденциа́льно; ***keep s.th. ~*** держа́ть в та́йне
**privation** [praɪ'veɪʃn] лише́ние, нужда́
**privatize** ['praɪvɪtaɪz] приватизи́ровать
**privilege** ['prɪvəlɪdʒ] привиле́гия; льго́та; **~d** привилегиро́ванный
**privy** ['prɪvɪ]: ***~ to*** посвящённый в (В)
**prize**[1] [praɪz]: ***~ open*** вскрыва́ть [-ры́ть], взла́мывать [-лома́ть]
**prize**[2] [~] **1.** пре́мия, приз; трофе́й; *in lottery* вы́игрыш; **2.** удосто́енный пре́мии; **3.** высоко́ цени́ть; **~fighter** боксёр-профессиона́л; **~ winner** призёр; лауреа́т
**pro** [prəʊ] *pl.* **pros**: ***the ~s and cons*** до́воды за и про́тив
**probab|ility** [prɒbə'bɪlətɪ] вероя́тность *f*; **~le** ['prɒbəbl] вероя́тный
**probation** [prə'beɪʃn] испыта́тельный срок; *law* усло́вное освобожде́ние
**probe** [prəʊb] *med.* **1.** зонд; **2.** зонди́ровать; *into problem* глубоко́ изуча́ть [-чи́ть]
**problem** ['prɒbləm] пробле́ма; вопро́с; (*difficulty*) тру́дность *f*; *math.* зада́ча; **~atic(al** □) [prɒblə'mætɪk(əl)] проблемати́чный
**procedure** [prə'siːdʒə] процеду́ра
**proceed** [prə'siːd] отправля́ться да́льше; приступа́ть [-пи́ть] (***to*** к Д); (*act*) поступа́ть [-пи́ть]; продолжа́ть [-до́лжить] (***with*** В); ***~ from*** исходи́ть (из Р); **~ing** [-ɪŋ] посту́пок; ***~s*** *pl. law* судопроизво́дство; (*scientific publication*) запи́ски *f/pl.*, труды́ *m/pl.*; **~s** ['prəʊsiːdz] дохо́д, вы́ручка
**process** ['prəʊses] **1.** проце́сс (*a. law*); ***in the ~*** в хо́де; ***in the ~ of construction*** стро́ящийся; **2.** *tech.* обраба́тывать [-бо́тать]; **~ing** [-ɪŋ] *of data, etc.* обрабо́тка; *of food* перерабо́тка; **~ion** [-ʃn] проце́ссия; **~or** [-ə] *comput.* проце́ссор

P

**proclaim** [prə'kleɪm] провозглаша́ть [-ласи́ть]; *war, etc.* объявля́ть [-ви́ть]
**proclamation** [prɒklə'meɪʃn] объявле́ние, провозглаше́ние
**procrastinate** [prəʊ'kræstɪneɪt] (*delay*) *v/i.* оття́гивать [-яну́ть], (*put off*) откла́дывать [отложи́ть]; (*drag out*) тяну́ть
**procure** [prə'kjʊə] *v/t.* дост(ав)а́ть
**prod** [prɒd] **1.** тычо́к, толчо́к; **2.** ты́кать (ткнуть); толка́ть [-кну́ть]; *fig.* подстрека́ть [-кну́ть]
**prodigal** ['prɒdɪgl] расточи́тельный; ***the* ♀ *Son*** блу́дный сын
**prodig|ious** [prə'dɪdʒəs] □ удиви́тельный; (*huge*) грома́дный; **~y** ['prɒdɪdʒɪ] чу́до; ***child* ~** вундерки́нд
**produc|e 1.** [prə'dju:s] (*show*) предъявля́ть [-ви́ть]; (*proof, etc.*) представля́ть [-а́вить]; производи́ть [-вести́]; *film, etc.* [по]ста́вить; *sound* изд(ав)а́ть; **2.** ['prɒdju:s] проду́кция; проду́кт; **~er** [prə'dju:sə] *of goods* производи́тель *m*; *thea.* режиссёр; *cine.* продю́сер
**product** ['prɒdʌkt] проду́кт; изде́лие; **~ion** [prə'dʌkʃn] произво́дство; проду́кция; *thea.* постано́вка; ***mass* ~** ма́ссовое произво́дство; **~ive** [prə'dʌktɪv] □ производи́тельный, *fig.* продукти́вный; *soil* плодоро́дный; *writer* плодови́тый; **~ivity** [prɒdʌk'tɪvətɪ] (*efficiency*) продукти́вность *f*, (*rate of production*) производи́тельность *f*
**profane** [prə'feɪn] (*desecrate*) оскверня́ть [-ни́ть]
**profess** [prə'fes] (*declare*) заявля́ть [-ви́ть]; (*claim*) претендова́ть на (В); ***I don't ~ to be an expert on this subject*** я не счита́ю себя́ специали́стом в э́той о́бласти; **~ion** [prə'feʃn] профе́ссия; **~ional** [~ənl] **1.** □ профессиона́льный; **2.** специали́ст; профессиона́л (*a. sport*); **~or** [~sə] профе́ссор
**proffer** ['prɒfə] предлага́ть [-ложи́ть]
**proficien|cy** [prə'fɪʃnsɪ] овладе́ние; о́пытность *f*; уме́ние; **~t** [~ʃnt] □ уме́лый, иску́сный
**profile** ['prəʊfaɪl] про́филь *m*
**profit** ['prɒfɪt] **1.** *comm.* при́быль *f*; вы́года, по́льза; ***gain ~ from*** извле́чь *pf.* по́льзу из (Р); **2.** *v/t.* приноси́ть по́льзу (Д); *v/i.* **~ *by*** [вос]по́льзоваться (Т); извлека́ть по́льзу из (Р); **~able** [~əbl] при́быльный; вы́годный; поле́зный; **~eer** [prɒfɪ'tɪə] спекуля́нт; **~ sharing** уча́стие в при́были
**profound** [prə'faʊnd] □ глубо́кий; (*thorough*) основа́тельный; **~ly** о́чень, глубоко́
**profus|e** [prə'fju:s] □ оби́льный; ще́дрый; **~ion** [prə'fju:ʒn] изоби́лие
**progeny** ['prɒdʒənɪ] пото́мство
**prognosis** [prɒg'nəʊsɪs] прогно́з
**program(me)** ['prəʊgræm] **1.** програ́мма; **2.** программи́ровать; *comput.* **~er** [~ə] программи́ст
**progress 1.** ['prəʊgres] прогре́сс; продвиже́ние; *in studies* успе́хи *m/pl.*; ***be in ~*** развива́ться; вести́сь; **2.** [prə'gres] продвига́ться вперёд; [с]де́лать успе́хи; **~ive** [~sɪv] □ передово́й, прогресси́вный; *illness, disease* прогресси́рующий; **~ *taxation*** прогресси́вный нало́г
**prohibit** [prə'hɪbɪt] запреща́ть [-ети́ть]; **~ion** [prəʊɪ'bɪʃn] запреще́ние; **~ive** [prə'hɪbətɪv] □ запрети́тельный
**project 1.** ['prɒdʒekt] прое́кт (*a. arch.*); план; **2.** [prə'dʒekt] *v/t. light* броса́ть [бро́сить]; (*plan*) [с-, за]проекти́ровать; *v/i.* (*jut out*) вы́да(ва́)ться; **~ile** [prə'dʒektaɪl] снаря́д
**prolific** [prə'lɪfɪk] (***~ally***) *writer, etc.* плодови́тый
**prolix** ['prəʊlɪks] □ многосло́вный
**prologue** ['prəʊlɒg] проло́г
**prolong** [prə'lɒŋ] продлева́ть [-ли́ть]; *law* пролонги́ровать
**promenade** [prɒmə'nɑ:d] **1.** прогу́лка; ме́сто для прогу́лки; *along waterfront* на́бережная; *in park* алле́я; **2.** прогу́ливаться [-ля́ться]
**prominent** ['prɒmɪnənt] (*conspicuous*) □ ви́дный, заме́тный; (*jutting out*) выступа́ющий; *fig.* (*outstanding*) выдаю́щийся
**promiscuous** [prə'mɪskjʊəs] □ неразбо́рчивый; огу́льный; *sexually* сек-

P

суа́льно распу́щенный

**promis|e** ['prɒmɪs] **1.** обеща́ние; ***make a ~*** [по]обеща́ть; ***show great ~*** подава́ть больши́е наде́жды; **2.** обеща́ть *(im)pf., pf. a.* [по-]; **~ing** [-ɪŋ] □ *fig.* перспекти́вный; подаю́щий наде́жды

**promontory** ['prɒməntrɪ] мыс

**promot|e** [prə'məʊt] (*further*) спосо́бствовать *(im)pf., pf. a.* [по-] (Д); соде́йствовать *(im)pf., pf. a.* [по-] (Д); (*establish*) учрежда́ть [-ди́ть]; (*advance in rank, station, etc.*) повыша́ть по слу́жбе; *mil.* присво́ить (очередно́е) зва́ние (Р); **~ion** [prə'məʊʃn] *in position* повыше́ние; продвиже́ние

**prompt** [prɒmpt] **1.** □ бы́стрый; *reply* неме́дленный; **2.** побужда́ть [-уди́ть]; внуша́ть [-ши́ть]; (*suggest*) подска́зывать [-за́ть] (Д); **~ness** ['prɒmptnɪs] быстрота́; прово́рство

**promulgate** ['prɒmlgeɪt] обнаро́довать; провозглаша́ть [-аси́ть]

**prone** [prəʊn] □ (*face down*) (лежа́щий) ничко́м; **~ *to*** скло́нный к (Д); ***he is ~ to colds*** он легко́ простужа́ется

**prong** [prɒŋ] *agric.* **~s** *pl.* ви́лы *f/pl.*

**pronounce** [prə'naʊns] (*articulate*) произноси́ть [-нести́]; (*proclaim*) объявля́ть [-ви́ть]; (*declare*) заявля́ть [-ви́ть]

**pronunciation** [prənʌnsɪ'eɪʃn] произноше́ние

**proof** [pru:f] **1.** доказа́тельство; (*test*) испыта́ние; прове́рка; *typ.* корректу́ра; **2.** (*impervious*) непроница́емый; **~reader** корре́ктор

**prop** [prɒp] **1.** подпо́рка; *fig.* опо́ра; **2.** подпира́ть [-пере́ть]; **~ *against*** приставля́ть [-вить] к (Д); прислони́ть

**propagate** ['prɒpəgeɪt] размножа́ть(ся) [-о́жить(ся)]; (*spread*) распространя́ть(ся) [-ни́ть(ся)]

**propel** [prə'pel] продвига́ть вперёд; **~ *s.o. towards …*** подтолкну́ть *pf.* кого́-л. к (Д); **~ler** [~ə] пропе́ллер; *naut.* гребно́й винт

**propensity** [prə'pensətɪ] предрасполо́женность *f*; скло́нность *f*

**proper** ['prɒpə] □ (*own, peculiar*) сво́йственный, прису́щий; подходя́щий; пра́вильный; (*decent, seemly*) прили́чный; **~ty** [~tɪ] иму́щество, со́бственность *f*; (*quality*) сво́йство; ***intellectual ~*** интеллектуа́льная со́бственность

**prophe|cy** ['prɒfəsɪ] проро́чество; **~sy** [~saɪ] [на]проро́чить

**prophet** ['prɒfɪt] проро́к

**prophylactic** [prɒfɪ'læktɪk] **1.** профилакти́ческий; **2.** профила́ктика

**proportion** [prə'pɔ:ʃn] **1.** пропо́рция; соразме́рность *f*; (*size*) до́ля, часть *f*; **~s** *pl.* разме́ры *m/pl*; **2.** соразмеря́ть [-ме́рить]; **~al** [~l] пропорциона́льный

**propos|al** [prə'pəʊzl] предложе́ние; **~e** [prə'pəʊz] *v/t.* предлага́ть [-ложи́ть]; *v/i. marriage* сде́лать *pf.* предложе́ние; (*intend*) намерева́ться, предполага́ть; **~ition** [prɒpə'zɪʃn] (*offer*) предложе́ние

**propound** [prə'paʊnd] предлага́ть на обсужде́ние, выдвига́ть [-винуть]

**propriet|ary** [prə'praɪətrɪ]: **~ *rights*** права́ со́бственности; **~ *name*** фи́рменное назва́ние; **~or** [~ətə] владе́лец *m*, -лица *f*; **~y** [~ətɪ] уме́стность *f*, присто́йность *f*

**propulsion** [prə'pʌlʃn] движе́ние вперёд

**prosaic** [prə'zeɪɪk] (**~ally**) *fig.* прозаи́чный

**prose** [prəʊz] **1.** про́за; **2.** прозаи́ческий; *fig.* прозаи́чный

**prosecut|e** ['prɒsɪkju:t] пресле́довать в суде́бном поря́дке; **~ion** [prɒsɪ'kju:ʃn] суде́бное разбира́тельство; **~or** ['prɒsɪkju:tə] *law* обвини́тель *m*; ***public ~*** прокуро́р

**prospect 1.** ['prɒspekt] перспекти́ва, вид (*a. fig.*); **2.** [prə'spekt] *geol.* разве́д(ыв)ать (***for*** на В); **~ive** [prə'spektɪv] □ бу́дущий, ожида́емый; **~us** [~təs] проспе́кт

**prosper** ['prɒspə] *v/i.* процвета́ть; преуспева́ть; **~ity** [prɒ'sperətɪ] процвета́ние; благополу́чие; *fig.* рас-

P

цвéт; **~ous** ['prɒspərəs] состоя́тельный; процвета́ющий
**prostitute** ['prɒstɪtju:t] проститу́тка
**prostrat|e** ['prɒstreɪt] (*lying flat*) распростёртый; (*without srength*) обесси́ленный; **~ *with grief*** сло́мленный го́рем; **~ion** [~ʃn] *fig.* изнеможе́ние
**prosy** ['prəʊzɪ] □ *fig.* прозаи́чный; бана́льный
**protect** [prə'tekt] защища́ть [-ити́ть]; [пред]охраня́ть [-ни́ть] (***from*** от Р); **~ion** [prə'tekʃn] защи́та; **~ive** [~tɪv] защи́тный; предохрани́тельный; **~or** [~tə] защи́тник; (*patron*) покрови́тель *m*
**protest** **1.** ['prəʊtest] проте́ст; **2.** [prə'test] *v/t.* (*declare*) заявля́ть [-ви́ть], утвержда́ть; *v/i.* [за]протестова́ть
**Protestant** ['prɒtɪstənt] **1.** протеста́нт *m*, -ка *f*; **2.** протеста́нтский
**protestation** [prɒtə'steɪʃn] торже́ственное заявле́ние
**protocol** ['prəʊtəkɒl] протоко́л (*a. dipl.*)
**prototype** ['prəʊtətaɪp] прототи́п
**protract** [prə'trækt] тяну́ть (В *or* с Т); продолжа́ть [-до́лжить]; **~ed** затяжно́й
**protru|de** [prə'tru:d] выдава́ться нару́жу, торча́ть; **~ding** [~ɪŋ] выступа́ющий; **~ *eyes*** глаза́ навы́кате; **~sion** [~ʒn] вы́ступ
**protuberance** [prə'tju:bərəns] вы́пуклость *f*
**proud** [praʊd] □ го́рдый (***of*** Т)
**prove** [pru:v] *v/t.* дока́зывать [-за́ть]; *v/i.*; **~ *o.s. to be*** ока́зываться [-за́ться]
**proverb** ['prɒvɜ:b] посло́вица
**provide** [prə'vaɪd] *v/t.* снабжа́ть [-бди́ть]; предоставля́ть [-а́вить]; *law* ста́вить усло́вием; предусма́тривать [-мотре́ть]; *v/i.*: **~ *for one's family*** обеспе́чивать [-чить] свою́ семью́; **~d** (***that***) при усло́вии (что)
**providen|ce** ['prɒvɪdəns] провиде́ние; (*prudence*) предусмотри́тельность *f*; **~t** [~dənt] □ предусмотри́тельный
**provin|ce** ['prɒvɪns] о́бласть *f*; прови́нция; *fig.* сфе́ра де́ятельности; **~cial** [prə'vɪnʃl] **1.** провинциа́льный; **2.** провинциа́л *m*, -ка *f*
**provision** [prə'vɪʒn] снабже́ние; обеспече́ние; *law of contract, etc.* положе́ние; **~*s*** *pl.* проду́кты; **~al** [~ʒənl] □ предвари́тельный; ориентиро́вочный; вре́менный
**proviso** [prə'vaɪzəʊ] усло́вие
**provocat|ion** [prɒvə'keɪʃn] вы́зов; провока́ция; **~ive** [prə'vɒkətɪv] *behaviour* вызыва́ющий; *question, etc.* провокацио́нный
**provoke** [prə'vəʊk] (с)провоци́ровать; (*stir up*) возбужда́ть [-буди́ть]; (*cause*) вызыва́ть [вы́звать]; (*make angry*) [рас]серди́ть
**prowl** [praʊl] кра́сться; броди́ть
**proximity** [prɒk'sɪmətɪ] бли́зость *f*
**proxy** ['prɒksɪ] (*authorization*) полномо́чие; (*substitute*) замести́тель; **~ *vote*** голосова́ние по дове́ренности; дове́ренность *f*
**prude** [pru:d] ханжа́
**pruden|ce** ['pru:dns] благоразу́мие; (*forethought*) предусмотри́тельность *f*; осторо́жность *f*; **~t** [~nt] □ благоразу́мный; осторо́жный; **~ *housekeeper*** бережли́вая хозя́йка
**prudery** ['pru:dərɪ] ха́нжество
**prune**[1] [pru:n] черносли́в
**prune**[2] [~] *agric.* подреза́ть [-ре́зать], обреза́ть [обре́зать]; *fig.* сокраща́ть [-рати́ть]
**pry**[1] [praɪ] подгля́дывать [-яде́ть]; **~ *into*** сова́ть нос в (В)
**pry**[2] [~]: *Am.* **~ *open*** → ***prize***[1]
**psalm** [sɑ:m] псало́м
**pseudonym** ['sju:dənɪm] псевдони́м
**psychiatrist** [saɪ'kaɪətrɪst] психиа́тр
**psychic** ['saɪkɪk], **~al** [~kɪkl] □ психи́ческий
**psycholog|ical** [saɪkə'lɒdʒɪkl] психологи́ческий; **~ist** [saɪ'kɒlədʒɪst] психо́лог; **~y** [~dʒɪ] психоло́гия
**pub** [pʌb] паб, пивно́й бар
**puberty** ['pju:bətɪ] полова́я зре́лость *f*
**public** ['pʌblɪk] **1.** □ публи́чный, обще́ственный; госуда́рственный; коммуна́льный; **~ *convenience*** общ-

P

е́ственный туале́т; **~ *figure*** госуда́рственный де́ятель; **~ *opinion*** обще́ственнос мне́ние; **~ *house*** пивна́я; **~ *spirit*** обще́ственное созна́ние; **2.** пу́блика; обще́ственность *f*; **~ation** [pʌblɪ'keɪʃn] опубликова́ние; изда́ние; ***monthly* ~** ежеме́сячник; **~ity** [pʌb'lɪsətɪ] гла́сность *f*; (*advertising*) рекла́ма

**publish** ['pʌblɪʃ] [о]публикова́ть, изд(ав)а́ть; оглаша́ть [огласи́ть]; **~*ing house*** изда́тельство; **~er** [-ə] изда́тель *m*; **~s** *pl.* изда́тельство

**pucker** ['pʌkə] **1.** [с]мо́рщить(ся); *frown* [на]су́пить(ся); **2.** морщи́на

**pudding** ['pʊdɪŋ] пу́динг; ***black* ~** кровяна́я колбаса́

**puddle** ['pʌdl] лу́жа

**puff** [pʌf] **1.** *of wind* дунове́ние; *of smoke* клуб; **2.** *v/t.* (~ *out*) наду́(ва́)ть; **~*ed eyes*** распу́хшие глаза́ *m/pl.*; *v/i.* дуть поры́вами; пыхте́ть; **~ *away at*** попы́хивать (Т); **~ *out*** наду́(ва́)ться; **~paste** слоёное те́сто; **~y** ['pʌfɪ] запыха́вшийся; *eyes* отёкший; *face* одутлова́тый

**pug** [pʌg]: **~ *dog*** мопс

**pugnacious** [pʌg'neɪʃəs] драчли́вый

**pug-nosed** ['pʌgnəʊzd] курно́сый

**puke** [pju:k] **1.** рво́та; **2.** *v/i.* [вы́]рвать

**pull** [pʊl] **1.** тя́га (*a. fig.*); (*inhalation of smoke*) затя́жка; **2.** [по]тяну́ть; (*drag*) таска́ть, [по]тащи́ть; (~ *out*) выдёргивать [вы́дернуть]; (*tug*) дёргать [-рнуть]; **~ *down*** (*demolish*) сноси́ть [снести́]; **~ *out*** (*move away*) отходи́ть [отойти́]; *med.* **~ *through*** *fig.* спаса́ть [-сти́]; (*recover*) поправля́ться [-а́виться]; **~ *o.s. together*** взять *pf.* себя́ в ру́ки; **~ *up*** подтя́гивать [-яну́ть]; *car, etc.* остана́вливать(ся) [-нови́ть(ся)]

**pulley** ['pʊlɪ] *tech.* блок; шкив

**pullover** ['pʊləʊvə] пуло́вер

**pulp** [pʌlp] *of fruit* мя́коть *f*; *of wood* древе́сная ма́сса; *fig.* бесфо́рменная ма́сса

**pulpit** ['pulpɪt] ка́федра

**puls|ate** [pʌl'seɪt] пульси́ровать; би́ться; **~e** [pʌls] пульс; *tech.* и́мпульс

**pumice** ['pʌmɪs] пе́мза

**pummel** ['pʌml] [по]колоти́ть, [по]бить

**pump** [pʌmp] **1.** насо́с; **2.** кача́ть; **~ *out*** выка́чивать [вы́качать]; **~ *up*** нака́чивать [-ча́ть]

**pumpkin** ['pʌmpkɪn] ты́ква

**pun** [pʌn] **1.** каламбу́р; игра́ слов; **2.** [с]каламбу́рить

**punch** [pʌntʃ] **1.** *tech.* пробо́йник; *for perforating* компо́стер; (*blow with fist*) уда́р кулако́м; **2. ~** *hole* проби́(ва́)ть; [про]компости́ровать; (*hit with fist*) бить кулако́м

**punctilious** [pʌŋk'tɪlɪəs] педанти́чный; щепети́льный до мелоче́й

**punctual** ['pʌŋktʃʊəl] □ пунктуа́льный; **~ity** [pʌŋktʃʊ'ælətɪ] пунктуа́льность *f*

**punctuat|e** ['pʌŋktʃʊeɪt] ста́вить зна́ки препина́ния; *fig.* прерыва́ть [-рва́ть]; **~ion** [pʌŋktʃʊ'eɪʃn] пунктуа́ция; **~ *mark*** знак препина́ния

**puncture** ['pʌŋktʃə] **1.** *tyre* проко́л; *med.* пу́нкция; **2.** прока́лывать [-коло́ть]

**pungen|cy** ['pʌndʒənsɪ] острота́, е́дкость *f*; **~t** [-nt] о́стрый, е́дкий (*a. fig.*)

**punish** ['pʌnɪʃ] нака́зывать [-за́ть]; **~able** [-əbl] наказу́емый; **~ment** [-mənt] наказа́ние

**puny** ['pju:nɪ] кро́хотный; тщеду́шный

**pupil**[1] ['pju:pl] *of eye* зрачо́к

**pupil**[2] [~] учени́к *m*, -и́ца *f*

**puppet** ['pʌpɪt] ку́кла, марионе́тка (*a. fig.*); **~ show** ку́кольное представле́ние

**puppy** ['pʌpɪ] щено́к; *coll.* (*greenhorn*) молокосо́с

**purchas|e** ['pɜ:tʃəs] **1.** поку́пка, заку́пка; **2.** покупа́ть [купи́ть]; приобрета́ть [-рести́]; **~er** [-ə] покупа́тель *m*, -ница *f*; **~ing** [-ɪŋ]: **~ *power*** покупа́тельная спосо́бность

**pure** [pjʊə] □ чи́стый; **~bred** ['pjʊəbred] чистокро́вный, поро́дистый

**purgat|ive** ['pɜ:gətɪv] слаби́тельное; **~ory** [-trɪ] чисти́лище

**purge** [pɜ:dʒ] очища́ть [очи́стить]

P

**purify** ['pjʊərɪfaɪ] очищáть [очи́стить]
**purity** ['pjʊərɪtɪ] чистотá
**purl** [pɜːl] *of water* журчáть
**purple** ['pɜːpl] **1.** пурпу́рный; багрóвый; **2.** ***turn ~*** [по]багровéть
**purport** ['pɜːpət] смысл, суть *f*
**purpose** ['pɜːpəs] **1.** намéрение, цель *f*; целеустремлённость *f*; ***on ~*** намéренно, нарóчно; ***to the ~*** кстáти; к дéлу; ***to no ~*** напрáсно; **2.** имéть цéлью; намеревáться [намéриться]; **~ful** [-fl] □ целенапрáвленный; целеустремлённый; **~less** [-lɪs] □ бесцéльный; **~ly** [-lɪ] нарóчно
**purr** [pɜː] [за]мурлы́кать
**purse** [pɜːs] **1.** кошелёк; *Am.* (*handbag*) сýмочка; ***public ~*** казнá; **2.** *lips* подж(им)áть
**pursuance** [pə'sjuːəns]: выполнéние; ***in (the) ~ of one's duty*** при исполнéнии своúх обя́занностей
**pursu|e** [pə'sjuː] (*go after*) преслéдовать (В); (*work at*) занимáться [заня́ться] (Т); (*continue*) продолжáть [-дóлжить]; **~er** [-ə] преслéдователь *m*, -ница *f*; **~it** [pə'sjuːt] преслéдование; погóня *f*; *mst.* **~s** *pl.* заня́тие
**pus** [pʌs] *med.* гной
**push** [pʊʃ] **1.** толчóк; (*pressure*) давлéние; напóр; (*effort*) уси́лие; *of person* напóристость *f*; ***at a ~*** при необходи́мости; **2.** толкáть [-кнýть]; наж(им)áть (на В); продвигáть(ся) [-ви́нуть(ся)] (*a.* ***~ on***); ***~ into*** *fig.* заставля́ть [-áвить]; ***~ one's way*** протáлкиваться [протолкáться]; **~-button** *el.* нажи́мная кнóпка; **~chair** дéтская *or* прогýлочная (*invalid's* инвали́дная) коля́ска
**puss(y)** ['pʊs(ɪ)] кóшечка, ки́ска
**put** [pʊt] [*irr.*] **1.** класть [положи́ть]; [по]стáвить; сажáть [посади́ть]; *question, etc.* зад(ав)áть; *into pocket, etc.* совáть [сýнуть]; (*express*) выражáть [-азить]; (*explain*) объясня́ть [-ни́ть]; ***~ across a river***, *etc.* перевози́ть [-везти́]; ***~ back*** стáвить на мéсто; стáвить назáд; ***~ by money*** откладывать [отложи́ть]; ***~ down*** (*rebellion*) подавля́ть [-ви́ть]; (*write down*) запи́сывать [-сáть]; (*set down*) положи́ть, [по]стáвить; (*attribute*) припи́сывать [-сáть]; (***to*** Д); ***~ forth*** проявля́ть [-ви́ть]; *shoots* пускáть [пусти́ть]; ***~ in*** вставля́ть [-áвить]; всóвывать [всýнуть]; ***~ off*** (*defer*) откладывать [отложи́ть]; ***~ on*** *dress, etc.* надé(вá)ть; (*feign*) притворя́ться; (*exaggerate*) преувели́чивать [-чить]; *weight* прибавля́ть [-áвить]; ***~ out*** выкладывать [вы́ложить]; (*extend*) протя́гивать [-тянýть]; *fire* [по]туши́ть; ***~ through*** *tel.* соединя́ть [-ни́ть] (***to*** с Т); ***~ to*** прибавля́ть [-бáвить]; ***~ to death*** казни́ть (*im*)*pf.*; ***~ up*** *building* [по]стрóить, возводи́ть [-вести́]; *prices* повышáть [-ы́сить]; давáть [дать] пристáнище; **2.** *v/i.*: ***~ to sea*** [вы]ходи́ть в мóре; ***~ in*** *naut.* заходи́ть в порт; ***~ up at*** останáвливаться [останови́ться] в (П); ***~ up with*** *fig.* мири́ться с (Т)
**putrefy** ['pjuːtrɪfaɪ] [с]гнить; разлагáться [-ложи́ть]
**putrid** ['pjuːtrɪd] □ гнилóй; (*ill-smelling*) вонючий
**putty** ['pʌtɪ] **1.** замáзка; **2.** замáз(ывать)
**puzzle** ['pʌzl] **1.** недоумéние; загáдка, головолóмка; ***crossword ~*** кроссвóрд; **2.** *v/t.* озадáчи(ва)ть; стáвить в тупи́к; ***~ out*** разгадáть распýт(ывать); *v/i.* би́ться (***over*** над Т); **~r** [-ə] *coll.* головолóмка, крéпкий орéшек
**pygmy** ['pɪgmɪ] пигмéй
**pyjamas** [pə'dʒɑːməz] *pl.* пижáма
**pyramid** ['pɪrəmɪd] пирами́да
**python** ['pɑɪθn] питóн

P

# Q

**quack**[1] [kwæk] кря́кать [-кнуть]
**quack**[2] [~] (*sham doctor*) шарлата́н
**quadrangle** ['kwɒdræŋgl] четырёхуго́льник
**quadru|ped** ['kwɒdruped] четвероно́гое живо́тное; **~ple** ['kwɒdrupl] □ учетверённый
**quagmire** ['kwægmaɪə] трясина
**quail** [kweɪl] (*falter*) дро́гнуть *pf.*; (*funk*) [с]тру́сить
**quaint** [kweɪnt] причу́дливый, стра́нный, курьёзный
**quake** [kweɪk] [за]трясти́сь; [за-] дрожа́ть; дро́гнуть *pf.*; *stronger* содрога́ться [-гну́ться]
**quali|fication** [kwɒlɪfɪ'keɪʃn] квалифика́ция; (*restriction*) огово́рка, ограниче́ние; **~fy** ['kwɒlɪfaɪ] *v/t.* квалифици́ровать (*im*)*pf.*; огова́ривать [-вори́ть]; ограни́чи(ва)ть; (*modify*) уточня́ть [-ни́ть]; (*describe*) оце́нивать [-ни́ть] (***as*** Т); *v/i.* подгота́вливаться [-гото́виться] (***for*** к Д); **~ty** [~tɪ] ка́чество; сво́йство
**qualm** [kwɑːm] сомне́ние
**quandary** ['kwɒndərɪ]: ***be in a ~*** не знать как поступи́ть
**quantity** ['kwɒntətɪ] коли́чество; *math.* величина́; мно́жество
**quarantine** ['kwɒrəntiːn] **1.** каранти́н; **2.** подверга́ть каранти́ну; содержа́ть в каранти́не
**quarrel** ['kwɒrəl] **1.** ссо́ра, перебра́нка; **2.** [по]ссо́риться; **~some** □ [~səm] сварли́вый
**quarry** ['kwɒrɪ] **1.** карье́р, каменоло́мня; **2.** добы́(ва́)ть, разраба́тывать
**quart** [kwɔːt] ква́рта
**quarter** ['kwɔːtə] **1.** че́тверть *f*, четвёртая часть; (*three months*) кварта́л; (*place*) ме́сто, сторона́; **~s** *pl. mil.* каза́рмы *f/pl.*; *fig.* исто́чники *m/pl.*; ***from all ~s*** со всех сторо́н; ***~ past two*** че́тверть тре́тьего; **2.** дели́ть на четы́ре ча́сти; (*give lodgings*) *a. mil.* расквартиро́вывать [-ирова́ть]; **~ly** [~lɪ] **1.** кварта́льный; **2.** (*periodical*) ежекварта́льный журна́л
**quartet(te)** [kwɔː'tet] *mus.* кварте́т
**quartz** [kwɒːts] кварц; *attr.* ква́рцевый
**quash** [kwɒʃ] (*cancel*) отменя́ть, аннули́ровать (*im*)*pf.*; (*crush*) подавля́ть [-дави́ть]
**quaver** ['kweɪvə] **1.** дрожь *f*; *mus.* восьма́я но́та; **2.** говори́ть дрожа́щим го́лосом
**quay** [kiː] при́стань *f*
**queasy** ['kwiːzɪ]: □ ***I feel ~*** меня́ тошни́т
**queen** [kwiːn] короле́ва; *chess* ферзь *m*; *cards* да́ма
**queer** [kwɪə] стра́нный, эксцентри́чный; *sl.* (*a. su.*) гомосексуа́льный; гомосексуали́ст
**quench** [kwentʃ] *thirst* утоля́ть [-ли́ть]; *fire* [по]туши́ть; (*cool*) охлажда́ть [охлади́ть]
**querulous** ['kwerʊləs] □ ворчли́вый
**query** ['kwɪərɪ] **1.** вопро́с; (*doubt*) сомне́ние; вопроси́тельный знак; **2.** спра́шивать [спроси́ть]; выража́ть ['-рази́ть] сомне́ние
**quest** [kwest] по́иски *m/pl.*; ***in ~ of*** в по́исках
**question** ['kwestʃən] **1.** вопро́с; сомне́ние; пробле́ма; ***beyond*** (***all***) ***~*** вне вся́кого сомне́ния; ***in ~*** о кото́ром идёт речь; ***call into ~*** подверга́ть сомне́нию; ***settle a ~*** реши́ть *pf.* вопро́с; ***that is out of the ~*** об э́том не мо́жет быть и ре́чи; **2.** расспра́шивать [-роси́ть]; задава́ть вопро́с (Д); (*interrogate*) допра́шивать [-роси́ть]; подверга́ть сомне́нию; **~able** [~əbl] сомни́тельный; **~naire** [kwestʃə'neə] анке́та; *for polls, etc.* вопро́сник
**queue** [kjuː] **1.** о́чередь *f*, хвост; **2.** (*mst. ~* ***up***) станови́ться в о́чередь
**quibble** ['kwɪbl] **1.** (*evasion*) увёртка; спор из-за пустяко́в; **2.** (*evade*) уклоня́ться [-ни́ться]; (*argue*) спо́рить

из-за пустяко́в

**quick** [kwɪk] **1.** (*lively*) живо́й; (*fast*) бы́стрый, ско́рый; *hands*, *etc*. прово́рный; *ear* о́стрый; *eye* зо́ркий; **2.** чувстви́тельное ме́сто; ***cut to the ~*** задева́ть за живо́е; **~en** ['kwɪkən] *v/t*. ускоря́ть [-о́рить]; (*liven*) оживля́ть [-ви́ть]; *v/i*. ускоря́ться [-о́риться]; оживля́ться [-ви́ться]; **~ness** ['kwɪknɪs] быстрота́; оживлённость *f*; *of mind* сообрази́тельность *f*; **~sand** зыбу́чий песо́к *m/pl*.; **~silver** ртуть *f*; **~-witted** [~'wɪtɪd] нахо́дчивый

**quiet** ['kwaɪət] **1.** □ (*calm*) споко́йный, ти́хий; (*noiseless*) бесшу́мный; ***keep s.th. ~*** ума́лчивать [умолча́ть] (о П); **2.** поко́й; тишина́; ***on the ~*** тайко́м, втихомо́лку; **3.** успока́ивать(ся) [-ко́ить(ся)]

**quill** [kwɪl] пти́чье перо́; *of porcupine*, *etc*. игла́

**quilt** [kwɪlt] **1.** стёганое одея́ло; **2.** [вы́]стега́ть; **~ed** ['~ɪd] стёганый

**quince** [kwɪns] *fruit*, *tree* айва́

**quinine** [kwɪ'niːn] *pharm*. хини́н

**quintuple** ['kwɪntjʊpl] пятикра́тный

**quip** [kwɪp] острота́; ко́лкость *f*

**quirk** [kwɜːk] причу́да

**quit** [kwɪt] **1.** покида́ть [-и́нуть]; оставля́ть [-а́вить]; (*stop*) прекраща́ть [-ати́ть]; ***give notice to ~*** под(ав)а́ть заявле́ние об ухо́де; **2.** свобо́дный, отде́лавшийся (***of*** от Р)

**quite** [kwaɪt] вполне́, соверше́нно, совсе́м; (*rather*) дово́льно; ***~ a hero*** настоя́щий геро́й; **~ (*so*)!** так!, соверше́нно ве́рно!

**quits** [kwɪts]: ***we are ~*** мы с ва́ми кви́ты

**quiver** ['kwɪvə] [за]дрожа́ть, [за-] трепета́ть

**quiz** [kwɪz] **1.** (*interrogation*) опро́с; (*written or oral test*) прове́рка зна́ний; *entertainment* виктори́на; **2.** расспра́шивать [-роси́ть], опра́шивать [опроси́ть]

**quizzical** ['kwɪzɪkl] *look* насме́шливый

**quorum** ['kwɔːrəm] *parl*. кво́рум

**quota** ['kwəʊtə] до́ля, часть *f*, кво́та

**quotation** [kwəʊ'teɪʃn] цита́та; цити́рование

**quote** [kwəʊt] [про]цити́ровать

# R

**rabbi** ['ræbaɪ] равви́н

**rabbit** ['ræbɪt] кро́лик

**rabble** ['ræbl] сброд; чернь *f*

**rabid** ['ræbɪd] □ неи́стовый, я́ростный; бе́шеный

**rabies** ['reɪbiːz] бе́шенство

**race**[1] [reɪs] ра́са; (*breed*) поро́да

**race**[2] [~] **1.** состяза́ние в ско́рости; бег; го́нки *f/pl*.; ***horse ~s*** *pl*. ска́чки *f/pl*.; бега́ *m/pl*.; **2.** (*move at speed*) [по]мча́ться; *compete* состяза́ться в ско́рости; уча́ствовать в ска́чках *и т.п.*; **~course** ипподро́м; **~track** *sport* трек; *for cars*, *etc*. автомотодром

**racial** ['reɪʃl] ра́совый

**rack** [ræk] **1.** ве́шалка; *for dishes* суши́лка; (*shelves*) стелла́ж, по́лка; *rail*. ***luggage ~*** се́тка для веще́й; ***go to ~ and ruin*** пойти́ пра́хом; погиба́ть [-и́бнуть]; разоря́ться [-ри́ться]; **2.** ***~ one's brains*** лома́ть себе́ го́лову

**racket**[1] ['rækɪt] те́ннисная раке́тка

**racket**[2] [~] шум, гам; *Am*. рэ́кет; **~eer** [rækə'tɪə] афери́ст; *Am*. вымога́тель *m*, рэкети́р

**racy** ['reɪsɪ] □ пика́нтный; колори́тный; риско́ванный

**radar** ['reɪdɑː] рада́р; радиолока́тор

**radian|ce** ['reɪdɪəns] сия́ние; **~t** [~nt] □ (*transmitted by radiation*) лучи́стый; (*shining*, *resplendent*) сия́ющий, лучеза́рный

**radiat|e** ['reɪdɪeɪt] излуча́ть [-чи́ть]; **~ion** [reɪdɪ'eɪʃn] излуче́ние; **~or** ['reɪ-

dıeıtə] излуча́тель *m*; *mot.* радиа́тор; *for heating* батаре́я, радиа́тор
**radical** ['rædıkl] **1.** □ *pol.* радика́льный; (*fundamental*) коренно́й; **2.** *math.* ко́рень *m*; *pol.* радика́л
**radio** ['reıdıəʊ] **1.** ра́дио *n indecl.*; **~ show** радиопостано́вка; **~ set** радиоприёмник; **~therapy** рентгенотерапи́я; **2.** передава́ть по ра́дио; **~active** радиоакти́вный; **~ waste** радиоакти́вные отхо́ды; **~activity** радиоакти́вность *f*; **~graph** [-grɑːf] рентге́новский сни́мок
**radish** ['rædıʃ] ре́дька; (**red**) **~** реди́ска; **~es** *pl.* реди́с *collect.*
**radius** ['reıdıəs] ра́диус; **within a ~ of** в ра́диусе (Р)
**raffle** ['ræfl] **1.** *v/t.* разы́грывать в лотере́е; *v/i.* уча́ствовать в лотере́е; **2.** лотере́я
**raft** [rɑːft] **1.** плот; **2.** *timber* сплавля́ть [-а́вить]; **~er** [~ə] *arch.* стропи́ло
**rag** [ræg] тря́пка; **~s** *pl.* тряпьё, ве́тошь *f*; лохмо́тья *m/pl.*
**ragamuffin** ['rægəmʌfın] оборва́нец; у́личный мальчи́шка
**rage** [reıdʒ] **1.** я́рость *f*, гнев; (*vogue*) пова́льное увлече́ние; **it is all the ~** э́то после́дний крик мо́ды; **2.** [вз]беси́ться; *of storm, etc.* бушева́ть
**ragged** ['rægıd] □ неро́вный; *clothes* рва́ный
**ragout** ['ræguː] *cul.* рагу́
**raid** [reıd] **1.** *mil.* налёт; *by police* обла́ва; **2.** соверша́ть [-ши́ть] налёт на (В); *mil.* вторга́ться [вто́ргнуться] в (В)
**rail**¹ [reıl] **1.** (*hand~*) пери́ла *n/pl.*; (*fence*) огра́да; *rail* рельс; *naut.* по́ручень *m*; **go off the ~s** сойти́ *pf.* с ре́льсов; *fig.* сби́ться с *pf.* пути́; **2.** е́хать по желе́зной доро́ге
**rail**² [~] [вы́]руга́ть, [вы́]брани́ть (**at, against** В)
**railing** ['reılıŋ] огра́да; пери́ла *n/pl.*
**railroad** ['reılrəʊd] *chiefly Am.*, **railway** [~weı] желе́зная доро́га
**rain** [reın] **1.** дождь *m*; **2. it's ~ing** идёт дождь; *fig.* [по]сы́паться; **~bow** ра́дуга; **~coat** *Am.* дождеви́к, плащ; **~fall** коли́чество оса́дков; **~y** ['reını] дождли́вый; *fig.* **for a ~ day** на чёрный день *m*
**raise** [reız] (*often* **~ up**) поднима́ть [-ня́ть]; *monument* воздвига́ть [-ви́гнуть]; (*elevate*) возвыша́ть [-ы́сить]; (*bring up*) воспи́тывать [-ита́ть]; *laughter, suspicion, etc.* вызыва́ть [вы́звать]; *money* добы́(ва́)ть, собира́ть; *increase* повыша́ть [-вы́сить]
**raisin** ['reızn] изю́минка; *pl.* изю́м *collect.*
**rake**¹ [reık] **1.** *agric.* гра́бли *f/pl.*; **2.** *v/t.* сгреба́ть [-ести́]; разгреба́ть [-ести́]; *fig.* **~ for** тща́тельно иска́ть (В *or* Р)
**rake**² [~] пове́са, распу́тник
**rally** ['rælı] **1.** (*gather*) собира́ть(ся) [собра́ть(ся)]; *fig.* собра́ться *pf.* с си́лами; овладе́(ва́)ть собо́й; (*rouse*) воодушевля́ть [-шеви́ть]; (*recover*) оправля́ться [опра́виться]; **2.** *Am.* ма́ссовый ми́тинг; *sport* ра́лли
**ram** [ræm] **1.** бара́н; *astr.* Ове́н; **2.** [про]тара́нить; заби́(ва́)ть; **~ home** вдолби́ть *pf.* в го́лову
**rambl|e** ['ræmbl] **1.** прогу́лка; **2.** (*wander*) броди́ть; (*speak incoherently*) говори́ть бессвя́зно; **~er** [~ə] праздношата́ющийся; (*plant*) ползу́чее расте́ние; **~ing** [~ıŋ] бродя́чий; бессвя́зный; *town* беспоря́дочно разбро́санный; ползу́чий
**ramify** ['ræmıfaı] разветвля́ться [-етви́ться]
**ramp** [ræmp] скат, укло́н; **~ant** ['ræmpənt] *plants* бу́йный; *sickness, etc.* свире́пствующий; *fig.* (*unrestrained*) необу́зданный
**rampart** ['ræmpɑːt] крепостно́й вал
**ramshackle** ['ræmʃækl] ве́тхий; обветша́лый
**ran** [ræn] *pt. от* **run**
**ranch** [ræntʃ] ра́нчо *n indecl.* фе́рма
**rancid** ['rænsıd] □ прого́рклый
**ranco(u)r** ['ræŋkə] зло́ба
**random** ['rændəm] **1. at ~** наугáд, наобу́м; **2.** сде́ланный (вы́бранный *и т.д.*) наудáчу; случáйный
**rang** [ræŋ] *pt. от* **ring**
**range** [reındʒ] **1.** ряд; *of mountains*

R

цепь *f*; (*extent*) предéл, амплитýда; диапазóн (*a. mus.*); *mil.* (*shooting* ~) стрéльбище; **2.** *v/t.* выстрáивать в ряд; располагáть [-ложи́ть]; *v/i.* выстрáиваться в ряд, располагáться [-ложи́ться]; *of land* простирáться; (*wander*) броди́ть

**rank** [ræŋk] **1.** ряд; *mil.* шерéнга; (*status*) звáние, чин; категóрия; ***~ and file*** рядовóй состáв; *fig.* обыкновéнные лю́ди; **2.** *v/t.* стрóить в шерéнгу; выстрáивать в ряд; классифици́ровать (*im*)*pf.*; (*consider*) считáть; *v/i.* стрóиться в шерéнгу; равня́ться (***with*** Д); **3.** *vegetation* бу́йный

**rankle** ['ræŋkl] (*fester*) гнои́ться; причиня́ть [-ни́ть] гнев, боль *f*

**ransack** ['rænsæk] (*search*) [по-] ры́ться в (П); (*plunder*) [о]грáбить

**ransom** ['rænsəm] вы́куп

**rant** [rænt] разглагóльствовать

**rap** [ræp] **1.** лёгкий удáр; *at door, etc.* стук; *fig.* ***not a ~*** ни грóша; **2.** ударя́ть [удáрить]; [по]стучáть

**rapaci|ous** [rə'peɪʃəs] □ жáдный; *animal* хи́щный; **~ty** [rə'pæsɪtɪ] жáдность *f*; хи́щность *f*

**rape** [reɪp] **1.** изнаси́лование; **2.** [из]наси́ловать

**rapid** ['ræpɪd] **1.** □ бы́стрый, скóрый; **2.** ***~s*** *pl.* порóги *m/pl.*; **~ity** [rə'pɪdətɪ] быстротá скóрость *f*

**rapt** [ræpt] (*carried away*) восхищённый; (*engrossed*) поглощённый; **~ure** ['ræptʃə] востóрг, экстáз; ***go into ~s*** приходи́ть в востóрг

**rare** [reə] □ рéдкий; *air* разрежённый; *undercooked* недожáренный; ***at ~ intervals*** рéдко

**rarity** ['reərətɪ] рéдкость *f*; *thing* раритéт

**rascal** ['rɑːskl] мошéнник; *child coll.* плути́шка

**rash**[1] [ræʃ] □ опромéтчивый; необдýманный

**rash**[2] [~] *med.* сыпь *f*

**rasp** [rɑːsp] **1.** (*grating sound*) скрéжет; **2.** скрежетáть; ***~ing voice*** скрипу́чий гóлос

**raspberry** ['rɑːzbrɪ] мали́на

**rat** [ræt] кры́са; ***smell a ~*** [по]чу́ять недóброе

**rate**[1] [reɪt] **1.** нóрма; стáвка; (*tax*) мéстный налóг; разря́д; (*speed*) скóрость *f*; ***at any ~*** во вся́ком слу́чае; ***~ of exchange*** (валю́тный) курс; ***~ of profit*** нóрма при́были; ***interest ~*** процéнтная стáвка; ***birth ~*** рождáемость *f*; ***death ~*** смéртность *f*; **2.** оцéнивать [-ни́ть]; расцéнивать [-ни́ть]; *fin.* облагáться налóгом; ***~ among*** считáться среди́ (Р)

**rate**[2] [~] (*scold*) брани́ть [вы́бранить] [от]ругáть

**rather** ['rɑːðə] скорéе; предпочти́тельно; вернéе; довóльно; ***I had ~…*** я предпочёл бы …; *int.* ещё бы!

**ratify** ['rætɪfaɪ] ратифици́ровать (*im*)*pf.*; утверждáть [-рди́ть]

**rating** ['reɪtɪŋ] (*valuing*) оцéнка; су́мма налóга; класс; *in opinion poll* рéйтинг

**ratio** ['reɪʃɪəʊ] соотношéние, пропóрция; коэффициéнт

**ration** ['ræʃn] **1.** рациóн; паёк; **2.** норми́ровать вы́дачу (Р)

**rational** ['ræʃnl] □ рационáльный; разу́мный; **~ity** [ræʃə'nælətɪ] рационáльность *f*; разу́мность *f*; **~ize** ['ræʃnəlaɪz] (*give reasons for*) оправ-дывать [-дáть]; (*make mare efficient*) рационализи́ровать (*im*)*pf.*

**rattle** ['rætl] **1.** треск; *of window* дребезжáние; *of talk* трескотня́; (*baby's toy*) погрему́шка; **2.** [за]дребезжáть; *of train, etc.* [про]громыхáть; *of pots, etc.* [за]гремéть (Т); говори́ть без у́молку; ***~ off*** отбарабáнить *pf.*; **~snake** гремýчая змея́

**ravage** ['rævɪdʒ] **1.** опустошéние; **2.** опустошáть [-ши́ть], разоря́ть [-ри́ть]

**rave** [reɪv] брéдить (*a. fig.*), говори́ть бессвя́зно; (*rage*) неистовствовать; ***~ about*** быть без умá от (Р)

**ravel** ['rævl] *v/t.* запу́т(ыв)ать; распу́т(ыв)ать; *v/i.* запу́т(ыв)аться; (*a.* ***~ out***) расползáться по швам

**raven** ['reɪvn] вóрон

R

**ravenous** ['rævənəs] прожо́рливый; ***feel ~*** быть голо́дным как волк
**ravine** [rə'viːn] овра́г, лощи́на
**raving** ['reɪvɪŋ]: ***he's ~ mad*** он совсе́м спя́тил
**ravish** ['rævɪʃ] приводи́ть в восто́рг; **~ing** [~ɪŋ] восхити́тельный
**raw** [rɔː] □ сыро́й; *hide, etc.* необрабо́танный; (*inexperienced*) нео́пытный; *knee, etc.* обо́дранный; **~boned** худо́й, костля́вый; **~ material** сырьё
**ray** [reɪ] луч; *fig.* про́блеск
**rayon** ['reɪɒn] иску́сственный шёлк, виско́за
**raze** [reɪz]: ***~ to the ground*** разруша́ть до основа́ния
**razor** ['reɪzə] бри́тва; **~ blade** ле́звие бри́твы
**re...** [riː] *pref.* (*придаёт слову значения*:) сно́ва, за́ново, ещё раз, обра́тно
**reach** [riːtʃ] **1.** ***beyond ~*** вне преде́лов досяга́емости; ***within easy ~*** побли́зости; под руко́й; ***within ~*** *financially* досту́пный; **2.** *v/t.* достига́ть [-и́гнуть] (Р); доезжа́ть [дойти́] до (Р); *of forest, land, etc.* простира́ться [-стере́ться] до (Р); (*pass*) протя́гивать [-яну́ть]; (*get to*) дост(ав)а́ть до (Р); *v/i.* протя́гивать ру́ку (***for*** за Т)
**react** [rɪ'ækt] реаги́ровать; ***~ against*** *idea, plan, etc.* возража́ть [-зи́ть] (про́тив Р)
**reaction** [rɪ'ækʃn] реа́кция; **~ary** [~ʃənrɪ] **1.** реакцио́нный; **2.** реакционе́р
**read 1.** [riːd] [*irr.*] [про]чита́ть; (*study*) изуча́ть [-чи́ть]; (*interpret*) истолко́вывать [-кова́ть]; *of instrument* пока́зывать [-за́ть]; *of text* гласи́ть; ***~ to s.o.*** чита́ть кому́-л. вслух; **2.** [red] **a**) *pt. и pt. p. от* ***read 1.***; **b**) *adj.*: ***well-~*** начи́танный; **~able** ['~əbl] разбо́рчивый; интере́сный; (*legible*) чёткий; **~er** ['~ə] чита́тель(ница *f*) *m*; (*reciter*) чтец; *univ.* ле́ктор
**readi|ly** ['redɪlɪ] *adv.* охо́тно; без труда́; легко́; **~ness** [~nɪs] гото́вность *f*; подгото́вленность *f*
**reading** ['riːdɪŋ] чте́ние; (*interpretation*) толкова́ние, понима́ние; *parl.* чте́ние (законопрое́кта); **~ lamp** насто́льная ла́мпа; **~ room** чита́льный зал
**readjust** [riːə'dʒʌst] *tech.* отрегули́ровать; приспоса́бливать [-со́бить]; *of attitude situation, etc.* пересма́тривать [-смотре́ть]; **~ment** [~mənt] регулиро́вка; приспособле́ние
**ready** ['redɪ] □ гото́вый; *money* нали́чный; ***make*** (*или* ***get***) **~** [при]гото́вить(ся); **~-made** гото́вый
**reaffirm** [riːə'fɜːm] вновь подтвержда́ть
**reagent** [riː'eɪdʒənt] *chem.* реакти́в
**real** [rɪəl] □ действи́тельный; реа́льный; настоя́щий; ***~ estate*** недви́жимость *f*; **~ity** [rɪ'ælətɪ] действи́тельность *f*; **~ization** [rɪəlaɪ'zeɪʃn] понима́ние, осозна́ние; (*implementation*) осуществле́ние, реализа́ция (*a. comm.*); **~ize** ['rɪəlaɪz] представля́ть себе́; осуществля́ть [-ви́ть]; осозн(ав)а́ть; сообража́ть [-ази́ть]; реализова́ть (*im*)*pf.*
**realm** [relm] короле́вство; ца́рство; *fig.* сфе́ра; ***be in the ~ of fantasy*** из о́бласти фанта́зии
**reanimate** [riː'ænɪmeɪt] оживля́ть [-ви́ть]; воскреша́ть, [-еси́ть]
**reap** [riːp] [с]жать; *fig.* пож(ин)а́ть; **~er** ['~ə] *machine* жа́тка
**reappear** ['riːə'pɪə] сно́ва появля́ться
**reappraisal** [riːə'preɪzl] переоце́нка
**rear** [rɪə] **1.** *v/t.* воспи́тывать [-та́ть]; (*breed*) выра́щивать [вы́растить]; *v/i. of horse* станови́ться на дыбы́; **2.** за́дняя сторона́; *mil.* тыл; ***at the ~ of, in the ~ of*** позади́ (Р); **3.** за́дний; ты́льный; **~ admiral** контрадмира́л
**rearm** [riː'ɑːm] перевооружа́ть(ся) [-жи́ть(ся)]
**rearrange** [riːə'reɪndʒ] перестра́ивать [-стро́ить]; *timetable, etc.* изменя́ть [-ни́ть], переде́лывать [-лать]; *furniture* переставля́ть [-ста́вить]
**reason** ['riːzn] **1.** (*intellectual capability*) ра́зум, рассу́док; (*cause*) основа́ние, причи́на; (*sense*) смысл; ***by ~ of*** по причи́не (Р); ***for this ~*** поэ́тому;

R

***it stands to ~ that …*** я́сно, что …, очеви́дно, что …; **2.** *v/i.* рассужда́ть [-уди́ть]; **~ *out*** разга́дывать [-да́ть]; продýмать *pf.* до конца́; **~ *out of*** разубежда́ть [-еди́ть] в (П); **~able** [~əbl] □ (благо)разýмный; (*moderate*) уме́ренный; **~ing** [~ɪŋ] рассужде́ние

**reassure** [riːə'ʃʊə] успока́ивать [-ко́ить], ободря́ть [-ри́ть]

**rebate** ['riːbeɪt] *comm.* ски́дка; вы́чет

**rebel 1.** ['rebl] бунтовщи́к *m*, -и́ца *f*; (*insurgent*) повста́нец; *fig.* бунта́рь *m*; **2.** [~] (*a.* **~lious** [rɪ'beljəs]) мяте́жный; **3.** [rɪ'bel] восст(ав)а́ть; бунтова́ть [взбунтова́ться]; **~lion** [rɪ'beljən] восста́ние; (*riot*) бунт

**rebirth** [riː'bɜːθ] возрожде́ние

**rebound** [rɪ'baʊnd] **1.** отска́кивать [-скочи́ть]; **~ *on*** *fig.* обора́чиваться [оберну́ться] (про́тив Р); **2.** рикоше́т; отско́к

**rebuff** [rɪ'bʌf] **1.** отпо́р; ре́зкий отка́з; **2.** дава́ть о́тпор (Д)

**rebuild** [riː'bɪld] [*irr.* (***build***)] сно́ва [по] стро́ить; реконструи́ровать; перестра́ивать [-стро́ить]

**rebuke** [rɪ'bjuːk] **1.** упрёк; вы́говор; **2.** упрека́ть [-кнýть], де́лать вы́говор (Д)

**recall** [rɪ'kɔːl] **1.** *of diplomat, etc.* о́тзыв; ***beyond ~*** безвозвра́тно, бесповоро́тно; **2.** отзыва́ть [отозва́ть]; (*revoke*) отменя́ть [-ни́ть]; (*remind*) напомина́ть [-о́мнить]; (*call to mind*) вспомина́ть [-о́мнить] (В)

**recapture** [riː'kæptʃe] *territory* взять обра́тно; освобожда́ть [-боди́ть]; ***~ the atmosphere*** воссоздава́ть [-да́ть] атмосфе́ру

**recede** [rɪ'siːd] (*move back*) отступа́ть [-пи́ть]; (*move away*) удаля́ться [-ли́ться]

**receipt** [rɪ'siːt] (*document*) распи́ска, квита́нция; (*receiving*) получе́ние; *cul.* реце́пт; **~s** *pl.* прихо́д

**receive** [rɪ'siːv] получа́ть [-чи́ть]; *guests, etc.* принима́ть [-ня́ть]; *news, ideas* воспринима́ть [-ня́ть]; **~r** [~ə] получа́тель *m*, -ница *f*; *tel.* телефо́нная тру́бка; *radio* приёмник

**recent** ['riːsnt] □ неда́вний; све́жий; но́вый; ***in ~ years*** в после́дние го́ды; **~ly** [~lɪ] неда́вно

**receptacle** [rɪ'septəkl] вмести́лище

**reception** [rɪ'sepʃn] получе́ние; приём; **~ *desk*** *in hotel* регистрация; *in hospital* регистратýра; **~ist** [~ənɪst] регистра́тор

**receptive** [rɪ'septɪv] □ восприи́мчивый (к Д)

**recess** [rɪ'ses] *parl.* кани́кулы *f/pl.*; (*break*) переры́в; *arch.* ни́ша; ***~es*** *pl. fig.* глуби́ны *f/pl.*; **~ion** [~ʃn] *econ.* спад

**recipe** ['resəpɪ] *cul.* реце́пт

**recipient** [rɪ'sɪpɪənt] получа́тель *m*, -ница *f*

**reciproc|al** [rɪ'sɪprəkl] взаи́мный; обою́дный; **~ate** [~keɪt] отвеча́ть [-ве́тить] взаи́мностью; (*interchange*) обме́ниваться [-ня́ться]; **~ity** [resɪ'prɒsətɪ] взаи́мность *f*

**recit|al** [rɪ'saɪtl] чте́ние, деклама́ция; (*account*) повествова́ние, расска́з; *mus.* со́льный; **~ation** [resɪ'teɪʃn] деклама́ция; **~e** [rɪ'saɪt] [про]деклами́ровать

**reckless** ['reklɪs] □ безрассу́дный; опроме́тчивый; беспе́чный

**reckon** ['rekən] *v/t.* счита́ть; причисля́ть [-чи́слить] (***among*** к Д); счита́ть [счесть] за (В); **~ *up*** подсчита́ть *pf.*; *v/i.* (*consider*) счита́ть, ду́мать, предполага́ть [-ложи́ть]; **~ (*up*)*on*** *fig.* рассчи́тывать на (В); ***a man to be ~ed with*** челове́к, с кото́рым сле́дует счита́ться; **~ing** [~ɪŋ] подсчёт, счёт; распла́та

**reclaim** [rɪ'kleɪm] [по]тре́бовать обра́тно; *waste* утилизи́ровать; *land* осва́ивать [-во́ить]; *neglected land* рекультиви́ровать

**recline** [rɪ'klaɪn] отки́дывать(ся) [-и́нуть(ся)]; полулежа́ть

**recluse** [rɪ'kluːs] отше́льник *m*, -ица *f*

**recogni|tion** [rekəg'nɪʃn] (*realization*) осозна́ние; узнава́ние; призна́ние (Р); ***change beyond ~*** изменя́ться [-ни́ться] до неузнава́емости; ***gain ~*** доби́ться *pf.* призна́ния; **~ze** ['rek-

R

əgnaɪz] узн(ав)áть; призн(ав)áть

**recoil** [rɪˈkɔɪl] **1.** *mil.* отдáча; **2.** отскáкивать [-скочи́ть], отпря́нуть *pf.*; *of gun* отдавáть [-дáть]

**recollect** [rekəˈlekt] вспоминáть [вспóмнить] (В); ***as far as I can ~*** наскóлько я пóмню; **~ion** [rekəˈlekʃn] воспоминáние, пáмять *f* (***of*** о П)

**recommend** [rekəˈmend] рекомендовáть *(im)pf.*, *pf. a.* [по-], [по]совéтовать; **~ation** [rekəmenˈdeɪʃn] рекомендáция

**recompense** [ˈrekəmpens] **1.** вознаграждéние; компенсáция; ***as*** *or* ***in ~*** в кáчестве компенсáции (***for*** за В); ***2.*** вознаграждáть [-ради́ть]; отплáчивать [отплати́ть] (Д); *for a loss, etc.* компенси́ровать, возмещáть [-мести́ть]

**reconcil|e** [ˈrekənsaɪl] примиря́ть [-ри́ть] (***to*** с Т); улáживать [улáдить]; ***~ o.s.*** примиря́ться [-ри́ться]; **~iation** [rekənsɪlɪˈeɪʃn] примирéние; улáживание

**recon|aissance** [rɪˈkɒnəsns] *mil.* развéдка; **~noitre** [rekəˈnɔɪtə] производи́ть развéдку; развéд(ыв)ать

**reconsider** [riːkənˈsɪdə] пересмáтривать [-мотрéть]

**reconstruct** [riːkənsˈtrʌkt] восстанáвливать [-нови́ть]; перестрáивать [-стрóить]; **~ion** [-ˈstrʌkʃn] реконстру́кция; восстановлéние

**record 1.** [ˈrekɔːd] зáпись *f*; *sport* рекóрд; *of meeting* протокóл; ***place on ~*** запи́сывать [-сáть]; граммофóнная пласти́нка, диск; репутáция; ***~ library*** фонотéка; ***~ office*** госудáрственный архи́в; ***off the ~*** неофициáльно; ***on ~*** зарегистри́рованный; *attr.* рекóрдный; ***in ~ time*** в рекóрдно корóткое врéмя; **2.** [rɪˈkɔːd] [за]пи́сывать [-сáть], [за]регистри́ровать; **~er** [rɪˈkɔːdə] регистрáтор; (*instrument*) самопи́сец; **~ing** [-ɪŋ] зáпись *f* (*a. mus.*)

**recount** [rɪˈkaʊnt] расскáзывать [-зáть]

**recourse** [rɪˈkɔːs]: ***have ~ to*** прибегáть [-бéгнуть] к (Р)

**recover** [rɪˈkʌvə] *v/t.* получáть обрáтно; верну́ть *pf.*; *waste* утилизи́ровать, регенери́ровать; *v/i. from illness* оправля́ться [-áвиться]; **~y** [-rɪ] восстановлéние; выздоровлéние; ***economic ~*** восстановлéние нарóдного хозя́йства

**recreation** [rekrɪˈeɪʃn] óтдых; развлечéние

**recrimination** [rɪkrɪmɪˈneɪʃn] контрообвинéние

**recruit** [rɪˈkruːt] **1.** *mil.* новобрáнец; *fig.* новичóк; **2.** брать [взять] на воéнную слу́жбу; *new players* наб(и)рáть; *for work* [за]вербовáть

**rectangle** [ˈrektæŋgl] прямоугóльник

**recti|fy** [ˈrektɪfaɪ] (*put right*) исправля́ть [-áвить]; **~tude** [ˈrektɪtjuːd] прямотá, чéстность *f*

**rector** [ˈrektə] *univ.* рéктор; *eccl.* пáстор, свящéнник; **~y** [-rɪ] дом свящéнника

**recumbent** [rɪˈkʌmbənt] лежáчий

**recuperate** [rɪˈkjuːpəreɪt] восстанáвливать си́лы; оправля́ться [оправиться]

**recur** [rɪˈkɜː] (*be repeated*) повторя́ться [-и́ться]; (*go back to s.th.*) возращáться [-рати́ться] (***to*** к Д); *of ideas, event* приходи́ть снóва на ум, на пáмять; (*happen again*) происходи́ть вновь; **~rence** [rɪˈkʌrəns] повторéние; **~rent** [-rənt] □ повторя́ющийся; периоди́ческий; *med.* возврáтный

**recycling** [riːˈsaɪklɪŋ] переработка; повтóрное испóльзование

**red** [red] **1.** крáсный; ***~ herring*** *fig.* отвлечéние внимáния; ***♀ Cross*** Крáсный Крест; ***~ tape*** волоки́та, бюрократи́зм; **2.** крáсный цвет

**red|breast** [ˈredbrest] мали́новка; **~den** [ˈredn] [по]краснéть

**redeem** [rɪˈdiːm] (*make amends*) искупáть [-пи́ть]; (*get back*) выкупáть [вы́купить]; спасáть [-сти́]; **~er** [-ə] спаси́тель *m*

**red-handed** [redˈhændɪd]: ***catch a p. ~*** поймáть *pf.* когó-л. на мéсте преступлéния

**red-hot** [redˈhɒt] накалённый докрас-

R

на́; горя́чий; *fig.* взбешённый
**redirect** [riːdɪ'rekt] *letter* переадресо́вывать [-ва́ть]
**red-letter** [red'letə]: **~ *day*** счастли́вый день; кра́сный день календаря́
**redness** ['rednɪs] краснота́
**redouble** [riː'dʌbl] удва́ивать(ся) [удво́ить(ся)]
**redress** [rɪ'dres] **1.** *errors, etc.* исправле́ние; *law* возмеще́ние; **2.** исправля́ть [-а́вить]; возмеща́ть [-ести́ть]
**reduc|e** [rɪ'djuːs] *in size* понижа́ть [-и́зить]; *prices, etc.* снижа́ть [-и́зить]; доводи́ть [довести́] (***to*** до Р); *pain* уменьша́ть [уме́ньшить]; (*lessen*) сокраща́ть [-рати́ть]; уре́з(ы-в)ать; **~tion** [rɪ'dʌkʃn] сниже́ние, ски́дка; уменьше́ние; сокраще́ние; *of picture, etc.* уме́ньшенная ко́пия
**redundant** [rɪ'dʌndənt] □ изли́шний; ***be made*** **~** быть уво́ленным
**reed** [riːd] тростни́к; камы́ш
**reeducation** [riːedjʊ'keɪʃn] переобуче́ние
**reef** [riːf] *geogr. naut.* риф
**reek** [riːk] **1.** вонь *f*; за́тхлый за́пах; **2.** *v/i.* дыми́ться; (неприя́тно) па́хнуть (***of*** Т)
**reel** [riːl] **1.** кату́шка; *for film, etc.* боби́на; **2.** *v/i.* [за]кружи́ться, [за]верте́ться; (*stagger*) шата́ться [шатну́ться]; ***my head ~ed*** у меня́ закружи́лась голова́; *v/t.* [на]мота́ть; **~ *off*** разма́тывать [-мота́ть]; *fig.* отбараба́нить *pf.*
**reelect** [riːɪ'lekt] переизб(и)ра́ть
**reenter** [riː'entə] сно́ва входи́ть в (В)
**reestablish** [riːɪ'stæblɪʃ] восстана́вливать [-нови́ть]
**refer** [rɪ'fɜː]: **~ *to*** *v/t.* относи́ть [отнести́] (к Д); (*direct*) направля́ть [-ра́вить], отсыла́ть [отосла́ть] (к Д); (*hand over*) передава́ть на рассмотре́ние (Д); (*attribute*) припи́сывать [-са́ть]; *v/i.* (*allude to*) ссыла́ться [сосла́ться] на (В); (*relate*) относи́ться [отнести́сь] к (Д); **~ee** [refə'riː] *sport* судья́ *m*; *football* арби́тр (*a. fig.*); *boxing* ре́фери *m indecl.*; **~ence** ['refrəns] спра́вка; *in book* ссы́лка; (*testimonial*) рекоменда́ция; (*allusion*) упомина́ние; (*relationship*) отноше́ние; ***in* ~ *to*** относи́тельно (Р); **~ *book*** спра́вочник; **~ *library*** спра́вочная библиоте́ка; ***make* ~ *to*** ссыла́ться [сосла́ться] на (В)
**referendum** [refə'rendəm] рефере́ндум
**refill** [riː'fɪl] наполня́ть сно́ва; пополня́ть(ся) [-по́лнить(ся)]
**refine** [rɪ'faɪn] *tech.* очища́ть [очи́стить]; *sugar* рафини́ровать (*im*)*pf.*; *fig.* де́лать(ся) бо́лее утончённым; **~ (*up*)*on*** [у]соверше́нствовать; **~d** [-d] *person* рафини́рованный; *style, etc.* изы́сканный, утончённый; очи́щенный; **~ry** [-ərɪ] *for sugar* са́харный заво́д
**reflect** [rɪ'flekt] *v/t.* отража́ть [отрази́ть]; *v/i.* **~ (*up*)*on***: броса́ть тень на (В); (*meditate on*) размышля́ть [-ы́слить] о (П); (*tell on*) отража́ться [-рази́ться] на (В); **~ion** [rɪ'flekʃn] отраже́ние; отсве́т; размышле́ние, обду́мывание; *fig.* тень *f*
**reflex** ['riːfleks] рефле́кс
**reforest** [riː'fɒrɪst] восстана́вливать [-нови́ть] лес
**reform** [rɪ'fɔːm] **1.** рефо́рма; **2.** реформи́ровать (*im*)*pf.*; *of person* исправля́ть(ся); **~ation** [refə'meɪʃən] преобразова́ние; исправле́ние; *hist.* ***the* ♀** Реформа́ция; **~er** [-mə] рефо́рма́тор
**refraction** [rɪ'frækʃn] *phys.* рефра́кция, преломле́ние
**refrain**¹ [rɪ'freɪn] *v/i.* возде́рживаться [-жа́ться] (***from*** от Р)
**refrain**² [~] припе́в, рефре́н
**refresh** [rɪ'freʃ] освежа́ть [-жи́ть]; *with food or drink* подкрепля́ть(ся) [-пи́ться]; **~ment** [-mənt] еда́; питьё
**refrigerat|e** [rɪ'frɪdʒəreɪt] замора́живать [-ро́зить]; (*cool*) охлажда́ть(ся) [охлади́ть(ся)]; **~ion** [rɪfrɪdʒə'reɪʃn] замора́живание; охлажде́ние; **~or** [rɪ'frɪdʒəreɪtə] холоди́льник; *of van, ship, etc.* рефрижера́тор
**refuel** [riː'fjʊəl] *mot.* заправля́ться

R

[-áвиться] (горю́чим)
**refuge** ['refju:dʒ] убе́жище; ***take ~*** укрыва́ться [-ы́ться]; **~e** [refjʊ'dʒi:] бе́женец *m*, -нка *f*
**refund** [rɪ'fʌnd] возмеща́ть расхо́ды (Д); возвраща́ть [-рати́ть]
**refusal** [rɪ'fju:zl] отка́з
**refuse 1.** [rɪ'fju:z] *v/t.* отка́зываться [-за́ться] от (Р); отка́зывать [-за́ть] в (П); (*deny*) отверга́ть [отве́ргнуть]; *v/i.* отка́зываться [-за́ться]; **2.** ['refju:s] отбро́сы *m/pl.*; му́сор; ***~ dump*** сва́лка
**refute** [rɪ'fju:t] опроверга́ть [-ве́ргнуть]
**regain** [rɪ'geɪn] получа́ть обра́тно; сно́ва достига́ть; *strength* восстана́вливать [-нови́ть]
**regal** ['ri:gəl] □ короле́вский, ца́рственный
**regale** [rɪ'geɪl] *v/t.* угоща́ть [угости́ть]; *v/i.* наслажда́ться [-ди́ться]
**regard** [rɪ'gɑ:d] **1.** внима́ние; уваже́ние; ***with ~ to*** по отноше́нию к (Д); ***kind~s*** серде́чный приве́т; **2.** [по]смотре́ть на (В); (*consider*) счита́ть, рассма́тривать (***as*** как); (*concern*) каса́ться; относи́ться [отнести́сь] к (Д); ***as ~s …*** что каса́ется (Р); **~ing** [-ɪŋ] относи́тельно (Р); **~less** [-lɪs] *adv.*: ***~ of*** несмотря́ на (В), незави́симо от (Р)
**regent** ['ri:dʒənt] ре́гент
**regime** [reɪ'ʒi:m] режи́м
**regiment** ['redʒɪmənt] полк
**region** ['ri:dʒən] о́бласть *f* (*a. administrative*); райо́н; *large* регио́н; **~al** [-l] □ областно́й; райо́нный; региона́льный
**register** ['redʒɪstə] **1.** журна́л; (*written record*) за́пись *f*; *tech.*, *mus.* реги́стр; **2.** регистри́ровать(ся) (*im*)*pf.*, *pf. a.* [за-]; заноси́ть в спи́сок; *mail* посыла́ть заказны́м; (*show*) пока́зывать [-за́ть]
**registr|ar** [redʒɪ'strɑ:] регистра́тор; слу́жащий регистату́ры; **~ation** [redʒɪ'streɪʃn] регистра́ция; **~y** ['redʒɪstrɪ]: ***~ office*** загс
**regret** [rɪ'gret] **1.** сожале́ние; **2.** [по]жале́ть (***that …*** что …); сожале́ть о (П); **~ful** [-fl] □ по́лный сожале́ния; опеча́ленный; **~table** [-əbl] □ приско́рбный
**regular** ['regjʊlə] □ пра́вильный; регуля́рный (*army a.*), постоя́нный); **~ity** [regjʊ'lærətɪ] регуля́рность *f*
**regulat|e** ['regjʊleɪt] [у]регули́ровать, упоря́дочи(ва)ть; *tech.* [от-] регули́ровать; **~ion** [regjʊ'leɪʃn] регули́рование; (*rule*) пра́вило
**rehabilitation** [ri:əbɪlɪ'teɪʃn] реабилита́ция; трудоустро́йство; перевоспита́ние
**rehears|al** [rɪ'hɜ:sl] *thea.*, *mus.* репети́ция; **~e** [rɪ'hɜ:s] *thea.* [про]репети́ровать
**reign** [reɪn] **1.** ца́рствование; *fig.* власть *f*; **2.** ца́рствовать; *fig.* цари́ть
**reimburse** [ri:ɪm'bɜ:s] возвраща́ть [-рати́ть]; возмеща́ть [-мести́ть] расхо́ды (Д)
**rein** [reɪn] вожжа́; *fig.* узда́
**reindeer** ['reɪndɪə] се́верный оле́нь *m*
**reinforce** [ri:ɪn'fɔ:s] уси́ливать [уси́лить]; укрепля́ть [-пи́ть]; *mil.* подкрепля́ть [-пи́ть] (*a. fig.*); **~ment** [-mənt] усиле́ние; *mil.* подкрепле́ние
**reinstate** [ri:ɪn'steɪt] восстана́вливать [-нови́ть] (*в правах и т.д.*)
**reiterate** [ri:'ɪtəreɪt] повторя́ть [-ри́ть]
**reject** [rɪ'dʒekt] **1.** *idea*, *etc.* отверга́ть [отве́ргнуть]; (*refuse to accept*) отка́зываться [-за́ться] от (Р); *proposal* отклоня́ть [-ни́ть]; *goods* бракова́ть; **2.** ['ri:dʒekt] брак; ***~s*** бракова́нный това́р; **~ion** [rɪ'dʒekʃn] отка́з; брако́вка
**rejoic|e** [rɪ'dʒɔɪs] *v/t.* [об]ра́довать; *v/i.* [об]ра́доваться (***at, in*** Д); **~ing** [-ɪŋ] (*часто* **~ings** *pl.*) весе́лье
**rejoin** [rɪ'dʒɔɪn] возража́ть [-рази́ть]; **~der** [-də] отве́т; возраже́ние
**rejuvenate** [rɪ'dʒu:vəneɪt] омола́живать(ся) [омолоди́ть(ся)]
**relapse** [rɪ'læps] **1.** *law*, *med.* рециди́в; **2.** *into bad habits*, *etc.* верну́ться *pf.*; ***~ into silence*** (сно́ва) умолка́ть
**relate** [rɪ'leɪt] *v/t.* расска́зывать

R

[-за́ть]; (*connect*) свя́зывать [-за́ть], соотноси́ть; *v/i.* относи́ться [отнести́сь]; **~d** [-ɪd] (*connected*) свя́занный; состоя́щий в родстве́ (***to*** с Т)

**relation** [rɪ'leɪʃn] отноше́ние; связь *f*; родство́; ро́дственник *m*, -ица *f*; ***in ~ to*** по отноше́нию к (Д); **~ship** [-ʃɪp] связь; родство́

**relative** ['relətɪv] **1.** □ относи́тельный; (*comparative*) сравни́тельный; ***~ to*** относя́щийся к (Д); **2.** ро́дственник *m*, -ица *f*

**relax** [rɪ'læks] *v/t.* ослабля́ть [-а́бить]; *muscles* расслабля́ть [-а́бить]; *v/i.* [о]сла́бнуть; расслабля́ться [-а́биться]; **~ation** [rɪlæk'seɪʃn] ослабле́ние; расслабле́ние; (*amusement*) развлече́ние

**relay** ['rɪːleɪ] **1.** сме́на; *sport* эстафе́та; *attr.* эстафе́тный; *el.* реле́ *n indecl.*; **2.** *radio* ретрансли́ровать (*im*)*pf.*

**release** [rɪ'liːs] **1.** освобожде́ние; высвобожде́ние; избавле́ние; *of film* вы́пуск; **2.** (*set free*) освобожда́ть [-боди́ть]; высвобожда́ть [вы́свободить]; (*relieve*) избавля́ть [-а́вить]; (*issue*) выпуска́ть [вы́пустить]; (*let go*) отпуска́ть [-сти́ть]

**relegate** ['relɪgeɪt] отсыла́ть [отосла́ть], низводи́ть [-вести́]; направля́ть [-ра́вить] (***to*** к Д); *sport* переводи́ть [-вести́]

**relent** [rɪ'lent] смягча́ться [-чи́ться]; **~less** [-lɪs] □ безжа́лостный

**relevant** ['reləvənt] уме́стный; относя́щийся к де́лу

**reliab|ility** [rɪlaɪə'bɪlətɪ] надёжность *f*; достове́рность *f*; **~le** [rɪ'laɪəbl] надёжный; достове́рный

**reliance** [rɪ'laɪəns] дове́рие; уве́ренность *f*

**relic** ['relɪk] пережи́ток; рели́квия

**relief** [rɪ'liːf] облегче́ние; (*assistance*) по́мощь *f*; посо́бие; подкрепле́ние; *in shiftwork* сме́на; *geogr* релье́ф; ***to my ~*** к моему́ облегче́нию; ***~ fund*** фонд по́мощи

**relieve** [rɪ'liːv] облегча́ть [-чи́ть]; (*free*) освобожда́ть [-боди́ть]; (*help*) ока́зывать по́мощь *f* (Д), выруча́ть [вы́ручить]; *of shift* сменя́ть [-ни́ть]; (*soften*) смягча́ть [-чи́ть]; ***~ one's feelings*** отвести́ *pf.* ду́шу

**religion** [rɪ'lɪdʒən] рели́гия

**religious** [rɪ'lɪdʒəs] □ религио́зный; (*conscientious*) добросо́вестный

**relinquish** [rɪ'lɪŋkwɪʃ] *hope, etc.* оставля́ть [-а́вить]; *habit* отка́зываться [-за́ться]; ***~ one's rights*** уступа́ть [-пи́ть] права́

**relish** ['relɪʃ] **1.** вкус; при́вкус; *cul.* припра́ва; **2.** наслажда́ться [-ади́ться] (Т); получа́ть удово́льствие от (Р); придава́ть вкус (Д); ***eat with ~*** есть с аппети́том

**reluctan|ce** [rɪ'lʌktəns] нежела́ние; неохо́та, нерасположе́ние; **~t** [-nt] □ неохо́тный; (*offering resistance*) сопротивля́ющийся

**rely** [rɪ'laɪ]: ***~ (up)on*** полага́ться [-ложи́ться] на (В), наде́яться на (В); (*depend on*) зави́сеть от (Р)

**remain** [rɪ'meɪn] ост(ав)а́ться; ***it ~s to be seen*** э́то ещё вы́яснится; ещё посмо́трим; **~der** [-də] оста́ток

**remark** [rɪ'mɑːk] **1.** замеча́ние; ***I made no ~*** я ничего́ не сказа́ла; **2.** (*notice, say*) замеча́ть [-е́тить]; выска́зываться [вы́сказаться] (***on*** о П); **~able** [rɪ'mɑːkəbl] (*of note*) замеча́тельный; (*extraordinary*) удиви́тельный

**remedy** ['remədɪ] **1.** сре́дство, лека́рство; ме́ра (***for*** про́тив Р); **2.** (*put right*) исправля́ть [-а́вить]

**rememb|er** [rɪ'membə] по́мнить; (*recall*) вспомина́ть [-о́мнить]; ***~ me to ...*** переда́й(те) приве́т (Д); **~rance** [-brəns] (*recollection*) па́мять *f*, воспомина́ние; (*memento*) сувени́р

**remind** [rɪ'maɪnd] напомина́ть [-о́мнить] (Д; ***of*** о П *or* В); **~er** [-ə] напомина́ние

**reminiscence** [remɪ'nɪsns] воспомина́ние

**remiss** [rɪ'mɪs] □ неради́вый; небре́жный; хала́тный; **~ion** [rɪ'mɪʃn] (*forgiveness*) проще́ние; освобожде́ние от до́лга; (*abatement*) уменьше́ние; *med.* реми́ссия

**remit** [rɪ'mɪt] *goods* перес(ы)ла́ть;

R

*money* переводи́ть [-вести́]; (*abate*) уменьша́ть(ся) [уме́ньшить(ся)]; **~tance** [-əns] де́нежный перево́д
**remnant** ['remnənt] *of cloth* оста́ток; *of food* оста́тки
**remodel** [riː'mɒdl] перестра́ивать [-стро́ить]
**remonstrate** ['remənstreɪt] протестова́ть; увещева́ть (***with*** В)
**remorse** [rɪ'mɔːs] угрызе́ния (*n/pl.*) со́вести; раска́яние; **~less** [-lɪs] □ безжа́лостный
**remote** [rɪ'məʊt] □ отдалённый; да́льний; **~ *control*** дистанцио́нное управле́ние; ***I haven't got the ~st idea*** не име́ю ни мале́йшего поня́тия
**remov|al** [rɪ'muːvl] перее́зд; *of threat, etc.* устране́ние; *from office* смеще́ние; **~ *van*** фурго́н для перево́зки ме́бели; **~e** [rɪ'muːv] *v/t.* удаля́ть [-ли́ть]; уноси́ть [унести́]; передвига́ть [-и́нуть]; (*take off*) снима́ть [снять]; (*take away*) уб(и-) ра́ть; (*dismiss*) снима́ть [снять]; *v/i.* переезжа́ть [перее́хать]; **~ers** [-əz] *firm* трансаге́нтство; *personnel* перево́зчики
**remunerat|e** [rɪ'mjuːnəreɪt] вознагражда́ть [-ради́ть]; (*pay*) опла́чивать [оплати́ть]; **~ive** [rɪ'mjuː'nərətɪv] □ (*profitable*) вы́годный
**Renaissance** [rɪ'neɪsns] эпо́ха Возрожде́ния; Ренесса́нс; ♀ (*revival*) возрожде́ние
**render** ['rendə] (*service*) ока́зывать [оказа́ть]; (*represent*) изобража́ть [-рази́ть]; *mus.* исполня́ть [-о́лнить]; (*translate*) переводи́ть [перевести́]; (*give as due*) возд(ав)а́ть
**renew** [rɪ'njuː] возобновля́ть [-нови́ть]; **~al** [-əl] возобновле́ние
**renounce** [rɪ'naʊns] отка́зываться [-за́ться] от (Р); (*disown*) отрека́ться [отре́чься] от (Р)
**renovate** ['renəveɪt] восстана́вливать [-нови́ть]; обновля́ть [обнови́ть]
**renown** [rɪ'naʊn] сла́ва; изве́стность *f*; **~ed** [-d] □ просла́вленный, изве́стный
**rent**[1] [rent] проре́ха; дыра́
**rent**[2] [~] **1.** *for land* аре́ндная пла́та; *for apartment* кварти́рная пла́та; **2.** (*occupy for ~*) взять в наём; (*let for ~*) сдать в наём; **~al** [rentl] (*rate of rent*) аре́ндная пла́та
**renunciation** [rɪnʌnsɪ'eɪʃn] отрече́ние; отка́з (***of*** от Р)
**reopen** [riː'əʊpən] открыва́ть [-ры́ть] вновь; **~ *negotiations*** возобновля́ть [-нови́ть] перегово́ры
**repair** [rɪ'peə] **1.** почи́нка, ремо́нт; ***in good ~*** в испра́вном состоя́нии; **2.** [по]чини́ть, [от]ремонти́ровать; (*make amends for*) исправля́ть [-а́вить]
**reparation** [repə'reɪʃn] возмеще́ние; *pol.* репара́ция
**repartee** [repɑː'tiː] остроу́мный отве́т
**repay** [*irr.* (***pay***)] [rɪ'peɪ] (*reward*) отблагодари́ть (***for*** за В); отдава́ть долг (Д); возмеща́ть [-ести́ть]; **~ment** [-mənt] *of money* возвра́т; возмеще́ние
**repeal** [rɪ'piːl] аннули́ровать (*im*)*pf.*; отменя́ть [-ни́ть]
**repeat** [rɪ'piːt] **1.** повторя́ть(ся) [-ри́ть(ся)]; **2.** повторе́ние; **~ed** [-ɪd]: **~ *efforts*** неоднокра́тные уси́лия
**repel** [rɪ'pel] отта́лкивать [оттолкну́ть]; *mil.* отража́ть [-рази́ть], отбива́ть [-би́ть]
**repent** [rɪ'pent] раска́иваться [-ка́яться] (***of*** в П); **~ance** [-əns] раска́яние; **~ant** [-ənt] ка́ющийся
**repercussion** [riːpə'kʌʃn] *of sound* отзвук; *fig.* после́дствие
**repertoire** ['repətwɑː] репертуа́р
**repetition** [repɪ'tɪʃn] повторе́ние
**replace** [rɪ'pleɪs] ста́вить, класть обра́тно; (*change for another*) заменя́ть [-ни́ть]; (*take place of*) замеща́ть [-ести́ть], заменя́ть [-ни́ть]; **~ment** [-mənt] замеще́ние, заме́на
**replenish** [rɪ'plenɪʃ] пополня́ть [-о́лнить]; **~ment** [-mənt] пополне́ние (*a. mil.*)
**replete** [rɪ'pliːt] напо́лненный; насы́щенный
**replica** ['replɪkə] то́чная ко́пия
**reply** [rɪ'plaɪ] **1.** отве́т (***to*** на В); **2.** отвеча́ть [-е́тить]; (*retort*) возража́ть

R

[-рази́ть]
**report** [rɪ'pɔːt] **1.** (*account*) отчёт сообще́ние; *mil.* донесе́ние; *official* докла́д; (*hearsay*) молва́, слух; (***on*** о П); **2.** сообща́ть [-щи́ть] (В *or* о П); *mil.* доноси́ть [-нести́] о (П); сде́лать *pf.* докла́д; докла́дывать [доложи́ть]; **~ *for work*** яви́ться *pf.* на рабо́ту; **~er** [~ə] репортёр
**repos|e** [rɪ'pəʊz] о́тдых; передышка; **~itory** [rɪ'pɒsɪtrɪ] склад; храни́лище
**represent** [reprɪ'zent] представля́ть [-а́вить]; изобража́ть [-рази́ть]; *thea.* исполня́ть роль *f* (Р); **~ation** [~zən'teɪʃn] изображе́ние; *parl.* представи́тельство; *thea.* представле́ние; постано́вка; **~ative** [reprɪ'zentətɪv] **1.** □ (*typical*) характе́рный; *parl.* представи́тельный; **2.** представи́тель *m*, -ница *f*; ***House of* 2*s*** *pl. Am. parl.* пала́та представи́телей
**repress** [rɪ'pres] подавля́ть [-ви́ть]; **~ion** [rɪ'preʃn] подавле́ние
**reprimand** ['reprɪmɑːnd] **1.** вы́говор; **2.** де́лать вы́говор (Д)
**reprint** [riː'prɪnt] **1.** перепеча́тка; **2.** перепеча́тывать [-тать]
**reprisal** [rɪ'praɪzl] отве́тное де́йствие
**reproach** [rɪ'prəʊtʃ] **1.** упрёк, уко́р; **2.** (***~ a p. with a th.***) упрека́ть [-кну́ть] (кого́-л. в чём-л.)
**reprobate** ['reprəbeɪt] негодя́й, распу́тник
**reproduc|e** [riːprə'djuːs] воспроизводи́ть [-извести́]; (*beget*) размножа́ться [-о́житься]; **~tion** [~'dʌkʃn] воспроизведе́ние; *of offspring* размноже́ние; (*copy*) репроду́кция
**reproof** [rɪ'pruːf] вы́говор; порицание
**reprove** [rɪ'pruːv] де́лать вы́говор (Д)
**reptile** ['reptaɪl] пресмыка́ющееся
**republic** [rɪ'pʌblɪk] респу́блика; **~an** [~lɪkən] **1.** республика́нский; **2.** республика́нец *m*, -нка *f*
**repudiate** [rɪ'pjuːdɪeɪt] (*disown*) отрека́ться [-ре́чься] от (Р); (*reject*) отверга́ть [-ве́ргнуть]
**repugnan|ce** [rɪ'pʌgnəns] отвраще́ние; **~t** [~nənt] □ отта́лкивающий, отврати́тельный
**repuls|e** [rɪ'pʌls] *mil.* отбива́ть [-би́ть], отража́ть [отрази́ть]; (*alienate*) отта́лкивать [оттолкну́ть]; **~ive** [~ɪv] □ отта́лкивающий; омерзи́тельный
**reput|able** ['repjʊtəbl] □ уважа́емый; почте́нный; *company, firm, etc.* соли́дный; **~ation** [repjʊ'teɪʃn] репута́ция; **~e** [ri'pjuːt] репута́ция; **~ed** [rɪ'pjuːtɪd] изве́стный; (*supposed*) предполага́емый; ***be ~*** (***to be ...***) слыть за (В)
**request** [rɪ'kwest] **1.** тре́бование; про́сьба; **2.** [по]проси́ть (В *or* Р *or* о П)
**require** [rɪ'kwaɪə] (*need*) нужда́ться в (П); (*demand*) [по]тре́бовать (Р); **~d** [~d] ну́жный; (*compulsory*) обяза́тельный; **~ment** [~mənt] нужда́; тре́бование; потре́бность *f*; ***meet the ~s*** отвеча́ть тре́бованиям
**requisit|e** ['rekwɪzɪt] **1.** необходи́мый; **2. ~es** *pl.* всё необходи́мое, ну́жное; ***sports ~*** спорти́вное снаряже́ние; **~ion** [rekwɪ'zɪʃn] зая́вка, тре́бование
**requital** [rɪ'kwaɪtl] (*recompense*) вознагражде́ние; (*avenging*) возме́здие
**requite** [rɪ'kwaɪt] отпла́чивать [-лати́ть] (Д ***for*** за В); (*avenge*) [ото]мсти́ть за (В)
**rescue** ['reskjuː] **1.** освобожде́ние; спасе́ние; ***come to s.o.'s ~*** прийти́ кому́-л. на по́мощь *f*; **2.** освобожда́ть [-боди́ть]; спаса́ть [-сти́]; ***~ party*** гру́ппа спаса́телей
**research** [rɪ'sɜːtʃ] иссле́дование
**resembl|ance** [rɪ'zembləns] схо́дство (***to*** с Т); **~e** [rɪ'zembl] походи́ть на (В), име́ть схо́дство с (Т)
**resent** [rɪ'zent] возмуща́ться [-мути́ться]; негодовать на (В); обижа́ться [оби́деться] за (В); ***I ~ his familiarity*** меня́ возмуща́ет его́ фамилья́рность; **~ful** [~fl] □ оби́женный; возмущённый; **~ment** [~mənt] негодова́ние; чу́вство оби́ды
**reservation** [rezə'veɪʃn] огово́рка; *for game* запове́дник; *for tribes* резерва́ция; (*booking*) предвари́тельный зака́з; ***without ~*** без вся́ких огово́рок,

R

безоговóрочно
**reserve** [rɪ'zɜːv] **1.** запáс; *fin.* резéрвный фонд; резéрв; (*reticence*) сдéржанность *f*; скрытность *f*; **2.** сберегáть [-рéчь]; (*keep back*) приберегáть [-рéчь]; откладывать [отложи́ть]; (*book*) заказывать [-зáть]; *for business purposes* [за]брони́ровать; оставлять за собой; ***I ~ the right to …*** я оставляю за собой прáво …; **~d** [-d] □ скры́тный; закáзанный зарáнее
**reside** [rɪ'zaɪd] жить, проживáть; **~nce** ['rezɪdəns] местожи́тельство; *official* резидéнция; **~nt** [-dənt] **1.** проживáющий, живýщий; **2.** постоя́нный жи́тель *m*; *in hotel* постоя́лец
**residu|al** [rɪ'zɪdjʊəl] остáточный; **~e** ['rezɪdjuː] остáток; (*sediment*) осáдок
**resign** [rɪ'zaɪn] *v/t. right, etc.* отказываться [-зáться] от; *hope* оставля́ть [-áвить]; *rights* уступáть [-пи́ть]; ***~ o.s. to*** покоря́ться [-ри́ться] (Д); *v/i.* уходи́ть в отстáвку; **~ation** [rezɪg'neɪʃn] отстáвка; ухóд с рабóты
**resilien|ce** [rɪ'zɪlɪəns] упрýгость *f*, эласти́чность *f*; **~t** [-nt] упрýгий, эласти́чный; *person* жизнестóйкий
**resin** ['rezɪn] смолá
**resist** [rɪ'zɪst] сопротивля́ться (Д); противостоя́ть (Д); **~ance** [-əns] сопротивлéние; *to colds, etc.* сопротивля́емость *f*; **~ant** [-ənt] сопротивля́ющийся; ***heat-~*** жаростóйкий; ***fire-~*** огнеупóрный
**resolut|e** ['rezəluːt] □ реши́тельный; **~ion** [rezə'luːʃn] (*motion*) резолю́ция, реши́тельность *f*, реши́мость *f*; ***make a ~*** решáть [-ши́ть]
**resolve** [rɪ'zɒlv] **1.** *v/t. fig.* решáть [реши́ть]; *problem, etc.* разрешáть [-ши́ть]; *v/i.* решáть(ся) [реши́ть(ся)]; ***~ (up)on*** решáться [-ши́ться] на (В); **2.** решéние; **~d** [-d] пóлный реши́мости
**resonance** ['rezənəns] резонáнс
**resonant** ['rezənənt] □ звучáщий; резони́рующий; ***be ~ with*** быть созвýчным
**resort** [rɪ'zɔːt] **1.** (*health ~*) курóрт; (*expedient*) надéжда; ***in the last ~*** в крáйнем слýчае; **2.** ***~ to***: прибегáть [-éгнуть] к (Д); обращáться [-ати́ться] к (Д)
**resound** [rɪ'zaʊnd] [про]звучáть; оглашáть(ся) [огласи́ть(ся)]
**resource** [rɪ'sɔːs]: ***~s*** *pl.* ресýрсы *m/pl.*; возмóжность *f*; нахóдчивость *f*; **~ful** [-fl] □ нахóдчивый
**respect** [rɪ'spekt] **1.** (*esteem*) уважéние; (*relation*) отношéние; ***in this ~*** в э́том отношéнии; ***~s*** *pl.* привéт; **2.** *v/t.* уважáть, почитáть; ***you must ~ his wishes*** вы обя́заны считáться с егó пожелáниями; **~able** [-əbl] □ прили́чный, поря́дочный; респектáбельный; *part. comm.* соли́дный; **~ful** [-fl] □ вéжливый, почти́тельный; **~ing** [-ɪŋ] относи́тельно (Р); **~ive** [-ɪv] □ соотвéтствующий; ***we went to our ~ places*** мы разошли́сь по свои́м местáм; **~ively** [-ɪvlɪ] соотвéтственно
**respirat|ion** [respə'reɪʃn] дыхáние; вдох и вы́дох; **~or** ['respəreɪtə] респирáтор
**respite** ['respaɪt] переды́шка; (*reprieve*) отсрóчка
**respond** [rɪ'spɒnd] отвечáть [-éтить]; ***~ to*** реаги́ровать на; отзывáться [отозвáться] на (В)
**response** [rɪ'spɒns] отвéт; *fig.* óтклик; реáкция
**responsi|bility** [rɪspɒnsɪ'bɪlətɪ] отвéтственность *f*; **~ble** [rɪ'spɒnsəbl] отвéтственный (***for*** за В, ***to*** пéред Т)
**rest**[1] [rest] **1.** óтдых, покóй; (*stand*) подстáвка; опóра; **2.** *v/i.* отдыхáть [отдохнýть]; (*remain*) оставáться; (*lean*) опирáться [оперéться] (***on*** на В); ***~ against*** прислоня́ть [-ни́ть]; *fig.* ***~ (up)on*** оснóвываться [-овáться] на (П); *v/t.* давáть óтдых (Д)
**rest**[2] [~] остáток
**restaurant** ['restrɒnt] ресторáн; **~ car** вагóн-ресторáн
**restful** ['restfl] спокóйный
**restive** ['restɪv] □ стропти́вый, упря́мый
**restless** ['restlɪs] непосéдливый, неугомóнный; *night, etc.* беспокóйный
**restoration** [restə'reɪʃn] *arch., hist.*

R

реставра́ция; восстановле́ние
**restore** [rɪ'stɔː] восстана́вливать [-нови́ть]; (*return*) возвраща́ть [-рати́ть]; (*reconvert*) реставри́ровать (*im*)*pf*.; **~ to health** выле́чивать [вы́лечить]
**restrain** [rɪ'streɪn] сде́рживать [-жа́ть]; уде́рживать; *feelings* подавля́ть [-ви́ть]; **~t** [~t] сде́ржанность *f*; (*restriction*) ограниче́ние; (*check*) обузда́ние
**restrict** [rɪ'strɪkt] ограни́чи(ва)ть; **~ion** [rɪ'strɪkʃn] ограниче́ние
**result** [rɪ'zʌlt] **1.** результа́т, исхо́д; (*consequence*) сле́дствие; **2.** явля́ться [яви́ться] сле́дствием (**from** Р); **~ in** приводи́ть [-вести́] к (Д), конча́ться ['-читься]
**resum|e** [rɪ'zjuːm] (*renew*) возобновля́ть [-ви́ть]; (*continue*) продолжа́ть [-лжить]; **~ one's seat** верну́ться на своё ме́сто; **~ classes** возобнови́ть *pf*. заня́тия
**resurrection** [rezə'rekʃn] *of custom, etc*. воскреше́ние; **the** ♀ Воскресе́ние
**resuscitate** [rɪ'sʌsɪteɪt] *med*. приводи́ть [-вести́] в созна́ние
**retail** ['riːteɪl] **1.** ро́зничная прода́жа; **goods sold by ~** това́ры, продаю́щиеся в ро́зницу; *attr*. ро́зничный; **2.** продава́ть(ся) в ро́зницу
**retain** [rɪ'teɪn] (*preserve*) сохраня́ть [-ни́ть]; (*hold*) уде́рживать [-жа́ть]
**retaliat|e** [rɪ'tælɪeɪt] отпла́чивать [-лати́ть] (тем же); **~ion** [rɪtælɪ'eɪʃn] отпла́та, возме́здие; **in ~ for** в отве́т на
**retard** [rɪ'tɑːd] (*check*) заде́рживать [-жа́ть]; замедля́ть [-е́длить]; **~ed** [~ɪd]: **mentally ~ child** у́мственно отста́лый ребёнок
**retention** [rɪ'tenʃn] удержа́ние; сохране́ние
**retentive** [rɪ'tentɪv]: **~ memory** хоро́шая па́мять *f*
**reticent** ['retɪsnt] скры́тный; молчали́вый
**retinue** ['retɪnjuː] сви́та, сопровожда́ющие ли́ца
**retir|e** [rɪ'taɪə] *v/t*. увольня́ть с рабо́ты; *v/i*. выходи́ть в отста́вку; *because of age* уходи́ть [уйти́] на пе́нсию; (*withdraw*) удаля́ться [-ли́ться]; (*seclude o.s.*) уединя́ться [-ни́ться]; **~ed** [~d] (*secluded*) уединённый; отставно́й, в отста́вке; **~ement** [~mənt] отста́вка; ухо́д на пе́нсию; уедине́ние; **~ age** пенсио́нный во́зраст; **~ing** [~rɪŋ] скро́мный, засте́нчивый
**retort** [rɪ'tɔːt] **1.** ре́зкий (*or* нахо́дчивый) отве́т; возраже́ние; **2.** *to a biting remark* [от]пари́ровать; возража́ть [-рази́ть]
**retrace** [riː'treɪs] просле́живать [-еди́ть]; **~ one's steps** возвраща́ться тем же путём
**retract** [rɪ'trækt] отрека́ться [отре́чься] от (Р); *one's words, etc*. брать наза́д; (*draw in*) втя́гивать [втяну́ть]
**retraining** [riː'treɪnɪŋ] переподгото́вка
**retreat** [rɪ'triːt] **1.** отступле́ние (*part. mil*.); (*place of privacy or safety*) приста́нище; **2.** (*walk away*) уходи́ть [уйти́]; удаля́ться [-ли́ться]; *part. mil*. отступа́ть [-пи́ть]
**retrench** [rɪ'trentʃ] сокраща́ть [-рати́ть]; [с]эконо́мить
**retrieve** [rɪ'triːv] (*get back*) брать [взять] обра́тно; (*restore*) восстана́вливать [-нови́ть]; (*put right*) исправля́ть [-а́вить]
**retro…** ['retrəʊ] обра́тно…; **~active** [retrəʊ'æktɪv] име́ющий обра́тную си́лу; **~grade** ['retrəʊgreɪd] реакцио́нный; **~spect** ['retrəʊspekt] ретроспекти́ва; **~spective** [retrəʊ'spektɪv] □ ретроспекти́вный; *law* име́ющий обра́тную си́лу
**return** [rɪ'tɜːn] **1.** возвраще́ние; возвра́т; *fin*. оборо́т; дохо́д, при́быль *f*; результа́т вы́боров; **many happy ~s of the day** поздравля́ю с днём рожде́ния; **in ~** в обме́н (**for** на В); в отве́т; **by ~** *of post* с обра́тной по́чтой; **tax ~** нало́говая деклара́ция; **~ ticket** обра́тный биле́т; **2.** *v/i*. возвраща́ться [-рати́ться]; верну́ться *pf*.; *v/t*. возвраща́ть [-рати́ть]; верну́ть *pf*.; присыла́ть наза́д; (*reply*) отвеча́ть [-е́тить]; **~ s.o.'s kindness** отблагодари́ть за доброту́
**reunion** [riː'juːnɪən] *of friends, etc*.

R

встре́ча; *of family* сбор всей семьи́; (*reuniting*) воссоедине́ние
**revaluation** [riːvæljʊ'eɪʃn] переоце́нка; *of currency* ревальва́ция
**reveal** [rɪ'viːl] обнару́жи(ва)ть; *secret, etc.* откры́(ва́)ть; **~ing** [~ɪŋ] *fig.* показа́тельный
**revel** ['revl] пирова́ть; упи́(ва́)ться (***in*** T)
**revelation** [revə'leɪʃn] открове́ние (*a. eccl.*); (*disclosure*) разоблаче́ние; откры́тие
**revelry** ['revəlrɪ] разгу́л; (*binge*) пиру́шка; кутёж
**revenge** [rɪ'vendʒ] **1.** месть *f*; *sport* рева́нш; отме́стка; ***in ~ for*** в отме́стку за (B); **2.** [ото]мсти́ть за (B); **~ful** [~fl] мсти́тельный
**revenue** ['revənjuː] дохо́д; *of state* госуда́рственные дохо́ды; ***Internal***, (*Brt.*) ***Inland*** ♀ Нало́говое управле́ние
**reverberate** [rɪ'vɜːbəreɪt] отража́ть(ся) [отрази́ть(ся)]
**revere** [rɪ'vɪə] уважа́ть, почита́ть; **~nce** ['revərəns] почте́ние
**reverent** ['revərənt] почти́тельный; по́лный благогове́ния
**reverie** ['revərɪ] мечты́ *f/pl.*; мечта́ние
**revers|al** [rɪ'vɜːsl] измене́ние; обра́тный ход; *of judg(e)ment* отме́на; **~e** [rɪ'vɜːs] **1.** обра́тная сторона́; *of paper* оборо́т, оборо́тная сторона́ (*a. fig.*); (*opposite*) противополо́жное; **~s** *pl.* превра́тности *f/pl.*; **2.** обра́тный; противополо́жный; **3.** изменя́ть [-ни́ть]; повора́чивать наза́д; *mot.* дава́ть за́дний ход; *law* отменя́ть [-ни́ть]
**revert** [rɪ'vɜːt] *to former state or question* возвраща́ться [-рати́ться]
**review** [rɪ'vjuː] **1.** (*survey*) обзо́р; *law* пересмо́тр; (*journal*) обозре́ние; *of book* реце́нзия; **2.** пересма́тривать [-смотре́ть]; писа́ть реце́нзию о (П)
**revis|e** [rɪ'vaɪz] пересма́тривать [-смотре́ть]; (*correct*) исправля́ть [-а́вить]; **~ion** [rɪ'vɪʒn] пересмо́тр; (*reworking*) перерабо́тка; испра́вленное изда́ние
**reviv|al** [rɪ'vaɪvl] возрожде́ние; *of trade, etc.* оживле́ние; **~e** [rɪ'vaɪv] приходи́ть *or* приводи́ть в чу́вство; (*liven up*) оживля́ть(ся) [-ви́ть(ся)]; ожи(ва́)ть
**revoke** [rɪ'vəʊk] *v/t.* (*repeal*) отменя́ть [-ни́ть]; *promise* брать [взять] наза́д
**revolt** [rɪ'vəʊlt] **1.** восста́ние; бунт; **2.** *v/i.* восста́(ва́)ть (*a. fig.*); *v/t. fig.* отта́лкивать [оттолкну́ть]
**revolution** [revə'luːʃn] (*revolving*) враще́ние; (*one complete turn*) оборо́т; *pol.* револю́ция; **~ary** [~ʃənərɪ] **1.** революцио́нный; **2.** революционе́р *m*, -ка *f*; **~ize** [~aɪz] революционизи́ровать (*im*)*pf.*
**revolv|e** [rɪ'vɒlv] *v/i.* враща́ться; *v/t.* враща́ть; обду́м(ыв)ать; ***~ a problem in one's mind*** всесторо́нне обду́мывать пробле́му; **~er** [~ə] револьве́р; **~ing** [~ɪŋ] враща́ющийся; ***~ door*** враща́ющаяся дверь *f*
**reward** [rɪ'wɔːd] **1.** награ́да; вознагражде́ние; **2.** вознагражда́ть [-ради́ть]; награжда́ть [-ради́ть]; **~ing** [~ɪŋ]: ***~ work*** благода́рная рабо́та
**rewrite** [riː'raɪt] [*irr.* (***write***)] перепи́сывать [-са́ть]
**rhapsody** ['ræpsədɪ] рапсо́дия
**rheumatism** ['ruːmətɪzəm] ревмати́зм
**rhinoceros** ['raɪnɒsərəs] носоро́г
**rhubarb** ['ruːbɑːb] реве́нь *m*
**rhyme** [raɪm] **1.** ри́фма; (рифмо́ванный) стих; ***without ~ or reason*** нет никако́го смы́сла; ни с того́, ни с сего́; **2.** рифмова́ть(ся) (***with*** с T)
**rhythm** ['rɪθəm] ритм; **~ic(al)** [~mɪk(l)] ритми́чный, ритми́ческий
**rib** [rɪb] ребро́
**ribald** ['rɪbəld] гру́бый; непристо́йный; скабрёзный
**ribbon** ['rɪbən] ле́нта; *mil.* о́рденская ле́нта; ***tear to ~s*** изорва́ть в кло́чья
**rice** [raɪs] рис; *attr.* ри́совый
**rich** [rɪtʃ] □ бога́тый (***in*** T); (*splendid*) роско́шный; *soil* плодоро́дный; *food* жи́рный; *colo(u)r* со́чный; ***get ~*** разбогате́ть; **~es** ['rɪtʃɪz] *pl.* бога́тство; сокро́вища *n/pl.*
**rick** [rɪk] *agric.* скирда́
**ricket|s** ['rɪkɪts] *pl.* рахи́т; **~y** [~ɪ] рахити́чный; *chair. etc.* ша́ткий

**rid** [rɪd] [*irr.*] избавля́ть [-а́вить] (***of*** от Р); ***get ~ of*** отде́л(ыв)аться от (Р), избавля́ться [-а́виться] от (Р)
**ridden** ['rɪdn] *pt. p. om* ***ride***
**riddle**[1] ['rɪdl] зага́дка; ***ask a ~*** задава́ть зага́дку
**riddle**[2] [~] (*sieve*) **1.** си́то, решето́; **2.** изреше́чивать [-шети́ть]
**ride** [raɪd] **1.** *on horseback* езда́ верхо́м; *for pleasure* прогу́лка; **2.** [*irr.*] *v/i. in car, on horseback, etc.* е́здить, [по]е́хать; ката́ться верхо́м; *v/t.* [по]е́хать на (П); **~r** [~ə] вса́дник *m*, -ица *f*; *in circus* нае́здник *m*, -ица *f*
**ridge** [rɪdʒ] го́рный кряж, хребе́т; *on rooftop* конёк
**ridicul|e** ['rɪdɪkjuːl] **1.** осмея́ние, насме́шка; **2.** высме́ивать [вы́смеять]; **~ous** [rɪ'dɪkjʊləs] □ неле́пый, смешно́й; ***don't be ~!*** не говори́ ерунду́!
**riding** ['raɪdɪŋ] верхова́я езда́
**rife** [raɪf]: **~ *with*** изоби́лующий (Т)
**riffraff** ['rɪfræf] подо́нки, отбро́сы (о́бщества) *m/pl.*
**rifle** [raɪfl] винто́вка; *for hunting* ружьё; **~man** *mil.* стрело́к
**rift** [rɪft] тре́щина, рассе́лина; *fig.* разры́в; *geol.* разло́м
**rig** [rɪg] **1.** *naut.* osна́стка; *coll.* наря́д; (*oil ~*) бурова́я вы́шка; **2.** оснаща́ть [оснасти́ть]; *coll.* наряжа́ть [-яди́ть]; **~ging** ['rɪgɪŋ] *naut.* такела́ж, сна́сти *f/pl.*
**right** [raɪt] **1.** □ (*correct*) пра́вильный, ве́рный; (*suitable*) подходя́щий, ну́жный; пра́вый; ***be ~*** быть пра́вым; ***put ~*** приводи́ть в поря́док; **2.** *adv.* пря́мо; пра́вильно; справедли́во; как раз; **~ *away*** сра́зу, сейча́с же; **~ *on*** пря́мо вперёд; **3.** пра́во; справедли́вость *f*; пра́вда; ***by ~ of*** на основа́нии (Р); ***on*** (*or* ***to***) ***the ~*** напра́во; **4.** приводи́ть в поря́док; (*correct*) исправля́ть [-вить]; **~eous** ['raɪtʃəs] □ пра́ведный; **~ful** [~fl] □ справедли́вый; зако́нный; **~ly** [~lɪ] пра́вильно; справедли́во
**rigid** ['rɪdʒɪd] □ негну́щийся, неги́бкий, жёсткий; *fig.* суро́вый; непрекло́нный; ***be ~ with fear*** оцепене́ть от стра́ха; **~ity** [rɪ'dʒɪdətɪ] жёсткость *f*; непрекло́нность *f*
**rigo(u)r** ['rɪgə] суро́вость *f*; стро́гость *f*
**rigorous** ['rɪgərəs] □ *climate* суро́вый; *measures* стро́гий
**rim** [rɪm] ободо́к; (*edge*) край; *of wheel* обод; *of glasses* опра́ва
**rind** [raɪnd] *of fruit* кожура́; *of cheese, etc.* ко́рка
**ring**[1] [rɪŋ] **1.** (*of bells*) звон; звоно́к; **2.** [*irr.*] [за]звуча́ть; *at door* [по-] звони́ть; **~ *s.o. up*** позвони́ть *pf.* кому́-л. по телефо́ну; ***that ~s a bell*** э́то мне что́-то напомина́ет
**ring**[2] [~] **1.** кольцо́; круг; *sport* ринг; **2.** (*mst.* **~ *in, round, about***) окружа́ть [-жи́ть]; **~leader** зачи́нщик *m*, -ица *f*; **~let** ['rɪŋlɪt] коле́чко; ло́кон; **~ *road*** кольцева́я доро́га
**rink** [rɪŋk] като́к
**rinse** [rɪns] [вы]полоска́ть; *dishes* сполосну́ть *pf.*
**riot** ['raɪət] **1.** беспоря́дки *m/pl.*; *of colo(u)rs* бу́йство; ***run ~*** шу́мно весели́ться, разгуля́ться *pf.*; **2.** принима́ть уча́стие в беспоря́дках, волне́ниях; бу́йствовать
**rip** [rɪp] **1.** (*tear*) [по]рва́ть; **2.** проре́ха
**ripe** [raɪp] □ зре́лый (*a. fig.*); спе́лый; гото́вый; ***the time is ~ for …*** пришло́ вре́мя …; **~n** ['~ən] созре́(ва́)ть, [по]спе́ть
**ripple** ['rɪpl] **1.** рябь *f*, зыбь *f*; (*sound*) журча́ние; **2.** покрыва́ть(ся) ря́бью, журча́ть
**rise** [raɪz] **1.** повыше́ние; *of sun* восхо́д; *of road, etc.* подъём; *geogr.* возвы́шенность *f*; *of river* исто́к; **2.**, [*irr.*] поднима́ться [-ня́ться]; всходи́ть; *of river* брать нача́ло; **~ *to*** быть в состоя́нии, спра́виться с (Т); **~n** ['rɪzn] *pt. p. om* ***rise***
**rising** ['raɪzɪŋ] возвыше́ние; восста́ние; восхо́д
**risk** [rɪsk] **1.** риск; ***run a*** (*or* ***the***) **~** рискова́ть [-кну́ть]; **2.** (*venture*) отва́жи(ва)ться на (В); рискова́ть [-кну́ть] (Т); **~y** ['~ɪ] □ риско́ванный
**rit|e** [raɪt] обря́д, церемо́ния; **~ual** ['rɪtʃʊəl] **1.** ритуа́льный; **2.** ритуа́л
**rival** ['raɪvəl] **1.** сопе́рник *m*, -ница *f*;

R

*comm.* конкуре́нт; **2.** сопе́рничающий; **3.** сопе́рничать с (Т); **~ry** [-rɪ] сопе́рничество; соревнова́ние
**river** ['rɪvə] река́; **~bed** ру́сло реки́; **~mouth** у́стье реки́; **~side** бе́рег реки́; *attr.* прибре́жный
**rivet** ['rɪvɪt] **1.** заклёпка; **2.** заклёпывать [-лепа́ть]; *fig. attention* прико́вывать [-ова́ть] (В к Д)
**road** [rəʊd] доро́га; путь *m*; **~ *accident*** доро́жное происше́ствие, ава́рия; **~side** обо́чина; **~sign** доро́жный знак
**roam** [rəʊm] *v/t.* броди́ть по (Д); *v/i.* стра́нствовать
**roar** [rɔː] **1.** *of storm, lion* [за]реве́ть; *of cannon* [за]грохота́ть; **~ *with laughter*** пока́тываться со́ смеху; **2.** рёв; гро́хот
**roast** [rəʊst] **1.** [из]жа́рить(ся); **2.** жа́реный; **~ *meat*** жарко́е
**rob** [rɒb] [о]гра́бить; *fig.* лиша́ть [-ши́ть] (***of*** Р); **~ber** ['~ə] граби́тель *m*; **~bery** ['~ərɪ] грабёж
**robe** [rəʊb] *magistrate's* ма́нтия; (*bath* ~) хала́т
**robin** ['rɒbɪn] мали́новка
**robot** ['rəʊbɒt] ро́бот
**robust** [rəʊ'bʌst] □ кре́пкий, здоро́вый
**rock**[1] [rɒk] скала́; утёс; го́рная поро́да; **~ *crystal*** го́рный хруста́ль *m*
**rock**[2] [~] **1.** *mus.* рок; **2.** *v/t.* кача́ть [-чну́ть]; *strongly* [по]шатну́ть; *to sleep* убаю́к(ив)ать; *v/i.* кача́ться; **~ *with laughter*** трясти́ от сме́ха
**rocket** ['rɒkɪt] раке́та; *attr.* раке́тный
**rocking chair** кача́лка
**rocky** ['rɒkɪ] (*full of rocks*) камени́стый; скали́стый
**rod** [rɒd] *tech.* сте́ржень *m*; прут *m*; *for fishing* уди́лище; ***piston* ~** шток
**rode** [rəʊd] *pt. от* ***ride***
**rodent** ['rəʊdənt] грызу́н
**roe**[1] [rəʊ] *zo.* косу́ля
**roe**[2] [~] икра́; ***soft* ~** моло́ки *f/pl.*
**rogu|e** [rəʊg] моше́нник; плут; **~ish** ['rəʊgɪʃ] плутова́тый
**role** [rəʊl] *thea.* роль *f* (*a. fig.*)
**roll** [rəʊl] **1.** *of cloth, paper, etc.* руло́н; (*list*) спи́сок; *of thunder* раска́т; (*bread* ~) бу́лочка; *naut.* бортова́я ка́чка; **2.** *v/t.* ката́ть, [по]кати́ть; *dough* раска́тывать [-ката́ть]; *metal* прока́тывать [-ката́ть]; **~ *up*** свёртывать [сверну́ть]; ска́тывать; *v/i.* ката́ться, [по]кати́ться; валя́ться (***in*** в П); *of thunder* грохота́ть; **~er** ['rəʊlə] ро́лик; вал; **~ *skates*** ро́ликовые коньки́
**rollick** ['rɒlɪk] шу́мно весели́ться
**rolling** ['rəʊlɪŋ] (*hilly*) холми́стый; **~ *mill*** *tech.* прока́тный стан; **~ *pin*** скалка́; **~ *stone*** *person* перекати́поле
**Roman** ['rəʊmən] **1.** ри́мский; **~ *numeral*** ри́мская ци́фра; **2.** ри́млянин *m*, -янка *f*
**romance** [rəʊ'mæns] **1.** *mus.* рома́нс; (*tale*) рома́н (*a. love affair*); **2.** *fig.* приукра́шивать действи́тельность; фантази́ровать; стро́ить возду́шные за́мки; **3.** ♀ рома́нский
**romantic** [rəʊ'mæntɪk] (**~*ally***) **1.** романти́чный; **2. ~ist** [~tɪsɪst] рома́нтик; **~ism** [~tɪsɪzəm] романти́зм, рома́нтика
**romp** [rɒmp] вози́ться, шу́мно игра́ть
**roof** [ruːf] кры́ша; **~ *of the mouth*** нёбо; **~ing** [~ɪŋ] **1.** кро́вельный материа́л; **2.** кро́вля; **~ *felt*** толь *m*
**rook**[1] [rʊk] *bird* грач
**rook**[2] [~] *coll.* **1.** моше́нник; **2.** обма́нывать [-ну́ть]
**rook**[3] [~] *chess* ладья́
**room** [ruːm, rʊm] ко́мната; ме́сто; простра́нство; ***make* ~ *for*** освободи́ть ме́сто для (Р); **~mate** това́рищ по ко́мнате; **~y** ['ruːmɪ] □ просто́рный
**roost** [ruːst] **1.** насе́ст; **2.** уса́живаться на насе́ст; *fig.* устра́иваться на́ ночь; **~er** ['~ə] пету́х
**root** [ruːt] **1.** ко́рень *m*; ***get to the* ~ *of*** добра́ться *pf.* до су́ти (Р); ***take* ~** пуска́ть ко́рни; укореня́ться [-ни́ться]; **2. ~ *out*** вырыва́ть с ко́рнем (*a. fig.*); (*find*) разы́скивать [-ка́ть]; ***stand* ~*ed to the spot*** стоя́ть как вко́панный; **~ed** ['ruːtɪd] укорени́вшийся
**rope** [rəʊp] **1.** кана́т; верёвка; *mst. naut.* трос; *of pearls* ни́тка; ***know the* ~*s*** *pl.* знать все ходы́ и вы́ходы; ***show the* ~*s*** *pl.* вводи́ть [ввести́] в суть де́ла; **2.**

связывать верёвкой; привязывать канатом; (*mst.* ~ ***off***) отгородить канатом
**rosary** ['rəʊzərɪ] *eccl.* чётки *f/pl.*
**rose**[1] [rəʊz] роза; розовый цвет
**rose**[2] [~] *pt. от* ***rise***
**rosin** ['rɒzɪn] канифоль *f*
**rostrum** ['rɒstrəm] кафедра; трибуна
**rosy** ['rəʊzɪ] □ розовый; румяный; *fig.* радужный
**rot** [rɒt] **1.** гниение; гниль *f*; **2.** *v/t.* [с]гноить; *v/i.* сгни(ва)ть, [с]гнить
**rota|ry** ['rəʊtərɪ] вращательный; **~te** [rəʊ'teɪt] вращать(ся); (*alternate*) чередовать(ся); **~tion** [rəʊ'teɪʃn] вращение; чередование
**rotten** ['rɒtn] □ гнилой; испорченный; *a. sl.* отвратительный
**rouge** [ruːʒ] румяна *n/pl.*
**rough** [rʌf] **1.** □ (*crude*) грубый; (*uneven*) шершавый; шероховатый; (*violent*) бурный; (*inexact*) приблизительный; ~ ***and ready*** сделанный кое-как, наспех; грубоватый; **2.**: ~ ***it*** обходиться без обычных удобств; **~en** ['rʌfn] делать(ся) грубым, шероховатым; **~ly** ['~lɪ] грубо, приблизительно; ~ ***speaking*** грубо говоря; **~ness** ['~nɪs] шероховатость *f*, грубость *f*
**round** [raʊnd] **1.** □ круглый; круговой; ~ ***trip*** поездка в оба конца; **2.** *adv.* кругом, вокруг; обратно; (*often* ~ ***about***) вокруг да около; ***all year*** ~ круглый год; **3.** *prp.* вокруг, кругом (Р); за (В *or* Т); по (Д); **4.** круг; цикл; *of talks* тур; *sport* раунд; *doctor's* обход; **5.** *v/t.* закруглять [-лить]; огибать [обогнуть]; ~ ***up*** окружать [-жить]; *v/i.* закругляться [-литься]; **~about** ['raʊndəbaʊt] **1.** *way* окольный; **2.** *mot.* кольцевая транспортная развязка; *at fair* карусель *f*; **~ish** ['raʊndɪʃ] кругловатый; **~-up** *of cattle* загон скота; облава
**rous|e** [raʊz] *v/t.* (*waken*) [раз]будить; *fig.* возбуждать [-удить]; воодушевлять [-вить]; ~ ***o.s.*** встряхнуться *pf.*; *v/i.* просыпаться [-снуться]; **~ing** ['raʊzɪŋ] возбуждающий; *cheers* бурный
**rout** [raʊt] обращать в бегство
**route** [ruːt] путь *m*; маршрут
**routine** [ruː'tiːn] **1.** режим, порядок; рутина; **2.** рутинный
**rove** [rəʊv] скитаться; бродить
**row**[1] [rəʊ] ряд
**row**[2] [raʊ] *coll.* гвалт; (*quarrel*) ссора
**row**[3] [rəʊ] грести; **~boat** гребная лодка; **~er** ['rəʊə] гребец
**royal** ['rɔɪəl] □ королевский; великолепный; **~ty** [~tɪ] член(ы) королевской семьи; авторский гонорар
**rub** [rʌb] *v/t.* тереть; протирать [-тереть]; натирать [натереть]; ~ ***in*** втирать [втереть]; ~ ***out*** стирать [стереть]; ~ ***up*** [от]полировать; (*freshen*) освежать [-жить]; *v/i.* тереться (***against*** о В); *fig.* ~ ***along*** проби(-ва)ться с трудом
**rubber** ['rʌbə] каучук; резина; (*eraser*) резинка; (*contraceptive*) противозачаточное средство; презерватив; *cards* роббер; *attr.* резиновый
**rubbish** ['rʌbɪʃ] мусор, хлам; *fig.* вздор; глупости *f/pl.*
**rubble** ['rʌbl] (*debris*) обломки; щебень *m*
**ruby** ['ruːbɪ] рубин; рубиновый цвет
**rucksack** ['rʌksæk] рюкзак
**rudder** ['rʌdə] *naut.* руль *m*
**ruddy** ['rʌdɪ] ярко-красный; *cheeks* румяный
**rude** [ruːd] □ неотёсанный; грубый; невежливый; *fig. health* крепкий; ~ ***awakening*** неприятное открытие; горькое разочарование
**rudiment** ['ruːdɪmənt] *biol.* рудимент; **~s** *pl.* основы *f/pl.*; **~s of knowledge** элементарные знания
**rueful** ['ruːfl] □ печальный
**ruffian** ['rʌfɪən] громила, хулиган
**ruffle** ['rʌfl] **1.** *sew.* сборка; *on water* рябь *f*; **2.** *hair* [взъ]ерошить; *water* рябить; *fig.* нарушать спокойствие (Р), [вс]тревожить
**rug** [rʌg] плед; *on floor* ковёр, коврик; **~ged** ['rʌgɪd] неровный; шероховатый; *terrain* пересечённый; *features* грубые, резкие
**ruin** ['ruːɪn] **1.** гибель *f*; разорение; *of*

R

*hopes*, *etc*. круше́ние; *mst*. **~s** *pl*. разва́лины *f/pl*., руи́ны *f/pl*.; **2.** [по]губи́ть; разоря́ть [-ри́ть]; разруша́ть [-у́шить]; *dishono(u)r* [о]бесче́стить; **~ous** ['ru:ɪnəs] □ губи́тельный; разори́тельный; разру́шенный

**rul|e** [ru:l] **1.** пра́вило; правле́ние; власть *f*; *for measuring* лине́йка; ***as a ~*** обы́чно; **2.** *v/t*. управля́ть (Т); (*give as decision*) постановля́ть [-ви́ть]; ***~ out*** исключа́ть [-чи́ть]; *v/i*. ца́рствовать; **~er** ['ru:lə] прави́тель *m*

**rum** [rʌm] ром

**Rumanian** [ru:'meɪnɪən] **1.** румы́нский; **2.** румы́н *m*, -ка *f*

**rumble** ['rʌmbl] **1.** громыха́ние; гро́хот; **2.** [за]громыха́ть; [за]грохота́ть; *of thunder* [за]греме́ть

**rumina|nt** ['ru:mɪnənt] жва́чное; **~te** [-neɪt] *fig*. размышля́ть

**rummage** ['rʌmɪdʒ] *v/t*. переры́(ва́)ть; *v/i*. ры́ться; ***~ sale*** благотвори́тельная распрода́жа

**rumo(u)r** ['ru:mə] **1.** слух; молва́; **2.**: ***it is ~ed that …*** хо́дят слу́хи, что …

**rump** [rʌmp] огу́зок

**rumple** ['rʌmpl] (с)мять; *hair* [взъ]еро́шить

**run** [rʌn] **1.** [*irr*.] *v/i*. *com* бе́гать, [по]бежа́ть; [по]те́чь; *of colo(u)rs*, *etc*. расплы́(ва́)ться; *of engine* рабо́тать; *text* гласи́ть; ***~ across a p.*** случа́йно встре́тить (В); ***~ away*** убега́ть [убежа́ть]; ***~ down*** сбега́ть [сбежа́ть]; *of watch*, *etc*. остана́вливаться [-ови́ться]; истоща́ться [-щи́ться]; ***~ dry*** иссяка́ть [-я́кнуть]; ***~ for*** *parl*. выставля́ть свою́ кандидату́ру на (В); ***~ into*** впада́ть в (В); *debt* залеза́ть [-ле́зть]; *person* встреча́ть [-е́тить]; ***~ on*** продолжа́ться [-до́лжиться]; говори́ть без умо́лку; ***~ out, ~ short*** конча́ться [ко́нчиться]; ***~ through*** прочита́ть бе́гло *pf*.; *capital* прома́тывать [-мота́ть]; ***~ to*** (*reach*) достига́ть [-и́гнуть]; ***~ up to*** доходи́ть [дойти́] до (Р); **2.** *v/t*. пробега́ть [-бежа́ть] (расстоя́ние); *water* нали́(ва́)ть; *business* вести́; (*drive in*) вонза́ть [-зи́ть]; *department*, *etc*. руководи́ть; проводи́ть [-вести́] (Т, ***over*** по Д); *car* сбива́ть [сбить]; ***~ down*** *fig*. поноси́ть (В); (*tire*) переутомля́ть [-ми́ть]; ***~ over*** переезжа́ть [-е́хать], сби(ва́)ть; прочита́ть бе́гло *pf*.; ***~ up*** *prices* взду(-ва́)ть; *building* возводи́ть [-вести́]; ***~ up a bill at*** [за]должа́ть (Д); **3.** бег; пробе́г; *of mechanism* рабо́та, де́йствие; *of time* тече́ние, ход; ряд; (*outing*) пое́здка, прогу́лка; руково́дство; ***the common ~*** обыкнове́нные лю́ди *m/pl*.; *thea*. ***have a ~ of 20 nights*** идти́ два́дцать вечеро́в подря́д; ***in the long ~*** со вре́менем; в конце́ концо́в

**run|about** ['rʌnəbaʊt] *mot*. малолитра́жка; **~away** бегле́ц

**rung**[1] [rʌŋ] *pt*. *p*. *от* ***ring***

**rung**[2] [~] ступе́нька стремя́нки

**runner** ['rʌnə] бегу́н; *of sledge* по́лоз; *of plant* побе́г; **~-up** [~'rʌp] *sport* занима́ющий второ́е ме́сто

**running** ['rʌnɪŋ] **1.** бегу́щий; *track* беґово́й; ***two days ~*** два дня подря́д; **2.** бе́ганье; *of person* бег; *of horses* бега́ *m/pl*.; **~board** подно́жка; **~water** *in nature* прото́чная вода́; *in man-made structures* водопрово́д

**runway** ['rʌnweɪ] *ae*. взлётно-поса́дочная полоса́

**rupture** ['rʌptʃə] **1.** разры́в; (*hernia*) гры́жа; **2.** разрыва́ть [разорва́ть] (*a*. *fig*.); прор(ы)ва́ть

**rural** ['rʊərəl] □ се́льский, дереве́нский

**rush**[1] [rʌʃ] **1.** *bot*. тростни́к, камы́ш; ***~ mat*** цино́вка

**rush**[2] [~] **1.** (*influx*) наплы́в; ***~ hours*** *pl*. часы́ пик; **2.** *v/i*. мча́ться; броса́ться [бро́ситься]; носи́ться, [по-] нести́сь; ***~ into*** броса́ться необду́манно в (В); *v/t*. мчать

**rusk** [rʌsk] суха́рь *m*

**Russian** ['rʌʃn] **1.** ру́сский; **2.** ру́сский, ру́сская; ру́сский язы́к

**rust** [rʌst] **1.** ржа́вчина; **2.** [за]ржаве́ть

**rustic** ['rʌstɪk] (***~ally***) дереве́нский; (*simple*) просто́й; (*rough*) гру́бый

**rustle** ['rʌsl] **1.** [за]шелесте́ть; **2.** ше́лест, шо́рох

**rust|proof** ['rʌstpru:f] нержаве́ющий;

R

**~y** ['rʌstɪ] заржа́вленный, ржа́вый
**rut** [rʌt] колея́ (*a. fig.*)
**ruthless** ['ruːθlɪs] безжа́лостный
**rye** [raɪ] *bot.* рожь *f*; ~ **bread** ржано́й хлеб

# S

**sabbatical** [sə'bætɪkl]: ~ ***leave*** *univ.* академи́ческий о́тпуск
**saber**, *Brt.* **sabre** ['seɪbə] са́бля, ша́шка
**sable** ['seɪbl] со́боль *m*; (*fur*) собо́лий мех
**sabotage** ['sæbətɑːʒ] **1.** сабота́ж; **2.** саботи́ровать (В)
**sack**[1] [sæk] **1.** разграбле́ние; **2.** [раз]гра́бить
**sack**[2] [~] **1.** мешо́к; **2.** класть, ссыпа́ть в мешо́к; *coll.* (*dismiss*) увольня́ть [-лить]; **~cloth**, **~ing** ['sækɪŋ] мешкови́на
**sacrament** ['sækrəmənt] *act or rite* та́инство; (*Eucharist*) прича́стие
**sacred** ['seɪkrɪd] □ свято́й; свяще́нный; *mus.* духо́вный
**sacrifice** ['sækrɪfaɪs] **1.** же́ртва; (*offering to a deity*) жертвоприноше́ние; ***at a ~*** с убы́тками; **2.** [по-] же́ртвовать
**sacrilege** ['sækrɪlɪdʒ] святота́тство, кощу́нство
**sad** [sæd] □ печа́льный, гру́стный; ***in a ~ state*** в плаче́вном состоя́нии
**sadden** ['sædn] [о]печа́лить(ся)
**saddle** ['sædl] **1.** седло́; **2.** [о]седла́ть; *fig.* взва́ливать [-ли́ть] (***s.o. with sth.*** что́-нибудь на кого́-нибудь); обременя́ть [-ни́ть]
**sadism** ['seɪdɪzəm] сади́зм
**sadness** ['sædnɪs] печа́ль *f*, грусть *f*
**safe** [seɪf] **1.** □ невреди́мый; надёжный; безопа́сный; ***~ and sound*** цел и невреди́м; ***in ~ hands*** в надёжных рука́х; **2.** сейф; **~guard** **1.** гара́нтия; **2.** охраня́ть [-ни́ть]; гаранти́ровать
**safety** ['seɪftɪ] **1.** безопа́сность *f*; надёжность *f*; **2.** безопа́сный; ~ **belt** реме́нь *m* безопа́сности, привязно́й реме́нь *m*; ~ **pin** англи́йская була́вка; ~ **razor** безопа́сная бри́тва; ~ **valve** предохрани́тельный кла́пан
**saffron** ['sæfrən] шафра́н
**sag** [sæg] *of roof, etc.* оседа́ть [-се́сть], прогиба́ться [-гну́ться]; *of cheeks, etc.* обвиса́ть [-и́снуть]; ***her spirits ~ged*** она́ упа́ла ду́хом
**sage**[1] [seɪdʒ] мудре́ц
**sage**[2] [~] *bot.* шалфе́й
**said** [sed] *pt. и pt. p. от* ***say***
**sail** [seɪl] **1.** па́рус; пла́вание под паруса́ми; **2.** *v/i.* идти́ под паруса́ми; (*travel over*) пла́вать, [по]плы́ть, отплы́(-ва́)ть; *v/t.* (*control navigation of*) управля́ть; пла́вать по (Д); **~boat** па́русная ло́дка; **~ing** [~ɪŋ] пла́вание; ***it wasn't plain ~*** всё бы́ло не так про́сто; **~or** [~ə] моря́к, матро́с; ***be a*** (***good***) ***bad ~*** (не) страда́ть морско́й боле́знью; **~plane** планёр
**saint** [seɪnt] свято́й; **~ly** ['seɪntlɪ] *adj.* свято́й
**sake** [seɪk]: ***for the ~ of*** ра́ди (Р); ***for my ~*** ра́ди меня́
**sal(e)able** ['seɪləbl] хо́дкий (това́р)
**salad** ['sæləd] сала́т
**salary** ['sælərɪ] окла́д, за́работная пла́та
**sale** [seɪl] прода́жа; (*clearance ~*) распрода́жа; аукцио́н; ***be for ~, be on ~*** име́ться в прода́же
**sales|man** ['seɪlzmən] продаве́ц; *door-to-door* коммивояжёр; **~woman** продавщи́ца
**saline** ['seɪlaɪn] соляно́й; солёный
**saliva** [sə'laɪvə] слюна́
**sallow** ['sæləʊ] *complexion* нездоро́вый; желтова́тый
**salmon** ['sæmən] ло́со́сь *m*; *flesh* лососи́на

S

**salon** ['sælɒn]: ***beauty ~*** космети́ческий сало́н

**saloon** [sə'lu:n] зал; *naut.* сало́н; бар, пивна́я; *Brt.* (*car*) седа́н

**salt** [sɔ:lt] **1.** соль *f*; *fig.* остроу́мие; ***take s.th. with a grain of ~*** относи́ться к чему́-л. скепти́чески; **2.** солёный; **3.** [по]соли́ть; заса́ливать [-соли́ть]; **~ cellar** соло́нка; **~y** ['sɔ:ltɪ] солёный

**salutary** ['sæljʊtrɪ] □ благотво́рный; поле́зный для здоро́вья

**salut|ation** [sælju:'teɪʃn] приве́тствие; **~e** [sə'lu:t] **1.** *mil.* отда́ние че́сти; во́инское приве́тствие; *with weapons* салю́т; **2.** приве́тствовать; отдава́ть честь *f* (Д)

**salvage** ['sælvɪdʒ] **1.** *of ship, property, etc.* спасе́ние; (*what is saved*) спасённое иму́щество; (*scrap*) ути́ль *m*; *paper* макулату́ра; *naut.* подъём; **2.** спаса́ть [спасти́]

**salvation** [sæl'veɪʃn] спасе́ние; ***2 Army*** А́рмия спасе́ния

**salve** [sælv] **1.** успокои́тельное сре́дство; **2.** *conscience* успока́ивать [-ко́ить]

**salvo** ['sælvəʊ] *of guns* залп; *fig.* взрыв аплодисме́нтов

**same** [seɪm]: ***the ~*** тот же са́мый; та же са́мая; то же са́мое; ***all the ~*** тем не ме́нее, всё-таки; ***it is all the ~ to me*** мне всё равно́

**sample** ['sɑ:mpl] **1.** про́ба; обра́зчик, образе́ц; *fig.* приме́р; **2.** [по-] про́бовать; отбира́ть образцы́ (P); *wine, etc.* дегусти́ровать

**sanatorium** [sænə'tɔ:rɪəm] санато́рий

**sanct|ion** ['sæŋkʃn] **1.** (*permission*) разреше́ние; (*approval*) одобре́ние; *official* са́нкция; ***apply ~ against*** применя́ть [-ни́ть] са́нкции про́тив (P); **2.** санкциони́ровать (*im*)*pf*.; дава́ть [дать] согла́сие, разреше́ние; **~uary** [-tʃʊərɪ] (*holy place*) святи́лище; (*refuge*) убе́жище

**sand** [sænd] **1.** песо́к; (*~bank*) о́тмель *f*; *of desert* пески́ *m/pl.* **~s** *pl.* песча́ный пляж; **2.** (*sprinkle with ~*) посыпа́ть песко́м; (*polish*) протира́ть [-ере́ть] песко́м

**sandal** ['sændl] санда́лия; (*lady's a.*) босоно́жки *f/pl.*

**sandpaper** нажда́чная бума́га

**sandwich** ['sænwɪdʒ] **1.** бутербро́д, са́ндвич; **2.**: **~ *between*** втíскивать [-нуть] ме́жду (T)

**sandy** ['sændɪ] песча́ный; песо́чный; песо́чного цве́та

**sane** [seɪn] норма́льный; *fig.* здра́вый, разу́мный; здравомы́слящий

**sang** [sæŋ] *pt. от* ***sing***

**sanguine** ['sæŋgwɪn] жизнера́достный, сангвини́ческий

**sanitary** ['sænɪtrɪ] □ санита́рный; гигиени́ческий; **~ *napkin*** гигиени́ческая прокла́дка

**sanitation** [sænɪ'teɪʃn] санита́рные усло́вия; *for sewage* канализа́ция

**sanity** ['sænətɪ] психи́ческое здоро́вье; здра́вый ум

**sank** [sæŋk] *pt. от* ***sink***

**sap** [sæp] **1.** *of plants* сок; *fig.* жи́зненные си́лы *f/pl.*; **2.** истоща́ть [-щи́ть]; *confidence* подрыва́ть [подорва́ть]; **~less** ['sæplɪs] истощённый; **~ling** ['sæplɪŋ] молодо́е деревцо́

**sapphire** ['sæfaɪə] *min.* сапфи́р

**sappy** ['sæpɪ] со́чный; *fig.* по́лный сил

**sarcasm** ['sɑ:kæzəm] сарка́зм

**sardine** [sɑ:'di:n] сарди́н(к)а; ***packed like ~s*** как се́льди в бо́чке

**sardonic** [sɑ'dɒnɪk] (**~*ally***) сардони́ческий

**sash** [sæʃ] куша́к, по́яс

**sash window** подъёмное окно́

**sat** [sæt] *pt. и pt. p. от* ***sit***

**satchel** ['sætʃəl] сумка, ра́нец

**sateen** [sə'ti:n] сати́н

**satellite** ['sætəlaɪt] *celestial* спу́тник (*a. spacecraft*)

**satiate** ['seɪʃɪeɪt] пресыща́ть [-ы́тить]; насыща́ть [-ы́тить]; **~d** [-ɪd] сы́тый

**satin** ['sætɪn] атла́с

**satir|e** ['sætaiə] сати́ра; **~ical** [sə'tɪrɪkl] сатири́ческий; **~ist** ['sætərɪst] сати́рик; **~ize** [-raɪz] высме́ивать [вы́смеять]

**satisfaction** [sætɪs'fækʃn] удовлетворе́ние

S

**satisfactory** [sætɪs'fæktərɪ] удовлетвори́тельный
**satisfy** ['sætɪsfaɪ] удовлетворя́ть [-ри́ть]; *hunger, etc.* утоля́ть [-ли́ть]; *obligations* выполня́ть [вы́полнить]; (*convince*) убежда́ть [убеди́ть]
**saturate** ['sætʃəreɪt] *chem.* насыща́ть [-ы́тить]; пропи́тывать [-ита́ть]; ***we came home ~d*** пока́ мы добежа́ли до́ дому, мы промо́кли
**Saturday** ['sætədɪ] суббо́та
**sauce** [sɔːs] со́ус; (*gravy*) подли́вка; *coll.* (*impudence*) де́рзость *f*; **~pan** кастрю́ля; **~r** ['sɔːsə] блю́дце
**saucy** ['sɔːsɪ] *coll.* де́рзкий
**sauerkraut** ['saʊəkraʊt] ки́слая капу́ста
**sauna** ['sɔːnə] са́уна
**saunter** ['sɔːntə] **1.** прогу́ливаться; **2.** прогу́лка
**sausage** ['sɒsɪdʒ] (*frankfurter*) соси́ска; (*salami, etc.*) колбаса́; (*polony, saveloy*) сарде́лька
**savage** ['sævɪdʒ] **1.** □ ди́кий; (*cruel*) жесто́кий; (*ferocious*) свире́пый; **2.** дика́рь *m*, -арка *f*; *fig.* зверь *m*; **~ry** [~rɪ] ди́кость *f*; жесто́кость *f*
**save** [seɪv] спаса́ть [спасти́]; избавля́ть [-ба́вить] (***from*** от Р); *strength, etc.* сберега́ть [-ре́чь]; (*put by*) [с]копи́ть, откла́дывать [отложи́ть]; *time, money, etc.* [с]эконо́мить
**saving** ['seɪvɪŋ] **1.** □ (*redeeming*) спаси́тельный; **2.** (*rescue*) спасе́ние; **~s** *pl.* сбереже́ния *n/pl.*
**savings bank** сберега́тельная ка́сса
**savio(u)r** ['seɪvɪə] спаси́тель *m*; ***the*** ♀ Спаси́тель *m*
**savo(u)r** ['seɪvə] **1.** (*taste*) вкус; *fig.* при́вкус; **2.** (*enjoy*) смакова́ть; ***~ of*** па́хнуть (Т); *fig.* отдава́ть (Т); **~y** [~rɪ] вку́сный; пика́нтный, о́стрый
**saw**[1] [sɔː] *pt. om* ***see***
**saw**[2] [~] **1.** пила́; **2.** [*irr.*] пили́ть; **~dust** опи́лки *f/pl.*; **~mill** лесопи́лка; лесопи́льный заво́д; **~n** [sɔːn] *pt. p. om* ***saw***
**say** [seɪ] **1.** [*irr.*] говори́ть [сказа́ть]; ***that is to ~*** то́ есть, те; ***you don't ~!*** неуже́ли!; ***I ~!*** послу́шай(те)!; ***he is said to be …*** говоря́т, что он …; ***I dare ~ …*** наве́рно (вполне́) возмо́жно …; ***they ~ …*** говоря́т …; **2. *have one's ~*** вы́сказать *pf.* своё мне́ние, сказа́ть *pf.* своё сло́во; **~ing** ['seɪɪŋ] погово́рка
**scab** [skæb] *on a sore* струп
**scaffolding** ['skæfəldɪŋ] *arch.* леса́ *m/pl.*
**scald** [skɔːld] **1.** ожо́г; **2.** [о]шпа́рить; обва́ривать [-ри́ть]
**scale**[1] [skeɪl] **1.** *of fish, etc.* чешу́йка (*collect.*: чешуя́); *inside kettles, etc.* на́кипь *f*; **2.** *fish* [по]чи́стить; *of skin* шелуши́ться
**scale**[2] [~] (***a pair of***) **~s** *pl.* весы́ *m/pl.*
**scale**[3] [~] **1.** масшта́б; (*size*) разме́р; *in grading* шкала́; *mus.* га́мма; **2.**: ***~ up*** постепе́нно увели́чивать; ***~ down*** постепе́нно уменьша́ть в масшта́бе
**scallop** ['skɒləp] *mollusk* гребешо́к
**scalp** [skælp] ко́жа головы́; *hist.* скальп
**scamp** [skæmp] **1.** шалу́н; безде́льник; **2.** рабо́тать ко́е-как; **~er** [~ə] бежа́ть поспе́шно; ***~ away, off*** уд(и)ра́ть
**scandal** ['skændl] сканда́л; позо́р; (*gossip*) спле́тни *f/pl.*; ***it's a ~!*** позо́р!; **~ize** [~dəlaɪz] возмуща́ть [-ти́ть]; шоки́ровать *impf.*; **~ous** [~ləs] □ позо́рный; сканда́льный; (*defamatory*) клеветни́ческий; (*shocking*) ужа́сный
**scant, scanty** [skænt, 'skæntɪ] ску́дный; недоста́точный
**scapegoat** ['skeɪpgəʊt] козёл отпуще́ния
**scar** [skɑː] **1.** шрам; рубе́ц; **2.** *v/t.* покрыва́ться рубца́ми; ***his face was ~red*** лицо́ его́ бы́ло покры́то шрама́ми; *v/i.* [за]рубцева́ться
**scarc|e** [skeəs] недоста́точный; ску́дный; (*rare*) ре́дкий; *goods* дефици́тный; ***make o.s. ~*** убира́ться [убра́ться]; **~ely** ['~lɪ] едва́ ли, как то́лько; едва́; **~ity** ['~sətɪ] нехва́тка; ре́дкость *f*
**scare** [skeə] **1.** [на-, ис]пуга́ть; отпу́гивать [-гну́ть] (*a.* ***~ away***); **2.** испу́г; па́ника; **~crow** пу́гало; *a. fig.* чу́чело
**scarf** [skɑːf] шарф; (*head~*) плато́к, косы́нка
**scarlet** ['skɑːlɪt] **1.** а́лый цвет; **2.** а́лый;

S

**~ fever** скарлати́на
**scathing** ['skeɪðɪŋ] ре́зкий; язви́тельный
**scatter** ['skætə] разбра́сывать [-броса́ть] (*a.* **~ about, around**); рассыпа́ть(ся) [-ы́пать(ся)]; *clouds, etc.* рассе́ивать(ся) [-е́ять(ся)]; *crowd* разбега́ться [-ежа́ться]
**scenario** [sɪ'nɑːrɪəʊ] сцена́рий
**scene** [siːn] сце́на; вид; ме́сто де́йствия; **behind the ~s** за кули́сами (*a. fig.*); **make a ~** устро́ить *pf.* сце́ну, сканда́л; **~ry** ['siːnərɪ] *thea.* декора́ции *f/pl.*; пейза́ж
**scent** [sent] **1.** арома́т, за́пах; (*perfume*) духи́ *m/pl.*; *hunt.* след; чутьё; нюх; **follow the wrong ~** идти́ по ло́жному сле́ду; **2.** *danger, etc.* [по]чу́ять; [на]души́ть
**schedule** ['ʃedjuːl] **1.** *of charges* спи́сок, пе́речень *m*; *of work* гра́фик, план; (*timetable*) расписа́ние; **a full ~** больша́я програ́мма; **2.** составля́ть расписа́ние (Р); (*plan*) назнача́ть [назна́чить], намеча́ть [-е́тить]
**scheme** [skiːm] **1.** схе́ма; план; прое́кт; (*plot*) интри́га; **2.** *v/t.* [за]проекти́ровать; *v/i.* плести́ интри́ги
**schnitzel** ['ʃnɪtzl] шни́цель *m*
**scholar** ['skɒlə] учёный; (*holder of scholarship*) стипендиа́т; **~ly** [-lɪ] *adj.* учёный; **~ship** [-ʃɪp] учёность *f*, эруди́ция; (*grant-in-aid*) стипе́ндия
**school** [skuːl] **1.** шко́ла; **at ~** в шко́ле; **secondary** (*Am.* **high**) **~** сре́дняя шко́ла; **2.** [на]учи́ть; приуча́ть [-чи́ть]; **~boy** шко́льник; **~fellow** шко́льный това́рищ; **~girl** шко́льница; **~ing** ['skuːlɪŋ] обуче́ние в шко́ле; **~master** учи́тель *m*; **~mate** → **schoolfellow**; **~mistress** учи́тельница; **~room** кла́ссная ко́мната
**science** ['saɪəns] нау́ка
**scientific** [saɪən'tɪfɪk] (**~ally**) нау́чный
**scientist** ['saɪəntɪst] учёный
**scintillate** ['sɪntɪleɪt] и́скриться; сверка́ть [-кну́ть]; мерца́ть; **scintillating wit** блестя́щее остроу́мие
**scissors** ['sɪzəz] *pl.* (*a* **pair of ~**) но́жницы *f/pl.*
**sclerosis** [sklə'rəʊsɪs] *med.* склеро́з
**scoff** [skɒf] **1.** насме́шка; **2.** смея́ться (**at** над Т)
**scold** [skəʊld] [вы́-, от]руга́ть, [вы́-]брани́ть; отчи́тывать [-чита́ть]
**scone** [skɒn] бу́лочка
**scoop** [skuːp] **1.** сово́к; *for liquids* черпа́к, ковш; *in newspaper* сенсацио́нная но́вость *f*; **2.** заче́рпывать [-пну́ть]
**scooter** ['skuːtə] *child's* самока́т; *mot.* моторо́ллер
**scope** [skəʊp] кругозо́р; разма́х; охва́т; просто́р; *of activity* сфе́ра; **outside the ~** за преде́лами (**of** Р)
**scorch** [skɔːtʃ] *v/t.* обжига́ть [обже́чь]; [с]пали́ть; *coll.* бе́шено нести́сь; **~er** ['~ə] *coll.* (*hot day*) зно́йный день
**score** [skɔː] **1.** (*cut*) зару́бка; *sport* счёт; *mus.* партиту́ра; **~s** *pl.* мно́жество; **on the ~ of** по причи́не (Р); **on that ~** на э́тот счёт, по э́тому по́воду; **what's the ~?** како́й счёт?; **2.** отмеча́ть [-е́тить]; засчи́тывать [-ита́ть]; выи́грывать [вы́играть]; забива́ть гол; *mus.* оркестрова́ть (*im*)*pf.*; *chiefly Am.* [вы́]брани́ть; **~board** табло́ *n indecl.*
**scorn** [skɔːn] **1.** презре́ние; **2.** презира́ть [-зре́ть]; *advice* пренебрега́ть [-ре́чь]; **~ful** ['skɔːnfl] □ *pers.* надме́нный; *look, etc.* презри́тельный
**Scotch** [skɒtʃ] **1.** шотла́ндский; **2.** шотла́ндский диале́кт; (*whiskey*) шотла́ндское ви́ски; **the ~** шотла́ндцы *m/pl.*; **~man** шотла́ндец; *trademark* **~ tape** кле́йкая ле́нта, скотч; **~woman** шотла́ндка
**scot-free** [skɒt'friː] невреди́мый; (*unpunished*) безнака́занный
**scoundrel** ['skaʊndrəl] негодя́й, подле́ц
**scour**[1] ['skaʊə] *v/t.* [вы́]чи́стить; *pan* начища́ть [начи́стить]; *with water* промыва́ть [про]мы́ть
**scour**[2] ['~] *area* прочёсывать [-чеса́ть] (В); *v/i.* ры́скать (*a.* **about**)
**scourge** [skɜːdʒ] **1.** бич (*a. fig.*); бе́дствие; **2.** [по]кара́ть

**scout** [skaʊt] **1.** разве́дчик (*a. ae.*); ***Boy* ~*s*** *pl.* ска́уты *m/pl.*; **2.** производи́ть разве́дку; **~ *about for*** [по]иска́ть (В)
**scowl** [skaʊl] **1.** хму́рый вид; **2.** [на]хму́риться; **~ *at*** хму́ро посмотре́ть *pf.* на (В)
**scraggy** ['skrægɪ] то́щий
**scram** [skræm] *coll.*: **~!** убира́йся!
**scramble** ['skræmbl] **1.** [вс]кара́бкаться; боро́ться (***for*** за В); **~*d eggs*** *pl.* яи́чница-болту́нья; **2.** сва́лка, борьба́; кара́бканье
**scrap** [skræp] **1.** *of paper* клочо́к, кусо́чек; *of cloth* лоскуто́к; (*cutting*) вы́резка; (*waste*) лом; втори́чное сырьё; **~*s*** *pl.* оста́тки *m/pl.*; *of food* объе́дки *m/pl.*; **2.** (*throw away*) выбра́сывать [вы́бросить]
**scrap|e** [skreɪp] **1.** скобле́ние; *on knee, etc.* цара́пина; (*predicament*) затрудне́ние; **2.** скобли́ть; скрести́(сь); соскреба́ть [-ести́] (*mst.* **~ *off***); отчища́ть [-и́стить]; (*touch*) заде́(ва́)ть; **~ *together*** *money* наскрести́
**scrap iron** желе́зный лом
**scrappy** ['skræpɪ] отры́вочный
**scratch** [skrætʃ] цара́пина; ***start from* ~** начина́ть всё с нуля́; [о]цара́пать; **~ *out*** (*erase*) вычёркивать [вы́черкнуть]
**scrawl** [skrɔːl] **1.** кара́кули *f/pl.*; **2.** написа́ть *pf.* неразбо́рчиво
**scream** [skriːm] **1.** вопль *m*; крик; **~*s of laughter*** взры́вы сме́ха; **2.** пронзи́тельно крича́ть
**screech** [skriːtʃ] **1.** крик; визг; **2.** пронзи́тельно крича́ть; взви́згивать [-гнуть]
**screen** [skriːn] **1.** ши́рма; экра́н (*a. cine*); **~ *adaptation*** экраниза́ция; ***adapt for the* ~** экранизи́ровать; ***the* ~** кино́ *n indecl.*; **2.** (*protect*) прикры́(ва́)ть; заслоня́ть [-ни́ть]; *film* пока́зывать на экра́не; просе́ивать [-е́ять]; (*investigate*) проверя́ть [-е́рить]
**screw** [skruː] **1.** шуру́п; винт; **2.** приви́нчивать [-нти́ть] (*mst.* **~ *on***); **~ *together*** скрепля́ть винта́ми; **~ *up*** зави́нчивать [-нти́ть]; *one's face* [с]мо́рщить; **~*driver*** отвёртка
**scribble** ['skrɪbl] **1.** кара́кули *f/pl.*; **2.** написа́ть *pf.* небре́жно
**scrimp** [skrɪmp]: **~ *and save*** вся́чески эконо́мить
**script** [skrɪpt] *cine.* сцена́рий; **~*writer*** сценари́ст
**Scripture** ['skrɪptʃə]: ***Holy* ~** Свяще́нное писа́ние
**scroll** [skrəʊl] сви́ток; (*list*) спи́сок
**scrub**[1] [skrʌb] куст; **~*s*** *pl.* кустáрник; за́росль *f*
**scrub**[2] [~] мыть [вы́мыть]
**scrubby** ['skrʌbɪ] *plant* (*stunted*) ча́хлый
**scruffy** ['skrʌfɪ] гря́зный; неопря́тный
**scrup|le** ['skruːpl] сомне́ния *n/pl.*; **~*ulous*** ['skruːpjʊləs] □ щепети́льный; (*thorough*) скрупулёзный; (*conscientious*) добросо́вестный
**scrutin|ize** ['skruːtɪnaɪz] внима́тельно рассма́тривать [-мотре́ть]; *case, etc.* тща́тельно изуча́ть [-чи́ть]; **~*y*** ['skruːtɪnɪ] испыту́ющий взгляд;всесторо́нняя прове́рка; внима́тельное изуче́ние
**scud** [skʌd] *of clouds* нести́сь; *of yacht* скользи́ть
**scuffle** ['skʌfl] **1.** потасо́вка, дра́ка; **2.** [по]дра́ться
**sculptor** ['skʌlptə] ску́льптор
**sculpture** ['skʌlptʃə] **1.** скульпту́ра; **2.** [из]вая́ть; *in stone* высека́ть [вы́сечь]; *in wood* ре́зать [вы́резать]
**scum** [skʌm] пе́на; *fig.* подо́нки *m/pl.*
**scurf** [skɜːf] пе́рхоть *f*
**scurry** ['skʌrɪ] бы́стро бе́гать; суетли́во дви́гаться; снова́ть (туда́ и сюда́); ***they scurried for shelter*** они́ бро́сились в укры́тие
**scurvy** ['skɜːvɪ] *med.* цинга́
**scythe** [saɪð] коса́
**sea** [siː] мо́ре; *attr.* морско́й; ***be at* ~** *fig.* не знать, что де́лать; недоумева́ть; **~*faring*** ['siːfeərɪŋ] морепла́вание; **~*going*** ['siːgəʊɪŋ] *ship* морехо́дный
**seal**[1] [siːl] *zo.* тюле́нь *m*
**seal**[2] [~] **1.** печа́ть *f*; (*leaden* **~**) пло́мба; **2.** *letter* запеча́т(ыв)ать; скрепля́ть печа́тью; *room* опеча́т(ыв)ать

S

**sea level** у́ровень *m* мо́ря
**sealing** ['siːlɪŋ] *tech.* уплотне́ние; **~ wax** сургу́ч
**seam** [siːm] **1.** шов (*a. tech*); рубе́ц; *geol.* пласт; **2.** сши(ва́)ть
**sea|man** моря́к; матро́с; **~plane** гидросамолёт
**searing** ['sɪərɪŋ]: **~ *pain*** жгу́чая боль *f*
**search** [sɜːtʃ] **1.** по́иски *m/pl.*; *by police* о́быск; ро́зыск; ***in ~ of*** в по́исках (Р); **~ *party*** поиско́вая гру́ппа; **2.** *v/t.* иска́ть; обы́скивать [-ка́ть]; **~ *me!*** не име́ю поня́тия; *v/i.* разы́скивать [-ка́ть] (***for*** В); **~ing** [~ɪŋ] тща́тельный; *look* испыту́ющий; **~light** проже́ктор; **~ warrant** о́рдер на о́быск
**sea|shore** морско́й бе́рег; **~sick** страда́ющий морско́й боле́знью; **~side** побере́жье; взмо́рье; ***go to the ~*** пое́хать *pf.* на мо́ре; *attr.* примо́рский; **~ *resort*** морско́й куро́рт
**season** ['siːzn] **1.** вре́мя го́да; пери́од; сезо́н; ***holiday ~*** пери́од отпуско́в; ***apricots are in ~ now*** абрико́сы сейча́с созре́ли; ***with the compliments of the ~*** с лу́чшими пожела́ниями к пра́зднику; **2.** *v/t. food* приправля́ть [-а́вить]; *wood.* выде́рживать [вы́держать]; **~able** [~əbl] □ своевре́менный; по сезо́ну; **~al** [~znl] □ сезо́нный; **~ing** [~zənɪŋ] припра́ва; **~ ticket** сезо́нный биле́т
**seat** [siːt] **1.** *in car* сиде́нье; (*garden ~*) скамья́; *thea., etc.* ме́сто; ***take a ~*** сесть *pf.*; ***take one's ~*** занима́ть [-ня́ть] своё ме́сто; **2.** уса́живать [усади́ть]; (*hold*) вмеща́ть [вмести́ть]; **~ed** [~ɪd] сидя́щий; ***be ~*** сиде́ть, сади́ться [сесть]
**sea|weed** морска́я во́доросль *f*; **~worthy** го́дный к пла́ванию
**secede** [sɪ'siːd] отделя́ться [-ли́ться]; отка́лываться [отколо́ться]
**seclu|de** [sɪ'kluːd] изоли́ровать (***from*** от Р): **~ *o.s.*** уединя́ться [-ни́ться]; **~ded** [~ɪd] уединённый; изоли́рованный; **~sion** [~'kluːʒn] уедине́ние
**second** ['sekənd] **1.** □ второ́й; втори́чный; уступа́ющий (***to*** Д); ***on ~ thoughts*** по зре́лому размышле́нию; **2.** секу́нда; ***a split ~*** до́ля секу́нды; мгнове́ние; **3.** (*support*) подде́рживать [-жа́ть]; **~ary** [~rɪ] □ втори́чный; второстепе́нный; побо́чный; **~ *education*** сре́днее образова́ние; **~-hand** поде́ржанный; *information* из вторы́х рук; **~ *bookshop*** букинисти́ческий магази́н; **~ly** [~lɪ] во-вторы́х; **~-rate** второсо́ртный; *hotel* второразря́дный; *writer, etc.* посре́дственный
**secre|cy** ['siːkrəsɪ] *of person* скры́тность *f*, секре́тность *f*; **~t** ['siːkrɪt] **1.** □ та́йный, секре́тный; **2.** та́йна, секре́т; ***in ~*** секре́тно, тайко́м; ***be in on the ~*** быть посвящённым в секре́т; ***keep a ~*** храни́ть та́йну
**secretary** ['sekrətrɪ] секрета́рь *m*, *coll.* секрета́рша; мини́стр
**secret|e** [sɪ'kriːt] *med.* выделя́ть [вы́делить]; **~ion** [~'kriːʃn] выделе́ние
**secretive** ['siːkrətɪv] скры́тный
**section** ['sekʃn] (*cut*) сече́ние, разре́з; (*part*) часть *f*; *of orange* до́лька; *in newspaper* отде́л; *of book* разде́л; **~al** [~ʃənl] разбо́рный, секцио́нный
**sector** ['sektə] се́ктор
**secular** ['sekjʊlə] □ *noneccl.* све́тский; *of this world* мирско́й
**secur|e** [sɪ'kjʊə] **1.** □ (*safe*) безопа́сный; (*reliable*) надёжный; (*firm*) про́чный; уве́ренный; ***I feel ~ about my future*** я уве́рена в своём бу́дущем; **2.** (*make fast*) закрепля́ть [-пи́ть]; обеспе́чи(ва)ть; (*make safe*) обезопа́сить *pf*; (*get*) дост(ав)а́ть; **~ity** [~rətɪ] безопа́сность *f*; надёжность *f*; обеспе́чение; зало́г; **~ities** *pl.* це́нные бума́ги *f/pl.*
**sedate** [sɪ'deɪt] □ степе́нный
**sedative** ['sedətɪv] *mst. med.* успока́ивающее сре́дство
**sedentary** ['sedntrɪ] □ сидя́чий
**sediment** ['sedɪmənt] оса́док
**seduc|e** [sɪ'djuːs] соблазня́ть [-ни́ть]; **~tive** [sɪ'dʌktɪv] □ соблазни́тельный
**see** [siː] [*irr.*] *v/i.* [у]ви́деть; ***I ~*** я понима́ю **~ *about a th.*** [по]забо́титься о (П); **~ *through a p.*** ви́деть кого́-л. наскво́зь; *v/t.* [у]ви́деть; *film, etc.* [по]смотре́ть; замеча́ть [-е́тить]; пони-

S

мáть [-ня́ть]; посещáть [-ети́ть]; ***~ a p. home*** провожáть когó-нибудь домóй; ***~ off*** провожáть [-води́ть]; ***~ to*** позабóтиться (о П); заня́ться *pf.* (Т); ***~ a th. through*** доводи́ть [довести́] чтó-нибудь до концá; ***live to ~*** дожи́(-вá)ть до (Р)

**seed** [siːd] **1.** сéмя *n* (*a. fig*); *of grain* зернó; *collect.* семенá *n/pl.*; *of apple, etc.* зёрнышко; (*offspring*) *mst. Bibl.* потóмство; **2.** *v/t.* засевáть [засéять]; [по]сéять; **~ling** ['siːdlɪŋ] *agric.* сéянец; (*tree*) сáженец; ***~s*** *pl.* рассáда *collect.*; **~y** ['siːdɪ] напóлненный семенáми; (*shabby*) потрёпанный, обноси́вшийся; *coll.* не в фóрме; нездорóвый

**seek** [siːk] [*irr.*] *mst. fig.* искáть (Р); ***~ advice*** обращáться за совéтом; ***~ after*** добивáться (Р); ***~ out*** разы́скивать [-ыскáть]; оты́скивать [-кáть]

**seem** [siːm] [по]казáться; **~ing** ['~ɪŋ] □ кáжущийся; мни́мый; **~ingly** ['~ɪŋlɪ] пови́димому; **~ly** ['~lɪ] подобáющий; пристóйный

**seen** [siːn] *pt. p. om* ***see***

**seep** [siːp] просáчиваться [-сочи́ться]

**seesaw** ['siːsɔː] доскá-качéли *f/pl.*

**seethe** [siːð] бурли́ть; *fig.* кипéть

**segment** ['segmənt] *math.* сегмéнт, отрéзок; *of orange* дóлька; (*part*) кусóк, часть *f*

**segregate** ['segrɪgeɪt] отделя́ть [-ли́ть]

**seismic** ['saɪzmɪk] сейсми́ческий

**seiz|e** [siːz] (*take hold of*) хватáть [схвати́ть]; (*take possession of*) *of* захвáтывать [захвати́ть]; ухвати́ться за (В) *pf.* (*a. fig.*); *property* конфисковáть (*im*)*pf.*; *fig. of feeling* охвáтывать [-ти́ть]; **~ure** ['siːʒə] *med.* при́ступ

**seldom** ['seldəm] *adv.* рéдко, почти́ никогдá

**select** [sɪ'lekt] **1.** отбирáть [отобрáть]; *s.th. to match* подбирáть [подобрáть]; **2.** отбóрный; (*exclusive*) и́збранный; **~ion** [sɪ'lekʃn] вы́бор; подбóр; отбóр

**self** [self] **1.** *pron.* сам; себя́; *coll.* = ***myself*** *etc.* я сам *и т.д.*; **2.** *su.* (*pl.* **selves** [selvz]) ли́чность *f*; **~-assured** самоувéренный; **~-centered**, *Brt.* **-centred** эгоцентри́чный; **~-command** самообладáние; **~-conceit** самомнéние; **~-conscious** застéнчивый; **~-contained** *person* самостоя́тельный; *lodgings, etc.* отдéльный; *fig.* зáмкнутый; **~-control** самообладáние; **~-defence** (**-nse**): ***in ~*** присамозащи́те; **~-determination** самоопределéние; **~-evident** очеви́дный; **~-interest** своекоры́стие; **~ish** ['selfɪʃ] эгоисти́чный; **~-possession** самообладáние; **~-reliant** полагáющийся на самогó себя́; **~-seeking** своекоры́стный; **~-service** самообслу́живание; **~-willed** своевóльный

**sell** [sel] [*irr.*] прод(ав)áть; торговáть; ***~ off, ~ out*** распрод(ав)áть; **~er** ['selə] продавéц (-вщи́ца)

**semblance** ['sembləns] подóбие; вид; ***put on a ~ of ...*** притворя́ться [-ри́ться]

**semi...** ['semɪ...] полу...; **~final** полуфинáл

**seminary** ['semɪnərɪ] семинáрия

**semolina** [semə'liːnə] мáнная крупá; *cooked* мáнная кáша

**senate** ['senɪt] сенáт; *univ.* совéт

**senator** ['senətə] сенáтор

**send** [send] [*irr.*] пос(ы)лáть; отправля́ть [-áвить]; ***~ for*** пос(ы-) лáть за (Т); ***~ out*** *signal, etc.* посылáть [-слáть]; *invitations* разослáть [рассылáть]; ***~ up*** вызывáть повышéние (Р); ***~ word*** сообщáть [-щи́ть]; **~er** [~ə] отправи́тель *m*

**senile** ['siːnaɪl] стáрческий

**senior** ['siːnɪə] **1.** стáрший; ***~ partner*** *comm.* главá фи́рмы; **2.** стáрше; ***he is my ~ by a year*** он стáрше меня́ нá год; **~ity** [siːnɪ'ɒrətɪ] старшинствó

**sensation** [sen'seɪʃn] ощущéние; чу́вство; сенсáция; ***cause a ~*** вызывáть [-звать] сенсáцию; **~al** [~ʃənl] □ сенсациóнный

**sense** [sens] **1.** чу́вство; ощущéние; смысл; значéние; ***common ~*** здрáвый смысл; ***bring a p. to his ~s*** *pl. fig.* образу́мить *pf.* когó-л.; ***make ~*** имéть смысл; быть поня́тным; **2.** ощущáть

S

[ощути́ть], [по]чу́вствовать
**senseless** ['senslıs] □ бессмы́сленный; (*unconscious*) без созна́ния
**sensibility** [sensə'bılətı] чувстви́тельность *f*
**sensible** ['sensəbl] □ (благо)разу́мный; здравомы́слящий; (*that can be felt*) ощути́мый, заме́тный; ***be ~ of*** созн(ав)а́ть (В)
**sensitiv|e** ['sensətıv] □ чувстви́тельный (***to*** к Д); **~ity** [sensə'tıvətı] чувстви́тельность *f* (***to*** к Д)
**sensual** ['senʃʊəl] □ чу́вственный
**sent** [sent] *pt. и pt. p. от* ***send***
**sentence** ['sentəns] **1.** *law* пригово́р; *gr.* предложе́ние; ***serve one's ~*** отбыва́ть наказа́ние; **2.** пригова́ривать [-говори́ть]
**sententious** [sen'tenʃəs] дидакти́чный; нравоучи́тельный
**sentiment** ['sentımənt] чу́вство; (*opinion*) мне́ние; → ***~ality***; **~al** [sentı'mentl] сентимента́льный; **~ality** [sentımen'tælətı] сентимента́льность *f*
**sentry** ['sentrı] *mil.* часово́й
**separa|ble** ['sepərəbl] □ отдели́мый; **~te 1.** □ ['seprıt] отде́льный; осо́бый; *pol.* сепара́тный; **2.** ['sepəreıt] отделя́ть(ся) [-ли́ть(ся)]; (*part*) разлуча́ть(ся) [-чи́ть(ся)]; (*go different ways*) расходи́ться [разойти́сь]; **~tion** [sepə'reıʃn] разлу́ка; расстава́ние; **~tism** ['sepərətızəm] сепарати́зм; **~tist** ['sepərətıst] сепарати́ст
**September** [sep'tembə] сентя́брь *m*
**sequel** ['si:kwəl] *of story* продолже́ние; (*result, consequence*) после́дствие
**sequence** ['si:kwəns] после́довательность *f*; (*series*) ряд, цикл
**serenade** [serə'neıd] серена́да
**seren|e** [sı'ri:n] □ безо́блачный (*a. fig.*); я́сный; безмяте́жный; споко́йный; **~ity** [sı'renətı] споко́йность; безмяте́жность *f*; безо́блачность *f*
**serf** [sɜ:f] *hist.* крепостно́й
**sergeant** ['sɑ:dʒənt] *mil.* сержа́нт
**serial** ['sıərıəl] □ поря́дковый; сери́йный; после́довательный; ***~ number*** сери́йный но́мер
**series** ['sıəri:z] *sg. a. pl.* се́рия; (*number*) ряд; *of goods* па́ртия
**serious** ['sıərıəs] □ серьёзный; ***be ~*** серьёзно говори́ть; **~ness** [-nıs] серьёзность *f*
**sermon** ['sɜ:mən] про́поведь *f*
**serpent** ['sɜ:pənt] змея́; **~ine** [~aın] изви́листый
**servant** ['sɜ:vənt] слуга́ *m*; служа́нка; прислу́га; ***civil ~*** госуда́рственный слу́жащий
**serve** [sɜ:v] **1.** *v/t.* [по]служи́ть (Д); *dinner, ball in tennis, etc.* под(ав)а́ть; *in shops, etc.* обслу́живать [-жи́ть]; *law* вруча́ть [-чи́ть] (***on*** Д); *sentence* отбы́(ва́)ть; (***it***) ***~s him right*** так ему́ и на́до; ***~ out*** выда(ва́)ть, разд(ав)а́ть; *v/i.* [по]служи́ть (*a. mil.*) (*as* Т); **2.** *tennis*; пода́ча
**service** ['sɜ:vıs] **1.** слу́жба; *in hotel, etc.* обслу́живание; услу́га; (*a.* ***divine ~***) богослуже́ние; (*train, etc.* ~) сообще́ние; *tennis*: пода́ча; *tech.* техобслу́живание; ***the ~s*** *pl.* а́рмия, флот и вое́нная авиа́ция; ***be at a p.'s ~*** быть к чьим-либо услу́гам; ***~ station*** ста́нция техобслу́живания; **2.** *Am. tech.* [от]ремонти́ровать; **~able** ['sɜ:vısəbl] □ поле́зный; про́чный
**serviette** [sɜ:vı'et] салфе́тка
**servile** ['sɜ:vaıl] подобостра́стный
**servitude** ['sɜ:vıtju:d] ра́бство; ***penal ~*** ка́торжные рабо́ты, отбы́тие сро́ка наказа́ния
**session** ['seʃn] *parl.* се́ссия; *law, etc.* заседа́ние
**set** [set] **1.** [*irr.*] *v/t.* (*adjust*) [по]ста́вить; *place* класть [положи́ть]; помеща́ть (-ести́ть); *homework, etc.* зад(ав)а́ть; *cine.* вставля́ть в ра́му; уса́живать [усади́ть] (***to*** за В); *med.* вправля́ть [-а́вить]; ***~ a p. laughing*** [рас]смеши́ть кого́-л.; ***~ sail*** отпра́виться *pf.* в пла́вание; ***~ aside*** откла́дывать [отложи́ть]; ***~ store by*** высоко́ цени́ть (В); счита́ть ва́жным (В); ***~ forth*** излага́ть [изложи́ть]; ***~ off*** отправля́ться [-виться]; ***~ up*** учрежда́ть [-еди́ть]; устра́ивать; **2.** *v/i. astr.* заходи́ть [зайти́], сади́ться [сесть]; *of jelly*

S

засты́(ва́)ть; **~ about a th.** принима́ться [-ня́ться] за что́-л.; **~ out** → **~ off**; **~ to work** бра́ться [взя́ться] за рабо́ту; **~ o.s. up as** выдава́ть себя́ за (В); **3.** неподви́жный; *time* определённый; *rules* устано́вленный; *smile* засты́вший; (*rigid*) твёрдый; **hard ~** нужда́ющийся; **4.** набо́р; компле́кт; *of furniture* гарниту́р; (*tea ~, etc.*) серви́з; (радио-)приёмник; (*group*) круг; *tennis*; сет; *thea.* декора́ции

**setback** ['setbæk] заде́ржка; неуда́ча; *in production* спад

**settee** [se'tiː] куше́тка

**setting** ['setɪŋ] *of jewels* опра́ва; *thea.* декора́ции; *fig.* окружа́ющая обстано́вка; *of sun* захо́д

**settle** ['setl] *v/t.* поселя́ть [-ли́ть]; приводи́ть в поря́док; *nerves*; успока́ивать [-ко́ить]; *question* реша́ть [-и́ть]; (*arrange*) устра́ивать [-ро́ить], ула́живать [-а́дить]; заселя́ть [-ли́ть]; *bill* опла́чивать [-ати́ть]; *v/i.* (*often* **~ down**) поселя́ться [-ли́ться]; устра́иваться [-ро́иться]; уса́живаться [усе́сться]; приходи́ть к соглаше́нию; *of dust, etc.* оседа́ть [осе́сть]; *of weather* устана́вливаться [-нови́ться]; **~d** ['setld] постоя́нный; усто́йчивый; **~ment** ['setlmənt] (*agreement*) соглаше́ние; (*act*) урегули́рование; (*village, etc.*) поселе́ние; **reach a ~** достига́ть [-ти́чь] соглаше́ния; **~r** ['setlə] поселе́нец

**set-to** ['settʊ] сва́тка; *coll.* потасо́вка; *verbal* перепа́лка

**seven** ['sevn] семь; семёрка → **five**; **~teen(th)** [sevn'tiːn(θ)] семна́дцать [-тый]; **~th** ['sevnθ] **1.** □ седьмо́й; **2.** седьма́я ча́сть *f*; **~tieth** ['sevntɪɪθ] семидеся́тый; **~ty** ['sevntɪ] се́мьдесят

**sever** ['sevə] *v/t.* (*cut*) разреза́ть [-е́зать]; разрыва́ть [-зорва́ть] (*a. fig.*); *v li.* [по]рва́ть(ся)

**several** ['sevrəl] не́сколько (Р); (*some*) не́которые *pl.*; □ отде́льный; **they went their ~ ways** ка́ждый пошёл свое́й доро́гой; **~ly** по отде́льности

**sever|e** [sɪ'vɪə] (*strict, stern*) стро́гий, суро́вый (*a. of climate*); (*violent, strong*) си́льный; *competition* жесто́кий; *losses* кру́пный; **~ity** [sɪ'verətɪ] стро́гость *f*; суро́вость *f*

**sew** [səʊ] [*irr.*] [с]шить; **~ on** пришива́ть [-ши́ть]

**sewer** ['sjuːə] канализацио́нная труба́; **~age** ['sjuːərɪdʒ] канализа́ция

**sew|ing** ['səʊɪŋ] шитьё; *attr.* шве́йный; **~n** [səʊn] *pt. p. от* **sew**

**sex** [seks] пол; секс; **~ual** ['sekʃʊəl] □ полово́й; сексуа́льный

**shabby** ['ʃæbɪ] □ *clothes* потёртый; *building, etc.* убо́гий; *behavio(u)r* по́длый; *excuse* жа́лкий

**shack** [ʃæk] *Am.* лачу́га, хиба́рка

**shackle** ['ʃækl]: **~s** *pl.* (*fetters*) око́вы *f/pl.*

**shade** [ʃeɪd] **1.** тень *f*; (*hue*) отте́нок; (*lamp~*) абажу́р; *fig.* нюа́нс; *paint* те́ни *f/pl.*; **2.** заслоня́ть [-ни́ть]; затеня́ть [-ни́ть]; [за-] штрихова́ть

**shadow** ['ʃædəʊ] **1.** тень *f*; (*ghost*) при́зрак; **2.** (*follow*) та́йно следи́ть за (Т); **~y** [~ɪ] тени́стый; (*indistinct*) сму́тный, нея́сный

**shady** ['ʃeɪdɪ] тени́стый; *coll.* тёмный, сомни́тельный; *side* тенево́й

**shaft** [ʃɑːft] *tech.* вал

**shaggy** ['ʃægɪ] косма́тый

**shake** [ʃeɪk] **1.** [*irr.*] *v/t.* трясти́ (В *or* Т); тряхну́ть (Т) *pf.*; встря́хивать [-хну́ть]; *of explosion* потряса́ть [-сти́] (*a. fig.*); *faith* [по]колеба́ть; *finger, fist* [по]грози́ть; **~ hands** пожа́ть ру́ку друг дру́гу, обменя́ться рукопожа́тием; **~ one's head** покача́ть *pf.* голово́й; *v/i.* [за]трясти́сь; [за]дрожа́ть (**with, at** от Р); **2.** дрожь *f*, потрясе́ние; **~n** ['ʃeɪkən] **1.** *p. pt. от* **shake**; **2.** *adj.* потрясённый

**shaky** ['ʃeɪkɪ] □ *on one's legs* нетвёрдый; *hands* трясу́щийся; (*not firm*) ша́ткий; **my German is ~** я пло́хо зна́ю неме́цкий язы́к

**shall** [ʃæl] [*irr.*] *v/aux. вспом, глагол, образующий будущее (1-е лицо единственного и множественного числа:)* **I ~ do** я бу́ду де́лать, я сде́лаю

**shallow** ['ʃæləʊ] **1.** ме́лкий; *fig.* по-

S

вéрхностный; **2.**: ***the ~s*** мелковóдье

**sham** [ʃæm] **1.** притвóрный; поддéльный; **2.** притвóрство; поддéлка; притвóрщик *m*; **3.** *v/t.* симулúровать *(im)pf.*; *v/i.* притворя́ться [-рúться]

**shamble** ['ʃæmbl] волочúть нóги

**shambles** ['ʃæmblz] (*disorder*) беспоря́док

**shame** [ʃeɪm] **1.** стыд; позóр; ***for ~!*** сты́дно!; ***what a ~!*** какáя жáлость!; ***it's a ~ that …*** жаль, что …; ***put to ~*** [при]стыдúть; **2.** [при-] стыдúть; [о]срамúть; **~faced** ['ʃeɪmfeɪst] □ пристыжённый, виновáтый вид; **~ful** ['ʃeɪmfl] □ посты́дный; позóрный; **~less** ['ʃeɪmlɪs] □ бессты́дный

**shampoo** [ʃæm'puː] **1.** шампу́нь *m*; мытьё головы́; **2.** мыть шампу́нем

**shamrock** ['ʃæmrɒk] трилúстник

**shank** [ʃæŋk] *anat.* гóлень *f*

**shape** [ʃeɪp] **1.** фóрма; (*outline*) очертáние; **2.** *v/t.* созд(ав)áть; придавáть фóрму, вид (Д); *v/i.* [с]формировáться; **~less** [-lɪs] бесфóрменный; **~ly** [-lɪ] хорошó сложённый

**share** [ʃeə] **1.** дóля, часть *f*; (*participation*) учáстие; *fin.* áкция; ***go ~s*** *pl.* платúть пóровну; ***have no ~ in*** не имéть отношéния (к Д); **2.** *v/t.* [по]делúться (Т); *v/i.* учáствовать (***in*** в П); **~holder** акционéр

**shark** [ʃɑːk] акýла (*a. fig.*)

**sharp** [ʃɑːp] **1.** □ *com.* óстрый (*a. fig.*); *fig.* (*clear in shape*) отчётливый; *turn* крутóй; (*biting*) éдкий; *pain* рéзкий; *voice* пронзúтельный; *remark* кóлкий; *coll.* продувнóй; **2.** *adv.* крýто; тóчно; ***at 2 o'clock ~*** рóвно в два часá; ***look ~!*** живо!; **3.** *mus.* диéз; **~en** ['ʃɑːpən] [на]точúть; заостря́ть [-рúть]; **~ener** ['ʃɑːpənə] (*pencil ~*) точúлка; **~ness** ['ʃɑːpnɪs] остротá; рéзкость *f*; **~-sighted** зóркий; **~-witted** остроýмный

**shatter** ['ʃætə] разбивáть вдрéбезги; *hope* разрушáть [-рýшить]; *health* расстрáивать [-рóить]

**shave** [ʃeɪv] **1.** [*irr.*] [по]брúть(ся); *plank* [вы́]строгáть; **2.** бритьё; ***have a ~*** [по]брúться; ***have a close ~*** едвá избежáть опáсности; **~n** ['ʃeɪvn] бри́тый

**shaving** ['ʃeɪvɪŋ] **1.** бритьё; **~s** *pl.* стрýжки *f/pl.*; **~ cream** крем для бритья́

**shawl** [ʃɔːl] шаль *f*, головнóй платóк

**she** [ʃiː] **1.** онá; **2.** жéнщина; **she-…** сáмка; ***she-wolf*** волчúца

**sheaf** [ʃiːf] *agric.* сноп; *of paper* свя́зка

**shear** [ʃɪə] **1.** [*irr.*] *sheep* [о]стрúчь; *fig.* обдирáть как лúпку; **2. ~s** *pl.* (бóльшие) нóжницы *f/pl.*

**sheath** [ʃiːθ] нóжны *f/pl.*; **~e** [ʃiːð] вкладывать в нóжны

**sheaves** [ʃiːvz] *pl. от* **sheaf**

**shed**[1] [ʃed] [*irr*] *hair, etc.* [по]теря́ть; *tears, blood* пролú(вá)ть; *clothes, skin* сбрáсывать [сбрóсить]; ***~ new light on s.th.*** проливáть [-лúть] свет (на В)

**shed**[2] [~] сарáй

**sheen** [ʃiːn] блеск; *reflected* óтблеск

**sheep** [ʃiːp] овцá; **~ dog** овчáрка; **~ish** ['ʃiːpɪʃ] глуповáтый; рóбкий; **~skin** овчúна; ***~ coat, ~ jacket*** дублёнка, полушýбок

**sheer** [ʃɪə] (*absolute*) полнéйший; (*diaphanous*) прозрáчный; (*steep*) отвéсный; ***by ~ chance*** по чúстой случáйности; ***~ nonsense*** абсолю́тная чепухá; ***~ waste of time*** бесполéзная трáта врéмени

**sheet** [ʃiːt] простыня́; *of paper, metal* лист; *of water, snow* ширóкая полосá; **~ iron** листовóе желéзо; **~ lightning** зарнúца

**shelf** [ʃelf] пóлка; *of rock* устýп; *sea* шельф

**shell** [ʃel] **1.** (*nut~*) скорлупá; *of mollusc* рáковина; *of tortoise* пáнцырь *m*; *tech.* кóрпус; **2.** *eggs* очищáть [очúстить] от скорлупы́; *peas* лущúть; *mil.* обстрéливать [-ля́ть]; **~fish** моллю́ск

**shelter** ['ʃeltə] **1.** *bulding, etc.* прию́т (*a. fig.*), кров; убéжище (*a. mil.*); **2.** *v/t.* приютúть *pf.*; *v/i.* (*a.* **take~**) укры́(вá)ться; приютúться *pf.*

**shelve** [ʃelv] *fig.* отклáдывать в дóлгий я́щик

**shelves** [ʃelvz] *pl. от* **shelf**

**shepherd** ['ʃepəd] **1.** пастýх; **2.** *sheep*

S

пасти́; *people* [про]вести́
**sherry** ['ʃerɪ] хе́рес
**shield** [ʃi:ld] **1.** щит; защи́та; ***ozone*** ~ озо́нный слой; **2.** заслоня́ть [-ни́ть] (***from*** от Р)
**shift** [ʃɪft] **1.** *at work* сме́на; (*change*) измене́ние; (*move*) сдвиг; ***make ~ to*** ухитря́ться [-ри́ться]; дово́льствоваться (***with*** Т); **2.** *v/t.* [по-] меня́ть; перемеща́ть [-мести́ть]; *v/i.* изворáчиваться [изверну́ться]; перемеща́ться [-мести́ться]; ~ ***for o.s.*** обходи́ться без по́мощи; **~y** ['ʃɪftɪ] ско́льзкий, *fig.* изворо́тливый, ло́вкий; ~ ***reply*** укло́нчивый отве́т
**shilling** ['ʃɪlɪŋ] ши́ллинг
**shin** [ʃɪn] *anat.* го́лень *f*
**shine** [ʃaɪn] **1.** сия́ние; свет; блеск, гля́нец; **2.** [*irr.*] сия́ть; свети́ть; блесте́ть; (*polish*) [от]полирова́ть; *shoes* [по]чи́стить; *fig.* блиста́ть
**shingle** ['ʃɪŋgl] (*gravel*) га́лька
**shiny** ['ʃaɪnɪ] □ (*polished*) начи́щенный; *through wear* лосня́щийся; (*bright*) блестя́щий
**ship** [ʃɪp] **1.** су́дно, кора́бль *m*; **2.** (*carry*) перевози́ть [-везти́]; **~board**: *naut.* ***on*** ~ на корабле́; **~building** судострое́ние; **~ment** ['ʃɪpmənt] груз; погру́зка; **~owner** судовладе́лец; **~ping** ['ʃɪpɪŋ] (*loading*) погру́зка; (*transport*) перево́зка; торго́вый флот, суда́ *n/pl.*; (*ship traffic*) судохо́дство; **~wreck** **1.** кораблекруше́ние; **2.** потерпе́ть *pf.* кораблекруше́ние; **~yard** верфь *f*
**shirk** [ʃɜ:k] увиливать [-льну́ть] от (Р); **~er** ['ʃɜ:kə] ло́дырь *m*; увилива́ющий (от Р)
**shirt** [ʃɜ:t] руба́шка, соро́чка; *woman's also* блу́зка; **~sleeves**: ***in one's*** ~ без пиджака́
**shiver** ['ʃɪvə] **1.** дрожь *f*; **2.** [за]дрожа́ть
**shoal**[1] [ʃəʊl] мелково́дье; мель *f*
**shoal**[2] [~] *of fish* стáя, кося́к
**shock** [ʃɒk] **1.** *fig.* потрясе́ние; *med.* шок; **2.** *fig.* потряса́ть [-ясти́]; шоки́ровать; ~ ***absorber*** *mot.* амортиза́тор; **~ing** ['ʃɒkɪŋ] □ сканда́льный; ужа́сный; потряса́ющий
**shod** [ʃɒd] *pt. и pt. p. от* ***shoe***
**shoddy** ['ʃɒdɪ] *goods, etc.* дрянно́й
**shoe** [ʃu:] **1.** ту́фля; *heavy* башма́к; *above ankle* полуботи́нок; (*horse*~) подко́ва; **2.** [*irr.*] обу́(ва́)ть; подко́вывать [-кова́ть]; **~horn** рожо́к; **~lace** шнуро́к для боти́нок; **~maker** сапо́жник; ~ **polish** крем для о́буви
**shone** [ʃɒn] *pt. и pt. p. от* ***shine***
**shook** [ʃʊk] *pt. от* ***shake***
**shoot** [ʃu:t] **1.** *bot.* ростóк, побе́г; **2.** [*irr.*] *v/t.* стреля́ть; (*kill*) [за]стрели́ть *pf.*; (*execute by shooting*) расстре́ливать [-ля́ть]; *cine.* снима́ть [снять], засня́ть *pf.*; *v/i.* стреля́ть [вы́стрелить]; *of pain* дёргать; (*a.* ~ ***along, past***) проноси́ться [-нести́сь]; промелькну́ть *pf.*; промча́ться *pf.*; ~ ***ahead*** ри́нуться вперёд; **~er** ['ʃu:tə] стрело́к
**shooting** ['ʃu:tɪŋ] стрельба́; *hunt.* охо́та; *cine.* съёмка; ~ ***star*** па́дающая звезда́
**shop** [ʃɒp] **1.** магази́н; (*work*~) мастерска́я; ***talk*** ~ говори́ть о рабо́те со свои́ми колле́гами; **2.** де́лать поку́пки (*mst.* ***go ~ping***); **~keeper** владе́лец магази́на; **~per** ['~ə] покупа́тель *m*; **~ping** ['~ɪŋ]: ~ ***center*** (***-tre***) торго́вый центр; ~ **window** витри́на
**shore** [ʃɔ:] бе́рег; взмо́рье; побере́жье; ***on the*** ~ на́ берег, на берегу́
**shorn** [ʃɔ:n] *pt. p. от shear*
**short** [ʃɔ:t] коро́ткий; (*brief*) кра́ткий; *in height* невысо́кий; (*insufficient*) недоста́точный; (*not complete*) непо́лный; *answer* ре́зкий, сухо́й; *pastry* песо́чный; ***in*** ~ коро́че говоря́; вкра́тце; ***fall*** ~ ***of*** уступа́ть в чём-л.; *expectations, etc.* не опра́вдывать [-да́ть]; ***cut*** ~ прер(ы)ва́ть; ***run*** ~ иссяка́ть [-я́кнуть]; ***stop*** ~ ***of*** не доезжа́ть [дое́хать], не доходи́ть [дойти́] до (Р) (*a. fig.*); **~age** ['ʃɔ:tɪdʒ] нехва́тка, дефици́т; **~circuit** коро́ткое замыка́ние; **~coming** недоста́ток; изъя́н; ~ **cut** кратча́йший путь *m*; **~en** ['ʃɔ:tn] *v/t.* сокраща́ть [-рати́ть]; укора́чивать [-роти́ть]; *v/i.* сокраща́ться [-рати́ться]; укора́чиваться [-ро-

S

ти́ться]; **~hand** стеногра́фия; **~ly** ['ʃɔːtlɪ] *adv.* вско́ре; **~s** [-s] *pl.* шо́рты; **~-sighted** близору́кий; **~-term** краткосро́чный; **~ wave** коротково́лновый; **~-winded** страда́ющий одышко́й

**shot** [ʃɒt] **1.** *pt. и pt. p. от* ***shoot***; **2.** вы́стрел; *collect.* дробь *f*, дроби́нка (*mst.* ***small ~***); *pers.* стрело́к; *sport* ядро́; *stroke, in ball games* уда́р; *phot.* сни́мок; *med.* инъе́кция; ***have a ~*** сде́лать *pf.* попы́тку; *coll.* ***not by a long ~*** отню́дь не; **~gun** дробови́к

**should** [ʃʊd, ʃəd] *pt. от* ***shall***

**shoulder** ['ʃəʊldə] **1.** плечо́; **2.** взва́ливать на пле́чи; *fig.* брать на себя́; **~ blade** *anat.* лопа́тка; **~ strap** брете́лька; *mil.* пого́н

**shout** [ʃaʊt] **1.** крик; во́зглас; **2.** [за]крича́ть [кри́кнуть]; [на]крича́ть (***at*** на В)

**shove** [ʃʌv] **1.** толчо́к; **2.** толка́ть [-кну́ть]; ***~ off*** ста́лкивать [столкну́ть]; отта́лкивать [оттолкну́ть]

**shovel** ['ʃʌvl] **1.** (*spade*) лопа́та; *for use in home* сово́к; **2.** сгреба́ть лопа́той

**show** [ʃəʊ] **1.** [*irr.*] *v/t.* (*manifest*) ока́зывать [-за́ть]; (*exhibit*) выставля́ть [вы́ставить]; *interest, etc.* проявля́ть [-ви́ть]; (*prove*) дока́зывать [-за́ть]; ***~ in*** вводи́ть [ввести́]; ***~ up*** (*expose*) разоблача́ть [-чи́ть]; *v/i. coll.* (*appear*) появля́ться [-ви́ться]; ***~ off*** [по]щеголя́ть; пуска́ть пыль в глаза́; **2.** (*spectacle*) зре́лище; (*exhibition*) вы́ставка; (*outward appearance*) ви́димость *f*; *thea.* спекта́кль *m*; **~case** витри́на

**shower** ['ʃaʊə] **1.** ли́вень *m*; душ; ***take a ~*** принима́ть [-ня́ть] душ; **2.** ли́ться ли́внем; *fig.* осыпа́ть [осы́пать]; *questions* засыпа́ть [-пать]; **~y** ['ʃaʊərɪ] дождли́вый

**show|n** [ʃəʊn] *pt. p. от* ***show***; **~room** вы́ставочный зал; **~ window** *Am.* витри́на; **~y** ['ʃəʊɪ] показно́й

**shrank** [ʃræŋk] *pt. от* ***shrink***

**shred** [ʃred] **1.** *of cloth* лоскуто́к; *of paper* клочо́к; ***tear to ~s*** разорва́ть [разрыва́ть] в кло́чья; **2.** [*irr.*] ре́зать, рвать на клочки́; *cul.* [на]шинкова́ть

**shrewd** [ʃruːd] проница́тельный; *in business* де́льный, расчётливый

**shriek** [ʃriːk] **1.** визг, крик, вопль *m*; **2.** [за]вопи́ть, [за]визжа́ть

**shrill** [ʃrɪl] □ пронзи́тельный, ре́зкий

**shrimp** [ʃrɪmp] *zo.* креве́тка; *coll. pers.* сморчо́к

**shrine** [ʃraɪn] святы́ня

**shrink** [ʃrɪŋk] [*irr.*] (*become smaller*) сокраща́ться [-рати́ться]; *of wood, etc.* усыха́ть [усо́хнуть]; *of cloth* сади́ться [сесть]; *recoil* отпря́нуть

**shrivel** ['ʃrɪvl] смо́рщи(ва)ть(ся); съёжи(ва)ться

**shroud** [ʃraʊd] **1.** са́ван; *fig.* покро́в; **2.** оку́т(ыв)ать (*a. fig.*)

**shrub** [ʃrʌb] куст; ***~s*** *pl.* куста́рник

**shrug** [ʃrʌg] пож(им)а́ть плеча́ми

**shrunk** [ʃrʌŋk] *pt. и pt. p. от* ***shrink*** (*a.* ***~en***)

**shudder** ['ʃʌdə] **1.** дрожа́ть *impf.*; содрога́ться [-гну́ться]; ***I ~ to think*** я содрога́юсь при мы́сли об э́том; **2.** дрожь *f*

**shuffle** ['ʃʌfl] **1.** ша́ркать; *cards* [пере]тасова́ть; ***~ off*** *responsibility* перекла́дывать [переложи́ть] отве́тственность на други́х; **2.** ша́рканье; тасо́вка

**shun** [ʃʌn] избега́ть [-ежа́ть] (Р)

**shunt** [ʃʌnt] *fig. coll.* (*postpone*) откла́дывать [отложи́ть]

**shut** [ʃʌt] [*irr.*] **1.** закры́(ва́)ть(ся), затворя́ть(ся) [-ри́ть(ся)]; ***~ down*** (*close*) закрыва́ть [-ры́ть]; ***~ up!*** замолчи́!; **2.** закры́тый; **~ter** ['ʃʌtə] ста́вень *m*; *phot.* затво́р

**shuttle** ['ʃʌtl] (*device for weaving*) челно́к; ***~ service*** челно́чные ре́йсы; при́городный по́езд

**shy** [ʃaɪ] *animal* пугли́вый; *person* засте́нчивый

**shyness** ['ʃaɪnɪs] засте́нчивость *f*

**Siberian** [saɪ'bɪərɪən] **1.** сиби́рский; **2.** сибиря́к *m*, -я́чка *f*

**sick** [sɪk] **1.** больно́й (***of*** Т); чу́вствующий тошноту́; уста́вший (***of*** от П); ***I am ~ of …*** мне надое́ло (+ *inf.*, И); ***I feel ~*** меня́ тошни́т; **~en** ['sɪkən] *v/i.* заболе́(ва́)ть; [за]ча́хнуть;

S

***~ at*** чу́вствовать отвраще́ние к (Д); *v/t.* де́лать больны́м; вызыва́ть тошноту́ у (Р)

**sickle** ['sɪkl] серп

**sick|-leave**: ***I am on ~*** я на больни́чном; **~ly** ['sɪklɪ] боле́зненный; (*causing nausea*) тошнотво́рный; (*puny*) хи́лый; **~ness** ['sɪknɪs] боле́знь *f*; тошнота́; **~ pay** вы́плата по больни́чному листу́

**side** [saɪd] **1.** *com.* сторона́; бок; (*edge*) край; ***~ by ~*** бок о́ бок; ***to be on the safe ~*** на вся́кий слу́чай; ***on the one ~ … on the other ~*** с одно́й стороны́ … с друго́й стороны́; ***take the ~ of*** примыка́ть к той и́ли ино́й стороне́ (Р); **2.** *attr.* боково́й; *effect, etc.* побо́чный; **3.** ***~ with*** встать *pf.* на сто́рону (Р); **~board** буфе́т, серва́нт; **~car** *mot.* коля́ска мотоци́кла; **~light** *mot.* подфа́рник; **~long**: ***~ glance*** взгляд и́скоса; **~walk** *Am.* тротуа́р

**siding** ['saɪdɪŋ] *rail.* запа́сный путь *m*

**sidle** ['saɪdl] подходи́ть бочко́м

**siege** [siːdʒ] оса́да; ***lay ~ to*** осажда́ть [осади́ть]

**sieve** [sɪv] си́то

**sift** [sɪft] просе́ивать [-е́ять]; *fig.* [про]анализи́ровать

**sigh** [saɪ] **1.** вздох; **2.** вздыха́ть [вздохну́ть]

**sight** [saɪt] **1.** зре́ние; вид; взгля́д; (*spectacle*) зре́лище; *of gun* прице́л; ***~s*** *pl.* достопримеча́тельности *f/pl.*; ***catch ~ of*** ви́деть, заме́тить *pf.*; ***lose ~ of*** потеря́ть из ви́ду; **2.** уви́деть *pf.*; **~seeing** ['saɪtsiːɪŋ] осмо́тр достопримеча́тельностей

**sign** [saɪn] **1.** знак; при́знак; симпто́м; *over a shop* вы́веска; ***as a ~ of*** в знак (Р); **2.** *v/i.* подава́ть знак (Д); *v/t.* подпи́сывать [-са́ть]

**signal** ['sɪgnəl] **1.** сигна́л; **2.** [по]дава́ть сигна́л; подава́ть [-да́ть] знак; [про]сигна́лить

**signature** ['sɪgnətʃə] по́дпись *f*

**sign|board** вы́веска; **~er** ['saɪnə] лицо́ подписа́вшее како́й-либо докуме́нт

**signet** ['sɪgnɪt]: ***~ ring*** кольцо́ с печа́ткой

**signific|ance** [sɪg'nɪfɪkəns] значе́ние; **~ant** [-kənt] значи́тельный; *look* многозначи́тельный; ва́жный

**signify** ['sɪgnɪfaɪ] зна́чить, означа́ть

**signpost** доро́жный указа́тель *m*

**silence** ['saɪləns] **1.** молча́ние; тишина́; безмо́лвие; ***~!*** ти́хо!; **2.** заста́вить *pf.* молча́ть; заглуша́ть [-ши́ть]; **~r** [~ə] *mot.* глуши́тель *m*

**silent** ['saɪlənt] безмо́лвный; молчали́вый; (*noiseless*) бесшу́мный

**silk** [sɪlk] **1.** шёлк; **2.** (*made of silk*) шёлковый; **~en** ['sɪlkən] (*resembling silk*) шелкови́стый; **~worm** шелкови́чный червь *m*; **~y** ['sɪlkɪ] шелкови́стый

**sill** [sɪl] *of window* подоко́нник

**silly** ['sɪlɪ] □ глу́пый; ***don't be ~*** не валя́й дурака́

**silt** [sɪlt] **1.** ил; **2.** за́иливаться (*mst.* ***~ up***)

**silver** ['sɪlvə] **1.** серебро́; **2.** (*made of silver*) сере́бряный; **~y** [~rɪ] серебри́стый

**similar** ['sɪmɪlə] □ схо́дный (с Т), похо́жий (на В); подо́бный, аналоги́чный; **~ity** [sɪmə'lærətɪ] схо́дство; подо́бие

**simile** ['sɪmɪlɪ] сравне́ние

**simmer** ['sɪmə] ме́дленно кипе́ть; держа́ть на ме́дленном огне́

**simple** ['sɪmpl] просто́й; несло́жный; **~-hearted** простоду́шный; наи́вный; **~ton** [~tən] проста́к

**simpli|city** [sɪm'plɪsətɪ] простота́; простоду́шие; **~fy** ['sɪmplɪfaɪ] упроща́ть [-ости́ть]

**simply** ['sɪmplɪ] про́сто

**simulate** ['sɪmjʊleɪt] симули́ровать (*im*)*pf.*; притворя́ться [-ори́ться]

**simultaneous** [sɪml'teɪnɪəs] □ одновреме́нный; ***~ interpretation*** синхро́нный перево́д; ***~ interpreter*** перево́дчик-синхрони́ст

**sin** [sɪn] **1.** грех; **2.** согреша́ть [-ши́ть], [по]греши́ть

**since** [sɪns] **1.** *prp.* с (Р); **2.** *adv.* с тех пор; … тому́ наза́д; **3.** *cj.* с тех пор, как; так как; поско́льку

**sincer|e** [sɪn'sɪə] □ и́скренний; **~ely**:

S

***yours ~*** и́скренне Ваш, *formal* с глубо́ким уваже́нием; **~ity** [sɪn'serətɪ] и́скренность *f*
**sinew** ['sɪnjuː] сухожи́лие; **~y** [-ɪ] жи́листый
**sinful** ['sɪnfl] □ гре́шный
**sing** [sɪŋ] [*irr.*] [с]петь; ***~ s.o.'s praises*** петь кому-л. дифира́мбы
**singe** [sɪndʒ] опаля́ть [-ли́ть]
**singer** ['sɪŋgə] певе́ц *m*, певи́ца *f*
**single** ['sɪŋgl] **1.** □ еди́нственный; одино́чный; (*alone*) одино́кий; (*not married*) холосто́й, незаму́жняя; ***in ~ file*** гусько́м; **2.**: ***~ out*** отбира́ть [ото-бра́ть]; **~-breasted** однобо́ртный; **~-handed** самостоя́тельно, без посторо́нней по́мощи; **~-minded** целеустремлённый; **~t** ['sɪŋglɪt] ма́йка
**singular** ['sɪŋgjʊlə] необыча́йный; стра́нный; *gr.* еди́нственный; **~ity** [sɪŋgjʊ'lærətɪ] осо́бенность *f*, необыча́йность *f*
**sinister** ['sɪnɪstə] злове́щий
**sink** [sɪŋk] **1.** [*irr.*] *v/i.* (*fall*) опуска́ться [-сти́ться] (*a. of sun, etc.*); [за-, по-, у]тону́ть; *fig.* погружа́ться [-узи́ться]; (*subside*) оседа́ть [осе́сть]; ***~ or swim*** будь что бу́дет; *v/t.* затопля́ть [-пи́ть]; **2.** *in kitchen* ра́ковина
**sinless** ['sɪnlɪs] безгре́шный
**sinner** ['sɪnə] гре́шник *m*, -ица *f*
**sip** [sɪp] пить ма́ленькими глотка́ми
**siphon** ['saɪfn] сифо́н
**sir** [sɜː] *form of adress* су́дарь *m*; ♀ сэр
**siren** ['saɪərən] сире́на
**sirloin** ['sɜːlɔɪn] филе́йная часть
**sister** ['sɪstə] сестра́; **~-in-law** [-rɪnlɔː] сестра́ му́жа (жены́); **~ly** [-lɪ] се́стринский
**sit** [sɪt] [*irr.*] *v/i.* сиде́ть; *of assembly* заседа́ть; ***~ down*** сади́ться [сесть]; ***~ for*** *paint.* пози́ровать; ***~ for an examination*** сдава́ть экза́мен
**site** [saɪt] ме́сто, местоположе́ние; ***building ~*** строи́тельная площа́дка
**sitting** ['sɪtɪŋ] заседа́ние; **~ room** гости́ная
**situat|ed** ['sɪtjʊeɪtɪd] располо́женный; **~ion** [sɪtʃʊ'eɪʃn] положе́ние; ситуа́ция; (*job*) ме́сто
**six** [sɪks] **1.** шесть; **2.** шестёрка; **~teen** [sɪk'stiːn] шестна́дцать; **~teenth** [sɪk'stiːn0] шестна́дцатый; **~th** [sɪksθ] **1.** шесто́й; **2.** шеста́я часть *f*; **~tieth** ['sɪkstɪəθ] шестидеся́тый; **~ty** ['sɪkstɪ] шестьдеся́т
**size** [saɪz] **1.** величина́; *of books, etc.* форма́т; (*dimension*) разме́р (*a. of shoes, clothing*); **2.** ***~ up*** определи́ть взве́сить *fig.* oцени́ть *pf.*, поня́ть *pf.*
**siz(e)able** ['saɪzəbl] поря́дочного разме́ра
**sizzle** ['sɪzl] шкворча́ть, шипе́ть
**skat|e** [skeɪt] **1.** конёк (*pl.*: коньки́); **2.** ката́ться на конька́х; **~er** ['skeɪtə] конькобе́жец *m*, -жка *f*
**skein** [skeɪn] мото́к пря́жи
**skeleton** ['skelɪtn] *anat.* скеле́т; *tech.* о́стов, карка́с; ***~ key*** отмы́чка
**skeptic**, *Brt.* **sceptic** ['skeptɪk] ске́птик; **~al** [-tɪkl] □ скепти́ческий
**sketch** [sketʃ] **1.** эски́з, набро́сок; **2.** де́лать набро́сок, эски́з (Р); **~y** ['-ɪ] пове́рхностный
**ski** [skiː] **1.** (*pl.* **~** *или* **~s**) лы́жа; **2.** ходи́ть на лы́жах
**skid** [skɪd] **1.** *mot.* юз, зано́с; *of wheels* буксова́ние; **2.** *v/i.* буксова́ть; идти́ [пойти́] ю́зом; *of person* скользи́ть
**skillful**, *Brt.* **skilful** ['skɪlfl] □ иску́сный, уме́лый
**skill** [skɪl] мастерство́, уме́ние; **~ed** [-d] квалифици́рованный, иску́сный
**skim** [skɪm] *cream, scum, etc.* снима́ть [снять]; (*glide*) скользи́ть [-зну́ть] по (Д); (*read*) просма́тривать [-смотре́ть]; ***~ over*** бе́гло прочи́тывать; ***~med milk*** сня́тое молоко́
**skimp** [skɪmp] эконо́мить; [по]скупи́ться (***on*** на В); **~y** ['skɪmpɪ] □ ску́дный
**skin** [skɪn] **1.** ко́жа; (*hide*) шку́ра; *of apricot, etc.* кожура́; **2.** *v/t.* сдира́ть ко́жу, шку́ру с (Р); **~-deep** пове́рхностный; **~ diver** аквалангист; **~flint** скря́га *m*; **~ny** ['skɪnɪ] то́щий; **~-tight** в обтя́жку
**skip** [skɪp] **1.** прыжо́к, скачо́к; **2.** *v/i.* [по]скака́ть; *fig.* переска́кивать

S

[-скочи́ть] (**from** с [P]), (**to** на [B]); *v/t*. (*omit*) пропуска́ть [-сти́ть]
**skipper** ['skɪpə] капита́н
**skirmish** ['skɜːmɪʃ] *mil*. сты́чка (*a. fig*.)
**skirt** [skɜːt] **1.** (*waist-down garment or part of a dress*) ю́бка; *of coat* пола́; (*edge*) край, окра́ина; **2.** *v/t*. обходи́ть [обойти́]; объезжа́ть [-е́хать]
**skit** [skɪt] сати́ра, паро́дия
**skittle** ['skɪtl] ке́гля; ***play*** (***at***) **~*s*** *pl*. игра́ть в ке́гли; **~ alley** кегельба́н
**skulk** [skʌlk] кра́сться
**skull** [skʌl] че́реп
**sky** [skaɪ] не́бо (небеса́ *pl*.); ***praise to the skies*** расхва́ливать до небе́с; ***out of a clear ~*** как гром среди́ я́сного не́ба; **~lark 1.** жа́воронок; **2.** выки́дывать шту́чки; **~light** светово́й люк; **~line** горизо́нт; *of buildings, etc*. очерта́ние; **~scraper** небоскрёб; **~ward**(**s**) ['skaɪwəd(z)] к не́бу
**slab** [slæb] плита́
**slack** [slæk] **1.** (*remiss*) небре́жный; *behavio(u)r* расхля́банный; (*loose*) сла́бый; (*slow*) ме́дленный; *rope, etc*. сла́бо натя́нутый; (*a. comm*.) вя́лый; **2.** *naut. of rope* слаби́на; **~s** *pl*. брю́ки *f/pl*.; **3.** = **~en** ['slækn] ослабля́ть [-а́бить]; [о]сла́бнуть; замедля́ть [-е́длить]
**slain** [sleɪn] *p. pt. om* ***slay***
**slake** [sleɪk] *thirst* утоля́ть [-ли́ть]
**slalom** ['slɑːləm] слало́м
**slam** [slæm] **1.** хло́панье; **2.** хло́пать [-пнуть] (T); захло́пывать(ся) [-пнуть(ся)]
**slander** ['slɑːndə] **1.** клевета́; **2.** [на-]клевета́ть; **~ous** [~rəs] □ клеветни́ческий
**slang** [slæŋ] сленг; жарго́н
**slant** [slɑːnt] склон, укло́н (*a. fig*.); то́чка зре́ния; **~ed** [~ɪd] (*biased*) тенденцио́зный; **~ing** [~ɪŋ] □ *adj*. наклонный; косо́й
**slap** [slæp] **1.** шлепо́к; ***~ in the face*** пощёчина; **2.** шлёпать [-пнуть]; *on back, etc*. хло́пать [-пнуть]
**slash** [slæʃ] **1.** разре́з; **2.** (*wound*) [по-]ра́нить; *with whip, etc*. [ис]полосова́ть [полосну́ть]
**slate** [sleɪt] сла́нец; *for roof* ши́фер
**slattern** ['slætən] неря́ха
**slaughter** ['slɔːtə] **1.** убо́й (скота́); *fig*. резня́, кровопроли́тие; **2.** [за-] ре́зать; забива́ть [-би́ть]; **~house** бо́йня
**Slav** [slɑːv] **1.** славяни́н *m*, -янка *f*; **2.** славя́нский
**slave** [sleɪv] **1.** раб *m*, -ыня *f*; *attr*. ра́бский; **2.** рабо́тать как ка́торжник
**slav|ery** ['sleɪvərɪ] ра́бство; **~ish** [~vɪʃ] □ ра́бский
**slay** [sleɪ] [*irr*.] уби́(ва́)ть
**sled** [sled], **sledge**[1] [sledʒ] са́ни *f/pl*.; *child's* са́нки *f/pl*.
**sledge**[2] [~] (*~ hammer*) кузне́чный мо́лот
**sleek** [sliːk] **1.** □ *animal's coat* гла́дкий и блестя́щий; *manner* вкра́дчивый
**sleep** [sliːp] **1.** [*irr*.] *v/i*. [по]спа́ть; ***~ like a log*** спать мёртвым сном; ***~ on it*** отложи́ть *pf*. до за́втра; *v/t*. дава́ть (кому́-нибудь) ночле́г; ***put to ~*** *animal* усыпля́ть [-пи́ть]; **2.** сон; **~er** ['~ə] спя́щий; *rail* спа́льный ваго́н; **~ing** ['~ɪŋ]: ***~ bag*** спа́льный мешо́к; ***~ pill*** табле́тка снотво́рного; ***~ car*** *rail*. спа́льный ваго́н; **~less** ['~lɪs] □ бессо́нный; **~walker** луна́тик; **~y** ['~ɪ] □ со́нный, *coll*. за́спанный
**sleet** [sliːt] мо́крый снег; **~y** ['sliːtɪ] сля́котный
**sleeve** [sliːv] рука́в; *tech*. му́фта; вту́лка
**sleigh** [sleɪ] са́ни *f/pl*.
**sleight** [slaɪt] (*mst*. ***~ of hand***) ло́вкость *f* (рук)
**slender** ['slendə] □ стро́йный; то́нкий; (*scanty*) ску́дный
**slept** [slept] *pt. u pt. p. om* ***sleep***
**sleuth** [sluːθ] *joc*. сы́щик, детекти́в
**slew** [sluː] *pt. om* ***slay***
**slice** [slaɪs] **1.** ло́моть *m*, *dim*. ло́мтик; (*part*) часть *f*; **2.** [на]ре́зать ло́мтиками
**slick** [slɪk] *coll*. гла́дкий; *Am*. хи́трый, ско́льзкий
**slid** [slɪd] *pt. u pt. p. om* ***slide***
**slide** [slaɪd] **1.** [*irr*.] скользи́ть [-зну́ть]; ката́ться по льду; вдвига́ть [-и́нуть],

всо́вывать [всу́нуть] (*into* в В); ***let things ~*** относи́ться ко всему́ спустя́ рукава́; **2.** *photo.* диапозити́в, слайд; **3.** скольже́ние; *for children* де́тская го́рка; (*land~*) о́ползень *m*; **~ rule** логарифми́ческая лине́йка

**slight** [slaɪt] **1.** □ (*thin and delicate*) то́нкий, хру́пкий; незначи́тельный; сла́бый; ***not the ~est idea*** ни мале́йшего представле́ния; **2.** (*disrespect*) пренебреже́ние; **3.** обижа́ть [-и́деть]; унижа́ть [-и́зить]

**slim** [slɪm] (*slender*) то́нкий, то́ненький; *person* стро́йный; ***~ hope*** сла́бая наде́жда

**slim|e** [slaɪm] (*mud*) жи́дкая грязь *f*; (*silt*) ил; **~y** ['slaɪmɪ] сли́зистый, ско́льзкий

**sling** [slɪŋ] **1.** *bandage* пе́ревязь; **2.** *throw* [*irr.*] швыря́ть [швырну́ть]

**slink** [slɪŋk] [*irr.*] кра́сться; ***~ off*** потихо́ньку отходи́ть [отойти́]

**slip** [slɪp] **1.** [*irr.*] *v/i.* скользи́ть; поскользну́ться *pf.*; *out of hands* выскольза́ть [вы́скользнуть]; *of wheels* буксова́ть; *v/t.* сова́ть [су́нуть]; *one's attention* ускольза́ть [-зну́ть]; ***~ a p.'s memory*** вы́лететь из головы́ (Р); ***~ on (off)*** наде́(ва́)ть, сбра́сывать [сбро́сить]; **2.** скольже́ние; *of paper* поло́ска; про́мах; оши́бка; *in writing* опи́ска; (*petticoat*) комбина́ция; (*pillowcase*) на́волочка; ***give a p. the ~*** ускольза́ть [-зну́ть] от (Р); ***~ of the tongue*** огово́рка; **~per** ['slɪpə] ко́мнатная ту́фля; **~pery** ['slɪpərɪ] ско́льзкий; (*not safe*) ненадёжный; **~shod** ['slɪpʃɒd] неря́шливый; (*careless*) небре́жный; **~t** [slɪpt] *pt. и p. pt. от* ***slip***

**slit** [slɪt] **1.** разре́з; щель *f*; **2.** [*irr.*] разре́зать в длину́

**sliver** ['slɪvə] *of wood* ще́пка; *of glass* оско́лок

**slogan** [sləʊgən] ло́зунг

**slop** [slɒp] **1.**: **~s** *pl.* помо́и *m/pl.*; **2.** (*spill*) проли́(ва́)ть; расплёскивать(-ся) [-еска́ть(ся)]

**slop|e** [sləʊp] **1.** накло́н, склон, скат; **2.** клони́ться; име́ть накло́н; **~ing** ['~ɪŋ] пока́тый

**sloppy** ['slɒpɪ] (*slovenly*) неря́шливый; (*careless*) небре́жный; сентимента́льный

**slot** [slɒt] щель *f*; про́резь *f*; паз; (*place or job*) ме́сто

**sloth** [sləʊθ] лень *f*, ле́ность *f*; *zo.* лени́вец

**slot machine** иго́рный (торго́вый) автома́т

**slouch** [slaʊtʃ] **1.** [с]суту́литься; *when sitting* [с]го́рбиться; ***~ about, around*** слоня́ться без де́ла; **2.** суту́лость *f*

**slovenly** ['slʌvnlɪ] неря́шливый

**slow** [sləʊ] **1.** ме́дленный; медли́тельный; (*dull in mind*) тупо́й; *trade* вя́лый; *watch* отст(ав)а́ть; **2.** (*a.* ***~ down, up***) замедля́ть(ся) [заме́длить(ся)]; **~poke** (*or chiefly Brt.* **~coach**) копу́ша; **~-witted** тупо́й, тупова́тый

**slug** [slʌg] слизня́к

**slugg|ard** ['slʌgəd] лежебо́ка *m/f.*; **~ish** ['slʌgɪʃ] ме́дленный, вя́лый

**sluice** [slu:s] шлюз

**slum** [slʌm] *mst.* **~s** *pl.* трущо́бы

**slumber** ['slʌmbə] **1.** дремо́та; сон; **2.** дрема́ть; спать

**slump** [slʌmp] **1.** *of prices, demand* ре́зкое паде́ние; **2.** ре́зко па́дать; *into a chair, etc.* тяжело́ опуска́ться

**slung** [slʌŋ] *pt. и pt. p. от* ***sling***

**slunk** [slʌŋk] *pt. и pt. p. от* ***slink***

**slur** [slɜ:] **1.** *in speech* невня́тная речь; *on reputation, etc.* пятно́; **2.** *v/t.* говори́ть невня́тно; ***~ over*** ума́лчивать [-молча́ть], опуска́ть [-сти́ть]; *fig. coll.* сма́зывать [сма́зать]

**slush** [slʌʃ] сля́коть *f*; та́лый снег

**sly** [slaɪ] □ хи́трый; лука́вый; ***on the ~*** тайко́м

**smack**[1] [smæk]: ***~ of*** име́ть (при́-) вкус; па́хнуть (Т)

**smack**[2] [~] **1.** (*kiss*) зво́нкий поцелу́й; (*slap*) шлепо́к; **2.** *lips* чмо́кать [-кнуть]; хло́пать [-пнуть] (Т); шлёпать [-пнуть]

**small** [smɔ:l] *com.* ма́ленький, небольшо́й; *mistakes, etc.* ме́лкий; незначи́тельный; ***~ change*** ме́лочь *f*; ***~ fry*** ме́лкая рыбёшка; ***~ of the back***

S

*anat.* поясни́ца; ***in the ~ hours*** под у́тро; в предрассве́тные часы́; **~ arms** *pl.* стре́лковое ору́жие; **~pox** *med.* о́спа; **~ talk** лёгкий, бессодержа́тельный разгово́р; све́тская болтовня́
**smart** [smɑːt] **1.** □ *blow* ре́зкий, си́льный; (*clever*) ло́вкий; у́мный; (*stylish*) элега́нтный; (*witty*) остроу́мный; (*fashionable*) мо́дный; **2.** боль *f*; **3.** боле́ть, садни́ть; *fig.* страда́ть; **~ness** ['smɑːtnɪs] наря́дность *f*, элега́нтность *f*; ло́вкость *f*
**smash** [smæʃ] **1.** *v/t. enemy* сокруша́ть [-ши́ть] *a. fig.*; разбива́ть вдре́безги; *v/i.* разби́(ва́)ться; ста́лкиваться [столкну́ться] (***into*** с Т); **~-up** (*collision*) столкнове́ние; катастро́фа
**smattering** ['smætərɪŋ] пове́рхностное зна́ние; небольшо́е коли́чество чего́-то
**smear** [smɪə] **1.** пятно́; мазо́к (*a. med.*); **2.** [на]ма́зать, изма́з(ыв)ать
**smell** [smel] **1.** за́пах; *sense* обоня́ние; **2.** [*irr.*] [по]чу́вствовать за́пах; *of animal* [по]чу́ять (В); (*a.* **~ *at***) [по]ню́хать (В); **~ *of*** па́хнуть (Т)
**smelt**[1] [smelt] *pt. и pt. p. om* ***smell***
**smelt**[2] [~] выплавля́ть [вы́плавить]
**smile** [smaɪl] **1.** улы́бка; **2.** улыба́ться [-бну́ться]
**smirk** [smɜːk] ухмыля́ться [-льну́ться]
**smite** [smaɪt] [*irr.*] (*afflict*) поража́ть [-рази́ть]; ***she was smitten with sorrow*** она́ была́ уби́та го́рем
**smith** [smɪθ]: ***black~*** кузне́ц
**smithereens** ['smɪðə'riːnz]: ***break into ~*** разбива́ть [-би́ть] вдре́безги
**smithy** ['smɪðɪ] ку́зница
**smitten** ['smɪtn] *pt. p. om* ***smite***
**smock** [smɒk] *child's* де́тский хала́тик; *woman's* же́нская [крестья́нская) блу́за
**smoke** [sməʊk] **1.** дым; ***have a ~*** покури́ть *pf.*; ***go up in ~*** ко́нчиться *pf.* ниче́м; **2.** кури́ть; [на]дыми́ть; (*emit ~*) [за]дыми́ться; *tobacco, etc.* выку́ривать [вы́курить] (*a.* **~ *out***); **~-dried** копчёный; **~less** ['~lɪs] бezды́мный; **~r** ['~ə] куря́щий; *rail coll.* ваго́н для куря́щих; **~stack** дымова́я труба́
**smoking** ['sməʊkɪŋ] куря́щий; **~ compartment** *rail.* купе́ для куря́щих; **~ room** ко́мната для куре́ния
**smoky** ['sməʊkɪ] ды́мный; наку́ренный
**smolder**, *Brt.* **smoulder** ['sməʊldə] тлеть
**smooth** [smuːð] **1.** □ гла́дкий; *take-off, etc.* пла́вный; (*calm*) споко́йный; (*ingratiating*) вкра́дчивый; (*flattering*) льсти́вый; **2.** пригла́живать [-ла́дить]; **~ *out*** разгла́живать [-ла́дить]; *fig.* (*a.* **~ *over***) смягча́ть [-чи́ть]; *differences* сгла́живать [-а́дить]
**smote** [sməʊt] *pt. om* ***smite***
**smother** ['smʌðə] [за]души́ть; *anger, etc.* подави́ть *pf.*
**smudge** [smʌdʒ] **1.** [за]па́чкать(ся); **2.** гря́зное пятно́
**smug** [smʌg] самодово́льный
**smuggle** ['smʌgl] занима́ться контраба́ндой; провози́ть контраба́ндой; **~r** [~ə] контрабанди́ст *m*, -ка *f*
**smut** [smʌt] **1.** (*soot*) са́жа, ко́поть *f*; (*fungus, crop disease*) головня́; (*obscene language*) непристо́йность *f*; ***a talk ~*** нести́ похабщину
**smutty** ['smʌtɪ] □ гря́зный
**snack** [snæk] лёгкая заку́ска; ***have a ~*** перекуси́ть; **~ bar** заку́сочная
**snag** [snæg] *fig.* препя́тствие; ***there's a ~*** в э́том загво́здка
**snail** [sneɪl] *zo.* ули́тка; ***at a ~'s pace*** ме́дленно как черепа́ха
**snake** [sneɪk] *zo.* зме́я
**snap** [snæp] **1.** (*noise*) щелчо́к; треск; (*fastener*) кно́пка, застёжка; *coll.* (*photo*) сни́мок; *fig.* (*zest*) жи́вость; ***cold ~*** внеза́пное похолода́ние; **2.** *v/i.* (*break*) [с]лома́ться; (*make a sharp noise*) щёлкать [-кнуть]; (*snatch*) ухва́тываться [ухвати́ться] (***at*** за В); *of a dog, a. fig.* огрыза́ться [-зну́ться] (***at*** на В); (*break, as a string, etc.*) [по-]рва́ться; (*close, as a fastener*) защёлкивать [защёлкнуть]; *phot.* де́лать сни́мок (Р); **~ *out of it!*** бро́сь(те)!, встряхни́тесь!; **~ *up*** (*buy up*) раскупа́ть [-пи́ть]; **~dragon** льви́ный зев;

S

~ **fastener** кно́пка (застёжка); ~**pish** ['snæpɪʃ] □ раздражи́тельный; ~**py** ['snæpɪ] *coll.* энерги́чный; живо́й; ***make it ~ !*** поживе́е; ~**shot** *phot.* сни́мок

**snare** [sneə] **1.** сило́к; *fig.* лову́шка, западня́; **2.** лови́ть [пойма́ть] сило́ками *m/pl.*

**snarl** [snɑːl] **1.** рыча́ние; **2.** [про-] рыча́ть; *fig.* огрыза́ться [-зну́ться]

**snatch** [snætʃ] **1.** рыво́к; (*a grab*) хвата́ние; (*fragment*) обры́вок; кусо́чек; **2.** хвата́ть [схвати́ть]; (~ *away*) вырыва́ть [-рвать]; ~ ***at*** хвата́ться [схвати́ться] за (В); ~ ***up*** подхва́тывать [-хвати́ть]

**sneak** [sniːk] **1.** *v/i.* (*move stealthily*) кра́сться; ~ ***up*** подкра́дываться [-ра́сться]; *v/t.* (*take in a furtive way, as a look, a smoke, etc.*) стащи́ть *pf.*, укра́сть *pf.*; **2.** (*telltale*) я́бедник *m*, -ица *f*; ~**ers** ['sniːkəz] *pl. Am.* полуке́ды *f/pl.*; (*running shoes*) кроссо́вки *f/pl.*

**sneer** [snɪə] **1.** (*contemptuous smile*) презри́тельная усме́шка; насме́шка; **2.** насме́шливо улыба́ться; насмеха́ться, глуми́ться (***at*** над Т)

**sneeze** [sniːz] **1.** чиха́нье; **2.** чиха́ть [чихну́ть]

**snicker** ['snɪkə] хихи́кать [-кнуть]; *of horses* ржать

**sniff** [snɪf] *v/t.* [по]ню́хать; *of dog* учу́ять; *v/i.* шмы́гать [-гну́ть] но́сом

**snigger** ['snɪgə] → ***snicker***

**snip** [snɪp] **1.** (*piece cut off*) обре́зок; кусо́к; (*cut*) надре́з; **2.** (*trim*) подреза́ть [-ре́зать]; (*cut out*) выре́зывать [вы́резать]

**sniper** ['snɑɪpə] сна́йпер

**snivel** ['snɪvl] хны́кать; (*after crying*) всхли́пывать [-пнуть]; *coll.* распуска́ть со́пли

**snob** [snɒb] сноб; ~**bery** ['snɒbərɪ] сноби́зм

**snoop** [snuːp] подгля́дывать, выню́хивать, чужи́е та́йны

**snooze** [snuːz] *coll.* **1.** лёгкий, коро́ткий сон; **2.** дрема́ть, вздремну́ть *pf.*

**snore** [snɔː] [за]храпе́ть

**snorkel** ['snɔːkl] шно́ркель *m*

**snort** [snɔːt] фы́ркать [-кнуть]; *of horse* [за]храпе́ть

**snout** [snaʊt] *pig's* ры́ло; *dog's, etc.* мо́рда

**snow** [snəʊ] **1.** снег; **2.** ***it is ~ing*** идёт снег; ***be covered with ~*** быть занесённым сне́гом; ***be ~ed under with work*** быть зава́ленным рабо́той; ~**ball** снежо́к; ~**drift** сугро́б; ~**fall** снегопа́д; ~**flake** снежи́нка; ~ **plow**, *Brt.* ~ **plough** снегоочисти́тель *m*; ~**storm** вью́га; ~**-white** белосне́жный; ~**y** ['snəʊɪ] □ сне́жный

**snub** [snʌb] **1.** *fig.* оса́живать [осади́ть]; **2.** пренебрежи́тельное обхожде́ние; ~**-nosed** курно́сый

**snug** [snʌg] □ ую́тный; ~**gle** ['snʌgl] (ла́сково) приж(им)а́ться (***up to*** к Д)

**so** [səʊ] так; ита́к; таки́м о́бразом; ***I hope ~*** я наде́юсь, что да; ***Look, it's raining. ~ it is.*** Смотри́, идёт дождь. Да, действи́тельно; ***you are tired, ~ am I*** вы уста́ли и я то́же; ~ ***far*** до сих пор

**soak** [səʊk] *v/t.* [за]мочи́ть; (*draw in*) впи́тывать [впита́ть]; *v/i.* промока́ть; ~ ***in*** пропи́тываться [-пита́ться]; ~ ***through*** проса́чиваться [-сочи́ться]; ***get ~ed to the skin*** промо́кнуть до ни́тки

**soap** [səʊp] **1.** мы́ло; **2.** намы́ли(ва)ть; ~ **dish** мы́льница; ~**suds** мы́льная пе́на; ~**y** ['səʊpɪ] □ мы́льный

**soar** [sɔː] (*fly high*) пари́ть; *of birds* взмыва́ть [-ыть]; *of prices* подска́кивать [-кочи́ть]

**sob** [sɒb] **1.** всхлип; рыда́ние; **2.** [за]рыда́ть; разрыда́ться *pf.*

**sober** ['səʊbə] **1.** □ тре́звый (*a. fig.*); **2.** *fig.* отрезвля́ть [-ви́ть]; ***have a ~ing effect*** [по]де́йствовать отрезвля́юще; ~ ***up*** протрезвля́ться [-ви́ться]

**so-called** [səʊ'kɔːld] так называ́емый

**sociable** ['səʊʃəbl] □ общи́тельный

**social** ['səʊʃl] **1.** □ обще́ственный; социа́льный; ~ ***security*** социа́льное обеспе́чение; **2.** вечери́нка

**socialism** ['səʊʃəlɪzəm] социали́зм

**society** [sə'saɪətɪ] о́бщество; *comm.*

S

компа́ния; (*the public, the community*) обще́ственность *f*; (*association*) объедине́ние
**sociology** [səʊsɪ'ɒlədʒɪ] социоло́гия
**sock** [sɒk] носо́к
**socket** ['sɒkɪt] *of eye* впа́дина; *for bulb* патро́н; *for wall* розе́тка; *tech.* ште́псельное гнездо́
**soda** ['səʊdə] со́да; (*drink*) газиро́ванная вода́
**sodden** ['sɒdn] промо́кший
**soft** [sɒft] □ *com.* мя́гкий; не́жный; ти́хий; нея́ркий; (*unmanly*) изне́женный; (*weak in mind*) *coll.* придуркова́тый; **~ drink** безалкого́льный напи́ток; **~en** ['sɒfn] смягча́ть(ся) [-чи́ть(ся)]; **~hearted** мягкосерде́чный; **~ware** *comput.* програ́ммное обеспе́чение
**soggy** ['sɒgɪ] сыро́й; пропи́танный водо́й
**soil** [sɔɪl] **1.** (*earth*) по́чва, земля (*a. fig. country*); **2.** (*dirty*) [за]па́чкать(ся)
**solace** ['sɒlɪs] утеше́ние
**solar** ['səʊlə] со́лнечный; **~ eclipse** со́лнечное затме́ние
**sold** [səʊld] *pt. u pt. p. от* **sell**
**solder** ['sɒldə] **1.** припо́й; **2.** пая́ть; запа́ивать [запая́ть]
**soldier** ['səʊldʒə] солда́т
**sole**[1] [səʊl] □ еди́нственный; (*exclusive*) исключи́тельный
**sole**[2] [~] **1.** *of foot* ступня́; *of shoe* подмётка; **2.** ста́вить подмётку на (В)
**sole**[3] [~] *zo.* ка́мбала
**solely** ['səʊllɪ] исключи́тельно, еди́нственно
**solemn** ['sɒləm] □ *event, etc.* торже́ственный; серьёзный; (*pompous*) напы́щенный; **~ity** [sə'lemnətɪ] торже́ственность *f*; **~ize** ['sɒləmnaɪz]: **~ a marriage** сочета́ть бра́ком
**solicit** [sə'lɪsɪt] *help, etc.* проси́ть; **~or** [~ə] *law Brt.* адвока́т, юриско́нсульт; **~ous** [~əs] □ (*considerate*) забо́тливый; **~ of** стремя́щийся к (Д); **~ude** [~juːd] забо́тливость *f*, забо́та
**solid** ['sɒlɪd] **1.** □ твёрдый; (*firm*) про́чный; (*unbroken*) сплошно́й; масси́вный; (*sound, reliable*) соли́дный; (*dependable*) надёжный; (*unanimous*) единогла́сный; (*united*) сплочённый; **a ~ hour** це́лый час; **on ~ ground** *fig.* на твёрдой по́чве; **~ gold** чи́стое зо́лото; **2.** *phys.* твёрдое те́ло; **~arity** [sɒlɪ'dærətɪ] солида́рность *f*
**soliloquy** [sə'lɪləkwɪ] моноло́г
**solit|ary** ['sɒlɪtrɪ] □ (*lonely*) одино́кий; (*secluded*) уединённый; **~ude** [~tjuːd] одино́чество, уедине́ние
**solo** ['səʊləʊ] со́ло *n indecl.*; **~ist** ['səʊləʊɪst] соли́ст *m*, -ка *f*
**solu|ble** ['sɒljʊbl] раствори́мый; *fig.* (*solvable*) разреши́мый; **~tion** [sə'luːʃn] (*process*) растворе́ние; (*result of process*) раство́р
**solv|e** [sɒlv] реша́ть [реши́ть], разреша́ть [-ши́ть]; **~ent** ['~vənt] **1.** *fin.* платёжеспособный; *chem.* растворя́ющий; **2.** раствори́тель *m*
**somb|er**, *Brt.* **~re** ['sɒmbə] □ мра́чный; угрю́мный; *clothes* тёмный
**some** [sʌm, səm] не́кий; како́й-то; како́й-нибудь; не́сколько; не́которые; о́коло (Р); **~ 20 miles** миль два́дцать; **in ~ degree, to ~ extent** до изве́стной сте́пени; **~body** ['sʌmbədɪ] кто́-то; кто́-нибудь; **~how** ['sʌmhaʊ] ка́к-то; ка́к-нибудь; **~ or other** так или ина́че; **~one** ['sʌmwʌn] → **somebody**
**somersault** ['sʌməsɔːlt] кувырка́ние; *in air* са́льто *n indecl.*; **turn ~s** *pl.* кувырка́ться, [с]де́лать са́льто, **turn a ~** кувыркну́ться *pf.*
**some|thing** ['sʌmθɪŋ] что́-то; что́нибудь; кое-что́; **~ like** приблизи́тельно; что́-то вро́де (Р): **is ~ the matter?** что́-нибудь не в поря́дке?; **~time** когда́-то, когда́-нибудь, когда́-либо; **~times** иногда́; **~what** слегка́, немно́го; до не́которой сте́пени; **~where** где́-то, куда́-то; где́-нибудь, куда́-нибудь
**son** [sʌn] сын, *dim.* сыно́к; (*pl.*: сыновья́; *rhet.*: сыны́)
**sonata** [sə'nɑːtə] сона́та
**song** [sɒŋ] песня, *dim.* пе́сенка; рома́нс; *coll.* **for a ~** за бесце́нок; **~bird** пе́вчая пти́ца

S

**son-in-law** зять *m*
**sonorous** ['sɒnərəs] □ звýчный
**soon** [su:n] скóро, вскóре; рáно; ***as ~ as*** как тóлько; **~er** ['su:nə] скорée; ***no ~ … than*** едвá …, как; ***no ~ said than done*** скáзано – сдéлано; ***the ~ the better*** чем скорée, тем лýчше
**soot** [sʊt] сáжа; кóпоть *f*
**soothe** [su:ð] успокáивать [-кóить] (*a. fig.*); *fig.* утешáть [утéшить]
**sooty** ['sʊtɪ] □ закопчённый; чёрный как сáжа
**sophist|icated** [sə'fɪstɪkeɪtɪd] изы́сканный; *person* свéтский, искушённый; *machinery* слóжный; *argument* изощрённый
**soporific** [sɒpə'rɪfɪk] снотвóрное
**sordid** ['sɔ:dɪd] □ *condition* убóгий; *behavio(u)r, etc.* гнýсный
**sore** [sɔ:] **1.** □ (*tender*) чувстви́тельный; *point* болéзненный; (*painful*) больнóй, воспалённый; (*aggrieved*) оби́женный; ***she has a ~ throat*** у неё боли́т гóрло; **2.** боля́чка; *from rubbing* натёртое мéсто; (*running ~*) гноя́щаяся рáн(к)а
**sorrel** ['sɒrəl] *bot.* щáвель *m*
**sorrow** ['sɒrəʊ] гóре, печáль *f*; (*regret*) сожалéние; ***to my great ~*** к моемý вели́кому сожалéнию; **~ful** ['sɔrəʊfʊl] печáльный, скóрбный
**sorry** ['sɒrɪ] □ пóлный сожалéния; **~?** *mst. Brt.* прости́те, не расслы́шал(а), *coll.* что?; (***I am***) (***so***) **~!** мне óчень жаль! виновáт!; ***I feel ~ for you*** мне вас жаль; ***I'm ~ to say that …*** к сожалéнию, я …; ***say ~*** извиня́ться [-ни́ться]
**sort** [sɔ:t] **1.** род, сорт; ***people of all ~s*** *pl.* лю́ди вся́кого разбóра; ***~ of*** *coll.* как бýдто; ***be out of ~s*** *pl.* быть не в дýхе; плóхо чýвствовать себя́; **2.** сортировáть; ***~ out*** разбирáть [разобрáть]; рассортирóвывать [-ировáть]
**so-so** ['səʊsəʊ] *coll.* так себé, невáжно
**SOS** [esəʊ'es] СОС: сигнáл бéдствия в áзбуке мóрзе
**souffle** ['su:fleɪ] суфлé *n indecl.*
**sought** [sɔ:t] *pt. и pt. p. от* ***seek***
**soul** [səʊl] душá (*a. fig.*); (*person*) человéк, душá
**sound**[1] [saʊnd] □ (*healthy*) здорóвый, крéпкий, (*firm*) прóчный; (*sensible*) здрáвый; *in mind* нормáльный; *comm.* надёжный; *sleep* глубóкий: ***be ~ asleep*** крéпко спать
**sound**[2] [~] **1.** звук, шум; *mus.* звучáние; **2.** звучáть (*a. fig.*); разд(ав)áться; *fig.* [про]зонди́ровать; *patient's chest* выслýшивать [вы́слушать]; ***~ barrier*** звуковóй барьéр; **~ing** ['saundɪŋ] *naut.* промéр глубины́ воды́; **~less** [~lɪs] □ беззвýчный; **~proof** звуконепроницáемый; **~track** звуковóе сопровождéние
**soup** [su:p] суп; **~ plate** глубóкая тарéлка; **~ spoon** столóвая лóжка
**sour** ['saʊə] □ ки́слый; (*bad-tempered*) раздражи́тельный; ***~ cream*** сметáна; *fig.* угрю́мый; ***turn ~*** закисáть [-и́снуть]; прокисáть [-и́снуть]
**source** [sɔ:s] истóк; истóчник (*mst. fig.*)
**south** [saʊθ] **1.** юг; **2.** ю́жный; **~east 1.** юго-востóк; **2.** юго-востóчный (*a.* ***~ern***)
**souther|ly** ['sʌðəlɪ], **~n** ['sʌðən] ю́жный; **~ner** ['sʌðənə] южáнин, южáнка
**southernmost** сáмый ю́жный
**southward**, **~ly** ['saʊθwəd, ~lɪ], **~s** [~dz] *adv.* к ю́гу, на юг
**south|west 1.** юго-зáпад; **2.** югозáпадный (*a.* ***~erly, ~ern***); **~wester** юго-зáпадный вéтер
**souvenir** [su:və'nɪə] сувени́р
**sovereign** ['sɒvrɪn] **1.** суверéнный; **2.** госудáрь *m*; монáрх; (*coin*) соверéн; **~ty** [~tɪ] суверенитéт
**Soviet** ['səʊvɪet] **1.** совéт; **2.** совéтский
**sow**[1] [saʊ] *zo.* свинья́; (*breeding ~*) свиномáтка
**sow**[2] [səʊ] [*irr.*] [по]сéять; засевáть [засéять]; **~n** [səʊn] *pt. p. от* ***sow***[2]
**soya beans** ['sɔɪə] сóевые бобы́ *m/pl.*
**spa** [spɑ:] курóрт с минерáльными истóчниками
**space** [speɪs] пространство; мéсто; промежýток; *of time* срок; *attr.* кос-

S

мúческий; **~craft** космúческий корáбль *m*
**spacing** ['speɪsɪŋ]: ***type s.th. in double ~*** печáтать чéрез два интервáла
**spacious** ['speɪʃəs] простóрный; обшúрный; вместúтельный
**spade** [speɪd] лопáта; **~s** *cards* пúки *f/pl.*; **~work** предварúтельная (кропотлúвая) рабóта
**spaghetti** [spə'getɪ] *pl.* спагéтти *indecl.*
**span** [spæn] **1.** *of bridge* пролёт; корóткое расстоя́ние úли врéмя; **2.** перекрывáть [-кры́ть] стрóить мост чéрез (В); измеря́ть [-éрить]
**spangle** ['spæŋgl] **1.** блёстка; **2.** украшáть блёстками; *fig.* усéивать [усéять] пядя́ми
**Spaniard** ['spænjəd] испáнец *m*, -нка *f*
**spaniel** ['spænjəl] спаниéль *m*
**Spanish** ['spænɪʃ] испáнский
**spank** [spæŋk] *coll.* **1.** шлёпать [-пнуть]; отшлёпать; **2.** шлепóк
**spanking** ['spæŋkɪŋ] *breeze* свéжий
**spare** [speə] **1.** □ (*reserve*) запаснóй; (*surplus*) лúшний, свобóдный; (*thin*) худощáвый; **~ *time*** свобóдное врéмя *n*; **2.** (**~** *part*) запаснáя часть *f*; **3.** *life* [по]щадúть; (*grudge*) [по]жалéть; (*save*) [с]берéчь; *time* уделя́ть [-лúть]; (*save from*) избавля́ть [-áвить] от (Р)
**sparing** ['speərɪŋ] □ эконóмный; (*frugal*) скýдный; ***he is ~ of praise*** он скуп на похвалы́
**spark** ['spɑːk] **1.** úскра (*a. fig.*); **2.** [за]-искрúться; **~(ing) plug** *mot.* зажигáтельная свечá
**sparkle** ['spɑːkl] **1.** úскра; (*process*) сверкáние; **2.** [за]úскриться, [за]-сверкáть; ***sparkling wine*** игрúстое винó
**sparrow** ['spærəʊ] воробéй
**sparse** [spɑːs] □ рéдкий; (*scattered*) разбрóсанный; **~ly** [-lɪ]: **~ *populated*** малонаселённый
**spasm** [spæzəm] спáзма, сýдорога; **~ *of coughing*** прúступ кáшля; **~odic** (**al** □) [spæz'mɒdɪk(əl)] сýдорожный
**spat** [spæt] *pt. и pt. p. от* ***spit***
**spatter** ['spætə] бры́згать [-знуть]; *with mud* забры́згать, обры́згать гря́зью; (*spill*) расплёскивать [-плескáть]
**spawn** [spɔːn] **1.** икрá; **2.** метáть икрý; *multiply* [рас]плодúться
**speak** [spiːk] [*irr.*] *v/i.* говорúть; [по]-говорúть (***with, to*** с Т); разговáривать; **~ *out*** выскáзываться [вы́сказаться] откровéнно; **~ *up*** говорúть грóмко; (*express, as opinion, etc.*) выскáзывать [вы́сказать]; *v/t. the truth, etc.* говорúть [сказáть]; **~er** ['spiːkə] выступáющий; доклáдчик; орáтор; *parl.* спúкер
**spear** [spɪə] **1.** копьё; острогá; **2.** пронзáть копьём; *fish* бить острогóй
**special** ['speʃl] □ специáльный; (*exceptional*) осóбенный; осóбый; **~ *delivery*** срóчная доставка; **~ *powers*** чрезвычáйные полномóчия; **~ist** [-ʃəlɪst] специалúст; **~ity** [speʃɪ'ælətɪ] → ***specialty***; **~ize** ['speʃəlaɪz] специализúровать(ся) (*im*)*pf.* (в П *or* по Д); **specialty** ['speʃəltɪ] осóбенность *f*; специáльность *f*
**species** ['spiːʃiːz] вид; разновúдность *f*; ***human ~*** человéческий род
**speci|fic** [spə'sɪfɪk] (***~ally***) характéрный; специфúческий; осóбый; (*definite*) определённый; **~ *gravity*** удéльный вес; **~fy** ['spesɪfaɪ] оговáривать [-ворúть]; тóчно определя́ть; (*stipulate*) предусмáтривать [-мотрéть], обуслáвливать [-слóвить]; **~men** ['spesɪmən] образéц, обрáзчик; экземпля́р
**specious** ['spiːʃəs] □ *excuse* благовúдный; показнóй
**speck** [spek] *of dirt, dust, etc.* пя́тнышко; *of colo(u)r* крáпинка
**spectacle** ['spektəkl] (*show*) зрéлище; **~s** [-z] *pl.* (*glasses*) очкú *n/pl.*
**spectacular** [spek'tækjʊlə] □ эффéктный; *coll.* потрясáющий
**spectator** [spek'teɪtə] зрúтель *m*, -ница *f*
**spect|er**, *Brt.* **~re** ['spektə] прúзрак
**spectrum** ['spektrəm] спектр
**speculat|e** ['spekjʊleɪt] (*consider*) размышля́ть [-ы́слить]; *fin.* спеку-

S

ли́ровать (***in*** T); **~ion** [spekjʊ'leɪʃn] размышле́ние; (*supposition*) предположе́ние; *fin.* спекуля́ция; **~ive** ['spekjʊlətɪv] (*given to theory*) умозри́тельный; *fin.* спекуляти́вный; **~or** ['spekjʊleɪtə] спекуля́нт

**sped** [sped] *pt. u pt. p. om* ***speed***

**speech** [spiːtʃ] речь *f*; **~less** ['spiːtʃlɪs] немо́й; онеме́вший; ***I was~*** я лиши́лся да́ра ре́чи

**speed** [spiːd] **1.** ско́рость *f*, быстрота́; *mot.* ско́рость *f*; ***at full ~*** на по́лной ско́рости; **2.** [*irr.*] *v/i.* [по-] спеши́ть; бы́стро идти́; ***~ by*** промча́ться *pf.* ми́мо; *v/t.* ***~ up*** ускоря́ть [-о́рить]; **~ing** ['~ɪŋ] *mot.* превыше́ние ско́рости; **~ limit** разреша́емая ско́рость *f*; **~ometer** [spiː'dɒmɪtə] *mot.* спидо́метр; **~y** ['spiːdɪ] □ бы́стрый

**spell**[1] [spel] **1.** (коро́ткий) пери́од; ***a cold ~*** пери́од холо́дной пого́ды; ***for a ~*** на вре́мя; ***rest for a ~*** немно́го передохну́ть *pf.*

**spell**[2] [~] писа́ть, произноси́ть по бу́квам; *fig.* (*signify*, *bode*) сули́ть

**spell**[3] [~] ча́ры *f/pl.*; очарова́ние; **~bound** очаро́ванный

**spelling** ['spelɪŋ] правописа́ние; орфогра́фия

**spelt** [spelt] *chiefly Brt. pt. u pt. p. om* ***spell***

**spend** [spend] [*irr.*] *money* [по]тра́тить, [из]расхо́довать; *time* проводи́ть [-вести́]; **~thrift** ['spendθrɪft] мот, расточи́тель *m*, -ница *f*

**spent** [spent] **1.** *pt. u pt. p. om* ***spend***; **2.** *adj.* (*exhausted*) истощённый; измо́танный

**sperm** [spɜːm] спе́рма

**spher|e** [sfɪə] шар; сфе́ра; *celestial* небе́сная сфе́ра; *fig.* о́бласть *f*, сфе́ра; по́ле де́ятельности; **~ical** ['sferɪkl] □ сфери́ческий

**spice** [spaɪs] **1.** спе́ция, пря́ность *f*; *fig.* при́вкус; при́месь *f*; **2.** приправля́ть [-а́вить]

**spick and span** ['spɪkən'spæn] (*spotlessly clean*) сверка́ющий чистото́й; с иго́лочки

**spicy** ['spaɪsɪ] □ пря́ный; *fig.* пика́нтный

**spider** ['spaɪdə] *zo.* пау́к

**spike** [spaɪk] **1.** (*point*) остриё; *on shoe* шип; *bot.* ко́лос; **2.** снабжа́ть шипа́ми; (*pierce*) пронза́ть [-зи́ть]

**spill** [spɪl] [*irr.*] *v/t.* проли́(ва́)ть; *powder* рассыпа́ть [-ы́пать]; *v/i.* проли́(-ва́)ться

**spilt** [spɪlt] *pt. u pt. p. om* ***spill***

**spin** [spɪn] **1.** [*irr.*] *yarn* [с]прясть; (*~ round*) крути́ться; [за]кружи́ть(ся); верте́ться; ***~ when fishing*** лови́ть ры́бу спи́ннингом; ***my head is ~ning*** у меня́ кру́жится голова́; ***~ a yarn*** расска́зывать исто́рию/небыли́цы; ***~ round*** оберну́ться *pf.*; **2.** круже́ние; бы́страя езда́

**spinach** ['spɪnɪdʒ] шпина́т

**spinal** ['spaɪnl] спинно́й; ***~ column*** позвоно́чный столб, спинно́й хребе́т; ***~ cord*** спинно́й мозг

**spine** [spaɪn] *anat.* позвоно́чник; *bot.* колю́чка; **~less** ['~lɪs] *fig.* бесхребе́тный

**spinning| mill** пряди́льная фа́брика; **~ wheel** пря́лка

**spinster** ['spɪnstə] (*old maid*) ста́рая де́ва; *law* (*unmarried woman*) незаму́жняя же́нщина

**spiny** ['spaɪnɪ] (*prickly*) колю́чий

**spiral** ['spaɪərəl] **1.** □ спира́льный; ***~ staircase*** винтова́я ле́стница; **2.** спира́ль *f*

**spire** ['spaɪə] *arch.* шпиль *m*

**spirit** ['spɪrɪt] **1.** *com.* дух, душа́; (*ghost*) привиде́ние; (*enthusiasm*) воодушевле́ние; (*alcohol*) спирт; ***~s*** *pl.* (***high*** припо́днятое, ***low*** пода́вленное) настрое́ние; спиртны́е напи́тки *m/pl.*; **2.** ***~ away, off*** та́йно похища́ть; **~ed** [~ɪd] (*lively*) живо́й; (*courageous*) сме́лый; (*energetic*) энерги́чный; ***~ argument*** жа́ркий спор; **~less** [~lɪs] вя́лый; ро́бкий; безжи́зненный

**spiritual** ['spɪrɪtʃʊəl] □ духо́вный; **~ism** [~ɪzəm] спирити́зм

**spit**[1] [spɪt] **1.** (*spittle*) слюна́; плево́к; *fig.* подо́бие; **2.** [*irr.*] плева́ть [плю́нуть]; *of fire* рассыпа́ть и́скры; *of cat* шипе́ть; *of rain* мороси́ть; ***the***

**~ting image of s.o.** то́чная ко́пия кого́-л.
**spit²** [~] *geogr.* коса́, о́тмель *f*; *cul.* ве́ртел
**spite** [spaɪt] **1.** зло́ба, злость *f*; ***in ~ of*** не смотря́ на (В); **2.** досажда́ть [досади́ть]; **~ful** ['spaɪtfʊl] зло́бный
**spitfire** ['spɪtfaɪə] вспы́льчивый челове́к
**spittle** ['spɪtl] слюна́; плево́к
**splash** [splæʃ] **1.** бры́зги *f/pl.* (*mst.* ***~es*** *pl.*); плеск; **2.** бры́згать [-знуть]; забры́згать *pf.*; плеска́ть(ся) [-сну́ть]
**spleen** [spliːn] *anat.* селезёнка; *fig.* раздраже́ние
**splend|id** ['splendɪd] □ великоле́пный, роско́шный; **~o(u)r** [~də] блеск, великоле́пие
**splice** [splaɪs] *rope* сплета́ть [сплести́]; *wood* соединя́ть [-ни́ть]; *tape, etc.* скле́ивать [-ить]
**splint** [splɪnt] *med.* ши́на; ***put an arm in a ~*** накла́дывать ши́ну на (В); **~er** ['splɪntə] **1.** *of stone* оско́лок; *of wood* ще́пка; *in skin* зано́за; **2.** расщепля́ть(ся) [-пи́ть(ся)]; раска́лываться [-коло́ться]
**split** [splɪt] **1.** (*crack, fissure*) тре́щина; щель *f*; *fig.* раско́л; **2.** расщеплённый; раско́лотый; **3.** [*irr.*] *v/t.* раска́лывать [-коло́ть]; расщепля́ть (-пи́ть); (*divide*) [по]дели́ть; ***~ hairs*** вдава́ться в то́нкости; спо́рить о пустяка́х; ***~ one's sides laughing*** надрыва́ться от сме́ха; *v/i.* раска́лываться [-коло́ться]; раздели́ться *pf.*; (*burst*) ло́паться [ло́пнуть]; **~ting** ['splɪtɪŋ] *headache* ужа́сный
**splutter** ['splʌtə] → ***sputter***
S
**spoil¹** [spɔɪl] **1.** (*a.* ***~s*** *pl.*) добы́ча
**spoil²** [~] [*irr.*] [ис]по́ртить; *food* [ис]по́ртиться; *child* [из]балова́ть
**spoke¹** [spəʊk] *of wheel* спи́ца; *of ladder* ступе́нька, перекла́дина
**spoke²** [~] *pt. от* ***speak***; **~n** ['spəʊkən] *pt. p. от* ***speak***; **~sman** ['spəʊksmən] представи́тель *m*
**sponge** [spʌndʒ] **1.** гу́бка; **2.** *v/t.* вытира́ть или мыть гу́бкой; ***~ up*** впи́тывать гу́бкой; *v/i. fig.* парази́т; жить на чужо́й счёт; **~ cake** бисквит; **~r** ['spʌndʒə] нахле́бник (-ница)
**spongy** ['spʌndʒɪ] гу́бчатый
**sponsor** ['spɒnsə] **1.** спо́нсор; (*guarantor*) поручи́тель *m*, -ница *f*; **2.** руча́ться [поручи́ться] за (В); рекомендова́ть; финанси́ровать
**spontaneous** [spɒn'teɪnɪəs] □ *behavio(u)r, talk* непосре́дственный, непринуждённый; спонта́нный; ***~ generation*** самозарожде́ние
**spook** [spuːk] привиде́ние; **~y** ['~ɪ] жу́ткий
**spool** [spuːl] *in sewing machine* шпу́лька; *in tape-recorder* боби́на; *of film, etc.* кату́шка
**spoon** [spuːn] **1.** ло́жка; **2.** черпа́ть ло́жкой; **~ful** ['spuːnfl] ло́жка (ме́ра)
**spore** [spɔː] спо́ра
**sport** [spɔːt] **1.** спорт; *attr.* спорти́вный; (*amusement, fun*) развлече́ние, заба́ва; (*good ~*) *sl.* молоде́ц; ***~s*** *pl.* спорти́вные и́гры *f/pl.*; ***~s ground*** спорти́вная площа́дка; **2.** *v/i.* игра́ть, весели́ться, резви́ться; *v/t. coll.* щеголя́ть (Т); **~sman** ['spɔːtsmən] спортсме́н
**spot** [spɒt] **1.** *com.* пятно́; *small* кра́пинка; (*place*) ме́сто; *coll.* (*small quantity*) немно́жко; ***be in a ~*** быть в тру́дном положе́нии; ***on the ~*** на ме́сте; сра́зу, неме́дленно; **2.** [за-, пере]па́чкать; (*detect*) обнару́жи(ва)ть; *coll.* (*identify*) опозн(ав)а́ть; **~less** ['spɒtlɪs] □ безупре́чный; незапя́тнанный; **~light** проже́ктор; *fig.* центр внима́ния; **~ty** ['spɒtɪ] пятни́стый; *face* прыщева́тый
**spouse** [spaʊz] супру́г *m*, -а *f*
**spout** [spaʊt] **1.** *water* струя́; *of teapot, etc.* но́сик; **2.** ли́ться струёй; бить струёй; *coll.* (*speak*) разглаго́льствовать
**sprain** [spreɪn] **1.** *med.* растяже́ние; **2.** растя́гивать [-тяну́ть]
**sprang** [spræŋ] *pt. от* ***spring***
**sprawl** [sprɔːl] (*a.* ***~ out***) растя́гивать(ся) [-ну́ть(ся)]; *in a chair* разва́ливаться [-ли́ться]; *bot.* бу́йно разраста́ться

**spray**[1] [spreɪ] **1.** водяна́я пыль *f*; бры́зги *f/pl.*; (*instrument*) пульвериза́тор, распыли́тель *m* (*a.* **~er**); **2.** распыля́ть [-ли́ть]; опры́скивать [-скать], обры́зг(ив)ать

**spray**[2] [~] (*cluster, bunch*) кисть *f*, гроздь *f*

**spread** [spred] **1.** [*irr.*] *v/t.* (*a.* **~ out**) расстила́ть [разостла́ть]; *news* распространя́ть [-ни́ть]; *butter* нама́з(ыв)ать (Т); *wings* расправля́ть [-а́вить]; **~ the table** накры́(ва́)ть на стол; *v/i. of fields* простира́ться; *of fire, etc.* распространя́ться [-ни́ться]; **2.** *pt. и pt. p. от* **spread 1.**; **3.** распростране́ние; протяже́ние

**spree** [spriː] весе́лье; (*drinking*) кутёж; **go on a shopping ~** отпра́виться по магази́нам; накупи́ть вся́кой вся́чины

**sprig** [sprɪg] ве́точка, побе́г

**sprightly** ['spraɪtlɪ] (*lively*) живо́й, оживлённый, (*cheerful*) весёлый; бо́дрый

**spring** [sprɪŋ] **1.** (*leap*) прыжо́к, скачо́к; (*mineral ~, etc.*) родни́к, ключ; (*a.* **~time**) весна́; *tech.* пружи́на; *of vehicle* рессо́ра; *fig.* моти́в; **2.** [*irr.*] *v/t.* (*explode*) взрыва́ть [взорва́ть]; **~ a leak** дава́ть течь *f*; *v/i.* (*jump*) пры́гать [-гнуть]; *to one's feet* вска́кивать [вскочи́ть]; *bot.* появля́ться [-ви́ться]; **~ aside** отскочи́ть *pf.* в сто́рону; **~ up** *fig.* возника́ть [-ни́кнуть]; **~ board** трампли́н; **~ tide** весна́; **~y** ['sprɪŋɪ] □ упру́гий

**sprinkl|e** ['sprɪŋkl] *liquid* бры́згать [-знуть]; обры́згивать [-знуть]; *sand, sugar* посыпа́ть [-ы́пать]; **~ing** [~ɪŋ]: **a ~** немно́го

**sprint** [sprɪnt] *sport* **1.** спринт; **2.** *sport* бежа́ть с максима́льной ско́ростью на коро́ткую диста́нцию; **he ~ed past us** он промча́лся ми́мо

**sprout** [spraʊt] **1.** *of plant* пуска́ть ростки́; *of seeds* прораста́ть [-расти́]; **2.** *bot.* ростóк, побе́г

**spruce**[1] [spruːs] □ (*neat*) опря́тный; (*smart*) наря́дный

**spruce**[2] [~] *bot.* ель *f*

**sprung** [sprʌŋ] *pt. и pt. p. от* **spring**

**spry** [spraɪ] (*lively*) живо́й; (*nimble*) подви́жный

**spun** [spʌn] *pt. и pt. p. от* **spin**

**spur** [spɜː] **1.** шпо́ра; *fig.* побужде́ние; **act on the ~ of the moment** де́йствовать не разду́мывая; **2.** пришпо́ривать; побужда́ть [-уди́ть]; **~ on** спеши́ть; *fig.* подстёгивать [-егну́ть]

**spurious** ['spjʊərɪəs] □ подде́льный; фальши́вый

**spurn** [spɜːn] отверга́ть, отказа́ться *pf.* с презре́нием

**spurt** [spɜːt] **1.** *of liquid* бить струёй; *of flame* выбра́сывать [вы́бросить]; **2.** *water* струя́; (*gust*) поры́в ве́тра; *sport* рыво́к (*a. fig.*)

**sputter** ['spʌtə] **1.** бры́зги *f/pl.*; шипе́ние; **2.** *of fire* [за]треща́ть, [за]шипе́ть; бры́згаться слюно́й при разгово́ре; говори́ть бы́стро и бессвя́зно

**spy** [spaɪ] **1.** шпио́н *m*, -ка *f*; **2.** шпио́нить, следи́ть (**on** за Т); (*notice*) заме́тить *pf.*

**squabble** ['skwɒbl] **1.** перебра́нка, ссо́ра; **2.** [по]вздо́рить

**squad** [skwɒd] *of workers* брига́да; отря́д; (*a. mil.*) гру́ппа, кома́нда (*a. sport*); **~ car** *Am.* патру́льная маши́на; **~ron** ['skwɒdrən] *mil.* эскадро́н; *ae.* эскадри́лья; *naut.* эска́дра

**squalid** ['skwɒlɪd] □ убо́гий

**squall** [skwɔːl] **1.** *of wind* шквал; вопль *m*, крик; **2.** [за]вопи́ть

**squander** ['skwɒndə] прома́тывать [-мота́ть], [рас]транжи́рить

**square** [skweə] **1.** □ квадра́тный; *shoulders, right angles, etc.* прямо́й; (*fair, honest*) прямо́й, че́стный; **2.** квадра́т; (*town ~*) пло́щадь *f*; **3.** *v/t.* де́лать прямоуго́льным; (*pay*) опла́чивать [оплати́ть]; (*bring into accord*) согласо́вывать [-сова́ть]; *v/i.* согласо́вываться [-сова́ться]

**squash** [skwɒʃ] **1.** фрукто́вый напи́ток; (*crush*) да́вка, толчея́; **2.** разда́вливать [-дави́ть]

**squat** [skwɒt] **1.** призе́мистый; **2.** сиде́ть на ко́рточках; **~ down** присе́сть *pf.* на ко́рточки

**squawk** [skwɒːk] **1.** *bird's* пронзи́тельный крик; **2.** пронзи́тельно крича́ть
**squeak** [skwiːk] [про]пища́ть; *of shoes, etc.* скрипе́ть
**squeal** [skwiːl] [за]визжа́ть; *sl.* доноси́ть [донести́]
**squeamish** ['skwiːmɪʃ] □ (*too scrupulous*) щепети́льный; оби́дчивый; *about food, etc.* привере́дливый; (*fastidious*) брезгли́вый
**squeeze** [skwiːz] **1.** сж(им)а́ть; (*clench*) сти́скивать [-снуть]; *lemon, etc.* выжима́ть [вы́жать]; *fig. money* вымога́ть (***from*** у Р); **2.** сжа́тие; пожа́тие; давле́ние; да́вка; **~r** ['skwiːzə] выжима́лка
**squelch** [skweltʃ] хлю́пать
**squint** [skwɪnt] коси́ть; *at the sun* [со]щу́риться
**squirm** [skwɜːm] изви́(ва́)ться, [с]ко́рчиться
**squirrel** [skwɪrəl] бе́лка
**squirt** [skwɜːt] **1.** струя́; *coll.* (*a nobody*) вы́скочка *m/f.*; **2.** бры́згать [-знуть]; бить то́нкой струёй
**stab** [stæb] **1.** уда́р; **2.** *v/t. to death* зака́лывать [заколо́ть]; *v/i.* (*wound*) наноси́ть уда́р (***at*** Д)
**stabili|ty** [stə'bɪlətɪ] усто́йчивость *f*, *fin.* стаби́льность *f*; про́чность *f*; **~ze** ['steɪbəlaɪz] стабилизи́ровать (*im*)*pf.*; **~zer** ['steɪbəlaɪzə] *tech.* стабилиза́тор
**stable**[1] ['steɪbl] □ усто́йчивый; *situation, etc.* стаби́льный
**stable**[2] [~] коню́шня
**stack** [stæk] **1.** *of hay* стог; *of wood* шта́бель *m*; *of books* сто́пка; ку́ча; **2.** скла́дывать [сложи́ть]
**stadium** ['steɪdɪəm] *sport* стадио́н
**staff** [stɑːf] **1.** (*flag~*) дре́вко; (*body of employees*) штат, персона́л; ***editorial~*** редколле́гия; **2.** набира́ть [-ра́ть] персона́л; укомплекто́вывать [-това́ть]
**stag** [stæg] *zo.* оле́нь-саме́ц
**stage** [steɪdʒ] **1.** сце́на, подмо́стки *m/pl.*; *for singer, etc.* эстра́да; *fig.* ста́дия, эта́п; **2.** [по]ста́вить; **~ manager** режиссёр
**stagger** ['stægə] *v/i.* шата́ть(ся) [(по)шатну́ться]; *v/t. fig.* потряса́ть [-ясти́]; поража́ть [порази́ть]; **~ing** [~ɪŋ] потряса́ющий
**stagna|nt** ['stægnənt] □ *water* стоя́чий; **~te** [stæg'neɪt] заста́иваться [застоя́ться]; *fig. mst. econ.* быть в состоя́нии засто́я
**staid** [steɪd] □ уравнове́шенный, степе́нный; сде́ржанный
**stain** [steɪn] **1.** пятно́ (*a. fig.*); **2.** [за]па́чкать; *fig.* [за]пятна́ть; ***~ed glass*** цветно́е стекло́; ***~ed-glass window*** витра́ж; **~less** ['steɪnlɪs] *steel* нержаве́ющий
**stair** [steə] ступе́нька; ***~s*** *pl.* ле́стница; **~case**, **~way** ле́стница; ле́стничная кле́тка
**stake** [steɪk] **1.** *wooden* кол; (*bet*) ста́вка; ***be at~*** *fig.* быть поста́вленным на ка́рту; **2.** *money* ста́вить (***on*** на В)
**stale** [steɪl] □ несве́жий; *air* спёртый; *joke* изби́тый; *bread* чёрствый; *news* устаре́вший
**stalemate** ['steɪlmeɪt] *chess* пат; *fig.* тупи́к
**stalk** [stɔːk] **1.** сте́бель *m*; *of leaf* черено́к; **2.** *v/i.* ва́жно ше́ствовать, го́рдо выступа́ть
**stall** [stɔːl] **1.** *for animals* сто́йло; *in market mst. Brt.* прила́вок; кио́ск, ларёк; *thea.* ме́сто в парте́ре; **2.**: ***the engine ~ed*** мото́р загло́х
**stallion** ['stælɪən] жеребе́ц
**stalwart** ['stɔːlwət] ро́слый, кре́пкий; *supporter* сто́йкий
**stamina** ['stæmɪnə] выно́сливость *f*
**stammer** ['stæmə] **1.** заика́ться [-кну́ться]; запина́ться [запну́ться]; **2.** заика́ние
**stamp** [stæmp] **1.** штамп, ште́мпель *m*, печа́ть *f*, *fig.* отпеча́ток, печа́ть *f*; *for letter* ма́рка; *of feet* то́панье; ***~ collector*** филатели́ст; **2.** [про]штампова́ть; [по]ста́вить ште́мпель *m*, печа́ть *f*; то́пать ного́й
**stampede** [stæm'piːd] **1.** пани́ческое бе́гство; **2.** обраща́ть(ся) в пани́ческое бе́гство
**stand** [stænd] **1.** [*irr.*] *v/i. com.* стоя́ть; проста́ивать [-стоя́ть]; (*~ still*) оста-

S

на́вливаться [-нови́ться]; (~ *fast*) держа́ться; усто́ять *pf.*; ~ ***against*** [вос]проти́виться, сопротивля́ться (Д); ~ ***aside*** [по]сторони́ться; ~ ***by*** прису́тствовать; *fig.* быть наготове; подде́рживать; [-жа́ть]; ~ ***for*** быть кандида́том (Р); стоя́ть за (В); зна́чить; ~ ***out*** выделя́ться [вы́делиться] (***against*** на П); ~ ***over*** остава́ться нерешённым; ~ ***up*** вст(ав)а́ть, поднима́ться [-ня́ться]; ~ ***up for*** защища́ть [-ити́ть]; **2.** *v/t.* [по]ста́вить; (*bear*) выде́рживать [вы́держать], выноси́ть [вы́нести]; *coll* (*treat*) угоща́ть [угости́ть] (Т); **3.** остано́вка; сопротивле́ние; то́чка зре́ния; стенд; кио́ск; пози́ция; ме́сто; (*support*) подста́вка; (*rostrum*) трибу́на; ***make a ~ against*** сопротивля́ться (Д)

**standard** ['stændəd] **1.** зна́мя *n*, флаг; но́рма, станда́рт; образе́ц *m*; ~ ***of living*** жи́зненный у́ровень *m*; **2.** станда́ртный; образцо́вый; **~ize** [-aɪz] стандартизи́ровать (*im*)*pf.*

**standby** ['stændbaɪ] **1.** опо́ра; **2.** *tech.*, *fin.* резе́рвный

**standing** ['stændɪŋ] **1.** (*posture*, *etc.*) стоя́чий; *permanent* постоя́нный; **2.** (*rank*, *reputation*) положе́ние; (*duration*) продолжи́тельность *f*

**stand|offish** [stænd'ɒfɪʃ] за́мкнутый; надме́нный; **~point** то́чка зре́ния; **~still** остано́вка; ***the work came to a ~*** рабо́та останови́лась; ***bring to a ~*** останови́ть, засто́порить

**stank** [stæŋk] *pt. om* **stink**

**stanza** ['stænzə] строфа́

**staple** ['steɪpl] основно́й; ~ ***diet*** осно́ва пита́ния

**star** [stɑː] **1.** звезда́ (*a. fig.*); *fig.* судьба́; ***the ♀s and Stripes*** *pl. Am.* национа́льный флаг США; ***thank one's lucky ~s*** благодари́ть судьбу́; **2.** игра́ть гла́вную роль *f*

**starboard** ['stɑːbəd] *naut.* пра́вый борт

**starch** [stɑːtʃ] **1.** крахма́л; **2.** [на]крахма́лить

**stare** [steə] **1.** при́стальный взгляд; **2.** смотре́ть при́стально; уста́виться *pf.*; (***at*** на В)

**stark** [stɑːk] (*stiff*) окочене́лый; (*utter*) соверше́нный; *adv.* соверше́нно

**starling** ['stɑːlɪŋ] скворе́ц

**starry** ['stɑːrɪ] звёздный

**start** [stɑːt] **1.** нача́ло; *of train*, *etc.* отправле́ние; *sport* старт; ***give a ~*** вздро́гнуть *pf.* ***give s.o. a ~*** испуга́ть кого́-л.; ***give s.o. a ~ in life*** помо́чь *pf.* кому́-л. встать на́ ноги; **2.** *v/i. at a sound*, *etc.* вздра́гивать [-ро́гнуть]; *from one's seat*, *etc.* вска́кивать [вскочи́ть]; отправля́ться в путь; *sport* стартова́ть (*im*)*pf.*; нач(ин)а́ться; *v/t.* (*set going*) пуска́ть (пусти́ть); *sport* дава́ть старт (Д); *fig.* нач(ин)а́ть; учрежда́ть [-еди́ть]; побужда́ть [-уди́ть] (~ ***a p. doing*** кого́-л. де́лать); **~er** ['stɑːtə] *mot.* стартёр

**startl|e** [stɑːtl] (*alarm*) трево́жить (*take aback*) поража́ть [порази́ть]; [ис-, на]пуга́ть; **~ing** ['stɑːtlɪŋ] порази́тельный

**starv|ation** [stɑː'veɪʃən] го́лод; голода́ние; **~e** [stɑːv] голода́ть; умира́ть с го́лоду; мори́ть го́лодом; ~ ***for*** *fig.* жа́ждать (Р)

**state** [steɪt] **1.** состоя́ние; (*station in life*) положе́ние; госуда́рство (*pol. a.* ♀); (*member of federation*) штат; *attr.* госуда́рственный; ***get into a ~*** разне́рвничаться *pf.*, разволнова́ться *pf.*; ~ ***of emergency*** чрезвыча́йное положе́ние; **2.** заявля́ть [-ви́ть]; констати́ровать (*im*)*pf.*; [с]формули́ровать; (*set forth*) излага́ть (изложи́ть); **~ly** [-lɪ] вели́чественный; **~ment** [-mənt] утвержде́ние; официа́льное заявле́ние; *fin.* отчёт; **~room** *naut.* отде́льная каю́та; **~sman** ['steɪtsmən] госуда́рственный де́ятель *m*

**static** ['stætɪk] *el.* стати́ческий; неподви́жный; (*stable*) стаби́льный

**station** ['steɪʃn] **1.** *radio*, *el.*, *rail.* ста́нция; (*building*) вокза́л; **2.** размеща́ть [-ести́ть] (*a. mil.*); **~ary** ['steɪʃənrɪ] неподви́жный; стациона́рный; **~ery** [~] канцеля́рские това́ры *m/pl.*

S

**statistics** [stə'tɪstɪks] стати́стика
**statue** ['stætʃuː] ста́туя
**stature** ['stætʃə] рост; масшта́б, кали́бр
**status** ['steɪtəs] положе́ние; **~ quo** ста́тус-кво
**statute** ['stætʃuːt] стату́т; зако́н; законода́тельный акт; *pl.* уста́в
**staunch** [stɔːntʃ] *supporter* ве́рный; непоколеби́мый
**stay** [steɪ] **1.** пребыва́ние, визи́т; *law* отсро́чка; **2.** *v/t. law* приостана́вливать [-нови́ть]; *v/i.* (*remain*) ост(ав)а́ться; *as guest at hotel, etc.* остана́вливаться [-нови́ться], жить (***at*** в П), [по]гости́ть
**stead** [sted]: ***in a person's ~*** вме́сто кого́-нибудь; **~fast** ['stedfɑːst] сто́йкий, непоколеби́мый
**steady** ['stedɪ] **1.** □ (*balanced*) усто́йчивый; *look, etc.* при́стальный; (*regular*) постоя́нный; равноме́рный; (*stable*) уравнове́шенный; **2.** де́лать(ся) усто́йчивым; приводи́ть в равнове́сие; *adv.* **~!** осторо́жно!
**steak** [steɪk] *of beef* бифште́кс; (*fillet ~*) вы́резка
**steal** [stiːl] [*irr.*] *v/t.* [с]ворова́ть, [у]кра́сть; *v/i.* кра́сться, прокра́дываться [-ра́сться]
**stealth** [stelθ]: ***by ~*** укра́дкой, тайко́м; **~y** ['stelθɪ] □ та́йный; бесшу́мный; ***~ glance*** взгляд укра́дкой; ***~ steps*** краду́щиеся шаги́
**steam** [stiːm] **1.** пар; **2.** *attr.* парово́й; **3.** *v/i.* (*move by steam*) *of train* идти́; *of ship* пла́вать; [по]плы́ть; ***get ~ed up*** запоте́ть *pf.*; *fig.* [вз]волнова́ться; *v/t.* вари́ть на пару́; пари́ть; выпа́ривать [вы́парить]; **~er** ['stiːmə] *naut.* парохо́д; *cul.* скорова́рка; **~y** ['stiːmɪ] насы́щенный па́ром; *glass* запоте́вший
**steel** [stiːl] **1.** сталь *f*; **2.** стально́й (*a.* ***~y***); ***~ o.s. for*** собра́ть всё своё му́жество; ожесточа́ться [-чи́ться]; **~works** сталелите́йный заво́д
**steep** [stiːp] круто́й; *coll. price* сли́шком высо́кий
**steeple** ['stiːpl] шпиль *m*; *with bell* коло́кольня; **~chase** ска́чки с препя́тствиями
**steer** [stɪə] пра́вить рулём; *naut., etc.* управля́ть (Т); **~ing** ['~ɪŋ]: ***~ wheel*** *naut.* штурва́л; *mot.* рулево́е колесо́, *coll.* бара́нка; **~sman** ['stɪəzmən] рулево́й
**stem**[1] [stem] **1.** *bot.* сте́бель *m*; *gr.* осно́ва; **2.** *v/i.* (*arise*) происходи́ть [-изойти́]
**stem**[2] [~] (*stop, check*) заде́рживать [-жа́ть]
**stench** [stentʃ] злово́ние
**stencil** ['stensl] трафаре́т
**stenographer** [ste'nɒgrəfə] стеногра́фист *m*, -ка *f*
**step**[1] [step] **1.** шаг (*a. fig.*); похо́дка; *of stairs* ступе́нька; (*footboard*) подно́жка; *fig.* ме́ра; ***it's only a ~ from here*** отсю́да руко́й пода́ть; ***~ by ~*** постепе́нно; ***a rushed ~*** необду́манный шаг; ***take ~s*** принима́ть [-ня́ть] ме́ры; ***tread in the ~s of*** *fig.* идти́ по стопа́м (Р); ***~s*** *pl.* стремя́нка; **2.** *v/i.* шага́ть [шагну́ть], ступа́ть [-пи́ть]; ходи́ть, идти́ [пойти́]; ***~ aside*** посторони́ться *pf.*; ***~ back*** отступи́ть *pf.* наза́д, отойти́ *pf.*; ***~ up*** *v/t.* (*increase*) повыша́ть [-ы́сить]
**step**[2] [~]: **~daughter** па́дчерица; **~father** о́тчим; **~mother** ма́чеха
**steppe** [step] степь *f*
**stepping-stone** ка́мень *m* для перехо́да через руче́й; ***~ to success*** ступе́нь к успе́ху
**stepson** па́сынок
**stereo** ['sterɪəʊ] стереофони́ческий (проигрыватель *m or* радиоприёмник)
**stereotype** ['sterɪətaɪp] стереоти́п
**steril|e** ['steraɪl] беспло́дный; (*free from germs*) стери́льный; **~ity** [ste'rɪlətɪ] бесплóдие; стери́льность *f*; **~ize** ['sterəlaɪz] стерилизова́ть (*im*)*pf.*
**sterling** ['stɜːlɪŋ]: ***the pound ~*** фунт сте́рлингов
**stern**[1] [stɜːn] □ стро́гий, суро́вый
**stern**[2] [~] *naut.* корма́
**stevedore** ['stiːvədɔː] до́кер; порто́вый гру́зчик

**stew** [stjuː] **1.** [с]туши́ть(ся); **2.** тушёное мя́со; ***be in a ~*** волнова́ться, беспоко́иться
**steward** ['stjʊəd] *naut., ae.* стю́ард, бортпроводни́к; **~ess** ['stjʊədɪs] стюарде́сса, бортпроводни́ца
**stick**[1] [stɪk] па́лка; (*walking ~*) трость *f*; ***~s*** *for fire* хво́рост
**stick**[2] [~] [*irr.*] *v/i.* прикле́и(ва)ться, прилипа́ть [-ли́пнуть]; (*become fixed*) застрева́ть [-ря́ть]; завяза́ть [-я́знуть]; *at home* торча́ть; ***~ to*** приде́рживаться [-жа́ться] (Р); ***~ at nothing*** не остана́вливаться ни пе́ред чем; ***~ out, ~ up*** торча́ть; стоя́ть торчко́м; *v/t.* вка́лывать [вколо́ть]; *fork, etc.* втыка́ть [воткну́ть]; *stamp* накле́ивать [-е́ить]; прикле́и(ва)ть; *coll.* (*bear*) терпе́ть, вы́терпеть *pf.*; ***~ing plaster*** лейкопла́стырь *m*
**sticky** ['stɪkɪ] ли́пкий, кле́йкий; ***come to a ~ end*** пло́хо ко́нчить *pf.*
**stiff** [stɪf] □ жёсткий, неги́бкий; *lock, etc.* туго́й; тру́дный; *relations* натя́нутый; ***~ with cold*** окочене́ть *pf.* от хо́лода; **~en** ['stɪfn] *of starch, etc.* [за]густе́ть
**stifle** ['staɪfl] задыха́ться [задохну́ться]; *rebellion* подавля́ть [-ви́ть]
**stigma** ['stɪgmə] *fig.* пятно́, клеймо́
**still** [stɪl] **1.** *adj.* ти́хий; неподви́жный; **2.** *adv.* ещё, всё ещё; **3.** *cj.* всё же, одна́ко; **4.** (*make calm*) успока́ивать [-ко́ить]; **~born** мертворождённый; **~ life** натюрмо́рт; **~ness** ['stɪlnɪs] тишина́
**stilted** ['stɪltɪd] *style* высокопа́рный
**stimul|ant** ['stɪmjʊlənt] *med.* возбужда́ющее сре́дство; *fig.* сти́мул; **~ate** [-leɪt] (*excite*) возбужда́ть [-уди́ть]; стимули́ровать (*a. fig.*); поощря́ть [-ри́ть]; **~ating** стимули́рующий, вдохновля́ющий; **~us** [-ləs] сти́мул
**sting** [stɪŋ] **1.** (*organ*) жа́ло; (*bite*) уку́с; о́страя боль *f*; *fig.* ко́лкость *f*; **2.** [*irr.*] [у]жа́лить; *of nettle* жечь(ся); (*smart, burn*) садни́ть; *fig.* уязвля́ть [-ви́ть]
**sting|iness** ['stɪndʒɪnɪs] ска́редность *f*; **~y** ['stɪndʒɪ] скупо́й
**stink** [stɪŋk] **1.** вонь *f*; **2.** [*irr.*] воня́ть
**stint** [stɪnt] **1.** (*fixed amount*) но́рма; **2.** (*keep short*) ограни́чи(ва)ть; [по]скупи́ться на (В); ***she doesn't ~ herself*** она́ себе́ ни в чём не отка́зывает
**stipulat|e** ['stɪpjʊleɪt] ста́вить усло́вия; обусло́вливать [-вить]; ***the ~d sum*** оговорённая [-вить]; су́мма; **~ion** [stɪpjʊ'leɪʃn] усло́вие
**stir** [stɜː] **1.** шевеле́ние; (*excitement*) сует́а, сумато́ха; движе́ние; *fig.* оживле́ние; ***create a ~*** наде́лать *pf.* мно́го шу́ма; **2.** *leaves, etc.* шевели́ть(ся) [-льну́ть(ся)]; *tea, etc.* [по]меша́ть; [вз]волнова́ть; ***~ up*** (*excite*) возбужда́ть [-уди́ть]; разме́шивать [-ша́ть]
**stirrup** ['stɪrəp] стре́мя *n* (*pl.*: стремена́)
**stitch** [stɪtʃ] **1.** *sew.* стежо́к; *in knitting* петля́; *med.* шов; **2.** [с]шить, проши́(ва́)ть
**stock** [stɒk] **1.** (*supply*) запа́с; ***live ~*** поголо́вье скота́, скота́, скот; ***capital ~*** уставно́й капита́л; ***take ~ of*** де́лать переучёт (Р), производи́ть инвентариза́цию; *fig.* крити́чески оце́нивать; **2.** *size* станда́ртный; *joke, etc.* изби́тый; **3.** (*supply*) снабжа́ть [-бди́ть]
**stock|breeder** животново́д; **~broker** биржево́й ма́клер; бро́кер; **~ exchange** фо́ндовая би́ржа; **~holder** *Am.* акционе́р
**stocking** ['stɔkɪŋ] чуло́к
**stock|taking** переучёт, инвентариза́ция; **~y** ['stɒkɪ] корена́стый
**stoic** ['stəʊɪk] **1.** сто́ик; **2.** сто́ический
**stole** [stəʊl] *pt. от* ***steal***; **~n** ['stəʊlən] *pt. p. от* ***steal***
**stolid** ['stɒlɪd] □ флегмати́чный
**stomach** ['stʌmək] **1.** желу́док; живо́т; ***it turns my ~*** от э́того меня́ тошни́т; **2.** *fig.* переноси́ть [-нести́]
**stone** [stəʊn] **1.** ка́мень *m*; *of fruit* ко́сточка; ***leave no ~ unturned*** [с]делать всё возмо́жное; **2.** ка́менный; **3.** броса́ть ка́мни, броса́ться камня́ми; *fruit* вынима́ть ко́сточки из (Р); **~-deaf** соверше́нно глухо́й; **~ware** гонча́рные изде́лия *n/pl.*
**stony** ['stəʊnɪ] камени́стый; *fig.* ка́менный

S

**stood** [stʊd] *pt. u pt. p. от* ***stand***
**stool** [stuːl] (*seat*) табуре́тка; (*f(a)eces*) стул
**stoop** [stuːp] **1.** *v/i.* наклоня́ться [-ни́ться], нагиба́ться [нагну́ться]; (*be bent*) [с]суту́литься; *fig.* унижа́ться [уни́зиться] (***to*** до P); *v/t.* суту́лить; **2.** суту́лость *f*
**stop** [stɔp] **1.** *v/t.* затыка́ть [заткну́ть] (*a.* **~ *up***), заде́л(ыв)ать; *tooth* [за]пломби́ровать; (*prevent*) уде́рживать [-жа́ть]; (*cease*) прекраща́ть [-крати́ть]; (*halt*) остана́вливать [-нови́ть]; **~ *it!*** прекрати́!; *v/i.* перест(ав)а́ть; (*stay*) остана́вливаться [-нови́ться]; (*finish*) прекраща́ться [-рати́ться]; конча́ться [ко́нчиться]; **2.** остано́вка; па́уза; заде́ржка; *tech.* упо́р; *gr.* (*a.* ***full* ~**) то́чка; **~page** ['stɒpɪdʒ] остано́вка, прекраще́ние рабо́ты; *tech.* про́бка, засоре́ние; **~per** ['stɒpə] про́бка; **~ping** ['stɒpɪŋ] (зубна́я) пло́мба
**storage** ['stɔːrɪdʒ] хране́ние; *place* склад
**store** [stɔː] **1.** запа́с; склад; *Am.* магази́н; (*department* **~**) универма́г; ***in* ~** нагото́ве; про запа́с; **2.** храни́ть на скла́де; (*put by*) запаса́ть [-сти́]; **~house** склад; *fig.* сокро́вищница; **~keeper** *Am.* хозя́ин магази́на
**stor(e)y** ['stɒrɪ] эта́ж
**stork** [stɔːk] а́ист
**storm** [stɔːm] **1.** бу́ря; *at sea* шторм; *mil.* штурм; ***a* ~ *in a teacup*** бу́ря в стака́не воды́; **2.** бушева́ть; *mil.* штурмова́ть (*a. fig.*); **~y** ['~ɪ] □ бу́рный (*a. fig.*); штормово́й
**story** ['stɔːrɪ] (*account*) расска́з, исто́рия; *lit.* расска́з; *longer* по́весть *f*; *cine.* сюже́т; *in newspaper* статья́
**stout** [staʊt] **1.** □ *thing* кре́пкий, про́чный; (*sturdy*) пло́тный; (*fat*) ту́чный; (*brave*) отва́жный; **2.** кре́пкое тёмное пи́во
**stove** [stəʊv] печь *f*, пе́чка; (ку́хонная) плита́
**stow** [stəʊ] (*pack*) укла́дывать [уложи́ть]; **~away** *naut.* безбиле́тный пассажи́р
**straggl|e** ['strægl] *of houses* быть разбро́санным; (*drop behind*) отст(ав)а́ть; **~ing** [-ɪŋ] разбро́санный; беспоря́дочный
**straight** [streɪt] **1.** *adj.* прямо́й; че́стный; (*undiluted*) неразба́вленный; ***put* ~** приводи́ть в поря́док; **2.** *adv.* пря́мо; сра́зу; **~en** ['streɪtn] выпрямля́ть(ся) [вы́прямить(ся)]; **~ *out*** приводи́ть в поря́док; **~forward** [~'fɔːwəd] □ че́стный, прямо́й, откровенный
**strain**¹ [streɪn] поро́да; сорт; черта́ хара́ктера
**strain**² [~] напряже́ние; *tech.* (*force*) нагру́зка; растяже́ние (*a. med.*); *mus. mst.* **~s** *pl.* напе́в, мело́дия; **2.** *v/t.* натя́гивать [натяну́ть]; напряга́ть [-я́чь]; (*filter*) проце́живать [-еди́ть]; (*exhaust*) переутомля́ть [-ми́ть]; *med.* растя́гивать [-яну́ть]; *v/i.* напряга́ться [-я́чься]; тяну́ться (***after*** за T); тяну́ть изо всех сил (***at*** B); [по]стара́ться; **~er** ['streɪnə] (*colander*) дуршла́г; (*sieve*) си́то; цеди́лка
**strait** [streɪt] проли́в; **~s** *pl.* затрудни́тельное положе́ние; **~ened** ['streɪtnd]: ***be in* ~ *circumstances*** оказа́ться *pf.* в стеснённом положе́нии
**strand** [strænd] *of hair* прядь *f*; *of cable* жи́ла; **~ed** [~ɪd]: ***be* ~** *fig.* оказа́ться *pf.* без средств
**strange** [streɪndʒ] □ стра́нный; (*alien*) чужо́й; (*unknown*) незнако́мый; **~r** ['streɪndʒə] незнако́мец *m*, -мка *f*; посторо́нний (челове́к)
**strangle** ['strængl] [за]души́ть
**strap** [stræp] **1.** *on watch, etc.* ремешо́к; (*shoulder* **~**) брете́лька; *mil.* пого́н; **2.** стя́гивать ремнём
**stratagem** ['strætədʒəm] уло́вка; хи́трость *f*
**strateg|ic** [strə'tiːdʒɪk] (**~*ally***) стратеги́ческий; **~y** ['strætədʒɪ] страте́гия
**strat|um** ['strɑːtəm], *pl.* **~a** [~tə] *geol.* пласт; *social* слой
**straw** [strɔː] **1.** соло́ма; соло́минка; ***the last* ~** после́дняя ка́пля; **2.** соло́менный; **~berry** ['~brɪ] клубни́ка; (*a.* ***wild* ~**) земляни́ка
**stray** [streɪ] **1.** сбива́ться с пути́, заблу-

S

ди́ться *pf.*; забрести́ *pf.*; *of thoughts, affections* блужда́ть; **2.** (*a.* **~ed**) заблуди́вшийся; бездо́мный; *dog, cat* бродя́чий; *bullet* шальна́я пу́ля
**streak** [stri:k] поло́ска; *fig.* черта́; **~s of grey** про́седь *f*
**stream** [stri:m] **1.** поток (*a. fig.*); (*brook*) руче́й; (*jet*) струя́; **2.** *v/i.* [по]те́чь; *poet.* струи́ться; *of flag, etc.* развева́ться
**streamline** *v/t.* придава́ть [прида́ть] обтека́емую фо́рму; упроща́ть [упрости́ть]; *fig.* рационализи́ровать
**street** [stri:t] у́лица; *attr.* у́личный; **not up my ~** не по мое́й ча́сти; **~ lamp** у́личный фона́рь *m*; **~car** *Am.* трамва́й
**strength** [streŋθ] си́ла; *of cloth, etc.* про́чность *f*; *of alcohol, etc.* кре́пость *f*; **on the ~ of** на основа́нии (Р); **~en** ['streŋθən] *v/t.* уси́ли(ва)ть; укрепля́ть [-пи́ть]; *v/i.* уси́ли(ва)ться
**strenuous** ['strenjuəs] энерги́чный; *day, work* напряжённый, тяжёлый
**stress** [stres] **1.** напряже́ние (*a. tech.*); (*accent*) ударе́ние; **2.** подчёркивать [-черкну́ть]; ста́вить ударе́ние на (П)
**stretch** [stretʃ] **1.** *v/t.* (**~** *tight*) натя́гивать [-яну́ть]; (*make wider or longer*) растя́гивать [-яну́ть]; *neck* вытя́гивать [вы́тянуть]; протя́гивать [-яну́ть]; (*mst.* **~ out**); **~ a point** допуска́ть [-сти́ть] натя́жку, преувели́чи(ва)ть; *v/i.* тяну́ться; растя́гиваться [-яну́ться]; **2.** растя́гивание; напряже́ние; *of road* отре́зок; натя́жка; преувеличе́ние; (*level area*) простра́нство; промежу́ток вре́мени; **~er** ['stretʃə] носи́лки *f/pl.*
**strew** [stru:] [*irr.*] посыпа́ть [посы́пать]; (*litter, scatter*) разбра́сывать [-роса́ть]
**stricken** ['strɪkən] *pt. p. om* **strike**
**strict** [strɪkt] (*exact*) то́чный; (*severe*) стро́гий
**stride** [straɪd] **1.** [*irr.*] шага́ть [шагну́ть]; **~ over** переша́гивать [-гну́ть]; **2.** большо́й шаг; **take (s.th.) in one's ~** *fig.* легко́ добива́ться своего́; легко́ переноси́ть [-нести́]
**strident** ['straɪdnt] □ ре́зкий, скрипу́чий; пронзи́тельный
**strike** [straɪk] **1.** забасто́вка; **be on ~** бастова́ть; **2.** [*irr.*] *v/t.* ударя́ть [уда́рить]; *coins, etc.* [от]чека́нить; *fig.* поража́ть [порази́ть]; находи́ть [найти́]; *a bargain* заключа́ть [-чи́ть]; *a pose* принима́ть [-ня́ть]; **~ up** *acquaintance* познако́миться; *v/i. of clock* [про]би́ть; [за]бастова́ть; **~ home** *fig.* попа́дать в са́мую то́чку; **~r** ['straɪkə] забасто́вщик (-ица)
**striking** ['straɪkɪŋ] □ порази́тельный; **~ changes** рази́тельные переме́ны
**string** [strɪŋ] **1.** верёвка; бечёвка; *mus.* струна́; *of pearls* ни́тка; **~s** *pl. mus.* стру́нные инструме́нты *m/pl.*; **pull ~s** испо́льзовать свои́ свя́зи; **2.** [*irr.*] *beads* нани́зывать [-за́ть]; **~ band** стру́нный орке́стр
**stringent** ['strɪndʒənt] *rules* стро́гий; (*which must be obeyed*) обяза́тельный
**strip** [strɪp] **1.** сдира́ть [содра́ть] (*a.* **~ off**); *bark* обдира́ть [ободра́ть]; разде́(ва́)ть(ся); *of rank, etc.* лиша́ть [лиши́ть] (**of** Р); (*rob*) [о]гра́бить; **2.** полоса́, поло́ска; **landing ~** взлётно-поса́дочная полоса́
**stripe** [straɪp] полоса́; *mil.* наши́вка
**strive** [straɪv] [*irr.*] [по]стара́ться; стреми́ться (**for, after** к Д); **~n** ['strɪvn] *pt. p. om* **strive**
**strode** [strəʊd] *pt. om* **stride**
**stroke** [strəʊk] **1.** уда́р (*a. med.*); *of pen, etc.* штрих; *of brush* мазо́к; **at one ~** одни́м ма́хом; **~ of luck** уда́ча; **2.** [по-] гла́дить
**stroll** [strəʊl] **1.** прогу́ливаться [-ля́ться]; **2.** прогу́лка
**strong** [strɒŋ] □ *com.* си́льный; про́чный; *tea, etc.* кре́пкий; *cheese* о́стрый; *argument* убеди́тельный; **a ~ point** си́льная сторона́; **~hold** *fig.* опло́т; **~-willed** реши́тельный; упря́мый
**strove** [strəʊv] *pt. om* **strive**
**struck** [strʌk] *pt. u pt. p. om* **strike**
**structure** ['strʌktʃə] структу́ра (*a. phys.*); *social* строй; *arch.* строе́ние

(*a. phys.*), сооруже́ние
**struggle** ['strʌgl] **1.** боро́ться; вся́чески стара́ться; би́ться (***with*** над Т); **~ *through*** с трудо́м пробива́ться; **2.** борьба́
**strung** [strʌŋ] *pt. и pt. p. от* ***string***
**stub** [stʌb] **1.** *of cigarette* оку́рок; *of pencil* огры́зок; **2.** *one's toe* ударя́ться [уда́риться] (***against*** о В)
**stubble** ['stʌbl] стерня́; *of beard* щети́на
**stubborn** ['stʌbən] □ упря́мый; непода́тливый; *efforts, etc.* упо́рный
**stuck** [stʌk] *pt. и pt. p. от* ***stick***; ***~up*** *coll.* высокоме́рный; зано́счивый
**stud** [stʌd] **1.** (*collar~*) за́понка; (*press-~*) кно́пка; *on boots* шип; **2.** усе́ивать [усе́ять] (Т)
**student** ['stju:dnt] студе́нт *m*, -ка *f*
**studied** ['stʌdɪd] *answer, remark* обду́манный; *insult* преднаме́ренный; умы́шленный
**studio** ['stju:dɪəʊ] сту́дия; *artist's* ателье́ *n indecl.*, мастерска́я
**studious** ['stju:dɪəs] □ наро́чи́тый; приле́жный
**study** ['stʌdɪ] **1.** изуче́ние; (*research*) иссле́дование; (*room*) кабине́т; *paint.* этю́д, эски́з; **2.** учи́ться (Д); изуча́ть [-чи́ть]; иссле́довать (*im*)*pf.*
**stuff** [stʌf] **1.** материа́л; вещество́; (*cloth*) ткань *f*, мате́рия; ***~ and nonsense*** чепуха́; **2.** *v/t.* (*fill*) наби́(ва́)ть; *cul.* фарширова́ть; начиня́ть [-ни́ть]; (*shove into*) засо́вывать [засу́нуть]; (*overeat*) объеда́ться [объе́сться]; **~ing** ['stʌfɪŋ] наби́вка; *cul.* начи́нка; **~y** ['stʌfɪ] □ спёртый, ду́шный
**stumble** ['stʌmbl] спотыка́ться [-ткну́ться]; *in speech* запина́ться [запну́ться]; **~ *upon*** натыка́ться [наткну́ться] на (В)
**stump** [stʌmp] **1.** *of tree* пень *m*; *of tail, etc.* обру́бок; *of cigarette* оку́рок; **2.** *v/t. coll.* ста́вить в тупи́к; *v/i.* тяжело́ ступа́ть; **~y** ['stʌmpɪ] призе́мистый
**stun** [stʌn] оглуша́ть [-ши́ть] (*a. fig.*); *fig.* ошеломля́ть [-ми́ть]
**stung** [stʌŋ] *pt. и pt. p. от* ***sting***
**stunk** [stʌŋk] *pt. и pt. p. от* ***stink***
**stunning** ['stʌnɪŋ] *coll.* сногсшиба́тельный
**stunt** [stʌnt] трюк
**stup|efy** ['stju:pɪfaɪ] ошеломля́ть [-ми́ть]; поража́ть [порази́ть]; *with drug* одурма́нить; **~id** ['stju:pɪd] □ глу́пый, тупо́й; **~idity** [stju:'pɪdətɪ] глу́пость *f*
**sturdy** ['stɜ:dɪ] си́льный, кре́пкий; здоро́вый; *thing* про́чный
**sturgeon** [stɜ:dʒən] осётр; *cul.* осетри́на
**stutter** ['stʌtə] заика́ться
**stye** [staɪ] *on eyelid* ячме́нь *m*
**style** [staɪl] стиль *m*; (*fashion*) мо́да; фасо́н; ***life ~*** о́браз жи́зни
**stylish** ['staɪlɪʃ] □ мо́дный; элега́нтный, *coll.* сти́льный
**suave** [swɑ:v] гла́дкий; обходи́тельный; мя́гкий в обраще́нии
**sub...** [sʌb] *mst.* под...; суб...
**subconscious** [sʌb'kɒnʃəs] **1.** подсозна́тельный; **2.** подсозна́ние; подсознательное
**subdivision** [sʌbdɪ'vɪʒn] подразделе́ние; *of a group a.* се́кция
**subdue** [səb'dju:] (*conquer, subjugate*) покоря́ть [-ри́ть]; подавля́ть [-ви́ть] (*reduce*) уменьша́ть [уме́ньшить]
**subject** ['sʌbdʒɪkt] **1.** подчинённый; подвла́стный; *fig.* **~ *to*** подлежа́щий (Д); ***she is ~ to colds*** она́ подве́ржена просту́дам; **2.** *adv.*: **~ *to*** при усло́вии (Р); **3.** *pol.* по́дданный; *in school* предме́т; *of novel* сюже́т; (*a.* ***~ matter***) те́ма; ***drop the ~*** перевести́ *pf.* разгово́р на другу́ю те́му; **4.** [səb'dʒekt] подчиня́ть [-ни́ть]; *fig.* подверга́ть [-е́ргнуть]
**subjugate** ['sʌbdʒʊgeɪt] (*entral*(*l*)) порабоща́ть [-бори́ть]; покоря́ть [-ри́ть]
**sublease** [sʌb'li:s] субаре́нда
**sublime** [sə'blaɪm] □ возвы́шенный
**submachine** [sʌbmə'ʃi:n]: **~ *gun*** автома́т
**submarine** [sʌbmə'ri:n] *naut.* подво́дная ло́дка, субмари́на
**submerge** [səb'mɜ:dʒ] погружа́ть(ся) [-узи́ть(ся)]; затопля́ть [-пи́ть]

**submiss|ion** [səb'mɪʃn] подчине́ние; поко́рность *f*; *of documents*, *etc*. представле́ние; **~ive** [səb'mɪsɪv] □ поко́рный

**submit** [səb'mɪt] (*give in*) покоря́ться [-ри́ться] (Д); (*present*) представля́ть [-а́вить]

**subordinate** **1.** [sə'bɔːdɪnət] подчинённый; *gr*. прида́точный; **2.** [~] подчинённый (-ённая); **3.** [sə'bɔːdineit] подчиня́ть [-ни́ть]

**subscribe** [səb'skraɪb] *v/t*. (*donate*) [по]же́ртвовать; *v/i*. подде́рживать [-жа́ть] (***to*** В); *magazine*, *etc*. подпи́сываться [-са́ться] (***to*** на В); **~r** [~ə] подпи́счик *m*, -чица *f*; *tel*. абоне́нт

**subscription** [səb'skrɪpʃn] подпи́ска; *to series of concerts*, *etc*. абонеме́нт; *to club* чле́нские взно́сы

**subsequent** ['sʌbsɪkwənt] □ после́дующий; **~ly** впосле́дствии

**subservient** [səb'sɜːvɪənt] подобостра́стный; (*serving to promote*) соде́йствующий (***to*** Д)

**subsid|e** [səb'saɪd] *of temperature* спада́ть [спасть]; *of water* убы́(ва́)ть; *of wind* утиха́ть [ути́хнуть]; *of passions* уле́чься *pf*.; **~iary** [səb'sɪdɪərɪ] **1.** □ вспомога́тельный; **2.** филиа́л, дочéрняя компа́ния; **~ize** ['sʌbsɪdaɪz] субсиди́ровать (*im*)*pf*.; **~y** ['sʌbsɪdɪ] субси́дия

**subsist** [səb'sɪst] (*exist*) существова́ть; жить (***on*** на В); (*eat*) пита́ться (***on*** Т); **~ence** [~əns] существова́ние; ***means of ~*** сре́дства к существова́нию

**substance** ['sʌbstəns] вещество́; (*gist*) су́щность *f*, суть *f*; (*content*) содержа́ние

**substantial** [səb'stænʃl] □ суще́ственный, ва́жный; (*strongly made*) про́чный; (*considerable*) значи́тельный; *meal* сы́тный

**substantiate** [səb'stænʃɪeɪt] обосно́вывать [-нова́ть]; дока́зывать справедли́вость (Р); (*confirm*) подтвержда́ть [-рди́ть]

**substitut|e** ['sʌbstɪtjuːt] **1.** заменя́ть [-ни́ть]; *at work* замеща́ть [-ести́ть] (***for*** В); **2.** заме́на; (*thing*) суррога́т; **~ion** [sʌbstɪ'tjuːʃn] заме́на

**subterfuge** ['sʌbtəfjuːdʒ] увёртка, уло́вка

**subterranean** [sʌbtə'reɪnɪən] □ подзе́мный

**subtle** ['sʌtl] □ то́нкий; утончённый; (*elusive*) неулови́мый

**subtract** [səb'trækt] *math*. вычита́ть [вы́честь]

**suburb** ['sʌbɜːb] при́город; предме́стье; (*outskirts*) окра́ина; **~an** [sə'bɜːbən] при́городный

**subvention** [səb'venʃn] субве́нция, дота́ция

**subversive** [sʌb'vɜːsɪv] *fig*. подрывно́й

**subway** ['sʌbweɪ] подзе́мный перехо́д; *Am. rail*. метро́(полите́н) *n indecl*.

**succeed** [sək'siːd] [по]сле́довать за (Т); (*take the place of*) быть прее́мником (Р); достига́ть це́ли; (*do well*) преуспе́(ва́)ть

**success** [sək'ses] успе́х; (*good fortune*) уда́ча; **~ful** [sək'sesfl] □ успе́шный; уда́чный; *person* уда́чливый; *businessman* преуспева́ющий; **~ion** [~'seʃn] после́довательность *f*; (*series*) ряд; ***in ~*** оди́н за други́м; подря́д; **~ive** [~'sesɪv] □ после́дующий, сле́дующий; **~or** [~'sesə] *at work* прее́мник *m*, -ница *f*; *to throne* насле́дник *m*, -ница *f*

**succinct** [sək'sɪnkt] кра́ткий, сжа́тый

**succulent** ['sʌkjʊlənt] со́чный

**succumb** [sə'kʌm] *to temptation*, *etc*. подд(ав)а́ться (***to*** Д); *to pressure*, *etc*. не выде́рживать [вы́держать] (***to*** Р)

**such** [sʌtʃ] тако́й; *pred*. тако́в, -а́ *и т.д*.; ***~ a man*** тако́й челове́к; ***~ as*** тако́й, как …; как наприме́р

**suck** [sʌk] соса́ть; выса́сывать [вы́сосать] (*a*. ***~ out***); вса́сывать [всоса́ть] (*a*. ***~ in***); **~er** ['sʌkə] *Am. coll*. проста́к; **~le** ['sʌkl] корми́ть гру́дью; **~ling** ['sʌklɪŋ] грудно́й ребёнок; *animal* сосу́н(о́к)

**suction** ['sʌkʃn] **1.** *tech*. вса́сывание; **2.**

S

*attr.* всáсывающий
**sudden** ['sʌdn] □ внезáпный; ***all of a ~*** внезáпно, вдруг
**suds** [sʌdz] *pl.* мы́льная пéна
**sue** [sjuː] *v/t.* предъявля́ть [-ви́ть] иск кому́-л.; *v/i.* возбужда́ть дéло (***for*** о П)
**suede** [sweɪd] зáмша
**suffer** ['sʌfə] *v/i.* [по]страдáть (***from*** от Р *or* Т); *v/t.* (*undergo, endure*) [по]терпéть; **~er** [~rə] страдáлец *m*, -лица *f*; **~ing** [~rɪŋ] страдáние
**suffice** [sə'faɪs] хватáть [-ти́ть], быть достáточным; ***~ it to say that*** достáточно сказáть, что …
**sufficient** [sə'fɪʃnt] □ достáточный
**suffocate** ['sʌfəkeɪt] *v/t.* [за]души́ть; *v/i.* задыхáться [задохну́ться]
**suffrage** ['sʌfrɪdʒ] избирáтельное прáво
**sugar** ['ʃʊgə] **1.** сáхар; ***granulated ~*** сáхарный песóк; ***lump ~*** (сáхар-) рафинáд; **2.** сáхарный; **3.** *tea, etc.* положи́ть сáхар; **~y** [~rɪ] *fig.* при́торный, слащáвый
**suggest** [sə'dʒest] (*propose*) предлагáть [-ложи́ть]; *solution* подскáзывать [-зáть]; наводи́ть на мысль *f* о (П); [по]совéтовать; **~ion** [~ʃən] совéт, предложéние; (*hint*) намёк; **~ive** [~ɪv] □ (*giving food for thought*) наводя́щий на размышлéние; (*improper*) непристóйный; *joke* двусмы́сленный
**suicide** ['suːɪsaɪd] самоуби́йство; ***commit ~*** покóнчить *pf.* с собóй
**suit** [suːt] **1.** (*a.* ***~ of clothes***) костю́м; *cards* масть *f*; *law* судéбное дéло, иск; **2.** *v/t.* (*adapt*) приспосáбливать [-осóбить] (***to, with*** к Д); соотвéтствовать (Д); удовлетвори́ть; (*be convenient or right*) устрáивать [-рóить]; подходи́ть [подойти́] (Д); ***~ yourself*** поступáй как знáешь; *v/i.* (*be appropriate*) подходи́ть, годи́ться; **~able** ['suːtəbl] □ подходя́щий; соотвéтствующий; **~case** чемодáн
**suite** [swiːt] *mus.* сюи́та; *in hotel* нóмер-лю́кс; *of furniture* гарниту́р
**suited** ['suːtɪd] подходя́щий
**sulfur**, *Brt.* **sulphur** ['sʌlfə] *chem.* сéра; **~ic** [sʌl'fjuərɪk] сéрный
**sulk** [sʌlk] **1.** [на]ду́ться; быть не в ду́хе; **2.**: ***~s*** [~s] *pl.* плохóе настроéние; **~y** ['sʌlkɪ] □ наду́тый
**sullen** ['sʌlən] угрю́мый, мрáчный; *sky* пáсмурный
**sultry** ['sʌltrɪ] □ ду́шный, знóйный
**sum** [sʌm] **1.** су́мма; итóг; ***in ~*** кóротко говоря́; ***~s*** *pl.* арифмéтика; **2.** (*a.* ***~ up***) *math.* склáдывать [сложи́ть]; *fig.* подводи́ть итóг
**summar|ize** ['sʌməraɪz] сумми́ровать (*im*)*pf.*; подводи́ть [-вести́] итóг; написáть *pf.* резюмé; **~y** [~rɪ] свóдка; аннотáция, резюмé *n indecl.*
**summer** ['sʌmə] лéто; ***in ~*** лéтом; **~y** [~ri] лéтний
**summit** ['sʌmɪt] верши́на (*a. fig.*); *pol.* сáммит, встрéча в верхáх; *fig.* предéл
**summon** ['sʌmən] соз(ы)вáть (собрáние *и т. п.*); *law* вызывáть [вы́звать]; **~s** [~z] вы́зов в суд; *law* судéбная повéстка
**sumptuous** ['sʌmptʃʊəs] роскóшный; пы́шный
**sun** [sʌn] **1.** сóлнце; **2.** сóлнечный; **3.** грéть(ся) на сóлнце; **~bathe** загорáть; **~burn** загáр; *painful* сóлнечный ожóг
**Sunday** ['sʌndɪ] воскресéнье
**sundown** захóд сóлнца
**sundry** ['sʌndrɪ] рáзный; ***all and ~*** все без исключéния
**sunflower** ['sʌnflaʊə] подсóлнечник
**sung** [sʌŋ] *pt. p. om* ***sing***
**sunglasses** *pl.* тёмные очки́ *n/pl.*
**sunk** [sʌŋk] *pt. p. om* ***sink***
**sunken** [sʌŋkən] *fig.* впáлый
**sun|ny** ['sʌnɪ] □ сóлнечный; **~rise** восхóд сóлнца; **~set** захóд сóлнца, закáт; **~shade** зóнт(ик) от сóлнца; **~shine** сóлнечный свет; ***in the ~*** на сóлнце; **~stroke** *med.* сóлнечный удáр; **~tan** загáр; **~tanned** загорéлый
**super…** ['suːpə] *pref.*: пéре…, пре…; сверх…; над…; су́пер…
**super** ['suːpə] замечáтельный; **~!** здóрово!
**superb** [suː'pɜːb] великолéпный, превосхóдный

**super|cilious** [suːpəˈsɪlɪəs] □ высокомéрный; **~ficial** [suːpəˈfɪʃl] □ повéрхностный; **~fluous** [suːˈpɜːfluəs] ли́шний, изли́шний; **~human** сверхчеловéческий; **~intend** [suːpərɪnˈtend] (*watch*) надзирáть за (T); (*direct*) руководи́ть (T); **~intendent** [-ənt] руководи́тель *m*
**superior** [suːˈpɪərɪə] **1.** □ *in rank* вы́сший, стáрший; *in quality* превосхóдный; превосходя́щий (***to*** B); ***~ smile*** надмéнная улы́бка; **2.** начáльник; *eccl.* настоя́тель *m*, -ница *f*; *of a convent* ***Mother/Father ~*** игýменья/игýмен; **~ity** [suːpɪərɪˈɒrətɪ] *of quality, quantity, etc.* превосхóдство; *of rank* старшинствó
**super|lative** [suːˈpɜːlətɪv] **1.** □ высочáйший; величáйший; **2.** *gr.* превосхóдная стéпень *f*; **~man** [ˈsuːpəmæn] суперме́н; **~market** [ˈsuːpəmɑːkɪt] универсáм (= *универсальный магазин самообслуживания*); **~sede** [suːpəˈsiːd] (*replace*) заменя́ть [-ни́ть]; (*displace*) вытесня́ть [вы́теснить]; *fig.* (*overtake*) обгоня́ть [обогнáть]; **~sonic** [suːpəˈsɒnɪk] сверхзвуковóй; **~stition** [suːpəˈstɪʃn] суевéрие; **~stitious** [-ˈstɪʃəs] суевéрный; **~vene** [-ˈviːn] слéдовать за чéм-либо; **~vise** [ˈsuːpəvaɪz] надзирáть (T); **~vision** [suːpəˈvɪʒn] надзóр; **~visor** [ˈsuːpəvaɪzə] надзиратель *m*, -ница *f*
**supper** [ˈsʌpə] ýжин; ***the Last ~*** Тáйная Вéчеря
**supplant** [səˈplɑːnt] вытесня́ть [вы́теснить] (B)
**supple** [ˈsʌpl] ги́бкий (*a. fig.*)
**supplement 1.** [ˈsʌplɪmənt] (*addition*) дополнéние; *to a periodical* приложéние; **2.** [-ˈment] дополня́ть [допóлнить]; **~ary** [sʌlɪˈmentərɪ] дополни́тельный, добáвочный
**supplier** [səˈplaɪə] поставщи́к
**supply** [səˈplaɪ] **1.** снабжáть [-бди́ть] (***with*** T); *goods* поставля́ть [-áвить]; *information, etc.* предоставля́ть [-áвить]; **2.** снабжéние; постáвка; (*stock*) запáс; **supplies** *pl.* (*food*) продовóльствие; ***~ and demand*** спрос и предложéние
**support** [səˈpɔːt] **1.** поддéржка; *phys., tech.* опóра (*a. fig.*); **2.** подпирáть [-перéть]; *a candidature, etc.* поддéрживать [-жáть]; *one's family, etc.* содержáть
**suppose** [səˈpəʊz] (*assume*) предполагáть [-ложи́ть]; (*imagine*) полагáть; *coll.* ***~ we do so?*** а éсли мы э́то сдéлаем?; ***he's ~d to be back today*** он дóлжен сегóдня вернýться
**supposed** [səˈpəʊzd] □ предполагáемый; **~ly** [səˈpəʊzɪdlɪ] предположи́тельно; я́кобы
**supposition** [sʌpəˈzɪʃn] предположéние
**suppress** [səˈpres] *uprising, yawn, etc.* подавля́ть [-ви́ть]; (*ban*) запрещáть [-ети́ть]; *laugh, anger, etc.* сдéрживать [-жáть]; **~ion** [səˈpreʃn] подавлéние
**suprem|acy** [suːˈpreməsɪ] превосхóдство; **~e** [suːˈpriːm] □ *command, etc.* верхóвный; (*greatest*) высочáйший
**surcharge** [ˈsɜːtʃɑːdʒ] (*extra charge*) приплáта, доплáта
**sure** [ʃʊə] □ *com.* вéрный; (*certain*) увéренный; (*safe*) безопáсный; надёжный; *Am.* **~!** конéчно; ***make ~ that ...*** вы́яснить *pf.*, убеди́ться *pf.*, провéрить *pf.*; **~ly** [ˈʃʊəlɪ] несомнéнно
**surf** [sɜːf] прибóй
**surface** [ˈsɜːfɪs] повéрхность *f*; ***on the ~*** *fig.* чи́сто внéшне; на пéрвый взгляд; ***~ mail*** обы́чной пóчтой
**surfing** [ˈsɜːfɪŋ] сéрфинг
**surge** [sɜːdʒ] **1.** волнá; **2.** *of waves* вздымáться; *of crowd* подавáться [-дáться] вперёд; *of emotions* [на-] хлы́нуть *pf.*
**surg|eon** [ˈsɜːdʒən] хирýрг; **~ery** [ˈsɜːdʒərɪ] хирурги́я; оперáция; *Brt.* приёмная (врачá); ***~ hours*** приёмные часы́
**surgical** [ˈsɜːdʒɪkl] □ хирурги́ческий
**surly** [ˈsɜːlɪ] □ неприве́тливый; хмýрый; угрю́мый
**surmise** [səˈmaɪz] **1.** предположéние; **2.** предполагáть [-ложи́ть]

**surmount** [sə'maʊnt] преодолé(вá)ть, превозмогáть [-мóчь]
**surname** ['sɜːneɪm] фами́лия
**surpass** [sə'pɑːs] *expectations, etc.* превосходи́ть [-взойти́]
**surplus** ['sɜːpləs] **1.** изли́шек; (*remainder*) остáток; **2.** изли́шний; ли́шний
**surprise** [sə'praɪz] **1.** удивлéние; *event, present, etc.* неожи́данность *f*, сюрпри́з; *attr.* неожи́данный; **2.** удивля́ть [-ви́ть]; (*take unawares*) заставáть врасплóх
**surrender** [sə'rendə] **1.** сдáча; капитуля́ция; **2.** *v/t.* сда(вá)ть; *one's rights* откáзываться [-зáться] от (Р); *v/i.* сд(ав)áться
**surround** [sə'raʊnd] окружáть [-жи́ть]; **~ing** [~ɪŋ] окружáющий; **~ings** [~ɪŋz] *pl.* окрéстности *f/pl.*; (*environment*) средá, окружéние
**survey** [sɜː'veɪ] **1.** (*look at, examine*) обозрé(вá)ть; осмáтривать [осмотрéть]; производи́ть [-вести́] топографи́ческую съёмку; **2.** ['sɜːveɪ] осмóтр; (*study*) обзóр; топографи́ческая съёмка; *attr.* обзóрный; **~or** [sə'veɪə] землемéр; топóграф
**surviv|al** [sə'vaɪvl] выживáние; (*relic*) пережи́ток; **~e** [sə'vaɪv] *v/t.* пережи́(вá)ть *mst. pf.*; *v/i.* оставáться в живы́х, вы́жи(вá)ть; *of custom* сохраня́ться [-ни́ться]; **~or** [sə'vaɪvə] остáвшийся в живы́х
**susceptible** [sə'septəbl] □ восприи́мчивый (***to*** к Д); (*sensitive*) чувстви́тельный; (*easily enamo(u)red*) влюбчивый
**suspect** [səs'pekt] **1.** подозревáть, заподáзривать [-дóзрить] (***of*** в П); *the truth of, etc.* сомневáться [усомни́ться] в (П); (*think*) предполагáть; **2.** ['sʌspekt] подозри́тельный; подозревáемый
**suspend** [sə'spend] подвéшивать [-éсить]; (*stop for a time*) приостанáвливать [-нови́ть]; врéменно прекращáть; **~ed** [~ɪd] подвеснóй; **~ers** [~əz] *pl. Am.* подтя́жки *f/pl.*
**suspens|e** [sə'spens] напряжённое внимáние; (*uneasy uncertainty*) состоя́ние неизвéстности, неопределённости; ***in ~*** напряжённо, в напряжéнии; **~ion** [sə'spenʃn] прекращéние; ***~ bridge*** вися́чий мост
**suspici|on** [sə'spɪʃn] подозрéние; *trace, nuance* оттéнок; **~ous** [~ʃəs] □ подозри́тельный
**sustain** [sə'steɪn] (*support*) подпирáть [-перéть], поддéрживать [-жáть] (*a. fig.*); *law* подтверждáть [-рди́ть]; выдéрживать [вы́держать]; (*suffer*) выноси́ть [вы́нести], испы́тывать [испытáть]
**sustenance** ['sʌstɪnəns] пи́ща; срéдства к существовáнию
**swaddle** ['swɒdl] [с-, за]пеленáть
**swagger** ['swægə] ходи́ть с вáжным ви́дом; (*brag*) [по]хвáстать (*a.* -ся)
**swallow**¹ ['swɒləʊ] *zo.* лáсточка
**swallow**² [~] глотóк; глотáть; проглáтывать [-лоти́ть]
**swam** [swæm] *pt. om* ***swim***
**swamp** [swɒmp] **1.** болóто, топь *f*; **2.** затопля́ть [-пи́ть], заливáть; **~y** ['swɒmpɪ] болóтистый
**swan** [swɒn] лéбедь *m*
**swap** [swɒp] *coll.* **1.** обмéнивать(ся) [-ня́ть(ся)]; [по]меня́ть(ся); **2.** обмéн
**swarm** [swɔːm] **1.** *of bees* рой; *of birds* стáя; толпá; **2.** *of bees* рои́ться; кишéть (***with*** Т); ***crowds ~ed into the cinema*** толпá хлы́нула в кинотеáтр
**swarthy** ['swɔːðɪ] смýглый
**sway** [sweɪ] **1.** качáние; (*influence*) влия́ние; **2.** качáть(ся) [качну́ть(ся)]; *fig.* [по]влия́ть, склони́ть на свою стóрону
**swear** [sweə] [*irr.*] (*take an oath*) [по]кля́сться (***by*** Т); (*curse*) [вы́-] ругáться; **~word** ругáтельство
**sweat** [swet] **1.** пот; **2.** [*irr.*] *v/i.* [вс]потéть; исполня́ть тяжёлую рабóту; *v/t.* заставля́ть потéть; ***~ blood*** *coll.* рабóтать как вол; **~er** ['swetə] сви́тер; **~y** ['swetɪ] пóтный
**Swede** [swiːd] швéд *m*, -ка *f*
**swede** [~] *bot.* брю́ква
**Swedish** ['swiːdɪʃ] швéдский
**sweep** [swiːp] **1.** [*irr.*] мести́, подме-

та́ть [-ести́]; *chimney* [по]чи́стить; (*rush*) проноси́ться [-нести́сь] (*a.* ~ ***past, along***); ~ ***s.o. off his feet*** вскружи́ть кому́-л. го́лову; **2.** *of arm* взмах; (*curve*) изги́б; ***make a clean*** ~ (***of***) отде́л(ыв)аться (от Р); ~**er** ['swi:pə]: ***road*** ~ подмета́тельная маши́на; ~**ing** ['swi:pɪŋ] □ *gesture* широ́кий; *accusation* огу́льный; *changes* радика́льный, широкомасшта́бный; ~**ings** [-z] *pl.* му́сор

**sweet** [swi:t] **1.** □ сла́дкий; *air* све́жий; *water* пре́сный; *person* ми́лый; ***have a*** ~ ***tooth*** быть сластёной; **2.** конфе́та; ~**s** *pl.* сла́сти *f/pl.*; ~**en** ['swi:tn] подсла́щивать [-ласти́ть]; ~ ***the pill*** позолоти́ть *pf.* пилю́лю; ~**heart** возлю́бленный (-енная)

**swell** [swel] **1.** [*irr.*] *v/i.* [о-, при-, рас]пу́хнуть; *of cheek* разду́(ва́)ться; *of wood* набуха́ть [-у́хнуть]; *of sound* нараста́ть [-сти́]; *v/t.* (*increase*) увели́чи(ва)ть; **2.** *coll.* (*fashionable*) шика́рный; (*excellent*) великоле́пный; **3.** *coll.* франт; ~**ing** ['swelɪŋ] о́пухоль *f*; *slight* припу́хлость *f*

**swelter** ['sweltə] изнемога́ть от жары́

**swept** [swept] *pt. и pt. p. от* ***sweep***

**swerve** [swɜ:v] свора́чивать [сверну́ть] в сто́рону; *of car, etc.* ре́зко сверну́ть *pf.*

**swift** [swɪft] □ бы́стрый, ско́рый; ~**ness** ['~nɪs] быстрота́

**swill** [swɪl] **1.** (*slops*) помо́и *m/pl.*; **2.** [про]полоска́ть, опола́скивать [-лосну́ть] (*a.* ~ ***out***)

**swim** [swɪm] **1.** [*irr.*] пла́вать, [по-] плы́ть; перепл(ы́(ва́)ть (*a.* ~ ***across***); ***my head*** ~***s*** у меня́ голова́ кру́жится; **2.** пла́вание; ***be in the*** ~ быть в ку́рсе де́л; ~**mer** ['~ə] пловéц *m*, -вчи́ха *f*; ~**ming** [-ɪŋ] пла́вание; ~ ***pool*** пла́вательный бассе́йн; ~ ***trunks*** пла́вки; ~**suit** купа́льный костю́м

**swindle** ['swɪndl] **1.** обма́нывать [-ну́ть], наду́(ва́)ть; **2.** обма́н, надува́тельство; ~**r** [~ə] моше́нник

**swine** [swaɪn] *coll. fig.* свинья́

**swing** [swɪŋ] **1.** [*irr.*] кача́ть(ся) [качну́ть(ся)]; *hands* разма́хивать; *feet* болта́ть; (*hang*) висе́ть; **2.** кача́ние; разма́х; взмах; ритм; каче́ли *f/pl.*; ***in full*** ~ в по́лном разга́ре; ***go with a*** ~ проходи́ть о́чень успе́шно; ~ ***door*** дверь *f*, открыва́ющаяся в любу́ю сто́рону

**swipe** [swaɪp] уда́рить; *joc.* (*steal*) стащи́ть

**swirl** [swɜ:l] **1.** *in dance, etc.* кружи́ть(ся); *of dust, etc.* клуби́ться; *of water* крути́ться; **2.** водоворо́т

**Swiss** [swɪs] **1.** швейца́рский; **2.** швейца́рец *m*, -рка *f*; ***the*** ~ *pl.* швейца́рцы *m/pl.*

**switch** [swɪtʃ] **1.** *el.* выключа́тель *m*; *radio, TV* переключа́тель *m*; **2.** (*whip*) хлеста́ть [-стну́ть]; *el.* переключа́ть [-чи́ть] (*often* ~ ***over***) (*a. fig.*); *fig.* ~ ***the conversation*** переводи́ть [-вести́] разгово́р (на В); ~ ***on*** *el.* включа́ть [-чи́ть]; ~ ***off*** выключа́ть [вы́ключить]; ~**board** *tel.* коммута́тор

**swollen** ['swəʊlən] *pt. p. от* ***swell***

**swoon** [swu:n] **1.** о́бморок; **2.** па́дать в о́бморок

**swoop** [swu:p] (*a.* ~ ***down***), ри́нуться; (*suddenly attack*) налета́ть [-ете́ть] (***on*** на В)

**sword** [sɔ:d] шпа́га; меч

**swore** [swɔ:] *pt. от* ***swear***

**sworn** [swɔ:n] *pt. p. от* ***swear***; *adj. enemy* закля́тый

**swum** [swʌm] *pt. p. от* ***swim***

**swung** [swʌŋ] *pt. и pt. p.от* ***swing***

**syllable** ['sɪləbl] слог

**syllabus** ['sɪləbəs] уче́бный план

**symbol** ['sɪmbl] си́мвол, усло́вное обозначе́ние; ~**ic(al)** [sɪm'bɒlɪk(l)] символи́ческий; ~**ism** ['sɪmbəlɪzəm] символи́зм

**symmetr|ical** [sɪ'metrɪkl] □ симметри́чный; ~**y** ['sɪmətrɪ] симметри́я

**sympath|etic** [sɪmpə'θetɪk] (~***ally***) сочу́вственный; ~**ize** ['sɪmpəθaɪz] [по]сочу́вствовать (***with*** Д); ~**y** ['sɪmpəθɪ] сочу́вствие (***with*** к Д)

**symphony** ['sɪmfənɪ] симфо́ния

**symptom** ['sɪmptəm] симпто́м

**synchron|ize** ['sɪŋkrənaɪz] *v/i.* совпада́ть по вре́мени; *v/t. actions* синхро-

S

низи́ровать (*im*)*pf*.; **~ous** [~nəs] □ синхро́нный
**syndicate** ['sɪndɪkət] синдика́т
**synonym** ['sɪnənɪm] сино́ним; **~ous** [sɪ'nɒnɪməs] синоними́ческий
**synopsis** [sɪ'nɒpsɪs] кра́ткое изложе́ние, сино́псис
**synthe|sis** ['sɪnθesɪs] си́нтез; **~tic** [sɪn'θetɪk] синтети́ческий
**syringe** [sɪ'rɪndʒ] шприц
**syrup** ['sɪrəp] сиро́п
**system** ['sɪstəm] систе́ма; **~atic** [sɪstə'mætɪk] (***~ally***) системати́ческий

# T

**tab** [tæb] *for hanging garment* ве́шалка; *mil*. наши́вка, петли́ца
**table** ['teɪbl] стол; (*list of data, etc.*) табли́ца; ***~ of contents*** оглавле́ние; **~cloth** ска́терть *f*; **~ d'hôte** ['tɑ:bl'dout] табльдо́т; о́бщий стол; **~lamp** насто́льная ла́мпа; **~spoon** столо́вая ло́жка
**tablet** ['tæblɪt] *med*. табле́тка; *of soap* кусо́к; мемориа́льная доска́
**table tennis** насто́льный те́ннис
**taboo** [tə'bu:] табу́ *n indecl*.
**tacit** ['tæsɪt] □ подразумева́емый; молчали́вый; **~urn** ['tæsɪtɜ:n] □ неразгово́рчивый
**tack** [tæk] **1.** гво́здик с широ́кой шля́пкой; (*thumb~*) *Am*. кно́пка; **~ing** *sew*. намётка; **2.** *v/t*. прикрепля́ть гво́здиками и́ли кно́пками; *sewing* смётывать [смета́ть]
**tackle** ['tækl] **1.** (*equipment*) принадле́жности *f/pl*.; *for fishing* снасть *f*; **2.** (*deal with*) энерги́чно бра́ться за (В); *problem* би́ться над (Т)
**tact** [tækt] такт, такти́чность *f*; **~ful** ['tæktfʊl] такти́чный
**tactics** ['tæktɪks] *pl*. та́ктика
**tactless** ['tæktlɪs] □ беста́ктный
**tag** [tæg] **1.** би́рка, этике́тка; *fig*. изби́тое выраже́ние; ***price ~*** це́нник; **2.**: ***~ along*** сле́довать по пята́м; тащи́ться сза́ди
**tail** [teɪl] **1.** хвост; *of coat* фа́лда; пола́; *of coin* обра́тная сторона́; ***heads or ~s?*** орёл или ре́шка?; **2.** *v/t*. (*follow*) сле́довать, тащи́ться (***after*** за Т); *Am. coll. of police* высле́живать [вы́следить]; *v/i*. тяну́ться верени́цей; ***~ off*** (*fall behind*) отст(ав)а́ть; **~coat** фрак; **~light** *mot*. за́дний фона́рь *m*/свет
**tailor** ['teɪlə] портно́й; **~-made** сде́ланный по зака́зу
**take** [teɪk] **1.** [*irr.*] *v/t*. брать [взять]; *medicine, etc*. принима́ть [-ня́ть]; [съ]есть; [вы́]пить; *seat* занима́ть [заня́ть]; *phot*. снима́ть [снять]; *time* отнима́ть [-ня́ть]; ***I ~ it that*** я полага́ю, что …; ***~ in hand*** взять *pf*. в свои́ ру́ки; ***~ o.s. in hand*** взять *pf*. себя́ в ру́ки; ***~ pity on*** сжа́литься *pf*. над (Т); ***~ place*** случа́ться [-чи́ться], происходи́ть (произойти́); ***~ a rest*** отдыха́ть (отдохну́ть); ***~ a hint*** поня́ть *pf*. намёк; ***~ a seat*** сади́ться [сесть]; ***~ a taxi*** брать [взять] такси́; ***~ a view*** выска́зывать свою́ то́чку зре́ния; ***~ a walk*** [по]гуля́ть, прогу́ливаться [-ля́ться]; ***~ down*** снима́ть [снять]; запи́сывать [-са́ть]; ***~ for*** принима́ть [-ня́ть] за (В); ***~ from*** брать [взять] у Р; ***~ in*** (*deceive*) обма́нывать [-ну́ть]; (*understand*) поня́ть *pf*.; ***~ off*** *coat, etc*. снима́ть [снять]; ***~ out*** вынима́ть [вы́нуть]; ***~ to pieces*** разбира́ть [разобра́ть]; ***~ up*** бра́ться [взя́ться] за (В); *space, time* занима́ть [заня́ть], отнима́ть [отня́ть]; **2.** *v/i*. (*have the intended effect*) [по]де́йствовать; (*be a success*) име́ть успе́х; ***~ after*** походи́ть на (В); ***~ off*** *ae*. взлета́ть [-ете́ть]; ***~ over*** принима́ть дела́ (***from*** от Р); ***~ to*** пристрасти́ться к (Д) *pf*.; привяза́ться к (Д) *pf*.; **~n** ['teɪkən] *pt. p. om* ***take***; ***be ~ ill*** заболе́(ва́)ть; **~-off**

T

['teɪ'kɔf] (*impersonation*) подража́ние; *ae.* взлёт
**takings** ['teɪkɪŋz] *pl. comm.* вы́ручка; сбор
**tale** [teɪl] расска́з, по́весть *f*; (*false account*) вы́думка; (*unkind account*) сплётня; ***tell ~s*** сплётничать
**talent** ['tælənt] тала́нт; **~ed** [~ɪd] тала́нтливый
**talk** [tɔːk] **1.** разгово́р, бесе́да; ***~s*** *pl. pol.* перегово́ры; ***there is ~ that …*** говоря́т, что …; **2.** [по]говори́ть; разгова́ривать; [по]бесе́довать; **~ative** ['tɔːkətɪv] разгово́рчивый; **~er** ['tɔːkə] **1.** говоря́щий; говорли́вый челове́к
**tall** [tɔːl] высо́кий; ***~ order*** чрезме́рное тре́бование; ***~ story*** *coll.* небыли́ца; неправдоподо́бная исто́рия
**tally** ['tælɪ] соотве́тствовать (***with*** Д)
**tame** [teɪm] **1.** □ *animal* ручно́й, приручённый; (*submissive*) поко́рный; (*dull*) ску́чный; **2.** прируча́ть [-чи́ть]
**tamper** ['tæmpə]: ***~ with*** тро́гать; копа́ться; *document* подде́л(ыв)ать (В); ***someone has ~ed with my luggage*** кто́-то копа́лся в моём багаже́
**tan** [tæn] **1.** (*sun~*) зага́р; **2.** загора́ть
**tang** [tæŋ] (*taste*) ре́зкий при́вкус; (*smell*) за́пах
**tangent** ['tændʒənt] *math.* каса́тельная; ***go*** (*a.* ***fly***) ***off at a ~*** ре́зко отклони́тся *pf.*
**tangerine** [tændʒə'riːn] мандари́н
**tangible** ['tændʒəbl] □ осяза́емый, ощути́мый
**tangle** ['tæŋgl] **1.** пу́таница, неразбери́ха; **2.** запу́т(ыв)ать(ся)
**tank** [tæŋk] цисте́рна; бак; *mil.* танк, *attr.* та́нковый; ***gas(oline) ~***, *Brt.* ***petrol ~*** бензоба́к
**tankard** ['tæŋkəd] высо́кая кру́жка
**tanker** ['tæŋkə] *naut.* та́нкер; *mot.* автоцисте́рна
**tantalize** ['tæntəlaɪz] дразни́ть; [за-, из]му́чить
**tantrum** ['tæntrəm] *coll.* вспы́шка гне́ва *или* раздраже́ния; ***throw a ~*** закати́ть *pf.* исте́рику
**tap**[1] [tæp] **1.** *for water, gas* кран; **2.**: ***~ for money*** выпра́шивать де́ньги у Р; ***~ for information*** выу́живать [-удить] информа́цию
**tap**[2] [~] **1.** [по]стуча́ть; [по]хло́пать; **2.** лёгкий стук; **~ dance** чечётка
**tape** [teɪp] тесьма́; *sport* фи́нишная ле́нточка; магни́тная ле́нта; ***sticky ~*** ли́пкая ле́нта; **~ measure** ['teɪpmeʒə] руле́тка; *of cloth* сантиме́тр
**taper** ['teɪpə] *v/i.* су́живаться к концу́; *v/t.* заостря́ть [-ри́ть]
**tape recorder** магнитофо́н
**tapestry** ['tæpəstrɪ] гобеле́н
**tar** [tɑː] **1.** дёготь *m*; *for boats* смола́; **2.** [вы́]смоли́ть
**tardy** ['tɑːdɪ] □ (*slow-moving*) медли́тельный; (*coming or done late*) запозда́лый
**target** ['tɑːgɪt] цель *f* (*a. fig.*); мише́нь *f* (*a. fig.*)
**tariff** ['tærɪf] тари́ф
**tarnish** ['tɑːnɪʃ] *fig.* [о]поро́чить; *v/i. of metal* [по]тускне́ть; ***~ed reputation*** запя́тнанная репута́ция
**tarpaulin** [tɑː'pɔːlɪn] брезе́нт
**tart**[1] [tɑːt] откры́тый пиро́г с фру́ктами; сла́дкая ватру́шка
**tart**[2] [~] ки́слый, те́рпкий; *fig.* ко́лкий
**tartan** ['tɑːtn] шотла́ндка
**task** [tɑːsk] (*problem*) зада́ча; (*job*) зада́ние; ***set a ~*** дать *pf.* зада́ние; ***take to ~*** отчи́тывать [-ита́ть]; **~ force** *mil.* операти́вная гру́ппа
**taste** [teɪst] **1.** вкус; ***have a ~ for*** люби́ть, знать толк (в П); **2.** [по]про́бовать; *fig.* испы́тывать [-пыта́ть]; ***~ sweet*** быть сла́дким на вкус; **~ful** ['teɪstfl] □ (сде́ланный) со вку́сом; изя́щный; **~less** [~lɪs] безвку́сный
**tasty** ['teɪstɪ] □ вку́сный
**tatter|ed** ['tætəd] изно́шенный, изо́рванный; ***~s*** *pl.* лохмо́тья *n/pl.*; ***tear to ~s*** разорва́ть в кло́чья; *fig.* разбива́ть [-би́ть] в пух и прах
**tattle** ['tætl] болтовня́
**tattoo** [tə'tuː] (*design on skin*) татуиро́вка
**taught** [tɔːt] *pt. и pt. p. от* ***teach***
**taunt** [tɔːnt] **1.** насме́шка, ко́лкость *f*; **2.** говори́ть ко́лкости (Д), дразни́ть

**taut** [tɔːt] (*stretched tight*) ту́го натя́нутый; *nerves* взви́нченный
**tawdry** ['tɔːdrɪ] □ безвку́сный; крича́щий
**tawny** ['tɔːnɪ] рыжева́то-кори́чневый
**tax** [tæks] **1.** нало́г (***on*** на В); ***income ~*** подохо́дный нало́г; ***~ evasion*** уклоне́ние от упла́ты нало́га; ***value added ~*** нало́г на доба́вочную сто́имость *f*; **2.** облага́ть нало́гом; *one's strength* чрезме́рно напряга́ть; ***~ s.o.'s patience*** испы́тывать чьё-л. терпе́ние; ***~ a p. with a th.*** обвиня́ть [-ни́ть] кого́-л. в чём-л.; **~ation** [tæk'seɪʃn] обложе́ние нало́гом; взима́ние нало́га
**taxi** ['tæksɪ] = **~cab** такси́ *n indecl.*
**taxpayer** ['tækspeɪə] налогоплате́льщик
**tea** [tiː] чай; ***make (the) ~*** зава́ривать [-ри́ть] чай
**teach** [tiːtʃ] [*irr.*] [на]учи́ть, обуча́ть [-чи́ть]; *a subject* преподава́ть; **~er** ['tiːtʃə] учи́тель *m*, -ница *f*; *univ.* преподава́тель *m*, -ница *f*
**teacup** ['tiːkʌp] ча́йная ча́шка
**team** [tiːm] **1.** *sport* кома́нда; *of workers* брига́да; ***~ spirit*** чу́вство ло́ктя; **2.**: ***~ up*** сотру́дничать; **~work** совме́стная рабо́та
**teapot** ['tiːpɒt] ча́йник (для зава́рки)
**tear**[1] [teə] **1.** [*irr.*] дыра́, проре́ха; **2.** [по]рва́ться; разрыва́ть(ся) [разорва́ть(ся)]; *fig.* раздира́ть(ся); (*go at great speed*) [по]мча́ться; ***country torn by war*** страна́, раздира́емая войно́й
**tear**[2] [tɪə] слеза́ (*pl.* слёзы)
**tearful** ['tɪəfl] □ слезли́вый; *eyes* по́лный слёз
**tease** [tiːz] **1.** челове́к, лю́бящий поддра́знивать; **2.** *coll.* дразни́ть; подшу́чивать; **~r** [~ə] *coll.* головоло́мка
**teat** [tiːt] сосо́к
**technic|al** ['teknɪkl] □ техни́ческий; **~ality** [teknɪ'kælətɪ] техни́ческая дета́ль *f*; форма́льность *f*; **~ian** [tek'nɪʃn] те́хник
**technique** [tek'niːk] те́хника; ме́тод, спо́соб
**technology** [tek'nɒlədʒɪ] техноло́гия; технологи́ческие нау́ки *f/pl.*
**tedious** ['tiːdɪəs] □ ску́чный, утоми́тельный
**tedium** ['tiːdɪəm] утоми́тельность *f*; ску́ка
**teem** [tiːm] изоби́ловать, кише́ть (***with*** Т)
**teenager** ['tiːneɪdʒə] подро́сток; ю́ноша *m* / де́вушка *f* до двадцати́ лет
**teeth** [tiːθ] *pl. от* **tooth**; **~e** [tiːð]: ***the child is teething*** у ребёнка проре́заются зу́бы
**teetotal(l)er** [tiː'təʊtlə] тре́звенник
**telecommunications** [telɪkəmjuːnɪ'keɪʃnz] *pl.* сре́дства да́льней свя́зи
**telegram** ['telɪgræm] телегра́мма
**telegraph** ['telɪgrɑːf] **1.** телегра́ф; **2.** телеграфи́ровать (*im*)*pf.*; **3.** *attr.* телегра́фный
**telephone** ['telɪfəʊn] **1.** телефо́н; **2.** звони́ть по телефо́ну; **~ booth** телефо́н-автома́т; **~ directory** телефо́нный спра́вочник
**telescop|e** ['telɪskəʊp] телеско́п; **~ic** [telɪs'kopɪk] телескопи́ческий; ***~ aerial*** выдвижна́я анте́нна
**teletype** ['telɪtaɪp] телета́йп
**televis|ion** ['telɪvɪʒn] телеви́дение
**telex** ['teleks] те́лекс
**tell** [tel] [*irr.*] *v/t.* говори́ть [сказа́ть]; (*relate*) расска́зывать [-за́ть]; (*distinguish*) отлича́ть [-чи́ть]; ***~ a p. to do a th.*** веле́ть кому́-л. что́-л. сде́лать; ***~ off*** *coll.* [вы́]брани́ть; *v/i.* (*affect*) сказы́ваться [сказа́ться]; (*know*) знать; ***how can I ~?*** отку́да мне знать?; **~er** ['telə] *esp. Am.* касси́р (в ба́нке); **~ing** ['telɪŋ] □ многоговоря́щий, многозначи́тельный; **~tale** ['telteɪl] я́беда *m & f*
**telly** ['telɪ] *chiefly Brt. coll.* те́лик
**temper** ['tempə] **1.** *steel* закаля́ть [-ли́ть] (*a. fig.*); **2.** нрав; (*mood*) настрое́ние; (*irritation, anger*) раздраже́ние, гнев; ***he has a quick ~*** он вспы́льчив; **~ament** ['temprəmənt] темпера́мент; **~amental** [temprə'mentl] □ темпера́ментный; **~ate** ['tempərət] □ *climate* уме́ренный; *behavio(u)r* сде́ржанный; **~ature**

T

['temprətʃə] температу́ра
**tempest** ['tempɪst] бу́ря; **~uous** □ [tem'pestʃʊəs] бу́рный (*a. fig.*)
**temple**[1] [templ] храм
**temple**[2] [~] *anat.* висо́к
**tempo** ['tempəʊ] темп
**tempor|ary** ['temprərɪ] □ вре́менный; **~ize** [~raɪz] стара́ться вы́играть вре́мя, тяну́ть вре́мя
**tempt** [tempt] искуша́ть [-уси́ть], соблазня́ть [-ни́ть]; (*attract*) привлека́ть [-е́чь]; **~ation** [temp'teɪʃn] искуше́ние, собла́зн; **~ing** ['~tɪŋ] □ зама́нчивый, соблазни́тельный
**ten** [ten] **1.** де́сять; **2.** деся́ток
**tenable** ['tenəbl]: ***not a ~ argument*** аргуме́нт, не выде́рживающий кри́тики
**tenaci|ous** [tɪ'neɪʃəs] □ це́пкий; ***~ memory*** хоро́шая па́мять *f*; **~ty** [tɪ'næsətɪ] це́пкость *f*, насто́йчивость *f*
**tenant** ['tenənt] *of land* аренда́тор; *of flat* квартира́нт
**tend** [tend] *v/i.* быть скло́нным (***to*** к Д); *v/t.* ***prices ~ to rise during the holiday season*** в пери́од отпуско́в це́ны обы́чно повыша́ются; уха́живать за (Т); присма́тривать [-мотре́ть]; *tech.* обслу́живать [-и́ть]; **~ency** ['tendənsɪ] тенде́нция; *of person* скло́нность *f*
**tender** ['tendə] **1.** □ *com.* не́жный; ***~ spot*** больно́е (уязви́мое) ме́сто; **2.** *comm.* те́ндер; **3.** предлага́ть [-ложи́ть]; *documents* представля́ть [-а́вить]; *apologies, etc.* приноси́ть [-нести́]; **~-hearted** [~'hɑːtɪd] мягкосерде́чный; **~ness** [~nɪs] не́жность *f*
**tendon** ['tendən] *anat.* сухожи́лие
**tendril** ['tendrəl] *bot.* у́сик
**tenement** ['tenəmənt]: ***~ house*** многокварти́рный дом
**tennis** ['tenɪs] те́ннис
**tenor** ['tenə] *mus.* те́нор; (*general course*) тече́ние, направле́ние; *of life* укла́д; (*purport*) о́бщий смысл
**tens|e** [tens] **1.** *gr.* вре́мя *n*; **2.** натя́нутый; *muscles, atmosphere, etc.* напряжённый; **~ion** ['tenʃn] напряже́ние; натяже́ние; *pol.* напряжённость *f*
**tent** [tent] пала́тка, шатёр
**tentacle** ['tentəkl] *zo.* щу́пальце
**tentative** ['tentətɪv] □ (*trial*) про́бный; (*provisional*) предвари́тельный
**tenterhooks** ['tentəhʊks]: ***be on ~*** сиде́ть как на иго́лках; ***keep s.o. on ~*** держа́ть кого́-л. в неизве́стности
**tenth** [tenθ] **1.** деся́тый; **2.** деся́тая часть *f*
**tenure** ['tenjʊə] пребывание в должности; пра́во владе́ния землёй; срок владе́ния
**tepid** ['tepɪd] □ теплова́тый; *fig.* прохла́дный
**term** [tɜːm] **1.** (*period*) срок; *univ.* семе́стр; *ling.* те́рмин; *school* че́тверть; ***~s*** *pl.* усло́вия; ***be on good*** (***bad***) ***~s*** быть в хоро́ших (плохи́х) отноше́ниях; ***come to ~s*** прийти́ *pf.* к соглаше́нию; **2.** (*call*) наз(ы)ва́ть; (*name*) [на]именова́ть
**termina|l** ['tɜːmɪnl] **1.** □ коне́чный; **2.** *el.* кле́мма, зажи́м; *Am. rail.* коне́чная ста́нция; ***air ~*** аэровокза́л; ***bus ~*** автовокза́л; **~te** [~neɪt] конча́ть(ся) [ко́нчить(ся)]; ***~ a contract*** расто́ргнуть *pf.* контра́кт; **~tion** [tɜːmɪ'neɪʃn] оконча́ние; коне́ц
**terminus** ['tɜːmɪnəs] *rail., bus* коне́чная ста́нция
**terrace** ['terəs] терра́са; ***~s*** *pl. sport* трибу́ны стадио́на; **~d** [~t] располо́женный терра́сами
**terrestrial** [te'restrɪəl] □ земно́й
**terrible** ['terəbl] □ ужа́сный, стра́шный
**terri|fic** [tə'rɪfɪk] (***~ally***) *coll.* потряса́ющий, великоле́пный; **~fy** ['terɪfaɪ] *v/t.* ужаса́ть [-сну́ть]
**territor|ial** [terɪ'tɔːrɪəl] □ территориа́льный; **~y** ['terətrɪ] террито́рия
**terror** ['terə] у́жас; (*violence*) терро́р; **~ize** [~raɪz] терроризова́ть (*im*)*pf.*
**terse** [tɜːs] □ (*concise*) сжа́тый
**test** [test] **1.** испыта́ние (*a. fig.*); про́ба; контро́ль *m*; *in teaching* контро́льная рабо́та; (*check*) прове́рка; *attr.* испыта́тельный; про́бный; ***nuclear ~s***

T

я́дерные испыта́ния; **2.** подверга́ть испыта́нию, прове́рке
**testament** ['testəmənt] *law* завеща́ние; ***Old*** (***New***) ♀ Ве́тхий (Но́вый) заве́т
**testify** ['testɪfaɪ] *law* дава́ть показа́ние (***to*** в по́льзу Р, ***against*** про́тив Р); свиде́тельствовать (***to*** о П)
**testimon|ial** [testɪ'məʊnɪəl] рекоменда́ция, характери́стика; **~y** ['testɪmənɪ] *law* свиде́тельские показа́ния; *fig.* свиде́тельство
**test pilot** лётчик-испыта́тель *m*
**test tube** *chem.* проби́рка
**tête-à-tête** [teɪtɑː'teɪt] с гла́зу на́ глаз
**tether** ['teðə]: ***come to the end of one's ~*** дойти́ *pf.* до ру́чки
**text** [tekst] текст; **~book** учéбник
**textile** ['tekstaɪl] **1.** тексти́льный; **2.** ***~s*** *coll.* тексти́ль *m*
**texture** ['tekstʃə] *of cloth* текстýра; *of mineral, etc.* структýра
**than** [ðæn, ðən] чем, не́жели; ***more ~ ten*** бо́льше десяти́
**thank** [θæŋk] **1.** [по]благодари́ть (В); ***~ you*** благодарю́ вас; **2.** ***~s*** *pl.* спаси́бо!; ***~s to*** благодаря́ (Д); **~ful** ['~fl] □ благода́рный; **~less** ['~lɪs] □ неблагода́рный
**that** [ðæt, ðət] **1.** *pron.* тот, та, то; те *pl.*; (*a.* э́тот *и т. д.*); кото́рый *и т. д.*; **2.** *cj.* что; чтобы
**thatch** [θætʃ]: ***~ed roof*** соло́менная кры́ша
**thaw** [θɔː] **1.** о́ттепель *f*; (*melting*) та́яние; **2.** *v/i.* [рас]та́ять; (*a.* ***~ out***) отта́ивать [отта́ять]
**the** [ðə, … ðr, … ðɪː] [ði: *перед гласными* ði, *перед согласными* ðə] **1.** *определённый артикль*; **2.** *adv.* ***~ … ~ …*** чем …, тем …
**theat|er**, *Brt.* **theatre** ['θɪətə] теа́тр; *fig.* аре́на; ***operating ~*** операцио́нная; ***~ of war*** теа́тр вое́нных де́йствий; **~rical** □ [θɪ'ætrɪkl] театра́льный (*a. fig.*); сцени́ческий
**theft** [θeft] воровство́; кра́жа
**their** [ðeə] *poss. pron.* (*от* ***they***) их; свой, своя́, своё, свои́ *pl.*; **~s** [ðeəz] *poss. pron. pred.* их, свой *и т.д*
**them** [ðəm, ðem] *pron.* (*косвенный падеж от* ***they***) их, им
**theme** [θiːm] те́ма
**themselves** [ðəm'selvz] *pron. refl.* себя́, -ся; *emphatic* са́ми
**then** [ðen] **1.** *adv.* тогда́; пото́м, зате́м; ***from ~ on*** с тех пор; ***by ~*** к томý вре́мени; **2.** *cj.* тогда́, в тако́м слу́чае; зна́чит; **3.** *adj.* тогда́шний
**thence** *lit* [ðens] оттýда; с того́ вре́мени; *fig.* отсю́да, из э́того
**theology** [θɪ'ɒlədʒɪ] богосло́вие
**theor|etic(al)** □ [θɪə'retɪk(l)] теорети́ческий; **~ist** ['θɪərɪst] теоре́тик; **~y** ['θɪərɪ] тео́рия
**there** [ðeə] там, тудá; ***~!*** (ну) вот!; ***~ she is*** вон она́; ***~ is, ~ are*** [ðə'riz, ðə'raː] есть, име́ется, име́ются; **~about(s)** [ðeərə'baʊt(s)] побли́зости; (*approximately*) о́коло э́того, приблизи́тельно; **~after** [ðeər'ɑːftə] по́сле того́; **~by** ['ðeə'baɪ] посре́дством э́того, таки́м о́бразом; **~fore** ['ðeəfɔː] поэ́тому; сле́довательно; **~upon** ['ðeərə'pɒn] сра́зу же; тут; всле́дствие того́
**thermo|meter** [θə'mɒmɪtə] термо́метр, гра́дусник; **~nuclear** [θɜːməʊ'njʊklɪə] термоя́дерный; **~s** ['θɜːməs] (*or* ***~ flask***) те́рмос
**these** [ðiːz] *pl. от* ***this***
**thes|is** ['θiːsɪs], *pl.* **~es** [~siːz] те́зис; диссерта́ция
**they** [ðeɪ] *pers. pron.* они́
**thick** [θɪk] **1.** □ *com.* то́лстый; *fog, hair, etc.* густо́й; *voice* хри́плый; *coll.* (*stupid*) глу́пый; ***that's a bit ~*** э́то уж сли́шком; **2.** *fig.* гу́ща; ***in the ~ of*** в са́мой гу́ще Р; **~en** ['θɪkən] утолща́ть(ся) [утолсти́ть(ся)]; *of darkness, fog, etc.* сгуща́ть(ся) [сгусти́ть(ся)]; **~et** ['θɪkɪt] ча́ща; *of bushes* за́росли *f/pl.*; **~-headed** тупоголо́вый, тупоу́мный; **~ness** ['θɪknɪs] толщина́; (*density*) густота́; **~set** [θɪk'set] *person* корена́стый; **~-skinned** (*a. fig.*) толстоко́жий
**thie|f** [θiːf], *pl.* **~ves** [θiːvz] вор; **~ve** [θiːv] *v/i.* ворова́ть
**thigh** [θaɪ] бедро́

T

**thimble** ['θɪmbl] напёрсток
**thin** [θɪn] **1.** □ *com*. то́нкий; *person* худо́й, худоща́вый; *hair* ре́дкий; *soup* жи́дкий; **2.** де́лать(ся) то́нким, утонча́ть(ся) [-чи́ть(ся)]; [по]реде́ть; [по]худе́ть
**thing** [θɪŋ] вещь *f*; предме́т; де́ло; **~s** *pl*. (*belongings*) ве́щи *f/pl*.; (*luggage*) бага́ж; (*clothes*) оде́жда; *for painting, etc*. принадле́жности *f/pl*.; ***the ~ is that*** де́ло в том, что ...; ***the very ~*** как раз то, что ну́жно; ***~s are getting better*** положе́ние улучша́ется
**think** [θɪŋk] [*irr*.] *v/i*. [по]ду́мать (***of, about*** о П); *abstractly* мы́слить; (*presume*) полага́ть; (*remember*) вспомина́ть [вспо́мнить] (***of*** о П); (*intend*) намерева́ться (+ *inf*.); (*devise*) приду́м(ыв)ать (***of*** В); *v/t*. счита́ть [счесть]; ***~ a lot of*** высоко́ цени́ть; быть высо́кого мне́ния о (П)
**third** [θɜːd] **1.** тре́тий; **2.** треть *f*
**thirst** [θɜːst] **1.** жа́жда (*a. fig*.); **2.** жа́ждать (***for, after*** Р) (*part. fig*.); **~y** ['~ɪ]: ***I am ~*** я хочу́ пить
**thirt|een** [θɜː'tiːn] трина́дцать; **~eenth** [θɜː'tiːnθ] трина́дцатый; **~ieth** ['θɜːtɪɪθ] тридца́тый; **~y** ['θɜːtɪ] три́дцать
**this** [ðɪs] *demonstrative pron*. (*pl*. ***these***) э́тот, э́та, э́то; э́ти *pl*.; ***~ morning*** сего́дня у́тром; ***one of these days*** как-нибу́дь, когда́-нибудь
**thistle** ['θɪsl] чертополо́х
**thorn** [θɔːn] *bot*. шип, колю́чка; **~y** ['θɔːnɪ] колю́чий; *fig*. тяжёлый, терни́стый
**thorough** ['θʌrə] □ основа́тельный, тща́тельный; (*detailed*) дета́льный, подро́бный; **~ly** *adv*. основа́тельно, доскона́льно; **~bred** чистокро́вный; **~fare** у́лица, магистра́ль *f*; "***No ~***" "Прое́зда нет"
**those** [ðəʊz] *pl*. *om* ***that***
**though** [ðəʊ] *conj*. хотя́; да́же е́сли бы, хотя́ бы; *adv*. тем не ме́нее, одна́ко; всё-таки; ***as ~*** как бу́дто, сло́вно
**thought** [θɔːt] **1.** *pt*. *u pt*. *p*. *om* ***think***; **2.** мысль *f*; мышле́ние; (*contemplation*) размышле́ние; (*care*) забо́та; внима́тельность *f*; **~ful** ['θɔːtfl] □ заду́мчивый; (*considerate*) забо́тливый; внима́тельный (***of*** к Д); **~less** ['θɔːtlɪs] □ (*careless*) беспе́чный; необду́манный; невнима́тельный (***of*** к Д)
**thousand** ['θaʊznd] ты́сяча; **~th** ['θaʊznθ] **1.** ты́сячный; **2.** ты́сячная часть *f*
**thrash** [θræʃ] [вы́]поро́ть; избива́ть [-би́ть]; *fig*. (*defeat*) побежда́ть [-еди́ть]; ***~ out*** тща́тельно обсужда́ть [-уди́ть]; **~ing** ['θræʃɪŋ]: ***give s.o. a good ~*** основа́тельно поколоти́ть *pf*. кого́-л.
**thread** [θred] **1.** ни́тка, нить *f*; *fig*. нить *f*; *of a screw, etc*. резьба́; **2.** *needle* продева́ть ни́тку в (В); *beads* нани́зывать [-за́ть]; **~bare** ['θredbeə] потёртый, изно́шенный; потрёпанный; *fig*. (*hackneyed*) изби́тый
**threat** [θret] угро́за; **~en** ['θretn] *v/t*. (при)грози́ть, угрожа́ть (Д ***with*** Т); *v/i*. грози́ть
**three** [θriː] **1.** три; **2.** тро́йка → ***five***; **~fold** ['θriːfəʊld] тройно́й; *adv*. втройне́; **~-ply** трёхслойный
**thresh** [θreʃ] *agric*. обмолоти́ть *pf*.
**threshold** ['θreʃhəʊld] поро́г
**threw** [θruː] *pt*. *om* ***throw***
**thrice** [θraɪs] три́жды
**thrift** [θrɪft] бережли́вость *f*, эконо́мность *f*; **~y** ['θrɪftɪ] □ эконо́мный, бережли́вый
**thrill** [θrɪl] **1.** *v/t*. [вз]волнова́ть; приводи́ть в тре́пет, [вз]будора́жить; *v/i*. (за)трепета́ть (***with*** от Р); [вз]волнова́ться; **2.** тре́пет; глубо́кое волне́ние; не́рвная дрожь *f*; **~er** ['θrɪlə] детекти́вный *or* приключе́нческий рома́н *or* фильм, три́ллер; **~ing** ['θrɪlɪŋ] захва́тывающий; *news* потряса́ющий
**thrive** [θraɪv] [*irr*.] *of business* процвета́ть; *of person* преуспева́ть; *of plants* разраста́ться; **~n** ['θrɪvn] *pt*. *p*. *om* ***thrive***
**throat** [θrəʊt] го́рло; ***clear one's ~*** отка́шливаться [-ляться]
**throb** [θrɒb] **1.** пульси́ровать; си́льно би́ться; **2.** пульса́ция; бие́ние, *fig*. тре́пет

**throes** [θrəʊz]: ***be in the ~ of*** в хо́де, в проце́ссе
**throne** [θrəʊn] трон, престо́л
**throng** [θrɒŋ] **1.** толпа́; **2.** [с]толпи́ться; (*fill*) заполня́ть [-о́лнить]; ***people ~ed to the square*** наро́д толпо́й вали́л на пло́щадь *f*
**throttle** ['θrɒtl] (*choke*) [за]души́ть; (*regulate*) дроссели́ровать
**through** [θru:] **1.** че́рез (В); сквозь (В); по (Д); *adv.* наскво́зь; от нача́ла до конца́; **2.** *train*, *etc.* прямо́й; ***be ~ with s.o.*** порва́ть с ке́м-л.; ***put ~*** *tel.* соедини́ть *pf.* (с Т); **~out** [θru:'aʊt] **1.** *prp.* че́рез (В); по всему́, всей ...; **2.** повсю́ду; во всех отноше́ниях
**throve** [θrəʊv] *pt. om* ***thrive***
**throw** [θrəʊ] **1.** [*irr.*] броса́ть [бро́сить], кида́ть [ки́нуть]; *discus*, *etc.* мета́ть [метну́ть]; **~ *away*** выбра́сывать ['-росить]; (*forgo*) упуска́ть [-сти́ть]; **~ *over*** перебра́сывать [-бро́сить]; **~ *light on s.th.*** пролива́ть [-ли́ть] свет на (В); **2.** бросо́к; броса́ние; **~n** [~n] *pt. p. om* ***throw***
**thru** *Am.* = ***through***
**thrush** [θrʌʃ] дрозд
**thrust** [θrʌst] **1.** толчо́к; *mil.* уда́р; **2.** [*irr.*] (*push*) толка́ть [-кну́ть]; (*poke*) ты́кать [ткнуть]; **~ *o.s. into*** *fig.* втира́ться [втере́ться] в (В); **~ *upon a p.*** навя́зывать [-за́ть] (Д)
**thud** [θʌd] глухо́й звук *or* стук
**thug** [θʌg] головоре́з
**thumb** [θʌm] **1.** большо́й па́лец (руки́); **2.** *book* перели́стывать [-ста́ть]; **~ *a lift*** *coll.* голосова́ть (на доро́ге)
**thump** [θʌmp] **1.** глухо́й стук; тяжёлый уда́р; **2.** стуча́ть [-у́кнуть]
**thunder** ['θʌndə] **1.** гром; **2.** [за]греме́ть; *fig.* мета́ть гро́мы и мо́лнии; **~bolt** уда́р мо́лнии; **~clap** уда́р гро́ма; **~ous** ['θʌndərəs] □ (*very loud*) громово́й, оглуша́ющий; **~storm** гроза́; **~struck** *fig.* как гро́мом поражённый
**Thursday** ['θɜ:zdɪ] четве́рг
**thus** [ðʌs] так, таки́м о́бразом
**thwart** [θwɔ:t] *plans*, *etc.* меша́ть, расстра́ивать [-ро́ить]; ***be ~ed at every turn*** встреча́ть препя́тствия на ка́ждом шагу́
**tick**¹ [tɪk] *zo.* клещ
**tick**² [~] **1.** *of clock* ти́канье; **2.** *v/i.* ти́кать
**tick**³ [~] *mark* га́лочка; **~ *off*** отмеча́ть га́лочкой
**ticket** ['tɪkɪt] **1.** биле́т; ***price ~*** этике́тка с ценой́; ***cloakroom ~*** номеро́к; ***round trip*** (*Brt.* ***return***) **~** обра́тный биле́т; **~ *office*** биле́тная ка́сса
**tickl|e** ['tɪkl] (по)щекота́ть; **~ish** [~ɪʃ] □ *fig.* щекотли́вый
**tidal** ['taɪdl]: **~ *wave*** прили́вная волна́
**tidbit** [tɪdbɪt], *Brt.* **titbit** ['tɪtbɪt] ла́комый кусо́чек; *fig.* пика́нтная но́вость *f*
**tide** [taɪd] **1.** ***low ~*** отли́в; ***high ~*** прили́в; *fig.* те́чение; направле́ние; **2.** *fig.* **~ *over*: *will this ~ you over till Monday?*** Э́то вам хва́тит до понеде́льника?
**tidy** ['taɪdɪ] **1.** опря́тный; аккура́тный; *sum* значи́тельный; **2.** уб(и)ра́ть; приводи́ть в поря́док
**tie** [taɪ] **1.** га́лстук; *sport* ничья́; **~s** *pl.* (*bonds*) у́зы *f/pl.*; **2.** *v/t. knot*, *etc.* завя́зывать [-за́ть]; *together* свя́зывать [-за́ть]; *v/i.* сыгра́ть *pf.* вничью́
**tier** [tɪə] я́рус
**tiff** [tɪf] *coll.* размо́лвка
**tiger** ['taɪgə] тигр
**tight** [taɪt] □ туго́й; туго натя́нутый; (*fitting too closely*) те́сный; *coll.* (*drunk*) подвы́пивший; *coll.* **~ *spot*** *fig.* затрудни́тельное положе́ние; **~en** ['taɪtn] стя́гивать(ся) [стяну́ть(ся)] (*a.* **~ *up***); *belt*, *etc.* затя́гивать [-яну́ть]; *screw* подтя́гивать [-яну́ть]; **~-fisted** скупо́й; **~s** [taɪts] *pl.* колго́тки
**tigress** ['taɪgrɪs] тигри́ца
**tile** [taɪl] **1.** *for roof* черепи́ца; *for walls*, *etc.* облицо́вочная пли́тка, *decorative* изразе́ц; **2.** покрыва́ть черепи́цей; облицо́вывать пли́ткой
**till**¹ [tɪl] ка́сса
**till**² [~] **1.** *prp.* до Р+; **2.** *cj.* пока́
**till**³ [~] *agric.* возде́л(ыв)ать (В); [вс]паха́ть
**tilt** [tɪlt] **1.** накло́нное положе́ние, на-

клóн; ***at full ~*** на пóлной скóрости; **2.** наклоня́ть(ся) [-ни́ть(ся)]
**timber** ['tɪmbə] лесоматериáл, строевóй лес
**time** [taɪm] **1.** *com.* врéмя *n*; (*suitable ~*) порá; (*term*) срок; ***at the same ~*** в то же врéмя; ***beat ~*** отбивáть такт; ***for the ~ being*** покá, на врéмя; ***in*** (*or* ***on***) ~ вóвремя; ***next ~*** в слéдующий раз; ***what's the ~?*** котóрый час?; **2.** (удáчно) выбирáть врéмя для P; **~ limit** предéльный срок; **~r** ['taɪmə] тáймер; **~ly** ['taɪmlɪ] своеврéменный; **~-saving** экономя́щий врéмя; **~table** *rail* расписáние
**timid** ['tɪmɪd] □ рóбкий
**tin** [tɪn] **1.** óлово; (*container*) консéрвная бáнка; **2.** консерви́ровать
**tinfoil** ['tɪnfɔɪl] фольгá
**tinge** [tɪndʒ] **1.** слегкá окрáшивать; *fig.* придавáть оттéнок (Д); **2.** лёгкая окрáска; *fig.* оттéнок
**tingle** ['tɪŋgl] испы́тывать *или* вызывáть покáлывание (в онемéвших конéчностях), пощи́пывание (на морóзе), звон в ушáх *и т. п.*
**tinker** ['tɪŋkə] вози́ться (***with*** с Т)
**tinkle** ['tɪŋkl] звя́кать [-кнуть]
**tin|ned** [tɪnd] консерви́рованный; **~ opener** консéрвный нож
**tinsel** ['tɪnsl] мишурá
**tint** [tɪnt] **1.** крáска; (*shade*) оттéнок; **2.** слегкá окрáшивать; *hair* подкрáшивать
**tiny** ['taɪnɪ] □ óчень мáленький, крóшечный
**tip**[1] [tɪp] (тóнкий) конéц, наконéчник; *of finger, etc.* кóнчик
**tip**[2] [~] **1.** информáция; (*hint*) намёк; (*advice*) рекомендáция, оснóванная на малодоступной информáции; **2.** давáть на чай (Д); давáть информáцию (Д), рекомендáцию
**tip**[3] [~] опроки́дывать [-и́нуть]
**tipple** ['tɪpl] *coll.* вы́пи(вá)ть, пить
**tipsy** ['tɪpsɪ] подвы́пивший
**tiptoe** ['tɪptəʊ]: ***on ~*** на цы́почках
**tire**[1] (*Brt.* ***tyre***) ши́на; ***flat ~*** спýщенная ши́на
**tire**[2] [taɪə] утомля́ть [-ми́ть]; устá(вá)ть; **~d** [~d] устáлый; **~less** ['~lɪs] неутоми́мый; **~some** ['~səm] утоми́тельный; (*pesky*) надоéдливый; (*boring*) скýчный
**tissue** ['tɪʃuː] ткань *f* (*a. biol.*); **~ paper** папирóсная бумáга
**title** ['taɪtl] заглáвие, назвáние; (*person's status*) ти́тул; звáние; **~ holder** *sport* чемпиóн; **~ page** ти́тульный лист
**titter** ['tɪtə] **1.** хихи́канье; **2.** хихи́кать [-кнуть]
**tittle-tattle** ['tɪtltætl] сплéтни *f/pl.*, болтовня́
**to** [tə, … tʊ, … tuː] *prp. indicating direction, aim* к (Д); в (В); на (В); *introducing indirect object, corresponds to the Russian dative case*: **~ *me*** *etc.* мне *и т. д.*; ***~ and fro*** *adv.* взад и вперёд; *показатель инфинитива*: ***~ work*** рабóтать; ***I weep ~ think of it*** я плáчу, дýмая об э́том
**toad** [təʊd] жáба; **~stool** погáнка
**toast** [təʊst] **1.** грéнок; (*drink*) тост; **2.** дéлать грéнки; поджáри(ва)ть; *fig.* (*warm o.s.*) грéть(ся); пить за (В); **~er** [~ə] тóстер
**tobacco** [tə'bækəʊ] табáк; **~nist's** [tə'bækənɪsts] табáчный магази́н
**toboggan** [tə'bɒgən] **1.** сáни *f/pl.*; *children's* сáнки; **2.** катáться на саня́х, сáнках
**today** [tə'deɪ] сегóдня; настоя́щее врéмя; ***from ~*** с сегóдняшнего дня; ***a month ~*** чéрез мéсяц
**toe** [təʊ] пáлец (на ногé); *of boot, sock* носóк
**toffee** ['tɒfɪ] ири́ска; *soft* тянýчка
**together** [tə'geðə] вмéсте
**togs** [tɒgs] *pl. coll.* одéжда
**toil** [tɔɪl] **1.** тяжёлый труд; **2.** уси́ленно труди́ться; тащи́ться, идти́ с трудóм
**toilet** ['tɔɪlɪt] туалéт; **~ paper** туалéтная бумáга
**token** ['təʊkən] знак; ***as a ~ of*** в знак чегó-то; ***~ payment*** символи́ческая плáта
**told** [təʊld] *pt. и pt. p. от* ***tell***
**tolera|ble** ['tɒlərəbl] □ терпи́мый; (*fairly good*) снóсный; **~nce** [~rəns]

T

терпи́мость *f*; **~nt** [-rənt] □ терпи́мый; **~te** [-reɪt] [вы-, по]терпе́ть, допуска́ть [-сти́ть]
**toll** [təʊl] (*tax*) по́шлина, сбо́р; *fig*. дань *f*; **~gate** ме́сто, где взима́ются сбо́ры; заста́ва
**tom** [tɒm]: **~ *cat*** кот
**tomato** [tə'mɑːtəʊ], *pl*. **~es** [~z] помидо́р, тома́т
**tomb** [tuːm] моги́ла
**tomboy** ['tɒmbɔɪ] сорване́ц (о де́вочке)
**tomfoolery** [tɒm'fuːlərɪ] дура́чество
**tomorrow** [tə'mɒrəʊ] за́втра
**ton** [tʌn] *metric* то́нна
**tone** [təʊn] **1.** *mus*., *paint*., *fig*. тон; интона́ция; **2.**: **~ *down*** смягча́ть(ся) [-чи́ть]; **~ *in with*** гармони́ровать (с Т)
**tongs** [tɒŋz] *pl*. щипцы́ *m/pl*., кле́щи, *a*. клещи́ *f/pl*.
**tongue** [tʌŋ] язы́к; ***hold your ~!*** молчи́(те)!
**tonic** ['tɒnɪk] *med*. тонизи́рующее сре́дство; **~ water** то́ник
**tonight** [tə'naɪt] сего́дня ве́чером
**tonnage**['tʌnɪdʒ]*naut*.тонна́ж; (*freight carrying capacity*) грузоподъёмность *f*; (*duty*) тонна́жный сбор
**tonsil** ['tɒnsl] *anat*. гла́нда, минда́лина
**too** [tuː] та́кже, то́же; *of degree* сли́шком; о́чень; (*moreover*) бо́лее того́; к тому́ же; ***there was ground frost last night, and in June ~!*** вчера́ но́чью – за́морозки на по́чве, и э́то ию́не!
**took** [tʊk] *pt*. *om* ***take***
**tool** [tuːl] (рабо́чий) инструме́нт; *fig*. ору́дие
**toot** [tuːt] **1.** гудо́к; **2.** дать гудо́к; *mot*. просигна́ли(зи́рова)ть
**tooth** [tuːθ] (*pl*. **teeth**) зуб; **~ache** зубна́я боль *f*, **~brush** зубна́я щётка; **~less** ['tuːθlɪs] □ беззу́бый; **~paste** зубна́я па́ста
**top** [tɒp] **1.** ве́рхняя часть *f*; верх; *of mountain* верши́на; *of head*, *tree* маку́шка; (*lid*) кры́шка; *leafy top of root vegetable* ботва́; ***at the ~ of one's voice*** во весь го́лос; ***on ~*** наверху́; ***on ~ of all this*** в доверше́ние всего́; в доба́вок ко всему́; **2.** вы́сший, пе́рвый; *speed*, *etc*. максима́льный; **3.** (*cover*) покры́(-ва́)ть; *fig*. (*surpass*) превыша́ть [-ы́сить]
**topic** ['tɒpɪk] те́ма; ***~al*** [~kl] актуа́льный, злободне́вный
**top-level**: **~ *negotiations*** перегово́ры на вы́сшем у́ровне
**topple** ['tɒpl] [с]вали́ть; опроки́дывать(ся) [-и́нуть(ся)] (*a*. **~ *over***)
**topsy-turvy** ['tɒpsɪ'tɜːvɪ] □ (перевёрнутый) вверх дном
**torch** [tɔːtʃ] фа́кел; ***electric ~*** электри́ческий фона́рь *m*; *chiefly Brt*. (*flashlight*) карма́нный фона́рик
**tore** [tɔː] *pt*. *om* ***tear***
**torment** **1.** ['tɔːment] муче́ние, му́ка; **2.** [tɔː'ment] [из-, за]му́чить
**torn** [tɔːn] *pt*. *p*. *om* ***tear***
**tornado** [tɔː'neɪdəʊ] торна́до (*indecl*.); смерчь *m*; (*hurricane*) урага́н
**torpedo** [tɔː'piːdəʊ] **1.** торпе́да; **2.** торпеди́ровать (*im*)*pf*. (*a. fig*.)
**torpid** ['tɔːpɪd] □ (*inactive*, *slow*) вя́лый, апати́чный
**torrent** ['tɒrənt] пото́к (*a*. *fig*.)
**torrid** ['tɒrɪd] жа́ркий, зно́йный
**tortoise** ['tɔːtəs] *zo*. черепа́ха
**tortuous** ['tɔːtʃʊəs] (*winding*) изви́листый; *fig*. (*devious*) укло́нчивый, неи́скренний
**torture** ['tɔːtʃə] **1.** пы́тка (*a*. *fig*.); **2.** пыта́ть; [из-, за]му́чить
**toss** [tɒs] (*fling*) броса́ть [бро́сить]; *in bed* беспоко́йно мета́ться; *head* вски́дывать [-и́нуть]; *coin* подбра́сывать [-ро́сить] (*mst*. **~ *up***)
**tot** [tɒt] (*child*) малы́ш
**total** ['təʊtl] **1.** □ (*complete*) по́лный, абсолю́тный; *war* тота́льный; *number* о́бщий; **2.** су́мма; ито́г; ***in ~*** в ито́ге; **3.** подводи́ть ито́г, подсчи́тывать [-ита́ть]; (*amount to*) составля́ть в ито́ге; (*equal*) равня́ться (Д); **~itarian** [təʊtælɪ'teərɪən] тоталита́рный; **~ly** [~lɪ] по́лностью, соверше́нно
**totter** ['tɒtə] идти́ нетвёрдой похо́дкой; (*shake*) шата́ться [(по)шатну́ться]; (*be about to fall*) разруша́ться
**touch** [tʌtʃ] **1.** (*sense*) осяза́ние; (*con-

*tact*) прикоснове́ние; *fig.* конта́кт, связь *f*; ***a ~*** (*a little*) чу́точка; (*a trace*) при́месь *f*; *of illness* лёгкий при́ступ; штрих; **2.** тро́гать [тро́нуть] (В) (*a. fig.*); прикаса́ться [-косну́ться], притра́гиваться [-тро́нуться] к (Д); *fig. subject, etc.* каса́ться [косну́ться] (Р); затра́гивать [-ро́нуть]; ***be ~ed*** *fig.* быть тро́нутым; ***~ up*** подправля́ть [-а́вить]; **~ing** ['tʌtʃɪŋ] тро́гательный; **~y** ['tʌtʃɪ] □ оби́дчивый

**tough** [tʌf] **1.** *meat, etc.* жёсткий (*a. fig.*); (*strong*) про́чный; *person* выно́сливый; *job, etc.* тру́дный; **2.** хулига́н; **~en** ['tʌfn] де́лать(ся) жёстким

**tour** [tʊə] **1.** пое́здка, экску́рсия, тур; *sport, thea.* турне́ *n indecl.*; *a. thea.* гастро́ли *f/pl.*; **2.** соверша́ть путеше́ствие *или* турне́ по (Д); путеше́ствовать (***through*** по Д); гастроли́ровать; **~ist** ['tʊərɪst] тури́ст *m*, -ка *f*; ***~ agency*** туристи́ческое аге́нтство

**tournament** ['tʊənəmənt] турни́р

**tousle** ['taʊzl] взъеро́ши(ва)ть, растрёпывать (-репа́ть)

**tow** [təʊ] *naut* **1.** букси́р; ***take in ~*** брать на букси́р; ***with all her kids in ~*** со все́ми детьми́; **2.** букси́ровать

**toward(s)** [tə'wɔːdz, twɔːdʒ] *prp.* (*direction*) по направле́нию к (Д); (*relation*) к (Д), по отноше́нию к (Д); (*purpose*) для (Р), на (В)

**towel** ['taʊəl] полоте́нце

**tower** ['taʊə] **1.** ба́шня; **2.** возвыша́ться (***above, over*** над Т) (*a. fig.*)

**town** [taʊn] **1.** го́род; **2.** *attr.* городско́й; ***~ council*** городско́й сове́т; ***~ hall*** ра́туша; **~ dweller** горожа́нин *m*, -нка *f*; **~sfolk** ['taʊnzfəʊk], **~speople** ['taʊnzpiːpl] *pl.* горожа́не *m/pl.*

**toxic** ['tɒksɪk] токси́ческий

**toy** [tɔɪ] **1.** игру́шка; **2.** *attr.* игру́шечный; **3.** игра́ть, забавля́ться; ***~ with*** (*consider*) поду́мывать

**trace** [treɪs] **1.** след; (*very small quantity*) следы́, незначи́тельное коли́чество; **2.** (*draw*) [на]черти́ть; (*locate*) высле́живать [вы́следить] (В); (*follow*) просле́живать [-еди́ть] (В)

**track** [træk] **1.** след; (*rough road*) просёлочная доро́га; (*path*) тропи́нка; *for running* бегова́я доро́жка; *for motor racing* трек; *rail* колея́; ***be on the right*** (***wrong***) ***~*** быть на пра́вильном (ло́жном) пути́; **2.** следи́ть за (Т); просле́живать [-еди́ть] (В); ***~ down*** высле́живать [вы́следить] (В)

**tract** [trækt] простра́нство, полоса́ земли́; *anat.* тракт; ***respiratory ~*** дыха́тельные пути́

**tractable** ['træktəbl] *person* сгово́рчивый

**tract|ion** ['trækʃn] тя́га; ***~ engine*** тяга́ч; **~or** ['træktə] тра́ктор

**trade** [treɪd] **1.** профе́ссия; ремесло́; торго́вля; **2.** торгова́ть (***in*** Т; ***with*** с Т); (*exchange*) обме́нивать [-ня́ть] (***for*** на В); ***~ on*** испо́льзовать (*im*)*pf.*; **~mark** фабри́чная ма́рка; **~r** ['treɪdə] торго́вец; **~sman** ['treɪdzmən] торго́вец; (*shopkeeper*) владе́лец магази́на; **~(s) union** [treɪd(z)'juːnɪən] профсою́з

**tradition** [trə'dɪʃn] (*custom*) тради́ция, обы́чай; (*legend*) преда́ние; **~al** [-ʃənl] □ традицио́нный

**traffic** [træfɪk] **1.** движе́ние (у́личное, железнодоро́жное *и т. д.*); (*vehicles*) тра́нспорт; (*trading*) торго́вля; ***~ jam*** зато́р у́личного движе́ния; **~ lights** *pl.* светофо́р; **~ police** ГАИ (госуда́рственная автомоби́льная инспе́кция)

**tragedy** ['trædʒədɪ] траге́дия

**tragic(al)** □ ['trædʒɪk(l)] траги́ческий, траги́чный

**trail** [treɪl] **1.** след; (*path*) тропа́; **2.** *v/t.* (*pull*) тащи́ть, волочи́ть; (*track*) идти́ по сле́ду (Р); *v/i.* тащи́ться, волочи́ться; *bot.* ви́ться; **~er** ['treɪlə] *mot.* прице́п, тре́йлер

**train** [treɪn] **1.** по́езд; (*retinue*) сви́та; *film star's* толпа́ (покло́нников); ***by ~*** по́ездом; ***freight ~*** това́рный соста́в; ***suburban ~*** при́городный по́езд, *coll.* электри́чка; ***~ of thought*** ход мы́слей; **2.** (*bring up*) воспи́тывать [-та́ть]; приуча́ть [-чи́ть]; (*coach*) [на]тренирова́ть(ся); обуча́ть [-чи́ть]; *lions, etc.* [вы́]дрессирова́ть

**trait** [treɪt] (характе́рная) черта́
**traitor** ['treɪtə] преда́тель *m*, изме́нник
**tram** [træm], **~car** ['træmkɑː] трамва́й, ваго́н трамва́я
**tramp** [træmp] **1.** (*vagrant*) бродя́га *m*; (*hike*) путеше́ствие пешко́м; *of feet* то́пот; звук тяжёлых шаго́в; **2.** тяжело́ ступа́ть; тащи́ться с трудо́м; то́пать; броди́ть; **~le** ['træmpl] (*crush underfoot*) топта́ть; тяжело́ ступа́ть; **~ down** зата́птывать [-топта́ть]
**trance** [trɑːns] транс
**tranquil** ['træŋkwɪl] □ споко́йный; **~(l)ity** [træŋ'kwɪlətɪ] споко́йствие; **~(l)ize** ['træŋkwɪlaɪz] успока́ивать(ся) [-ко́ить(ся)]; **~(l)izer** ['træŋkwɪlaɪzə] транквилиза́тор
**transact** [træn'zækt] заключа́ть [-чи́ть] сде́лку, вести́ дела́ с (Т); **~ion** [~'zækʃn] сде́лка; **~s** *pl*. (*proceedings*) труды́ *m/pl*. нау́чного о́бщества
**transatlantic** [trænzət'læntɪk] трансатланти́ческий
**transcend** [træn'send] выходи́ть [вы́йти] за преде́лы; *expectations*, *etc*. превосходи́ть [-взойти́], превыша́ть [-ы́сить]
**transfer 1.** [træns'fɜː] *v/t*. переноси́ть [-нести́], перемеща́ть [-мести́ть]; *ownership* перед(ав)а́ть; *to another job*, *town*, *team*, *etc*. переводи́ть [-вести́]; *v/i*. *Am*., *of passengers* переса́живаться [-се́сть]; **2.** ['trænsfɜː] перено́с; переда́ча; *comm*. трансфе́рт; перево́д; *Am*. переса́дка; **~able** [træns'fɜːrəbl] с пра́вом переда́чи; переводи́мый
**transfigure** [træns'fɪgə] видоизменя́ть [-ни́ть]; *with joy*, *etc*. преобража́ть [-рази́ть]
**transfixed** [træns'fɪkst]: **~ with fear** ско́ванный стра́хом
**transform** [træns'fɔːm] превраща́ть [-врати́ть]; преобразо́вывать [-зова́ть]; **~ation** [~fə'meɪʃn] преобразова́ние; превраще́ние; **~er** [~'fɔːmə] трансформа́тор
**transfusion** [træns'fjuːʒn]: **blood ~** перелива́ние кро́ви
**transgress** [trænz'gres] *v/t*. *law*, *etc*. преступа́ть [-пи́ть]; *agreement* наруша́ть [-у́шить]; *v/i*. (*sin*) [со]греши́ть; **~ion** [~'greʃn] просту́пок; *of law*, *etc*. наруше́ние
**transient** ['trænzɪənt] → ***transitory***; *Am*., *a*. (*temporary guest/lodger*) вре́менный жиле́ц; челове́к/скита́лец, и́щущий себе рабо́ту
**transit** ['trænzɪt] прое́зд; *of goods* перево́зка; транзи́т; **he is here in ~** он здесь прое́здом
**transition** [træn'zɪʃn] перехо́д; перехо́дный пери́од
**transitory** ['trænsɪtrɪ] □ мимолётный; преходя́щий
**translat|e** [træns'leɪt] переводи́ть [-вести́] (**from** с Р, **into** на В); *fig*. (*interpret*) [ис]толкова́ть; объясня́ть [-ни́ть]; **~ion** [~'leɪʃn] перево́д; **~or** [~leɪtə] перево́дчик *m*, -чица *f*
**translucent** [trænz'luːsnt] полупрозра́чный
**transmission** [trænz'mɪʃn] переда́ча (*a. radio & tech.*); *radio*, *TV* трансля́ция
**transmit** [trænz'mɪt] перед(ав)а́ть (*a. radio*, *TV*, *a.* трансли́ровать); *heat* проводи́ть *impf*.; **~ter** [~ə] переда́тчик (*a. radio*, *TV*)
**transparent** [træns'pærənt] □ прозра́чный (*a. fig.*)
**transpire** [træn'spaɪə] *fig*. вы́ясниться *pf*., оказа́ться *pf*.; *coll*. случа́ться [-чи́ться]
**transplant** [træns'plɑːnt] **1.** переса́живать [-сади́ть]; *fig*. *people* переселя́ть [-ли́ть]; **2.** ['trænsplɑːnt] *med*. переса́дка
**transport 1.** [træn'spɔːt] перевози́ть [-везти́]; транспорти́ровать *im*(*pf*.); *fig*. увлека́ть [-е́чь]; восхища́ть [-ити́ть]; **2.** ['trænspɔːt] тра́нспорт; перево́зка; *of joy*, *delight*, *etc*. **be in ~s** быть вне себя́ (**of** от Р); **~ation** [trænspɔː'teɪʃn] перево́зка, транспортиро́вка
**transverse** ['trænzvɜːs] □ попере́чный; **~ly** поперёк

**trap** [træp] **1.** лову́шка, западня́ (*a. fig.*); капка́н; **2.** *fig.* (*lure*) замани́ть *pf.* в лову́шку; ***fall into a ~*** попа́сть *pf.* в лову́шку; (*fall for the bait*) попа́сться *pf.* на у́дочку; **~door** опускна́я дверь *f*

**trapeze** [trəˈpiːz] трапе́ция

**trappings** [ˈtræpɪŋz] *pl.* (*harness*) сбру́я; *fig.* ***the ~ of office*** вне́шние атрибу́ты служе́бного положе́ния

**trash** [træʃ] хлам; (*waste food*) отбро́сы *m/pl.*; *fig.* дрянь *f*; *book* макулату́ра; (*nonsense*) вздор, ерунда́; **~y** [ˈtræʃɪ] □ дрянно́й

**travel** [ˈtrævl] **1.** *v/i.* путеше́ствовать; е́здить, [по]е́хать; (*move*) передвига́ться [-и́нуться]; *of light, sound* распространя́ться (-ни́ться); *v/t.* объезжа́ть [-е́здить, -е́хать]; проезжа́ть [-е́хать] (… *км в час и т. п.*); **2.** путеше́ствие; *tech.* ход; (пере)движе́ние; **~(l)er** [~ə] путеше́ственник *m*, -ица *f*

**traverse** [trəˈvɜːs] **1.** пересека́ть [-се́чь]; (*pass through*) проходи́ть [пройти́] (В); **2.** попере́чина

**travesty** [ˈtrævəstɪ] паро́дия

**trawler** [ˈtrɔːlə] тра́улер

**tray** [treɪ] подно́с

**treacher|ous** [ˈtretʃərəs] □ (*disloyal*) преда́тельский, вероло́мный; (*unreliable*) ненадёжный; **~ *weather*** кова́рная пого́да; **~y** [~rɪ] преда́тельство, вероло́мство

**treacle** [ˈtriːkl] па́тока; (*chiefly Brt., molasses*) мела́сса

**tread** [tred] **1.** [*irr.*] ступа́ть [-пи́ть]; ***~ down*** зата́птывать [затопта́ть]; ***~ lightly*** *fig.* де́йствовать осторо́жно, такти́чно; **2.** по́ступь *f*, похо́дка; *of stairs* ступе́нька; *of tire*, *Brt. tyre* проте́ктор

**treason** [ˈtriːzn] (госуда́рственная) изме́на

**treasure** [ˈtreʒə] **1.** сокро́вище; **2.** храни́ть; (*value greatly*) дорожи́ть; **~r** [~rə] казначе́й

**treasury** [ˈtreʒərɪ]; сокро́вищница; *Brt.* ***the* ≗** Казначе́йство

**treat** [triːt] **1.** *v/t. chem.* обраба́тывать [-бо́тать]; *med.* лечи́ть; (*stand a drink, etc.*) угоща́ть [угости́ть] (***to*** Т); (*act towards*) обраща́ться [обрати́ться] с (Т), обходи́ться [обойти́сь] с (Т); *v/i.* **~ *of*** рассма́тривать [-мотре́ть], обсужда́ть [-уди́ть] (В); ***~ for … with*** лечи́ть (от Р, Т); **2.** (*pleasure*) удово́льствие, наслажде́ние; ***this is my ~*** за всё плачу́ я!; я угоща́ю!

**treatise** [ˈtriːtɪz] нау́чный труд

**treatment** [ˈtriːtmənt] *chem., tech.* обрабо́тка (Т); *med.* лече́ние; (*handling*) обраще́ние (***of*** с Т)

**treaty** [ˈtriːtɪ] догово́р

**treble** [ˈtrebl] **1.** □ тройно́й, утро́енный; **2.** тройно́е коли́чество; *mus.* ди́скант; **3.** утра́ивать(ся) [утро́ить(ся)]

**tree** [triː] де́рево; ***family ~*** родосло́вное де́рево

**trellis** [ˈtrelɪs] решётка; шпале́ра

**tremble** [ˈtrembl] [за]дрожа́ть, [за]трясти́сь (***with*** от Р)

**tremendous** [trɪˈmendəs] □ грома́дный; стра́шный; *coll.* огро́мный, потряса́ющий

**tremor** [ˈtremə] дрожь *f*; **~s** *pl.* подзе́мные толчки́

**tremulous** [ˈtremjʊləs] □ дрожа́щий; (*timid*) тре́петный, ро́бкий

**trench** [trentʃ] кана́ва; *mil.* транше́я, око́п

**trend** [trend] **1.** направле́ние (*a. fig.*); *fig.* (*course*) тече́ние; (*style*) стиль *m*; (*tendency*) тенде́нция; **2.** име́ть тенде́нцию (***towards*** к Д); склоня́ться

**trendy** [ˈtrendɪ] *coll.* сти́льный; мо́дный

**trespass** [ˈtrespəs] зайти́ *pf.* на чужу́ю террито́рию; (*sin*) соверша́ть просту́пок; (*encroach*) злоупотребля́ть [-би́ть] (***on*** Т); ***~ on s.o.'s time*** посяга́ть на чьё-л. вре́мя

**trial** [ˈtraɪəl] (*test, hardship*) испыта́ние, про́ба; *law* суде́бное разбира́тельство; суд; *attr.* про́бный, испыта́тельный; ***on ~*** под судо́м; ***give a. p. a ~*** взять кого́-л. на испыта́тельный сро́к

**triang|le** [ˈtraɪæŋgl] треуго́льник; **~ular** [traɪˈæŋgjʊlə] □ треуго́льный

T

**tribe** [traɪb] пле́мя *n*; *pej.* компа́ния; братва́

**tribune** ['trɪbjuːn] (*platform*) трибу́на; (*person*) трибу́н

**tribut|ary** ['trɪbjʊtərɪ] *geogr.* прито́к; **~e** ['trɪbjuːt] дань *f* (*a. fig.*); ***pay ~ to*** *fig.* отдава́ть до́лжное (Д)

**trice** [traɪs]: ***in a ~*** вмиг, ми́гом

**trick** [trɪk] **1.** (*practical joke*) шу́тка, *child's* ша́лость *f*; *done to amuse* фо́кус, трюк; уло́вка; (*special skill*) сноро́вка; ***do the ~*** подействовать *pf.*, дости́чь *pf.* це́ли; **2.** (*deceive*) обма́нывать [-ну́ть]; наду́(ва́)ть; **~ery** ['trɪkərɪ] надува́тельство, обма́н

**trickle** ['trɪkl] течь стру́йкой; (*ooze*) сочи́ться

**trick|ster** ['trɪkstə] обма́нщик; **~y** ['trɪkɪ] □ (*sly*) хи́трый; (*difficult*) сло́жный, тру́дный; ***~ customer*** ско́льзкий тип

**tricycle** ['traɪsɪkl] трёхколёсный велосипе́д

**trifl|e** ['traɪfl] **1.** пустя́к; ме́лочь *f*; ***a ~*** *fig., adv.* немно́жко; **2.** *v/i.* занима́ться пустяка́ми; относи́ться несерьёзно к (Д); ***he is not to be ~d with*** с ним шу́тки пло́хи; *v/t.* ***~ away*** зря тра́тить; **~ing** ['traɪflɪŋ] пустя́чный, пустяко́вый

**trigger** ['trɪgə] **1.** *mil.* спусково́й крючо́к; **2.** (*start*) дава́ть [дать] нача́ло; вызыва́ть ['-звать] (В)

**trill** [trɪl] **1.** трель *f*; **2.** выводи́ть трель

**trim** [trɪm] **1.** *figure* аккура́тный, ла́дный; *garden* приведённый в поря́док; **2.** *naut.* (у́гол наклоне́ния су́дна) диффере́нт; ***in good ~*** в поря́дке; **3.** *hair, etc.* подреза́ть [-е́зать], подстрига́ть [-и́чь]; *dress* отде́л(ыв)ать; *hedge* подра́внивать [-ровня́ть]; **~ming** ['trɪmɪŋ] *mst.* ***~s*** *pl.* отде́лка; *cul.* припра́ва, гарни́р

**trinket** ['trɪŋkɪt] безделу́шка

**trip** [trɪp] **1.** пое́здка; экску́рсия; **2.** *v/i.* идти́ легко́ и бы́стро; (*stumble*) спотыка́ться [споткну́ться] (*a. fig.*); *v/t.* подставля́ть подно́жку (Д)

**tripartite** [traɪ'pɑːtaɪt] *agreement* трёхсторо́нний; состоя́щий из трёх часте́й

**tripe** [traɪp] *cul.* рубе́ц

**triple** ['trɪpl] тройно́й; утро́енный; **~ts** ['trɪplɪts] *pl.* тро́йня *sg.*

**tripper** [trɪpə] *coll.* экскурса́нт

**trite** [traɪt] □ бана́льный, изби́тый

**triumph** ['traɪəmf] **1.** триу́мф; торжество́; **2.** (*be victorious*) побежда́ть [-ди́ть]; (*celebrate victory*) торжествова́ть, восторжествова́ть *pf.* (***over*** над Т); **~al** [traɪ'ʌmfl] триумфа́льный; **~ant** [traɪ'ʌmfənt] победоно́сный; торжеству́ющий

**trivial** ['trɪvɪəl] □ ме́лкий, пустяко́вый; тривиа́льный

**trod** [trɒd] *pt. от* ***tread***; **~den** ['trɔdn] *pt. p. от* ***tread***

**trolley** ['trɒlɪ] теле́жка; *Am. streetcar* трамва́й; ***~bus*** тролле́йбус

**trombone** [trɒm'bəʊn] *mus.* тромбо́н

**troop** [truːp] **1.** (*group*) гру́ппа, толпа́; **2.** дви́гаться толпо́й; ***~ away, ~ off*** удаля́ться [-ли́ться]; ***we all ~ed to the museum*** мы всей гру́ппой пошли́ в музе́й; ***~s*** *pl.* войска́ *n/pl.*

**trophy** ['trəʊfɪ] трофе́й

**tropic** ['trɒpɪk] тро́пик; ***~s*** *pl.* тро́пики *m/pl.*; **~al** □ [~pɪkəl] тропи́ческий

**trot** [trɒt] **1.** *of horse* рысь *f*; бы́стрый шаг; ***keep s.o. on the ~*** не дава́ть кому́-л. поко́я; **2.** бежа́ть трусцо́й

**trouble** ['trʌbl] **1.** (*worry*) беспоко́йство; (*anxiety*) волне́ние; (*cares*) забо́ты *f/pl.*, хло́поты *f/pl.*; (*difficulties*) затрудне́ния *n/pl.*; беда́; ***get into ~*** попа́сть *pf.* в беду́; ***take the ~*** стара́ться, прилага́ть уси́лия; **2.** [по]беспоко́ить(ся); трево́жить; [по]проси́ть; утружда́ть; ***don't ~!*** не утружда́й(те) себя́!; **~some** [~səm] тру́дный, причиня́ющий беспоко́йство; **~shooter** [~ʃuːtə] авари́йный монтёр; уполномо́ченный по урегули́рованию конфли́ктов

**troupe** [truːp] *thea.* тру́ппа

**trousers** ['traʊzəz] *pl.* брю́ки *f/pl.*

**trout** [traʊt] форе́ль *f*

**truant** ['truːənt] *pupil* прогу́льщик; ***play ~*** прогу́ливать уро́ки

**truce** [truːs] переми́рие

**truck** [trʌk] **1.** (*barrow*) теле́жка; *Am.*

T

(*motorvehicle*) грузови́к; *Brt. rail.* грузова́я платфо́рма; **2.** *mst. Am.* перевози́ть на грузовика́х
**truculent** ['trʌkjʊlənt] (*fierce*) свире́пый; (*cruel*) жесто́кий; агресси́вный
**trudge** [trʌdʒ] идти́ с трудо́м; таска́ться, [по]тащи́ться; ***I had to ~ to the station on foot*** пришло́сь тащи́ться на ста́нцию пешко́м
**true** [tru:] ве́рный, пра́вильный; (*real*) настоя́щий; ***it is ~*** э́то пра́вда; ***come ~*** сбы́(ва́)ться; ***~ to life*** реалисти́ческий; (*genuine*) правди́вый; *portrait, etc.* как живо́й
**truism** ['tru:ɪzəm] трюи́зм
**truly** ['tru:lɪ] ***he was ~ grateful*** он был и́скренне благода́рен; ***Yours ~*** (*at close of letter*) пре́данный Вам
**trump** [trʌmp] **1.** (*card*) ко́зырь *m*; **2.** бить козырно́й ка́ртой
**trumpet** ['trʌmpɪt] **1.** труба́; ***blow one's own ~*** расхва́ливать себя́; **2.** [за-, про]труби́ть; *fig.* раструби́ть *pf.*; **~er** [~ə] труба́ч
**truncheon** ['trʌntʃən] *policeman's* дуби́нка
**trunk** [trʌŋk] *of tree* ствол; *anat.* ту́ловище; *elephant's* хо́бот; *Am. mot.* бага́жник; (*large suitcase*) чемода́н; ***pair of ~s*** трусы́; **~ call** *tel.* вы́зов по междугоро́дному телефо́ну; **~ road** магистра́ль *f*
**trust** [trʌst] **1.** дове́рие; ве́ра; *comm.* конце́рн, трест; ***on ~*** на ве́ру; в креди́т; ***position of ~*** отве́тственное положе́ние; **2.** *v/t.* [по]ве́рить (Д); доверя́ть [-е́рить] (Д ***with*** В); *v/i.* полага́ться [положи́ться] (***in, to*** на В); наде́яться (***in, to*** на В); ***I ~ they will agree*** наде́юсь, они́ соглася́тся; **~ee** [trʌs'ti:] опеку́н; попечи́тель *m*; довери́тельный со́бственник; **~ful** ['trʌstfl] □, **~ing** ['trʌstɪŋ] □ дове́рчивый; **~worthy** [~wɜ:ðɪ] заслу́живающий дове́рия; надёжный
**truth** [tru:θ] пра́вда; (*verity*) и́стина; **~ful** ['tru:θfl] □ *person* правди́вый; *statement, etc. a.* ве́рный
**try** [traɪ] **1.** (*sample*) [по]про́бовать; (*attempt*) [по]пыта́ться; [по]стара́ться; (*tire, strain*) утомля́ть [-ми́ть]; *law* суди́ть; (*test*) испы́тывать [испыта́ть]; ***~ on*** примеря́ть [-е́рить]; ***~ one's luck*** попыта́ть *pf.* сча́стья; **2.** попы́тка; **~ing** ['traɪɪŋ] тру́дный; тяжёлый; (*annoying*) раздража́ющий
**T-shirt** ['ti:ʃɜ:t] ма́йка (с коро́ткими рукава́ми), футбо́лка
**tub** [tʌb] (*barrel*) ка́дка; (*wash~*) лоха́нь *f*; *coll.* (*bath~*) ва́нна
**tube** [tju:b] труба́, тру́бка; *Brt.* (*subway*) метро́ *n indecl.*; *of paint, etc.* тю́бик; ***inner ~*** *mot.* ка́мера
**tuber** ['tju:bə] *bot.* клу́бень *m*
**tuberculosis** [tju:bɜ:kjʊ'ləʊsɪs] туберкулёз
**tubular** ['tju:bjʊlə] □ тру́бчатый
**tuck** [tʌk] **1.** *on dress* скла́дка, сбо́рка; **2.** де́лать скла́дки; засо́вывать [-су́нуть]; (*hide*) [с]пря́тать; ***~ in shirt*** запра́вить *pf.*; *to food* упи́сывать; ***~ up*** *sleeves* засу́чивать [-чи́ть]
**Tuesday** ['tju:zdɪ] вто́рник
**tuft** [tʌft] *of grass* пучо́к; *of hair* хохо́л
**tug** [tʌg] **1.** (*pull*) рыво́к; *naut.* букси́р; **2.** тащи́ть [тяну́ть]; (*a.* ***tug at***) дёргать [дёрнуть]
**tuition** [tju:'ɪʃn] обуче́ние
**tulip** ['tju:lɪp] тюльпа́н
**tumble** ['tʌmbl] **1.** *v/i.* (*fall*) па́дать [упа́сть]; (*overturn*) опроки́дываться [-и́нуться]; *into bed* повали́ться; ***~ to*** (*grasp, realize*) разгада́ть *pf.*, поня́ть *pf.*; **2.** паде́ние; **~down** полуразру́шенный; **~r** [~ə] (*glass*) стака́н
**tummy** ['tʌmɪ] *coll.* живо́т; *baby's* живо́тик
**tumo(u)r** ['tju:mə] о́пухоль *f*
**tumult** ['tju:mʌlt] (*uproar*) шум и кри́ки; сумато́ха; си́льное волне́ние; **~uous** [tju:'mʌltʃʊəs] шу́мный, бу́йный; взволно́ванный
**tuna** ['tju:nə] туне́ц
**tune** [tju:n] **1.** мело́дия, моти́в; ***in ~*** *piano* настро́енный; ***in ~ with*** сочета́ющийся, гармони́рующий; ***out of ~*** расстро́енный; ***sing out of ~*** фальши́вить; **2.** настра́ивать [-ро́ить]; (*a.* ***~ in***) *radio* настра́ивать (***to*** на В); **~ful** ['tju:nfl] □ мелоди́чный

T

**tunnel** ['tʌnl] **1.** туннéль *m* (*a.* тоннéль *m*); **2.** проводи́ть туннéль (под Т, сквозь В)

**turbid** ['tɜːbɪd] (*not clear*) му́тный; *fig.* тумáнный

**turbot** ['tɜːbət] пáлтус

**turbulent** ['tɜːbjʊlənt] бу́рный (*a. fig.*); *mob*, *etc.* бу́йный

**tureen** [tə'riːn] су́пница

**turf** [tɜːf] дёрн; (*peat*) торф; (*races*) скáчки *f/pl.*; ***the ~*** ипподрóм

**Turk** [tɜːk] ту́рок *m*, турчáнка *f*

**turkey** ['tɜːkɪ] индю́к *m*, индéйка *f*

**Turkish** ['tɜːkɪʃ] **1.** турéцкий; ***~ delight*** рахáт-луку́м; **2.** турéцкий язы́к

**turmoil** ['tɜːmɔɪl] смятéние; волнéние; беспоря́док

**turn** [tɜːn] **1.** *v/t.* (*round*) вращáть, вертéть; *head*, *etc.* поворáчивать [поверну́ть]; (*change*) превращáть [-рати́ть]; (*direct*) направля́ть [-рáвить]; ***~ a corner*** заверну́ть *pf.* за у́гол; ***~ down*** *suggestion* отвергáть [-éргнуть]; (*fold*) загибáть [загну́ть]; ***~ off*** *tap* закры́(вá)ть; *light*, *gas*, *etc.* выключáть [вы́ключить]; ***~ on*** *tap* откры́(вá)ть; включáть [-чи́ть]; ***~ out*** выгоня́ть [вы́гнать]; *of job*, *etc.* увольня́ть [уво́лить]; *goods* выпускáть (вы́пустить); ***~ over*** перевёртывать [-верну́ть]; *fig.* перед(ав)áть; ***~ up*** *collar*, *etc.* поднимáть; **2.** *v/i.* вращáться, вертéться; поворáчиваться [поверну́ться]; станови́ться [стать]; превращáться [-рати́ться]; ***~ pale, red, etc.*** побледнéть *pf.*, покраснéть *pf.*, *и т. д.*; ***~ about*** оборáчиваться [оберну́ться]; ***~ in*** (*inform on*) доноси́ть [-нести́]; (*go to bed*) ложи́ться спать; ***~ out*** окáзываться [-зáться]; ***~ to*** приниMáться [-ня́ться] за (В); обращáться [обрати́ться] к (Д); ***~ up*** появля́ться [-ви́ться]; ***~ upon*** обращáться [обрати́ться] прóтив (Р); **3.** *su.* поворóт; изги́б; перемéна; услу́га; *of speech* оборóт; *coll.* (*shock*) испу́г; ***at every ~*** на кáждом шагу́, постоя́нно; ***in ~s*** по óчереди; ***it is my ~*** моя́ óчередь *f*; ***take ~s*** дéлать поочерёдно; ***in his ~*** в свою́ óчередь; ***do s.o. a good ~*** оказáть *pf.* комý-л. услу́гу; ***~er*** ['tɜːnə] тóкарь *m*

**turning** ['tɜːnɪŋ] *of street*, *etc.* поворóт; ***~ point*** *fig.* поворóтный пункт; перелóм; *fig.* кри́зис

**turnip** ['tɜːnɪp] *bot.* рéпа

**turn|out** ['tɜːnaʊt] *econ.* вы́пуск, проду́кция; числó учáствующих на собрáнии, голосовáнии, и. т. д.; ***~over*** ['tɜːnəʊvə] *comm.* оборóт; *of goods* товарооборóт; ***~stile*** ['tɜːnstaɪl] турникéт

**turpentine** ['tɜːpəntaɪn] скипидáр

**turquoise** ['tɜːkwɔɪz] *min.* бирюзá; бирюзóвый цвет

**turret** ['tʌrɪt] бáшенка

**turtle** ['tɜːtl] *zo.* черепáха

**tusk** [tʌsk] *zo.* би́вень *m*

**tussle** ['tʌsl] потасóвка; дрáка

**tussock** ['tʌsək] кóчка

**tutor** ['tjuːtə] **1.** (*private teacher*) репети́тор; *Brt. univ.* предподаватель *m*, -ница *f*; **2.** давáть чáстные урóки; обу́чать [-чи́ть]; ***~ial*** [tjuː'tɔːrɪəl] *univ.* консультáция

**tuxedo** [tʌk'siːdəʊ] *Am.* смóкинг

**twaddle** ['twɒdl] **1.** пустáя болтовня́; **2.** пустослóвить

**twang** [twæŋ] **1.** *of guitar* звон; (*mst.* ***nasal ~***) гнусáвый гóлос; **2.** звенéть

**tweak** [twiːk] **1.** щипóк; **2.** ущипну́ть

**tweed** [twiːd] твид

**tweezers** ['twiːzəz] *pl.* пинцéт

**twelfth** [twelfθ] двенáдцатый

**twelve** [twelv] двенáдцать

**twent|ieth** ['twentɪɪθ] двадцáтый; ***~y*** ['twentɪ] двáдцать

**twice** [twaɪs] двáжды; вдвóе; ***think ~*** хорошó обду́мать

**twiddle** ['twɪdl] *in hands* вертéть; (*play*) игрáть (Т); ***~ one's thumbs*** *fig.* бездéльничать

**twig** [twɪg] вéточка, прут

**twilight** ['twaɪlaɪt] су́мерки *f/pl.*

**twin** [twɪn] близнéц; ***~ towns*** горoдá-побрати́мы

**twine** [twaɪn] **1.** бечёвка, шпагáт; **2.** [с]вить; *garland* [с]плести́; *of plants* обви́(вá)ть(ся)

**twinge** [twɪndʒ] при́ступ бóли; ***~ of***

T

***conscience*** угрызе́ния со́вести *f/pl.*
**twink|le** ['twiŋkl] **1.** мерца́ние, мига́ние; *of eyes* и́скорки; **2.** [за]мерца́ть; мига́ть; искри́ться; **~ling** [~ıŋ]: ***in the ~ of an eye*** в мгнове́ние о́ка
**twirl** [twɜːl] верте́ть, крути́ть
**twist** [twıst] **1.** круче́ние; (*~ together*) скру́чивание; *of road, etc.* изги́б; *fig.* (*change*) поворо́т; *of ankle* вы́вих; **2.** [с]крути́ть; повора́чивать [-верну́ть], [с]ви́ться; сплета́ть(ся) [-ести́(сь)]; ***~ the facts*** искажа́ть [-ази́ть] фа́кты
**twit** [twıt] *coll.* болва́н
**twitch** [twıtʃ] **1.** подёргивание; **2.** подёргиваться
**twitter** ['twıtə] **1.** ще́бет; **2.** [за]щебета́ть (*a. of little girls*), чири́кать [-кнуть]; ***be in a ~*** дрожа́ть
**two** [tuː] **1.** два, две; дво́е; па́ра; ***in ~*** на́двое, попола́м; ***put ~ and ~ together*** смекну́ть в чём де́ло *pf.*; ***the ~ of them*** они́ о́ба; **2.** дво́йка; → ***five***; ***in ~s*** попа́рно; **~-faced** [~'feist] *fig.* двули́чный; **~fold** ['tuːfəʊld] **1.** двойно́й; **2.** *adv.* вдво́е; **~pence** ['tʌpəns] два пе́нса; **~-stor(e)y** двухэта́жный; **~-way** двусторо́нний
**type** [taıp] **1.** тип; *of wine, etc.* сорт; *typ.* шрифт; ***true to ~*** типи́чный; **2.** печа́тать на маши́нке; **~writer** пи́шущая маши́нка
**typhoid** ['taıfɔıd] (*a.* ***~ fever***) брюшно́й тиф
**typhoon** [taı'fuːn] тайфу́н
**typhus** ['taıfəs] сыпно́й тиф
**typi|cal** ['tıpıkl] типи́чный; **~fy** [~faı] служи́ть типи́чным приме́ром для (Р)
**typist** ['taıpıst] машини́стка; ***shorthand ~*** (машини́стка)-стенографи́ст(ка)
**tyrann|ical** [tı'rænıkəl] □ тирани́ческий; **~ize** ['tırənaız] тира́нить; **~y** ['tırənı] тирани́я
**tyrant** ['taırənt] тира́н
**tyre** ['taıə] → ***tire***
**tzar** [zɑː] → ***czar***

# U

**ubiquitous** [juː'bıkwıtəs] □ вездесу́щий *a. iro.*
**udder** ['ʌdə] вы́мя *n*
**UFO** ['juːfəʊ] НЛО
**ugly** ['ʌglı] □ уро́дливый, безобра́зный (*a. fig.*); ***~ customer*** ме́рзкий/опа́сный тип
**ulcer** ['ʌlsə] я́зва
**ulterior** [ʌl'tıərıə]: ***~ motive*** за́дняя мысль *f*
**ultimate** ['ʌltımıt] □ после́дний; коне́чный; (*final*) оконча́тельный; **~ly** [~lı] в конце́ концо́в
**ultra...** ['ʌltrə] *pref.* сверх..., у́льтра...
**umbrage** ['ʌmbrıdʒ]: ***take ~ at*** обижа́ться [оби́деться] на (В)
**umbrella** [ʌm'brelə] зо́нтик; ***telescopic ~*** складно́й зо́нтик
**umpire** ['ʌmpaıə] **1.** *sport* судья́ *m*, арби́тр; **2.** суди́ть
**un...** [ʌn] *pref.* (*придаёт отрицательное или противоположное значение*) не..., без...
**unable** [ʌn'eıbl] неспосо́бный; ***be ~*** быть не в состоя́нии, не [с]мочь
**unaccountabl|e** [ʌnə'kaʊntəbl] □ необъясни́мый, непостижи́мый; **~y** [~blı] по непоня́тной причи́не
**unaccustomed** [ʌnə'kʌstəmd] не привы́кший; (*not usual*) непривы́чный
**unacquainted** [ʌnə'kweıntıd]: ***~ with*** незнако́мый с (Т); не зна́ющий (Р)
**unaffected** [ʌnə'fektıd] □ (*genuine*) непритво́рный, и́скренний; (*not affected*) не(за)тро́нутый (***by*** Т)
**unaided** [ʌn'eıdıd] без посторо́нней по́мощи
**unalterable** [ʌn'ɔːltərəbl] □ неизме́нный
**unanimous** [juː'nænıməs] □ едино-

дýшный; *in voting* единоглáсный

**unanswerable** [ʌn'ɑːnsərəbl] □ *argument* неопровержи́мый

**unapproachable** [ʌnə'prəʊtʃəbl] □ (*physically inaccessible*) непристýпный; *person* недостýпный

**unasked** [ʌn'ɑːskt] непрóшеный; ***I did this ~*** я э́то сдéлал по своéй инициати́ве

**unassisted** [ʌnə'sɪstɪd] без посторóнней пóмощи, самостоя́тельно

**unassuming** [ʌnə'sjuːmɪŋ] скрóмный, непритязáтельный

**unattractive** [ʌnə'træktɪv] непривлекáтельный

**unauthorized** [ʌn'ɔːθəraɪzd] неразрешённый; *person* посторóнний

**unavail|able** [ʌnə'veɪləbl] не имéющийся в нали́чии; отсýтствующий; ***these goods are ~ at present*** э́тих товáров сейчáс нет; **~ing** [~lɪŋ] бесполéзный

**unavoidable** [ʌnə'vɔɪdəbl] неизбéжный

**unaware** [ʌnə'weə] не знáющий, не подозревáющий (***of*** P); ***be ~ of*** ничегó не знать о (П); не замечáть [-éтить] (P); **~s** [~z]: ***catch s.o. ~*** заставáть [-стáть] когó-л. врасплóх

**unbalanced** [ʌn'bælənst] неуравновéшенный (*a. mentally*)

**unbearable** [ʌn'beərəbl] □ невыноси́мый, нестерпи́мый

**unbecoming** [ʌnbɪ'kʌmɪŋ] □ (*inappropriate*) неподходя́щий; (*unseemly*) неподобáющий; *clothes* не идýщий к лицý

**unbelie|f** [ʌnbɪ'liːf] невéрие; **~vable** ['ʌnbɪ'liːvəbl] □ невероя́тный

**unbend** [ʌn'bend] [*irr.* (**bend**)] выпрямля́ть(ся) [вы́прямить(ся)]; *fig.* станови́ться непринуждённым; **~ing** [~ɪŋ] □ *fig.* чи́стый; *fig.* непреклóнный

**unbias(s)ed** [ʌn'baɪəst] □ беспристрáстный

**unbind** [ʌn'baɪnd] [*irr.* (**bind**)] развя́зывать [-зáть]

**unblemished** [ʌn'blemɪʃt] чи́стый; *fig.* незапя́тнанный

**unblushing** [ʌn'blʌʃɪŋ] беззастéнчивый

**unbolt** [ʌn'bəʊlt] отпирáть [-перéть]

**unbounded** [ʌn'baʊndɪd] □ неограни́ченный; беспредéльный

**unbroken** [ʌn'brəʊkn] (*whole*) неразби́тый; *record* непоби́тый; (*uninterrupted*) непреры́вный

**unburden** [ʌn'bɜːdn]: ***~ o.s.*** изливáть [-ли́ть] дýшу

**unbutton** [ʌn'bʌtn] расстёгивать [расстегнýть]

**uncalled-for** [ʌn'kɔːldfɔː] непрóшенный; неумéстный

**uncanny** [ʌn'kænɪ] □ сверхъестéственный; жýткий, пугáющий

**uncared** [ʌn'keəd]: ***~-for*** забрóшенный

**unceasing** [ʌn'siːsɪŋ] □ непрекращáющийся, беспреры́вный

**unceremonious** [ʌnserɪ'məʊnɪəs] бесцеремóнный

**uncertain** [ʌn'sɜːtn] неувéренный; *plans, etc.* неопределённый; неизвéстный; ***it is ~ whether he will be there*** неизвéстно, бýдет ли он там; ***~ weather*** перемéнчивая погóда; **~ty** [~tɪ] неувéренность *f*; неизвéстность *f*; неопределённость *f*

**unchanging** [ʌn'tʃeɪndʒɪŋ] □ неизмéнный

**uncharitable** [ʌn'tʃærɪtəbl] □ немилосéрдный; ***~ words*** жестóкие словá

**unchecked** [ʌn'tʃekt] беспрепя́тственный; (*not verified*) непровéренный

**uncivil** [ʌn'sɪvl] невéжливый; **~ized** [ʌn'sɪvɪlaɪzd] нецивилизóванный

**uncle** ['ʌŋkl] дя́дя *m*

**unclean** [ʌn'kliːn] □ нечи́стый

**uncomfortable** [ʌn'kʌmfətəbl] неудóбный; *fig.* нелóвкий

**uncommon** [ʌn'kɒmən] □ (*remarkable*) необыкновéнный; (*unusual*) необы́чный; (*rare*) рéдкий

**uncommunicative** [ʌnkə'mjuːnɪkətɪv] неразговóрчивый, сдéржанный; скры́тный

**uncomplaining** [ʌnkəm'pleɪnɪŋ] безрóпотный

U

**uncompromising** [ʌn'kɒmprəmaɪzɪŋ] □ бескомпроми́ссный
**unconcerned** [ʌnkən'sɜːnd]: ***be ~ about*** относи́ться равноду́шно, безразли́чно (к Д)
**unconditional** [ʌnkən'dɪʃənl] □ безогово́рочный, безусло́вный
**unconquerable** [ʌn'kɒŋkrəbl] □ непобеди́мый
**unconscious** [ʌn'kɒnʃəs] □ (*not intentional*) бессозна́тельный; потеря́вший созна́ние; ***be ~ of*** не созн(ав)а́ть Р; ***the ~*** подсозна́ние; **~ness** [-nɪs] бессозна́тельное состоя́ние
**unconstitutional** [ʌnkɒnstɪ'tjuːʃnl] □ противоре́чащий конститу́ции; неконституцио́нный
**uncontrollable** [ʌnkən'trəʊləbl] □ неудержи́мый; неуправля́емый
**unconventional** [ʌnkən'venʃənl] □ (*free in one's ways*) чу́ждый усло́вности; (*unusual*) необы́чный; эксцентри́чный; (*original*) нешабло́нный
**uncork** [ʌn'kɔːk] отку́пори(ва)ть
**uncount|able** [ʌn'kaʊntəbl] бесчи́сленный; **~ed** [-tɪd] несчётный
**uncouth** [ʌn'kuːθ] (*rough*) гру́бый
**uncover** [ʌn'kʌvə] *face, etc.* откры́(ва́)ть; снима́ть кры́шку с (Р); *head* обнажа́ть [-жи́ть]; *fig. plot, etc.* раскрыва́ть [-ы́ть]
**uncult|ivated** [ʌn'kʌltɪveɪtɪd] *land* невозде́ланный; *plant* ди́кий; *person* неразвито́й; некульту́рный
**undamaged** [ʌn'dæmɪdʒd] неповреждённый
**undaunted** [ʌn'dɔːntɪd] □ (*fearless*) неустраши́мый
**undecided** [ʌndɪ'saɪdɪd] □ нерешённый; (*in doubt*) нереши́тельный
**undeniable** [ʌndɪ'naɪəbl] □ неоспори́мый; несомне́нный
**under** ['ʌndə] **1.** *adv.* ни́же; внизу́; вниз; **2.** *prp.* под (В, Т); ни́же (Р); ме́ньше (Р); при (П); **3.** *pref.* ни́же..., под..., недо...; **4.** ни́жний; ни́зший; **~bid** [ʌndə'bɪd] [*irr.* (***bid***)] предлага́ть бо́лее ни́зкую це́ну, чем (И); **~brush** [-brʌʃ] подле́сок; **~carriage** [-kærɪdʒ] шасси́ *n indecl.*; **~clothing** [-kləʊðɪŋ] ни́жнее бельё; **~cut** [-kʌt] сбива́ть це́ну; **~done** [ʌndə'dʌn] недожа́ренный; *cake* непропечённый; **~estimate** [ʌndər'estɪmeɪt] недооце́нивать [-и́ть]; **~fed** [-fed] недоко́рмленный, истощённый от недоеда́ния; **~go** [ʌndə'gəʊ] [*irr.* (***go***)] испы́тывать [испыта́ть]; *criticism, etc.* подверга́ться [-е́ргнуться] (Д); **~graduate** [ʌndə'grædʒʊət] студе́нт *m*, -ка *f*; **~ground** [-graʊnd] **1.** подзе́мный; *pol.* подпо́льный; **2.** метро́(полите́н) *n indecl.*; (*movement*) подпо́лье; **~hand** [ʌndə'hænd] **1.** та́йный, закули́сный; **2.** *adv.* та́йно, за спино́й; **~lie** [ʌndə'laɪ] [*irr.* (***lie***)] лежа́ть в осно́ве (Р); **~line** [ʌndə'laɪn] подчёркивать [-черкну́ть]; **~mine** [ʌndə'maɪn] подрыва́ть [подорва́ть]; **~neath** [ʌndə'niːθ] **1.** *prp.* под (Т/В); **2.** *adv.* вниз, внизу́; **~rate** [ʌndə'reɪt] недооце́нивать [-и́ть]; **~secretary** [ʌndə'sekrətrɪ] замести́тель *m*, помо́щник мини́стра (в А́нглии и США); **~signed** [ʌndə'saɪnd] нижеподписа́вшийся; **~stand** [ʌndə'stænd] [*irr.* (***stand***)] *com.* понима́ть [поня́ть]; подразумева́ть (***by*** под Т); ***make o.s. understood*** уме́ть объясни́ться; **~standable** [ʌndə'stændəbl] поня́тный; **~standing** [ʌndə'stændɪŋ] понима́ние; взаимопонима́ние; (*agreement*) договорённость *f*; ***come to an ~*** договори́ться *pf.*; **~state** [ʌndə'steɪt] преуменьша́ть [-ме́ньшить]; **~stood** [ʌndə'stʊd] *pt. u pt. p. om* ***understand***; **~take** [ʌndə'teɪk] [*irr.* (***take***)] предпринима́ть [-ня́ть]; (*make o.s. responsible for*) брать на себя́; обя́зываться (-за́ться); **~taker** [-teɪkə] содержа́тель *m* похоро́нного бюро́; **~taking** [ʌndə'teɪkɪŋ] предприя́тие; **~tone** [-təʊn]: ***in an ~*** вполго́лоса; **~value** [ʌndə'væljuː] недооце́нивать [-и́ть]; **~wear** [-weə] ни́жнее бельё; **~write** [ʌndə'raɪt] [*irr.* (***write***)] [за]страхова́ть; **~writer** [-raɪtə] поручи́тель-гара́нт; страхова́тель *m*
**undeserved** [ʌndɪ'zɜːvd] □ незаслу́женный
**undesirable** [ʌndɪ'zaɪərəbl] □ неже-

U

ла́тельный; *moment*, *etc*. неудо́бный, неподходя́щий
**undisciplined** [ʌn'dɪsɪplɪnd] недисциплини́рованный
**undiscriminating** [ʌndɪs'krɪmɪneɪtɪŋ] неразбо́рчивый
**undisguised** [ʌndɪs'gaɪzd] □ откры́тый, я́вный; незамаскиро́ванный
**undivided** [ʌndɪ'vaɪdɪd] □ неразделённый; *attention* по́лный
**undo** [ʌn'duː] [*irr*. (***do***)] *string*, *etc*. развя́зывать [-за́ть]; *buttons*, *zip* расстёгивать [расстегну́ть]; (*destroy*) погуби́ть *pf*.; **~ing** [~ɪŋ]: ***that was my ~*** это погуби́ло меня́
**undoubted** [ʌn'daʊtɪd] несомне́нный, бесспо́рный
**undreamed-of**, **undreamt-of** [ʌn'dremtɒv] невообрази́мый, неожи́данный
**undress** [ʌn'dres] разде́(ва́)ть(ся); **~ed** [~st] неоде́тый
**undue** [ʌn'djuː] □ (*excessive*) чрезме́рный
**undulating** ['ʌndjʊleɪtɪŋ] *geogr*. холми́стый
**unduly** [ʌn'djuːlɪ] чересчу́р, чрезме́рно
**unearth** [ʌn'ɜːθ] вырыва́ть из земли́; *fig*. (*discover*) раска́пывать [-копа́ть]; **~ly** [ʌn'ɜːθlɪ] (*not terrestrial*) неземно́й; (*supernatural*) сверхъесте́ственный; (*weird*) стра́нный; *time* чересчу́р ра́нний (час)
**uneas|iness** [ʌn'iːzɪnɪs] беспоко́йство, трево́га; **~y** [ʌn'iːzɪ] □ беспоко́йный, трево́жный
**uneducated** [ʌn'edjʊkeɪtɪd] необразо́ванный
**unemotional** [ʌnɪ'məʊʃənl] бесстра́стный; неэмоциона́льный
**unemploy|ed** [ʌnɪm'plɔɪd] безрабо́тный; **~ment** [~mənt] безрабо́тица
**unending** [ʌn'endɪŋ] □ несконча́емый, бесконе́чный
**unendurable** [ʌnɪn'djʊərəbl] нестерпи́мый
**unequal** [ʌn'iːkwəl] □ нера́вный; *length*, *weight* разли́чный; ***be ~ to*** не в си́лах; *task*, *etc*. не по плечу́; **~led** [~d] непревзойдённый
**unerring** [ʌn'ɜːrɪŋ] □ безоши́бочный
**uneven** [ʌn'iːvn] □ неро́вный; *temper* неуравнове́шенный
**uneventful** [ʌnɪ'ventfl] □ без осо́бых собы́тий/приключе́ний
**unexpected** [ʌnɪks'pektɪd] □ неожи́данный
**unexposed** [ʌnɪk'spəʊzd] *film* неэкспони́рованный
**unfailing** [ʌn'feɪlɪŋ] □ ве́рный, надёжный; *interest* неизме́нный; *patience*, *etc*. неистощимый, беспреде́льный
**unfair** [ʌn'feə] □ несправедли́вый; *play*, *etc*. нече́стный
**unfaithful** [ʌn'feɪθfl] □ неве́рный; (*violating trust*) вероло́мный; *to the original* нето́чный
**unfamiliar** [ʌnfə'mɪlɪə] незнако́мый; *surroundings* непривы́чный
**unfasten** [ʌn'fɑːsn] *door* открыва́ть [-ы́ть]; *buttons*, *etc*. расстёгивать [расстегну́ть]; *knot* развя́зывать [-за́ть]; **~ed** [~d] расстёгнутый; *door* неза́пертый
**unfavo(u)rable** [ʌn'feɪvərəbl] □ неблагоприя́тный; *reports*, *etc*. отрица́тельный
**unfeeling** [ʌn'fiːlɪŋ] □ бесчу́вственный
**unfinished** [ʌn'fɪnɪʃt] незако́нченный
**unfit** [ʌn'fɪt] него́дный, неподходя́щий; ***~ for service*** него́ден к вое́нной слу́жбе
**unflagging** [ʌn'flægɪŋ] □ неослабева́ющий
**unfold** [ʌn'fəʊld] развёртывать(ся) [-верну́ть(ся)]; *plans*, *secret*, *etc*. раскры́(ва́)ть
**unforeseen** [ʌnfɔː'siːn] непредви́денный
**unforgettable** [ʌnfə'getəbl] □ незабыва́емый
**unfortunate** [ʌn'fɔːtʃənɪt] несча́стный; неуда́чный; (*unlucky*) неуда́чливый; **~ly** [~lɪ] к несча́стью; к сожале́нию
**unfounded** [ʌn'faʊndɪd] необосно́-

ванный
**unfriendly** [ʌn'frendlɪ] недружелю́бный; неприве́тливый
**unfruitful** [ʌn'fru:tfl] □ неплодоро́дный; *fig.* беспло́дный
**unfurl** [ʌn'fɜ:l] развёртывать [разверну́ть]
**ungainly** [ʌn'geɪnlɪ] нескла́дный
**ungodly** [ʌn'gɔdlɪ]: нечести́вый; ***he woke us up at an ~ hour*** он разбуди́л нас безбо́жно ра́но
**ungovernable** [ʌn'gʌvənəbl] □ неуправля́емый; *temper, etc.* неукроти́мый, необу́зданный
**ungracious** [ʌn'greɪʃəs] □ (*not polite*) неве́жливый
**ungrateful** [ʌn'greɪtfl] □ неблагода́рный
**unguarded** [ʌn'gɑ:dɪd] □ неохраня́емый, незащищённый; *fig.* неосторо́жный
**unhampered** [ʌn'hæmpəd] беспрепя́тственный
**unhappy** [ʌn'hæpɪ] □ несча́стный
**unharmed** [ʌn'hɑ:md] *thing* неповреждённый; *person* невреди́мый
**unhealthy** [ʌn'helθɪ] □ нездоро́вый, боле́зненный; *coll.* (*harmful*) вре́дный
**unheard-of** [ʌn'hɜ:dɒv] неслы́ханный
**unhesitating** [ʌn'hezɪteɪtɪŋ] □ реши́тельный; **~ly** [~lɪ] не коле́блясь
**unholy** [ʌn'həʊlɪ] поро́чный; *coll.* жу́ткий, ужа́сный
**unhoped-for** [ʌn'həʊptfɔ:] неожи́данный
**unhurt** [ʌn'hɜ:t] невреди́мый, це́лый
**uniform** ['ju:nɪfɔ:m] **1.** □ одина́ковый; (*alike all over*) единообра́зный, одноро́дный; **2.** фо́рма, фо́рменная оде́жда; **~ity** [ju:nɪ'fɔ:mətɪ] единообра́зие, одноро́дность *f*
**unify** ['ju:nɪfaɪ] объединя́ть [-ни́ть]; унифици́ровать (*im*)*pf.*
**unilateral** [ju:nɪ'lætrəl] односторо́нний
**unimaginable** [ʌnɪ'mædʒɪnəbl] □ невообрази́мый
**unimportant** [ʌnɪm'pɔ:tənt] □ нева́жный
**uninhabit|able** [ʌnɪn'hæbɪtəbl] неприго́дный для жилья́; **~ed** [~tɪd] *house* нежило́й; необита́емый
**uninjured** [ʌn'ɪndʒəd] непострада́вший; невреди́мый
**unintelligible** [ʌnɪn'telɪdʒəbl] □ непоня́тный; *hand writing* неразбо́рчивый, нево́льный
**unintentional** [ʌnɪn'tenʃənl] □ ненаме́ренный, неумы́шленный
**uninteresting** [ʌn'ɪntrəstɪŋ] □ неинтере́сный
**uninterrupted** [ʌnɪntə'rʌptɪd] □ непреры́вный, беспреры́вный
**uninvit|ed** [ʌnɪn'vaɪtɪd] неприглашённый; *pej.* незва́ный; ***come ~*** прийти́ *pf.* без приглаше́ния; **~ing** [~tɪŋ] непривлека́тельный; *food* неаппети́тный
**union** ['ju:nɪən] сою́з; (*trade ~*) профсою́з; **♀ Jack** брита́нский национа́льный флаг
**unique** ['ju:ni:k] еди́нственный в своём ро́де, уника́льный
**unison** ['ju:nɪzn] унисо́н; гармо́ния; в по́лном согла́сии; ***act in ~*** де́йствовать сла́женно
**unit** ['ju:nɪt] *mil.* часть *f*, подразделе́ние; *math.* едини́ца; *tech.* агрега́т; ***~ furniture*** секцио́нная ме́бель; **~e** [ju:'naɪt] *in marriage* сочета́ть у́зами бра́ка; соединя́ть(ся) [-ни́ть(ся)]; объединя́ть(ся) [-ни́ть(ся)]; **~y** ['ju:nətɪ] еди́нство
**univers|al** [ju:nɪ'vɜ:sl] □ *agreement, etc.* всео́бщий; всеми́рный; *mst. tech.* универса́льный; **~e** ['ju:nɪvɜ:s] мир, вселе́нная; **~ity** [ju:nɪ'vɜ:sətɪ] университе́т
**unjust** [ʌn'dʒʌst] □ несправедли́вый; **~ified** [ʌn'dʒʌstɪfaɪd] неопра́вданный
**unkempt** [ʌn'kempt] (*untidy*) беспоря́дочный; неопря́тный; *hair* растрёпанный
**unkind** [ʌn'kaɪnd] □ недо́брый
**unknown** [ʌn'nəʊn] неизве́стный; ***~ to me*** *adv.* без моего́ ве́дома
**unlace** [ʌn'leɪs] расшнуро́вывать [-ова́ть]

U

**unlawful** [ʌn'lɔːfl] □ незако́нный
**unless** [ən'les, ʌn'les] *cj.* е́сли не
**unlike** [ʌn'laɪk] **1.** непохо́жий на (В); ***it's quite ~ her*** э́то совсе́м на неё не похо́же; **2.** *prp.* в отли́чие от (Р); **~ly** [ʌn'laɪklɪ] неправдоподо́бный, невероя́тный; маловероя́тный; ***his arrival today is ~*** маловероя́тно, что он прие́дет сего́дня
**unlimited** [ʌn'lɪmɪtɪd] неограни́ченный
**unload** [ʌn'ləʊd] выгружа́ть [вы́грузить], разгружа́ть [-узи́ть]; *mil. a weapon* разряжа́ть [-яди́ть]
**unlock** [ʌn'lɒk] отпира́ть [отпере́ть]; **~ed** [~t] неза́пертый
**unlooked-for** [ʌn'lʊktfɔː] неожи́данный, непредви́денный
**unlucky** [ʌn'lʌkɪ] □ неуда́чный, несчастли́вый; ***I was ~*** мне не повезло́; ***be ~*** (*bring ill-luck*) приноси́ть несча́стье
**unmanageable** [ʌn'mænɪdʒəbl] □ неуправля́емый; *child, problem* тру́дный
**unmanly** [ʌn'mænlɪ] нему́жественный; не по-мужски́; трусли́вый
**unmarried** [ʌn'mærɪd] нежена́тый, холосто́й; *woman* незаму́жняя
**unmask** [ʌn'mɑːsk] *fig.* разоблача́ть [-чи́ть]
**unmatched** [ʌn'mætʃt] не име́ющий себе́ ра́вного, непревзойдённый
**unmerciful** [ʌn'mɜːsɪfl] безжа́лостный
**unmerited** [ʌn'merɪtɪd] незаслу́женный
**unmistakable** [ʌnmɪs'teɪkəbl] □ ве́рный, очеви́дный; несомне́нный; (*clearly recognizable*) легко́ узнава́емый
**unmitigated** [ʌn'mɪtɪgeɪtɪd] несмягчённый; *fig.* отъя́вленный, по́лный, абсолю́тный
**unmoved** [ʌn'muːvd] оста́вшийся равноду́шным; бесчу́вственный; ***he was ~ by her tears*** её слёзы не тро́нули его́
**unnatural** [ʌn'nætʃrəl] □ неесте́ственный; (*contrary to nature*) противоесте́ственный
**unnecessary** [ʌn'nesəsrɪ] □ нену́жный, ли́шний; (*excessive*) изли́шний
**unnerve** [ʌn'nɜːv] обесси́ливать; лиша́ть прису́тствия ду́ха, реши́мости
**unnoticed** [ʌn'nəʊtɪst] незаме́ченный
**unobserved** [ʌnəb'zɜːvd] незаме́ченный
**unobtainable** [ʌnəb'teɪnəbl]: ***~ thing*** недосту́пная вещь *f*
**unobtrusive** [ʌnəb'truːsɪv] ненавя́зчивый
**unoccupied** [ʌn'ɒkjʊpaɪd] неза́нятый
**unoffending** [ʌnə'fendɪŋ] безоби́дный
**unofficial** [ʌnə'fɪʃl] неофициа́льный
**unopened** [ʌn'əʊpənd] неоткры́тый; *letter* нераспеча́танный
**unopposed** [ʌnə'pəʊzd] не встреча́ющий сопротивле́ния
**unpack** [ʌn'pæk] распако́вывать [-ова́ть]
**unpaid** [ʌn'peɪd] *debt* неупла́ченный; *work* неопла́ченный
**unparalleled** [ʌn'pærəleld] бесприме́рный; *success, kindness* необыкнове́нный
**unpardonable** [ʌn'pɑːdɔnəbl] □ непрости́тельный
**unperturbed** [ʌnpə'tɜːbd] невозмути́мый
**unpleasant** [ʌn'pleznt] □ неприя́тный; **~ness** [~nɪs] неприя́тность *f*
**unpopular** [ʌn'pɒpjʊlə] □ непопуля́рный; ***make o.s. ~*** лиша́ть [-ши́ть] себя́ популя́рности
**unpractical** [ʌn'præktɪkəl] непракти́чный
**unprecedented** [ʌn'presɪdəntɪd] □ беспрецеде́нтный; *courage* бесприме́рный
**unprejudiced** [ʌn'predʒʊdɪst] □ непредубеждённый; непредвзя́тый
**unprepared** [ʌnprɪ'peəd] □ неподгото́вленный; без подгото́вки
**unpretentious** [ʌnprɪ'tenʃəs] □ скро́мный, без прете́нзий
**unprincipled** [ʌn'prɪnsəpld] бесприн-

U

ци́пный
**unprofitable** [ʌn'prɒfɪtəbl] невы́годный; *enterprise* нерента́бельный
**unpromising** [ʌn'prɒmɪsɪŋ] малообеща́ющий; ***the crops look ~*** вряд ли бу́дет хоро́ший урожа́й
**unproved** [ʌn'pru:vd] недока́занный
**unprovoked** [ʌnprə'vəʊkt] неспровоци́рованный
**unqualified** [ʌn'kwɒlɪfaɪd] неквалифици́рованный; некомпете́нтный; *denial*, *etc.* безоговоро́чный; *success*, *etc.* реши́тельный; безграни́чный
**unquestionable** [ʌn'kwestʃənəbl] несомне́нный, неоспори́мый
**unravel** [ʌn'rævəl] распу́т(ыв)ать (*a. fig.*); (*solve*) разга́дывать [-да́ть]
**unreal** [ʌn'rɪəl] нереа́льный
**unreasonable** [ʌn'ri:znəbl] □ не(благо)разу́мный; безрассу́дный; *price*, *etc.* чрезме́рный
**unrecognizable** [ʌn'rekəgnaɪzəbl] □ неузнава́емый
**unrelated** [ʌnrɪ'leɪtɪd] *people* не ро́дственники; *ideas*, *facts*, *etc.* не име́ющий отноше́ния; не свя́занные (ме́жду собо́й)
**unrelenting** [ʌnrɪ'lentɪŋ] □ неумоли́мый; ***it was a week of ~ activity*** всю неде́лю мы рабо́тали без переды́шки
**unreliable** [ʌnrɪ'laɪəbl] ненадёжный
**unrelieved** [ʌnrɪ'li:vd]: ***~ boredom*** необлегчённая ску́ка; ***~ sadness*** неизбы́вная грусть *f*
**unremitting** [ʌnrɪ'mɪtɪŋ] □ беспреры́вный; *pain*, *etc.* неослабева́ющий
**unreserved** [ʌnrɪ'zɜ:vd] □ *seat*, *etc.* незаброни́рованный; *support*, *etc.* безоговоро́чный
**unrest** [ʌn'rest] *social*, *political* волне́ния, беспоря́дки; (*disquiet*) беспоко́йство
**unrestrained** [ʌnrɪs'treɪnd] □ *behavio(u)r* несде́ржанный; *anger*, *etc.* необу́зданный
**unrestricted** [ʌnrɪs'trɪktɪd] □ неограни́ченный
**unrewarding** [ʌnrɪ'wɔ:dɪŋ] неблаго да́рный
**unripe** [ʌn'raɪp] незре́лый, неспе́лый
**unrival(l)ed** [ʌn'raɪvld] непревзойдённый; не име́ющий сопе́рников
**unroll** [ʌn'rəʊl] развёртывать [-верну́ть]
**unruffled** [ʌn'rʌfld] *sea*, *etc.* гла́дкий; *person* невозмути́мый
**unruly** [ʌn'ru:lɪ] непослу́шный; непоко́рный; бу́йный
**unsafe** [ʌn'seɪf] □ (*not dependable*) ненадёжный; (*dangerous*) опа́сный
**unsal(e)able** [ʌn'seɪləbl] *goods* нехо́дкий
**unsanitary** [ʌn'sænɪtərɪ] антисанита́рный
**unsatisfactory** [ʌnsætɪs'fæktərɪ] □ неудовлетвори́тельный
**unsavo(u)ry** [ʌn'seɪvərɪ] невку́сный; неприя́тный; (*offensive*) отврати́тельный
**unscathed** [ʌn'skeɪðd] невреди́мый
**unscrew** [ʌn'skru:] отви́нчивать(-ся) [-нти́ть(ся)]; вывёртывать [-вернуть]
**unscrupulous** [ʌn'skru:pjʊləs] □ беспринци́пный; неразбо́рчивый в сре́дствах
**unseasonable** [ʌn'si:zənəbl] □ (*ill-timed*) несвоевре́менный; не по сезо́ну
**unseemly** [ʌn'si:mlɪ] неподоба́ющий; (*indecent*) непристо́йный
**unseen** [ʌn'si:n] (*invisible*) невиди́мый; (*not seen*) неви́данный
**unselfish** [ʌn'selfɪʃ] □ бескоры́стный
**unsettle** [ʌn'setl] *person* расстра́ивать [-ро́ить]; **~d** [~d] *weather* неусто́йчивый; *problem*, *etc.* нерешённый; *bill* неопла́ченный
**unshaken** [ʌn'ʃeɪkən] непоколеби́мый
**unshaven** [ʌn'ʃeɪvn] небри́тый
**unshrinkable** [ʌn'ʃrɪŋkəbl] безуса́дочный
**unsightly** [ʌn'saɪtlɪ] неприглядный
**unskil(l)|ful** [ʌn'skɪlfl] □ неуме́лый, неиску́сный; **~ed** [ʌn'skɪld] неквалифици́рованный
**unsociable** [ʌn'səʊʃəbl] необщи́тельный

**unsolicited** [ʌnsə'lɪsɪtɪd] непро́шенный
**unsophisticated** [ʌnsə'fɪstɪkeɪtɪd] безыску́сный, бесхи́тростный; просто́й, простоду́шный
**unsound** [ʌn'saʊnd] □ *health* нездоро́вый; *views* не(доста́точно) обосно́ванный; *judg(e)ment* ша́ткий; лишённый про́чности
**unsparing** [ʌn'speərɪŋ] □ (*unmerciful*) беспоща́дный; (*profuse*) ще́дрый; **~ efforts** неуста́нные уси́лия
**unspeakable** [ʌn'spi:kəbl] □ невырази́мый; (*terrible*) ужа́сный
**unstable** [ʌn'steɪbl] □ неусто́йчивый; *phys.*, *chem.* нестóйкий
**unsteady** [ʌn'stedɪ] □ → **unstable**; *hand* трясу́щийся; *steps* нетвёрдый; ша́ткий; непостоя́нный
**unstudied** [ʌn'stʌdɪd] невы́ученный; есте́ственный, непринуждённы
**unsuccessful** [ʌnsək'sesfl] □ неуда́чный, безуспе́шный; неуда́чливый
**unsuitable** [ʌn'su:təbl] □ неподходя́щий
**unsurpassed** [ʌnsə'pɑ:st] непревзойдённый
**unsuspect|ed** [ʌnsəs'pektɪd] □ неожи́данный; **~ing** [~ɪŋ] неподозрева́емый (***of*** о П)
**unsuspicious** [ʌnsə'spɪʃəs] □ *person* неподозрева́ющий; дове́рчивый
**unswerving** [ʌn'swɜ:vɪŋ] □ неукло́нный
**untangle** [ʌn'tæŋgl] распу́т(ыв)ать
**untarnished** [ʌn'tɑ:nɪʃt] *reputation* незапя́тнанный
**untenable** [ʌn'tenəbl] *theory etc.* несостоя́тельный
**unthink|able** [ʌn'θɪŋkəbl] немы́слимый; **~ing** [~ɪŋ] □ безду́мный; опроме́тчивый
**untidy** [ʌn'taɪdɪ] □ неопря́тный, неаккура́тный; *room* неу́бранный
**untie** [ʌn'taɪ] развя́зывать [-за́ть]; *one thing from another* отвя́зывать [-за́ть]
**until** [ən'tɪl] **1.** *prp.* до (Р); ***not ~ Sunday*** не ра́нее воскресе́нья; **2.** *cj.* (до тех пор) пока́ … (не) …
**untimely** [ʌn'taɪmlɪ] несвоевре́менный; ***~ death*** безвре́менная кончи́на
**untiring** [ʌn'taɪərɪŋ] □ неутоми́мый
**untold** [ʌn'təʊld] (*not told*) нерасска́занный; (*incalculable*) несме́тный, несчётный
**untouched** [ʌn'tʌtʃt] нетро́нутый
**untroubled** [ʌn'trʌbld]: необеспоко́енный; ***~ life*** безмяте́жная жизнь *f*
**untrue** [ʌn'tru:] □ неве́рный; ***this is ~*** э́то непра́вда
**untrustworthy** [ʌn'trʌstwɜ:ðɪ] не заслу́живающий дове́рия
**unus|ed 1.** [ʌn'ju:zd] (*new*) не бы́вший в употребле́нии; (*not used*) неиспо́льзованный; **2.** [ʌn'ju:st] непривы́кший (***to*** к Д); **~ual** [ʌn'ju:ʒʊəl] □ необыкнове́нный, необы́чный
**unvarnished** [ʌn'vɑ:nɪʃt] *fig.* неприкра́шенный
**unvarying** [ʌn'veərɪɪŋ] □ неизменя́ющийся, неизме́нный
**unveil** [ʌn'veɪl] *statute*, *monument* откры́(ва́)ть
**unwanted** [ʌn'wɒntɪd] *child* нежела́нный; нену́жный
**unwarranted** [ʌn'wɒrəntɪd] □ неразрешённый; неопра́вданный; *criticism*, *etc.* незаслу́женный
**unwavering** [ʌn'weɪvərɪŋ] □ непоколеби́мый; ***~ look*** при́стальный взгляд
**unwell** [ʌn'wel]: нездоро́вый; ***he is ~*** ему́ нездоро́вится; ***feel ~*** нева́жно (пло́хо) себя́ чу́вствовать
**unwholesome** [ʌn'həʊlsəm] неблаготво́рный; (*harmful*) вре́дный
**unwieldy** [ʌn'wi:ldɪ] □ *carton*, *etc.* громо́здкий
**unwilling** [ʌn'wɪlɪŋ] □ нескло́нный, нежела́ющий; нерасполо́женный; ***be ~ to do s.th.*** не хоте́ть что́-то сде́лать
**unwise** [ʌn'waɪz] □ неразу́мный
**unwittingly** [ʌn'wɪtɪŋlɪ] нево́льно, непреднаме́ренно
**unworthy** [ʌn'wɜ:ðɪ] □ недосто́йный
**unwrap** [ʌn'ræp] развёртывать(ся) [-верну́ть(ся)]

U

**unyielding** [ʌn'jiːldɪŋ] □ неподатливый, неуступчивый

**unzip** [ʌn'zɪp] расстёгивать [-егнуть]; ***come ~ped*** расстегнуться *pf*.

**up** [ʌp] **1.** *adv*. вверх, наверх; вверху, наверху; выше; *fig*. ***be ~ to the mark*** быть в форме, на высоте; ***be ~ against a task*** стоять перед задачей; ***~ to*** вплоть до (Р); ***it is ~ to me*** (***to do***) мне приходится (делать); ***what's ~?*** *coll*. что случилось?, в чём дело?; ***what is he ~ to?*** чем он занимается?; **2.** *prp*. вверх по (Д); по направлению к (Д); ***~ the river*** вверх по реке; **3.** *su*. ***the ~s and downs*** *fig*. превратности судьбы; **4.** *vb*. *coll*. поднимать [-нять]; *prices* повышать [-ысить]

**up|braid** [ʌp'breɪd] [вы]бранить; **~bringing** ['ʌpbrɪŋɪŋ] воспитание; **~date** [ʌp'deɪt] модернизировать; *person* держать в курсе дела; **~heaval** [ʌp'hiːvl] *earthquake*, *etc*. сдвиг; *fig*. глубокие (революционные) перемены; **~hill** [ʌp'hɪl] (идущий) в гору; *fig*. тяжёлый; **~hold** [ʌp'həʊld] *irr*. *support* поддерживать [-жать]; **~holster** [ʌp'həʊlstə] оби(ва)ть; **~holstery** [~stərɪ] обивка

**up|keep** ['ʌpkiːp] содержание; *cost* стоимость *f* содержания; **~lift** **1.** ['ʌplɪft] душевный подъём; **2.** [ʌp'lɪft] поднимать [-нять]

**upon** [ə'pɒn] → ***on***

**upper** ['ʌpə] верхний; высший; ***gain the ~ hand*** одерживать [одержать] верх (над Т); **~most** [~məʊst] самый верхний; наивысший; ***be ~ in one's mind*** стоять на первом месте, быть главным

**uppish** ['ʌpɪʃ] *coll*. надменный

**upright** ['ʌpraɪt] □ прямой (*a*. *fig*.), вертикальный; *adv*. *a*. стоймя; **~ piano** пианино *n indecl*.

**up|rising** ['ʌpraɪzɪŋ] восстание; **~roar** ['ʌprɔː] шум, *coll*. гам; **~roarious** [ʌp'rɔːrɪəs] □ (*noisy*) шумный; (*funny*) ужасно смешной

**up|root** [ʌp'ruːt] вырывать с корнем; *fig*. ***I don't want to ~ myself again*** я не хочу снова переезжать; **~set** [ʌp'set] [*irr*. (***set***)] (*knock over*) опрокидывать(ся) [-инуть(ся)]; *person*, *plans*, *etc*. расстраивать [-роить]; **~shot** ['ʌpʃɒt] итог, результат; ***the ~ of it was that …*** кончилось тем, что …; **~side ~ down** [ʌpsaɪd'daʊn] вверх дном; **~stairs** [ʌp'steəz] вверх (по лестнице), наверх(у); **~start** ['ʌpstɑːt] выскочка *m/f*; **~stream** [ʌp'striːm] вверх по течению; **~-to-date** [ʌptə'deɪt] современный; ***bring s.o. ~*** вводить [ввести] когол. в курс дела; **~turn** [ʌp'tɜːn] сдиг к лучшему; улучшение; **~ward(s)** ['ʌpwədz] вверх, наверх; ***~ of*** свыше, больше

**urban** ['ɜːbən] городской; **~e** [ɜː'beɪn] вежливый; (*refined*) изысканный; (*suave*) обходительный

**urchin** ['ɜːtʃɪn] мальчишка *m*

**urge** [ɜːdʒ] **1.** (*try to persuade*) убеждать [-едить]; подгонять [подогнать] (*often* ***~ on***); **2.** стремление, желание, толчок *fig*.; **~ncy** ['ɜːdʒənsɪ] (*need*) настоятельность *f*; (*haste*) срочность *f*; настойчивость *f*; **~nt** ['ɜːdʒənt] □ срочный; настоятельный, настойчивый

**urin|al** ['jʊərɪnl] писсуар; **~ate** [~rɪneɪt] [по]мочиться; **~e** [~rɪn] моча

**urn** [ɜːn] урна

**us** [əs, … ʌs] *pers*. *pron*. (*косвенный падеж от* ***we***) нас, нам, нами

**usage** ['juːzɪdʒ] употребление; (*custom*) обычай

**use** **1.** [juːs] употребление; применение; пользование; (*usefulness*) польза; (*habit*) привычка; (***of***) ***no ~*** бесполезный; ***come into ~*** войти в употребление; ***for general ~*** для общего пользования; ***what's the ~ …?*** какой смысл …?, что толку …?; **2.** [juːz] употреблять [-бить]; пользоваться (Т); воспользоваться (Т) *pf*.; использовать (*im*)*pf*.; (*treat*) обращаться с (Т), обходиться [обойтись] с (Т); ***I ~d to do*** я, бывало, часто делал; **~d** [juːst]: ***~ to*** привыкший к (Д); **~ful** ['juːsfl] □ полезный; пригодный; ***come in ~*** пригодиться; **~less** ['juːslɪs] □ бесполезный; непригодный, не-

го́дный; **~r** ['juːzə] по́льзователь *m*; (*customer*) потреби́тель *m*; *of library, etc.* чита́тель *m*
**usher** ['ʌʃə] (*conduct*) проводи́ть [-вести́]; (**~ *in***) вводи́ть [ввести́]; **~ette** [~'ret] билетёрша
**usual** ['juːʒʊəl] □ обыкнове́нный, обы́чный
**usurp** [juː'zɛːp] узурпи́ровать (*im*)*pf.*; **~er** [juː'zɜːpə] узурпа́тор
**utensil** [juː'tensl] (*mst. pl.* **~s**) инструме́нт; посу́да; ***kitchen ~s*** ку́хонные принадле́жности *f/pl.*
**utility** [juː'tɪlətɪ] (*usefulness*) поле́зность *f*; ***public utilities*** коммуна́льные услу́ги/предприя́тия
**utiliz|ation** [juːtəlaɪ'zeɪʃn] испо́льзование, утилиза́ция; **~e** ['juːtəlaɪz] испо́льзовать (*im*)*pf.*, утилизи́ровать (*im*)*pf.*
**utmost** ['ʌtməʊst] кра́йний, преде́льный; ***do one's ~*** сде́лать *pf.* всё возмо́жное; ***at the ~*** са́мое бо́льшее
**utter** ['ʌtə] **1.** □ *fig.* по́лный; соверше́нный; **2.** *sounds* изд(ав)а́ть; *words* произноси́ть [-нести́]; **~ance** [~ərəns] выска́зывание; ***give ~ to*** выска́зывать [-сказать]; *emotion* дать вы́ход (Д)
**U-turn** ['juːtɜːn] *mot.* разворо́т

# V

**vacan|cy** ['veɪkənsɪ] (*emptiness*) пустота́; (*unfilled job*) вака́нсия; *in hotel* свобо́дная ко́мната; **~t** ['veɪkənt] □ неза́нятый, вака́нтный; пусто́й; *look, mind, etc.* отсу́тствующий
**vacat|e** [və'keɪt] *house, hotel room, etc.* освобожда́ть [-боди́ть]; **~ion** [və'keɪʃn, *Am.* veɪ'keɪʃən] *univ.* кани́кулы *f/pl.*; *Am.* (*holiday*) о́тпуск; ***be on ~*** быть в о́тпуске
**vaccin|ate** ['væksɪneɪt] *med.* [с]де́лать приви́вку; **~ation** [væksɪ'neɪʃn] приви́вка; **~e** ['væksiːn] вакци́на
**vacillate** ['væsəleɪt] колеба́ться
**vacuum** ['vækjʊəm] *phys.* ва́куум (*a. fig.*); **~ cleaner** пылесо́с; **~ flask** те́рмос; **~-packed** в ва́куумной упако́вке
**vagabond** ['vægəbɒnd] бродя́га *m*
**vagrant** ['veɪgrənt] бродя́га *m*
**vague** [veɪg] неопределённый, нея́сный, сму́тный; ***I haven't the ~st idea of …*** я не име́ю ни мале́йшего представле́ния о (П)
**vain** [veɪn] □ (*useless*) тще́тный, напра́сный; (*conceited*) тщесла́вный; ***in ~*** напра́сно, тще́тно; **~glorious** [veɪn'glɒːrɪəs] тщесла́вный; (*boastful*) хвастли́вый
**valet** ['vælɪt, 'vælei] камерди́нер
**valiant** ['vælɪənt] *rhet.* хра́брый, до́блестный
**valid** ['vælɪd] *law* действи́тельный (*a. of ticket, etc.*), име́ющий си́лу; *of an argument, etc.* ве́ский, обосно́ванный
**valley** ['vælɪ] доли́на
**valo(u)r** ['vælə] *rhet.* до́блесть *f*
**valuable** ['væljʊəbl] **1.** □ це́нный; **2. ~s** *pl.* це́нности *f/pl.*
**valuation** [væljʊ'eɪʃn] оце́нка
**value** ['væljuː] **1.** це́нность *f*; *comm.* сто́имость *f*; *math.* величина́; ***put*** (*or* ***set***) ***little ~ on*** невысоко́ цени́ть; **2.** оце́нивать [-и́ть] (В); цени́ть (В); дорожи́ть (Т); **~less** ['væljuːlɪs] ничего́ не сто́ящий
**valve** ['vælv] *tech.* ве́нтиль *m*, кла́пан (*a. anat.*)
**van** [væn] автофурго́н; *rail.* бага́жный *or* това́рный ваго́н
**vane** [veɪn] (*weathercock*) флю́гер; *of propeller* ло́пасть *f*
**vanguard** ['vængɑːd]: ***be in the ~*** быть в пе́рвых ряда́х; *fig.* авангард
**vanilla** [və'nɪlə] вани́ль
**vanish** ['vænɪʃ] исчеза́ть [-е́знуть]
**vanity** ['vænətɪ] тщесла́вие; **~ bag** (су́мочка-)космети́чка
**vanquish** ['væŋkwɪʃ] побежда́ть

V

[-еди́ть]
**vantage** ['vɑːntɪdʒ]: ~ ***point*** удо́бное для обзо́ра ме́сто; вы́годная пози́ция
**vapid** ['væpɪd] □ пло́ский; пре́сный; *fig.* неинтересный
**vaporize** ['veɪpəraɪz] испаря́ть(ся) [-ри́ть(ся)]
**vapo(u)r** ['veɪpə] пар
**varia|ble** ['veərɪəbl] **1.** □ непостоя́нный, изме́нчивый; **2.** *math.* переме́нная величина́; **~nce** [~rɪəns]: ***be at ~*** расходи́ться во мне́ниях; быть в противоре́чии; **~nt** [~rɪənt] вариа́нт; **~tion** [veərɪ'eɪʃn] измене́ние; *mus.* вариа́ция
**varie|d** ['veərɪd] □ → ***various***; **~gated** ['vɛərigeɪtɪd] разноцве́тный, пёстрый; **~ty** [və'raiəti] разнообра́зие; (*sort*) сорт, разнови́дность *f*; ряд, мно́жество; ***for a ~ of reasons*** по ря́ду причи́н; ~ ***show*** варьете́; эстра́дное представле́ние
**various** ['veərɪəs] ра́зный, (*of different sorts*) разли́чный; разнообра́зный; **~ly** [~lɪ] по-ра́зному
**varnish** ['vɑːnɪʃ] **1.** лак; *fig.* (*gloss*) лоск; **2.** покрыва́ть ла́ком
**vary** ['veərɪ] (*change*) изменя́ть(ся) [-ни́ть(ся)]; (*be different*) разни́ться; *of opinion* расходи́ться [разойти́сь]; (*diversify*) разнообра́зить
**vase** [vɑːz] ва́за
**vast** [vɑːst] □ обши́рный, грома́дный
**vat** [væt] чан; бо́чка, ка́дка
**vault** [vɔːlt] **1.** свод; (*tomb, crypt*) склеп; (*cellar*) подва́л, по́греб; **2.** (*a.* ~ ***over***) перепры́гивать [-гнуть]
**veal** [viːl] теля́тина; *attr.* теля́чий
**veer** [vɪə] *of wind* меня́ть направле́ние; *views, etc.* изменя́ть [-ни́ть]; ***the car ~ed to the right*** маши́ну занесло́ впра́во
**vegeta|ble** ['vedʒtəbl] **1.** о́вощ; **~*s*** *pl.* зе́лень *f*, о́вощи *m/pl.*; **2.** *oil* расти́тельный; овощно́й; ~ ***garden*** огоро́д; ~ ***marrow*** кабачо́к; **~rian** [vedʒɪ'teərɪən] **1.** вегетариа́нец *m*, -нка *f*; **2.** вегетариа́нский; **~tion** [vedʒɪ'teɪʃn] расти́тельность *f*
**vehemen|ce** ['viːəməns] си́ла; стра́стность *f*; **~t** [~t] си́льный; стра́стный; *protests, etc.* бу́рный
**vehicle** ['viːɪkl] автомаши́на, авто́бус *и т. д.* (*любое транспортное средство*); *fig.* сре́дство; *med.* перено́счик
**veil** [veɪl] **1.** вуа́ль *f*; *of mist* пелена́; *fig.* заве́са; ***bridal ~*** фата́; **2.** закрыва́ть вуа́лью; *fig.* завуали́ровать; *in mist* оку́тывать
**vein** [veɪn] ве́на; *geol.* жи́ла; *fig.* жи́лка; (*mood*) настрое́ние
**velocity** [vɪ'lɒsətɪ] ско́рость *f*
**velvet** ['velvɪt] ба́рхат; *attr.* ба́рхатный; **~y** [~ɪ] ба́рхатный (*fig.*); бархати́стый
**vend|or** ['vendə] (у́личный) продаве́ц *m*, -вщица *f*
**veneer** [və'nɪə] фане́ра; *fig.* фаса́д
**venerable** ['venərəbl] □ почте́нный; *eccl. title* преподо́бный
**venereal** [və'nɪərɪəl] венери́ческий
**Venetian** [və'niːʃn] венециа́нский; ~ ***blinds*** жалюзи́ *n indecl.*
**vengeance** ['vendʒəns] месть *f*
**venom** ['venəm] (*part.* змеи́ный) яд (*a. fig.*); *fig.* зло́ба; **~ous** [~əs] □ ядови́тый (*a. fig.*)
**vent** [vent] **1.** вентиляцио́нное отве́рстие; (*air ~*) отду́шина; ***give ~ to*** изли́(-ва́)ть (В); **2.** *fig.* изли́(ва́)ть (В), дава́ть вы́ход (Д)
**ventilat|e** ['ventɪleɪt] прове́три(ва)ть; *fig., of question* обсужда́ть [-уди́ть], выясня́ть [вы́яснить]; **~ion** [ventɪ'leɪʃn] вентиля́ция
**venture** ['ventʃə] **1.** риско́ванное предприя́тие; ***at a ~*** науга́д; ***joint ~*** совме́стное предприя́тие; **2.** рискова́ть [-кну́ть] (Т); отва́жи(ва)ться на (В) (*a.* ~ ***upon***)
**veracious** [və'reɪʃəs] правди́вый
**veranda(h)** [və'rændə] вера́нда
**verb|al** ['vɜːbl] □ слове́сный; (*oral*) у́стный; *gr.* отглаго́льный; **~atim** [vɜː'beɪtɪm] досло́вно, сло́во в сло́во; **~ose** [vɜː'bəʊs] □ многосло́вный
**verdict** ['vɜːdɪkt] *law* верди́кт; ***what's your ~, doctor?*** каково́ Ва́ше мне́ние, до́ктор?

V

**verdure** ['vɜːdʒə] зéлень *f*
**verge** [vɜːdʒ] **1.** (*edge*) край; *of forest* опýшка; *of flower bed* бордю́р; *fig.* грань *f*; ***on the ~ of*** на грáни (Р); **2.**: ***~ (up)on*** гранúчить с (Т)
**veri|fy** ['verɪfaɪ] проверя́ть [-éрить]; (*bear out*) подтверждáть [-рдúть]; **~table** ['verɪtəbl] □ настоя́щий, úстинный
**vermin** ['vɜːmɪn] *coll.* вредúтели *m/pl.*; (*lice, etc.*) паразúты *m/pl.*
**vermouth** ['vɜːməθ] вéрмут
**vernacular** [və'nækjʊlə] *language* роднóй; мéстный диалéкт
**versatile** ['vɜːsətaɪl] разносторóнний; (*having many uses*) универсáльный
**verse** [vɜːs] стихú *m/pl.*; (*line*) строкá; (*stanza*) строфá; **~d** [vɜːst] óпытный, свéдущий; ***she is well ~ in English history*** онá хорошó знáет англúйскую истóрию
**version** ['vɜːʃn] вариáнт; (*account of an event, etc.*) вéрсия; (*translation*) перевóд
**vertebral** ['vɜːtɪbrəl]: ***~ column*** позвонóчник
**vertical** ['vɜːtɪkəl] □ вертикáльный; *cliff, etc.* отвéсный
**vertigo** ['vɜːtɪgəʊ] головокружéние
**verve** [vɜːv] энтузиáзм; подъём
**very** ['verɪ] **1.** *adv.* óчень; ***the ~ best*** сáмое лýчшее; **2.** *adj.* настоя́щий, сýщий; (*in emphasis*) сáмый; ***the ~ same*** тот сáмый; ***the ~ thing*** úменно то, что нýжно; ***the ~ thought*** ужé однá мысль *f*, самá мысль *f*; ***the ~ stones*** дáже кáмни *m/pl.*
**vessel** ['vesl] сосýд (*a. anat.*); *naut.* сýдно, корáбль *m*
**vest** [vest] жилéт; *chiefly Brt.* мáйка
**vestibule** ['vestɪbjuːl] вестибю́ль *m*
**vestige** ['vestɪdʒ] (*remains*) след, остáток; ***there is not a ~ of truth in this*** в э́том нет и дóли прáвды
**veteran** ['vetərən] **1.** ветерáн; **2.** *attr.* стáрый, (*experienced*) óпытный
**veterinary** ['vetrɪnərɪ] **1.** ветеринáр (*mst.* ***~ surgeon***); **2.** ветеринáрный
**veto** ['viːtəʊ] **1.** вéто *n indecl*; **2.** налагáть [-ложúть] вéто на (В)
**vex** [veks] досаждáть [досадúть], раздражáть [-жúть]; **~ation** [vek'seɪʃn] досáда, неприя́тность *f*; **~atious** [vek'seɪʃəs] досáдный; **~ed** ['vekst] *person* раздосáдованный; *question* спóрный; больнóй
**via** ['vaɪə] чéрез (В)
**viable** ['vaɪəbl] жизнеспосóбный
**vial** ['vaɪəl] пузырёк
**vibrat|e** [vai'breit] вибрúровать; **~ion** [~ʃn] вибрáция
**vice**[1] [vaɪs] порóк
**vice**[2] [~] *chiefly Brt.* → ***vise***
**vice**[3] [~] *pref.* вúце…; ***~ president*** вúце-президéнт
**vice versa** [vaɪsɪ'vɜːsə] наоборóт
**vicinity** [vɪ'sɪnətɪ] (*neighbo[u]rhood*) окрéстность *f*; блúзость *f*; ***in the ~*** недалекó (***of*** от Р)
**vicious** ['vɪʃəs] □ порóчный; злой; ***~ circle*** порóчный круг
**vicissitude** [vɪ'sɪsɪtjuːd]: *mst.* ***~s*** *pl.* преврáтности *f/pl.*
**victim** ['vɪktɪm] жéртва; **~ize** [~tɪmaɪz] (*for one's views, etc.*) преслéдовать
**victor** ['vɪktə] победúтель *m*; **~ious** [vɪk'tɔːrɪəs] □ победонóсный; **~y** ['vɪktərɪ] побéда
**video** ['vɪdɪəʊ] вúдео; **~camera** видеокáмера; **~cassette** видеокассéта; **~recorder** видеомагнитофóн, *coll.* вúдик
**vie** [vaɪ] сопéрничать
**view** [vjuː] **1.** вид (***of*** на В); пóле зрéния; (*opinion*) взгляд; (*intention*) намéрение; ***in ~ of*** ввидý Р; ***on ~*** (вы́ставленный) для обозрéния; ***with a ~ to*** *or* ***of*** + *ger.* с намéрением (+ *inf.*); ***have in ~*** имéть в видý; **2.** (*examine*) осмáтривать [осмотрéть]; (*consider*) рассмáтривать [-мотрéть]; (*look at*) [по]смотрéть на (В); **~point** тóчка зрéния
**vigil|ance** ['vɪdʒɪləns] бдúтельность *f*; **~ant** [~lənt] □ бдúтельный
**vigo|rous** ['vɪgərəs] □ сúльный, энергúчный; **~(u)r** ['vɪgə] сúла, энéргия
**vile** [vaɪl] □ мéрзкий, нúзкий
**villa** ['vɪlə] вúлла
**village** ['vɪlɪdʒ] селó, дерéвня; *attr.* сéльский, деревéнский; **~r** [~ə] сéльский (-кая) жúтель *m* (-ница *f*)

**villian** ['vɪlən] злодéй, негодя́й
**vim** [vɪm] энéргия, си́ла
**vindic|ate** ['vɪndɪkeɪt] (*prove*) докáзывать [-зáть]; (*justify*) опрáвдывать [-дáть]; **~tive** [vɪn'dɪktɪv] □ мсти́тельный
**vine** [vaɪn] виногрáдная лозá; **~gar** ['vɪnɪgə] ýксус; **~ growing** виногрáдарство; **~yard** ['vɪnjəd] виногрáдник
**vintage** ['vɪntɪdʒ] сбор виногрáда; винó урожáя определённого гóда; ***~ wine*** мáрочное винó
**violat|e** ['vaɪəleɪt] *law, promise, etc.* нарушáть [-ýшить]; (*rape*) [из]наси́ловать; **~ion** [vaɪə'leɪʃn] нарушéние
**violen|ce** ['vaɪələns] си́ла; наси́лие; ***outbreak of ~*** беспоря́дки *m/pl.*; **~t** [~nt] □ (*strong*) си́льный, мóщный, нéистовый; *quarrel, etc.* я́ростный; *of death* наси́льственный
**violet** ['vaɪələt] фиáлка, фиолéтовый цвет
**violin** [vaɪə'lɪn] скри́пка
**viper** ['vaɪpə] гадю́ка
**virgin** ['vɜːdʒɪn] **1.** дéвственница; ***the Blessed ♀*** Дéва Мари́я, Богорóдица; **2.** □ дéвственный (*a.* **~al**); **~ity** [və'dʒɪnətɪ] дéвственность *f*
**Virgo** ['vɜːgəʊ] *in the zodiac* Дéва
**viril|e** ['vɪraɪl] (*sexually potent*) вири́льный; пóлный энéргии, мýжественный; **~ity** [vɪ'rɪlətɪ] мýжественность *f*; (*potency*) мужскáя си́ла
**virtu|al** ['vɜːtʃʊəl] □ факти́ческий; **~e** ['vəːtjuː] добродéтель *f*; (*advantage*) достóинство; ***in*** *or* ***by ~ of*** благодаря́; в си́лу (P); **~ous** ['vɜːtʃʊəs] □ добродéтельный; (*chaste*) целомýдренный
**virulent** ['vɪrʊlənt] *of poison* смертéльный; *of illness* свирéпый; опáсный; *fig.* злóбный
**virus** ['vaɪərəs] ви́рус; *attr.* ви́русный
**visa** ['viːzə] ви́за; ***entry*** (***exit***) **~** въезднáя (выезднáя) ви́за
**viscount** ['vaɪkaʊnt] викóнт
**viscous** ['vɪskəs] □ вя́зкий; *liquid* тягýчий, густóй
**vise** [vaɪs] *tech.* тиски́ *m/pl.*
**visibility** ['vɪzə'bɪlətɪ] □ ви́димость *f*
**visible** ['vɪzəbl] *apparent, evident* ви́димый; *conspicuous, prominent* ви́дный; *fig., obvious* я́вный, очеви́дный
**vision** ['vɪʒn] (*eyesight*) зрéние; (*mental picture*) ви́дение; *fig.* проницáтельность *f*; ***field of ~*** пóле зрéния; ***my ~ of the events is different*** моё ви́дение э́тих собы́тий инóе; **~ary** ['vɪʒənərɪ] прови́дец *m*, -дица *f*; (*one given to reverie*) мечтáтель *m*, -ница *f*
**visit** ['vɪzɪt] **1.** *v/t. person* навещáть [-ести́ть]; *museum, etc.* посещáть [-ети́ть]; *v/i.* ходи́ть в гóсти; (*stay*) гости́ть; **2.** посещéние, визи́т; **~ing** [~ɪŋ]: ***~ card*** визи́тная кáрточка; ***~ hours*** приёмные часы́; **~or** ['vɪzɪtə] посети́тель *m*, -ница *f*, гость *m*, -я *f*
**vista** ['vɪstə] перспекти́ва (*a. fig.*); (*view*) вид
**visual** ['vɪʒʊəl] зри́тельный; нагля́дный; ***~ aids*** нагля́дные посóбия; **~ize** [~aɪz] представля́ть себé, мы́сленно ви́деть
**vital** ['vaɪtl] □ жи́зненный; (*essential*) насýщный, сущéственный; *person, style* живóй; **~s, ~ parts** *pl.* жи́зненно вáжные óрганы *m/pl.*; **~ity** [vaɪ'tælətɪ] жи́зненная си́ла; энéргия; жи́вость *f*; ***the child is full of ~*** ребёнок пóлон жи́зни
**vitamin** ['vaɪtəmɪn, *Brt.* 'vɪtəmɪn] витами́н; ***~ deficiency*** авитаминóз
**vivaci|ous** [vɪ'veɪʃəs] живóй, темперáментный; **~ty** [vɪ'væsətɪ] жи́вость *f*
**vivid** ['vɪvɪd] □ *fig.* живóй, я́ркий
**vixen** ['vɪksn] лисá, лиси́ца
**vocabulary** [və'kæbjʊlərɪ] словáрь *m*, спи́сок слов; *person's* запáс слов
**vocal** ['vəʊkl] □ голосовóй; (*talkative*) разговóрчивый; *mus.* вокáльный; ***~ cords*** голосовы́е свя́зки
**vocation** [vəʊ'keɪʃn] призвáние; профéссия; **~al** [~l] □ профессионáльный
**vogue** [vəʊg] мóда; популя́рность *f*; ***be in ~*** быть в мóде
**voice** [vɔɪs] **1.** гóлос; ***at the top of one's ~*** во весь гóлос; ***give ~ to*** выражáть [вы́разить] (В); **2.** выражáть [вы́разить]

V

**void** [vɔɪd] **1.** пусто́й; лишённый (***of*** Р); *law* недействи́тельный; **2.** пустота́; пробе́л
**volatile** ['vɒlətaɪl] *chem.* лету́чий; *fig.* изме́нчивый
**volcano** [vɒl'keɪnəʊ] (*pl.* **volcanoes**) вулка́н
**volition** [və'lɪʃn] во́ля
**volley** ['vɒlɪ] *of shots* залп; *fig. of questions, etc.* град; **~ball** волейбо́л
**voltage** ['vəʊltɪdʒ] *el.* напряже́ние
**voluble** ['vɒljʊbl] разгово́рчивый, говорли́вый
**volum|e** ['vɒljuːm] объём; (*book*) том; (*capacity*) ёмкость *f*, вмести́тельность *f*; *fig. of sound, etc.* си́ла, полнота́; ~ ***control*** *radio, T.V.* регуля́тор зву́ка; **~inous** [və'luːmɪnəs] □ объёмистый; обши́рный
**volunt|ary** ['vɒləntrɪ] □ доброво́льный; **~eer** [vɒlən'tɪə] **1.** доброво́лец; **2.** *v/i.* вызыва́ться [вы́зваться] (***for*** на В); идти́ доброво́льцем; *v/t. help, etc.* предлага́ть [-ложи́ть]
**voluptu|ary** [və'lʌptʃʊərɪ] сластолю́бец; **~ous** [~ʃʊəs] сладостра́стный
**vomit** ['vɒmɪt] **1.** рво́та; **2.** [вы́]рвать: ***he is ~ing*** его́ рвёт
**voraci|ous** [və'reɪʃəs] □ прожо́рливый, жа́дный; ~ ***reader*** ненасы́тный чита́тель; **~ty** [və'ræsətɪ] прожо́рливость *f*
**vortex** ['vɔːteks] *mst. fig.* водоворо́т; *of wind mst. fig.* вихрь
**vote** [vəʊt] **1.** голосова́ние; (*vote cast*) го́лос; пра́во го́лоса; во́тум; (*decision*) реше́ние; ***cast a ~*** отдава́ть го́лос (***for*** за В; ***against*** про́тив Р); ***~ of no confidence*** во́тум недове́рия; ***put to the ~*** поста́вить *pf.* на голосова́ние; **2.** *v/i.* голосова́ть (*im*)*pf.*, *pf. a.* [про-] (***for*** за В; ***against*** про́тив Р); *v/t.* голосова́ть (*im*)*pf.*, *pf. a.* [про-]; **~r** ['vəʊtə] избира́тель *m*, -ница *f*
**voting** ['vəʊtɪŋ] **1.** голосова́ние; **2.** избира́тельный; ~ ***paper*** избира́тельный бюллете́нь
**vouch** [vaʊtʃ]: ~ ***for*** руча́ться [поручи́ться] за (В); **~er** ['vaʊtʃə] (*receipt*) распи́ска; *fin.* ва́учер
**vow** [vaʊ] **1.** обе́т, кля́тва; **2.** *v/t.* [по]кля́сться в (П)
**vowel** ['vaʊəl] гла́сный
**voyage** [vɔɪɪdʒ] **1.** путеше́ствие водо́й, пла́вание; **2.** путеше́ствовать мо́рем
**vulgar** ['vʌlgə] □ (*unrefined*) вульга́рный; (*low*) по́шлый; (*common*) широко́ распространённый
**vulnerable** ['vʌlnərəbl] □ *fig. position* уязви́мый; *person* рани́мый
**vulture** ['vʌltʃə] *zo.* гриф; *fig.* стервя́тник

# W

**wad** [wɒd] *of cotton, paper* комо́к; *of banknotes* па́чка
**waddle** ['wɒdl] ходи́ть вперева́лку
**wade** [weɪd] *v/t.* переходи́ть вброд; *v/i.* проб(и)ра́ться (***through*** по Д *or* че́рез В)
**wafer** ['weɪfə] *relig.* обла́тка; ва́фля
**waffle** ['wɒfl] *cul.* ва́фля
**waft** [wɒft, wɑːft] **1.** *of wind* дунове́ние; *of air* струя́; **2.** доноси́ться [-нести́сь]
**wag** [wæg] **1.** (*joker*) шутни́к; **2.** маха́ть [махну́ть] (Т); *of dog* виля́ть [вильну́ть] хвосто́м; ~ ***one's finger*** грози́ть па́льцем
**wage**[1] [weɪdʒ]: ~ ***war*** вести́ войну́
**wage**[2] *mst.* **~s** [weɪdʒɪz] *pl.* за́работная пла́та, зарпла́та; ~ ***freeze*** замора́живание за́работной пла́ты
**wag(g)on** ['wægən] пово́зка, теле́га; *rail. Brt.* това́рный ваго́н, *open* ваго́н-платфо́рма
**waif** [weɪf] *homeless* бездо́мный ребёнок; беспризорного; *neglected* за-

бро́шенный ребёнок
**wail** [weɪl] **1.** вопль *m*; вой; (*lament*) причита́ние; *of wind* завыва́ние; **2.** [за]вопи́ть; выть, завы́(ва́)ть; причита́ть
**waist** [weɪst] та́лия; ***stripped to the ~*** го́лый по по́яс; **~coat** ['weiskout, 'weskət] *chiefly Brt.* (*vest*) жиле́т
**wait** [weɪt] *v/i.* ждать (***for*** B *or* P), ожида́ть (***for*** P), подожда́ть *pf.* (***for*** B *or* P); (*часто*: ***~ at table***) обслу́живать [-жи́ть] (B); ***well, we'll have to ~ and see*** что ж, поживём-уви́дим; ***I'll ~ up for you*** я не ля́гу, подожду́ тебя́; *v/t.* выжида́ть [вы́ждать] (B); **~er** ['weɪtə] официа́нт
**waiting** ['weɪtɪŋ] ожида́ние; **~ room** приёмная; *rail.* зал ожида́ния
**waitress** ['weɪtrɪs] официа́нтка
**waive** [weɪv] *a claim, right, etc.* отка́зываться [-за́ться] от (P)
**wake** [weik] **1.**: ***hunger brought disease in its ~*** го́лод повлёк за собо́й эпиде́мию; **2.** [*irr.*] *v/i.* бо́дрствовать; (*mst.* ***~ up***) просыпа́ться [просну́ться]; *fig.* пробужда́ться [-уди́ться]; *v/t.* [раз]буди́ть; *fig.* пробужда́ть [-уди́ть]; *desire, etc.* возбужда́ть [-уди́ть]; **~ful** ['weɪkfl] □ бессо́нный; (*vigilant*) бди́тельный; **~n** ['weikən] → ***wake*** *2*
**walk** [wɔːk] **1.** *v/i.* ходи́ть, идти́ [пойти́]; (*stroll*) гуля́ть, прогу́ливаться; ***~ away*** отходи́ть [отойти́]; ***~ in(to)*** входи́ть [войти́]; ***~ off*** уходи́ть [уйти́]; ***~ out*** выходи́ть [вы́йти]; ***~ over*** (*cross*) переходи́ть (перейти́); ***~ up*** подходи́ть [-дойти́]; **2.** ходьба́; (*gait*) похо́дка; прогу́лка пешко́м; (*path*) тропа́, алле́я; ***~ of life*** сфе́ра де́ятельности; профе́ссия
**walking** ['wɔːkɪŋ] **1.** ходьба́; **2.**: ***~ dictionary*** ходя́чая энциклопе́дия; **~ stick** трость *f*
**walk|out** ['wɔːk'aut] забасто́вка; **~over** лёгкая побе́да
**wall** [wɔːl] **1.** стена́; (*side, unit*) сте́нка; ***drive s.o. up the ~*** доводи́ть кого́-л. до исступле́ния; **2.** обноси́ть стено́й; ***~ up*** заде́л(ыв)ать (*дверь и т. п.*)
**wallet** ['wɒlɪt] бума́жник
**wallflower** желтофио́ль *f*; *fig.* де́вушка, оста́вшаяся без партнёра (на та́нцах, и т. д.)
**wallop** ['wɒləp] *coll.* [по]би́ть, [по-, от]колоти́ть
**wallow** ['wɒləʊ] валя́ться
**wallpaper** обо́и *m/pl.*
**walnut** ['wɔːlnʌt] *bot.* гре́цкий оре́х
**walrus** ['wɔːlrəs] *zo.* морж
**waltz** [wɔːls] **1.** вальс; **2.** танцева́ть вальс
**wan** [wɒn] □ бле́дный, ту́склый
**wander** ['wɒndə] броди́ть; блужда́ть (*a. of gaze, thoughts, etc.*)
**wane** [weɪn]: ***be on the ~*** *of moon* убы́(ва́)ть, быть на уще́рбе; *of popularity, etc.* уменьша́ться [-ши́ться], снижа́ться [-и́зиться]
**wangle** ['wæŋgl] заполучи́ть хи́тростью; *coll.* вы́клянчить
**want** [wɒnt] **1.** (*lack*) недоста́ток (***of*** P *or* в П); (*powerty*) нужда́; (*need*) потре́бность *f*; **2.** *v/i.* ***be ~ing***: ***he is ~ing in patience*** ему́ недостаёт терпе́ния; ***~ for*** нужда́ться в (П); *v/t.* [за]хоте́ть (P *a.* B); [по]жела́ть (P *a.* B); нужда́ться в (Д); ***he ~s energy*** ему́ недостаёт эне́ргии; ***what do you ~?*** что вам ну́жно?; ***you ~ to see a doctor*** вам сле́дует обрати́ться к врачу́; **~ed** [~ɪd] (в объявле́ниях) тре́буется, *law* разы́скивается
**wanton** ['wɒntən] □ (*debauched*) распу́тный; *of cruelty* бессмы́сленный
**war** [wɔː] **1.** война́; *fig.* борьба́; ***be at ~*** воева́ть с (T); ***make ~*** вести́ войну́ ([***up***]***on*** с T); **2.** *attr.* вое́нный; ***~ memorial*** па́мятник солда́там, поги́бшим на войне́
**warble** ['wɔːbl] *of birds* издава́ть тре́ли; *of person* залива́ться пе́сней
**ward** [wɔːd] **1.** находя́щийся под опе́кой; *hospital* пала́та; **2. ~** (***off***) *blow* отража́ть [отрази́ть], *danger, illness* отвраща́ть [-рати́ть]; **~er** ['wɔːdə] *in prison* надзира́тель; тюре́мный контролёр; **~robe** ['wɔːdrəʊb] платяно́й шкаф; (*clothes*) гардеро́б
**ware** [weə] *in compds.* посу́да; **~s** *pl.*

това́р(ы *pl.*) изде́лия
**warehouse** ['weəhaʊs] склад
**war|fare** ['wɔːfeə] война́, веде́ние войны́; **~head** [~hed] боеголо́вка
**warm** [wɔːm] **1.** □ тёплый (*a. fig.*); *fig.* горя́чий; *person* серде́чный; **2.** тепло́; **3.** [на-, ото-, со]гре́ть, нагре́(-ва́)ть(ся), согре́(ва́)ться (*a.* ~ ***up***); ***his words ~ed my heart*** его слова́ согре́ли мою́ ду́шу; **~th** [~θ] тепло́; теплота́ (*a. fig.*)
**warn** [wɔːn] предупрежда́ть [-реди́ть] (***of, against*** о П); *caution* предостерега́ть [-стере́чь] (***of against*** от Р); **~ing** ['wɔːnɪŋ] предупрежде́ние; предостереже́ние
**warp** [wɔːp] *of wood* [по]коро́бить(ся); *fig.* извраща́ть [-рати́ть]; (*distort*) искажа́ть [искази́ть]; ***~ed mind*** извращённый ум
**warrant** ['wɒrənt] **1.** (*justification*) оправда́ние; *fin.* гара́нтия, руча́тельство; (~ *to arrest*) о́рдер на аре́ст; **2.** опра́вдывать [-да́ть]; руча́ться [поручи́тьсяэ́ за (В); (*guarantee*) гаранти́ровать (*im*)*pf.*; **~y** [~ɪ] гара́нтия; руча́тельство
**warrior** ['wɒrɪə] *poet.* во́ин
**wart** [wɔːt] борода́вка
**wary** ['weərɪ] □ осторо́жный
**was** [wəz, … wɒz] *pt. om* ***be***
**wash** [wɒʃ] **1.** *v/t. floor, dishes* [вы́-, по]мы́ть; *face* умы́ть *pf.*; *wound, etc.* промы́(ва́)ть; *clothes* [вы́]стира́ть; *v/i.* [вы́]мыться, умы́ться *pf.*; стира́ться; ***that won't ~*** *coll.* не пройдёт; э́тому никто́ не пове́рит; **2.** мытьё; сти́рка; (*articles for washing*) бельё; *of waves* прибо́й; ***mouth ~*** полоска́ние; **~basin** ра́ковина; **~er** ['wɒʃə] (*washing machine*) стира́льная маши́на; *tech.* ша́йба, прокла́дка; **~ing** ['wɒʃɪŋ] **1.** мытьё; сти́рка; (*articles*) бельё; **2.** стира́льный; ~ ***powder*** стира́льный порошо́к
**washroom** ['wɒʃrʊm] *Am. euph.* (*lavatory*) убо́рная
**wasp** [wɒsp] оса́
**waste** [weɪst] **1.** (*loss*) потеря́; (*wrong use*) изли́шняя тра́та; (*domestic*) отбро́сы *m/pl.*; *tech.* отхо́ды *m/pl.*; ***lay ~*** опустоша́ть [-ши́ть]; ~ ***of time*** напра́сная тра́та вре́мени; **2.**: **~land** пусты́рь *m*, *plot of ground* пу́стошь *f*; **3.** *v/t. money, etc.* [по-, рас]тра́тить зря; *time* [по]теря́ть; *v/i. resources* истоща́ться [-щи́ть-ся]; **~ful** ['weɪstfl] □ расточи́тельный; ~ **paper** испо́льзованная нену́жная бума́га; *for pulping* макулату́ра; **~paper basket** корзи́на для нену́жных бума́г
**watch**[1] [wɒtʃ] (*wrist~*) нару́чные часы́ *m/pl.*; ва́хта
**watch**[2] *v/i.*: ~ ***for*** *chance, etc.* выжида́ть [вы́ждать] (В); ~ ***out!*** осторо́жно!; *v/t.* (*look at*) смотре́ть; (*observe*) наблюда́ть, следи́ть за (Т); **~dog** сторожева́я соба́ка; **~ful** [~ful] бди́тельный; **~maker** часовщи́к; **~man** [~mən] вахтёр
**water** ['wɔːtə] **1.** вода́; **~s** *pl.* во́ды *f/pl.*; ***drink the ~s*** пить минера́льные во́ды; ***throw cold ~ on s.o.*** охлади́ть *pf.* пыл, отрезви́ть *pf.*; *attr.* водяно́й; во́дный; водо…; **2.** *v/t.* поли́(ва́)ть; *animals* [на]пои́ть; (*a.* ~ ***down***) разбавля́ть водо́й; *fig.* чересчу́р смягча́ть; *v/i. of eyes* слези́ться; ***it makes my mouth ~*** от э́того у меня́ слю́нки теку́т; **~colo(u)r** акваре́ль; **~fall** водопа́д; ~ **heater** (*kettle*) кипяти́льник
**watering** ['wɔːtərɪŋ]: ~ **can** ле́йка; ~ **place** *for animals* водопо́й; (*spa*) куро́рт на во́дах
**water| level** у́ровень воды́; ~ **lily** водяна́я ли́лия, кувши́нка; ~ **main** водопрово́дная магистра́ль; **~melon** арбу́з; ~ **polo** во́дное по́ло *n indecl.*; **~proof 1.** непромока́емый; **2.** непромока́емый плащ *m*; ~ **supply** водоснабже́ние; **~tight** водонепроница́емый; *fig. of alibi, etc.* неопровержи́мый; **~way** во́дный путь *m*; фарва́тер; **~works** *pl. a.*, *sg.* систе́ма водоснабже́ния; **~y** ['wɔːtərɪ] водяни́стый
**wave** [weɪv] **1.** волна́; *of hand* знак, взмах; **2.** *v/t.* [по]маха́ть, де́лать знак (Т); *hair* зави́(ва́)ть; ~ ***a p. away*** де́лать знак кому́-либо, что́бы он удали́лся; отстраня́ть [-ни́ть] жéстом; ~ ***aside***

W

*fig.* отмáхиваться [-хнýться] от (Р); *v/i. of flags* развевáться; *of hair* вúться; *of corn, grass* колыхáться; *of boughs* качáться; **~length** длинá волны́

**waver** ['weɪvə] [по]колебáться; *of flames* колыхáться [-хнýться]; *of troops, voice* дрóгнуть *pf.*

**wavy** ['weɪvɪ] волнúстый

**wax**[1] [wæks] воск; *in ear* сéра; *attr.* восковóй

**wax**[2] [~] [*irr.*] *of moon* прибы́(вá)ть

**way** [weɪ] *mst.* дорóга, путь *m*; (*direction*) сторонá, направлéние; мéтод, спóсоб; (*custom, habit*) обы́чай, привы́чка; (*a.* **~s** *pl.*) óбраз жúзни; поведéние; ***~ in, out*** вход, вы́ход; ***in a ~*** в извéстном смы́сле; ***in many ~s*** во мнóгих отношéниях; ***this ~*** сюдá; ***by the ~*** кстáти, мéжду прóчим; ***by ~ of*** в кáчестве (Р); (*through*) чéрез; ***in the ~*** *fig.* поперёк дорóги; ***on the ~*** в путú, по дорóге; ***out of the ~*** находя́щийся в сторонé; (*unusual*) необы́чный; необыкновéнный; ***under ~*** на ходý; в пугú; ***give ~*** уступáть [-пúть] (Д); ***have one's ~*** добивáться своегó; настáивать на своём; ***keep out of s.o.'s ~*** избегáть когó-л; ***lead the ~*** идтú впередú, [по]вестú; ***lose the ~*** заблудúться *pf.*; **~lay** [weɪ'leɪ] [*irr.* (***lay***)] подстерегáть [-рéчь]; **~side** **1.** обóчина; **2.** прúдорожный; **~ward** ['weɪwəd] □ своенрáвный

**we** [wɪ, … wiː] *pers. pron.* мы

**weak** [wiːk] □ слáбый; **~en** ['wiːkən] *v/t.* ослабля́ть [-áбить]; *v/i.* [о]слабéть; **~ling** ['wiːklɪŋ] физúчески слáбый *or* слабовóльный человéк; **~ly** [-lɪ] *adv.* слáбо; **~ness** [-nɪs] слáбость *f*

**wealth** [welθ] богáтство; (*profusion*) изобúлие; **~y** ['welθɪ] □ богáтый

**wean** [wiːn] отнимáть от грудú; отучáть [-чúть] (***from, of*** от Р)

**weapon** ['wepən] орýжие (*a. fig.*)

**wear** [weə] **1.** [*irr.*] *v/t. hat, glasses, etc.* носúть; (*a.* ***~ away, down, off***) стирáть [стерéть]; изнáшивать (*fig.* изнуря́ть [-рúть] *mst.* ***~ out***); *v/i. clothes* носúться; ***~ on*** мéдленно тянýться; **2.** (*a.* ***~ and tear***, *part. tech.*) износ́; ***men's*** (***ladies'***) ***~*** мужскáя (жéнская) одéжда

**wear|iness** ['wɪərɪnɪs] устáлость *f*; утомлённость *f*; **~isome** [-səm] □ (*tiring*) утомúтельный; (*boring*) скýчный; **~y** ['wɪərɪ] **1.** утомлённый; **2.** утомля́ть(ся) [-мúть(ся)]; *v/i.* наскýчить *pf.*

**weasel** ['wiːzl] *zo.* лáска

**weather** ['weðə] **1.** погóда; ***be a bit under the ~*** невáжно себя́ чýвствовать; быть в плохóм настроéнии; **2.** *v/t. of rocks* изнáшивать [-носúть]; *a storm* выдéрживать [вы́держать] (*a. fig.*); *v/i.* выветриваться [вы́ветриться]; **~-beaten**, **~worn** *face* обвéтренный; *person* пострадáвший от непогóды; **~ forecast** прогнóз погóды

**weav|e** [wiːv] [*irr.*] [со]ткáть; [с]плестú; *fig. story* сочиня́ть [-нúть]; **~er** ['wiːvə] ткач *m*, ткачúха *f*

**web** [web] *spider's* паутúна; ***a ~ of lies*** паутúна лжи

**wed** [wed] *of woman* выходúть зáмуж (за В); *of man* женúться (*im*)*pf.* (на П); сочетáться брáком; **~ding** ['wedɪŋ] **1.** свáдьба; **2.** свáдебный; **~ding ring** обручáльное кольцó

**wedge** [wedʒ] **1.** клин; ***drive a ~ between*** *fig.* вби(вá)ть клин мéжду (Т); **2.** (*a.* ***~ in***) вклúнивать(ся) [-нить(ся)]; ***~ o.s. in*** втúскиваться [втúснуться]

**wedlock** ['wedlɒk] брак

**Wednesday** ['wenzdɪ] средá

**wee** [wiː] крóшечный, малю́сенький; ***~ hours*** предрассвéтные часы́

**weed** [wiːd] **1.** сорня́к; **2.** [вы́]полóть; **~killer** гербицúд; **~y** ['wiːdɪ] зарóсший сорнякóм; *coll. fig. person* тóщий, долговя́зый

**week** [wiːk] недéля; ***by the ~*** понедéльно; ***for ~s on end*** цéлыми недéлями; ***this day a ~*** недéлю томý назáд; чéрез недéлю; **~day** бýдний день *m*; **~end** [wiːk'end] суббóта и воскресéнье, уикéнд; **~ly** ['wiːklɪ] **1.** еженедéльный; **2.** еженедéльник

**weep** [wiːp] [*irr.*] [за]плáкать; **~ing**

W

['wiːpɪŋ] *person* пла́чущий; *willow* плаку́чий
**weigh** [weɪ] *v/t.* взве́шивать [-е́сить] (*a. fig.*); **~ anchor** поднима́ть я́корь; **~ed down** отягощённый; *v/i.* ве́сить; взве́шиваться [-е́ситься]; *fig.* име́ть вес, значе́ние; **~ (up)on** тяготе́ть над (T)
**weight** [weɪt] **1.** вес; (*heaviness*) тя́жесть *f*; (*object for weighing*) ги́ря; *sport* шта́нга; *of responsibility* бре́мя *n*; влия́ние; **2.** отягоща́ть [-готи́ть]; *fig.* обременя́ть [-ни́ть]; **~y** ['weɪtɪ] □ тяжёлый; тру́дный; *fig.* ва́жный, ве́ский
**weird** [wɪəd] (*uncanny*) таи́нственный; стра́нный
**welcome** ['welkəm] **1.** приве́тствие; **you are ~ to** + *inf.* я охо́тно позволя́ю вам (+ *inf.*); (**you are**) **~** не́ за что!; **~!** добро́ пожа́ловать!; **2.** (*wanted*) жела́нный; (*causing gladness*) прия́тный; **3.** (*greet*) приве́тствовать (*a. fig.*); (*receive*) раду́шно принима́ть
**weld** [weld] *tech.* сва́ривать [-и́ть]
**welfare** ['welfeə] *of nation* благосостоя́ние; *of person* благополу́чие; *Am.* социа́льная по́мощь *f*
**well¹** [wel] коло́дец; *fig.* исто́чник; (*stairwell*) пролёт; *tech.* бурова́я сква́жина; **2.** хлы́нуть *pf.*
**well²** [~wel] **1.** хорошо́; **~ off** состоя́тельный; **I am not ~** мне нездоро́вится; **2.** *int.* ну! *or* ну, …; **~-being** [~'biːɪng] благополу́чие; **~-bred** [~'bred] (хорошо́) воспи́танный; **~-built** [~'bɪlt] хорошо́ сложённый; **~-founded** [~'faʊndɪd] обосно́ванный; **~-kept** [~'kept] *garden* ухо́женный; *secret* тща́тельно храни́мый; **~-read** [~'red] начи́танный; *in history, etc.* хорошо́ зна́ющий; **~-timed** [~'taɪmd] своевре́менный; **~-to-do** [~tə'duː] состоя́тельный, зажи́точный; **~-worn** [~'wɔːn] поно́шенный; *fig.* изби́тый
**Welsh** [welʃ] **1.** уэ́льский, валли́йский; **2.** валли́йский язы́к; **the ~** валли́йцы *m/pl.*
**welter** ['weltə] *of ideas* сумбу́р
**went** [went] *pt. от* **go**
**wept** [wept] *pt. и pt. p. от* **weap**
**were** [wə, wɜː] *pt. pl. от* **be**
**west** [west] **1.** за́пад; **2.** за́падный; **3.** *adv.* к за́паду, на за́пад; **~ of** к за́паду от (P); **~erly** ['westəlɪ], **~ern** ['westən] за́падный; **~ward(s)** ['westwəd(z)] на за́пад
**wet** [wet] **1.** дождли́вая пого́да; **don't go out in the ~** не выходи́ под дождь; **2.** мо́крый; *weather* сыро́й; дождли́вый; "**~ Paint**" "окра́шено"; **get ~ through** насквозь промо́кнуть *pf.*; **3.** [*irr.*] [на]мочи́ть, нама́чивать [-мочи́ть]
**whale** [weɪl] кит
**wharf** [wɔːf] прича́л, при́стань *f*
**what** [wɒt] **1.** что?; ско́лько …?; **2.** то, что; что; **~ about … ?** что но́вого о …?; ну как …?; **~ for?** заче́м?; **~ a pity …** кака́я жа́лость …; **3. ~ with …** из-за (P), отча́сти от (P); **4.** како́й; **~(so)ever** [wɔt(sou)'evə] како́й бы ни; что бы ни; **there is no doubt whatever** нет никако́го сомне́ния
**wheat** [wiːt] пшени́ца
**wheel** [wiːl] **1.** колесо́; *mot.* руль *m*; **2.** *pram, etc.* ката́ть, [по]кати́ть; **~ into** вка́тывать [-ти́ть]; **~ round** повора́чивать(ся) [поверну́ть(ся)]; **~barrow** та́чка; **~chair** инвали́дная коля́ска
**wheeze** [wiːz] хрипе́ть; дыша́ть с при́свистом
**when** [wen] **1.** когда́?; **2.** *conj.* когда́, в то вре́мя как, как то́лько; тогда́ как
**whenever** [wen'evə] вся́кий раз когда́; когда́ бы ни
**where** [weə] где, куда́; **from ~** отку́да; **~about(s)** **1.** [weərə'baʊt(s)] где?; **2.** ['weərəbaʊt(s)] местонахожде́ние; **~as** [weər'æz] тогда́ как; поско́льку; **~by** [weə'baɪ] посре́дством чего́; **~in** [weər'ɪn] в чём; **~of** [weər'ɒv] из кото́рого; о кото́ром; о чём; **~upon** [weərə'pɒn] по́сле чего́
**wherever** [weər'evə] где бы ни; куда́ бы ни
**wherewithal** [weəwɪ'ðɔːl] необходи́мые сре́дства *n/pl.*
**whet** [wet] [на]точи́ть; *fig.* возбуж-

W

да́ть [-уди́ть]
**whether** ['weðə] … ли; **~ or not** так и́ли ина́че; в любо́м слу́чае
**which** [wɪtʃ] **1.** кото́рый?; како́й?; **2.** кото́рый; что; **~ever** [~'evə] како́й уго́дно, како́й бы ни …
**whiff** [wɪf] *of air* дунове́ние, струя́; (*smell*) за́пах; *of pipe*, *etc.* затя́жка
**while** [waɪl] **1.** вре́мя *n*, промежу́ток вре́мени; ***after a ~*** че́рез не́которое вре́мя; ***a little*** (***long***) ***~ ago*** неда́вно (давно́); ***in a little ~*** ско́ро; ***for a ~*** на вре́мя; *coll.* ***worth ~*** сто́ящий затра́ченного труда́; **2.** ***~ away*** *time* проводи́ть [-вести́]; **3.** (*a.* ***whilst*** [waɪlst]) пока́, в то вре́мя как; тогда́ как
**whim** [wɪm] при́хоть *f*, капри́з
**whimper** ['wɪmpə] [за]хны́кать
**whim|sical** ['wɪmzɪkl] ☐ прихотли́вый, причу́дливый; **~sy** ['wɪmzɪ] при́хоть *f*; причу́да
**whine** [waɪn] [за]скули́ть; [за]хны́кать
**whip** [wɪp] **1.** *v/t.* хлеста́ть [-стну́ть]; (*punish*) [вы́]сечь; *eggs*, *cream* сби(ва́)ть; ***~ out*** *gun*, *etc.* выхва́тывать ['-хватить]; ***~ up*** расшеве́ливать [-ли́ть]; подстёгивать [-стегну́ть]; *v/i.*: ***I'll just ~ round to the neighbo(u)rs*** я то́лько сбе́гаю к сосе́дям; **2.** плеть; кнут, (*a.* ***riding ~***) хлыст
**whippet** ['wɪpɪt] *zo.* го́нчая
**whipping** ['wɪpɪŋ] (*punishment*) по́рка
**whirl** [wɜːl] **1.** *of dust* вихрь *m*; круже́ние; ***my head is in a ~*** у меня́ голова́ идёт кру́гом; **2.** кружи́ть(ся); **~pool** водоворо́т; **~wind** смерч
**whisk** [wɪsk] **1.** (*egg ~*) мутóвка; **2.** *v/t. cream*, *etc.* сби(ва́)ть; (*remove*) смáхивать [-хну́ть]; *v/i. of mouse*, *etc.* ю́ркать [ю́ркнуть]; **~ers** ['wɪskəz] *pl. zo.* усы́ *m/pl.*; (*side-~*) бакенба́рды *f/pl.*
**whiskey**, *Brt.* **whisky** ['wɪskɪ] ви́ски *n indecl.*
**whisper** ['wɪspə] **1.** шёпот; **2.** шепта́ть [шепну́ть]
**whistle** ['wɪsl] **1.** свист; свисто́к (*a. instrument*); **2.** свисте́ть [сви́стнуть]
**white** [waɪt] **1.** *com.* бе́лый; (*pale*) бле́дный; ***~ coffee*** ко́фе с молоко́м; ***~ lie*** ложь *f* во слаце́ние; **2.** бе́лый цвет; *of eye*, *egg* бело́к; **~n** ['waɪtn] [по]бели́ть; (*turn white*) [по]беле́ть; **~ness** ['waɪtnɪs] белизна́; **~wash 1.** побе́лка; **2.** [по]бели́ть; *fig.* обеля́ть [-ли́ть]
**whitish** ['waɪtɪʃ] бел(ес)ова́тый
**Whitsun** ['wɪtsn] *relig.* Тро́ица
**whiz(z)** [wɪz] *of bullets*, *etc.* свисте́ть; ***~ past*** промча́ться *pf.* ми́мо
**who** [huː] *pron.* **1.** кто?; **2.** кото́рый; кто; тот, кто …; *pl.*: те, кто
**whoever** [huː'əvə] *pron.* кто бы ни …; (*who ever*) кто то́лько; кото́рый бы ни …
**whole** [həʊl] **1.** ☐ (*complete*, *entire*) це́лый, весь; (*intact*, *undamaged*) це́лый; ***~ milk*** це́льное молоко́; ***~ number*** це́лое число́; **2.** це́лое; всё *n*; ито́г; ***on the ~*** (*entity*, *totality*) в це́лом; **~-hearted** ☐ и́скренний, от всего́ се́рдца; **~sale 1.** (*mst.* ***~ trade***) о́птовая торго́вля; **2.** о́птовый; *fig.* (*indiscriminate*) огу́льный; ***~ dealer*** о́птовый торго́вец; **3.** о́птом; **~some** ['həʊlsəm] ☐ поле́зный, здравый
**wholly** ['həʊlɪ] *adv.* целико́м, всеце́лпо́лностью
**whom** [huːm] *pron.* (*винительный падеж от* ***who***) кого́ *и т. д.*; кото́рого *и т. д.*
**whoop** [huːp]: ***~ of joy*** ра́достный во́зглас; **~ing cough** ['huːpɪŋ kɒf] *med.* коклю́ш
**whose** [huːz] (*родительный падеж от* ***who***) чей *m*, чья *f*, чьё *n*, чьи *pl.*; *relative pron. mst.*: кото́рого, кото́рой: ***~ father*** оте́ц кото́рого
**why** [waɪ] **1.** *adv.* почему́?, отчего́?, заче́м?; **2.** *int.* да ведь …; что ж…
**wick** [wɪk] фити́ль *m*
**wicked** ['wɪkɪd] ☐ (*malicious*) злой, зло́бный; (*depraved*) бессо́вестный; (*immoral*) безнра́вственный
**wicker** ['wɪkə]: ***~ basket*** плетёная корзи́нка; ***~ chair*** плетёный стул
**wide** [waɪd] *a.* ☐ *and adv.* широ́кий; обши́рный; широко́; далеко́, далёко

(***of*** от Р); ~ ***awake*** бди́тельный; осмотри́тельный; ***three feet*** ~ три фу́та в ширину́, шириной в три фу́та; ~ ***of the mark*** далёкий от и́стины; не по существу́; ~**n** ['waɪdn] расширя́ть(ся) [-и́рить(ся)]; ~**spread** распространённый
**widow** ['wɪdəʊ] вдова́; ***grass*** ~ соло́менная вдова́; *attr.* вдо́вий; ~**er** [~ə] вдове́ц
**width** [wɪdθ] ширина́; (*extent*) широта́
**wield** [wi:ld] *lit.* владе́ть (Т); держа́ть в рука́х
**wife** [waɪf] жена́; (*spouse*) супру́га
**wig** [wɪg] пари́к
**wild** [waɪld] **1.** □ ди́кий; *flowers* полево́й; *sea* бу́рный; *behavio(u)r* бу́йный; ***be*** ~ ***about s.o. or s.th.*** быть без ума́/в ди́ком) восто́рге от кого́-л. *or* чего́-л.; ***run*** ~ расти́ без присмо́тра; ***talk*** ~ говори́ть не ду́мая; **2.** ~, ~**s** [~z] ди́кая ме́стность *f*; де́бри *f/pl.*; ~**cat strike** неофициа́льная забасто́вка; ~**erness** ['wɪldənɪs] пусты́ня, ди́кая ме́стность *f*; ~**fire** ***like*** ~ с быстрото́й мо́лнии; ~**fowl** дичь *f*
**wile** [waɪl] *mst.* ~**s** *pl.* хи́трость *f*; уло́вка
**wil(l)ful** ['wɪlfl] упря́мый, своево́льный; (*intentional*) преднаме́ренный
**will** [wɪl] **1.** во́ля; (*willpower*) си́ла во́ли; (*desire*) жела́ние; *law* (*testament*) завеща́ние; ***with a*** ~ энерги́чно; **2.** [*irr.*] *v/aux.*: ***he*** ~ ***come*** он придёт; **3.** завеща́ть (*im*)*pf.*; [по]жела́ть, [за]хоте́ть; ~ ***o.s. compel*** заставля́ть [-ста́вить] себя́
**willing** ['wɪlɪŋ] □ *to help, etc.* гото́вый (***to*** на В *or* + *inf.*); ~**ness** [~nɪs] гото́вность *f*
**willow** ['wɪləʊ] *bot.* и́ва
**wilt** [wɪlt] *of flowers* [за]вя́нуть; *of person* [по]ни́кнуть; раскиса́ть [-ки́снуть]
**wily** ['waɪlɪ] □ хи́трый, кова́рный
**win** [wɪn] [*irr.*] *v/t.* побежда́ть [-еди́ть]; выи́грывать; *victory* одержи́вать [-жа́ть]; *prize* получа́ть [-чи́ть]; ~ ***a p. over*** угова́ривать [-вори́ть]; склони́ть кого́-л. на свою́ сто́рону; *v/i.* выи́грывать [вы́играть]; оде́рживать побе́ду
**wince** [wɪns] вздра́гивать [вздро́гнуть]
**winch** [wɪntʃ] лебёдка; во́рот
**wind**[1] [wɪnd] ве́тер; (*breath*) дыха́ние; *of bowels, etc.* га́зы *m/pl.*; *mus.* духовы́е инструме́нты *m/pl.* ***let me get my*** ~ ***back*** подожди́, я отдышу́сь; ***get*** ~ ***of*** *s.th.* [по]чу́ять; узна́ть *pf.*, пронюха́ть *pf.*; ***second*** ~ второ́е дыха́ние
**wind**[2] [waɪnd] [*irr.*] *v/t.* нама́тывать [намота́ть]; обма́тывать [обмота́ть]; *of plant* обви́(ва́)ть; ~ ***up*** *watch* заводи́ть [завести́]; *comm.* ликвиди́ровать (*im*)*pf.*; *discussion, etc.* зака́нчивать [зако́нчить]; *v/i.* нама́тываться [намота́ться]; обви́(ва́)ться
**wind|bag** ['wɪndbæg] *sl.* болту́н; пустозво́н; ~**fall** пада́нец; *fig.* неожи́данное сча́стье
**winding** ['waɪndɪŋ] **1.** изги́б, изви́лина; (*act of* ~) нама́тывание; *el.* обмо́тка; **2.** изви́листый; ~ ***stairs*** *pl.* винтова́я ле́стница
**wind instrument** духово́й инструме́нт
**windmill** ветряна́я ме́льница
**window** ['wɪndəʊ] окно́; (*shop* ~) витри́на; ~ **dressing** оформле́ние витри́ны; *fig.* показу́ха *coll.*; ~**sill** [~sɪl] подоко́нник
**wind|pipe** ['wɪndpaɪp] *anat.* трахе́я; ~**shield**, *Brt.* ~**screen** *mot.* ветрово́е стекло́
**windy** ['wɪndɪ] □ ве́треный; *fig.* (*wordy*) многосло́вный; *chiefly Brt. coll.* ***get*** ~ стру́сить *pf.*
**wine** [waɪn] вино́; ~ **glass** бокал; рю́мка
**wing** [wɪŋ] (*a. arch.*) крыло́; *thea.* ~**s** *pl.* кули́сы *f/pl.*; ***take*** ~ полете́ть *pf.*; ***on the*** ~ в полёте; ***take s.o. under one's*** ~ взять *pf.* кого́-л. под своё кры́лышко
**wink** [wɪŋk] **1.** (*moment*) миг; *coll.* ***not get a*** ~ ***of sleep*** не сомкну́ть *pf.* глаз; **2.** морга́ть [-гну́ть], мига́ть [мигну́ть]; ~ ***at*** подми́гивать [-гну́ть] (Д); *fig.* (*connive*) смотре́ть сквозь па́льцы на (В)

**win|ner**['wɪnə] победи́тель *m*, -ница *f*; *in some competitions* призёр; лауреа́т; ***Nobel Prize*** ♀ лауреа́т Но́белевской пре́мии; **~ning** ['wɪnɪŋ] **1.** (*on way to winning*) выи́грывающий; побежда́ющий; (*having won*) вы́игравший, победи́вший; *fig.* (*attractive, persuasive*) обая́тельный (*a.* **~some** [-səm]); **2. ~s** *pl.* вы́игрыш

**wint|er**['wɪntə] **1.** зима́; *attr.* зи́мний; **2.** проводи́ть зи́му, [пере-, про]зимова́ть; **~ry** ['wɪntrɪ] зи́мний

**wipe** [waɪp] вытира́ть [вы́тереть]; *tears* утира́ть [утере́ть]; ***~ off*** стира́ть [стере́ть]; ***~ out*** (*destroy*) уничтожа́ть [-о́жить]; **~r** ['waɪpə] (*windshield ~, Brt. windscreen ~*) стеклоочисти́тель; *coll.* дво́рник

**wire** ['waɪə] **1.** про́волока; *el.* про́вод; *coll.* телегра́мма; **2.** [с]де́лать прово́дку; телеграфи́ровать (*im*)*pf.*; **~ netting** прово́лочная се́тка

**wiry** ['waɪərɪ] *person* жи́листый; *hair* жёсткий

**wisdom**['wɪzdəm] му́дрость *f*; ***~ tooth*** зуб му́дрости

**wise**[1] [waɪz] му́дрый; благоразу́мный; **~crack** *coll.* остро́та

**wise**[2] [~]: ***in no ~*** нико́им о́бразом

**wish** [wɪʃ] **1.** жела́ние; пожела́ние (*a. greetings*); **2.** [по]жела́ть (Р) (*a.* ***~ for***); ***~ well*** (***ill***) жела́ть добра́ (зла); **~ful**['wɪʃfl]: ***~ thinking*** *in context* принима́ть жела́емое за действи́тельное

**wisp** [wɪsp] *of smoke* стру́йка; *of hair* прядь *f*

**wistful** ['wɪstfl] □ заду́мчивый, тоскли́вый

**wit** [wɪt] *verbal felicity* остроу́мие; (*mental astuteness*) ум, ра́зум (*a.* **~s** *pl.*); остросло́в; ***be at one's ~'s end*** в отча́янии; ***I'm at my ~s end*** пря́мо ум за ра́зум захо́дит; ***be scared out of one's ~s*** испуга́ться до́ сме́рти

**witch** [wɪtʃ] колду́нья; ве́дьма; **~craft** колдовство́; **~hunt** охо́та за ве́дьмами

**with**[wɪð] с (Т), со (Т); (*because of*) от (Р); у (Р); при (П); ***~ a knife*** ножо́м, ***~ a pen*** ру́чкой

**withdraw** [wɪð'drɔː] [*irr.* (***draw***)] *v/t.* убира́ть; *quickly* одёргивать [-рнуть]; *money from banks* брать [взять]; брать наза́д; *from circulation* изыма́ть [изъя́ть]; *troops* выводи́ть [-вести]; *v/i.* удаля́ться [-ли́ться]; *mil.* отходи́ть [отойти́]; **~al** [-əl] изъя́тие; удале́ние; *mil.* отхо́д; вы́вод; **~n** *person* за́мкнутый

**wither** ['wɪðə] *v/i.* [за]вя́нуть; *of colo(u)r* [по]блёкнуть; *v/t. crops* погуби́ть *pf.*; ***~ed hopes*** увя́дшие наде́жды

**with|hold** [wɪð'həʊld] [*irr.* (***hold***)] (*refuse to give*) отка́зывать [-за́ть] в (П); *information* скры(ва́)ть (***from*** от Р); **~in** [~'ɪn] **1.** *lit. adv.* внутри́; **2.** *prp.* в (П), в преде́лах (Р); внутри́ (Р); ***~ call*** в преде́лах слы́шимости; **~out** [~'aʊt] **1.** *lit. adv.* вне, снару́жи; **2.** *prp.* без (Р); вне (Р); ***it goes ~ saying …*** само́ собо́й разуме́ется; **~stand** [~'stænd] [*irr.* (***stand***)] выде́рживать [вы́держать] про тивостоя́ть (Д)

**witness** ['wɪtnɪs] **1.** свиде́тель *m*, -ница *f*; очеви́дец *m*, -дица *f*; ***bear ~*** свиде́тельствовать (***to, of*** о П); **2.** свиде́тельствовать о (П); быть свиде́телем (Р); *signature, etc.* заверя́ть [-е́рить]

**wit|ticism** ['wɪtɪsɪzəm] остро́та; **~ty** ['wɪtɪ] □ остроу́мный

**wives** [waɪvz] *pl. от* ***wife***

**wizard** ['wɪzəd] волше́бник, маг

**wizened** ['wɪznd] *old lady* вы́сохший; *apple, etc.* смо́рщенный

**wobble** ['wɒbl] кача́ться, шата́ться

**woe** [wəʊ] го́ре; **~begone** ['wəʊbɪgɒn] удручённый

**woke** [wəʊk] *pt. от* ***wake***; **~n** ['woukən] *pt. p. от* ***wake***

**wolf** [wʊlf] **1.** волк; **2.** ***~ down*** есть бы́стро и с жа́дностью; на́спех проглоти́ть

**wolves** [wʊlvz] *pl. от* ***wolf***

**woman** ['wʊmən] же́нщина; ***old ~*** старуха; ***~ doctor*** же́нщина-врач; **~ish** [~ɪʃ] □ женоподо́бный, ба́бий; **~kind** [~'kaɪnd] *collect.* же́нщины *f/pl.*; **~ly** [~lɪ] же́нственный

**womb** [wuːm] *anat.* ма́тка; чре́во ма́тери

**women** ['wɪmɪn] *pl. от* ***woman***; **~folk**

[~fəʊk] же́нщины *f/pl.*
**won** [wʌn] *pt.* и *pt. p. от* **win**
**wonder** ['wʌndə] **1.** удивле́ние, изумле́ние; (*miracle*) чу́до; **2.** удивля́ться [-ви́ться] (***at*** Д); ***I ~*** интере́сно, хоте́лось бы знать; **~ful** [~fl] □ удиви́тельный, замеча́тельный
**won't** [wəʊnt] не бу́ду *и т. д.*; не хочу́ *и т. д.*
**wont** [~]: ***be ~*** име́ть обыкнове́ние
**woo** [wuː] уха́живать за (Т)
**wood** [wʊd] лес; (*material*) де́рево, лесоматериа́л; (*fire~*) дрова́ *n/pl.*; ***dead ~*** сухосто́й; *fig.* балла́ст; *attr.* лесно́й, деревя́нный; дровяно́й; **~cut** гравю́ра на де́реве; **~cutter** дровосе́к; **~ed** ['wʊdɪd] леси́стый; **~en** ['wʊdn] деревя́нный; *fig.* безжи́зненный; **~pecker** [~pekə] дя́тел; **~winds** [~wɪndz] деревя́нные духовы́е инструме́нты *m/pl.*; **~work** деревя́нные изде́лия *n/pl.*; *of building* деревя́нные ча́сти *f/pl.*; **~y** ['wʊdɪ] леси́стый
**wool** [wʊl] шерсть *f*; *attr.* шерстяно́й; **~gathering** ['wʊlgæðərɪŋ] *fig.* мечта́тельность; вита́ние в облака́х; **~(l)en** ['wʊlɪn] шерстяно́й; **~ly** ['wʊlɪ] **1.** (*like wool*) шерсти́стый; *thoughts* нея́сный; **2. *woollies*** *pl.* шерстяны́е изде́лия *n/pl.*; *esp.* бельё
**word** [wɜːd] **1.** *mst.* сло́во; разгово́р; (*news*) изве́стия, но́вости; (*promise*) обеща́ние, сло́во; **~*s*** *pl. mus.* слова́ *n/pl.*; *fig.* (*angry argument*) кру́пный разгово́р; ***in a ~*** одни́м сло́вом; ***in other ~s*** други́ми слова́ми; ***~ of hono(u)r*** че́стное сло́во; **2.** формули́ровать (*im*)*pf., pf. a.* [c-]; **~ing** ['wɜːdɪŋ] формулиро́вка
**wordy** ['wɜːdɪ] □ многосло́вный
**wore** [wɔː] *pt. от* ***wear 1***
**work** [wɜːk] **1.** рабо́та; труд; де́ло; заня́тие; *art, lit.* произведе́ние, сочине́ние; *attr.* работо…; рабо́чий; **~*s*** *pl.* механи́зм; (*construction*) строи́тельные рабо́ты *f/pl.*; (*mill*) заво́д; (*factory*) фа́брика; ***all in a day's ~*** де́ло привы́чное; ***be out of ~*** быть безрабо́тным; ***I'm sure it's his ~*** уве́рен, э́то де́ло его́ рук; ***set to ~*** бра́ться за рабо́ту; **2.** *v/i.* рабо́тать; занима́ться [-ня́ться] (*have effect*) де́йствовать; *v/t.* [*irr.*] *land, etc.* обраба́тывать [-бо́тать]; [*regular vb.*] *mine, etc.* разраба́тывать [-бо́тать]; *machine, etc.* приводи́ть в де́йствие; ***~ one's way*** *through crowd* проби́(ва́)ться, с трудо́м пробива́ть себе́ доро́гу (*both a. fig.*); ***~ off*** *debt* отраба́тывать [-бо́тать]; *anger* успока́иваться [-ко́иться]; ***~ out*** *problem* реша́ть [реши́ть]; *plan* разраба́тывать [-бо́тать]; *agreement* составля́ть [-вить]; [*a. irr.*]; ***~ up*** (*excite*) возбужда́ть; *coll.* взбудора́жи(ва)ть; ***don't get ~ed up*** споко́йно
**work|able** ['wɜːkəbl] осуществи́мый; приго́дный; приго́дный для обрабо́тки; **~aday** бу́дний; повседневный; **~day** (*time worked for payment*) трудоде́нь *m*; **~er** ['wɜːkə] *manual* рабо́чий; рабо́тник (-ица); **~ing** ['wɜːkɪŋ] рабо́чий; рабо́тающий; де́йствующий; ***in ~ order*** в рабо́чем состоя́нии; ***~ capital*** оборо́тный капита́л
**workman** ['wɜːkmən] рабо́тник; **~ship** мастерство́; (*signs of skill*) отде́лка
**work|shop** ['wɜːkʃɒp] мастерска́я; *in factory* цех
**world** [wɜːld] *com.* мир, свет; *attr.* миров́ой, всеми́рный; *fig.* ***a ~ of difference*** огро́мная ра́зница; ***come into the ~*** роди́ться, появи́ться *pf.* на свет; ***come up in the ~*** преуспе́(ва́)ть (в жи́зни); сде́лагь карье́ру; ***it's a small ~*** мир те́сен; ***champion of the ~*** чемпио́н ми́ра
**wordly** ['wɜːldlɪ] све́тский
**world power** мирова́я держа́ва
**worldwide** ['wɜːldwaɪd] всеми́рный
**worm** [wɜːm] **1.** червя́к, червь *m*; *med.* глист; **2.** вы́ве́дывать (вы́ведать), вы́пы́тывать [вы́пытать] (***out of*** у Р); ***~ o.s.*** *fig.* вкра́дываться [вкра́сться] (***into*** в В)
**worn** [wɔːn] *pt. p. от* **wear**; **~-out** [wɔːn'aʊt] изно́шенный; *fig.* изму́ченный
**worry** ['wʌrɪ] **1.** беспоко́йство; трево́га; (*care*) забо́та; **2.** беспоко́ить(ся); (*bother with questions, etc.*) надоеда́ть [-е́сть] (Д); (*pester*) пристава́ть к (Д);

[за]му́чить; ***she'll ~ herself to death!*** она́ совсе́м изведёт себя́!

**worse** [wɜːs] ху́дший; *adv.* ху́же; *of pain, etc.* сильне́е; ***from bad to ~*** всё ху́же и ху́же; **~n** ['wɜːsn] ухудша́ть(ся) [уху́дшить(ся)]

**worship** ['wɜːʃɪp] **1.** *relig.* богослуже́ние; **2.** поклоня́ться (Д); (*love*) обожа́ть; **~per** [-ə] покло́нник *m*, -ица *f*

**worst** [wɜːst] (самый) ху́дший, наиху́дший〉; *adv.* ху́же всего́; ***if the ~ comes to the ~*** в са́мом ху́дшем слу́чае; ***the ~ of it is that …*** ху́же всего то, что …

**worth** [wɜːθ] **1.** сто́ящий; заслу́живающий; ***be ~*** заслу́живать, сто́ить; **2.** цена́; сто́имость *f*; це́нность *f*; ***idea of little ~*** иде́я, не име́ющая осо́бой це́нности; **~less** ['wəːθlis] ничего́ не сто́ящий; не име́ющий це́нности; **~while** ['wəːθ'wail] *coll.* сто́ящий; ***be ~*** име́ть смысл; ***be not ~*** не сто́ить труда́; **~y** ['wɔːði] □ досто́йный (***of*** Р); заслу́живающий (***of*** В)

**would** [wʊd] (*pt. от* ***will***) *v/aux.*: ***he ~ do it*** он сде́лал бы э́то; он обы́чно э́то де́лал

**wound**[1] [wuːnd] **1.** ра́на, ране́ние; **2.** ра́нить (*im*)*pf.*; заде́(ва́)ть

**wound**[2] [waʊnd] *pt. и pt. p. от* ***wind***

**wove** ['wəʊv] *pt. от* ***weave***; **~n** ['wouvn] *pt. p. от* ***weave***

**wrangle** ['ræŋgl] **1.** препрека́ния *n/pl.*, **2.** препрека́ться

**wrap** [ræp] *v/t.* (*часто* ***~ up***) завёртывать [заверну́ть]; *in paper* обёртывать [оберну́ть]; заку́т(ыв)ать; *fig.* оку́т(ыв)ать; ***be ~ped up in*** *thought, etc.* быть погружённым в (В); *v/i.* ***~ up*** заку́т(ыв)аться; **~per** ['ræpə] обёртка; **~ping** ['ræpɪŋ] упако́вка; обёртка

**wrath** [rɔːθ] гнев

**wreath** [riːθ], *pl.* **~s** [riːðz] *placed on coffin* вено́к; гирля́нда; *fig. of smoke* кольцо́, коле́чко

**wreck** [rek] **1.** (*destruction*) *esp. of ship* круше́ние; ава́рия; катастрофа; *involving person, vehicle, etc.* разва́лина; **2.** *building, plans* разруша́ть [-у́шить]; *car* разби́ть *pf.*; ***be ~ed*** потерпе́ть *pf.* круше́ние; **~age** ['rekɪdʒ] (*remains*) обло́мки

**wrench** [rentʃ] **1.** (*spanner*) га́ечный ключ; ***give a ~*** дёрнуть *pf.*; **2.** вырыва́ть [-рвать]; *joint* выви́хивать [вы́вихнуть]; *fig.*, (*distort*) *facts, etc.* искажа́ть [исказить]; ***~ open*** взла́мывать [взлома́ть]

**wrest** [rest] вырыва́ть [вы́рвать] (***from*** у Р) (*a. fig.*); **~le** ['resl] *mst. sport* боро́ться; **~ling** [-lɪŋ] борьба́

**wretch** [retʃ]: ***poor ~*** бедня́га

**wretched** ['retʃɪd] □ несча́стный; (*pitiful*) жа́лкий

**wriggle** ['rɪgl] *of worm, etc.* изви́(ва́)ться; ***~ out of*** уклоня́ться [-ни́ться] от (Р), выкру́чиваться [вы́кутиться] из (Р)

**wring** [rɪŋ] [*irr.*] скру́чивать [-ути́ть]; *one's hands* лома́ть; (*a.* ***~ out***) *of washing, etc.* выжима́ть [вы́жать]; *money* вымога́ть (***from*** у Р); *confession* вы́рвать *pf.* (***from*** у Р)

**wrinkle** ['rɪŋkl] **1.** *in skin* морщи́на; *in dress* скла́дка; **2.** [с]мо́рщить(ся)

**wrist** [rɪst] запя́стье; ***~ watch*** ручны́е (*or* нару́чные) часы́ *m/pl.*

**write** [raɪt] [*irr.*] [на]писа́ть; ***~ down*** запи́сывать [-са́ть]; ***~ out*** *check, Brt. cheque, etc.* выпи́сывать [вы́писать]; ***~ off*** (*cancel*) спи́сывать [-са́ть]; **~r** ['raɪtə] писа́тель *m*, -ница *f*

**writhe** [raɪð] *with pain* [с]ко́рчиться

**writing** ['raɪtɪŋ] **1.** *process* писа́ние; (*composition*) письмо́; (литерату́рное) произведе́ние, сочине́ние; (*a.* ***hand~***) по́черк; ***in ~*** пи́сьменно; **2.** пи́сьменный; ***~ paper*** пи́счая бума́га

**written** ['rɪtn] **1.** *pt. p. от* ***write***; **2.** пи́сьменный

**wrong** [rɒŋ] **1.** □ (*not correct*) непра́вильный, оши́бочный; не тот (, кото́рый ну́жен); ***be ~*** быть непра́вым; ***go ~*** *of things* не получа́ться [-чи́ться], срыва́ться [сорва́ться]; (*make a mistake*) сде́лать *pf.* оши́бку; ***come at the ~ time*** прийти́ *pf.* не во́время; *adv.* непра́вильно, не так; **2.** неправота́; непра́вильность *f*; (*injustice, unjust* *action*) оби́да; несправедли́вость *f*; зло; ***know right from ~*** отлича́ть добро́ от зла; **3.** поступа́ть несправедли́во с (Т); обижа́ть [оби́деть]; **~doer** [-du:ə] гре́шник *m*, -ница *f*; престу́пник *m*, -ница *f*; правонаруши́тель; **~ful** ['rɒŋfl] □ (*unlawful*) незако́нный; (*unjust*) несправедли́вый

**wrote** [rəʊt] *pt. от* ***write***

**wrought** [rɔ:t] *pt. и pt. p. от* ***work 2*** [*irr.*]: ***~ iron*** ко́ваное желе́зо

**wrung** [rʌŋ] *pt. и pt. p. от* ***wring***

**wry** [raɪ] □ *smile* криво́й; *remark* переко́шенный; ирони́ческий

# X

**xerox** ['zɪərɒks] **1.** ксе́рокс; **2.** ксерокопи́ровать

**Xmas** ['krɪsməs, 'eksməs] → ***Christmas***

**X-ray** ['eksreɪ] **1.** рентге́новские лучи́ *m/pl.*; рентгенogra ́мма; **2.** просве́чивать [просвети́ть] рентгено́вскими лу́чами; [с]де́лать рентген

**xylophone** ['zaɪləfəʊn] ксилофо́н

# Y

**yacht** [jɒt] **1.** я́хта; **2.** плыть на я́хте; **~ing** ['jɒtɪŋ] па́русный спорт

**yankee** ['jæŋki] *coll.* я́нки *m indecl.*

**yap** [jæp] **1.** тя́вкать [-кнуть]; болта́ть

**yard**[1] [jɑ:d] двор

**yard**[2] [~] ярд; измери́тельная лине́йка; **~stick** *fig.* мери́ло, ме́рка

**yarn** [jɑ:n] пря́жа; *coll. fig.* расска́з; ***spin a ~*** плести́ небыли́цы

**yawn** [jɔ:n] **1.** зево́та; **2.** зева́ть [зевну́ть]; *fig.* (*be wide open*) зия́ть

**year** [jiə, jɜ:] год (*pl.* года́, го́ды, лета́ *n/pl.*); ***he is six ~s old*** ему́ шесть лет; **~ly** [-lɪ] ежего́дный

**yearn** [jɜ:n] тоскова́ть (***for, after*** по Д)

**yeast** [ji:st] дро́жжи *f/pl.*

**yell** [jel] **1.** пронзи́тельный крик; **2.** пронзи́тельно крича́ть, (*howl*) [за]вопи́ть

**yellow** ['jeləʊ] **1.** жёлтый; *coll.* (*cowardly*) трусли́вый; ***~ press*** жёлтая пре́сса; **2.** [по]желте́ть; **~ed** [-d] пожелте́вший; **~ish** [-ɪʃ] желтова́тый

**yelp** [jelp] **1.** лай, визг; **2.** [за]визжа́ть, [за]ла́ять

**yes** [jes] да; нет: ***you don't like tea? – Yes, I do*** Вы не лю́бите чай? – Нет, люблю́

**yesterday** ['jestədɪ] вчера́

**yet** [jet] **1.** *adv.* ещё, всё ещё; уже; до сих пор; да́же; тем не ме́нее; ***as ~*** пока́, до сих пор; ***not ~*** ещё не(т); **2.** *cj.* одна́ко, всё же, несмотря́ на э́то

**yield** [ji:ld] **1.** *v/t.* (*give*) приноси́ть [-нести́]; (*surrender*) сда(ва́)ть; *v/i.* уступа́ть [-пи́ть] (***to*** Д); подд(ав)а́ться; сд(ав)а́ться; **2.** *agric.* урожа́й; *fin.* дохо́д; **~ing** ['ji:ldɪŋ] □ *fig.* усту́пчивый

**yog|a** ['jəʊgə] (*system*) йо́га; **~i** [-gɪ] йог

**yog(h)urt** [jɒgət] йо́гурт

**yoke** [jəʊk] ярмо́ (*a. fig.*); и́го; *for carrying, buckets, pails, etc.* коромы́сло

**yolk** [jəʊk] желто́к

**you** [jə, … jʊ, … ju:] *pron. pers.* ты, вы; тебя́, вас; тебе́, вам (*часто* ***to ~***) *и т. д.*; ***~ and I*** (***me***) мы с ва́ми

**young** [jʌŋ] **1.** □ молодо́й; *person* ю́ный; **2. *the ~*** молодёжь *f*; *zo.* детёныши *m/pl.*; **~ster** ['jʌŋstə] подро́сток, ю́ноша *m*

**your** [jə, … jɔː] *pron. poss.* твой *m*, твоя́ *f*, твоё *n*, твои́ *pl.*; ваш *m*, ва́ша *f*, ва́ше *n*, ва́ши *pl.*; **~s** [jɔːz] *pron. poss. absolute form* твой *m*, твоя́ *f и т. д.*; **~self** [jɔː'self], *pl.* **~selves** [~'selvz] сам *m*, сама́ *f*, само́ *n*, са́ми *pl.*; себя́, -ся

**youth** [juːθ] *collect.* молодёжь *f*; (*boy*) ю́ноша *m*, мо́лодость *f*; ***in my ~*** в мо́лодости (*or* в ю́ности); **~ful** ['juːθfl] □ ю́ношеский; (*looking young*) моложа́вый

# Z

**zeal** [ziːl] рве́ние, усе́рдие; **~ous** ['zeləs] □ рья́ный, усе́рдный, ре́вностный

**zenith** ['zenɪθ] зени́т (*a. fig.*)

**zero** ['zɪərəʊ] нуль *m* (*a.* ноль *m*); ***10° below*** (***above***) ***~*** де́сять гра́дусов моро́за (тепла́) *or* ни́же (вы́ше) нуля́

**zest** [zest] (*gusto*) жар; ***~ for life*** жизнера́достность; любо́вь к жи́зни

**zigzag** ['zɪgzæg] зигза́г

**zinc** [zɪŋk] цинк; *attr.* ци́нковый

**zip** [zɪp] (*sound of bullets*) свист; *coll.* эне́ргия; ***~ code*** почто́вый и́ндекс; ***~ fastener*** = **~per** ['zɪpə] (застёжка-)-мо́лния

**zone** [zəʊn] зо́на (*a. pol.*); *geogr.* по́яс; (*region*) райо́н

**zoo** [zuː] зооса́д, зоопа́рк

**zoolog|ical** [zəʊə'lɒdʒɪkl] □ зоологи́ческий; ***~ gardens*** → ***zoo***; **~y** [zəʊ'ɒlədʒɪ] зооло́гия

**zoom** [zuːm] **1.** (*hum, buzz*) жужжа́ние; *ae.*, (*vertical climb*) свеча́, го́рка; **2.** [про]жужжа́ть; *ae.* [с]де́лать свечу́/го́рку; ***~ lens*** объекти́в с переме́нным фокусным расстоя́нием

# Appendix

# Important Russian Abbreviations

**авт.** ***автóбус*** bus
**АЗС** ***автозапрáвочная стáнция*** filling station
**акад.** ***академик*** academician
**АТС** ***автоматическая телефóнная стáнция*** telephone exchange
**АЭС** ***áтомная электростáнция*** nuclear power station

**б-ка** ***библиотéка*** library
**б.** ***бы́вший*** former, ex-
**БЦЭ** ***Большáя совéтская энциклопéдия*** Big Soviet Encyclopedia

**в.** ***век*** century
**вв.** ***векá*** centuries
**ВВС** ***воéнно-воздýшные си́лы*** Air Forces
**ВИЧ** ***ви́рус иммунодефици́та человéка*** HIV (human immunodeficiency virus)
**вм.** ***вмéсто*** instead of
**ВОЗ** ***Всеми́рная организáция здравоохранéния*** WHO (World Health Organization)
**ВС** ***Верхóвный Совéт*** *hist.* Supreme Soviet; ***вооружённые си́лы*** the armed forces
**вуз** ***вы́сшее учéбное заведéние*** university, college

**г** ***грамм*** gram(me)
**г.** ***1. год*** year **2.** ***гóрод*** city
**га** ***гектáр*** hectare
**ГАИ** ***Государственная автомоби́льная инспéкция*** traffic police
**ГАТТ** ***Генерáльное соглашéние по тамóженным тари́фам и торгóвле*** GATT (General Agreement on Tariffs and Trade)
**гг.** ***гóды*** years
**г-жа** ***госпожá*** Mrs
**ГИБДД** ***Госудáрственная инспéкция безопáсности дорóжного движéния*** traffic police
**глав...** *in compounds* ***глáвный*** chief, main
**главврáч** ***глáвный врач*** head physician
**г-н** ***господи́н*** Mr
**гос...** *in compounds* ***госудáрственный*** state, public
**гр.** ***граждани́н*** citizen
**ГУМ** ***Госудáрственный универсáльный магази́н*** department store
**дир.** ***дирéктор*** director
**ДК** ***Дом культýры*** House of Culture
**ДОБДД** ***Департáмент обеспечéния безопáсности дорóжного движéния*** traffic police
**доб.** ***добáвочный*** additional
**доц.** ***доцéнт*** lecturer, reader, assistant professor
**д-р** ***дóктор*** doctor

**ЕС** ***Европéйский союз*** EU (European Union)
**ЕЭС** ***Европéйское экономи́ческое сообщество*** EEC (European Economic Community)

**ж.д.** ***желéзная дорóга*** railroad, railway

**зав.** ***завéдующий*** head of ...
**загс** ***отдéл зáписей граждáнского состоя́ния*** registrar's (registry) office
**зам.** ***замести́тель*** deputy, assistant

**и др.** ***и други́е*** etc.
**им.** ***и́мени*** called
**и мн. др.** ***и мнóгие други́е*** and many (much) more
**ИНТЕРПОЛ** ***междунарóдная организáция уголóвной поли́ции*** INTERPOL
**и пр., и проч.** ***и прóчее*** etc

**ИТАР** ***Информацио́нное телегра́фное аге́нтство Росси́и*** ITAR (Information Telegraph Agency of Russia)
**и т.д.** ***и так да́лее*** and so on
**и т.п.** ***и тому́ подо́бное*** etc.

**к.** ***копе́йка*** kopeck
**кг** ***килогра́мм*** kg (kilogram[me])
**кв. 1.** ***квадра́тный*** square; **2.** ***кварти́ра*** apartment, flat
**км/час** ***киломе́тров в час*** km/h (kilometer per hour)
**колхо́з** ***коллекти́вное хозя́йство*** collective farm, kolkhoz
**коп.** ***копе́йка*** kopeck
**к.п.д.** ***коэффицие́нт поле́зного де́йствия*** efficiency
**КПСС** ***Коммунисти́ческая па́ртия Сове́тского Сою́за*** *hist.* C.P.S.U. (Communist Party of the Soviet Union)
**куб.** ***куби́ческий*** cubic

**л.с.** ***лошади́ная си́ла*** h.p. (horse power)

**МАГАТЭ** ***Междунаро́дное аге́нтство по а́томной эне́ргии*** IAEA (International Atomic Energy Agency)
**МБР** ***Министе́рство безопа́сности Росси́и*** Ministry of Security of Russia
**МВД** ***Министе́рство вну́тренних дел*** Ministry of Internal Affairs
**МВФ** ***Междунаро́дный валю́тный фонд*** IMF (International Monetary Fund)
**МГУ** ***Моско́вский госуда́рственный университе́т*** Moscow State University
**МИД** ***Министе́рство иностра́нных дел*** Ministry of Foreign Affairs
**МО** ***Министе́рство оборо́ны*** Ministry of Defence
**МОК** ***Междунаро́дный олимпи́йский комите́т*** IOC (International Olympic Committee)
**м.пр.** ***ме́жду про́чим*** by the way, incidentally; among other things
**МХАТ** ***Моско́вский худо́жественный академи́ческий теа́тр*** Academic Artists' Theater, Moscow

**напр.** ***наприме́р*** for instance
**№** ***но́мер*** number
**НА́ТО** ***Североатланти́ческий сою́з*** NATO (North Atlantic Treaty Organization)
**НЛО** ***неопо́знанный лета́ющий объе́кт*** UFO (unidentified flying object)
**н.э.** ***на́шей э́ры*** A.D.

**о.** ***о́стров*** island
**обл.** ***о́бласть*** region
**ОБСЕ** ***Организа́ция по безопа́сности и сотру́дничеству в Евро́пе*** OSCE (Organization on Security and Cooperation in Europe)
**о-во** ***о́бщество*** society
**оз.** ***о́зеро*** lake
**ОНО** ***отде́л наро́дного образова́ния*** Department of Popular Education
**ООН** ***Организа́ция Объединённых На́ций*** UNO (United Nations Organization)
**отд.** ***отде́л*** section, ***отделе́ние*** department
**ОПЕК** ***Организа́ция стран-экспортёров не́фти*** OPEC (Organization of Petroleum Exporting Countries)

**п.** ***пункт*** point, paragraph
**пер.** ***переу́лок*** lane
**ПК** ***персона́льный компью́тер*** PC (personal computer)
**пл.** ***пло́щадь*** *f* square; area (*a. math.*)
**проф.** ***профе́ссор*** professor
**р. 1.** ***река́*** river; **2.** ***рубль*** *m*

r(o)uble
**райко́м** ***райо́нный комите́т*** district commitee (*Sov.*)
**РИА** ***Росси́йское информацио́нное аге́нтство*** Information Agency of Russia
**РФ** ***Росси́йская Федера́цня*** Russian Federation

**с.г.** ***сего́ го́да*** (of) this year
**след.** ***сле́дующий*** following
**см** ***сантиме́тр*** cm. (centimeter)
**с.м.** ***сего́ ме́сяца*** (of) this month
**см.** ***смотри́*** see
**СМИ** ***Средства ма́ссовой информа́ции*** mass media
**СНГ** ***Содру́жество незави́симых госуда́рств*** CIS (Commonwealth of Independent States)
**СП** ***совме́стное предприя́тие*** joint venture
**СПИД** ***синдро́м преобретённого иммунодефици́та*** AIDS (acquired immune deficiency syndrome)
**ср.** ***сравни́*** cf. (compare)
**СССР** ***Сою́з Сове́тских Социалисти́ческих Респу́блик*** *hist.* U.S.S.R. (Union of Soviet Socialist Republics)
**ст.** ***ста́нция*** station
**стенгазе́та** ***стенна́я газе́та*** wall newspaper
**с., стр.** ***страни́ца*** page
**с.х.** ***се́льское хозя́йство*** agriculture
**с.-х.** **сельскохозя́йственный** agricultural
**США** ***Соединённые Шта́ты Аме́рики*** U.S.A. (United States of America)

**т** ***то́нна*** ton
**т. 1.** ***това́рищ*** comrade; **2.** ***том*** volume
**ТАСС** ***Телегра́фное аге́нтство Сове́тского Сою́за*** *hist.* TASS (Telegraph Agency of the Soviet Union)
**т-во** ***това́рищество*** company, association
**т. е.** ***то есть*** i.e. (that is)
**тел.** ***телефо́н*** telephone
**т.к.** ***так как*** cf. ***так***
**т. наз.** ***так называ́емый*** so-called
**тов.** → ***т. 1***
**торгпре́дство** ***торго́вое представи́тельство*** trade agency
**тт.** ***тома́*** volumes
**тыс.** ***ты́сяча*** thousand
**ул.** ***у́лица*** street

**ФБР** ***Федера́льное бюро́ рассле́дований*** FBI (Federal Bureau of Investigation)
**ФИФА** ***Междунаро́дная ассоциа́ция футбо́льных о́бществ*** FIFA (Fédération Internationale de Football)
**ФРГ** ***Федерати́вная Респу́блика Герма́ния*** Federal Republic of Germany
**ФСБ** ***Федера́льная Слу́жба Безопа́сности*** Federal Security Service

**ЦБР** ***Центра́льный банк Росси́й*** Central Bank of Russia
**ЦПКиО** ***Центра́льный парк культу́ры и о́тдыха*** Central Park for Culture and Recreation
**ЦРУ** ***Центра́льное разве́дывательное управле́ние*** CIA (Central Intelligence Agency)

**ЮАР** ***Ю́жно-Африка́нская Респу́блика*** South African Republic
**ЮНЕСКО** ***Организа́ция Объединённых на́ций по вопро́сам образова́ния, нау́ки и культу́ры*** UNESCO (United Nations Educational, Scientific and Cultural Organization)

# Important American and British Abbreviations

**AC** ***alternating current*** переме́нный ток
**A/C** ***account (current)*** теку́щий счёт
**acc(t).** ***account*** отчёт; счёт
**AEC** ***Atomic Energy Commission*** Коми́ссия по а́томной эне́ргии
**AFL-CIO** ***American Federation of Labor & Congress of Industrial Organizations*** Америка́нская федера́ция труда́ и Конгре́сс произво́дственных профсою́зов, АФТ/КПП
**AL, Ala.** ***Alabama*** Алаба́ма (штат в США)
**Alas.** ***Alaska*** Аля́ска (штат в США)
**a.m.** ***ante meridiem*** **(=** ***before noon*****)** до полу́дня
**AP** ***Associated Press*** Ассоши'йтед пресс
**AR** ***Arkansas*** Арка́нзас (штат в США)
**ARC** ***American Red Cross*** Америка́нский Кра́сный Крест
**Ariz.** ***Arizona*** Аризо́на (штат в США)
**ATM** ***automated teller machine*** банкома́т
**AZ** ***Arizona*** Аризо́на (штат в США)

**BA** ***Bachelor of Arts*** бакала́вр иску́сств
**BBC.** ***British Broadcasting Corporation*** Брита́нская радиовеща́тельная корпора́ция
**B/E** ***Bill of Exchange*** ве́ксель *m*, тра́тта
**BL** ***Bachelor of Law*** бакала́вр пра́ва
**B/L** ***bill of lading*** коносаме́нт; тра́нспортная накладна́я
**BM** ***Bachelor of Medicine*** бакала́вр медици́ны
**BOT** ***Board of Trade*** министе́рство торго́вли (Великобрита́нии)
**BR** ***British Rail*** Брита́нская желе́зная доро́га
**Br(it).** ***Britain*** Великобрита́ния; ***British*** брита́нский, англи́йский
**Bros.** ***brothers*** бра́тья *pl.* (в назва́ниях фирм)

**c. 1.** ***cent(s)*** цент (америка́нская моне́та); **2.** ***circa*** приблизи́тельно, о́коло; **3.** ***cubic*** куби́ческий
**CA** ***California*** Калифо́рния (штат в США)
**C/A** ***current account*** теку́щий счёт
**Cal(if).** ***California*** Калифо́рния (штат в США)
**Can.** ***Canada*** Кана́да; ***Canadian*** кана́дский
**CIA** ***Central Intelligence Agency*** Центра́льное разве́дывательное управле́ние, ЦРУ
**CID** ***Criminal Investigation Department*** кримина́льная поли́ция
**c.i.f.** ***cost, insurance, freight*** цена́, включа́ющая сто́имость, расхо́ды по страхова́нию и фрахт
**CIS** ***Commonwealth of Independent States*** содружество незави́симых госуда́рств, СНГ
**c/o** ***care of*** че́рез, по а́дресу (на́дпись на конве́ртах)
**Co.** ***Company*** о́бщество, компа́ния
**COD** ***cash*** (*am. collect*) ***on delivery*** нало́женный платёж, упла́та при доста́вке
**Colo.** ***Colorado*** Колора́до (штат в США)
**Conn.** ***Connecticut*** Конне́ктикут (штат в США)
**cwt** ***hundredweight*** хандредвейт

**DC 1.** ***direct current*** постоя́нный ток; **2.** ***District of Columbia*** федера́льный о́круг Колу́мбия (с америка́нской столи́цей)
**Del.** ***Delaware*** Де́лавэр (штат в США)
**dept.** ***Department*** отде́л; управле́ние; министе́рство; ве́домство
**disc.** ***discount*** ски́дка; ди́сконт, учёт векселе́й
**div.** ***dividend*** дивиде́нд
**DJ 1.** ***disc jockey*** диск-жоке́й; **2.** ***dinner jacket*** смо́кинг
**dol.** ***dollar*** до́ллар
**DOS** ***disk operating system*** ди́сковая операцио́нная систе́ма
**doz.** ***dozen*** дю́жина

**dpt.** ***Department*** отдéл; управлéние; министéрство; вéдомство

**E 1.** ***East*** востóк; ***Eastern*** востóчный; **2.** ***English*** англи́йский
**E. & O.E.** ***errors and omissions excepted*** исключáя оши́бки и прóпуски
**EC** ***European Community*** Европéйское Сóобщество, ЕС
**ECOSOC** ***Economic and Social Council*** Экономи́ческий и социáльный совéт, ООН
**ECU** ***European Currency Unit*** Европéйская дéнежная едини́ца, ЭКЮ
**EEC** ***European Economic Community*** Европéйское экономи́ческое сообщество, ЕЭС
**e.g.** ***exempli gratia*** (лат. = ***for instance***) напр. (наприме́р)
**Enc.** ***enclosure(s)*** приложéние (-ния)
**Esq.** ***Esquire*** эсквáйр (ти́тул дворяни́на, должностнóго лицá; обы́чно стáвится в письмé пóсле фами́лии)
**etc. & c.** ***et cetera, and so on*** и так дáлее
**EU** ***European Union*** Европéйский сою́з

**f** ***feminine*** жéнский; *gram.* жéнский род; ***foot*** фут, ***feet*** фу́ты; ***following*** слéдующий
**FBI** ***Federal Bureau of Investigation*** федерáльное бюрó расслéдований (в США)
**FIFA** ***Fédération Internationale de Football Association*** Международная федерáция футбóльных óбществ, ФИФА
**Fla.** ***Florida*** флори́да (штат в США)
**F.O.** ***Foreign Office*** министéрство инострáнных дел
**fo(l)** ***folio*** фóлио *indecl. n* (формáт в пол-листá); лист (бухгáлтерской кни́ги)
**f.o.b.** ***free on board*** франко-борт, ФОБ
**fr.** ***franc(s)*** фрáнк(и)
**FRG** ***Federal Republic of Germany*** Федерати́вная Респу́блика Гермáния, ФРГ
**ft.** ***foot*** фут, ***feet*** фу́ты

**g.** ***gram(me)*** грамм
**GA (Ga.)** ***Georgia*** Джóрджия (штат в США)
**GATT** ***General Agreement on Tariffs and Trade*** Генерáльное соглашéние по тамóженным тари́фам и торгóвле
**GB** ***Great Britain*** Великобритáния
**GI** ***government issue*** *fig.* америкáнский солдáт
**GMT** ***Greenwich Mean Time*** срéднее врéмя по гри́нвичскому меридиáну
**gr.** ***gross*** брýтто
**gr.wt.** ***gross weight*** вес брýтто

**h.** ***hour(s)*** час(ы́)
**HBM.** ***His (Her) Britannic Majesty*** Егó (Её) Бритáнское Вели́чество
**H.C.** ***House of Commons*** Палáта óбщин (в Великобритáнии)
**hf.** ***half*** полови́на
**HIV** ***human immunodeficiency virus*** ВИЧ
**HL** ***House of Lords*** палáта лóрдов (в Великобритáнии)
**HM** ***His (Her) Majesty*** Егó (Её) Вели́чество
**HMS** ***His (Her) Majesty's Ship*** корáбль англи́йского воéнно-морскóго флóта
**HO** ***Home Office*** министéрство вну́тренних дел (в А́нглии)
**HP, hp** ***horsepower*** лошади́ная си́ла (едини́ца мóщности)
**HQ, Hq** ***Headquarters*** штаб
**HR** ***House of Representatives*** палáта представи́телей (в США)
**HRH** ***His (Her) Royal Highness*** Егó (Её) Королéвское Высóчество
**hrs.** ***hours*** часы́

**IA, Ia.** ***Iowa*** Айóва (штат в США)
**IAEA** ***International Atomic Energy Agency*** Международное агéнтство по áтомной энéргии, МАГАТЭ
**ID** ***identification*** удостоверéние ли́чности
**Id(a).** ***Idaho*** А́йдахо (штат в США)
**i.e., ie** ***id est*** (лат. = ***that is to say***) т.е. (то есть)
**IL, Ill.** ***Illinois*** Иллинóйс (штат в США)

**IMF** ***International Monetary Fund*** Междунаро́дный валю́тный фонд ООН
**in.** ***inch(es)*** дю́йм(ы)
**Inc., inc.** ***incorporated*** объединённый; зарегистри́рованный как корпора́ция
**incl.** ***inclusive, including*** включи́тельно
**Ind.** ***Indiana*** Индиа́на (штат в США)
**inst.** ***instant*** с.м. (сего́ ме́сяца)
**INTERPOL** ***International Criminal Police Organization*** Междунаро́дная организа́ция уголо́вной поли́ции, ИНТЕРПОЛ
**IOC** ***International Olympic Committee*** Междунаро́дный олимпи́йский комите́т, МОК
**IQ** ***intelligence quotient*** коэффицие́нт у́мственных спосо́бностей
**Ir.** ***Ireland*** Ирла́ндия; ***Irish*** ирла́ндский

**JP** ***Justice of the Peace*** мирово́й судья́
**Jnr, Jr, jun., junr** ***junior*** мла́дший

**Kan(s).** ***Kansas*** Канза́с (штат в США)
**KB** ***kilobyte*** килоба́йт
**kg** ***kilogram(me)s.*** килогра́мм, кг
**km** ***kilometer, -tre*** киломе́тр
**kW, kw** ***kilowatt*** килова́тт
**KY, Ky** ***Kentucky*** Кенту́кки (штат в США)

**l.** ***litre*** литр
***L pound sterling*** фунт сте́рлингов
**La.** ***Louisiana*** Луизиа́на (штат в США)
**LA** *1.* ***Los Angeles*** Лос-Анджелес; **2.** ***Australian pound*** австрали́йский фунт (де́нежная едини́ца)
**lb., lb** ***pound*** фунт (ме́ра ве́са)
**L/C** ***letter of credit*** аккредити́в
**LP** ***Labour Party*** лейбори́стская па́ртия
**Ltd, ltd** ***limited*** с ограни́ченной отве́тственностью

**m. 1.** ***male*** мужско́й; **2.** ***meter, -tre*** метр; **3.** ***mile*** ми́ля; **4.** ***minute*** мину́та
**MA** ***Master of Arts*** маги́стр иску́сств
**Mass.** ***Massachusetts*** Массачу́сетс (штат в США)
**max.** ***maximum*** ма́ксимум
**MD** ***medicinae doctor*** (лат. = ***Doctor of Medicine***) до́ктор медици́ны
**Md.** ***Maryland*** Мэ́риленд (штат в США)
**ME, Me.** ***Maine*** Мэн (штат в США)
**mg.** ***milligram(me)(s)*** миллигра́мм
**Mich.** ***Michigan*** Мичига́н (штат в США)
**Minn.** ***Minnesota*** Миннесо́та (штат в США)
**Miss.** ***Mississippi*** Миссиси́пи (штат в США)
**mm.** ***millimeter*** миллиме́тр
**MO 1.** ***Missouri*** Миссу́ри (штат в США); **2.** ***money order*** де́нежный перево́д по по́чте
**Mont.** ***Montana*** Монта́на (штат в США)
**MP 1.** ***Member of Parliament*** член парла́мента; **2.** ***military police*** вое́нная поли́ция
**mph** ***miles per hour*** (сто́лько-то) миль в час
**Mr** ***Mister*** ми́стер, господи́н
**Mrs** *originally* ***Mistress*** ми́ссис, госпожа́
**MS 1.** ***Mississippi*** Миссиси́пи (штат в США); **2.** ***manuscript*** ру́копись *f*; **3.** ***motorship*** теплохо́д

**N** ***north*** се́вер; ***northern*** се́верный
**NATO** ***North Atlantic Treaty Organization*** Североатланти́ческий сою́з, НАТО
**NC, N.C.** ***North Carolina*** Се́верная Кароли́на (штат в США)
**ND, ND.** ***North Dakota*** Се́верная Дако́та (штат в США)
**NE 1.** ***Nebraska*** Небра́ска (штат в США); **2.** ***northeast*** се́веро-восто́к
**Neb(r).** ***Nebraska*** Небра́ска (штат в США)
**Nev.** ***Nevada*** Нева́да (штат в США)
**NH, N.H** ***New Hampshire*** Нью-хэ́мпшир (штат в США)
**NJ, N.J** ***New Jersey*** Нью-Дже́рси (штат в США)
**NM, N.M(ex).** ***New Mexico*** Нью-Ме́ксико (штат в США)
**nt.wt.** ***net weight*** вес не́тто, чи́стый вес

**NW** ***northwestern*** се́веро-за́падный
**NY, N.Y.** ***New York*** Нью-Йо́рк (штат в США)
**NYC, N.Y.C.** ***New York City*** Нью-Йо́рк (го́род)

**OH** ***Ohio*** Ога́йо (штат в США)
**OHMS** ***On His (Her) Majesty's Service*** состоя́щий на короле́вской (госуда́рственной или вое́нной) слу́жбе; служе́бное де́ло
**OK 1.** ***okay*** всё в поря́дке, всё пра́вильно; утверждено́, согласо́вано; **2.** ***Oklahoma*** Оклахо́ма (штат в США)
**Okla.** ***Oklahoma*** Оклахо́ма (штат в США)
**OR, Ore(g).** ***Oregon*** Орего́н (штат в США)
**OSCE** ***Organisation on Security and Cooperation in Europe*** Организа́ция по безопа́сности и сотру́дничеству в Евро́пе, ОБСЕ

**p** *Brt* ***penny, pence*** пе́нни, пенс
**p.** ***page*** страни́ца; ***part*** часть, ч.
**PA, Pa.** ***Pennsylvania*** Пенсильва́ния (штат в США)
**p.a.** ***per annum*** (лат.) в год; ежего́дно
**PC 1.** ***personal computer*** персона́льный компью́тер; **2.** ***police constable*** полице́йский
**p.c.** ***per cent*** проце́нт, проце́нты
**pd.** ***paid*** упла́чено; опла́ченный
**Penn(a).** ***Pennsylvania*** Пенсильва́ния (штат в США)
**per pro(c).** ***per procurationem (= by proxy)*** по дове́ренности
**p.m., pm** ***post meridiem (= after noon)*** ...часов (часа) дня
**PO 1.** ***post office*** почто́вое отделе́ние; **2.** ***postal order*** де́нежный перево́д по по́чте
**POB** ***post office box*** почто́вый абонеме́нтный я́щик
**POD** ***pay on delivery*** нало́женный платёж
**Pres.** ***president*** президе́нт
**Prof.** ***professor*** проф. профе́ссор
**PS** ***Postscript*** постскри́птум, припи́ска
**PTO., p.t.o.** ***please turn over*** см. н/об. (смотри́ на оборо́те)

**RAF** ***Royal Air Force*** вое́нно-возду́шные си́лы Великобрита́нии
**RAM** ***random access memory*** операти́вное запомина́ющее устро́йство, ОЗУ
**ref.** ***reference*** ссы́лка, указа́ние
**regd** ***registered*** зарегистри́рованный; заказно́й
**reg.ton** ***register ton*** реги́стровая то́нна
**Rev., Revd** ***Reverend*** преподо́бный
**RI, R.I.** ***Rhode Island*** Род-Айленд (штат в США)
**RN** ***Royal Navy*** вое́нно-морско́й флот Великобрита́нии
**RP** ***reply paid*** отве́т опла́чен

**S** ***south*** юг; ***southern*** ю́жный
**s 1.** ***second*** секу́нда; **2.** *hist.* ***shilling*** ши́ллинг
**SA 1.** ***South Africa*** Ю́жная А́фрика; **2.** ***Salvation Army*** А́рмия спасе́ния
**SC, S.C.** ***South Carolina*** Ю́жная Кароли́на (штат в США)
**SD, S.D(ak).** ***South Dakota*** Ю́жная Дако́та (штат в США)
**SE 1.** ***southeast*** ю́го-восто́к; ***southeastern*** ю́го-восто́чный; **2.** ***Stock Exchange*** фо́ндовая би́ржа (в Ло́ндоне)
**Soc.** ***society*** о́бщество
**Sq.** ***Square*** пло́щадь *f*
**sq.** ***square...*** квадра́тный
**SS** ***steamship*** парохо́д
**stg.** ***sterling*** фунт сте́рлингов
**suppl.** ***supplement*** дополне́ние, приложе́ние
**SW** ***southwest*** ю́го-за́пад; ***southwestern*** ю́го-за́падный

**t** ***ton*** то́нна
**TB** ***tuberculosis*** туберкулёз, ТБ
**tel.** ***telephone*** телефо́н, тел.
**Tenn.** ***Tennessee*** Те́ннесси (штат в США)
**Tex.** ***Texas*** Теха́с (штат в США)
**TU** ***trade(s) union*** тред-ю́нион профессиона́льный сою́з
**TUC** ***Trade Unions Congress*** конгре́сс (брита́нских) тред-юнио́нов

**UK** ***United Kingdom*** Соединённое Короле́вство (Англия, Шотла́ндия, Уэльс и Се́верная Ирла́ндия)

**UFO** ***unidentified flying object*** неопо́знанные лета́ющие объе́кты, НЛО

**UN** ***United Nations*** Объединённые На́ции

**UNESCO** ***United Nations Educational, Scientific, and Cultural Organization*** Организа́ция Объединённых На́ций по вопро́сам просвеще́ния, нау́ки и культу́ры, ЮНЕСКО

**UNSC** ***United Nations Security Council*** Сове́т Безопа́сности ООН

**UP** ***United Press*** телегра́фное аге́нтство „Ю́на́йтед Пресс"

**US(A)** ***United States (of America)*** Соединённые Шта́ты (Аме́рики)

**USW** ***ultrashort wave*** у́льтракоро́ткие во́лны, УКВ

**UT**, **Ut.** ***Utah*** Ю́та (штат в США)

**V** ***volt(s)*** во́льт(ы) В

**VA**, **Va.** ***Virginia*** Вирджи́ния (штат в США)

**VCR** ***video cassette recorder*** видеомагнитофо́н

**viz.** ***videlicet*** (лат.) а и́менно

**vol.** ***volume*** том

**vols** ***volumes*** тома́ *pl*

**VT**, **Vt.** ***Vermont*** Вермо́нт (штат в США)

**W 1.** ***west*** за́пад; ***western*** за́падный; **2.** ***watt*** ватт, Вт

**WA**, **Wash.** ***Washington*** Вашингто́н (штат в США)

**W.F.T.U.** ***World Federation of Trade Unions*** Всеми́рная федера́ция профессиона́льных сою́зов, ВФП

**WHO** ***World Health Organization*** Всеми́рная организа́ция здравоохране́ния, ВОЗ

**Wis(c).** ***Wisconsin*** Виско́нсин (штат в США)

**wt.**, **wt** ***weight*** вес

**WV**, **W Va.** ***West Virginia*** За́падная Вирги́ния (штат в США)

**WWW** ***World-Wide Web*** всеми́рная паути́на

**WY**, **Wyo.** ***Wyoming*** Вайо́минг (штат в США)

**Xmas** ***Christmas*** Рождество́

**yd(s)** ***yard(s)*** ярд(ы)

**YMCA** ***Young Men's Christian Association*** Христиа́нская ассоциа́ция молоды́х люде́й

**YWCA** ***Young Women's Christian Association*** Христиа́нская ассоциа́ция молоды́х (де́вушек)

# Russian Geographical Names

**Австра́лия** *f* Australia
**А́встрия** *f* Austria
**Азербайджа́н** *m* Azerbaijan
**А́зия** *f* Asia
**Алба́ния** *f* Albania
**А́льпы** *pl. the* Alps
**Аля́ска** *f* Alaska
**Аме́рика** *f* America
**А́нглия** *f* England
**Антаркти́да** *f the* Antarctic Continent, Antarctica
**Анта́рктика** *f* Antarctic
**Аргенти́на** *f* Argentina
**А́рктика** *f* Arctic (Zone)
**Арме́ния** *f* Armenia
**Атла́нтика** *f*, **Атланти́ческий океа́н** *m the* Atlantic (Ocean)
**Афганиста́н** *m* Afghanistan
**Афи́ны** *pl.* Athens
**А́фрика** *f* Africa

**Байка́л** *m* ( Lake) Baikal
**Балти́йское мо́ре** *the* Baltic Sea
**Ба́ренцево мо́ре** *the* Barents Sea
**Белору́ссия** *f* Byelorussia
**Бе́льгия** *f* Belgium
**Бе́рингово мо́ре** *the* Bering Sea
**Бе́рингов проли́в** *the* Bering Straits
**Болга́рия** *f* Bulgaria
**Бо́сния** *f* Bosnia
**Брита́нские острова́** *the* British Isles
**Брюссе́ль** *m* Brussels
**Будапе́шт** *m* Budapest
**Бухаре́ст** *m* Bucharest

**Варша́ва** *f* Warsaw
**Вашингто́н** *m* Washington
**Великобрита́ния** *f* Great Britain
**Ве́на** *f* Vienna
**Ве́нгрия** *f* Hungary
**Вене́ция** *f* Venice
**Во́лга** *f the* Volga

**Гаа́га** *f the* Hague
**Герма́ния** *f* Germany
**Гимала́и** *pl. the* Himalayas
**Гонко́нг** *m* Hong Kong
**Гренла́ндия** *f* Greenland
**Гре́ция** *f* Greece
**Гру́зия** *f* Georgia (Caucasus)

**Да́ния** *f* Denmark
**Днепр** *m* Dniepr
**Донба́сс** *m* (Доне́цкий бассе́йн) *the* Donbas, *the* Donets Basin
**Дуна́й** *m the* Danube

**Евро́па** *f* Europe
**Еги́пет** *m* [-пта] Egypt
**Енисе́й** *m the* Yenisei

**Иерусали́м** *m* Jerusalem
**Изра́иль** *m* Israel
**И́ндия** *f* India
**Ира́к** *m* Iraq
**Ира́н** *m* Iran
**Ирла́ндия** *f* Ireland; Eire
**Исла́ндия** *f* Iceland
**Испа́ния** *f* Spain
**Ита́лия** *f* Italy

**Кавка́з** *m the* Caucasus
**Казахста́н** *m* Kasakhstan
**Каи́р** *m* Cairo
**Камча́тка** *f* Kamchatka
**Кана́да** *f* Canada
**Каре́лия** *f* Karelia
**Карпа́ты** *pl. the* Carpathians
**Каспи́йское мо́ре** *the* Caspian Sea
**Кёльн** *m* Cologne
**Ки́ев** *m* Kiev
**Кипр** *m* Cyprus
**Коре́я** *f* Korea
**Крым** *m* [в -ý] *the* Crimea
**Кузба́сс** *m* Кузне́цкий бассе́йн *the* Kuzbas, *the* Kuznetsk Basin

**Ла́дожское о́зеро** Lake Ladoga
**Ла-Ма́нш** *m the* English Channel
**Ленингра́д** *m* Leningrad (*hist.*)
**Лива́н** *m* Lebanon
**Литва́** *f* Lithuania
**Ла́твия** *f* Latvia

**Ме́ксика** *f* Mexico
**Молдо́ва** *f* Moldova
**Монго́лия** *f* Mongolia
**Москва́** *f* Moscow

**Нева́** *f the* Neva
**Нидерла́нды** *pl. the* Netherlands
**Норве́гия** *f* Norway

**Нью-Йо́рк** *m* New York

**Палести́на** *f* Palestine
**Пари́ж** *m* Paris
**По́льша** *f* Poland
**Пра́га** *f* Prague

**Рейн** *m* Rhine
**Рим** *m* Rome
**Росси́йская Федера́ция** *f* Russian Federation
**Росси́я** *f* Russia
**Румы́ния** *f* Romania

**Санкт-Петербу́рг** *m* St. Petersburg
**Се́верный Ледови́тый океа́н** *the* Arctic Ocean
**Сиби́рь** *f* Siberia
**Стокго́льм** *m* Stockholm
**Соединённые Шта́ты Аме́рики** *pl. the* United States of America

**Те́мза** *f* the Thames
**Таджикиста́н** *m* Tajikistan
**Туркменистан** *f* Turkmenistan
**Ту́рция** *f* Turkey

**Узбекиста́н** *m* Uzbekistan
**Украи́на** *f the* Ukraine
**Ура́л** *m the* Urals

**Финля́ндия** *f* Finland
**Фра́нция** *f* France

**Чёрное мо́ре** *the* Black Sea
**Чечня́** *f* Chechnia
**Че́шская Респу́блика** *f the* Czech Republic

**Швейца́рия** *f* Switzerland
**Шве́ция** *f* Sweden

**Эдинбу́рг** *m* Edinburgh
**Эсто́ния** *f* Estonia

**Ю́жно-Африка́нская Респу́блика** *f the* South African Republic

# English Geographical Names

**Afghanistan** [æf'gænɪstɑːn] Афганистáн
**Africa** ['æfrɪkə] Áфрика
**Alabama** [ˌælə'bæmə] Алабáма (штат в США)
**Alaska** [ə'læskə] Аля́ска (штат в США)
**Albania** [æl'beɪnjə] Албáния
**Alps** [ælps] *the* Áльпы
**Amazon** ['æməzn] *the* Амазóнка
**America** [ə'merɪkə] Амéрика
**Antarctica** [ænt'ɑːktɪkə] *the* Антáртика
**Arctic** ['ɑːktɪk] *the* Áрктика
**Argentina** [ˌɑːdʒən'tiːnə] Аргенти́на
**Arizona** [ˌærɪ'zəʊnə] Аризóна (штат в США)
**Arkansas** ['ɑːkənsɔː] Аркáнзас (штат и рекá в США)
**Asia** ['eɪʃə] Áзия; ***Middle ~*** Срéдняя Áзия
**Athens** ['æθɪnz] г. Афи́ны
**Atlantic Ocean** [ətˌlæntɪk'əʊʃn] *the* Атланти́ческий океáн
**Australia** [ɒ'streɪljə] Австрáлия
**Austria** ['ɒstrɪə] Áвстрия

**Baikal** [baɪ'kæl] óзеро Байкáл
**Balkans** ['bɔːlkənz] *the* Балкáны
**Baltic Sea** [ˌbɔːltɪk'siː] *the* Балти́йское мóре
**Barents Sea** ['bæːrəntsiː] *the* Бáренцево мóре
**Belfast** [ˌbel'fɑːst] г. Бéлфаст
**Belgium** ['beldʒəm] Бéльгия
**Bering Sea** [ˌbeərɪŋ'siː] *the* Бéрингово мóре
**Berlin** [bɜː'lɪn] г. Берли́н
**Birmingham** ['bɜːmɪŋəm] г. Би́рмингем
**Black Sea** [ˌblæk'siː] *the* Чёрное мóре
**Bosnia** ['bɒznɪə] Бóсния
**Boston** ['bɒstən] г. Бостóн
**Brazil** [brə'zɪl] Брази́лия
**Britain** ['brɪtn] (***Great*** Велико) Британия
**Brussels** ['brʌslz] г. Брюссель
**Bucharest** [ˌbuːkə'rest] г. Бухарéст
**Bulgaria** [bʌl'geərɪə] Болгáрия
**Byelorussia** [bɪˌeləʊ'rʌʃə] Белорýссия, Беларýсь

**Cairo** ['kaɪrəʊ] г. Каи́р
**Calcutta** [kæl'kʌtə] г. Калькýтта
**California** [ˌkʌlɪ'fɔːnjə] Калифóрния (штат в США)
**Cambridge** ['keɪmbrɪdʒ] г. Кéмбридж
**Canada** ['kænədə] Канáда
**Cape Town** ['keɪptaʊn] г. Кéйптаун
**Carolina** [ˌkærə'laɪnə] Кароли́на (***North*** Сéверная, ***South*** Ю́жная)
**Caspian Sea** [ˌkæspɪən'siː] *the* Каспи́йское мóре
**Caucasus** ['kɔːkəsəs] *the* Кавкáз
**Ceylon** [sɪ'lɒn] о. Цéйлон
**Chechnia** ['tʃetʃnɪə] Чечня́
**Chicago** [ʃɪ'kɑːgəʊ, *Am.* ʃɪ'kɔːgəʊ] г. Чикáго
**Chile** ['tʃɪlɪ] Чи́ли
**China** ['tʃaɪnə] Китáй
**Colorado** [ˌkɒlə'rɑːdəʊ] Колорáдо (штат в США)
**Columbia** [kə'lʌmbɪə] Колýмбия (рекá, гóрод, админ. округ)
**Connecticut** [kə'netɪkət] Коннектикут (рекá и штат в США)
**Copenhagen** [ˌkəʊpn'heɪgən] г. Копенгáген
**Cordilleras** [ˌkɔːdɪ'ljeərəz] *the* Кордильеры (горы)
**Croatia** [krəʊ'eɪʃə] Хорвáтия
**Cuba** ['kjuːbə] Кýба
**Cyprus** ['saɪprəs] о. Кипр
**Czech Republic** [ˌtʃek rɪ'pʌblɪk] *the* Чéшская Респýблика

**Dakota** [də'kəʊtə] Дакóта ***North*** Сéверная, ***South*** Ю́жная (штáты в США)
**Danube** ['dænjuːb] р. Дунáй
**Delaware** ['deləweə] Дéлавер (штат в США)
**Denmark** ['denmɑːk] Дáния
**Detroit** [də'trɔɪt] г. Детрóйт
**Dover** ['dəʊvə] г. Дувр
**Dublin** ['dʌblɪn] г. Дýблин

**Edinburgh** ['edɪnbərə] г. Э́динбург
**Egypt** ['iːdʒɪpt] Еги́пет
**Eire** ['eərə] Э́йре
**England** ['ɪŋglənd] Áнглия
**Europe** ['jʊərəp] Еврóпа

**Finland** ['fɪnlənd] Финля́ндия
**Florida** ['flɒrɪdə] Фло́рида
**France** [frɑːns] Фра́нция

**Geneva** [dʒɪ'niːvə] г. Жене́ва
**Georgia** ['dʒɔːdʒjə] Джо́рджия (штат в США); Гру́зия
**Germany** ['dʒɜːmənɪ] Герма́ния
**Gibraltar** [dʒɪ'brɔːltə] Гибра́лтар
**Glasgow** ['glɑːzgəʊ] г. Гла́зго
**Greece** ['griːs] Гре́ция
**Greenwich** ['grenɪtʃ] г. Гри́н(в)ич

**Hague** ['heɪg] *the* г. Га́ага
**Harwich** ['hærɪdʒ] г. Ха́ридж
**Hawaii** [hə'waiiː] Гава́йи (о́стров, штат в США)
**Helsinki** ['helsɪŋkɪ] г. Хе́льсинки
**Himalaya** [ˌhɪmə'leɪə] *the* Гимала́и
**Hiroshima** [hɪ'rɒʃɪmə] г. Хиро́сима
**Hollywood** ['hɒlɪwʊd] г. Го́лливуд
**Hungary** ['hʌŋgərɪ] Ве́нгрия

**Iceland** ['aɪslənd] Исла́ндия
**Idaho** ['aɪdəhəʊ] А́йдахо (штат в США)
**Illinois** [ˌɪlə'nɔɪ] И́ллинойс (штат в США)
**India** ['ɪndjə] И́ндия
**Indiana** [ˌɪndɪ'ænə] Индиа́на (штат в США)
**Indian Ocean** [ˌɪndjən'əʊʃən] *the* Инди́йский океа́н
**Iowa** ['aɪəʊə] А́йова (штат в США)
**Iran** [ɪ'rɑːn] Ира́н
**Iraq** [ɪ'rɑːk] Ира́к
**Ireland** ['aɪələnd] Ирла́ндия
**Israel** ['ɪzreɪəl] Израи́ль
**Italy** ['ɪtəlɪ] Ита́лия

**Japan** [dʒə'pæn] Япо́ния
**Jersey** ['dʒɜːzɪ] о. Дже́рси
**Jerusalem** [dʒə'ruːsələm] г. Иерусали́м

**Kansas** ['kænzəs] Ка́нзас (штат в США)
**Kentucky** [ken'tʌkɪ] Кенту́кки (штат в США)
**Kiev** ['kiːev] г. Ки́ев
**Korea** [kə'rɪə] Коре́я
**Kosovo** ['kɒsəvəʊ] Ко́сово
**Kremlin** ['kremlɪn] Кремль
**Kuwait** [kʊ'weɪt] Куве́йт

**Latvia** ['lætvɪə] Ла́твия
**Libya** ['lɪbɪə] Ли́вия
**Lithuania** [ˌlɪθjuː'eɪnjə] Литва́
**Lisbon** ['lɪzbən] г. Лиссабо́н
**Liverpool** ['lɪvəpuːl] г. Ли́верпул
**London** ['lʌndən] г. Ло́ндон
**Los Angeles** [lɒs'ændʒɪliːz] г. Лос-А́нджелес
**Louisiana** [luːˌiːzɪ'ænə] Луизиа́на (штат в США)
**Luxembourg** ['lʌksəmbɜːg] г. Люксембу́рг

**Madrid** [mə'drɪd] г. Мадри́д
**Maine** [meɪn] Мэн (штат в США)
**Malta** ['mɔːltə] Ма́льта (о. и госуда́рство)
**Manitoba** [ˌmænɪ'təʊbə] Манитоба
**Maryland** ['meərɪlənd] Мэ́риленд (штат в США)
**Massachusetts** [ˌmæsə'tʃuːsɪts] Массачу́сетс (штат в США)
**Melbourne** ['melbən] г. Мельбурн
**Mexico** ['meksɪkəʊ] Ме́ксика
**Michigan** ['mɪʃɪgən] Ми́чиган (штат в США)
**Minnesota** [ˌmɪnɪ'səʊtə] Миннесо́та (штат в США)
**Minsk** [mɪnsk] г. Минск
**Mississippi** [ˌmɪsɪ'sɪpɪ] Миссиси́пи (река́ и штат в США)
**Missouri** [mɪ'zʊərɪ] Миссу́ри (река́ и штат в США)
**Moldova** [mɒl'dəʊvə] Молдо́ва
**Montana** [mɒn'tænə] Монта́на (штат в США)
**Montreal** [ˌmɒntrɪ'ɔːl] г. Монреа́ль
**Moscow** ['mɒskəʊ] г. Москва́
**Munich** ['mjuːnɪk] г. Мю́нхен

**Nebraska** [nə'bræskə] Небра́ска (штат в США)
**Netherlands** ['neðələndz] *the* Нидерла́нды
**Nevada** [nə'vɑːdə] Нева́да (штат в США)
**Newfoundland** ['njuːfəndlənd] о. Ньюфа́ундленд
**New Hampshire** [ˌnjuː'hæmpʃə] Нью-Хэ́мпшир (штат в США)
**New Jersey** [ˌnjuː'dʒɜːzɪ] Нью-Дже́рси (штат в США)
**New Mexico** [ˌnjuː'meksɪkəʊ] Нью-Ме́ксико (штат в США)

**New Orleans** [ˌnjuːˈɔːlɪənz] г. Но́вый Орлеа́н
**New York** [ˌnjuːˈjɔːk] Нью-Йо́рк (город и штат в США)
**New Zealand** [ˌnjuːˈziːlənd] Но́вая Зела́ндия
**Niagara** [naɪˈægərə] *the* р. Ниага́ра, Ниага́рские водопа́ды
**Nile** [naɪl] *the* р. Нил
**North Sea** [ˌnɔːθˈsiː] *the* Се́верное мо́ре
**Norway** [ˈnɔːweɪ] Норве́гия

**Ohio** [əʊˈhaɪəʊ] Ога́йо (река́ и штат в США)
**Oklahoma** [ˌəukləˈhəʊmə] Окла-хо́ма (штат в США)
**Oregon** [ˈɒrɪgən] Орего́н (штат в США)
**Oslo** [ˈɒzləʊ] г. Осло
**Ottawa** [ˈɒtəwə] г. Отта́ва
**Oxford** [ˈɒksfəd] г. О́ксфорд

**Pacific Ocean** [pəˌsɪfɪkˈəʊʃn] Ти́хий океа́н
**Pakistan** [ˌpɑːkɪˈstɑːn] Пакиста́н
**Paris** [ˈpærɪs] г. Пари́ж
**Pennsylvania** [ˌpensɪlˈveɪnjə] Пен-сильва́ния (штат в США)
**Philippines** [ˈfɪlɪpiːnz] *the* Фили-ппи́ны
**Poland** [ˈpəʊlənd] По́льша
**Portugal** [ˈpɔːtʃʊgl] Португа́лия
**Pyrenees** [ˌpɪrəˈniːz] *the* Пире-не́йские го́ры

**Quebec** [kwɪˈbek] г. Квебе́к

**Rhine** [raɪn] *the* р. Рейн
**Rhode Island** [ˌrəʊdˈaɪlənd] Род-А́йленд (штат в США)
**Rome** [rəʊm] г. Рим
**Romania** [ruːˈmeɪnjə] Румы́ния
**Russia** [ˈrʌʃə] Росси́я

**Saudi Arabia** [ˌsaʊdɪəˈreɪbɪə] Сау́-довская Ара́вия
**Scandinavia** [ˌskændɪˈneɪvjə] Скан-дина́вия
**Scotland** [ˈskɒtlənd] Шотла́ндия
**Seoul** [səʊl] г. Сеул
**Serbia** [ˈsɜːbɪə] Се́рбия
**Siberia** [saɪˈbɪərɪə] Сиби́рь
**Singapore** [ˌsɪŋəˈpɔː] Сингапу́р
**Spain** [speɪn] Испа́ния
**Stockholm** [ˈstɒkhəʊm] г. Сток-го́льм
**St Petersburg** [sntˈpiːtəzbɜːg] г. Санкт-Петербу́рг
**Stratford** [ˈstrætfəd] -on-Avon [ˈeivən] г. Стра́тфорд-на-Э́йвоне
**Sweden** [swiːdn] Шве́ция
**Switzerland** [ˈswɪtsələnd] Швей-ца́рия
**Sydney** [ˈsɪdnɪ] г. Си́дней

**Taiwan** [ˌtaɪˈwɑːn] Тайва́нь
**Teh(e)ran** [ˌteəˈrɑːn] г. Тегера́н
**Tennessee** [ˌtenəˈsiː] Теннеси́ (река́ и штат в США)
**Texas** [ˈteksəs] Те́хас (штат в США)
**Thames** [temz] *the* р. Те́мза
**Turkey** [ˈtɜːkɪ] Ту́рция

**Ukraine** [juːˈkreɪn] *the* Украи́на
**Urals** [ˈjʊərəlz] *the* Ура́льские го́ры
**Utah** [ˈjuːtɑː] Ю́та (штат в США)

**Venice** [ˈvenɪs] г. Вене́ция
**Vermont** [vɜːˈmɒnt] Вермонт (штат в США)
**Vienna** [vɪˈenə] г. Ве́на
**Vietnam** [ˌviːetˈnæm] Вьетна́м
**Virginia** [vəˈdʒɪnjə] ***West*** За́падная Вирджи́ния (штат в США)

**Warsaw** [ˈwɔːsɔː] г. Варша́ва
**Washington** [ˈwɒʃɪŋtən] Ва́шинг-тон (город и штат в США)
**Wellington** [ˈwelɪŋtən] г. Ве́ллинг-тон (столица Новой Зеландии)
**White Sea** [ˌwaɪtˈsiː] *the* Бе́лое мо́ре
**Wimbledon** [ˈwɪmbldən] г. Уи́мбл-дон
**Wisconsin** [wɪsˈkɒnsɪn] Виско́нсин (река́ и штат в США)
**Worcester** [ˈwʊstə] г. Ву́стер
**Wyoming** [waɪˈəʊmɪŋ] Вайо́минг (штат в США)

**Yugoslavia** [ˌjuːgəʊˈslɑːvjə] Юго-сла́вия

**Zurich** [ˈzʊərɪk] г. Цю́рих

# Numerals

## Cardinals

**0** ноль & нуль *m* naught, zero
**1** оди́н *m*, одна́ *f*, одно́ *n* one
**2** два *m*/*n*, две *f* two
**3** три three
**4** четы́ре four
**5** пять five
**6** шесть six
**7** семь seven
**8** во́семь eight
**9** де́вять nine
**10** де́сять ten
**11** оди́ннадцать eleven
**12** двена́дцать twelve
**13** трина́дцать thirteen
**14** четы́рнадцать fourteen
**15** пятна́дцать fifteen
**16** шестна́дцать sixteen
**17** семна́дцать seventeen
**18** восемна́дцать eighteen
**19** девятна́дцать nineteen
**20** два́дцать twenty
**21** два́дцать оди́н *m* (одна *f*, одно *n*) twenty-one
**22** два́дцать два *m*/*n* (две *f*) twenty-two
**23** два́дцать три twenty-three
**30** три́дцать thirty
**40** со́рок forty
**50** пятьдеся́т fifty
**60** шестьдеся́т sixty
**70** се́мьдесят seventy
**80** во́семьдесят eighty
**90** девяно́сто ninety
**100** сто (а *или* one) hundred
**200** две́сти two hundred
**300** три́ста three hundred
**400** четы́реста four hundred
**500** пятьсо́т five hundred
**600** шестьсо́т six hundred
**700** семьсо́т seven hundred
**800** восемьсо́т eight hundred
**900** девятьсо́т nine hundred
**1000** (одна́) ты́сяча *f* (а *или* one) thousand
**60140** шестьдеся́т ты́сяч сто со́рок sixty thousand one hundred and forty
**1 000 000** (оди́н) миллио́н *m* (а *или* one) million
**1 000 000 000** (оди́н) миллиа́рд *m* milliard, *Am.* billion

## Ordinals

**1st** пе́рвый first
**2nd** второ́й second
**3rd** тре́тий third
**4th** четвёртый fourth
**5th** пя́тый fifth
**6th** шесто́й sixth
**7th** седьмо́й seventh
**8th** восьмо́й eighth
**9th** девя́тый ninth
**10th** деся́тый tenth
**11th** оди́ннадцатый eleventh
**12th** двена́дцатый twelfth
**13th** трина́дцатый thirteenth
**14th** четы́рнадцатый fourteenth
**15th** пятна́дцатый fifteenth
**16th** шестна́дцатый sixteenth
**17th** семна́дцатый seventeenth
**18th** восемна́дцатый eighteenth
**19th** девятна́дцатый nineteenth
**20th** двадца́тый twentieth
**21st** два́дцать пе́рвый twenty-first
**22nd** два́дцать второ́й twenty-second
**23rd** два́дцать тре́тий twenty-third
**30th** тридца́тый thirtieth
**40th** сороково́й fortieth
**50th** пятидеся́тый fiftieth
**60th** шестидеся́тый sixtieth
**70th** семидеся́тый seventieth
**80th** восьмидеся́тый eightieth
**90th** девяно́стый ninetieth
**100th** со́тый (one) hundredth
**200th** двухсо́тый two hundredth
**300th** трёхсо́тый three hundredth
**400th** четырёхсо́тый four hundredth

**500th** пятисóтый five hundredth
**600th** шестисóтый six hundredth
**700th** семисóтый seven hundredth
**800th** восьмисóтый eight hundredth
**900th** девятисóтый nine hundredth
**1000th** ты́сячный (one) thousandth
**60 140th** шестьдесят ты́сяч сто сороковóй sixty thousand one hundred and fortieth
**1 000 000th** миллиóнный millionth

# American and British Weights and Measures

## 1. Linear Measure

**1 inch** (**in.**) дюйм = 2,54 см
**1 foot** (**ft**) фут = 30,48 см
**1 yard** (**yd**) ярд = 91,44 см

## 2. Nautical Measure

**1 fathom** (**fm**) морска́я саже́нь = 1,83 м
**1 cable('s) length** ка́бельтов = 183 м, в США = 120 морски́м саже́ням = 219 м
**1 nautical mille** (**n. m.**) *or* **1 knot** морска́я ми́ля = 1852 м

## 3. Square Measure

**1 square inch** (**sq. in.**) квадра́тный дюйм = 6,45 кв. см
**1 square foot** (**sq. ft**) квадра́тный фут = 929,03 кв. см
**1 square yard** (**sq. yd**) квадра́тный ярд = 8361,26 кв. см
**1 square rod** (**sq. rd**) квадра́тный род = 25,29 кв. м
**1 rood** (**ro.**) руд = 0,25 а́кра
**1 acre** (**a.**) акр = 0,4 га
**1 square mile** (**sq. ml**, *Am.* **sq. mi.**) квадра́тная ми́ля = 259 га

## 4. Cubic Measure

**1 cubic inch** (**cu. in.**) куби́ческий дюйм = 16,387 куб. см
**1 cubic foot** (**cu. ft**) куби́ческий фут = 28 316,75 куб. см
**1 cubic yard** (**cu. yd**) куби́ческий ярд = 0,765 куб. м
**1 register ton** (**reg. tn**) реги́стровая то́нна = 2,832 куб. см

## 5. British Measure of Capacity

*Dry and Liquid Measure*

Ме́ры жи́дких и сыпу́чих тел
**1 imperial gill** (**gl**, **gi.**) станда́ртный джилл = 0,142 л
**1 imperial pint** (**pt**) станда́ртная пи́нта = 0,568 л
**1 imperial quart** (**qt**) станда́ртная ква́рта = 1,136 л
**1 imperial gallon** (**Imp. gal.**) станда́ртный галло́н = 4,546 л

*Dry Measure*

**1 imperial peck** (**pk**) станда́ртный пек = 9,092 л
**1 imperial bushel** (**bu.**, **bsh.**) станда́ртный бу́шель = 36,36 л
**1 imperial quarter** (**qr**) станда́ртная че́тверть = 290,94 л

*Liquid Measure*

**1 imperial barrel** (**bbl.**, **bl**) станда́ртный ба́ррель = 1,636 гл

## 6. American Measure of Capacity

*Dry Measure*

**1 U.S. dry pint** америка́нская суха́я пи́нта = 0,551 л
**1 U.S. dry quart** америка́нская суха́я ква́рта = 1,1 л
**1 U.S. dry gallon** америка́нский сухо́й галло́н = 4,4 л
**1 U.S. peck** америка́нский пек = 8,81 л
**1 U.S. bushel** америка́нский бу́шель = 35,24 л

*Liquid Measure*

**1 U.S. liquid gill** америка́нский джилл (жи́дкости) = 0,118 л
**1 U.S. liquid pint** америка́нская пи́нта (жи́дкости) = 0,473 л
**1 U.S. liquid quart** америка́нская ква́рта (жи́дкости) = 0,946 л
**1 U.S. gallon** америка́нский галло́н (жи́дкости) = 3,785 л
**1 U.S. barrel** амсрика́нский ба́ррель = 119 л
**1 U.S. barrel petroleum** америка́нский ба́ррель не́фти = 158,97 л

## 7. Avoirdupois Weight

**1 grain** (**gr.**) гран = 0,0648 г
**1 dram** (**dr.**) дра́хма = 1,77 г
**1 ounce** (**oz**) у́нция = 28,35 г
**1 pound** (**lb.**) фунт = 453,59 г

**1 quarter** (**qr**) чéтверть = 12,7 кг, в США = 11,34 кг

**1 hundredweight** (**cwt**) цéнтнер = 50,8 кг, в США = 45,36 кг

**1 stone** (**st.**) стон = 6,35 кг

**1 ton** (**tn, t**) = 1016 кг (тж long ton: tn. l.), в США = 907,18 кг (тж short ton: tn. sh.)

## Some Russian First Names

**Алекса́ндр** *m*, Alexander
*dim*: Са́ня, Са́ша, Шу́ра, Шу́рик
**Алекса́ндра** *f*, Alexandra
*dim*: Са́ня, Са́ша, Шу́ра
**Алексе́й** *m*, Alexis
*dim*: Алёша, Лёша
**Анастаси́я** *f*, *coll.* Наста́сья, Anastasia
*dim*: На́стя, Настёна, Та́ся
**Анато́лий** *m* Anatoly
*dim*: То́лик, То́ля
**Андре́й** *m* Andrew
*dim*: Андре́йка, Андрю́ша
**А́нна** *f* Ann, Anna
*dim*: А́ннушка, Аню́та, Аня, Ню́ра, Ню́ша, Ню́ся
**Анто́н** *m* Antony
*dim*: Анто́ша, То́ша
**Антони́на** *f* Antoni(n)a
*dim*: То́ня
**Арка́дий** *m* Arcady
*dim*: Арка́ша, Адик
**Арсе́ний** *m* Arseny
*dim*: Арсю́ша
**Бори́с** *m* Boris
*dim*: Бо́ря, Бори́ска
**Вади́м** *m* Vadim
*dim*: Ди́ма, Ва́дик, Ва́дя
**Валенти́н** *m* Valentine
*dim*: Ва́ля
**Валенти́на** *f* Valentine
*dim*: Ва́ля, Валю́ша, Ти́на
**Вале́рий** *m* Valery
*dim*: Вале́ра, Ва́ля, Вале́рик
**Вале́рия** *f* Valeria
*dim*: Ле́ра, Леру́ся
**Варва́ра** *f* Barbara
*dim*: Ва́ря, Варю́ша
**Васи́лий** *m* Basil
*dim*: Ва́ся, Василёк
**Ве́ра** *f* Vera
*dim*: Веру́ся, Веру́ша
**Ви́ктор** *m* Victor
*dim*: Ви́тя, Витю́ша
**Викто́рия** *f* Victoria
*dim*: Ви́ка
**Влади́мир** *m* Vladimir
*dim*: Во́ва, Воло́дя
**Владисла́в** *m* Vladislav
*dim*: Вла́дя, Вла́дик, Сла́ва, Сла́вик
**Все́волод** *m* Vsevolod
*dim*: Се́ва
**Вячесла́в** *m* Viacheslav
*dim*: Сла́ва, Сла́вик
**Гали́на** *f* Galina
*dim*: Га́ля, Га́лочка
**Генна́дий** *m* Gennady
*dim*: Ге́на, Ге́ня, Ге́ша
**Гео́ргий** *m* **Его́р** *m* George, Egor
*dim*: Го́ша, Жо́ра/Его́рка
**Григо́рий** *m* Gregory
*dim*: Гри́ша, Гри́ня
**Да́рья** *f* Daria
*dim*: Да́ша, Дашу́ля, Да́шенька
**Дени́с** *m* Denis
*dim*: Дени́ска
**Дми́трий** *m* Dmitry
*dim*: Ди́ма, Ми́тя, Митю́ша
**Евге́ний** *m* Eugene
*dim*: Же́ня
**Евге́ния** *f* Eugenia
*dim*: Же́ня
**Екатери́на** *f* Catherine
*dim*: Ка́тя, Катю́ша
**Еле́на** *f* Helen
*dim*: Ле́на, Алёнка, Алёна, Алёнушка, Лёля
**Елизаве́та** *f* Elizabeth
*dim*: Ли́за, Ли́занька
**Заха́р** *m* Zachary
*dim*: Заха́рка
**Зинаи́да** *f* Zinaida
*dim*: Зи́на, Зину́ля
**Зо́я** *f* Zoe
*dim*: Зо́енька
**Ива́н** *m* John
*dim*: Ва́ня, Ваню́ша
**И́горь** *m* Igor
*dim*: Игорёк, Га́рик
**Илья** *m* Elijah, Elias
*dim*: Илю́ша
**Инноке́нтий** *m* Innokenty
*dim*: Ке́ша
**Ио́сиф** *m* **О́сип** *m* Joseph
*dim*: О́ся
**Ири́на** *f* Irene
*dim*: И́ра, Ири́нка, Ири́ша, Иру́ся
**Кири́лл** *m* Cyril
*dim*: Кири́лка, Кирю́ша
**Кла́вдия** *f* Claudia
*dim*: Кла́ва, Кла́ша, Кла́вочка
**Константи́н** *m* Constantine
*dim*: Ко́ка, Ко́стя
**Ксе́ния** *f* **Акси́нья** *f* Xenia

*dim*: Ксéня, Ксю́ша
**Кузьмá** *m* Cosmo
*dim*: Кýзя
**Лари́са** *f* Larisa
*dim*: Лари́ска, Лáра, Лóра
**Лев** *m* Leo
*dim*: Лёва, Лёвушка
**Леони́д** *m* Leonid
*dim*: Лёня
**Ли́дия** *f* Lydia
*dim*: Ли́да, Лидýся, Лидýша
**Любóвь** *f* Lubov (Charity)
*dim*: Лю́ба, Любáша
**Людми́ла** *f* Ludmila
*dim*: Лю́да, Лю́ся, Ми́ла
**Макáр** *m* Macar
*dim*: Макáрка, Макáрушка
**Макси́м** *m* Maxim
*dim*: Макси́мка, Макс
**Маргари́та** *f* Margaret
*dim*: Ри́та, Маргó(ша)
**Мари́на** *f* Marina
*dim*: Мари́нка, Мари́ша
**Мари́я** *f* **Мáрья** *f* Maria
*dim*: Мари́йка, Марýся, Мáня, Мáша, Мáшенька
**Марк** *m* Mark
*dim*: Маркýша, Маркýся
**Матвéй** *m* Mathew
*dim*: Матвéйка, Матю́ша, Мóтя
**Михаи́л** *m* Michael
*dim*: Михáлка, Ми́ша, Мишýля
**Надéжда** *f* Nadezhda (Hope)
*dim*: Нáдя, Надю́ша
**Натáлия** *f coll.* **Натáлья** *f* Natalia
*dim*: Натáша, Нáта, Натýля, Натýся, Тáта
**Ники́та** *m* Nikita
*dim*: Ни́ка, Ники́тка, Ники́ша
**Николáй** *m* Nicholas
*dim*: Ни́ка, Николáша, Кóля
**Ни́на** *f* Nina
*dim*: Нинýля, Нинýся
**Оксáна** *f* Oxana
*dim*: Ксáна
**Олéг** *m* Oleg
*dim*: Олéжка
**Óльга** *f* Olga
*dim*: Óля, Óлюшка, Олю́ша
**Пáвел** *m* Paul
*dim*: Пáвлик, Павлýша, Пáша
**Пётр** *m* Peter
*dim*: Петрýша, Пéтя
**Поли́на** *f* Pauline
*dim*: Поли́нка, Пóля, Пáша
**Раи́са** *f* Raisa
*dim*: Рáя, Раю́ша
**Ростислáв** *m* Rostislav
*dim*: Рóстик, Рóся, Слáва, Слáвик
**Руслáн** *m* Ruslan
*dim*: Руслáнка, Рýсик
**Светлáна** *f* Svetlana
*dim*: Светлáнка, Свéта
**Святослáв** *m* Sviatoslav
*dim*: Слáва
**Семён** *m* Simeon, Simon
*dim*: Сёма, Сéня
**Сергéй** *m* Serge
*dim*: Сергýня, Серёжа, Серж
**Станислáв** *m* Stanislav
*dim*: Стáсик, Слáва
**Степáн** *m* Stephen
*dim*: Степáша, Стёпа
**Степани́да** *f* Stephanie
*dim*: Стёша
**Тамáра** *f* Tamara
*dim*: Тóма
**Татьяна** *f* Tatiana
*dim*: Тáня, Таню́ша, Тáта
**Тимофéй** *m* Timothy
*dim*: Ти́ма, Тимóша
**Фёдор** *m* Theodore
*dim*: Фéдя, Федю́ля(ня)
**Фéликс** *m* Felix
*dim*: Фéля
**Фили́пп** *m* Philip
*dim*: Фи́ля, филю́ша
**Эдуáрд** *m* Edward
*dim*: Э́дик, Э́дя
**Э́мма** *f* Emma
*dim*: Э́ммочка
**Ю́лия** *f* Julia
*dim*: Ю́ля
**Ю́рий** *m* Yuri
*dim*: Ю́ра, Ю́рочка, Юрáша
**Я́ков** *m* Jacob
*dim*: Я́ша, Я́шенька, Яшýня
**Ярослáв** *m* Yaroslav
*dim*: Слáва (ик)

# Grammatical Tables

## Conjugation and Declension

The following two rules relative to the spelling of endings in Russian inflected words must be observed:

1. Stems terminating in г, к, х, ж, ш, ч, щ are never followed by ы, ю, я, but by **и, у, а**.

2. Stems terminating in ц are never followed by и, ю, я, but by **ы, у, а**.

Besides these, a third spelling rule, dependent on phonetic conditions, i.e. the position of stress, is likewise important:

3. Stems terminating in ж, ш, ч, ц can be followed by an o in the ending only if the syllable in question bears the stress; otherwise, i.e. in unstressed position, **е** is used instead.

## A. Conjugation

Prefixed forms of the perfective aspect are represented by adding the prefix in angle brackets, e.g.: <про>читáть = читáть *impf.*, прочитáть *pf.*

Personal endings of the present (and perfective future) tense:

| | | | | | | |
|---|---|---|---|---|---|---|
| 1st conjugation: | -ю (-у) | -ешь | -ет | -ем | -ете | -ют (-ут) |
| 2nd conjugation: | -ю (-у) | -ишь | -ит | -им | -ите | -ят (-ат) |

*Reflexive*:

| | | | | | | |
|---|---|---|---|---|---|---|
| 1st conjugation: | -юсь (-усь) | -ешься | -ется | -емся | -етесь | -ются (-утся) |
| 2nd conjugation: | -юсь (-усь) | -ишься | -ится | -имся | -итесь | -ятся (-атся) |

Suffixes and endings of the other verbal forms:

| | | | | |
|---|---|---|---|---|
| *imp.* | -й(те) | -и(те) | -ь(те) | |
| *reflexive* | -йся (-йтесь) | -ись (-итесь) | -ься (-ьтесь) | |
| | *m* | *f* | *n* | *pl.* |
| *p. pr. a.* | -щий(ся) | -щая(ся) | -щее(ся) | -щие(ся) |
| *g. pr.* | -я(сь) | -а(сь) | | |
| *p. pr. p.* | -мый | -мая | -мое | -мые |
| *short form* | -м | -ма | -мо | -мы |
| *pt.* | -л | -ла | -ло | -ли |
| | -лся | -лась | -лось | -лись |
| *p. pt. a.* | -вший(ся) | -вшая(ся) | -вшее(ся) | -вшие(ся) |
| *g. pt.* | -в(ши) | -вши(сь) | | |
| *p. pt. p.* | -нный | -нная | -нное | -нные |
| | -тый | -тая | -тое | -тые |
| *short form* | -н | -на | -но | -ны |
| | -т | -та | -то | -ты |

Stress:

a) There is *no change of stress unless the final syllable of the infinitive is stressed*, i. e. in all forms of the verb stress remains invariably on the root syllable accentuated in the infinitive, e.g.: пла́кать. The forms of пла́кать correspond to paradigm [3], except for the stress, which is always on пла́-. The imperative of such verbs also differs from the paradigms concerned: it is in **-ь(те)** provided their stem ends in **one consonant** only, e.g.: пла́кать – пла́чь(те), ве́рить – ве́рь(те); and in **-и(те)** (unstressed!) in cases of **two and more consonants** preceding the imperative ending, e.g.: по́мнить – по́мни(те). Verbs with a vowel stem termination, however, generally form their imperative in **-й(те)**: успоко́ить – успоко́й(те).

b) The prefix вы- in perfective verbs always bears the stress: вы́полнить (but *impf.*: выполня́ть). Imperfective (iterative) verbs with the suffix -ыв-/-ив- are always stressed on the syllable preceding the suffix: пока́зывать (but *pf.* показа́ть), спра́шивать (but *pf.* спроси́ть).

c) In the past participle passive of verbs in **-а́ть (-я́ть)**, there is usually a shift of stress back onto the root syllable as compared with the infinitive (see paradigms [1]–[4], [6], [7], [28]). With verbs in **-е́ть** and **-и́ть** such a shift may occur as well, very often in agreement with a parallel accent shift in the 2nd p.sg. present tense, e.g.: [про]смотре́ть: [про]смотрю́, смо́тришь – просмо́тренный; see also paradigms [14]–[16] as against [13]: [по]мири́ть: [по]мирю́, -и́шь – помирённый. In this latter case the short forms of the participles are stressed on the last syllable throughout: -ённый: -ён, -ена́, -ено́, -ены́. In the former examples, however, the stress remains on the same root syllable as in the long form: -'енный: -'ен, -'ена, -'ено, -'ены.

(*a*) present, (*b*) future, (*c*) imperative, (*d*) present participle active, (*e*) present participle passive, (*f*) present gerund, (*g*) preterite, (*h*) past participle active, (*i*) past participle passive, (*j*) past gerund.

Verbs in **-ать**

**1** <про>**чита́ть**

| | |
|---|---|
| (*a*), <(*b*)> | <про>чита́ю, -а́ешь, -а́ют |
| (*c*) | <про>чита́й(те)! |
| (*d*) | чита́ющий |
| (*e*) | чита́емый |
| (*f*) | чита́я |
| (*g*) | <про>чита́л, -а, -о, -и |
| (*h*) | <про>чита́вший |
| (*i*) | прочи́танный |
| (*j*) | прочита́в |

**2** <по>**трепа́ть**
(with л after б, в, м, п, ф)

| | |
|---|---|
| (*a*), <(*b*)> | <по>треплю́, -е́плешь, -е́плют |
| (*c*) | <по>трепли́(те)! |
| (*d*) | тре́плющий |
| (*e*) | – |
| (*f*) | трепля́ |
| (*g*) | <по>трепа́л, -а, -о, -и |
| (*h*) | <по>трепа́вший |
| (i) | <по>трёпанный |
| (j) | потрепа́в |

**3** <об>**глода́ть**
(with changing consonant:
г, д, з > ж
к, т > ч
х, с > ш
ск, ст > щ)

| | |
|---|---|
| (*a*), <(*b*)> | <об>глoжу́, -о́жешь, -о́жут |
| (*c*) | <об>гложи́(те)! |
| (*d*) | гло́жущий |
| (*e*) | – |
| (*f*) | гложа́ |
| (*g*) | <об>глода́л, -а, -о, -и |
| (*h*) | <об>глода́вший |
| (*i*) | обгло́данный |
| (*j*) | обглода́в |

| | |
|---|---|
| **4** | <по>**держа́ть** |
| | (with preceding ж, ш, ч, щ) |
| (*a*), <(*b*)> | <по>держу́, -е́ржишь, -е́ржат |
| (*c*) | <по>держи́(те)! |
| (*d*) | держа́щий |
| (*e*) | – |
| (*f*) | держа́ |
| (*g*) | <по>держа́л, -а, -о, -и |
| (*h*) | <по>держа́вший |
| (*i*) | поде́ржанный |
| (*j*) | подержа́в |

Verbs in **-авать**

| | |
|---|---|
| **5** | **дава́ть** |
| (*a*) | даю́, даёшь, даю́т |
| (*c*) | дава́й(те)! |
| (*d*) | даю́щий |
| (*e*) | дава́емый |
| (*f*) | дава́я |
| (*g*) | дава́л, -а, -о, -и |
| (*h*) | дава́вший |
| (*i*) | – |
| (*j*) | – |

Verbs in **-евать**

| | |
|---|---|
| | (*e.* = -ю́, -ёшь, *etc.*) |
| **6** | <на>**малева́ть** |
| (*a*), <(*b*)> | <на>малю́ю, -ю́ешь, -ю́ют |
| (*c*) | <на>малю́й(те)! |
| (*d*) | малю́ющий |
| (*e*) | малю́емый |
| (*f*) | малю́я |
| (*g*) | <на>малева́л, -а, -о, -и |
| (*h*) | <на>малева́вший |
| (*i*) | намалёванный |
| (*j*) | намалева́в |

Verbs in **-овать**

(and in **-евать** with preceding ж, ш, ч, щ, ц)

| | |
|---|---|
| **7** | <на>**рисова́ть** |
| | (*e.* = -ю́, -ёшь, *etc.*) |
| (*a*), <(*b*)> | <на>рису́ю, -у́ешь, -у́ют |
| (*c*) | <на>рису́й(те)! |
| (*d*) | рису́ющий |
| (*e*) | рису́емый |
| (*f*) | рису́я |
| (*g*) | <на>рисова́л, -а, -о, -и |
| (*h*) | <на>рисова́вший |
| (*i*) | нарисо́ванный |
| (*j*) | нарисова́в |

Verbs in **-еть**

| | |
|---|---|
| **8** | <по>**жале́ть** |
| (*a*), <(*b*)> | <по>жале́ю, -е́ешь, -е́ют |
| (*c*) | <по>жале́й(те)! |
| (*d*) | жале́ющий |
| (*e*) | жале́емый |
| (*f*) | жале́я |
| (*g*) | <по>жале́л, -а, -о, -и |
| (*h*) | <по>жале́вший |
| (*i*) | ...ённый (*e.g.*: одолённый) |
| (*j*) | пожале́в |

| | |
|---|---|
| **9** | <по>**смотре́ть** |
| (*a*), <(*b*)> | <по>смотрю́, -о́тришь, -о́трят |
| (*c*) | <по>смотри́(те)! |
| (*d*) | смо́трящий |
| (*e*) | – |
| (*f*) | смотря́ |
| (*g*) | <по>смотре́л, -а, -о, -и |
| (*h*) | <по>смотре́вший |
| (*i*) | ...о́тренный (*e.g.*: просмо́тренный) |
| (*j*) | посмотре́в |

| | |
|---|---|
| **10** | <по>**терпе́ть** |
| | (with л after б, в, м, п, ф) |
| (*a*), <(*b*)> | <по>терплю́, -е́рпишь, -е́рпят |
| (*c*) | <по>терпи́(те)! |
| (*d*) | терпя́щий |
| (*e*) | терпи́мый |
| (*f*) | терпя́ |
| (*g*) | <по>терпе́л, -а, -о, -и |
| (*h*) | <по>терпе́вший |
| (*i*) | ...ённый (*e.g.*: претерпенный) |
| (*j*) | потерпе́в |

| | |
|---|---|
| **11** | <по>**лете́ть** |
| | (with changing consonant: г, з > ж; к, т > ч; х, с > ш; ск, ст > щ) |
| (*a*), <(*b*)> | <по>лечу́, -ети́шь, -етя́т |
| (*c*) | <по>лети́(те) |
| (*d*) | летя́щий |

(*e*) –
(*f*) летя́
(*g*) <по>лете́л, -а, -о, -и
(*h*) <по>лете́вший
(*i*) ...енный (*e.g.*: ве́рченный)
(*j*) полете́в(ши)

Verbs in **-ереть**

**12** <по>**тере́ть**
(*st.* = -ешь, -ет, *etc.*)
(*a*), <(*b*)> <по>тру́, -трёшь, -тру́т
(*c*) <по>три́(те)!
(*d*) тру́щий
(*e*) –
(*f*) –
(*g*) <по>тёр, -ла, -ло, -ли
(*h*) <по>тёрший
(*i*) потёртый
(*j*) потере́в

Verbs in **-ить**

**13** <по>**мири́ть**
(*a*), <(*b*)> <по>мирю́, -ри́шь, -ря́т
(*c*) <по>мири́(те)!
(*d*) миря́щий
(*e*) мири́мый
(*f*) миря́
(*g*) <по>мири́л, -а, -о, -и
(*h*) <по>мири́вший
(*i*) помирённый
(*j*) помири́в(ши)

**14** <по>**люби́ть**
(with л after б, в, м, п, ф)
(*a*), <(*b*)> <по>люблю́, -ю́бишь, -ю́бят
(*c*) <по>люби́(те)!
(*d*) лю́бящий
(*e*) люби́мый
(*f*) любя́
(*g*) <по>люби́л, -а, -о, -и
(*h*) <по>люби́вший
(*i*) ...лю́бленный (*e.g.*: возлю́бленный)
(*j*) полюби́в

**15** <по>**носи́ть**
(with changing consonant see No 11)
(*a*), <(*b*)> <по>ношу́, -о́сишь, -о́сят
(*c*) <по>носи́(те)!
(*d*) но́сящий
(*e*) носи́мый
(*f*) нося́
(*g*) <по>носи́л, -а, -о, -и
(*h*) <по>носи́вший
(*i*) поно́шенный
(*j*) поноси́в

**16** <на>**кроши́ть**
(with preceding ж, ш, ч, щ)
(*a*), <(*b*)> <на>крошу́, -о́шишь, -о́шат
(*c*) <на>кроши́(те)!
(*d*) кроша́щий
(*e*) кроши́мый
(*f*) кроша́
(*g*) <на>кроши́л, -а, -о, -и
(*h*) <на>кроши́вший
(*i*) накро́шенный
(*j*) накроши́в

Verbs in **-оть**

**17** <за>**коло́ть**
(*a*), <(*b*)> <за>колю́, -о́лешь, -о́лют
(*c*) <за>коли́(те)!
(*d*) ко́лющий
(*e*) –
(*f*) –
(*g*) <за>коло́л, -а, -о, -и
(*h*) <за>коло́вший
(*i*) зако́лотый
(*j*) заколо́в

Verbs in **-уть**

**18** <по>**ду́ть**
(*a*), <(*b*)> <по>ду́ю, -у́ешь, -у́ют
(*c*) <по>ду́й(те)!
(*d*) ду́ющий
(*e*) –
(*f*) ду́я
(*g*) <по>ду́л, -а, -о, -и
(*h*) <по>ду́вший
(*i*) ...ду́тый (*e.g.*: разду́тый)
(*j*) поду́в

**19** <по>**тяну́ть**
(*a*), <(*b*)> <по>тяну́, -я́нешь, -я́нут
(*c*) <по>тяни́(те)!
(*d*) тя́нущий
(*e*) –
(*f*) –
(*g*) <по>тяну́л, -а, -о, -и
(*h*) <по>тяну́вший

(*i*) потя́нутый
(*j*) потяну́в

**20** <со>**гну́ть**
(*st.* = -ешь, -ет, *etc.*)
(*a*), <(*b*)> <со>гну́, -нёшь, -ну́т
(*c*) <со>гни́(те)!
(*d*) гну́щий
(*e*) –
(*f*) –
(*g*) <со>гну́л, -а, -о, -и
(*h*) <со>гну́вший
(*i*) со́гнутый
(*j*) согну́в

**21** <за>**мёрзнуть**
(*a*), <(*b*)> <за>мёрзну, -нешь, -нут
(*c*) <за>мёрзни(те)!
(*d*) мёрзнущий
(*e*) –
(*f*) –
(*g*) <за>мёрз, -зла, -о, -и
(*h*) <за>мёрзший
(*i*) ...нутый (*e.g.*: воздви́гнутый)
(*j*) замёрзши

## Verbs in **-ыть**

**22** <по>**кры́ть**
(*a*), <(*b*)> <по>кро́ю, -о́ешь, -о́ют
(*c*) <по>кро́й(те)!
(*d*) кро́ющий
(*e*) –
(*f*) кро́я
(*g*) <по>кры́л, -а, -о, -и
(*h*) <по>кры́вший
(*i*) <по>кры́тый
(*j*) покры́в

**23** <по>**плы́ть**
(*st.* = -ешь, -ет, *etc.*)
(*a*), <(*b*)> <по>плыву́, -вёшь, -ву́т
(*c*) <по>плыви́(те)!
(*d*) плыву́щий
(*e*) –
(*f*) плывя́
(*g*) <по>плы́л, -а́, -о, -и
(*h*) <по>плы́вший
(*i*) ...плы́тый (*e.g.*: проплы́тый)
(*j*) поплы́в

## Verbs in **-зти́, -зть** (**-сти**)

**24** <по>**везти́**
(-с[т]- = -с[т]-instead of -з- throughout)
(*st.* = -ешь, -ет, *etc.*)
(*a*), <(*b*)> <по>везу́, -зёшь, -зу́т
(*c*) <по>вези́(те)!
(*d*) везу́щий
(*e*) везо́мый
(*f*) везя́
(*g*) <по>вёз, -везла́, -о́, -и́
(*h*) <по>вёзший
(*i*) повезённый
(*j*) повезя́

## Verbs in **-сти́, -сть**

**25** <по>**вести́**
(-т- = -т- instead of -д- throughout)
(*st.* = -ешь, -ет, *etc.*)
(*a*), <(*b*)> <по>веду́, -дёшь, -ду́т
(*c*) <по>веди́(те)!
(*d*) веду́щий
(*e*) ведо́мый
(*f*) ведя́
(*g*) <по>вёл, -вела́, -о́, -и́
(*h*) <по>ве́дший
(*i*) поведённый
(*j*) поведя́

## Verbs in **-чь**

**26** <по>**влечь**
(*a*), <(*b*)> <по>влеку́, -ечёшь, -еку́т
(*c*) <по>влеки́(те)!
(*d*) влеку́щий
(*e*) влеко́мый
(*f*) –
(*g*) <по>влёк, -екла́, -о́, -и́
(*h*) <по>влёкший
(*i*) ...влечённый (*e.g.*: увлечённый)
(*j*) повлёкши

## Verbs in **-ять**

**27** <рас>**та́ять**
(*e.* = -ю́, -ёшь, -ёт, *etc.*)
(*a*), <(*b*)> <рас>та́ю, -а́ешь, -а́ют
(*c*) <рас>та́й(те)!
(*d*) та́ющий
(*e*) –
(*f*) та́я

(*g*) <рас>та́ял, -а, -о, -и
(*h*) <рас>та́явший
(*i*) ...а́янный (*e.g.*: обла́янный)
(*j*) раста́яв

**28** <по>**теря́ть**
(*a*), <(*b*)> <по>теря́ю, -я́ешь, -я́ют
(*c*) <по>теря́й(те)!
(*d*) теря́ющий
(*e*) теря́емый
(*f*) теря́я
(*g*) <по>теря́л, -а, -о, -и
(*h*) <по>теря́вший
(*i*) поте́рянный
(*j*) потеря́в

## B. Declension

### Noun

a) Succession of the six cases (horizontally): nominative, genitive, dative, accusative, instrumental and prepositional in the singular and (thereunder) the plural. *With nouns denoting animate beings (persons and animals) there is a coincidence of endings in the accusative and genitive both singular and plural of the masculine, but only in the plural of the feminine and neuter genders.* This rule also applies, of course, to adjectives as well as various pronouns and numerals that must in syntactical connections agree with their respective nouns.

b) Variants of the following paradigms are pointed out in notes added to the individual declension types or, if not, mentioned after the entry word itself.

**Masculine nouns:**

| | | *N* | *G* | *D* | *A* | *I* | *P* |
|---|---|---|---|---|---|---|---|
| **1** | ви́д | - | -а | -у | - | -ом | -е |
| | | -ы | -ов | -ам | -ы | -ами | -ах |

*Note*: Nouns in -ж, -ш, -ч, -щ have in the *g/pl.* the ending -ей.

| | | | | | | | |
|---|---|---|---|---|---|---|---|
| **2** | реб | **-ёнок** | -ёнка | -ёнку | -ёнка | -ёнком | -ёнке |
| | | -я́та | -я́т | -я́там | -я́т | -я́тами | -я́тах |
| **3** | слу́ча | **-й** | -я | -ю | -й | -ем | -е |
| | | -и | -ев | -ям | -и | -ями | -ях |

*Notes*: Nouns in -ий have in the *prpos/sg.* the ending -ии.
When *e.*, the ending of the *instr/sg.* is -ём, and of the *g/pl.* -ёв.

| | | | | | | | |
|---|---|---|---|---|---|---|---|
| **4** | про́фил | **-ь** | -я | -ю | -ь | -ем | -е |
| | | -и | -ей | -ям | -и | -ями | -ях |

*Note*: When *e.*, the ending of the *instr/sg.* is -ём.

**Feminine nouns:**

| | | | | | | | |
|---|---|---|---|---|---|---|---|
| **5** | рабо́т | **-а** | -ы | -е | -у | -ой | -е |
| | | -ы | - | -ам | -ы | -ами | -ах |
| **6** | неде́л | **-я** | -и | -е | -ю | -ей | -е |
| | | -и | -ь | -ям | -и | -ями | -ях |

*Notes*: Nouns in -ья have in the *g/pl.* the ending -ий (unstressed) or -éй (stressed), the latter being also the ending of nouns in -éя. Nouns in -я with preceding vowel terminate in the *g/pl.* in -й (for -ий see also No. 7). When *e.*, the ending of the *instr/sg.* is -ёй (-ёю).

| | | | | | | | |
|---|---|---|---|---|---|---|---|
| **7** | áрм**и** | **-я** | -и | -и | -ю | -ей | -и |
| | | -и | -й | -ям | -и | -ями | -ях |
| **8** | тетрáд | **-ь** | -и | -и | -ь | -ью | -и |
| | | -и | -ей | -ям | -и | -ями | -ях |

**Neuter nouns:**

| | | | | | | | |
|---|---|---|---|---|---|---|---|
| **9** | блюд | **-о** | -а | -у | -о | -ом | -е |
| | | -а | - | -ам | -а | -ами | -ах |
| **10** | пóл | **-е** | -я | -ю | -е | -ем | -е |
| | | -я́ | -éй | -я́м | -я́ | -я́ми | -я́х |

*Note*: Nouns in -ье have in the *g/pl.* the ending -ий. In addition, they do not shift their stress.

| | | | | | | | |
|---|---|---|---|---|---|---|---|
| **11** | учи́ли**щ** | **-е** | -а | -у | -е | -ем | -е |
| | | -а | - | -ам | -а | -ами | -ах |
| **12** | желáн**и** | **-е** | -я | -ю | -е | -ем | -и |
| | | -я | -й | -ям | -я | -ями | -ях |
| **13** | врé**м** | **-я** | -ени | -ени | -я | -енем | -ени |
| | | -ена́ | -ён | -ена́м | -ена́ | -ена́ми | -ена́х |

## Adjective

also ordinal numbers, etc.

*Notes*

a) Adjectives in **-ский** have no predicative (short) forms.

b) Variants of the following paradigms have been recorded with the individual entry words.

| | | *m* | *f* | *n* | *pl.* | |
|---|---|---|---|---|---|---|
| **14** | бéл | **-ый(-óй)** | **-ая** | **-ое** | **-ые** | long form |
| | | -ого | -ой | -ого | -ых | |
| | | -ому | -ой | -ому | -ым | |
| | | -ый | -ую | -ое | -ые | |
| | | -ым | -ой | -ым | -ыми | |
| | | -ом | -ой | -ом | -ых | |
| | | - | -á | -о (*a.* -ó) | -ы (*a.* -ы́) | short form |

| | | | | | | |
|---|---|---|---|---|---|---|
| **15** | си́н | **-ий** | **-яя** | **-ее** | **-ие** | |
| | | -его | -ей | -его | -их | |
| | | -ему | -ей | -ему | -им | |
| | | -ий | -юю | -ее | -ие | long form |
| | | -им | -ей | -им | -ими | |
| | | ем | -ей | -ем | -их | |
| | | -(ь) | -я́ | -е | -и | short form |
| **16** | стро́г | **-ий** | **-ая** | **-ое** | **-ие** | |
| | | -ого | -ой | -ого | -их | |
| | | -ому | -ой | -ому | -им | |
| | | -ий | -ую | -ое | -ие | long form |
| | | -им | -ой | -им | -ими | |
| | | -ом | -ой | -ом | -их | |
| | | - | -а́ | -о | -и (*а.* -и́) | short form |
| **17** | то́щ | **-ий** | **-ая** | **-ее** | **-ие** | |
| | | -его | -ей | -его | -их | |
| | | -ему | -ей | -ему | -им | |
| | | -ий | -ую | -ее | -ие | long form |
| | | -им | -ей | -им | -ими | |
| | | -ем | -ей | -ем | -их | |
| | | - | -а | -е (-о́) | -и | short form |
| **18** | оле́н | **-ий** | **-ья** | **-ье** | **-ьи** | |
| | | -ьего | -ьей | -ьего | -ьих | |
| | | -ьему | -ьей | -ьему | -ьим | |
| | | -ий | -ью | -ье | -ьи | |
| | | -ьим | -ьей | -ьим | -ьими | |
| | | -ьем | -ьей | -ьем | -ьих | |
| **19** | дя́дин | **-** | **-а** | **-о** | **-ы** | |
| | | -а | -ой | -а | -ых | |
| | | -у | -ой | -у | -ым | |
| | | - | -у | -о | -ы | |
| | | ым | -ой | -ым | -ыми | |
| | | -ом[1] | -ой | -ом | -ых | |

[1]) Masculine surnames in -ов, -ев, -ин, -ын have the ending -е.

## Pronoun

| | | | | | | |
|---|---|---|---|---|---|---|
| **20** | **я** | меня́ | мне | меня́ | мной (мно́ю) | мне |
| | **мы** | нас | нам | нас | на́ми | |
| **21** | **ты** | тебя́ | тебе́ | тебя́ | тобо́й (тобо́ю) | тебе́ |
| | **вы** | вас | вам | вас | ва́ми | вас |
| **22** | **он** | его́ | ему́ | его́ | им | нём |
| | **она́** | её | ей | её | е́ю (ей) | ней |
| | **оно́** | его́ | ему́ | его́ | им | нём |
| | **они́** | их | им | их | и́ми | них |

*Note*: After prepositions the oblique forms receive an н-prothesis, e.g.: для него́, с не́ю (ней).

| | | | | | | |
|---|---|---|---|---|---|---|
| 23 | **кто** | когó | комý | когó | кем | ком |
| | **что** | чегó | чемý | что | чем | чём |

*Note*: In combinations with ни-, не- a preposition separates such compounds, e.g. ничтó: ни от чегó, ни к чемý.

| | | | | | | |
|---|---|---|---|---|---|---|
| 24 | **мой** | моегó | моемý | мой | мои́м | моём |
| | **моя́** | моéй | моéй | мою́ | моéй | моéй |
| | **моё** | моегó | моемý | моё | мои́м | моём |
| | **мои́** | мои́х | мои́м | мои́ | мои́ми | мои́х |
| 25 | **наш** | нáшего | нáшему | наш | нáшим | нáшем |
| | **нáша** | нáшей | нáшей | нáшу | нáшей | нáшей |
| | **нáше** | нáшего | нáшему | нáше | нáшим | нáшем |
| | **нáши** | нáших | нáшим | нáши | нáшими | нáших |
| 26 | **чей** | чьегó | чьемý | чей | чьим | чьём |
| | **чья** | чьей | чьей | чью | чьей | чьей |
| | **чьё** | чьегó | чьемý | чьё | чьим | чьём |
| | **чьи** | чьих | чьим | чьи | чьи́ми | чьих |
| 27 | **э́тот** | э́того | э́тому | э́тот | э́тим | э́том |
| | **э́та** | э́той | э́той | э́ту | э́той | э́той |
| | **э́то** | э́того | э́тому | э́то | э́тим | э́том |
| | **э́ти** | э́тих | э́тим | э́ти | э́тими | э́тих |
| 28 | **тот** | тогó | томý | тот | тем | том |
| | **та** | той | той | ту | той | той |
| | **то** | тогó | томý | то | тем | том |
| | **те** | тех | тем | те | тéми | тех |
| 29 | **сей** | сегó | семý | сей | сим | сём |
| | **сия́** | сей | сей | сию́ | сей | сей |
| | **сиé** | сегó | семý | сиé | сим | сём |
| | **сии́** | сих | сим | сии́ | си́ми | сих |
| 30 | **сам** | самогó | самомý | самогó | сами́м | самóм |
| | **самá** | самóй | самóй | самý, самоё | самóй | самóй |
| | **самó** | самогó | самомý | самó | сами́м | самóм |
| | **сáми** | сами́х | сами́м | сами́х | сами́ми | сами́х |
| 31 | **весь** | всегó | всемý | весь | всем | всём |
| | **вся** | всей | всей | всю | всей | всей |
| | **всё** | всегó | всемý | всё | всем | всём |
| | **все** | всех | всем | все | всéми | всех |
| 32 | **нéсколько** | нéскольких | нéскольким | нéсколько | нéсколькими | нéскольких |

## Numeral

| | | | | | | |
|---|---|---|---|---|---|---|
| 33 | **оди́н** | одногó | одномý | оди́н | одни́м | однóм |
| | **однá** | однóй | однóй | однý | однóй | однóй |
| | **однó** | одногó | одномý | однó | одни́м | однóм |
| | **одни́** | одни́х | одни́м | одни́ | одни́ми | одни́х |

| | | | | | |
|---|---|---|---|---|---|
| **34** | **два** | **две** | **три** | **четы́ре** | |
| | двух | двух | трёх | четырёх | |
| | двум | двум | трём | четырём | |
| | два | две | три | четы́ре | |
| | двумя́ | двумя́ | тремя́ | четырьмя́ | |
| | двух | двух | трёх | четырёх | |
| **35** | **пять** | **пятна́дцать** | **пятьдеся́т** | **сто** | **со́рок** |
| | пяти́ | пятна́дцати | пяти́десяти | ста | сорока́ |
| | пяти́ | пятна́дцати | пяти́десяти | ста | сорока́ |
| | пять | пятна́дцать | пятьдеся́т | сто | со́рок |
| | пятью́ | пятна́дцатью | пятью́десятью | ста | сорока́ |
| | пяти́ | пятна́дцати | пяти́десяти | ста | сорока́ |
| **36** | **две́сти** | **три́ста** | **четы́реста** | **пятьсо́т** | |
| | двухсо́т | трёхсо́т | четырёхсо́т | пятисо́т | |
| | двумста́м | трёмста́м | четырёмста́м | пятиста́м | |
| | две́сти | три́ста | четы́реста | пятьсо́т | |
| | двумяста́ми | тремяста́ми | четырьмяста́ми | пятьюста́ми | |
| | двухста́х | трёхста́х | четырёхста́х | пятиста́х | |
| **37** | **о́ба** | **о́бе** | **дво́е** | **че́тверо** | |
| | обо́их | обе́их | двои́х | четверы́х | |
| | обо́им | обе́им | двои́м | четверы́м | |
| | о́ба | о́бе | дво́е | че́тверо | |
| | обо́ими | обе́ими | двои́ми | четверы́ми | |
| | обо́их | обе́их | двои́х | четверы́х | |

A
B
C
D
E
F
G
H
I
J
K
L
M
N
O
P
Q
R
S
T
U
V
W
X-Z